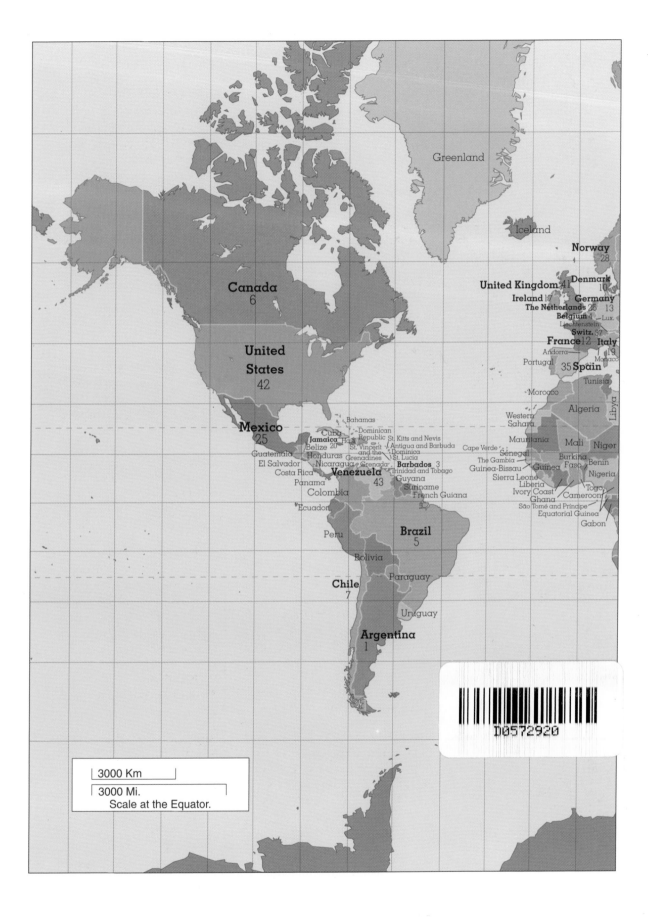

Greenland

Iceland

Norway
28

United Kingdom 41   Denmark
                                10
Ireland 17   Germany
The Netherlands 26   13
Belgium 4   Lux.
Liechtenstein
Switz. 37
France 12   Italy
Andorra   19
Portugal   35 Spain   Monaco

Canada
6

United
States
42

Mexico
25

Tunisia

Morocco

Western
Sahara

Algeria   Libya

Mauritania   Mali   Niger

Bahamas

Cuba   Dominican
Jamaica Haiti   Republic St. Kitts and Nevis
Belize 20   Antigua and Barbuda
Guatemala   St. Vincent   Dominica
El Salvador   and the   St. Lucia
Costa Rica Honduras   Grenadines   Barbados 3
Nicaragua   Grenada   Trinidad and Tobago
Panama   Venezuela   Guyana
        43   Suriname
Colombia   French Guiana

Cape Verde   Senegal
The Gambia   Guinea
Guinea-Bissau   Burkina
    Sierra Leone   Faso   Benin
        Liberia   Nigeria
        Ivory Coast   Togo
            Ghana   Cameroon
        São Tomé and Príncipe
            Equatorial Guinea
                Gabon

Ecuador

Peru

Brazil
5

Bolivia

Chile
7

Paraguay

Argentina
1

Uruguay

3000 Km

3000 Mi.
Scale at the Equator.

Business Today

EIGHTH EDITION

David J. Rachman
Department of Marketing
Bernard M. Baruch College of the City University of New York

Michael H. Mescon
Regents Professor of Human Relations
and Holder of the
Bernard B. and Eugenia A. Ramsey
Chair of Private Enterprise
Georgia State University

Courtland L. Bovée
Professor of Business Administration
C. Allen Paul Distinguished Chair
Grossmont College

John V. Thill
Chief Executive Officer
Communication Specialists of America

PRENTICE HALL
Upper Saddle River, New Jersey 07458

BUSINESS TODAY

Copyright © 1997 by Prentice-Hall, Inc.
A Simon & Schuster Company
Upper Saddle River, New Jersey 07458
(Previous editions published by McGraw-Hill, Inc.)

Illustration and Text Credits and Photo Credits appear on pages R21-R28 and on this page by reference.

This book was set in Bembo by York Graphic Services, Inc. The editors were Dan Loch, Karen Westover, and Ira C. Roberts; the design was done by John Odam Design Associates; the production supervisor was Annette Mayeski. The photo editor was Susan Holtz. Exhibits were rendered by Fine Line Illustrations, Inc. Von Hoffmann Press, Inc., was printer and binder.

ISBN 0-13-079968-8

Library of Congress Cataloging-in-Publication Data

Business today / David J. Rachman . . .[et al.].—8th ed.
    p.   cm.
    Includes bibliographical references (p.   ) and indexes.
    ISBN 0-13-079968-8
    1. Business.   2. Management—United States.   I. Rachman, David J.
IN PROCESS
658—dc20   95-19806

Prentice-Hall International (UK) Limited, London
Prentice-Hall of Australia Pty. Limited, Sydney
Prentice-Hall Canada, Inc., Toronto
Prentice-Hall Hispanoamericana, S.A., Mexico
Prentice-Hall of India Private Limited, New Delhi
Prentice-Hall of Japan, Inc., Tokyo
Simon & Schuster Asia Pte. Ltd., Singapore
Editora Prentice-Hall do Brasil, Ltda., Rio de Janeiro

Printed in the United States of America

10 9 8 7 6 5 4 3 2

Contents in Brief

Preface xxi

Contents

Part One	**Focus on Business Today** *opposite page 1*
Chapter 1	**Foundations of American Business** *opposite page 1*

Chapter 2	**International Business 30**

Chapter 3   **Ethical and Social Responsibilities of Business 60**

Chapter 4   **Forms of Business Enterprise 96**

Chapter 7

Organizing for Business 178

Chapter 8

The Production of Goods and Services 206

Part Three   **Managing Human Resources 238**

Chapter 9   **Human Relations 238**

Chapter 10   **Human Resources Management 268**

| Chapter 11 | **Union–Management Relations 304** |

Chapter 14

Distribution 404

Chapter 17

Accounting 504

Part Six	Finance 538
Chapter 18	**Money and Banking 538**

| Chapter 19 | **Financial Management 566** |

Chapter 20

Securities Markets 598

Part Seven	The Environment of Business 634
Chapter 21	**Government Regulation, Taxation, and Business Law 634**

Chapter 22	**Risk Management and Insurance 664**

Appendix A	**Career Guide: The Employment Search A1**

Preface

Literally millions of students have learned about business from *Business Today,* and its popularity continues. *Business Today* is relied on for its consistency of topics covered, content, currency, ancillary package, service, and commitment to students. *Business Today* presents a balanced view of business—the strengths, weaknesses, successes, failures, problems, and challenges. With its vast array of features, it gives students a solid underpinning for more advanced courses, and it explains the opportunities, rewards, and challenges of a business career.

Business Today, Eighth Edition, continues its respected tradition of excellence. Students not only read about business but also experience it firsthand in every chapter through a variety of highly involving activities that no other textbook can match. Students appreciate its up-to-date real-life examples, its carefully integrated in-depth coverage, its lively conversational writing style, and its eye-opening contemporary graphics. With its powerful Video Exercises, integration of international examples and concepts throughout the book, coverage of current events, exploration of important ethical and societal issues, activities that foster critical thinking, and wealth of assignments to improve students' business communication skills, this edition implements the guidelines for undergraduate business programs of the American Association of Collegiate Schools of Business.

The Eighth Edition has been extensively revised and updated, with two important goals in mind: (1) to provide a clear and complete description of the concepts underlying business, and (2) to illustrate with real-life examples and cases the remarkable dynamism and liveliness of business organizations and of the people who operate them. Every chapter in this edition has been improved and enriched to give students an even better learning experience.

INTEGRATED VIDEO EXERCISES TEACH IMPORTANT CONCEPTS

The ability to drive home a point—to excite the human mind and to stimulate action—is what makes videos so incredibly powerful. Now you can harness this power and bring the drama and immediacy of real-world business into your classroom. The high-quality videos that accompany this text allow students to meet, on location, a cross section of real people who work for some of the world's most fascinating companies—including small, medium, and large firms as well as nonprofit and international organizations. Most important, these videos enable you to challenge your students with the unique set of exercises placed at the end of each chapter.

Business Today videos and exercises do more than simply relate to end-of-chapter cases. Each video is integrated with chapter material, and the exercises are far more involving than simple discussion questions. Students are asked to react to the videos by responding to questions, making decisions, and taking the initiative to solve real business problems, Closely integrated with the content of the chapter,and offering instructors maximum flexibility in selecting various types of student assignments, the exercises for each video contain 10 labeled components: analysis, application, decision, comunication, integration, ethics, debate, teamwork, research, and role playing. These critically acclaimed videos and valuable exercises surpass those offered with any other text and are unparalleled in helping students understand how business principles and concepts in the chapter are applied in the workplace. Examples are

- China: An Economic Miracle?
- ServiceMaster Serves Up Motivation
- McDonald's Covers the World with Fast Food and Good Times
- Acuvue Commercial Gives Consumers a New Look at Contact Lenses

INTERNATIONAL EXAMPLES OFFER A GLOBAL PERSPECTIVE

When students enter the business world, they will most likely be facing competition not only from home but also from abroad. As it becomes harder and harder to separate the domestic business climate from the growing global economy, students have a vital need to understand international business. Thus today's business texts must have a global perspective, and *Business Today* integrates hundreds of international examples throughout its 22 chapters. These examples describe U.S. companies doing business overseas, as well as overseas organizations doing business in the United States and other countries. Specifically, coverage of international business includes

- A complete chapter (see Chapter 2) on international business
- A series of "Exploring Global Business" boxes throughout the book

- Cases such as "Ford Steers Toward Global Operations," "Pepperoni Wrapped in Red Tape," and "Flying High on Worldwide Horizontal Links."
- Numerous examples throughout the book that focus on international principles and practices
- "Video Exercises" focusing on multinational companies, such as McDonald's in Europe
- New "Mastering the Geography of Business" exercises at the end of each major part of the book
- Maps on the endpapers, with a coded system for locating many of the companies and countries discussed in the text

ETHICAL AND SOCIETAL MATERIAL EXPLORES TODAY'S MOST IMPORTANT ISSUES

Whether small enterprises or multinational corporations, companies throughout the world are attempting to resolve ethical dilemmas. Today's students need to understand social responsibility as it relates to the environment, consumers, employees, and investors. This edition includes a well-rounded chapter (see Chapter 3) that discusses ethical decision making on both the individual and the corporate levels.

This text fires students' enthusiasm and respect for business, but it doesn't pretend that business is without problems or critics. By pointing out ethical dilemmas and by reminding students of the responsibilities that accompany the rights of free enterprise, *Business Today* helps prepare the next generation of conscientious businesspeople. In addition, a series of "Thinking About Ethics" boxes appear throughout the book so that students can see that nearly every aspect of business presents ethical questions. Here are just a few of the social and ethical issues discussed in the book:

- AIDS in the workplace
- Employee drug testing
- English-only rules on the job
- Environmental pollution
- Glass ceiling
- Negligent hiring
- Computerized dialing systems
- Privacy versus company security
- Employee strikes versus public welfare
- Privacy and marketing databases
- Product liability
- Sexual harassment
- Insurance fraud

Business Today has no examples promoting alcohol. The authors certainly support companies' rights to market their products, but considering that many students taking this course are not of legal drinking age and that alcoholism among college students is increasing, the authors believe that an emphasis on alcoholic products in a textbook is inappropriate. *Business Today* also avoids tobacco examples (other than those instances in which tobacco products are the subject of critical discussion). The business literature offers thousands of great examples that students can relate to, and this edition takes advantage of those.

SPECIFIC ELEMENTS STIMULATE AND DEVELOP CRITICAL THINKING

National test results show a serious weakness in the ability of U.S. students to reason, analyze, interpret, synthesize, and solve problems. According to respected reports on the state of higher education by the National Commission on Excellence in Education, the National Institute of Education, and the Association of American Colleges, fostering students' ability to think critically should be one of the major focuses of an undergraduate education.

Moreover, labor forecasters predict that between now and the end of this century, the majority of the workforce in the United States will change jobs, change careers, or need retraining. Therefore, if students are to make a successful transition from the classroom to the workplace and maintain uninterrupted, rewarding employment, they must apply the critical thinking skills that will make them adaptable workers.

Critical thinking calls for skills such as observing, classifying, interpreting, criticizing, summarizing, analyzing, comparing, hypothesizing, collecting and organizing information, making decisions, and applying knowledge to new situations. Specific features in *Business Today* have been designed to stimulate critical thinking and to develop these vital skills more effectively than any other introductory business text. These features include the questions that conclude chapter-opening "On the Job: Facing Business Challenges" vignettes, end-of-chapter "On the Job: Meeting Business Challenges" case studies/simulations, chapter-ending review questions, chapter-ending "A Case for Critical Thinking" exercises, "Building Your Communication Skills" exercises, "Keeping Current Using *The Wall Street Journal*" exercises, part-ending "Mastering the Geography of Business" exercises, and experiential Video Exercises.

SMALL BUSINESS TAKES CENTER STAGE

More than any other recent group of students, today's business students have strong entrepreneurial interests. Although comparatively few will ever be self-employed, many will work for small enterprises. In either case, they have an obvious need to understand the risks, rewards, problems, and perils of small business. An entire chapter is devoted to this subject (see Chapter 5), and throughout this book, smaller businesses are used as examples.

RELIABLE AND EFFECTIVE PEDAGOGY SPARKS STUDENT LEARNING

Business Today includes an extraordinary number of pedagogical devices that simplify teaching, facilitate learning, maintain interest and enjoyment, and illustrate the practical application of chapter concepts. In short, these devices make this new edition the most effective teaching tool ever published for introductory business.

"On the Job: Facing Business Challenges" Introduces Each Chapter

As a glance at the table of contents will reveal, each chapter begins with "On the Job: Facing Business Challenges" a slice-of-life vignette that attracts student interest by vividly portraying business challenges faced by a real executive. The vignette closes with thought-provoking questions that help draw students into the chapter and that provide a rationale for studying the chapter. Throughout the chapter, references to the opening vignette help students see the connection between the chapter's content and the real world of business. The special dimension of reality provided by these vignettes helps students develop a genuine interest in the world of business, which is the first step in learning about it.

"On the Job: Meeting Business Challenges" Concludes Each Chapter

Each chapter concludes with an end-of-chapter case study/simulation that (1) elaborates on the actions taken by the executive featured in the opening vignette and (2) analyzes the results in light of the concepts presented in the chapter. Then the student takes over, playing a role in the executive's organization by making business decisions in four carefully chosen scenarios. These case studies/simulations include

- Microsoft: Struggling to Survive Success
- Johnson & Johnson: Keeping Employees in the Pink and the Company in the Black

- Nike: Running a Race That Never Ends
- Orville Redenbacher: Personality with a Pop
- Ben & Jerry's Homemade: Can a Company Be Both Profitable and Socially Responsible?

Special Feature Boxes Revolve Around Five Well-Integrated Themes

Special Feature boxes are strategically placed in every chapter to help make the world of business come alive. Based on extensive research in business literature, they further enhance the practical flavor of the book.

Focusing on Cultural Diversity

This series of boxes focuses student attention on how business is affected by the increasing diversity of the workforce—whether at home or abroad. Topics include "How to Avoid Business Blunders Abroad," Managing the Multinational Workforce," "Importing Japanese Teamwork," and "Organizations Learn the Value of Diversity."

Thinking about Ethics

These Special Feature boxes present current ethical issues in business. Topics include "Does Capitalism Cause Pollution?" "How Do Your Ethics Measure Up?" "Should Corporate Cultures Stress Only English on the Job?" "Employee Privacy versus Company Security," and "Healthy Competition or Unhealthy Control?"

Exploring Global Business

These boxes demonstrate to students the impact of international business on virtually every concept presented in this text. Topics include "Gift versus Bribe: When a Friendly Exchange Turns into Risky Business," "Merging Hand-Made Craftsmanship and World-Class Manufacturing," "Can Universal Appeal Overcome Cultural Differences?" "Toys 'R' Us Stores Play Santa Internationally," and "International Insurance: Don't Leave Home without It."

Understanding the High-Tech Revolution

This series of boxes exemplifies the ever-growing influence of technology on business. Topics include "Technology Helps Your Small Company Level the Playing Field," "Smart Factories and the Revival of U.S. Manufacturing," "Computerized Creativity in New-Product Design," "The Mixed Blessing of Advertising Technology," and "Cutting the Cables with Wireless Communications."

Gaining the Competitive Edge

These boxes exemplify timely issues of vital importance to contemporary business. Some of them offer "how-to" guidelines to demonstrate how business concepts can be applied in a practical way. Topics include "Managing the Changing Organization," "The Challenge of Organizing Today's Workforce," "Steps to an Effective Sales Presentation," and "How to Read an Annual Report."

Cases Present Challenging Business Problems

At the end of each chapter, "A Case for Critical Thinking" provides further illustration and practical application of key concepts. This classic device assists students in evaluating situations, using good judgment, learning to make decisions, and developing critical thinking skills. The case questions reinforce major points made in the chapter. Case topics include

- Mail Boxes Etc.: Putting a Stamp on the Market
- General Electric: New Management Techniques for Electrifying Performance
- Domino's Pizza: The Pizza Distribution Olympics: A Question of Dough . . .
- Minivans: Families Love the Convenience; Chrysler Loves the Profits
- Hub-and-Spoke Is Wheel of Fortune for Federal Express

New "Mastering the Geography of Business" Exercises Help Develop Geographic Literacy

Now that so many businesses are affected by global affairs, students need a stronger understanding of geography. You'll find a "Mastering the Geography of Business" exercise at the end of each major part in this text. Each of these new exercises describes a real-world business situation and asks students to complete an activity that requires geographic knowledge or research. The maps appearing on this book's endpapers can be useful in completing these exercises.

Special Exercises Build Communication Skills

The ability to communicate well—whether listening, speaking, reading, or writing—is a skill students must possess to have a successful career. Because of their extensive research and writing in the area of communication, the authors are especially equipped to help your students develop these skills. You'll find unique "Building Your Communication Skills" exercises near the end of each chapter. Students are called on to practice a wide range of communication activities, including one-on-one and group discussions, class debates, personal interviews, panel sessions, oral and written reports, and letter-writing assignments.

The Wall Street Journal Exercises Keep Students Current

To emphasize the link between today's business news and *Business Today,* a "Keeping Current Using *The Wall Street Journal*" exercise is provided at the end of each chapter. Students are asked to choose an article they are interested in and are provided a structure for analyzing the article in the context of the material covered in the chapter. These exercises offer interesting and useful ways to use *The Wall Street Journal* in the classroom and give students practice in the critical skill of interpreting business news.

Real-Life Examples Translate Theory into Practice

Educational experiments demonstrate that students learn more and are more interested in their studies when actual people, organizations, and events are presented. True-to-life examples also help prepare students for the world of work by showing them how theory translates into practice. One of the most important characteristics of *Business Today* is its realism. In addition to having a factual chapter-opening vignette and real cases, each chapter has abundant examples from businesses of every size and from a wide range of industries.

Learning Objectives Establish Benchmarks for Measuring Success

Each chapter begins with a list of objectives that summarizes exactly what students should learn as a result of studying the chapter. Organized to reflect the sequence of topics within the chapter, these objectives guide the learning process and help motivate students to master the material.

At the end of each chapter, the "Summary of Learning Objectives" restates the learning objectives and summarizes chapter highlights, a feature designed to reinforce learning of basic concepts.

Four-Way Approach Reinforces Business Terminology

Because business has its own special terminology, an important goal of this textbook is vocabulary development. First, each key term is printed in boldface within the text. Second, a definition appears in the margin adjacent to the term. Third, an alphabetical list of key terms appears at the end of each chapter, with convenient cross-references to the pages where terms are defined. Fourth, all marginal definitions are also assembled in an alphabetical Glossary at the end of the book. With this four-way method of vocabulary reinforcement, students should be able to learn the basic terminology of the course with ease.

New Career Guide Helps Students Prepare for Today's Workplace

The competition for jobs and promotions is increasing as we approach the twenty-first century, and at the same time, the stability of employment relationships is much less dependable. This edition of *Business Today* provides a special appendix for students: "Career Guide: The Employment Search." This new appendix helps students plan and research their pursuit of employment, but it doesn't stop there. It also guides students in their preparation of such documents as résumés and application letters. In addition, this new appendix discusses ways for students to build careers rather than simply hunt for jobs.

Readable Writing Style Motivates Students

The reading level of this book has been carefully monitored to ensure accessibility for students. The lucid writing style makes the material pleasing to read and easy to comprehend. Every line of text has been carefully edited to ensure that it reads clearly and that there is a smooth transition from one idea to the next.

New Magazine Layout and Full-Color Graphics Reflect State-of-the-Art Design

Business Today, Eighth Edition, looks the way it does for more than just artistic reasons. Students are used to reading popular magazines with lots of headings, paragraphs, and boxed material. Because of the pervasive influence of television and film, students expect to be visually stimulated while they learn. To accommodate today's media sophisticates, *Business Today* has been designed to resemble the layout of a magazine, to be engrossing and attractive, and yet to be businesslike and professional.

Because of a firm belief that effective design serves both to invite the reader's interest and to reinforce learning, striking new three-dimensional artwork and graphic examples have been created for this new edition. The art program—numerous exhibits and photographs—amounts to a course in itself. Combined with the instructive captions, the art serves as both a preview and a review of each chapter. Boxes, photos, and illustrations appear at the top or bottom of the page or in the margin to avoid interfering with students' attention and concentration.

COMPREHENSIVE RESEARCH PROVIDES A SOLID FOUNDATION

A successful textbook must be revised to reflect changes in the course for which the book is designed. For the Eighth Edition of *Business*

Today, over 500 professors of business contributed their viewpoints on trends in instructional methodology for the introductory business course. Their recommendations, as well as those of a distinguished panel of more than 20 academic and business experts, helped shape this new edition.

In addition, the authors conducted an exhaustive study of the literature of business, including hundreds of the very latest articles, reports, monographs, and books. As a glance at the extensive References and Credits sections near the end of this book will show, *Business Today* is the most carefully researched and documented introductory business textbook on the market. This attention to detail is in keeping with the goal of accurately portraying the changing nature and emerging trends of business.

CAREFUL PREPARATION OFFERS THE UNIQUE ADVANTAGE OF CURRENCY

For any textbook to meet the needs and expectations of both students and professors, it must reflect the rapid changes occurring every day in the business world. Extraordinary measures have been taken to ensure that *Business Today* is the most up-to-date textbook on the market, with more 1995 references than any other text. Topic coverage includes

- The trend toward competing on the basis of speed, quality, service, and customer satisfaction
- The attempts of entrepreneurs and governments to convert from planned to free-market economies in countries such as Poland and China
- The current status of NAFTA, GATT, and the European Union
- The growing use of multidomestic and transnational management approaches
- The trend toward more ethical business practices, including such issues as ethics officers, whistle-blowing, and ethics hot lines
- The rise in shareholder lawsuits
- The reemergence of the conglomerate in the 1990s, including comparisons with 1960s-style conglomerates
- The growing importance of the quality of work life, including its relationship to motivation
- The legality of employee-involvement programs such as union-management teams, including how Xerox used these teams to boost efficiency and quality and keep production jobs in the United States
- The growth of geodemographics—the newest and most promising technique for analyzing and segmenting the consumer market
- The emergence of electronic retailing, including direct-response television and computer-interactive retailing

- The popularity of selling over the Internet
- The move by Procter & Gamble toward everyday low pricing (EDLP) and away from massive trade discounts—the first major consumer-goods producer to do so
- The continuing influence of technology on business, including the information highway, multimedia, client/server technology, and the Internet
- The use of virtual reality systems to simulate new equipment designs, including an example from Caterpillar
- The interstate banking now allowed by the Interstate Banking and Efficiency Act of 1994
- The more than 700 government laboratories that are offering to partner with private companies to develop new products.
- The serious and growing problems of insurance fraud
- The cost-control efforts in the health-care industry, including Oregon's controversial rationing program

MASTER REFINEMENTS ENHANCE THE BOOK

The following list is a brief overview of some of the refinements made in *Business Today,* Eighth Edition. For a more detailed list of changes, see the beginning of each chapter in the Creative Lectures in the Instructor's Manual. Revisions in this edition include

- Rearranging the chapters in the first part of the book to reflect the growing importance of, and the increased focus on, international business and ethical and social responsibilities in business
- Updating dramatic changes in the global economy, with greater emphasis on ever-accelerating technological development, diversity in both the workforce and the consumer market, and the strategic value of information
- Updating the legislative and regulatory actions relating to social responsibility
- Discussing greater efforts toward workforce diversity
- Presenting information on why leveraged buyouts are risky and why their record is mixed
- Clarifying the definitions of public and private corporations to distinguish those that are owned by regular stockholders and those that are owned by governments
- Exploring the impact of social and economic factors on the development of small businesses
- Updating the crisis-management material to focus on Jack-in-the Box
- Strengthening coverage of cultural diversity, including how Japanese automakers adapted their team approaches when they opened U.S. plants

- Exploring how Swissair uses horizontal organization to conduct business around the world
- Clarifying the definition of corporate culture to include the roles played by values and norms
- Analyzing Victor Vroom's contribution to expectancy theory
- Introducing new information on changes in the workforce, including worker demographics, women in the workforce, and cultural diversity.
- Presenting information on assessment centers to show how companies can assess a candidate's abilities in a simulated workplace environment
- Broadening the discussion of health and safety programs to explain the role of OSHA in setting safety standards
- Updating the discussion of worker associations as a tool unions can use to build a long-term relationship with workers who may become interested in union representation in the future.
- Presenting marketing management, strategy, and segmentation in one integrated discussion to make the importance of these topics easier to grasp
- Adding new material to the discussion of marketing research: how research can help the marketing effort, the major types of marketing research (including exploratory, descriptive, and causal), and the four major steps in the research process (define the problem, design the research, collect the data, analyze the data)
- Examining the growing importance of service as a way of distinguishing increasingly similar basic products
- Addressing the issue of growing competition between national and private-label brands
- Tempering the discussion of physical distribution to deemphasize the technical and administrative complexity and to emphasize the growing strategic importance of physical distribution
- Updating the discussion of information systems to make it a more practical description of how companies use computers throughout the organization
- Updating and condensing the discussion of the evolving banking environment to delineate the impact of deregulation on competition
- Reworking and expanding "Government as Watchdog and Regulator" with sections covering the five major areas of regulation: competition, consumer rights, employee rights, investor rights, and the environment
- Adding a discussion of uncertainty avoidance, which covers such diverse tasks as marketing research and advanced information systems that lower the risk of decision making by increasing the flow of relevant information

INTEGRATED SUPPLEMENTARY MATERIALS MAKE *BUSINESS TODAY* A COMPLETE LEARNING PACKAGE

The supplementary package has been thoroughly revised, and several new elements have been added. The instructor's materials are not only comprehensive, but also totally integrated with the text.

Study Guide
Stanley Garfunkel, CUNY, Queensborough Community College
Dennis Guseman, California State University, Bakersfield

Creative Lectures (two-volume Instructor's Manual)
Judith G. Bulin, Monroe Community College

Test Bank (two volumes) and Computerized Test Bank
George Ruggiero
The Community College of Rhode Island

Guide for Non-Native Speakers to accompany Business Today
J. Marcia Le Roy, Englobus Communications and Development Group

PowerPoint Presentation Package
Ronald G. Cheek, University of New Orleans

Every Student's INTERNET RESOURCE GUIDE
Sara Amato, Central Washington State University

Business Week (selected readings on the PRIMIS system)

Acetate Transparency Program

The Business Today *Videodisc*

The Business Today *Integrated Video Series*

Career, Communication, and Critical Thinking: A Student Guide
Les R. Dlabay, Lake Forest College
William J. Hisker, St. Vincent College
Courtland L. Bovée, Grossmont College
John V. Thill, Communication Specialists of America

Software: *Testmaker* (Computerized Test Bank)
Threshold: A Competitive Management Simulation
PC CASE: Computerized Cases 2e
Computerized Instructor's Manual
Report Card: Classroom Management Software
SHOES: A Marketing Simulation
SIMEX, 3e

Contact your McGraw-Hill representative for eligibility and minimum order requirements for certain supplements.

ACKNOWLEDGMENTS

A key reason for the continued success of *Business Today* is an extensive market research effort. In this revision, the advice of hundreds of instructors around the country aided us in our attempt to create a textbook suited to the unique needs of the introductory business market. Our sincere thanks are extended to the individuals who responded to our market questionnaires.

We wish to extend a sincere appreciation to the professionals within the College Division of The McGraw-Hill Companies. The editorial, production, and design qualities of *Business Today,* Eighth Edition, are the result of

PART ONE

FOCUS ON BUSINESS TODAY

Chapter

1

Foundations of American Business

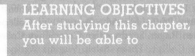

LEARNING OBJECTIVES
After studying this chapter, you will be able to

1 Explain what an economic system is

2 List the four factors of production

3 Name the three major types of economic systems and differentiate their identifying characteristics

4 Describe the relationship between profit and sales, and explain how profit motivates entrepreneurs

5 List three ways companies compete

6 Explain how supply and demand interact to influence prices

7 List the four major economic roles of the U.S. government

8 Identify six trends that will influence the economy in the years ahead

NFL Star Trades Shoulder Pads for Business Suits

Defensive players in the National Football League always showed a healthy respect for the running and catching abilities of Drew Pearson, a standout wide receiver for the Dallas Cowboys. Now his competitors in the business world are starting to show respect too.

Of course, Pearson didn't make an instant jump from football stardom to business stardom. His early efforts involved jobs commonly held by retired athletes (television broadcaster and assistant coach)—but Pearson wanted something more. As he put it: "I wanted to do something more productive during the week."

His chance came in 1986 in the form of Ken Shead, a recent all-star himself—as one of Xerox's top salespeople in the United States. Shead had been thinking about selling clothing and accessories with sports logos. He had a good idea but felt he needed a partner with a high profile that would get the company off the ground. Pearson's name and capacity for hard work and perseverance made him the perfect match. Pearson had already turned down numerous business offers as he neared the end of his NFL career, saying that star athletes get all kinds of opportunities to attach their names to various enterprises. He wanted to be an entrepreneur, not just a figurehead, and Shead's proposal fit the bill.

The new business, named Drew Pearson Companies (DPC), didn't exactly start off with a bang. While the pair and their other partners managed to generate $3 million in sales in the first 12 months, costs were so high that both men opted not to draw any salary that year. Like all new businesses, DPC faced a number of hurdles: getting its hands on enough money to finance operations and expansion, finding or making the right products to sell, and making sure it had channels of distribution to reach its customers. Pearson's celebrity status in Texas helped open some doors, but ultimately, DPC was given the same calculated scrutiny as all other new businesses.

If you were Drew Pearson, what would you do to help your company succeed? How could you take advantage of positive forces in a

The immense popularity and visibility of professional football combine to make NFL logos one of the hottest licensing properties around.

free-market economy? How would you minimize the impact of the negative ones? Would you be able to compete on something other than just price? What factors of production would you need, and how would you acquire them? In short, how would you repeat the success Pearson enjoyed on the playing field in the new field of business?[1]

SUCCESS IN A FREE-MARKET SYSTEM

Like hundreds of thousands of people before him, Drew Pearson recognized that the United States is a land of economic opportunity. The fact that he was even able to start a company is something that people in many other economies have never had the chance to do (at least until the last few years). Because Pearson's customers are free to buy or not buy his products, he has to offer more attractive products than his competitors offer. Moreover, by starting a new business, Pearson is running a substantial risk. Many businesses fail, even when the founder works hard and has a great product. Nevertheless, risk is what makes a success so much more enjoyable. We all have the chance to succeed—or fail—by our own efforts.

The Nature of Economic Systems

An **economic system** is a basic set of rules used to allocate a society's resources to satisfy its citizens' needs. The link between economy and society is crucial; every nation's economic system is shaped by its politics and social values. Yet even though every nation has a unique way of distributing resources, economic systems all have certain features in common and may be measured in similar ways.

Factors of Production

A society's resources are referred to by economists as the **factors of production.** One factor of production, **natural resources,** includes things that are useful in their natural state, such as land, forests, minerals, and water. The second, **labor,** consists of the human resources used to produce goods and services. (Note that you'll often hear the term *labor* used to refer specifically to unionized workers.) The third factor of production is **capital,** which includes the physical, human-made elements that can be used to produce goods and services, such as computers, robots, machines, tools, and buildings. (You'll also hear businesspeople refer to capital as the amount of money invested in a company or the amount of money available to invest.)

A fourth factor of production is entrepreneurship. **Entrepreneurs** are people like Drew Pearson, who develop ways to use the other factors of production more efficiently. They acquire materials, employ workers, and invest in capital goods. In some societies, entrepreneurs risk losing only their reputations or their positions if they fail. In the United States, entrepreneurs also risk losing their personal resources. On the other hand, U.S. entrepreneurs reap the benefits if they succeed. which motivates them to risk trying something new.

---

economic system *Means by which a society distributes its resources to satisfy its people's needs*

factors of production *Resources that a society uses to produce goods and services, including natural resources, labor, capital, and entrepreneurship*

natural resources *Land, forests, minerals, water, and other tangible assets usable in their natural states*

labor *Generally, the human resources used to produce goods and services; also used in a specific sense to refer to organized union workers*

capital *The physical, human-made elements used to produce goods and services, such as factories and computers; can also refer to the money invested in, or available to invest in, a business*

entrepreneurs *People who accept the risk of failure to organize the other three factors of production in order to produce goods and services more efficiently*

Accounting, marketing, production, personnel, government regulations, banking—the list of things today's businesspeople need to know about is long, to say the least. Well, you can add one more. For many companies today, advanced technology is as important as the bricks in the building and cash in the bank account. Technology has pervaded every aspect of the modern business operation, providing dramatic increases in productivity and competitiveness but also presenting some daunting training challenges.

Consider how computer and communications technology helps the Dovel Group, a Seattle-area provider of marketing services for companies in the computer and electronics industries. Company founder George Dovel runs the operation as a *virtual enterprise* that has no fixed organizational structure and no employees other than himself. For each client project, he assembles a team of specialists who can handle editing, graphic design, copywriting, or whatever other tasks are required. Technology is the link that holds everything together. As Dovel puts it: "My goal is to do top-notch work in the fastest way possible. Two factors make this goal possible: finding smart, flexible people to work with and

SUCCEEDING IN BUSINESS, ONE BYTE AT A TIME

thoughtfully applying technology to make us all more productive." In addition to the usual array of software for word processing and other functions, here are three key ways computer tools make the company's success possible:

- *Time management.* In service businesses, time translates directly into revenue. In fact, Dovel views time as his most important resource. "The only thing we can't replace or buy more of is time. An hour that slips away wasted is revenue lost forever." To squeeze the most out of every day, he uses a program called Above & Beyond, which charts out how he *should* spend each day, then analyzes how he actually *did* spend it. It's like budgeting, only with time instead of money.
- *Record and file management.* From academic research into marketing

topics to snippets of conversations to examples of good and bad advertising, Dovel and his team collect a constant stream of data and information. Keeping track of all this manually would consume enormous amounts of time, so the group created an index using database software. When someone needs everything on file about pricing, for instance, a few clicks with a mouse displays everything on that topic.

- *Long-distance communications.* Dovel has three computers in his office, all equipped with modems and software to tap into a variety of computer networks, including private corporate networks, commercial services such as CompuServe, and the Internet. This aspect of technology essentially erases the issue of geography. If an editor Dovel needs to work with is halfway across the country, he simply delivers the material electronically. In addition, it provides a great deal of personal flexibility. "More than once, I've sat on the beach with a laptop computer and worked on projects for clients hundreds or thousands of miles away. I still deliver the material via computer network as usual, so as far as they know, it looks like I'm sitting in my office the whole time. It's not a bad way to make a buck."

Although all economies rely on the same basic factors of production, not all are blessed with the same quantity and quality of resources. The United States and Canada are more fortunate than many countries and regions, having a wealth of land and raw materials, an industrious and well-educated workforce, a strong capital base, and an abundance of entrepreneurs. To a great extent, the prosperity of these two countries comes from their plentiful resources.

Increasingly, success in business rests on its **productivity,** on how efficiently a company can use the factors of production at its disposal. Productivity is addressed at all levels of an organization and in all business functions. Compaq (a computer company) and Southwest Airlines are among the most productive leaders in their industries, giving them a solid competitive advantage.

productivity *How efficiently available factors of production are used*

Economic Goals and Measurements
Each society's economic system reflects the country's history, traditions, aspirations, and politics. What works for one culture might not

An emphasis on productivity is one of the ways computer makers such as Dell work to keep prices competitive.

gross national product (GNP) *Total value of all the final goods and services produced by an economy over a given period of time; includes receipts from overseas operations of domestic companies, and excludes profits from foreign-owned businesses within a nation's borders*

gross domestic product (GDP) *Dollar value of all the final goods and services produced by an economy during a specified period (usually a year); includes profits from foreign-owned businesses within a nation's borders, and excludes receipts from overseas operations of domestic companies*

work as well for another. When measuring the success of different economic systems, the fairest approach is to apply the standards that are valued by the people of that culture. Such goals as economic stability, job security, and equality of income and opportunity are given higher priority in some cultures than others.

One of the measures traditionally used in the United States for keeping economic score is **gross national product (GNP),** the value of all outputs produced by domestically owned factors of production during a specified period (usually a year). GNP excludes profits from foreign-owned businesses within a nation's borders, and it includes receipts from overseas operations of domestic companies.[2]

You'll occasionally run across GNP figures, but since 1991, the United States (and virtually all other countries) now use a measure called **gross domestic product (GDP).** In contrast to GNP, GDP includes income from foreign-owned businesses within a nation's borders and excludes income from overseas operations of domestic companies. Put another way, GNP considers *who* is responsible for the production; GDP considers *where* the production occurs.

When GDP is compared over a number of years, patterns may appear. A rise in GDP is a sign of economic growth, indicating that the country has achieved at least one goal—a higher level of production, the benefits of which can be distributed to the people. GDP is also used to compare two or more economies. GDP figures can be adjusted for inflation and currency rates, but they may be misleading because of different population sizes. So economists often calculate

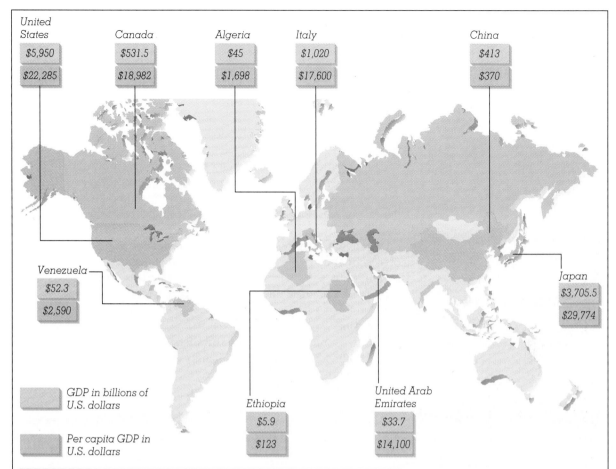

United States
$5,950
$22,285

Canada
$531.5
$18,982

Algeria
$45
$1,698

Italy
$1,020
$17,600

China
$413
$370

Venezuela
$52.3
$2,590

Japan
$3,705.5
$29,774

GDP in billions of U.S. dollars

Per capita GDP in U.S. dollars

Ethiopia
$5.9
$123

United Arab Emirates
$33.7
$14,100

per capita figures—a nation's total GDP divided by its population. With a GDP of roughly $6 trillion and a population of 260 million, the United States has a per capita GDP of about $23,000. Compare this with Canada, whose GDP of $531 billion (in U.S. dollars) and population of 28 million work out to a GDP per capita of $19,000 (in U.S. dollars).[3] Exhibit 1.1 compares GDP figures for a number of countries around the world. Keep in mind, however, that GDP measures strictly economic output. It can't tell you whether people are happier or healthier, nor does it measure a country's ability to keep producing in the future. For instance, value that results from harvesting natural resources boosts GDP in the short term, but the long-term impact may actually be decreased value if the resource can't be sustained or replaced.

In the United States, government policymakers and businesspeople use GDP to forecast trends and to analyze the economy's performance. Yet, even though GDP figures are widely used, many economists complain that they can be misleading for reasons other than differing population sizes. The GDP figures do not reflect the value of the **underground economy**—income from business activities that are legal but not reported to the government. In some less developed economies, underground sources of income make up a large portion of the GDP. Even in the United States, the underground economy is estimated to generate more than $500 billion a year.[4]

Exhibit 1.1
Total and Per Capita GDP in 10 Nations
The free-market system is one of the factors that has helped people in the United States develop one of the highest standards of living in the world, as measured by per capita GDP.

underground economy *Economic activity that is not reported, even though it is generated by legal activities*

bartering *Trading by exchanging goods or services directly rather than through a medium such as money*

Some critics also complain that the value of **bartering,** or trading, goods and services cannot easily be measured because money is not used in such transactions.

Types of Economic Systems

Regardless of exactly how they operate, all economic systems must deal with the same basic questions: How should limited economic resources be used to satisfy society's needs? What goods and services should be produced? Who should produce them? How should these goods and services be divided among the population? Such questions are addressed differently by the three main economic systems: capitalism, communism, and socialism (see Exhibit 1.2). The best way to distinguish between these systems is in terms of the freedom they give individuals to own the factors of production and to pursue their own economic interests. (Keep in mind that even though capitalism, communism, and socialism are referred to here as economic systems, they can be political and social systems as well.)

capitalism *Economic system based on economic freedom and competition*

Exhibit 1.2
Types of Economic Systems
Socialist economic systems are similar to capitalism in many respects, whereas communism is quite different in nearly all respects.

Capitalism

The U.S. economic system is **capitalism,** which permits a high degree of individual freedom. Capitalism owes its philosophical origins to eighteenth-century philosophers such as Adam Smith, who ad-

Factors	Capitalism	Communism	Socialism
Careers and employment	Every individual has right to choose occupation and place of employment.	Limited freedom in selecting occupations and places of employment; nearly everyone works for state.	Individuals free to select occupations and employment of their choice within state-controlled economy.
Business ownership	Private ownership of business and industry encouraged and sanctioned by government.	All industries and virtually all farms owned by state.	Major utilities, transportation, mining, and communications owned by government; mixture of private and public ownership.
Competition	Competition encouraged by state; monopolies forbidden unless government-regulated.	No competition, because government owns and controls all businesses and industries.	Competition encouraged in smaller businesses but restricted in key industries (usually owned by state).
Government planning	Business makes decisions independently of government but must conform to rules and regulations.	Master plan for major economic and business decisions.	Management of key industries must follow government plans.
Consumer choice	Goods and services sold at prices based on supply and demand; wide assortment available.	Limited choice of goods; prices (higher) determined by state.	Goods and services sold at prices based on supply and demand; wide assortment available.
Labor unions	Large-scale union participation with right to bargain collectively.	Labor unions function as information channels for communist party; no power to negotiate wages, hours, or benefits.	Large-scale union participation with right to bargain collectively.
Taxation	Medium taxation; right to influence by vote.	Heavy taxation in form of sales tax and large cost margins.	Heavy taxation; right to influence by vote.
Profits	All net profits kept by individual(s) incurring risk in business.	All "profits" (margins) go to state.	Businesses not owned by state may earn reasonable profits.

vanced the theory of **pure capitalism.** In the ideal capitalist economy, all production and allocation decisions are made by private holders of property or money. The market itself serves as a self-correcting mechanism, an "invisible hand," to ensure the production of the goods that society wants in the quantities that society wants, without anyone's ever issuing an order of any kind.[5] In reality, however, the government must sometimes intervene. Because the government can use its power to affect prices and wages or to change the way resources are allocated, the economic system of the United States may be called **mixed capitalism.**

pure capitalism Capitalism in its ideal state, in which all resource allocations are controlled by the unfettered operation of the free market

Even under mixed capitalism, private individuals are allowed to determine what is produced, by whom, and for whom. The pursuit of private gain is regarded as a worthwhile goal that ultimately benefits society as a whole. Other countries with variations of this economic system include Canada, Germany, and Japan.

mixed capitalism Economic system in which operation of the free market is influenced to some degree by government involvement

Capitalist economies like these operate under a **free-market system.** Thus, they are often called **market economies.** In essence, having a free-market system means that if you have something to sell, whether it's tractor parts or investment advice, you're free to charge any price you want and to sell to anyone willing to pay that price. Similarly, as a consumer, you're free to buy whatever you want and can afford from whomever you choose. The nature of the business conducted in such an economy is called **free enterprise.**

free-market system Economic system in which the way people spend their money determines which products will be produced and what those products will cost

market economies Economic systems in which goals are achieved by the action of the free market, with a minimum of government intervention

In a free-market system, independent entrepreneurs and entrepreneurial leaders of existing businesses play an important role. They look for unfulfilled needs and bring together the resources required to meet those needs. Therefore, business is a major partner in U.S. society.

free enterprise The nature of business in a free-market system

Communism

The system that allows individuals the least degree of economic freedom is **communism,** which is characterized by (1) state ownership of the factors of production and (2) planned resource allocation. The second feature is so important in these economies that they are frequently called planned economies. In a **planned economy,** social equality is a major goal, and private enterprise is generally regarded as wasteful and exploitative. Planned economies exist in such countries as North Korea and Cuba.

communism Economic system in which all productive resources are owned and operated by the government, to the elimination of private property

planned economy Economic system in which resource-allocation decisions are made by the central government

The degree to which communism is actually practiced varies from country to country. In its purest form, almost all factors of production are under state control. Private ownership is restricted largely to personal and household items. Resource allocation is handled through rigid centralized planning by a handful of government officials who decide what goods to produce, how to produce them, and to whom they should be distributed.

Planned economies have advantages and disadvantages. Unemployment and inflation can be controlled more easily. On the other hand, without the opportunity to get ahead, entrepreneurs like Drew Pearson have little incentive to develop new products or more efficient ways of doing things. As a consequence, goods and services that people in the United States take for granted are often difficult to ob-

Many people blame business for creating the lion's share of our pollution problems. According to conventional wisdom, greedy companies think nothing of exploiting the earth in their quest for profits. They'll dump toxic wastes in the rivers, strip the forests bare, dig huge open pits in the ground, and spew all sorts of vile stuff into the air. Oil spills and other high-profile incidents confirm the public's perception that the free-enterprise system and the protection of the environment are inherently at odds.

Fed up with big business, some people are pressing for stronger environmental rules and regulations and for tougher enforcement of laws already on the books. They argue that government intervention is required to stem the environmental abuses of capitalism. So, if capitalism causes pollution and if government intervention is the answer, you'd expect communist and former communist countries to be models of environmental purity, wouldn't you?

Yet these countries have some of the worst pollution in the world. Major cities in the former Soviet Union routinely dump untreated sewage and industrial wastes into the

DOES CAPITALISM CAUSE POLLUTION?

handiest body of water. The Volga River has so much oil floating on its surface that passengers on river boats are warned not to toss cigarettes in.

The picture is equally grim in Eastern Europe. The Polish railroad tracks are so damaged by acid rain that trains are not allowed to go over 24 miles an hour. Also, 95 percent of the water in Poland is unfit for human consumption; 65 percent can't even be used for industrial purposes because it's so toxic that it would destroy heavy metals used by industry. In what was formerly East Germany, 40 percent of the population suffers ill effects from air pollution; visitors have been known to vomit from simply breathing the air; and people often use their headlights in midday to see through the smog. In Slovakia

and the Czech Republic, the top 12 inches of much of the finest farmland is toxic, poisoned by overuse of fertilizers. Air pollution has destroyed 300,000 acres of forest; there's nothing left for 350 miles but stumps and skeletons of dying trees. The same problems haunt the cities and countryside in China, Bulgaria, Hungary, Romania, and the former Yugoslavia.

In other words, pollution is an expected by-product of industrialization and population growth, regardless of the economic or political systems in place in any particular country. In fact, when an economy is struggling, both consumers and government officials have limited opportunity to even think about environmental problems; they're focused on surviving from day to day.

So how can we fight pollution? The answer lies in having adequate government controls in place to prevent abuses, reducing consumption whenever possible, maintaining a strong economy that provides both businesses and consumers with enough income to afford the cost of safeguarding the environment, and listening to those consumers who are demanding more environmentally sensitive products.

tain in planned economies. For example, in some ex-Soviet cities, the typical wait for an apartment is 15 years.[6]

Although pure communism still has its supporters, the economic record of real-world communism is dismal. Because of such economic failure and the associated social unrest, many of the planned economies around the world are trying to shift in the direction of free-market policies. Poland is among the most promising of these. In the four years after communist rule ended there, entrepreneurs had started 1.5 million businesses. The country is one of the few in Eastern Europe to show any economic growth, and Polish businesspeople have proven to be smart, aggressive, and remarkably adept at adjusting to a more competitive market environment. Malgorzata Partala has established a successful clothing company with stores throughout Poland and is already setting her sights on Russia, another country struggling to convert to a free-market economy.[7]

In China, even as hardline communists battle to prevent political reform, the country's businesspeople are taking steady steps toward a more market-based economy. Transforming a planned economy into one based on free-market principles is a huge task, but China is making progress. Its economy has grown by an average of 9 percent per year for the last 15 years, and a million millionaires have emerged in a country that long shunned the pursuit of private wealth.[8]

Even so, such small steps aren't nearly enough for many businesspeople in Hong Kong. After 1997, Hong Kong will cease to be a British colony and will fall under the control of communist China. As a result, hundreds of thousands of businesspeople and their families are leaving Hong Kong.[9]

Socialism

The third major type of economic system is **socialism,** which lies somewhere between capitalism and communism in the degree of economic freedom that it permits. Like communism, socialism involves a relatively high degree of government planning and some government ownership of land and capital resources. Unlike communism, government involvement is limited to industries considered vital to the common welfare, such as transportation, utilities, medicine, steel, and communications. In these industries, the government owns or controls all the facilities and determines what will be produced and how the output will be distributed. Private ownership is permitted in industries that are not considered vital, and both businesses and individuals are allowed to benefit from their own efforts. However, taxes are high in socialist states because the government absorbs the costs of medical care, education, subsidized housing, and other social services.

Although socialist systems have a much better economic record than communist systems, they too have been leaning more in the direction of free-market economies. Countries from Great Britain to Mexico to Argentina have been selling off state-owned enterprises, including telephone companies and national airlines. Sweden, one of the most committed socialist countries in the world, has been forced to trim its generous social programs and push for more market-based competition among businesses. As prime minister Carl Bildt puts it: "You can only be a caring society if you've got a strong economy."[10]

ECONOMIC FORCES AFFECTING BUSINESS

Countries around the world are becoming more capitalistic because they're impressed with the prosperity that seems to accompany the free-market system. By and large, people in capitalistic countries enjoy higher standards of living than people in communist or socialist societies.

As we take a closer look at economic forces, it's important to recognize that you can view the business world at two levels. **Macroeconomics** looks at the economy as a whole, whereas **microeconomics** considers the actions of and the influences on specific parts

Yang Yian's nickname—Millionaire Yang—gives you an idea of the success he has had as one of China's new entrepreneurs.

socialism *Economic system characterized by public ownership and operation of key industries combined with private ownership and operation of less vital industries*

macroeconomics *Study of the economy as a whole*

microeconomics *Study of specific entities in the economy, such as households, companies, or industries*

of the economy, such as households, companies, or industries. For instance, a national unemployment trend is a macroeconomic issue, but unemployment in the auto industry is a microeconomic issue. Some of the issues you'll explore in this book are on the macroeconomic level (giving you the "big picture"); others are on the microeconomic level (concerning specific industries or companies).

The Profit Motive

profit Money left over after expenses and taxes have been deducted from revenue generated by selling goods or services

One of the foundations of free-market economies is **profit,** the difference between what it costs to produce and market something and what customers are willing to pay for it. If it costs you $1.00 to make a sandwich and you can sell the sandwich for $1.50, your gross profit is 50 cents. When Drew Pearson and his colleagues plan new products, the profit motive is a key force behind their actions.

Over the long term, profit is the primary goal of most business enterprises. However, many businesses at times choose to sacrifice short-term profits for the sake of long-term goals. This strategy helps explain the success of Japanese imports in U.S. markets. Many Japanese companies have been willing (and able) to postpone initial profits in order to keep their prices lower and thereby penetrate the U.S. market to a greater degree. As you can imagine, this is not an easy strategy to implement; you need deep pockets and patient investors.

Scarcity and Opportunity Cost

scarcity Shortage of desirable resources

One fact of economic life is that most resources are scarce. Only so much land, so many workers, and so much capital are available. Even the number of a business's potential customers is limited, and certainly their dollars are. Because of such **scarcity**—a shortage of desired resources—individuals and businesses are sometimes required to make hard economic choices. For example, if it's Friday night and you have $20 in your pocket, do you spend it on a good dinner? Do you use it to go shopping? Do you save it for future use? You may choose any of these options, but as soon as you spend that $20, it's gone—you can't do anything else with it.

opportunity cost Value of using a resource; measured in terms of the value of the next best alternative for using that resource

This simple concept is called **opportunity cost.** Say that you decided to spend the $20 on dinner. Not only would that decision cost you $20, but it would also cost you the opportunity of buying something else. Even if a friend invited you to dinner so that you could save your $20, the time you spend at dinner would not be available for other pursuits. In other words, whenever resources are limited, the decision to use some of those resources means that they will not be available for other, perhaps more worthwhile, uses. The true cost of making an economic decision to attend college, for example, is not only the cost of tuition but also the value of the next best alternative that can't be chosen, such as to buy a new car or to take a trip to Australia.

Competition

competition Rivalry between two or more suppliers who are pursuing the same customers

Just as scarcity is an economic fact of life, so is **competition,** the situation in which two or more suppliers of a product are rivals in the pursuit of the same customers. If you set out to sell a product or service in a free-market society, chances are that someone else will be trying to sell something similar. Because potential customers are free to buy where they please, you must compete with your rivals for those customers. You might choose to compete in one of three ways: price, quality, or innovation.

Competition and Price

Evidence of price competition is everywhere you look. Fast-food restaurants sell special meal deals at reduced prices, carmakers offer rebates and discounts, stereo stores offer to beat any other price in town—these are examples of trying to gain a competitive advantage through price. When markets become filled with competitors and products start to look alike, price becomes a company's key competitive weapon.

Competing on price seems an obvious and easy choice to make, but the consequences can be devastating to individual companies and to entire industries. During a three-year period in the early 1990s, price wars caused the U.S. airline industry to lose more money than it had made since the Wright brothers' first flight. It's an astonishing statistic: losing more money in 3 years than the industry had made in almost 90. Things got so bad by 1993 that a presidential commission was established to find ways to help the airlines. Still, they seem trapped; in the summer of 1994, fare wars pushed prices down another 30 percent.[11]

The harsh truth of many price wars is that sooner or later, everybody will be selling at a loss. Companies that are vulnerable to price wars are desperately looking for ways to survive. They seem to have only two alternatives: They can structure their company in a way that lets them produce goods or services at a lower cost, or they can find ways to add unique value to their products so that they can compete on something other than price, such as quality, service, or innovation.

Competition, Quality, and Service

Instead of cutting prices, a business may decide to compete for customers by offering higher-quality goods or better service than its rivals offer. Best Buy, a major consumer electronics retailer, gained a competitive advantage by taking its salespeople off commission and putting them on straight salary. The salespeople were less inclined to push customers toward specific purchases, a service improvement that consumers appreciate.[12]

A business that competes on the basis of quality or service may well end up with a total profit that's equal to or greater than the profit of a business that competes on price. This possibility provides a practical incentive for businesses to maintain high standards, and it increases the choices available to consumers. For instance, Best Buy doubled its revenues in three years. Its customers spend less per visit

Service stations that have installed self-service credit-card readers attract customers who enjoy the speed and convenience of paying at the pump.

than customers at archrival Circuit City ($115 versus $250), but Best Buy comes out ahead in the number of transactions per day at each store (500 versus 190). In other words, the soft-sell approach pulls in an average of $57,500 per day, compared with Circuit City's $47,500.[13]

Competition and Innovation

In addition to encouraging variations in quality and price, the free-market system also encourages immense variety in the types of goods and services offered to the public. Changes in popular taste, technology, the economy, and the competitive environment are constantly creating new business opportunities. The possibility of profit, however remote, attracts entrepreneurs willing to risk their time or money. The result is an astonishing tendency toward innovation and diversity of businesses. Almost anything you might want to buy—any product or service, no matter how obscure—is probably sold somewhere. Most of the competition in advanced free-market economies is **monopolistic competition,** in which a large number of sellers (none of which dominates the market) offer products that can be distinguished from competing products in at least some small way.

Supply and Demand

As we have seen, the competitive strategies of rival businesses influence prices in a free-market system. These competitive strategies are usually influenced by the forces of supply and demand. In economic terms, **supply** refers to the quantities of a good or service that producers will provide on a particular date at various prices. **Demand** refers to the amount of a good or service that consumers will buy at that time at various prices.

On the surface, the theory of supply and demand seems little more than common sense. Consumers would buy more when the price is low and less when the price is high. Producers would offer more when the price is high and less when the price is low. In other words, the quantity supplied and the quantity demanded would continuously interact, and the balance between them at any given moment would be reflected by the current price on the open market.

However, a quick look at any real-life market situation shows you that pricing isn't that simple. To a large degree, pricing depends on the type of product being sold. When the price of gasoline goes up, consumers may cut down a little, but most won't stop driving, even if the price were to double. In the same way, you're not going to stop taking your medicine just because the price goes up—and you wouldn't take more just because the price happened to go down. Moreover, from a producer's perspective, a drop in price can lead to more production, not less. Assume that you need sales of $10,000 a day just to keep your factory open and that you've been selling an average of 2,000 products a day priced at $5. If the price you can charge the market drops to $4, you'll try to increase sales to 2,500 products a day to maintain the $10,000 level.

Nevertheless, in broad terms, supply and demand regulate a free-market system by determining what is produced and in what amounts. For example, a movie studio might produce more comedies if ticket

---

monopolistic competition *Situation in which many sellers offer products that differ from competing products in at least some small way*

supply *Specific quantity of a product that the seller is able and willing to provide at various prices at a given time*

demand *Specific quantity of a product that consumers are willing and able to buy at various prices at a given time*

sales for similar films are brisk. On the other hand, it might decide to produce fewer comedies and more action adventure movies if attendance at comedies lags. The result of such decisions—in theory, at least—is that consumers will get what they want and producers will earn a profit by keeping up with public demand.

Price from the Buyer's Point of View

The forces of supply and demand determine the market price for products and services. Say that you're shopping for blue jeans, and the pair you want is priced at $35. This is more than you can afford, so you don't make the purchase. When the store puts them on sale the following week for $18, however, you run right in and buy a pair.

But what if the store had to buy the jeans from the manufacturer for $20. It would have made a profit selling them to you for $35, but it would lose money selling them for $18. What if the store asks to buy more from the manufacturer at $10 or $15 but the manufacturer refuses? Is there a price that will make both the supplier and the customer happy? The answer is yes—the price at which the number of jeans demanded equals the number supplied.

This relationship is shown in Exhibit 1.3. A range of possible prices is listed vertically at the left of the graph, with the lowest at the bottom and the highest at the top. Quantity of blue jeans is represented along the horizontal axis. The points plotted on the line labeled **D** indicate that on a given day the store would sell 10 pairs of jeans if they were priced at $35, 15 pairs if they were priced at $30, and so on. The line that describes this relationship between price and quantity demanded is a **demand curve.** (Demand curves are not necessarily curved; they may be straight lines.)

Price from the Seller's Point of View

Now, think about the situation from the retailer's point of view. In general, the more profit the store can make on a particular item, the more of that item it will want to sell. This relationship can also be depicted graphically. Again, look at Exhibit 1.3. The line labeled **S** shows that the store would be willing to offer 30 pairs of jeans at $35, 25 pairs at $30, and so on. The store's willingness to carry the item increases as the price it can charge and its profit potential per item increase. In other words, as price goes up, quantity supplied goes up (aside from the special situations described earlier; this set of curves would look much different for insulin or heating oil). The line tracing the relationship between price and quantity supplied is called a **supply curve.**

As much as the store would like to sell 30 pairs of jeans at $35, you and your fellow consumers are likely to want only 10 pairs at that price. If the store offered 30 pairs, therefore, it would probably be stuck with some that it would have to mark down. How does the store avoid this problem? It looks for the point at which the demand curve and the supply curve intersect, the point at which the intentions of buyers and sellers coincide. The point marked **E** in Exhibit 1.3 shows that when jeans are priced at $25, consumers are willing to buy 20 pairs of them and the store is willing to sell 20 pairs. In other words, at the price of $25, supply and demand are in balance.

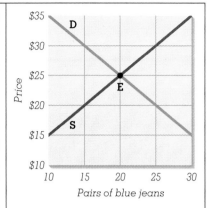

Exhibit 1.3

The Relationship Between Supply and Demand

In a free-market system, prices aren't set by the government; nor do producers alone have the final say. Instead, prices reflect the interaction of supply (**S**) *and demand* (**D**)*. The equilibrium price* (**E**) *is established when the amount of a product that producers are willing to sell at a given price equals the amount that consumers are willing to buy at that price.*

demand curve *Series of points on a graph showing the relationship between price and quantity demanded*

supply curve *Series of points on a graph showing the relationship between price and quantity supplied*

The price at this point is known as the **equilibrium price.**

Note that this intersection represents both a specific price—$25 in our example—and a specific quantity of goods—here, 20 pairs of jeans. It is also tied to a specific point in time. Note also that it is the mutual interaction between demand and supply that determines the equilibrium price. In a purely free-market economy, no outside interference disrupts that interaction.

As time passes, equilibrium points between supply and demand may shift. In the blue-jeans business, clothing styles may change or other retailers may mark down their jeans and attract your customers. When supply and demand shift, you need to reevaluate the profit potential of the jeans and adjust your buying and pricing policies accordingly.

Circular Flow

So far, this discussion has focused on the economic forces that affect individuals and businesses. However, some economic forces affect society as a whole. Perhaps the most important force affecting all of society is **circular flow,** which describes the movement of all resources within an economy. Just as the bloodstream carries oxygen to the body's cells and carbon dioxide from those cells back to the lungs, the economy carries goods and services, which are exchanged for money (see Exhibit 1.4):

1. Goods and services flow from businesses to households; households generate a return flow of money as compensation for these goods. Goods and services also flow from businesses to other businesses.
2. Governments provide goods and services (such as roads, courts, and education) to households and businesses, which send a return flow of money in the form of taxes.
3. At the same time, households provide services to businesses in the form of labor and receive a return flow of money in the form of wages and salaries.

The flow of money also involves saving and investing. As a group, people in the United States have historically saved approximately

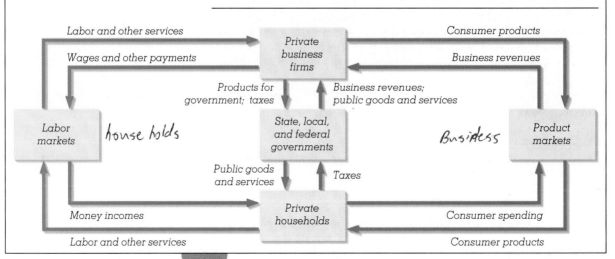

5 percent of their household income. This money is invested in bank accounts, stocks, bonds, and other forms of savings. Much of it eventually wends its way through the banking system and securities markets and ends up in businesses, where it can be used for capital improvements. Many economists are concerned because people in the United States tend to save a smaller percentage of their incomes than people in other industrial countries. This tendency means that U.S. companies have a relatively harder time financing expansion. To make matters worse, the household savings rate in the United States has declined in the last few years.[14]

As business becomes more international in scope, the flow of capital, labor, raw materials, and goods and services is taking on a global dimension. Companies in the United States employ foreign labor, build plants in other countries, sell their products abroad, and obtain capital from foreign investors. As a result, the flow of money is becoming increasingly dependent on decisions and events over which U.S. companies have relatively little control. Thus U.S. prosperity—or lack of it—depends on what happens in places like Japan, Germany, Saudi Arabia, Australia, Poland, China, Mexico, and Canada.

The Multiplier Effect

The circular-flow diagram shows that all elements of the U.S. economy are linked. Because of the interrelationships, any change in one part of the economic system creates changes elsewhere. If the U.S. government decides to purchase some missiles to defend the nation's borders, some missile-plant workers will have more income. If some of these workers decide to spend the extra income on new boats, boatbuilders will have more income. The boatbuilders, in turn, might spend this income on beer, and the brewers might spend it on cars. The **multiplier effect** is how all economic decisions ripple through the system (see Exhibit 1.5). Money never stays in one place, and every market decision has an impact on other markets.

The multiplier effect operates in the opposite direction as well, which can be devastating. When U.S. government defense spending began to drop in the late 1980s, California lost an estimated 330,000 aerospace and defense industry jobs. The industry accounts for 13 percent of all jobs in California (20 percent or more in Los Angeles and Orange counties), and it's not hard to imagine the impact of cutting off that many personal incomes.[15] Virtually every sector of the economy and society is affected, from housing to food to education.

THE ROLE OF GOVERNMENT

Although the market system generally works well, it's far from perfect. If left unchecked, the economic forces that make capitalism succeed may also create severe problems for some groups or individuals. The solution to these problems often requires government intervention. This intervention takes four basic forms: enforcing rules and regulations, providing public goods and transfer payments, fostering competition, and contributing to economic stability.

multiplier effect Chain reaction whereby a change in one economic variable affects other variables, resulting in a ripple of changes throughout an economic system

Exhibit 1.5

Multiplier Effect

All economic decisions ripple through the economy. Spending 75 percent of each additional amount of revenue in each cycle would yield a series of spending cycles like this one. Keep in mind that the multiplier can work the other way, too—as it did when the government cut spending on missiles and other military hardware.

Hypothetical spending cycles	Amount spent (in billions)		Cumulative amount spent (in billions)
First cycle: Government buys $100 billion worth of missiles.	$100	Missiles	$100
Second cycle: Missile workers have more income, spend it on $75 billion worth of new boats.	$75	Boats	$175
Third cycle: Boatbuilders have more income, spend it on $56 billion in beer.	$56	Beer	$231
Fourth cycle: Brewery workers buy $42 billion worth of new cars.	$42	Cars	$273
Fifth cycle: Autoworkers spend $32 billion on air travel.	$32	Air travel	$305
Sixth cycle: Airline personnel buy $24 billion worth of bicycles.	$24	Bicycles	$329
Seventh cycle and beyond: Additional spending adds another $71 billion in sales.	$71	Additional	$400

Enforcing Rules and Regulations

The federal government creates thousands of new rules and regulations every year.[16] Moreover, state and local governments are adding their own provisions to the body of rules that limit what businesses and consumers can and cannot do. For the most part, these regulations just keep piling up, since relatively few of them are ever officially rescinded. So the hand of government affects business activities, from applying for permits and licensing to start a business, all the way through to the design of packaging and advertising. Some legislation, such as the Clean Air Act and the Nutrition Labeling and Education Act, forced businesses to enact changes that cost millions and perhaps billions of dollars. The burden of regulation falls particularly hard on small companies, which often lack the legal and administrative resources to keep up with new rules.

Government rules and regulations restrict the freedom of the marketplace. As a consumer, you can't buy some medications without a doctor's prescription; you can't buy alcoholic beverages without a certificate proving that you're old enough; and you can't buy certain products lacking safety features, such as cars without seatbelts and medication without childproof tops. Some goods (such as endangered animal species) and services (such as contract murder) aren't legally available at all.

Companies and individuals are also required to share their profits with the government. Whether those profits take the form of corporate earnings, stock dividends, personal wages, or winnings from a lottery, they are taxed, and the money is used by the government.

Just as government bodies create new regulations year after year, they sometimes seek to remove existing regulations through the process of **deregulation.** Deregulation can have a dramatic impact on an industry. Look at U.S. telephone service. Before the U.S. government broke up AT&T in 1984 (Bell Atlantic, BellSouth, Nynex, and the other regional Bell companies all used to be part of AT&T), no one was allowed to compete with AT&T for long-distance service. At the same time, AT&T was not allowed to sell computers and other products except for telephones. Deregulation changed all that. Long-distance phone service is now one of the most highly competitive industries in the country, and AT&T is a leading supplier of computers and other high-technology products.[17]

deregulation *Process of removing existing regulations*

Providing Public Goods and Transfer Payments

Although everybody hates to pay taxes, most of us are willing to admit they're a necessary evil. If the government didn't take your tax money and buy national defense, would you be inclined to invest in a missile of your own? Similarly, it might not be practical to rely on individual demand to provide police and fire protection, to build roads, or to launch satellites. Instead, the government steps in and supplies such **public goods.**

public goods *Goods or services that can be supplied more efficiently by government than by individuals or businesses*

In addition, U.S. society recognizes that some individuals aren't capable of supplying enough labor to provide themselves a decent standard of living. Individuals could each contribute voluntarily to care for these people, but the government takes care of that. The government collects "contributions" in the form of taxes from those who are capable of supporting themselves and distributes the money to the less self-sufficient in the form of **transfer payments** such as Social Security, food stamps, welfare, and unemployment compensation. The individuals who receive these allocations are usually not required to provide any goods or services in return.

transfer payments *Payments by government to individuals that are not made in return for goods and services*

Fostering Competition

Because competition generally benefits the U.S. economy, the United States has laws to ensure that no single enterprise becomes too powerful. The theoretical ideal is **pure competition,** in which no single firm or group of firms in an industry is large enough to influence prices and thereby distort the workings of the free-market system.

pure competition *Situation in which so many buyers and sellers exist that no single buyer or seller can control the price of a product or the number of units sold*

In practice, however, pure competition works better in some industries than in others. Compare the dry-cleaning business with the auto industry. The nature of dry cleaning is such that small, independent firms operating on a local level are efficient. This is not the case in the auto industry, where economies of scale (cost efficiencies made possible by making or buying thousands of identical or similar products) favor large manufacturers. An industry of this type, dominated by just a few producers, is called an **oligopoly.** Although oligopolies themselves are not illegal, the law prohibits oligopolists from artificially setting prices by agreeing among themselves. In addition, the government has the power to prevent combinations of firms that would reduce competition and lead to oligopolistic conditions in an industry.

oligopoly *Market dominated by a few producers*

For the world. By the world.

Boeing is America's leading exporter, and has been for the last three years. Airlines in more than 140 countries fly Boeing airplanes. But we are a major *customer* as well as a major *supplier*. For example, we buy goods and services from some 30,000 firms with facilities and employees in every state in the U.S. and in 31 nations around the world.

For information on Boeing's role in the global economy, write to Corporate Communications, FW, PO Box 3707, MS 10-06, Seattle, WA 98124-2207.

BOEING

The commercial aircraft industry, led by Seattle-based Boeing, is an example of an oligopoly market.

monopoly *Market in which there are no direct competitors so that one company dominates*

antitrust laws *Federal regulations that prohibit most monopolies*

Restrictions are also imposed to prevent the development of a monopoly in any particular industry or market. A **monopoly** is a company that has total control over products and prices and keeps other companies from competing. (Some monopolies, such as utilities, are legal but closely regulated.) Because true monopolies undermine the principle of competition, they are prohibited by federal **antitrust laws** and have been a subject of continuing government concern since the turn of the century.

A number of factors apart from government intervention help prevent the development of oligopolies and monopolies. In many instances, consumers and businesses can find substitute goods or services if the prices in one industry are too high. When the price of copper went up, the telecommunications industry turned to new technology (fiber optics) that didn't depend on copper wire and cable. Even if there are no domestic substitutes, consumers and businesses can often purchase foreign products, thereby discouraging oligopolists from raising prices.

In fact, many foreign governments prefer to have only one or two major companies in industries where economies of scale provide a distinct advantage. They argue that the larger firms will have a better chance of competing in the world market. U.S. producers facing this type of competition from abroad argue against strict enforcement of antitrust laws. Some even advocate the development of a national industrial policy that would cultivate specific industries and technologies vital to international competitiveness. Under such a policy, the government would foster cooperation among U.S. companies so that they would be better able to compete on a global scale.

Contributing to Economic Stability

An economy never stays exactly the same size. Instead, it grows and contracts in response to the combined effects of such factors as technological breakthroughs, changes in investment patterns, shifts in consumer attitudes, world events, and basic economic forces. Since 1854 economists have charted more than 30 distinct cycles of growth and decline in our economy. On the average, the periods of expansion have lasted about three years, while the periods of contraction, or **recession,** have averaged 11 months, creating an upward trend overall.[18]

These up-and-down swings are known as the **business cycle.** Although such swings are natural and to some degree predictable, they cause hardship. Once consumers start to buy less, factories must produce less, so companies must lay off workers, who in turn buy less—and so on. In an attempt to avoid such problems and to foster economic stability, the government adjusts the tax system, interest rates, and the total amount of money circulating in our economy. These government actions have two facets: **Fiscal policy** involves changes in the government's revenues and expenditures to stimulate or dampen the economy. **Monetary policy** involves adjustments to the nation's money supply by increasing or decreasing interest rates. In the United States, monetary policy is controlled primarily by the Federal Reserve Board, a group of appointed government officials who oversee the country's central banking system. (Monetary policy is discussed more fully in Chapter 18.)

Employment and Unemployment

When the U.S. economy is strong, it has historically been able to employ about 95 percent of the people who are willing and able to work. During downturns in the business cycle, however, unemployment may become a major economic and social problem. The most extreme case in this century came during the Great Depression of the 1930s, when unemployment affected as much as 25 percent of the labor force. Today's welfare programs did not exist then, so most of the unemployed and their families went hungry. Since then, the United States has been able to maintain higher levels of employment, largely through the decisions of fiscal policy. For half a century now, whenever business activity has fallen off and large numbers of people have lost their jobs, people in the United States have encouraged government to borrow and spend money in order to keep businesses in operation and people employed.

Unfortunately, despite the past effectiveness of such fiscal policy, recent economic conditions make it more difficult to intervene in the business cycle. The government is already spending far more than it's taking in—on the order of several hundred billion dollars every year. This budget deficit raises several concerns. First, when the government borrows to finance various programs, it competes with busi-

recession *Period during which national income, employment, and production all fall*

business cycle *Fluctuations in the rate of growth that an economy experiences over a period of several years*

fiscal policy *Use of government revenue collection and spending to influence the business cycle*

monetary policy *Actions taken by the Federal Reserve Board to influence the economy by controlling the money supply; the Fed's primary tool is the manipulation of interest rates*

ness and personal borrowing. The nation has only so much money available for investment, and if the government, businesses, and consumers are all trying to borrow the same funds, somebody loses out. When government borrowing crowds out business and private borrowing, the economy suffers a decline in both capital and consumer spending. This, in turn, has a depressing effect on the GDP.[19] The second major concern is the amount of the GDP that must be used to pay interest on government debt. If you've ever run up a big balance on a credit card and been forced to pay substantial interest charges every month, you understand what a financial drain these interest payments can be.

In spite of these concerns, however, some experts support the controversial position that the deficit isn't as harmful to the economy as most people think. Moreover, people employed by government programs or as a result of government spending will be putting money into the economy, helping a wide variety of businesses. The deficit question is a great illustration of how complex the study of national and global economies really is.

Inflation and Disinflation

inflation Economic condition in which prices rise steadily throughout the economy

disinflation Economic condition in which the rate of inflation declines

Inflation is a steady rise of the prices of goods and services throughout the economy. When prices in the overall economy decline, economists use the term **disinflation.** The main influence on inflation and disinflation is monetary policy, which is why the Federal Reserve keeps a close eye on interest rates. When it raised interest rates several times during 1994, for instance, the Fed was trying to keep inflation in check by controlling access to credit.[20]

Although prices in the overall economy tend to increase year after year, not all industries and product categories necessarily follow this trend. Technological advancements can generate dramatic price reductions over time. In the personal-computer industry, for instance, prices tend to drop so much that some people put off buying as long as possible, knowing that products will almost always get cheaper. Price wars have fueled the decline in computer prices from time to time, but the fundamental fact remains that advancements in technology have made computers much less expensive. Pet food is another good example. Over the decade from 1984 to 1994, H. J. Heinz Pet Products cut the prices it charged retailers by 22 percent. Fortunately for Heinz, it has managed to cut its production costs by 30 percent.[21]

cartel Association of producers that attempts to control a market and keep prices high by limiting output and dividing market shares among the members

In contrast, prices in a particular industry can also increase faster than average. In the petroleum industry, for example, the Organization of Petroleum Exporting Countries (OPEC) can decide to limit production. With so much of the world's oil production under OPEC's influence, prices the world over are affected by this **cartel**—a producers' group that tries to control prices by controlling production levels.

SHIFTS IN THE ECONOMIC CLIMATE

The role of government is a reasonably constant fact of economic life—as are such economic forces as the profit motive, scarcity and opportunity costs, competition, supply and demand, circular flow, and the multiplier effect. Businesspeople take such factors into account when planning how to operate a business, even though they can't control the economic impact. By matching data from recent trends with fundamental economic forces, forecasters try to project trends into the future (see Exhibit 1.6). At the same time, however, businesspeople must cope with unexpected shifts in the economy, which have occurred throughout our nation's history and will undoubtedly continue into the future.

The History of Our Economy's Growth

The first economic base in the United States was the small family farm. People grew enough food for their families and used any sur-

	1994	2010
Our planet		
World population	5.607 billion	7.32 billion
World economy	$26 trillion	$48 trillion
World trade	$4 trillion	$16.6 trillion
Consumer inflation	4.3 percent	2.5 percent
Average income per capita		
Developed countries	$16,610	$22,802
Emerging market nations	$950	$2,563
Number of nations	192	202
Number of people living in poverty	2.7 billion	3.9 billion
Number of AIDS cases	20 million	38 million
Average number of children per woman	3.2	2.7
Average life expectancy		
Men	63	67
Women	67	71
Work and play		
World telephone lines		
Wired	607 million	1.4 billion
Wireless	34 million	1.3 billion
Personal computers		
Worldwide	150 million	278 million
Desktop computers	132 million	230 million
Mobile computers	18 million	47 million
Communications satellites	1,100	2,260
Cars produced annually		
Developed countries	20 million	30 million
Emerging market nations	8 million	30 million
McDonald's restaurants	14,000	30,000
Credit-card transactions	1.5 trillion	2 trillion
Air-travel miles	1.5 trillion	3 trillion
U.S. golf courses	14,648	16,800
Movie screens		
United States	25,105	74,114
Worldwide	86,902	162,766
U.S. gambling revenues	$39.5 billion	$125.6 billion
What we'll pay		
Dollar's value abroad	1.0	9.33
U.S. single-family home	$153,000	$287,000
Wharton School of Business M.B.A.	$ 84,200	$257,200
Mercedes E320 Sedan	$ 43,975	$ 70,600
Ford Contour	$ 13,310	$ 21,000

Exhibit 1.6
Facing the Future
Businesspeople can use predictions such as these to devise strategies and get their companies ready for the future.

plus to trade for necessary goods provided by independent crafts-people and merchants. Business operated on a small scale, and much of the population was self-employed. With fertile, flat terrain and adequate rainfall, farmers soon prospered, and their prosperity spread to the townspeople who served them.

In the early nineteenth century, people began making greater use of the rivers, harbors, and rich mineral deposits. Excellent natural resources helped businesspeople accumulate the capital they needed to increase production. Saving played an important role in the European tradition, and in the United States, this tradition contributed to the habit of putting something aside today for the tools needed tomorrow.

By the mid-nineteenth century, the United States had begun the transition from a farm-based economy to an industrial economy. Entrepreneurs brought together the capital, technology, and labor required for heavy industrialization. The scale of business began to shift. Independent craftspeople were replaced by large-scale factories in which each person did one simple task over and over. The trend toward mass production and the division of labor was fueled by the arrival of millions of new workers who came to the United States from abroad.

As businesses increased in size, they increased in power. More and more industrial assets were concentrated in fewer and fewer hands, putting smaller competitors, workers, and consumers at a disadvantage. By popular mandate, the government passed laws and regulations to prevent the abuse of power by big business. At the same time, workers began to organize into unions to balance the power of their employers. The Great Depression of the 1930s further strengthened the hand of government and labor as people lost confidence in the power of business to pull the country out of hard times.

World War II and the postwar reconstruction revived the economy and renewed the trend toward large-scale enterprises. The government, accustomed to playing a major role in the war effort, continued to exert a large measure of control over business and the economy. Stimulated by a boom in world demand and an expansive political climate, the country prospered throughout the 1960s.

Then, as Western Europe and Japan gradually grew stronger, the United States entered an era of diminishing growth. Ironically, the United States had supplied its foreign competitors with the resources and know-how to stake a claim in the world marketplace. Inflation soared while the economy stagnated. The Vietnam War dulled U.S. optimism and made people question the wisdom of both big business and big government.

Throughout the 1980s, competition from abroad continued to increase. Business responded with an often ruthless effort to regain its competitive edge. Entire industries virtually disappeared. Some giant corporations gobbled one another up; others splintered into fragments. Hundreds of thousands of jobs were eliminated. During this period of upheaval, a subtle shift occurred. Small companies began reasserting their role in the economy, generating new jobs to employ some of the workers abandoned by large corporations.

Now, as the country approaches the twenty-first century, U.S. businesses have reasserted themselves through improved product quality and a focus on productivity. The computer industry, one of the largest segments of the global economy, is led by U.S. companies. The U.S. auto industry has pushed itself through a remarkable turnaround and is poised for a positive future. The vast U.S. service sector is also reaching around the world, offering banking, telecommunications, and other services to a growing list of customers.

The Challenges Ahead

The U.S. economy has by no means reached the limits of its potential. It still has natural resources, labor, and capital that can be used more productively, and U.S. businesspeople seem to have an unlimited capacity for the kind of entrepreneurial vision that allows people like Drew Pearson to bring resources together to create needed goods and services as well as new jobs.

The next century will provide new problems and opportunities for companies and their employees. Forces you'll need to consider range from the global economy to competing on speed, quality, and customer satisfaction. A whole range of factors are already changing the ways companies do business, and they promise to continue changing the business environment for years to come.

The Global Economy

The economies of the world will continue to merge as multinational corporations continue to invest overseas and expand through international partnerships. The lines between exports and imports will blur as companies become more international in scope. It's already difficult to define just what an "American car" means, when so many parts come from other countries. The United States will continue to face strong competition from Western Europe, Japan, and newly industrialized countries such as Taiwan, Korea, and Singapore. At the same time, the growth of free-market economies in Eastern Europe, the former Soviet Union, and Latin America will continue providing U.S. businesses with new opportunities as well as new challenges. Third World countries will continue to supply raw materials and basic commodities. *The challenge:* Without resorting to the sorts of trade restrictions that would harm consumers or increase tensions among nations, the United States must find ways to keep businesses healthy and workers employed. To remain competitive, businesses must continue their efforts to control costs and boost quality.

Accelerating Technological Development

As older industries are transferred to lower-wage regions of the globe, the United States will rely more heavily on technology as its chief competitive weapon. New fields such as biotechnology, information systems, robotics, lasers, fiber optics, and composite materials will serve as the mainsprings of economic

As a result of the high-tech revolution, employees need continual training on new technologies. This technician at Lawrence Livermore National Labs in Livermore, California, is learning how to operate a laser fusion system.

growth. Developments will occur rapidly in these fields, putting a premium on our ability to respond quickly and reap a profit before a particular level of technology becomes obsolete. With the help of computers and sophisticated telecommunications equipment, employees will be increasingly free to work in scattered locations. *The challenge:* In the process of adopting new technology, businesses must consider the needs of their employees, their customers, and society in general in order to minimize the negative impact of change.

Social, Ethical, and Environmental Concerns

All businesses are forces that extend beyond simple economics. They affect the lives of people everywhere, and business leaders will continue to consider a wide variety of social, ethical, and environmental issues. Many people, both inside and outside the business world, expect businesses to behave in ways that benefit, or at least don't actively harm, society. As businesses become more complex through global expansion and technological change, they face an increasing variety of ethical issues, from the marketing of unhealthy products to the tactics used in computing financial results. Environmental issues are high on the list of consumer concerns, and rightly or wrongly, business gets blamed for causing many environmental troubles. The horrific pollution problems in former communist countries illustrate that in a sense, a healthy environment and a healthy economy are not only compatible but interdependent. Businesses can expect continued pressure from both environmental groups and government regulators. *The challenge:* Businesses must find ways to behave in socially and ethically responsible ways that also minimize environmental impact—while maintaining acceptable profit and employment levels.

A Diverse Workforce and a Diverse Consumer Market

Consider the view that for years, U.S. business strategy and practice were based on a model of white men running companies that sold products to white women who stayed at home raising the children. Although such a view is oversimplified, it's eye-opening to look back at predictions made in the 1950s for life in the 1990s and beyond. All kinds of technological breakthroughs were envisioned, but nearly all the visionaries missed the profound social changes of the last several decades. Women, ethnic minorities, and immigrants are rising through the ranks of corporations and starting their own businesses, although not as fast as many people would like to see. The traditional family of a stay-at-home wife with two or three children now represents less than half of all U.S. households. Stepfamilies will be the most common type of household by 2000. In London, fewer than 30 percent of households have children.[22] These changes affect both the way businesses are run and the markets they sell products to. *The challenge:* To succeed in the face of growing cultural diversity, businesses must find effective ways to lead diverse groups of employees and sell their products to a diverse consumer market.

The Strategic Value of Information

Businesspeople realize that the more they know about their customers and their competitors, the greater their chances of success. Businesses around the world spend billions of dollars on computer-based information systems in an attempt to collect, organize, and use information more effectively. The benefits of successful information management include more accurate identification of potential customers, more efficient marketing, and greater customer satisfaction. *The challenge:* Businesses must find cost-effective ways to manage information without overloading the people who need to use it, without getting lost in meaningless data, and without being controlled by it.

Competing on Speed, Quality, and Customer Satisfaction

One of the most perplexing business issues in a highly competitive market is that customers have numerous products to choose from, most or all of which will be perfectly satisfactory. Someone shopping for a car or a personal computer, for instance, can choose from dozens of brands, and nearly all will meet the person's needs. From a business management perspective, you face the tough challenge of getting and keeping customers when your basic product isn't all that different from your competitor's. For many businesses, the secret will be to compete on the basis of *time* (getting products to market sooner), *quality* (doing a better job of meeting customer expectations), and *customer satisfaction* (making sure buyers are happy with every aspect of the purchase, from the shopping experience until they're through using the product). *The challenge:* To compete on these factors, businesses must have skill, motivation, and drive from the top of the company to the bottom, excelling in every function while making as few mistakes as possible.

SUMMARY OF LEARNING OBJECTIVES

1 Explain what an economic system is.
An economic system is a society's way of producing, distributing, and marketing the goods and services desired by its population.

2 List the four factors of production.
Natural resources, labor, capital, and entrepreneurship are the four factors of production.

3 Name the three major types of economic systems and differentiate their identifying characteristics.
Under capitalism, the factors of production are owned by individuals, who make the business decisions. Citizens have a high degree of economic freedom but also face considerable economic risk. Under communism, the government owns all factors of production and makes all the business decisions. Distinctions between rich and poor are minimized. Under socialism, the state owns and operates certain key industries but allows private ownership of many businesses. Relatively high taxes permit the government to provide many social services.

4 Describe the relationship between profit and sales, and explain how profit motivates entrepreneurs.
Profit is the amount left over after expenses are deducted from revenues. The profits of the business add to its value and increase the entrepreneur's financial reward.

5 List three ways companies compete.
Companies compete on the basis of price, quality and service, and innovation.

6 Explain how supply and demand interact to influence prices.
In the simplest sense, supply and demand affect price in the following manner: When price goes up, the quantity demanded goes down, but the supplier's incentive to produce more goes up. When price goes down, the quantity demanded increases, whereas the quantity supplied may (or may not) decline. When the interests of buyers and sellers are in balance, an equilibrium price is established. There is more to price than simple notions of supply and demand, however, as the examples of medicine and gasoline illustrate.

7 List the four major economic roles of the U.S. government.

The U.S. government enforces rules and regulations, provides public goods and transfer payments, fosters competition, and contributes to economic stability.

8 Identify six trends that will influence the economy in the years ahead.

The six trends identified in the chapter are (1) the increasingly global nature of the economy; (2) the accelerating pace of technological change and its positive and negative effects; (3) continued public and government scrutiny of business's social, ethical, and environmental performance; (4) the challenges of meeting the needs of a diverse workforce and a diverse consumer market; (5) the increasing strategic value of information; and (6) the need to compete on the basis of speed, quality, and customer satisfaction.

On his way from football star to business executive, Drew Pearson kept taking tough hits—only instead of NFL defensive backs, he now had to contend with banks, competitors, suppliers, and the other forces at work in the economy. However, he and partner Ken Shead are a testament to the power of dogged determination. They never gave up, overcoming each obstacle that appeared in their path, pushing for every advantage they could find. By 1993 the company was generating nearly $80 million in annual sales and had become the largest black-owned licensed sports and character apparel manufacturer in the world.

DPC's specialty is hats. The company sold 24 million of them in 1993, and its sales continue to grow. So if you wear an athletic logo or cartoon character on your head, chances are it's a DPC product. As a licensed manufacturer, DPC faces some particular business challenges, foremost among them just getting the licenses. The National Football League, the National Basketball Association, Major League Baseball, the National Hockey League, and companies such as Disney and Warner Brothers are very careful about granting rights to their logos. In fact, DPC is one of only six companies to hold licenses with all four major professional sports organizations. Pearson notes that every license is hard to get "because it's a treasured and valued commodity." Major League Baseball, for instance, turns down 80 percent of the applications it receives every year, so DPC's success isn't something to take lightly.

It took DPC nearly a year of presentations and negotiations to secure a deal with Disney, a company flooded by licensing requests. Now DPC is Disney's top headwear licensee and the first to sell Disney hats aimed at adults. The NFL arrangement relied on Pearson's NFL connections to a large degree. Before hooking up with DPC, the NFL's licensing arm wasn't doing business with any minority-owned companies. Pearson and Shead saw an opportunity and persuaded former Dallas Cowboys owner Hank Schramm to approach his colleagues at the NFL offices.

Retail distribution is another valuable part of DPC's story. Without a link to the consumer, manufacturers have no way to sell their products. Through years of hard work and dependable performance, DPC is now carried by some of the most respected retailers in the country, including Marshall Field, J. C. Penney, and Wal-Mart, in addition to many sporting goods stores.

With a solid record under their belts, Pearson and his DPC team continue to push into new markets with new products. They're developing unique brand names to increase consumer awareness, and they're even sponsoring contests among college students to come up with new hat designs. Like all athletes and business-people, Drew Pearson knows that success has to be achieved over and over again, year after year.

Your Mission: You are a member of the executive team at Drew Pearson Companies, helping your colleagues make the decisions that will keep the company growing into the future. Using what you know about business in a free-market economy—and your own experience as a consumer—decide how the company should respond to the following scenarios. Like real business decisions, some of these scenarios have more than one good answer; just be sure you can defend the answer you choose.

1. Competition is getting fierce in the market for logo and character hats. Some companies have resorted to competing on price, but you're not sure what to do. Which of the following courses sounds best for DPC over the long term?

a. Produce a better-quality hat, one that will last through years of normal wear and tear. Customers shouldn't mind paying more for that level of quality.

b. Make sure your hats stand out from the competition in terms of design, whether it's classy and subdued or wild and even outrageous. Hats are fashion statements, after all.

c. You really don't have much choice when competitors are cutting prices; you'll have to follow suit or lose lots of business.

2. Celebrity endorsers are an important marketing force in athletic apparel. Which of the following people makes the most sense as DPC's spokesperson for a new line of hats with NFL logos? Be ready to explain your answer.

a. A young player who's made a name for himself on—and off—the field; he's well known, but some of his name recognition comes from a reputation as a wild party animal.

b. A very popular player nearing the end of his playing career.

c. The mascot of one of the NFL teams.

3. Like every other product category, sports hats can be influenced by the multiplier effect. Which of the following events in the economy is likely to generate the most product sales for you?

a. The awarding of a major league baseball franchise to the Tampa–St. Petersburg area, which has been trying to get a team for years

b. The Summer Olympics

c. An NFL Super Bowl

4. Information plays a key role in all your business decisions; the more and better information you have, the better decisions you can make. Which of the following approaches to collecting information would be the most beneficial in laying out DPC strategy for the next year or two?

a. Keeping a close eye on the progress of less popular sports that have a chance of breaking into the mainstream, such as soccer

b. Watching what competitors do to see what kind of products DPC should come out with next

c. Regularly interviewing people in your target markets to see what kind of products they like and dislike[23]

KEY TERMS

antitrust laws (18)
bartering (6)
business cycle (19)
capital (2)
capitalism (6)
cartel (20)
circular flow (14)
communism (7)
competition (10)
demand (12)
demand curve (13)
deregulation (17)
disinflation (20)
economic system (2)
entrepreneurs (2)
equilibrium price (14)

factors of production (2)
fiscal policy (19)
free enterprise (7)
free-market system (7)
gross domestic product (GDP) (4)
gross national product (GNP) (4)
inflation (20)
labor (2)
macroeconomics (9)
market economies (7)
microeconomics (9)
mixed capitalism (7)
monetary policy (19)
monopolistic competition (12)
monopoly (18)
multiplier effect (15)

natural resources (2)
oligopoly (17)
opportunity cost (10)
planned economy (7)
productivity (3)
profit (10)
public goods (17)
pure capitalism (7)
pure competition (17)
recession (19)
scarcity (10)
socialism (9)
supply (12)
supply curve (13)
transfer payments (17)
underground economy (5)

REVIEW QUESTIONS

1. How is capitalism different from communism and socialism in the way it achieves key economic goals?

2. The U.S. economic system is actually a form of modified capitalism. What are the benefits and drawbacks of this system (as opposed to pure capitalism) for the average citizen?

3. How do scarcity and opportunity cost affect the businessperson?

4. What role does competition play in a free-market economy?

5. Define the demand curve, the supply curve, and the equilibrium price.

6. What role does the multiplier effect play in an economic system?

7. What happens when an economy shifts from a period of high inflation to a period of disinflation?

8. What major change in the American economy appeared during the mid-nineteenth century, and what were some of its effects?

PROGRAMMING HIS WAY TO THE TOP OF THE U.S. ECONOMY

Perhaps no other person in the world illustrates the potential rewards for success in a free-market economy more than Microsoft co-founder and CEO Bill Gates. Gates dropped out of college in 1975 to start his company with high-school pal Paul Allen. Twenty years later, the company they formed sells nearly $4 billion worth of software, is the largest software company in the world, and controls 44 percent of the PC software market. Gates's fortunes rose with the company's; he's now the richest person in the United States, with a personal worth of around $7 billion. (Allen left the company in 1983 and has since used his own sizable Microsoft stock fortune to buy a slew of advanced-technology companies and the Portland Trailblazers basketball team.)

The notion of supply and demand has played a key role in Microsoft's success. Because the company is the supplier of the MS-DOS operating system software, customers and other software companies have had to play by Microsoft's rules. Compatibility is the name of the game in PC software, and for the most part, anybody who wants to be successful must be compatible with Microsoft.

Through the multiplier effect, Microsoft's success has affected the economy all around its base in Redmond, Washington (a suburb of Seattle). At one point, sources estimated that stock options for Microsoft employees had created 2,000 millionaires within the company. Needless to say, 2,000 millionaires can have a positive effect on a city's economy. Several software companies have been started by ex-Microsoft employees, further adding to the region's economy.

Various government agencies have shaped Microsoft's progress as well. On the one hand, the U.S. Justice Department attempted to sue the company over alleged violations of the federal antitrust laws. The case was settled in 1994, with Microsoft agreeing to what it called minor changes in its licensing practices. On the other hand, the company has actively sought increased protection from software pirates around the world. Software is extremely easy to copy, and many countries don't have the same legal protections for product creators that the United States has. So although the antitrust suit has been an expensive distraction, Microsoft clearly stands to benefit from government intervention on the software piracy issue.

In the future, expect to run across Microsoft products if you travel the information superhighway. Gates plans to be there when computers, telephones, and television converge in a massive information and communication network. Expect him to continue using the forces at work in the free-market system to ensure his company's sustained success.

1. Would Gates and Microsoft have been as successful if they had tried to start out in a country other than the United States? Explain your answer.
2. Would you consider Microsoft a monopoly? Why or why not?
3. How is Microsoft affected by the U.S. government's manipulation of the value of the dollar?

Examine how the various economic forces affect a business operation by interviewing the owner or manager of a local business. If that is not possible, consult the journals and periodicals available in your library and select an article that profiles a business. Consider the following: profit motive, scarcity and opportunity cost, competition, and supply and demand. Present a brief discussion of your findings to several class members or write a brief summary, as directed by your instructor. Be prepared to discuss the method you used to locate information for the analysis.

In the past decade, the following business developments have had a dramatic impact on sectors of the economy. Choose one of these factors. Then in recent issues of *The Wall Street Journal,* find three or more articles related to the topic you've chosen.

- The increasingly global economy
- Accelerating technological development
- Social, ethical, and environmental concerns
- Workforce diversity
- Consumer diversity
- The strategic value of information
- Competing on speed, quality, or customer satisfaction

1. What effects of this development are mentioned in the articles you've chosen?
2. What is the impact (or the expected impact) of this development on employment? What groups are most likely to be affected?
3. How do you think this development will affect the industry or job field that you hope to enter?

CHINA: AN ECONOMIC MIRACLE?

Synopsis

The People's Republic of China has long been an intriguing puzzle for U.S. companies. Many view it as a source of cheap land and cheap labor; many have dreams about selling products to even a small fraction of China's 1.2 billion citizens. On the other hand, China's hard-line communist government and its high-profile human-rights abuses (such as the killings in Beijing's Tiananmen Square in 1989) give pause to many people in the United States—some of whom think we should do no business with China at all. One issue that no one disputes is the magnitude of the Chinese economy; if it continues to grow at recent rates, it will be one of the largest economies in the world within a few years. This video program ponders whether this growth is good for the United States, and it examines how China has been able to make such tremendous progress in the last 10 to 15 years.

Exercises

ANALYSIS

1. Why does the McCann-Erickson advertising-agency manager say that he can't run the same television commercial across China? How does this situation compare with advertising in the United States?

2. What are the economic implications of the heavily subsidized rent paid by the family you see in the video? Who pays the real cost when families rent apartments for $1.40 a month?

3. Japanese management consultant Kenichi Ohmae says in the video that Guangdong province could become another of Asia's "Tigers." What countries does this comment refer to?

4. Why does the program say that China has an emperor when, in fact, nobody has such a title in the country today?

5. Looking at Hong Kong's location on a world map, what conclusions might you draw about its rise to become the tenth largest trading nation in the world?

APPLICATION

How might U.S. companies benefit from the principles of Confucius that are expressed in the video program? Are U.S. companies already applying those principles?

DECISION

Pick a company whose products you use as a consumer. Would you recommend that those products be exported to China? Why or why not? If the product does seem like a good fit, would it sell better in the urban market or in the less developed areas in the west?

COMMUNICATION

Many ads produced in the United States are difficult to translate for use in other nations because they rely on word play that doesn't work in other languages or they refer to U.S. events and ideas that consumers elsewhere may not know about. Find an ad running in the United States that you think might be difficult to translate, and explain how you would simplify it to ease the translation into Chinese.

INTEGRATION

Look ahead to the material on franchising in Chapter 5. Does China seem like a good place to use the franchising alternative, or would it be better to use an approach that gives you greater hands-on control? Explain your answer.

ETHICS

When U.S. consumers buy products that are manufactured in Chinese factories that are considered unsafe by U.S. standards, are those consumers committing ethical violations by supporting the unsafe factory conditions? Explain your answer.

DEBATE

Should we take a hard line on what we consider human-rights violations in China or overlook things we don't like in order to help open up China and bring it more in line with the rest of the world?

TEAMWORK

China used to share with Russia the distinction of being a global communist superpower. Russia has rejected communism, but its economy has gone downhill in recent years. China continues to embrace communism, and its economy has grown dramatically. In a team of four (two students for Russia and two for China), research the recent economic performance of the two countries, and find out why they seem to be going in different directions.

RESEARCH

The Chinese economy slowed down considerably within a year or two of the time this program was produced. Do the library research needed to find out how the country is doing today.

ROLE PLAYING

In a group with three other students, one of you plays the role of a U.S. marketing manager trying to convince Chinese distributors that they should sell your product to Chinese consumers. The other three students play the distributors, who challenge various points in the sales pitch. The marketing manager can choose whatever product he or she wants to try selling.

Chapter

2

International Business

After opening Pizza Huts for PepsiCo's restaurant division in Africa, Eastern Europe, Scandinavia, and the Middle East, Andrew Rafalat figured he could start a Pizza Hut from scratch on the moon if he had to. The moon, maybe—but Moscow was something else. "Setting up a business here was like setting up an island in an ocean," Rafalat explained. "You hoped it would survive the storm." No one could know how severe a storm was coming—or when. Before the Soviet Union broke into separate republics, before the Communist party lost power, and before Russia began moving aggressively toward capitalism, Western companies like Pizza Hut were eyeing the region's potential.

Russia was only one of many markets outside the United States where Pizza Hut wanted to expand during the 1980s. Today millions of customers in Germany, Brazil, Israel, Poland, Thailand, France, and every place in between can enjoy U.S.-style pizza at local Pizza Hut outlets. However, the road to global growth wasn't always smooth, as Andrew Rafalat found out.

Consider the Moscow experience. Pepsi-Cola was the first foreign consumer product to cross the iron curtain. Encouraged by this success, PepsiCo wanted to introduce other staples of the U.S. diet through its restaurant and snack-food divisions, which include Pizza Hut, KFC, Taco Bell, and Frito-Lay.

After lengthy negotiations, PepsiCo arranged a complex $3 billion deal that involved a lot more than pizza. In addition to opening the restaurants, PepsiCo agreed to build and equip 28 new bottling plants (in addition to the 26 already there). These plants would buy concentrate from PepsiCo and pay for it using vodka and revenue from some oil tankers (rather than rubles). At the time, this peculiar form of payment was necessary because rubles could not be exchanged for dollars, which meant that money made in what was then the U.S.S.R. was good only in the U.S.S.R.—a big problem for a U.S. company.

When Rafalat finally arrived in Moscow to open the two Pizza Huts, he faced a seemingly endless series of obstacles. Even though the restaurant equipment was imported from the West, setting things

Pepperoni Wrapped in Red Tape

Pizza Hut brought American-style pizza to Russia.

up was difficult because the local transportation system was unpredictable. Supplies were lost for weeks. Lining up ingredients was difficult because the food distribution system was disorganized. Of course, there was also the problem of hiring and training 300 Muscovites to staff the restaurants. The biggest problem for Rafalat, though, was the government red tape. A person needed a master's degree in bureaucratic intrigue to cope with the system. "It seemed impossible," said Rafalat. "I had a problem even knowing whom to call."[1]

THE DYNAMICS OF INTERNATIONAL BUSINESS

Like Pizza Hut, more and more enterprises are becoming global in scope, reaching out for opportunities to buy, sell, and manufacture goods and services throughout the world. The shift to a worldwide focus poses obvious problems for managers like Andrew Rafalat, who must cope with unfamiliar ways of doing business. On a broader level, it also poses problems for government policymakers.

Honda's manufacturing plant in Marysville, Ohio, is only one of many facilities in the United States owned and operated by companies based outside the country. The role of government in promoting and regulating international trade has become increasingly complex as more companies cross national borders to make and sell products.

What should national objectives be with respect to international business? When countries negotiate international trade agreements, should they try to promote the interests of domestic companies and protect them from foreign competitors? It was once assumed that the national interest and the interests of U.S. corporations were one and the same. "What's good for America is good for General Motors, and vice versa" was once a fairly accurate statement. Now the issue is much more complex. Nearly 40 percent of the General Motors workforce works in non-U.S. operations, which provide 90 percent of the company's net income. At the same time, foreign-owned factories employ roughly 10 percent of U.S. manufacturing workers, and they provide the United States with some of its favorite products. For the past few years, one of the most popular cars in the United States has been the Honda Accord, a "Japanese import" manufactured not in Tokyo but in Marysville, Ohio. If the U.S. government tries to protect GM from Honda, is it doing the country a favor? Should the U.S. government look out for its own corporations, workers, or consumers? Can a policy be devised to serve all three equally well?

Why Nations Trade

International trade occurs because no single country has the resources to produce everything well. Traditional explanations for nations' achieving international success in particular industries refer to the theory of **comparative advantage,** a country's ability to specialize in making and selling products it can produce more efficiently than other countries because of its natural and human resources. Comparative advantage has nothing to do with the actual costs involved

comparative advantage *Nation's ability to produce an item more efficiently than other nations because of its natural and human resources*

in production; it concerns the use of resources, such as low-cost labor or huge reserves of oil, to produce a product more efficiently than a nation that lacks those resources. If a country can use less of its resources (oil, labor, and so on) to produce a particular product, it has comparative advantage over a country that must use more of its resources to produce the same product.

In contrast, an **absolute advantage** is a nation's ability to produce a particular item using fewer resources (per unit of output) than any other nation. China can be seen as having an absolute advantage in the production of hand-made toys because of the country's lower labor costs. Still, China's absolute advantage doesn't restrict other countries from exploiting their own comparative advantages to make the same product. The United States might have a comparative advantage in the production of hand-made toys because of unique manufacturing techniques that speed up the process.[2]

However, these two concepts don't explain how many nations are able to compete successfully on a global level in industries that don't depend on naturally occurring raw materials or large labor pools. To explain this phenomenon, Harvard Business School professor Michael E. Porter points to the theory of **national competitive advantage,** the ability of a country's industries to innovate and upgrade to a higher level of technology and productivity. According to this theory, a nation can be competitive in the world market by making the best use of innovation and technology.

Consider the Dutch flower industry. Researchers found that the Dutch didn't become international leaders in cut flowers because they have the ideal climate. The country's national competitive advantage was achieved by establishing research centers to study flower cultivation, packaging, and shipping. Today the Netherlands has a thriving $3 billion flower industry and provides nearly 60 percent of the world's cut flowers.[3]

Because no nation can make everything it needs, each nation trades the goods it makes most efficiently for goods that other countries produce more efficiently. In this way, specialization expands the total supply of goods and reduces their total cost. However, for political reasons, most countries try to remain reasonably self-sufficient in certain essential industries. For example, the United States does not want to become totally dependent on foreign oil because of concerns that the supply might be interrupted in the event of a conflict with oil-producing nations.

The Growing Importance of World Markets

Never before have organizations been able to cross national borders so easily or so inexpensively, thanks to the high speed and low cost of today's communication, transportation, and information systems. Companies are no longer confined to the resources or the market potential of a single country. Today companies all over the world are able to look to other countries for product components, raw materials, and human resources. At the same time, they're working to bring new or existing products to market in other countries.[4]

Initially, most U.S. companies approached these growing foreign

absolute advantage Nation's ability to produce a particular product with fewer resources (per unit of output) than any other nation

national competitive advantage Ability of a nation's industries to be innovative and move to a higher level of technology and productivity

markets from bases in the United States. However, as international business became an increasingly important source of sales and profits, U.S. companies began to open foreign branches and sales offices, staffed by local workers. One step led to another, and soon U.S. companies were adding production and assembly operations abroad to minimize transportation expenses, capitalize on lower labor costs, and take advantage of local raw materials. These companies became **multinational corporations (MNCs),** businesses with operations in several countries. The country where a company is headquartered is the *home country*; any nation outside the home country where the company does business is the *host country*.

multinational corporations (MNCs) Companies with operations in more than one country

When deciding where to locate various company functions, global managers make the best use of the resources in home and host countries, which improves the efficiency of the corporation as a whole. Marketing and sales activities might be located close to the customers. Toronto-based Bata, the world's largest maker of footwear, operates in 68 countries. Local managers in each country monitor local fashions and customer needs, and then manufacture and market Bata shoes to the tastes of people in each host country.[5] Some companies might locate research and design facilities near a pool of skilled engineers and scientists and put factories where labor rates are low and transportation is readily available. Based solely on economics, these decisions might or might not serve the national interests of the corporation's home country.

International Business Economics

The world economy is dynamic, and at any given time, a country may be buying more of one type of product or selling more of another. **Importing** is buying goods or services from a supplier in another country; **exporting** is selling products outside the country in which they are produced. As Exhibit 2.1 illustrates, the United States exports more food and agricultural products than it imports, but it imports more manufactured goods and more mineral fuels and related products than it exports. The level of a country's imports and exports forms an important part of international business economics.

importing Purchasing goods or services from another country and bringing them into one's own country

exporting Selling and shipping goods or services to another country

The Balance of Trade

The U.S. **balance of trade** is determined by the relationship between the value of its imports and the value of its exports. In years when the United States exports more than it imports, the balance of trade is favorable, creating a **trade surplus:** People in other countries buy more from the United States than it buys from them, and money flows into the U.S. economy. When U.S. imports exceed exports, the balance of trade is unfavorable, creating a **trade deficit:** The United States is buying more from other countries, so money is flowing from the U.S. economy into those other countries' economies.

balance of trade Relationship between the value of the products a nation exports and those it imports

trade surplus Positive trade balance created when a country exports more than it imports

trade deficit Negative trade balance created when a country imports more than it exports

As Exhibit 2.2 illustrates, the U.S. balance of trade varies from year to year. One reason for the variation is the change in the value of the dollar compared with the value of other currencies. When the

PART ONE | FOCUS ON BUSINESS TODAY

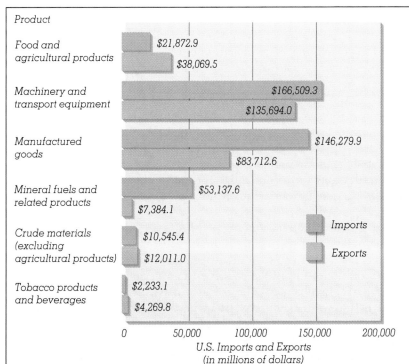

Product

Food and agricultural products — Imports $21,872.9; Exports $38,069.5

Machinery and transport equipment — Imports $166,509.3; Exports $135,694.0

Manufactured goods — Imports $146,279.9; Exports $83,712.6

Mineral fuels and related products — Imports $53,137.6; Exports $7,384.1

Crude materials (excluding agricultural products) — Imports $10,545.4; Exports $12,011.0

Tobacco products and beverages — Imports $2,233.1; Exports $4,269.8

U.S. Imports and Exports
(in millions of dollars)

Imports / Exports

Exhibit 2.1
Leading U.S. Imports and Exports
The United States actively partici-pates in global trade by import-ing products from other countries and exporting products to other countries.

dollar is extremely high against other currencies, products from other countries seem relatively inexpensive in the United States, and U.S. products seem relatively expensive overseas. As U.S. consumers buy more of the relatively inexpensive imported goods and consumers overseas buy less of the relatively expensive U.S. goods, the trade deficit grows. However, when the situation is reversed and U.S. con-sumers buy fewer imported goods while people in other countries buy more U.S. exports, the trade deficit narrows and may even turn into a trade surplus.

Bear in mind that the gap between imports and exports does not necessarily mean that U.S. companies are not competitive in the world market. In many cases, they've simply moved some of their opera-tions. The overseas subsidiaries of U.S. companies produce and sell

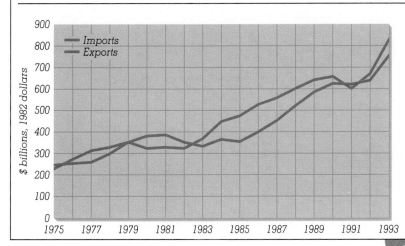

Exhibit 2.2
The U.S. Balance of Trade
When the United States imports more than it exports, it experi-ences a trade deficit. However, when the United States exports more than it imports, it experi-ences a trade surplus.

abroad more than $700 billion a year in products that are not counted as U.S. exports. If one-seventh of this production were shifted here and exported, the trade deficit would be wiped out.[6] Another offsetting factor is that many of the products imported into the United States are made by U.S.-owned companies operating abroad. AT&T and Texas Instruments are among the largest exporters in Taiwan, and General Electric is the largest private employer in Singapore. These companies have set up factories to make components in countries where wage rates are low. When the parts are shipped back to the United States for assembly, they are called imports. This sourcing pattern accounts for a substantial portion of the U.S. trade imbalance with Mexico, Taiwan, South Korea, and Singapore.[7]

The Balance of Payments

The **balance of payments** is the broadest indicator of international trade, measuring the total flow of money into a country minus the flow of money out of the country over a period of time (usually one year) (see Exhibit 2.3). The balance of payments includes not only the balance of trade but also payments of foreign aid by governments and direct investments in assets. For example, when a U.S. company buys all or part of a company based in another country, that investment is counted in the balance of payments but not in the balance of trade. Similarly, when foreign companies buy U.S. companies, stocks, bonds, or real estate, those transactions are part of the balance of payments.

For most of the 1980s, foreign investments in the United States exceeded U.S. investments overseas. In the 1990s, however, the United States has been attracting a lower level of investments from abroad than it did in the 1980s. One reason is relatively low interest rates in the United States compared with higher rates overseas, which means that investors can earn a better return in other countries. Then, too, all sorts of interesting new investment opportunities have opened up throughout the world. Business investments in Eastern Europe and in the former Soviet Union are drawing funds from all around the

balance of payments *Sum of all payments one nation has made to other nations minus the payments it has received from other nations during a specified period of time*

Exhibit 2.3
The U.S. Balance of Payments
During most of the 1980s, more money flowed out of the United States than in.

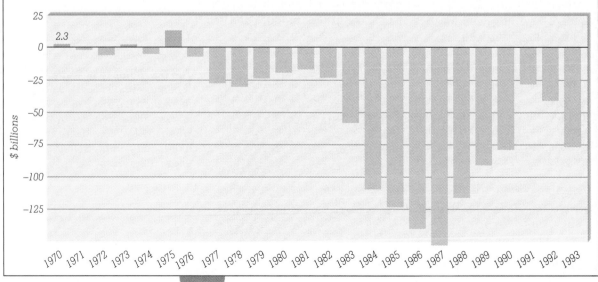

world, including from PepsiCo and its Pizza Hut subsidiary.[8] Meanwhile, the growing economies of the Pacific Rim, including China, are bringing in more foreign investment.[9] The Latin American countries are also soaking up capital as they sell off state-owned businesses to private investors.[10]

GOVERNMENT ACTIONS RELATING TO INTERNATIONAL BUSINESS

How the United States or any other country fares in its international economic relationships depends to a great extent on government actions that affect trade, foreign investment, and currency values. Basically, the national objective is to devise policies that balance the interests of U.S. companies, U.S. workers, and U.S. consumers. Other countries, of course, are trying to do the same thing. As you might expect, the many players involved in world trade sometimes have conflicting goals.

Protectionist Measures

Every country has the right to control its participation in the global marketplace. Motivated by **protectionism,** many countries erect legal fences aimed at shielding their industries from foreign competition. Much of the world's trade is restricted in one way or another as a result of protectionist measures.[11] The main types of protectionism are tariffs, quotas, subsidies, restrictive standards, and retaliatory measures.

protectionism Government policies aimed at shielding a country's industries from foreign competition

Tariffs

Tariffs are taxes levied against goods imported into a country. Tariffs can be a significant source of government revenue. Most of the time, however, tariffs are protective; that is, they make goods brought into a country more expensive, thereby giving domestic producers a cost advantage. Although countries see tariffs as a way to protect their own industries, consumers who want to buy imported goods wind up paying a higher price.[12]

tariffs Taxes levied on imports

During the depression years of the 1930s, many countries tried to protect jobs at home by imposing higher and higher tariffs. However, those tariffs stifled world trade and contributed to the downward spiral of the world economy. To avoid repeating the problem, the United States led a movement after World War II to reduce tariffs throughout the world. The effort resulted in an international agreement that has sharply reduced tariffs. This agreement, known as the General Agreement on Tariffs and Trade, is discussed in detail later in the chapter.

Quotas

As reliance on tariffs declined, many countries adopted other techniques to discourage imports. One of the most common is to impose **quotas,** which limit the number of specific items that may be imported. This limit tends to raise the ultimate price paid by con-

quotas Fixed limits on the quantity of imports a nation will allow for a specific product

sumers for items covered by quotas. For example, U.S. consumers pay twice the world price for sugar because of limitations on importing sugar; Japanese consumers pay seven to eight times the world price for rice because of limitations on importing rice.[13] Apparel and agriculture are two of the industries protected by the 3,600 product quotas set by the United States.[14] Often quotas are negotiated; one trading partner "voluntarily" agrees to limit its exports to another country. Japan, for example, voluntarily restricts the number of autos as well as the number of computerized metal-cutting tools it sells to the United States.

In the most extreme form, a quota becomes an **embargo,** which prohibits trade in certain products or with specific countries altogether. The embargo against Vietnam is one example. For 19 years, U.S. companies weren't permitted to do business with Vietnam. When the embargo was lifted in 1994, U.S. companies quickly entered this growing market: Coca-Cola and PepsiCo began distributing their soft drinks, Mobil Oil teamed up with Japanese companies to drill for oil off Vietnam's coast, and General Electric began negotiating to sell jet engines, medical equipment, and locomotives.[15] Although some embargoes are politically motivated, most are imposed to protect domestic industries or for health or safety reasons. To protect its dairy industry, Canada forbids the importation of oleomargarine. The U.S. ban on toys with lead paint is motivated by health concerns.

embargo *Total ban on trade with a particular nation or in a particular product*

Now that the United States has lifted its embargo against Vietnam, many U.S. companies are actively promoting their products to Vietnamese consumers and businesses.

Subsidies

Rather than restrict imports, some countries prefer to subsidize domestic producers so that their prices will be substantially lower than import prices. The idea is often to help build up an industry until it is strong enough to compete on its own. The European Airbus, for example, is a subsidized joint venture in aircraft manufacturing supported by Germany, France, England, and Spain. By far the greatest amount of money goes to agricultural subsidies; major industrial countries spend $240 billion a year subsidizing their farmers. These subsidies benefit the huge farm industries in the United States and Europe, but the United States is seeking to reduce agricultural price supports as part of a movement away from such protectionist measures.

Restrictive Standards

One way to keep imports out is to establish standards that give domestic producers an edge. Many countries require special licenses for doing certain kinds of business and then make it difficult for companies from other countries to obtain a license. In Brazil import licenses are withheld for any domestically made product, effectively blocking 90 percent of imports.[16] Other countries require imports to pass special tests, which complicates the process of selling a product in that country.

In addition, some countries set standards for the percentage of a product's components that must be bought from domestic suppliers. Brazilian laws prevent Whirlpool from buying components such as electronic controls from suppliers in the United States or Asia; instead, the company must buy from Brazilian suppliers, who often charge up to six times as much as overseas suppliers. These costs are passed along to consumers in Brazil, in the form of higher prices for appliances made inside the country.[17]

Retaliatory Measures

Like other countries, the United States has legal weapons to strike back against countries that engage in what are deemed to be unfair trade practices. Under Section 301 of the Trade Act of 1988, the president is legally obligated to retaliate against foreign producers that use questionable tactics in approaching the U.S. market. The United States is particularly quick to act against companies that sell goods below cost or at lower prices in the United States than in their home country. This practice, known as **dumping,** puts pressure on U.S. companies to cut their own prices in order to maintain sales.

dumping Charging less than the actual cost or less than the home-country price for goods sold in other countries

If a U.S. company presses for action and can support the dumping claim, the government typically responds by imposing an antidumping duty on the import, which effectively raises its price to the U.S. level and protects U.S. producers. More than 40 countries have similar antidumping laws, which can have far-reaching effects on local economies. For example, European countries set high duties on aspartame, a low-calorie sweetener, to prevent dumping by NutraSweet, the U.S. maker. With the added duties, Nutrasweet found exporting aspartame to Europe too expensive. So the company opened a factory in France and began production there, which boosted the local economy by employing French workers.[18]

The Pros and Cons of Protectionism

Is protectionism a good idea or a bad idea? Some of the arguments for protectionism are as follows:

1. Building in a preference for a country's home industries can boost local economies and save local jobs.
2. Protectionism shields domestic industries from head-to-head competition with overseas rivals.

On the other hand, many less developed countries that once imposed trade barriers to shield their emerging industries are now opening up their markets because trade restrictions were stifling their economies. The United States has been walking a fine line between free trade and protectionism. Both the executive and legislative branches of the government are involved in trade policy, and they have historically viewed trade issues from different perspectives. Since World War II, U.S. presidents, looking at the overall long-term economic picture, have advocated a reduction in trade barriers. Congress, however, has tended toward protectionism, responding to pressure from manufacturers and workers in their districts who fear the immediate threats of competition and possible loss of jobs.

Still, study after study has shown that in the long run, protectionism hurts everyone. Some of the arguments against protectionism are as follows:

1. Consumers pay the price for protectionism. As discussed earlier, farm subsidies and other measures translate into higher price tags. Existing U.S. trade barriers are estimated to cost U.S. consumers $80 billion a year in higher prices for imports.[19] Moreover, U.S. consumers pay $40 billion more for fabrics and clothing than they would without restrictions.[20]
2. The cost of saving jobs in specific industries is enormous. Each job saved in the dairy industry, for example, costs consumers $220,000 annually. Other annual costs range from $30,000 (for jobs in the rubber-footware industry) to $750,000 (for jobs in the steel industry).[21]
3. The jobs that are saved in industries threatened by imports may be offset by jobs lost in other sectors of the economy. Protectionism can hurt workers in companies that distribute or sell foreign goods. Companies that depend on imported parts may have to cut back on production and employment if they can't obtain what they need from overseas suppliers.
4. U.S. companies could be crippled by protectionist measures, since many businesses depend on imported components, materials, or equipment. Such U.S. multinationals as General Motors, IBM, and General Electric, which import nearly $80 billion in items from their overseas plants and affiliates, would be severely hampered by tariffs or quotas.[22]

5. A loophole exists for every "protectionist fix." When the United States limited imports of cotton from China, Chinese companies got around the barrier by switching to cotton blends.[23]

Trade Agreements and Trade Finance

To prevent trade disputes from escalating into full-blown trade wars and to ensure that international business is conducted in a fair and orderly fashion, the countries of the world have created a number of agreements to facilitate and finance global trade. Philosophically, most of these agreements support the basic principle of **free trade.** They agree that each nation ultimately benefits if it trades freely, because it is exchanging the goods and services it produces most efficiently for goods and services it produces less efficiently.

free trade International trade unencumbered by restrictive measures

The General Agreement on Tariffs and Trade

The General Agreement on Tariffs and Trade (GATT) is a worldwide trade pact that was first established in the aftermath of World War II. GATT is actually two things: a constantly evolving trade treaty and an administrative organization of about 300 people in Geneva representing the 117 member nations that have signed the treaty. Over the years, each GATT country has sent representatives to a series of meetings about trade problems. The guiding principle has been one of nondiscrimination: Any trade advantage a GATT member gives to one country must be given to all GATT members, and no single GATT nation can be singled out for punishment.

GATT has been successful in reducing tariff barriers on manufactured goods, which have fallen from an average of 40 percent in pre-GATT days to 5 percent today. The latest GATT agreement, which was signed in 1994 for 1995 implementation, cut worldwide tariffs by an average of one-third and brought agricultural products under GATT rules for the first time.[24] However, this round of GATT talks, known as the Uruguay Round, didn't succeed in lowering foreign trade barriers against a number of service industries, including banking and entertainment. Hollywood's movie and television studios were particularly disappointed because they were seeking to expand by sending U.S.-made films and programming abroad.[25]

Even as tariffs have fallen, other nontariff barriers have emerged to take their place. In fact, 80 percent of all trade barriers these days are permitted under GATT. Many of these barriers are used by industrialized countries to protect local workers against the loss of jobs to lower-wage workers in other countries. As companies shift labor-intensive operations to China, Hungary, and other nations where wages are comparatively low, the issue of employment in industrialized countries will remain a key problem in world trade.[26]

Trading Blocs

One way to encourage trade is through **trading blocs,** regional groupings of countries within which trade barriers have been removed. Although specific rules vary from group to group, trading blocs generally promote trade inside the region and, at the same time,

trading blocs Organizations of nations that remove barriers to trade among their members and that establish uniform barriers to trade with nonmember nations

create uniform barriers against goods and services entering the region from nonmember countries.

One of the largest trading blocs is the European Union (EU). Originally formed in 1957, the EU started as a loose alliance of six trading partners: France, West Germany (now Germany), Italy, Belgium, the Netherlands, and Luxembourg. Later, the number expanded to 12 by admitting Great Britain, Denmark, Greece, Ireland, Portugal, and Spain; additional expansion is likely.[27] Inside the bloc, the nations are working to do away with hundreds of local regulations, variations in product standards, and protectionist measures that limit trade between EU countries. Eliminating barriers means the nations of the EU can function as a single market, with trade flowing as it does between states in the United States.

With a combined GNP of approximately $5 trillion and a population of 360 million, the EU has become a commanding force in the world economy. The EU also has a close economic relationship with seven neighboring Western European countries (Austria, Finland, Iceland, Liechtenstein, Norway, Sweden, and Switzerland) that belong to the European Free Trade Association (EFTA), another trading bloc. The pact between the two groups formed the European Economic Area, which has significant clout because its countries account for about two-thirds of the world's trade.[28]

The United States, Canada, and Mexico formed a powerful trading bloc by signing the North American Free Trade Agreement (NAFTA), which took effect in 1994. Although the agreement was controversial, the three countries have begun phasing out all the tariffs and quotas that formerly restricted trade within the bloc. This process paves the way for freer flow of goods, services, and capital within the three-nation region. In the future, NAFTA may be expanded to include other countries in Central and South America.

As soon as NAFTA was in place, General Motors, Ford, and Chrysler moved quickly to export cars to Mexico; General Motors just as quickly brought into the U.S. more cars made in Mexican plants.[29] Caterpillar, the U.S.-based earth-moving-equipment manufacturer, also increased its exports to Mexico. Similarly, Wal-Mart, Kmart, and many other U.S. companies opened operations in Mexico, attracted by the opportunity to reach Mexican consumers. However, despite the easing of trade restrictions, businesses that cross national borders in North America still have to comply with local laws governing product labeling and other details.[30]

In Asia, six nations have formed the Association of Southeast Asian Nations Free Trade Area to boost regional trade. This trading bloc consists of Brunei, Indonesia, Malaysia, the Philippines, Singapore, and Thailand; Vietnam and Laos are also interested in joining. In addition, Japan is strengthening its trading ties with Korea, Hong Kong, Taiwan, and Singapore. Cen-

The European Union has negotiated with Japan for voluntary export restraints that limit the number of imported Japanese vehicles, including these Toyotas. However, if the EU restricts the sales of cars made by Japanese-owned plants inside the trading bloc, the automakers may cut back on new investment in Europe.

tral and South American countries are also active in trading blocs, including the Latin America Integration Association.

Some economists are apprehensive about the growing importance of regional trading blocs. One fear is that the world is splitting into three camps, revolving around the Americas, Europe, and Asia. This division might undermine GATT and ultimately diminish world trade. Poorer nations, particularly, might suffer if they do not fall conveniently into one of the "big three" economic regions. Another fear is that some countries' industries won't be successful in exporting because they've been sheltered from global competition for too long. Moreover, the restrictions that trading blocs place on products imported from nonmember nations might escalate protectionism. On the other side of this issue, the growth of global commerce and the availability of customers and suppliers within a trading bloc can be a boon to smaller or younger nations trying to build a strong economy. Also, member countries can reach a wider market with far fewer hassles than before.[31]

International Trade Finance

One of the major problems of international trade is that some less developed countries are too poor to participate to any great extent in the world economy. They lack both the capital to develop their own industrial potential and the money to pay for much-needed imports. Two international organizations—the International Monetary Fund (IMF) and the World Bank—are especially helpful in channeling funds to these nations.

The IMF, founded in 1945 and now affiliated with the United Nations, lends money to countries that are having trouble with their balance of payments. The World Bank, officially known as the International Bank for Reconstruction and Development, was founded to finance reconstruction following World War II. It now provides low-interest loans for specific projects. Both the IMF and the World Bank are funded by contributions from 135 member nations. The bulk of the funds come from the United States, Western Europe, and Japan.

In addition to the IMF and the World Bank, a number of regional development banks help nations in particular areas. The European Bank for Reconstruction and Development funnels loans from Western Europe to Eastern Europe; the Asian Development Bank of Manila is funded primarily by Japan to make loans to emerging economies in Asia; and the Inter-American Development Bank, which is dominated by the United States, provides money for loans to nations in Latin America.

Apart from these quasi-governmental banks, the private banking system is also involved in international lending, although many banks are no longer as willing to make loans to less developed countries because the countries have had problems repaying loans. The international debt of developing countries now totals $1.3 trillion. Strapped with large loan repayments, the indebted nations are unable to pay for imports and industrial development. Some U.S. banks have forgiven a percentage of the loans. As a result, Mexico cut its debt payments by $4 billion a year between 1989 and 1994. However, the unintended effect on many other poor countries is the difficulty the United States is having in paying off its share of the Third World write-offs.[32]

Economic Summit Meetings

Apart from participating in formal organizations that facilitate world trade, some countries also hold occasional economic summit meetings with key trading partners. These policy-making sessions are generally attended by the finance ministers of the countries involved, and they usually deal with such issues as exchange rates and trade imbalances. Because they are attended by high-ranking government officials, the meetings are influential in shaping trade relationships. In recent years, the United States has increasingly relied on such meetings to resolve perplexing trade problems within the Group of Five (the United States, Great Britain, France, Germany, and Japan), the Group of Seven (the Group of Five plus Canada and Italy), and the Group of Ten (the Group of Seven plus Belgium, the Netherlands, Sweden, and Switzerland, which joined later).

U.S. Measures Governing Foreign Trade

In addition to promoting world trade through international groups, the United States has established domestic agencies and policies that help U.S. companies compete abroad. Over 15 federal agencies, including the Commerce Department, the Small Business Administration, and the Agriculture Department, are together spending more than $2 billion to help promote exports.[33] Companies based in the United States can also receive financial support for their export activities through the Export-Import Bank of the United States, known as Eximbank. Eximbank arranges loans that enable customers in other countries to buy U.S. goods and services, guarantees repayment of loans made to U.S. exporters, and arranges insurance to cover exporters against nonpayment by overseas customers.[34]

Companies interested in doing business abroad are affected by a number of U.S. laws passed to encourage participation in international trade. For instance, the Webb-Pomerene Export Trade Act of 1918 allows U.S. companies to cooperate in developing export markets without running afoul of the antitrust laws that limit joint activities in the United States. The Export Trading Companies Act of 1982 further eased antitrust rules for companies involved in international business. This act allows companies and banks to form export trading companies to market products abroad. In 1988 Congress enacted a sweeping trade bill that gives the president power to block any foreign purchase of U.S. companies that might endanger U.S. security. The act also requires the government to investigate the trade practices of countries that maintain numerous barriers to imports from the United States.

As an added incentive to exporting, the government grants tax benefits to companies engaged in international business. Companies are allowed to set up **foreign sales corporations (FSCs),** which are marketing subsidiaries that can exempt some of their income taxes on profits from exports. The federal government offers insurance

foreign sales corporations (FSCs)
Tax-sheltered subsidiaries of U.S.-based corporations that engage in exporting

against some of the political and economic risks associated with doing business abroad. The government-sponsored Foreign Credit Insurance Association and the Overseas Private Investment Corporation offer coverage for losses due to *expropriation* (the takeover of a business by a foreign government), war, revolution, insurrection, credit defaults, and currency-exchange problems.

All U.S. companies that do business in other countries have to comply with the Foreign Corrupt Practices Act. This U.S. law outlaws actions such as bribing government officials in other nations to approve or speed deals. It does allow certain payments, including small payments to officials for expediting routine government actions. Critics of this U.S. law complain that payoffs are a routine part of world trade, so forbidding U.S. companies to follow suit cripples their ability to compete. Others counter that U.S. exports haven't been affected by this law and say that companies can conduct business abroad without violating antibribery rules. Until more nations agree on what practices should be made illegal, U.S. companies operating overseas will continue to tread lightly around the issue of questionable payments.[35]

When it comes to encouraging overseas companies to do business in the United States, most of the action occurs on the state and local level. Most of the states and many of the major cities have agencies that try to persuade foreign companies to open regional facilities that will employ U.S. workers. Tuscaloosa, Alabama, for example, fought hard to be selected as the site of the first Mercedes-Benz factory in the United States after competing against sites in 30 states. The plant will hire 1,500 workers and create more area jobs in related industries.[36]

Adjustments in Currency Values

Perhaps the most potent weapon the federal government has used to help U.S. companies compete internationally is lowering the value of the dollar relative to the value of foreign currencies, a practice known as *devaluation*. This adjustment in currency values makes U.S. products cheaper abroad and increases the price of imports in the United States (see Exhibit 2.4).

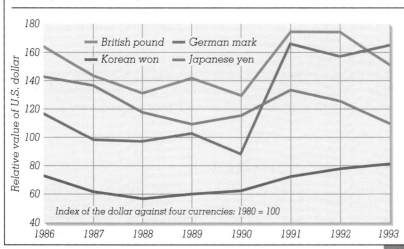

Exhibit 2.4
The Value of the Dollar
This chart indexes the dollar's value against the currencies of Germany, Great Britain, Japan, and Korea.

Because each country has its own currency, trade between countries involves an exchange of currencies. When a company in one country sells its products abroad, the price must be converted from one currency to another. For example, every time a Japanese trading company buys a ton of soybeans from the United States, it must obtain U.S. dollars to pay for them. It may do so by exchanging Japanese yen for dollars at one of the international banks that handle **foreign exchange,** the conversion of one currency into an equivalent amount of another currency. The number of yen, francs, or pounds that must be exchanged for every dollar, mark, or lira is known as the **exchange rate** between those two currencies.

International traders operate under a **floating exchange rate system,** a flexible system governed by the forces of supply and demand, which is reflected in foreign-exchange markets around the world (in banks and elsewhere). Exchange rates change rapidly because supply and demand are always changing. The relationships between the rates are determined in part by what is happening in local economies. If Italy's economy is suffering from severe inflation and unemployment, the value of Italian currency will be lower than the currency values in countries not experiencing economic turmoil.

When the U.S. dollar is strong—that is, relatively high in value—more units of foreign currency are required to purchase each dollar, a situation that tends to lower U.S. exports and raise U.S. imports. Conversely, a weak dollar boosts exports and dampens imports. The exchange rate also affects the prices for supplies, payroll, and other items that companies have to pay for when they operate in another country. For example, one-quarter of the revenues earned by the executive recruiting firm Ridenour & Associates comes from international business. Although the firm deals in services rather than in goods, exchange rates are important to its profitability. For every executive placed, the firm receives a commission of 30 percent of that manager's total first-year compensation. The commission is paid in the local currency, which the firm converts to U.S. dollars. At one time, placing an executive with a German firm at a salary of 200,000 Deutsche marks would have generated a fee of $32,856. When the mark was worth more relative to the dollar, the same placement would have brought a fee of $33,078.[37]

The foreign-exchange value of currency issued by countries that have not joined the International Monetary Fund can't easily be determined, which complicates international trade with those countries. Also, some nations don't allow their currencies to cross into other nations. In such situations, a company can turn to **countertrade**, a trading practice in which the company accepts locally produced products instead of cash in exchange for imported products.

THE GLOBAL CORPORATION

Although government policies have set the stage for the expansion of world trade, the real action has occurred because thousands of companies and individuals acting independently have realized that operating on a global basis is both necessary and beneficial. If you

What if a customer can't pay cash? As much as 30 percent of the world's trade is completed without cash, either because a national trade imbalance must be corrected or because currency isn't allowed to leave the country. Rather than forgo the sale, many companies turn to countertrade, a practice which the U.S. government doesn't officially encourage—or discourage. Still, many U.S. companies have successfully used countertrade to fuel exports.

Countertrade can be quite complex. Just ask Dan West, director of countertrade for Monsanto, who worked out a way for his company to sell valves in an Eastern European country. West accepted a shipment of wooden and metal chair frames, ball bearings, and garden tractors equivalent in value to the valves that Monsanto shipped abroad. He negotiated to sell these Eastern European items in England, France, and Canada, and then converted the cash from these sales to U.S. dollars. Although this deal was anything but easy, it allowed Monsanto to avoid receiving payment in a currency that isn't

THE BOOM IN GLOBAL BARTER

generally traded worldwide.

Sometimes countertrade is a good way to cover financial obligations that customers can't meet. N–Ren International, a small engineering and construction firm based in Brussels, expected to receive $60 million for building a fertilizer plant in Madagascar. However, when the plant was nearly complete, the Madagascar government said it could no longer pay N–Ren in cash because it had to cover its increasing national debt. Instead, N–Ren accepted cloves in exchange for its services. N–Ren got to keep the money it made from selling the spice, and the company's exporting success over the next five years earned enough profits to cover

the payments not received for the plant.

In addition to Monsanto, McDonnell Douglas, Rockwell International, General Motors, PepsiCo, and Dow Chemical are among the many U.S. companies that use countertrade to expand into markets around the world. PepsiCo, in fact, has successfully used countertrade to build a strong competitive position in Russia, India, and Mexico. Through countertrade, PepsiCo has been able to sell 40 million cases of soft drinks in the former Soviet Republics, an amount expected to double in the coming decade.

Despite the advantages of countertrade, this technique carries some risk. Goods received in trade are sometimes difficult to sell, and facilities set up in other countries may turn into competitors later on. Countertrade agreements can also be complicated and time-consuming to complete, sometimes to the point of eating away the profits. Nevertheless, for a company interested in taking advantage of every sales opportunity, this approach can be a competitive advantage in the global marketplace.

work for a U.S. manufacturer, the chances are three out of four that some of your toughest competitors will be companies based in other countries.[38] The chances are also good that your employer will sell or produce at least some products abroad, particularly if you work for a large corporation. At last count, some 100,000 U.S. firms were involved in international business in one way or another.[39] Dozens of large U.S. corporations have invested heavily in overseas operations and look to those markets for future sales and profit growth (Exhibit 2.5). At the same time, more companies based in other countries are entering the U.S. market.

Forms of International Business Activity

Any company can become involved in world trade through a range of activities that reflect an increasing level of ownership, financial commitment, and risk. Many companies first expand into international trade through importing and exporting. Four other forms of international business activity are licensing, franchising, joint ventures, and wholly owned facilities.

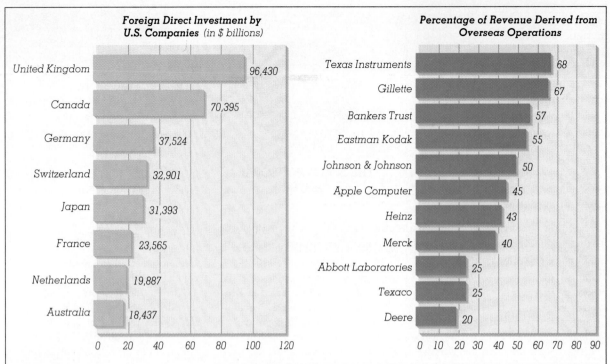

Foreign Direct Investment by U.S. Companies (in $ billions)

Country	$ billions
United Kingdom	96,430
Canada	70,395
Germany	37,524
Switzerland	32,901
Japan	31,393
France	23,565
Netherlands	19,887
Australia	18,437

Percentage of Revenue Derived from Overseas Operations

Company	Percentage
Texas Instruments	68
Gillette	67
Bankers Trust	57
Eastman Kodak	55
Johnson & Johnson	50
Apple Computer	45
Heinz	43
Merck	40
Abbott Laboratories	25
Texaco	25
Deere	20

Exhibit 2.5

U.S. Involvement in International Business

These charts show the areas of the world that have attracted the most investment dollars and the U.S. companies that derived a large portion of their revenues from operations in other countries.

licensing *Agreement to produce and market another company's product in exchange for a royalty or fee*

Importing and Exporting

One of the most common forms of international business is importing or exporting merchandise. Importing is particularly prevalent in the retailing industry. Companies like Kmart have legions of buyers who scour the world for merchandise to import. Smaller companies, like the corner gift shop, also handle imported goods, although they may purchase them through wholesalers in the United States rather than directly from suppliers abroad.

The level of U.S. exports has jumped 121 percent since 1978 as more U.S. companies enter global markets—providing more than 10 million U.S. manufacturing jobs.[40] Companies that want to export their products may do so directly by calling on potential customers overseas, or they may rely on intermediaries here or abroad. Working through someone with connections in the target country is particularly attractive to smaller companies and to those with little experience in international business. Many countries now have foreign trade offices that help importers and exporters interested in doing business within their borders. In addition, the International Trade Administration of the U.S. Department of Commerce offers a variety of services, including political and credit-risk analysis, advice on entering other markets, and tips on financing sources. It also introduces U.S. companies to overseas business and government contacts and to potential importers, buyers, and agents.

Licensing

Another approach to international business is **licensing,** where an agreement entitles one company to produce or market another company's product in return for a royalty or fee. A U.S. business might obtain the rights to manufacture and sell a Scandinavian skin lotion in the United States, using the Scandinavian formula and packaging design. The U.S. company would be responsible for maintaining the quality of the product and for advertising, promoting, and distributing the item. In exchange for the product rights, the U.S. company would pay the Scandinavian company a percentage of its income from sales of the product.

Licensing deals can also work the other way, with the U.S. company acting as the licensor and the overseas company as the licensee. The U.S. firm would avoid the shipping costs, trade barriers, and uncertainties associated with trying to enter other markets, but it would still receive a portion of the revenue from overseas sales.

Franchising

Expanding through *franchising* arrangements is similar in many ways to licensing. The franchisee obtains the rights to duplicate a specific product—perhaps a restaurant, photocopy shop, or videotape rental store—and the company selling the franchise obtains a royalty fee in exchange. McDonald's and KFC are just two of the multinationals that have used this approach to reach consumers overseas, and smaller companies are following suit. For example, Ziebart Tidy-Car, which franchises car-improvement outlets from its headquarters in Michigan, has arranged to open more than 300 outlets in 40 countries.[41] By franchising its operations, a firm can minimize the costs and risks of global expansion and avoid violating trade restrictions.

Joint Ventures and Strategic Alliances

Joint ventures and strategic alliances offer another practical approach to international business. Two or more companies share the investment costs as well as the profits of the venture, and each brings nec-

One way Mister Donut expands globally is by franchising its operations in other countries. This franchise in Japan stresses the taste and appeal of American-style coffee and donuts.

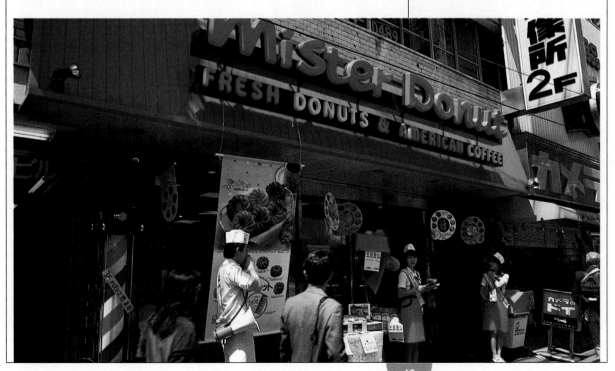

essary skills to the business. McCormick & Company, the giant spice-maker based in Maryland, has used joint ventures and strategic alliances to do business in China as well as in other countries. Similarly, Comshare, a management software company in Michigan, has linked up with Software AG of Far East, the second largest software company in Japan, to pool efforts in developing Japanese-language versions of its computer accounting programs.[42]

In some countries, a joint venture may be the only logical form of business because of local restrictions on direct investment. Many countries will not allow foreign companies to own facilities outright, so to do business at all, you must have a local partner. This was the case when Pizza Hut first opened in Moscow. Since private ownership of any business was forbidden at that time, Pizza Hut's local partner was the City of Moscow.

Wholly Owned Facilities

The most comprehensive form of international business is a wholly owned operation run in another country, without the financial participation of a local partner. Many U.S. firms currently do business this way, as do companies based in other countries. These operations vary in form, size, and purpose. Some are started from scratch; others are acquired from local owners. Some are small sales offices; others are full-scale manufacturing facilities. Some are set up to exploit the availability of raw materials; others take advantage of low wage rates or provide the most direct access to markets in other countries. In almost all cases, at least part of the workforce is drawn from the local population.

Colgate-Palmolive, like many other U.S. companies, locates facilities in other countries so that it can be closer to those local markets. This Colgate-Palmolive factory in Durban, South Africa, draws its workforce from surrounding areas.

Take Levi Strauss, the world's most famous brand of blue jeans. The company's global network of wholly owned manufacturing and distribution facilities provides over 50 percent of the company's net income. Although Levi Strauss's San Francisco headquarters maintains tight control of its international operations, the company relies heavily on local managers to find the right approach to meeting the tastes of home markets. Interestingly enough, though, what works in one market can often be translated into another. The Dockers line of casual slacks, which provides over $550 million in annual sales in North America, combines ideas from the company's Argentinian and Japanese units.[43]

Overseas Investment in the United States

While U.S. companies are opening facilities overseas, companies based abroad are also moving into the U.S. market by acquiring U.S. companies or building new facilities. Such investments total more than $400 billion and will continue to grow (see Exhibit 2.6).[44] These facilities boost the U.S. economy through the addition of jobs and demand for local supplies and services. Although Japanese-owned op-

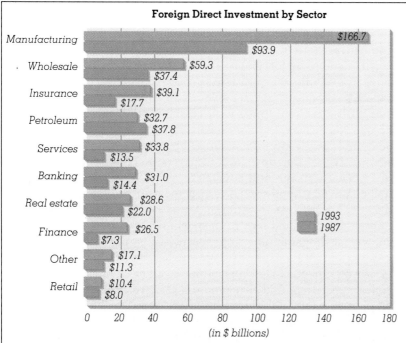

Foreign Direct Investment by Sector

Manufacturing — $166.7 / $93.9
Wholesale — $59.3 / $37.4
Insurance — $39.1 / $17.7
Petroleum — $32.7 / $37.8
Services — $33.8 / $13.5
Banking — $31.0 / $14.4
Real estate — $28.6 / $22.0
Finance — $26.5 / $7.3
Other — $17.1 / $11.3
Retail — $10.4 / $8.0

(1993 / 1987)

0 20 40 60 80 100 120 140 160 180
(in $ billions)

Exhibit 2.6

Where Overseas Companies Invest in the United States
U.S. manufacturing is by far the most attractive industry for investors from abroad.

erations are common in some areas of the country, British, Canadian, and German companies all employ more U.S. workers than do Japanese firms.

Companies from all over the world are doing business in the United States. Some, like Northern Telecom and Unilever, have owned U.S. facilities for years. Northern Telecom is a fast-growing telecommunications company based in Canada that employs 22,000 people in the United States—almost as many workers as it employs in Canada.[45] Unilever is a Dutch–British company with a long-time U.S. presence through its ownership of Lever Brothers, maker of laundry detergents, margarines, and other consumer products.[46]

With increased investment in U.S. facilities, many products that appear to have been made abroad are actually produced in the United States. For example, 6.5 million Japanese-brand television sets are manufactured in the United States; only 230,000 are imported from Japan for sale in the United States.[47] Similarly, carmakers from around the world—including Mazda, Honda, Nissan, and BMW—both make and sell some of their most popular models in the United States. This approach not only reduces the cost of bringing products to an attractive market but also builds goodwill in the host country.

Management of the Global Corporation

Managing operations in more than one country can be tricky. Traditionally, multinational companies have used a *multidomestic management* approach that allows their local units to act independently. In each country, the local organization is self-contained and acts much like a separate domestic business might act. Multidomestic management allows local managers to respond quickly to the needs and pressures in the host countries. For example, each of the 100 companies

CHAPTER 2 | INTERNATIONAL BUSINESS

51

owned by Asea Brown Boveri, a Swedish-Swiss maker of power equipment and industrial goods, deals in its own way with local governments, workers, unions, and customers.

The rapid pace of global expansion has pushed many multinationals to adopt *transnational management,* an approach in which the company coordinates the activities of all its units to achieve worldwide goals—without losing local flexibility. In essence, every part of the company shares the same goals, and top management balances the overall use of resources with the opportunities available in every country. At the same time, local managers are responsible for day-to-day operations in the host countries.

Unilever uses transnational management to coordinate the efforts of 500 companies in 75 countries. Local managers have the freedom to make decisions and take independent action within their companies and, at the same time, are expected to work toward the overall goals set by top managers. This approach helps Unilever apply what it learns in one country to operations in other countries. Sometimes Unilever managers find that products that sell well in one country can be successfully introduced in other countries, although they realize that a few products (such as steak and kidney pie in the United Kingdom) are uniquely national and therefore not appropriate for other markets.[48]

Cultural Differences and How to Handle Them

Unilever, like other multinational corporations, recognizes that each country has its own local tastes and cultural customs. As more companies compete globally, the odds are increasing that you will be involved in international business at some point in your career. Regardless of whether you work for a U.S. company or one that has its headquarters in another country, you'll need to develop skills in dealing with people from other countries. The best approach you can take is to recognize and respect the differences that distinguish members of other cultures.

People from other cultures differ in their social values, their ideas of status, their decision-making habits, their attitude toward time, their use of space, their body language, and their manners. These differences can lead to misunderstandings in international business relationships, particularly if language differences exist as well. Take the signal for *no.* People in the United States and Canada shake their heads back and forth; people in Bulgaria nod up and down; people in Japan move their right hands; people in Sicily raise their chins. To avoid confusion, a businessperson who wants to complete a deal in one of these countries must understand the meaning of these signals.

Although cultural differences pose significant barriers to communication, these problems can be resolved if people maintain an open mind. The best way to prepare yourself to do business with people from another culture is to study that culture in advance. Learn everything you can about the culture's history, religion, politics, and customs—especially its business customs. Who makes decisions? How are negotiations usually conducted? Is gift giving expected? What is the proper attire for a business meeting? In addition, seasoned inter-

Doing business in another country can be extremely tricky. Here are some issues to consider when you conduct business abroad.

The Importance of Packaging

Numerous problems result from the failure to adapt packaging for other cultures. Sometimes only the color of the package needs to be altered to enhance a product's sales. White, for instance, symbolizes death in Japan and much of Asia; green represents danger or disease in Malaysia. Obviously, using the wrong color in these countries might produce negative reactions.

The Language Barrier

Some product names travel poorly. For instance, the gasoline company Esso found out that its name means "stalled car" in Japan. However, some company names have traveled well. Kodak may be the most famous example. A research team deliberately developed this name after searching for a word that was pronounceable everywhere but had no specific meaning anywhere.

Problems with Promotions

In its U.S. promotion, one company

HOW TO AVOID BUSINESS BLUNDERS ABROAD

had effectively used this sentence: "You can use no finer napkin at your dinner table." The U.S. company decided to use the same commercials in England because, after all, the British do speak English. To the British, however, the word *napkin* or *nappy* actually means "diaper." The ad could hardly be expected to boost sales of dinner napkins in England.

Local Customs

Social norms vary greatly from country to country and it is difficult for any outsider to be knowledgeable about all of them, so local input is vital. For example, one firm promoted eyeglasses in Thailand with commercials featuring animals wearing glasses. However, in Thailand animals are considered a low form of

life; humans would never wear anything worn by an animal.

Translation Problems

The best translations of an advertising message convey the concept of the original but do not precisely duplicate the original. PepsiCo learned this lesson when it reportedly discovered that its slogan "Come alive with Pepsi" was translated into German as "Come alive out of the grave with Pepsi." In Asia, the slogan was once translated as "Bring your ancestors back from the dead."

The Need for Research

Proper market research may reduce or eliminate most international business blunders. Market researchers can uncover needs for product adaptations, potential name problems, promotional requirements, and useful market strategies. Good research may even uncover potential translation problems.

As you can see, doing business in other cultures can be risky if you're unprepared. However, awareness of differences, consultation with local people, and concern for host-country feelings can reduce problems and save money.

national businesspeople suggest the following techniques for improving intercultural communication:

- *Deal with the individual.* Don't stereotype the other person or react with preconceived ideas. Regard the person as an individual first, not as a representative of another culture.
- *Be alert to the other person's customs.* Expect him or her to have differing values, beliefs, expectations, and mannerisms.
- *Be aware that gestures and expressions mean different things in various cultures.* The other person's body language may not mean what you think, and he or she may read unintentional meanings into your message. Clarify your true intent by repetition and examples. Ask questions and listen carefully.
- *Adapt your style to the other person's.* If the other person appears to be direct and straightforward, follow suit. If not, adjust your behavior to match.
- *Show respect.* Learn how respect is communicated—through gestures, eye contact, and so on—in various cultures.

1 Differentiate between absolute, comparative, and national competitive advantage.

A country with an absolute advantage can produce a particular product with fewer resources than any other nation. A country with a comparative advantage can produce a particular product more efficiently than other countries because of its natural and human resources. A country with a national competitive advantage has the ability to innovate and upgrade to a higher level of technology and productivity, which makes it more competitive in the world market.

2 Distinguish between the balance of trade and the balance of payments.

The balance of trade is the total value of exports minus the value of imports over a specific period. The balance of payments is the total flow of money into the country minus the flow of money out of the country.

3 Identify five techniques that countries use to protect their domestic industries.

Five of the most common forms of protectionism are tariffs, quotas, subsidies, restrictive standards, and retaliatory measures.

4 Outline the arguments for and against protectionism.

People who support protectionism believe that building in a preference for a country's home industries can boost local economies and save local jobs. It can also shield domestic industries from head-to-head competition with overseas rivals. The people who argue against protectionism point to results such as the higher consumer prices, the high cost of saving jobs, the possibility of losing jobs in other sectors of the economy, the damage done to U.S. companies that depend on imports, and the existence of many loopholes.

5 Explain how trading blocs and the GATT affect trade.

Trading blocs are regional groupings of countries within which trade barriers have been removed. These alliances ease trade between bloc members and strengthen barriers for nonmembers. The General Agreement on Tariffs and Trade (GATT) is a worldwide trade agreement among more than a hundred nations seeking to reduce certain trade barriers and increase world trade.

6 Define foreign exchange and discuss the effect of a weaker U.S. dollar on U.S. companies that do business in other countries.

Foreign exchange is the conversion of one currency into an equivalent amount of another currency. When the dollar falls in value relative to other currencies, U.S. products become cheaper on the world market. Because U.S. products cost less, demand rises, and U.S. companies can export more. At the same time, imports become expensive, which puts U.S. products at an advantage. Profits also increase when earnings in other currencies are converted to dollars.

7 List five forms of international business activity.

Importing and exporting, licensing, franchising, joint ventures and strategic alliances, and wholly owned facilities are five of the most common forms of international business activity.

8 Identify six ways to improve communication in an international business relationship.

To improve international communication, you can learn as much as you can about the other person's culture; keep an open mind and avoid stereotyping; be sensitive to the other person's customs; anticipate misunderstandings and guard against them; adapt your style to match the other person's style; learn how to show respect in another culture.

PepsiCo's strategy in Russia was to blanket the region with Pizza Huts; running a couple of isolated restaurants in Moscow simply wouldn't be profitable enough to justify the effort. Given this ambitious plan, the first two restaurants represented a chance to establish a model that could be duplicated in other parts of the country.

Andrew Rafalat's job, then, was not only to get the two Moscow Pizza Huts up and running but also to lay the foundation for future expansion. He started with the Moscow City government. Under Soviet law at the time, foreign companies could not hold a majority interest in a Soviet business, and ownership of private property by Soviet citizens was still restricted. So Pizza Hut had to operate through joint ventures with government entities—in this case, the City of Moscow, which owned 51 percent of the two restaurants.

Next, Rafalat had to find sites for the first two Pizza Huts. Government officials offered two cellars on the outskirts of Moscow. Rafalat pointed out that succeeding in the restaurant business generally involves putting the outlets where the people are. He eventually wrangled two reasonably decent spots, one with the capacity to seat 325 people; the other, 120 people. After an initial rush of heavy business, the two restaurants were ex-

pected to serve between 3,000 and 5,000 customers per day. The typical U.S. Pizza Hut serves approximately 1,200 customers, whereas the European average is 2,000 per day.

Although Rafalat originally planned to rely totally on local supplies to equip, furnish, and stock the restaurants, he quickly discovered that this plan was not practical at the start. Nothing was available. Although he soon found local sources for pizza ingredients, he initially had to import nearly everything from the West, from building materials to pizza ovens. Local transportation, however, was unpredictable. After waiting weeks for his first shipments, Rafalat had more success routing shipments from London to Helsinki, Finland, and then trucking them south to the Pizza Hut warehouse in Moscow.

Rafalat also needed to hire and train roughly 300 people—managers, chefs, and other kitchen and restaurant help. He needed to teach them to make pizza, of course, but more important, he had to teach them about customer service, then an unknown concept in Russia. Five Pizza Hut managers from the West spent almost two months giving the Moscow employees a crash course in how to operate a restaurant. They discovered that competition excited the employees; everything from folding pizza boxes to sprinkling on the cheese became a team sport, a game to win. By the time the restaurants opened, team spirit among the staff was high; the employees were having *fun,* and so were the customers, who had never seen a cheerful restaurant employee before.

However, Rafalat's biggest problem was coping with the many layers of government bureaucracy. Although some members of the government were eager to encourage capitalism and foreign investment, many traditionalists still clung to the communist doctrine and were extremely suspicious of Westerners. Rafalat eventually discovered that many of his problems with the government could

be solved with a slice or two of "complimentary" pizza.

Finally, after three years of hard work, Rafalat opened Moscow's first two Pizza Huts. When he saw hundreds of people lined up to get in, he worried whether the restaurants would make it through the week. However, there was plenty of pizza to go around—and one outlet served so much pizza that it quickly became one of the highest-volume restaurants in the worldwide PepsiCo chain. Rafalat trained local managers to take over, and went on to become the regional operations manager for Pizza Hut in Eastern Europe.

Your Mission: When Rafalat took the assignment in Moscow, he asked you to come along as his aide. "You have a knack for figuring out how to get things done, and that will come in handy," he said. Handle the following assignments, using your common sense and the principles discussed in this chapter.

1. Andrew Rafalat wants to develop local sources for ingredients for dough, cheese, tomato sauce, and vegetable and meat toppings. How should you proceed?

a. Call the manager of the McDonald's in Moscow and ask how that chain is handling the problem of obtaining ingredients.

b. Seek help from the officials in the City of Moscow who are your joint venture partners. Perhaps they can use their connections to obtain the necessary ingredients through official channels.

c. Pass the word among your Muscovite employees that you are prepared to buy from local sources through unofficial channels and pay a premium over the state prices in order to obtain consistent quality and delivery.

2. Soon after you open, a government sanitation official closes both Pizza Huts, claiming that you have not filed the required papers, that your employees have not been properly tested for disease, and that you are using dirty vegetables. How can you cope?

a. Invite the official who closed the restaurants to return for a closer look. While the inspector is there, subtly indicate that you believe friendly officials should be rewarded with Western currency.

b. Try to comply with all the requirements as quickly as possible.

c. Use PepsiCo's influence with highly placed officials to get the restaurants reopened immediately.

3. Your restaurants accept both rubles and Western currencies. How-ever, the value of the ruble has been dropping as a result of Russia's economic changes. As long as you buy ingredients from the West with Western currency and sell pizza in Moscow for rubles, your profits are at the mercy of currency fluctuations. As the ruble falls, so do your profits. Until you can buy from local sources, what should you do?

a. Raise prices across the board.

b. Accept only rubles.

c. Accept only Western currencies.

4. You have been asked to help find an apartment for a PepsiCo manager relocating to Moscow. Your govern-ment contacts have pulled strings to get a three-bedroom apartment with a private bath. However, the apartment has no lightbulbs, no drainpipe under the sink, and no stove. What should you do?

a. Complain to the city officials and ask them to fix the problems.

b. Thank the city officials for their help in finding such a nice apartment and ask for their advice on correcting these few "minor" things.

c. Ask the people at the U.S. embassy to get the names of reliable service people and sources of household appliances and supplies.[49]

KEY TERMS

absolute advantage (33)
balance of payments (36)
balance of trade (34)
comparative advantage (32)
countertrade (46)
dumping (39)
embargo (38)
exchange rate (46)

exporting (34)
floating exchange rate system (46)
foreign exchange (46)
foreign sales corporations (44)
free trade (41)
importing (34)
licensing (48)
multinational corporations (MNCs) (34)

national competitive advantage (33)
protectionism (37)
quotas (37)
tariffs (37)
trade deficit (34)
trade surplus (34)
trading blocs (41)

REVIEW QUESTIONS

1. What is the balance of trade, and how does it relate to the balance of payments?

2. What is a multinational corporation?

3. Why do countries join trading blocs?

4. What is dumping, and how does the United States respond to this practice?

5. How does the International Monetary Fund differ from the World Bank and the Export-Import Bank?

6. What is a floating exchange rate?

7. How can a company use licensing agreements to enter world markets?

8. How does multidomestic management differ from transnational management?

FORD STEERS TOWARD GLOBAL OPERATIONS

Henry Ford, the man behind the Model T, was among the first U.S. executives to move aggressively into overseas markets. Decades later, the company he founded is moving full speed ahead to integrate its U.S. and European operations as the first step toward forging a global organization. The next step is to have the company's operations in Asia and Latin America work more closely together. The ultimate goal: to design and build a car that can be sold—with minor alterations to fit local needs—in any market in the world.

The idea of a "world car" is hardly new. The first time Ford tried this idea was in the 1960s. The company planned a front-wheel-drive economy car to be sold in the United States and abroad. When Ford discovered that the car cost more to build than some of the company's larger models, it canceled plans for the U.S. version. The next attempt was in the early 1980s with the compact Ford Escort. This model was intended for both Europe and the United States, but Ford's European and U.S. engineering groups couldn't agree on a single version. That's why the version sold in Europe had little in common with the version sold in the United States.

Ford's third attempt came in the 1990s with the Mondeo, a car named to evoke the word for *world* in several languages. Built in Belgium, the Mondeo was introduced in Europe 18 months before the two U.S. versions, the Ford Contour and the Mercury Mystique, which are built in Kansas City. Because the European version was seen as too conservative for U.S. car buyers, the styling was changed for the U.S. version. Although Ford spent $5.5 billion to design and produce the Mondeo, the company expects the model to be profitable.

The "Ford 2000" plan is driving the move toward a global organization that can use the facilities in each location to best advantage. Small front-wheel-drive cars are to be created and produced in Europe, for instance, because this type of car is extremely popular there. In turn, Ford can use the same design and manufacturing process as a base for making small cars to be sold in the U.S. market, with styling adjusted to local tastes. In the United States, four vehicle project centers will be designing larger cars and trucks that can be sold (and possibly manufactured) around the world.

Alex Trotman, chairman of Ford, is pushing for this global approach because he sees how much the company can save by engineering a car just once. "We are using resources around the world more than we have in the past," he says. "We're avoiding duplication." Trotman also wants Ford to be able to adapt the best methods for making cars, regardless of where these techniques originate. Building on these strengths will help Ford push more aggressively into rapidly growing markets such as China, India, and Southeast Asia.

However, some experts are skeptical that the results of this global approach will be as Trotman expects. "We are dealing with different cultures, different manufacturing processes, different government regulations, five hours' difference in time," observes one U.S. car executive. "How do you run operations from that philosophical and physical distance?" Lee Iacocca, former president of Ford and retired chairman of Chrysler, is also doubtful. "Can one product group make decisions for both continents? I don't think it can be done," he says. "I keep reading about the global economy and changing communications, but you still see different desires in England than in the U.S." Critics may disagree with Trotman's approach, but he's set a course to steer Ford toward a truly global organization by the turn of the century.

1. Why would Ford want to build small cars in Europe, where they're popular, rather than importing them from the United States to sell in Europe?

2. What advantages and disadvantages might the company find if it used licensing to introduce the Ford name in India?

3. Do you agree with Lee Iacocca's assessment of variations in local tastes? Give an example to support your answer.

As directed by your instructor (either in a group of three or four students or on your own), select a U.S.-made good or service that you think might be appropriate for customers outside the United States. Next, choose a country that you believe would be a good place to market that product. Finally, develop a strategy for marketing your selected product in the country of your choice.

• Using the library as a resource, write a brief profile of your chosen country; include its geographical location, population, form of government, monetary unit, language, literacy rate, per capita income, and status of communication (number of television sets, radios, newspapers, and magazines).

• In addition to the information in your profile, identify other factors that would influence the marketing of your selected product in your chosen country. Such factors might include packaging or product color, brand name, potential applications, and social customs.

• Prepare a brief presentation outlining how you would present this product in your chosen country. Would any changes need to be made in the product to bring it to this new market? Would advertising aimed at the U.S. audience be appropriate in the country you've chosen? What competition do you think your product would face?

Find a *Wall Street Journal* article describing an experience of a U.S. company or division that conducts business outside the United States. As an alternative, look for an article describing how a company or division based in another country has started doing business in the United States.

1. Describe in your own words the company's experience. Was it positive, negative, or mixed? Why?

2. What cultural or business differences did the company encounter? What problems did these differences create for the company? What did the company do to overcome the obstacles?

3. Did the company achieve its objectives? What, if any, major changes did it have to make in its plans? What conclusions can you draw from this company's particular experience with international trade?

BUY AMERICAN?

Synopsis

This video addresses both sides of the issue of whether buying foreign goods is harmful to U.S. workers.

Exercises

ANALYSIS

1. Why did U.S. sales of Japanese cars increase so dramatically over the last several decades? Do the union workers in this video address this issue?

2. What sort of response did you have to the textile industry commercial at the beginning of this video program? Did it change your views about buying clothing? Why or why not?

3. Why do some experts claim that a closed economy leads to fewer choices for consumers? If this claim is true, do you consider a reduction in choices an acceptable trade-off in light of saving jobs?

4. What effect does foreign competition appear to have had on the quality of automobiles manufactured by U.S. companies?

5. Why do you suppose the major Japanese car companies have built assembly plants here in the United States?

APPLICATION

Assume you're an executive in the U.S. subsidiary of a German company that sells power tools in the United States. Your company is battling a "buy American" movement in the tool market, led by an editor at one of the major trade journals in the industry. Use what you've learned about international trade issues to draft a letter to this editor, explaining why a strict "buy American" policy is not good for the country overall or for individual tool buyers.

DECISION

Assume that your parents work for a U.S. automaker and that you're in the market for a new car. The car you really want is a Honda Accord, which is a direct competitor of such U.S. cars as the Ford Taurus and Mercury Sable. Will you buy the Accord? If so, what will you say to your parents if they question your loyalty or patriotism?

COMMUNICATION

The "buy American" movement usually bases its pleas on patriotism and the need to protect jobs in this country. Try to frame a "buy American" message on economic arguments, rather than emotional ones. Write a

one-page flyer explaining why it makes economic sense for U.S. citizens to buy U.S. products.

INTEGRATION

The Case for Critical Thinking in Chapter 13 discusses the minivan market. It raises at least one issue that might explain why the workers in the GM plant in Tarrytown were losing their jobs. Read the case and reconsider the Tarrytown issue. Are those workers really losing their jobs because people are buying foreign cars? (The GM minivans shown in the Tarrytown video are a key issue here.)

ETHICS

If buying foreign cars leads to lost jobs in the U.S. auto industry, at least in the short term, do U.S. citizens have a moral obligation to refrain from buying those foreign cars?

DEBATE

Organize a debate on the issue of freedom of choice versus the desire to preserve U.S. jobs. One side should take the position that there is a direct link between buying American products and saving American jobs. The other side should voice the view held by most economists and trade experts, that closing off an economy leads to fewer and less attractive choices for consumers.

TEAMWORK

In a team of four students, find out how many cars and trucks the major U.S. automakers export to Japan, China, Germany, and France. Are the companies having more trouble in some countries than in others? Why?

RESEARCH

Conduct library research to find the latest available data on the trade balance between the United States and Japan. Where does the United States stand overall in its trade balance with Japan? Which U.S. industries have improved in the last two or three years? Which have fallen further behind?

ROLE PLAYING

Form a team with three other students. One of you will play a role similar to that of the union leader shown in the video (the man who demonstrated his belief in buying American by forbidding union members from parking foreign cars in the union parking lot. The student's job is to convince the three other students (all playing the roles of union members) that buying foreign cars is an attack on the autoworkers' union. At least one of the three "union member" students should attempt to raise such issues as consumer choice, competitiveness, and managerial decision making—factors that may also endanger union jobs.

Chapter

3

Ethical and Social Responsibilities of Business

1 Identify four stakeholder groups to which business has a responsibility

2 Name three kinds of pollution and outline actions to control them

3 List the four rights of consumers

4 State the responsibilities of the Equal Employment Opportunity Commission

5 Define sexism and describe gender issues that can influence discrimination in the workplace

6 Discuss two general ways that businesses may cheat investors

7 Distinguish between ethical dilemmas and ethical lapses

8 List and explain four philosophical approaches to resolving ethical questions in business

Can a Company Be Both Profitable and Socially Responsible?

Ben & Jerry's Homemade makes more than premium ice cream; it makes an unusual effort to operate a business as a force for social change. The company has earned a nationwide reputation as an organization that stands apart in today's highly competitive, money-driven business environment. Making a profit seems to be less important to the founders than meeting the needs of employees and the surrounding community. From the start, the company culture has emphasized people, fun, and adventure.

Co-founders Ben Cohen and Jerry Greenfield intended to start an ice cream parlor, and once the business got going, they planned to sell it and move on. However, something always forced them to grow, such as a new competitor or the need to replace or fix equipment. Almost in spite of itself, the ice cream parlor became a growth company.

However, growth brought both higher profits and financial controls. The company was becoming less fun and more "businesslike." Cohen and Greenfield didn't want the company to become like other corporations. So four years after starting the company, the two founders decided on a way to run it so that Ben & Jerry's Homemade would be a force for social change. They envisioned the company as being held in trust for the community. Growth and profit would be a means to increased social responsibility, which would justify being more businesslike.

The co-founders' social-responsibility goals are demonstrated in many ways. Of pretax profits, 7.5 percent goes to support social causes (the national average is 1.5 percent). The company is a leader in corporate recycling and environmental programs. Products not only are associated with peace, justice, and the environment but also support these causes financially. For example, a percentage of sales from Peace Pops goes to promoting world peace. Rain Forest Crunch is made with nuts from the South American rain forest, which supports the native people and gives them a financial incentive to nurture the forest rather than harvest it for lumber.

The Ben & Jerry's Homemade recipe for success combines premium ice cream and a commitment to social responsibility.

Today the company is a multimillion-dollar corporation, and double-digit growth is once again challenging the culture and commitment to social change. The company now employs hundreds of people, and not all of them share Cohen and Greenfield's idealism. The two founders worry that some managers have become too profit-oriented and that new projects are being evaluated primarily for their ability to generate profit. What does it mean for a company to be socially responsible? Can a large corporation balance the desire to be socially responsible with the need to remain profitable?[1]

FOUNDATIONS OF SOCIAL RESPONSIBILITY

As Ben Cohen and Jerry Greenfield realize, each company functions as part of an interactive system of relationships with individuals and groups in society. However, the ideal relationship between businesses and society is a matter of debate. Managerial decisions and actions have increasingly come under scrutiny as academics, social activists, and managers try to determine what a business's responsibility should be for activities that affect society, both positively or negatively. Another issue being debated is how much responsibility businesses should bear for reducing or solving social problems.

social responsibility Concept that a business needs to look beyond its own goals and recognize other obligations to society

These two issues form the core of a concept known as **social responsibility,** which argues that a company has a greater obligation to society beyond the pursuit of profit or other goals. Yes, businesses must be profitable to survive, but beyond profit, what does a business owe to society? The answer depends, in part, on its stakeholders.

Business and Its Stakeholders

stakeholders Individuals or groups to whom business has a responsibility

A business has many **stakeholders:** groups that are affected by (or affect) a business's operations. Stakeholders include employees, consumers, investors, and society at large. If a company's management consistently ignores social responsibilities and shortchanges its stakeholders, the business will suffer and eventually fold. Investors who are unhappy with the company's performance will invest elsewhere. Workers whose needs are not met will quit and find other jobs. Customers whose tastes and values are ignored will spend their money on other things. If the concerns of society are disregarded, the voters will clamor for laws to limit offensive business activities.

Most business executives sincerely try to respond to the needs of these four groups. Generally speaking, their efforts are successful. However, stakeholder interests sometimes conflict, which means managers face choices as they try to reconcile competing interests. When trying to ensure profits, for example, a manager might be tempted to compromise product quality. Would the choice be justified? No, but it isn't always easy to know what's best. On the other hand, 29 states have passed *constituency statutes,* which allow corporate directors to look beyond shareholder interests and consider the interests of employees, the community, and other stakeholders as well.[2]

To determine whether its activities and operations are socially responsible, a business can perform a **social audit,** a systematic evaluation and reporting of the company's performance in the area of social responsibility. Ben & Jerry's Homemade asks an outsider to conduct a social audit once a year, and it announces the results in its annual report to shareholders. This social audit shows the impact of Ben & Jerry's operations on its employees, customers, communities, suppliers, and shareholders.

One way to balance social responsibility and stakeholder interests is to appoint a high-level manager who will coordinate company-wide efforts. McDonald's created the post of vice president of environmental affairs, which is held by Mike Roberts. Roberts and a task force have worked with the nonprofit Environmental Defense Fund to reduce the huge stream of waste from McDonald's 11,000 restaurants by 80 percent within a few years. At least 42 major changes in restaurant operations are involved—everything from composting food scraps to replacing plastic spoons with a biodegradable starch-based alternative. From now on, the entire company will view waste reduction as a top priority, along with quickness, cleanliness, and quality service. McDonald's plans to spend $100 million annually on waste-reduction efforts and expects its suppliers to incur additional costs as well.[3]

Companies are also doing more *cause-related marketing,* in which they contribute a portion of the profit from sales of a product to a worthy cause. Ben & Jerry's uses this technique to promote its Rain Forest Crunch brittle. A percentage of the profits goes into a fund to protect the Amazon rain forest. For many companies, social responsibility extends to *philanthropy,* the donation of money, time, goods, or services to charitable, humanitarian, or educational institutions. Corporations donate over $5.6 billion to charity each year, and many executives also donate their time to community affairs.[4]

The Evolution of Social Responsibility

Social responsibility is a concept with decades-old roots. In the nineteenth century, the prevailing view among U.S. industrialists was that business had only one responsibility: to make a profit. Railroad tycoon William Vanderbilt summed up this attitude when he said, "The public be damned. I'm working for the shareholders."[5] Although some businesses were concerned with the impact their products and operations had on customers, employees, shareholders, and the community, others put profit over every other consideration. *Caveat emptor* was the rule of the day—"Let the buyer beware." If you bought a product, you paid the price and took the consequences. No consumer groups or government agencies would help you if the product was defective or caused harm; if you tried to sue the company, chances were you would lose.

By the early twentieth century, reformers were pushing politicians and government regulators to protect citizens from the abuses of big business. Muckrakers and crusading journalists used the power of the pen to stir up public indignation and agitate for reform. For example, after reading Upton Sinclair's novel *The Jungle,* which described

social audit *Periodic assessment and reporting of what a business is doing to be socially responsible*

Exhibit 3.1

**Early Government Regulations
Pertaining to Business**

*Despite their reputation for relent-
lessly pursuing profits, many
early tycoons were also philan-
thropists. For example, Andrew
Carnegie, a pioneer in the steel
industry, donated money to build
public libraries in towns throughout the United States. Nevertheless, government regulations
were needed to ensure fair business practices.*

Government regulation	Date	Effect
Interstate Commerce Act	1887	Regulated business practices, specifically railroad operations and shipping rates.
Sherman Antitrust Act	1890	Fostered competition by preventing monopolies and noncompetitive mergers.
Pure Food and Drug Act	1906	Encouraged purity of food and drugs, specifically those transported across state lines.
Meat Inspection Act	1906	Encouraged purity of meat and meat products, specifically those transported across state lines.
Federal Trade Commission Act	1914	Controlled illegal trade practices through the creation of the Federal Trade Commission.
Clayton Antitrust Act	1914	Eliminated price discrimination that gave large businesses an advantage over smaller firms.

unclean conditions in the meat-packing industry, President Theodore
Roosevelt pushed for passage of the Pure Food and Drug Act of
1906. In addition, laws were passed to limit the power of monopolies and prevent unfair business practices, among other reforms (see
Exhibit 3.1).

The Great Depression, which started in 1929, led to more disen-
chantment with business. With 25 percent of the workforce unemployed, people lost their faith in unbridled capitalism, and pressure
mounted for government to fix the system. At the urging of President Franklin D. Roosevelt, Congress passed laws in the 1930s and
1940s to protect workers, consumers, and investors. These laws established the Social Security system, allowed employees to join unions
and bargain collectively, set a minimum hourly wage, and limited the
length of the workweek. New laws prevented unfair competition and
false advertising, and started the Securities and Exchange Commission to protect investors.

Public confidence in U.S. business revived during World War II,
and throughout the 1950s, the relationship among business, government, and society was relatively tranquil. However, the climate shifted
in the 1960s, as activism exploded on four fronts: environmental protection, national defense, consumerism, and civil rights. These movements have drastically altered the way business is conducted in the
United States. Many of the changes have been made willingly by socially responsible companies, others have been forced by government
action, and still others have come about because of pressure from citizen groups.

Despite the efforts of various groups, many people say that
U.S. businesses should do much more for society. Approximately two
out of three people believe that U.S. business is not doing enough to
provide job security for employees, help the community, keep the environment clean, price products fairly, and behave ethically.[6] The problem, some argue, is inherent in the "me first" nature of capitalism. In
the ideal capitalist society, because people are free to pursue their own
interests, they will all look out for themselves, and society as a whole

will benefit. According to this argument, the "invisible hand" of the market—Adam Smith's concept—will juggle everyone's interests more effectively than government action. However, in the real world of capitalism, gaining rights for U.S. workers and consumers has taken 100 years of protest and pressure.[7]

These days investors and social activists are driving businesses to look even beyond their own operations and police the practices of their suppliers.[8] The drive for higher profits does motivate some businesses to take actions that don't benefit society, but an increasing number of businesses are adding social responsibility to their list of corporate goals. Management expert Peter Drucker contends that businesses should, in fact, view social problems as opportunities to satisfy consumer needs—in a profitable way.[9]

Practical Limitations on Social Responsibility

Undertaking socially responsible activities takes money. Just how much money is unclear, because no single source of information exists on business's expenditures for socially desirable activities.

Look just at pollution control: The Environmental Protection Agency estimates that the United States devotes 2 percent of its GDP to protect and clean up the environment; that figure is expected to increase to almost 3 percent, or $46 billion, by the year 2000. Is that too much? Can the country afford it? The answer depends on your priorities, but as a percentage of GDP, the amount is comparable to what other industrialized nations are spending. To help you put the figure in perspective, consider that people in the United States spend roughly the same amount on illegal drugs each year, twice as much on clothing, and six times as much on defense.[10]

Although socially responsible programs are welcomed by many stakeholders, companies do not have unlimited resources. No business has the luxury of paying "whatever it takes," for years or decades, to save lives or to protect the environment. If a company spends $1 million to save a few lives by cleaning its wastewater more thoroughly, it may not have another $1 million to spend on other safety measures to save more lives. Deciding how to spend limited resources is a juggling act that every business faces, and it comes from the push and pull of trying to satisfy a diverse group of stakeholders.

BUSINESS AND THE ENVIRONMENT

The difficulty of balancing profits and social responsibility becomes apparent when you consider the case of Bofors Nobel, a manufacturer of paint pigments. The company disposed of manufacturing wastes on 68 wooded acres behind its plant in Muskegon, Michigan. When the government ordered the firm to clean up the site, the estimated cost came to $60 million. With annual sales of only $30 million, Bofors opted to close its doors.[11] Now the company is out of business, its customers are scrambling to line up new sources of pigment, the employees are out of work, and the toxic waste remains. In a situation like this, there are no winners.

The Pervasiveness of Pollution

pollution *Threats to the physical environment caused by human activities in an industrial society*

Toxic wastes are not the only form of **pollution** threatening our environment. Our air, our water, and our land are all threatened by economic progress, and the pollution of one may taint another. Pollution is pervasive and global: Industrialized and developing nations alike are grappling with these issues.

Air Pollution

As a resident of the United States, the chances are two out of three that you breathe air that fails to meet the standards of the Environmental Protection Agency (EPA).[12] Air quality is bad enough to cause 50,000 premature deaths each year, bad enough to add an extra $10 to $25 billion annually to the nation's health-care bills,[13] and potentially bad enough to jeopardize the ecological balance and make the earth uninhabitable.

The most noticeable form of air pollution is probably smog, which is produced by the interaction of sunlight and hydrocarbons (gases released when fossil fuels are burned). Another sort of air pollutant is acid rain, created when emissions from coal-burning factories and electric utility plants react with air. Acid rain has been blamed for damaging lakes and forests in southeastern Canada and the northeastern United States.

Apart from contributing to acid rain, coal emissions may also contribute to a greenhouse effect. The heated gases form a layer of unusually warm air around the earth, which traps the sun's heat and prevents the earth's surface from cooling. Some scientists believe that the greenhouse effect will eventually change the earth's climate, including a general increase in temperature, changes in rainfall, and a rise in the level of the oceans.

Another long-term threat is the depletion of the earth's protective ozone layer caused by chlorofluorocarbons (CFCs), which have been widely used as industrial cleansers, refrigerants, and ingredients in insulation and foam packaging. Scientists fear that if the ozone layer deteriorates, the effects of the sun's rays may be magnified, increasing the incidence of a deadly form of skin cancer. In addition, experts worry about airborne toxins that are emitted during some manufacturing processes. Large companies release some 2.7 billion pounds of these chemical wastes into the air each year, and small companies probably add much more.[14] Although the effects of many of these substances are unknown, some are carcinogenic (cancer-causing). Second-hand tobacco smoke has also been classified by the EPA as a carcinogen, a move that is nudging more employers toward a smoke-free workplace.[15]

In the past, ozone-depleting chlorofluorocarbons (CFCs) were widely used in refrigerators. These days Whirlpool and other manufacturers have abandoned CFCs in favor of more efficient cooling technologies that don't harm the ozone layer.

Water Pollution

Our air is not the only part of our environment to suffer. Approximately 10 percent of our river and lake water is polluted.[16] In some areas, the harbors and coastal waters are in trouble as well. This pollution comes from a variety of sources: manufacturing facilities, mining and construction sites, farms, and city sewage systems. Although dramatic accidents like the *Exxon Valdez* oil spill in Alaskan waters are widely publicized, the main threat is the careless day-to-day disposal of wastes from thousands of individual sources.

Land Pollution

Even if all wastewater were purified before being discharged, our groundwater would still be endangered by leakage from the millions of tons of hazardous substances that have been buried underground or dumped in improper storage sites. The cost for cleaning up U.S. toxic-waste sites could eventually exceed $500 billion.[17] Many of these sites were created years ago by companies that carelessly— but legally—disposed of substances that are now known to be unhealthy. Cleaning up these wastes will be extremely difficult and expensive.

Government and Industry Response

Today an overwhelming majority of people in the United States consider themselves environmentalists. In fact, by a ratio of 6 to 1, they want to reduce pollution even if it means paying higher prices.[18] Politicians and businesspeople are well aware of this, and they're responding accordingly.

Concern for the environment has been growing since the 1960s, when **ecology,** or the balance of nature, became a popular cause. In 1963 federal, state, and local governments began enacting laws and regulations to reduce pollution. (See Exhibit 3.2 for a brief summary of major federal legislation.) The legislation underlying federal efforts to control pollution is the National Environmental Policy Act of 1969, which established a structure for coordinating all federal environmental programs. This act was followed by a presidential order in December 1970 establishing the Environmental Protection Agency (EPA) to regulate air and water pollution by manufacturers and utilities, supervise auto-pollution control, license pesticides, control toxic substances, and safeguard the purity of drinking water.

The 1990 Clean Air Act uses a free-market approach, allowing companies to choose their own strategies for battling pollution. In certain cities, companies can buy and sell pollution rights. Each company is given an allowable "pollution quota" based on such factors as its size and industry. If a company voluntarily reduces pollution below its limit, it can sell its "credits" to another company. Although granting companies the right to pollute might seem counterproduc-

Exhibit 3.2

Major Federal Environmental Legislation
Since the early 1960s, major federal legislation aimed at the environment has focused on cleaner air, cleaner water, and reduced toxic waste.

Legislation	Date	Effect
National Environmental Policy Act	1969	Established a structure for coordinating all federal environmental programs.
Order of Administrative Reorganization	1970	Established Council on Environmental Quality to advise president on environmental policy and to review environmental impact statements. Led to formation of Environmental Protection Agency.
Air pollution		
Clear Air Act and amendments	1963, 1965, 1970, 1977, 1990	Assisted states and localities in formulating control programs. Set federal standards for auto-exhaust emissions. Set maximum permissible pollution levels. Authorized nationwide air-pollution standards and limitations to pollutant discharge. Required scrubbers in new coal-fired power plants. Directed EPA to prevent deterioration of air quality in clean areas. Set schedule and standards for cutting smog, acid rain, hazardous factory fumes, and ozone-depleting chemicals.
Solid-waste pollution		
Solid Waste Disposal Act and amendments	1965, 1984	Authorized research and assistance to state and local control programs. Regulated treatment, storage, transportation, and disposal of hazardous waste.
Resource Recovery Act	1970	Subsidized pilot recycling plants. Authorized nationwide control programs.
Resource Conservation and Recovery Act	1976	Directed EPA to regulate hazardous-waste management.
Surface Mining and Reclamation Act	1976	Controlled strip mining and restoration of reclaimed land.

tive, it encourages them to clean up their operations as quickly and as thoroughly as possible.[19]

Today's carrot-and-stick approach is prodding businesses toward stricter compliance by rewarding effective measures for pollution control and handing out stiffer penalties for offenders.[20] At the same time, businesses and governmental regulators recognize that the health threat posed by a given industrial pollutant must be weighed against the economic cost of limiting or eliminating its use. Many activities that cause pollution also produce socially desirable results. The waste dumps, factories, power plants, and pesticides that threaten the environment almost always meet a legitimate social need. Long-term solutions lie in giving business the motive and opportunity to find alternative ways to meet those needs.

One of the most promising new directions is emphasizing prevention as opposed to correction. Pioneering companies are reducing the flow of pollutants into the environment—and lowering their cleanup bills—by using alternative materials, changing production techniques, redesigning products, and recycling wastes. Since 1975, 3M has launched 2,500 projects aimed at reducing pollution; rather

Legislation	Date	Effect
Water pollution		
Federal Water Pollution Control Act and amendments	1956, 1972	Authorized grants to states for water-pollution control. Gave federal government limited authority to correct pollution problems. Authorized EPA to set and enforce water-quality standards.
Water Quality Act	1965	Provided for adoption of water-quality standards by states, subject to federal approval.
Water Quality Improvement Act	1970	Strengthened federal authority over water pollution. Provided for federal cleanup of oil spills.
Safe Drinking Water Act	1974	Set standards for drinking-water quality.
Clean Water Act	1977	Ordered control of toxic pollutants by 1984 using best available, economically feasible technology.
Water Quality Act	1987	Extended grants for sewage-treatment projects. Required states to control pollution due to rainfall runoff from farm and urban areas, forestry, and mining sites.
Other pollutants		
Federal Insecticide, Fungicide and Rodenticide Act and amendments	1947, 1967, 1972	To protect farmers, outlawed fraudulent sales claims. Required registration of poisonous products. Provided authority to license users of pesticides.
Pesticide Control Act and amendments	1972, 1975	Required pesticides shipped across state lines to be certified effective and harmless to crops, animal feed, animals, and humans. Set deadline for registration, classification, and licensing of many pesticides.
Noise Control Act	1972	Required EPA to set standards for major sources of noise and to advise Federal Aviation Administration on standards for airplane noise.
Toxic Substances Control Act	1976	Required chemicals testing. Authorized EPA to restrict the use of harmful substances.
Comprehensive Environmental Response, Compensation, and Liability Act	1980	"Superfund Act" created trust fund to clean up hazardous-waste sites. Set schedules and preferences for cleanup activities.
Oil Pollution Act	1990	Set up liability trust fund. Extended operations for preventing and containing oil pollution.

than costing a lot of money, these projects have actually saved $1 billion.[21] This movement toward *green marketing,* changing existing products and creating new, environmentally safe products, is accelerating. However, until recently, many people were confused by terms such as *recyclable* and *biodegradable,* which are commonly used in promoting "green" products. Now that the Federal Trade Commission (FTC) has issued more precise definitions for these words, manufacturers have a better idea of what they can say—and consumers have a better idea of what a product promises.

Progress Toward Cleaner Air

Our air is gradually becoming cleaner, thanks to government standards and industry's efforts to comply. The EPA spends $24 billion a year implementing the Clean Air Act; companies spend some $35 million per year to combat air pollution.[22] Cars account for 40 percent of our smog problem and are 96 percent cleaner than they were before 1970.[23] Factory emissions that contribute to smog and acid rain have declined. An agreement among 24 nations to limit the production of chlorofluorocarbons should help reduce the threat to the ozone layer. The fight against toxic chemical emissions is getting a boost from the passage of the Emergency Planning and Community Right-to-Know Act, which requires businesses to report the amount of toxic chemicals they release into the air, land, and water.

In 1990 Congress passed a series of tough amendments to the 1970 Clean Air Act. The legislation calls for cuts in smog, acid rain, toxic emissions, and ozone-depleting chemicals by phasing in improvements through 2005. Unlike previous laws, this one applies to small companies as well as large ones, covering local dry cleaners, bakeries, and other seemingly innocent businesses that can pollute the air. Instead of requiring companies to reduce pollution to virtually zero, this law requires them to achieve whatever level of purity can be attained using the best technology available. This provision puts an end to a controversy over the meaning of "negligible health risk" that has tied up the implementation of previous laws.

Experts project that by 2005, the 1990 law should knock out 75 to 90 percent of the pollutants being released into the air.[24] However, the cost may run as high as $25 billion per year. Opponents of the measure say that profits and jobs will be lost and that the economy will suffer. On the other hand, given the circular flow of money, one company's expenditures become another company's revenues, so the net economic effect may not be all that severe.[25]

An increasingly popular method of assessing potential pollution problems is through life-cycle analysis. Companies study the environmental effects of their products at every stage, from gathering materials and manufacturing to distribution, use, and disposal. Consultants can help in this process. Says Paul Willer of Andersen Consulting: "In the past, you sold a turbine and forgot it to the end of its natural life. Now you perform diagnostic tests while the turbine is in operation, you replace the parts, and you extend the product's life. This is more economical and environmental."[26]

The Battle for Cleaner Water

Since the passage of the Water Quality Act of 1965, the U.S. government has invested over $50 billion in the fight against water pollution; state and local governments have contributed at least half again as much. Much of this money has been used to upgrade sewage systems to handle wastes from homes and businesses. These improvements have helped clean up harbors, lakes, and rivers that formerly served as cheap dumping grounds for raw sewage.

Industry has also made a major investment in treating wastewater. Factories that used to dump toxic chemicals into nearby waterways are discouraged from doing so by the National Pollutant Discharge Elimination System, which requires any company that pumps fluid into a river or lake to obtain a permit. Even though this system has effectively stopped "point-source" pollution from industry, it does nothing to control nonpoint pollution—the runoff from farms and streets that accounts for 65 percent of the stream pollution in the United States.[27]

The War on Toxic Waste

For years many industrial wastes were routinely dumped in landfills, where protective barriers (if any) could not be counted on to prevent dangerous chemicals from leaking into the soil and the water supply. In 1980 Congress established the so-called Superfund to clean up the most hazardous of these dumps, and funding so far has reached $15.2 billion. When a site is targeted for cleanup, the EPA encourages the parties responsible for the pollution to pay the bill. If an agreement can't be reached, the Superfund pays for the cleanup, and the EPA tries to recover the costs by suing the companies most responsible for the damage. These companies, in turn, may sue others that were involved in owning, operating, or sending wastes to the site. All too often, the effort to parcel out responsibility leads to lawsuits involving hundreds of companies, tying up the cleanup effort for years. Companies generally end up paying about 60 percent of the cleanup costs; the government pays the rest. Each site costs an average of $30 million to restore.[28]

Results to date are discouraging. In just over 10 years, only a small number of sites were removed from the Superfund list.[29] There's a question, however, about whether the groundwater in some sites can ever be restored to drinking-water purity—the standard imposed by a 1986 amendment to the Superfund law. Some 19 locations that improved after initial treatment have subsequently reverted to a contaminated state. A more practical approach, some argue, would simply be to contain the damage, since only 11 percent of the sites pose a potential health threat to residents in a finite area.[30]

Although old sites will be a continuing problem far into the future, industry is making progress in reducing and preventing pollution.[31] For one thing, more companies are now dumping wastes in their own controlled and environmentally sound sites, and fewer are leaving their wastes to independent disposal firms, which are notorious for illegal dumping. In addition, manufacturers are trying out several other methods of eliminating or neutralizing their hazardous by-products. Some use high-temperature incineration, some recycle wastes, some give their wastes to other companies that can use them (sometimes getting in return wastes *they* can use), some neutralize wastes biologically, and some have redesigned their manufacturing processes so that they don't produce the wastes in the first place.

consumerism *Movement that pressures businesses to consider consumer needs and interests*

BUSINESS AND CONSUMERS

The activism of the 1960s that awakened business to its environmental responsibilities also made companies more sensitive to consumers. Crusaders such as Ralph Nader, author of *Unsafe at Any Speed,* shocked the public with exposés about poorly designed, unsafe, and unhealthful products. This gave rise to **consumerism,** a movement that put pressure on businesses to consider consumer needs and interests. Consumerism prompted many businesses to create consumer-affairs departments to handle customer complaints, and state and local agencies set up bureaus to offer consumer information and

Legislation	Date	Effect
		Food and drugs
Federal Food, Drug, and Cosmetic Act	1938	Put cosmetics and therapeutic products under Food and Drug Administration's jurisdiction. Outlawed false and misleading labeling.
Delaney Amendment to the Food, Drug, and Cosmetic Act	1958	Banned chemicals found to induce cancer from use as food additives.
Color Additives Amendment	1960	Mandated disclosure of coloring added to foods.
Kefauver-Harris Drug Amendments to the Food, Drug, and Cosmetic Act	1962	Required manufacturers to test safety and effectiveness before marketing drugs and to show common or generic drug name on label.
Wholesome Meat Act	1967	Strengthened inspection standards for slaughterhouses of red-meat animals.
Orphan Drug Act and amendments	1983, 1985	Set incentives and granted exclusive marketing rights to promote the development of drugs for rare diseases and conditions.
Drug Price Competition/Patent Term Restoration Act	1984	Shortened application process for approval of generic versions of certain drugs.
Nutrition Education and Labeling Act	1990	Required specific, uniform product labels detailing nutritional information. Outlawed certain claims when key information is not shown.
Food, Agriculture, Conservation, and Trade Act	1990	Prevented pesticides banned in United States from being exported to other countries.
		Misbranding and false or harmful advertising
Federal Hazardous Substances Act	1960	Required warning labels on items with dangerous chemicals.
Cigarette Labeling Act	1965	Mandated warnings on cigarette packages and in ads.
Fair Packaging and Labeling Act	1966, 1972	Required honest, informative package labeling. Labels must show origin of product, quantity of contents, uses or applications.
Public Health Cigarette Smoking Act	1970	Banned radio and TV cigarette ads. Strengthened required warning on packaging.
Country of Origin Labeling Act	1985	Required clothing to be labeled with country of origin.

assistance. At the federal level, President John F. Kennedy announced a "bill of rights" for consumers, laying the foundation for a wave of consumer-oriented legislation (see Exhibit 3.3). These rights include the right to safety, the right to be informed, the right to choose, and the right to be heard.

The Right to Safety

The U.S. government imposes many safety standards, which are enforced primarily by the Consumer Product Safety Commission (CPSC), an agency created in 1972 to monitor the safety of some 15,000 products sold to consumers. Standards for some products, such as automobiles, drugs, foods, and medical devices, are established and monitored by special agencies. In addition, state and local agencies have regulations of their own.

Theoretically, companies that don't comply with these rules are forced to take corrective action. However, many consumer advocates complain that some unsafe products slip through the cracks because regulatory agencies lack the resources to do an effective job. Roger

Legislation	Date	Effect
Sales practices		
Land Sales Disclosure Act	1968	Protected consumers from unfair practices in sales of land conducted across state lines.
Trade Regulation Rule	1972	Set a 72-hour cooling-off period to allow consumers to cancel sales made door-to-door.
Magnuson-Moss Warranty Act	1975	Required complete written warranties in ordinary language. Required warranties to be available before purchase.
Product safety		
Flammable Fabrics Act	1953, 1967	Prohibited interstate shipment of apparel or fabric made of flammable materials. Set stronger standards for clothing flammability.
Child Protection and Toy Safety Act	1969	Greater protection from toys with dangerous mechanical or electrical hazards.
Consumer Product Safety Act	1972	Created Consumer Product Safety Commission.
Credit protection		
Truth-in-Lending Act (Consumer Protection Credit Act)	1968	Required creditors to disclose finance charge and annual percentage rate. Limited cardholder liability for unauthorized use.
Fair Credit Reporting Act	1970	Required credit-reporting agencies to set process for assuring accuracy. Required creditors who deny credit to tell consumers the source of information.
Equal Credit Opportunity Act and amendment	1974, 1978	Prohibited discrimination in granting credit on the basis of gender, marital status, race, color, religion, age, and source of income.
Fair Credit Billing Act	1974	Set process for disputing credit billing errors.
Fair Debt Collection Practices Act	1978	Outlawed deceptive, unfair collection practices.

Burrows is the lone CPSC inspector in San Diego, California, one of the 10 largest U.S. cities. Burrows not only investigates all complaints received by the local CPSC office but also spot-checks to be sure the city's 27,000 retailers are selling safe products. His investigations of accidents involving all-terrain vehicles and lawn darts were instrumental in the nationwide banning of those products.[32]

Even without government action, manufacturers are motivated to meet safety standards by the threat of product-liability suits and declining sales. A poor safety record can hurt a company's reputation. Consider the case of the Audi 5000 sedan, which reportedly was prone to sudden, violent acceleration when the transmission was put into drive. After a report on the problem was aired on "60 Minutes," Audi's sales plunged by almost half in two years. Although Audi initially blamed the problem on inept drivers, it was ultimately forced to recall the car and modify the transmission. The firm discontinued the Audi 5000S and introduced new models, but according to industry experts, "It'll take five years to repair the damage" to Audi's reputation.[33]

The Right to Be Informed

One possible way to protect the safety of consumers is to explain any product risks on the label. If the danger is great enough, a warning label is required by law, as in the case of cigarettes. However, warning labels can be a mixed blessing for consumers. To some extent, the presence of a warning protects the manufacturer from product-liability suits, but the label may not deter people from using the product. The warning labels on toys are a case in point. Every year, roughly 12,000 children are seriously injured by toys, many of which are clearly labeled "Not recommended for children under three years of age."[34]

Regardless of whether a product is harmful, however, consumers have a right to know what is in it and how to use it. At the same time, they have a right to know the costs of goods or services and the details of any purchase contracts. Over the years, the government has created a variety of rules and regulations that prevent companies from making false or misleading claims about the ingredients, features, or prices of their products and services.

The federal agencies responsible for labeling (the Food and Drug Administration, the Federal Trade Commission, and the Agriculture Department) are more aggressively protecting consumer rights. Research shows that nearly three-quarters of shoppers read food labels when deciding whether to buy a product the first time, so labels are an important ingredient in informing consumers.[35] The Nutrition Education and Labeling Act of 1990 became the basis for reregulating food labeling: The surgeon general's office led an interagency task force to revamp the warning labels on alcohol, the FDA cracked down on the use of false or misleading claims on labels, the FTC investigated the claims made by liquid-diet manufacturers, and the Agriculture Department developed new standards for labeling meat and poultry.

These agencies are concerned not only with safety but also with accurate information. The FDA has pushed for consistency in serving sizes (so that consumers can compare equal quantities), it has clarified label language (so that consumers will know what terms such as *ultralight* really mean), and it has investigated the accuracy of health claims (so that consumers can identify which products are truly good for them). The FDA has taken action against companies that were making misleading claims about "fresh" foods and about products labeled "low in cholesterol," "light," or "high in fiber."[36]

The Right to Choose

Business responds very well to the right to choose: The number of products available to consumers is truly amazing. But how far should this right extend? Are we entitled to choose products that are harmful—cigarettes and liquor, for example? Or sugar-coated cereal? Or rock music with suggestive lyrics? To what extent are we entitled to learn about these products? Should beer and wine ads be eliminated from television, as ads for other types of alcoholic beverages have been? Should advertising aimed at children be banned?

These are some of the issues that consumer groups are concerned about. No clear answers have been found. Generally speaking, however, business is sensitive to these issues. Recent public concern about drunk driving, for example, has led the liquor industry to encourage responsible drinking. Similarly, the movie industry has instituted a rating system to help the public gauge whether a film is appropriate for a particular audience. Most U.S. businesspeople would rather help consumers make informed choices than be told what choices they can offer.

The Right to Be Heard

A final consumer right is the right to be heard. Again, most businesses are extremely responsive to this issue. Over half of all companies with sales of over $10 million have toll-free consumer information numbers.[37] For example, Procter & Gamble, Scott Paper, Gillette, and many other makers of personal-care and household products print toll-free hot-line numbers on product packages. Actively encouraging feedback from customers gives these businesses the information they need to correct problems and make informed decisions about changing existing products and offering new ones.

Consumers can often make their viewpoints heard by working through advocacy groups such as the Consumer Federation of America, the National Consumers League, Mothers Against Drunk Driving, and the American Association of Retired Persons. These organizations, and hundreds of others that represent special interests, have the resources to lobby lawmakers and influence public opinion.

The Food and Drug Administration protects consumers' rights by regulating the nutritional information that Healthy Choice and other food manufacturers must provide on product labels and in advertising.

They can also put pressure directly on businesses by staging demonstrations or boycotts.

The right to be heard also covers a broad range of complaints about discrimination against customers. More than 4,000 African American customers complained to the U.S. Justice Department about racial discrimination by some Denny's restaurants. Among their complaints: being asked to pay for meals in advance (although other customers weren't asked to do this) and receiving slower service than other customers. Flagstar, the chain's owner, responded by making a public apology, paying $46 million to settle the claims, and setting up a seven-year plan to increase the number of minority franchisees and suppliers.[38]

BUSINESS AND WORKERS

Over the past 20 years, dramatic changes have occurred in the attitudes and composition of the workforce. These changes have forced businesses to modify their recruiting, training, and promotion practices.

The Push for Equality in Employment

The United States has always stood for economic freedom and the individual's right to pursue opportunity. Unfortunately, until the past few decades, many people were targets of economic **discrimination,** relegated to low-paying, menial jobs and prevented from taking advantage of many opportunities solely on the basis of their ethnic background, race, gender, age, disability, religion, or other characteristics unrelated to the ability to do a particular job.

The burden of discrimination has fallen on **minorities,** groups such as African Americans, Hispanics, Asian Americans, immigrants, people with disabilities, and people who are elderly. In a social or economic sense, women are a minority as well. Even though they outnumber men in our society, women have also traditionally suffered economic discrimination.

Job discrimination, in particular, has been a vicious cycle. Because they could not hope for better jobs, many minority-group members have had little incentive to seek an education. Because they have not been adequately educated, many have not been able to qualify for those jobs that might have been available to them. Exhibit 3.4 shows how discrimination has affected the job opportunities of key minorities.

Discrimination runs counter to the ideal of equal opportunity for all. This is a particular problem when a growing percentage of the U.S. workforce is made up of people from diverse cultural and ethnic backgrounds. As a result, government and businesses are both working to fight discrimination.

Government Action

Congress, the executive branch of the government, and the courts all play a vital role in shaping the country's position on civil rights. In

discrimination *In a social and economic sense, denial of opportunities to individuals on the basis of some characteristic that has no bearing on their ability to perform in a job*

minorities *In a social and economic sense, categories of people that society at large singles out for discriminatory, selective, or unfavorable treatment*

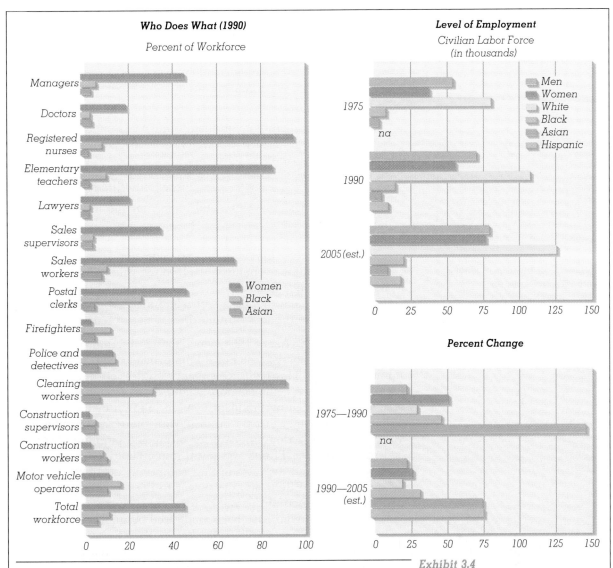

Who Does What (1990)

Percent of Workforce

Managers
Doctors
Registered nurses
Elementary teachers
Lawyers
Sales supervisors
Sales workers
Postal clerks
Firefighters
Police and detectives
Cleaning workers
Construction supervisors
Construction workers
Motor vehicle operators
Total workforce

Legend: Women, Black, Asian

Scale: 0 20 40 60 80 100

Level of Employment

Civilian Labor Force (in thousands)

1975
na

1990

2005 (est.)

Legend: Men, Women, White, Black, Asian, Hispanic

Scale: 0 25 50 75 100 125 150

Percent Change

1975—1990
na

1990—2005 (est.)

Scale: 0 25 50 75 100 125 150

Exhibit 3.4
How Discrimination Has Affected Employment of Minorities
Discrimination has resulted in continuing low levels of employment for minorities and has narrowed their choice of career.

-

affirmative action *Activities undertaken by businesses to recruit and promote women and minorities, based on an analysis of the workforce and the available labor pool*

addition, state and local governments have their own programs and policies for helping minorities. However, whereas some people want to create special programs to help minorities move up the economic ladder, others prefer to minimize the government's intervention.

Affirmative action is the set of actions taken by businesses to recruit and promote members of minority groups. Its proponents believe that equal opportunity can best be achieved if minority groups are temporarily given special benefits. They argue that minorities deserve and require preferential treatment to boost opportunities and to make up for years of discrimination. The opponents of affirmative action believe that individuals should be judged on their own merits, regardless of race, gender, religion, or age. They argue that creating special opportunities for women and minorities creates a double standard that infringes on the rights of other workers and forces companies to hire, promote, and retain people who are not necessarily the best choice from a business standpoint. These affirmative-action opponents believe that government and business should instead promote economic growth, which will create more jobs for all.

Although points of disagreement remain about how far affirmative action should go, there is broad consensus on the basics. Here is a brief summary of what employers can and cannot do:

- *Voluntary affirmative action.* Companies can adopt voluntary programs to hire and promote qualified women and minorities to correct an imbalance in their workforce, even if there is no evidence of past discrimination.
- *Mandatory affirmative action.* The federal courts can impose mandatory affirmative-action plans in cases where employers have clearly discriminated against women and minorities and have refused to take corrective action.
- *Quotas.* In cases where companies have discriminated against minorities, a federal court can impose rigid numerical hiring and promotion **quotas** for minorities. However, voluntary quota plans remain legally questionable.
- *Layoffs.* Companies cannot lay off white males with job seniority in order to save the jobs of minorities with less seniority.

quotas *Fixed numbers of minority-group members to be hired*

The Civil Rights Act of 1964, which forbids discrimination in employment, also established the Equal Employment Opportunity Commission (EEOC). This regulatory agency battles job discrimination on the basis of race, color, religion, gender, or national origin. A presidential order issued by President Lyndon Johnson in 1965 requires all private companies that do business with the government to develop affirmative-action programs for hiring and promoting women and minorities. The EEOC was given responsibility for monitoring these programs and for investigating complaints of job-related discrimination. The EEOC has the power to file legal charges against companies that discriminate and to force them to compensate individuals or groups who have been victimized by unfair practices.

In recent years, the Civil Rights Act of 1991 has paved the way for workers to sue companies for discrimination and has given women powerful legal tools against job bias. Government actions have also helped minority-owned businesses. In 1990 the Pilot Mentor Protege Program (a section of the Defense Authorization Act of 1991) became law. This program aims to increase the number of qualified U.S. Department of Defense subcontractors by reimbursing prime contractors that adopt a minority-owned firm and offer technical and managerial assistance. By increasing the subcontractor's capability, the prime contractor is helping create its own supplier base, a plan applauded by all.[39]

Business's Response
Since passage of the 1964 Civil Rights Act, most businesses have taken an active role in complying with government requirements to set up affirmative-action programs to recruit members of minority groups and train them for jobs. With the passage of the 1991 civil rights legislation, companies have been given the incentive to train their managers and set up employment policies to ensure freedom from bias in the workplace.

Although business has many reasons for its commitment to affirmative action, the most important is that the policy has worked. By and large, companies have had positive experiences with the people who have been hired and promoted under these programs. Furthermore, cultural diversity is rapidly becoming a fact of business life. By the end of the 1990s, 85 percent of the new hires will be women, African Americans, Hispanics, or Asian Americans. White males will become a minority of the workforce, and employers who discriminate against women and minorities will be at a serious competitive disadvantage in attracting talented people.[40]

These days, successful and socially responsible organizations are viewing workforce diversity as an opportunity to expand the pool of people who can contribute to the organization. Minorities make up more than half of Levi Strauss & Company's workforce, but the company continues to push for more women and minorities in top management. At Nike, a series of recruiting programs has helped the company double the percentage of minority employees in just three years.[41] Minority-owned businesses are being helped by companies, too. Burger King is investing more than $100 million in programs to support minority suppliers and franchise owners.[42]

Gender Issues

Although men do face some sexual discrimination in the workplace, women are more likely than men to feel the effects of **sexism,** discrimination on the basis of gender. However, women have made significant strides toward overcoming sexism on the job, thanks to a combination of affirmative action and changing societal attitudes. In the 1950s, only 20 percent of college undergraduates were women; today, women earn more B.A. degrees than men, and their most frequent major is business. Roughly a third of all professional degrees are earned by women, versus 5 percent in 1960. In addition, 30 percent of all working women are professionals or managers, the same proportion as men.[43]

As women have moved into higher-paying occupations, the gap between their earnings and men's earnings has narrowed from 64 percent in 1980 to 76 percent today.[44] Despite their progress, however, women continue to earn significantly less than men, even when they compete in the same occupations, as Exhibit 3.5 illustrates. Women are more likely than men to work part-time or on an intermittent basis, so they may lag behind their male peers on the career ladder. Also, many of the top-paying positions are held by men in their 50s and 60s who began their careers in the years before the women's movement.

Many women see a **glass ceiling,** or wall of subtle discrimination, barring them from moving up into the highest ranks. Only 3 of every 100 top jobs in the largest U.S. companies are held by women, about the same number as a decade ago.[45] Women may be denied promotions because managers assume they are less interested in the job and more tied to their family than their male associates are. Indeed, this is the case for some women: 82 percent of a group of 1,000 professional women said in a recent poll that they would choose a

sexism Discriminating against a person on the basis of gender

glass ceiling Invisible barrier of subtle discrimination that keeps women out of the top positions in business

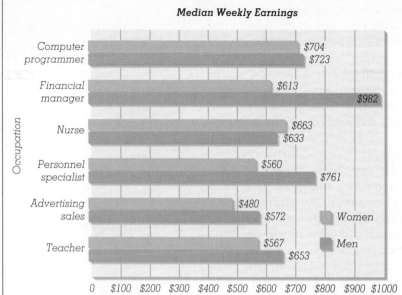

Median Weekly Earnings

Exhibit 3.5
Women's Earnings Versus Men's Earnings
Despite more than 30 years of fighting for equal opportunity, women still earn less than men in almost every field.

Occupation	Women	Men
Computer programmer	$704	$723
Financial manager	$613	$982
Nurse	$663	$633
Personnel specialist	$560	$761
Advertising sales	$480	$572
Teacher	$567	$653

career path with flexible full-time work hours and more family time but slower career advancement over one with inflexible hours and faster advancement.[46] Still, many women are forcing companies to confront gender bias in the executive suite as well as in the corporate boardroom, where 90 percent of the directors in the largest companies are white males.[47]

Meanwhile, blue-collar women are grappling with another type of career-versus-family issue—fetal protection. Some major corporations have traditionally barred women of childbearing age from jobs involving hazardous chemicals that might cause birth defects. Women argued that these fetal-protection policies effectively shut them out of 20 million higher-paying industrial jobs. In 1991 the Supreme Court ruled that fetal-protection policies are an illegal form of sex discrimination. The court's ruling will give women, not companies, the final decision about whether they should take assignments that might be harmful to their unborn children.

The burden of caring for children as well as for other family members has been lightened by the Family and Medical Leave Act. Signed into law in 1993, the law mandates 12 weeks of unpaid leave for new parents or workers caring for seriously ill relatives, and it has benefited both women and men. In addition, more than 70 percent of large U.S. companies offer some form of child-care assistance, although some may offer nothing more than lists of child-care providers. One family-friendly company is Fel-Pro, an automotive-parts producer in Skokie, Illinois, that offers a subsidized day-care center and a summer camp. "We are not a charity," says co-chairman David Weinberg. "We are enhancing profits by keeping employees satisfied."[48]

Another sensitive issue in the workplace is **sexual harassment.** As defined by the EEOC, sexual harassment takes two forms: the obvious request for sexual favors with an implicit reward or punishment related to work, and the more subtle creation of a sexist environment

sexual harassment *Unwelcome sexual advance, request for sexual favors, or other verbal or physical conduct of a sexual nature within the workplace that affects a person's job prospects or job performance* in which employees are made to feel uncomfortable by off-color jokes, lewd remarks, and posturing. Research shows that 50 to 85 percent of all working women experience some sexual harassment during their careers; 90 percent of the top 500 U.S. firms have received complaints of sexual harassment. Moreover, 5 out of 10 men say they've done or said something at work that could be considered sexual harassment by a female colleague.[49]

This issue has received renewed attention since 1991, when Anita Hill publicly charged Clarence Thomas, now a U.S. Supreme Court justice, with sexual harassment.[50] What constitutes sexual harassment? Recent court cases involving women use the "reasonable woman" standard. If a reasonable woman would find a situation objectionable, the court deems it sexual harassment. Another important factor is whether the employer has an effective internal grievance procedure that allows employees to complain without suffering repercussions.

Honeywell, Corning, and Du Pont are among the companies that have supported antiharassment programs with employee training, detailed handbooks, and workshops. AT&T says that 19 out of 20 complaints received are valid, and the company warns that employees can be fired for acts of sexual harassment. Rather than offering separate training, AT&T offers voluntary classes on workplace diversity, believing the approach has more impact.[51]

Live Action Training is a performance group in San Diego that is hired by corporate clients to raise employee awareness of sexual harassment problems. By acting out hypothetical situations, such as this encounter, the group provokes discussions about sexual harassment in the workplace.

People with Disabilities

In 1990 people with a wide range of physical and mental difficulties got a boost from the passage of the federal Americans with Disabilities Act (ADA), which guarantees equal opportunities for an estimated 50 million to 75 million people who have or have had a condition that might handicap them. As defined by the 1990 law, *disability* is a broad term that protects not only those with obvious physical handicaps but also those with less visible conditions, such as cancer, heart disease, diabetes, epilepsy, AIDS, drug addiction, alcoholism, and emotional illness. In most situations, employers can't legally require job applicants to pass a physical examination as a condition of employment. The law also forbids terminating the employment of people who have serious drinking or drug problems unless their chemical dependency prevents them from performing the essential functions of their jobs.

This legislation also requires that all businesses serving the public make their services and facilities accessible to people with disabilities. This requirement means that restaurants, hotels, stores, airports, buses, taxis, banks, sports stadiums, and so forth must try to accommodate people who are disabled. A hotel, for example, must equip 5 percent of its rooms with flashing lights or other "visual alarms" for people with hearing impairments.[52] In addition, the rights of workers with disabilities are protected by the Vocational Rehabilitation Act of 1973. This law requires that companies working under U.S. government contracts worth at least $2,500 set up affirmative-action programs and arrange physical access for workers with disabilities.

Occupational Safety and Health

Every 18 seconds, someone in the United States is injured on the job; every 50 minutes, someone is killed in a work-related accident; every year, more than 70,000 people die from diseases directly related to their work.[53] Obviously, some jobs are more dangerous than others, as you see in Exhibit 3.6. Concern about workplace hazards mounted during the activist 1960s, resulting in passage of the Occupational Safety and Health Act of 1970, which set mandatory standards for safety and health and which established the Occupational Safety and Health Administration (OSHA) to enforce them.

OSHA is charged not only with preventing accidents but also with eliminating "silent killers": work-related diseases (such as black lung among coal miners) and injury from the toxic effects of chemicals and other harmful substances. OSHA employees investigate complaints and review company records to identify firms with higher-than-average accident rates. The usual penalty for safety violations is a fine. If the violation was intentional, OSHA turns the case over to the Justice Department for criminal prosecution. However, in the 1980s, OSHA referred only 30 cases, and the Justice Department prosecuted only 4 of them. No corporate executive has ever served in prison for federal safety violations that resulted in a worker's death, although six executives have been sentenced under state convictions.[54]

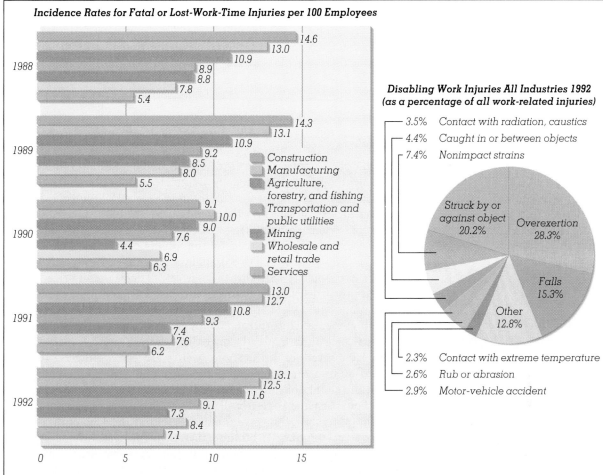

Incidence Rates for Fatal or Lost-Work-Time Injuries per 100 Employees

1988
14.6
13.0
10.9
8.9
8.8
7.8
5.4

1989
14.3
13.1
10.9
9.2
8.5
8.0
5.5

1990
9.1
10.0
9.0
7.6
4.4
6.9
6.3

1991
13.0
12.7
10.8
9.3
7.4
7.6
6.2

1992
13.1
12.5
11.6
9.1
7.3
8.4
7.1

0   5   10   15

Construction
Manufacturing
Agriculture, forestry, and fishing
Transportation and public utilities
Mining
Wholesale and retail trade
Services

Disabling Work Injuries All Industries 1992 (as a percentage of all work-related injuries)

— 3.5% Contact with radiation, caustics
— 4.4% Caught in or between objects
— 7.4% Nonimpact strains

Struck by or against object 20.2%
Overexertion 28.3%
Falls 15.3%
Other 12.8%

— 2.3% Contact with extreme temperature
— 2.6% Rub or abrasion
— 2.9% Motor-vehicle accident

Exhibit 3.6
Accidents on the Job
Construction and manufacturing jobs are the most dangerous. Service workers are the least likely to be injured at work.

Even without government supervision, many companies are working to improve the health and safety of their employees, motivated both by genuine concern and by costly workers' compensation claims. Alcoa, the big aluminum company, has improved its safety record by 25 percent in three years, saving an estimated $10,000 to $12,000 for every accident it prevents.[55]

BUSINESS AND INVESTORS

In addition to its other responsibilities, a business must also keep in mind its responsibility to those who have invested in the company. Although a growing number of investors are concerned about the ethics of the companies in which they invest, most are chiefly interested in the company's financial performance. Thus, the company's major responsibility to investors is to make money on their behalf. Any action that cheats the investors out of their rightful profits is unethical. However, a business can also fail in its responsibilities to shareholders by being too concerned about profits.

Cheating the Investor

Investors can be cheated in many ways. However, most scams fall into one of two categories: misrepresenting the potential of the investment or diverting the earnings or assets so that the investor's rightful return is reduced.

Misrepresenting the Investment

Every year tens of thousands of people are the victims of investment scams. Lured by promises of high returns, people sink more than a billion dollars per year in nonexistent oil wells, gold mines, and other fraudulent operations touted by complete strangers over the telephone.[56] One fraudulent investment in the early 1990s involved Operation Desert Storm. Shortly after Iraq invaded Kuwait, regulators raided 32 telemarketing firms in Los Angeles, Dallas, and Salt Lake City, charging con artists with touting phony oil and gas deals. Some 3,500 investors put a total of $50 million into these investments, trusting the promoters' claims that the war would drive up oil prices. One retired postal worker, for example, invested $31,250 in gas wells that were supposed to yield $625 per month and did indeed receive a few monthly checks. Unfortunately, though, the operation was a **Ponzi scheme,** meaning that early investors were paid with money raised from later investors. In fact, the wells were either plugged or not owned by the company making the offer, and the scheme collapsed when the supply of new investors dried up.[57]

A Ponzi scheme is clearly illegal, but other ways of misrepresenting the potential of an investment fall within the law. With a little "creative accounting," a business that is in financial trouble can be made to look reasonably good to all but the most astute investors. Companies have some latitude in their reports to shareholders, and some firms are more conscientious than others in representing their financial performance.

Diverting Earnings or Assets

Business executives may also take advantage of the investor by using the company's earnings or resources for personal gain. Managers have many opportunities to indirectly take money that rightfully belongs to the shareholders. Perhaps the most common approach is to cheat on the expense account. Padding invoices and then splitting the overcharge with the supplier is another common ploy. Another possibility is selling company secrets to competitors or using inside information to play the stock market.

Incidents of **insider trading**—the use of nonpublic knowledge gained from one's position in a company to benefit from fluctuations in stock prices—have been publicized in recent years. Although insider trading is illegal, it is difficult to police. Say you're an accountant for a major corporation. You know the company is about to report a large, unexpected loss. When the news breaks, the price of the stock will undoubtedly fall. You could protect yourself by selling the stock you own before the word gets out. Who would know the difference? Who would care? Consider the people who might buy your shares; chances are *they* would care. Consider the other shareholders,

Ponzi scheme *Form of fraud in which money received from later investors is used to pay off the earlier investors*

insider trading *Employee's or manager's use of unpublicized information gained in the course of his or her job to benefit from fluctuations in the stock market*

Your company has sent you to an African country to conduct business. You think you've clinched the deal, but then your contact asks you for a "gift" of money to ensure that the deal goes through. Deciding how to handle such situations requires knowing the customs of the country you're doing business in.

Most non-Western countries, especially those in Africa and Asia, have three traditions built around exchanges of gifts: the inner circle, the future-favors system, and the gift exchange. The savvy businessperson who can tap into these traditions will not only clinch today's deal but also establish long-term business relationships—without compromising integrity.

In these cultures, people see themselves as belonging to an inner circle that consists of relatives, friends, and close colleagues. Members of the inner circle are devoted to mutual protection and prosperity; everyone else is an outsider. Obviously, people prefer to conduct business with insiders, people they know and trust.

In a system of future favors, a gift or service obligates the recipient to

GIFT VERSUS BRIBE: WHEN A FRIENDLY EXCHANGE TURNS INTO RISKY BUSINESS

return the favor in the future—with interest. Once the favor is returned, the original giver becomes obligated to repay this greater favor. This system of obligations becomes a lifelong relationship, one that can provide access to the inner circle and that can serve as the basis of business dealings.

A third tradition is the practice of giving and receiving gifts to fuel a long-term sequence of gift exchanges. As expert Jeffrey A. Fadiman noted: "The gifts are simply catalysts. Under ideal circumstances the process should be unending, with visits, gifts, gestures, and services flowing back and forth among participants throughout their lives."

By participating in the traditional exchange of gifts and favors and becoming part of an inner circle, Western businesspeople can build trust, gain access to local markets, and minimize risk in a foreign environment. However, it's important to distinguish gifts from bribes. One clue is the size of the request—the smaller the amount, the less likely it is to be a bribe. Another clue is the person the money is to be paid to. If it is supposed to go to a third party—especially someone in power—it is more likely to be a bribe.

Many large U.S. corporations have developed clever and legal strategies for handling requests for payoffs. Instead of making private payments to individuals, they offer donations to build hospitals and schools, they provide engineering or other expert services for public works, or they donate jobs—all with the goal of creating goodwill in the host nation. In the process, they gain a reputation for providing social services instead of paying bribes, and the foreign officials who arrange the donations increase their prestige.

---

the investors who actually own the company even though they have no day-to-day involvement with it. Would it be fair for you to profit while they did not?

Overdoing the Quest for Profits

Most executives would agree that insider trading is damaging to shareholders—but what about trying to maximize profits? How can that be bad? Few companies knowingly break laws in an attempt to gain competitive advantage. Many companies, on the other hand, have taken questionable steps in their zeal to maximize profits. Should a company bribe a foreign official? You might say no, but be aware that bribery is a custom in many cultures. The Foreign Corrupt Practices Act explicitly outlaws bribes paid by U.S. companies to higher-level foreign officials or to political parties and candidates.[58] However, "grease" payments to lower-level officials such as customs agents are permitted. As a manager, where would you draw the line between higher- and lower-level officials?

What about spying on competitors? When does legitimate research become unethical or illegal? Not long ago, Johnson & Johnson was ordered to pay $113 million to 3M for analyzing a sample of a soon-to-be-launched 3M material used in making casts for broken bones. J&J received the sample from a disgruntled 3M employee who offered to explain the technology for $20,000. Although J&J did not pay for any information, the company was able to use the sample in developing a similar product. What J&J should have done, according to one security expert, was report the situation to 3M and call the FBI.[59]

The push for higher sales has backfired at a number of companies in recent years, including Sears, Roebuck. Investigating a rising number of consumer complaints about Sears auto centers, California officials found that employees were under orders to aggressively sell products such as brakes and shock absorbers. An additional 43 states also charged Sears with unfair business practices. At an estimated cost of $60 million, Sears settled the charges, and CEO Edward Brennan acknowledged management's responsibility for setting up goals and compensation systems that led to the problem.[60]

None of the executives involved in these cases profited personally; their chief concern was to improve the financial performance of the company. Some might argue that these executives were guilty of nothing worse than loyalty to their company, or that their competitors were doing the same thing, or that the rules they broke were trivial. Do you think these executives were right or wrong?

BUSINESS APPROACHES TO ETHICAL BEHAVIOR

When you think about a business's approach to social responsibility, you probably think of the programs set up or plans made by the business as a whole. However, the business does not take action or make decisions; only individuals within the business can do so. The sense of right and wrong that each decision maker brings to the workplace, therefore, influences the steps a company takes toward social responsibility.

What is right and what is wrong? This is a central question in **ethics,** the study of individual decisions made in the context of a system of moral standards or rules of conduct. Someone may make a decision that complies with the law and, at the same time, seems unethical because it falls short of the broader set of moral principles expected by society. In the words of Shirley Peterson, head of the ethics program at Northrop, a major defense contractor: "Compliance is what you have to do; ethics is what you should do."[61]

Surveys show that people think unethical behavior is common in business. Eight out of ten upper-level managers think people are either occasionally or frequently unethical in their business dealings. Worse, nearly one in four believes that ethical standards get in the way of career success.[62] "Often what we do is not what we would like to do," says one small-business owner. "Many business questions are more a matter of survival than ethics."[63]

ethics *Study of individual choices made in the framework of certain rules of conduct or moral standards*

As an ethics officer for Northrop, a large defense contractor, Shirley Peterson helps set standards for ethical behavior that guide individual decisions and actions throughout the company.

Ethical Dilemmas and Ethical Lapses

Ethical questions can be divided into two general categories. The first is the **ethical dilemma,** in which an issue has two conflicting but arguably valid sides. A classic ethical dilemma in business is whether tobacco companies should be allowed to advertise. Allowing them to do so encourages unhealthy behavior, but not allowing them to advertise could violate their right to freedom of speech and hurt their ability to sell a legal product. The common theme in all ethical dilemmas is the conflict between the rights of two or more important groups of people. The number of potential ethical dilemmas a business faces increases with the number of stakeholders.

An **ethical lapse** occurs when an individual makes an unethical decision. Be careful not to confuse ethical dilemmas (which are unresolved interpretations of ethical issues) with ethical lapses (which are cases of unethical behavior). A liquor company's decision to advertise a product that contributes to alcoholism is an ethical dilemma, but an auto executive's decision to accept bribes from dealers in exchange for allocating more stock of a fast-selling car model is an ethical lapse.

ethical dilemma *Situation in which both sides of an issue can be supported with valid arguments*

ethical lapse *Situation in which an individual makes an unethical decision*

Philosophical Bases for Ethical Decisions

Guided by written policies and unwritten standards as well as the example set by top managers, every individual in a corporation makes choices with moral implications. If everyone behaves ethically, the organization as a whole will act in a responsible manner. The trick, then, is for each person to think through the consequences of his or her actions and make the "right" choice.

The trouble lies in determining what is right in any given situation. One approach is to measure each act against certain absolute standards. In our culture, these standards are generally derived from Judeo-Christian teachings: "Thou shalt not lie"; "Thou shalt not steal"; "Thou shalt not bear false witness against thy neighbor"; "Do unto others as you would have them do unto you." These principles provide the foundation for our laws and regulations.

However, rules have their limitations. Some situations defy clear-cut distinctions. In such situations, three other philosophical approaches are useful in identifying the most ethical course of action: utilitarianism, individual rights, and justice.[64]

Utilitarianism

According to the concept of **utilitarianism,** the right decision is the one that produces the greatest good for the greatest number of people. Using this approach, you try to figure out the impact of all the alternative actions on everyone concerned and then choose the alternative that creates the most good for the most people. You would reject alternatives that catered to narrow interests or failed to satisfy the needs of the majority. The value of this approach depends on your skill in estimating the effect of your decisions. The challenge is in coming up with a decision that would benefit the most people.

utilitarianism *Philosophy used in making ethical decisions that aims to achieve the greatest good for the greatest number*

individual rights *Philosophy used in making ethical decisions that aims to protect human dignity*

Individual Rights

Another approach is to be guided by a belief in the importance of **individual rights.** Because a belief in another person's rights implies that you have a duty to protect those rights, you would reject any decision that violated those rights. You would not deceive people or trick them into acting against their own interests. You would respect their privacy and their right to express their opinion. You would not force people to act in a way that was contrary to their religious or moral beliefs. You would not punish a person without a fair and impartial hearing. Although you might be guided by a desire to achieve the greatest good for the greatest number of people, you would reject any choice that violated the rights of even one person. In an era when individual workers expect and demand their rights, this philosophy is becoming a practical necessity. When dealing with issues related to AIDS or drug testing, for example, companies are trying to honor the individual's right to privacy without jeopardizing the group's rights to a safe working environment.

Justice

justice *Philosophy used in making ethical decisions that aims to ensure the equal distribution of burdens and benefits*

When making ethical decisions, you might also apply the principles of **justice.** These principles include a belief that people should be treated fairly and impartially, that rules should be applied consistently, and that people who harm others should be held responsible and should make restitution. A just decision, then, is one that is fair, impartial, and reasonable in light of the rules that apply to the situation.

These three approaches are not mutually exclusive alternatives. On the contrary, most people combine them to reach decisions that will satisfy as many people as possible without violating any person's rights or treating anyone unjustly. Still, wanting to be a good, ethical corporate citizen isn't enough; a business has to actively take steps to become more ethical.

The Effort to Become More Ethical

Most companies are concerned about ethical issues, and many are trying to develop approaches for improving their ethics. Listen to Melisse Shaban, general manager of Aveda, a cosmetics manufacturer in Minneapolis, Minnesota: "People—employees and customers—want the opportunity to do the right thing, so it's the job of a company to make it easier for individuals to make a choice." Ethical behavior starts at the top, where a strong leadership position by the CEO and other senior managers sets the tone for people throughout the company. Robert Dunn, vice president of corporate affairs for Levi Strauss & Company, explains the company's management vision: "Ethics at Levi Strauss is not an option, it's a ground rule, a part of every decision. If there is a conflict, ethical values must prevail."[65]

In addition to strong management leadership, companies can take specific steps to encourage ethical behavior. Three out of four large companies have adopted a written **code of ethics,** which defines the values and principles that should be used to guide decisions.[66] Many also run training programs to teach employees how to deal

code of ethics *Written statement setting forth the principles that should guide an organization's decisions*

The solutions to many day-to-day questions in business are not simply right or wrong. Rather, they fall into a gray area. To demonstrate the perplexing array of moral dilemmas faced by business-people, here is a nonscientific test. In the space at the end of each statement, mark 0 if you strongly disagree, 1 if you disagree, 2 if you agree, and 3 if you strongly agree.

1. A company can withhold negative information about a product to complete a big sale as long as the negative aspect isn't dangerous or life-threatening. _____

2. Managers must sometimes overlook contract and safety violations in order to get on with the job. _____

3. Employees cannot possibly keep completely accurate expense records. Therefore, they may sometimes find they have to give approximate figures. _____

4. On occasion, an employee may need to withhold embarrassing information from the boss. _____

5. Employees should do what managers suggest, even though they may have doubts about whether it's the right thing to do. _____

6. Sometimes employees have to conduct personal business on company time. _____

HOW DO YOUR ETHICS MEASURE UP?

7. Taking a friend to lunch and charging it to the company as a business expense is acceptable as long as the bill is reasonable and doing so doesn't become a regular habit. _____

8. I would quote a "hopeful" shipping date to get an order. _____

9. Employees can make long-distance calls to friends and family from the office when the telephone is not being used for company business. _____

10. Management must be goal-oriented. Therefore, the end usually justifies the means. _____

11. If providing heavy entertainment and twisting company policy a bit would win a large contract, I would authorize it. _____

12. Exceptions to company policy and procedures are a way of life. _____

13. Inventory controls should be designed to report "underages" rather than "overages" in goods received. _____

14. Occasional use of the company's photocopying machine for personal or community activities is acceptable. _____

15. Taking home company property (pencils, paper, tape, and the like) for personal use is an accepted fringe benefit. _____

If your total score is	You are
0	A possible saint
1–5	Bishop material
6–10	Excellent in ethical development
11–15	Good in ethical development
16–25	Average in ethical development
26–35	Deficient in ethical development
36–44	In trouble
45	A possible jailbird

with ethical dilemmas. Some companies screen potential employees for honesty *before* they are hired.

More companies are creating official positions to deal with ethical issues. Roughly 20 percent of large corporations have appointed corporate ethics officers to oversee corporate-wide efforts to act in an ethical manner.[67] At Nynex, for example, Graydon Wood serves as the telephone company's top ethical officer—even though Wood has no background in ethics. "You don't need to know about Aristotle to be an ethics officer," Wood says. "You're trying to do what's best for the greatest number of people, and not hurt anyone in the process." Wood and an ethics policy committee drafted Nynex's ethics code, refined it with the help of lower-level managers in three states, and then sent the code to all managers. He also established a hot line for employees to call in allegations of wrongdoing and discuss ethical issues.[68]

Ethics hot lines encourage *whistle-blowing,* an employee's disclosure of illegal, unethical, wasteful, or harmful practices by the company. However, whistle-blowing brings along with it high costs: Public accusation of wrongdoing hurts the business's reputation, requires attention from managers who must investigate, and damages employee morale. Fear of negative publicity sometimes causes a company to fire or transfer an employee who reports possible ethical violations. Still, companies that are sincerely interested in operating ethically do work hard to respond appropriately to whistle-blowing.

SUMMARY OF LEARNING OBJECTIVES

1 **Identify four stakeholder groups to which business has a responsibility.**
Companies have a responsibility to society, to consumers, to employees, and to investors.

2 **Name three kinds of pollution and outline actions to control them.**
Air, water, and land pollution are all significant problems. The government passed the National Environmental Policy Act of 1969 and set up the Environmental Protection Agency to regulate the disposal of hazardous wastes and clean up polluted areas. Also, many companies have acted to reduce the pollution they produce and to safely dispose of hazardous wastes.

3 **List the four rights of consumers.**
Consumers have the right to safety, the right to be informed, the right to choose, and the right to be heard.

4 **State the responsibilities of the Equal Employment Opportunity Commission.**
The EEOC is responsible for seeing that employers do not discriminate on the basis of race, color, gender, religion, or national origin. The EEOC also investigates and takes action on complaints of job discrimination.

5 **Define sexism and describe gender issues that can influence discrimination in the workplace.**
Sexism is discrimination on the basis of gender. Gender issues that influence discrimination are the gap between male and female pay, the glass ceiling, fetal protection, the need to care for family, and sexual harassment.

6 **Discuss two general ways that businesses may cheat investors.**
Investors are cheated (1) when companies or individuals misrepresent the value of an investment and (2) when companies divert earnings or assets for their personal use, thus reducing the amount available to investors.

7 **Distinguish between ethical dilemmas and ethical lapses.**
An ethical dilemma is an issue with two conflicting but arguably valid sides. An ethical lapse occurs when an individual makes an unethical decision.

8 **List and explain four philosophical approaches to resolving ethical questions in business.**
When resolving ethical questions, companies may apply standards based on religious teachings, the principles of utilitarianism (the greatest good for the greatest number of people), individual rights (respect for human dignity), and justice (fair distribution of society's benefits and burdens).

Ben Cohen and Jerry Greenfield realized that their company was no longer what it had been. They had hundreds of employees, and stock had been sold publicly, making the company responsible not only to the community and employees but to stockholders as well. Even internal communication had changed. Monthly staff meetings for all employees had always been a part of the Ben & Jerry culture. In the old days, employees split into small groups, talked over problems, and came back with solutions. Now the meetings had become one-way communications, with managers talking at the employees.

Cohen and Greenfield wanted to make some changes. First, they wanted management to be more responsive to employees, for they believed that communication had not kept pace with the other changes growth had brought to the company. Even though Ben & Jerry's promoted social causes, sales were based on the quality of the product. They believed that the excellent product would not continue to exist without better communication. Second, they wanted to put more power in the hands of lower management and to make life more enjoyable for everyone at the company.

Before making any changes, Cohen called a staff meeting and asked the employees what they considered to be the most pressing problems facing Ben & Jerry's. As in the old days, the employees talked over the problems and came back with some answers. The most pressing problem expressed was the need for a clearly stated direction. Employees felt caught between the managers, who wanted the company to grow and become more businesslike, and the co-founders, who wanted the company to be a force for social change.

In response, company managers first developed a comprehensive strategy that stressed growth and profits. Disturbed, Cohen and Greenfield pressed for more emphasis on social responsibility. In the end, the co-founders got their social agenda, but the company also had to tend to business.

The revised plan yielded an improved Ben & Jerry's. The company now had a clearly stated direction: Produce a product of the highest quality, demonstrate social responsibility, and remain economically viable. The company's position regarding its commitment to product quality and to social goals remained true to the vision of Cohen and Greenfield. The employees, still an important part of the organization, were given more room for input and discussion on business decisions.

Even as the company moved forward, some controversies emerged. Ben & Jerry's promotes the idea of employee ownership. However, employees now own less than 1 percent of the company's stock, although the co-founders have become millionaires. This imbalance is being addressed by a stock-option plan started in 1994. In addition, the push for increased production to fuel company growth has raised concerns about safety issues related to back injuries, chemical burns, and other injuries.

However, Ben & Jerry's success has allowed the firm to show stronger support for social issues. For instance, the company has opened three Russian stores, which donate 10 percent of their profits to local charities. In addition, a program called "Partnershops" helps establish Ben & Jerry's franchises that donate part or all of their profits to local charities; in turn, the charities are involved in the stores' operation. These and other programs help Ben & Jerry's Homemade balance profits and social change.

Your Mission: As an assistant to founders Ben Cohen and Jerry Greenfield, you are responsible for helping them keep the company on track with its new direction. Consider the following scenarios, and decide how you will act:

1. A group of the company's employees recently approached you with a concern about one of the social causes the company supports through the Ben & Jerry Foundation. They were opposed to the cause and did not want the company to support it. Of the following, what would be your best response?

a. You do not believe all employees need to support all the social causes. You tell employees that the Ben & Jerry Foundation is responsible for allocating the donated funds to social programs they choose.

b. You take the issue back to the employees. You call a staff meeting and have the employees vote on which social causes the company should support.

c. The employees have approached you in a very responsible manner and you feel obligated to act on their concerns. You ask the board to withdraw support for this cause.

2. A new ice cream promoting a healthy ozone layer has been proposed. Ingredients for the product are produced exclusively by environmentally sound practices, so the product is more expensive to manufacture than competing products. A preliminary review indicates the product would pay for itself but would generate no profit. What should you do?

a. The ice cream meets the company's social and product goals. You want to launch it, since other products will make up for the lack of profit.

b. You are being disloyal to the stockholders if you do not maximize profits with every decision. You withdraw support for the product.

c. You decide to compromise the product by changing some of the environmentally sound ingredients to reduce the cost. This approach may dilute the social message, but you need to keep the shareholders in mind.

3. A congressional bill has been proposed to limit the fat content of manufactured foods. If passed, this bill will affect your ice cream products. What do you do?

a. You hire a professional lobbyist, who attempts to prevent the bill from becoming law. You believe people can decide for themselves what to eat and have the right to choose which foods they buy.

b. You share the government's concern for consumer health. You develop a strategy for reducing the fat content of all Ben & Jerry's ice creams.

c. You support the effort to reduce fat, but you also believe in consumer choice. You propose an alternative bill to require accurate labeling of food containers.

4. As the environment becomes more important to both the government and the consumer, what is Ben & Jerry's responsibility as a manufacturer?

a. Ben & Jerry's must take full responsibility for reducing waste, no matter what the cost. To counteract the pollution already in the environment, businesses must use safer resources, regardless of the effect on profit.

b. In addition to meeting all government standards, Ben & Jerry's must decide which actions will yield the most benefit for the least money.

c. Complying with government regulations is all that any company can do. Like other firms, Ben & Jerry's has a hard time keeping up with government requirements, regardless of other actions the company may want to take.[69]

KEY TERMS

affirmative action (77)
code of ethics (88)
consumerism (72)
discrimination (76)
ecology (68)
ethical dilemma (87)
ethical lapse (87)
ethics (86)

glass ceiling (79)
individual rights (88)
insider trading (84)
justice (88)
minorities 76)
pollution (66)
Ponzi scheme (84)

quotas (78)
sexism (79)
sexual harassment (80)
social audit (63)
social responsibility (62)
stakeholders (62)
utilitarianism (87)

REVIEW QUESTIONS

1. How has business's sense of social responsibility evolved since the turn of the century?
2. What are some of the things business has done to protect the environment from the dangers of pollution?
3. In what way do you think the consumer movement might actually benefit business?

4. In what ways is business legally accountable for helping achieve equal opportunity for minorities?
5. What are the responsibilities of the Occupational Safety and Health Administration, and how does the agency carry out its mission?
6. What is insider trading, and how does it harm an investor in a company?

7. How do individuals employ philosophical principles in making ethical business decisions?
8. What is whistle-blowing, and how can companies learn from it?

DIALING UP SOCIAL RESPONSIBILITY

Working Assets is a telephone service with a conscience. What other telephone service offers customers the opportunity to pay less for long-distance calls and simultaneously show support for social causes? No other telephone service is endorsed by both Ralph Nader and Gloria Steinem, prints its bills on completely recycled paper with soy-based ink, and plants 17 trees for each ton of paper it uses. No other service offers Free Speech Days (monthly free calls to selected government officials) and Citizen Letters (monthly letters sent to government officials and corporate executives).

More than 130,000 customers use the services of Working Assets, which was founded by Laura S. Scher and Peter Barnes in 1988. Working Assets is a long-distance reseller, buying phone time at budget rates from bigger telephone companies and then reselling it to customers. In addition to offering low rates for all long-distance calls, the company offers extra discounts when customers place calls to fellow customers.

Although the ability to save on long-distance calls is one reason customers sign up, what sets Working Assets apart from AT&T, MCI, and Sprint is its agenda of social responsibility. The company donates 1 percent of its revenues to nonprofit causes such as civil rights and environmental groups. Every year customers are asked to vote on which causes to support in the coming year.

The main tool that Working Assets uses to communicate with its customers is the monthly billing statement. "No one else thinks of the bill as a product," explains CEO Scher. "They think of the bill as a transaction. This is the crux of our whole operation, and this is where we have fun."

The bill gives customers the chance to support social causes by rounding up what they owe in any month. For example, if a bill is $26.85, the customer can choose to pay $30 (or any amount higher than what's being billed). "It's like the penny jar next to the cash register," Scher says. Just as grocery-store customers can drop coins into charity canisters at the checkout, Working Assets customers can add something to their monthly bills, knowing this extra amount will go to a good cause — and is deductible on their income taxes as a charitable contribution. Roughly $50,000 is raised every month through such contributions.

The bill also invites customers to call (free on the first Monday of every month) or authorize sending a letter to some government figure or business executive (a $3 charge per month), urging action on a particular issue. As many as 25,000 Working Assets customers participate in any given month. Recent campaigns have sent messages to McDonald's, supporting vegetable burgers; to the governor of California, opposing measures that would penalize immigrants; and to the head of the Envi-ronmental Protection Agency, protesting toxic-waste incinerators near schools. "Now we have a lobbying tool as opposed to just a fund-raising tool," says Scher.

To date, the company has donated more than $3 million to dozens of causes. Co-founders Scher and Barnes are moving aggressively to expand their customer base so that they can tackle more issues more effectively. "The more customers we get, the more money we give to nonprofit groups and the more political clout we get," says Barnes. However, being socially aware doesn't mean giving up the profit focus of a well-managed business. Says Scher, "In some ways we've created an ideal company — one that is able to meet both a financial and a social bottom line."

1. Which of the four basic consumer rights does Working Assets appear to be promoting with its Citizen Letters and Free Speech Day offers? Do you agree with this approach? Why or why not?

2. Is Working Assets acting responsibly by encouraging customers to round up their bills and pay more so that the company can donate money to social causes? Explain your answer.

3. What do you think customers should do when they don't want to support the monthly cause that Working Assets features in its billing statement?

As directed by your instructor, call or write a local business or franchise operation and request a copy of its code of ethics. As an alternative, visit the periodical section of your library and locate such a code in a business magazine or professional journal article dealing with business ethics. With a group of three other students, evaluate the code. Consider what the code says about the rights of workers, shareholders, and consumers. Who is protected by this code? How does the company balance its obligations to stakeholders with its goals of making products and generating profits?

From recent issues, find a *Wall Street Journal* article related to one or more of the following ethical/social-responsibility challenges faced by businesses:

- Environmental issues, such as air and water pollution, acid rain, and hazardous-waste disposal
- Employee or consumer safety measures
- Consumer information/education
- Employment discrimination/affirmative action
- Investment ethics
- Industrial spying and theft of trade secrets
- Fraud, bribery, and overcharging
- Company codes of ethics

1. What was the nature of the ethical challenge or social-responsibility issue presented in the article?

2. What stakeholder group(s) are affected? What lasting effects will be felt by (a) the company and (b) these stakeholder group(s)?

3. Does the article report any wrongdoing by a company or agency official? Was the action illegal, unethical, or questionable? What course of action would you recommend the company or agency take to correct or improve matters now?

WHEN IN ROME, SHOULD YOU REALLY DO AS THE ROMANS DO?

Synopsis

As global business grows, so does the challenge of global business ethics. As complex as ethics can be inside a single country, ethical questions become much more difficult as soon as you cross the border into another country. The key problem with global ethics is the difference in ethical standards from one country to the next. This video addresses the problem of conflicting standards and values, and it presents several intriguing—and very realistic—ethical dilemmas. A panel made up of ethics experts, international business executives, and business students discuss these dilemmas and expose the complexity of global ethical questions. The scenarios these people discuss are more than just academic exercises; they occur regularly in the world of global business.

Exercises

ANALYSIS

1. Why are colleges and universities putting more emphasis on business ethics?

2. Is it possible to teach ethics to adults, or are a person's behavioral patterns basically in place by the time he or she reaches adulthood?

3. If a global business situation involves conflicts between two countries' value systems, whose should prevail?

4. Is it proper for one country to "preach" its value system and ethical standards to the rest of the world?

5. What is your school's responsibility in terms of the overall topic of business ethics?

APPLICATION

Make the pesticide decision described in the video; then explain how you would handle whichever decision you reach. In other words, if you decide to sell the pesticide, explain what steps you'll take.

DECISION

Let's say your company is in a desperate financial condition, and if sales don't improve soon, you'll have to lay off dozens of employees. The economy is in dire shape as well, and you know that few of the laid-off employees will find other jobs. You're faced with a global ethics question on a big sales opportunity that could turn the company around. In any situation like this, what are some of the general questions you should ask yourself before making the decision?

COMMUNICATION

Assume that you're the CEO of a company that has just established a code of ethics. Write a memo to all employees, describing the code (make up any details you need) and emphasizing the company's position in terms of following and enforcing the new code.

INTEGRATION

Turn back to Chapter 1 and review the description of per-capita incomes around the world. Do you think that these variations in economic prosperity around the world have an impact on global ethical challenges?

ETHICS

Nations in the Third World are often criticized by people in the United States and other developed countries for such environmentally unsound practices as cutting down rain forests.

However, these less developed countries make a good point when they respond that the vast majority of the world's pollution is generated by a comparatively small collection of industrialized countries. As one of the world's premier polluters, does the United States have any right to criticize, say, Brazil's destruction of the Amazon rain forest?

DEBATE

Some U.S. executives say that the Foreign Corrupt Practices Act (FCPA) puts them at a serious disadvantage in certain cases. One could even argue that the FCPA creates another ethical problem in that the U.S. companies that can't compete successfully may have to lay off employees, pay lower dividends to investors, and so on. Option A: In a formal debate format, argue either for or against the FCPA. Option B: Take either side and state your case in a brief report.

TEAMWORK

In a team of three or four students, research the Michael Milken case and write a one-page summary of the situation, including both the charges against him and his defense in response to those charges.

RESEARCH

Do the research necessary to write a one-paragraph update on the status of U.S. business involvement in either South Africa or the People's Republic of China.

ROLE PLAYING

One student plays the role of the CEO of a company whose international sales manager has recently crossed an ethical line in securing a deal (make up whatever details you need; you might find it easiest to base this role play on one of the scenarios from the video). Several other students play company directors. Together, decide how you will respond.

Chapter

4

Forms of Business Enterprise

Pulling off a wedding is no piece of cake, if you'll pardon the pun. In addition to ordering the cake, you have to plan the guest list, select sites for the service and reception, coordinate wardrobes, order massive quantities of food and drink, and attend to dozens of other details.

That's a big job, to be sure, but now imagine you're arranging the marriage of the sixth largest and ninth largest banks in the United States. Of course, companies aren't usually driven into each other's arms with the same passion that joins married couples, but the things that make a marriage work are rather similar to the things that make a corporate merger work. They include shared goals, compatible cultures, open communication, and the mundane but all-important tasks of simply coexisting day after day under the same roof.

When Chemical Bank (the number 6 bank) and Manufacturers Hanover (number 9) decided to join forces, Chemical CEO (chief executive officer) Walter Shipley and his counterpart at Manufacturers, John McGillicuddy, knew it would be a massive undertaking. Perhaps most important was the relationship between Shipley and McGillicuddy. Here were two of the most powerful players in the corporate world, each accustomed to running his own show. The new company, however, would need only one CEO; after the merger, one of the two men would no longer be top dog.

The tone these two executives set in their relationship would filter down through the two organizations, guiding the way employees felt about the merger. Employees often bear the brunt of mergers. Like executives, they can lose their jobs if the new company has more people than it needs. Unlike executives, they don't have much say in the merger decision.

Beyond the people issues, Shipley and McGillicuddy and their crews had to address financial questions, customer concerns, and a host of operational details. One good example is the corporate computer system. Computers are the nervous systems of every modern bank, but should the new computer system adopt Chemical's setup or Manufacturers'? Such issues may seem obscure and not very critical, but they can make or break a merger.

And You Thought Planning a Wedding Was a Headache

Successfully merging teams of people was one of the biggest challenges facing Chemical Bank when it merged with Manufacturers Hanover.

If you were Shipley or McGillicuddy, how would you help prepare for the merger? What steps would you take to make sure the new company would be successful? How would you handle the issues of executive power transfers, employee relationships, customers, and all the operational questions, from what to call the new company to which of the two computer systems to use?[1]

HOW TO CATEGORIZE COMPANIES BY INDUSTRY SECTOR

What do you know about companies like Chemical Bank, Exxon, or the convenience store on the corner? Is it the kind of company you respect? Would you like to work there? Would you invest your money in it? Would you feel comfortable buying its products or services? To answer those questions, you need to figure out what makes the company tick.

Most companies can be categorized by industry sector. As Exhibit 4.1 illustrates, **service businesses** include wholesale and retail trade, finance and insurance, transportation and utilities, and other services, such as the banking services dispensed by a firm such as Chemical Bank. **Goods-producing businesses** include manufacturing, construction, mining, and agriculture. Broadly speaking, companies in these two major sectors of the economy differ in their growth rate, cycle of business, cost structure, company size, and geographic focus.

The relationship between services and the production of goods is not a battle for dominance. The two sectors are complementary parts of a whole, each dependent on the other. Producers need service businesses to buy and distribute products, and service businesses depend on the production of goods for survival. What would a clothing manufacturer do without department stores? How could McDonald's dish up all those burgers without beef, buns, and grills?

In fact, the line between services and producers has blurred somewhat. Consider IBM, for example. Few IBM employees are involved in physically building a good. Most perform service tasks, such as interacting with individual customers, designing systems for them, or

service businesses *Businesses that provide intangible products or perform useful labor on behalf of another*

goods-producing businesses *Businesses that produce tangible products*

Exhibit 4.1

Sectors of the U.S. Economy
The service sector provides more than 70 percent of the revenues produced in the United States.

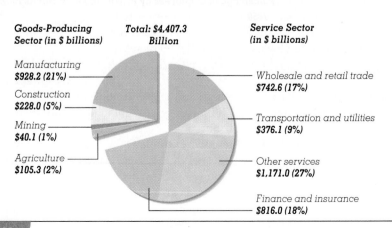

Goods-Producing Sector (in $ billions)

Total: $4,407.3 Billion

Service Sector (in $ billions)

Manufacturing **$928.2 (21%)**

Construction **$228.0 (5%)**

Mining **$40.1 (1%)**

Agriculture **$105.3 (2%)**

Wholesale and retail trade **$742.6 (17%)**

Transportation and utilities **$376.1 (9%)**

Other services **$1,171.0 (27%)**

Finance and insurance **$816.0 (18%)**

finding out what they need. Such activity ultimately results in selling a good, so you can't call it a service. However, the activity itself does not actually produce a good, so you can't call it manufacturing either. The distinction between a good and a service is fuzzy here because what is produced cannot be separated from what is performed.[2]

Growth of the Service Sector

Service occupations now account for more than 70 percent of the U.S. national income. Every recent economic recovery gained momentum from the service sector, the segment of the economy that delivers services rather than goods. The service sector has created over 44 million jobs in the last three decades. Many of these new jobs went to women and minorities entering the workforce.[3] Most of the new jobs created in the United States by the end of the century will be in services, although a frequent complaint about these service jobs is that they often don't pay as well as manufacturing jobs and don't provide as much room for personal or professional growth. Service businesses now employ roughly 70 percent of the 130 million or so people at work in the United States (see Exhibit 4.2). Manufacturing jobs make up most of the rest, with agriculture employing just a small fraction of all workers. Experts foresee 107.4 million service jobs in 2005, compared with 25.2 million in manufacturing.[4] The manufacturing sector, by the way, has added very few net jobs over the last 20 years.[5]

Services have always played an important part in the U.S. economy, accounting for half of all employment as long ago as 1940. In the last decade or two, however, services became an increasingly vital force for several reasons:

- *Economic prosperity increases the demand for services.* The 76 million baby boomers in the United States (people born between 1946 and 1964) are in their peak earning years. These consumers find themselves with more disposable income and look for services to help them invest, travel, relax, and stay fit. Similar trends are taking place in other parts of the world. For example, people over age 35

Exhibit 4.2

Shifts in Employment by Industry Sector
Since the end of World War II, the service sector has been responsible for creating virtually all job growth in the U.S. economy.

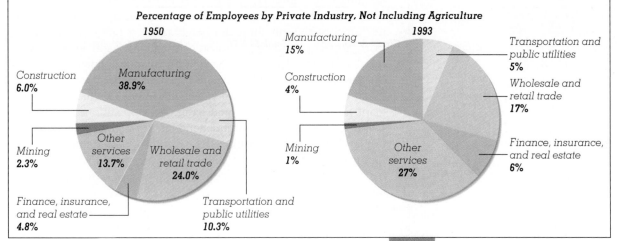

Percentage of Employees by Private Industry, Not Including Agriculture

1950

Manufacturing 38.9%
Construction 6.0%
Mining 2.3%
Other services 13.7%
Wholesale and retail trade 24.0%
Finance, insurance, and real estate 4.8%
Transportation and public utilities 10.3%

1993

Manufacturing 15%
Construction 4%
Mining 1%
Other services 27%
Transportation and public utilities 5%
Wholesale and retail trade 17%
Finance, insurance, and real estate 6%

are crowding into exercise centers, sports clubs, and sporting goods stores across Europe, trying to get in shape and feel better about themselves.[6]

- *Population patterns in the United States continue to change.* There are more elderly people, more single people living alone, and fewer traditional families. The number of women in the workforce grew 213.7 percent in the four decades after World War II, compared with a 51.5 percent increase in the number of working men.[7] As a result, there are more two-career households than ever before. This trend creates opportunities for service companies that can help couples with all the tasks they no longer have time for, including lawn maintenance, food service, and child care.

- *The number and complexity of goods needing service are increasing.* Computers, VCRs, CD players, recreational vehicles, and security systems are examples of products that can require specialized installation, repair, or user training. In the office, automation products ranging from laser printers to fax machines need expert attention. Factories use robots, automated test equipment, and computer-controlled production lines that require extensive support services.

- *Businesses need help in a complex global economy.* The need for business services continues to change and expand, for several reasons: Corporate restructurings can leave firms without adequate internal services, the continued growth of global marketing and manufacturing requires more international support services, and the business of business just keeps getting more complicated.[8]

- *Technology creates new service opportunities.* Many technological advances, from automated teller machines to the information superhighway, create services that couldn't have been offered before.

The service sector is a rich and varied part of the economy. You can make some sense of it by breaking it down into related segments: retailing and wholesaling, finance and insurance, transportation and utilities, and a final group that contains all other service businesses:

- *Retailing and wholesaling.* The slowest-growing sector of the service industry—retailing and wholesaling—is also the largest in sales volume and total number of employees. Retailers employ more than one in six U.S. residents, or over 19 million workers. In fact, retailing is the third largest employer in the United States.[9] In this category, you find many small, family-run businesses like the corner grocery, the gift shop, the neighborhood café, and the candy store. You also find the wholesale distributors and brokers who serve as intermediaries between producers and retailers.

- *Finance and insurance.* The financial-services sector contains a relatively even mix of large and small businesses. On the one hand, giant insurance companies and banks have operations around the world; on the other hand, independent insurance agents, real estate brokers, and local banks operate within well-defined regions. Companies with fewer than 500 employees account for roughly half of the sector's employment and slightly less than half of its sales.[10]

- *Transportation and utilities.* This sector includes GTE, AT&T, and the regional telephone companies; electricity, water, and natural gas suppliers; and companies such as UPS, American Airlines, and Santa Fe Pacific that move people and packages around the world. Transportation and utilities have not grown much in terms of employment over the past decade or two. Deregulation has caused considerable turmoil in such industries as telecommunications and airlines. This segment of the service sector is dominated by large companies. Airlines, electric utilities, and telecommunications companies are **capital-intensive businesses,** meaning getting into the business and creating products require significant amounts of capital. It takes a great deal of money to buy airplanes, build power plants, or construct nationwide telephone networks. Small businesses simply lack the funds.

capital-intensive businesses *Businesses that require large investments in capital assets*

- *Other services.* The most rapidly growing service area is the group of "other" services, which includes such diverse businesses as beauty parlors, repair shops, private schools, health services, hotels, amusement parks, theaters, and business and professional services. Employment in these businesses has more than doubled since the 1950s.[11] By and large, this sector is composed of **labor-intensive businesses,** those that rely to a significant degree on human effort or skill in the creation of the product. The most important factor of production is labor, supplied in many cases by the owner of the business. In most labor-intensive businesses, the **barriers to entry** are relatively low; in other words, you don't need a lot of special knowledge, facilities, employees, or capital to open shop. All you need is a good idea, a little money, and a willingness to work. As a consequence, you see many small firms in this sector.

labor-intensive businesses *Businesses in which labor costs are more important than capital costs*

barriers to entry *Factors that make it difficult to launch a business in a particular industry*

Production's Revival

In the early 1980s, the goods-producing sector was plagued by recession, unfavorable exchange rates between the dollar and foreign currencies, tough international competition, and relatively lackluster productivity. Producers regained much of their momentum by the early 1990s, however, largely as a result of better management. From computers to cars, producers slashed costs and improved product quality and customer service.

Historically, the goods-producing sector has been more global in scope than the service sector. The 10 largest U.S. exporters together ship well over $100 billion worth of goods to other countries every year.[12] Service firms such as Chemical Bank are counting on overseas sales to make up an increasing percentage of their business.

The U.S. manufacturing sector has rebounded in recent years by abandoning old factories or upgrading them with new technology that emphasizes quality and productivity.

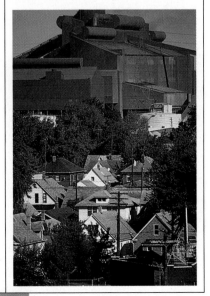

Manufacturing

Manufacturing is by far the largest category in the goods-producing sector, and it has improved most dramatically in recent years. By almost every measure—quality, sales, profits, international market share—U.S. factories are proving that they have what it takes to succeed. Large companies dominate the manufacturing sector.[13] Nevertheless, small businesses play an important role in the manufacturing sector, both as suppliers to large manufacturers and as pioneers of new technology. Many of the most exciting scientific developments of recent years have come from small high-tech companies involved in such fields as biotechnology, computers, robotics, and lasers.

Construction

Construction is one of the most cyclical businesses in the economy, responding to general economic conditions and to fluctuations in interest rates. When rates are high, the cost of borrowing money to build and buy property increases, so construction declines. The outlook for the industry in the 1990s is cloudy because the United States has an oversupply of commercial buildings. Unlike manufacturing, construction is made up largely of small, local businesses. Firms with under 100 employees account for two-thirds of the volume.[14]

Mining

Mining is another volatile business, subject to big swings in profitability depending on global economic conditions and on supply-and-demand relationships. One reason for this volatility is that mining is a **commodity business** with little distinction between one unit of production and another. Regardless of who produces it, oil is oil, gold is gold, copper is copper. Companies cannot do much to differentiate their products, so they are forced to compete on the basis of price. When the supply of commodity products exceeds demand, the producers all cut their prices, and profits fall throughout the industry. In recent years, the global supply of many minerals has increased because developing nations have expanded their mining capacity in order to build an export base. This expansion has depressed profits for the mining sector as a whole.

Agriculture

Like mining, agriculture is a commodity business, so profitability hinges on supply-and-demand relationships. As more and more developing nations become more self-sufficient in food production, U.S. farmers have seen their profits shrink along with their export market. At the same time, farming has become more capital-intensive as the price of equipment and land has increased.

The pressure of profits has forced many of the less successful farmers to sell out to larger concerns. Over the next several years, the number of commercial farms is expected to decline, and the average size of each farm is expected to increase.[15] Although farm employment represents only a small fraction of total employment in the United States, the health of the nation's farms ripples throughout the economy, affecting equipment makers, banks, and rural retailers.

HOW TO CATEGORIZE COMPANIES BY FORM OF OWNERSHIP

Figuring out where a company fits in the industrial scheme of things gives you a general idea of its characteristics. Another way to get a feel for what makes a company tick is to look at its form of ownership. The three most common forms of business ownership are sole proprietorship, partnership, and corporation. As Exhibit 4.3 illustrates,

commodity business *Business in which products are undifferentiated, with the result that price becomes the chief competitive weapon; usually applied to basic goods such as minerals and agricultural products*

Exhibit 4.3
Prevalence and Profits of the Three Forms of Business Ownership
Sole proprietorships are the most common type of business in the United States, accounting for 72 percent of all enterprises. However, corporations account for 72 percent of the profits earned by U.S. businesses.

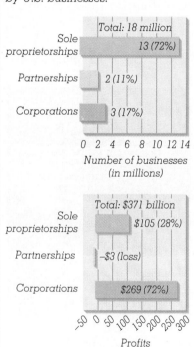

corporations tend to be larger-scale operations, accounting for the lion's share of total receipts in all eight of the economy's industrial subsectors. However, proprietorships are more numerous, particularly in the service sector.

Each form of business ownership has a characteristic internal structure, legal status, size, and field to which it is best suited. Each has key advantages and disadvantages for the owners, and each offers employees a distinctive working environment with its own risks and rewards. Exhibit 4.4 contrasts the characteristics of the three forms of business.

Exhibit 4.4
Characteristics of the Forms of Business Ownership
The "best" form of ownership depends on the objectives of the people involved in the business.

Aspect	Form of ownership		
	Sole proprietorship	Partnership	Corporation
Tax treatment	Profits and losses flow directly to the owners, are taxed at personal rates.	Profits and losses flow directly to the partners, are taxed at personal rates. Partners share income and losses equally unless the partnership agreement specifies otherwise.	Profits and losses are taxed at corporate rates. Profits are taxed again at personal rates when they are distributed to the investors as dividends.
Owner's control	Owner has complete control.	General partnerships: Partners have control of the business; each partner is entitled to equal control unless the partnership agreement specifies otherwise. Limited partnerships: The general partner controls the business; limited partners don't participate in the management.	Ownership and management of the business are separate. Individual shareholders in public corporations are not involved in daily management decisions; in private or closely held corporations, owners are more likely to participate in managing the business.
Owner's liability	Owner assumes unlimited personal liability for the business.	General partnerships: Partners assume unlimited liability for the business. Limited partnerships: Partners are liable only for the amount of their investment.	Investors' liability is limited to the amount of their investment.
Liquidity of owner's investment	Owner must generally sell the business to get his or her investment out of it.	Partners must generally sell their share in the business to recoup their investment.	Shareholders in public corporations may trade their shares on the open market; shareholders in private corporations must find a buyer for their shares to recoup their investment.
Ease of formation	No expenses or formalities apart from obtaining necessary business licenses.	No formalities or expenses needed apart from obtaining necessary licenses; however, advisable to have an attorney develop a written partnership agreement.	Must follow procedures established by the state in which the business is incorporated; expense and complexity of incorporation vary from state to state. Public corporations must also comply with requirements of their stock exchanges.
Life span of the business	May be limited to the life span of the owner.	Depends on the terms of partnership agreement.	Unlimited.

Sole Proprietorships

A **sole proprietorship** is a business owned by one person, although it may have many employees. It is the easiest and least expensive form of business to start. Many farms, retail establishments, and small service businesses are sole proprietorships, as are many home-based businesses (such as caterers and housekeeping services).

Advantages of Sole Proprietorships

Sole proprietorship has a number of advantages. One is ease of establishment. All you have to do to launch a sole proprietorship is to obtain any necessary licenses, open your doors, and start selling your goods or services. Once you're under way, you have the satisfaction of working for yourself. You can make your own decisions—what hours to work, whom to hire, what prices to charge, whether to expand, and whether to shut down. Best of all, you can keep all the profits, and these profits are taxed at the personal-income rate, not the higher corporate rate.

You also have the advantage of privacy. As a sole proprietor, you do not have to reveal your performance or plans. Although you may need to provide financial information to a banker if you need a loan, and you must provide certain financial information when you file tax returns, you do not have to prepare any reports for outsiders as you would if you owned a corporation.

Disadvantages of Sole Proprietorships

Although a sole proprietorship can theoretically be any size, most are relatively small businesses. The majority have annual revenue below $25,000. [16] The small scale of most sole proprietorships reflects their limited financial resources. A single person starting a company generally has less capital than a group of people and may also have more difficulty getting a loan. Furthermore, a sole proprietor may have to pay more for credit, because lending institutions are likely to charge higher interest rates to small companies than to large corporations.

In some cases, the sole proprietor's independence may be a drawback because it often means that the business depends on the talents and managerial skills of one person. If problems crop up, the sole proprietor may not recognize them or may be too proud to seek help, especially given the high cost of hiring experienced managers and professional consultants.

The major disadvantage is the proprietor's **unlimited liability.** From a legal standpoint, the owner and the business are one and the same. Any legal damages or debts incurred by the business are the owner's responsibility. As a sole proprietor, you might have to sell personal assets, such as your family's home, to satisfy a business debt. If someone sues you over a business matter, you might lose everything you own.

A final disadvantage is that sole proprietorships often have a limited life. Some sole proprietors pass their business on to their heirs as part of their estate. However, the owner's death may mean the demise of the business, particularly if the owner's skills are crucial to the operation.

Partnerships

If starting a business on your own seems a little intimidating, you might decide to share the risks and rewards by going into business with a partner. In that case, you would form a **partnership**—a legal association of two or more people as co-owners of a business for profit. You and your partners would share the profits and losses of the business and perhaps the management responsibilities as well. Your partnership might remain a small, two-person operation, or it might grow into an international business with thousands of employees, as some accounting and consulting firms have done.

There are three basic types of partnerships. In a **general partnership,** all partners are legally equal and are liable for the business's debts. In a **limited partnership,** however, one or more people act as general partners and run the business. The remaining partners are passive investors (that is, they are not involved in managing the business). These partners are called limited partners because their liability is limited to the amount of their capital contribution. They cannot be sued for more money than they invested in the business. In a **master limited partnership (MLP),** firms act like corporations, selling partner units on a recognized stock exchange. MLPs have advantages similar to those of corporations (limited liability, unlimited life, and transferable ownership); moreover, if 90 percent of their gross income is passive (typically, rental income or other income not requiring the physical efforts of the owners), they pay no corporate taxes (since profits are paid to stockholders who pay taxes at individual rates).

Advantages of Partnerships

Proprietorships and partnerships have some of the same advantages. Like proprietorships, partnerships are easy to form, although it's wise to get a lawyer's advice on the partnership agreement—the legal document that spells out the partners' rights and responsibilities. Partnerships also provide the same tax advantages as proprietorships, since profits are taxed at personal-income-tax rates rather than corporate rates.

In a couple of respects, partnerships are superior to sole proprietorships, largely because there's strength in numbers. When you have several people putting up their money and pooling their talents, you can start a more ambitious enterprise and increase your chances of success, assuming, of course, that you have picked good partners. As a partner, you may also have better luck than a sole proprietor in obtaining financing, since you and your partners are all legally responsible for paying off the debts of the group. Finally, by forming a partnership you increase the chances that the organization will endure since new partners can be drawn into the business to replace those who die or retire. The founders of the accounting firm KPMG Peat Marwick died many years ago, but their firm, which was founded

partnership Unincorporated business owned and operated by two or more persons under a voluntary legal association

general partnership Partnership in which all partners have the right to participate as co-owners and are individually liable for the business's debts

limited partnership Partnership composed of one or more general partners and one or more partners whose liability is usually limited to the amount of their capital investment

master limited partnership (MLP) Business partnership that acts like a corporation, trading partnership units on listed stock exchanges; if 90 percent of income is passive, MLPs are taxed at individual rates

Tom and Kate Chappell are partners in their business, Tom's of Maine, a manufacturer of all-natural health and beauty products.

in 1897, continues. Provisions for handling the departure and addition of partners are usually covered in the partnership agreement.

Disadvantages of Partnerships

A fundamental drawback of a general partnership arrangement is the unlimited liability of the active partners. If one of your partners makes a serious business or professional mistake and is sued by a disgruntled client, you are financially accountable. You stand to lose everything you own. At the same time, you are responsible for any debts incurred by the partnership. Even though malpractice insurance or business-risk insurance offers some financial protection, you pay a premium for your peace of mind. Faced with the risk of unlimited liability, many lawyers, doctors, and accountants are forming professional corporations rather than partnerships.

Another disadvantage of partnerships is the potential for interpersonal problems. Difficulties often arise because each partner wants to be responsible for managing the organization. Electing a managing partner to lead the organization may diminish the conflicts, but disagreements are still likely to arise. Moreover, the partnership may have to face the question of what to do with unproductive partners. Finally, in the ranks of the aspiring partners, competition is often fierce. The junior employees are vying for a limited number of partnership slots, and they view each other as rivals. This situation may give rise to political maneuvering or create a pressure-cooker environment in which everyone is working 80-hour weeks in hopes of looking good.

Corporations

A **corporation** is a legal entity with the power to own property and conduct business. The corporation's legal status and obligations exist independently of its owners, unlike the case with sole proprietorships and partnerships. The modern corporation evolved in the nineteenth century when large sums of capital were needed to build railroads, coal mines, and steel mills. Such endeavors required so much money that no single individual or group of partners could hope to raise it all. The solution was to sell shares in the business to numerous investors, who would get a cut of the profits in exchange for their money. These investors got a chance to vote on certain issues that might affect the value of their investment, but they were not involved in managing day-to-day operations. To protect the investors from the risks associated with such large undertakings, their liability was limited to the amount of their investment.

It was a good solution, and the corporation quickly became a vital force in the nation's economy. As rules and regulations developed to define what corporations could and could not do, corporations acquired the legal attributes of people. Like you, a corporation can receive, own, and transfer property; make contracts; and sue and be sued.

The relationship between a corporation and its **shareholders,** or owners, is a source of enormous strength. Since ownership and management are separate, the owners may get rid of the managers (in

corporation *Legally chartered enterprise with most of the legal rights of a person, including the right to conduct a business, to own and sell property, to borrow money, and to sue or be sued*

shareholders *Owners of a corporation*

PART ONE | FOCUS ON BUSINESS TODAY

theory, at least), if the owners vote to do so. Conversely, because shares of the company (known as **stock**) may be bequeathed or sold to someone else, the company's ownership may change drastically over time while the company and its management remain intact (as long as the company is economically sound). The corporation's unlimited life span, combined with its ability to raise capital, gives it the potential for significant growth.

A company need not be large to incorporate. Most corporations, like most businesses, are relatively small, and most small corporations are privately held. The big ones, however, are *really* big. The 500 largest corporations in the United States, as listed by *Fortune* magazine, have combined sales of over $2 trillion and employ well over 10 million

stock *Shares of ownership in a corporation*

GAINING THE COMPETITIVE EDGE

Where's the best place to start your career—in a large corporation, a small company, or a business of your own? Many students have a negative view of work in a large corporation, but the majority of people who actually work in those companies enjoy their jobs. Working for a small company or striking out on your own does have some advantages, of course. However, the following advantages of working for a well-managed large company are hard to ignore:

1. *Experienced people who can teach you a thing or two.* Large corporations are likely to employ dozens of people who specialize in your field. You'll have a chance to learn about the diverse niches that might appeal to you. Your opportunities to find a mentor will be far greater than they might be in a small company that employs only a few people in any given specialty.

2. *A broad range of activities and locations.* If you think variety is the spice of life, a big corporation may be just the ticket. Most have formal rotation programs to help new employees gain firsthand experience in various parts of the business. You'll have the chance to broaden your expertise and see which functions are your favorites. Since most Fortune 500 companies have operations in many locations, you may also have the chance to move from city to city, or even to another country.

PLACES TO WORK: IS BIGGER BETTER?

3. *Major budget and program responsibility early on.* Because Fortune 500 companies operate on such a large scale, you may find yourself managing a significant program with a big budget before you know it. Outlays that would be enormous in a small company are routine in a larger operation. At the same time, mistakes are not such a big deal, since major corporations do not have all their eggs in one basket. If you gamble and lose, you won't sink the company. This freedom helps you to learn to take sensible risks.

4. *Formal training.* Most large corporations offer extensive training to get their new recruits started on the right foot. In some organizations, you can learn as much on the job as you would in a graduate business program—and get paid for doing it.

5. *More resources to do the job.* Success often depends on the tools you have to work with. In a big corporation, you are likely to have advanced information systems, state-of-the-art

equipment, a well-trained staff, and a large enough budget to get the job done. These resources will enable you to accomplish things you could not hope to achieve in a smaller organization.

6. *A chance to work on significant projects.* Big companies do big things, and being part of that action can be exciting. Whether you're involved in building a new hotel in Hong Kong or designing state-of-the-art telecommunications systems, you can participate in something on a grand scale. Furthermore, being associated with a large, well-known organization can open doors that might otherwise be closed to you. It's amazing how responsive people become when they know that you represent a powerful company.

7. *Opportunities for advancement.* Your chances of being promoted at a big company are greater than they are at a small company because there are more slots to move into. Since most large companies are committed to promoting from within, you will have the inside track. You will also have the benefit of a professional human resources department that will help you formulate and achieve your career goals.

8. *Excellent pay and benefits.* With few exceptions, big companies pay higher salaries and provide better benefits than small companies. Money may not be what motivates you, but it certainly helps pay the bills.

people. Even after years of layoffs and cutbacks, General Motors alone has three-quarters of a million employees; if all of them lived in one place, it would be one of the 12 largest cities in the United States.[17]

Types of Corporations

Corporations have evolved into various types. The first distinction is whether a corporation is government-owned, quasi-government, or private. **Government-owned corporations** are formed by federal or state governments for a specific public purpose, such as running local school districts, making student loans, or developing major land areas (such as the Tennessee Valley Authority's building an extensive dam system in the Tennessee River Valley). **Quasi-government corporations** are public utilities having a government-granted monopoly to provide electricity, local phone service, water, and natural gas. The companies on the Fortune 500 list are almost all **private corporations**—that is, companies owned by private individuals or companies. These investors buy stock on the open market, which gives private corporations access to large amounts of capital. In return, the shareholders receive the chance to share in the profits if the corporation succeeds.

Corporations may be either not-for-profit or for-profit corporations. **Not-for-profit corporations** pursue goals other than economic ones, such as those targeted by charitable, educational, and fraternal organizations. The Public Broadcasting System (PBS), the American Heart Association, and Harvard University are all not-for-profit corporations. **For-profit corporations** are formed to earn money for their owners.

Corporations that are **publicly traded** (called open corporations) actively sell stock on the open market. Both private and quasi-government corporations may be publicly traded, such as Ford Motor and Commonwealth Edison (which supplies power to the Chicago area). Corporations that are **not publicly traded** (called closed corporations) withhold their stock from public sale, preferring to finance any expansion out of their own earnings or to borrow from some other source. By withholding their stock from public sale, the owners retain complete control over their operations and protect their businesses from unwelcome takeover attempts. Such famous companies as Hallmark, United Parcel Service, and Hyatt Hotels have opted to remain closed corporations. **Professional corporations** are not publicly traded, and their shareholders offer professional services (such as medical, legal, and engineering services). Popular because of their ability to set up beneficial pension and insurance plans, professional corporations are replacing partnerships in some parts of the country.

Another type of corporation, known as the **S corporation** (or subchapter S corporation), is a cross between a partnership and a corporation. Income and deductions from the business flow directly to

Electricity is a product offered in some parts of the country by quasi-government corporations and in other parts by private companies, such as Pacific Gas & Electric in California.

government-owned corporations *Corporations formed and owned by a government body for a specific public purpose*

quasi-government corporations *Public utilities having a monopoly to provide basic services*

private corporations *Companies owned by private individuals or companies*

not-for-profit corporations *Incorporated institutions whose owners have limited liability and that exist to provide a social service rather than to make a profit*

the owners and are taxed at personal-income-tax rates, just as they are in a partnership. At the same time, the shareholders in an S corporation, like the shareholders in a regular corporation, have limited liability. S corporations can be extremely attractive under certain circumstances, but their freedom of operation is limited by a number of restrictions. For example, an S corporation can have no more than 35 shareholders; it cannot own more than 80 percent of the stock of another corporation; and it cannot derive more than 25 percent of its income from passive sources such as rent, interest, or royalties.

Companies can now combine the advantages of S corporations and limited partnerships without having to abide by the restrictions of either. **Limited liability companies** (LLCs) allow firms to pay taxes like partnerships while protecting shareholders from personal liability beyond their investments. Moreover, LLCs are not restricted to 35 shareholders. In addition, members' participation in management is not restricted (as it is in limited partnerships). Unlike a corporation, however, an LLC's existence is restricted to 30 years.[18]

Finally, not all corporations are independent entities. **Subsidiary corporations** are partially or wholly owned by another corporation known as a **parent company,** which supervises the operations of the subsidiary. A **holding company** is a special type of parent company that owns other companies for investment reasons and usually exercises little operating control over these subsidiaries. Exhibit 4.5 summarizes some of these distinctions between types of corporations.

Corporations can also be classified according to where they do business. An *alien corporation* operates in the United States but is incorporated in another country. A *foreign corporation,* sometimes called an *out-of-state corporation,* is incorporated in one state (frequently the state of Delaware, where incorporation laws are lenient) but does business in several other states where it is registered. A *domestic corporation* does business only in the state where it is chartered.

Corporate Structure and Governance

Although a corporation's shareholders own the business, they are rarely involved in managing it, particularly if the corporation is publicly traded. Instead, they elect a board of directors to represent them. The directors, in turn, select and monitor the top officers, who actually run the company (see Exhibit 4.6).

Shareholders. Theoretically, the shareholders (who can be individuals, other companies, nonprofit organizations, pension funds, and mutual funds) are the ultimate governing body of the corporation, but in practice, most individual shareholders in large corporations—where the shareholders may number in the millions—accept the recommendations of management. Indeed, the more shareholders there are, the less tangible influence each one has on the corporation. However, some shareholders have more influence than others. For one thing, some people own stock that carries no voting rights, and others own shares that are worth one vote each. Furthermore, some people (or organizations) own more shares with voting rights than others do; a person with 1,000 voting shares, for example, has 1,000 votes and 10 times the impact of a person with only 100 voting shares.

for-profit corporations Companies formed to earn money for their owners

publicly traded corporations Corporations that actively sell stock on the open market; also called open corporations

not publicly traded corporations Corporations that withhold their stock from public sale; also called closed corporations

professional corporations Companies whose shareholders offer professional services (medical, legal, engineering) and set up beneficial pension and insurance plans

S corporation Corporations with no more than 35 shareholders that may be taxed as a partnership; also known as a subchapter S corporation

limited liability companies (LLCs) Organizations that combine the benefits of S corporations and limited partnerships without the drawbacks of either

subsidiary corporations Corporations whose stock is owned entirely or almost entirely by another corporation

parent company Company that owns most, if not all, of another company's stock and that takes an active part in managing that other company

holding company Company that owns most, if not all, of another company's stock but that does not actively participate in the management of that other company

Type	Definition	Example
Government-owned corporation	Business formed by federal or state government for a specific purpose	TVA
Quasi-government corporation	Public utilities with a monopoly on providing basic public services	Commonwealth Edison
Private corporation	Business owned by private individuals or companies	General Motors
Not-for-profit corporation	Service or arts institution in which no stockholder or trustee shares in the profits or losses and which is exempt from corporate income taxes	Harvard University
For-profit corporation	Company in business to make a profit	IBM
Professional corporation	Business whose partners offer professional services (medical, legal, engineering) and can set up beneficial pension and insurance packages	La Jolla Medical Group, Inc.
S corporation	Corporation with no more than 35 owners, whose profits are taxed at personal-income-tax rates rather than at corporate-income-tax rates	Inland Asphalt
Limited liability company	Business that reaps the benefits of S corporations and limited partnerships without the drawbacks	Realatech
Parent company	Operating company that owns or controls subsidiaries through the ownership of voting stock	Sears, Roebuck
Holding company	Corporation organized for the purpose of owing stock in and managing one or more corporations; differs from a parent company in that it generally does not conduct operations of its own	Intermark
Subsidiary corporation	Corporation that is entirely, or almost entirely, owned by another corporation, known as a parent company or holding company	Seven-Up

Exhibit 4.5

Major Types of Corporations
The most visible corporations are the large, private ones, such as General Motors, IBM, and Coca-Cola, but other types are also common.

institutional investors *Organizations that own many shares of stock; typical examples are banks, mutual funds, pension funds, insurance companies, foundations*

proxy *Document authorizing another person to vote on behalf of a shareholder in a corporation*

board of directors *Group of people, elected by the shareholders, who have the ultimate authority in guiding the affairs of a corporation*

In the last 20 years, **institutional investors,** such as pension funds, insurance companies, mutual funds, and college endowment funds, have accumulated an increasing share of the stock in the nation's corporations. They now own over half the stock in scores of Fortune 500 companies.[19] These large institutional investors want the value of their stock to increase, and they are beginning to play a more powerful role in governing the corporations in which they own shares.[20]

At least once a year, all the owners of voting shares are invited to a meeting to choose directors, select an independent accountant to audit the company's financial statements, and attend to other business. Some states limit the type of issues on which shareholders may vote; thus the shareholders effectively have little or no voice in management. Shareholders who cannot attend the annual meeting in person vote by **proxy,** signing and returning a slip of paper that authorizes management to vote on their behalf.

Board of Directors. As a practical matter, the **board of directors,** which supposedly represents the shareholders, is responsible for guiding corporate affairs and selecting corporate officers. The board has the power to vote on major management decisions, such as building a new factory, hiring a new president, or buying a new subsidiary. Depending on the size of the company, the board might have anywhere from 3 to 35 directors, although 15 to 25 is the typical range. In some corporations, several of the directors may be inside directors, people who are also employees of the company. The outside directors are typically major stockholders, executives of other firms, or influential people connected with the company's industry.

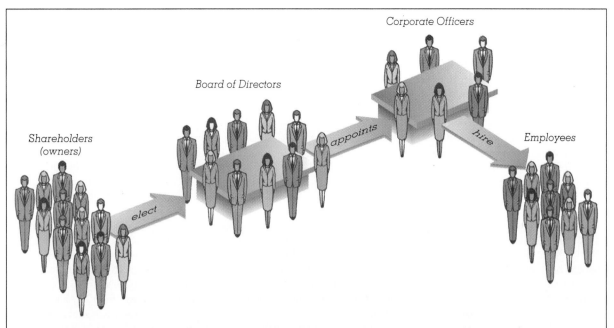

Shareholders (owners)   elect   Board of Directors   appoints   Corporate Officers   hire   Employees

The board's actual involvement in running a corporation varies from one company to another. Some boards are strong and independent and serve as a check on the company's management; others act as a "rubber stamp," simply approving management's recommendations. Assertive boards are becoming more common these days, partly because board members recognize that they can be held financially responsible if they fail to perform their duties. This fact came as a rude shock to the directors of Trans Union Corporation, who accepted a takeover bid without soliciting competing offers for the company. The Delaware Supreme Court ruled that the directors had been too hasty in accepting the first bid and had therefore deprived the shareholders of money they might have received if other offers had been encouraged. The directors agreed to pay the shareholders $13.5 million of the $23.5 million settlement.[21]

Officers. The real power in a corporation often lies with the **chief executive officer,** or **CEO,** who is responsible for establishing the policies of the company at the direction of the board. The chief executive officer may also be the chairman of the board, the president of the corporation, or both. In many instances, the CEO picks a slate of directors that includes friends and business associates and submits their names to the shareholders for approval. Since the directors in these companies owe their position on the board to the CEO, they tend to be loyal. However, in the past few years, boards at Pillsbury, General Motors, and IBM have replaced their CEOs when the directors agreed that the shareholders' interests were being compromised by company management.[22]

Advantages of Corporations

No other form of business ownership can match the success of the corporation in bringing together money, resources, and talent; in ac-

Exhibit 4.6
The Corporate Framework
Theoretically, the corporate framework resembles a democracy, in which shareholders vote to elect representatives (members of the board of directors) who will establish corporate policy and select competent managers to direct the employees. Actually, the real power in a corporation often lies with the top executives, who suggest a roster of board members for shareholder approval.

chief executive officer (CEO) *Person appointed by a corporation's board of directors to carry out the board's policies and supervise the activities of the corporation*

As one of the most culturally diverse—and culturally tolerant—nations on earth, the United States is a good training ground for managers who need to lead multicultural workforces. Even this wonderful learning opportunity, though, can't always prepare managers for international assignments. So the question arises: Who should lead a U.S. company's business units in other countries? It actually breaks down to two questions for most U.S. multinationals: Who should be in charge in each country, and who should be in charge of multiple-country regions, such as Europe or Southeast Asia?

Most U.S. companies have switched from routinely moving U.S. executives to overseas posts to moving them only when their specific technical skills can't be found in the country in question. In fact, U.S. citizens now account for fewer than 2 percent of the people employed outside of the United States by U.S. companies. Most companies prefer to hire locally to get people who are more in tune with local

CAN UNIVERSAL APPEAL OVERCOME CULTURAL DIFFERENCES?

markets, closer to customers, and more readily accepted by the local business community. Another factor that companies have to consider is the expense of temporarily moving U.S. managers to overseas posts. For instance, it costs four times as much to move a U.S. manager to Egypt than to hire an Egyptian locally.

The second key question—who to put in charge of multiple-country regions—raises some sticky issues. Although we might tend to view Europeans as fairly similar from a cultural standpoint, the reality is often far different. French businesspeople tend to have little patience

for the Swedish style of consensus management (in which everybody gets to have a say, and the company doesn't move forward until everybody agrees on the plan). British employees aren't wild about working for a German boss. Who should be in charge of a region that covers these four countries, and possibly many others? One solution is to pick a manager from Holland or Switzerland, who might be viewed as more neutral, or to pick somebody from the United States.

By the way, are you looking for a career in international management? Many multinational companies are hiring graduates from specialized business schools such as the American Graduate School of International Management in Arizona, the University of South Carolina's International Business Program, and France's INSEAD. If you possess a skill that U.S. companies need overseas (particularly marketing and production), a foreign language, and an internationally oriented education, you stand a much better chance of getting that dream job.

---

cumulating assets; and in creating wealth. The corporation has certain significant advantages that make it the best vehicle for accomplishing these tasks. One of these advantages is the corporation's limited liability. Although a corporate entity can assume tremendous liabilities, it is the corporation that is liable rather than any of the private shareholders. Say you buy stock in a company that goes bankrupt. You may lose the money you invested in the stock, but you are not legally responsible for paying the company's debts. Of course, the board members and company management may be liable if they have acted irresponsibly or illegally.

liquidity Asset's ease of conversion to cash

Private corporations also have the advantage of **liquidity,** which means that investors can easily convert their stock into cash by selling it on the open market. This option makes buying stock in a private corporation attractive to many investors because getting your money out of a sole proprietorship or a partnership can be extremely difficult. A corporation's unlimited life span is another important advantage. It allows a firm to make long-range plans and to recruit, train, and motivate the best employees.

Disadvantages of Corporations
Corporations are not without some disadvantages. Publicly owned companies are required by the government to follow certain rules

112

and to publish information about their finances and operations. These reporting requirements increase the pressure on corporate managers to achieve short-term growth and earnings targets in order to satisfy shareholders and attract potential investors. In addition, having to disclose financial information increases the company's vulnerability to competitors and to those who might want to take over the company. The paperwork and costs associated with incorporation can also be burdensome, particularly if you plan to sell stock. The complexity varies from state to state, but regardless of where you live, it is wise to consult an attorney and an accountant before incorporating.

Although the tax rates for small corporations have declined in recent years, incorporated businesses still suffer from relatively *high taxes* when compared with unincorporated businesses. All corporations (with the exception of S corporations) pay a tax of 34 percent on annual profits between $75,000 and $100,000. In addition, shareholders must pay income taxes on their share of the company's profits received as dividends. Thus corporate profits are taxed twice, whereas the profits in a sole proprietorship or partnership are taxed only once, and at a lower rate.

MERGERS AND ACQUISITIONS

Regardless of what form a business takes—be it a sole proprietorship, a partnership, or a corporation—the chances are reasonably good

Large multinational corporations such as Sony have the resources needed to acquire smaller companies with breakthrough technologies or other attributes that might be of interest.

that its form will evolve over time. Companies of all sizes and types achieve a variety of objectives by merging, dividing, and restructuring. A look at the Fortune 500 during the tumultuous 1980s illustrates the point. Almost 40 percent of the corporations listed at the start of the 1980s merged with or were acquired by other firms. Standard Brands, for example, was acquired by Nabisco, which was acquired by R. J. Reynolds, which in turn was acquired by KRK (Kohlberg Kravis Roberts). Of the 313 Fortune 500 corporations that survived the decade, 67 underwent radical restructuring, generally by purging themselves of secondary businesses. Mobil Oil sold off its nonenergy divisions; Colgate-Palmolive pruned its health-care businesses; and General Mills sold its toy, fashion, and retailing units.[23]

Types of Mergers

The terms most often used to describe all this activity are *mergers, acquisitions,* and *leveraged buyouts.* The difference between a merger and an acquisition is fairly technical, having to do with how the financial transaction is structured. Basically, in a **merger,** two or more companies combine to create a new company by pooling their interests, as when Chemical Bank and Manufacturers Hanover agreed to join forces. In an **acquisition,** one company buys another company (or parts of another company) and emerges as the controlling corporation. The acquiring company also assumes all the debts and contractual obligations of the company it acquires. The flip side of an acquisition is a **divestiture,** in which one company sells a portion of its business to another company. In the late 1980s, many acquisitions were **leveraged buyouts (LBOs).** In an LBO, one or more individuals purchase the company (or a division of the company) with borrowed funds, using the assets of the company they're buying to secure (or guarantee repayment of) the loan. The term *leverage* is borrowed from physics, where a lever allows you to lift more than you can lift on your own. The loans are then repaid out of the company's earnings, through the sale of assets, or with stock.

Leveraged buyouts sound great on paper, but they can be very risky. The problem with debt, as you probably know all too well, is that it requires regular payments of principal and interest. The debt payments are added to the regular demands on a company's cash— salaries, rent, supplies, and so forth—which reduces its operating flexibility. It often doesn't take much to push a highly leveraged company over the edge. Price wars, recessions, and new competitors are just three of the factors that can put so much financial pressure on a leveraged company that it is unable to make its regular payments. With much of its cash tied up in debt payments, a company might not have the room to respond when competitors cut prices. The result is a snowball effect, where its higher prices lead to fewer sales, which leads to even less revenue, which makes it even less able to cut prices, and so on.

Mergers and acquisitions represent relatively radical ways in which companies are combined. On a more modest scale, businesses often join forces in alliances to accomplish specific purposes. In a **joint venture,** two or more companies combine forces to work on a proj-

merger *Combination of two or more companies in which the old companies cease to exist and a new enterprise is created*

acquisition *Combination of two companies in which one company purchases the other and remains the dominant corporation*

divestiture *Sale of part of a company*

leveraged buyouts (LBOs) *Situations in which individuals or groups of investors purchase companies with the debt secured by the companys' assets*

joint venture *Enterprise supported by the investment of two or more parties for mutual benefit*

ect. The joint venture may be dissolved fairly quickly if the project is limited in scope, or it may endure for many years. Corning Glass Works and PPG Industries have worked together in a joint venture for over 50 years to create glass architectural materials.[24] A **consortium** is similar to a joint venture, but it involves the combined efforts of several companies. The David Sarnoff Research Center, General Electric's NBC, France's Thomson S. A., and the Netherlands' Philips Electronics formed an international consortium to design a system for high-definition television (HDTV). As one of five groups submitting proposals to the FCC for testing, their aim was to offer consumers razor-sharp television pictures.[25]

Cooperatives also serve as a vehicle for joint activities. In a cooperative, a group of people or small companies with common goals work collectively to obtain greater bargaining power and to benefit from economies of scale. Like large companies, these co-ops can buy and sell things in quantity; but instead of distributing a share of the profits to stockholders, co-ops divide profits among their members.

How Mergers Occur

About 95 percent of all mergers and acquisitions are friendly deals.[26] The ones that make the headlines, however, are usually the **hostile takeovers,** where one party fights to gain control of a company against the wishes of the existing management. If the "raider" succeeds in taking over the target company, the existing managers are generally dismissed. Needless to say, they fight tooth and nail to stave off their attacker.

A hostile takeover can be launched in two ways: the tender offer and the proxy fight. In a **tender offer,** the raider offers to buy a certain number of shares of stock in the corporation at a specific price. The price offered is generally more than the current stock price, so the shareholders are motivated to sell. The raider hopes to get enough shares to take control of the corporation and replace the existing board of directors and management. In a **proxy fight,** the raider launches a public relations battle for shareholder votes, hoping to enlist enough votes to oust the board and management. Proxy fights sound easy enough, but they are tough to win. The insiders have certain advantages: They know how to get in touch with shareholders, and they can use money from the corporate treasury in their campaign. In one study of 60 major proxy fights, researchers found that incumbent managers won 70 percent of the time.[27]

Even friendly mergers and takeovers can be risky, however. Joining two companies is a complex process involving every aspect of both companies. Executives have to agree on how power will be transferred and shared. Marketing departments often need to figure out how to blend advertising campaigns and sales forces. Mergers in particular often entail layoffs, transfers, and other employment changes. Experts list five steps companies should take to help smooth the transition from two companies to one:[28]

- *Don't rush.* The accounting and consulting giant Arthur Andersen spent three years getting to know the people and operations of

consortium *Group of companies working jointly to promote a common objective or engage in a project of benefit to all members*

cooperatives *Associations of people or small companies with similar interests, formed to obtain greater bargaining power and other economies of scale*

hostile takeovers *Situations in which an outside party buys enough stock in a corporation to take control against the wishes of the board of directors and corporate officers*

tender offer *Invitation made directly to shareholders by an outside party who wishes to buy a company's stock at a price above the current market price*

proxy fight *Attempt to gain control of a takeover target by urging shareholders to vote for directors favored by the acquiring party*

Asahi Shinwa, a Japanese firm it planned to buy. The companies understood and trusted each other by the time the acquisition took place.

- *Investigate your potential partner.* A company is a complex thing, and potential problems can lie buried in financial details, pending lawsuits, customer-satisfaction issues, and other areas. BankAmerica rushed into a buyout of Security Pacific, unaware that it was buying a pile of problem loans as part of the deal.
- *Use the best in each company.* The best mergers are the combination of two strong companies that complement each other. The idea is to build the new company out of the best parts of both, whether it's technologies, product lines, customer bases, management, or policies and practices.
- *Be honest with employees.* Mergers and acquisitions can be traumatic for employees. Some may lose their jobs; others may find their jobs moved across the state or across the country. Being honest with people helps them prepare for the changes.
- *Take care of the people you want to keep.* If people are afraid they'll get lost in the commotion of a merger or acquisition, they are likely to look for new jobs elsewhere. The transition is hectic and worrisome; if the good people are kept happy during this time, they're more likely to stay.

One Hundred Years of Mergers and Acquisitions

Companies have been combining in various configurations since the early days of U.S. business history. Mergers tend to happen in waves, in response to changes in the economy. One of the biggest waves of merger activity occurred between 1881 and 1911, when capitalists created giant monopolistic **trusts,** buying enough stock of competing companies in basic industries like oil and steel to control the market. These trusts were **horizontal mergers,** or combinations of competing companies performing the same functions. The purpose of a horizontal merger is to achieve the benefits of economies of scale and to fend off competition. The rise of a government antitrust movement and the dissolution of Standard Oil in 1911 marked the end of this wave, although in recent years, the horizontal merger has reappeared as the government has reexamined its approach to analyzing mergers.

A second great wave occurred in the boom decade of the 1920s. This era was marked by the emergence of **vertical mergers,** in which a company involved in one phase of an industry absorbs or joins a company involved in another phase of the same industry. The aim of a vertical merger is often to guarantee access to supplies or to markets.

A third wave of mergers occurred in the late 1960s and early 1970s, when corporations acquired strings of unrelated businesses, often in an attempt to moderate the risks of a volatile economy. These **conglomerate mergers** were designed to augment a company's growth and diversify its risks. Theoretically, when one business was down, another would be up, thus creating a balanced performance picture for the company as a whole. Some of these conglomerates had hundreds

trusts *Monopolistic arrangements established when one company buys a controlling share of the stock of competing companies in the same industry*

horizontal mergers *Combinations of companies that are direct competitors in the same industry*

vertical mergers *Combinations of companies that participate in different phases of the same industry*

conglomerate mergers *Combinations of companies that are in unrelated businesses, designed to augment a company's growth and diversify risk* of companies at their peaks. Many of the superconglomerates of the late 1960s have been dismantled or slimmed down for a variety of reasons: to streamline operations, to build up capital for other endeavors, or to get rid of unprofitable subsidiaries.

Another wave of mergers occurred in the 1980s, a decade in which an incredible $3.7 trillion was spent on mergers, acquisitions, and leveraged buyouts.[29] Although many of these deals were made to improve the operations of the companies involved, the chance to make a quick profit was the motive in many cases. When the decade began, many companies were actually worth more than the combined value of all their stock. A clever takeover artist could borrow money, buy enough stock to control the company, sell off pieces of the company to repay the debt, and still come out with money left over. The mergers of this decade peaked in 1988 (see Exhibit 4.7).

The mergers occurring in the 1990s are in sharp contrast to the bids by raiders in the 1980s. Today most of the deals are being made by large corporations for strategic purposes. Instead of using debt to take over and dismantle a company for a quick profit, corporate buyers are using cash and stock to selectively acquire businesses that will enhance their position in the marketplace. After trying for several years to make a dent in the market for personal-finance software against dominant leader Intuit, Microsoft gave up in 1994 and just bought Intuit. To help counter the growing influence of huge hospital companies (which are driving prices down as they buy in bigger and bigger quantities), drug makers are merging to gain size and strength. Software developers Adobe Systems and Aldus figured they could gain more market share working together, so they merged in 1994 as well. Strategic mergers are reaching across borders, too, as U.S. companies buy their way into markets in Argentina, Norway, China, Singapore, Brazil, and other countries.[30]

A new breed of conglomerate builders began to emerge in the mid-1990s as well. Betting that the conglomerate concept from the 1960s wasn't fundamentally flawed but just poorly managed in many cases, they focused on increasing productivity in all operations and mutual support between related businesses.[31]

The Debate over Mergers and Acquisitions

The rash of mergers and acquisitions that occurred in the 1980s kindled a heated debate that continues even with the new style of deals in the 1990s. Opponents argued that these mergers create an immense burden of high-risk corporate debt and divert investment from productive assets. Instead of building new plants or developing new products, said critics, companies borrow huge sums to finance an endless game of "musical ownership."

In many cases, the critics' warnings proved to be well-founded. A number of companies that took on heavy loads of debt to finance acquisitions subsequently went under or faced severe financial hardships. Some of the prominent companies in this group include the Campeau retailing empire (the Allied Stores and Federated Department Stores, which included Bloomingdale's, Stern's, and Jordan Marsh), Borden, Burlington Industries, Goodyear, and Marriott. At

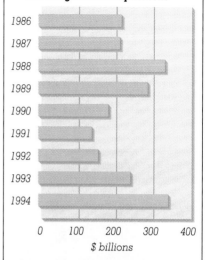

Volume of Announced U.S. Mergers and Acquisitions

Exhibit 4.7
Merger and Acquisition Activity in Recent Years
The decade of the deal climaxed in 1988. Activity began to pick up again in 1992.

one point in the early 1990s, Goodyear was paying over $1 million *per day* in interest (it has rebounded in the years since).[32]

Critics also pointed out that mergers and acquisitions entail high costs for individuals and communities. Even in friendly deals, there are bound to be losers: executives whose careers come to a crashing halt, workers who are laid off through no fault of their own, communities that suddenly find themselves with empty factories because operations are consolidated elsewhere, and consumers who face higher prices when competition diminishes. Another particularly bitter issue was the amount of money that raiders were making on deals that resulted in layoffs and other hardships for thousands of people.

Apart from the deal makers, few people lamented the transition from the finance-driven deals of the 1980s to the strategy-driven deals of the 1990s. However, the mergers of the 1980s had their good points. Shareholders benefited from all the merger activity, which boosted stock prices and fueled big increases in the market value of takeover targets. In addition, the fear of becoming takeover targets forced many companies to become more efficient.

Merger and Acquisition Defenses

During the 1980s wave, when many takeovers were uninvited and even openly hostile, corporate boards and executives devised a number of schemes to defend themselves against unwanted takeovers. Every corporation that sells stock to the general public is potentially vulnerable to takeover by any individual or company that buys enough shares to gain a controlling interest. The ultimate takeover defense is to "take a company private," which means buying back your own stock and taking the company off the market. Of course, this radical action requires that holders of your stock be willing to sell and that you either have enough cash on hand to buy all the stock back or are willing to engage in a leveraged buyout. It also means that you've cut off the stock market as a future means of generating cash, so it's not a move that many corporations make.

Companies that want or need to remain publicly traded can take several measures to discourage takeovers. Perhaps the most dramatic is the **poison pill,** which is a plan to make the company less valuable in some way to the potential raider. Poison pills are set up to be triggered by a takeover attempt; the idea is to discourage the takeover from actually happening. A good example is a special sale of newly issued stock to current stockholders only, at prices below the stock's current market price. Such action increases the number of shares the raider has to buy, making the deal more expensive.

Another plan is designed to benefit a company's top executives but can also serve the same purpose as a poison pill to a limited degree. A **golden parachute** is a series of guarantees to those executives that if they leave or are forced out after a takeover, they will receive

Many people displaced by corporate mergers and acquisitions get back on their feet by starting their own small businesses.

poison pill *Defense against hostile takeovers; the basic idea is to make the company less attractive in some way to the potential raider*

golden parachute *Generous compensation packages guaranteed to executives in the event they lose their jobs after a takeover*

PART ONE | FOCUS ON BUSINESS TODAY

generous compensation packages, often totaling many millions of dollars per executive.

The **shark repellent** tactic is more direct; it is simply a requirement that stockholders representing a large majority of shares must approve of any takeover attempt. Such a plan is viable only if the management team has the support of the majority of shareholders, of course.

Last, if a company feels it is unable to fight off a takeover on its own, it can try to convince a **white knight**—a friendly buyer—to take it over before a raider can. White knights usually agree to leave the current management team in place and to let the company continue to operate in an independent fashion.

shark repellent Direct takeover defense in which the company's board requires a large majority of voting shares to approve any takeover attempt

white knight Friendly buyer who agrees to take over a company to prevent a raider from taking it over

SUMMARY OF LEARNING OBJECTIVES

1 Identify the two broad sectors of the U.S. economy and the eight subsectors.

The economy consists of (1) the service sector, which includes wholesale and retail trade, finance and insurance, transportation and utilities, and other services; and (2) the goods-producing sector, which includes manufacturing, construction, mining, and agriculture.

2 List five factors that have contributed to the growth of the service sector.

In recent years, the service sector has expanded because economic prosperity has increased the demand for services, population patterns in the United States continue to change, the number and complexity of goods needing service are increasing, businesses find themselves needing more services to help them deal with a complex global economy, and technology keeps creating new service opportunities.

3 Discuss the three basic forms of business ownership.

A sole proprietorship is a business owned by a single person. A partnership is an association of two or more people who share in the ownership of an enterprise. The dominant form of business is the corporation, a legally chartered entity having many of the same rights and duties as a person.

4 List five advantages and four disadvantages of forming a sole proprietorship.

Sole proprietorships have five advantages: (1) they are easy to establish, (2) they provide the owner with control and independence, (3) the owner reaps all the profits, (4) income is taxed at personal rates, and (5) the company's plans and financial performance remain private. The four main disadvantages of a sole proprietorship are (1) the company's financial resources are usually limited, (2) management talent may be thin, (3) the owner is liable for the debts and damages incurred by the business, and (4) the business may cease when the owner dies.

5 Explain the difference between a general and a limited partnership.

A general partnership is owned by general partners who are equally liable for the business's debts. A limited partnership is owned by at least one general partner, who runs the business, and limited partners, who are passive investors and generally liable for no more than the amount of their investment.

6 List the three groups that govern a corporation and describe the role of each.

Shareholders are the basis of the corporate structure. They elect the board of directors, who in turn elect the officers of the corporation. The corporate officers carry out the policies and decisions of the board. In practice, the shareholders and board members often follow the lead of the chief executive officer.

7 Cite four advantages of corporations.

Corporations have the power to raise large sums of capital. They offer the shareholders protection from liability, they provide liquidity for investors, and they have an unlimited life span.

8 Describe the five waves of merger activity.

The earliest mergers, occurring from 1881 to 1911, were horizontal mergers, combining two companies that compete in the same industry. A second wave of mergers occurred in the 1920s. These were vertical mergers, combining two companies that participate in different phases of the same industry. The 1960s and 1970s introduced a third wave of mergers known as conglomerate mergers, in which unrelated companies are combined. The mergers of the 1980s focused on the purchase of undervalued companies, which were then dismantled and sold off piece by piece. The most recent wave of mergers, occurring in the 1990s, can be described as strategic, with large corporations acquiring businesses that will enhance their market position.

When Walter Shipley of Chemical Bank and John McGillicuddy of Manufacturers Hanover set out to merge their two companies, they were taking a course that was anything but assured. Most corporate mergers fail to meet their goals. From clashes at the top to the tiniest operational details, mergers are fraught with traps.

The Chemical-Manufacturers story, however, is a promising exception to the rule. The steps the two companies made before the merger, and the steps the united company took after, offer helpful guidelines for any two merger partners. The things these two companies did right started right at the top. Shipley, McGillicuddy, and their respective boards decided that McGillicuddy would run the combined company until his retirement at the beginning of 1993; then Shipley took over from there. By avoiding a power struggle at the top, the two men set a cooperative tone for both organizations' employees. Throughout the executive ranks, Shipley and McGillicuddy worked hard to woo key managers and keep them on board through the transition.

Another smart move was combining the best parts each bank had to offer. The new enterprise (which took on Chemical's name) picked up Manufacturers' state-of-the-art computer system, its effective policies for picking loan customers, and its impressive list of corporate clients. The old Chemical pitched in with its pervasive network of retail branches and its expertise at loan syndication (selling pieces of a huge corporate loan to other banks).

Like families and other social units, companies have particular cultures. Issues as seemingly minor as whether employees are on a first-name basis with top executives can become important factors to consider when merging two corporate cultures. Chemical's approach was not to force either bank's original culture on the new entity, but to build a new culture for the new bank. As Shipley puts it: "We are reexamining how we do everything."

The degree to which Chemical has succeeded becomes even more apparent when you compare its case with another major banking merger that happened at about the same time. When California-based BankAmerica took over neighboring Security Pacific, it rushed into the deal and got more than it bargained for (or less, actually). BankAmerica's two biggest mistakes appeared to be (1) not reviewing Security Pacific's financial situation closely enough and (2) not paying enough attention to Security Pacific's best executives and employees. As a result of the first mistake, BankAmerica ended up with a pile of problem loans that it didn't know Security Pacific was carrying. The second problem led to many of Security Pacific's most productive loan officers' leaving, feeling that they were being ignored by BankAmerica management. Moreover, the merger and subsequent consolidation threw 16,000 people out of work, so it was painful all the way around.

Chemical, however, appears to be in great shape for the future. The old Chemical Bank had net income of $430 million in 1990, the last full year before the merger. In 1992, the first full postmerger year, the new company enjoyed net income of $1.086 billion. Its Texas operations are poised to take advantage of increased U.S.-Mexico business resulting from the North American Free Trade Agreement. Like all great marriages, it's standing on solid ground and eager to face the future.

Your Mission: You're one of the Chemical executives on a team planning the acquisition of Phoenix First National, a bank serving small businesses and consumers in Phoenix and surrounding communities in central Arizona. Phoenix First National is highly respected in the area, both by competitors and customers. It isn't as technologically advanced as some other banks, but its customer service is second to none. Some customers, in fact, have been using the bank all their lives. On the negative side, the bank's reluctance to adopt newer technologies has left it relatively inefficient. It hasn't made a profit in three years. The following issues come up during the planning phase of the acquisition:

1. Assume that some of Chemical's existing branches don't have customer-service reputations as good as those at Phoenix First. How might you be able to take advantage of Phoenix First's expertise in this area and apply it throughout Chemical's other operations?

a. After the acquisition, put Phoenix First's CEO in charge of all of Chemical's retail banking operations.

b. Send Chemical branch managers to Phoenix First for two-week training sessions to see how the Phoenix operation works with customers.

c. There's not really any way to take advantage of Phoenix First's expertise because it applies only in the local Phoenix market.

2. Both Phoenix First and Chemical's existing Texas subsidiary (which operates under the name Texas Commerce) have branches in New Mexico. After the acquisition, how should you handle the overlap?

a. Let them keep operating as is; by competing against each other, they'll become more efficient.

b. Texas Commerce was part of the Chemical family before Phoenix First, so it should be allowed to take over the Phoenix First operations in New Mexico.

c. With the management teams from Phoenix First, Texas Commerce, and Chemical's head office, decide which of the two banks is best able to manage the New Mexico operations; then assign the territory as appropriate.

3. By introducing some of the computer techniques Chemical uses to process accounts, you figure you could reduce Phoenix First's costs by enough to make it solidly profitable. Unfortunately, this would involve laying off 10 percent of the bank's clerical staff. What should you do?

a. You need these people to keep working until the new computer systems are in place, so don't tell them their jobs are disappearing until the last possible minute.

b. Don't lay the people off; the disruption this action would cause in their lives is not worth the bank's profits.

c. If the bank continues to operate at a loss, eventually all employees might lose their jobs. Don't walk in from New York with the answer in hand, however. Sit down with the people in Phoenix, explain the problem, and ask for their help in coming up with creative ideas.

4. Phoenix First's current CEO is the granddaughter of the bank's founder and a leading figure in the local business community. She's resisting the takeover, even though the bank's board has agreed to it, because she doesn't want to lose control to some giant bank from New York City.

a. She has a point; the fact that Phoenix First is so highly regarded in its local market is evidence that she should be allowed to keep running things her way.

b. Her bank may be popular, but it's not profitable. If she resists, she should be replaced by someone willing to adopt newer practices that will keep the bank from going under.

c. Some compromise needs to be worked out. Her relationship with the community is valuable, and so is Chemical's operating expertise. Maybe she could agree to cede control of the bank's internal operations but not its marketing and customer service, for instance.[33]

acquisition (114)
barriers to entry (101)
board of directors (110)
capital-intensive businesses (101)
chief executive officer (CEO) (111)
commodity business (102)
conglomerate mergers (116)
consortium (115)
cooperatives (115)
corporation (106)
divestiture (114)
for-profit corporations (109)
general partnership (105)
golden parachute (118)
goods-producing businesses (98)
government-owned corporations (108)
holding company (109)
horizontal mergers (116)

hostile takeovers (115)
institutional investors (110)
joint venture (114)
labor-intensive businesses (101)
leveraged buyouts (LBOs) (114)
limited liability companies (LLCs) (109)
limited partnership (105)
liquidity (112)
master limited partnership (MLP) (105)
merger (114)
not-for-profit corporations (108)
not publicly traded corporations (109)
parent company (109)
partnership (105)
poison pill (118)

private corporations (108)
professional corporations (109)
proxy (110)
proxy fight (115)
publicly traded corporations (109)
quasi-government corporations (108)
S corporation (109)
service businesses (98)
shareholders (106)
shark repellent (119)
sole proprietorship (104)
stock (107)
subsidiary corporations (109)
tender offer (115)
trusts (116)
unlimited liability (104)
vertical mergers (116)
white knight (119)

REVIEW QUESTIONS

1. What factors have contributed to the revival of the manufacturing sector?
2. What is a sole proprietorship? Why is it the most common type of business in the United States?
3. Define unlimited liability and explain why it's a risk for a sole proprietor.
4. Define a partnership. In what fields are partnerships typical?
5. Discuss the advantages and disadvantages of partnerships.
6. Explain the difference between a private and a government-owned corporation.
7. To what extent do shareholders control the activities of a corporation?
8. What are the two techniques used to conduct a hostile takeover?

SHAREHOLDER PROTECTION OR LEGAL OPPORTUNISM?

Reporting financial results is getting to be a nerve-wracking task for many U.S. corporations. If quarterly or annual revenues and profits don't meet expectations—and stock prices drop as a result—corporations stand a good chance of being hit by lawsuits from shareholders. The idea behind these lawsuits is that if shareholders had known the company wasn't performing as well as they thought it was, they could have sold their shares earlier, before the price dropped.

The issue stems from the corporation's responsibility to communicate with its shareholders. Some of this communication is done directly, through quarterly and annual reports. In other cases, the communication is indirect, as when corporate officers talk to groups of financial analysts. These analysts (who usually work for banks, mutual fund companies, or stockbrokers) study what the corporations have to say and then issue recommendations and projections for the stock. If the future seems rosy, analysts will tell people (through newsletters, advice to stock brokers, appearances on financial television shows, and other avenues) that the stock price is likely to go up as the company's fortunes improve. On the other hand, if analysts question the company's prospects, they may tell people to sell the stock now because it's probably headed downhill. In any case, the perceptions shareholders develop about the stocks they own influence their expectations. If they bought on the idea that the stock would go up, they naturally expect it to go up.

This communication process places a heavy responsibility on corporate executives. To avoid creating false impressions (either positive or negative), they have to be very careful about what they tell shareholders and analysts. Naturally, they want to share good news with the world because this helps drive up the price of their company's stock. On the other hand, they have to be honest about bad news or potentially bad news to avoid misleading people. Similarly, if analysts and the public get *too* excited about a company's prospects, the excitement is likely to drive the price higher than it really should be. Sooner or later, it will come crashing down to where it should have been in the first place. You can see that the challenge is to keep the public's perception of the stock's value in line with its real value, based on the company's performance.

When perceptions are out of line with reality, people look for somebody to blame. Did the company mislead investors by hiding bad news? Did analysts overstate growth estimates? Did investors simply jump on a hot stock and mindlessly drive it too high? Increasingly, blame is being pinned on the corporation, as shareholders take them to court. Software developer Legent Computer was sued within hours of announcing quarterly earnings that were below expectations. A federal judge eventually threw the case out for lack of evidence, but not before it took a heavy toll on the company. Legent staffers had to provide 290,000 pages of documents, top executives had to spend much of their time preparing for trial—not running the business—and the whole affair cost the company several million dollars.

While these lawsuits might sound like angry shareholders fighting back after losing money in the stock market, that's not always the case. Several law firms across the country scan newspapers, looking for company announcements that don't meet projections. The lawyers then run ads trying to alert all shareholders in the company of a pending *class-action lawsuit* against the company (a suit filed on behalf of more than one person). In other words, it's not angry shareholders looking for lawyers; it's lawyers looking for shareholders.

As many as 40 percent of these law-suits are thrown out of court, as Legent's was. In many other cases, corporations settle out of court, even when they claim to be innocent, simply to avoid the years of distracting and expensive litigation. The settlements average $4.5 million each, and law firms' average cut of the money is 39 percent, or $1.8 million, so it's easy to see why some lawyers are eager to find these cases. The lucrative business is under review, though, as both the Securities and Exchange Commission and Congress are looking for ways to protect corporations from frivolous lawsuits.

1. What steps could corporations take to reduce the chances of attracting shareholder lawsuits?
2. Why don't shareholders just vote management out of their jobs if they're not happy with the corporation's financial results?
3. Do you think law firms should be able to hunt for cases to file, rather than waiting for shareholders to come to them asking for help? Why or why not?

Some critics believe that growth in the service sector has contributed to the decline of industry in the United States. Using information from the text, as well as from other resources, examine the increase in service-related businesses and the factors leading to their growth. Consider the interrelationship between businesses in the goods-producing and service sectors. Be prepared to discuss both the advantages and disadvantages of a growing service sector for the overall economy.

• As a class, divide into groups of two and discuss the pros and cons of this issue. Alternate taking a positive or negative position with your partner.
• Following discussion with your partner, develop with the class a chart listing the contrasting points of view.

Find an article or series of articles in recent issues of *The Wall Street Journal* illustrating one of the following business developments:

• Merger
• Acquisition
• Divestiture
• Hostile takeover
• Leveraged buyout
• Consortium or joint venture

1. Explain in your own words what steps or events led to this development.
2. What results do you expect this development to have on (a) the company itself, (b) consumers, (c) the industry the company is part of? Write down and date your answers.
3. Follow your story in *The Wall Street Journal* over the next month (or longer, as your instructor requests). What problems, opportunities, or other results are reported? Were they anticipated at the time of the initial story, or did they seem to catch industry analysts by surprise? How well did you do at predicting the results in your answers to question 2?

CASH IN TRASH

Synopsis

This video explores the economics of recycling and whether or not recycling makes financial sense.

Exercises

ANALYSIS

1. Can smaller companies use the McDonald's closed-loop approach to recycling? Why or why not?
2. Why has the U.S. approach of leaving it up to the market been unsuccessful so far?
3. Should cities across the country even bother to continue with recycling programs if there is no market for the materials they collect? Why or why not?
4. Is recycling a concern only for companies in the manufacturing sector? Why or why not?
5. In what sector of the economy would you put recycling firms? Explain your answer.

APPLICATION

Choose one recyclable material and outline a plan to increase demand for goods made from this material. Address three topics in your plan: the range of goods that can be made from the recycled material, how effectively these goods compete with goods made from nonrecycled materials, and how you could promote your recycled products to likely customers.

DECISION

If you were the McDonald's executive in charge of recycling and a group of business owners approached you about participating in McDonald's closed-loop program, what issues would you consider before you make a decision?

COMMUNICATION

Write a two-minute speech that could be given to an association of small-business owners, encouraging them to buy recycled office supplies. Be ready to address the concern many will have about the cost and quality of recycled products.

INTEGRATION

Review the discussion of social responsibility in Chapter 3. Do you think companies or consumers have a responsibility to buy products made from recycled materials, given that increased demand for such products is

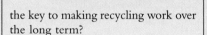

the key to making recycling work over the long term?

ETHICS

Closed-loop recycling systems make sense for big companies such as McDonald's that consume huge amounts of paper and other materials. However, if the closed-loop approach proves unfeasible for smaller companies, would McDonald's be doing the country a disservice by pushing to keep the government out of recycling? In other words, is McDonald's placing its needs above the needs of other companies and consumers?

DEBATE

One key to the successful Taiwan program is a limited degree of government intervention. However, free-market advocates in this country are likely to try to block any attempt to get the government involved in a na-

tional closed-loop system. On the other hand, the U.S. government already intervenes in a wide variety of industries, from price guarantees for milk producers to import protection for textile mills, so we don't really have a purely free-market economy anyway. Debate the wisdom of getting the government more involved in the recycling business.

TEAMWORK

In a team of three or four students, research the process for recycling a particular material (such as glass). Follow the material from the point of consumption (consumers' homes, for instance) back to the recycling facilities and from there to wherever the material is used in the production of new products. Summarize and illustrate visually the key steps in the process.

RESEARCH

Find out whether any progress has been made in the effort to get consumers and organizations to buy more recycled products. If progress has been made, what were the driving forces—government regulation, public pressure, consumer awareness, or improved economics (such as lower prices for recycled goods)?

ROLE PLAYING

Form a team with three other students. One will play the role of a business owner who has seen this news report and decided that it isn't worth the time and trouble to recycle. After all, says this person, why should the company spend time and money separating materials for recycling when recycling doesn't seem to make economic sense anyway? A second student will play a consumer who still believes in recycling. A third student will play a consumer who has never bothered to recycle at all. The fourth student will play a recycling advocate who tries to convince the business owner and the nonrecycling consumer that recycling is the sensible, responsible thing to do.

Chapter

5

Small Businesses, New Ventures, and Franchises

LEARNING OBJECTIVES

After studying this chapter, you will be able to

1 Differentiate between lifestyle businesses and high-growth ventures

2 Discuss the impact of social and economic factors on the development of small businesses

3 List four important functions of small businesses in the economy

4 Identify three ways of getting into business for yourself

5 Name 10 topics that should be covered in a formal business plan

6 Describe nine sources of financing available for new businesses

7 Identify five managerial activities that are important to the success of a small business

8 Explain the pros and cons of owning a franchise

How to Keep Your Feet on the Ground While Turning an Industry Upside Down

The idea for Staples occurred to Tom Stemberg when he arrived for a job interview at a warehouse club, one of those vast discount barns that sell everything from tomato paste to computers. As Stemberg made his way through the store toward the executive offices, he noticed that the office-supply section looked like it had been plundered by savages. The devastation told him that the merchandise was moving fast.

Lights flashed. Why not create a warehouse club for office supplies, a Toys "Я" Us for grown-ups that would offer low prices on everything from rubber bands to office furniture? With 12 years as a grocery executive behind him, Stemberg could see that big stores with low prices would transform the office-supply business, just as supermarkets had transformed the grocery business. He pictured customers wheeling shopping carts down wide, brightly lit aisles, loading up on items that, for economy's sake, were frequently bundled three or more to a package. Merchandise would be piled high on metal shelves, and the aisles would be numbered and identified with bright red signs to indicate product categories. Rows of checkout counters would welcome the departing shoppers, and boxes of candy and other impulse items would tempt the buyers waiting to pay.

Stemberg's market research confirmed his hunch that the office-products industry was both attractive and ripe for change. The potential market was huge ($100 billion in annual sales) and growing rapidly (11 percent per year). Better yet, a whole category of customers (small businesses) was getting a bad deal on price. While large corporations were buying their office supplies at quantity discounts from wholesalers and manufacturers, small businesses were paying full price at retail office-supply stores or ordering goods through catalogs at slightly reduced prices. Therefore, a company like General Motors might spend $4 for a dozen yellow pads, whereas a small business might spend $11.50.

What Stemberg hoped to do was give those small businesses and individuals the same kind of price break that General Motors was

Superstores such as Staples recognized that traditional retail stores were not meeting many shoppers' needs.

getting. He knew how to do this: Using his experience building a chain of high-volume, low-priced food warehouses, he would buy directly from manufacturers, cut out the wholesalers, keep his costs down with a no-frills approach, and pass the savings along to the customers.

To make the concept work, however, he would need to open a number of stores in a short period of time. That would take both money and workers. He would also need to persuade office-supply manufacturers to deal with him directly, a move that would upset their relationships with wholesalers. How could he raise the funds required for rapid expansion? How could he attract a group of managers capable of building a major business from scratch? How could he gain the cooperation of office-products suppliers?[1]

THE WORLD OF SMALL BUSINESS

A quick look up and down a typical commercial street is enough to tell you that small businesses are an important element in the U.S. economy. However, determining just *how* important is surprisingly tricky, partly because there's no single reliable source of data on small businesses and partly because *small* is a relative term. A manufacturing firm with 500 employees might be considered small if it competes against much larger companies, but a retail establishment with 500 employees might be classified as big compared with its competitors. For official purposes, the Small Business Administration (SBA) defines a **small business** as a firm that is independently owned and operated, not dominant in its field, and relatively small in terms of annual sales and number of employees compared with other firms in its industry. From a practical standpoint, any company with fewer than 500 employees is generally considered small. The SBA says that small businesses account for 42 percent of all goods and services sold in the country and 47 percent of private-sector jobs.[2]

Small businesses are of two distinct types: Roughly 80 to 90 percent are modest operations with little growth potential (although some have attractive income potential for the solo businessperson). The self-employed consultant working part-time from a home office, the corner florist, and the neighborhood pizza parlor fall into this category of **lifestyle businesses,** organizations built around the personal and financial needs of an individual or a family.[3] Lifestyle businesses aren't designed to grow into large enterprises.

In contrast to lifestyle businesses, some small firms, such as Staples was when it started, are small simply because they are new. These **high-growth ventures** aim at outgrowing their small-business status as quickly as possible. Usually run by a team rather than by one

Small businesses, such as these retail shops in Dexter, Maine, provide nearly half of all private-sector jobs in the United States.

individual, they often obtain a sizable supply of investment capital and then attempt to introduce new products or services to a large market.

Trends Affecting Small Businesses

America's small-business roots run deep. The country was originally founded by people involved in small businesses—the family farmer, the shopkeeper, the craftsperson. Successive waves of immigrants carried on the tradition, launching restaurants and laundries, driving taxicabs, and opening newsstands and bakeries. These small businesses are the cornerstone of our economic system.

Yet despite our independent heritage, we have become a nation of employees. In 1800 some 80 percent of the working population was self-employed. By 1992, the 10 million people in this country who were self-employed made up only about 8 percent of the workforce.[4] The trend away from self-employment began after the Civil War, when big business emerged as the primary economic force. Aided by improvements in transportation and communication, large producers were able to achieve **economies of scale,** which are the savings resulting from manufacturing, marketing, or buying large quantities of an item. These large producers could manufacture goods at lower costs than their smaller rivals, so they were able to charge lower prices. The small, independent businesses could not compete. As scores of them closed their doors, the dominant firms became increasingly powerful, making it virtually impossible for new rivals to enter many industries.[5]

In the last couple of decades, however, the trend toward bigness has slowed. To some extent, this trend reflects the economy's shift toward services, where economies of scale are often elusive and starting new businesses is usually easier. Even in the manufacturing sector, however, small firms have often been able to hold their own against larger rivals. In many industries, the advent of computer-aided manufacturing equipment has enabled small plants to operate just as efficiently as larger ones, eliminating the large-scale producer's advantage in economies of scale. Because of their simpler organization and management structure, these small plants can often provide customized service or deliver goods more quickly than their larger rivals.

At the same time, a number of other factors have encouraged more people to leave the corporate world and form businesses of their own. Demographic trends have had something to do with it. Baby boomers have reached their 30s and 40s, the prime age for starting businesses. Furthermore, many of these people are frustrated by their career progress. With so many baby boomers competing for the same positions in big companies, the odds of rising to the top are getting slimmer. Add the fact that many big companies have been laying off middle managers, and you get a large pool of frustrated, experienced people looking for a better option.

The increasing diversity of the workforce has also been a factor, with more women and minorities moving up in the corporate world—then often moving out into the small-business world. Women now

small business *Company that is independently owned and operated, that is not dominant in its field, and that meets certain criteria for number of employees or annual sales revenue*

lifestyle businesses *Small businesses intended to provide the owner with a comfortable livelihood*

high-growth ventures *Small businesses intended to achieve rapid growth and high profits on investment*

economies of scale *Savings from manufacturing, marketing, or buying large quantities/*

Jacqueline Clark, president and founder of A Choice Nanny, is one of the 6.5 million U.S. women who own businesses.

own or control 6.5 million small companies in the United States and are starting new businesses at nearly twice the rate that men are. In fact, 10 percent of the U.S. workforce now works for women-owned businesses. Similar advances are showing up in other segments of the population, too. From 1979 to 1994, for instance, the number of businesses owned by Hispanic Americans doubled, from 225,000 to more than a half million. Some of these people are responding to the same urges that have always driven entrepreneurs; others look to small-business ownership as a way around the career roadblocks they perceive in the traditional corporate world.[6]

For an idea of the boom in small business, consider this fact: The number of people who try to start businesses in the United States now exceeds the number who are getting married or starting families.[7] Small business is clearly a big deal in the U.S. economy. Although much of the new business activity occurred in urban population centers, small businesses sprang up throughout the country, as Exhibit 5.1 indicates.

The Men and Women Who Build Businesses

Could you or should you join the thousands of men and women who start new businesses every year? It's not for everyone. Laid-off executives who are used to running multibillion-dollar enterprises sometimes have trouble adjusting to the unglamorous details of daily life in a small business. Many miss the support services they enjoyed in large corporations. Perhaps the biggest hurdle for the majority of new small-business owners is the constant challenge to sell, sell, sell.[8]

For the most part, those who take the plunge are ordinary people rather than glamorous adventurers. Most start with relatively small sums of money and operate informally from their homes, at least for

Exhibit 5.1
Regional Variations in Business Start-Ups
Throughout the 1990s, new businesses sprang up from coast to coast. As you might expect, the areas with the most rapid population growth were also the areas with the most new-business activity.

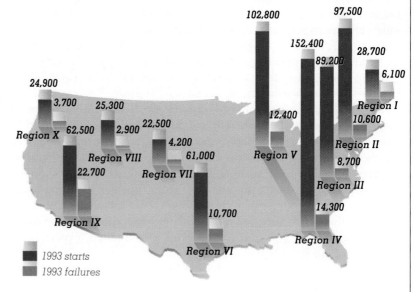

Note: All numbers have been rounded to the nearest hundred. Business starts listed here are incorporations and do not include sole proprietorships or partnerships. Business failures listed here are establishments that ceased operations with creditors.

130

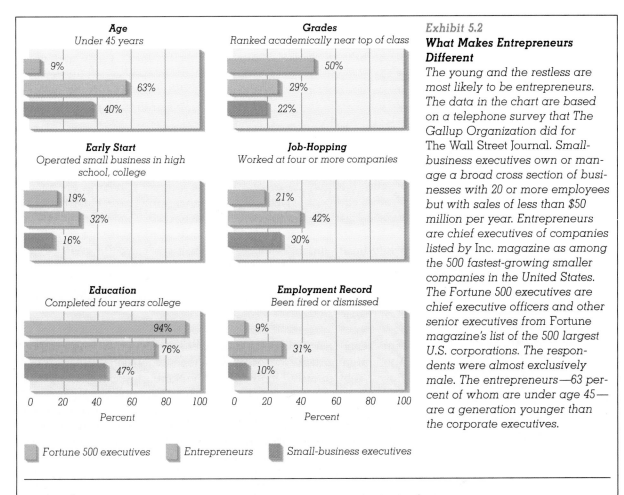

Age
Under 45 years

9%
63%
40%

Grades
Ranked academically near top of class

50%
29%
22%

Early Start
Operated small business in high school, college

19%
32%
16%

Job-Hopping
Worked at four or more companies

21%
42%
30%

Education
Completed four years college

94%
76%
47%

Employment Record
Been fired or dismissed

9%
31%
10%

0 20 40 60 80 100
Percent

0 20 40 60 80 100
Percent

Fortune 500 executives   Entrepreneurs   Small-business executives

Exhibit 5.2

What Makes Entrepreneurs Different

The young and the restless are most likely to be entrepreneurs. The data in the chart are based on a telephone survey that The Gallup Organization did for The Wall Street Journal. Small-business executives own or manage a broad cross section of businesses with 20 or more employees but with sales of less than $50 million per year. Entrepreneurs are chief executives of companies listed by Inc. magazine as among the 500 fastest-growing smaller companies in the United States. The Fortune 500 executives are chief executive officers and other senior executives from Fortune magazine's list of the 500 largest U.S. corporations. The respondents were almost exclusively male. The entrepreneurs—63 percent of whom are under age 45—are a generation younger than the corporate executives.

a while.[9] As Exhibit 5.2 illustrates, these people have diverse backgrounds in terms of education and business experience. One common factor is a willingness to work long hours. Three out of four people who start their own company spend at least 50 hours a week on the job; a quarter of them put in 70 hours or more.[10]

Roughly two-thirds of the new business founders begin **start-up companies**; that is, they start from scratch rather than buying an existing operation or inheriting the family business. Before going into business for themselves, most company founders are employed by small businesses rather than major corporations.[11] They are likely to draw on their experience in an industry or profession for their idea. Nearly all attribute their success to doing an ordinary thing especially well, as opposed to coming up with an extraordinary idea.[12]

start-up companies New ventures

The Economic Role of Small Businesses

People who build businesses perform a valuable service for the rest of us. Small businesses play a number of important roles in our economy.

Providing Jobs

Stop and think for a minute about the people you know who have jobs. Where do they work? For big companies? For the government?

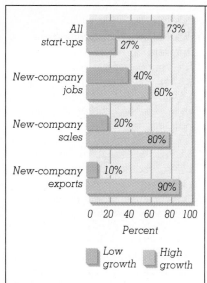

All start-ups: 73%, 27%
New-company jobs: 40%, 60%
New-company sales: 20%, 80%
New-company exports: 10%, 90%

Percent: 0 20 40 60 80 100

Low growth   High growth

Exhibit 5.3

The Role of High-Growth Companies

Although they account for a relatively small share of all new businesses, the companies that grow rapidly are responsible for more of the newly created jobs, sales, and exports.

Or for small businesses? If you're typical, at least a third of your friends and relatives work for companies that employ fewer than 100 people, and the percentage is growing.[13] As Exhibit 5.3 illustrates, most of that growth has occurred in the new high-growth ventures like Staples. In fact, in the five years from 1988 to 1992, 70 percent of the job growth happened in just 4 percent of the companies in business during that time period.[14]

The jobs created by small businesses differ from those created by big companies in several key respects. For one thing, small businesses generally pay less in terms of both cash compensation and employee benefits. Roughly 25 percent of these jobs are part-time. They tend to be filled by employees who are either younger or older than the average big-company employee. Many of these employees have never worked before; many others have been out of work for a long time before finally finding a job with a small company. On average, employees in small businesses have less formal education than their counterparts in large companies. By hiring workers who don't quite fit the corporate mold, small businesses serve as an important safety net in our society.[15]

Introducing New Products and Services

Another important way small businesses contribute to economic growth is by fostering innovation. The National Science Foundation estimates that 98 percent of the nation's "radical" new-product developments spring from small firms, a staggering percentage given the fact that small companies spend less than 5 percent of the nation's research-and-development money.[16] Among the contributions that small businesses have made are the safety razor, the self-winding wristwatch, the helicopter, stainless steel, and the plain-paper copier.

Supplying the Needs of Large Corporations

Besides providing new products and jobs, small businesses fill an important role in the operation of large corporations, acting as distributors, servicing agents, and suppliers. In fact, some of the most successful companies in the country have based their business strategy on the use of small, outside suppliers. Consider Liz Claiborne, one of the leading firms in the fashion industry: The company has no factories, and all its garments are made on contract by outside suppliers, which gives Liz Claiborne the flexibility to change its designs quickly—an important competitive edge in the fickle world of fashion.[17]

Providing Specialized Goods and Services

Finally, many small businesses exist because they meet consumers' special needs. If you want to rent a Santa Claus suit, buy an odd piece of sheet music, or get your watch fixed, you naturally turn to a small business for help. Big companies tend to shy away from businesses of this type because the demand isn't sufficient to make mass production worthwhile.

Cross Colours has taken the clothing industry by storm in the last several years by offering street-inspired garments that weren't readily available from other sources, many with African color schemes and designs. The company started out targeting African Americans but has grown by leaps and bounds and is now one of the most respected firms in the entire industry.[18]

THE JOB OF BUILDING A BUSINESS

Suppose you decide to join the ranks of business owners. What are your chances of success? You may have heard some depressing statistics about the number of new ventures that fail. Some reports say your chances of success are only one in three; others claim that the odds are even worse, stating that 85 percent of all new ventures fail within 10 years. New analysis by Dun & Bradstreet (D&B), a company that specializes in analyzing the business environment, says the true failure rate is much lower if you remove the operations that it doesn't consider "genuine businesses." For instance, a free-lancer who writes one article for a magazine and then stops writing would be counted as a failed business under the traditional measurement (which is based on tax returns, by the way). D&B says that the failure rate for real businesses in only about 1 percent per year and that two-thirds of all new businesses survive for at least several years.[19]

Finding an Opportunity

If you decide to take the risk, there are three ways to get into business for yourself: Start from scratch, buy an existing operation, or obtain a franchise. Starting from scratch is the most common route, and probably the most difficult as well. Most of the people who succeed do so because they have enough experience to minimize the risks. They start with something they know how to do and capitalize on an existing network of professional or industry contacts. Hillary Sterba and Nancy Novinc started their tool-engineering company, S&N Engineering, with a combined 26 years of experience in that industry and even more years of business experience in general.[20]

Not all entrepreneurs start with that much experience, however. Many start with less experience but an innovative idea or a better way to do something other companies are already doing (see Exhibit 5.4). *Fortune* magazine recently identified 40 entrepreneurs, mostly in their 30s, who have already built companies with sales of $40 million a year or more. Together, these 40 superstars had combined sales of $17 billion and employed 64,000 people.[21]

Another option is buying an existing business. This approach tends to reduce the risks—provided, of course, that you check the company out carefully. When you buy a business, you instantly acquire a known product or service and a system for producing it. You don't have to go through the painful period of building a reputation, establishing a clientele, and hiring and training employees. Financing the venture is generally much easier; lenders are reassured by the history and assets of the going concern. With these major details already settled, you can concentrate on making improvements.

Obtaining a franchise is another alternative. The franchiser's name, product, and system are already established, and you can build on that

Exhibit 5.4

How to Get Good Ideas for New Businesses

When looking for ideas for new companies, think in terms of what people want but can't get. According to the experts, "inventing a fancy gizmo first and then finding out later that no one wants it is a waste of time."

Concept	Explanation	Example
Upgrade	Take a basic product and enhance it.	Designer blue jeans, gourmet cookies
Downgrade	Take a quality product and reduce its cost and price.	No-frills motels, budget rental cars
Bundle	Combine products to provide double benefits.	Laundromats that sell food or beverages
Unbundle	Take a product that has multiple features and offer only one of those features independently.	Term life insurance that has no savings value
Transport	Move a product that sells well in one area to another area.	Ethnic restaurants
Mass-market	Take a product that has been used for a specific purpose and find a larger audience for it.	Industrial cleaners repackaged for consumer markets
Narrowcast	Aim for a narrow portion of a large market	Cable TV service for rural markets
Think big	Offer the broadest possible selection of a general category of goods.	Electronics "supermarkets"
Think small	Offer a complete selection of a specific type of product.	Bookstore that sells only mystery novels
Compete on price	Offer more value for the same price, the same value for a lower price, or lower quality at a far lower price.	Warehouse stores

base. However, owning a franchise is no guarantee that your business will succeed. According to one study, your chances are no better with a franchise operation than with a start-up.[22]

Deciding on a Form of Ownership

Once you have identified a promising opportunity, you need to decide on the form of business you will use. You can choose a sole proprietorship, a partnership, or a corporation, depending on your needs and the advantages and disadvantages of each (see Exhibit 5.5). For each type of organization, certain legal formalities must be met.

The sole proprietorship can be started by opening a checking account for the business, obtaining invoices and other forms, and accumulating the cash to pay a month's rent. You may also have to obtain a business license and take care of other legal details, depending on the type of business.

To start a partnership, you need two additional things: a partnership agreement, which spells out the basic outlines of your arrangement with your partner or partners, and a buy/sell agreement, which defines what will happen if one of the partners dies.

For a corporation, you must choose the state in which you want to incorporate, file incorporation papers, form a board of directors, name officers, and also set up a stock-redemption plan, which serves the same functions as the buy/sell agreement in a partnership.

Form of ownership	Advantage	Disadvantage
Sole proprietorship	Ease of formation and dissolution Control and freedom Secrecy of operations Tax advantages	Limited potential for big profits Restricted financial resources Reliance on owner for all managerial skills Unlimited liability Life of business limited to owner's interest or life span
Partnership	Ease of formation Tax advantages Ownership opportunities for skilled persons Legal standing in case of disputes Increased capital and credit sources Ability to continue despite changes in ownership	Unlimited liability of general partners Ever-present danger of interpersonal conflict between partners Potential for aggressive competition among employees for partnership status Lack of clear-cut management responsibility
Corporation	Limited liability for shareholders (owners) Investment liquidity Unlimited life span	Requirements for public disclosure Costs to establish and dissolve Tax rates

The best form of business for you depends on your circumstances: your financial situation, the type of business you're starting, the number of employees, the risks involved, and your tax position. For advice on this issue, it is generally worthwhile to consult a lawyer or an accountant who specializes in this area. Regardless of whether you form a sole proprietorship, a partnership, or a corporation, you need to obtain various licenses and permits. Requirements differ from state to state and from business to business. For information, contact the Internal Revenue Service or the chamber of commerce in your area.

Developing a Business Plan

One of the first steps you should take toward starting a new business is to develop a written business plan that explains what you're going to do. Preparing such a plan will help you decide how to turn your idea into reality, and if you need outside financing, the plan will also help you persuade lenders and investors to back your business. Your business plan may be relatively informal if you're starting out on a small scale and using your own money, but at a minimum, it should describe the basic concept of the business and outline specific goals, objectives, and resource requirements.

Although the business plan has a simple, straightforward purpose, it requires a great deal of thought. Before you even open your doors, you have to make important decisions about personnel, marketing, facilities, suppliers, and distribution. A formal plan, suitable for use with banks or investors, should cover the following points (keep in mind that your audience wants short, concise information, not lengthy volumes):[23]

1. *Summary.* In one or two pages, describe your product or service and its market potential. Describe your company and its princi-

ples, highlighting those things that will distinguish your firm from the competitors. Summarize your financial projections and expected return on investment. Also indicate how much money you need and for what purpose.

2. *Company and industry.* Give full background information on the origins and structure of your venture and the characteristics of its industry.
3. *Products or services.* Give a complete but concise description, focusing on the unique attributes of your products or services.
4. *Market.* Provide data that will persuade the investor that you understand your market and can achieve your sales goals.
5. *Marketing strategy.* Provide projections of sales and market share, and outline a strategy for identifying and contacting customers, setting prices, servicing customers, advertising, and so forth.
6. *Design and development plans.* If your product requires design or development, describe the nature and extent of what needs to be done, including costs and possible problems.
7. *Operations plan.* Provide information on the facilities, equipment, and labor needed, including background on principals, directors, and key management personnel.
8. *Overall schedule.* Show development of the company in terms of completion dates for major aspects of the business plan.
9. *Critical risks and problems.* Identify all negative factors and discuss them honestly.
10. *Financial information.* Include a detailed budget of start-up and operating costs, as well as projections for income, expenses, and cash flow for the first three years of business.

Although a business plan makes sense from a theoretical point of view, it's important to point out that many businesses, and even many successful businesses, don't have an active plan in place. In fact, 41 of the 100 fastest-growing companies on *Inc.* magazine's annual list in one recent year had no business plan at all. Only 28 of the remaining 59 had a formal plan that included the elements in the previous list.[24] One of the biggest reasons is lack of time. Writing a traditional business plan can take months, and many entrepreneurs simply can't take that much time away from running their companies. Also, it's easy to overanalyze a potential business idea and end up frozen in place at the starting line. However, just because these businesses don't have formal, written plans doesn't mean the owners haven't spent a great deal of time planning and analyzing.

Obtaining Financing

With your business plan in hand, you can begin the search for financing. The most common sources of funds for new businesses fall into two basic categories: debt and equity. **Debt** must be repaid; **equity**—capital funds obtained by selling shares of ownership in the company—does not have to be repaid. However, equity does entitle the investor to a piece of your company and a share of future profits. Most businesses are financed with a mix of debt and equity.

debt *Funds obtained by borrowing*

equity *Capital funds obtained by selling shares of ownership in the company*

Once the business is launched, it will have a continuing need for money. You can't expect to obtain all the financing you need in one fell swoop. Although a few businesses do grow entirely through internally generated funds, most need repeated transfusions from outside lenders or investors.

Say that you're just starting out. How much money will you need, and where should you turn first for capital? The answer depends on the size and type of business you want to launch. Retail and service businesses generally require less start-up cash than manufacturing companies or high-tech research-and-development ventures. On average, though, nearly half of small businesses are launched with less than $20,000, as Exhibit 5.6 indicates.[25] Even entrepreneurs who found high-growth firms begin with a modest pool of capital. As Exhibit 5.6 also shows, finding the money was usually no problem. Sixty percent of the time, the founders reached into their own pockets.

Bank Loans and Other Sources of Debt

The second most common source of funds is bank loans, although banks are often reluctant to back new ventures. Most banks expect you to put up 25 to 50 percent of the money yourself, and they demand both collateral and personal guarantees to back the loan.[26] In addition, banks typically charge small businesses relatively high interest—two or three points above the prime rate available to large corporate clients. In periods when interest rates in general are high, this practice may impose a severe burden on small companies. It pays to shop around for the most attractive rate. Banks have differing loan criteria and business objectives. Some cultivate small businesses and offer attractive interest rates or special services. It doesn't hurt to apply at two banks simultaneously.

If you apply to several banks and are turned down by all of them, you may be able to qualify for a loan backed by the Small Business Administration (SBA). To get an SBA-backed loan, you apply to a regular bank, which actually provides the money; the SBA guaran-

Cost of Launching New Businesses

Capital	Percentage of businesses
Under $5,000	18
$5,000-$10,000	14
$10,000-$20,000	16
$20,000-$50,000	25
$50,000-$100,000	15
$100,000-$250,000	8
$250,000-$500,000	2
$500,000 or more	1
NA	1

Sources of Funding for New Businesses

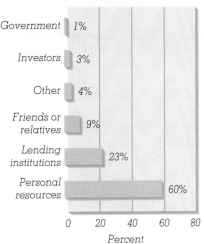

Exhibit 5.6

How Much It Costs to Launch a Business and Where the Money Comes From

Most new businesses are started with relatively little money. The founders generally use their own savings to get under way.

tees to repay 85 to 90 percent of the loan if you fail to do so. The average SBA-backed loan is about $100,000; the upper limit is $750,000. In addition to operating its loan guarantee program, the SBA provides a limited number of direct loans to minorities, women, and veterans.[27]

From the businessperson's standpoint, SBA-backed loans are especially attractive because they generally have longer repayment terms than conventional bank loans—nine years as opposed to two or three. A longer repayment term translates into lower monthly payments. Unfortunately, demand for SBA loans vastly outstrips the agency's supply of capital. As a consequence, getting an SBA loan is difficult. In a typical year, only about 17,000 businesses are lucky enough to qualify.[28]

One of the best ways to borrow money for a small business is to obtain credit from suppliers. Say that you want to open a store. You might be able to persuade a potential supplier to provide your initial inventory on credit. The supplier's risk is minimal in a deal like this; if you don't sell the product, the supplier can take it back. Later, you can ease your financial situation by negotiating liberal payment terms with your vendors or by using the money that others owe you to secure a loan.

Private Investors

Wealthy individuals are one of the most promising sources of equity financing, funding some 30,000 start-up companies every year.[29] However, finding a so-called angel may be difficult. Bankers, accountants, brokers, financial planners, and other entrepreneurs are often able to provide leads. One organized listing of private investors is the Venture Capital Network, a nonprofit corporation based in New Hampshire, which uses a computer to match investors and entrepreneurs.

Venture Capitalists

In addition to looking for private investors, many high-growth ventures attempt to attract the interest of **venture capitalists,** investment specialists who raise pools of capital to fund ventures that are likely to succeed. The investment funds available to venture-capital firms come from corporations, wealthy individuals, pension funds, and other pools of capital, such as university endowments.

venture capitalists (VCs) Investment specialists who provide money to finance new businesses or turnarounds in exchange for a portion of the ownership, with the objective of making a considerable profit on the investment

Venture capitalists, or VCs as they're called in entrepreneurial circles, do not simply lend money to a small business as a bank would. Instead, they provide capital in return for an ownership interest, which may amount to half of the stock or more. They often become involved in helping run the business. In a typical scenario, the venture-capital firm buys part of the stock in the company at a low price—say, 50 cents a share—then, when the company goes public, the VC sells at a much higher price.

The problem with venture capital is that it's extremely hard to find. VCs fund fewer than 5,000 companies each year, and many of those companies are established firms ripe for expansion rather than raw start-ups. To catch the eye of a typical venture capitalist, you need a business with pizzazz that has the potential to reach $50 million in sales within five years and provide an annualized rate of return of 20 to 40 percent over five to seven years—VCs are aggressive investors.[30]

If your business doesn't fit the profile of a high-powered venture-capital firm, you might be able to raise money from one of the investment firms created by the Small Business Administration. Small Business Investment Companies (SBICs) and Special Enterprise Small Business Investment Companies (SESBICs), which finance minority-owned businesses, are similar in operation to venture-capital firms, but they tend to make smaller investments and are willing to consider businesses that VCs may not want to finance. They are federally licensed, shareholder-owned investment companies that have borrowed money at lower-than-market rates from the SBA to put into new ventures.

Corporate Sources

Yet another source of funding is big business. Companies like IBM, Motorola, and Eastman Kodak are making direct investments in small businesses.[31] In addition, many other large companies provide equity funding through investment pools run by venture capitalists.

In general, the large corporation's interests differ from the venture capitalist's. Apart from hoping for a profitable investment, most large companies want to gain access to promising technology, with the possible goal of acquiring the operation. Corporate investors often provide more than money. They sometimes share their marketing expertise or provide distribution capabilities that the new venture lacks.

State and Local Government Programs

Increasingly, state and local governments hoping to boost their economies and create jobs have launched hundreds of programs to help small businesses. Most now have some sort of small-company financing, and more than half offer venture-capital funds aimed at start-ups as well as research-and-development grants.[32]

In a related development, many state and local economic-development offices and universities are forming **incubator** facilities to nurture fledgling businesses. In a typical incubator, new companies can lease space at bargain rates and share secretaries, reception-ists, telephone equipment, financial and accounting advice, marketing support, and credit-checking services. Some incubators are open to businesses of all types, but many specialize. For example, the Spokane Business Incubation Center operates the Kitchen Center, where small food-processing companies can share a commercial kitchen.[33] These facilities can make a big difference to the success of a start-up business. According to the National Business Incubation Association, 8 out of 10 businesses that are nurtured in incubators succeed.[34]

incubator Facility set up to nurture businesses during their early growth phases

Business incubators, such as this one in Spokane, Washington, help new companies get off to a successful start.

going public *Act of raising capital by selling company shares to the public for the first time*

Public Stock Offerings

After a high-growth venture has been operating for a few years, it has the option of raising capital by **going public,** or selling stock in the company on the open market. Going public achieves two purposes: (1) it raises money for the company, and (2) it enables the founder and other early equity investors to make money by selling at a profit the stock they obtained at low prices.

Although the potential rewards for going public are enormous, problems exist as well. Success depends on the public demand for stock in new companies, which varies considerably from year to year. Another problem is the expense. Typically, when a company goes public, it might raise $10 million but spend $330,000 on various fees and printing costs and another $800,000 on underwriting commissions. Unless your company is profitable and has annual sales of $15 million to $20 million or more, going public is not a viable option. Only about 5 percent of small businesses raise capital in this fashion.[35]

Managing the Business

Assuming that you obtain adequate financing to start or buy your own business, your next job is to run it. You may find yourself working 12-hour days week in and week out—with no boss to blame for your miseries! It is common for small-business owners not only to put out the product—be it chopsticks, videotapes, homemade bread, or legal advice—but also to function as sales representative, secretary, personnel manager, financial planner, public-relations expert, and janitor. Exhibit 5.7 shows where the time goes in a typical entrepreneur's week. With all the details to attend to, it's easy for the owner of a small business to lose sight of the big picture. Here are some of the broad managerial tasks that can make or break a small business.

Planning the Activities of the Business

You can find plenty of successful entrepreneurs who claim to have done very little formal planning, but even the most intuitive of them have *some* idea of what they're trying to accomplish and how they

Exhibit 5.7

How Entrepreneurs Spend Their Time

The men and women who found companies are jacks-of-all-trades, but their top priorities are selling and producing the product.

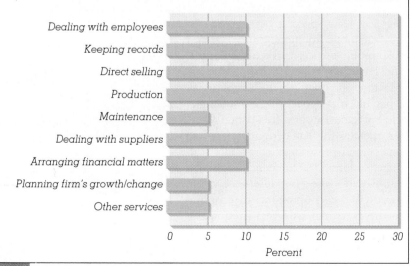

When small companies look at the resources and skills of their larger competitors, the sight can be more than a little daunting. With sales forces that span the globe, trained support staffs and technical specialists, and big travel and marketing budgets, big companies seem to have the playing field tilted dramatically in their direction. However, the tilt isn't quite as severe as you might think. Technology is helping small companies compete more and more effectively.

Imagine you're a management consultant who helps companies find ways to operate more efficiently. You're good at what you do, but you also face competition from some awfully big accounting and consulting firms, some with offices all over the world. How can little old you hope to compete? You can magnify yourself with technology, that's how.

Start with the way you communicate with clients and potential clients. Let's say you have a client in Denver, but you're based in Miami. One of your big competitors is trying to woo this client away from you. Naturally, this competitor has a branch office right there in Denver, so somebody just walks down the

TECHNOLOGY HELPS YOUR SMALL COMPANY LEVEL THE PLAYING FIELD

street to visit your client. Nevertheless, you don't have to be shut out. Using the new videoconferencing feature built into your personal computer, you can stay in close audio-visual contact with your client. You can even conduct training sessions long-distance. When you need to send or receive anything, your choices include Federal Express (which itself is strongly driven by technology), the Internet (for computer files), and, of course, regular phone and fax lines. You can hang onto the client because you're just as good as the big competitor—and your fees are lower because you don't have rented office space all over the world to support.

What about getting new clients, though? The big companies can

surely beat you to the punch with flashy advertising campaigns. Not so fast. Your knowledge of technology will keep you in the running here as well. To begin with, you can carefully screen and select clients using a variety of electronic information sources, all available through your computer. By selecting your prospects with care and learning all about them before making a sales pitch, you increase your chances of success.

When it's time to make that sales presentation, your big foes have nothing on you. Using the multimedia resources on your computer, you craft a presentation that mixes charts and graphs, flowcharts, video clips from current clients, and music and sound effects to emphasize important points. You play this entire show through a liquid crystal display (LCD) projection system that dazzles your audience with colorful animation. Your computer and display equipment are small enough to fit in your briefcase, so you can make this presentation anywhere potential clients can be found.

Sounds like the big competitors should be afraid of *you,* don't you think?

---

hope to do it. Before you rush in to supply a product, you need to be sure that a market exists. No amount of hard work can make a bad idea into a profitable one: The health-food store in a meat-and-potatoes neighborhood and the child-care center in a retirement community are probably doomed from the beginning.

You must also try to foresee some of the problems that might arise and figure out how to cope with them. What will you do if one of your suppliers suddenly goes out of business? Can you locate another supplier quickly? What if the neighborhood suddenly starts to change —even for the better? An influx of wealthier neighbors may cause such a steep increase in rent that your business must move. Also, tough competition may move into the neighborhood along with the fatter pocketbooks. Do you have an alternative location staked out? What if fashions suddenly change? Can you switch quickly from, say, hand-painted T-shirts to some other kind of shirt?

Marketing for the New Business
Marketing is especially important in a new business, because the company's ultimate success depends on building a customer base. Mar-

keting encompasses a number of important activities, such as product development, pricing, distribution, and promotion, which are discussed in detail in Chapters 12 through 15.

In terms of product development, small companies often have an edge over larger organizations because they can react more quickly. If a demand for broccoli pizzas arises tomorrow, a small restaurant can make them up almost as quickly as "Pop" can run out to the supermarket for the new ingredients and "Mom" can think of a way to incorporate them into the old family recipe. A chain, on the other hand, would probably not get wind of the new demand for months and would then need time to study the concept, formulate a new recipe, order ingredients in quantity, ship them to each outlet, and so on.

When it comes to prices, however, small companies may be at a disadvantage compared with larger firms. Because of their larger volume of business, big firms may have lower costs per unit and thus be able to charge lower prices. To set prices at the optimum level, you have to analyze your competition, your area, your costs, and your profit requirements. Once you've set those prices, you have to remain tuned in to changing conditions in the marketplace so that you don't get caught with too little demand for your supply or with too little reward for your risks.

Choosing the ideal outlet for your product is another problem. To build a distribution network, you must persuade wholesalers or retailers to carry your product. When Richard Worth was trying to get stores to carry his Frookies cookies, he agreed to stage promotional events to draw customers into stores.[36]

Monitoring and Controlling Operations

In addition to marketing your product, you need to develop an effective record-keeping system that will handle customer files, billing, production and inventory data, employee information, and basic accounting functions. As "Understanding the High-Tech Revolution" points out, many small businesses are using personal computers to boost efficiency and effectiveness.

Coping with Red Tape

No business operates in a vacuum—and like all other enterprises, new businesses are subject to the pressures and requirements of our society's legal and regulatory system. If you need a trademark, a company brand, or a patent, or if you are thinking of becoming incorporated, you will definitely need legal help. Many other situations also require the help of a lawyer.

Likewise, you'll be coping with government regulations, many of which were written with larger businesses in mind but are applied to small businesses anyway. Disposing of hazardous wastes, for example, may be difficult for small companies, which typically lack their own waste-treatment facilities. Similarly, small businesses are struggling to comply with the recently passed Americans with Disabilities Act, which is designed to ensure that disabled consumers receive the same level of services as other customers. Although small businesses have more time to comply with the law than large firms do, they may be required to make costly modifications to their facilities or prove that doing so would pose an economic hardship. One regulation, for example, requires that restaurants must either be accessible to the disabled or offer home delivery. Another requires that store aisles be wide enough to accommodate wheelchairs and that shelves be low enough so that a person in a wheelchair can reach the merchandise.

Adjusting to Growth

One of the most difficult management problems you may face in a new business is success. Trouble often occurs when the founder—fundamentally an "idea person"—assumes the role of manager. Many people who are good at launching companies lack the skills needed to manage them over the long run. The person who excels during the start-up phase may not be able to delegate work well or may have problems figuring out how to expand the business.

Even if the person is flexible enough to adjust to changing conditions, there is a lot to learn as a company grows. Arranging additional financing, hiring new people, adding new products, computerizing the record keeping—all these activities are demanding.

THE FRANCHISE ALTERNATIVE

One way to avoid some of the management headaches associated with starting a business is to invest in a **franchise,** an approach that enables you to use a larger company's trade name and sell its products or services in a specific territory. In exchange for this right, the **franchisee** (you, the small-business owner) pays an initial fee (and often monthly royalties as well) to the **franchiser** (the corporation).

Franchises are of three basic types. In a *product franchise,* the franchisee pays the franchising company for the right to sell trademarked goods, which are purchased from the franchiser and resold by the franchisee. Car dealers and gasoline stations fall into this category. In a *manufacturing franchise,* like a soft-drink bottling plant, the franchisee is licensed by the parent company to produce and distribute its products, using supplies purchased from the franchiser. In a *business-format franchise,* the franchisee buys the right to open a business using the franchiser's name and format for doing business. The fast-food chains typify this form of franchising.

If you are an average American, you already know something about franchises. In our economy, they are a factor of rising importance, as Exhibit 5.8 suggests. We buy our houses from franchised real estate brokers, get our hair cut in franchised beauty salons, and drive cars purchased from franchised dealers. The soda pop we drink is bottled by franchisers, and the food we eat is sold by franchises such as McDonald's, Wendy's, Pizza Hut, and Kentucky Fried Chicken. Fran-

franchise Business arrangement in which an individual obtains rights from a larger company to sell a well-known product or service

franchisee Person or group to whom a corporation grants an exclusive right to the use of its name in a certain territory, usually in exchange for an initial fee plus monthly royalty payments

franchiser Corporation that grants a franchise to an individual or group

This Subway franchise in Mexico City is part of one of the largest franchise systems in the world.

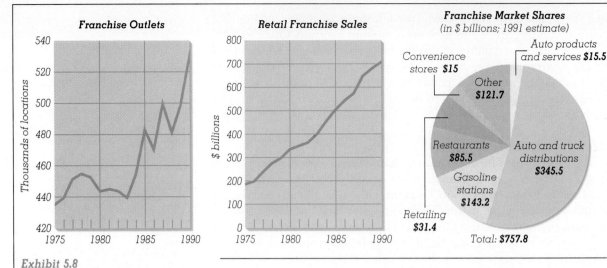

Franchise Outlets

Thousands of locations / 1975–1990

Retail Franchise Sales

$ billions / 1975–1990

Franchise Market Shares
(in $ billions; 1991 estimate)

Convenience stores **$15**

Auto products and services **$15.5**

Other **$121.7**

Restaurants **$85.5**

Gasoline stations **$143.2**

Auto and truck distributions **$345.5**

Retailing **$31.4**

Total: **$757.8**

Exhibit 5.8

The Growth of Franchising

Both the number and revenues of franchises have increased dramatically over the past decade.

chises account for about one-third of all retail sales in the United States and employ millions of people. With sales growing at five times the rate of the GDP, franchises will be responsible for half of all retail sales by the year 2000.[37]

Franchising is not a new phenomenon. It has been around since the nineteenth century, when such companies as Singer and International Harvester established dealerships throughout the world. Early in this century, Coca-Cola, General Motors, and Metropolitan Life Insurance Company (among others) used franchises to distribute or sell their products. However, the real boom in franchising began in the late 1950s, with the proliferation of hotels and motels such as Holiday Inn and of fast-food establishments such as Baskin-Robbins and Dunkin' Donuts.

The 1980s saw a proliferation of service-oriented franchises that catered to the needs of busy baby boomers: day-care centers, cleaning services, auto-maintenance centers, and video-rental stores. The 1980s also saw a shift in the type of people buying franchises. It used to be that the typical franchisee expected to own and operate one store, but more and more franchisees are entering the business with broader ambitions. Their aim is to own a number of outlets and delegate day-to-day operations to employees.[38]

The 1990s are bringing an increase in corporate franchising, with giant companies like PepsiCo operating a collection of franchise chains such as KFC, Pizza Hut, and Taco Bell. You can also expect to see franchisers reaching overseas to sustain their customary growth rate, particularly if they have already saturated much of the domestic market. McDonald's opened 634 new locations in 1993 alone, many in overseas locations.[39]

Advantages of Franchising

Why is franchising so popular? According to the president of the International Franchise Association, franchising has triple benefits: "The franchiser wins because he builds a strong foundation for his company. The franchisee wins because he can take advantage of the fran-

Your franchise business is hot. You've sold hundreds, perhaps thousands, of franchise packages across the country. One day you walk past a world map, and a light goes on in your head—what if you could expand all over the globe? Many U.S. franchisers are doing it, and have done so for years, in fact. Roughly 450 of the 3,000 franchise chains in the United States have set up shop in other countries. McDonald's is the long-time leader in this global adventure, with nearly a third of its 13,000 restaurants in other countries.

In large part because of McDonald's success, U.S. franchise operations are viewed quite positively by potential partners in other countries. However, expanding beyond our shores is a lot more complicated than expanding a franchise business here at home. It takes money to get

MOVING AROUND THE WORLD WITH FRANCHISING

started, since you have to go through most of the same steps you took to get started in the United States, from registering your trademark to scouting locations to selecting local suppliers. In addition, it's hard work. Sunil Dewan, who's in charge of international franchising for the Ponderosa steak restaurant chain, puts it this way: "We're on the road almost constantly." The "road" Dewan is talking about stretches from Thailand to Dubai, by the way.

Your chances of international franchise are best when you have:

• A sound and profitable business already in operation in the United States
• The finances to invest in expansion for months or years before you break even—and lots and lots of patience
• People who can take over and manage franchises
• The ability to listen and the willingness to adapt

How can you find the ideal candidates for your franchise business? Most of them will find you, actually. Roughly 90 percent of all candidates approach the franchiser. The International Franchise Association holds conferences around the world that give franchisers a chance to meet potential partners. For a small fee, the U.S. Commerce Department will line up interviews in 48 countries with aspiring franchisees.

chiser's proven business system. And the general public benefits from the consistency of the product or service."[40]

The biggest winners are generally the franchisers, who are able to expand their businesses through franchised outlets without depleting their own capital. Franchisers not only expand their business using other people's money but also receive regular income from franchisees, who pass on a percentage of their gross revenues and help pay for advertising and promotional costs.

Investing in a franchise can also be good for the franchisee, because the risk is reasonably low. When you invest in a franchise, you know that you are getting a viable business, one that has "worked" many times before. You also have the advantage of instant name recognition and mass advertising. An independent hamburger stand can't afford a national TV advertising campaign, but McDonald's, Burger King, and Wendy's can.

In addition to giving you a proven formula, buying a franchise helps you solve one of the biggest problems that small businesses face: lack of money. Franchisers generally use a number of methods to make sure the franchisee is on firm financial footing. First, before approving prospective franchisees, the franchiser weeds out those whose own finances are in unacceptable shape; a franchiser will not grant a franchise unless the applicant has enough money for start-up costs. (The franchiser, unlike many independent proprietors, has enough experience to estimate start-up costs realistically.) The investment required varies from a few thousand dollars to upward of a million, depending on the franchise. The initial investment covers such franchiser services as site-location studies, market research, training, and technical assistance, as well as the costs associated with building or leasing the structure, decorating the building, purchasing supplies, and operating the business for 6 to 12 months.

Few franchisees are able to write a check for the amount of the total investment. Most obtain a loan to cover at least part of the cost. In some cases, the lender is actually the franchiser. Approximately one-quarter of *Entrepreneur Magazine*'s list of top 500 franchisers offer some sort of financial assistance to their franchisees.[41]

Besides financial aid and advice, the franchiser gives a new franchisee training in how to run a business. Many franchise organizations offer advice on advertising, taxes, and other business matters, as well as offering instructions in the day-to-day operation of the franchise. The Dwyer Group, a Texas-based franchiser of cleaning and maintenance businesses, supports its 2,000 franchisees with a marketing staff reachable by telephone 14 hours and day and numerous field-support managers who meet in person with franchisees.[42]

Disadvantages of Franchising

Although franchising offers many advantages, it is not the ideal vehicle for everyone. For one thing, owning a franchise is no guarantee of wealth. It may be the safest way to get into business, but it is not necessarily the cheapest. According to some analysts, it costs 10 to 30 percent more to buy a franchise than to open a business independently.[43] In addition, not all franchises are hugely profitable operations. Some franchisees barely survive, in fact.

One of the most significant financial variables is the monthly payment, or royalty, that must be turned over to the franchiser. The fees vary widely, from nothing at all to 20 percent of sales. High royalties are not necessarily bad—if the franchisee gets ongoing assistance in return.

Another drawback of franchises is that many of them allow individual operators very little independence. Franchisers can prescribe virtually every aspect of the business, down to the details of employees' uniforms and the color of the walls. Franchisees may be required to buy the products they sell directly from the franchiser at whatever price the franchiser feels like charging. Franchisers may also make important decisions without consulting franchisees. In recent years, a growing number of disgruntled franchisees have filed lawsuits or formed associations in an attempt to even the balance of power.

Evaluating the Franchise

The best way to protect yourself from a poor franchise investment is to study the opportunity very carefully before you commit yourself. Since 1978 the Federal Trade Commission has required franchisers to disclose information about their operations to prospective franchisees. By studying this information, you can determine the financial condition of the franchiser and ascertain whether it has been involved in lawsuits with franchisees. Before signing a franchise agreement, it's

Exhibit 5.9

1. Are your legal responsibilities as a franchisee clear? Are your family members similarly obligated?
2. Who is responsible for selecting the location of your business?
3. Is the name or trademark of your franchise legally protected? Can the franchiser change or modify the trademark without consulting you?
4. Has the franchiser made any oral promises that are not reflected in the written franchise agreement?
5. What are your renewal rights? What conditions must you meet to renew your agreement?
6. Do you have exclusive rights to a given territory, or could the franchiser sell to additional franchisees who would become your competitors?
7. Under what terms are you allowed or required to terminate the franchise agreement? What becomes of the lease and assets if the agreement is terminated? Are you barred from opening a similar business?
8. Under what terms and conditions are you permitted or required to sell some or all of your interests in the franchise?
9. Are you required to buy supplies from the franchiser or other specified suppliers? Under what circumstances can you choose your own suppliers?
10. Has your attorney studied the written franchise agreement? Does it conform to the requirements of the Federal Trade Commission?

Ten Questions to Ask Before Signing a Franchise Agreement

A franchise agreement is a legally binding contract that defines the relationship between the franchisee and the franchiser. Because the agreement is drawn up by the franchiser, the terms and conditions generally favor the franchiser. You don't necessarily have to agree to everything on the first go-around. Maybe you can negotiate a better deal. Before signing the franchise agreement, be sure to consult an attorney.

wise to consult an attorney. Exhibit 5.9 suggests some points to consider as you study the package of information on the franchise.

Another good source of information about a franchise is other franchisees. You might want to spend a few months working for someone who already owns a franchise you're interested in. At a minimum, you should find out what other franchisees think of the opportunity. If they had it to do over again, would they still invest?

SUMMARY OF LEARNING OBJECTIVES

1 Differentiate between lifestyle businesses and high-growth ventures.
Most small businesses are lifestyle businesses, intended to provide the owner with a comfortable living. High-growth ventures, on the other hand, are businesses with ambitious sales, profit, and growth objectives.

2 Discuss the impact of social and economic factors on the development of small businesses.
The expansion of the small-business sector in recent years reflects a shift to services, a relative decline in the advantages afforded by large-scale manufacturing, the aging of the baby-boom generation, and an increase in the number of women and minorities in the workforce.

3 List four important functions of small businesses in the economy.
Small businesses provide jobs, introduce new goods and services, supply the needs of large corporations, and provide specialized goods and services.

4 Identify three ways of getting into business for yourself.
You can start a new company from scratch, buy a going concern, or invest in a franchise.

5 Name 10 topics that should be covered in a formal business plan.
A formal business plan should (1) summarize your business concept, (2) describe the company and its industry, (3) explain the product, (4) analyze the market, (5) describe your marketing strategy, (6) discuss design and development plans, (7) explain your operations plan, (8) provide an overall schedule, (9) identify risks and potential problems, and (10) provide detailed financial information.

6 Describe nine sources of financing available for new businesses.

New businesses may be financed through personal savings, commercial-bank loans or loans from the Small Business Administration, credit from suppliers, private investors, venture capitalists, Small Business Investment Companies and Special Enterprise Small Business Investment Companies, corporate sources, state and local programs, and public stock offerings.

7 Identify five managerial activities that are important to the success of a small business.

Success depends on planning the activities of the business, marketing, monitoring and controlling operations, coping with red tape, and adjusting to growth.

8 Explain the pros and cons of owning a franchise.

A franchisee has the advantages of wide name recognition and mass advertising, financial help, and training and support. However, owning a franchise involves considerable start-up expense, monthly payments to the franchiser, and constraints on the franchisee's independence.

Tom Stemberg knew his idea for a chain of office-supply superstores was a good one, but he didn't realize *how* good until he started looking for money. One of his first calls was to Leo Kahn, an old adversary from Stemberg's supermarket days. One of the country's leading supermarket entrepreneurs, Kahn had recently sold his food-store chains for $80 million and, at age 68, was looking for new investments to liven up his retirement. Despite his previous rivalry with Stemberg in Boston's supermarket price wars, Kahn agreed to put $500,000 in capital for the new venture and to serve as chairman of the board.

Stemberg and Kahn refined the idea for Staples and prepared a detailed business plan, which they circulated to venture capitalists. Although most would-be entrepreneurs have trouble raising money, Stemberg and Kahn received dozens of offers. "We could easily have raised $100 million," Stemberg recalls. What excited the venture capitalists was the "rightness" of the idea. As one investor said: "A lot of retail start-ups come by, but most of them are a twist on an old theme or a better presentation. Not Staples—it was an entirely new retailing category." Stemberg turned down most of the offers but accepted $4 million in start-up funds in exchange for 50 percent of the company, with commitments for $31 million later on.

With his money problems solved, he was ready to build a management team. Because he expected the business to grow rapidly, Stemberg wanted people who had worked for large-scale operations. He also wanted people with practical, hands-on experience in retailing, people who understood costs and customers. Not surprisingly, he turned to his contacts in the grocery business. Many of Staples's top people are, like Stemberg, graduates of the management-training program at Jewel Companies. Although many of the people he recruited held high-paying executive positions, Stemberg persuaded them that joining Staples would enable them to get in on the ground floor of a company with enormous potential. In addition to offering competitive salaries, he promised his team stock in the company, which could be extremely valuable if Staples went public.

Before Stemberg could open his first store, however, he needed merchandise to stock the shelves. His plans called for a deep inventory of some 5,000 items, ranging from paper and pencils to coffee machines and computers—everything a small company might need to set up shop and run a business. However, vendors of office supplies were leery of doing business directly with Staples. Many major manufacturers didn't want to upset their relationships with their wholesalers, who would be cut out of the distribution chain by Staples. The wholesalers, in turn, were reluctant to sell to the company, because Staples demanded price discounts in exchange for volume orders. Furthermore, the wholesalers' customers—the retailers—would be hurt by Staples's low prices. In fact, several retailers threatened to stop doing business with wholesalers that supplied Staples. Meanwhile, the wholesalers were putting similar pressure

---

on the manufacturers to prevent them from selling to Staples.

The manufacturers' reluctance to sell directly to Stemberg threatened the profitability of his entire concept, which depends on shortening the distribution chain to save on costs. To combat their fears, Stemberg and his vice president of merchandising, Paul Korian, invited a group of 100 major office-products manufacturers to a breakfast meeting. After hearing a presentation on the company's prospects and probable impact on the office-supply business, many of the manufacturers were convinced that Staples would revolutionize the industry and that cooperating with the firm would be the most profitable course.

Time has clearly validated Tom Stemberg's idea. Office-supply superstores have grown rapidly across the country. Staples has been growing every year since it opened, although not as quickly as an imitator called Office Depot, which now claims the number one spot in the industry. Stemberg is pushing into Canada and Europe and sees a bright future for the industry he helped create.

Your Mission: You are a new recruit in Staples's management-training program. In addition to learning the business from the ground up, you handle special projects for Staples's top executives. They have asked for your help in analyzing the following issues:

1. Although Staples has grown—and grown profitably—Stemberg wants to consider getting additional capital to help with expansion plans in Europe. The company went public in 1987, so some funds have been raised through the stock market. Stemberg has asked you to weigh some of the advantages and disadvantages of various funding alternatives and to recommend the one you prefer. Here are the options:
  a. Getting bank loans
  b. Offering more stock to the public

c. Using a combination of debt and equity

2. When Stemberg opened the first Staples store, he was disappointed that more customers didn't show up. Perhaps he shouldn't have been surprised, however. Most of the store's target customers—owners and office managers of small businesses—aren't used to shopping for office supplies in a warehouse. Stemberg must persuade them to visit his stores. Stemberg has asked for your advice on how to get the owners and office managers of small businesses to come in for an initial visit. Which of the following options do you recommend?

  a. Encourage Staples managers and employees to join organizations where they might meet the target customers. By attending meetings, the Staples team could make contacts with local businesspeople and introduce them to the company's advantages.
  b. Blanket local areas with radio, TV, and newspaper ads to introduce as many people as possible to Staples.
  c. Buy a list of the small businesses located within reasonable driving distance of each store and call them on the phone. Explain the Staples concept, ask how much the business spends on various supplies, and follow up with a free coupon for something the company uses often.

3. Good ideas are quickly imitated. Before Stemberg could say "paper clip," he was confronted with competition from "me-too" office-supply warehouses. What strategy should he pursue in competing with the clones?
  a. Expand as quickly as possible into as many geographic areas as possible in hopes of nailing down the best locations and developing an initial base of loyal customers before competitors can get up and running.
  b. Working from the store's original base in Boston, expand the chain throughout the heavily populated corridor from Washington, D.C.,

through New England. Concentrate on getting established in this area so that Staples will have a significant advantage when competitors try to move in. With the Northeast in hand, expand selectively into other metropolitan areas where small businesses are doing well.
  c. When competition surfaces, fight back by starting price wars and increasing the company's advertising and marketing budgets.

4. Stemberg has asked you to investigate the advantages and disadvantages of franchising the Staples concept. Which of the following points would you emphasize most strongly in your report to him?
  a. Franchising would be a good way for Staples to expand rapidly throughout the country. Franchisees would supply much of the money and labor required to open stores in all the major metropolitan areas, thereby enabling the company to get a jump on the competition and nail down the best locations.
  b. Franchising would limit Stemberg's control over the quality and consistency of Staples stores and might jeopardize the company's long-term competitiveness.
  c. Franchising would be beneficial overseas; the participation of foreign partners would help Staples overcome legal barriers to international expansion and would enhance the company's understanding of foreign markets.[44]

debt (136)
economies of scale (129)
equity (136)
franchise (143)

franchisee (143)
franchiser (143)
going public (140)
high-growth ventures (129)

incubator (139)
lifestyle businesses (129)
small business (129)
start-up companies (131)
venture capitalists (138)

REVIEW QUESTIONS

1. What qualities usually characterize the men and women who run successful small businesses, and why?
2. Why have small businesses been started in record numbers in recent years?
3. Where can small-business owners look for new opportunities?

4. In what ways do small businesses complement big businesses in our economy?
5. Why do many new businesses fail, and how might such failures be avoided?
6. What are the principal sources of financing for new businesses?

7. What are the motives that encourage big businesses to support start-up companies?
8. How does a franchise operation work, and what are some of its advantages and disadvantages for the franchisee?

A CASE FOR CRITICAL THINKING

PUTTING A STAMP ON THE MARKET

Suppose you had a bright idea for a service business—a convenient place where people could rent a postal box, mail packages, buy office supplies and stamps, make copies, collect telephone messages, duplicate keys, and send documents electronically by telex or fax. Say you did some market research and found that people liked the idea, and you thought you could make a decent living by opening such a center. Being ambitious, you thought you might even open a bunch of centers. After all, if one is good, aren't two better? And why stop at two? Why not open centers in every town and neighborhood throughout the country? You had a few reservations, though. There was nothing patentable about your idea. Anybody with a little capital could duplicate your service. If you were successful, people might imitate you and grab the best locations before you could afford to expand. So what should you do?

Anthony DeSio, chief executive officer of Mail Boxes Etc. (MBE), solved the problem by franchising. By 1994, he had sold franchises for over 2,000 MBE centers scattered across the country from Alaska to Florida. DeSio estimates that the U.S. market can accommodate up to 20,000 centers of the MBE type, and he plans to lock up a dominant position before rivals such as Postal-Annex + can beat him to the punch. He has also expanded internationally, with franchise operations in more than 20 countries.

During the expansion phase, MBE's primary source of revenues is the sale of franchises. Over 17 percent of its 1994 income came from franchise fees, in fact. The company also receives royalties from franchisees and revenue from selling equipment and supplies to franchisees. This reliance on internal sources of income is a point of concern for some observers because it indicates that the company is not actually supporting itself yet through sales to customers.

As the MBE network matures and growth slows, however, DeSio anticipates that royalties and revenue from selling equipment and supplies will replace franchise fees as the main source of company income. It could be a major challenge.

DeSio believes that building a nationwide network will eventually provide MBE with a major advantage over independent competitors. Economies of scale have already helped bring down the cost of operations. The centralized purchasing and shipping department obtains supplies and equipment in large quantities at reduced prices, and it passes the savings on to individual franchisees. The headquarters design-and-construction staff helps local owners plan their centers more efficiently and get good deals from national suppliers on cabinetry and fixtures. The MBE administration and franchise-support departments provide customized computer software to help franchisees manage their accounting and inventory control.

PART ONE | FOCUS ON BUSINESS TODAY

DeSio believes that in the long run, MBE's success will depend on strong, positive relationships between the company's executive office and the franchise owners. He has created seven regional franchise advisory councils to obtain feedback from the field. DeSio also supports the franchisees with training programs. He has opened two company-owned stores to experiment with new ideas and test new products and services. These include selling airline tickets and serving as drop-off centers for consumer electronics products that need repair.

1. Do you think DeSio was wise to rely on franchising to expand his business, or should he have attempted to retain ownership of all the stores? Explain your answer.

2. What are the pros and cons of starting your own mail-and-business-services center versus buying an MBE franchise?

3. What are the risks of relying so heavily on franchising fees during the growth stage of the business?

BUILDING YOUR COMMUNICATION SKILLS

Using the section titled "Obtaining Financing" as a resource, investigate one of the sources of funding that is available to new-business ventures. Either by letter or in a personal interview, contact a local financial institution or a state, local, or federal business adviser to find out what type of financing is available for new businesses. The reference section of your local library might also have information regarding local funding sources. Be sure to note the requirements necessary to obtain funding from each source. (For example, are sources limited to a specific type of business?) As directed by your instructor, prepare a brief report summarizing your findings and present it to the class.

KEEPING CURRENT USING *THE WALL STREET JOURNAL*

Scan issues of *The Wall Street Journal* for articles describing problems or successes faced by small businesses in the United States. Clip or copy three or more articles that interest you.

1. What problem or opportunity does each article present? Is it an issue that faces many businesses, or is it specific to one industry or region?
2. What could a potential small-business owner learn about the risks and rewards of business ownership from reading these articles?
3. Have you ever considered starting a business? What impact did these articles have on your interest? Why?

The Influence of Immigration on Business

The United States is a country of immigrants, from the early wanderers who came across the Bering Strait into what is now Alaska to the people who are fleeing Hong Kong in anticipation of China's taking over the once-British colony. Patterns of immigration have changed over time, often affected by geography and sometimes resulting from events in other parts of the world or from changes in U.S. immigration laws.

Immigration has produced distinct concentrations of ethnic and racial groups across the United States. For instance, the seven states with the highest concentration of African Americans are all in the South, whereas 65 percent of all Hispanic Americans live in states located in three corners of the country: California, Florida, and New York.[45] Geography is a major cause of the Hispanic migration into California and Florida, whereas other factors are probably responsible for the settlement of Hispanic Americans in New York.

The ethnic and racial makeup of a city or state can have a profound effect on business, from the employment opportunities an area offers to the types of products businesses can successfully sell. Consider the makeup of the city or town you're living in, and answer the following questions. You may need to visit the library to conduct some research.

1. What role do you think geography played in creating the ethnic and racial composition of your city? Is the geographic connection direct and obvious (such as people from Asia moving to Hawaii and the West Coast), or is the influence of geography less direct (such as Hispanic populations settling in Idaho and Washington state)?

2. How are businesses in your city affected by ethnic and racial composition? Consider investigating businesses such as restaurants and clothing stores. You might also examine employment patterns in your area.
3. On a map of the world, identify the countries that produced your city's population. If you can't narrow your city's population to specific countries, identify regions or continents.

RAY KURZWEIL: FINANCING THE FUTURE

Synopsis

In many respects, Ray Kurzweil represents the classic inventor/entrepreneur. On the one hand, he has a vision of technology helping humankind; from a computer that can read text for blind persons to a sophisticated synthesizer that lets a solo musician replicate the sounds of many different instruments. On the other hand, he knows that it's impossible to succeed without investment capital and strong business skills. This video introduces Kurzweil and a number of his inventions, and it chronicles his efforts to secure financing for each new creation.

It also explains how ideas for new products come to him, including a meeting with musician Stevie Wonder that led to Kurzweil's foray into electronic music.

Exercises

ANALYSIS

1. Using the checklist in the chapter, do you think you have what it takes to succeed as a small-business owner?

2. How do you suppose Kurzweil finds new opportunities?

3. With the products described in the video, would franchising ever make sense for Kurzweil?

4. With respect to the amount of time it takes one of his inventions to return any profits, does equity or debt financing make more sense?

5. Which would be riskier: one of Kurzweil's high-tech breakthroughs or a new neighborhood dry cleaner? Explain your answer.

APPLICATION

The voice-input technology shown in the video might have quite a few ap-plications in the business world. List as many potential uses for it as you can and in each case explain how the technology would increase productivity or quality or decrease costs.

DECISION

Let's say you're the chief financial officer at Xerox, and Ray Kurzweil is approaching you again to invest in his latest project. What are some of the factors you should think about before making the decision to invest?

COMMUNICATION

Identify a new product that you've seen recently, either in person or in an advertisement. Assume you're about to

sell it to a potential customer; write a 30-second oral description of the product and its benefits.

INTEGRATION

Referring to the discussion of the service sector in Chapter 2, how might Kurzweil's various ventures participate in the service sector?

ETHICS

Is it ethical for Kurzweil to approach investors for money for new projects, even though only one of his existing product ideas has made any money so far?

DEBATE

Some might say that a talent such as Kurzweil's should be applied to more important problems than Stevie Wonder's need for a new keyboard. Option A: In a formal debate format, argue either for or against this statement. Option B: Take either side and state your case in a brief summary report.

TEAMWORK

In a team of four students, two of the students should propose a new product idea, describing the target customers and the benefits the product brings to them. The other two students should look for holes in their logic and point out ways to improve the proposal.

UPDATE RESEARCH

Do the research necessary to write a one-paragraph update on the current status of Ray Kurzweil's various business enterprises.

ROLE PLAYING

One student should play the role of an entrepreneur pitching a new business to two other students, who are playing the role of potential investors. The new business idea doesn't have to be something high-tech like Kurzweil's; a new dry-cleaning business or similar "low-tech" concept would be fine as well.

PART TWO
OPERATING A BUSINESS

Chapter 6
The Fundamentals of Management

Chapter 7
Organizing for Business

Chapter 8
The Production of Goods and Services

Chapter

The
Fundamentals
of Management

LEARNING OBJECTIVES
After studying this chapter, you will be able to

1 Discuss the three categories of managerial roles

2 Describe the three levels of management

3 Distinguish between the three types of managerial skills

4 List the four steps in the management process

5 Discuss how strategic, tactical, and operational plans are developed and used

6 Cite three leadership styles and explain why no one style is best

7 Identify the four steps in the control cycle

8 List five measures that companies can take to better manage crises

A t Microsoft, shrewd business deals and sheer luck propelled the pioneering software company into a leading role at the center of the ever-changing, hotly competitive computer industry. However, success brought its own management problems. Spectacular 50 percent annual growth left Microsoft unwieldy and disorganized, even as software companies such as Lotus and Novell were taking aim at its market share. Computer technology continued to evolve at a rapid pace, consumers grew more demanding, and rival programmers worked around the clock to create new and better applications. For founder and chief executive officer Bill Gates, managing Microsoft required heroic effort.

Visionary leadership was largely the reason for Microsoft's wild success. When Gates dropped out of Harvard to found the company in 1975, personal computers were toys for the "hard-core technoid," as he once described himself. Nevertheless, Gates envisioned a computer in every home and in every office, with Microsoft software in every computer. He made an early alliance with computer giant IBM, putting Microsoft's basic operating program into 80 percent of the United States's 50 million personal computers. He also led Microsoft boldly into Europe and Asia. His charisma and technical knowledge motivated Microsoft employees, who investigated new data-storage technologies and broadened software offerings for home and office.

As the company grew, good ideas were no longer enough. Gates found he was so busy that he could hardly handle day-to-day operational details, much less develop the vision he needed to stay ahead of the competition in the twenty-first century. Organization was lacking, and planning became an afterthought. Time after time, his company targeted a new market only to introduce a mediocre product the first time out. Gates personally took charge of five important product lines but then couldn't find the time to tailor them to customer needs. Projects died. Customers got angry.

Gates also worried about something that threatened his leadership: He feared losing touch with his employees, the people who put his

Struggling to Survive Success

Bill Gates is moving Microsoft into the twenty-first century through effective management techniques and a visionary outlook on technology

One of the interpersonal roles managers fulfill is that of figurehead. Vice chairman Roger Enrico represented PepsiCo at this public introduction of a line of Pepsi clothing.

management *Process of coordinating organizational resources to meet a goal*

roles *Behavioral patterns*

hierarchy *Pyramid-like organizational structure comprising top, middle, and lower management*

top managers *Those at the top of an organization's management hierarchy, having the most power and responsibility in the organization*

vision into action. In the relaxed atmosphere of Microsoft, talking shop with the CEO was an important morale booster as well as a way to introduce employees to company values. Gates relished personal contact with employees, but their number had grown into the thousands, and they were spread around the world.

Although Gates had always made the big decisions at Microsoft, more decisions were needed, and he was already working in excess of 65 hours a week. How could he plan for the long term and still manage daily affairs effectively? What could he do to reach the staff and spread his vision? How could he ensure Microsoft's success through the year 2000 and beyond?[1]

THE SCOPE OF MANAGEMENT

Microsoft's Bill Gates would be the first to admit that management is needed in every type of organization. It is the force that unites everything in a business enterprise and sets everything in motion. **Management** is the coordination of an organization's resources (land, labor, capital, and information) to meet a goal. Certain basic principles of that coordination apply to virtually every type of organization, regardless of size or purpose. An auto plant, a city government, a baseball team, a typing service—all require management. Whenever people work together to achieve a goal, someone makes decisions about who will do what, when they will do it, and what resources they will use.

Managerial Roles

In the course of coordinating the organization's work, managers build a network of relationships. They maintain relationships with bosses, peers, and employees that can be described as **roles,** or behavioral patterns. These managerial roles fall into three categories:

- *Interpersonal roles.* As *figureheads* managers represent the firm by performing ceremonial duties, such as officiating at company functions, attending employee weddings, and greeting visitors. As *leaders* they hire, train, motivate, and encourage employees while guiding them toward achieving organizational goals. As *liaisons* managers link groups and individuals both inside and outside the company (such as suppliers, competitors, government agencies, consumers, special-interest groups, and interrelated work groups).
- *Informational roles.* Some of the most important managerial roles are informational ones. As *monitors* managers seek useful information, questioning people inside and outside the organization about important issues. As *disseminators* they distribute information to employees as well as to other managers at all levels. In addition, as *spokespeople* managers transmit information to outsiders, whether through board meetings, correspondence, or outside contacts.
- *Decisional roles.* Managers use the information they gather to make better decisions. As *entrepreneurs* managers try to improve their units by seeking new ways of using resources and technologies. As *dis-*

turbance handlers they resolve unexpected problems that threaten organizational goals (such as reacting to an economic crisis). As *resource allocators* they decide how organizational resources will be used to meet planned objectives. As *negotiators* managers bargain with many individuals and groups, including suppliers, employees, and unions.[2]

Managers continually change roles as they cope with daily challenges and unexpected situations. However, certain roles may be emphasized more than others, depending on a manager's organizational level.

Managerial Hierarchy

In all but the smallest organizations, more than one manager is necessary to oversee the activities of other employees. That's why most companies form a management **hierarchy**—a pyramid structure with top, middle, and bottom management levels. More managers are at the bottom level than at the top, as illustrated in Exhibit 6.1. However, in today's leaner companies, fewer levels separate managers at the top and bottom.

Top managers are the upper-level managers who have the most power and who take overall responsibility for the organization. An example is the chief executive officer (CEO), who sets the organization's goals, makes long-range plans, establishes major policies, and represents the company to the outside world. Some companies group several top managers into an office of the president or an office of the chair. For example, the office of the chairman at cosmetics maker Avon Products includes the chairman, the vice chairman, and the executive vice president for North America.[3]

Middle managers report to top-level managers. Managers at this level develop plans for implementing the broad goals set by top managers, and they coordinate the work of first-line managers. At the middle level are plant managers, division managers, branch managers, and other similar positions.

At the bottom of the management hierarchy are **first-line managers** (or *supervisory managers*). These managers oversee the work of operating employees and put into action the plans developed at higher levels. Positions at this level include supervisor, department head, and office manager. As more and more companies cut costs and decentralize, middle-management jobs are being eliminated, and greater authority is being given to first-line managers. This increased responsibility is driving many first-line managers to improve their education and their managerial skills.[4]

Managerial Skills

Whatever the type or size of the organization, managers employ three basic kinds of skills: technical, human relations, and conceptual. Because managers accomplish their goals primarily by working with and through others, all levels of management need human relations skills. However, the need for technical and conceptual skills varies according to management level. As managers rise through the hierarchy,

middle managers *Those in the middle of the management hierarchy, who implement the goals of top managers and coordinate the work of first-line managers*

first-line managers *Those at the bottom of the management hierarchy, who supervise the operating employees; also called supervisory managers*

Exhibit 6.1
The Management Hierarchy
Separate job titles are used to designate the three basic levels in the management hierarchy.

Top Managers

President
Vice president
General
Pope
College chancellor

Middle Managers

Head of accounting
Factory manager
Army captain
Cardinal
Dean of business

First-line Managers

Supervisor
Sergeant
Pastor
Chair of the marketing department

they may need to strengthen their abilities in one or more of these skill areas; fortunately, these skills can be successfully learned.[5]

A top-level manager (such as a president) spends a lot of time analyzing information (say, about industry trends and the economic climate) and making decisions based on that information. In addition, top managers are constantly communicating with people to obtain information and to convey decisions. So they rely heavily on both conceptual and human relations skills, and they rely less on technical skills.

Managers at the middle level assist the exchange of information between top managers and first-line managers. Planning, decision making, and problem solving are also part of the middle manager's efforts to implement directives from top management and to cope with problems uncovered by first-line managers. As a result, middle managers rely heavily on human relations skills, and they rely more on technical skills than on conceptual skills.

A first-line manager supervises and communicates with the employees who are doing the technical work of the organization. For instance, the shift supervisor of a large restaurant would spend most of her time working alongside the serving staff and the kitchen staff, showing them what to do, motivating them, and working toward goals set by the owner (top management) and the restaurant manager (middle management). Given their position in the hierarchy, first-line managers rely more on technical and human relations skills than on conceptual skills.

Technical Skills

technical skills Ability and knowledge to perform the mechanics of a particular job

A person who knows how to operate a machine, prepare a financial statement, program a computer, or pass a football has **technical skills;** that is, he or she has the knowledge and the ability to perform the mechanics of a particular job. First-line managers such as production supervisors often understand a technical skill well enough to train employees in their jobs and to keep higher-level managers informed about problems in the production process. However, in certain companies, managers without the relevant technical skills may supervise such highly trained employees as computer programmers, engineers, and accountants.

administrative skills Technical skills in information gathering, data analysis, planning, organizing, and other aspects of managerial work

Regardless of whether they have the technical skills to perform the jobs they supervise, all managers must have some technical managerial skills, or **administrative skills,** such as the ability to make schedules, gather information, analyze data, plan, and organize. Although many technical skills are not readily transferable from one industry to another, administrative skills can often be applied in a wide range of industries. If you're trained to operate textile-cutting machines, you would probably be unable to use your skills in the restaurant business. If you're a manager in a garment business, however, you might be able to use your administrative skills in another type of manufacturing business.

Human Relations Skills

human relations skills Skills required to understand other people and to interact effectively with them

All the skills required to understand other people, work effectively with them, and get them working together as a team are **human re-**

lations skills. Because their main job is getting things done with and through people, managers need human relations skills in countless situations. Before employees can work together productively, managers work hard to instill a shared confidence that everyone in the organization is able and willing to work toward common goals. Managers need good human relations skills to inspire the kind of trust that encourages all employees to try new things and to offer new ideas.[6]

One human relations skill needed by managers at all levels is **communication,** exchanging information. Communication keeps internal operations running smoothly and fosters good relationships with people outside the organization. Of course, successful communication is a two-way street. Effective managers are always attuned to the way people react to what's being said, and they listen carefully to what other people say. This two-way communication builds trust and connects people throughout the company.[7]

Effective managers also know how to choose the most appropriate **communication media,** or channels of communication. They understand that the choice of whether to use oral communication (face-to-face conversation, group meetings, telephone calls, telephone or video conferences, or videotapes) or written communication (letters, memos, reports, or electronic-mail messages sent by computer) depends on the nature of the message. Complex, nonroutine messages are best communicated orally, because the listener can pick up important information from the speaker's body signals (such as facial expression or hand motions). In contrast, simpler, routine messages are more likely to be generally understood without such nonverbal cues.[8]

Oral Communication. Speaking and listening—oral communication—take up a substantial part of any business day. Within the firm, managers participate in meetings, presentations, conferences, and chats with employees at all levels so that they can quickly obtain the latest information on key issues.[9] Outside the firm, sales talks, interviews, speeches, and press conferences require managers to use oral communication to achieve organizational goals.

Managers often choose oral over written communication because of the nonroutine nature of their work. Face-to-face conversations allow participants to check nonverbal cues by watching each other's expressions, hearing each other's voices, and observing each other's intensity. Even telephone conversations allow listeners to detect voice intensity and to find out whether the message has been understood; however, telephone calls lack the eye contact, head nods, and other body signals that are part of face-to-face conversations. The more important and unusual the message, the more reason to choose oral communication. However, some volatile situations are best handled

communication Exchange of information

communication media Channels of communication

Managers choose oral communication when they need to communicate complex, nonroutine messages. This manager is briefing sales personnel at the Takashimaya Department Store in Tokyo.

through written communication to keep things on an unemotional level.[10]

Written Communication. Written communication is a good choice for routine and simple messages as well as for more complicated and volatile ones. Within any organization, memos, progress reports, job descriptions, and other written communications circulate constantly. A company's goals, plans, and results are recorded in the form of summaries of meetings, financial statements, and any number of other written documents. At the same time, written communication is essential for presenting an organization to the outside world. Letters, annual reports, sales brochures, and advertisements all play an important role in shaping a company's public image.

The ability to communicate effectively in writing is a valuable skill at all levels of management. Here are a few basic suggestions:

- *Gear your message to your audience.* When explaining how a computer works, for instance, you would use one writing style for an elementary-school magazine and another for a sales brochure directed to potential buyers.
- *Write simply and clearly.* Long, needlessly complex sentences can slow the reader and hide the message you're trying to put across.
- *Be objective.* If you are not careful about balancing the message, the reader may reject it as biased and unreliable.

Conceptual Skills

Managers need **conceptual skills** to see the organization as a whole and to understand the relationships among its parts. Managers like Microsoft's Bill Gates use their conceptual skills to gain perspective, acquire and analyze information, see connections, find both problems and opportunities, come to conclusions, formulate plans, and make decisions.

Decision Making. A key managerial activity requiring conceptual skill is **decision making,** the process of identifying a decision situation, analyzing the problem, considering the alternatives, arriving at a decision, taking action, and assessing the results. As you can see, decision making has six distinct steps:

1. *Recognize the need for a decision.* Managers continually scan the organization's environment for changes that create problems to solve or opportunities to pursue.
2. *Analyze and define the problem or opportunity.* Managers diagnose causes and define exactly what must be decided.
3. *Develop alternatives.* Managers generate a number of possible solutions or courses of action.
4. *Select desired alternatives.* After considering the advantages and disadvantages of each alternative, managers select the most promising course of action (which may be a combination of several alternatives).
5. *Implement the chosen alternative.* Through careful planning and sensitivity for those implementing and those affected by the decision, managers translate the chosen alternative into action.
6. *Evaluate the results.* Managers monitor the results of decisions to see whether the chosen alternative works, whether any new prob-

---

conceptual skills *Ability to understand the relationship of parts to the whole*

decision making *Process of identifying a decision situation, analyzing the problem, weighing the alternatives, arriving at a decision, taking action, and evaluating the results*

lem or opportunity arises because of the decision, and whether a new decision must be made.[11]

However, following the decision process does not guarantee a right decision. When Quaker Oats decided to acquire the company that owned Gaines Foods (pet food), the logic behind the decision was sound, but the results were a nightmare. Quaker had one of its worst fiscal years in a decade. Quaker managers overestimated the benefits of acquiring Gaines, and they did not predict that becoming number 2 in pet food would make them the number 1 target in the industry. Competitors responded aggressively, forcing Quaker to defend its market share, and Quaker's pet-food business was badly injured. Soon afterward, executives decided to reformulate Quaker's dog foods as part of a long-term plan for future growth.[12]

Types of Decisions. Management decisions are of two types. *Programmed decisions* are routine, recurring decisions made according to a predetermined system of decision rules. *Nonprogrammed decisions* are unique and nonroutine, so they cannot be made according to any set procedures or rules. Managers make decisions based on varying amounts of information, so their decisions have varying degrees of possible success or failure.

Managers make decisions under four possible conditions: (1) When managers have all the information necessary, they feel confident about the success of those decisions, so they make decisions with *certainty*. (2) When managers have good information but not all the information they need, their decisions have a greater possibility of failure, so they make decisions with some *risk*. (3) When managers have incomplete information, they are required to make assumptions that might be wrong, so they make decisions with *uncertainty*.[13] (4) When managers have unclear objectives, poorly defined alternatives, and little or no information, the possibility that their decision will fail is the greatest, so they make decisions with *ambiguity*—the most difficult and risky condition for decision making.[14]

THE MANAGEMENT PROCESS

Managers in every type of organization have the same set of functions. Even managers of the smallest organizations go through these four basic steps when starting and maintaining a business: (1) planning, (2) organizing, (3) leading, and (4) controlling. As you read the following descriptions of the management process, keep in mind that various levels of management have different responsibilities in each phase of the process.

The Planning Function

Without a doubt, planning is the first management function, the one on which all others depend. Managers engaged in **planning** establish objectives and goals for the organization and determine the best ways to achieve them. They consider budgets, schedules, data about the industry and the general economy, the company's existing resources, and resources that may realistically be obtained. An important aspect of planning is the careful evaluation of basic assumptions. Just because a business has developed along certain lines in response to previous conditions doesn't mean that another way might not be appropriate, given today's conditions. Managers need strong conceptual skills to carry out planning activities.

Goals and Objectives

An organization's **mission** is its overall purpose. It answers the question, What is the organization supposed to do? A **mission statement** sets the organization's purpose into words and defines the organization's scope of operations, allowing everyone to channel energies in the same direction.[15] For example, spice maker McCormick established this mission statement:

> The primary mission of McCormick & Company is to expand its worldwide leadership position in the spice, seasoning and flavoring markets.[16]

Through the planning process, the company's mission is supported by goals and objectives. Although these terms are often used interchangeably, a **goal** is a broad, long-range target of the organization, and an **objective** is a specific short-range target. A **plan** is a sys-

planning Establishing objectives and goals for an organization and determining the best ways to accomplish them

mission Overall purpose of an organization

mission statement Putting the organization's mission into words

goal Broad, long-range target or aim

objective Specific, short-range target or aim

plan Systematic set of actions designed to achieve goals and objectives

strategic goals Goals focusing on broad organizational issues

PART TWO | OPERATING A BUSINESS

tematic set of actions that will help the organization achieve its goals and objectives. Goals and plans are used at three organizational levels.

Levels of Goals

To be effective, managers set organizational goals that are specific, measurable, relevant, challenging, attainable, and time-limited. Setting appropriate goals increases employee motivation, provides standards by which individual and group performance can be measured, guides employee activity, and clarifies management's expectations.

Top managers set **strategic goals,** which focus on broad issues and apply to the company as a whole. These goals encompass eight major areas of concern: market standing, innovation, human resources, financial resources, physical resources, productivity, social responsibility, and profit.[17] Middle managers set **tactical objectives,** which focus on departmental issues and describe the results necessary to achieve the organization's strategic goals. First-line managers set **operational objectives,** which focus on short-term issues and describe the results necessary to achieve both the tactical objectives and the strategic goals.

Goals are not ends in themselves, but the means to ends. By accomplishing your goals, you help your managers achieve their goals. Achieving operational objectives helps achieve tactical objectives, which in turn helps achieve strategic goals.

Levels of Plans

By establishing organizational goals, managers set the stage for the actions needed to achieve those goals. If you don't plan your actions, the chances of reaching company goals are slim. Each level of goals has a corresponding level of plans for how those goals will actually be achieved.[18]

Strategic plans are the actions designed to achieve strategic goals. Strategic plans are usually long-term, defining actions over a period of two to five years. They are laid out by top managers, who consult with board members and middle managers. **Tactical plans** are the actions designed to achieve tactical objectives and to support strategic plans. Tactical plans usually lay out actions for the next one to three years. They are developed by middle managers, who consult with first-line managers before committing to top management. **Operational plans** are the actions designed to achieve operational objectives and to support tactical plans. Operational plans usually define actions for less than one year. They are developed by first-line managers, who consult with middle managers.

Coordinating the three levels of plans is essential. For example, when Timex realized that consumers were more interested in style than in durability, top managers defined a bold new direction for the company. They set a strategic goal of regaining the market share they had lost to competitors such as Swatch, and they developed a strategic plan to target health- and fashion-conscious consumers. The tactical objective was to sell to amateur athletes, and the tactical plan was to interview amateur athletes to find out what these consumers wanted. The operational objective was to give consumers what they

Joseph Paquette, Jr., CEO of Philadelphia Electric, is one of several top managers who set the company's mission and use the planning process to support that mission. He explains his company's plans at the annual shareholders' meeting.

tactical objectives *Objectives that focus on departmental issues and describe the results necessary to achieve the organization's strategic goals*

operational objectives *Objectives that focus on short-term issues and describe the results needed to achieve tactical objectives and strategic goals*

strategic plans *Actions designed to accomplish strategic goals, usually defined for periods of two to five years and developed by top managers*

tactical plans *Actions designed to achieve tactical objectives and to support strategic plans, usually defined for a period of one to three years and developed by middle managers*

operational plans *Actions designed to achieve operational objectives and to support tactical plans, usually defined for less than one year and developed by first-line managers*

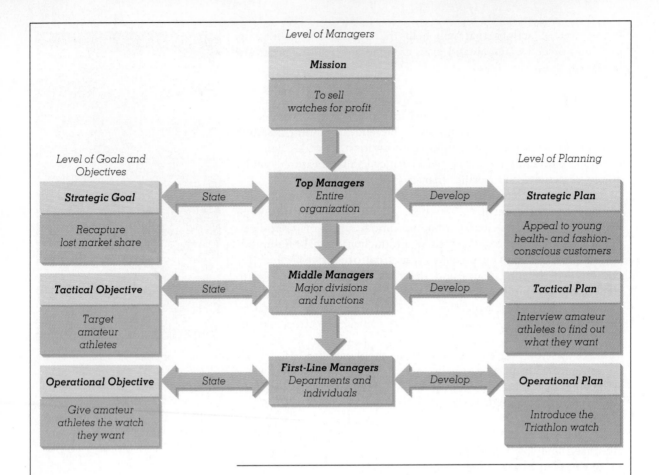

Level of Managers

Mission
To sell
watches for profit

Level of Goals and Objectives

Level of Planning

Strategic Goal
Recapture
lost market share

State ← **Top Managers** Entire organization → Develop

Strategic Plan
Appeal to young
health- and fashion-
conscious customers

Tactical Objective
Target
amateur
athletes

State ← **Middle Managers** Major divisions and functions → Develop

Tactical Plan
Interview amateur
athletes to find out
what they want

Operational Objective
Give amateur
athletes the watch
they want

State ← **First-Line Managers** Departments and individuals → Develop

Operational Plan
Introduce the
Triathlon watch

Exhibit 6.2
Managerial Planning at Timex
When managers at Timex responded to competition from companies such as Swatch, they set clear goals and objectives and then carefully developed plans to achieve them. The result was the Triathlon watch, offering sport-chic style as well as the ability to time activities such as swimming, biking, and running.

organizing *Process of arranging resources to carry out the organization's plans*

wanted, and the operational plan was to introduce a watch that could clock swimming, biking, and running: the Triathlon watch. The company was so successful with the Triathlon watch that it developed watches for skiers, aerobics enthusiasts, sailors, and fishers. Clearly, Timex's goals and planning contributed to the overwhelming success of its sport-chic watches.[19] Exhibit 6.2 shows the relationship among the three levels of management, the goals and objectives set by each level, and the plans developed by each level.

The Organizing Function

Like the planning function, the organizing function requires that a manager have strong conceptual skills. **Organizing** is the process of arranging resources to carry out the organization's plans. At this stage, managers think through all the activities that employees carry out—from programming the organization's computers and driving its trucks to mailing its letters—and all the facilities and equipment that employees need to complete those tasks. They also give other people the ability to work toward organizational goals by determining who should have the authority to make decisions, to perform or supervise activities, and to distribute resources.

A major problem managers face in organizing is figuring out the specific jobs needed to achieve the company's goals and objectives and then **staffing** the jobs, or selecting people who can do what must be done. Determining how to reward employees, how to help them develop their skills, and how to evaluate their work performance is also part of this function.

staffing Process of matching the right people with the right jobs

More and more companies are replacing individuals with teams as the building blocks of organizations. A **team** is two or more people working together to achieve a specific objective. Teams may be formed at any level of the organization. They may be formal and permanent (established as part of the regular structure), they may be informal and temporary (created to increase employee participation in a specific project), or they may be anything in between, depending on each organization's unique situation.

team Two or more people working together to achieve a specific objective

Teams are a powerful management tool: They directly involve employees in decision making, which increases the power of employees in the organization and improves the flow of information between employees and managers. Thus teams appear to increase employee satisfaction, organizational productivity, and product quality. In addition, the broadening of employee tasks makes the organization more flexible.[20] Some authorities point to the success of organizations based on team spirit rather than on the ingenuity of one top executive, believing teams should be valued more than maverick geniuses.[21]

Generally, top managers establish the structure for the organization as a whole, and they select the people who fill the upper-level positions. Middle managers have similar responsibilities, but usually for just one division or unit. First-line managers seldom set up organizational structure, but they typically play an important role in the organizing function by hiring and training operational employees.

This formal team at Rockwell International works together to find ways of improving production and quality.

Organizing is particularly challenging because any organization is likely to undergo constant change. Longtime employees leave, and new employees arrive. Equipment breaks down or becomes obsolete, and replacements are needed. The public's tastes and interests change, and the organization has to reevaluate its plans and activities. Shifting political and economic trends can lead to employee cutbacks—or perhaps expansion. Every month (perhaps every week), the organization faces new situations, and so management's organizing tasks are never finished.

The Leading Function

Into the positions and relationships determined by the organizing process come individuals from differing backgrounds, each with unique interests, ambitions, and personal goals. To meld all the people in the organization into a productive work team, the manager applies the third major management function, **leading,** the process of influencing and motivating people to work effectively and willingly

leading Process of influencing and motivating people to work toward organizational goals

When Japanese automakers decided to build automobile manufacturing plants in the United States, they knew they'd have to build a new kind of team approach as well. Although the Japanese carmakers used advanced manufacturing technology to build quality cars, their real edge over U.S. automakers came from the way the people who built the cars worked together. So the managers at Honda, Nissan, Mazda, and Toyota sought to recreate their team success when they opened U.S. plants.

The team production process planned for these Japanese-owned plants required close cooperation between employees and managers, a dramatic departure from the less cooperative relationship between labor and management in many U.S.-owned plants. To encourage closer relations in the Japanese-owned plants, the managers and employees shared the same dining facilities and often wore the same company-owned uniforms. Activities like Toyota's "personal touch" program,

IMPORTING JAPANESE TEAMWORK

which subsidizes after-hours socializing between Japanese and U.S. employees, helped bring together people on all levels.

Some aspects of the Japanese team approach had to be modified to be more acceptable to U.S. employees. At Nissan's U.S. plants, for example, employees do not have to wear the company uniform. Although all Nissan employees in Japan participate in morning exercises, this program has been dropped from the U.S. plants' schedules. At the same time, key elements of the Japanese team approach have not been changed. Managers in the Japanese-owned plants consult

with the people on the assembly line when considering production issues, and employees have a say in other plant processes as well.

More than 10 Japanese-owned plants are located in what is called "Japan's Auto Alley," a stretch from Michigan to Tennessee with a combined manufacturing capacity of over 2 million vehicles a year. Since the first Honda facility opened in Marysville, Ohio, the benefits of the transplanted team approach have been evident: The quality of the Hondas made in the United States rivals—or exceeds—the quality of the same models built in Japan. However, the real sign of the success of the Japanese approach to teamwork can be seen in auto plants owned by Chrysler and other U.S. carmakers. Many of these plants have restructured their assembly processes to resemble the Japanese system, and about one-third of the unionized employees working in the restructured plants now belong to some type of team.

---

motivating Giving employees a reason to do the job and to perform at their peak

leadership Skill of persuading others to achieve organizational goals by showing how things are done and by setting an example in behavior and spirit

transactional leadership Traditional view of management involving motivating employees to perform at expected levels, structuring employee roles and tasks, and linking rewards with goal achievement

toward company goals. Like the other management functions, leading requires strong human relations skills.

Effective managers are good at **motivating,** giving employees a reason to do the job and to put forth their best performance (see Chapter 9). They also demonstrate **leadership,** the ability to influence the attitudes and actions of others both through the demonstration of specific tasks and through the manager's own behavior and spirit. The combination of motivating employees and showing leadership is often called *directing*.

Leadership Traits

When early researchers studied leadership, they looked for specific characteristics, or *traits,* common to all good leaders. At the time, they were unable to prove any link between particular traits and leadership ability. However, later research found that leaders who have specific traits, such as decisiveness and self-confidence, are likely to be more effective.[22]

Leadership has traditionally been viewed as (1) motivating employees to perform at *expected* levels, (2) providing the structure necessary to clarify employee tasks and activities, and (3) linking employee self-interest—through rewards—with goal achievement. This traditional view is called **transactional leadership.** However, organizations also need leaders who can motivate employees to perform *better than expected*, inspire employees to look *beyond* their own self-interest, and spur employees to work toward an exciting but challenging future vision. This second view is called **transformational leadership,** and it requires managers who can demonstrate charisma and consideration for employees.[23]

To be an effective manager, you need both transactional and transformational leadership skills.[24] Consider the leadership of Joan T. Bok as head of the New England Electric System in Massachusetts. Bok worked her way up to chairperson by using her transactional leadership skills (to guide employees in meeting everyday customer needs) and her transformational leadership skills (to inspire employees to work toward a future of increased environmental awareness and diverse energy sources). "I like being innovative, thinking about tomorrow's world," says Bok. "When you do that, a different wisdom comes into decision making."[25]

transformational leadership Beyond the traditional view of management, involving motivating performance above expected levels, inspiring employee concern for broader issues, and spurring employees to work toward a challenging future vision

Leadership Styles

Leadership style is the way authority is used by a manager to lead others. Every manager, from the baseball manager to the university chancellor, has a definite style. The three broad categories of leadership style are autocratic, democratic, and laissez-faire:

- *The autocratic style.* **Autocratic leaders** make decisions without consulting others. This style can be highly effective when quick decisions are critical, but only when the leader can enforce those decisions. However, critics of the autocratic style maintain that these managers could be more objective, could motivate employees better, and could be more open to the ideas of others. This style was popular for many years and is still favored by some managers.

autocratic leaders Managers who do not involve others in decision making

- *The democratic style.* **Democratic leaders** delegate authority and involve employees in decision making. Although they welcome employee participation and open communication, they are responsible for the final decision. Democratic leaders provide relatively little supervision and are most effective when managing highly skilled professionals. Although decision making can be slow, and the leader may end up having little control over employees, democratic leadership is increasingly popular.[26] For example, Semco used democratic leadership to get its employees more involved in company decisions. This approach helped Semco become Brazil's largest manufacturer of marine and food-processing machinery.[27]

democratic leaders Managers who delegate authority and involve employees in decision making

- *The laissez-faire style.* The French term *laissez faire* can be translated as "leave it alone," or, more roughly, as "hands off." **Laissez-faire leaders** take the role of consultant, encouraging employees' ideas and offering insights or opinions when asked. However, the laissez-faire style may fail if the group pursues goals that do not match the organization's. Today this approach has been adapted to self-leadership and employee empowerment.

laissez-faire leaders Managers who lead by taking the role of consultant, leaving the actual decision making up to employees

According to Ronald Pilenzo, president of the Society for Human Resource Management, the move toward more democratic and laissez-faire styles is occurring because "workers of today are different. They have more education, are more self-directed or want to be, and want to control their working conditions. This requires a more participatory or nondirective approach for the manager who wants to get results."[28] As Microsoft's Bill Gates knows, no one leadership style works every time. Think of leadership styles as existing along a continuum (a range) of possible leadership behaviors, as suggested by Exhibit 6.3.

Approaches to Management

One manager may use all three leadership styles, but at different times. In fact, each situation may call for a different style. The best approach depends on the leader's personality, the employees' skills and backgrounds, and the problems that the company is facing at any particular moment. A number of contingencies (possible events) may cause the situation to change. For example, the firm may start making new products, or it may face new competition. Adapting management principles to current business circumstances is called **contingency leadership** (or *situational management*).

A company that has a regular system for involving its employees in decision making is using **participative management.** In contrast to individual leadership styles, participative management is an overall approach adopted by the organization. It has been widely and successfully used in Japan, and some U.S. companies have practiced it for many years.

Many companies see the participative approach to management as an important tool. Participative management works when employees have knowledge and experience that can make a positive contribution to the decision-making process. The success of participative management depends on managers who are willing to involve others and lead them in productive meetings and group problem-solving sessions. Although participative management does improve human relations, its major value is in improving productivity and quality while reducing costs.[29]

For example, Max De Pree, chairman of Herman Miller, believes in participative management. Every employee of the business-furniture manufacturer is well informed about the company's suc-

contingency leadership *Leadership style promoting the flexibility to adopt the style most appropriate to current business conditions; also called* situational management

participative management *System for involving employees in a company's decision making*

Exhibit 6.3
Continuum of Leadership Behavior
Leadership style is a continuum, ranging from boss-centered to employee-centered. Situations that require managers to exercise greater authority fall toward the boss-centered end of the continuum. Other situations call for a manager to give workers leeway to function more independently.

Boss-centered Leadership						Employee-centered Leadership
Use of authority by the manager						Area of freedom for workers
Manager makes decision, announces it.	Manager "sells" decision.	Manager presents ideas, invites questions.	Manager presents tentative decision subject to change.	Manager presents problems, gets suggestions, makes decisions.	Manager defines limits, asks group to make decision.	Manager permits workers to function within defined limits.

cesses and problems—from factory employees to the chairman himself. The company stresses open communication, and employees are able to go straight to the top with complaints and ideas. All employees participate in company profits, and all are appraised quarterly. Thanks to participative management, Herman Miller enjoys low absenteeism, low turnover, reduced costs, and solid profits.[30]

The Contolling Function

In management, **controlling** means monitoring progress toward organizational goals, resetting the course (if goals or objectives change in response to shifting conditions), and correcting deviations (if goals or objectives are not being attained). Managers use their technical skills for the controlling function, comparing where they are with where they should be. If everything is operating smoothly, controls permit managers to repeat acceptable performance. If results are below expectations, controls help managers take any necessary action.

controlling Process of measuring progress against goals and objectives and correcting deviations if results are not as expected

The controlling function is important for **total quality management (TQM),** a comprehensive approach that involves building quality into every organizational process as a way of improving customer satisfaction. Also known as *total quality control,* TQM requires that every person at every level accept responsibility for meeting quality standards. In the past, many companies inspected finished products and reworked or discarded items that didn't meet quality standards. Today many firms use planning to set quality goals for every department, use controlling to check progress toward quality goals, and then use the results to set standards for continuous quality improvement. For example, Toyota sets standards for every aspect of its business, from guaranteeing damage-free delivery and improving dealer sales and service to designing and producing better cars and accessories. The carmaker uses a quality audit to determine where quality falls below preset standards, and it offers quality counseling to help determine solutions.[31]

total quality management (TQM) Comprehensive management approach that builds quality into every organizational process as a way of improving customer satisfaction; also called total quality control

Controlling is strongly tied to the planning function. Managers get information about results through reports from employees as well as from outside sources. Then they compare the results with the goals and objectives that were set during planning. When necessary, they take corrective action by changing plans, reorganizing, or redirecting efforts. Using a continuous control process, managers can spot and correct problems before they become more serious.

The Control Cycle

Controlling is a continuous four-step cycle that involves all levels of management (see Exhibit 6.4). In the first step, top managers set **standards,** criteria for measuring the performance of the organization as a whole. Control standards must be linked to strategic goals, or the company may end up controlling the wrong tasks. Examples of specific standards include the following:

standards Criteria against which performance may be measured

- Increase the profit margin from 17 percent to 20 percent.
- Produce 1,500 circuit boards monthly with fewer than 1 percent failures.
- Make 20 sales calls each week.

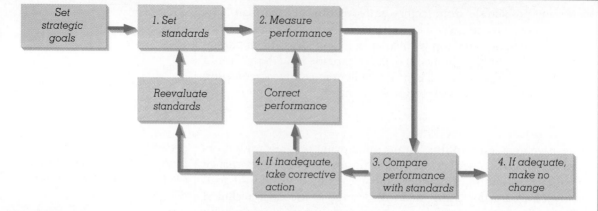

Exhibit 6.4
The Control Cycle
The control cycle has four basic steps: (1) based on strategic goals, top managers set the standards by which the organization's overall performance will be measured; (2) managers at all levels measure performance; (3) actual performance is compared with the standards; (4) appropriate corrective action is taken (if performance meets standards, nothing other than encouragement is needed; if performance falls below standards, corrective action may include improving performance, establishing new standards, changing plans, reorganizing, or redirecting efforts).

management by objectives (MBO)
Control method in which managers are motivated to achieve results by the opportunity to structure personal objectives and make plans that mesh with the organization's goals

Consider how founder James E. Casey built six messengers and two bicycles into the giant United Parcel Service by setting standards. Excellent customer service was his goal, and he set strict performance standards for his delivery people. Some of the 138 standards involve emotional stability and neat appearance. Also, drivers are not to scuffle, splash pedestrians with mud, or drive on people's lawns.[32]

In the second step of the control cycle, managers assess performance, using both quantitative (specific, numerical) and qualitative (subjective) performance measures. In the third step, managers compare performance with the established standards and search for the cause of any discrepancies. If the performance meets the standards, the fourth step is to make no changes. However, if the performance falls short, the fourth step is to take corrective action, which may be done by adjusting performance or by reevaluating standards.

Management by Objectives

Another well-known method of controlling performance is **management by objectives (MBO),** a technique that motivates managers to achieve results by offering the opportunity to establish personal objectives and plans that mesh with the organization's strategic goals. Because managers collaborate in setting goals and plans, they are motivated to work hard toward achieving the goals. An MBO program has four phases (see Exhibit 6.5):

1. The organization's strategic goals are clearly communicated to everyone. These goals are set by top managers, who consult with middle managers.
2. Middle managers meet with first-line managers (and sometimes nonmanagers) to agree on personal objectives. Each first-line manager writes an individual plan of action geared to achieving these personal goals, which in turn support the organization's strategic goals.
3. First-line managers meet periodically with middle managers to discuss progress toward meeting the personal objectives that have been set. If goals are not being met, the plans (or objectives) may be changed.
4. Managers at every level meet annually, semiannually, or quarterly with their supervisors to judge whether personal goals are being

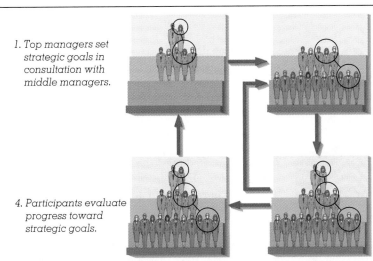

1. Top managers set strategic goals in consultation with middle managers.

2. Middle managers and supervisory managers set objectives.

3. Participants meet with middle managers to discuss progress toward objectives.

4. Participants evaluate progress toward strategic goals.

Exhibit 6.5
Management by Objectives
The MBO system has four phases. This cycle is refined and repeated as managers at all levels try to mesh personal work goals with the organization's objectives.

met. This cycle of setting and refining goals and plans keeps the organization on track toward its strategic goals.

Xerox and many other companies use the MBO process, which is most effective when top management is actively involved. Also, the program has more chance of success when managers participate in setting goals rather than being assigned goals. In addition, personal goals that are specific and able to be objectively measured help avoid any bias. Moreover, effective companies try to minimize MBO paperwork because a blizzard of forms can discourage participants.[33]

CRISIS MANAGEMENT

The most important goal of any business is to survive, but any number of problems may arise, some threatening the very existence of the company. An ugly fight for control of a company, a product failure, a breakdown in routine operations (as a result of fire, for example), or an environmental accident—any surprising event may develop into a serious and crippling crisis. Managers can help determine their company's future through **crisis management,** the handling of such unusual and serious problems. For example, experts hailed the way Johnson & Johnson coped with two Tylenol poisoning scares. The company moved quickly to remove capsules from stores and to publicize the first problem. As a result, the effects of that scare had been almost completely overcome by the time of the second incident.

Speedy, open communication can make all the difference. Top managers of the Jack in the Box hamburger chain took many of the right steps after a food-poisoning problem that sickened hundreds of customers in three Western states: The chain threw away 20,000 pounds of hamburger meat, changed meat suppliers, publicized a toll-free telephone number for customer complaints, and changed cooking procedures. However, initial statements by top managers denied responsibility for the problem and criticized the chain's meat supplier.

crisis management System for minimizing the harm that might result from some unusually threatening situations

Moreover, two weeks passed before Jack in the Box offered to pay the hospital costs of stricken customers. Although the company began an apologetic ad campaign only days after the problem was uncovered, the damage was done, and many nervous customers took their business elsewhere.[34]

Companies that experience a crisis for which they are ill prepared appear to make a series of similar mistakes. First, warnings about possible problems are ignored at one or more management levels. Then when the crisis hits, the company does the worst thing it could do: It denies the severity of the problem, or it denies its own role in the problem. Finally, when the company is forced to face reality, it takes hasty, poorly conceived action.

A better approach is to prepare for a crisis before it occurs. Experts stress that the first 24 hours of a crisis are critical. The first move is to determine the extent of the problem and then communicate truthfully with the public and with the company's employees. Simultaneously, pull the offending product from store shelves, stop the offending action, or bring the source of the problem (whatever it is) under control to the extent possible.

Responding to a crisis is much easier when management has prepared for problems by actively looking for signs of a disaster in the making.[35] Many farsighted companies have set up crisis teams composed of people who respond well under stress. These teams identify where their companies are most vulnerable, studying past mistakes committed by their own companies and by others. Next, they prepare **contingency plans,** actions the company can take to cope with unexpected or unpredictable events. Created with the company's strategic goals in mind, these plans outline steps that can prevent or counter the most serious threats and help the company recover quickly.[36]

After a flood that ruined $500,000 worth of merchandise, Christine Bierman, president of Colt Safety, developed plans for preventing similar disasters. One plan called for stacking boxes on shelves that are 36 inches above the floor.

contingency plans *Actions the company can take to cope with unforeseen events*

The best-prepared companies hold drills, simulating crisis conditions. During the Los Angeles riots that followed a jury acquittal of four police officers in the beating of Rodney King, Arco's crisis team knew what to do for their 132 stations in the area because procedures had been spelled out in the company's crisis management plan. Although developed for disasters such as refinery fires, gas explosions, and earthquakes, the plan was methodically executed by Arco's crisis team, effectively controlling the extent of damage, injury, and loss of life.[37]

1 Discuss the three categories of managerial roles.

A manager's roles fall into three categories. Interpersonal roles include dealing with people as figurehead, leader, and liaison. Informational roles include handling information as monitor, disseminator, and spokesperson. Decisional roles include analyzing and making choices as entrepreneur, disturbance handler, resource allocator, and negotiator.

2 Describe the three levels of management.

Top managers take overall responsibility for the organization. Middle managers have the task of implementing the broad goals set by top management as well as coordinating the work of first-line managers. First-line managers supervise the work of operating employees.

3 Distinguish between the three types of managerial skills.

Managers make use of technical skills, including administrative skills, which involve having the knowledge and the ability to perform a specific job; human relations skills, including communication, which involve understanding other people and working effectively with them; and conceptual skills, including decision making, which involve the ability to see the organization as a whole and to understand the relationships among its parts.

4 List the four steps in the management process.

The four steps in the management process are planning, organizing, leading, and controlling.

5 Discuss how strategic, tactical, and operational plans are developed and used.

Strategic plans usually cover two to five years and are designed by top managers to achieve strategic goals. Tactical plans are then laid out to achieve tactical objectives and to support strategic plans. They are usually made for one to three years by middle managers, who consult with first-line managers before reporting to top management. Operational plans are laid out to achieve operational objectives and to support tactical plans. They cover a period of less than one year and are designed by first-line managers, who consult with middle managers.

6 Cite three leadership styles, and explain why no one style is best.

Three leadership styles are autocratic, democratic, and laissez-faire. Each may be best in a different situation: authoritative when quick decisions are needed, democratic when employee participation in decision making is desirable, and laissez-faire when fostering creativity is a priority. Leaders should be flexible enough to respond with the best approach for the situation.

7 Identify the four steps in the control cycle.

The control cycle consists of (1) setting standards based on the strategic goals of the organization, (2) measuring performance, (3) comparing actual performance with established standards, and (4) taking corrective action if necessary (providing encouragement if performance meets standards, correcting performance if performance falls short of standards, or reevaluating standards if they exceed acceptable performance).

8 List five measures that companies can take to better manage crises.

During a crisis, an organization should (1) move quickly to explain the problem to the public and to the company's employees and (2) control the source of the problem to the extent possible. Before the crisis occurs, the company may (3) set up a crisis team of people who react well under stress, (4) prepare contingency plans to deal with the most serious threats, and (5) hold drills under simulated crisis conditions.

As projects slipped behind schedule and competitors stepped up their attacks, Microsoft chief executive officer Bill Gates knew he had to take himself out of day-to-day operations. Microsoft had great ideas, but it was failing to plan and implement effectively. Now the company's reputation was on the line.

So Gates got help. He turned over daily operations to a three-person office of the president, which freed Gates for more creative work: envisioning products for the twenty-first century and planning for the company's long-term future. Then he reorganized the company into three major groups: products, sales and support, and operations. This new organization was designed to increase the company's efficiency and its responsiveness to customer needs. However, Gates didn't want to lose the entrepreneurial spirit that characterized the company's early years. The organization structure was planned around small, self-sufficient working groups that encouraged individual employees to feel greater responsibility for their work.

Even though Gates could now effectively lead his managers, he was still concerned that his growing staff might lose touch with him and his strategic goals. He didn't have to look far for the solution: Microsoft established an electronic network that soon linked 12,000 employees across 27 countries. This network includes an electronic-mail system that lets virtually any employee communicate directly with the CEO. Dozens do daily, and Gates tries to respond the same day he receives a message. Employees feel they have direct access to the top. They say Gates's messages are blunt and sometimes sarcastic — but always entertaining. By staying in touch with every level and every employee at Microsoft, Gates ensures that his vision is acknowledged and understood by everyone at Microsoft.

Gates's vision and drive have helped Microsoft achieve a commanding lead in the race for market share. As many as 85 percent of all personal computers now run on Microsoft operating programs. Moreover, Gates is boldly moving the company into new frontiers. One promising area is the office of the future, in which equipment such as computers, copiers, printers, and fax machines would be linked together to more efficiently create and move documents. Gates is also looking at ways of marrying the computer and the television set to create a combination entertainment-information device. Although Microsoft's future growth will not be as explosive as it was in the early years, Gates knows that effective management on all levels is what will keep the company on top.

Your Mission: You work in the Microsoft unit that's developing complex software to let companies tie all their computers together into one network. Although you started as a programmer, you have been a manager for several years and are no longer an expert on the latest technical developments. In the following situations, choose the best responses.

1. You're nearing a critical deadline and an employee keeps missing his objectives. He promises to do too much and then winds up pleading for more time and resources. He's a recent college graduate with lots of theory but little practical experience. How do you react?

a. You have already sent a memo stressing the importance of deadlines. You should privately reprimand this employee and inspire better performance.

b. The employee clearly has enthusiasm and technical skills but may lack the conceptual skills needed in this situation. You can help by talking with him and sharing your experience and perspective.

c. Ask the employee to explain the hours and resources he spent on the project as well as the methods he used. Then have him pinpoint his least effective and least efficient areas so that he can work on his problems.

2. Gates has just left a meeting with your programmers and seems more agitated than usual. During the meeting, one programmer flipped a football, another nonchalantly paged through a magazine, and a third directly answered the CEO's criticism with little show of respect. In response, Gates called parts of one program "stupid." You're already behind schedule, and you don't need the CEO breathing down your neck. What should you do?

a. You were intimidated at the meeting because you didn't understand all the technical talk. Put in some time studying programming again so that you can follow the technical discussion and be able to defend your people.

b. Try to persuade Gates to go through you instead of going straight to your programmers. This approach would give you more control.

c. Gates encourages employees to speak up, and so should you. Talk with your programmers about what they thought of the meeting.

3. Your boss wants you to speak to a magazine reporter about a program your group is developing. You know you'll be asked about product development delays in your department. What is your single best response?

a. Don't deny that you've put extra time into your product, but explain that the company has broadened its focus from new-product innovation to include a total quality approach.

b. You have the information the reporter needs, so you are in charge of the interview. Prepare statements that promote your products. Avoid answering questions that are embarrassing.

c. Develop a friendly relationship with the reporter so that he or she will see things from a favorable point of view. Suggest that you meet for lunch, and be sure to pay the bill. Try to avoid talking about specifics.

4. You have been asked to set up a computer-networking program for company headquarters. The program your group is working on isn't complete. Other companies also offer such software, and you might use products from several companies to create the system. You don't want to embarrass yourself—and perhaps the whole company—by installing a system that doesn't work well or by relying on a rival company's software. What's your best response?

a. Your job is to install a networking program, so do it. Use the best available resources, and if Microsoft can provide part of the system, so much the better.

b. Put off installing the networking program until after you can complete the software your department is developing.

c. Announce that you'll use your own software; then tell your programmers to drop everything else until they've perfected the new program. If you succeed, everyone will be a winner.[38]

KEY TERMS

administrative skills (158)
autocratic leaders (167)
communication (159)
communication media (159)
conceptual skills (160)
contingency leadership (168)
contingency plans (172)
controlling (169)
crisis management (171)
decision making (160)
democratic leaders (167)
first-line managers (157)
goal (162)
hierarchy (156)
human relations skills (158)

laissez-faire leaders (167)
leadership (166)
leading (165)
management (156)
management by objectives (MBO) (170)
middle managers (157)
mission (162)
mission statement (162)
motivating (166)
objective (162)
operational objectives (163)
operational plans (163)
organizing (164)
participative management (168)
plan (162)

planning (162)
roles (156)
staffing (165)
standards (169)
strategic goals (162)
strategic plans (163)
tactical objectives (163)
tactical plans (163)
team (165)
technical skills (158)
top managers (156)
total quality management (TQM) (169)
transactional leadership (166)
transformational leadership (167)

REVIEW QUESTIONS

1. What is management? Why is it so important?
2. Why are human relations skills important to managers at all levels?
3. Why do managers need good communication skills?

4. What are the elements of decision making?
5. How do goals and objectives differ?
6. What does the control cycle do for businesses?

7. How does transactional leadership differ from transformational leadership?
8. What is the goal of crisis management?

A CASE FOR CRITICAL THINKING

NEW MANAGEMENT TECHNIQUES FOR ELECTRIFYING PERFORMANCE AT GE

Aircraft engines, major appliances, broadcasting, financial services, medical systems—in these areas and many others, General Electric businesses held first or second place in worldwide market share. The huge firm employed more than 200,000 people, and its revenues topped $50 billion. Some units were struggling, but overall profits rose year after year. In short, GE looked for all the world like a highly successful business.

Even so, despite GE's achievements, chief executive officer John F. (Jack) Welch, Jr., believed that a new management approach was needed. For years, managers had simply handed down orders without inviting employee comment. As long as company goals were met, such autocratic methods weren't questioned, even when they discouraged employees from contributing their ideas. Looking at the challenges ahead, Welch reasoned that continuing GE's success into the twenty-first century would require the creativity and the talents of every person who worked at GE—managers and employees alike.

However, moving toward participative management would require a major change in the company's management style. Instead of giving orders, GE managers would have to be more democratic. They would need to learn how to coach and how to energize their employees. Moreover, to tap the ideas of people from the top to the bottom of the company, the managers would also have to find ways of including employees in the decision-making process at every level.

As Welch thought about what the GE of the future would look like, he decided to encourage, in his own words, "speed, simplicity, and self-confidence" and to give every person in every department "the freedom to be creative." He felt that the way to improve productivity was by "getting people involved and excited about their jobs." At the same time, he realized that this approach would fail if GE employees didn't change their thinking.

Some employees had become so used to the autocratic management style of the past that they lacked the self-confidence to speak up or to question their managers. Others had simply stopped offering ideas when they saw that their managers didn't react well to employee initiative. In Welch's eyes, GE employees needed more fire and zest to propel GE toward higher revenues, productivity, and profits.

To encourage a more productive employee-management relationship, Welch introduced the Workout program. Several times a year, the heads of each GE facility meet with up to 100 people drawn from various levels and functions. The facility's top manager outlines several challenges to be addressed, and the group works on its own to develop plans for meeting those challenges. Although the top manager must approve all ideas before they are implemented, most are innovative and cost-efficient, and few ideas are rejected.

Welch also encouraged employees to question any unnecessary practices that might hold the company back from peak performance. By challenging their bosses, employees are able to expose and clear away outdated methods of doing things. In addition, encouraging employees to speak up and be heard increases the employees' self-confidence.

Finally, Welch provided extensive leadership training to help GE managers learn and practice new leadership skills and approaches. He also changed the standards by which managers are evaluated, to reflect the new emphasis. Promotions now go to managers who achieve company goals by sharing ideas with and from employees, by having the self-confidence to delegate work, by being honest in their communications, and by making and implementing decisions more quickly. Managers who achieve company goals by forcing performance out of their employees are not promoted.

Transforming GE managers into more participative leaders has not been an overnight process. Still, Welch is already reporting a change in spirit among people at all levels, and he sees a significant rise in productivity as well. Armed with this new management style—and renewed employee enthusiasm—GE is well positioned to meet coming challenges.

1. How does the Workout program encourage a nondirective management approach?
2. Do you think GE's increasingly participative management style is responsible for its continued growth? Why or why not?
3. Is Welch's leadership style transactional or transformational? Explain your answer.

GARY DAVID GOLDBERG: FROM CAVEMAN TO LEADING-EDGE MANAGER

Synopsis

The list of successful Hollywood executives who lived for a time in a cave is probably rather short, but at the top of that list you would surely find Gary David Goldberg. This video chronicles his days from a care-free cave dweller in Greece to his current role as the head of Ubu Productions, creator and producer of some of the most successful television shows on the air. It provides a backstage look at the creation and shooting of "Family Ties," a phenomenally successful show that now reaps riches in syndication. However, the video is more than an insider's look at a TV program. It also explains Goldberg's management philosophies and practices, from sharing the enormous wealth his shows generate to insisting that his employees be given an on-site day-care center so that they can more easily balance the demands of work and family life.

Exercises

ANALYSIS

1. Which managerial skills did you see Goldberg using?

2. For the production of a TV show, which set of skills is most important? Explain your answer.

3. Would Goldberg be an effective CEO of a major corporation, such as IBM or Toyota?

4. How would you describe Goldberg's leadership style?

5. Explain how management by objectives (MBO) could be used to produce a TV show.

APPLICATION

How might a manager in a less glamorous business, such as a steel mill, apply Goldberg's creative, share-the-wealth management style?

DECISION

Assume that in a last-minute script-tuning session with his writers, Goldberg finds himself in disagreement with the entire staff regarding a scene change. He thinks the group's idea is out of character with the show's established tone, but he doesn't want to cause long-term friction by overriding their decisions. If you were in his shoes, what would you do?

COMMUNICATION

Just as many employees need day care for their children, some need care facilities for elderly relatives. Assume Ubu wants to add an elder-care facility; write a one-page memo to Paramount's chief financial officer, explaining why the facility is needed.

INTEGRATION

Chapter 1 identifies three general types of competition. Which of these apply to the products created by Ubu Productions? Who are Ubu's competitors?

ETHICS

Goldberg seems to exhibit little tolerance for employees who can't or won't perform up to his expectations. Is this really fair in all cases? After all, people have different levels of intelligence and experience.

DEBATE

Assume that other managers in the entertainment business are pressuring Goldberg to stop paying his people so much, saying that not all shows are as profitable as his, so not all production companies can afford the salary increases that usually occur at Ubu. Option A: In a formal debate format, take either Goldberg's position or the position of one of the managers pressuring him to stop paying so much. Option B: Take either position and state your case in a brief report.

TEAMWORK

In a team of five or six students, outline an episode of a currently popular TV show. When you're finished, share with the class how your team handled the four managerial functions of planning, directing, organizing, and controlling.

RESEARCH

Do the research necessary to write one paragraph on either (a) how Goldberg and Ubu are doing these days or (b) how much money "Family Ties" currently makes in syndication.

ROLE PLAYING

One student plays Goldberg, a second plays an actor, and a third plays a writer. The actor refuses to do a scene created by the writer, saying that it is embarrassing. Goldberg needs to mediate the dispute and get the team working together again.

Chapter

7

Organizing for Business

From IBM to Independence

How do you build a new, independent organization after years of control by a gigantic, global parent? That was the challenge facing top executives at Lexmark International. The original factory in Lexington, Kentucky, was a division of IBM, manufacturing electric typewriters renowned for their durability and useful features. In later years, after IBM introduced the personal computer, the division also made keyboards and printers. Then IBM decided to get out of the typewriter and printer business. An investment firm bought the division in 1991, along with the right to use the IBM name on its products until 1996.

The new company was called Lexmark, a name formed by combining *lex* (derived from *lexicon,* a dictionary or a particular vocabulary) and *mark* (from the idea of making a mark on paper, like a printer). Marvin L. Mann, a 32-year veteran of IBM, was appointed CEO. In turn, he recruited other IBM executives to head production, research and development, human resources, and sales and marketing. Together, they were responsible for planning the transition from operating as one of many IBM divisions to operating as an independent company making $1.8 billion in sales to customers all over the world.

Lexmark started life with more than 5,000 employees but soon slimmed down to 4,100 by offering payouts to people who agreed to leave the company voluntarily. The company inherited a well-trained and motivated workforce from parent IBM, and it shared IBM's commitment to high quality and strict ethical standards. However, Mann wanted some things at Lexmark to be different from the way they were under IBM. He was concerned that the new company would have a hard time putting creative ideas in motion if employees on the shop floor had to go through layers of management to talk with decision makers at the top. He also wanted to speed up decision making by avoiding the delays IBM experienced when managers from different departments challenged each other's proposals. Finally, he wanted Lexmark employees to risk trying new things without fearing that they would be punished for failures.

Lexmark has transformed itself from a typewriter manufacturer to a computer printer manufacturer

organization *Group of people whose interactions are structured into goal-directed activities*

organization structure *Formal patterns designed by managers to define work tasks and individual jobs, to establish reporting relationships, and to coordinate all organizational tasks*

organization chart *Diagram showing how employees and tasks are grouped and where the lines of communication and authority flow*

Exhibit 7.1
Organization Chart for a Large Consumer-Products Company
At first glance, organization charts may look very similar. In fact, the traditional model of an organization is a triangle or pyramid in which numerous boxes form the base and lead up to fewer and fewer boxes on higher levels, ultimately arriving at one box at the top. A glance at a company's organization chart reveals who has authority over whom, who is responsible for whose work, and who is accountable to whom.

Mann and his management team were well aware that these changes wouldn't be easy—altering the way employees work together and even modifying the way ideas flow upward and downward. If the new company was to thrive on its own, managers and employees alike would have to forget the IBM way and build an entirely new organization. How could Mann set up a structure that would unleash his employees' creativity and entrepreneurial spirit? In what way could he arrange work tasks to manufacture printers more efficiently? How could he streamline Lexmark to allow the company to respond quickly to changes in customer needs and shifts in competitive pressures?[1]

DEFINING ORGANIZATION STRUCTURE

As Marvin Mann knows well, a company's strategy is supported by its organization. Whereas strategic planning defines *what* a company will do, organization structure defines *how* a company's tasks are divided and *how* its resources are deployed. An **organization** is a group of people whose activities and interactions are structured into goal-directed activities. Whether their activity is playing a sport to win or producing computers to sell, group members work together to achieve the organization's goals.

Organization structure results from the formal patterns designed by managers as they (1) define work tasks and individual jobs, (2) establish reporting relationships, and (3) coordinate all tasks so that the organization can achieve its overall goals. To define an organization's structure, managers use a diagram known as an **organization chart,** which shows the way employees and tasks are grouped and how the lines of communication and authority flow (see Exhibit 7.1).

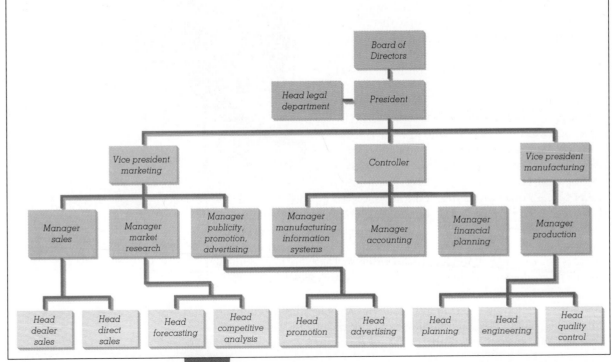

Organization structure is important because it lets employees know where and how they fit into an organization, enabling them to work together toward company goals and to feel satisfied with their contributions to the organization. Structure is also the only way to turn strategic plans into action. Without some kind of structure, managers would be unable to coordinate the organization's work, and the best-laid plans would never be carried out. Like Lexmark, companies around the world are realizing that sound organization structure can be a true competitive advantage.[2]

Consider Glenn and Leonard Wood's small but successful business, Wood Brothers' Race Shop, in Stuart, Virginia. The company is home for three Thunderbirds that are used to race (at over 200 miles per hour) on the professional stock-car circuit. The Wood brothers have been producing championship racing cars since 1950, and that kind of success doesn't happen by chance. In part, such an accomplishment comes from technical skill and mechanical know-how. It also comes from good organization.

In the organization Glenn designed, his younger brother Leonard serves as chief mechanic. Under Leonard's direction, Glenn's sons Eddie and Len regularly take the cars apart and rebuild them from the inside out; then Leonard fine-tunes things until he's satisfied. Eddie is also responsible for sealing and smoothing the cars' sheet-metal exteriors (after Leonard has gone over every inch in his never-ending battle to reduce wind resistance). Len works with Leonard on the engines, once they've been built or rebuilt to Leonard's precise specifications by Tommy Turner (who lives in a town nearby). Kim Wood, Glenn's daughter, keeps the company's books.

When explaining the success of his shop, Glenn Wood says, "There's no secret. Everybody always does the best they can."[3] In reality, Glenn's too modest about his family business. His organization structure works: It assigns everyone a specific job, and everyone knows how and where his or her job fits. It clearly shows who makes the decisions, and it coordinates each task so that everybody can work toward reaching the company's goals.

The organization chart for Wood Brothers' Race Shop shows all the jobs necessary to produce a championship racing car. It also shows who does each job and who each worker reports to (see Exhibit 7.2). For larger businesses, many of the boxes in the organization chart represent workers performing the same function, as in Exhibit 7.1.

Of course, no one structure will fit every organization, but all companies have one, and each company designs its structure to accomplish its organizational goals. Some companies design relatively rigid structures that follow the pyramid shape of the management hierarchy discussed in Chapter 6, where a broad base of employees is supervised by several levels of managers. Other organizations design structures that have fewer levels and are much less rigid—or design structures with no levels at all.[4]

Workers at White Flower Farm in Litchfield, Connecticut, have to be experts in their fields. They also need to know how their tasks fit into the organization as a whole, who makes which decisions, and how everyone can work together to reach company goals.

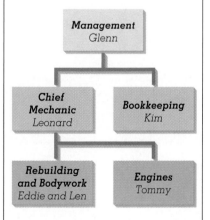

Exhibit 7.2
Organization Chart for Wood Brothers' Race Shop
Even a small business may have an organization chart, indicating the responsibilities of the various members.

For instance, Semco, a Brazilian manufacturer, uses a circular chart consisting of three concentric circles. The tiny center circle contains the five top managers, who coordinate all company activities. Surrounding this is a second circle containing the heads of Semco's eight divisions. Around the second circle is a third, the largest of the three, which contains all employees who handle the research, design, sales, and production tasks.[5]

DESIGNING THE FORMAL ORGANIZATION

The term *formal* means that the organization structure is specifically designed by management to accomplish strategic goals. Thus the formal organization is the official design for accomplishing tasks that lead to goal achievement. (An informal organization structure also exists in every organization and is discussed later in the chapter.) When management writes a description of the way a company is supposed to work and draws up an organization chart, the organizational plan has been *formalized*; that is, the structure is recorded in a form that can be seen by other people and can be used to guide the work of managers and employees.[6]

To design a company's organization structure, managers have traditionally considered three phases: (1) vertical organization (defining individual jobs to complete the tasks necessary to accomplish the planned work), (2) departmentalization (grouping jobs into departments and larger units), and (3) horizontal organization (coordinating all tasks). All three elements are needed to keep the company on track toward achieving its goals. In successful companies, every employee (from president to assembly-line worker) understands who makes the decisions, how the work is divided, and how everyone functions together to achieve strategic goals.

Vertical Organization

Vertical organization links activities at the top of the organization with those at the middle and lower levels in order to achieve organizational goals.[7] After top managers set the mission and organizational goals, they define the individual tasks necessary to achieve those goals, and they hire people to perform the tasks and to help them accomplish their mission.

Division of Labor

Because businesses perform a wide variety of tasks, managers often subdivide the work into distinct jobs to be accomplished efficiently. This process is called **division of labor.** In 1776 Scottish economist Adam Smith found that if each of 10 workers went through every step needed to make a pin, the entire group could make 200 pins a day. However, if each worker performed only a few steps and no one made a pin from start to finish, the same 10 workers could make 48,000 pins a day. Few employees have the skills to perform every

vertical organization *Structure linking activities at the top of the organization with those at the middle and lower levels*

division of labor *Specialization in or responsibility for some portion of an organization's overall work tasks; also called* work specialization

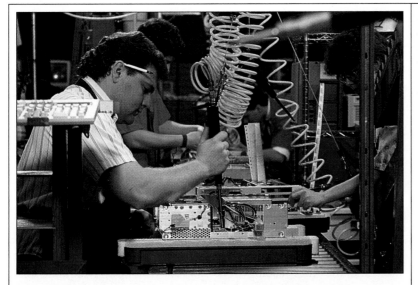

Employees at Dell Computer in Austin, Texas, have to be experts in their fields. They also need to know how their tasks fit into the organization as a whole, who makes which decisions, and how everyone can work together to reach company goals.

task a company needs, so division of labor (or *work specialization*) is one way that organizations can function.

Dividing labor can improve organization efficiency because each worker performs tasks that are well defined and that require specific skills. When employees concentrate on the same specialized tasks, they can perfect their skills, and they can perform their tasks more quickly. Also, managers can hire people whose skills fit the tasks, and they can cut the time needed to learn work responsibilities by not asking employees to shift from task to task.

However, organizations can overdo specialization. If a task is defined too narrowly, employees become bored with performing the same tiny, repetitive job over and over. Also, they feel unchallenged and alienated. As a result, managers must think carefully about how specialized or how broad each task should be. In fact, more and more organizations are balancing specialization and employee motivation by breaking work down according to overall processes or group tasks rather than individual tasks. In turn, group members share responsibility for the results, and they decide how to break down a complex task.[8] For instance, at Saginaw Plant 6, a General Motors plant in Michigan, workers in groups known as cells share responsibility for manufacturing certain parts in the most efficient way.[9]

An organization functions more smoothly if employees know not only what to do and when to do it but also who makes decisions about the work. So when managers plan the division of labor for their organization, they also plan to grant the right amount of authority to those who need it to complete the job.

Authority, Responsibility, and Accountability

In organizations, employees are assigned **responsibility** for their jobs; that is, they are obligated to perform those duties and to achieve those goals and objectives associated with their jobs. As employees work toward organizational goals, they report their results to supervisors

responsibility Obligation to perform the duties and to achieve the goals and objectives associated with a particular position and justify any outcomes that fall below expectations. This reporting is called **accountability.** Managers ensure that tasks are accomplished by exercising **authority,** the power to make decisions, issue orders, carry out actions, and allocate resources to achieve organizational goals. A glance at a company's organization chart reveals who has authority over whom, who is responsible for which tasks, and who is accountable to whom.

The organization chart in Exhibit 7.2 shows authority, responsibility, and accountability in Wood Brothers' Race Shop. The boxes representing Eddie, Len, and Tommy are on the same row, indicating that those people are equals in the Wood Brothers' organization. The lines going up from their boxes to Leonard's indicate that Leonard gives them instructions and oversees their work. Although Kim's box is on the same row as Leonard's, the fact that she, as bookkeeper, has no authority over Eddie, Len, and Tommy is indicated by the absence of any lines from their boxes to hers. Glenn's box at the top of the chart and the lines leading from it show that he has ultimate authority and responsibility. He directly supervises both Kim and Leonard and, through Leonard, indirectly supervises Eddie, Len, and Tommy. Thus vertical structure helps managers delegate authority through the chain of command, it defines the span of management, and it determines whether decision making will be centralized or decentralized.

Delegation

Except in the smallest businesses, no one person can oversee and control all the work. **Delegation** is the assignment of work and of the authority and responsibility to do that work. On paper, delegation is a fairly simple, straightforward matter. In practice, however, it can be far more complicated. First, although managers can transfer the authority and the responsibility for tasks, they cannot transfer the ultimate accountability for results.[10] Consider, for example, Joseph Hazelwood, captain of the *Exxon Valdez,* who was held accountable and had to stand trial for his ship's oil spill off Alaska, even though he wasn't at the helm during the accident.

Second, managers determine how much authority and responsibility their employees need to do their jobs properly:

1. If workers are told to drill a hole, they must be given the authority to get a drill from the company's equipment room.
2. If salespeople are responsible for satisfying customers, they should have the authority to exchange unwanted merchandise without an elaborate procedure.
3. If managers are responsible for increasing production, they must have the authority to hire and fire employees, to raise salaries, or to rearrange work.

As you can see, delegation works only when authority matches responsibility.

Third, authority can be delegated only to *willing* recipients. A manager can't delegate to an employee who refuses to take on responsibility or authority. Employees sometimes resist delegation because

THE ABCs OF ABB'S ORGANIZATION STRUCTURE

What kind of organization structure is appropriate for a corporation with 1,300 subsidiaries and 210,000 employees spread around the world? Percy Barnevik faced this challenge when he engineered the merger of Sweden's Asea and Switzerland's Brown Boveri into Zurich-based ABB, Asea Brown Boveri. ABB is a global organization producing electrical power equipment, robots, locomotives, and other industrial goods. Barnevik needed an organization design that would allow all ABB subsidiaries to concentrate on meeting customer needs. At the same time, the organization structure would have to enhance corporate performance in diverse global environments.

To start, Barnevik embraced decentralization with a vengeance. He pushed responsibility, authority, and accountability as far down the hierarchy as possible to put decision making in the hands of the ABB people closest to the customers they served. Next he created an organization design he calls a "multidomestic corporation." In addition to departmentalizing by matrix, which means every employee reports to both a country manager and a business sector man-

ager, Barnevik created a series of 100 national companies.

The top managers of each national company were directed to act as though they managed a domestic company, and they assumed the responsibility for dealing with their local governments, unions, and customers. Manufacturing was also decentralized so that goods would be produced in the customer's country whenever possible. This structure has allowed each national company to develop a local identity that attracts domestic orders as well as export orders.

For example, ABB's Combustion Engineering unit in the United States serves customers around the world. In South Korea, Combustion Engineering is building nuclear

power plants. The subsidiary operates as a U.S. company, so it must comply with U.S. legal and regulatory guidelines. Moreover, despite its Swiss ownership, Combustion Engineering also enjoys the support of the U.S. government, which can be particularly helpful in trade negotiations.

Thanks to this organization design, ABB subsidiaries are able to reap the benefits of acting locally while taking advantage of the parent company's resources.

Although decentralization has helped subsidiaries focus on the needs of their customers, Barnevik has also applied centralization to coordinate activities that cut across company (and country) lines. He has designated key research-and-development labs in Germany, Switzerland, and Sweden as "centers of excellence." Rather than duplicate research activities in individual subsidiaries, Barnevik has these labs conduct research that benefits the entire corporation. The money he saves as a result of such efficiencies is plowed back into research so that overall R&D expenditures remain sufficiently high to fuel ABB's long-term growth.

they lack motivation, training, or self-confidence. However, with training, support, and practice, most employees will want to accept delegated authority and responsibility.[11] In fact, in today's changing workplace, employees are becoming more and more involved in the day-to-day workings of companies. They are eager for more responsibility and want the authority to do what they feel is necessary to meet work goals.

Fourth, authority can be delegated only by willing managers. When managers delegate authority, they give up a portion of their control over people, tasks, and results. Some managers find it difficult to give up authority, resorting to *micromanagement,* an excessive degree of personal involvement in and control over the daily actions of their employees. However, organizations would not be able to function if managers tried to complete every task personally rather than delegating authority.[12] That's why more managers are learning to empower employees and give them the support they need to accomplish work on their own.

chain of command *Pathway for the flow of authority from one management level to the next*

Chain of Command. Every vertical structure has an identifiable flow of authority and communication. By linking tasks, authority, and responsibility, the vertical structure establishes the **chain of command,** the unbroken line of authority that connects each level of management to the next. The chain of command establishes who has the authority to give directions and who reports to whom. Two basic principles are associated with the chain of command: (1) each employee is held accountable to only one manager, and (2) the line of authority in an organization is clearly defined for every employee.

Line and Line-and-Staff Organization. The simplest and most common chain-of-command system is known as **line organization** because it establishes a clear line of authority flowing from the top down. Everyone knows who is responsible to whom, and the ultimate authority is easily identified. The organization chart in Exhibit 7.2 represents this pattern.

Even in a small organization such as The Daily Aztec, the student newspaper at San Diego State University, everyone has to know his or her position in the chain of command. At the top of the chain is Cathy Hendrie (right), who is editor-in-chief.

Businesses structured according to line organization enjoy a number of practical advantages. Because managers know when and where they can make decisions, line authority tends to speed decision making, simplify discipline, and clarify the communication channels. In addition, the simplicity of line organization sometimes results in lower expenses.

On the other hand, line organization has two important disadvantages. First, the technical complexity of a firm's activities may require specialized knowledge that individual managers don't have and can't easily acquire. Second, growth may extend the chain of command to the point that communication and decision making take too long to travel up and down the line.

A more elaborate system has developed out of the need to combine specialization with management control. Traditionally, the line organization manages the primary activities of the organization. In **line-and-staff organization,** managers in the chain of command are supplemented by functional groupings of people known as **staff,** who provide advice and specialized services. Staff personnel are not in the line organization's chain of command (see Exhibit 7.3). The main advantage of line-and-staff organization is that it gives line managers access to the support of specialized staff experts.

line organization *Chain-of-command system that establishes a clear line of authority flowing from the top down*

line-and-staff organization *Organization system that has a clear chain of command but that also includes functional groups of people who provide advice and specialized services*

staff *Functional experts who supplement the line organization by providing advice and specialized services*

span of management *Number of people under one manager's control; also known as span of control*

Span of Management

The number of people a manager directly supervises is called a **span of management** or *span of control.* When a large number of people report directly to one person, he or she has a wide span of management. When only a few people report, the span is narrow. Fewer managers are required when each has a wide span of control. The question, however, is how many people a manager can effectively oversee.

No formula exists for determining the ideal span of management.

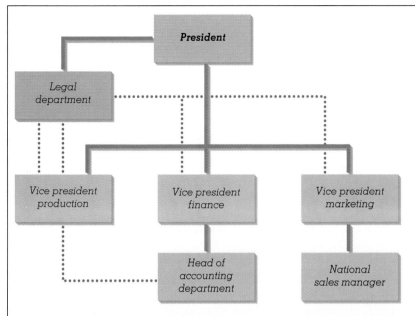

Exhibit 7.3
Simplified Line-and-Staff Structure
A line-and-staff organization divides employees into those who are in the direct line of command (from the top level of the hierarchy to the bottom) and those who provide staff (or support) services to line managers at various levels but who report directly to top management.

President

Legal department

Vice president production

Vice president finance

Vice president marketing

Head of accounting department

National sales manager

How well people work together is more important than the number of people reporting to one person. Still, several factors affect the number of people a manager can effectively supervise, including the manager's personal skill and leadership ability, the skill of the workers, the motivation of the workers, and the nature of the job. In general, highly skilled employees don't require as much supervision as less skilled employees. The manager of an organization made up almost exclusively of professionals or scientists may, therefore, have a wide span of management.[13]

When a manager supervises a large number of people, such as all the cashiers working on a particular supermarket shift, the span of management is fairly wide.

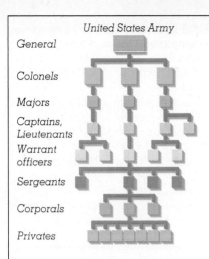

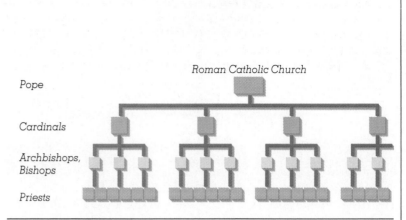

The span of management determines the number of hierarchical levels in a company, or whether the vertical structure is tall or flat. A **tall structure** has a narrow span and many hierarchical levels. For example, General Motors has 22 levels of management between the top and the bottom of its hierarchy, and Ford has 17 layers. A **flat structure** has a wide span of management and few hierarchical levels (see Exhibit 7.4). Compared with GM and Ford, Toyota's organization structure is much flatter because it has only 7 layers between top and bottom.[14] Generally, tall structures cost more because more managers must be paid, and the many layers delay communication and decision making. Also, pinpointing responsibility for specific tasks can be more difficult in a tall structure.[15]

To counteract the problems inherent in tall structures and to improve productivity, many companies have been **downsizing,** reducing the layers of middle management, expanding spans of management, and shrinking the size of the workforce. At General Electric a decade ago, as many as 10 layers of people separated top management from employees on the shop floor, but today only 5 levels separate CEO Jack Welch from the shop employees.[16] Similarly, when Lexmark was a division of IBM, 8 layers separated assembly-line workers from top management; today, the independent company has only 4 layers.

Centralization Versus Decentralization

The hierarchical level at which decisions are made is determined by how centralized or decentralized the authority is. **Centralization** focuses decision authority near the top of the organization. **Decentralization** pushes decision authority down to lower organization levels.

Centralization has several advantages: It simplifies vertical coordination (since decisions essentially trickle down from above), it uses top management's richer experience and broader view of organizational goals, and by focusing power at the top of the vertical structure, it encourages strong leadership. Decentralization, on the other hand, has advantages also: By pushing decision making down to lower levels of management, decentralization eases the burden on top ex-

Unprecedented change is challenging U.S. businesses. Companies are trying to adapt to deregulation, rapid technological change, takeover threats, and intense competition from abroad. On the other hand, change is itself being sought by some companies as a way to compete. At PepsiCo, CEO Wayne Calloway's biggest worry is complacency, so he forces change by moving managers back and forth across company divisions. Whether reacting to change or seeking it out, companies can use several organizational techniques to manage it. Among the most common are restructuring and downsizing, but managers are also using intrapreneurs, new ventures, and corporate culture to manage change.

Restructuring
Rather than just rearranging boxes on the organization chart or changing individual work tasks, more companies are restructuring entire work processes. In this fundamental restructuring, known as *reengineering,* the organization rethinks a group of tasks that has become irrelevant and creates a new, more productive process that works better for the company and its customers.

For example, Hallmark recently reengineered the process it uses to create new products. The company reduced from two years to just a few months the time needed to get a new product to market. This change enables Hallmark to respond more quickly to shifting consumer tastes.

MANAGING THE CHANGING ORGANIZATION

Used this way, restructuring is not a short-term fix for some specific problem but a long-term method of handling change and instilling flexibility.

Downsizing
To reduce costs and to be nimble enough to manage rapid change, companies are also reducing the number of people they employ. However, unless managers reexamine work processes before eliminating people, downsizing will fail. Downsizing without restructuring work process can lead to an organization so nervous about who will be laid off next that employees begin to think only of themselves and become unwilling to take risks that might benefit the firm.

To achieve the lean, mean structure firms need to compete effectively in today's environment, companies can downsize by (1) cutting unnecessary work, (2) putting quality first, (3) questioning long-held assumptions, (4) empowering people, (5) communicating, and (6) taking care of survivors.

Other Approaches
Companies can encourage change and innovation by supporting intrapreneurs, entrepreneurs within the organization. Intrapreneurs use corporate resources to start their own product line under the corporate umbrella. For example, S. C. Johnson & Son (maker of Johnson Wax and Raid bug spray) has set up a $250,000 seed fund available to anyone at the company with a promising new-product idea.

Some companies encourage intrapreneurial spirit in separate new-venture units. For instance, Colgate-Palmolive's new-venture unit works on such specialized products as a deodorizing pad for cat litter boxes and a cleaning solution for teenagers' dental retainers. The General Foods Culinova Group is leading its parent into the refrigerated take-out food business.

Finally, many companies are encouraging innovative change by giving their employees more freedom. Hewlett-Packard, for example, allows its engineers access to company labs around the clock. In addition, it allows researchers to devote 10 percent of company time to exploring their own ideas, without fear of penalty for failure. Using these methods and more, the most successful companies these days are those that successfully manage change.

ecutives and offers lower-level employees more challenge. Also, because decisions don't have to be referred up the hierarchy, decision making in a decentralized organization tends to be faster.[17] At Campbell Soup, for example, decentralization puts regional managers closer to their customers so that they can respond quickly to changing customer needs.[18]

So which is better? The most recent trend has been toward decentralization in order to improve effectiveness by speeding decision making, freeing top management, and accelerating response to the changing environment. However, this trend does not mean that all companies should decentralize. McDonald's has clearly shown how size and centralization can be a competitive advantage.[19] Each organization has to look at its own situation to determine the correct hierarchical level of decision making.

Departmentalization

departmentalization *Grouping people within an organization according to function, division, teams, matrix, or network*

Departmentalization groups people into departments and then groups departments into larger units to achieve goals. By specifying how people will be grouped, departmentalization influences how the organization operates; for example, it dictates the number of managers needed to link each department in the hierarchy with the one above and below. Because people in one department might share office space, equipment, and budget resources, departmentalization dictates how resources are distributed. By encouraging a shared view (or group perspective), departmentalization helps individuals see how their efforts help the department. One danger is that people may become more concerned with their own department's goals than with other departments' goals, so managers must encourage cross–unit coordination (discussed later in this chapter under "Horizontal Organization").[20]

Departments can be organized by function (what people do), by division (such as product, process, customer, or geography), according to teams (including project managers), into a matrix (combining both function and division), and by network (electronically connecting separate companies that perform specific business functions). However, remember that more than one type of departmentalization may be used in a single organization.

Function

departmentalization by function *Grouping workers according to their similar skills, resource use, and expertise*

Organizing departments according to what people do is **departmentalization by function.** Workers are grouped according to their skills, resource use, and expertise. Common functional departments include operations, marketing, human resources, finance, research and development, and accounting.[21]

Companies develop their own patterns to suit the particular functions they must carry out. As seen in Exhibit 7.5, *Time* magazine has four main functional departments: editorial, advertising, production, and circulation. Each department works more or less independently, having its own managers and personnel, budget, work schedules, and so on. The contact among departments is only on certain levels and for specific purposes. For instance, the director of advertising might consult with the production director on the number of advertising pages, but an individual ad salesperson would be unlikely to have direct dealings with the production staff.

Functional departmentalization allows efficient use of resources, encourages the development of in–depth skills, provides a clear career path, centralizes decision making so that top management can provide unified direction, and enhances communication and coordination within departments (since all activities are basically related). However, functional departmentalization can allow barriers to grow

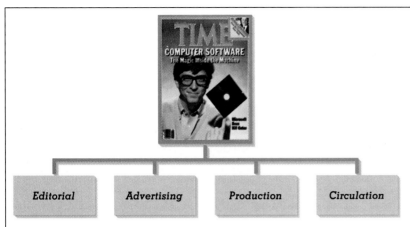

Exhibit 7.5
Departmentalization by Function
Departmentalization by function divides employees into groups according to their job functions, allowing specialists to have direct authority in their area of expertise. For example, instead of assigning a word-processing operator to each department head, a company might have a word-processing pool under the supervision of an expert in office automation.

Editorial	Advertising	Production	Circulation

between departments, can slow response to environmental change (because innovation and change require the involvement of several departments), and can sometimes overstress specialization and division of labor (thus alienating employees).[22]

Division

Departmentalization by division groups departments according to similarities in product, process, customer, or geography. In a divisional structure, each division is a self-contained unit with all the major functional resources it requires to achieve its goals (see Exhibit 7.6). Thus it has little need to rely on other divisions. For example, a functional structure would group all accountants in one department and all engineers in another. In contrast, a divisional structure would place functional groups for accounting and engineering in each division.[23]

departmentalization by division
Grouping departments according to similarities in product, process, customer, or geography

One difference between functional and divisional structure is the level at which decisions are made. In a functional structure, differences between engineering and accounting would have to be solved by top management. In a divisional structure, the solution comes lower in the hierarchy, at the divisional level.[24]

As mentioned earlier, *Time* magazine has a functional structure that groups people into departments according to skills and resources. In turn, *Time* is owned by Time Warner and is part of the organization's Publishing division (which produces magazines and books). Other

Exhibit 7.6
Departmentalization by Division
Campbell Soup reorganized its businesses into three divisions so that managers can more efficiently research and satisfy customer needs. Each division has all the functions needed to conduct business separately from the other divisions.

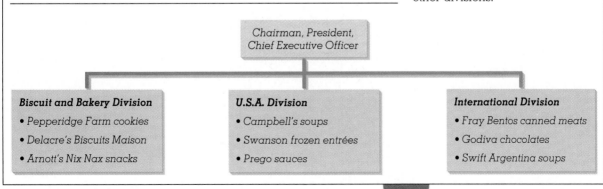

Chairman, President, Chief Executive Officer

Biscuit and Bakery Division
- Pepperidge Farm cookies
- Delacre's Biscuits Maison
- Arnott's Nix Nax snacks

U.S.A. Division
- Campbell's soups
- Swanson frozen entrées
- Prego sauces

International Division
- Fray Bentos canned meats
- Godiva chocolates
- Swift Argentina soups

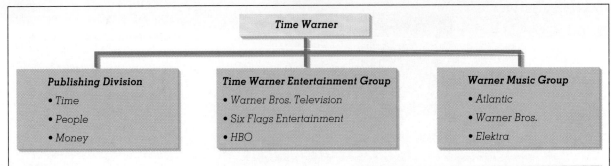

Time Warner		
Publishing Division • Time • People • Money	**Time Warner Entertainment Group** • Warner Bros. Television • Six Flags Entertainment • HBO	**Warner Music Group** • Atlantic • Warner Bros. • Elektra

Exhibit 7.7

Product Divisions

Time Warner employees are grouped according to what they produce, which brings together people of diverse skills to produce a specific product or service.

product divisions *Divisional structure based on products*

process divisions *Divisional structure based on the major steps of a production process*

customer divisions *Divisional structure that focuses on customers or clients*

geographic divisions *Divisional structure based on location*

Time Warner divisions are the Warner Music Group (recorded music), and Time Warner Entertainment Group (films, television, and theme parks) (see Exhibit 7.7). Time Warner uses a structure based on **product divisions,** grouping companies that make similar products into appropriate divisions.

A divisional structure based on the major steps of a production process has **process divisions.** For example, a table manufacturing company might have three divisions, one for each phase of manufacturing a table. Division 1 would size and shape the wood; division 2 would drill and rough-finish the pieces; and division 3 would assemble and finish the table (see Exhibit 7.8). Astra/Merck, a company that markets anti-ulcer and high-blood-pressure drugs, is organized around six process divisions, including drug development and distribution. "A functional organization wasn't likely to support our strategic goals to be lean, fast, and focused on the customer," explains Robert C. Holmes, director of strategic planning for Astra/Merck.[25]

Some organizations create **customer divisions** to concentrate on specific groups of customers. This approach is useful when the company serves different types of customers. For example, Johnson & Johnson devotes a separate division to each of its three main types of customers for health-care products: (1) consumer, (2) pharmaceutical, and (3) professional markets (see Exhibit 7.9). These customer divisions allow Johnson & Johnson employees to focus on the needs of each division's customers.

When a company is spread over a national or international area and differences from region to region are important enough to merit special attention, departments can be grouped by geographic location. **Geographic divisions** allow companies greater responsiveness to local customs, styles, product preferences, and the like. Note, how-

Exhibit 7.8

Process Divisions

Because process divisions allow employees to specialize in particular tasks, the production overall is more efficient.

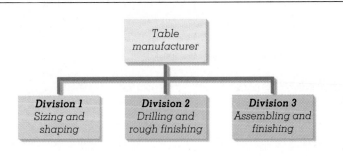

Table manufacturer		
Division 1 Sizing and shaping	**Division 2** Drilling and rough finishing	**Division 3** Assembling and finishing

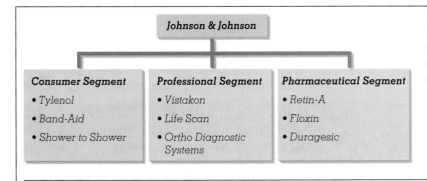

Exhibit 7.9
Customer Divisions
*Customer divisions lead employ-
ees to focus on customer needs
and customer service.*

ever, that a company doesn't have to use geographic divisions just because it does business across a large geographic area. Today's high-speed communication devices allow executives at corporate headquarters to oversee the operations of far-flung branch offices with an efficiency that was impossible a generation ago.

Quaker Oats, for example, has two main geographic divisions: (1) U.S. and Canadian Grocery Products and (2) International Grocery Products. Each division is further subdivided to allow the company to focus on the needs of customers in specific regions (see Exhibit 7.10). People in those geographic divisions pay close attention to local and regional issues.

Divisional departmentalization offers several advantages. Divisions can react quickly to change because they don't need to coordinate with other divisions, which makes the organization more flexible. This structure can improve service because each division focuses on a limited number of products, processes, customers, or locations. Top managers can focus on problem areas more easily, and managers can gain valuable experience by dealing with the various functions in their divisions.[26]

However, divisional departmentalization can mean duplication of resources, which increases costs. Also, the coordination between one division and others can be poor: employees within a division may focus too narrowly on divisional goals and neglect the organization's overall goals. Finally, divisions may compete with one another for employees, money, and other resources, causing rivalries that hurt the organization as a whole.[27]

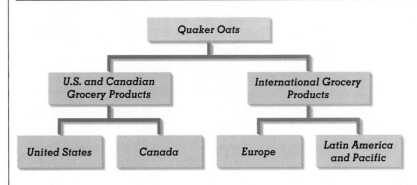

Exhibit 7.10
Geographic Divisions
*Geographic divisions such as
those established by Quaker Oats
allow employees to concern
themselves with local and
regional issues.*

Teams

As more companies push responsibility and authority to lower levels, many have changed to **departmentalization by teams,** in which functional employees are assigned to teams that handle specific tasks such as resolving problems between departments. Some companies take this type of departmentalization a step further by organizing **self-managing teams,** in which members are responsible for all aspects of a production process or a particular operation. For example, at FourGen Technologies Software, members of each self-managing team make their own decisions about how to complete work assignments, and they handle some managerial duties, such as scheduling product revisions and restructuring teams when needed.[28]

Team departmentalization can help organizations stay flexible and responsive. It can also motivate employees to be more creative, to develop a broader view, and to coordinate across functions. For example, to improve its services to policyholders, Aid Association for Lutherans (AAL) reorganized its huge insurance enterprise from a functional structure into a team structure. The transformation eliminated three layers of management and cut personnel by 10 percent. At the same time, the teams handled 10 percent more transactions, achieving AAL's goal of speeding up the processing of cases.[29]

Of course, team departmentalization can lead to conflicts and dual loyalties among team members. Because of the need for team meetings, teams may actually reduce efficiency. Also, teams may decentralize decision making too much, causing top managers to feel out of control and leading team members to focus on team goals rather than strategic goals.[30]

Matrix

Departmentalization by matrix permanently assigns employees to both a functional group and a project team (see Exhibit 7.11), using functional and divisional patterns simultaneously. Matrix departmentalization helps organizations build in-depth skills in functional departments and at the same time be adaptable to changing environmental demands. However, excellent communication and coordi-

Exhibit 7.11
Departmentalization by Matrix
In a matrix structure, each employee is assigned to both a functional group (with a defined set of basic functions, such as production manager) and a project team (which consists of members of various functional groups working together on a project, such as bringing out a new consumer product).

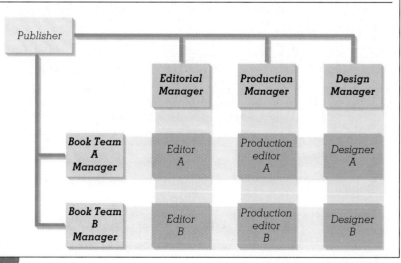

nation are needed to avoid potential problems, such as employees' reporting to two supervisors who disagree about what should be done. Among the companies that have used matrix departmentalization are Procter & Gamble, Lockheed, and Dow Chemical.[31]

Under **project management,** employees are assigned to a functional group but temporarily leave their position in the organization's permanent hierarchy when they are assigned to a specific project. Project teams disband when their tasks are completed. Merck, a U.S. pharmaceutical firm, has a system that guarantees good ideas won't be lost during the long product-development process. Merck assigns a project manager to each promising research effort. This manager guides the product through the entire process and across innumerable departments from research to final government approval. It is the project manager who persuades scientists from diverse disciplines to commit their time and budget to each project, which increases loyalty for the product and encourages unity among team members.[32]

project management Assigning employees to a functional group but also temporarily assigning them to a specific project

Network

Departmentalization by network is a method of electronically connecting separate companies that perform selected tasks for a small headquarters organization. Engineering, marketing, research, and accounting are no longer part of one organization; they are essentially separate organizations working under contract. The network approach is especially appropriate for international operations, allowing every part of the business to draw on resources no matter where in the world they may be.

departmentalization by network Electronically connecting separate companies that perform selected tasks for a small headquarters organization

Lewis Galoob Toys in California, for example, is able to compete with Hasbro, Mattel, and other industry giants because it uses network departmentalization. A few hundred employees in Galoob's main office control the company's contracts with outsiders, who handle toy design, engineering, manufacturing, distribution, and other key functions.

Some companies have experimented with an internal version of network structure. For instance, Digital Equipment Corporation's nine customer divisions contract with central company units that offer engineering, manufacturing, and other resources as needed.[33]

Network structure is extremely flexible because of the ability to hire whatever services are needed and then change them after a short time. The organization can continually redefine itself, and employees have greater job variety and job satisfaction. However, this approach lacks hands-on control, since the functions are not in one location or company. Also, if a network company goes out of business or fails to deliver, such a development can cause severe problems for the central organization. Finally, strong employee loyalty and team spirit are less likely to develop.[34]

Horizontal Organization

Organizations must have systems for coordinating information and communication among employees in various departments at various

horizontal organization *Structure to coordinate activity by facilitating communication and information exchange across departments*

information systems *All written and electronic forms of sharing information, processing data, and communicating ideas*

task force *Group of people from several departments who are temporarily brought together to address a specific issue*

managerial integrator *Manager who coordinates activities of several functional departments but belongs to none*

levels. **Horizontal organization** coordinates activity by facilitating communication and information exchange across departments without the need to go up and down the vertical chain of command. Horizontal organization also provides the opportunity for employees to share views, which strengthens their willingness to understand, support, and implement innovative ideas. Without horizontal organization, every problem, every decision, and every piece of information would have to travel through the vertical hierarchy, effectively isolating departments from one another and paralyzing companies.

Three ways organizations achieve horizontal coordination are through information systems, task forces and teams, and managerial integrators:[35]

- *Information systems.* All written and electronic forms of sharing information, processing data, and communicating ideas are **information systems.** They include internal written communications (reports, bulletins, and memos) as well as electronic communication devices (computers, electronic mail, and teleconferences).[36] Electronic systems offer the ability to quickly process and communicate vast amounts of information, thus greatly enhancing horizontal coordination. Digital Equipment Corporation, for example, has an internal network that links 95,000 users and 35,000 computers spanning 33 countries. Any DEC employee can send a message to any other employee at any time, regardless of geographic or organization location.[37]

- *Teams and task forces.* A **task force** is a group of people from several departments who are temporarily brought together to address a specific issue or problem. At Oryx Energy (an independent Dallas gas producer), massive efforts to change the corporation's character were carried out by teams that unearthed problems and suggested solutions. Each team had between 8 and 10 members, and only 2 or 3 were from the department being studied. Oryx's teams not only succeeded in changing the company from a paper-swamped operation to a dynamic organization but also saved the company $75 million a year.[38] In most cases, task forces make recommendations to senior managers, who make the final decision about implementation. Members of task forces and teams help coordinate the organization's activities by sharing information with their own departments.[39]

- *Managerial integrators.* A **managerial integrator** is a manager who coordinates the activities of several functional departments without officially being a member of any. These managers often have titles such as project manager, product manager, brand manager, program manager, or branch manager. The functional department managers retain line authority over their employees, so even though integrating managers have authority over the project, product, brand, program, or branch, they have no authority over the employees working on it. However, when integrating managers use their human relations skills to resolve problems that arise between departments, they improve the horizontal coordination of their projects.[40]

196

The amount of vertical and horizontal organization defines the character of a company. An organization that emphasizes vertical structure maintains tight control over hierarchical levels, defines jobs rigidly, sets up many specific rules, centralizes authority, and communicates through the vertical hierarchy. However, an organization that emphasizes horizontal structure loosens the control, allows tasks to be redefined to fit employee or environmental needs, decentralizes authority and decision making, and encourages horizontal communication. Many organizations try to strike a balance between vertical and horizontal structures so that they can benefit from the best features of both.[41]

New Approaches to Work

Every day companies face large and small changes in customer needs, employee needs, competitive pressures, technology, government regulation, and other areas. To gain the flexibility they need to survive in this dynamic environment, an increasing number of companies are combining vertical and horizontal organization to create new approaches to organizing work. After all, with change a constant concern, managers can't find the time every day to figure out how each job in the organization should be adjusted. Instead of carving work up into small, discrete tasks that are assigned to people with narrow sets of skills, human resource experts are now looking at ways to keep work whole, provide all the information needed to complete the work, and empower employees to take responsibility for the end result. This approach allows employees at all levels to be more self-reliant, and it gives them the opportunity to show what they can do (developing a well-rounded set of skills that will prepare them for a wider range of work challenges through the years).

Look at the European Collision Center, a small auto-body shop in Cambridge, Massachusetts. Rather than requiring technicians to specialize in small, specific parts of the overall process, owner Wayne Stevenson allows workers to stay with one car from the time it enters the shop until the time it leaves. Workers have been trained to do everything needed to restore the auto body, and Stevenson offers yearly training to keep workers' skills up to date. Keeping the work whole—not chopping it up into small parts that are passed through a series of workers—lets workers finish what they start and take pride in the completed project. Customers evidently like it too—Stevenson's business has doubled in each of the past five years.[42]

With such new approaches to organizing work, employees have more control over what they do, when they do it, and how they do it. Managers are more like coaches than dictators, offering ideas and helping solve problems when they arise. One increasingly popular method of organizing work is around teams that tackle individual projects. Team members with the appropriate skills are assigned (or invited) to work on a project. Each member takes responsibility for working cooperatively to accomplish the project's goals; then the team disbands, and its members join teams that are tackling other projects. The key to this fluid organization of work is technology, which allows information to flow throughout the company so that everyone is aware of the goals, the schedules, the resources, and the changes that influence every task.[43]

UNDERSTANDING THE INFORMAL ORGANIZATION

Although the vertical and horizontal organizations formally define the relationships among employees, every company has an **informal organization,** the network of interactions that develop on a personal level among the workers (see Exhibit 7.12). Although the relationships among people in the formal and informal organizations may be the same, they often aren't, because employees who do not work together in a formal sense may informally form personal relationships. As a result of these relationships, natural leaders emerge who have the contacts to get things done. Whether the power of natural leaders is granted to them by their peers or by their influence with management, it benefits the organization.[44]

The informal organization also provides employees with an opportunity for social interaction, and it serves as an outlet for stress, tension, and anxiety. It can smooth the way for communication and provide information that managers use in decision making. At the same time, the informal organization can create conflicting loyalties, and it can work against company values if the informal group does not share those values. In addition, the informal organization can encourage resistance to management plans as well as complaints, poor-quality work, and absenteeism. Information is spread within the informal organization through the grapevine.

informal organization *Interactions that are not defined by the formal structure but that influence how the organization accomplishes its goals*

Exhibit 7.12
Informal Organization
In addition to its formal organization structure, every company has an informal organization. These networks of social connections are often formed without regard for hierarchy or departmentalization.

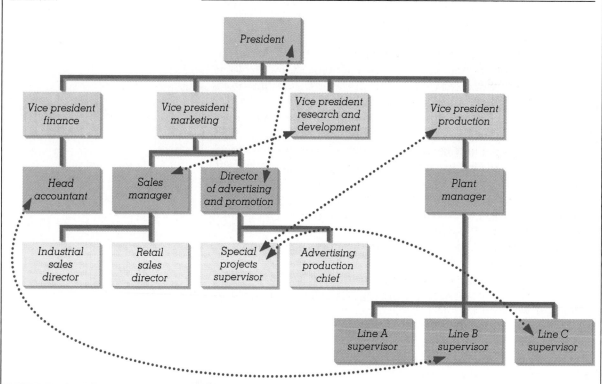

Grapevines

The **grapevine** is the communication network of the informal organization. Grapevines relay news unofficially by bypassing the formal chain of command. They may convey either personal or business information. Grapevines also exist among companies and within industries. Employees with personal connections to someone in a competing or client company may spread information before it is publicized. In many cases, such gossip simply makes work less boring. Sometimes, however, it contributes to the spread of damaging rumors.

Smart managers make good use of the grapevine, which sometimes provides factual tips about both internal and external matters, such as employee attitudes or outsiders' perceptions of the company. The challenge is to figure out when the grapevine's information is accurate and when it is misleading.

grapevine Communication network of the informal organization

Office Politics

The term *office politics* refers to the complex struggle for power and recognition that takes place in any organization. Office politics operate outside the official organizational structure. Such political relations come into play when employees try to advance their careers by bringing their own abilities and achievements to the attention of higher-level managers.

Although office politics can be seen as the manipulation of other people in an attempt to gain power, such political action can also be useful. Highly motivated workers tend to be very productive, and when many employees scramble for recognition, quite a few wind up producing at a high level. In addition, although ruthlessness and power struggles are one aspect of office politics, simple courtesy and leadership are another. In the long run, those who demonstrate the ability to work productively with others are most likely to get ahead. Developing productive working relationships is the purpose of two time-honored processes: networking and mentorship.

Networking

Networking is the art of making and using contacts, both inside and outside the organization you work for. Networking is the way people find out about jobs that aren't advertised in the newspaper; it's the way they learn about new developments in their field before the public does. Many managers move ahead quickly in their careers because of the relationships they've built through networking.[45]

The three keys to successful networking are visibility, familiarity, and image. *Visibility* means making your presence known. The more people who meet you, the more you are likely to be remembered. *Familiarity* means letting people get to know you. Exposing your skills, attitudes, and opinions takes courage, but people will be more willing to deal with you if they know how you think. *Image* means giving the impression that you are competent and pleasant to deal with. An optimistic, enthusiastic approach to business—and to life—is magnetic.[46]

networking Seeking to broaden one's effectiveness in an organization or industry by forming relationships with others in the same and related fields mentor Experienced member of an organization who serves as a guide and protector to a lower-level employee

At Textron, a major U.S. defense contractor, an apprenticeship program gives less experienced employees the opportunity to learn new job skills and explore career options in the organization through a relationship with a knowledgeable mentor.

corporate culture Set of values and norms that guides and influences the attitudes and behavior of employees and managers within a company

intrapreneurs Employees who have the entrepreneurial spirit to develop innovative ideas within the organization

Mentors

Another way to develop productive working relationships is by learning from a **mentor**, an experienced manager or employee who guides you through the corporate maze. Mentors have deep knowledge of the business and a useful network of industry colleagues. In addition, they can explain office politics and serve as a role model for appropriate business behavior.

Your mentor won't always be your boss. Relationships with mentors often develop informally between the individuals involved; however, some companies have formal mentoring programs. In one such program, women employees at Xerox can visit for a few hours every month with any of the women executives participating in the program and discuss work or career issues.[47] The less experienced employees gain from their mentors' advice and ideas; the mentors themselves gain new contacts for their networks as well as personal satisfaction.

Corporate Culture

Corporate culture is the set of values (defining what is prized) and norms (defining what is acceptable) that shapes employee attitudes and behavior. It serves as a guidepost by which employees may judge what the company wants from them, how they should approach problems, and what types of solutions will be acceptable. It also sets the tone for ethical and socially responsible behavior, showing employees what is considered right and wrong. As an element of the informal organization, corporate culture can't be directly observed. However, it can be communicated through stories about past successes, awards and ceremonies marking special events, company slogans, and corporate symbols such as flags and logos.[48]

General Electric has been working hard to create a corporate culture in which employees willingly take the initiative to suggest improvements that can help the company compete more effectively. Changing from a closed culture that discouraged individual initiative to an open atmosphere that leads to creativity and challenge isn't easy. Such a change is a long process that requires ongoing employee education and conditioning.[49] For GE and many other companies, however, a corporate culture focused on creativity, individual initiative, and high performance is a key ingredient in a strong organization structure. In fact, many companies use corporate culture to nurture the efforts of **intrapreneurs,** employees with entrepreneurial spirit who pursue innovative ideas within the organization. Intrapreneurs have the freedom and the resources to pursue their new ideas on company time, so they can help their companies find new ways of satisfying customer needs, overcoming competitive challenges, and meeting overall goals.

1 Discuss the three purposes of organization structure.

Managers use organization structure to divide labor and assign formal tasks to individuals and groups, to define the span of management and the lines of authority, and to coordinate all organizational tasks.

2 Describe the problems associated with specialization.

Specializing too much can alienate employees by giving them small, repetitious tasks that seem unchallenging and boring.

3 Explain how departmentalization facilitates goal achievement.

Departmentalization breaks work into smaller tasks, grouping people into departments and grouping departments into larger units to achieve goals. It dictates how the organization operates and how resources are distributed, facilitating individual efforts within each department.

4 List five types of departmentalization.

The five types of departmentalization are (1) by function, (2) by division, (3) according to teams, (4) by matrix, and (5) by network.

5 Discuss how vertical organization differs from horizontal organization.

Emphasizing vertical structure imposes tight control over hierarchical levels, leads to routine jobs that are rigidly defined, requires exacting organizational rules, centralizes authority, and limits communication to the vertical path. Emphasizing horizontal structure loosens control, leads to varied jobs that can be redefined to fit employees or environmental needs, decentralizes authority, pushes decision making down the hierarchy, and coordinates communication and information exchange across departments.

6 Explain three methods of horizontal organization.

The three most common methods of horizontal organization are information systems, teams and task forces, and managerial integrators. All three methods facilitate communication and information exchange across departmental boundaries.

7 Discuss the positive and negative aspects of the informal organization.

The positive aspects of informal organization include providing employees with an opportunity for social interaction; providing an outlet for stress, tension, and anxiety; facilitating organizational communication; providing managers with information; and helping leaders get things done through personal contacts. The negative aspects of informal organization include creating conflicting loyalties, counteracting company values, and encouraging resistance to management plans.

8 Define corporate culture and explain how it is communicated.

Corporate culture is the set of values and norms that shapes employee attitudes and behavior. It can be communicated through stories about past successes, awards and ceremonies marking special events, company slogans, and corporate symbols.

ON THE JOB: MEETING BUSINESS CHALLENGES AT LEXMARK INTERNATIONAL

Marvin Mann knew that Lexmark's move from IBM to independence would require an entirely new organization structure. Under the IBM system, eight layers had separated assembly-line workers from top management, and employees had to approach manager after manager to get the necessary approvals for changes or new projects. Coming up with new products took time, too. Two or three years might pass from the time an idea was proposed (say, for a new printer) until the first printer rolled off the assembly line. Meanwhile, aggressive competitors like Hewlett-Packard, Apple, Canon, and Epson would be moving quickly to bring out new printers packed with clever features that customers desired.

To start, Mann reorganized Lexmark according to product, creating four groups that each focused on a set of related products. Next, he cut the number of layers separating top management from assembly-line workers from eight to four. This action helped speed up communication and decision making throughout the company. Mann also abandoned the IBM method of studying and debating proposals for months before making decisions, giving more power to managers and employees at every level. "Our people have a lot more freedom to get things done than before," he observes.

Instead of a rigid hierarchical structure, Mann formed teams to tackle routine problems as well as special situations. For example, a team of assembly-line workers assumed complete responsibility for designing a more efficient laser-printer production process. When all members of the team were satisfied that the new production process would work, they signed their names to the proposal—and were given the authority to implement the change.

Similarly, teams of people from manufacturing, finance, marketing, and other departments are totally responsible for designing and producing new products. Because the departments coordinate their efforts from the start, they can get a new product to market in about half the time they needed under the IBM system. What's more, they've been able to double the number of products under development without adding more designers.

With these organizational changes in place, Lexmark was able to introduce an ambitious new-product program only months after leaving the IBM family. The company revamped its existing printers and came up with a new line of laser printers, which were praised by computer magazines for their simplicity, reliability, and print quality. At the same time, workers (not managers) set and then achieved a goal of 100 percent accuracy in making and shipping the 50 million items Lexmark produces every year. As a result of these and many other initiatives, sales are strong, manufacturing costs are down, and quality is up. No wonder Mann sees the typing on the wall for a bright future ahead.

Your Mission: Marvin Mann has asked you, a consultant specializing in organization structure, to offer suggestions that will help the company organize for success. Select the best solution for each of these situations:

1. Mann asks you about the span of management in a production unit that will be manufacturing a new portable laser printer. He wants your opinion on whether the assembly-line workers in this unit should be supervised using a wide or narrow span of management. What advice would you offer?

a. Use a narrow span of management to allow managers to keep a close watch on the manufacturing process. After all, the company has to be able to catch and correct any problems quickly when making a new product.

b. Use a wide span of management to allow workers the same degree of responsibility and accountability as in other Lexmark units. The workers are just as concerned as the managers about the quality of the new products.

c. Start with a narrow span of management to maintain tight control when the unit begins making the new product. Later, after the managers have solved any initial problems, switch to a wider span of management.

2. For the past few days, a rumor about layoffs has been spreading through the Lexmark grapevine. Even though the rumor is untrue, many employees are beginning to worry about their jobs. What do you suggest Mann do?

a. Mann should prepare a straightforward message about the facts of the situation. Next, he should use every available method to communicate with all employees, including memos, face-to-face meetings, and so on.

b. Mann should prepare a brief memo that denies the rumored layoffs and wastes no time with muddying details. A reassuring word from the CEO is all that's needed to stop a false rumor.

c. Tell Mann to ignore the rumor. No matter what he says, employees will believe that the rumor must have some basis in fact. Because the threat of layoffs is unfounded, talk will eventually die down.

3. The head of human resources comes to you for ideas about how to handle a newly hired manager who has difficulty delegating to her workers. This work group has done well in the past, but the new manager is afraid that any problems will make her look bad. To avoid mistakes, she tries to control everything her workers do. What's the best advice you can offer?

a. Until the new manager sees the kind of work her employees are capable of, she won't trust them to do their jobs without close supervision. Intervening now won't help; time is the best solution for this problem.

b. Let this manager's boss suggest that she start delegating by defining the tasks to complete, setting performance goals, monitoring progress toward the goals, and coaching when workers need her support. Then she'll see how well her workers handle their tasks without close supervision.

c. Let this manager's boss stress that delegation is the only way to get things done in a large organization. He should explain that he has to delegate to the people below him, because he can't do everybody's work, and she has to delegate to the people below her if anything is to be accomplished.

4. As Lexmark grows, it will be hiring new managers at all levels. Mann asks for your thoughts about how to help these managers learn the organization's procedures as well as the ins and outs of getting things done. What do you recommend?

a. Set up a mentor program to match an experienced manager with every new manager who's hired. The mentor can explain the formal and informal organization, offer tips about office politics, and answer any questions.

b. Set up a special task force to work with new hires. The task force should have a representative from every department to answer questions and explain their roles in the organization.

c. Give new managers a copy of the organization chart. They'll solve their own problems by asking workers and colleagues for help, and they'll soon gain a better understanding of how the business really operates.[50]

accountability (184)
authority (184)
centralization (188)
chain of command (186)
corporate culture (200)
customer divisions (192)
decentralization (188)
delegation (184)
departmentalization (190)
departmentalization by division (191)
departmentalization by function (190)
departmentalization by matrix (194)
departmentalization by network (195)

departmentalization by teams (194)
division of labor (182)
downsizing (188)
flat structure (188)
geographic divisions (192)
grapevine (199)
horizontal organization (196)
informal organization (198)
information systems (196)
intrapreneurs (200)
line-and-staff organization (186)
line organization (186)
managerial integrator (196)
mentor (200)

networking (199)
organization (180)
organization chart (180)
organization structure (180)
process divisions (192)
product divisions (192)
project management (195)
responsibility (183)
self-managing teams (194)
span of management (186)
staff (186)
tall structure (188)
task force (196)
vertical organization (182)

1. Why is organization structure important?
2. Discuss the three phases of organization structure.
3. Under what circumstances should an organization set up geographic divisions?

4. Why would you expect a manager of a group of nuclear physicists to have a wide span of management?
5. What are the characteristics of tall organizations and flat organizations? Is the U.S. Navy a tall organization or a flat one? How do you know?

6. Why would horizontal organization promote innovation?
7. Should organizations emphasize horizontal or vertical organization? Why?
8. How can using the informal organization help a manager be more effective?

FLYING HIGH ON WORLDWIDE HORIZONTAL LINKS

Every top manager faces the dual challenge of efficiently arranging activities and coordinating all jobs so that the organization's goals can be achieved. This task is even more complex for an organization that conducts business in many countries. Employees may be separated from their counterparts in other countries by hundreds or thousands of miles, yet they are expected to work together toward common goals, such as increasing company profits or gaining market share. Strong horizontal organization is needed to improve communication and information interchange among the people in these far-flung locations; without it, employees will not be able to understand their roles in the organization or perform as expected.

Imagine the horizontal organiza-tion needed to coordinate activities at Swissair, a Zurich-based airline that serves the European continent and selected global capitals, including several U.S. cities. Swissair's reputation for customer satisfaction is put to the test every hour of every day, as its planes take off and land in airports around the world. In a typical year, the airline carries 8 million passengers. Otto Loepfe, Swissair's president, knew that horizontal organization was the key to improving coordination among the 18,000 employees and managers who worked all over the globe.

For years, Swissair operated a centralized organization, using functional departmentalization to manage planning, scheduling, and other activities. In addition, the airline used geographical departmentalization to organize its worldwide sales force. However, no one was directly responsible for the flight routes, and decisions often moved slowly when issues involved two or more departments.

Expansion brought other problems, as well. For instance, when the airline was smaller, nearly everyone had been able to make frequent customer contact. However, since Swissair had grown and added routes, Loepfe saw that comparatively few managers now met the customer, even though customer contact was vital if the airline was to understand and meet the needs of its passengers. To solve these problems, Loepfe changed his organization structure.

In the structure Loepfe established, route managers hold key integrating roles. These route managers are responsible for meeting customer needs on several routes, and they influence but do not have direct authority over the types of aircraft used on their routes, the meals served, the schedules, and even the hotels where the crews stay. Even though route managers are accountable for the overall cost of their routes, Loepfe does not measure their performance on the basis of profitability. He has adopted this policy because many Swissair routes are interdependent, feeding traffic to and from key destinations, and the company sometimes elects to maintain certain routes even if they are temporarily unprofitable.

Given their responsibilities, route managers must frequently consult with top managers in Zurich, and Loepfe has smoothed this process by flattening the organization. In the old organization, a country manager was separated by three layers of management from the president. Now a route manager is only one layer away from the president, so information can be exchanged more quickly. However, Loepfe didn't simply transfer managers into these new positions. Instead, he required people to apply for them; the manager of North America had to apply for the position of route manager of North America, even though the new position included many of the tasks already handled under the old position.

Loepfe knows that some difficulties may lie ahead, including increased competitive pressure and the worldwide impact of airline deregulation. So he has carefully designed Swissair's organization structure to help the airline efficiently serve its customers on every route, positioning Swissair for high-flying customer satisfaction and profits well into the next century.

1. Why is the route manager considered a managerial integrator?
2. How do you think functional departmentalization might be used to organize activities conducted at Swissair's central headquarters?
3. How would you use information systems to improve Swissair's horizontal coordination?

BUILDING YOUR COMMUNICATION SKILLS

Either as an individual or with a classmate, examine the formal organizational structure of a business or an institution (such as a hospital, college, or public service agency). If you are unable to obtain an organization chart for this business or institution, you might find it useful to create one using the information you can gather by observing operations or talking with managers.

• Using information from the text, determine the division of labor, the form of departmentalization, and the centralization of your chosen business or institution.
• Describe the organization in a written or an oral presentation. Compare the structure with that of businesses or organizations examined by other class members. Is any organization taking a new approach to organizing work? Is the new approach effective?

KEEPING CURRENT USING *THE WALL STREET JOURNAL*

Choose an article from *The Wall Street Journal* that describes a company's restructuring.

1. What changes were made in the company's organization structure or corporate culture?
2. What reasons are given for the changes? If no reasons are given, what is your best guess about the reasons for the changes?
3. What effects have the organizational changes had on the company, its customers, and its products? If the changes are just now being implemented or announced, what results does the company expect the restructuring to have?

SPRINGFIELD REMANUFACTURING COMPANY TEAMS UP FOR SUCCESS

Synopsis

Innovative management is often associated with high technology and celebrity entrepreneurs, but this video shows that enlightened management works just as well in the unglamorous business of overhauling truck engines. Springfield Remanufacturing Company (SRC) tripled its sales in six years after it adopted a management system that patterns business efforts after Americans' love of a good game. SRC bases its game of business on three principles: First, everyone is on the same team; the company is owned by its managers and employees. Second, everyone learns how to keep score; even entry-level workers are taught how to read financial statements so that they can see how well the company is doing. Third, everyone has a stake in the company's success; as the company prospers and the value of its stock climbs, so does the financial health of the managers and employees who own it.

Exercises

ANALYSIS

1. What type of organization is operating at SRC?
2. Explain the role of authority in a team-oriented organization.
3. Using the chapter's clues for identifying a corporate culture, how would you describe the culture at SRC?
4. What role could intrapreneurship play at SRC, and how might it be encouraged?
5. Would SRC's structure tend to be more centralized or decentralized?

APPLICATION

One of the reasons SRC's employee-involvement approach works is that employees see long-term benefit in learning how to read financial statements, work extra hours when needed, and so on. How might this concept be applied to a business such as a convenience store, in which employees rarely work for more than a few years? In a page or less, outline how SRC's approach could be applied by the owner of a convenience store.

DECISION

Assume that SRC has decided to purchase a company and make it a division. However, this company has a traditional, centralized corporate culture that emphasizes top-down control, not teamwork and participation. Identify the problems that SRC might encounter as it tries to infuse the new division with the SRC culture.

COMMUNICATION

Write a three-minute introductory speech that you would present to the employees and managers of the new division, describing SRC's culture and the company's reasons for introducing it to the new division.

INTEGRATION

Which of the three leadership styles described in Chapter 6 seems to be the norm at SRC?

ETHICS

Teamwork in the SRC style can be a boon to productivity and employee satisfaction, but it is sometimes hard for individual accomplishments to stand out in such an environment. A good sports analogy is the fate of linemen on a football team; they slug it out game after game for the benefit of the team but rarely get any individual glory. In this sense, is a strong emphasis on teamwork really fair?

DEBATE

Many people view the education of employees in corporate finance as a necessary part of the teamwork approach used at SRC. Some people, however, say that becoming well versed in corporate finance is too great a burden for some employees, particularly those who aren't all that interested in the business and just want to do a good day's work and not worry about anything else. Option A: In a formal debate format, take either side of this issue. Option B: Take either position and state your case in a brief summary report.

TEAMWORK

With three or four other students, develop a short presentation that teaches financial novices how to read an income statement. Chapter 17 offers an introduction to income statements, and you may want to use other sources as well.

RESEARCH

Do the research necessary to write a one-paragraph update on either (a) the book that Bo Burlingham was writing, including its title, whether it is still in print, and any reviews it received in the business press or (b) SRC's current status.

ROLE PLAYING

One student plays the production manager, who is announcing to two other students (playing the role of production-line employees) that the company has received a large order that would require canceling the Thanksgiving holiday if the company accepts it. One employee wants to take the order; the other doesn't.

Chapter

8

The Production of Goods and Services

Staying on the Road to Higher Sales

When Japanese manufacturers began selling heavyweight motorcycles in the United States in the early 1970s, Harley-Davidson remained calm. The Milwaukee company controlled 99.7 percent of the market and saw no reason to panic. After all, if your customers love your product so much that they tattoo your logo on their chests, can't you count on their loyalty?

The answer is no. The Harley was no longer the superb machine it once was. It leaked oil, vibrated wildly, and broke down frequently. Harley's older customers patiently rebuilt their motorcycles, but younger riders were not so forgiving. They increasingly chose the trouble-free, smooth-riding motorcycles that Honda, Yamaha, Suzuki, and Kawasaki imported. By the time its market share had slipped to 23 percent, Harley began leaking red ink along with engine oil.

In an effort to compete more effectively, Harley decided to focus on quality production during the 1980s. The company changed its design and manufacturing systems to stress quality and reliability, and it carefully controlled the number of motorcycles produced so that the quality could be maintained. This turnaround reestablished Harley's worldwide reputation for superior quality. Customers liked the new motorcycles, and sales began to climb.

By the early 1990s, market share had returned to 64 percent, a number that could have been higher if the company hadn't presold its entire output by the middle of every year. With $1.2 billion in sales, Harley's biggest problem now was to make enough motorcycles to keep up with soaring demand in the United States and abroad. Dealers were frustrated because they couldn't give customers what they wanted. As dealer Debra Meyers put it: "People don't understand. Not only can't they have the color they want, they can't have the bike. Period."

The last thing Harley CEO Richard F. Teerlink wanted was to frustrate dealers and customers. Although he recognized that higher production would lead to higher sales and profits, he refused to increase output at the risk of damaging the company's new reputation

Harley-Davidson's focus on quality delights its worldwide base of loyal customers.

for quality. Faced with a sea of clamoring customers and anxious dealers, how could Teerlink boost Harley's production while keeping a firm grip on the quality that had brought the company back to its dominant position in the motorcycle industry? What could the CEO do to monitor the production process and keep it on track and on time? How could he make Harley flexible enough to handle the constant change needed to compete with rivals all over the globe?[1]

THE QUEST FOR COMPETITIVENESS

The managers at Harley-Davidson recognize that the foundation of any business is **production,** the transformation of resources into goods or services that people need or want. A great deal of attention has been focused on the production function in recent years, as companies around the world try to increase their competitive strengths through higher quality, greater efficiency, faster production, and lower costs.

At the core of production is the **conversion process,** the sequence of events in which resources are converted into products. It can be diagrammed simply (see Exhibit 8.1):

$$Input \rightarrow transformation \rightarrow output$$

This formula applies to both intangible services and tangible goods. For example, a consultant's knowledge about a company and ability to communicate (input) can be transformed through analysis into specific advice about running a company (output). For a shirtmaker to produce a shirt, the resources that are input to be converted—cloth, thread, and buttons—are tangible; the form of the output that people want, the shirt, is tangible too.

Two basic types of conversion exist. One type, called an **analytic system,** breaks raw materials into one or more distinct products, which may or may not resemble the original material in form and function. In meat packing, for example, a steer is divided into hide,

production *Transformation of resources into forms that people need or want*

conversion process *Sequence of events (input → transformation → output) for transforming materials into goods and services*

analytic system *Production process that breaks incoming materials into various component products.*

Exhibit 8.1
The Conversion Process
Production of goods or services is basically a process of conversion. Input (the basic ingredients or skills) is transformed (by the application of labor, equipment, and capital) into output (the desired product).

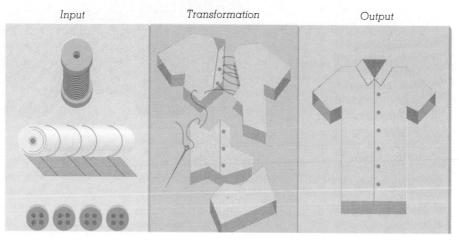

Input	Transformation	Output

bone, steaks, and so on. The second type of conversion, the **synthetic system,** combines two or more materials to form a single product. In steel manufacturing, iron is combined with small quantities of other minerals at high temperatures to make steel.

The ultimate goal of production in all business endeavors is to make a profit. When competition is fierce and prices can't be raised to increase profits, smart businesspeople seek production **effectiveness,** increasing competitiveness by emphasizing efficiency, quality, and human relations.

The Industrial Revolution

Throughout most of human history, people have sought ways of improving production **efficiency**—they have tried to lower costs by getting the optimum output from each resource used in the production process. For example, the feudal system provided a more efficient division of labor than nomadic life or small tribal settlements. Then a series of technological advances in England starting 200 years ago brought about even more efficient production and ushered in a period known as the industrial revolution.

The first of these technological advances was **mechanization,** the use of machines to do work previously done by people. Adding to mechanization's efficiency was **standardization,** or the production of uniform, interchangeable parts. Henry Ford introduced the technological advance with the most wide-ranging influence, the **assembly line,** where an item is put together as it progresses past a number of workstations at which each employee performs a specific task.

As manufacturers became more adept at integrating mechanization, standardization, and the assembly line into the production process, they turned their attention toward eliminating as much costly manual labor as possible through **automation,** the process of performing a mechanical operation with the absolute minimum of human intervention. In automated production, people put machines into operation and monitor or regulate them and inspect their output. Beyond that, the machines do the work.

These four advances in production efficiency allowed the development of **mass production.** Manufacturing uniform goods in great quantities has cut prices, made products available to more people, and helped raise the standard of living in countries where mass production has been implemented.

The Second Industrial Revolution

At Deere & Company's tractor plant in Waterloo, Iowa, a conveyor belt sends freshly cut gears humming toward another assembly area. At one point, a mechanized arm seizes a roughly cut cogwheel, swings away from the belt, and inserts the gear into a device that polishes it smooth. At the other end of the device, another arm retrieves a finished gear and replaces it on the conveyor belt. Before this plant opened, several employees would have polished the unfinished gears.

synthetic system *Production process that combines two or more materials or components to create finished products; the reverse of an analytic system*

effectiveness *Increasing competitiveness through efficiency, quality, and improved human relations*

efficiency *Minimizing cost by maximizing the level of output from each resource*

mechanization *Use of machines to do work previously done by people*

standardization *Uniformity in goods or parts, making them interchangeable*

assembly line *Series of workstations at which each employee performs a specific task in the production process*

automation *Process of performing a mechanical operation with the absolute minimum of human intervention*

mass production *Manufacture of uniform products in great quantities*

Today, however, the polishing job is done more cheaply and precisely by computer-controlled machines and robots.[2]

What do developments like these mean? Many experts have compared them with the original industrial revolution because recent advances in production technology and processes are dramatically increasing efficiency. However, the second industrial revolution includes more than the efficiency of improved technology. Forward-looking companies now consider the structure and process of manufacturing to be strategic weapons, not merely ways to cut costs and boost efficiency.[3] Thus, they are pursuing effectiveness through efficiency in production technology, in process design, and in materials management, as well as through quality assurance and improved human relations.

In addition, operations effectiveness yields another powerful competitive strength: time. Because companies such as Xerox, Wal-Mart, Toyota, and Ford can now design and produce new products faster and can perform ongoing business functions more quickly, they have a big advantage over their slower competitors. For example, Siemens Medical Electronics in Danvers, Massachusetts, used advanced technology to cut almost half the time needed to develop a new product—and saved thousands of dollars in costs.[4]

Advances in Production Technology

More and more U.S. companies are refitting and reorganizing their factories to join the revolution. The most visible advances in production technology have been computers and **robots**—programmable machines that work with tools and materials to perform various tasks. Toyota, for instance, uses robots to handle dirty, noisy jobs (such as sanding car bodies) as well as for delicate tasks such as aligning car hoods with engine compartments.[5]

However, robots aren't always the answer. At Apple Computer's factory, for instance, five automated guided vehicles (AGVs) have been replaced by an even more efficient system called an HGV—the human-guided vehicle—because continually rerouting the AGVs to keep up with changes in the factory's layout was a problem.[6] The use of advanced technology helps improve efficiency under certain conditions:[7]

- When manual operations are highly concentrated in one area
- When a job is so difficult or tedious that no one wants to do it
- When many injuries occur in one area of the factory

One of the worst mistakes a company can make is to automate a series of tasks that have been performed manually without first examining the underlying process. If the basic process creates the wrong products or involves needless steps, there is no sense in automating it without cleaning it up first. In fact, just fixing the manual process can often improve productivity. When Corning Glass Works examined the manufacturing process at two of its factories, it discovered that 115 of the 235 processing steps were no longer necessary. It eliminated the steps, which cut production time from four weeks to three days—without automating the plants.[8]

robots *Programmable machines that can complete a variety of tasks by working with tools and materials*

PART TWO | OPERATING A BUSINESS

Computer-Aided Design and Engineering. The starting point for the production of anything—by any means—is designing the product. Computers have become an important part of the design phase. For example, **computer-aided design (CAD)** is the use of computer graphics in the design of products. A related process is **computer-aided engineering (CAE),** the use of computer-generated three-dimensional images and computerized calculations to allow engineers to test products. Using CAE, engineers can subject proposed products to changing temperatures, various stresses, and even simulated accidents, without ever building preliminary models. Using CAE saves time and money, and improves quality too. For example, when Boeing engineers designed the new 777 airplane, they corrected problems and tried new ideas on their computer screens, without building an actual model.[9] Thanks to computers and other technology, a product can now be perfected—or a bad idea abandoned—before production.

Computer-Aided Manufacturing. The use of computers to control production machines (robots, inspection devices, AGVs, and the like) is called **computer-aided manufacturing (CAM).** Good CAM systems increase the output, speed, accuracy, and dependability of assembly lines. Combinations of CAD and CAM are rapidly becoming significant factors at all sorts of companies, including Levi Strauss (jeans), La-Z-Boy (recliners), and Bally (shoes). Oneida uses CAD/CAM to design and produce forks, knives, and spoons. What used to take the company 70 weeks to do now takes about half as long and sometimes even less.[10]

Computer-Integrated Manufacturing. The highest level of computerization in operations management is **computer-integrated manufacturing (CIM),** in which all the elements of design, engineering, and production, including CAD and CAM, are integrated in computer networks that communicate across departments.[11] For many companies, CIM is a better route to competitive success than the massive automation schemes attempted in the past.[12] Inviting customer input throughout the process can boost quality and customer satisfaction as well.[13]

CIM is a key component of "the factory of the future." For example, the Fanuc plant in Japan has a small crew working with machines by day to manufacture parts for robots and machine tools. By night, the factory works alone. Robots unload raw materials, and other robots work them into simple shapes that can be used by the computer-controlled machining center (which can change its tools, reposition the part, and cut away unwanted portions of the part like a sculptor forming a figure). One person monitors all activity on closed-circuit television screens and corrects problems simply by typing commands on a computer keyboard.[14]

computer-aided design (CAD) *Use of computer graphics in the development of products or processes*

computer-aided engineering (CAE) *Use of computers to test products without building an actual model*

computer-aided manufacturing (CAM) *Use of computers to control production machines*

Designers at Ford use computer-aided design systems to plan new car models in great detail.

computer-integrated manufacturing (CIM) *Computer-based systems that coordinate and control all the elements of design and production, including CAD and CAM*

New Process Designs

Advances in technology have been accompanied by changes in the way the production process is organized. Mass-production methods have traditionally been geared toward large factories with several assembly lines, each producing a single product. Today, however, producers have turned to flexible manufacturing and the focused factory for greater productivity.

Flexible Manufacturing. One of the most recent changes in the production process has been the development of an alternative to **hard manufacturing,** using specialized production equipment that is locked into place. Generally, hard manufacturing is associated with **repetitive manufacturing,** in which the same thing is done over and over. It is economical only if similar items are produced at a steady rate. The mass production of everything from televisions to garden tools can fall into this category.

If hard manufacturing is repetitive, it may benefit from long-term savings on **setup costs,** the expenses incurred each time a manufacturer begins a production run of a different type of item. However, because hard manufacturing usually involves producing one unchangeable product design in large volume, its applications in many of today's markets are limited. In addition, the initial investment is high, because hard manufacturing requires specialized equipment for each of the operations involved in making a single item. Only after much production on a massive scale is the cost of that specialized equipment recouped. For example, Harley-Davidson, invested $4.8 million in hard manufacturing to make a particular motorcycle —only to have to dismantle the operation when demand for that product faded.[15]

One alternative is **flexible manufacturing** (also called *soft manufacturing* or *FMS,* for *flexible manufacturing system*), in which computer-controlled machines such as a machining center adapt to differing versions of similar operations (see Exhibit 8.2). With flexible manufacturing, changing from one product design to another requires only a few signals from the computer, not a complete refitting of the machinery. For example, a General Electric plant that produces over 1 million electric meters a year can easily be reprogrammed to produce any one of 2,000 variations.[16] With such flexibility, producers can outmaneuver less agile competitors by moving swiftly into profitable new fields, moving out when those fields begin to decline, and quickly adapting products to meet emerging customer needs.[17]

A flexible manufacturing system is particularly desirable for a **job shop,** which makes dissimilar items or produces at so irregular a rate that repetitive operations won't help. Most small machine shops are examples. The specialized equipment they produce is not churned out in any great quantity, and their customers often require customized features. The flexibility provided by computerization is also making some repetitive manufacturers more like job shops. For example, although Deere has a long tradition of repetitive manufacturing, one of its plants can turn out some 5,000 types of tractors—including one with a 15-gear transmission, one with fewer gears, and one without so much as a radio.[18]

---

hard manufacturing *Use of specialized production equipment that cannot readily be moved*

repetitive manufacturing *Repeated, steady production of identical goods or services*

setup costs *Expenses incurred each time a producer organizes resources to begin producing goods or services*

flexible manufacturing *Production use of computer-controlled machines that can adapt to various versions of the same operation; also called* soft manufacturing

job shop *Firm that produces dissimilar items or that produces its goods or services at intervals*

212

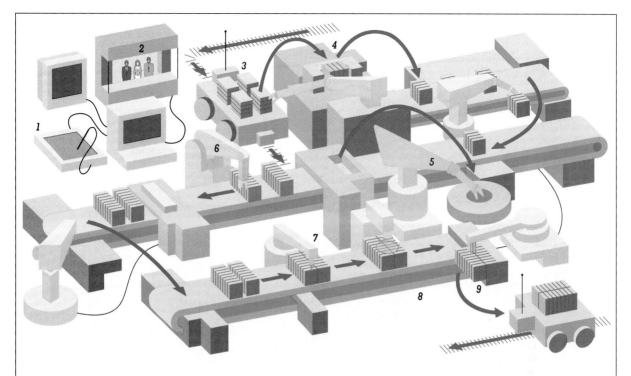

1. *A fully automated flexible manufacturing system begins with an electronic drafting board that transmits data to the electronic "foreman" of the system.*

2. *Managers keep track of the robots' work simply by consulting remote terminals for daily output data.*

3. *In response to a computer command, an AGV is loaded automatically in the storage area and brings the parts to the assembly line. A wire under the floor sends low-frequency radio signals that establish the carrier's path.*

4. *A programmed pick-and-place robot picks up pieces from the carrier, fits them into the lathe, and places them on the conveyor belt.*

5. *The various machining tools needed for this operation are supplied by a revolving holder. The central controller directs the lathe to choose the appropriate tool for each cutting step.*

6. *An assembly robot puts the parts together. Because assembly operations are often quite complex, robots of this type are more difficult to develop than some of the other kinds.*

7. *A welding robot, which fixes the parts in place, is a good example of flexible automation in action: The robot has been programmed to make all the different welds required on this product.*

8. *An inspection device, a camera plus a semiconductor chip, checks the finished item against standards.*

9. *Another pick-and-place robot puts the finished products on an AGV, which will bring them to shipping.*

Although a growing number of U.S. factories are taking advantage of flexible manufacturing, such systems do have limitations.[19] The products made by an FMS system require similarly sized machines, accuracy, power, tolerance, and, often, standardized parts. Also, developing a flexible system requires a long period of planning and development before any payoff is realized, so managers seeking short-term profits might be tempted to avoid the investment required by flexible manufacturing systems.[20]

The Focused Factory. One advantage of flexible manufacturing is that plants can be smaller, more specialized, and closer to important markets, which are also key characteristics of the **focused factory.** Instead of trying to produce in one location everything for every

Exhibit 8.2
Fully Automated Flexible Manufacturing System
A flexible manufacturing system uses computer-controlled robots throughout the production process. It is capable of switching rapidly from production of one item to production of another.

focused factory *Manufacturing facility that deals with only one narrow set of products*

Say you need a pager to keep in touch with your home or office. You don't want just any pager, though—you want the right color (after all, you do have to wear it), and you want it to play a discrete musical sequence when a call arrives. In short, you want a product created for your unique needs. Where can you find somebody to make just the pager you want? Pagers are mass-produced gadgets that roll off production lines by the thousands. You can't expect anybody to customize one for you, at least not without waiting for weeks and spending hundreds or thousands of dollars for it—can you?

For your customized pager, you can call Motorola's pager factory in Boynton Beach, Florida. How long will it take? Motorola can usually have your pager built within an hour and a half. (If you think that's fast, the plant's director of manufacturing, Sherita Ceasar, says the company is close to building a custom pager while the customer is still on the phone placing the order!) Then, depending on where you live, the unit will be in your hands the same day, or the next day at the latest.

Manufacturing that is this fast and still this flexible is no small accomplishment. Moreover, it provides a strong dose of hope for the future of

SMART FACTORIES AND THE REVIVAL OF U.S. MANUFACTURING

U.S. industry. Motorola's Boynton Beach facility joins an elite group of U.S. manufacturing plants that are racing past their global rivals (including the vaunted Japanese automation marvels) in the quest to deliver high-quality products in a hurry, often with customization for individual clients.

The force behind this industrial renaissance is the microprocessor, the computer-on-a-chip device that controls just about everything from toasters to automobile engines these days. In factories such as Motorola's, microprocessors route customer orders, direct robots, and control the flow along assembly lines. However, this isn't the hands-off, robotic automation often associated with flexible manufacturing systems (FMS). Humans play the central role here, making split-second decisions and

performing precision assembly work that robots stumble over.

Unlike the huge, complex, and expensive FMS installations that characterized manufacturing technology in the 1980s, Motorola's plant and others like it are built around teams of highly trained employees and agile computer systems. The idea is not to produce thousands of identical products one after the other, but to customize products as much as possible for every customer. Because information flow is so vital when you're building in small batches or even individual units, software has become more important than machinery in these factories.

An IBM manufacturing manager calls the microprocessor "America's secret weapon" in the global marketplace. In fact, some of Japan's massive, automated factories that inspired awe and even fear just a few years ago are now starting to look like a disadvantage. Not only does their complexity create all kinds of operating problems, but they have trouble responding to the growing demand for customized products. The best sign of how well U.S. manufacturers are doing these days is the number of overseas visitors trooping through U.S. factories to see what this secret weapon is all about.

market, the focused factory concentrates on a narrower set of products for a particular market.

Focused factories have been established for two reasons. First, it is difficult for a factory to do *everything* well. Management must decide what it needs to do particularly well—say, cut delivery time—and deemphasize something less important. Second, competence comes from simplicity and repetition. A focused factory with clear objectives and support from top management as well as sufficient experience is likely to be efficient and therefore competitive.[21] In fact, some experts say that giant factories are just too unwieldy to manage; smaller factories are easier to control and, with FMS, can respond more quickly to changes in the marketplace.[22]

Materials Management
Modern companies like Harley-Davidson are also attempting to become more efficient and profitable by taking a closer look at the way

they handle **inventory,** the goods and materials they stock for the production process and for sales to final customers. Every company needs a system of **inventory control,** some way of determining the right quantities of supplies and products to have on hand and some way to keep track of where those items are. Inventory control also means protecting inventories. Taking pains to purchase materials efficiently or to stockpile finished products is pointless if the materials or products are lost or damaged in storage.

One of the main issues in materials management is inventory size. Large inventories take advantage of economies of scale and allow customer demand to be met quickly, but they also tie up the company's money. That's why companies want to limit inventories—sometimes to practically nothing. However, whittling down supplies too much carries its own dangers. It is just as costly, if not more so, to stop production while waiting for supplies. Thus, a major goal of materials management is to shorten and stabilize **lead times,** the periods that elapse between the placement of a supply order and the receipt of materials. The challenge is to have enough inventory to keep production going while tying up a minimum of money.

Material Requirements Planning. One technique used to control inventory is called **material requirements planning (MRP),** which helps a manufacturer get the correct materials where they are needed on time and without unnecessary stockpiling. A computer calculates when certain materials are needed, when they should be ordered, and when they should be delivered so that they won't cost too much to store. Some companies produce only those products already ordered and have little difficulty determining how much inventory they will need throughout production. Other companies, however, cannot predict as precisely, so their estimation of inventory materials becomes more complicated.[23]

MRP can help companies that make complicated products. For example, a job shop's products are always changing, so the parts and materials required for production are always changing. Nevertheless, each part must be in the right place at the right time. What's more, there may be subassemblies such as motors or circuit boards that also require careful scheduling in order to be in the right place when required. Computer-based MRP is valuable in coordinating the delivery of various materials, each subassembly, and finished products.

Just-in-Time Systems. Many manufacturers have implemented an inventory control method known as the **just-in-time (JIT) system.** This is another method of achieving the goal sought through MRP—having only the right amounts of materials arrive at precisely the times they are needed—but it adds the human element by stressing teamwork in the production process. The purpose of JIT is to eliminate waste by using small inventories that require less storage space, less accounting, and less investment. Moreover, JIT is geared for continual and constant improvement. The JIT system grew out of the Japanese *kanban* system, in which cards are used to keep various operations informed about what they should be doing to maintain a smooth production flow.[24]

A JIT system requires careful preplanning, which has some indirect benefits. For instance, reducing stocks of parts to practically noth-

inventory *Goods held on hand for the production process or for sales to final customers*

inventory control *Method of determining the right quantity of various items to have on hand and of keeping track of their location, use, and condition*

lead times *Periods that elapse between placement of a purchase order and receipt of materials from the supplier*

material requirements planning (MRP) *Method of getting the correct materials where they are needed for production and doing it on time and without unnecessary stockpiling*

just-in-time (JIT) system *Continuous process of inventory control that, through teamwork, seeks to deliver a small quantity of materials where and when they are needed*

Coleman, which makes lanterns, coolers, and camping stoves, adopted a just-in-time system as a way of reducing inventory costs and the need for storing work in progress. Paul Grimes works in the Wichita, Kansas, plant, which uses JIT to turn out more products without more employees.

ing ("zero inventory") requires factories to keep production flowing smoothly from beginning to end without any holdups. A constant flow requires good teamwork: No one wants to be caught slowing the flow or holding up production. On the other hand, JIT places a tremendous burden on suppliers, such as the steel companies that supply an auto factory, because they must be able to meet the production schedules of their customers.

Organizations that use JIT report enormous returns on their investment. St. Luke's Episcopal Hospital in Houston saved $1.5 million over three years when it closed its enormous supplies warehouse and set up "stockless distribution." Rather than storing and handling thousands of items, the hospital receives daily deliveries from Baxter International (the nation's largest hospital supplier), whose computers communicate directly with St. Luke's inventory management system. Each day Baxter gathers the needed materials and delivers directly to each area inside the hospital.[25]

Manufacturing Resource Planning. Advanced inventory control methods such as MRP and JIT have caused some dramatic shifts in corporate management. For example, in the past, employees spent hours maintaining inventory records, some of which were only 60 percent accurate.[26] Today many companies are integrating inventory management with production activities through **manufacturing resource planning (MRP II),** a computer-based system that manages production planning and control by integrating information gathered from financial, accounting, personnel, marketing, and other departments.

However, unless every employee conscientiously updates the system, the information may become outdated and inaccurate. Handled with painstaking discipline, the software can simulate what might happen in the plant under various conditions, thus allowing managers to perform "what if" analyses.[27] For example, Compaq Computer used MRP II software to determine whether it had enough capacity and

manufacturing resource planning (MRP II) *Computer-based system that integrates data from all departments to manage production planning and control*

PART TWO | OPERATING A BUSINESS

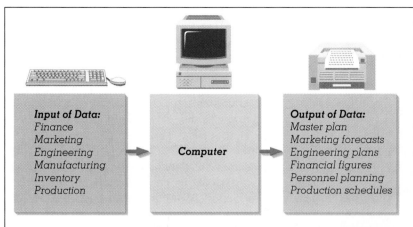

Exhibit 8.3
MRP II
An MRP II computer system gives managers in every department easy access to data from all other departments, which in turn makes it easier to generate—and adhere to—the organization's overall plans, forecasts, and schedules.

Input of Data:
Finance
Marketing
Engineering
Manufacturing
Inventory
Production

Computer

Output of Data:
Master plan
Marketing forecasts
Engineering plans
Financial figures
Personnel planning
Production schedules

parts to build 10,000 personal computers—and what would be needed to build up to 30,000 more.[28] MRP II can also integrate a company's activities, both in the plant and in the office (see Exhibit 8.3). With MRP II, every department works from the same data. Moreover, the system can track each step of production, allowing managers throughout the company to consult other managers' inventories, schedules, and plans. An MRP II system linked with computer-aided design can automatically begin the process of ordering the parts and materials needed to produce a new product. In addition, with MRP II, people on the factory floor can draw on data once reserved for top executives, such as inventory levels, back orders, and unpaid bills.

Quality Assurance

Efficiency and productivity alone are not enough to ensure a company's competitive standing. Quality is also important. During the 1970s, some major U.S. industries let quality levels slip drastically, and many customers defected to imported products. For example, as much as one-third of the market share for U.S. automobiles went to Japanese firms during that time. Experts in Detroit said that the average sticker price of a U.S.-built car was once inflated by as much as 25 percent to pay for costs directly related to low quality, including surplus scrap, rejected parts, inspections, repairs, and warranties.[29] Just to make up for poor quality, the typical U.S. company spent 10 to 20 percent of its revenue on everything from product testing to defending itself against product-liability suits.[30]

Recently, however, some U.S. industries, including the automobile industry, have greatly improved their attention to quality. The traditional means for doing so is **quality control,** measuring quality against some standard after the good or service has been produced and weeding out defects. With some quality-control systems, employees check and test output at random—every tenth item, every hundredth, and so on—and report on all the rejects, telling how many there were in a given period and why they were thrown out or reworked. Quality control, however, is only part of the picture.

A more comprehensive approach is **quality assurance,** a system of companywide policies, practices, and procedures to assure that qual-

quality control Routine checking and testing of a finished product for quality against some standard

quality assurance System of policies, practices, and procedures implemented throughout the company to create and produce quality goods and services

North American Lighting in Flora, Illinois, uses quality assurance to identify and correct problems in its automobile headlamp components before they are assembled. This system allows the company to uncover and correct any defects before the headlamps are attached to new cars.

statistical process control (SPC)
Monitoring the production process using control charts

statistical quality control (SQC)
Use of random sampling to test the quality of production output

ity is built into every product so that each meets preset quality standards. Quality assurance includes quality control as well as doing the job right the first time by designing tools and machinery properly, demanding quality parts from suppliers, training employees better, and encouraging them to take pride in their work. Henry J. Heinz, founder of the food giant, described the essence of this effort years ago: "Doing common things uncommonly well."[31]

Quality assurance also includes the now widely used concept of **statistical process control,** in which the *process* of production is monitored through the use of control charts so that managers can see whether production is proceeding consistently as planned or whether product quality varies.[32] Another quality-assurance concept is **statistical quality control (SQC),** a system designed to solve the types of quality problems that crop up in industries where the production process is so complex that thousands of tests have to be conducted to ensure quality at all levels. Statistical quality control applies the same method that Gallup polls use to determine popular opinion: If you carefully select a handful of representative parts, you can figure out an approximate truth about the whole.

Statistical quality control increases efficiency because inventories decline, work moves more smoothly, and costs drop. Moreover, managers may also learn of other problems when they focus on quality. For instance, quality expert W. Edwards Deming once suggested that employees at Pontiac Engine Plant No. 18 track problems that were cropping up with some connecting-rod bolts. Sure enough, they discovered that all the defects originated from one supplier, and that contract was immediately terminated. At that one plant, statistical quality control increased the proportion of acceptable products coming off the production line from 60 percent to 96 percent, and scrap rates and inventories fell.[33]

Total Quality Management. The highest level of quality awareness is the concept of total quality management (TQM), defined in Chapter 6 as a comprehensive approach that involves building quality into every organizational process as a way to improve customer satisfaction. Leading manufacturers such as Hewlett-Packard, Toyota, Fiat, and Ciba-Geigy employ TQM, and the concept applies equally well to service businesses, nonprofit organizations, and government agencies.[34] For example, the U.S. Navy has implemented TQM programs in a wide range of locations. Instead of relying solely on quality control in the Cherry Point naval aviation depot in North Carolina, Navy officials found that TQM helped the facility reduce the number of defects from as many as 10 per aircraft serviced to as few as 1 for every two planes.[35]

Here's what R. L. Heidke, vice president and director of corporate quality for Eastman Kodak, says of TQM: "We have found that the principles of TQM which we practice at Eastman Kodak Company are just as applicable to hospitals, schools, and local government.

We believe the basics of TQM are universal, and they include customer focus, teamwork, analytical approach to process management and decision making, management leadership, and continuous improvement. Application of these principles is not something one does in addition to their regular work, it is the way they do their work."[36]

Quality Standards and Awards. Companies that do business in Europe have to leap an extra quality hurdle. All goods and services sold in Europe must meet the requirements of ISO 9000, a set of international quality standards that establishes a minimum level of acceptable quality. Set by the International Organization for Standardization, ISO 9000 focuses on internal production and process issues that affect quality, but it doesn't measure quality in terms of customer satisfaction or business results.[37]

Organizations that want to improve quality can also follow the guidelines of various national or state quality awards. The European Quality Award, for example, honors outstanding performance in quality leadership, customer satisfaction, and business results. In Japan, the Deming Prize is a highly regarded industrial quality award. The Canada Awards for Business Excellence looks at total quality management as well as entrepreneurship and innovation. In the United States, the Malcolm Baldrige National Quality Award honors the quality achievements of U.S. companies. Delaware, Florida, Maine, New York, and Wyoming are just some of the states that have instituted quality awards to encourage higher quality levels.[38] Even if an organization doesn't want to actually apply for an award, quality can be improved by simply measuring performance against the award's standards—and fixing any problems uncovered by this process.

Improving Human Relations

Companies can boost the bottom line by improving human relations so that employees approach their work more intelligently, are happier, and work harder.[39] **Methods improvement** examines jobs with an eye to improving the efficiency level.[40] It includes such considerations as changing operation sequences, balancing work loads, training employees, simplifying materials handling, and applying **ergonomics,** the study of human characteristics in designing and arranging the most effective and safest tasks, equipment, and environments.[41]

In addition to improved efficiency, companies are interested in how employees relate to their jobs. Job rotation, for instance, may provide challenges for employees and increase personal esteem as they develop new skills. Job enlargement, expanding an employee's tasks, may be the answer to oversimplification. Similarly, job enrichment expands tasks as well as responsibility, providing a sense of achievement, recognition, and growth.[42]

Another way of providing more job satisfaction is by using **quality circles,** in which a small group of employees meets regularly to find solutions to quality, safety, and production problems. When properly structured, quality circles and similar problem-solving teams not only improve the final product but also help create a sense of unity among all the employees of the company.

For example, as part of its well-publicized "Quality Is Job One"

methods improvement *Examining all aspects of a job or task in order to improve efficiency levels*

ergonomics *Study of human performance in relation to the tasks performed, the equipment used, and the environment*

quality circles *Regularly scheduled meetings of a small group of employees to come up with solutions to quality, safety, and production problems*

campaign, Ford set up quality circles at its Louisville, Kentucky, plant. Trucks from the plant had consistently rated lowest on Ford's quality scale. Under threat of a permanent plant shutdown, managers and employees agreed on a series of changes, some directly related to production issues. One assembly-line employee suggested turning some bolts to face up instead of down so that the bolts could be tightened easily from above. Management created the position of "quality upgrader," to track such problems as loose bolts and poorly fitting parts while the assembly line continues running. Also, the plant was spruced up and kept spotless, and employees who once had to sit on spare parts to eat lunch now enjoy picnic tables throughout the plant. Morale improved, and absenteeism dropped to 1 percent from a high on some days of more than 6 percent. These changes helped Ford halve warranty costs, reduce the number of defects per truck, and become more competitive.[43]

Quality circles have been more successful in Japan than they have been in the United States. Management professor Peter Drucker attributes this difference to the fact that U.S. companies haven't adopted statistical quality control to the extent that Japanese firms have. Without the constant monitoring and feedback that statistical quality control provides, the efforts and contributions of quality circles can be difficult to measure, and the lack of feedback can frustrate both employees and managers.[44]

Competitiveness in Service Operations

Although efficiency has received stronger emphasis in the manufacturing industries, its potential has not been lost on the service industries. Some services, though, may never be suited to mass production. For instance, few would be reassured by the image of a patient on a hospital assembly line, with robot-doctors performing the steps of a standardized appendectomy. However, service industries such as fast-food chains, hotels, accounting firms, car-rental agencies, and even some real estate firms use mass-production principles ingeniously. As in a Model T factory, each step and procedure is standardized, and equipment performs each task efficiently.

Quality, both of product and of human relations, is also an issue outside assembly-line industries. Darla Mendales, vice president of corporate quality management at Fidelity Investments, is working to ensure that her company's services meet customer expectations. Her efforts range from fast, courteous phone service to simpler application forms. Her task is complex because, as a colleague notes, a shift to customer satisfaction is difficult for a system that has always emphasized speed and efficiency. However, Mendales is making impressive strides as she gradually persuades other managers to define quality in terms of customer satisfaction.[45]

Computerized infant-monitoring equipment has improved productivity and the quality of health care at Stanford Hospital's newborn intensive care unit. The sensors automatically detect any changes in the infants' vital signs and alert nurses so that they can respond.

Toward World-Class Manufacturing

Companies like Harley-Davidson are constantly reminded that they compete in a global economy; more companies are seeking growth by selling in other countries, which puts pressure on the companies in those markets. To compete globally, companies are increasingly pursuing *world-class manufacturing,* a term used to describe a level of quality and operational effectiveness that puts a company among the top performers worldwide. As an executive at Convex Computer notes: "If you are in a worldwide business, you had better be world-class."[46]

Compare the performance of Nucor, an upstart steel producer, with that of Bethlehem Steel, one of the country's oldest and largest producers. An innovative Nucor plant in Crawfordsville, Indiana, produces roughly 1 million tons of steel a year with about 400 employees. In contrast, the Burns Harbor Bethlehem Steel plant, also in Indiana, produces 4 1/2 times as much steel, but needs 15 times as many employees to do so. Not surprisingly, Nucor's efficiency has yielded profits while Bethlehem and other "Big Steel" companies are hurting.[47]

More and more world-class manufacturers are improving quality by using **benchmarking,** the process of comparing an organization's

benchmarking *Process of comparing a company's processes and products with standards set by the world's best and then matching or exceeding those standards*

MERGING HAND-MADE CRAFTSMANSHIP AND WORLD-CLASS MANUFACTURING

Can advanced technology share a factory with old-fashioned craftsmanship? Rolls-Royce has proven that the answer is yes. The legendary British company is renowned for its luxurious Rolls-Royce and Bentley cars and limousines. At its peak, the company was selling more than 3,000 vehicles a year in Great Britain and international markets, with the lowest-priced car costing well over $100,000.

However, like General Motors, Ford, Chrysler, and Toyota, Rolls-Royce saw its car sales stall in the early 1990s when the world economy faltered. To remain competitive, Michael J. Donovan, one of Rolls-Royce's managing directors, realized that the company had to cut production costs and improve productivity. Donovan and other top managers came up with a plan to combine the two factories into one and cut time out of the 50 days needed to manufacture each car. Using cross-functional teamwork and benchmarking, they also set out to meet or exceed the highest international standards of automobile manufacturing.

Top executives slashed the number of management layers in the factory from seven to four and reduced the workforce from 5,700 to 2,400 through voluntary retirements and buyouts. Next, they redesigned the factory to create 16 manufacturing zones. Every zone operated as a "factory within a factory" to manufacture its part of the product on time and within budget. Each of the 10 or so teams in each zone was composed of production employees, engineers, and any other employees needed to accomplish the team's tasks. Teams were given freedom to complete their work as they saw fit, and they

quickly found ways of speeding up production while boosting quality beyond the already high levels.

The new arrangement pleases Paul Simm, who used to sit at one of the workstations on the assembly line and handle the same task over and over. Now Simm is a member of a team that assembles V-8 engines, and he puts together much of each engine he touches. "It's more interesting; I've got more responsibility, and in the end you've got something with your name on it," Simm says. "That certainly helps improve quality. If there's a problem, it's going to come back to you."

Despite the streamlined production methods, hand-crafted quality has not disappeared from the Rolls-Royce factory. Metalworkers still craft each stainless steel front grille and hood ornament by hand. At a customer's request, the woodworking shop will make a dashboard in any type of wood. Even with the hand crafting, Rolls-Royce has been able to reduce production time to 30 days and retain the painstaking attention to detail and quality that made the company famous.

---

processes and products with the world's best and then working to meet or beat those standards. These companies know that using benchmarks from other industries can help them make improvements that go beyond what their competitors are doing. For example, manufacturers might measure their production standards against the performance of Toyota, IBM, and Hewlett-Packard, considered among the best in the world.

Production and the Natural Environment

Today's production managers spend a significant amount of time on environmental concerns. Virtually every aspect of a company's operations has the potential to pollute. Factories can generate air pollution, water pollution, solid-waste-disposal problems, excessive noise, and other undesirable elements. Service businesses can't escape the environmental issue either; even if their processes don't generate pollution, just the presence of hundreds of people in an office building can create problems.

Since pollution control is often expensive, many of these environmental problems pit nature against the bottom line. However, an increasing number of manufacturers are discovering that they can win on both counts. Reynolds Metals saved $30 million in pollution-control equipment and reduced emissions by 65 percent when it switched to water-based inks in its packaging plants. Clairol, which used to flush production pipes with water, now cleans them with foam balls. This change netted $240,000 a year in reduced disposal costs and cut wastewater discharge by 70 percent.[48]

PRODUCTION AND OPERATIONS MANAGEMENT

Despite all the recent advances in production technology and methods, someone must still take overall responsibility for this important aspect of a company's existence. **Production and operations management (POM)** is the coordination of an organization's resources for manufacturing goods or producing services. Like other types of management, POM involves the basic functions of planning, organizing, directing, and controlling. In addition, the production and operations manager must oversee creation of the product.

POM is growing as one of the business world's most dynamic areas of specialization. For one thing, it is becoming the focus of many companies' efforts to become more competitive and profitable. The field is challenging because (1) it's undergoing rapid change; (2) it involves many activities, from interpreting market research (determining what kinds of goods and services should be produced) to production planning and control of the production process; and (3) it applies to all kinds of companies, regardless of size or product. Once regarded as a second-class career track for business-school graduates, production management is enjoying a surge in popularity. Leading schools such as MIT, Northwestern, Cornell, and Purdue have added or upgraded courses and degree programs in manufacturing.[49]

production and operations management (POM) *Coordination of an organization's resources in order to manufacture its goods or produce its services*

Like all other types of management, POM requires careful consideration of the company's goals, the strategies for attaining those goals, and the standards against which results will be measured. It also involves an understanding of future demand, possible product changes, and the resources needed to respond to customer or competitor shifts.

One long-term issue that must be resolved early is the location of production facilities. Although being near low-cost resources and transportation was once of overriding importance, today such considerations as local living standards and the qualifications of the local workforce enter into the decision (see Exhibit 8.4). Look at the availability of labor, for instance. Firms that need highly trained accountants, engineers, or computer scientists often locate near university communities such as Boston. On the other hand, if most of the jobs can be filled by unskilled or semiskilled employees, firms can choose locations where such labor is available at a relatively low cost.

Another consideration is access to transportation and resources. A company that must bring bulky materials to a plant or ship cumbersome products out has to be close to highways and rail lines. Advanced telecommunications and overnight delivery now make it possible for some service industries and the service components of manufacturing industries to operate away from industrial areas—in such locations as Greenwood, South Carolina, where the George W. Park Seed Company is based.

In the shorter term, top managers must clarify what they expect

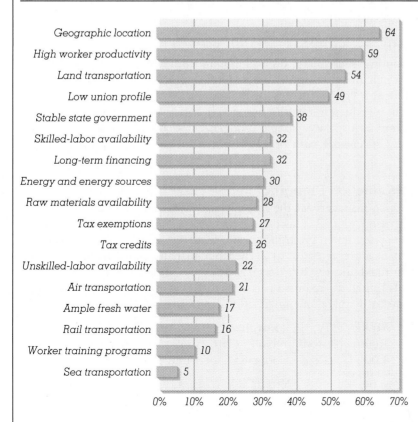

Exhibit 8.4
Important Factors in Site Selection
This chart shows the results of a survey measuring the importance of various factors in site selection. Shown is the percentage of 1,000 executives who rated a given factor "vitally important."

production forecasting *Estimating how much of a company's goods and services must be produced in order to meet future demand*

from production and operations. To do so, they start with **production forecasting,** which deals specifically with the question of how much to produce in a certain time span. Using past sales figures and educated guesses about the future behavior of the economy and of competitors, managers estimate future demand for the company's products. (When a company is beginning to produce new products and has no history to rely on, managers usually adapt information about related products and markets.) These estimates are used to plan, budget, and schedule the use of resources.

PRODUCTION CONTROL

production control *Production planning, routing, scheduling, dispatching, and follow-up and control in an effort to achieve efficiency and high quality*

For an idea of the wide range of activities involved in one part of POM, consider **production control,** a set of steps leading to the efficient production of a high-quality product. The manufacture of complex goods is not simply a matter of adding part A to part B to part C and so forth until a product emerges ready to ship. Automobiles, for example, are assembled from subunits that vary from car to car. A system is needed to ensure that the correct engine, the right tires, and the proper trim reach each car at the precise point in the assembly process at which they are to be added. In the production of complex services, too, someone needs to track the various elements and employees involved. For example, in the development of computer software, someone has to make sure that parts of the program written by various people mesh well and that the user manual is accurate too.

Production-control procedures vary from company to company. Most manufacturing processes, however, have five steps: planning, routing, scheduling, dispatching, and following up and controlling. When many resources and complex procedures are involved, production control may become complicated. To get a feeling for the complexities, follow the five steps taken by an imaginary small company as it makes a simple product, wooden tables. The company has just received a rush order for 500 white and 500 unpainted tables.

Production Planning

bill of materials *Listing of all parts and materials in a product that are to be made or purchased*

Once managers set the larger goals, they move on to plan the production process. This is no small task, as the imaginary table company illustrates. From industrial and design engineers, the production manager receives lists of all the labor, machinery, and materials needed to make the 1,000 tables that have been ordered. A **bill of materials** lists all the required parts and materials and specifies whether they are to be made or purchased:

Make	Purchase
1,000 table tops	4,000 dowels (one to fasten each leg)
4,000 table legs	50 gallons of white paint

The next step is to determine the quantity of these materials already on hand. The production manager discovers that the company has enough wood and paint but only 2,000 dowels. So an order for an

224

additional 2,000 dowels must be placed with a supplier who can deliver on time.

Routing

Routing, the second step in production control, is the task of specifying the sequence of operations and the path through the facility that work will take. The way production is routed depends on the type of product and the layout of the plant (see Exhibit 8.5). The three main classifications are process, assembly-line, and fixed-

routing *Specifying the sequence of operations and the path the work will take through the production facility*

Exhibit 8.5
Routing and Production Layouts
The way a company routes the sequence of operations and the path the work will take (see Figure A) depends on the layout of the plant (see Figures A, B, and C below and on next page).

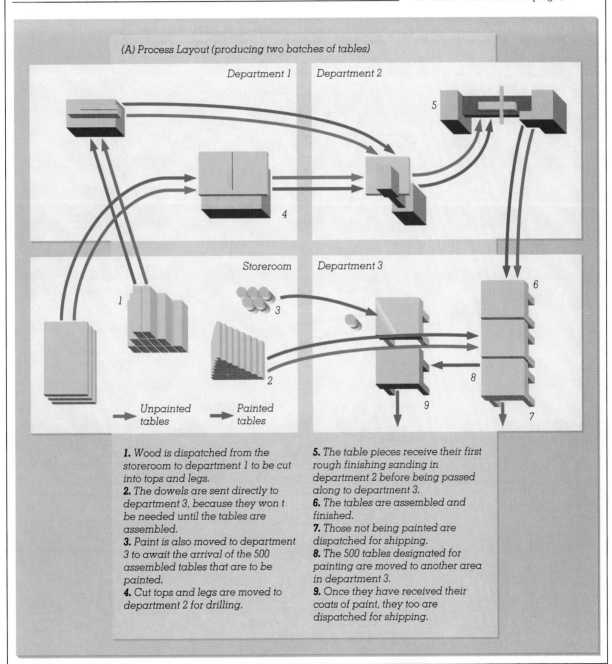

(A) Process Layout (producing two batches of tables)

Department 1   Department 2

Storeroom   Department 3

→ Unpainted tables   → Painted tables

1. Wood is dispatched from the storeroom to department 1 to be cut into tops and legs.
2. The dowels are sent directly to department 3, because they won t be needed until the tables are assembled.
3. Paint is also moved to department 3 to await the arrival of the 500 assembled tables that are to be painted.
4. Cut tops and legs are moved to department 2 for drilling.

5. The table pieces receive their first rough finishing sanding in department 2 before being passed along to department 3.
6. The tables are assembled and finished.
7. Those not being painted are dispatched for shipping.
8. The 500 tables designated for painting are moved to another area in department 3.
9. Once they have received their coats of paint, they too are dispatched for shipping.

Exhibit 8.5 (continued)

(B) Assembly-Line Layout (registering for college classes)

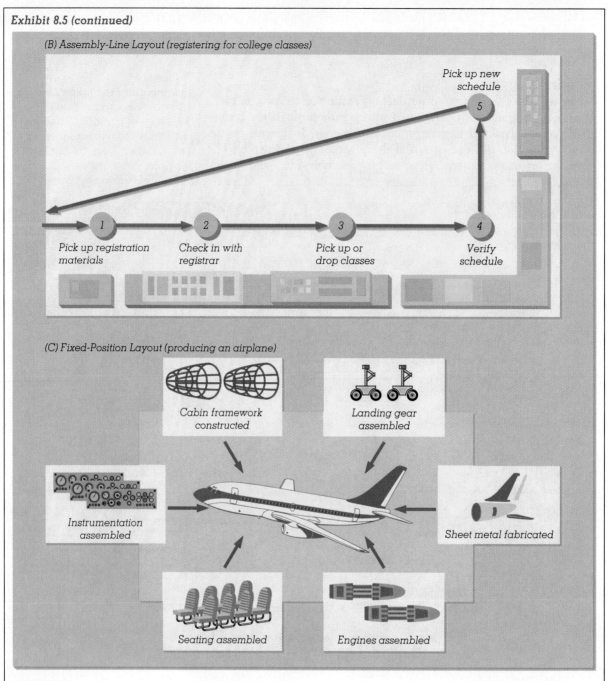

(C) Fixed-Position Layout (producing an airplane)

Routing: Steps in the sequence of operations

Production layouts:
The type of production layout that a company chooses depends on the goods or services it is producing.

(A) A process layout is arranged according to the specialized employees and materials involved in various phases of the production process.

(B) In an assembly-line layout, the developing product moves in a continuous sequence from one workstation to the next.

(C) A fixed-position layout requires employees and materials to be brought to the product.

position layouts.[50] They apply to both the manufacture of goods and the production of services.

Process Layout

The table-manufacturing company has three departments, each handling a different phase of the table's manufacture and each equipped with specialized tools, machines, and employees. Department 1 cuts wood into desired sizes and shapes. Department 2 does drilling and rough finishing. Department 3 assembles and finishes. This is a **process layout,** because it concentrates in one place everything needed to complete one phase of the process. The table tops and legs are routed from department 1, where they are made, to department 2 to have the dowel holes drilled and to be rough-finished, and then to department 3 for assembly, finishing, and painting.

Although the production process is straightforward under this system, materials handling is not. The table tops and legs are routed first to department 1 and then to department 2, but the dowels and paint are routed directly from inventory to department 3 (see Exhibit 8.5A). There, all 1,000 tables are assembled, but only 500 are painted.

Process layout is frequently used in service industries as well. A college, for example, may have a language department, a business department, a science department, and so on, each with its own supply of professors and classrooms. As students are processed into college graduates, they travel from one department to the next for exposure to a specific set of ideas.

Assembly-Line Layout

An alternative to process layout is the **assembly-line layout,** in which the main production process occurs along a line, and products in progress move from one workstation to the next. Materials and subassemblies of component parts may feed into the main line at several points, but the flow of production is continuous. Automobile and personal-computer manufacturers are just two of many industries that typically use this layout (see Exhibit 8.5B).

Some production of services is also organized this way. When students register for college classes in person, for example, the various clerks and registrars are stationed in some sort of line. Students proceed from one station to the next, acquiring the various documents that enable them to put together a schedule. Many colleges, such as the University of Washington in Seattle, have automated this process by allowing students to register for classes by phone. Piles of paper are replaced by the school's computer system, which guides callers through the registration process.

Fixed-Position Layout

Companies that produce such hard-to-move products as large aircraft and buildings use a **fixed-position layout,** in which the product

process layout Method of arranging equipment so that production tasks are carried out in discrete locations containing specialized equipment and personnel

The Jaguar plant in Brownslane, England, uses a process layout to locate in one place all the operations and materials needed for each step in the production process. The employees in this section of the plant use the same parts and operations to assemble components for car door panels.

assembly-line layout Method of arranging equipment in which production is a flow of work proceeding along a line of workstations

fixed-position layout Method of arranging equipment in which the product is stationary and equipment and personnel come to it

stays in one place and the employees and equipment are brought to it. This approach saves the expense and difficulty of moving the product (and the danger of damaging it). It also means that planning when to bring in employees and equipment is more difficult. A building contractor, for example, must plan carefully to avoid bringing in the cement trucks needed to pour the foundation before the bulldozers have finished grading the site (see Exhibit 8.5C).

Many services use fixed-position production as well. Home and landscape maintenance requires a fixed-position layout, and so does intensive care in a hospital. The patient stays in one place, and the nurses, doctors, food, drugs, and other supplies are all transported there.

Scheduling

scheduling *Process of determining how long each production operation takes and then setting a starting and ending time for each*

In any production process, managers must use **scheduling,** determining how long each operation takes and setting a starting and ending time for each. This is not easy, even in businesses as simple as the table company in the example. Here is what the table manufacturer's production manager has to consider in order to construct a schedule: If department 2 can drill 4,000 dowel holes in a day, then all 4,000 legs and all 1,000 table tops should arrive in department 2 on the same day. If department 1 can make 1,000 table tops and 1,000 legs a week, it should start on the legs three weeks before it starts to cut the tops, or all the parts won't be ready for departments 2 and 3 at the same time. If the entire order is to be shipped at the same time and as soon as possible, department 3 should paint the first 500 tables as they are assembled and finished so that the paint will be dry by the time the last 500 are completed. The schedule must also show how much time will elapse before the job reaches department 3— that is, how much time department 3 has available to work on other jobs before this one arrives.

Although this project is complicated enough, many are far more complicated. That's why many production managers chart each project's various steps. Earlier this century, Henry L. Gantt developed a technique for charting the steps to be taken and the time required. Exhibit 8.6 is a **Gantt chart,** which is basically a bar chart showing the amount of time required to accomplish each part of a manufacturing process. At a glance, managers can see whether they are on schedule, ahead of schedule, or behind schedule compared with what they had planned.

Gantt chart *Bar chart used to control schedules by showing how long each part of a production process should take and when it should take place*

In every process or project, one combination of tasks affects the elapsed time more than any other. For instance, at the table factory, producing the legs is one of the tasks in this sequence; if the legs take longer than expected, they will slow down the entire operation. On the other hand, the production schedule for the table tops is less critical—the tops could slip by up to two weeks and still be done by the time the legs are all done. The legs, then, are said to be on the *critical path,* whereas the tops aren't. Identifying the critical path is important because it shows managers where the highest-priority tasks are. Scheduling based on the critical path is called the **critical path method (CPM)** because it focuses on the particular sequence of

critical path method (CPM) *Scheduling method that estimates the smallest amount of time in which a project can be completed by projecting the time needed for completion of the longest sequence of tasks (the critical path)*

PART TWO | OPERATING A BUSINESS

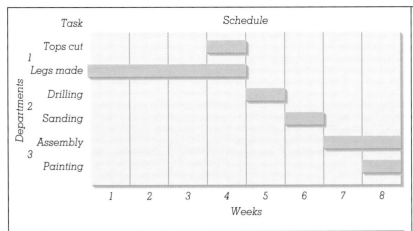

Task   Schedule

Departments

1
   Tops cut
   Legs made

2
   Drilling
   Sanding

3
   Assembly
   Painting

Weeks

Exhibit 8.6
A Gantt Chart: Scheduling a Complicated Table Order
A chart like this enables a production manager to see immediately the dates on which production steps must be started and completed if goods are to be delivered on schedule. Some steps may overlap to save time. For instance, after three weeks of cutting table legs, cutting table tops begins. This overlap ensures that the necessary legs and tops are completed at the same time and can move on together to the next stage in the manufacturing process.

tasks that is expected to take the longest time, thus determining when the project can be completed.

Consider the manufacture of shoes in Exhibit 8.7. At the beginning of the process, three parallel paths deal with heels, soles, and tops. All three processes must be finished before the next phase (sewing tops to soles and heels) can be started. However, one of the three paths—the tops—takes 33 days, whereas the other two take only 18 and 12 days. The shoe tops, then, are on the critical path because they will delay the entire operation if they fall behind schedule. In contrast, soles can be started up to 21 days after starting the tops without slowing down production. (This free time in the soles schedule is called *slack time;* managers can choose to produce the soles anytime during the 33-day period required by the tops.)

The production manager uses CPM to estimate the least possible amount of time in which the whole operation can be completed, basing this estimate on the projected time needed to complete the entire critical path. CPM can also help managers balance work loads. For instance, the shoe manager might have the sole people finish their work as soon as possible and then help the tops people with their work, which would speed up the entire process.

Exhibit 8.7
A CPM Chart: Manufacture of Shoes
In the manufacture of shoes, the critical path involves receiving, cutting the pattern, dyeing the leather, sewing the tops, sewing the tops to soles and heels, finishing, packaging, and shipping—a total of 62 time units.

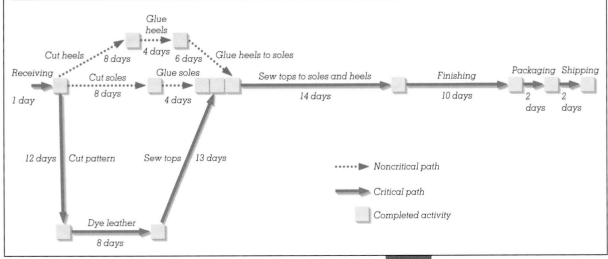

program evaluation and review technique (PERT) *Scheduling method similar to the critical path method but relying on statistical estimates of how long each task should take*

dispatching *Issuing work orders and routing papers to department heads and supervisors*

Another scheduling method, the **program evaluation and review technique (PERT),** is similar to CPM but is better suited to processes and projects in which managers can't predict task durations with complete confidence. Like CPM, PERT also focuses on the order in which tasks must occur. However, in place of a single time projection for each task, PERT uses four figures: an *optimistic* estimate (if things go well), a *pessimistic* estimate (if they don't go well), a *most likely* estimate (how long the task usually takes), and an *expected* time estimate, an average of the other three estimates.[51]

Dispatching

Dispatching is issuing work orders and distributing papers to department supervisors. These orders specify the work to be done and the schedule for its completion. In the case of the table manufacturer, the production manager would dispatch orders to the storeroom, requesting delivery of the needed materials (wood, dowels, paint) to the appropriate departments and machines before the scheduled starting time. Dispatching is considerably more difficult in industries employing fixed-position layouts. In hospitals, for example, dispatching is vital if patients are to receive timely care with the most efficient use of facilities.

Following Up and Controlling

Once the schedule has been set and the orders dispatched, a production manager cannot just sit back and assume that the work will get done correctly and on time. Even the best scheduler may misjudge the time needed to complete an operation, and production may be delayed by accidents, mechanical breakdowns, or supplier problems. So the production manager needs a system for handling delays and preventing a minor disruption from growing into chaos. A successful system is based on good communication between the employees and the production manager.

Suppose a machine breakdown causes department 2 of the table company to lose half a day of drilling time. If the schedule is not altered to direct other work to department 3, the employees and equipment in department 3 will sit idle for some time. If department 2 informs the production manager of its machine problem right away, the production manager can immediately reschedule some fill-in work for department 3.

In addition to such a follow-up system, production managers generally need a formal system for making sure the products meet quality standards. Traditionally, this was done by checking and testing completed components and products using quality-control techniques. Today, however, many companies use quality assurance and total quality management to build quality into the production process itself. In every industry, paying careful attention to every phase of production can improve effectiveness and, therefore, competitiveness and profits.

1 Diagram the conversion process.

The conversion process is input → transformation → output.

2 Cite the four technological advances that made mass production possible.

Mass production became possible after the development of mechanization, standardization, the assembly line, and automation.

3 Explain the use of flexible manufacturing and the focused factory as alternatives to hard manufacturing.

Hard manufacturing is using specialized production equipment that is locked into place. In contrast, flexible manufacturing uses computer-controlled machines to adapt the factory to differing versions of similar operations. The focused factory concentrates on a narrow set of products for a particular market, so manufacturers can make changes more rapidly.

4 Explain the use of material requirements planning, just-in-time systems, and manufacturing resource planning for more effective materials management.

Material requirements planning (MRP) determines when materials are needed, when they should be ordered, and when they should be delivered. Just-in-time systems (JIT) limit the quantity of materials on hand by making them available only when they are actually required for the production process. Manufacturing resource planning (MRP II) is a computerized system that brings together data from all parts of a company (including financial and design departments) to better manage production planning and control.

5 Differentiate between quality control and quality assurance.

Quality control focuses on measuring finished products against some preset standard and weeding out defects. Quality assurance, on the other hand, is a system of companywide policies, practices, and procedures to build quality into a product and assure that each product meets quality standards.

6 Define the five basic steps in production control.

(1) Planning is the analysis of what to produce and how much to produce, as well as where and how to produce it. (2) Routing is figuring out how production will proceed. (3) Scheduling adds the time element to the production process. (4) Dispatching is sending production orders. (5) Following up and controlling is seeing that everything proceeds according to plan, as well as figuring out how to cope with problems as they arise.

7 Identify the three main production layouts.

In a process layout, the developing product is sent from one department to another for a certain type of processing; specialized equipment and employees are stationed in each department. In an assembly-line layout, the product in progress proceeds along a continuous line of workstations. In a fixed-position layout, the product stays in one place, and the employees and equipment are brought to it.

8 Describe three techniques for improving scheduling.

Scheduling may be improved by using (1) the Gantt chart, which is a bar chart indicating the expected duration of specific tasks; (2) the critical path method (CPM), which identifies the sequence of tasks expected to take the longest in order to control the project completion time; and (3) the program evaluation and review technique (PERT), which is based on several statistical estimates of how long tasks can be expected to take.

Even though Harley-Davidson had regained its reputation for building dependable motorcycles, higher demand created a new dilemma for CEO Richard Teerlink: how to increase production and boost sales without sacrificing quality. Even though motorcycle enthusiasts in Europe, Japan, and Australia were eager to buy, Harley agreed to limit international exports to 30 percent of all sales until production caught up with demand in North America. Now Teerlink turned his attention to production and operations, the areas that had fueled Harley's return to prominence in the late 1980s.

Following Honda's lead, Harley installed the JIT system of inventory management. Among other things, JIT lowered the number of parts and supplies held in waiting, so Harley could spend more on research to improve quality and to speed up the manufacturing process. Harley adapted to JIT by changing everything from its purchasing practices to the layout of its factories. It also

forged closer relationships with a smaller group of suppliers who could deliver high-quality parts on time. Because Harley was using fewer suppliers, it was able to place larger orders and qualify for bulk discounts.

In addition, Harley redesigned its production machinery and created more standardized parts for multiple bike models. With this approach, the company could build individual models in smaller batches, which allowed for more frequent product upgrades. The smaller batches also cut down on the number of defective parts.

Now Teerlink decided that Harley had to do more. He appointed a vice president of continuous improvement to oversee further reductions in waste, defects, and variability. He also moved Harley deeper into flexible manufacturing, and he set up a create-demand team, a production team, and a product-support team to tap the knowledge of people who had experience in a variety of functions.

This emphasis on quality and world-class manufacturing has kept Harley well ahead of second-place Honda. Revamping its production and operations processes has even positioned Harley to turn the tables on Japanese companies: Harley-Davidson is now the best-selling imported motorcycle in Japan.

Your Mission: Teerlink has hired you as an operations consultant to evaluate Harley's manufacturing systems and to help plot its strategy for the future. For each of the following situations, choose the best response:

1. Harley doesn't automate any part of its operations without evaluating the underlying processes, fixing any problems, and then deciding whether automation makes sense. At a recent meeting with production staff, you ask for ideas about automating tasks that are still done manually. Which one of the following areas would you recommend that Harley automate?

a. A machining area where employees make a wide variety of unique tools and fixtures for use on the production line

b. The assembly area where gas tanks are attached to the cycle frames and where employees are complaining that they have to do the same simple job over and over again

c. The department where incoming parts (some of which are quite heavy and hard to handle) are unpacked and directed to the appropriate locations on the production line

2. The company's employees continually offer suggestions on improving quality, but you want to implement only those related to quality assurance rather than quality control. Which one of the following suggestions should you accept?

a. Have an inspector measure the time it takes to start the engines on finished motorcycles when the bikes are driven off the assembly line.

b. Find out why the stitching in some seat covers is breaking after a few months of use; then ask the manufacturer concerned to fix the problem.

c. Survey dealers to find out how often the factory ships the wrong owner's manual with a motorcycle; ask if this error rate is acceptable.

3. Harley's managers are well aware of the impact that employee attitudes and motivation have on quality and productivity. When studying several other manufacturing firms, managers have uncovered a number of approaches to getting employees involved and making sure they are satisfied with their work. Considering both cost and effectiveness, which of the following involvement/motivation programs do you think Harley should adopt?

a. Rotate employees through all the factory jobs, from engineering and design all the way through shipping, clerical work, and even janitorial work. Employees will better appreciate the challenges each job entails, and the result will be a more cohesive workforce with a greater sense of teamwork.

b. Encourage employees to start quality circles throughout the plant, and make sure they link their efforts to the company procedures for statistical quality control.

c. Adapt (b) so that employees start quality circles, but do not require the statistical reporting element; too much attention to tracking and monitoring will demoralize employees who feel that their every move is being watched and criticized.

4. One phase of the motorcycle-assembly process is split into three parallel task groups, each taking care of one general area of the motorcycle. The assembly line continues in a single line after the three parallel tasks are done (similar to the three parallel task groups in Exhibit 8.7). Considering the individual task times and critical path analysis, where should you assign several people whose old jobs in another factory have been eliminated?

Task	Time Required
Preparing stereo	15 minutes
Preparing saddle bags	5 minutes
Preparing mirrors	6 minutes
Preparing fog lights	10 minutes
Inspecting paint-job quality	45 minutes
Cutting wires to length	9 minutes
Installing connectors	18 minutes
Testing for continuity	10 minutes

a. Task group 1: Preparing accessories, which includes the stereo, the saddle bags, the mirrors, and the fog lights

b. Task group 2: Inspecting paint, which is done entirely by an automated electro-optical inspection robot

c. Task group 3: Assembling the electrical harness, which includes cutting wires to length, adding connectors, and testing for continuity[52]

KEY TERMS

analytic system (208)
assembly line (209)
assembly-line layout (227)
automation (209)
benchmarking (221)
bill of materials (224)
computer-aided design (CAD) (211)
computer-aided engineering (CAE) (211)
computer-aided manufacturing (CAM) (211)
computer-integrated manufacturing (CIM) (211)
conversion process (208)
critical path method (CPM) (228)
dispatching (230)
effectiveness (209)
efficiency (209)
ergonomics (219)

fixed-position layout (227)
flexible manufacturing (212)
focused factory (213)
Gantt chart (228)
hard manufacturing (212)
inventory (215)
inventory control (215)
job shop (212)
just-in-time (JIT) system (215)
lead times (215)
manufacturing resource planning (MRP II) (216)
mass production (209)
material requirements planning (MRP) (215)
mechanization (209)
methods improvement (219)
process layout (227)
production (208)

production and operations management (POM) (222)
production control (224)
production forecasting (224)
program evaluation and review technique (PERT) (230)
quality assurance (217)
quality circles (219)
quality control (217)
repetitive manufacturing (212)
robots (210)
routing (225)
scheduling (228)
setup costs (212)
standardization (209)
statistical process control (SPC) (218)
statistical quality control (SQC) (218)
synthetic system (209)

1. How does material requirements planning (MRP) differ from manufacturing resource planning (MRP II)?

2. Why is an effective system of inventory control important to every manufacturer?

3. What are the benefits of JIT systems?

4. Why have companies moved beyond quality control to quality assurance and total quality management?

5. What is benchmarking, and why do manufacturers use it?

6. Why is production and operations management particularly important today?

7. What is involved in each step of production control?

8. What factors need to be considered when selecting a site for a production facility?

A CASE FOR CRITICAL THINKING

PROFIT FORMULAS INCLUDE PEOPLE

At many companies, production problems arise when top management tries to impose changes from above: Employees may refuse to operate machinery or may intentionally slow down the work; the definitions of occupational roles may be confused; and systems may be designed without consideration for the people who will run them. None of this has to happen, however. From conception of change through implementation, a policy of frank and open communication among top executives, managers, and employees will smooth the road for all concerned.

James Lewis, president of Continental Container Systems (a division of Continental Can Company in Chicago), is credited with making the company profitable by installing process technology and by using effective people management. "To explain Continental's commitment to a future in manufacturing, we started 'communication circles,' which have gradually evolved into quality circles. To further show management's resolve, we established a no-layoff policy for the shop. We treat shop-floor employees as fixed assets." The result was an older, more experienced workforce adapting to process changes quickly and easily.

Of course, planning helps smooth the transition to new technology. In Germany, human resource managers at the European electronics giant Siemens review the production capacity and technology changes being planned, and then they determine the skills and abilities that the manufacturing workforce will need to operate the new equipment. Most Siemens employees remain with the company throughout their work lives, so they generally need additional training to handle advanced machinery. Siemens managers estimate that upgrading an employee's technical competence requires 5 to 7 years, so they now look as far as 10 years in the future when considering the skills that their production workforce will need.

Planning for new equipment is also having positive effects at General Motors. "Although GM is not yet the lowest-cost producer of motor vehicles, CIM [computer-integrated manufacturing] coupled with HIM [human-integrated manufacturing] will bring this about," predicts Gerald L. Elson, executive director of artificial intelligence. The HIM program emphasizes training; while old machinery is being torn out, employees are being trained to use the new tools being installed.

Companies are even revamping their organization structures so that they can improve production quality and productivity through employee involvement. Del Norte, a Texas-based maker of electronic security systems, has a new three-tier organization structure. The first tier is a quality steering committee that sets and communicates the company's direction. The second tier is a corrective team of middle managers and supervisors who support the work teams, share information across all departments, and form special teams of employees to tackle problems that touch more than one function. The third tier consists of the work teams that actually perform all production tasks.

Rewarding employee involvement is also important. Consolidated Edison of New York, a utility company, runs its *Employee Suggestion Awards Program.* Employees can receive as much as $15,000, based on how much money is actually saved as a result of the suggestion. "Most ideas are really solutions to problems that employees encounter regularly in the process of doing their jobs," says Laurie Hanson, Con Ed spokesperson. "How often have we all said, 'there's got to be a better way to do this'? But if we find a better way, no one—except maybe a nearby co-worker doing the same job—hears about it. Certainly supervisors or managers don't hear about it. This program helps correct that oversight."

If employees are treated with respect and are provided a good working environment, they respond. "Declining productivity was never a blue-collar problem," said Bruce Bumpus, vice president of Zymark Corporation, which makes robotic systems in the Boston area. Thus, executives are beginning to brief production employees (even on financial and sales information), and management is beginning to listen to employees—to the benefit of all.

1. How should manufacturing employees be involved in the development of JIT systems?
2. Besides increasing employee involvement and providing technical training, what can be done to improve human relations in a production facility?
3. In any attempt to improve human relations, is it possible for management to involve employees too much?

BUILDING YOUR COMMUNICATION SKILLS

Many phases of production, from design to inspection, have become computerized. With your class, or in small groups of three or four students, discuss the personnel issues that you believe have arisen as a result of this technological revolution in business. You might draw a chart that depicts the positive and negative results of technology on human resource management. Develop a consensus opinion (or a written summary) regarding the various issues discussed.

• How has technology affected the job market? Are jobs being enhanced or replaced by computers?
• Consider pride in process. Has computerized production created a feeling of distance from the end product for some employees?
• How have companies involved employees in an effort to improve morale and make them feel more involved?

KEEPING CURRENT USING *THE WALL STREET JOURNAL*

Find an article in *The Wall Street Journal* that describes a problem or an innovation in one of the following areas:

• Quality assurance or total quality management
• Production control
• Technology in manufacturing
• Manufacturing layout
• Manufacturing cost or time

1. What are the causes of the problem or reasons for the innovation?
2. How will the problem or innovation affect the company's employees? Costs? Competitive position?
3. What career opportunities or problems are suggested by this development?

Why Is the Silicon Valley in California Rather Than Colorado or Kentucky?

 Comparing geographic information about companies and industries can lead to some interesting questions. For instance, why are so many high-tech companies located in California's Silicon Valley (an area encompassing San Jose, Santa Clara, Palo Alto, and surrounding cities south of San Francisco)? For some industries, patterns of location and development seem fairly obvious. Florida has an ideal climate for citrus trees. Various cities along the East, West, and Gulf Coasts have excellent natural harbors, which aided the development of a healthy shipping industry in those areas. Sometimes studying physical geography leads you to answers fairly quickly.

In other industries, however, the geographic connection seems weaker. For instance, why is so much of the insurance industry centered in Hartford, Connecticut? Why is Washington's manufacturing output (measured in dollar value) more than twice as high as Maryland's when the two states have similar populations?[53] Why are the three largest U.S. steel producers headquartered in Ohio and Pennsylvania when most iron ore (source of the primary ingredient in steel) is mined in Minnesota, Michigan, Utah, and Missouri?

Exploring these geographic patterns helps you understand how industries develop and how they affect local and regional economies and societies. Choose one of these five industries and then answer the questions that follow:

- Computer software
- Automobiles
- Commercial passenger aircraft
- Carpeting
- Poultry processing

1. Where did the industry start in the United States?
2. Who are the biggest competitors today?
3. Where are they located?
4. What influence has geography had on the industry's growth?
5. How strong is the influence of physical geography compared with the influence of other factors (such as where an industry pioneer happened to be living or where the cost for labor happened to be less expensive)?

SEPTOR DISCOVERS THE HUMAN SIDE OF AUTOMATION

Synopsis

Factory automation has often been seen as—and sold as—an automatic cure-all for quality and productivity problems. After all, the theory goes, if people are making the mistakes and causing the problems, the mistakes and problems will disappear when people are replaced by automated machinery. In reality, however, automation does not always cure the problem. This video shows how Septor, a U.S. auto-parts manufacturer, learned that removing human input can cause enormous problems of its own. The video compares Septor's factory with a Japanese factory that uses identical equipment, only minus the automation. In the Japanese factory, highly trained technicians and engineers keep a close eye on the machinery and solve any problems that arise. In Septor's highly computerized factory, however, even a simple problem freezes production because the few employees, who have been reduced to passive caretakers, aren't even paying attention.

Exercises

ANALYSIS

1. How can we reconcile the apparent need for automation with the desire to keep as many people as possible employed?
2. From what you've seen in the video, what conclusions might you make about the differences between U.S. and Japanese management practices?
3. Why do you suppose these differences exist?
4. Should U.S. manufacturers try to closely copy Japanese manufacturing methods?
5. Did this factory appear to be using hard or soft manufacturing?

APPLICATION

The situation at Septor demonstrates the need for trained employees to be involved in even the most advanced production facilities. This need also applies to service businesses that rely on automation, such as the information systems used by an insurance company to process claims. Assume you work for this insurance company; draw up some brief guidelines for making sure that employees stay involved in the process.

DECISION

In both manual and automated production facilities, managers sometimes have to stop production because of quality problems. The key factor in the decision to stop production is the minimum acceptable quality level, which is the lowest that quality can drop and still be acceptable. List the points you would have to consider when defining a minimum acceptable quality level for a manufacturer such as Septor.

COMMUNICATION

Just as lower-level employees at the Springfield Remanufacturing Company in the Chapter 7 video exercise had to learn the basics of corporate finance, employees in manufacturing companies such as Septor often have to learn statistical quality-control methods in order to improve quality and productivity. Draft a three-minute speech to the production employees, explaining why this is an important subject for them to learn.

INTEGRATION

Referring to what you learned about motivation in Chapter 6, list several ways that the employees in the Septor plant might be motivated to pay closer attention to the machinery.

ETHICS

The issue of replacing employees with computers (or machinery of any kind) has long troubled some observers of the business world. The problem stretches back to the earliest days of the industrial revolution and promises to remain a key issue as companies struggle to increase productivity. Is it fair to replace a good employee with a machine?

DEBATE

When faced with the problem shown at Septor, some managers would be tempted simply to punish the employees who erred. Option A: In a formal debate format, argue for or against doing so. Option B: Take either position and state your case in a brief report.

TEAMWORK

In a team of four students, outline a plan for automating a job that one of you now holds or has held in the past. One student should serve as devil's advocate when the plan is finished, searching for flaws.

RESEARCH

Do the research necessary to write a one-page summary on either (a) current trends in employee training among U.S. manufacturers or (b) the current balance of trade between the United States and Japan, in terms of manufactured goods.

ROLE PLAYING

One student plays the role of a salesperson from a company that sells factory automation equipment, such as robots. The other student plays a manufacturing manager who is skeptical of the true benefits of automated production. The salesperson tries to convince the manager that, if implemented correctly, automation has much to offer.

PART THREE

MANAGING HUMAN RESOURCES

Chapter 9
Human Relations

Chapter 10
**Human Resources
Management**

Chapter 11
**Union-Management
Relations**

Chapter

Human
Relations

LEARNING OBJECTIVES

After studying this chapter,
you will be able to

1 List the three main components of good human relations within an organization

2 Explain how the five
levels in Maslow's hierarchy
of needs relate to employee
motivation

3 Identify the two factors
affecting employee
motivation in Herzberg's
Two-factor theory

4 List three basic assumptions of expectancy theory

5 Discuss the use of the
four forms of reinforcement

6 Describe how Theory X,
Theory Y, and Theory Z link
employee motivation and
management style

7 Explain how changes in
the workforce have
complicated the challenge of
motivating employees

8 Discuss the use of goal
setting, behavior
modification, training and
retraining, and improved
quality of work life as
motivational techniques

Putting the Backbone Back into Steel

Skeptics laughed when they heard that F. Kenneth Iverson wanted to beat the system by opening his own steel mill. How could a tiny firm named Nucor produce material more cheaply than so-called Big Steel? After World War II, the U.S. steel industry boomed until it was larger than all the other nations' steel industries put together. These skeptics pointed out that expensive labor alone would prevent Iverson from cutting costs enough for Nucor to compete. In fact, union contracts guaranteed steelworkers wages that were half again higher than those in other industries.

Despite the skeptics, Iverson was determined to act fast. His company was a successful maker of steel roof joists (beams used to support roofs). However, his main supplier, United States Steel (now known as USX), was raising prices and charging more for steel than Iverson could get for his finished joists. If he didn't do something soon, his company would be extinct.

Looking below the surface of Big Steel, Iverson saw complacent operations trapped in webs of bureaucracy. He saw management rewarding itself with favorable employment contracts, often ignoring the needs of shop workers. The employees resented managers who insulated themselves from mill operations with layers of supervision, who preferred to dictate rather than lead, and who enjoyed extras such as country club memberships, separate cafeterias, and private rest rooms. So Big Steel employees had turned to unions, which negotiated good salaries and benefits.

For their part, plant managers saw unions enforcing restrictive work rules that increased production costs. In turn, higher production costs drove up the prices that customers paid for steel. Supervisors also complained that unions pampered employees, who seemed more concerned about racking up their paid sick leave than about the quality of the steel leaving the factory.

Iverson concluded that the problem with Big Steel wasn't the high cost of labor; it was the declining productivity of an alienated workforce. If employees could only be motivated by managers sensitive to their needs, they would perform enthusiastically and produce steel more efficiently. Then Nucor could afford to make steel at a cost that would allow the company to make a profit. Furthermore, Iverson be-

Nucor workers have raised their productivity level well above the average in the steel industry.

lieved that employees would be less inclined to seek union representation if his company used the right motivation techniques.

Iverson had to attract employees to his new mill with nothing more than a promise, and he had to convince them that he was sincere. How could he get employees to join and then stay with his company when they were guaranteed higher salaries at union shops? How could he motivate them to produce steel at rock-bottom cost when they traditionally viewed such efforts as benefiting management only?[1]

HUMAN RELATIONS WITHIN AN ORGANIZATION

As F. Kenneth Iverson realizes, motivation is just one part of human relations. The term **human relations** refers to the ways people interact with one another. This chapter looks at the ways individuals interact within a business organization. In that setting, human relations are determined by organizational culture and management practices, as well as by other more general forces.

The Roles of the Organization and Management

Most organizations and their managers realize the importance of maintaining good human relations. A climate of openness and trust encourages better performance and more loyalty from employees. For example, everyone at Walt Disney Productions—including the president—wears a name tag with first name only. At Microsoft, employees at any level are invited to send electronic mail to CEO Bill Gates, who personally reads and answers every message.[2] This kind of open atmosphere can only have a positive effect on human relations. In addition, when employees are satisfied with the interpersonal component of their jobs, productivity usually improves.

The Components of Good Human Relations

Three components are particularly important to good human relations: leadership, communication, and motivation. The first component is leadership, the ability to influence people to work toward accomplishing a goal. A leader's approach is determined by the demands of the situation, by the needs and personalities of his or her employees, and by the culture of the organization. Managers need to distinguish between authority—the ability to *make* someone do something—and leadership—the ability to *inspire* someone to do something. The manager who inspires enthusiasm and who works hard alongside employees is usually more effective than the boss who invokes authority and takes all the credit for the group's accomplishments.

A second component of good organizational human relations is communication. Through speaking, listening, writing, and reading, managers and employees not

human relations *Ways two or more people interact with one another*

Anita Roddick, founder and chief executive of The Body Shop, inspires her employees to work toward organizational goals as well as for the good of the community.

only share crucial job-related information but also build interpersonal networks and patterns of interaction. Effective business communication is clear and, at the same time, incorporates courtesy and respect. One study found that 90 percent of the people who report good communication with their bosses are satisfied with their jobs.[3]

A third factor contributing to good organizational human relations is **motivation,** the force that moves individuals to take action. In some cases, fear of management or of losing a job may move someone to take action, but it's much less effective than encouraging the employee's own sense of direction, creativity, and pride in doing a good job. That's why effective managers take into account employees' individual needs and show them how those needs can be satisfied within the organization's framework (see Exhibit 9.1).

A concept closely related to motivation is **morale,** a person's attitude toward both the job and the organization. Employee perception of the workplace affects morale. Traditionally, managers believed that performance was determined by real conditions, such as sufficient resources, competent employees, efficient systems, and clear goals. Today, managers realize that *perceived* conditions—fairness, clarity, appreciation, responsiveness, involvement—significantly affect performance as well. Employees perform better when they feel positive about perceived conditions. Positive conditions include the following:[4]

- *Fairness.* The company is not driven by office politics; promotions are based on merit.
- *Clarity.* Organizational, work-group, and individual goals are clearly defined.
- *Appreciation.* Employees believe that they are of value to the organization.
- *Responsiveness.* Employees believe that managers are concerned with employee needs and problems.
- *Involvement.* Employees believe that they are contributing to organizational goals.

A person who has good morale is more likely to be cheerful, enthusiastic, loyal, and more productive. However, morale is only one element of motivation. To better understand motivation, consider the following theories of motivation and the specific challenges of motivating today's workforce.

motivation *Force that moves someone to take action*

morale *How an employee sees the job or the organization*

Exhibit 9.1
The Motivation Process
The key to effective motivation is to demonstrate to employees that their individual needs dovetail with the needs of the organization.

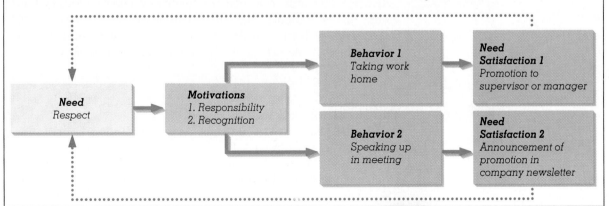

MOTIVATION THEORY

Motivation has been a topic of interest to managers for more than a hundred years. One of the earliest managers to think about the link between employee morale and motivation was Robert Owen, a nineteenth-century Scottish industrialist. He reduced working hours, provided meal facilities, improved employee housing, and introduced other innovations at his textile mill in New Lanark, Scotland. Although Owen's factory became a showplace of productivity, his methods weren't widely copied by other managers; it was not until the turn of the century that business owners began thinking about methods for motivating rather than driving employees to produce.[5]

Scientific Management

scientific management *Management perspective that focuses on the scientific study of work situations to improve efficiency*

Frederick W. Taylor, a machinist and engineer from Philadelphia, became interested in employee efficiency and motivation late in the nineteenth century, when he worked for Midvale Steel. He developed **scientific management,** a management approach that seeks to improve employee efficiency through the scientific study of work. Taylor believed in division of labor, and he used time-and-motion studies to break work processes into individual tasks that were both efficient and easy to measure. He then determined a reasonable level of productivity for each task and established a quota (or minimum goal) that he expected each employee to reach. In his view, people were motivated almost exclusively by money, so he set up pay systems that rewarded employees when they were productive.

piecework system *Practice of paying employees a certain amount for each unit produced*

Under Taylor's **piecework system,** employees who just met or fell short of the quota were paid a certain amount for each unit produced. Those who produced more were paid at a higher rate for *all* units produced, not just for those that exceeded the quota; this pay system gave employees a strong incentive to boost productivity. When Taylor went on to introduce his system of scientific management at Bethlehem Steel, the results were profitable for everyone. The average steelhandler's wage rose from $1.15 to $1.85 a day, and productivity increased so sharply that handling costs were cut by more than half.

Because scientific management concentrated on money as the prime motivator, it failed to take into account other motivational elements, such as opportunities for personal satisfaction or individual initiative. So scientific management can't explain why a person whose spouse makes a good living will still want to work or why a Wall Street lawyer will take a hefty pay cut to serve in government. Soon other researchers began looking beyond money to discover what else motivated people.

The Hawthorne Studies

Between 1924 and 1932, researchers conducted landmark motivation studies at Western Electric's Hawthorne plant in Cicero, Illinois. In an early study of the effect of the work environment on employee productivity, lighting was altered in one workroom but kept constant in a second workroom. When the researchers raised lighting levels in the first room, productivity went up in both; when they lowered lighting levels in that room, productivity still went up in both—even when the lighting was reduced to the level of moonlight.[6]

These researchers later studied the group behavior that developed among men who worked on switchboard equipment. They discovered that the employees established their own **group norms,** or standards of behavior, for what the correct output should be. The group sneered at overproducers as "rate busters" and underproducers as "rate chiselers." This group pressure was effective; the employees were more concerned with the approval of their peers than with earning more money.[7]

The earlier work-environment studies baffled researchers, because employee productivity improved whether or not changes had been introduced. The researchers concluded that this improvement was simply a result of participating in the research—of being asked for opinions and ideas, of being listened to. This phenomenon came to be known as the **Hawthorne effect.** Later researchers who conducted experiments and carefully reviewed the Hawthorne results have not been convinced that the Hawthorne effect exists.[8] However, in the later group-behavior study, the Hawthorne researchers clearly showed that peer pressure in the informal organization has at least as much power to motivate employees as the formal organization.

Maslow's Hierarchy of Needs

In 1943 psychologist Abraham Maslow proposed the theory that behavior is determined by a variety of needs. He organized these needs into five categories and then arranged the categories in a hierarchy (see Exhibit 9.2). The most basic needs (food, water, shelter) were at the bottom of this hierarchy, and the more advanced needs (esteem, self-actualization) were toward the top. A human being, according to Maslow, is a "perpetually wanting animal." When lower-level needs have been satisfied, at least in part, a person tries to satisfy needs on the next level.[9]

All the requirements for basic survival—food, clothing, shelter, and so on—fall into the category of *physiological needs.* These basic needs must be satisfied before the person can consider other needs. Today, physiological needs are so readily fulfilled by most wage earners that

group norms Standards of behavior that all members of a given group accept

Hawthorne effect Improvement in performance as a by-product of attention, a theory developed during the Hawthorne studies of productivity

Exhibit 9.2
Maslow's Hierarchy of Needs
According to Maslow, needs on the lower levels of the hierarchy must be satisfied before higher-level needs can be addressed.

more advanced needs tend to be more motivating. For example, when the bare essentials have been taken care of, the person is motivated to fulfill the need for security. Such *safety needs* may be satisfied through health insurance, pension plans, job security, and safe working conditions.

Beyond safety needs, human beings have a powerful need to associate with others, to give and receive love, and to feel a sense of belonging. As shown by the way employees responded to group norms in the Hawthorne studies, these *social needs* can have a definite influence on actions. People also have *esteem needs*—they need a sense of personal worth and integrity. In addition, they need the respect of others, a respect based on competence and achievement. These needs are closely related to the idea of status, which is one's rank or importance in the eyes of others. The opportunity to fulfill these needs can be a powerful motivator.

Maslow defined the need for *self-actualization* as the need to become everything one is capable of. This need is the highest and most difficult to fulfill. Employees who reach this point work not simply to make money or to impress others but also because they feel their work is worthwhile and satisfying in itself.

Although Maslow's hierarchy is a convenient way to classify human needs, it would be a mistake to view it as a rigid sequence. Each level of needs does not have to be completely satisfied before a person can be motivated by a higher need. Indeed, at any one time, most people are motivated by a combination of needs.

Two-Factor Theory

In the 1960s, Frederick Herzberg and his associates undertook their own study of human needs. They asked accountants and engineers to describe specific aspects of their jobs that made them feel satisfied or dissatisfied, and then analyzed the results. They found that two entirely different sets of factors were associated with satisfying and dissatisfying work experiences (see Exhibit 9.3). What Herzberg called **hygiene factors** were associated with dissatisfying experiences. These potential sources of dissatisfaction include company policies, working conditions, and job security.

Management may lessen dissatisfaction by improving hygiene factors that concern employees, but such improvements won't influence satisfaction. On the other hand, managers can help employees feel more motivated and, ultimately, more satisfied, by paying attention to **motivators** such as achievement, recognition, responsibility, and other personally rewarding factors. Herzberg's theory is related to the hierarchy of needs: The motivators closely resemble Maslow's higher-level needs, and the hygiene factors resemble the lower-level needs.

Should managers such as Nucor's Iverson concentrate on motivators or on hygiene factors? It depends. A skilled, well-paid, middle-class, middle-aged employee may be motivated to perform better if motivators are supplied. However, a young or elderly unskilled employee who earns low wages or an employee who is insecure will probably still need the support of strong hygiene factors to reduce dissatisfaction before the motivators can be effective.[10]

hygiene factors *Aspects of the work environment that are associated with dissatisfaction*

motivators *Factors of human relations in business that may increase motivation*

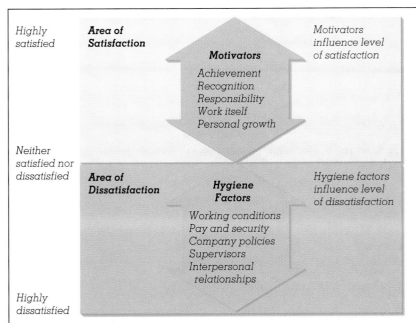

Highly
satisfied

**Area of
Satisfaction**

Motivators

Achievement
Recognition
Responsibility
Work itself
Personal growth

*Motivators
influence level
of satisfaction*

Neither
satisfied nor
dissatisfied

**Area of
Dissatisfaction**

*Hygiene
Factors*

Working conditions
Pay and security
Company policies
Supervisors
Interpersonal
relationships

*Hygiene factors
influence level
of dissatisfaction*

Highly
dissatisfied

Exhibit 9.3
Two-Factor Theory
*Hygiene factors such as company
policies and working conditions
can influence employee dissatisfaction. On the other hand, motivators such as opportunities for
achievement and recognition can
influence employee satisfaction.*

Expectancy Theory

Another motivation theory that has been examined in recent years
was proposed by Victor Vroom and later modified by David Nadler
and Edward Lawler, among others.[11] According to this **expectancy
theory,** the amount of effort that individuals will expend on a task
depends on the expected outcomes. Employees take into account
(1) how well they think they will do on the task (Can I do it?),
(2) whether they think they will be rewarded for that performance
(If I do it, what will I get?), and (3) whether the reward will be worth
the amount of effort required (Will it be worth my while?).

An important aspect of this theory is that it sees motivation as
varying from individual to individual. Each employee is likely to have
his or her own view of the difficulty of a task, the value of the reward, and the connection between the two. On the basis of this model
of expectancy, Nadler and Lawler suggest that managers can improve
employee performance by (1) determining the rewards valued by each
employee, (2) determining the desired level of performance from each
employee, (3) making performance levels attainable, (4) linking rewards to performance, and (5) making sure the reward is adequate.

*expectancy theory Idea that the
amount of effort an employee expends
will depend on the expected outcome*

Reinforcement Theory

Reinforcement theory, pioneered by psychologist B. F. Skinner
during the 1930s, holds that the way people behave is directly related
to the consequences of their actions. According to this theory, if people find that their actions result in a pleasant outcome, they will probably repeat those actions. On the other hand, if the consequences are
not pleasant—or are distinctly unpleasant—people are unlikely to
repeat those actions.[12]

*reinforcement theory Theory that
people repeat actions that produce pleasant outcomes and do not repeat actions
that produce unpleasant outcomes*

Forms of Reinforcement

A manager can encourage or discourage employee behavior through the use of *reinforcement,* a response that directly follows a particular action. If the reinforcement results in pleasant consequences, the employee is likely to repeat the action; if the consequences are not pleasant, the employee is unlikely to repeat the action. Reinforcement theory includes four forms of reinforcement: positive reinforcement and negative reinforcement are used to encourage certain behaviors; extinction and punishment are used to discourage certain behaviors (see Exhibit 9.4).[13]

Positive reinforcement offers pleasant consequences, such as a gift or praise, for completing or repeating a desired action. Experts recommend the use of positive reinforcement because it emphasizes the desired behavior rather than the unwanted behavior. In contrast, *negative reinforcement* (also known as avoidance learning) allows people to avoid unpleasant consequences by behaving in the desired way. Imagine, for example, that employees know they will have to work late if they don't finish a report on time—but they don't have to work late if they finish on time. In this case, employees can avoid working late (unpleasant consequences) by finishing on time (desired behavior).

Extinction discourages a specific behavior by not offering a reward. For instance, managers who want employees to ask questions only at the end of a meeting can ignore any questions that are asked before the end. Because they don't get a reaction, employees will be discouraged from asking questions at inappropriate times, and that behavior will become extinct.

Another way to discourage behavior is through *punishment,* in which the manager responds to an employee's action with unpleasant consequences. Managers at China's Xian Department Store use punishment to change the behavior of salesclerks. Each month, the managers review customer complaints and select employees for the "40 Worst" list. These employees' undesirable behaviors range from ignoring customers to throwing things at them. Managers then post signs indicating which clerks are the worst in the store.[14] Punishment has been criticized because it doesn't necessarily change behavior over the long term and because it doesn't offer an acceptable action in place of the behavior that is to be changed.

Exhibit 9.4
Approaches to Reinforcement
According to reinforcement theory, employee behavior can be shaped by positive reinforcement, negative reinforcement, extinction, and punishment.

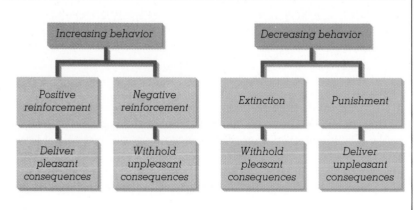

Reinforcement Schedules

What timetable for reinforcement works best? The answer depends on whether you want to change behavior quickly or over a long period. For changing behavior quickly, try offering a reward every time the employee acts in the desired way. Steven Ettridge, president of Temps & Company in Washington, D.C., reinforces his salespeople's efforts continuously. He gives each salesperson 50 cents for every call made to find new customers for the temporary-help agency. Ettridge believes that this system encourages salespeople to keep making calls even when they don't make a sale right away. However, continuous reinforcement doesn't work well when used over a long period, and employees quickly stop the behavior when rewards stop.[15]

In most cases, offering occasional rewards for the desired behavior works better. Because employees know they will be rewarded—but they don't know when—they are likely to keep doing their best for some time. Think about what happens when a manager inspects a department's work once a week, but employees aren't told the exact day on which the manager will appear. The employees will probably work hard every day because they want to be praised for their work on the day the manager actually appears.

Motivation and Management Style

The motivation of employees is highly related to the attitudes of managers toward them. Over the years, a number of management styles have come into and gone out of vogue.

Theory X and Theory Y

In the 1960s, psychologist Douglas McGregor identified a certain set of assumptions as underlying most management thinking. He labeled this set of assumptions **Theory X:**

1. The average person dislikes work and will avoid it if possible.
2. Because of the dislike for work, the average person must be forced, controlled, directed, or threatened with punishment in order to be motivated to work toward achieving organizational goals.
3. The average person prefers to be directed, wishes to avoid responsibility, has relatively little ambition, and wants security.

According to McGregor, Theory X–oriented managers believe that employees can be motivated only by the fear of losing their jobs or by external rewards. This management style emphasizes physiological and safety needs and tends to ignore the higher-level needs in Maslow's hierarchy.

To counteract this management focus on lower-level needs, McGregor proposed another set of assumptions for managers. He based these assumptions, called **Theory Y,** on Maslow's higher-level needs:

1. The average person does not dislike work. It is as natural as play or rest.
2. External control and the threat of punishment are not the only ways to motivate people to meet organizational goals. The average

Theory X *Set of managerial assumptions about employee motivations focusing on lower-level needs*

Theory Y *Set of managerial assumptions about employee motivations focusing on higher-level needs*

General Electric applies Theory Y in its global operations. Here, GE managers in an Outward Bound workshop practice team-building skills to achieve a common goal.

person naturally works toward goals to which she or he is committed.

3. How deeply a person is committed to organization objectives depends on the rewards for achieving them.
4. Under favorable conditions, the average person learns not only to accept responsibility but also to seek it.
5. Many people are capable of using imagination, cleverness, and creativity to solve problems that arise within an organization.
6. Especially in modern industrial life, the average person's intellectual potential is only partially realized.

Theory Y–oriented managers believe that employees can be motivated by the opportunity to be creative, to work hard for a cause they believe in, and to satisfy needs beyond the basic need to pay the rent.

The assumptions behind Theory X emphasize authority; the assumptions behind Theory Y emphasize growth and self-direction. It was McGregor's belief that although some employees need the strong direction demanded by Theory X, those who are ready to realize their social, esteem, and self-actualization needs will not work well under Theory X assumptions.[16]

Theory Z

Theory Z *Human relations approach that emphasizes involving employees at all levels and treating them like family*

Another perspective on motivation was developed by William Ouchi, who studied management practices in Japan and the United States. Ouchi's **Theory Z** assumes that the best management involves employees at all levels and treats employees like family. This theory combines elements of both U.S. and Japanese management techniques, and it is often seen in U.S. companies that have adopted a Japanese approach to business.

Theory Z satisfies the lower-level needs in Maslow's hierarchy by looking after employee welfare. It also satisfies middle-level needs by using the group process to make decisions. In addition, it satisfies higher-level needs by inviting employees to take individual responsibility. Managers who adopt Theory Z believe that employees with a sense of identity and belonging are more likely to perform their jobs conscientiously and will try more enthusiastically to achieve company goals.

Can management techniques based on Japanese practices effectively motivate people in the United States? In Japanese firms, everyone participates in decision making, and duties are rotated to avoid boredom, extreme specialization, and rigidity. Surviving in a small, densely populated, resource-poor land has made teamwork and compromise essential for the Japanese. People in the United States, on the other hand, have a tradition of individualism and self-reliance. Even so, some U.S. firms are already using Theory Z. Some Procter & Gamble plants have instituted partially self-governing work groups, and Hewlett-Packard keeps employee turnover down during economic slumps by making sure all employees—not just those in the lowest-paid positions—work shorter hours and give up certain privileges.[17]

THE CHALLENGE OF MOTIVATING EMPLOYEES IN THE 1990s

Nucor's F. Kenneth Iverson isn't the only one concerned with motivating employees. Managers trying to motivate employees today are faced with a number of challenges that make their task especially difficult. These challenges relate to the changing nature of the workforce, the changing economy, and the changing corporate culture.

The Changing Workforce

The workforce in North America is undergoing significant changes that over the next decade will require major alterations in how managers keep employees happy and productive on the job. Some of the most significant trends affecting the makeup of the workforce include the following:

- The population and the labor force is growing, but slowly. By 2000, the U.S. workforce will increase by only 1 percent annually.
- The pool of young employees is shrinking. In 1988 employees aged 16 to 24 accounted for 18 percent of the U.S. workforce; that number had declined to 15 percent by 1992.
- The average age of the U.S. workforce will rise to 39 by the turn of the century; by that time, nearly half the population will be over 45 years old.
- More women are entering the U.S. workforce. By 2000, some 80 percent of women aged 25 to 44 will be working.
- Immigrants represent the largest share of the increase in both population and workforce since World War I—4 million to 7 million by 2000.
- Women, minorities, and immigrants will form more than 80 percent of the net additions to the U.S. labor force between now and 2000.[18]

Three of the most significant trends include the aging of the workforce, the swelling ranks of women in the workforce, and the increasing cultural diversity in the workforce.

The Aging of the Workforce

The baby boomers—people born between 1946 and 1964—are so numerous that they tend to distort most statistics. When these 76 million people began entering the workforce, the average age of U.S. employees fell. Now that they are approaching mid-career, the average age is again rising. This aging labor pool and the declining number of young employees are largely due to baby boomers' decisions to marry later, to postpone or forgo starting a family, and to have fewer children.

Because of their sheer numbers, competition for jobs and promotions among baby boomers is likely to remain strong. For those who are eager to get ahead, the continual corporate restructuring and downsizing limits opportunities still further. Management may have a hard time helping baby-boom employees feel satisfied with their jobs in the face of shrinking promotion possibilities. How companies manage to do so, according to analyst Anne Fisher, "could make the difference between ending up leaner and more competitive or just ending up leaner."[19]

Many employees in their 30s and 40s want more from their jobs than just a good paycheck and satisfying work. They are trying to balance their careers and family lives. They want flexible work schedules and a choice of career paths to help them in this balancing act. As the baby boomers enter their 50s and 60s, they will be viewing their jobs and work environment differently. They'll seek employee stock-ownership plans and other means for giving them more involvement in the company as well as a comfortable retirement to look forward to. They'll also want to learn new skills and have the chance to apply their talents and experience.[20]

The 38 million twenty-somethings now entering the workforce are also motivated by satisfying work, but they want more out of life than just work. "This is the most difficult generation ever to manage," says Marilyn Moats Kennedy, a career consultant. "The traditional appeals—money, prestige—have no appeal. They are much less easily motivated than people motivated by money. They want to do their job, get home and have a life."[21]

Women in the Workforce

The consequences of increasing numbers of women employees are even broader (see Exhibit 9.5). Because of the growing number of two-career households, it's no longer easy to transfer an employee to another part of the country. Nor can employers assume that employees of either gender will be willing—or able—to sacrifice family needs in order to work overtime. Child care, for example, has become a critical issue. In 1992 nearly 23 million women with children under 17 were in the U.S. labor force.[22]

Employment decisions must increasingly take into account the needs of *all* family members. To help employees balance the demands of work and family, businesses can offer child-care assistance, parental leave, flexible work schedules, telecommuting (home-based employees linked to the office by computer), and other solutions, which are explored later in this chapter.

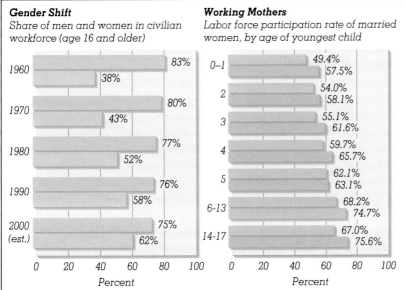

Gender Shift
Share of men and women in civilian workforce (age 16 and older)

Year	Men	Women
1960	83%	38%
1970	80%	43%
1980	77%	52%
1990	76%	58%
2000 (est.)	75%	62%

Percent

Working Mothers
Labor force participation rate of married women, by age of youngest child

Age of youngest child		
0–1	49.4%	57.5%
2	54.0%	58.1%
3	55.1%	61.6%
4	59.7%	65.7%
5	62.1%	63.1%
6–13	68.2%	74.7%
14–17	67.0%	75.6%

Percent

Exhibit 9.5
Women and Mothers in the Workforce
The participation of women in the workforce is expected to reach 62 percent by 2000, and more and more of those women are mothers with children at home.

Increasing Cultural Diversity

A growing percentage of the U.S. workforce is made up of members from diverse cultural and ethnic backgrounds (see Exhibit 9.6). These employees bring with them a wide range of work skills, traditions, and attitudes toward work that can affect their behavior on the job. Some come from indigenous groups within North America; others are recently arrived immigrants. The challenge for managers is to communicate with this diverse workforce and foster cooperation and harmony among employees. If they can do this, they'll gain a source of ideas that can be "the key to innovative survival in the years to come," says Paul J. Giddens of Georgia-Pacific.[23]

Some companies have tackled the situation head-on by instituting management-training programs for dealing with cultural diversity.

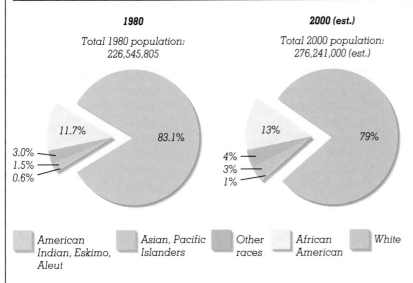

1980
Total 1980 population: 226,545,805

- 11.7%
- 3.0%
- 1.5%
- 0.6%
- 83.1%

2000 (est.)
Total 2000 population: 276,241,000 (est.)

- 13%
- 4%
- 3%
- 1%
- 79%

American Indian, Eskimo, Aleut | Asian, Pacific Islanders | Other races | African American | White

Exhibit 9.6
Minorities in the Workforce
African American, Asian American, and other minority employees are making up a greater proportion of the U.S. workforce.

Successful organizations believe that workforce diversity presents an opportunity to expand the pool of people who can contribute to the organization. In fact, recent studies confirm that culturally diverse work groups come up with more innovative and effective solutions to business problems than do groups lacking such diversity. These results are encouraging more companies to go beyond what is required by law and to take steps that will promote a culturally diverse workforce.

However, despite the benefits of cultural diversity, managing such a workforce sometimes requires managers to take extra steps. The training in cultural diversity (used by a growing number of organizations) is accomplished through seminars, videotapes, workshops, even games. Burger King and Price Waterhouse, among many others, have used a board game called *The Diversity Game* to raise managers' awareness of diversity issues.

Improving cultural diversity in the workforce has become such an important goal that some companies

ORGANIZATIONS LEARN THE VALUE OF DIVERSITY

have set up programs to measure results and hold managers accountable. Gannett, the parent of *USA Today*, requires managers to set specific goals for achieving workforce diversity, buying from minority suppliers, and other targets. At Mobil Oil, the presidents of each subsidiary meet with the company chairman once a year to explain their plans for improving diversity; progress is monitored by Mobil's vice president of employee relations.

Even successful companies can benefit from workforce diversity. Consider the situation found by Nadia Ali when she was hired as U.S. southwest district manager for

the gift and engraving retail chain Things Remembered. Half of her local customers spoke Spanish, but many of the employees in the southwest stores spoke only English, so they couldn't communicate with their Spanish-speaking customers. Ali decided that the employees and managers she hired in the future would have to be able to speak conversational Spanish. She also arranged for current employees to take Spanish lessons, a program paid for by headquarters.

By increasing the workforce diversity in her district, Ali was able to better serve her customers and in turn boost district sales. Employees got more out of their jobs and didn't leave as quickly as in the past. What had been a frustrating situation for both customers and employees was transformed into a situation that benefited everybody. As more organizations expand their operations to other areas or pursue customers in other lands, cultural diversity in the workforce will be recognized as a vital prerequisite for doing business in today's global business environment.

Hundreds of companies have used a series of seven 30-minute videotapes titled "Valuing Diversity" (produced by Copeland Griggs with funding from major corporations) to sensitize managers to stereotypes, introduce them to typical types of misunderstandings, and give them suggestions for making the most of what employees from varying backgrounds have to offer. The program covers not only ethnicity and culture but also gender, age, race, disability, and sexual orientation. In addition, many companies are instituting programs to encourage employees to be tolerant of cultural and language differences.

At Digital Equipment Corporation, a program called "Valuing Differences" has been in place for several years. It is based on the philosophy that "people work best when they feel valued, and that people feel more valued when their differences—their unique attributes—are taken into account."[24] Among other companies that have made a major commitment to diversity management are Apple Computer, Avon, Corning, du Pont, Hewlett-Packard, Honeywell, Pacific Bell, Procter & Gamble, US West, and Xerox.[25] Many of these companies have orientation programs for new minority employees, encourage the formation of support groups or networks, and sponsor cultural-awareness activities.

The Changing Economy

The way business is conducted in the United States is evolving daily. Changes in markets, competition, financing, workforce demographics, technology, organization, management, and ideas and beliefs are transforming all aspects of business life. In turn, these changes are influencing the overall economy in which employees, managers, and organizations operate.

One major change concerns the relationship between organizations and the people they employ. In the past, hardworking, loyal employees could expect job security and the chance to advance. Now, companies under pressure may lay off employees as a cost-cutting measure sparked by takeovers, mergers, and recessions. In the past, the average person worked for two companies during a lifetime; today, the average person changes jobs every three to seven years.[26]

Not surprisingly, these layoffs have employees fearing for their jobs. Certainly, such anxiety affects their productivity and weakens company loyalty. In fact, a Time/CNN poll found that 57 percent of those surveyed believed companies to be less loyal to employees today than they were 10 years ago, and 63 percent said that employees are less loyal to their companies.[27] One manufacturing manager sums up the situation this way: "Loyalty will return only when management discovers that employees are a valuable resource—more valuable than capital equipment—and begins to treat employees accordingly."[28]

In addition, the shift from a manufacturing economy to a service economy has displaced many production employees. At the same time, companies are installing more sophisticated equipment, which in turn requires more skilled operators. This technological change is making it difficult for former production employees and less skilled employees to qualify for jobs in upgraded factories unless they receive special training. Managers are also asking employees to find ways of continuously improving products and production methods, which puts more pressure on employees.

Even as some employees have to hunt longer and harder for the jobs they want, many companies are scrambling to find qualified employees among the shrinking labor pool. That's why top applicants are being wooed with hiring bonuses, flexible work schedules, job training, and other incentives. Business is also assuming responsibility for training and retraining employees to meet the needs of the changing workplace. These economic changes mean that, more than ever before, remaining competitive demands a serious investment in human resources at every level.

The Changing Corporate Culture

In light of the changes in both the workforce and the economy, corporate cultures have been changing. When promotions are fewer and slower in coming, cultures have to downplay the importance of job advancement as the main source of job satisfaction. Otherwise, turnover will become an even more crucial problem as employees change jobs in a continuing effort to climb to the top. One solution is to offer a career path that combines horizontal as well as vertical

SHOULD CORPORATE CULTURES STRESS ONLY ENGLISH ON THE JOB?

When Frances Arreola read the memo announcing that employees should speak only English on the job, she was outraged. Arreola, a lens inspector for Signet Amoralite, a lens-manufacturing firm in southern California, remembers having been punished and humiliated by elementary-school teachers for speaking in her native Spanish. She is now fluent in both English and Spanish but feels that the English-only rules stressed in some corporate cultures constitute discrimination.

Over half of Signet Amoralite's 900 employees are Asian, Filipino, or Hispanic, and the company defends the English-only rule on the grounds that "speaking in another language that friends and associates cannot fully understand can lead to misunderstandings, is impolite, and can even be unsafe." The company claims that the English-only requirement is not written policy, just a guideline, and violating it carries no punishment.

Nevertheless, this policy—and ones like it at hundreds of companies throughout the United States—is incorporated into the corporate culture, and it is considered by critics to violate federal laws against discrimination on the basis of national origin. According to Equal Employment Opportunity Commission rules, employers can establish language restrictions only when such restrictions are required by valid business necessities.

Managers are caught in the middle. On the one side are employees who are disturbed by co-employees speaking to each other in a language they don't understand and who consider this behavior rude. On the other side are employees who feel they have a right to speak in a more familiar language as long as it doesn't affect their work. What is a manager to do?

The best solution, according to experts, is to offer cultural-sensitivity training that will eliminate misconceptions on both sides and create a more open corporate culture. Native English speakers often assume that nonnative speakers don't want to make the effort to learn and use English. More commonly, however, nonnative speakers are highly motivated to learn English because they believe it will improve their chances for advancing in the work world. "They tend to speak English as often as they can," says Michael Adams, who helps run cultural-sensitivity programs for employees at the University of California at San Francisco. "When they speak another language, it's done in order to help a fellow employee understand something."

Colleagues may empathize if they step into the nonnative speaker's shoes. They can be asked to imagine traveling overseas and encountering someone from their home country. What language would they converse in? Would that be rude, or would it simply be more comfortable? An increasing number of companies have found that training can help improve understanding and reduce tensions between culturally diverse employees in a single corporate culture.

advancement. "Employees shouldn't think just in terms of moving up all the time, but should consider lateral moves to improve skills and knowledge of the company," says Frank Spaulding, vice president of Household International, a financial-services giant.[29]

Corporate culture will also have to become more open. Honest communication during restructuring, for example, can keep rumors from getting out of control, improve morale, and allow employees to concentrate on performance. If employees are too concerned about job security, they will be less willing to think creatively and to take risks. Thus organizations will need to find ways of supporting and encouraging creativity and risk taking. Saturn Electronics & Engineering, based in Rochester Hills, Michigan, uses its corporate culture to motivate everyone from factory employees to top executives. "It's a very young company so we were able to form a new culture, not change an old one," says owner Wallace K. Tsuha, Jr. "We really stress teamwork. We're all in this together—fairly."[30]

As you can see, the changing workforce, the changing economy, and the changing corporate culture can all influence motivation. Even though studies and theories help us think about motivation, companies themselves must respond to the challenge of devising techniques to motivate employees to do their best—and beyond.

MOTIVATIONAL TECHNIQUES

What can organizations do to motivate people? When asked which motivators were most important, employees identified the techniques in the proportions shown in Exhibit 9.7. Today's employees are motivated by more than just good pay; satisfaction of higher-level needs is equally important. Many young people now entering the job market are less driven by professional success and more concerned with personal fulfillment. To them, leisure time, family ties, and nonmaterial satisfactions are as important as work.[31]

Another problem is how to motivate employees to stick with difficult or dirty jobs, a problem that Nucor had to face. So did Nissan, whose Japanese factories needed to attract and retain employees. Nissan's solution was to improve the factory environment so that the work would be easier, cleaner, and more efficient. The carmaker also installed robots to take over more dangerous or complex tasks. Employees benefited from these changes, says Katsutoshi Aihara, a union official: "At the end of the day, there are many fewer cases of muscle aches and backaches."[32]

To motivate people, employers must go beyond traditional incentives. Many now boost motivation through goal setting, behavior modification, training and retraining, better quality of work life, flexible schedules, telecommuting, and work and job sharing.

Goal Setting

Some employees are highly motivated by clear and challenging—but achievable—goals. In Nucor's goal-setting program, employees re-

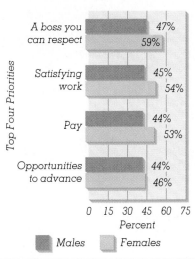

What Matters Most on the Job
Workers were asked which factors about a job are extremely important.

Top Four Priorities

A boss you can respect — 47% (Males), 59% (Females)
Satisfying work — 45% (Males), 54% (Females)
Pay — 44% (Males), 53% (Females)
Opportunities to advance — 44% (Males), 46% (Females)

Percent: 0 15 30 45 60 75

■ Males   ■ Females

Exhibit 9.7
Motivating Forces for Today's Employees
This graph shows the results of a survey of employees who were asked to identify the motivators that were most important to them.

ceive bonuses when they achieve the goal of producing more than the standard amount of steel. Of course, each individual's goals have to be coordinated with the overall organizational goals. However, individual goals are fewer in number, narrower in scope, and cover shorter time spans than organizational goals. They also involve less uncertainty and risk than organizational goals.[33]

Bear in mind that goal setting won't work as a motivational technique unless employees participate in setting their own goals. If goals are imposed from above, the advantage of this technique—bringing the employees' higher-level needs into play—will be lost, and employees will feel manipulated. Furthermore, effective goal-setting programs allow employees to find out whether they are in fact meeting their goals. Management by objectives, a goal-setting program discussed in Chapter 6, motivates employees because of the participation in setting goals and the ability to check progress.

Behavior Modification

behavior modification *Systematic use of rewards and punishments to change human behavior*

The idea behind **behavior modification,** a technique based on the reinforcement theory of motivation, is simple: Change employee actions by systematically encouraging actions that are desirable and discouraging those that are not. Managers start by determining which actions are desirable and which they want to change. Then they use the appropriate method of reinforcement to encourage employees to make the change.

Studies have found that offering praise and recognition for an employee's efforts is more effective than offering punishment (whether in the form of reprimand, ridicule, or sarcasm). Praise as a means of behavior modification has been used successfully by 3M, Ford, AT&T, PepsiCo, and other corporations. When Emery Air Freight set a goal

Don Carlton, president of Texas-based Radian, uses positive reinforcement to reinforce behaviors that help the company achieve its goals. He recognized the cost-cutting efforts of Allana M. Coffey, manager of facilities administration, by presenting her with the firm's Corporate Achievement Award.

of answering all customer inquiries within 90 minutes, each customer-service representative was asked to record, on a log sheet, the actual time it took to answer each inquiry. If an employee's performance improved, he or she was praised by the supervisor. Those who didn't improve were praised for their honesty and accuracy in filling out their log sheets and were then reminded of the 90-minute goal. After a few days of such feedback, customer-service reps were meeting the 90-minute goal 90 percent of the time.[34]

A number of companies use rewards of various kinds to reinforce the behavior of hardworking employees. These rewards may take the form of gifts, certificates or medals, dinners, trips, and other forms of recognition. Omni Hotels gives on-the-spot commendations to employees who go above and beyond the call of duty to help guests. As they earn such commendations, employees become eligible for medals, cash prizes, and the chance to attend a gala celebration for Omni Service Champions.[35]

Training and Retraining

In today's economy, many people feel threatened by the possibility of losing their jobs. This insecurity can lead to lower motivation and threaten organizational productivity. Job worries may also lead to personal problems that can interfere with an individual's work performance.

One way to motivate these employees is to sponsor training that will sharpen skills or to offer retraining that will give employees entirely new skills. Manufacturing employees may learn to operate robots and other automated equipment instead of tightening bolts; service employees may learn to sell instead of manage. At Collins & Aikman, a carpet manufacturer, classes were offered so that employees could learn math and other skills needed to operate computerized weaving equipment.[36] Although some people may not adjust easily to training or retraining, most appreciate the opportunity to become more useful to their companies or to the economy as a whole.

Better Quality of Work Life

Although dividing work into tiny specialized tasks helped managers deal with uneducated employees early in this century, that approach doesn't make as much sense today. Highly specialized jobs rarely satisfy today's better-educated and more sophisticated employees, some of whom know more about the technical aspects of their work than their supervisors do. As a result, many organizations are working to improve the **quality of work life (QWL),** the environment created by work and job conditions.[37] An improved QWL benefits both the individual and the organization: Employees gain the chance to use their special abilities and improve their skills, and the organization gains a more motivated employer.

A common way of improving QWL is through **job enrichment,** which reduces specialization and makes work more meaningful by expanding each job's responsibilities. For example, truck drivers who work for Ryder System not only deliver Xerox copying machines

quality of work life (QWL) Overall environment that results from job and work conditions

job enrichment Reducing work specialization and making work more meaningful by adding to the responsibilities of each job

but also set them up, test them, and train customers to use them.[38] How do employees feel when their jobs are expanded to include new duties? One man who had been a boilermaker with Gulf Oil for 28 years was unhappy when he was reassigned to help employees in other crafts. He resented the change because he could not take pride in performing unfamiliar tasks such as pipe fitting or welding. "When you're not doing the thing you've been trained to do," he says, "it has to affect your identity."[39] At the other extreme is a woman who spent 17 years performing one tedious step on a check-processing line at a Chicago bank and was then given a new, less specialized job. Now she uses a computer to perform most of the steps necessary to process and deposit checks. "I like it because you see the package from beginning to end," she says. "It's better to be part of the whole thing. Everyone should have change in their life."[40]

Flexible Schedules

The changing workforce is changing lifestyles and needs. Two-career couples with children must perform miracles of scheduling and routing to make sure that the kids get to school or to the baby-sitter and still get themselves to work on time; single parents have half the resources and twice the problem. Moreover, many employees are going back to school or working at second jobs. No wonder so many people applaud **flextime,** a scheduling system that allows employees to choose their own hours within certain limits. For instance, a company may require everyone to be at work between 10:00 A.M. and 2:00 P.M., but employees may arrive or depart whenever they want as long as they work a total of eight hours every day. The sense of control they get from arranging their own work schedules is in itself motivating for many people.

One national poll found that 78 percent of working adults would prefer to have flexible hours, even if it meant slower career advancement, in order to spend more time with their families.[41] In response to this employee need, more and more companies are offering flextime. In fact, a survey of 259 major employers found that 42 percent already offered flextime.[42] For example, 70 of the 240 part-time employees at Quill, a company in Illinois that markets office products and computers, have chosen to work on flexible schedules that suit their own personal and work demands.[43]

Flextime is more widespread in white-collar businesses that do not have to maintain standard customer-service hours. Flextime is not usually an option for employees on production teams, in retail stores, or in many offices where employees have to be on hand to wait on customers or answer calls. Among other drawbacks to flextime are (1) supervisors' feeling uncomfortable and less in control when employees are coming and going, and (2) co-workers' possibly resenting flextimers and assuming they take their jobs less seriously.

Telecommuting

Someone who works from home using computers and telecommunications equipment to stay in touch with his or her employer's of-

flextime *Scheduling system in which employees are allowed certain options regarding time of arrival and departure*

fices is **telecommuting.** Telecommuting has many advantages. Employee productivity may rise up to 20 percent, and the company's office-space costs are reduced. Telecommuting may also allow a company to keep an employee who might otherwise leave for more flexible work arrangements elsewhere.[44] Employees like this option because they can set their own hours, reduce job-related expenses such as commuting costs, and have more time with their families.

Of course, only certain types of jobs lend themselves to telecommuting; a printer who runs giant color presses can't do that from home. In addition, some home-based workers find they miss interacting with colleagues. When Apple Computer started a telecommuting program, it expected, but didn't get, a large response. Many people simply didn't want to work at home, and others were reluctant to give up the social environment of the office.[45] Furthermore, setting up a home-based office can be expensive, especially if a fax machine and other communication equipment are used. Some telecommuters have found that they actually put in longer hours or that they encounter too many distractions, such as young children requiring attention. Most telecommuters, however, find that the benefits outweigh the drawbacks.

telecommuting *Working from home and communicating with the company's main office via computer and other devices*

Work Sharing and Job Sharing

Two techniques can be used to improve morale when there is a mismatch between the amount of work available and the amount of work desired by the employee. **Work sharing,** which is more common in an economic downturn, distributes the hardships among a company's entire workforce by slicing a few hours off everybody's workweek and cutting pay. **Job sharing** lets two employees share a single full-time job and split the salary and benefits.

Advances in technology now allow millions of U.S. workers to enjoy the benefits of full- or part-time telecommuting from home.

work sharing *Slicing a few hours off everybody's workweek and cutting pay to minimize layoffs*

job sharing *Splitting a single full-time job between two employees for their convenience*

When a company adopts work sharing instead of laying people off, nearly everyone stands to gain. Employees are less anxious about being unemployed and are thus willing to spend more money, which helps local merchants stay in business. Because most employees keep their jobs rather than being "bumped" from one job to another by those employees with seniority, quality remains high. When business surges forward again, companies that have instituted work sharing are better equipped to meet the stepped-up demand because they do not have to call back old employees or train new ones. Employees are also more willing to put in long hours for a company that helps them through a tough spell.

Job sharing, by contrast, is a voluntary solution to the needs of working parents, employees going back to school, and the like. It is usually offered to people who already work for the company but need to cut back their hours; rather than lose a good employee or go to the trouble of finding and training someone new, the company finds a way to split responsibilities.

At Steelcase, the giant office-furniture manufacturer in Grand

Rapids, Michigan, a job-sharing program has been in place since 1982. Job sharers must have been full-time employees with the company for at least one year, and the job must have no supervisory or budgetary responsibilities. The two people sharing a job are expected to put in a combined 40-hour workweek, and each receives 50 percent of the job's benefits. For instance, two women who share a recruiting position in the marketing department each work two and a half days a week; they meet for lunch on Wednesdays to compare notes.[46]

Other Motivational Techniques

One popular motivational technique is employee **empowerment,** giving employees more say in the actual workings of the company, usually by offering them greater decision-making power. Empowerment gives employees greater responsibility and greater accountability for the company's performance. This involvement also leads to a deeper sense of satisfaction when employees' ideas and work contributions help achieve the company's goals, an especially important consideration when a company must continually improve its products and processes.

Federal Express has been a pioneer in the field of employee empowerment. FedEx employees are involved in hiring and advancement decisions within their areas. They also serve on quality-assurance teams, elect representatives to work with management on operations and human resources issues, and can take any grievances to a review board of their own choosing. These and other means of inviting participation forge a team spirit that increases motivation.[47]

Federal Express empowers its teams to find and fix problems throughout the company. This team identified a billing problem, tracked it to its source, and implemented a solution that saved the company $2.1 million a year.

As more organizations move toward team structures, they need motivational techniques geared to group efforts. One such approach is **gain sharing,** in which dollar rewards are tied to team performance. Gain-sharing bonuses are usually given on a monthly basis (as opposed to long-term profit sharing) and are tied to goals in areas that employees can directly influence, such as sales, payroll costs, customer satisfaction, and material costs.[48]

Employee stock options are another monetary incentive for increasing employee involvement. The goal of such plans is to demonstrate to employees the connection between performance and financial reward. This kind of monetary incentive is discussed in greater detail in Chapter 10.

In some cases, companies seek out new owners—their own employees. *Employee-owned businesses* can sometimes be the best solution if the alternative is a shutdown. Located in Westlake, Ohio, Manco is an employee-owned company that manufactures consumer mailing materials, duct tape, and office supplies. Everyone in the firm keeps track of the company's daily sales, shipments, and billings via large charts posted in the company cafeteria. Employees enjoy the satisfaction of directly controlling their company, and they benefit from the most effective of all motivational techniques: a stake in their own success.[49]

gain sharing *Motivational program that offers monetary rewards based on short-term team performance*

1 List the three main components of good human relations within an organization.
Leadership, communication, and motivation are the major elements that contribute to good human relations.

2 Explain how the five levels in Maslow's hierarchy of needs relate to employee motivation.
Physiological needs, the most basic requirements for human life, are seldom strong motivators for modern wage earners. Safety (or security) needs can be met through job security and pension plans. Social needs, which drive people to seek membership in informal groups, may be more important than financial considerations. Esteem needs, which relate to feelings of self-worth and respect from others, are met by motivational techniques of recognition. Self-actualization needs may be met by giving employees the opportunity to expand their skills and take on additional responsibility.

3 Identify the two factors affecting employee motivation in Herzberg's two-factor theory.
Hygiene factors—such as company policy, working conditions, and job security—have a bad effect on motivation only if they are deficient. Motivators—achievement, recognition, and responsibility—are related positively to increases in productivity.

4 List three basic assumptions of expectancy theory.
The three basic assumptions of expectancy theory are (1) the employee's perception of task difficulty (Can I do it?), (2) the employee's perception of the reward (If I do it, what will I get?), and (3) the employee's perception of the connection between the two (Will it be worth my while?).

5 Discuss the use of the four forms of reinforcement.
Reinforcement theory includes four forms of reinforcement: Positive reinforcement and negative reinforcement are used to encourage certain behaviors; extinction and punishment are used to discourage certain behaviors.

6 Describe how Theory X, Theory Y, and Theory Z link employee motivation and management style.
Theory X and Theory Y describe two opposite sets of assumptions about employees' motives for working; Theory X emphasizes management authority, and Theory Y emphasizes employee growth and self-direction. Theory Z, which describes human relations within U.S. companies that have adopted certain Japanese management techniques, assumes that employees are part of a family and that their needs therefore deserve consideration.

7 Explain how changes in the workforce have complicated the challenge of motivating employees.
Because of changes in the workforce, managers need to find new ways of keeping employees happy and productive on the job. Baby boomers feel blocked from advancing, and they want more participation in work decisions. People in their 20s who are entering the workforce want a balance between work and home life. The influx of women has created a need for more flexible arrangements to accommodate family requirements outside the job and a change in the ability to relocate employees. The increasing cultural diversity means that employees bring a wide range of work skills, traditions, and attitudes to their work, which can affect their behavior on the job.

8 Discuss the use of goal setting, behavior modification, training and retraining, and an improved quality of work life as motivational techniques.
Some companies motivate their employees by allowing them to set clear and challenging personal goals that support organizational goals. With behavioral modification, managers seek to change employee behavior by systematically encouraging actions that are desirable and discouraging those that are not. Employers can motivate employees who are worried about job security by sponsoring training that will sharpen skills or by offering retraining that will give employees entirely new skills. An improved quality of work life leads to better work and job conditions that give employees the chance to use their special abilities and build their skills.

As critics shook their heads, F. Kenneth Iverson opened a tiny steel mill, challenging Big Steel's domination of the U.S. marketplace. Cynics said Iverson's company, Nucor, would collapse under the weight of the industry's sky-high wage scale. Iverson, on the other hand, believed he could pull off his nervy scheme by motivating employees properly.

Iverson opened his first mills in rural areas where industry was still largely nonunion. He hired farm youths with more determination than knowledge of steel, and he put each in a small work group dedicated to a specific task in the steel-making process. Iverson encouraged employees to think of their work groups as small businesses of their own. Then he added a series of motivational programs.

The financial reward for each employee included hefty bonuses scaled to production achieved by the work groups. Employees in teams that produced more than the standard amount of steel could earn twice the standard base wage through performance bonuses. These production bonuses were posted daily on bulletin boards and paid weekly to stimulate goal-oriented individuals.

Employees also received bonuses based on return-on-assets-employed. On top of the bonuses, 10 percent of pretax earnings was paid to employees in a profit-sharing plan. Plant managers receive bonuses tied to the company's overall performance. Nucor took attitude surveys to develop personnel policies, hospitalized employees got benefits from the first day, and the company offered tuition assistance for children of employees.

Nucor also introduced punishments. An employee who arrived 15 minutes late lost a whole day's production bonus. The whole week's bonus was lost if the employee was a half hour late. Moreover, employees were not paid if their group's machinery broke down. People supported such rules because they helped groups earn their maximum bonuses.

Subsequent events proved Iverson correct in his approach to motivation. Today his $2.2 billion company produces 980 tons of steel per employee per year, far better than the industry average of 420. Including bonuses, Nucor's millworkers routinely earn $45,000, more than many unionized employees earn. What's more, Nucor has remained highly profitable while larger steel companies have undergone painful downsizing.

Starting with one small North Carolina mill, Iverson built Nucor into the nation's ninth largest steel producer. These days the company is known around the world for its motivational techniques. Nucor's success proves that motivated employees make a difference.

Your Mission: You are Nucor's vice president for human resources. Consider the following problems and suggest how company policies might be altered to avoid human relations conflicts that result from rapid growth:

1. Although employees are basically pleased with Nucor's bonus structure, they are still powerless to alter the structure to fit specific situations at specific plants. What would you suggest to empower employees in this area?

a. Let employees know they already have it a lot better than their counterparts in other companies, and be sure they understand that anyone making trouble over this issue will be fired immediately.

b. Have managers organize groups of shop workers to meet regularly and make suggestions to higher management for modifying the bonus structure under certain conditions.

c. Let individual employees submit suggestions in writing to upper management so that everyone will feel included and empowered.

2. In a recent attitude survey, a large number of employees complained about growing boredom on the job. You suspect this boredom may be related to the narrowness and repetitiveness of the tasks assigned. Moreover, you fear there may be a connection between this boredom and the lower productivity figures you've been hearing about lately. What should Nucor do?

a. Alert managers to the growing boredom problem, and have them cut the bonuses of any employees who appear to be slacking off.

b. Ask a group of employees to immediately redesign tasks and suggest job enrichment programs to combat the boredom problem.

c. Appoint a team of managers and employees to determine whether narrow, repetitious tasks are at the core of the problem. If so, the team can suggest ways of overcoming this problem.

3. One employee has been consistently late to work in the morning, usually one-half to one hour. He never complains about losing some or all of his week's bonus, and once he arrives, he is one of the most highly motivated and productive employees in the plant. When asked, he explains that he is a widower with three young children. By the time he feeds and dresses them and drives them to school each morning, he often misses the 8:00 starting time at work. What should you do?

a. Leave it alone. The man's problems are his own, not Nucor's. Since the employee is abiding by the rules and not complaining about losing his bonuses, things are working out fine.

b. Tell the employee that because of his special circumstances, he can come in late. He won't lose any more bonuses unless he comes in after 9:00.

c. Appoint a team to see how many other employees might benefit from flextime. If the numbers warrant it, have the team look into how flextime might be used with the work teams already in place.

4. A few employees at one plant are angry that Nucor has not revealed details of its latest investments in technology, which may hurt company earnings and reduce bonuses for the coming year. Nucor managers have said that the technology will lead to profits in future years, and they refuse to talk publicly about the technology because they fear this information could help competitors. How should managers handle this situation?

a. Set up meetings in every plant to discuss the new technology and the need for continued secrecy. Encourage employees to talk about other areas of disagreement. Then respond to these concerns directly and honestly.

b. Don't back down from maintaining secrecy about the new technology. Competitive threats are a real concern that employees should never underestimate. Suggest that complainers look for jobs elsewhere.

c. Tell a few employees, in confidence, the facts about the new technology. Swear them to secrecy and ask them to reassure their co-workers that the technology is a step in the right direction and will ultimately result in higher profits.[50]

KEY TERMS

behavior modification (256)
empowerment (260)
expectancy theory (245)
flextime (258)
gain sharing (261)
group norms (243)
Hawthorne effect (243)
human relations (240)

hygiene factors (244)
job enrichment (257)
job sharing (259)
morale (241)
motivation (241)
motivators (244)
piecework system (242)
quality of work life (QWL) (257)

reinforcement theory (245)
scientific management (242)
telecommuting (259)
Theory X (247)
Theory Y (247)
Theory Z (248)
work sharing (259)

REVIEW QUESTIONS

1. What does scientific management see as the primary tool for motivation? Is this approach practical today?
2. Why were the Hawthorne studies important?
3. What are the practical implications of Maslow's hierarchy? What are its limitations?

4. How do Theories X and Y relate to Theory Z?
5. What challenges do companies face when managing a diverse workforce?
6. What is reinforcement theory, and what are the four forms of reinforcement?

7. What is quality of work life, and how does it influence employee motivation?
8. What is employee empowerment?

THE PIZZA DISTRIBUTION OLYMPICS: A QUESTION OF DOUGH . . .

. . . the kind you spend as well as the kind you knead and spread in a pizza pan. Domino's Pizza Distribution Olympics was management's brainstorm for recognizing employee achievement and encouraging high, uniform work standards at the same time. This special event takes place every July and features employee competition in events ranging from forming dough balls and driving pizza trucks to slicing vegetables and balancing an accounting ledger.

The Olympics began as a way of recognizing the essential, but often unsung, efforts of Domino's subsidiary, Domino's Pizza Distribution. This unit was formed to provide Domino's retail stores worldwide with vegetables, toppings, napkins, uniforms—and, of course, dough. However, Domino's franchisees aren't obligated to buy from the subsidiary. That's why the subsidiary works hard to please the stores it serves.

Domino's founder Tom Monaghan once called the Distribution unit his "secret weapon" because of its contribution to Domino's success. However, keeping employee morale high was difficult, in part because the subsidiary's work was virtually unknown outside the company. However, Valerie Russell, an accountant at company headquarters, believed participation in the Olympics would not only highlight the importance of every individual's job but also act as a means of monitoring and improving work standards by making performance competitive.

The three-day Olympics event is now companywide. Each department in the Distribution subsidiary holds competitions to qualify team members for the Olympics. The local winners are flown to headquarters to compete for valuable prizes, such as cash, rings, and vacations. Contestants have a good time and, at the same time, they demonstrate work practices that lead to faster or more efficient performance. After the competition, Domino's managers meet with the champions to discuss how the winning procedures, methods, and techniques can help improve everyone's job performance.

The dough event, for example, yielded unexpected dividends. Management observed that contestants were using a number of techniques and achieving varying results when they prepared pizza dough. So the Domino's managers picked the brains of the best dough makers to create a manual detailing the specifics of dough production. This manual helps employees in every Domino's unit make good dough every time by following the procedures outlined by the chain's winning dough makers.

Dough makers haven't been the only personnel inspired to better performance. Also rising to the occasion was the Florida-based truck driver who times himself whenever he loads his truck (and the many others like him who were stimulated to make a special effort by special recognition).

1. Domino's budgets more than $1 million yearly for the games. What does the company gain in return?

2. What effect does the pooling of expertise have on employee morale and performance?

3. Do the Pizza Olympics appeal to lower-level or higher-level employee needs?

With a small group of three or four students (preferably students you don't know well), select a ready-made assembly project that can be completed in one or two hours. This can be a jigsaw puzzle, a plastic model, or some other similar craft project. As you work, consider the process that your group goes through to complete the project. How did you decide on the project? Did your group select a leader, or was leadership a shared responsibility? How did you delegate responsibilities in the project? After you complete the project, write a brief summary of the activities of your group as they relate to the following factors: human relations, leadership, communication, motivation, and morale. As a class, share and discuss the experiences of each group.

Select one or two articles from recent issues of *The Wall Street Journal* that relate to employee motivation or morale.

1. What is the problem, solution, or trend described in the article(s), and how does it influence employee attitudes or motivation?

2. Does this problem relate to just one company's experience, or does it have broader implications? Who is affected by it now, and who do you think might be affected by it in the future?

3. What challenges and opportunities does this development offer management in this company or industry? The employees?

SERVICEMASTER SERVES UP MOTIVATION

Synopsis

One of the most difficult motivation challenges in any industry is to find ways of boosting morale and pride among employees who handle custodial chores. This was the situation faced by ServiceMaster, a company that has built a thriving business out of cleaning offices, schools, and other facilities. ServiceMaster hires, trains, and supervises custodial workers, then uses motivational techniques such as its "Olympic" games to instill a sense of pride and accomplishment. Although some employees are concerned about the religious overtones of the company's approach, others say that ServiceMaster has helped them do their best.

Exercises

ANALYSIS

1. Which of Herzberg's hygiene factors do you think might have the greatest effect on ServiceMaster employees?

2. Which of Herzberg's motivators do you think the company is applying to boost motivation?

3. What effect might positive feedback from teachers, students, and parents have on the ServiceMaster employees who clean a local school?

4. Why does ServiceMaster see employee training as part of motivation?

5. To which level (or levels) of Maslow's hierarchy of needs does the Olympic competition seem to appeal?

APPLICATION

Could you use an Olympic game program to help motivate employees of a real estate brokerage firm? If so, explain what kind of competitions you would plan; if not, suggest another way of motivating brokers to sell more houses.

DECISION

Empowering employees can unleash creativity and enthusiasm that makes employees feel good about their contributions and helps the company be more successful. However, not every employee suggestion is appropriate. As a ServiceMaster supervisor, what should you consider before deciding whether an employee can change the methods being used to complete certain work tasks?

COMMUNICATION

You've decided that the ServiceMaster employee's suggested changes to work

methods aren't appropriate. Now plan what you'll say when you talk with this employee. Limit your remarks to no more than three minutes, and make up any details you need.

INTEGRATION

Would the ServiceMaster supervisors who work directly with custodial employees put the most emphasis on technical, human relations, or conceptual skills described in Chapter 6? Why?

ETHICS

In the interest of fairness, should the ServiceMaster Olympic games include supervisors and corporate officials as well as workers?

DEBATE

Should every employer be required to allow employees to make flextime arrangements if they choose? Option A: In a formal debate format, argue for or against the idea of universal availability of flextime. Option B: Take either position and state your case in a brief summary report.

TEAMWORK

In a team of five students, identify ways that ServiceMaster can help satisfy its employees at all five levels of Maslow's hierarchy. You may choose to work on each level as a team or to assign one level to each student.

RESEARCH

Do the research necessary to write a one-paragraph update on either (a) ServiceMaster's current status or (b) how competitors motivate their employees.

ROLE PLAYING

Two students play the role of ServiceMaster employees seeking a job-sharing arrangement because of family pressures that make holding a full-time job difficult. Their manager, played by a third student, has to be convinced that job sharing will work. Assume that the job is cleaning a law firm's downtown offices during overnight hours.

Chapter

10

Human Resources Management

Keeping Employees in the Pink and the Company in the Black

Does a healthier workforce translate into healthier profits? This was one of the key issues facing Johnson & Johnson CEO Ralph S. Larsen and his predecessor, James E. Burke, as they considered the challenge of keeping employees satisfied and productive by successfully managing the company's human resources. Johnson & Johnson had expanded throughout the world, employing more than 70,000 people to research, manufacture, and market health-care products in dozens of countries.

Employee health was a major concern for several reasons. Studies showed that over 30 percent of Johnson & Johnson's employees were smokers, and an internal report revealed that smokers had a 45 percent greater rate of absenteeism than nonsmokers. Smokers also contributed disproportionately to the company's medical expenses (30 percent higher than nonsmokers), an ominous statistic at a time when health-care costs were rising at nearly twice the rate of inflation.

Another problem confronting J&J was the effect of changing demographics on employees. Employees increasingly fell into one of three groups: they were part of two-career couples with children; they were responsible for an aging parent; or they were single mothers or fathers. A survey of 10,000 J&J employees revealed that they were frustrated by their inability to meet all their obligations, both to their families and to their employer. Many stated that they had difficulty finding day care, especially sick-child and infant care, and almost 20 percent responded that they could not afford day care even if they could have located a suitable provider.

Although these employees felt torn between family pressures and employment roles, they found little help at work. Most stated that their managers were unsympathetic about the dilemma. Balancing their work and family obligations took its toll on employees, who reported higher levels of stress, greater absenteeism, and lower job satisfaction.

For guidance on these issues, the CEOs turned to Johnson & Johnson's operating document, the corporate credo written by Robert Wood Johnson, son of a founding Johnson brother and chairman of the company for 25 years. Johnson ranked the company's obligation

Johnson & Johnson encourages its employees to develop healthier lifestyles by participating in the company's Live for Life wellness program.

to its employees ahead of its responsibility to its shareholders and second only to its commitment to its customers. This credo would serve as a blueprint for successful human resources management.

So how could J&J top managers promote health in the workplace? How could they help J&J employees balance family and career obligations? What programs could be established to more effectively meet the personal and professional needs of their employees? What effect would such programs have on the company's bottom line?[1]

THE PROCESS OF HUMAN RESOURCES MANAGEMENT

As Johnson & Johnson's managers know, employees are an important component of every business. More and more companies consider employees their most valuable asset, and such attitudes have fueled the rising emphasis on obtaining the people a company needs and then overseeing their training and development, motivation, evaluation, and compensation. This specialized function, formerly referred to as *personnel management,* is now termed **human resources management** to reflect the importance of a well-chosen and well-managed workforce in achieving company goals.

human resources management Specialized function of planning how to obtain employees, oversee their training, evaluate them, and compensate them

Human resources management is becoming more complex in the 1990s, and its role is increasingly viewed as a strategic one. The workforce, the economy, and corporate culture are being transformed at an accelerating pace; changes in technology alone have already created crucial mismatches between employees' skills and employers' needs. Furthermore, these changes are taking place within a social environment in which employees' rights, privacy, and health risks are but a few of the factors at stake.

Human resources managers must figure out how to attract qualified employees from a shrinking pool of entry-level employees; how to train less educated, poorly skilled employees; how to keep experienced employees when they have fewer opportunities for advancement; and how to lay off employees equitably in an era of downsizing and economic recession. They must also retrain employees to enable them to cope with increasing automation and computerization, manage increasingly complex (and expensive) employee benefits programs, fit workplace policies to changing workforce demographics and employee needs, and cope with the challenge of meeting government regulations in hiring practices and equal opportunity in employment.

In addition, human resources executives are increasingly required to take a global perspective, providing for employees who travel to and work in other countries. Fluor, a California-based engineering and construction firm with more than 22,000 employees worldwide, has some 500 international human resources professionals who administer payroll, benefits, and training programs, and coordinate recruiting and staffing at operations in 80 countries.[2] Given the growing importance and complexity of human resources problems, it's scarcely surprising that all but the smallest businesses employ specialists to deal with them.

What exactly do human resources departments do? Human resources staff members plan how to meet a company's human resources needs, recruit and select employees, train and develop employees and managers, and appraise employee performance. The staff also administers pay and employee benefits and oversees changes in employment status (promotion, reassignment, termination or resignation, retirement). Overall, the human resources department keeps the organization running smoothly at every level, easing the integration of people from a variety of cultures and backgrounds so that all work cooperatively toward the common goals.[3] This chapter explores each of these human resources responsibilities, beginning with planning.

Human Resources Planning

The first step in staffing business organizations, as in any other management endeavor, is to plan (see Exhibit 10.1). As one human resources staff director explains, a company must have "people on hand at the right time and in the right place to make a thing go."[4]

Exhibit 10.1
Steps in Human Resources Planning
Careful attention to each phase of this sequence helps ensure that a company will have the right human resources when it needs them.

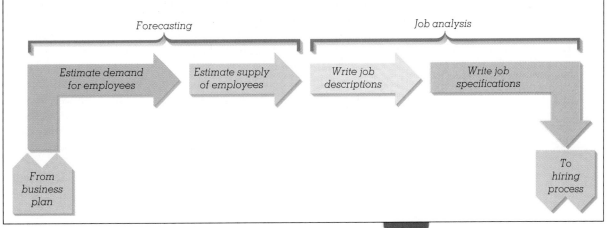

Planning is a critical step. A miscalculation could leave a company without enough employees to keep up with demand, resulting in lost business because customers or clients go elsewhere.

Yet if a company expands its staff too rapidly, profits may be eaten up by payroll, or the firm may have to lay off people who were just recruited and trained at considerable expense. Some of the most spectacular surges and slumps in staffing have occurred in the U.S. electronics industry. When Silicon Valley firms anticipated greatly increased demand for electronic components, they hired large numbers of new employees, only to lay them off a short time later because business didn't boom as expected. That's why the ability to forecast future staffing needs is a key part of human resources planning.

Forecasting

Supply and demand are factors in human resources planning, just as they are in more general business planning. Forecasting begins with estimates of *demand,* the numbers and kinds of employees that will be needed at various times. For example, a shoe chain that is planning to open another store within six months would estimate that it needs an additional store manager and an assistant manager as well as part-time salespeople. Although the chain might start looking immediately for someone as highly placed as the manager, hiring salespeople might be postponed until just before the store opens.

The next task is to estimate the *supply* of available employees. In many cases, that supply is within the company already—perhaps just needing training to fill future requirements. The shoe chain may well find that the assistant manager at an existing store can be promoted to manage the new store, and one of the current salespeople can be named assistant manager. If existing employees cannot be tapped for new positions, the human resources manager must determine how to find people outside the company who have the necessary skills. The shoe chain may have to look outside for the new manager, assistant manager, and additional salespeople, which would mean hiring them and providing training in the store's operations.

The Changing Labor Market. Every business needs to know whether enough people with the required skills are available in the general workforce. Keeping track of the labor market is not easy, because it is undergoing substantial change. Although fewer jobs are available for factory employees in traditional "smokestack" industries such as steel manufacturing, the demand for people with skills in engineering, computer technology, and many other technical areas is mushrooming. Nurses are in short supply. In fact, National Medical Enterprises, a major U.S. hospital company, has gone so far as to recruit nurses from Ireland, Scandinavia, and China.[5] The United States is also seeing a shortage of experienced tool and die makers, despite pay that can reach $80,000 a year.[6] Companies are having difficulty finding qualified people to fill jobs in a wide range of categories (see Exhibit 10.2).

What's more, the gap is widening between what employers will require of new employees in the years ahead and the actual skills of these employees. Many of the new jobs created in the United States

	Some difficulty	Great difficulty
Job categories experiencing labor shortages today		
Percentage of companies reporting difficulty recruiting now		
Secretarial/clerical	39	9
Skilled crafts	35	9
Technical	51	13
Professional	50	11
Sales	29	3
Administrative	31	2
Supervisory/management	45	3
Job categories where labor shortages are expected in five years		
Percentage of companies expecting difficulty in future recruiting		
Secretarial/clerical	32	21
Skilled crafts	28	18
Technical	36	27
Professional	41	22
Sales	27	8
Administrative	35	6
Supervisory/management	42	11

Exhibit 10.2
Labor Shortages
Employers are having difficulty finding qualified applicants in a wide variety of job categories.

in the next 10 years will require higher education or technical training. As more organizations expand into global markets, they need managers and employees with technical skills, as well as the ability to adapt to other cultures and the foresight to spot local, national, and international trends.[7] At the same time, many employees don't have the basic mathematics, reading, and writing skills for today's jobs. Phoenix Specialty Manufacturing found that some of its employees didn't have the mathematical ability to calculate measurements in terms of thousandths of an inch; others couldn't read a shipping label.[8]

Three influences are changing the labor market in the 1990s: (1) fewer qualified employees are available in some professions; (2) a need is growing for people who can be effective in other cultures; and (3) the basic skills of some employees are inadequate. In response, a growing number of U.S. businesses, such as Kodak and Motorola, are working more closely with schools to prepare students at all levels for future jobs. They're also offering training and development courses on their own, as discussed later in this chapter.

Strategic Staffing Techniques. Human resources planners must also take into account today's fluid business conditions. To avoid drastic overstaffing or understaffing, many companies are turning to part-time and temporary employees, who are easily added when business picks up and are easily let go when it slows down again. General Motors and other downsized corporations have avoided adding new permanent employees by hiring temporary employees only when they're needed.[9]

*Filene's, like most other depart-
ment stores, hires part-time temporary employees to help out during the winter holidays, when
business is brisk. When business
slows down again, these employees are usually laid off or scheduled to work fewer hours.*

The part-time labor force has increased by leaps and bounds in
recent years, particularly the segment made up of "involuntary" part-
timers. These are people who want full-time jobs but who are forced
to settle for part-time. Between 1970 and 1990, the number of such
involuntary part-timers grew by 121 percent; they now make up more
than 6 million of the 21 million part-time U.S. workers. The number of voluntary part-timers increased by 69 percent during the same
period. A growing number of businesses trying to save money and
increase flexibility have built their workforces around part-time employees, whose schedules can be rearranged to suit the company's
needs.[10]

A large percentage of the workforce is also made up of temporary
employees. In 1983 only 0.5 percent of all U.S. workers were hired
through temporary-help agencies; today 1.4 percent are hired through
such agencies.[11] Some 85 percent of U.S. firms enlist the services of
temporary agencies. "Temps" can perform tasks ranging from the
repetitive and boring to the highly technical and demanding. In fact,
some 20 percent are highly skilled professionals, constituting the
fastest-growing segment.[12] Although temps have traditionally received
no company benefits, that situation is changing. In an effort to attract
high-quality temps, many companies (and temporary-help agencies)
are providing at least some benefits.[13]

Job Analysis

If you were the owner of a small business, it might make sense for
you to hire employees on an informal basis, since you would be in
a good position to know the requirements of all the jobs in your
company. However, in large organizations like Johnson & Johnson,
where hundreds or thousands of employees are performing a wide
variety of jobs, management needs a more formal and objective
method of evaluating job requirements. That method is called **job
analysis.**

job analysis Process by which jobs are
studied to determine the tasks and dynamics involved in performing them

Several questions must be asked in job analysis: What tasks are involved in the job (what does the person do all day)? What qualifications and skills are needed to do the job? In what kind of setting

PART THREE | MANAGING HUMAN RESOURCES

does the job take place? (Some jobs, such as sales, require extensive public contact; others, such as factory work, do not.) Does the job entail much time pressure (such as daily newspaper reporting) or little time pressure (such as attending to children in a day-care center)?

To obtain the information needed for a job analysis, human resources experts start by asking employees or supervisors for information. They also observe employees directly, perhaps using a stopwatch or videotape to monitor someone's work activities. Some employers even ask employees to keep daily diaries describing exactly what they do during the workday.

After job analysis has been completed, the human resources manager develops a **job description,** a specific statement of the tasks involved in the job and the conditions under which the holder of the job will work. The manager may also develop a **job specification,** a statement describing the skills, education, and previous experience that the job requires. Exhibit 10.3 presents a description and a specification for the same job.

Recruiting and Selecting New Employees

The next step is to match the job specification with an actual person or selection of people. This is done through **recruiting,** the process of attracting suitable candidates for an organization's jobs. **Recruiters** are specialists on the human resources staff who are responsible for obtaining these candidates. They consider people already working for the company; they seek referrals from employees or colleagues in the industry; they advertise in newspapers and work through public and private employment agencies; they visit union hiring halls or college campuses; and they may try to attract people who work for other companies.

When recruiters have difficulty finding qualified candidates in the immediate area, they become more creative in their efforts. They may advertise in areas where a similar business has recently closed or downsized, enter into cooperative arrangements with vocational schools that offer training in desired skills, or look abroad for people with the needed skills.

The Hiring Process

After exploring at least one—but usually more—of these recruitment channels to assemble a pool of applicants, the human resources department may spend weeks and sometimes months on the hiring process. Most companies go through the same basic stages in the hiring process as they sift through applications to come up with the person or people they want.

The first stage is to select a small number of qualified candidates from the total number of applications received. A person may be chosen on the basis of a standard application form that all candidates fill out or on the basis of a **résumé,** a summary of education, experience, and personal data compiled by the applicant. Sometimes both sources of information are used.

The second stage in the hiring process is to interview each candidate to clarify her or his qualifications and to fill in any missing in-

job description Statement of the tasks involved in a given job and the conditions under which the holder of the job will work

job specification Statement describing the kind of person who would be best for a given job—including the skills, education, and previous experience that the job requires

recruiting Process of attracting appropriate applicants for an organization's jobs

recruiters Members of the human resources staff who are responsible for obtaining new job candidates

résumé Summary of education, experience, and personal data compiled by the applicant for a job

SUNNYVALE GENERAL HOSPITAL

Job Description and Specifications

Job Title: *Job Analyst*   **Job Code:** *166.088*

Date: *September 1, 1995*   **Job Location:** *Human Resources Department*

Supervisor: *Anitra Jacobson*

Job Description:

Job Summary
Collects and develops job analysis information through interviews, questionnaires, observation, or other means. Provides other human resources specialists with needed information.

Job Duties
Designs job analysis schedules and questionnaires. Collects job information. Writes job descriptions and job specifications. Performs other duties as assigned by supervisors.

Working Conditions
Works mostly in an office setting. Travels to hospital clinics in county from one to three days per month. Travels around each work site collecting job information.

Job Specifications:

Skill Factors
Education: College degree required.

Experience: At least one year as job analyst trainee, recruiter, or other professional assignment in personnel area.

Communication: Oral and written skills should demonstrate ability to summarize job data succinctly.

Effort Factors
Physical Demands: Limited to those normally associated with clerical jobs: sitting, standing, and walking.

Mental Demands: Extended visual attention is needed to observe jobs. Initiative and ingenuity are mandatory since job receives only general supervision. Ability to analyze and synthesize large amounts of abstract information into job descriptions, job specifications, and job standards is essential.

formation. Another goal of the interview is to get an idea of the applicant's personality and ability to work well with others. Depending on the type of job at stake, candidates may also be asked to move to a third stage, taking a test or a series of tests.

After the initial interviews, the best candidates may be asked to meet with someone in the human resources department who will conduct a more probing interview. These candidates will also be interviewed by the person who will supervise the new employee. The supervisor, sometimes in consultation with her or his boss and the human resources department, goes on to the fourth stage by evaluating the candidates. The fifth stage is to check the references of the top few candidates. In the sixth stage, the supervisor selects the most suitable person for the job. Now the search is over—provided the candidate accepts the offer.

The following sections look more closely at two of these stages, interviewing and testing. Both can play a crucial role in hiring decisions, although testing in particular is controversial. Then you'll get a glimpse of the legal land mines that human resources managers must avoid in the course of screening job applicants and making hiring decisions.

Interviewing

Useful interviews follow established, standardized procedures tailored to the company's needs. If you were a member of the human resources department preparing to interview a candidate, you would provide a comfortable, private environment for the meeting, allow sufficient time, and develop a set of questions based on the applicant's résumé and application. Thorough preparation helps you set the stage for a productive discussion with the candidate.

During the course of the interview, keep the conversation focused on job-related issues in order to determine whether the person is right for the job and whether the job is right for the person. Ask about the applicant's background and work experience, professional goals, and related skills and interests. The questions in Exhibit 10.4 are typical.

Good interviewers have mastered the skills of building trust and rapport. They create a relaxed atmosphere that puts applicants at ease and encourages communication. They also realize the importance of listening carefully and of being nonjudgmental. These interviewing skills help you gather the important information needed for hiring decisions.[14]

Testing

One much-debated aspect of the hiring process is testing—not just the tests that prospective employers give job applicants, but any devices that they may use to evaluate employees when making job decisions. Tests are used to gauge abilities, aptitude, intelligence, interests, and sometimes even physical condition and personality.

Many companies rely on preemployment testing to determine whether applicants are suited to the job and will be worth the expense of hiring and training. Companies use three main procedures: job-skills testing, psychological testing, and drug testing. Job-skills tests are the most common type. They are designed to assess competency

Exhibit 10.3 (opposite page)
Sample Job Description and Job Specification
A job description lists the tasks the job involves and the conditions under which those tasks are performed. A job specification spells out the characteristics—skills, education, and experience—of the ideal candidate for the job.

Employment history

- Why do you wish to change employment?
- What do you like the least about your current position?
- What goals do you expect to achieve in your current job that you have not already accomplished?

The new position

- What are your expectations of this position?
- What do you anticipate being the most challenging aspects of this job?
- What can you contribute to this position?
- What would be your first goal in this position?
- How would you handle a 10 percent budget cut in your area of responsibility?

Career goals

- What are your long-term goals?
- How have you moved from each stage in your career to the next?
- What factors are most important to you in terms of job satisfaction?
- When do you anticipate a promotion?

Company "fit"

- Are you a team player or are you more satisfied working alone?
- Do you praise the contributions of others?
- What characteristics do you believe an outstanding employee should possess? A peer? A supervisor?
- How would you handle a "problem" employee?
- How would you deal with a colleague who has competed with you for a position, feels better qualified than you, and now works for you?

The U.S. Bureau of the Census uses job-skills testing to assess how well applicants can transcribe data, an important part of the job.

or specific abilities needed to perform a job. Thus, secretaries might be given a word-processing test, and people applying for jobs requiring physical dexterity might be given a test for eye-hand coordination. Some companies use *assessment centers* to simulate work assignments in an officelike setting and test management candidates on such elements as decision making and interpersonal skills.

Psychological tests usually take the form of questionnaires filled out by job applicants either with pencil and paper or using a computer. These tests can be used to assess overall intellectual ability, attitudes toward work, interests, managerial potential, or personality characteristics. Morse Shoe, a Massachusetts-based retailer, reduced its losses from theft by one-third after its applicants began taking tests designed to predict honesty, punctuality, and conscientiousness.[15] People who favor psychological testing say that it can predict how well employees will actually perform on the job. However, critics say that such tests are ineffective and potentially discriminatory. Any human resources manager who uses preemployment testing must choose well-validated tests, administer them to all candidates for the same position, and never rely on test results as the sole basis for hiring decisions.

Drug testing is being used by an increasing number of employers in the private sector. Studies have shown that drug users have greater absenteeism rates, are involved in significantly more on-the-job accidents, and incur much higher medical costs than employees who use no drugs. To avoid the increased costs and reduced productivity associated with drug abuse in the workplace (estimated to cost industry some $100 billion a year), employers frequently require applicants to be tested for drug use. According to a survey by the American Management Association, more than 60 percent of U.S. firms conduct drug testing; of those, 96 percent will not hire applicants who test positive.[16] Because drug testing is surrounded by legal controversy, it is one of the issues addressed in the next section.

Hiring and the Law

Federal and state laws and regulations govern many aspects of the hiring process. In particular, employers must be careful to avoid discrimination in the wording of their application forms, in interviewing, and in testing. They must also worry about obtaining sufficient information about employees to avoid becoming the target of a negligent-hiring lawsuit. For example, a trucking company would check applicants' driving records to avoid hiring a new driver with poor driving skills.

Application forms typically include questions about a person's job experience and may also include questions about matters that are not strictly job-related (outside activities and so on). Questions about unrelated factors such as marital status, age, and religion violate the Equal Employment Opportunity Commission's regulations because they may lead to discrimination. The exception is when such information relates to a bona fide occupational qualification that arises out of the nature of the specific job. Despite these rules, some standard application forms ordered from business stationers still include such questions; companies that use these forms may, therefore, be unwittingly violating the law.[17] Since the Immigration Reform and Control Act was passed in 1986, employers must also be wary of asking too few questions. Almost all U.S. companies are forbidden to hire illegal aliens and must verify that the newly hired are legally eligible to work. The act also prohibits discrimination in hiring on the basis of national origin or citizenship status, resulting in a sticky situation for many employers trying to determine their applicants' citizenship.

If you're interviewing a candidate, ask only about matters that are related to the job. Even though the Family Support Act of 1988 requires employers to withhold child support from wages, companies who ask about an applicant's child-support obligations may be liable for state and federal penalties.[18] In addition, questions about whether the person is married or has children, whether he or she owns or rents a home, what caused a physical disability, whether the person belongs to a union, whether he or she has ever been arrested, and when the applicant attended school (because the answer would indicate the applicant's age) aren't allowed.

The question of whether to use psychological testing has become more complex in recent years. As the result of a Supreme Court ruling that tests are unlawful if they discriminate, employers have to be sure that their tests accurately measure qualities related to job performance and that test scores are not the principal basis for hiring decisions. Furthermore, the Americans with Disabilities Act (ADA) outlaws the use of testing to screen out applicants with medical problems before a job offer has been made. As a result, using psychological tests to deny a job to someone whose mental state may pose a threat to the health or safety of co-workers and customers may bring an employer into conflict with the ADA.[19] Since these are difficult determinations, some employers prefer not to use psychological tests at all.

The legal aspects of drug testing vary from state to state and continue to change. Some states prohibit drug testing by private employers, whereas others severely limit the situations in which testing can be used. The U.S. government mandates that certain government employees and employees of federal contractors undergo drug screening. It is important to make sure that applicants sign a waiver consenting to the testing, that the testing be conducted reliably and accurately, and that the results be kept confidential. Those who test positive should be given an opportunity for a retest. Before institut-

EMPLOYEE PRIVACY VERSUS COMPANY SECURITY

Companies have the right—and, to some extent, the obligation—to protect themselves against lawsuits and theft, their employees against unsafe conditions, and their customers against unhealthy and faulty products. No one argues with these goals. However, some people have criticized the methods companies use to protect that right.

For example, should employers be allowed to test job applicants and employees to ensure that they won't expose companies to undue risk? Many companies are concerned about employee abuse of drugs and alcohol, which can impair productivity and pose a safety hazard to others. Although some states have laws restricting drug testing, firms frequently try to screen out substance abusers by testing prospective (and sometimes current) employees. However, critics charge that a company's right to know is offset by an employee's "right to be let alone," in the now historic words of U.S. Supreme Court Justice Louis D. Brandeis. Such testing, say the critics, is an invasion of employee privacy, especially since it relates to what employees do when they're not on the job.

What complicates the issue is that the tests, although increasingly accurate, generally cannot distinguish between the alcohol in cough syrup and the alcohol in cocktails. Furthermore, tests may detect marijuana as long as 30 days after its use, and eating three poppy-seed bagels can produce enough morphine in the body to result in a positive test. In short, someone who is not under the influence of an illegal substance may test positive for it.

Another important privacy issue pertains to AIDS (acquired immune deficiency syndrome). Although medical experts have repeatedly em-

phasized that AIDS cannot be transmitted by food handling or casual contact, some people are fearful when they learn that a co-worker is AIDS-infected. Employees who have AIDS or related conditions are now covered by laws protecting the disabled, but they have little or no insulation against discrimination by co-workers. Given this emotional environment, employees want assurances that their medical records will be handled in confidence. At the same time, more companies are educating their employees about the realities of AIDS and other medical conditions.

It is difficult to fault companies for trying to make their products safer and their work sites more secure. However, few companies have adopted formal policies regarding employee privacy, which leaves room for abuse. Many employee-privacy issues have yet to be tested in court, and privacy laws vary from state to state. At this point, therefore, only one thing is clear: Finding a balance between employer and employee rights is likely to be one of the most debated workplace issues of the 1990s.

ing any kind of physical test, a company should determine whether such testing is really necessary.

Despite the legal hurdles companies must overcome to find out about potential employees, they are facing greater accountability for the actions of employees on the job resulting from negligent hiring. For example, violence in the workplace is an increasing threat that can harm employees and customers, hurt productivity, and lead to expensive lawsuits and higher health-care costs.[20] In one case, McDonald's was ordered to pay damages to a mother and her three-year-old son who had been assaulted by a McDonald's employee in one of the company's fast-food outlets in Denver. It was discovered that the employee, who had been hired as part of a special employment program for the mentally and physically disabled, had a previous conviction for child molestation. McDonald's was held negligent for having failed to fully investigate the man's past—despite the fact that he had been recommended by the state Department of Social Services, which had withheld the information about the conviction.[21]

This and similar cases emphasize the need for employers to conduct thorough background checks on job applicants, including verifying all educational credentials and previous jobs, accounting for any large time gaps between jobs, and checking references. Background checks are particularly important for jobs in which employees are in a position to possibly harm others. In these situations, the human resources department has to weigh the need for uncovering information against a respect for the privacy of applicants.

Training and Development

In one way or another, every new employee needs training. Each company has its own way of doing even routine procedures. To make sure that all new employees understand the company's goals, policies, and procedures, most large organizations and many small ones have well-defined **orientation** programs. Although they vary, such programs usually include these topics:[22]

orientation Session or procedure for acclimating a new employee to the organization

- Company background and structure, including the chain of command
- Employment policies, including overtime requirements, paydays, termination procedures, and the like
- Standards of employee conduct, such as dress codes and smoking policies
- Benefit programs, including insurance benefits, pension plans, and vacation policies
- Job duties and responsibilities

The new employee's supervisor typically spends time making her or him feel comfortable, introducing co-workers, and giving a tour of the facilities. This attention helps reduce any anxiety the newcomer might feel, setting him or her on the right track from the beginning. It also helps new employees figure out where they fit in the organization.

Many companies also offer training (and retraining), because employee competence has a direct effect on productivity and profits.

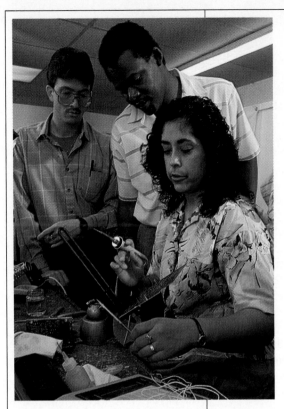

Goodwill Industries, a nonprofit organization, offers electronics-assembly classes to give workers the skills they need to qualify for high-tech industrial jobs.

Johnson & Johnson, for instance, retrained its managers to be more sensitive toward employees' conflicting obligations to work and to family. Training may take place at the work site (where an experienced employee oversees the trainee's on-the-job efforts) or in a classroom (where an expert lectures groups of employees). Often a training program simply teaches the specific skills of a particular job, but some programs go beyond to help employees acquire polish, confidence, and job-related abilities such as public speaking.

More employers are providing basic language and mathematics instruction for their employees. According to one source, every fifth person now hired by U.S. industry lacks basic reading and math skills, and functional illiteracy costs business over $6 billion annually in lost productivity.[23] The literacy problem is so pervasive that 93 percent of large corporations surveyed are offering or plan to offer some form of basic-skills courses to employees.[24]

Some companies are tackling the training problem in a different way: by contributing to or working with the public schools. A recent poll of Fortune 500 companies found that 78 percent of those responding contribute money to schools, 64 percent offer materials or equipment, and 50 percent encourage their employees to tutor or teach at schools.[25] An increasing number of businesses are entering into school partnerships, in which they adopt local schools. Phoenix Mutual Life Insurance has adopted schools in Hartford, Connecticut, where company employees tutor children and provide other services. Another approach is to work with vocational schools to provide necessary training. Near Seattle, the Applied Technology Center operated by two community colleges contracts with companies such as Honeywell and Boeing to train employees in specific skills, such as electronics assembly.[26]

Motorola, a leader in mobile communications, gives 40 hours of training every year to employees and managers at every level from the assembly line to the executive suite. Moreover, the company plans to quadruple the hours spent in training by 2000. Its Motorola University not only trains and retrains 100,000 employees worldwide but also helps educate schoolchildren and suppliers. The ambitious program ranges from basic-skills training (to ensure that all employees can read and write English at a seventh-grade level, at least) to advanced engineering programs. This ambitious commitment to training is paying off in improved productivity and product quality.[27]

Managers, too, must continue learning throughout their professional lives if they are to stay effective in the face of ever-changing management challenges. To address such needs, many organizations arrange for management training and development programs to sharpen their managers' skills. General Electric, McDonald's, IBM, and Xerox are four corporate giants with extensive management-development programs. Nearly 1,000 GE managers attend the com-

Training employees is always necessary and often expensive. Whether the subject is algebra or advertising strategy, people often learn things long before they actually need to apply them. So when it's time to use this information on the job, most people have forgotten much of what they learned. Moreover, managers are concerned about the expense of pulling people off their jobs and sending them to sit in training rooms so that they can learn new information and skills. For example, Hewlett-Packard used to spend $5 million every time it brought its worldwide sales force together to learn about new products.

Now, along with other leading-edge companies, HP is responding to such problems by completely redefining the way it trains employees. Rather than separating training from the actual job, innovators are working to make learning a part of the job. One key to this approach is changing the emphasis from the teaching process to the learning process—and computers are playing an important role.

IT SURE WOULD BE NICE TO LEARN ALGEBRA THIS WAY

As the world's largest management-consulting firm, Andersen Consulting believes that its most important asset is the accumulated knowledge of its workforce. As the firm's 27,000 consultants work with clients around the world, they add to Andersen's storehouse of experience. However, the company's global reach presents a huge challenge: How can someone in Chicago share her skills with someone in Frankfurt or Tokyo? Andersen Consulting uses The Knowledge Xchange system, a worldwide, computerized learning network that stores the company's accumulated knowledge and skills, letting any Andersen consultant tap into this vast treasure chest. Rather

than sitting in classrooms learning about all the various things the company can teach them, the consultants get the information they need when they need it. For instance, if someone has to learn about a particular manufacturing technology for a client project, he or she can quickly identify who else in the company has experience in that area and then see what they've learned about it.

In a similar approach, HP's learning network—dubbed the Hewlett-Packard Interactive Network (HPIN)—brings instructors and learners together for live sessions, even when the participants are located around the globe. In addition to making the learning process more effective, the computer network has cut that $5 million new-product training cost to just $85,000. The salespeople who need to learn about new products spend far less time traveling and sitting in classrooms, so they can spend more time doing what they're supposed to do—selling those new products.

---

pany's annual New Manager's Program, which is held in locations all over the world.[28]

Appraising Employee Performance

When should an employee be given a raise in pay? When should someone be promoted, demoted, transferred, or let go? The answers to such questions can be obtained by evaluating the employee's performance—but how should an employee's work be evaluated?

Many companies have developed **performance appraisal** systems to objectively evaluate employees according to set criteria. Such systems promote fairness because their standards are usually job-related ("Rhonda turns in weekly reports on time" rather than "Rhonda's always bustling around the office, so she must be doing an efficient job"). When performance appraisals are used, the standards are written down so that both employee and supervisor understand what is expected and are therefore able to determine whether the work is being done adequately. Most formal systems also require regular, writ-

performance appraisal Evaluation of an employee's work according to specific criteria

| Name _____ | Title _____ | Service Date _____ | Date _____ |

Location _____ Division _____ Department _____

Length of Time in Present Position   Period of Review   Appraised by _____

_____ From: _____ To: _____   Title of Appraisor _____

Area of Performance	Comment	Rating
Job Knowledge and Skill *Understands responsibilities and uses background for job. Adapts to new methods/techniques. Plans and organizes work. Recognizes errors and problems.*		5 4 3 2 1
Volume of Work *Amount of work output. Adherence to standards and schedules. Effective use of time.*		5 4 3 2 1
Quality of Work *Degree of accuracy–lack of errors. Thoroughness of work. Ability to exercise good judgment.*		5 4 3 2 1
Initiative and Creativity *Self-motivation in seeking responsibility and work that needs to be done. Ability to apply original ideas and concepts.*		5 4 3 2 1
Communication *Ability to exchange thoughts or information in a clear, concise manner. Dealing with different organizational levels of clientele.*		5 4 3 2 1
Dependability *Ability to follow instructions and directions correctly. Performs under pressure. Reliable work habits.*		5 4 3 2 1
Leadership Ability/Potential *Ability to guide others to the successful accomplishment of a given task. Potential for developing subordinate employees.*		5 4 3 2 1

5. Outstanding   *Employee who consistently exceeds established standards and expectations of the job.*

4. Above Average   *Employee who consistently meets established standards and expectations of the job. Often exceeds and rarely falls short of desired results.*

3. Satisfactory   *Generally qualified employee who meets job standards and expectations. Sometimes exceeds and may occasionally fall short of desired expectations. Performs duties in a normally expected manner.*

2. Improvement Needed   *Not quite meeting standards and expectations. An employee at this level of performance is not quite meeting all the standard job requirements.*

1. Unsatisfactory   *Employee who fails to meet the minimum standards and expectations of the job.*

I have had the opportunity to read this performance appraisal.

How long has this employee been under your supervision?

Signature   Date

Signature of Supervisor   Date

Exhibit 10.5

Sample Performance Appraisal Form

Many companies use printed forms like this one to make sure performance appraisals are as objective as possible.

ten evaluations of each employee's work (see Exhibit 10.5). These evaluations provide a record of the employee's performance, which may protect the company in cases of disputed terminations. Finally, many performance appraisal systems require the employee to be rated by several people (including more than one supervisor and perhaps several co-workers). This practice further promotes fairness by correcting for the possible bias that might influence one person's appraisal.

The biggest problem with appraisal systems is finding a way to measure performance. Productivity is the ultimate criterion, but it's not always easy to measure. In a production job, the person who types the most pages of acceptable copy or who assembles the most defect-free microprocessors in a given amount of time is clearly the most productive. However, how does an employer evaluate the productivity of the registration clerk at a hotel or the middle manager at a large television station? Although the organization's overall productivity can be measured (number of rooms booked per night, number of viewers per hour), often the employer can't directly relate the results to any one employee's efforts. Thus, additional criteria, such as rating of the organization by customers, the behavior of the employee toward co-workers and customers, job knowledge, motivation, and skills, are needed to help judge employee performance.

THE ROLE OF COMPENSATION

In return for their services, employees receive **compensation,** a combination of payments, benefits, and employer services. Although it isn't the only factor in motivating employees, proper compensation plays an important role. In fact, many people use compensation as a yardstick for measuring their success in the world of work.

compensation Payment to employees for their work

Wage and Salary Administration

On what basis should employees be paid? How much should they be paid? When should they be paid? These questions relate to wage and salary administration, one of the major responsibilities of the human resources department.

Wages Versus Salaries

Many blue-collar and some white-collar employees receive compensation in the form of **wages,** which are based on a calculation of the number of hours the employee has worked or the number of units he or she has produced. Sometimes compensation is based on a combination of both time and productivity. Wages provide a direct incentive to an employee: The more hours worked or the more pieces completed, the higher the employee's pay. Employers in the United States must comply with the Fair Labor Standards Act of 1938, which sets a minimum hourly wage for most employees and mandates overtime pay for employees who work longer than 40 hours a week.

wages Cash payment based on a calculation of the number of hours the employee has worked or the number of units the employee has produced

Employees whose output is not always directly related to the number of hours they put in or the number of pieces produced are paid **salaries.** Salaries, like wages, base compensation on time, but the unit of time is a week, two weeks, a month, or a year. Salaried employees such as managers and professionals normally receive no pay for the extra hours they sometimes put in; overtime is simply part of their obligation. However, they do get a certain amount of leeway in their working time.

salaries Weekly, monthly, or yearly cash compensation for work

Both wages and salaries are, in principle, based on the contribution of a particular job to the company. Thus, a sales manager, who

comparable worth *Concept of equal pay for jobs that are equal in value to the organization and require similar levels of education, training, and skills*

is responsible for bringing in sales revenue, is paid more than her or his secretary, who handles administrative tasks but doesn't sell or supervise. In recent years, human resources managers have grappled with the concept of **comparable worth,** which seeks equal pay for jobs that are equal in value to the organization.[29] Under a comparable-worth system, men and women who perform jobs that entail similar levels of education, training, and skills receive the same pay. Advocates of laws mandating comparable worth want to ensure that wages for jobs traditionally held by women are brought in line with the value they contribute to the organization. However, opponents say that comparable-worth laws would increase labor costs and require new, more complex methods of setting compensation.

In 1991 the average U.S. employee received pay of $24,575.[30] Pay varies widely by position, industry, and location. A credit manager can command better pay in New York City than in Salt Lake City, for example. Among the best-paid employees in the world are chief executive officers of large American corporations. In 1993 CEO pay at the largest U.S. companies averaged nearly $2 million (including stock options and other long-term compensation).[31] Over the decade of the 1980s, CEO pay jumped 212 percent, compared with a mere 78 percent increase in company earnings per share of Standard & Poor's 500 companies.[32] Employees are baffled and angry that chief executives are making big money while massive layoffs continue. Increasingly, critics are asking for a reassessment of how CEO compensation is set and are demanding that the fortunes of the people on top be more closely tied to the successes and failures of the company itself.

Incentive Programs

Johnson & Johnson and many other companies around the world are concerned with productivity. To encourage employees to be more productive, companies often provide CEOs, managers, sales representatives, and other employees with **incentives** linked to reaching certain individual or group levels of production or profitability. In other words, achievements, not just activities, are made the basis for payment.

Bonuses and Commissions. For both salaried and wage-earning employees, one type of incentive compensation is the **bonus,** a payment in addition to the regular wage or salary. Some firms pay an annual year-end bonus (amounting to a certain percentage of each employee's earnings) as an incentive to reduce turnover during the year. Other cash bonuses are tied to company performance. Although such bonuses were once reserved for the executive and management levels, they are becoming increasingly available to employees at other levels as well.[33] **Commissions** are payments made as a percentage of sales made. Used mainly for sales staff, they may be the sole compensation or may be an incentive payment in addition to a regular salary.

Profit Sharing and Gain Sharing. Employees may be rewarded for staying with a company and encouraged to work harder through **profit sharing,** a system whereby employees receive a portion of the company's profits. Depending on the company, profits may be dis-

incentives *Cash payments to employees who produce at a desired level or whose unit (often the company as a whole) produces at a desired level*

bonus *Cash payment in addition to the regular wage or salary, which serves as a reward for achievement*

commissions *Payments to employees who achieve a certain percentage of sales made*

profit sharing *System for distributing a portion of the company's profits to employees*

tributed quarterly, semiannually, or annually. For example, Chrysler recently gave 65,000 unionized employees profit-sharing checks averaging $4,300 when it reported year-end record profits.[34] Another option is to put off payment until the employee retires, is disabled, or leaves the company—provided the employee has worked the minimum number of years called for in the plan.

Gain sharing is similar to profit sharing, but the rewards are tied to cost savings from meeting specific goals for improving productivity, quality, and so on. At AT&T Universal Card Services, gain sharing is based on how quickly and accurately employees process credit-card requests and handle other tasks.[35] The success of such programs often depends on how closely incentives are linked to actions within the employee's control.

One approach to gain sharing, often referred to as **pay for performance,** requires employees to accept a lower base pay but receive rewards if they reach production targets or other goals. When such a plan was launched at Long John Silver's 1,000 company-owned fast-food restaurants, hourly wages actually increased by more than $.75 in the first quarter.[36] Other companies that have had success with pay-for-performance programs include Corning, Nordstrom, and Monsanto. However, similar programs have sometimes failed; in general, when the goals are unattainable or not specific, employees may become demoralized.[37]

Knowledge-Based Pay. An approach to compensation being explored by some companies is **knowledge-based pay,** or skill-based pay, which is keyed to employees' knowledge and abilities rather than to their job per se. Alcoa, TRW, and Westinghouse are just a few of the companies that have developed knowledge-based pay programs. Typically, the pay level at which a person is hired is pegged to his or her current level of skills; as the employee acquires new skills, the pay level goes up. Knowledge-based pay systems are designed to reduce staffing requirements, increase teamwork, and increase flexibility (because a single employee may have the skills to perform a variety of jobs).[38] Such programs also motivate employees who have little opportunity for promotion.

Employee Benefits and Services

Companies regularly provide **employee benefits,** financial benefits other than wages, salaries, and incentives. Starbucks Coffee offers a variety of benefits, including medical and dental insurance, vacation and holiday pay, stock options, discounts on Starbucks merchandise, and a free pound of Starbucks coffee every week. The benefits package is available to part-time as well as full-time employees, which helps Starbucks attract and retain good people at every level.[39] Executives often receive a special set of additional benefits referred to as **perks,** or perquisites, which include such niceties as company cars and club memberships. Exhibit 10.6 lists some of the most popular executive perks.

The amount of money allotted for employee benefits has been rising steadily. According to U.S. Chamber of Commerce statistics, companies paying an average annual wage of $32,299 spend $12,402 on

gain sharing *Plan for rewarding employees not on the basis of overall profits but in relation to achievement of goals such as cost savings from higher productivity*

pay for performance *Accepting a lower base pay in exchange for bonuses based on meeting production or other goals*

knowledge-based pay *Pay keyed to an employee's acquisition of skills; also called* skill-based pay

employee benefits *Compensation other than wages, salaries, and incentive programs*

perks *Special class of employee benefits made available to a company's most valuable employees*

Exhibit 10.6
Executive Perks
Here are the top 10 perks offered by companies to their CEOs and company presidents.

Overall ranking	Percentage of all companies
1. Company car/limousine for business use	64
2. Disability coverage	58
3. Entertainment expense account	56
4. Telephone credit cards	55
5. Company car for personal use	47
6. Supplemental life insurance	46
7. Car telephone	36
8. Physical exams	35
9. Tax preparation assistance	29
10. Club membership (dining/social)	27

employee benefits, more than a third of the total pay (see Exhibit 10.7).[40] Benefits and services for salaried employees typically cost even more. Still, companies like Starbucks provide benefits because benefits encourage employees to stay.

Many types of benefits and services are provided. Some, such as Social Security and unemployment insurance are mandatory; others, such as health-care coverage, are optional. Only the benefits most commonly provided by an employer are described here. Be aware, however, that benefits and services are undergoing considerable change to meet the shifting needs of the workforce. Today's workforce is much less homogeneous than in the past, and the two-career family has far different needs for benefits. Instead of two sets of insurance benefits, for example, such a family may prefer one spouse to receive insurance and the other to receive day-care assistance. In addition, a growing number of employers, including Warner Brothers and Lotus Development, offer health-care coverage for partners of gay employees, and some companies extend these partner benefits to unmarried heterosexual employees, as well.[41]

Exhibit 10.7
The Benefits Package
An employee who earns an hourly wage of $11.58 typically receives additional benefits worth over $4.53.

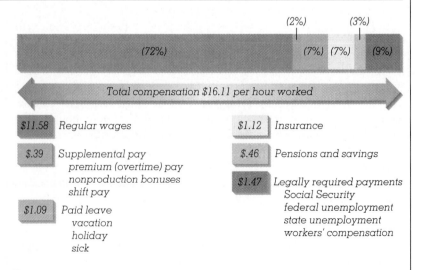

(2%) (3%)

(72%) (7%) (7%) (9%)

Total compensation $16.11 per hour worked

$11.58	Regular wages
$.39	Supplemental pay premium (overtime) pay nonproduction bonuses shift pay
$1.09	Paid leave vacation holiday sick

$1.12	Insurance
$.46	Pensions and savings
$1.47	Legally required payments Social Security federal unemployment state unemployment workers' compensation

Insurance Plans and Unemployment Benefits

Although it is entirely optional, insurance is the most popular employee benefit. Most businesses offer substantial compensation in the form of life and health insurance; dental plans, disability insurance, and long-term-care insurance are also gaining in popularity. Often a company will negotiate a group insurance plan for employees and pay most of the premium costs. However, health-care coverage has become much more costly in recent years; in 1991 U.S. employers paid $196 billion for employee health care.[42] Faced with exploding costs, many companies now require employees to pay part of their insurance premiums or more of the actual doctor bills.

Under the terms of the Social Security Act of 1935, employers in all 50 states finance special **unemployment insurance** to benefit employees who are laid off or (to a lesser extent) who quit their jobs. Each employer pays into a state fund a tax corresponding to the number of people in the industry who have been on the unemployment rolls. An employee who becomes unemployed for reasons not related to performance is entitled to collect benefits. The amount of the benefit is usually tied to the employee's total earnings during the previous year, but both the amount of the payment and the length of time it is available vary from state to state. Employees in certain industries—notably automobile, steel, rubber, and glass—receive additional benefits (called supplemental unemployment benefits) from either the company or the union.

Retirement Benefits

In the past, few people were able to save enough money in the course of their working years for their retirement. The main purpose of the Social Security Act was to provide those who could not accumulate enough retirement money with the basic support they would need in later life. However, over the years, nearly everyone who works regularly has become eligible for Social Security payments during retirement. This income is paid for by the Social Security tax, part of which is withheld by the employer from employees' wages and part paid by the employer.

A variety of company-sponsored **pension plans** have been developed over the past few decades as a way of providing additional retirement security. The number of employees covered by pension plans increased steadily until 1979. Then the cost and complexity of such plans increased so dramatically that some employers began canceling them (see Exhibit 10.8).[43] Most pension plans are funded by money that is set aside on a regular basis to pay retirement benefits in the future. In one popular type of pension plan, employees make regular contributions out of their paychecks, and the company matches some portion (usually 50 percent) of the amount. However, with employees earning higher pension payments and living longer after retirement, many companies are finding that their pension claims for the foreseeable future have grown nearly as large as their total assets.

Pension Guarantees. Some retirees find themselves in tight economic circumstances. If their pensions were cut off—if a former em-

unemployment insurance *Government-sponsored program for assisting employees who are laid off or, to a lesser extent, who quit their jobs*

pension plans *Company-sponsored programs for providing retirees with income*

Exhibit 10.8
Who Offers Pension Plans?

The larger the organization, the more likely it is to offer an employer- or union-provided pension plan. The graph shows what percentage of employees are covered by pension plans at U.S. organizations varying in size from under 25 to over 1,000 workers.

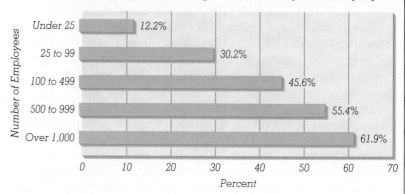

Percentage of Employees Covered by Pension Plans *(by size of company)*

Number of Employees:
- Under 25 — 12.2%
- 25 to 99 — 30.2%
- 100 to 499 — 45.6%
- 500 to 999 — 55.4%
- Over 1,000 — 61.9%

Percent: 0, 10, 20, 30, 40, 50, 60, 70

ployer went out of business or declared bankruptcy, or if the pension fund ran out of money—many of these people would be in trouble. Recognizing this situation, Congress passed the Employee Retirement Income Security Act of 1974 (ERISA), which set up a federal agency to insure the assets of pension plans. This act guarantees that, with some exceptions and limitations, retirement benefits will be paid no matter what happens to the company or the plan. It also sets standards for managing pension funds and requires public disclosure of a plan's operations.

Current Pension Issues. Strapped for cash, a number of companies have become creative about substituting other assets for cash payments to retirees. Despite ERISA rulings that companies must pay at least 75 percent of pension funds in cash, companies sometimes ignore these requirements. Some employees are offered the option of stocks and bonds instead of cash. United States Steel (now USX), for example, once met its pension-plan obligations with a special type of stock that can't be sold, thereby saving $333 million in cash and linking its pension plan to the corporation's future success. Although this tactic conserves company cash, it threatens the arm's-length relationship that companies are supposed to have with their retirement funds.[44]

Employee Stock-Ownership Plans

Another employee benefit being offered by a number of companies is the **employee stock-ownership plan (ESOP).** In an ESOP, a company places a certain amount of its stock in trust for all or some of its employees, with each employee entitled to a certain share. If the company does well, the ESOP may be a substantial employee benefit. An additional advantage of the ESOP is that it's free to the employee and nearly so to the employer (because companies offering such programs are eligible for a federal tax credit).

Such plans work well for some companies but not for others. When W. L. Gore & Associates (a chemical-fabrication company in Delaware) started its ESOP, 5,000 employees (called "associates") owned company stock. The company was growing 25 percent a year, and associates felt like part of the management team. Said one associate: "I

employee stock-ownership plan (ESOP) *Program enabling employees to become owners or part owners of a company*

want to make sure this company works, and I feel I'm a part owner because I have a lot to say about my area of expertise."

At the other end of the spectrum, when Dan River (a textile manufacturer in Virginia) started its ESOP, about 8,000 employees owned 70 percent of the stock. However, the company was firmly in the hands of the managers and outside investors (who owned 30 percent of the company) because the ESOP plan was set up for its tax advantages, and employee involvement in operations was ignored. As one employee complained: "The company stamps its cartons with a big 'D' and 'employee-owned.' But most of the people realize that they don't own anything. They're just paying the bill for these big management people to own the company."[45]

Family Benefits

More and more working parents are looking for such benefits as unpaid leave to take care of a new baby and day-care assistance once the parent returns to work. Johnson & Johnson provides on-site child care at two of its facilities, and it provides family-care leave of up to one year. Such family benefits are proving helpful (not only to employees but also to companies) in the form of higher employee morale and productivity as well as lower absenteeism. Although gaining momentum, the concept of family benefits is only getting started. Now, 1 out of 10 companies provides child-care assistance of some sort, from handing out lists of local community services to providing day-care facilities on the premises; a few, such as the American Bankers Insurance Group in Miami and Target Stores in Minneapolis, have even built satellite schools for children of employees. About 40 percent of U.S. firms offer some form of maternity leave, and a growing number are expanding their programs to give fathers paternity leave (although few men are taking advantage of such leave, primarily out of concern over damage to their careers).[46]

A related family issue is care for aging parents. An estimated 20 percent of large corporations offer some form of elder-care assistance, ranging from referral services that help find care providers to dependent-care allowances.[47] Some companies will even agree to move elderly relatives when they transfer an employee to another location. For instance, du Pont moved one employee's in-laws from New York to North Carolina, where the employee was transferred. NationsBank has also moved older relatives of employees who have been transferred.[48]

Other Employee Benefits

Although sometimes overlooked, paid holidays, sick pay, premium pay for working overtime or unusual hours, and paid vacations are important benefits. Companies handle holiday pay in various ways; a company with a liberal policy on paid holidays usually emphasizes this fact in its employment advertising. Sick-day allowances also vary from company to company, although sick days are usually limited to curb excessive absenteeism. To provide incentives for employee loyalty, most companies grant employees longer paid vacations if the employees have been with the organization for a prescribed number of years. Among the many other benefits that companies sometimes offer are sabbaticals and tuition loans, personal computers and company cars, financial counseling and legal services, club and association memberships, assistance with buying a home, and paid expenses for spouses who travel with employees.

One benefit, guaranteed by the Family and Medical Leave Act to employees of companies that employ 50 or more, is the right to take up to 12 weeks of unpaid leave during a 12-month period for family reasons and medical emergencies. Employees can take leave to care for a newborn or adopted child, to take care of a serious illness in the employee's family, or to take care of the employee's own illness. Companies must allow employees to return to the same job (or an equivalent one) after the leave.[49]

Flexible Benefits

Until recently, most employee benefits came as a package with a particular job. Once hired, the employee got whatever insurance, paid holidays, pension plan, and other benefits the company had set up. A newer approach allows employees to pick their benefits—up to a certain dollar amount—to meet their particular needs. An employee with a young family might want extra life or health insurance, for example, and might feel no need for a pension plan. A single employee might pass up life insurance and choose a tax-deferred retirement plan. Another employee might "buy" an extra week or two of vacation time by giving up some other benefit.

About 25 percent of large companies have taken this flexible "cafeteria" approach to employee benefits. Given the varied lifestyles and needs of the 1990s workforce, more companies (even small businesses) are setting up flexible benefits plans. The type of company that might best adopt such a plan would be one experiencing rapid growth, one with few skilled employees, one in an industry where the competition for employees is strong, one that already has generous benefits, or one with a diverse group of employees.[50]

Health and Safety Programs

Health and safety programs reduce potential suffering and keep health-related losses to a minimum, which is why they're a major concern for human resources managers. By educating employees in safety procedures, setting and enforcing safety regulations, and redesigning work environments to minimize the potential for death, injury, and illness, businesses can make the workplace safer for employees and, at the same time, cut health-related losses. Some companies go beyond the requirements set by the Occupational Safety and Health Administration (OSHA), a federal agency that sets standards for employee safety, although some small employers are so preoccupied with survival that they may not even meet minimum safety requirements.[51]

Some two-thirds of companies with at least 50 employees are taking a more active role in maintaining employee health. Wellness and fitness programs encourage employees to eat sensibly, stop smoking, control stress, and exercise. The results have been impressive. Mutual Benefit Life Insurance found that employees who used the fitness

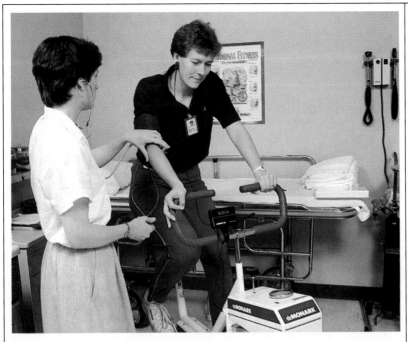

Many companies maintain on-site medical facilities to help their workers stay healthier and remain productive. At this Northern Telecom plant in North Carolina, a nurse uses stress testing to assess employee fitness.

center at its Newark, New Jersey, headquarters missed an average of 2.5 workdays a year (compared with 4.25 missed days for employees who didn't use the facilities), and their medical claims averaged $313 a year (compared with $1,086 for nonusers).[52] Johnson & Johnson has had similar success with its Live for Life program. Participants receive an individualized health-risk profile and are encouraged to watch their diets, exercise, and give up smoking. The wellness program includes on-site gyms and healthy foods in the cafeteria.[53] Some large companies go further, providing at-work medical care for employees. Southern California Edison, for example, has eight primary-care clinics, two first-aid stations, and a corporate pharmacy for its 57,000 employees. Using its own doctors and buying drugs at wholesale rates keeps Edison's health-care costs under control.[54]

A number of companies have also instituted an **employee assistance program (EAP)** for employees with personal problems, especially drug or alcohol dependence. Such programs have been reported to reduce (on the average) absenteeism by 66 percent, health-care costs by 86 percent, sickness benefits by 33 percent, and work-related accidents by 65 percent.[55] Participation in EAPs is voluntary and confidential. Employees are given in-house counseling or are referred to outside therapists or treatment programs.

employee assistance program (EAP)
Company-sponsored counseling or referral plan for employees with personal problems

CHANGES IN EMPLOYMENT STATUS

Sometimes, despite the most rigorous planning, recruiting, selecting, and training, an employee leaves the job for which she or he was hired. The employee may decide to retire or may resign voluntarily because the job proves unsatisfying or because a better opportunity arises. On the other hand, the company may take the initiative in making the change—either reassigning, promoting, or laying off the

Exhibit 10.9
Why People Leave Their Jobs
In a recent exit survey of federal government employees, young professionals identified these reasons as the single most important factor in their decision to leave.

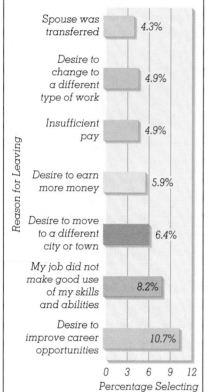

Reason for Leaving

Reason	Percentage
Spouse was transferred	4.3%
Desire to change to a different type of work	4.9%
Insufficient pay	4.9%
Desire to earn more money	5.9%
Desire to move to a different city or town	6.4%
My job did not make good use of my skills and abilities	8.2%
Desire to improve career opportunities	10.7%

0   3   6   9   12
Percentage Selecting as Most Important

employee. Exhibit 10.9 shows why some people leave their jobs. Whatever the reason, losing an employee usually means going to the trouble and expense of finding a replacement, whether from outside or from within the company.

Promoting and Reassigning Employees

When someone leaves the company or is promoted to a position of more responsibility, the company has to find someone else for the open job. Many companies prefer to look inside for such candidates. In part, this "promote from within" policy allows the company to benefit from the training and experience of its own workforce. It also rewards employees who have worked hard and demonstrated the ability to handle additional tasks. Also, morale is usually better when the company promotes from within because employees see that they can advance.

A potential pitfall of promotion is that a person may be given a job beyond his or her competence. It isn't uncommon for someone who is good at one kind of job to be made a manager, a position that requires a completely different set of skills. Someone who consistently racks up the best sales in the company, for example, is not necessarily the person who should be promoted to sales manager. If the promotion is a mistake, the company not only loses its sales leader but also risks losing the employee altogether. People who can't perform well in a new job generally become demoralized and lose confidence in the abilities they do have. At the very least, support and training are needed to help promoted employees perform well in their new jobs.

One big issue these days is *relocation* of promoted and reassigned employees. In the past, companies transferred some employees fairly often, especially those being groomed for higher management positions. Now, however, fewer and fewer employees are willing to accept transfers. One reason is that many more couples have two careers; if one spouse is transferred, either the other has to leave his or her job, or the couple has to accept a "commuter" marriage, in which they see each other only on weekends and vacations. Changing values are another factor; many employees today are as committed to community activities and to nearby family members as to their career advancement. Economics is often a factor as well. It's expensive to sell and buy houses (especially if real estate values in the new location are higher than in the old one), and the cost of one spouse's quitting a job and being unemployed for a few months may not be offset by the raise that typically accompanies a transfer.[56]

Companies have traditionally helped transfer employees by providing house-hunting trips; temporary living expenses; and moving, storage, and transportation expenses. In addition, many corporations are now helping spouses find good jobs in new locations, assisting transferees with home sales, and sometimes reimbursing them for spouses' lost wages and for financial losses arising from selling and buying houses. Many companies are also reconsidering their transfer policies and asking employees to transfer only when it is absolutely necessary.

Today's flatter organizations offer fewer opportunities for upward advancement. As a result, one of the challenges of human resources managers is retaining talented and ambitious people. One approach used by companies such as PepsiCo and Hughes Aircraft is the *lateral transfer*, a sideways move from one department to another, as in the move from electrical engineering to quality control. Other companies offer employees challenging tasks in unfamiliar areas to help broaden their experience. Overseas assignments, academic sabbaticals, and career-development programs are among the other approaches being used to motivate employees and managers who have fewer chances for upward movement.[57]

Terminating Employment

A company invests time, effort, and money in each new employee it recruits and trains. This investment is lost when an employee is removed by **termination**—permanently laying the employee off because of cutbacks or firing the employee for poor performance. Many companies facing a downturn in business have avoided large-scale layoffs by cutting administrative costs (curtailing travel, seminars, and so on), freezing wages, postponing new hiring, or encouraging early retirement. Sometimes, however, a company has no alternative but to reduce the size of its workforce, leaving the human resources department with the task of handling layoffs and their resulting effects on both the terminated and remaining employees.

termination Act of getting rid of an employee through layoffs or firing

Layoffs

Layoffs are the termination of employees for economic or business reasons unrelated to employee performance. Companies were once free to lay off whomever they pleased. Recently, however, some laid-off employees have sued, charging that they were unfairly singled out because of age, gender, religion, or race. Even employers that schedule layoffs on the basis of **seniority,** or length of time with the company, have found themselves in court. The reason? The so-called last-hired, first-fired principle (that is, the employees most recently hired are the first to be laid off) means that women and minorities are more likely to be the ones laid off, since in most cases they have only recently been hired in significant numbers.

layoffs Termination of employees for economic or business reasons

seniority Longevity in a position or company, frequently used as a basis for making human resources decisions (compensation, termination, and so on)

An alternative is a layoff system that evaluates each employee according to criteria (reliability, communication skills, and so on) picked by both employees and supervisors. Each employee accumulates a certain number of points under this system, and those with the fewest points are let go in the event of layoffs. This method has been used in a number of large companies.[58]

To help ease the pain of layoffs, many companies are now providing laid-off employees with job-hunting assistance. Although **outplacement** aids such as résumé-writing courses, career counseling, office space, and secretarial help are most often offered to laid-off executives, even middle managers and blue-collar employees often receive this type of help. When McDonnell Douglas reduced its St. Louis headquarters workforce by 5,000, its human resources department not only provided outplacement support centers equipped

outplacement Job-hunting and other assistance that a company provides to laid-off employees

with computers, phones, and career advisers but also sponsored a job fair and ran radio ads touting the high quality of laid-off employees to potential employers.[59]

Nevertheless, as well as affecting those who have been notified that they will be leaving, layoffs also influence both the morale and the productivity of the employees who are staying. Many of those who remain feel overworked and nervous about future layoffs. Says L. Marshall Stellfox, partner in a New York City human resources consulting firm: "Companies can help bolster sagging morale if they tell their remaining employees truthfully about the status of job security and their opportunity for promotion."[60]

Some companies have adopted no-layoff, or guaranteed-employment, policies. Employees may still be fired for not doing their jobs, but in an economic downturn, they may be shifted to other types of jobs, perhaps at reduced pay, or given the chance to participate in work-sharing programs. At Honda's plant in Marysville, Ohio, layoffs have been avoided by slowing down the production lines; Volkswagen cut its workweek to four days to avoid layoffs.[61] Ethically, such policies are a good idea, but they have practical benefits as well: Employees tend to be more loyal and more motivated because they know they will not work themselves out of a job. Cleveland's Lincoln Electric discovered such benefits in its guaranteed-employment policy. When its factory employees (dubbed "Lincoln's leopards") volunteered to make sales calls and to pay their own expenses to get the company through hard times, they brought in $10 million in sales.[62] Why offer lifetime employment? Answers Hallmark's CEO Irving Hockaday, Jr.: "We believe that we have to manage for the long term, protect our people from cyclical, changing markets, and if they know we're going to do that, they will help us solve the problem."[63]

Firings and Employment at Will

It has long been illegal for a U.S. company to fire an employee because he or she is a would-be union organizer, has filed a job-safety complaint, or is of a particular race, religion, gender, or age. Beyond these restrictions, the courts have traditionally held that any employee not covered by a contract may be fired "at will." **Employment at will** is the ability of the employer to keep or terminate employees as it wishes. Recently, however, a number of legal decisions have begun to alter this doctrine. The most far-reaching decisions have held that there may be an implied contract between employer and employee requiring that any firing be done "fairly." Some commentators on the subject have called this notion "the right to a job."

Employees have won **wrongful discharge** suits against former employers by arguing that documents issued by the company (employee handbooks, for example) state that no employee may be fired without proper warning and an opportunity to remedy whatever problems may exist. Some fired employees have even argued that their being called "permanent" employees by the company should protect them from firing—or at least from unfair firing. The question of fairness is difficult to pin down, but most companies losing court cases did so because they fired the employee with inadequate warning that the employee's job was on the line and with little or no explanation

employment at will Employer's right to keep or terminate employees as it wishes

wrongful discharge Firing an employee with inadequate advance notice or explanation of why. Before firing anyone, managers need to ask, "Has this employee been properly warned and notified? Have both the warning and the grounds for dismissal been clearly noted in the employee's record?"

Wrongful discharge cases have been plentiful in light of the massive layoffs in recent years. Analysts say that a former employee has an 86 percent chance of winning a wrongful discharge suit brought against a private business, with an average damage award of $650,000.[64] To avoid such suits, many companies are requiring employees to sign an "employment at will" statement acknowledging that they may be fired at any time at the company's discretion. Some companies are also describing the employment-at-will policy in application forms or company handbooks. Blue Cross and Blue Shield of Michigan, for example, says that any employee "can be terminated at any time without reason." It avoids implied promises by referring to employees as "regular" or "full-time" rather than "permanent."[65] Such official disclaimers may help protect a company's right to fire employees, even though they might be offensive to employees.

Retiring Employees

The U.S. population is aging rapidly. For the business community, an aging population presents two challenges. The first is to give job opportunities to people who are willing and able to work but who happen to be past the traditional retirement age. Many older citizens are concerned about their ability to live comfortably on fixed retirement incomes. Others simply prefer to work. The second challenge is to encourage some older employees to retire early. As the baby-boom generation ages, it will be pushing hard for higher-level jobs held by older executives.

Mandatory Retirement

For several decades, many companies and industries had **mandatory retirement** policies that made it necessary for people to quit working as soon as they turned a certain age. The federal Age Discrimination in Employment Act, passed in 1967, outlawed discrimination against anyone between the ages of 40 and 65. Despite the law, some employees have involuntarily been retired. They are beginning to seek relief in the courts, and they are winning. Chase Manhattan Bank was ordered to pay more than half a million dollars in back pay and employee benefits to three former executives. These employees had been between the ages of 49 and 55 when they were forced to retire, and they were replaced by younger, lower-paid employees.[66] More than 13,000 such cases are being filed with the EEOC each year.

In 1986 Congress amended the Age Discrimination in Employment Act to prohibit mandatory retirement for most employees. As a corollary, employers are also forbidden to stop benefit contributions or accruals because of age. Under federal law, those who complain of age discrimination are also granted the right to a jury trial. This right means that many more cases will probably be decided in the employees' favor; juries are usually sympathetic to the problems of

mandatory retirement *Required dismissal of an employee who reaches a certain age*

employees who have been asked to go because they are "too old." As a result, 9 out of 10 age-discrimination cases are settled out of court.[67]

Early Retirement

One method a company may use to trim its workforce is simply to offer its employees (often those nearing retirement) financial incentives to resign, such as enhanced retirement benefits or one-time cash payments. Inducing employees to depart by offering them financial incentives is known as a **worker buyout.** Although this method is more expensive than firing or laying off employees, it has several advantages. The morale of the remaining employees is preserved, because they feel less threatened about their own security. Also, because those who participate in the buyout are usually senior staff members, younger employees see their chances for promotion rise.

Nevertheless, early retirement incentives can create substantial long-term financial burdens for a company. It's interesting to note that despite the law forbidding mandatory retirement, early retirements are on the rise. One survey found that two-thirds of U.S. employees now retire before age 65.[68] It seems that many people who are eligible for early retirement often take advantage of it in order to pursue new interests or to start a new business.

worker buyout *Distribution of financial incentives to employees who voluntarily depart, usually undertaken in order to shrink the payroll*

1 Discuss the six main functions of human resources departments.
Human resources departments engage in planning, recruiting and selecting new employees, training and developing employees, appraising employee performance, compensating employees, and accommodating changes in employment status.

2 Identify the six stages in the hiring process.
The stages in the hiring process are (1) narrowing down the number of qualified candidates, (2) interviewing, (3) administering employment tests (optional), (4) evaluating candidates, (5) conducting reference checks, and (6) selecting one candidate for the job.

3 Explain why companies use training and development programs.
Companies use orientation training to help new employees learn procedures, policies, and goals. They use job-skills training to teach employees how to perform specific work tasks, and they use basic-skills training in mathematics and language to help employees master skills for working with each other and with customers and suppliers. Management-development programs help new and experienced managers sharpen their skills.

4 State two general ways of compensating employees.
Employees are compensated through payments such as wages and salaries and through benefits and services.

5 Describe the two possible components of employee pay.
Wages (for hourly employees) or salaries (for nonhourly employees) are the most typical component of employee pay. Some employees also receive incentive payments (bonuses, commissions, profit sharing, and gain sharing), which are cash payments tied to employee or company performance in order to encourage higher and performance.

6 Explain six employee benefits and services.
Insurance plans, including unemployment benefits, are the most popular type of benefit; they help protect employees who lose their income through illness or changing economic conditions, and they provide for survivors if an employee dies. Retirement benefits are also popular as a means of helping people save for later years. Employee stock-ownership plans (ESOPs), in which employees receive shares of the company's stock, give employees a stake in the company. Family-benefit programs include maternity and paternity leave, child-care assistance, and elder-care assistance. Flexible benefit plans allow employees to choose the unique combination of benefits that suit their needs. Health and safety programs, including fitness and wellness programs, help keep employees at peak productivity.

7 Describe five ways an employee's status may change.
An employee's status may change through promotion to a higher-level position, through reassignment to a similar or lower-level position, through termination (removal from the company's payroll), through voluntary resignation, or through retirement.

8 Distinguish between the two reasons that employers may terminate employment.
Employment may be terminated through layoffs or firings. Layoffs occur because the company is restructuring, has changed management or ownership, or is in distress, and they may be temporary. Firings, however, are permanent removals of employees because of poor performance.

Ralph Larsen and James Burke understood that effective human resources management was the key to the satisfied and highly productive workforce so necessary to Johnson & Johnson's future success. The first step to improved productivity was to help employees meet their dual responsibilities to family and job. To start, the company opened a child-care center at its corporate headquarters in New Brunswick, New Jersey, and a second center at its nearby Somerset office. Child-care costs at these centers are limited to 10 percent of an employee's disposable income.

Under its Balancing Work and Family Program, J&J helps employees locate resources and referrals for child care and elder care. It also goes beyond the bare legal minimum, allowing employees to take family-care leave of up to one year after the arrival of a newborn or adopted child and letting employees arrange a flexible work schedule to attend an ailing family member.

In addition, Johnson & Johnson managers participated in training to sensitize them to work and family issues. To underscore the company's commitment to family care, human resources managers added a new sentence to the company credo: "We must be mindful of ways to help our employees with their family responsibilities." This commitment to helping employees better manage family pressures boosted productivity by reduc-

ing absenteeism, tardiness, and stress. In addition, the company's work-family policies helped attract and keep qualified employees in a tightening labor market.

Productivity was also enhanced by a wellness program, Live for Life, designed to emphasize steps employees can take to maintain and improve their health. The program sets four goals for employees: they should quit smoking, eat more fruit and fewer fatty foods, exercise regularly, and buckle their seatbelts. At J&J headquarters, employees can work out in a gym, select "healthy heart" foods in the cafeteria, and check their weight in rest rooms. To encourage participation, employees are eligible to win prizes for meeting their goals. Over 35 J&J locations now have fitness centers and wellness programs, and 75 percent of the workforce participates.

The results have been impressive. Smoking among employees has been reduced to less than 20 percent, a decline of more than one-third. Live for Life costs J&J $225 a year for each employee, but lower absenteeism and reduced health costs have saved $378 per employee.

Live for Life was so successful that J&J formed a new company, Johnson & Johnson Health Management, to market the Live for Life program. The new company assists with fitness center design and management, and it orchestrates health-promotion campaigns in such areas as smoking cessation, nutrition, and stress management. Live for Life is available at 60 leading corporations and medical centers that together employ more than 850,000 people.

Your Mission: Ralph S. Larsen wants to keep costs low while improving quality. As vice president for human resources, your mission is to create employee programs that reflect Larsen's vision of a leaner, more streamlined Johnson & Johnson by maintaining the loyalty, well-being, and productivity of employees. How

would you handle the following situations?

1. One of Larsen's biggest challenges is revitalizing J&J's consumer-goods operations in the United States. To boost sales, J&J introduced new products such as No More Tears Baby Sunblock, Tylenol Chewables, and Johnson's Creamy Baby Oil. Because it is the consumer-products sales team that will ultimately place these items on supermarket shelves, Larsen has asked you to use human resources methods to increase the effectiveness of the sales force. You devise a list of three steps that you should take. Which should you implement first?

a. Conduct a job analysis of the sales department to ensure that the components needed for a well-coordinated, effective sales effort are in place.

b. Have all salespeople participate in a one-week training program to refamiliarize them with J&J products and to boost their assertiveness.

c. Review the sales force's employee performance appraisals and conduct new appraisals if necessary. Weed out weak employees and promote those who have demonstrated their ability to sell.

2. Johnson & Johnson's Acuvue disposable contact lenses have become the leading soft contact lens in the United States, so Johnson & Johnson Vision Products is doubling the size of its facility. B. D. Walsh, president of Johnson & Johnson Vision Products, asks for advice on evaluating applicants for new manufacturing positions. Walsh is looking for employees with a high degree of manual dexterity who have experience working on an assembly line. He gives you a list of the three selection methods he intends to use, but he is uncertain about weighting them. Which method should be given highest priority in the employee-selection process?

a. Job applications
b. Interviews
c. Performance tests

3. Walsh is concerned that some assembly-line employees abuse drugs and alcohol, which might lead them to inadvertently jeopardize the health of customers and undermine the reputation of the Acuvue brand. Walsh wants to institute drug testing and asks you for suggestions about how tests might be administered. What do you recommend?

a. You suggest testing only those employees who are suspected of substance abuse.

b. You sympathize with people who resent having to take a drug test. You suggest testing only those assembly-line employees whose carelessness could harm the customer.

c. You believe the only fair way to administer a drug test is to test everyone at Johnson & Johnson Vision Products. You suggest that Walsh set an example and volunteer to take the first test.

4. Larsen wants you to review the Live for Life program and the Balancing Work and Family program to determine where costs can be cut. You draw up a preliminary list of suggestions. After reviewing them, you forward one to Larsen's office. Which one do you choose?

a. Statistics show that the voluntary Live for Life program saves J&J more than $100 for each person enrolled. Require that all employees participate so that the company can save even more.

b. Raise the percentage that employees pay for child care to 25 percent of their disposable income.

c. Offer employees on family-care leave the option of working at least 15 hours a week at home on a flexible schedule.[69]

KEY TERMS

bonus (286)
commissions (286)
comparable worth (286)
compensation (285)
employee assistance program (EAP) (293)
employee benefits (287)
employee stock-ownership plan (ESOP) (290)
employment at will (296)
gain sharing (287)
human resources management (270)

incentives (286)
job analysis (274)
job description (275)
job specification (275)
knowledge-based pay (287)
layoffs (295)
mandatory retirement (297)
orientation (281)
outplacement (295)
pay for performance (287)
pension plans (289)
performance appraisal (283)

perks (287)
profit sharing (286)
recruiters (275)
recruiting (275)
résumé (275)
salaries (285)
seniority (295)
termination (295)
unemployment insurance (289)
wages (285)
worker buyout (298)
wrongful discharge (296)

REVIEW QUESTIONS

1. What are the major forecasting challenges for human resources managers?
2. What is the purpose of conducting a job analysis? What are some of the techniques used for gathering information?
3. What are the major legal pitfalls in the hiring process?
4. What methods are companies us-

ing to deal with the lack of basic skills in the employee pool?
5. What is the purpose of using incentive programs as part of the compensation package?
6. Why are more companies offering family benefits and flexible benefits?
7. What effect has downsizing had on promotion and reassignment of

employees? On termination procedures?
8. What are some of the problems facing employees who are nearing retirement?

A FURNACE NAMED AMANDA

John Scheel watches proudly as orange molten iron is heated to precisely 3,700 degrees and is then sent down a brick-lined path to the waiting torpedo tank car. "A cast in a blast furnace is like a religious experience," says Scheel, senior blast-furnace engineer for Armco. It is Scheel who must ensure that the raw materials—iron ore, limestone, and coke—combine at exactly the right temperature to be converted into pig iron, the main ingredient of steel. Also, it is because of Scheel that, since 1982, Armco's fuel costs have dropped 17 percent and the cost of producing a ton of iron has decreased more than 25 percent. For Armco, Scheel is a pivotal employee.

Symbolized by silicon chips and robots, manufacturing is becoming more and more impersonal in many industries. Despite this push toward automation, managers can still point to a few people whose unique skills mean success for their employers—even though their number is dwindling as technology advances. Pivotal personnel are found on factory floors rather than in boardrooms, and their knowledge comes more often from hands-on experience than from classroom education. Although CEOs and management teams generally make the critical decisions, "once those decisions are made, the crucial part of accomplishing a project comes with the pivotal jobs," says Tsun-yan Hsieh, who studied the role of pivotal jobs for the management-consulting firm of McKinsey & Company.

In addition to his engineering degree, Scheel has an MBA in finance and international business, and he writes poetry—not exactly your basic steelworker. Nevertheless, he is singlemindedly devoted to Armco's blast furnace, which is named Amanda. He keeps photographs of Amanda both in his apartment and in the local restaurant in which he has an ownership stake. Already working 12-hour days, Scheel is often found at the furnace late at night (even at two o'clock in the morning on Christmas). "The process runs you, you don't run the process," says Scheel. Nevertheless, he also says his work is like "being an orchestra conductor."

Scheel enthusiastically takes extra steps to keep Amanda running smoothly. Not only has he created a computer system to monitor the makeup of the iron Amanda produces, but he has devised a computer warning system that can detect potential problems before any damage can be done. He has also developed a process for accurately regulating the amount of coal slurry that goes into Amanda (which Armco has patented and now sells to other steelmakers). In addition, Scheel tracks late coal shipments by phone; he clears jammed ore dumpers by banging them with a shovel; and he persuades fellow employees to accept new technology.

"With his background and ability, John could be working in several places other than a steel mill," says Glenn D. Easterling, one of Scheel's supervisors. Lucky for Armco, however, John Scheel is filling a pivotal role working with a furnace named Amanda.

1. Do you think employers can easily replace pivotal employees when they leave or retire? Will companies of the future be able to find pivotal employees? Explain.
2. How important do you think salary and bonuses are to specially skilled employees such as John Scheel?
3. Does lack of official recognition seem to be a problem for pivotal employees such as Scheel? Are such employees likely to resent the high-profile executives in the boardroom?

Use job analysis to evaluate the specific requirements of a position you are interested in. Develop a job description and a job specification for a particular position you would like to hold. With the members of your class, generate a list of items that should be included in the job analysis. To obtain information about the career you've chosen, you might interview a person working in that field, interview a human resources manager with a company who employs people in that field, or use reference books that provide information about your desired job and career.

Locate one or more articles in *The Wall Street Journal* that illustrate how a company or industry is adapting to changes in its workforce. (Examples include retraining, literacy or basic-skills training, flexible benefits, and benefits aimed at working parents or people who care for aging relatives.)

1. What employee needs or changes in the workforce caused the company (or industry) to adapt?
2. Was the company (industry) forced to change for some financial or legal reason, or did it move voluntarily to meet the need or adapt to the change? Why?
3. What other changes in the workforce or in employee needs do you think this company or industry is likely to face in the next few years? Explain your reasons for making this

JOB TRAINING: DOES IT LEAD TO MORE AND BETTER JOBS?

Synopsis

All employees need some kind of training, even if it's only an orientation covering company policies. But what about the training needs of unemployed workers? Can teaching new job skills help prospective employees find and keep good jobs? This video looks at how two training programs—one for auto technicians, one for stone cutters—are helping build workers' skills and self-confidence. Despite such costly efforts, retrained workers may be frustrated in their efforts to find good-paying jobs, in part because layoffs have reduced employment opportunities in many companies. On the other hand, training programs give people the knowledge they need to compete for the jobs that are available. Even after they're hired, the need for training doesn't end. Managers and employees alike need continued training and development to keep up with technological changes in their industries.

Exercises

ANALYSIS

1. How should the General Motors training program evaluate the performance of trainees who are assigned to work on a car?

2. Should job-training programs also teach basic interview skills that workers need during a job search?

3. What kind of job-skills test would you ask applicants for an auto-technician job to take?

4. Who's in a better position to write a job description: a manager who oversees that job or someone with experience in the job?

5. As an employee, would you prefer benefits such as health-care insurance or an equivalent increase in your wages? Do you think every employee would agree with you?

APPLICATION

How can job training help a small company that uses an unusual production process find and hire skilled workers?

DECISION

Assume you own a small but growing auto-repair business that has been asked to donate materials and equipment to a job-training program for auto technicians. What would you need to know before deciding whether to participate?

COMMUNICATION

You've made a decision about contributing to the job-training program. Now plan what you'll say during a two-minute telephone conversation in which you tell the program director what you've decided.

INTEGRATION

Should a construction supervisor with no knowledge of stone carving use an autocratic, democratic, or laissez-faire leadership style (described in Chapter 6) to manage a crew of experienced stone carvers?

ETHICS

Is it ethical to raise unemployed workers' hopes by training them for jobs that may or may not exist? List at least two points on both sides of this ethical issue.

DEBATE

In the video, a job-training expert says that if the United States has the world's most sophisticated workers, it can attract the world's most sophisticated jobs. Option A: In a formal debate format, debate this issue. Option B: Take either position and write a brief report summarizing your arguments.

TEAMWORK

In a team of three students, identify at least three local companies that might be interested in hiring graduates of an appliance-repair training program. Then develop a short presentation that explains to the employers the benefits of hiring these graduates.

RESEARCH

Research the type of job-training programs offered by local schools, churches, or nonprofit groups in your area. What kinds of job skills do these programs teach? Are graduates able to find jobs?

ROLE PLAYING

One student should assume the role of human resources director at a large construction company. Another student should play the role of a non-profit-agency head who is trying to persuade the human resources director to allow two of the company's most experienced stone cutters to teach at a three-month job-skills training program.

Chapter

11

Union–Management Relations

Negotiating a Radically New Contract

Richard LeFauve of General Motors and Donald Ephlin of United Auto Workers had been adversaries for years. LeFauve represented management (white collars, planners, order-givers) and Ephlin represented labor (blue collars, strong backs, order-takers) as they faced one another from opposite sides of the negotiating table. However, when LeFauve became president of GM's Saturn division, both men agreed that a drastic change was needed in the relationship between management and labor. Facing aggressive Japanese automakers, both men believed that management *and* labor had a lot to lose unless an altogether new relationship could be forged.

LeFauve recognized that GM was battling fierce competition. Honda, Toyota, and Nissan had aggressively entered the U.S. market, reducing GM's share to about 35 percent. Customers believed that buying GM meant they were getting less car for their money, and GM was finding it increasingly difficult to compete on cost alone. For one thing, Japanese companies could build a car in about 100 hours, including suppliers' labor. General Motors took twice as long, and LeFauve saw union work rules as one cause of low productivity. At some plants, union jobs were divided into more than 100 classifications, so an entire assembly line might be shut down while a lone electrician rewired a faulty outlet. Disagreement over employees' seniority rights, job security, and wage increases threatened successive contract negotiations as GM tried in vain to streamline production rules. LeFauve believed that changes were necessary to keep the company competitive.

Saturn is a runaway success with customers as well as a symbol of cooperation between labor and management.

Yet Ephlin saw union members facing more than the possibility of losing market share. Employees were concerned with personal security: More than 230,000 union jobs had already disappeared because of foreign competition, and at least 83,000 more were expected to vanish as Japanese carmakers stepped up production in nonunion U.S. factories. Pride was also at stake. Auto plants in the United States were averaging 82 defects for every 100 cars, whereas plants in Japan averaged only 65. Union autoworkers blamed the problem on managers who were more interested in production schedules and quotas than in raising employee proficiency. Ephlin noted that Japanese autoworkers received an average of 370 hours of job training, whereas their U.S. counterparts received perhaps 46 hours. Ephlin believed that change was necessary to improve the skills and job security of his union members.

Both LeFauve and Ephlin were facing some of the most crucial questions in their long careers. How could management persuade labor to streamline production rules for the good of the company? How could labor persuade management to look beyond purely financial goals? Most important, could management and labor become teammates instead of adversaries?[1]

LABOR ORGANIZATIONS IN THE U.S. ECONOMY

As managers with Saturn and the United Auto Workers (UAW) are well aware, certain unavoidable differences of interest exist between employees and the companies that employ them. On the one hand, owners and managers of businesses have a right to use their resources as they see fit in order to increase productivity and profits. On the other hand, employees have a right to job security, safe and comfortable working conditions, and pay that rewards their contributions to the organization. In the best of times and in the most enlightened companies, these two sets of needs can often be met simultaneously. In uncertain times, however, when the economy slows down and competition speeds up, the needs of employees and management can differ. Because of this potential for conflict, employees form **labor unions,** organizations that seek to protect employee interests by negotiating with employers for wages and benefits, working hours, and working conditions.

Management sells a product, and employees sell their own labor, the services they can perform for the employer. Naturally, both want to get the best possible price. Just as the price that a company charges for a product is affected by the forces of supply and demand, so is

labor unions *Organizations of employees formed to protect and advance their members' interests*

Union members are seeking more involvement in the companies for which they work. At Xerox, union members have made suggestions that helped the company boost efficiency and quality while saving money.

PART THREE | MANAGING HUMAN RESOURCES

the price that employees charge for their services. A labor union alters the supply-and-demand equation by representing most or all of the employees—the supply of labor—that the company needs. By using their combined bargaining strength, employees can put more pressure on management than they could as individuals. An individual employee can easily be replaced, but the entire workforce cannot.

A History of Unions

In 1792 a group of shoemakers held a meeting in Philadelphia to discuss matters of common interest. The result of their modest assembly was the formation of the first known union in the United States. During the next several decades, other unions appeared. They were chiefly local **craft unions,** made up of skilled artisans belonging to a single profession or craft and concerned only with trade-related matters.

craft unions Unions made up of skilled artisans belonging to a single profession or practicing a single craft

In the 1840s and 1850s, as improved transportation cut shipping costs, created a national market, and made employees more mobile, local craft unions banded together into national craft unions. In 1869 several national craft unions joined forces as the Knights of Labor. Over the next two decades, membership in this national union reached 700,000. However, several member unions became dissatisfied with the leadership's emphasis on moral betterment instead of improvements in wages and working conditions. Furthermore, the 1886 Haymarket Riot—during which a bomb exploded among Chicago police trying to break up a labor rally—turned public opinion against the labor movement, of which the Knights were the most visible symbol. By 1890 control of the union movement had passed to a rival group, the American Federation of Labor (AFL), founded in 1886. The AFL dominated the labor movement for the next 40 years.

During the 1930s, labor unions expanded their membership enormously, especially among unskilled employees. They benefited greatly from legislation passed during President Franklin D. Roosevelt's four terms in office. (The most significant laws relating to unions, many dating from this era, are described in Exhibit 11.1.) They also benefited from the work of an unofficial Committee for Industrial Organization, which was set up within the AFL in 1935. Its goal was to organize **industrial unions** representing both skilled and unskilled employees from all parts of a particular industry.

industrial unions Unions representing both skilled and unskilled employees from all phases of a particular industry

The committee organized the auto and steel industries, boosting AFL membership to over 4 million. But three years later, the AFL formally expelled the committee. The craft unionists who controlled the AFL viewed the industrial unions as a threat. The committee became a fully independent federation of industrial unions and changed its name to the Congress of Industrial Organizations (CIO).

During World War II, full employment helped unions grow even more. In exchange for a no-strike pledge, unions were able to win many concessions from management. After the war, labor's demands for wage increases erupted into a series of severe strikes. In 1947 legislators in Washington responded by enacting the Labor-Management Relations Act (known informally as the Taft-Hartley Act), which re-

Legislation	Provision
Norris–La Guardia Act of 1932	Limits companies' ability to obtain injunctions against union strikes, picketing, membership drives, and other activities
National Labor Relations Act of 1935 (Wagner Act)	Prohibits employers from interfering with employees' right to form, join, or assist labor organizations; from interfering with labor organizations by dominating them or by making financial contributions to them; from discouraging membership in labor organizations by discriminating against members in employment or by requiring promises not to join union as condition of employment; from refusing to bargain collectively with the labor organization chosen by employees to represent them; from discharging employees because they have testified or filed charges against their employer under this act
Labor-Management Relations Act of 1947 (Taft-Hartley Act)	Amends Wagner Act to restrict unions (declares closed shop illegal, requires 60-day notice before strike or lockout, empowers federal government to issue injunctions to prevent strikes that would endanger national interest); declares jurisdictional strikes (in disputes between unions), featherbedding, refusal to bargain in good faith, and secondary boycotts illegal; requires union officers to certify that they are not Communists; requires unions to submit financial reports to secretary of labor; allows unions to sue employers for contract violations; permits employers to petition National Labor Relations Board for elections under certain circumstances
Landrum-Griffin Act of 1959	Aims to control union corruption by penalizing bribery of union officials by employers; closing loopholes in law forbidding secondary boycotts; prohibiting hot-cargo clauses in employment contracts, which give unions the right not to handle goods of a company whose employees are on strike; requiring all unions to file constitutions and bylaws with the secretary of labor; requiring all unions to publish financial records open to inspection by members; making union officials more personally responsible for unions' financial affairs, making embezzlement of union funds a federal offense, and forbidding union loans of more than $2,000 to officers; denying convicted felons the right to hold union office for five years following release from prison; giving every union member an equal right to vote on issues, attend meetings, and speak freely; forbidding unions from raising dues unless a majority of members votes for the increase by secret ballot; giving union members the right to sue unions; requiring that members be formally charged and given fair hearing before being fired, expelled, or punished in any way by the union

Exhibit 11.1

Key Legislation Relating to Unions

Most major labor legislation was enacted in the 1930s and 1940s.

stricted some of the organizing practices used by labor, such as making union membership a condition of employment.

In 1955 the AFL and the CIO merged their 16 million members. In the next few years, disclosures of union corruption and other problems prompted Congress to act to curb such abuses. Federal legislation passed in 1959 gave union members specific rights and required unions to report on their internal affairs. Since then, union membership has declined for a number of reasons, but in some industries, unions continue to hold considerable clout.

The Labor Movement Today

Unions now represent only 16 percent of nonfarm workers in the United States, down from a peak of over 35.5 percent in 1945 (see Exhibit 11.2). The decline has also been felt in some other countries. British trade unions lost a quarter of their members in the last decade; Japan's most powerful union split in half following its failure to prevent the privatization of the Japanese National Railway.[2] However, unions still cover, on average, 53 percent of all workers in the major industrial countries.[3]

A key reason for the decline in union membership is a massive shift in industry. In many countries, older, less efficient industries are falling victim to more efficient, lower-cost foreign competitors. During the 1970s and 1980s, a fifth of large unionized companies in the United States went bankrupt, unable to compete against companies with lower wage costs.[4] Other unionized companies have closed

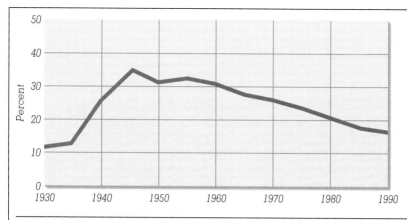

Exhibit 11.2
Union Membership Among Nonagricultural Employees
The influence of labor unions has declined since they first gained strength in the 1930s and peaked in the 1940s and 1950s. However, union efforts to organize government employees, health-care personnel, and other groups may slow or stop the decline in membership.

plants, moved manufacturing overseas, and automated jobs that were previously performed by unionized labor.

Look at the trends in union membership among manufacturing employees and at the issues being raised. The United Auto Workers represents employees at General Motors, Ford, and Chrysler, as well as at aerospace, agriculture, and other companies. In 1969 the UAW represented more than 1.5 million employees; now it represents just 835,000. In the past, the big issue was higher wages; today, important issues include job security, health-care costs, and plant closings.[5] Similarly, the United Steelworkers of America saw its membership drop from 1.2 million in 1980 to 560,000 in 1993. Here, too, current issues go beyond pay and benefits; the union is bargaining for no-layoff guarantees, labor involvement at all levels, and more job training.[6]

Even though heavy industry is on the decline in the United States, high-tech and service industries are on the rise, and unions are working to organize in those industries as well as in government. In fact, the percentage of unionized employees in government has grown to about 37 percent in the past decade. In comparison, the percentage of nonfarm private-sector workers in unions is 12 percent.[7]

The coming of a global economy has also brought changes to the labor movement. As manufacturing jobs move out of the United States, some U.S. unions are expanding their efforts to other countries. For example, the United Electrical Workers lost nearly 20 percent of its membership when some manufacturers shifted production to Mexican plants. The union followed the jobs and began to support union organizing efforts at General Electric's Mexican factories.[8]

Why Employees Join

Today's employees have a variety of reasons for seeking union representation. They're likely to express a preference for union membership if[9]

- They are deeply dissatisfied with their current job and employment conditions
- They believe that unionization can be helpful in improving those job conditions
- They are willing to overlook the generally negative stereotype of unions held by the population as a whole

According to recent studies, the employees most likely to be interested in joining a union are women, minorities, and low-wage employees.[10] At Farris Fashions in Brinkley, Arkansas, employees receive relatively low pay and minimal benefits. So, when the Amalgamated Clothing and Textile Workers Union approached them about unionizing, 70 percent signed the cards required to hold an election.[11]

At the same time, polls have found that many employees believe that unions tend to stifle individual initiative and are not necessary to ensure fair treatment from employers; about half of those polled believe that unions make it harder for companies to stay in business.[12] The companies that have most successfully resisted unionization seem to have adopted participative management styles and an enhanced sense of responsibility toward employees. Nevertheless, even the best working conditions are no guarantee that employees won't seek union representation. For instance, although Federal Express is renowned for treating its employees well, pilots still voted to join the Air Line Pilots Association. The vote revealed the pilots' job-security fears and their concern over reduced opportunities for advancement.[13]

How Unions Are Structured

national union *Nationwide organization made up of locals that represent employees in locations around the country*

A **national union** is a nationwide organization composed of many local unions that represent employees in specific locations; examples are Donald Ephlin's United Auto Workers of America (which represents GM employees) and the United Steelworkers of America. In contrast, *international unions* have members in more than one country, such as the United States and Canada. **Locals,** or local unions, each represent employees in a specific geographic area or facility; an example is Local 1853, which represents GM's Saturn employees.

locals *Relatively small union groups, usually part of a national union or a labor federation, that represent members who work in a single facility or in a certain geographic area*

A national union is responsible for such activities as organizing new areas or industries, negotiating industrywide contracts, assisting locals with negotiations, administering benefits, lobbying Congress, and lending assistance in the event of a strike. In return, local unions send representatives to the national delegate convention, submit negotiated contracts to the national union for approval, and provide financial support in the form of dues. They have the power to negotiate with individual companies or plants and to undertake their own membership activities.

labor federation *Umbrella organization of national unions and unaffiliated local unions that undertakes large-scale activities on behalf of their members and that resolves conflicts between unions*

The AFL-CIO is a **labor federation** consisting of a variety of national unions and of local unions that are not associated with any other national union. The AFL-CIO's two primary roles are to promote the political objectives of the labor movement and to provide assistance to member unions in their collective-bargaining efforts.[14] In addition, the AFL-CIO provides research and technical support to members and will arbitrate disputes between competing unions.

shop steward *Union member and employee who is elected to represent other union members and who attempts to resolve employee grievances with management*

Each local union is a hierarchy with a broad base of *rank-and-file* members, the employees the union represents. These members pay an initiation fee, pay regular dues, and vote to elect union officials. Each department or facility also has or elects a **shop steward,** who works in the facility as a regular employee and serves as a go-between with supervisors when a problem arises. In large locals and in locals that

PART THREE | MANAGING HUMAN RESOURCES

represent employees at several locations, an elected full-time **business agent** visits the various work sites to negotiate with management and enforce the union's agreements with those companies.

National and international unions, and labor federations, have a full complement of officers and often a sizable staff of experts. The organizers who go out seeking to set up new locals are an essential element at this level. Delegates elected by the locals attend regularly scheduled national conventions to elect the officers and approve changes to the umbrella organization's constitution.

How Unions Organize

Union organizers generally start by visiting with employees, although dissatisfied employees may also approach the union (see Exhibit 11.3). The organizers survey employees by asking questions such as "Have you ever been treated unfairly by your supervisor?" Employees who express interest are sent information about the union along with **authorization cards,** sign-up cards used to designate the union as their bargaining agent. If 30 percent or more of the employees in the group sign the union's authorization cards, the union may ask management to recognize it. Usually, however, unions do not seek to become the group's bargaining agent unless a majority of the employees sign.

Often the company's management is unwilling to recognize the union at this stage. Then the union can ask the National Labor Relations Board (NLRB) to supervise a **certification** election, the process by which a union becomes the official bargaining agent for a company's employees. During the organizing period before an election, the union and the company's managers explain their views to the employees. Of course, both must take care that their actions are within federal legal and regulatory guidelines. Then the vote is held. If a majority of the affected employees choose to make the union their bargaining agent, the union becomes certified. If not, that union and all other unions have to wait a year before trying again.

business agent Full-time union staffer who negotiates with management and enforces the union's agreements with companies

authorization cards Sign-up cards designating a union as the signer's preferred bargaining agent

certification Process by which a union is officially recognized by the National Labor Relations Board as the bargaining agent for a group of employees

Exhibit 11.3
The Union-Organizing Process
This diagram summarizes the steps a labor union takes when organizing a group of employees and becoming certified to represent them in negotiations with management. The certification election is necessary only if management is unwilling to recognize the union.

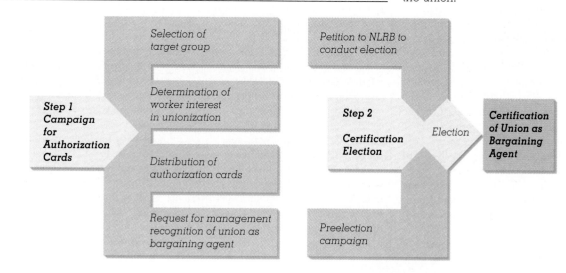

Selection of target group

Determination of worker interest in unionization

Distribution of authorization cards

Request for management recognition of union as bargaining agent

Step 1
Campaign for Authorization Cards

Petition to NLRB to conduct election

Preelection campaign

Step 2
Certification Election

Election

Certification of Union as Bargaining Agent

Why Unions Are Challenged or Removed

Once a company becomes aware that a union is seeking a certification election, management may mount an active campaign to point out the disadvantages of unionization. A company is not allowed, however, to make specific threats or promises about how it will respond to the outcome of the election, and it is not allowed to change general wages or working conditions until the election has been concluded.

Even when a union wins a certification election, there's no guarantee that it will represent a particular group of employees forever. Sometimes employees become dissatisfied with their union and no longer wish to be represented by it. When this happens, the union members can take a **decertification** vote to take away the union's right to represent them. If the majority votes for decertification, the union is removed as bargaining agent. Although still infrequent, decertification elections have increased since the mid-1970s, now accounting for 20 percent of all representation elections (as opposed to half that in 1977). During the 1980s, unions lost 75 percent of all de-

decertification *Process employees use to take away a union's official right to represent them*

GAINING THE COMPETITIVE EDGE

THE CHALLENGE OF ORGANIZING TODAY'S WORKFORCE

It's not easy being a union organizer these days—not that it ever was. However, with today's diverse workforce and declining interest in union membership among employees in some industries, union organizers have to be even more creative when it comes to recruiting members. Some organizers work patiently behind the scenes to attract members over the long term. Others try to quickly rally support before management finds out what's going on.

The International Ladies Garment Workers Union (ILGWU) uses the long-term approach to attract the more than 100,000 immigrants who work in garment shops in Los Angeles, El Paso, and New York City. Such employees speak little English, usually do not understand their legal rights, and are afraid to do anything that might jeopardize their jobs. So ILGWU organizers get involved with community groups where they can patiently counsel employees on their rights under immigration and labor law. They also teach the employees English as a second language. The union then offers "associate membership" with dues often as low as $1 a

month. Eventually some of the associate members win formal union representation at their shops.

Organizers for the United Steelworkers, on the other hand, use a different tactic for reaching beyond the union's traditional manufacturing base to work with office employees. Of course, observers note that organizing office employees can be a tough transition for some of the seasoned organizers used to dealing with disgruntled laborers in steel mills. That's exactly why the Steelworkers hired Katie Gohn. One of the union's newest organizers, Gohn is a 41-year-old former secretary with a business degree. She'd never

even set foot in a steel mill, but more important to Gohn's success was learning union organizing strategies. To accomplish that, she spent four months at the AFL-CIO's Organizing Institute and served as apprentice on half a dozen organizing campaigns before starting out to organize an office on her own. Unlike the ILGWU's long-term approach to new immigrant employees in the garment industry, Gohn pursues office employees with intense campaigns that last only a few days.

Gohn often puts in 14-hour days, eats in her motel room, and surveys employees to find issues appealing to them. She calls on other women and on ethnic organizers to help reach the diverse workforce. During one year with the Steelworkers, Gohn spent only six weeks at home, and during some campaigns she has gone without sleep for three days at a time. Even so, her 17-year-old daughter and her husband (who's a member of the Teamsters) support her work as an organizer. Winning over today's workforce may not be easy, but union organizers are still convinced that the challenge is worthwhile.

certification elections. Possible reasons for union losses include the following:[15]

- The increase in foreign competition has forced management to emphasize productivity.
- The unions have failed to deliver higher wages, more benefits, and better job security.
- The National Labor Relations Board has shown more concern for employee interests.
- The nature of work has changed; employees are better educated; and the percentage of women and part-time employees has increased.
- Nonunion industries have grown.
- The relationship between employer and employees has improved.

THE COLLECTIVE-BARGAINING PROCESS

As long as a union has been certified as the bargaining agent for a group of employees, its main job is to negotiate employment contracts with management in a process known as **collective bargaining.** Together, union and management negotiators forge the human resources policies that will apply to the unionized employees—and other employees covered by the contract—for a certain period.

Most labor contracts are a compromise between the desires of union members and of management. The union pushes for the best possible deal for its members, and management tries to negotiate agreements that are best for the company (and the shareholders, if a corporation is publicly held). Both sides have tools they can use to influence the other during the collective-bargaining process. Exhibit 11.4 illustrates the process described here.

Preparing to Meet

Before meeting with management, the union negotiating team must thoroughly understand the needs of its members as well as the company's situation. Sometimes the union hires investment bankers and

collective bargaining Process used by unions and management to negotiate work contracts

Exhibit 11.4
The Collective-Bargaining Process
Contract negotiations go through the four basic steps shown here.

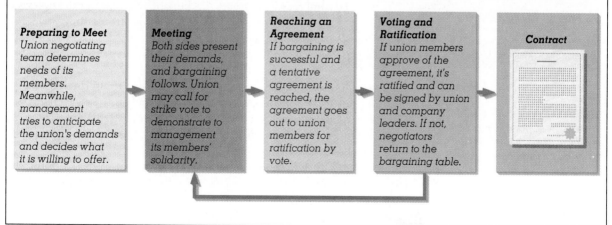

Preparing to Meet
Union negotiating team determines needs of its members. Meanwhile, management tries to anticipate the union's demands and decides what it is willing to offer.

Meeting
Both sides present their demands, and bargaining follows. Union may call for strike vote to demonstrate to management its members' solidarity.

Reaching an Agreement
If bargaining is successful and a tentative agreement is reached, the agreement goes out to union members for ratification by vote.

Voting and Ratification
If union members approve of the agreement, it's ratified and can be signed by union and company leaders. If not, negotiators return to the bargaining table.

Contract

consultants to analyze the company's business situation in advance.[16] The management side, meanwhile, tries to anticipate the union's needs and demands and determines what it is willing to offer. These estimates are often withheld from the other side at the beginning of negotiations, because each side is trying to outguess the other. Both may come to the bargaining table with extreme positions from which they can fall back during actual bargaining. Management may offer a contract with no wage gains, for instance, and the union may demand an outrageous pay increase. Neither realistically expects these demands to be met.

Before or during negotiations, the union may show strength by calling a strike vote. This vote may not signal an actual strike; it is called merely to demonstrate that the members are solidly behind their negotiating team and to remind management that a strike is possible when the current contract expires.

Meeting and Reaching an Agreement

When the negotiating teams actually sit down together, management's chief negotiator may be the vice president in charge of industrial relations or someone hired from the outside. The union's chief negotiator may be the local's business agent or a negotiator supplied by national headquarters. Although insiders might be expected to know more about their side's needs, outsiders often do a better job in tough negotiations because their nerves are less likely to become frayed in grueling bargaining sessions. Near the end of negotiations, meetings may last 12 to 15 hours—and calm discussion may give way to personal insults. However, labor and management negotiators generally try to remain composed and reasonable, especially in an era when cooperation between management and labor is necessary to combat competition from overseas companies.

Once the negotiating teams have assembled, they state their opening positions, and each side discusses them point by point. Labor usually wants additions to the current contract. Management counters with the changes it wants, sometimes including **givebacks,** concessions made by union members to rescind promised increases in wages or benefits that the company says will hurt its competitive position. In a cooperative atmosphere, the real issues behind the demands gradually come to light. For example, management may begin by demanding the right to determine the sizes of work crews when all it really wants is smaller crews; the union is unlikely to give up total control over crew sizes, which is a key element of its power, but may agree to certain reductions. After many stages of bargaining, each party presents its package of terms. Any gaps between labor and management demands are then dealt with.

What if one side or the other simply refuses to discuss a point? If one side is unwilling even to talk, the other side can ask the NLRB to rule on whether the topic is one that can be omitted (a **permissive subject**)—such as health insurance for retired employees—or

Negotiations over provisions in union contracts generally take time. Navistar International and the United Auto Workers talked for 14 consecutive days before agreeing on a contract that limited layoffs, boosted retirement benefits, increased pay, and improved health-care benefits.

givebacks *Concessions made by union members to give up promised increases in wages or benefits because the company believes the higher costs will hurt its competitive position*

permissive subject *Topic that may be omitted from collective bargaining*

one that must be discussed (a **mandatory subject**)—such as wages, hours, and health-care benefits.

If negotiations reach an impasse, outside help may be needed. The most common alternative is **mediation**—bringing in an impartial third party to study the situation and make recommendations for resolution of the differences. Mediators are generally well-respected community leaders whom both sides will listen to. However, the mediator can only offer suggestions, and his or her solutions are not binding. When a legally binding settlement is needed, the negotiators may submit to **arbitration,** a process through which an impartial arbitrator listens to both sides and then makes a judgment by accepting one side's view. In *compulsory arbitration,* the parties are required by a government agency to submit to arbitration; in *voluntary arbitration,* the parties agree on their own to use arbitration to settle their differences.

Voting and Ratifying a Contract

The contract that is constructed and agreed to during the collective-bargaining sessions then goes to the union members for **ratification,** a vote to accept or reject the contract in its entirety. If the contract is accepted, it has been ratified, and union and company leaders sign it. If the contract is rejected, the negotiators return to the bargaining table to try to bring the contract more in line with the employees' wishes.

Ratification procedures vary among unions. Some unions use representatives of different groups of employees with special interests to help secure ratification. When a companywide agreement is negotiated, many unions first send a proposed agreement to a council of lower-level union officers. However, union constitutions usually require that all employees covered by an agreement have an opportunity to approve contract settlements.[17]

WHEN NEGOTIATIONS BREAK DOWN

The vast majority of management-union negotiations are settled quickly, easily, and in a businesslike manner. This was not always the case. In the early days of unionism, conflicts often arose over such basic issues as money and working conditions, and both sides used pressure tactics that are now illegal. To defy management, the unions used threats of property damage, violence against employees siding with management, and sabotage of plants and equipment. To try to prevent the spread of unionism, management used the **yellow-dog contract,** an agreement (later forbidden by the Norris–La Guardia Act) that forced employees to promise not to join or remain in a union, and the **blacklist,** a secret list circulated among employers to keep union organizers from getting jobs. These tactics were outlawed in the 1930s. Nevertheless, today both sides are able to draw on many powerful options when negotiations or mediation procedures break down.

---

mandatory subject *Topic that must be discussed in collective bargaining*

mediation *Process for resolving a labor-contract dispute in which a neutral third party meets with both sides and attempts to steer them toward a solution*

arbitration *Process for resolving a labor-contract dispute in which an impartial third party studies the issues and makes a binding decision*

ratification *Process by which union members vote on a contract negotiated by union leaders*

yellow-dog contract *Agreement forcing employees to promise, as a condition of employment, not to join or remain in a union; forbidden by the Norris–La Guardia Act*

blacklist *Secret list circulated among employers to keep people such as union organizers from getting jobs*

Labor's Options

Strikes and picket lines are perhaps labor's best-known tactics, but a number of others are also used. In a **slowdown,** for example, employees continue to do their jobs, but at a snail's pace. When contract negotiations at A. E. Staley Manufacturing stalled, the company imposed tougher working conditions such as 12-hour shifts. In response, members of Local 837 of the Allied Industrial Workers of America in Decatur, Illinois, started a slowdown that affected the company's production of corn oil, soft-drink sweeteners, and other products.[18] It's important to note that employees who participate in slowdowns are not protected under the National Labor Relations Act and thus may be disciplined by management. Other union tactics include boycotts and the judicious use of financial influence, political influence, and publicity.

slowdown Decreasing employee productivity to pressure management

Strikes and Picket Lines

The most powerful weapon that organized labor can use is the **strike,** a temporary work stoppage aimed at forcing management to accept union demands. The basic idea behind the strike is that, in the long run, it costs management more in lost earnings to resist union demands than to give in. An essential part of the strike is **picketing:** Union members positioned at entrances to company premises march back and forth with signs and leaflets, trying to persuade nonstriking employees to join them and to persuade customers and others to stop doing business with the company. One union will often honor another's picket line, so that even a relatively small union can shut down an employer. For example, striking department-store employees can close down a business if union truckers won't cross their picket line to make deliveries.

strike Temporary work stoppage by employees who want management to accept their union's demands

picketing Strike activity in which union members march before company entrances to persuade nonstriking employees to walk off the job and to persuade customers and others to cease doing business with the company

Since the early 1980s, the number of strikes in the United States has dropped dramatically. One reason for this decline is that many companies are able to continue operating throughout a strike, either because they are highly automated or because union jobs can be performed by management and temporary employees. Companies can often (but not always) hold out longer than the strikers can. In addition, nonstriking employees sometimes show little regard for picket lines, perhaps because of the uncertain outlook for jobs, perhaps because of the general decline in union popularity. Also, the Taft-Hartley Act allows for a **cooling-off period,** an 80-day period during which a strike (or threatened strike) is suspended by order of the president of the United States and the courts because of the potential for jeopardizing "national health and safety." This cooling-off period provides an opportunity for both sides to negotiate.

cooling-off period Eighty-day period allowed by the Taft-Hartley Act during which a strike is suspended by order of the president of the United States and the courts to protect public health and safety

Boycotts

A less direct but equally powerful weapon is the **boycott,** in which union members and sympathizers refuse to buy or handle the product of a target company. Millions of union members form an enormous bloc of purchasing power, which may be able to pressure management into making concessions. One of the best-known boycotts of the past couple of decades was the grape boycott organized by

boycott Union activity in which members and sympathizers refuse to buy or handle the product of a target company

César Chávez in the early 1970s. In order to pressure California growers into accepting the United Farm Workers (UFW) as the bargaining agent for previously unorganized farm laborers, he and his colleagues persuaded an estimated 17 million people in the United States to stop buying grapes. Eventually, the California legislature passed the country's first law guaranteeing farmworkers the right to hold union elections, and today the UFW has about 100,000 members.[19]

A 1988 Supreme Court decision paved the way for more aggressive boycotting activities by clarifying the legality of *secondary boycotts,* or boycotts of companies that do business with the targeted union employer. Such boycotts are now legal if they do not involve coercive tactics or picketing. One of the first unions to take advantage of this ruling was the United Paper Workers International. Already embroiled in a year-long strike against International Paper, the union immediately began boycotts against two banks that finance International Paper. Members handed out leaflets in front of the banks, urging customers not to do business there. For International Paper employees, the ploy was ultimately unsuccessful.[20]

SHOULD EMPLOYEES STRIKE WHEN THE PUBLIC WELFARE IS AT STAKE?

Striking employees fighting for higher wages, job security, or other issues often make the headlines when they disrupt work operations. However, even though strikes create difficulties for management, most of the time they cause only minor inconveniences for the public. In some industries, however, a massive strike can have devastating effects on large segments of the population.

The 1994 Teamsters strike against Roadway Express (a trucking carrier) hurt employees and customers as well as the company. The company, which employs 18,000 unionized employees, lost millions in revenue every day of the strike. Roadway's president, Michael Wickham, had to lay off about 20 percent of the workforce, a layoff that could be permanent. "This strike did not have to happen. It shouldn't have happened. The impact on employees is long-term. That's inexcusable," said Wickham during the strike. Worse, customers were forced to switch to other truckers or to use other forms of transportation—and many said they wouldn't return to a unionized carrier. If customers continue to stay away, more jobs could be in jeopardy.

When union members vote for or against a strike, they face the dilemma of choosing between their own needs and the needs of thousands of innocent bystanders. Consider, for example, the 6,000 Greyhound bus drivers who walked off the job in early 1990. Greyhound is the only nationwide bus company, and people in nearly 10,000 communities depend on it for public transportation. In nearly half of those communities, the strike completely halted bus service. Although Greyhound eventually replaced most of the striking drivers, it could no longer afford to service many small communities along marginally profitable routes. For people like Geneva Fisher, a 66-year-old widow who lives in Tipton, Missouri, the strike's effect was quite discouraging. Fisher doesn't drive and has relied on Greyhound for frequent trips to visit her sister in Sedalia. Without Greyhound, she has to do most of her visiting by phone.

Perhaps the people who face the most difficult choice in a possible strike situation are unionized hospital employees. Currently, fewer than 20 percent of the country's 3.6 million hospital employees belong to unions, but that percentage may soon increase. A Supreme Court ruling has paved the way for labor unions to more easily organize hospital employees, including doctors and clerical employees.

However, hospital workers don't have to walk out on patients. Before hospital management and unionized nurses at Danbury Hospital in Danbury, Connecticut, finally agreed on a new contract, the union was ready to hold an "informational picket" in which off-duty employees walk in front of the hospital carrying signs that explain their views. Such action doesn't affect patient care, but it does allow employees to make a public statement about the issues.

Financial and Political Influence

Many unions have huge financial assets, including the more than $500 billion in their members' pension funds, which they may use to exert influence. In the International Paper strike, union organizers threatened to withdraw union funds from banks that shared directors with International Paper. They were also able to persuade other unions, such as the American Federation of State, County, and Municipal Employees, to make similar threats.[21] However, the threats didn't work at International Paper—the strike ended with 2,300 union members being permanently replaced.

Unions may also exercise significant political power by endorsing candidates and encouraging union members to vote for those candidates. They often raise funds for candidates as well. The Committee on Political Education (COPE), founded by the AFL–CIO in 1955, solicits funds from union members for distribution to candidates who favor labor's positions. In one recent period, eight union political action committees (PACs) each contributed more than $500,000 to candidates; the Teamsters PAC alone gave $5.5 million. The direct participation of union members in the electoral process may be even more effective. More than a fifth of the delegates to the 1992 Democratic presidential nominating convention were union members.[22]

Publicity

Labor can also press its case using a publicity campaign mounted not only against the target company but also against all companies affiliated with it. After J. P. Stevens fought 20 years (using both legal and illegal means) to prevent any direct effort toward organizing its employees, the Amalgamated Clothing and Textile Workers Union unleashed ads, letters, phone calls, and news releases about the company's lenders, major shareholders, and outside board members. At long last, even though J. P. Stevens had become the number 1 antiunion employer in the United States, the company relented under the pressure of the union's publicity campaign.[23]

Management's Options

As powerful as the union's tactics may be, companies are not helpless when it comes to fighting back. Management can use a number of legal methods to pressure unions when negotiations break down.

Strikebreakers and Management-Run Operations

strikebreakers People who cross a picket line to work

When union members walk off their jobs, management can legally replace them with **strikebreakers,** people who cross the picket line to work. (Union members brand them as "scabs.") Management is even allowed to hire permanent replacements for strikers if necessary to keep a business operating. Greyhound Lines kept its nationwide bus system rolling by hiring 3,000 permanent replacements for the 6,000 unionized drivers who walked off the job in 1990. Other companies that took on permanent replacements in recent years include

Colt Industries, the *Chicago Tribune,* and the New York *Daily News.*[24] However, organized labor is fighting back by lobbying for laws that forbid companies from hiring permanent replacements for striking employees.

Another way for management to put pressure on unions when negotiations break down is to substitute middle managers and supervisory personnel for the striking employees. In some industries, management is able to hold out during strikes by depending on their computers. At AT&T, many operations are now computerized, so the ratio of employees to supervisors has shifted from 5:1 to 2:1 over the past 20 years, making it easier for supervisors to take over during a strike. However, this type of victory comes at a price. During one strike at AT&T, more than 2,000 cases of vandalism were reported as employees took out their frustration on the new electronic "scabs." In recent years, however, both the Communications Workers of America and the International Brotherhood of Electrical Workers have worked closely with AT&T to redesign the work environment and give employees more say in the organization.[25]

This strike by the UAW protested excessive overtime at the Buick City General Motors plant in Michigan, which supplies parts for GM plants all over the United States. Management negotiated with the union to settle the strike by agreeing to hire more production employees.

lockouts *Management activities in which union members are prevented from entering a business during a strike, to force union acceptance of management's last contract proposal*

Lockouts

The United States Supreme Court has upheld the use of **lockouts,** in which management locks out union employees in order to pressure a union to accept a contract proposal. A lockout is legal only if union and management have come to an impasse in negotiations. During a lockout, the company may hire temporary replacements as long as it has no anti-union motivation and negotiations have been amicable.[26]

Although the lockout is rarely used in major industries today, some instances still occur. After the United Auto Workers started a limited strike at Caterpillar, which makes earth-moving and construction equipment, the company responded with a lockout. Five months went by without progress. Then Caterpillar announced that employees who returned to work would be covered by the terms of the company's most recent offer. Those who didn't return would be permanently replaced. Because jobs were scarce and some UAW members had already begun crossing picket lines, the union ended the strike and the employees returned to their jobs.[27] Another example is the Timex lockout of employees in a Dundee, Scotland, plant. The plant had been unprofitable in recent years; labor and management had long battled over wages, benefits, and layoffs. Union employees went on strike, Timex locked them out, and the company finally closed the plant six months later.[28]

Injunctions

An **injunction** is a court order directing someone to do something or to refrain from doing it. Management used this weapon without

injunction *Court order directing someone to do something or not do something*

restriction in the early days of unionism, when companies typically sought injunctions to order striking employees back to work on the grounds that the strikers were interfering with business. Today injunctions are legal only in certain cases. For example, the president of the United States has the right, under the Taft-Hartley Act, to obtain a temporary injunction to halt a strike deemed harmful to the national interest. When Jimmy Carter was president, he invoked the Taft-Hartley Act to get striking miners in the bituminous coal industry back to work, stating that coal production was in the national interest. However, coal workers disobeyed the court, so the judge lifted his order.

Industry Pacts and Organizations

Some industries have copied the united-front strategy of the AFL-CIO by forging mutual-assistance pacts: They temporarily agree to abandon competition in order to assist a competitor singled out for a strike. Such agreements provide a form of strike insurance to help the company hold out against union demands. Certain industries have also formed national organizations such as the National Association of Manufacturers to counterbalance the national union organizations. These organizations try to coordinate industrywide strategy and to keep wage and benefit levels even among companies. They also lobby for legislation to protect management against union demands.

THE COLLECTIVE-BARGAINING AGREEMENT

Signing a collective-bargaining agreement (or contract) between union and management doesn't mark the end of negotiations. Rather, it lays the groundwork for discussions that will continue throughout the life of the contract to iron out unspecified details of the various contract issues.

Basic Contract Issues

As Saturn's LeFauve and the UAW's Ephlin recognize, most labor contracts cover similar issues. Whether a union represents teachers, hospital employees, miners, or assembly workers, the issues of common concern are union security and management rights, compensation, job security, work rules, and employee safety and health.

Union Security and Management Rights

Once a union has been established, the contracts it negotiates begin with a provision guaranteeing the security of the union. This provision is included because unions want a firm institutional base from which to work.

Ideally, a union would like to see all employees under its jurisdiction, but such a **closed shop,** compelling employees to join the union as a condition of being hired, is illegal under the Taft-Hartley Act. The next best alternative for labor is the **union shop,** which allows an employer to hire new people at will, but after a probationary period—usually 30 days—the employees must join the union. Another

closed shop *Workplace in which union membership is a condition of employment*

union shop *Workplace in which the employer may hire new people at will but only for a probationary period, after which they must join the union*

PART THREE | MANAGING HUMAN RESOURCES

States with right-to-work laws

alternative is the **agency shop,** which requires nonunion employees who benefit from agreements negotiated by the union to pay service fees to that union. The opposite of a closed shop is an **open shop,** in which employees are not required to join the union or pay dues, although they may join voluntarily. Certain states, mostly in the Sunbelt and the West, have passed **right-to-work laws,** which give employees the explicit right to keep a job without joining a union (see Exhibit 11.5).

agency shop Workplace requiring nonunion employees who are covered by agreements negotiated by the union to pay service fees to that union

Compensation
A collective-bargaining agreement addresses several issues relating to employee compensation. The most common issues are wage rates, cost-of-living adjustments, profit sharing, and employee benefits.

open shop Workplace in which union membership is voluntary and employees need not join or pay dues

Wage Rates. Until recently, unions negotiated similar wages for members working for all companies in a particular industry or at all plants within a particular company. This practice is referred to as **pattern bargaining.** Until 15 years ago, union assemblers at all General Motors, Ford, and Chrysler plants earned wages that were within 3 cents an hour of each other.[29] However, many companies began breaking away from patterns in their industries and negotiating separately with the unions. In particular, the major steel companies have abandoned pattern bargaining, as have several of the largest railroads, coal companies, and meat packers.[30]

right-to-work laws Laws giving employees the explicit right to keep a job without joining a union

pattern bargaining Negotiating similar wages and benefits for all companies within a particular industry

Two primary factors have prompted the recent changes in the way unions negotiate wage rates: economic recessions and tough foreign competition. Many unions have agreed to contracts freezing wages at current levels or cutting wages or benefits in return for job-security guarantees. The reasoning is that it's better to have a job at a lower wage than to have no job at all. That's what happened at Rubbermaid's plant in Wooster, Ohio, where the Rubber Workers

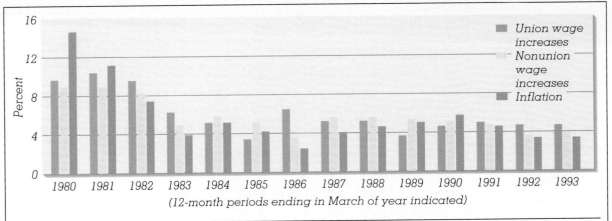

Exhibit 11.6
Wages, Inflation, and Unions
In recent years, union wage increases have been smaller than nonunion wage increases and in many cases have not even kept pace with inflation.

two-tier wage plans *Compensation agreements in which new employees are put on a wage scale lower than that of veteran employees*

cost-of-living adjustment (COLA) *Clause in a union contract ensuring that wages will rise in proportion to inflation*

Local 302 accepted givebacks in exchange for some measure of job security. Because of the union's concessions, the company stopped shifting production and jobs to nonunionized plants where costs were lower.[31]

During the 1980s recessions, some unions agreed to **two-tier wage plans,** in which the pay scale of new employees differed from that of senior employees. Although this strategy was widely used by industries struggling to compete, it later came under fire because of the morale problems it created for lower-paid newcomers. As a result of such concessions, givebacks, and otherwise small wage increases negotiated over the past decade, union wages have sometimes increased at a slower rate than nonunion wages—and sometimes more slowly than the cost of living (see Exhibit 11.6). Today union wage gains are at the lowest point in the past few decades, although union employees still average 23 percent higher wages than nonunion employees.[32]

COLAs. In 1950 the United Auto Workers and General Motors adopted an innovative policy. To guarantee that employees' pay would keep pace with inflation, their contract adopted a **cost-of-living adjustment (COLA)** clause. During the term of the contract, employees' wages would automatically be increased in proportion to inflation in the general economy. By 1976 over 60 percent of employees covered by labor contracts benefited from COLA provisions.[33]

COLAs have been popular because they seem to maintain employees' buying power without any particular effort in negotiating contracts or raising productivity. In reality, however, some analysts have identified major flaws. For one thing, COLAs are believed to magnify the effects of inflation in the general economy, especially when inflation jumps suddenly, as it did during the oil crises of the 1970s. The cost of COLAs is also less predictable than standard wage agreements and therefore complicates management's strategic planning. In the climate of the mid-1980s, when unions and management began trying to work together to save industries and when the inflation rate remained low, COLAs lost some of their appeal. By 1991 only 34 percent of employees covered by labor contracts received COLA increases.[34]

Profit Sharing. Although profit sharing is not a new idea, it has attracted increased attention in recent years. Today approximately

16 percent of all full-time employees in medium and large private companies are included in profit-sharing plans.[35] Some plans provide employees with deferred income they may claim on retirement as an incentive to produce more in the present. Others provide cash payments to employees each time the company's profits are determined.

Both management and unions are increasingly looking at profit sharing as a means of reducing wage inflation and increasing productivity. However, labor has some apprehension about the income risks associated with profit sharing. In fact, the AFL-CIO recently advised its affiliates to make profit sharing the smallest part of any total economic package they negotiate.[36] In addition, union negotiators are developing innovative bargaining strategies to protect employees when profits are down. The United Steelworkers, for example, agreed to a wage-cut profit-sharing arrangement with LTV Steel, with the wage cuts treated as loans to be repaid from future profits. In addition, just in case future profits turn out to be insufficient to satisfy the debt, the contract requires LTV to issue interest-bearing stock to employees for the unpaid balance.[37]

Employee Benefits. Management can also avoid increasing basic wage rates in labor contracts by providing additional benefits. In particular, unions have been stressing higher pensions. However, employers are fighting these demands because in the past few years, they have had to absorb large increases in Social Security taxes and unemployment compensation rates. Employers have also been pushing for employees to pay more of the $100 billion that medical insurance costs companies every year. Unfortunately, the skyrocketing costs of medical insurance have made employee benefits a prime area of union-management contention in recent years.

Job Security

In the face of continuing corporate cutbacks, deregulation, and competition from importers and nonunionized domestic companies, unions have been stressing job security over wage increases. In fact, job security is *the* issue of the 1990s. Unions sometimes demand **lifetime security,** protection for employees against temporary layoffs due to economic slowdowns and against permanent layoffs due to closing outmoded plants or expanded subcontracting (getting another company to do work previously done in-house).

Automation can also pose a threat to job security. Unions are demanding that management give them advance notice of any attempts to introduce new equipment that would cost their members jobs, and they are demanding that employees already on the job not be laid off because of automation. Two unions acutely aware of the potential of automation for reducing the number of jobs have been the Communications Workers of America (CWA) and the International Brotherhood of Electrical Workers (IBEW), which represent nearly 90 percent of the telephone workforce. Both unions negotiated the creation of labor-management "technology committees" at AT&T, through which both unions and management discuss the introduction of new equipment. The CWA has also arranged retraining programs so that members can learn high-technology skills ranging from computer programming to the repair of electronic equipment.[38]

lifetime security *Arrangement that gives employees some protection against temporary layoffs during an economic slowdown and against job loss during a downsizing or plant closing*

This General Motors Assembly Center in Hamtramck, Michigan, where Cadillacs are made, is one of the many GM plants covered by a UAW contract that offers higher layoff and retirement pay. The contract allows GM management to move workers to other plants if it decides to close a factory.

work rules *Policies set during collective bargaining that govern what type of work union members will do and the conditions under which they will work*

featherbedding *Practice of requiring employees to be kept on the payroll for work they don't do or for work that isn't necessary*

In large industries often plagued by job insecurity, such as the automotive industry, unions tend to focus on job guarantees. However, with the U.S. auto industry bracing for tough economic times and intense competition, unions are more willing to accept "income" guarantees and better retirement packages in lieu of jobs. In 1990 the United Auto Workers won unprecedented job-security provisions in a contract with the Big Three automakers. Under the pact, many of the companies' 450,000 blue-collar employees received 85 percent of their regular take-home pay for three years if they took "preretirement leave" or were laid off.[39] The pattern continued into 1993, when General Motors signed a new three-year contract with the UAW that boosted layoff and retirement pay even further in exchange for the freedom to move employees to other plants when the carmaker decides to close a plant.[40]

Work Rules and Job Descriptions

High on the list of issues that Saturn's LeFauve and the UAW's Ephlin had to grapple with were traditional work rules and restrictive job classifications, both of which tend to reduce productivity. **Work rules** are definitions of the types of work that covered employees may do and of the working conditions they must have. In the past, unions used narrow work rules to preserve jobs. For example, a union may specify in its contract that 20 employees are needed to complete a particular work task, even though two will sit idle. The practice of requiring employees to be paid for work they don't do or for work that isn't needed is known as **featherbedding.** In the past 20 years, however, management and unions both have realized that for productivity to be increased, some fundamental changes had to be made in work rules.

After tough negotiations, unions representing employees at Chrysler agreed to change many job definitions. A welder who had been kept on the payroll for many years to handle occasional welding jobs was dismissed, and one of the maintenance employees was trained to handle the welding jobs. Under the old rules, only an electrician could unplug one of the plant's sewing machines; now anyone can do that. The result of the joint union-management effort has been the rescue of a doomed plant, increased production, and savings of $6.4 million a year—even without automation.[41]

Employee Safety and Health

Most union contracts have provisions covering employees' safety and health, although the contracts rarely do more than restate federal regulations already in force. However, the combination of escalating health-care costs and greater awareness of environmental hazards has given rise to important new demands in labor negotiations. Some current issues include concern over injuries due to repetitive motions in typing or assembly activities and exposure to radiation emitted by computer display terminals.[42]

Administration of the Agreement

Once a collective-bargaining agreement goes into effect, it is up to management and union representatives to make it work. **Grievances,** or complaints of management violation of some aspect of the contract, inevitably arise. Grievances typically come up when employees feel that they have been passed over for promotion, aren't getting a fair share of overtime, or are being asked to work too much overtime.

A contract's grievance procedures protect the employees' right to **due process,** which is a system of procedures and mechanisms for ensuring equity and justice on the job. Under the Fifth Amendment, "No person shall . . . be deprived of life, liberty, or property, without due process of law." Since most employees covered by a collective-bargaining agreement have a "property interest" in their employment, they can't be disciplined or terminated without an explanation and an opportunity to present their side of the story.

Although grievance procedures vary somewhat from contract to contract, grievances are usually referred first to the union's shop steward, who discusses them with the employee's immediate supervisor. If these discussions fail, the problem may then be discussed by the union's chief steward and the company's department head. The next step in the process brings together the union grievance committee and the company human resources (or personnel) manager. If they fail to solve the grievance, it is then up to the union business agent and the company plant manager to try to resolve the issue.

If the employee's complaint still cannot be satisfied, it goes to an *arbitrator,* whose powers are defined in the contract and whose ruling is usually final. Arbitration is generally considered a last resort because it removes control from both union and management, and it may be complicated and expensive. As a result, there has been a shift to *grievance mediation,* in which a neutral third party meets with both sides and attempts to steer them toward a solution to the problem.

Although grievance procedures are still an important aspect of contract administration, today's competitive environment has caused labor to focus less on grievances and more on cooperation and teamwork. GM's Saturn division is just one example of a team effort between labor and management that should minimize conflicts and promote cooperation.

UNION-MANAGEMENT RELATIONS IN A CHANGING ENVIRONMENT

Economic pressures have brought new approaches to the twin goals of maintaining the health of U.S. companies and protecting the rights of employees. To survive against foreign competitors, whose labor costs are often much lower, unions and management alike have developed some new strategies.

Plant Shutdowns and Bankruptcy

Companies sometimes decide to close an inefficient factory so that they can institute sweeping improvements in a new one, and they are

grievances Employee complaints about management's violating some aspect of a labor contract

due process System of procedures and mechanisms for ensuring equity and justice on the job

sometimes forced to close a factory because business is bad. Regardless of the reason, a factory closing may cause a wide variety of problems. Some are foreseeable, such as unemployment and economic problems for the local area. Less obvious problems are alcoholism, drug abuse, depression, marital stress, and other psychological difficulties among laid-off employees. Most plants close with little advance notice, and employees bear the brunt of the problems.

Manufacturers in nearly every European country must let employees know about closings in advance; German companies, for example, must give notice 12 months in advance.[43] Until recently, however, U.S. companies didn't have to tell employees before they closed any factories. The Plant-Closing Notification Act of 1988 changed that. In effect since 1989, the law requires companies to give employees at least 60 days' notice of impending plant closings or layoffs.

If business is bad enough, a company may file for bankruptcy in order to relieve some of the pressure from creditors. When Texas Air acquired Continental Airlines, it declared Continental bankrupt and then reopened the company as a nonunion carrier with much lower wages. Other companies used this tactic as well, which led to federal legislation that limits the use of bankruptcy in labor relations.

Employee Rights in Nonunion Companies

In the effort to reduce union influence and power, management has taken another approach: granting its nonunionized employees many of the same benefits enjoyed by union members. These benefits include salaries competitive with those earned by union members, liberal work rules, and seniority privileges. One study showed that 30 percent of all nonunion employers had established formal grievance procedures to settle disputes between management and employees. A *peer-review system,* for example, allows an unhappy employee to appeal to a board of employees and managers. The board listens to both sides, gathers information, and then votes on a decision, which is final.[44]

Another factor in the changing balance of power between labor and management is the changing role of government. Laws now mandate health and safety standards on the job, and a variety of federal and local laws forbid discrimination on the basis of race, gender, or age (see Exhibit 11.7). Recent legislation has also clarified employers' responsibility for pension plans, and the minimum-wage law has been steadily expanded to include all employees.

Employee Ownership

Faced with more mergers and plant closings, concern about mounting job losses has led unions to pursue a number of innovative means for helping unionized companies remain competitive. These options have ranged from placing union representatives on company boards to increasing employee stock ownership to actually engineering employee buyouts.

In many cases, unions have granted givebacks in exchange for enhanced employee-ownership programs that give employees a bigger

Issue	Legislation/court ruling	Source
Privacy	Limits on employee data that government may disclose to employers	Federal Privacy Act of 1974, 10 states
	Limits on use of lie-detector tests for job applicants	20 states
	Employee rights to access personnel files	9 states
	Limits on use of arrest records in hiring	12 states
Safety and health	Broad requirements for guaranteeing a safe and healthful workplace	Occupational Safety and Health Act of 1970, 24 states
	Protections for mine workers	Federal Mine Safety and Health Act of 1977
Pension and other benefit plans	Funding, vesting, and other standards	Employee Retirement Income Security Act of 1974, various states
Wages and working conditions	Provisions for national minimum wage, 40-hour workweek for regular pay, and other working conditions	Fair Labor Standards Act of 1938, state wage and hour laws (all states)
Union security	Limits on employers' ability to discharge and discipline employees for union activity	National Labor Relations Act of 1935
	Protection of union security in railroad industry	Railway Labor Act of 1926
Right to know	Requirement that companies divulge information on hazardous substances used in workplace	25 states
Whistle-blowers	Protection for corporate and government employees who expose wrongdoing	21 states
Employment at will	Limits on employment-at-will doctrine, which holds that employees may be fired at any time without cause	Court decisions in 30 states
Plant shutdowns	Requirement that employees receive 60 days advance notice of plant shutdowns or massive layoffs	Plant-Closing Notification Act of 1988
Discrimination	Broad protection against discrimination in hiring, promotion, and discharge	Civil Rights Act of 1964
	Protection for older employees against age discrimination	Age Discrimination in Employment Act of 1967
	Prohibition of any mandatory retirement age	19 states
	Prohibition of policies mandating retirement before age 70	1986 amendment to Age Discrimination in Employment Act of 1967
	Limits on discrimination on the basis of marital status and sexual orientation	Various states and localities
	Limits on gender discrimination in pay	Equal Pay Act of 1963
	Requirements of equal pay for comparable work	Some federal court decisions
	Increased protection against bias and harassment, allowing trials by jury and increasing cash awards for damages and reimbursement costs	Civil Rights Act of 1991
	Limits on discrimination against employees or qualified job applicants with certain physical or mental impairments	Americans with Disabilities Act (ADA) of 1990

Exhibit 11.7
Guaranteeing Employee Rights
Nonunion as well as union employees have benefited from a number of state and federal legislative actions as well as court decisions guaranteeing employee rights in the United States.

say in how a company is run. Labor representatives now sit on the boards of Kaiser Aluminum, Wheeling–Pittsburgh Steel, and many smaller companies. Unions are encouraging employees to learn more about the business end of their industry and are fighting for greater employee access to companies' financial records. According to one steel industry labor expert, "Being an effective union today is having an understanding of the core business the union is in and communicating that understanding to members."[45]

Many unions favor employee stock–ownership plans (ESOPs), described in Chapter 10. In 1990 some 10,000 companies had such

The 54,000 employees who work for United Airlines have a bigger stake in their company's success now that they've assumed ownership of the unionized carrier.

plans. With ESOPs, employees have been able to gain partial or complete ownership of roughly 1,500 companies.[46] For example, Avis's 13,000 employees have ownership control of the car-rental company. Most attempts by unions to buy companies have been unsuccessful, but the machinist union did succeed in purchasing Chase Brass & Copper from Standard Oil, and the maritime unions were able to purchase WFI Industries, a family-owned tugboat company.[47]

Employee-Involvement Programs

An increasing number of companies are forging closer partnerships with unions and their members by inviting involvement in all aspects of their businesses. Xerox is only one example of a company that has remade itself with the help of unionized employees. To compete with overseas rivals, management needed to cut $3 million from the cost of manufacturing certain photocopier parts. After members of the Amalgamated Clothing and Textile Workers Union came up with ways to save $2.9 million at Xerox's Webster, New York, plant, the company agreed to continue production there rather than shifting to a company factory in Mexico. Management and union members also worked in teams to determine the best way to complete each production task and to improve quality. The result? "The cost of building *product X* is competitive with what others can build it for, and we think we've built a better one," says Joe Laymon, Xerox's director of corporate industrial relations.[48]

Even as more companies establish employee-management teams to solve problems or deal with workplace issues, the use of such groups has been brought into question by a recent ruling from the National Labor Relations Board. Electromation, an electronic-component maker in Elkhart, Indiana, organized committees to study cost-cutting measures that would affect wages and bonuses. The Teamsters Union was trying to establish itself at Electromation, and it protested the company's employee-management committees to the NLRB, arguing that such activities were illegal under the National Labor Relations Act of 1935. Because management set up the committees, told committee members what to study (such as issues that concerned terms of employment), provided meeting space, and gave employees paid time off from their regular duties to participate, the NLRB ruled that Electromation had illegally established a management-dominated labor organization.

Experts say that companies can avoid problems by allowing employee-involvement teams to deal only with subjects such as efficiency and productivity, not with pay practices, working conditions, or other subjects that are generally covered by collective-bargaining agreements. In addition, management by itself can't determine the size or structure of these teams, set the meeting times and places, or dictate the topics to be examined. Finally, companies can avoid problems by inviting all employees to participate—perhaps by establishing a "committee of the whole" so that employees who take part aren't representing nonparticipating employees; team members can rotate so that everyone has a chance to have a say.[49]

New Directions for Unions

Unions are beginning to pursue new issues and different employees, and they are doing so in new and different ways. In high-tech companies, unions are making headway with employees who face layoffs and delays in pay increases when employers get caught in an economic squeeze. Unions are also actively recruiting women by offering them more leadership roles and by emphasizing such concerns as child care and a higher minimum wage.[50]

One analyst believes that unions must do the following in order to stay healthy between now and the end of the century:[51]

- Win job guarantees—perhaps not lifetime jobs but at least guarantees that employees will get other jobs in the company before being laid off.
- Make imaginative pay deals that exchange a piece of the profits for traditional wages and benefits.
- Communicate with members to find out how they feel and to let them know the facts of economic life.
- Accept new technology that will make employers more competitive and therefore more stable sources of jobs.
- Attract new members from the service industries, perhaps by hiring more female union executives and organizers.

Some unions have already begun experimenting. The National Union of Hospital and Health Care Employees has found that hard facts may be more persuasive with today's employees than rallies and pep talks. The union uses its union pension funds to finance projects that use organized labor. In addition, it's offering insurance to selected groups of employees who sign up as associate members, with the hope that the associate members will someday become full-fledged unionists. *Worker associations* are union-backed organizations that offer help on workplace issues other than compensation. For example, members of AIM (Associate ILGWU Members) in New York are affiliated with the International Ladies Garment Workers Union (ILGWU) and receive services such as English classes, computer courses, skills training, and legal help with immigration, disability, and sexual harassment issues.[52]

More fundamentally, faced with a basic change in the relationship between management and labor, unions have started reconsidering their position and have begun emphasizing the benefits that they can provide to employers as well as to employees. For one thing, unions can provide skilled employees who are less likely to quit; they offer a source of responsible labor.[53] Unions have also been stressing their ability to help train people and upgrade their skills. Additionally, they have tried to expand their appeal to members by offering such non-traditional services as free legal advice and low-interest credit cards.[54]

1 Identify two main types of labor unions.

Craft unions, which developed first, are composed of people who perform a particular type of work. Industrial unions organize people who perform different types of work within a single industry, such as the automobile and steel industries.

2 Outline the organizational structure of unions.

National unions are composed of local unions; labor federations are composed of national unions and unaffiliated local unions. Each local has a hierarchy consisting of rank-and-file members, an elected president, elected shop stewards, and perhaps a business agent. National unions and federations consist of delegates elected by the local unions, who in turn elect officers; staff experts and organizers are hired to carry out the unions' programs.

3 Identify the two main steps unions take to become the bargaining agent for a group of employees.

First, unions distribute authorization cards, which designate the union as bargaining agent. If at least 30 percent (but usually a majority) of the target group sign the cards, the union asks management to recognize it. Second, if management is unwilling, the union asks the National Labor Relations Board to sponsor a certification election. If a majority of the employees vote in favor of being represented by the union, the union wins.

4 Describe the four main stages in collective bargaining.

The first stage is preparing to meet. The second stage is actually negotiating. The third stage is forming a tentative agreement. The fourth stage is ratifying the proposed contract.

5 Identify four options that unions have if negotiations with management break down.

Unions can conduct strikes, organize boycotts, exercise financial and political influence, and use publicity to pressure management into complying with union proposals.

6 Identify four options that management has if negotiations with the union break down.

To pressure a union into accepting its proposals, management may continue running the business with strikebreakers and managers, institute a lockout of union members, seek an injunction against a strike or other union activity, or seek a pact with other companies in the industry.

7 List five general issues that may be addressed in a labor contract.

Among the issues that may be subject to negotiation are union security and management rights, compensation, job security, work rules, and employee safety and health.

8 Describe five major ways that management and unions are responding to changes in the structure of the economy.

First, management has tried using plant shutdowns and bankruptcy to void burdensome labor contracts. Second, as a result of legislation, court rulings, and changing management philosophies, companies have given nonunionized employees most of the same rights and benefits that unions demanded in the past. Third, employees sometimes become owners of a company to safeguard their jobs. Fourth, companies are inviting employees to become more involved in the company's operations through special programs. Fifth, unions have experimented with new organizing tactics designed to make them more appealing to groups of employees who have not traditionally belonged to unions.

Saturn could be viewed as one of the most expensive and risky experiments in the history of U.S. manufacturing: $5 billion for a mile-long factory to produce a car that, as one dealer said, "drives and feels like a Honda." To Richard LeFauve and Donald Ephlin, it was the beginning of a new relationship between management and labor. Although parts of the agreement between General Motors and the United Auto Workers have been implemented in other industries, Saturn's agreement was the first to combine so many ideas in one pact.

Instead of the traditional boss-worker structure, managers and employees are joined into teams and committees to make decisions by consensus. These groups decide everything about Saturn's operation, including who does what job, who goes on vacation when, how to engineer component parts, how to market the car, and even the company's long-range strategy. For the first time, labor is involved in decisions concerning product, personnel, and profits. Union representatives helped choose an advertising agency and helped select which GM dealers would sell the car. Union employees are paid a salary instead of an hourly wage, and 80 percent of them—determined by seniority—cannot be laid off, except in the case of some catastrophic event. Even then, the joint management-labor committees can reduce the hours of operation or even stop production to prevent layoffs.

For its part, the UAW agreed to streamline the production process. The key change was a reduction in job classifications from more than 100 to a maximum of 6:1 for production employees and up to 5 for skilled employees. This change, combined with state-of-the-art production processes and equipment, helped boost productivity. The union also agreed to an initial 20 percent cut in compensation in exchange for the salaries and management-style bonuses employees now receive. Future salary levels are decided by consensus of the Strategic Advisory Committee (the highest group of decision makers in the Saturn hierarchy), and these levels are based on the average hourly rates at all U.S. manufacturing plants, including those owned by Japanese companies. Finally, in an effort to tear down the walls between management and labor, all employees park in the same parking lots and eat in the same cafeterias.

In contrast to the 597-page UAW contract covering all other GM operations, which must be renegotiated every three years, the 28-page Saturn agreement is known as a living document, and it never expires. However, it can be altered at any time, as long as both parties agree. Some other plants have been the scene of angry confrontations between labor and management as GM closes some factories and takes other steps to cut costs. The Saturn plant, on the other hand, has generally avoided such problems because its contract allows both sides to be flexible in dealing with issues as they arise. Whether the UAW will let GM negotiate a similar contract for future plants is an open question; so far, GM contracts have generally followed the pattern bargaining of the industry.

Still, Saturn's success shows that union and management are capable of working together so that both benefit. These days, 6,000 Saturn employees produce more than 300,000 cars a year, and the car has earned a reputation for quality. That success has both Chrysler and Ford looking carefully at the model of cooperation that the UAW and GM have established.

Your Mission: You serve as a labor relations consultant to United Auto Workers officials and to Local 1853, which represents Saturn workers. You're familiar with other contracts in the industry, and you are helping the union with long-term planning. How would you handle the following situations?

1. When Saturn's profits are low, employees lose because their pay depends, in part, on company profit. Given these circumstances, what would be the best approach for the UAW when negotiating at other GM plants?

a. Press for a Saturn-type agreement at all GM plants.

b. Negotiate a more traditional contract at other GM plants, and wait for the Saturn agreement to prove its viability.

c. Ignore Saturn; it's an experiment that doesn't relate to GM's other plants, mainly because no other plant incorporates the state-of-the-art design and manufacturing processes found at Saturn.

2. A few of the decisions made by Saturn committees have turned out to be bad ones. Management says that poorly trained union representatives serving on those committees are to blame. Union employees, on the other hand, say that management team members agreed to proposals made by union members and that all committee decisions were reached by consensus. What should the UAW do?

a. Try to force changes in the consensus process so that union members can't be blamed for poor group decisions.

b. Press for better business-management education for all team members so that they will be better able to understand complex business problems.

c. Gain greater union representation on all committees. This approach has been suggested by some UAW members who believe that the poor decisions were a result of the disproportionate influence of managers on the committees.

3. Relations between Saturn managers and the production-line employees have been so smooth that some employees are questioning the union's value. A group has asked for your help in planning a decertification vote. The request leaves you in an uncomfortable position. How should you respond?

a. You don't want the union to think you're undercutting its efforts, so you should tell the group to make plans without your support.

b. Explain that a decertification attempt might jeopardize the cooperative situation at Saturn. Suggest that the group approach union leaders to discuss these concerns, and offer to talk with the leaders yourself if the group cannot make contact on its own.

c. Tell the group that the union is committed to their success and that they should remain loyal to it.

4. Saturn's daily operations are smooth. However, you know that it's crucial to have a plan in place for emergency situations—fire, flooding, and so on. Which of the following would be the best approach to take?

a. During a crisis, fast, decisive action is absolutely necessary. Consequently, there simply isn't time to get employees or the union leadership involved. Management should have free rein to act according to their own instincts in the event of an emergency.

b. Although there isn't always time to get input from everyone, the union shouldn't be shut out completely. The best idea would be to involve both GM and UAW personnel in planning escape routes and other actions.

c. The union watches out for the safety of the employees during normal times, so it should have the responsibility to do so during a crisis as well. Let union leaders handle any problems that arise.[55]

agency shop (321)
arbitration (315)
authorization cards (311)
blacklist (315)
boycott (316)
business agent (311)
certification (311)
closed shop (320)
collective bargaining (313)
cooling-off period (316)
cost-of-living adjustment (COLA) (322)
craft unions (307)
decertification (312)

due process (325)
featherbedding (324)
givebacks (314)
grievances (325)
industrial unions (307)
injunction (319)
labor federation (310)
labor unions (306)
lifetime security (323)
locals (310)
lockouts (319)
mandatory subject (315)
mediation (315)
national union (310)

open shop (321)
pattern bargaining (321)
permissive subject (314)
picketing (316)
ratification (315)
right-to-work laws (321)
shop steward (310)
slowdown (316)
strike (316)
strikebreakers (318)
two-tier wage plans (322)
union shop (320)
work rules (324)
yellow-dog contract (315)

REVIEW QUESTIONS

1. Why do employees choose to join labor unions? Why do they not join labor unions?
2. What factors have contributed to the current decline in union membership?
3. What are grievances, and how are they resolved?

4. How does a closed shop differ from a union shop, an agency shop, and an open shop?
5. What employee compensation issues can be addressed by a union contract?
6. How do employee-involvement programs work, and what potential problems do they bring up?

7. How do arbitration and mediation differ?
8. What is a cooling-off period, and what does it accomplish?

A CASE FOR CRITICAL THINKING

A NIGHTMARE AT NORDSTROM

For more than 60 years, United Food and Commercial Workers Local 1001 represented employees at Nordstrom's Seattle-area department stores. Although the classy national chain was staffed by some 30,000 employees, fewer than 2,000 salespeople were union members. Only stores in Seattle and Tacoma were unionized, which didn't create any major problems—until the summer of 1989.

During contract negotiations, management proposed optional

union membership in response to employee complaints about mandatory union dues. When Seattle Local 1001 put the proposal to a vote, the 250 or so members who showed up voted overwhelmingly to reject the idea. Nevertheless, Nordstrom stood its ground, causing negotiations to break down.

Joe Peterson, head of the local, was convinced that management wanted to throw out the union. So he put up the fight of his life, stirring dissension in Washington as well as in nonunionized stores as far away

as southern California and Virginia. It didn't take long for Peterson to show that a local union leader can play tough against a major corporation. "The company vastly underestimated our resolve to protect not only this contract but the other retail contracts" in the area, Peterson insisted.

In a surprise move, the union decided not to strike but to fight with negative publicity. The union set up a toll-free telephone number for employee complaints. The common gripe was about being pressured to work "off the clock" when attending store meetings, writing thank-you notes to customers, and delivering merchandise to customers. A union inquiry uncovered 825 current and former salespeople who claimed the company owed them millions of dollars in back wages. Peterson informed the press, which started covering the story.

The state of Washington's Department of Labor and Industries (DLI) investigated and ordered Nordstrom to change its practices and pay back wages. Joe Demarte, Nordstrom's vice president of personnel, claimed the union used its inquiry as a publicity stunt: "For the DLI, it was a routine audit and a routine report, but the union had the press there."

Anti-union salespeople at Nordstrom were upset by the union's actions, and they began organizing to decertify the union. "All the salespeople here operate as entrepreneurs," said John Rockwood, a shoe salesman in one of the Seattle stores. As for the DLI's report, he said: "It's petty little timekeeping stuff. We make twice as much money as anybody else in the industry. We just haven't kept meticulous records as to the time we have actually spent working for the company."

To resolve the off-the-clock issue, Nordstrom mailed a settlement form to current sales employees so that they could enter detailed information about the amount of time they worked. In all, the company paid out just under $3 million in claims. The union, however, calculated that Nordstrom owed employees as much as $300 million in back pay, and filed a lawsuit in state court in February 1990. Nordstrom settled the lawsuit in 1993 by agreeing to back pay estimated at $15 million.

The union also charged Nordstrom with drumming up anti-union sentiment and aiding the anti-union forces. In August 1990, Nordstrom agreed to settle with the NLRB all charges of unfair labor practices. Yet its battle with the union raged on. More charges were filed, but the NLRB cleared Nordstrom of allegations of unfair labor practices. By early 1991, a group of Nordstrom employees had collected enough signatures to petition for an election to decertify the union as bargaining agent for the Seattle-area employees. When the election was held, the majority of employees voted for decertification.

Nordstrom saw the victory as confirmation that its employees no longer wanted union representation. After all, union members received the same wages and benefits as the store's nonunion salespeople elsewhere. The following year, Local 367 withdrew its representation of employees at the Tacoma store, the last organized store, rather than face a decertification vote.

1. When negotiations between Nordstrom's management and union leaders broke down over the optional union-membership issue, why do you think the union chose to fight back with negative publicity instead of with a strike?
2. What could the union have done to make membership more attractive to the employees in Nordstrom's Seattle and Tacoma stores?
3. What effect might union decertification in Seattle-area stores have on Nordstrom and its employees?

Choose one or two articles from *The Wall Street Journal* illustrating one of the following aspects of labor-management relations:

• Union organizing
• Collective-bargaining negotiations
• Strikebreakers or lockouts
• Employee layoffs and plant closings
• Union givebacks and concessions
• Government-mandated labor practices

1. What are the major issues described in the article?

2. From the information presented in the article, what seem to be the major sources of disagreement between management and labor, the major reasons behind a drive to unionize, or the major issues surrounding the government-mandated labor practices?

3. Are the issues or problems still unresolved, or has some kind of agreement or solution been reached? If so, what are the terms of the agreement? What did each side gain? What did each side concede? If you were a member of the union involved, what would be your reaction to this agreement?

People Are the Same Everywhere, Aren't They?

Companies that expand across national or cultural borders sometimes run into barriers they don't expect in human resources management. For example, Japanese automakers were surprised when they tried to get workers in their new U.S. plants to join in for daily warm-up exercises. Even though the activity is commonplace in Japan, it simply didn't catch on in the United States.

When companies operate across national and cultural borders, understanding cultural expectations and norms is crucial to effective management. Some of the concepts to consider involve personal space, conversational formalities (or lack thereof), friendliness, willingness to "job hop," respect for authority figures, and awareness of social class distinctions.

You can identify a number of potentially important workplace issues by exploring a country's general culture. Egyptians, for instance, address each other by first names only in informal, private settings. When in public, however, even good friends may add titles when addressing each other. Egyptians tend to be more conscious of social classes than are people in the United States. Also, they place great value on visiting friends and relatives.[56]

Assume that you're the president of a financial-services firm based in Indianapolis and that you're ready to expand overseas. To ease your first attempt at international expansion, you're trying to find a country with workplace characteristics most similar to those in the United States. Gather as much relevant information as you can about the following four countries, choose the one with work styles that feel most like those of the United States, and explain your choice. (Your instructor may want you to do this as a group exercise):

• England
• France
• South Korea
• Mexico

LABOR DAY: LABOR AND MANAGEMENT TRY NEW ROLES AS COLLABORATORS

Synopsis

This video presents an unusual collaboration between management and organized labor—on a picket line. In this particular case, managers of several unionized grocery stores and the grocery workers' union are teaming up against a number of nonunion stores in the area. The nonunion stores are a threat to the union stores because their prices are lower, a situation made possible by lower, nonunionized wages. The union is concerned that if the nonunion stores run the union stores out of business, union workers will lose jobs. On the other hand, the nonunion stores view the union-management collaboration as unfair and possibly illegal. In addition to this particular struggle, the video also highlights a new attitude found among many unions these days, an attitude of working with, rather than against, management.

Exercises

ANALYSIS

1. How are consumers likely to react to pleas such as the one made by the union-management coalition?
2. What effect has unionization had on this community overall?
3. Why don't the managers of the union stores simply kick the union out and replace them with cheaper, nonunion labor?
4. Why did the union decide to work with management?
5. Should the grocery workers' union apply this model nationwide (i.e., should every local join forces with store managers to drive out nonunion stores)?

APPLICATION

Try to find any two groups that could benefit from the sort of cooperation demonstrated by the union grocery stores and the grocery union. Describe their current relationship, what they could do to cooperate, and the benefits each would get from such cooperation.

DECISION

As a consumer, whose side would you take if one of the union members pictured in the video called and asked you to stop shopping at nonunion stores?

COMMUNICATION

Put yourself in the position of the head of the grocery union, and write a "telepicketing" message that union members could use to sway consumers. People don't want to spend

much time listening to a phone pitch; make sure the core of your message can be communicated in a minute or less.

INTEGRATION

What if the union-management boycott campaign doesn't work, and the Piggly Wiggly stores in the video stay in business? Referring to the description of competition in Chapter 1, outline ways that the union stores can compete with the nonunion stores. Keep in mind that the union stores' prices will be higher because of the union wages.

ETHICS

Assume that the union-management campaign works, and Piggly Wiggly and the other nonunion stores go out

of business. What if the managers of remaining (union) stores decide to stop cooperating with the union once their common enemy (the nonunion stores) is out of the picture? Would such a shift on management's part be ethical?

DEBATE

The video raised, but didn't resolve, a key ethical issue: Is it fair for union stores to join together with unions in an effort to drive nonunion stores out of business? After all, it is perfectly legal to own and manage a nonunion store. Option A: In a formal debate format, support or reject the fairness of picketing against the nonunion stores.
Option B: Take either position and state your case in a brief report.

TEAMWORK

The union movement tends to provoke strong emotional reactions from some people. In a team of four or five students, conduct an informal survey of friends, relatives, and other people that you can reach conveniently. The entire team should first develop a brief questionnaire that will uncover feelings toward unions and then split up the task of polling people.

RESEARCH

Do the research necessary to write a one-paragraph update on either (a) the status of the class-action lawsuit discussed in the video or (b) trends in union membership in the service sector of the U.S. economy.

ROLE PLAYING

One student plays the role of the union members in the video who were telephoning local residents, asking them to avoid shopping at the nonunion stores. Another student plays a resident who is sympathetic to the union's cause, and a third plays a resident who happens to have just lost his or her job at a nonunion store that recently closed because of the boycott.

PART FOUR

MARKETING

Chapter

12

Marketing and Consumer Behavior

LEARNING OBJECTIVES
After studying this chapter
you will be able to

1 Explain what marketing is

2 Describe the four forms of utility created by marketing

3 Explain the importance of quality and customer service in competitive marketing

4 Outline the three steps in the strategic planning process

5 Define market segmentation and list the methods most often used to segment markets

6 Specify the four basic components of the marketing mix

7 Describe the five steps in the buyer's decision process

8 List the four steps in the marketing research process

Running a Race That Never Ends

Manufacturers of athletic shoes are running their own race, a race that never seems to end. Nike, however, was named after the Greek goddess of victory for a good reason, and the company has no intention of letting the competition run away. Started by former collegiate sprinter Philip Knight and his University of Oregon coach, Bill Bowerman, Nike stressed technology and high-performance products from the very beginning. An experiment with urethane rubber and a waffle iron got it all started, and serious runners loved the new waffle-soled shoes. By 1981 Knight and his company had about half of the U.S. athletic-shoe market, outpacing established overseas competitors such as Adidas and Puma.

In the 1980s, Nike offered over 140 models of shoes. As the running boom of the 1970s faded, Knight knew he had to look beyond high-performance running shoes to expand the company's sales. He identified other segments in the sports market, including basketball and tennis players, and with products designed specifically for these athletes, Nike continued to prosper.

The 1980s brought a new twist to the market, however. Serious athletes weren't the only people interested in athletic shoes. Capitalizing on the aerobic-exercise boom, younger rival Reebok boldly poured on the speed, taking the lead by 1986 on the strength of its innovative aerobics shoes. Two years later, Reebok's share of the market was 27 percent, and Nike's share had tumbled from around 50 percent to 23 percent. Then the aerobics fad was followed by another important change in the U.S. shoe market. Athletic shoes became fashionable footwear. People who had no intention of being serious athletes, or even serious exercisers, adopted athletic shoes as their favorite footwear. Again Reebok was ahead of Nike in responding to this shift. First, actress Cybill Shepherd arrived at the Emmy Awards ceremony wearing an elegant evening gown and blazing orange Reeboks. Then, on a poster for his hit movie *Back to the Future,* Michael J. Fox dashed through time wearing Reeboks. What started as a product for dedicated runners had turned into a product for dedicated followers of fashion.

Runners are one of Nike's key target markets.

Despite impressive technology, its own series of celebrity endorsements, and award-winning advertising, Nike lost its footing in the late 1980s, and Reebok streaked ahead. By 1988 Reebok was selling 75 million pairs of shoes annually, compared with Nike's 50 million. However, the scrappy Knight fought back with new products and an emphasis on style and fashion. Nike regained the lead and has held it by a slim margin into the mid-1990s.

The race continues. If you were Phil Knight, what would you do to keep Nike on top while defending against competitors? How would you help Nike meet the ever-changing demands of consumer tastes and advances in shoe technology? How would you define your market and identify areas of potential growth? What message would you want to communicate to your audience, and how would you get that message across?[1]

MARKETING FUNDAMENTALS

Nike's Phillip Knight knows how important marketing is. By this point in your life, you already know quite a bit about marketing. People have been trying to sell you things for years, and you've learned something about their techniques—advertisements, price markdowns, special contests, tantalizing displays of merchandise. Despite marketing's high visibility, the term is difficult to define. The American Marketing Association (AMA) recently evaluated 25 definitions before agreeing on the meaning of the word. According to AMA's definition, **marketing** is planning and executing the conception, pricing, promotion, and distribution of ideas, goods, and services to create exchanges that satisfy individual and organizational objectives.[2]

As this definition implies, marketing encompasses a wide range of activities. If you set out to handle all of a firm's marketing functions, you would be very busy indeed. In fact, in most large organizations, each division has its own marketing department, staffed by a legion of specialists. Some of them conduct research to determine what consumers want to buy; some use that research to design new products and services; others make decisions on how to price the firm's offerings; still others handle the transportation, storage, and distribution of the goods; and, finally, some are responsible for advertising, sales promotion, publicity, and personal selling. Marketing is involved in all decisions related to determining a product's characteristics, price, production quantities, market-entry date, sales, and customer service.

Although we generally think of marketing in connection with selling tangible products for a profit, the AMA definition applies to services and ideas as well. Social activists, religious leaders, politicians, universities, and charities of all types rely on the principles of marketing to "sell" themselves and their causes to the public. **Place marketing** describes efforts to market geographic areas ranging from neighborhoods to entire countries. **Idea marketing** involves concepts that provide intellectual or spiritual benefits to the customer. The term *product* is used in this text to refer to any "bundle of value" that can be exchanged in a marketing transaction.

marketing *Process of planning and executing the conception, pricing, promotion, and distribution of ideas, goods, and services to create exchanges that satisfy individual and organizational objectives*

place marketing *Efforts to market neighborhoods, cities, states, regions, and even entire countries*

idea marketing *Marketing of concepts that provide intellectual or spiritual benefits*

You might not think of it as marketing, but promoting yourself in a job interview is one of the most common marketing activities in business today.

The Role of Marketing in Society

Take another look at the AMA definition of marketing. Notice that it involves an exchange between two parties—the buyer and the selling organization—both of whom obtain satisfaction from the transaction. This definition suggests that marketing plays an important role in society by helping people satisfy their needs and wants and by helping organizations determine what to produce.

Needs and Wants

A **need** represents a difference between your actual state and your ideal state. You're hungry, and you don't want to be hungry; you need to eat. These needs create the motivation to buy products and are therefore at the core of any discussion of marketing.

Your **wants** are based on your needs, but they are more specific. Producers do not create needs, but they do shape your wants by exposing you to alternatives. For instance, when you need some food, you may want a Snickers bar or an orange. A fundamental goal of marketing is to direct the customer's basic need for various products into the desire to purchase specific brands.

need Difference between a person's actual state and his or her ideal state; provides the basic motivation to make a purchase

wants Things that are desirable in light of a person's experiences, culture, and personality

Exchanges and Transactions

When you participate in the **exchange process,** you trade something of value (usually money) for something else of value, whether you're buying dinner, a car, or a college education. When you make a purchase, you cast your vote for that item and encourage the producer of that item to make more of it. In this way, supply and demand are balanced, and society obtains the goods and services that are most satisfying.

exchange process Act of obtaining a desired object from another party by offering something in return

transaction *Exchange between parties*

When the exchange actually occurs, it takes the form of a **transaction.** Party A gives party B $1.29 and gets a medium Coke in return. A trade of values takes place. Most transactions in an advanced society involve money, but money is not necessarily required. When you were a child, perhaps you traded your peanut butter sandwich for bologna and cheese in a barter transaction.

The Four Utilities

utility *Power of a good or service to satisfy a human need*

To encourage the exchange process, marketers enhance the appeal of their products and services by adding four types of **utility,** or value to the customer (see Exhibit 12.1). **Form utility** refers to the characteristics of the product—its shape, size, color, function, and style.

form utility *Consumer value created when a product's characteristics are made more satisfying*

The producers of Softsoap, for example, enhanced the appeal of hand soap by producing it in liquid form and dispensing it through a pump, making it more pleasant to use and thereby increasing its form utility. In other cases, marketers try to make their products available when and where customers want to buy them, creating **time utility** and **place utility.** The final form of utility is **possession utility**—the satisfaction that buyers get when they actually possess a product, both legally and physically.

time utility *Consumer value added by making a product available at a convenient time*

place utility *Consumer value added by making a product available in a convenient location*

The Evolution of Marketing

Marketing has changed dramatically since the turn of the century, when a firm could rely on a good, solid product to sell itself. Increasing competition, shifts in consumer attitudes, and the growth of mass media have all contributed to the evolution of marketing (see Exhibit 12.2).

possession utility *Consumer value created when someone takes ownership of a product*

The Production Era

Until the 1930s, many business executives viewed marketing simply as an offshoot of production. Product design was based more on the demands of mass-production techniques than on customer wants and needs. Manufacturers were generally able to sell all that they produced; they could comfortably limit their marketing efforts to taking orders and shipping goods. The production era had **sellers' markets** in many industries, meaning that demand for products exceeded

sellers' markets *Situations in which demand for products exceeds supply, which may tempt marketers to pay less attention to customer satisfaction*

Exhibit 12.1

Examples of the Four Utilities
The utility of a good or service has four aspects, each of which enhances the product's value to the consumer.

Types of utility	Example of utility
Form utility	Sunkist Fun Fruits appeal to youngsters because of their imaginative shapes—numbers, dinosaurs, letters, spooks, animals. The bite-sized fruit snacks are both functionally and psychologically satisfying.
Time utility	LensCrafters has captured a big chunk of the market for eyeglasses by providing on-the-spot, one-hour service.
Place utility	By offering home delivery, Domino's has achieved a major position in the pizza market and prompted competitors to follow suit.
Possession utility	TEST, Inc., a manufacturer of materials-testing equipment for the aerospace industry, allows customers to try its $100,000 machine free of charge on a 90-day trial basis.

Production Era	Sales Era	Marketing Era
		Research customer needs
		Employ the marketing concept
	Advertise	Advertise
	Develop sales force	Develop sales force
Take orders	Take orders	Take orders
Deliver goods/perform services	Deliver goods/perform services	Deliver goods/perform services

Industrial Revolution	1930s	World War II	Today

supply. Henry Ford, for example, focused on ways to produce automobiles more quickly and inexpensively, confident that people would buy them. When customers asked for a choice of color, Ford reportedly replied: "They can have any color they want, as long as it's black." Ford wasn't necessarily ignoring customer demands; he simply knew that a single color made car production much more efficient.

The Sales Era

As production capacity increased in the late 1920s, the markets for manufactured goods became more competitive. Business leaders, realizing that they would have to persuade people to buy all the goods they could make, expanded their marketing activities. To stimulate demand for their products, they spent more on advertising. They also began to develop trained sales forces that could seek out and sell to the thousands of potential customers across the country.

In spite of their increasing marketing sophistication, most companies were still overlooking the needs of the marketplace during this era. Instead of asking what the consumer wanted, they were producing what the company could make and getting their sales force to create demand. They were thinking primarily in terms of the company and its abilities rather than in terms of the consumer's needs.

The Marketing Era

The 1950s were the start of the marketing era, during which companies began to practice marketing in its current form. The development of efficient production techniques earlier in the century laid the groundwork for plentiful supplies of most products. This led to **buyers' markets** in many cases; that is, supply exceeded demand. The method of achieving business success shifted from pushing products on customers to finding out what buyers wanted and then filling that need.

The notion of marketing continued to evolve, and businesspeople started talking about the **marketing concept,** stressing customer needs and wants that lead to long-term profitability and the integration of marketing with other parts of the company (see Exhibit 12.3).[3] The marketing concept came into existence in the 1960s and continues to develop and expand, although its application is not universal. Many companies continue to operate in the sales era, and some even operate with production-era values.

Exhibit 12.2
The Evolution of Marketing
Marketing has changed dramatically, evolving from the old-fashioned concept of simply producing the merchandise and making it available for customers to today's highly competitive marketing strategies, which involve aggressively seeking market niches and consumer needs to fill.

buyers' markets *Situations in which supply exceeds demand and marketers need to pay close attention to customers' needs*

marketing concept *Approach to business management that stresses not only customer needs and wants but also long-term profitability and the integration of marketing with other functional units within the organization*

Exhibit 12.3

The Marketing Concept

The marketing concept integrates every part of the company while placing emphasis on customer satisfaction and long-term profitability.

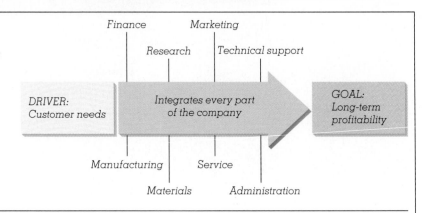

Finance   Marketing

Research   Technical support

DRIVER: Customer needs

Integrates every part of the company

GOAL: Long-term profitability

Manufacturing   Service

Materials   Administration

With the marketing concept, the emphasis on long-term profitability is key. If your only interest is making a fast buck, it doesn't make sense for you to invest in research laboratories, support personnel, service facilities, and the other elements often needed to satisfy customers. On the other hand, if you want to be financially healthy 5, 10, or 20 years from now, it is perfectly sensible to make these investments.

Competitive Marketing and Customer Satisfaction

In addition to paying more attention to customers, companies have also been giving more thought to the competition. Just as Nike must keep tabs on Reebok, companies can no longer succeed simply by satisfying customers if competitors are satisfying them just as well. What companies seek is a **competitive advantage,** something that sets them apart from their rivals and makes their product more appealing to customers.

A competitive advantage may be established in two ways: (1) by offering a lower price for a similar product or (2) by offering a product that does a better job of meeting customer needs.[4] With the first approach, success lies in driving down costs so that a company can create and deliver a product less expensively than its competitors can. Wal-Mart has become the nation's largest retailer by keeping its operating costs far below its major competitors', giving it the opportunity to beat them on price.[5]

The second approach is known as **product differentiation,** in which you find ways, other than price, to make your products stand out from the competition.[6] The goal is to satisfy customers in a way that your competitors can't. This approach involves paying close attention to quality and customer service.

As a consumer, you probably think that the need to focus on customer satisfaction is obvious: Doesn't every company want to satisfy its customers? However, achieving quality and good customer service is a lot easier said than done. What if the customers at your McDonald's franchise don't like to wait in line? You want to keep them happy, so you add more employees to take orders and cook food. The additional employees cost money, however. Now what do you do? Raise prices and risk losing business to your competitors? Keep your prices the same and accept lower profits—or in extreme

competitive advantage Quality that makes a product more desirable than similar products offered by the competition

product differentiation Features that distinguish one company's product from another company's similar product

cases, no profits at all? The challenge is to deliver quality products and great customer service at competitive prices, and it's not an easy challenge by any means.

What Do Quality and Customer Service Really Mean? The term **quality** can mean many different things, but from a marketing perspective, it is the degree to which a product meets customer expectations and specifications.[7] In other words, it's more than just reliability, appearance, or other individual factors. People want cars that won't break down, of course, but they always want cars that are safe, comfortable, and a pleasure to drive. Keep in mind that there is an appropriate level of quality, too; it's sometimes easy to go overboard. It would be impressive to build a car that lasts 100 years, but nobody expects that level of reliability—and nobody will pay for it, either.

Just as quality has a particular meaning in marketing today, so too does customer service. The customer-service department used to be little more than an office that handled customer complaints. Today's top companies realize that everybody should be involved in customer service, from the CEO to the cleaning staff. From this perspective, **customer service** encompasses everything a company does to satisfy its customers and to help them realize the greatest possible value from the goods and services they are purchasing.[8]

The Importance of Quality and Customer Service. Satisfying customers is hard work. Is it worth the trouble? Consider the advantages companies gain when they satisfy their customers:

- *Building customer loyalty.* When customers are satisfied with a particular supplier, they are far less likely to defect to other suppliers. Research in the auto industry showed that customers who liked the cars they own are much more likely to buy from that manufacturer again.[9] Efforts to establish long-term customer loyalty are called **relationship marketing.**
- *Differentiating your products.* In an increasing number of product categories, most businesses provide products that will satisfy the buyer's basic demands. For instance, you can choose from dozens of brands of personal computers, and most will get the job done for you. Given this *product parity,* how can a business stand out from the crowd? For many, the answer is superior customer service.
- *Decreasing marketing costs.* Customer service can dramatically lower your company's marketing costs, for two important reasons: Winning a new customer can cost up to five times as much as keeping an existing customer, and satisfied customers help sell products for you when they tell their family, friends, and colleagues about your company. Also, research suggests that dissatisfied customers may tell as many as 20 other people about their bad experiences.[10] You can see that not satisfying customers can put you at a huge disadvantage.
- *Increasing prices and profits.* Delivering better products and better customer service may cost you more initially, but the payoff is often quite positive. Firms perceived to offer superior customer service find they can charge as much as 10 percent more than their competitors, and these companies boast average profit margins that are 12 times higher. Similarly, companies whose product quality is

quality *Degree to which a product meets customer expectations and requirements*

customer service *Efforts a company makes to satisfy its customers and to help them realize the greatest possible value from the products they are purchasing*

relationship marketing *Focus on fostering long-term customer loyalty*

in the top one-third of their markets command prices 5 to 6 percent higher than companies in the bottom one-third.[11]

Intuit, the maker of such popular software products as the Quicken personal-finance package, has an interesting interpretation of customer satisfaction. The company doesn't consider customer satisfaction its ultimate goal, but rather sees it as the *minimum* it needs to do just to stay in business. Intuit tries to go beyond satisfying with what it calls "wowing" the customer, or creating "enthusiasm and delight."[12]

STRATEGIC MARKETING PLANNING

Successful marketing rarely happens without careful planning. *Strategic marketing planning* is a three-step process: examining your past performance, assessing new opportunities, and then developing a marketing strategy to exploit those opportunities (see Exhibit 12.4). The purpose of strategic marketing planning is to help you identify and create competitive advantage.[13] Most companies document the results of their planning efforts in a document called the *marketing plan*. Here's a closer look at the three stages.

Stage 1: Review Your Current Performance

Unless you're starting a new business, your company has a history of marketing performance. Maybe your sales have slowed down in the past year, maybe you've had to cut prices so much that you're barely breaking even, or maybe things are going quite well and you have lots of cash to spend on new marketing activities. Reviewing where you are and how you got there is a critical step in planning, because you can't fix problems or build on your strengths unless you know what they are.

The complexity of this step depends on the complexity of your business. A giant multinational firm such as Xerox or British Petroleum has to review the performance of dozens of product lines and geographic divisions. At the other extreme, small businesses may have just a handful of products to think about. The important point is to understand how well each product is doing in each market where you sell it.

Stage 2: Assess Your Opportunities

Once you've reviewed your progress thus far, the next question is where to go from here. Successful companies are always on the look-

Exhibit 12.4
The Strategic Marketing Planning Process
Strategic marketing planning involves the three steps of examining your performance, assessing new opportunities, and then developing a marketing strategy.

Stage 1
Examine past/current performance

Stage 2
Assess new opportunities

Stage 3
Develop a marketing strategy

out for new opportunities, which can be divided into four groups: (1) selling more of your existing products in current markets, (2) creating new products for your current markets, (3) selling your existing products in new markets, and (4) creating new products for new markets.[14] These four groups are listed in order of increasing risk; trying new products in unfamiliar markets usually is the riskiest choice of all.

Choosing an opportunity involves three steps: analyzing the external environment to uncover both constraints and possible opportunities, assessing your capabilities and limitations, and then setting your marketing objectives.

Analyzing the External Environment

Economic conditions, social trends, technology, competition, laws and regulations, and the natural environment all have a profound impact on a firm's marketing options. The external environment can create entirely new markets, destroy old markets, and generally present an endless parade of problems and opportunities for marketers.

Economic Forces. Marketers are keenly aware of the importance of such broad economic trends as gross domestic product, interest rates, inflation, unemployment, personal income, and savings rates. In tough times, consumers postpone the purchase of expensive items like major appliances, automobiles, and homes. They cut back on travel, entertainment, and luxury goods. Conversely, when the economy is good, consumers open their pocketbooks and satisfy their pent-up demand for higher-priced goods and services. By being aware of these trends, marketers can adjust the firm's inventory levels and juggle their marketing activities to respond to the customer's buying mood.

Social Trends. Planners also study the social and cultural environment to determine shifts in consumer values. If social trends are running against a product, the producer might need to increase its advertising budget to educate consumers about the product's benefits. Alternatively, it might modify the product to respond to changing tastes. Economic forces can affect social trends as well. During recessions some people might view flashy cars and expensive clothes as irresponsible wastes of money, making these products less attractive to the consumer market overall.

Technology. Technology is a double-edged sword, providing both risks and opportunities. When semiconductor technology made the personal computer possible, thousands of companies popped up out of nowhere to provide software, services, supplies, and accessories. On the other hand, the market for typewriters, mechanical-drafting equipment, and a host of other mature products is shrinking as a result of the computer's advances. When technology changes, marketing approaches must often be revised to cope with new competitors, new market segments, and new product features.

Competition. Knowing the competition is an essential ingredient in any marketing plan. If you own a Burger King franchise, your success obviously depends on what McDonald's and Wendy's do. To some extent, you are at the mercy of Taco Bell, Kentucky Fried Chicken, and Pizza Hut as well. On any given day, your customers might de-

As these signs in Chinatown (Los Angeles) attest, competition in many consumer markets is intense.

cide to satisfy their hunger in any number of ways—they might even fix themselves a sandwich. A successful marketing plan identifies sources of competitive advantage you might have and builds a marketing program around them.

Laws and Regulations. Like every other function in business today, marketing is controlled by laws at the local, state, national, and international levels. From product design to pricing to advertising, virtually every task you'll encounter in marketing is affected in some way by laws and regulations. The range and diversity of marketing law make it a career specialty all on its own, but here are several points you should know:

- *Regulations can alter or even destroy entire industries, but they can also create tremendous opportunities.* For example, the Nutrition Education and Labeling Act of 1990 (which actually didn't take full effect until 1994) forced food marketers to include standardized nutrition labels on their products. This requirement cost the manufacturers millions of dollars but was a bonanza for the laboratories that conduct food testing. One lab president even jokingly referred to the law as the "National Laboratories Employment Act."[15]

- *Regulations can be an expensive burden to business, but they can also provide welcome relief.* Small companies in particular can be hit hard by the complexity and cost of following regulations. On the other hand, regulations can protect honest marketers from unscrupulous competitors. When the Chinese government imposed rules on medical advertising for accuracy and scientific supportability, advertising executive Kenny Ho explained that his clients welcomed the changes.[16]

- *Regulations can vary widely from one country to the next.* A great example is advertising that openly compares one product with its competitors' products. The U.S. government encourages this sort of advertising, but some other countries prohibit it entirely.

Natural Environment. Changes in the natural environment can affect marketers, both positively and negatively. Interruptions in the supply of raw materials can upset even the most carefully conceived marketing plans. Floods, droughts, and cold weather can affect the price and availability of many products as well as the behavior of target customers. When an unusually stormy summer hit the Pacific Northwest in 1993, many businesses that cater to outdoor activities watched sales drop sharply. George McConnell of McConnell's Boat House in Mukilteo, Washington, says that even wind affects his boating and fishing equipment business. When the wind blows boats away from people's favorite fishing spots, they give up and go home.[17]

Recognizing Your Capabilities and Limitations

In addition to surveying external factors to find opportunities and potential pitfalls, marketers must look within their own companies to determine their strengths and weaknesses. Various marketing strategies require differing financial resources, production capabilities, distribution networks, and promotion capabilities.

The manufacturer with the lowest production costs is in a better position to compete on the basis of price than a competitor with high production costs, whereas a company with wide distribution has a natural advantage in promoting products through mass advertising. Southwest Airlines boasts lower operating costs than rivals such as American and United, and it uses that advantage to offer lower prices on its flights.[18]

Setting Objectives

When you have an opportunity in mind, you're ready to set your marketing objectives. Good objectives are specific and measurable. Establishing a goal to "increase sales in the future" is not a good objective; it doesn't say by how much or by what date. On the other hand, a goal to "increase sales 25 percent by the end of next year" provides a clear target and a reference against which progress can be measured. Objectives should also be challenging enough to be motivating. As Mitchell Leibovitz of the Pep Boys auto-parts chain says: "If you want to have ho-hum performance, have ho-hum goals."[19] A common marketing objective is to achieve a certain level of **market share,** which is a firm's portion of the total sales in a market.

market share Measure of a firm's portion of the total sales in a market

Stage 3: Develop the Marketing Strategy

With an objective as your guide, you're ready to define a **marketing strategy,** which consists of three elements: a choice of *target markets,* the p*osition* you'd like to achieve in those markets, and a *marketing mix* to help you get there. The following sections give you a closer look at each of the three parts.

marketing strategy Overall plan for marketing a product

Target Markets

Who should your customers be? It might sound like an obvious question, but it is sometimes one of the toughest questions a business faces, primarily because most businesses can identify more opportunity than they have the resources to pursue. Should you try to sell to everybody who's a potential consumer or just to one subgroup? All the consumers or businesses who might be interested in a product—and have the ability to pay for it—make up the **market** for that product. The **consumer market** consists of individuals or households that purchase goods and services for personal use. The **organizational market** is made up of three main subgroups: the industrial/commercial market (companies that buy goods and services to produce their own goods and services), the reseller market (wholesalers and retailers), and the government market (federal, state, and local agencies).[20]

market People who need or want a product and who have the money to buy it

consumer market Individuals who buy goods or services for personal use

organizational market Customers who buy goods or services for resale or for use in conducting their own operations

Understanding Market Segmentation. Since a market contains all the customers who might be interested in a certain type of product, does that mean you should try to sell the same product to every one of those potential buyers? It depends on the nature of the market and the customers. Think about jeans, for instance. Consumers of all ages are interested in jeans, but they aren't all interested in the same kinds of jeans. A parent buying jeans for a four-year-old daughter, a teenager, and a retiree who buys jeans for gardening will have different purchase criteria, including fit, color, brand name, durability, and comfort. You won't have much success if you try to sell the same product to these three people.

In contrast, if your product is gasoline, the parent, the teenager buying jeans for school, and the retiree will have very similar purchase criteria (level of service at the gas station might be the only significant difference). Because your customers want the same basic features and benefits from your product, you can be successful selling the same product to all three groups. In fact, just think how silly it would be to see a brand of gasoline aimed specifically at parents or at teenagers.

market segmentation *Division of a market into subgroups of buyers that are likely to respond in consistent ways*

The fact that different groups of buyers often want different types of products leads to the idea of **market segmentation.** This is the process of dividing a market into smaller subsets of consumers or organizations with similar characteristics, behavior, and needs. Each of these **market segments** can then be targeted using a particular combination of products, advertising, and other marketing efforts. The most important issue in segmentation is *buyer response.* The parent and the teenager will respond differently to your marketing efforts. If you know how each group is likely to respond, you can design marketing programs that maximize sales to both groups.

market segments *Groups of individuals or organizations within a market that share certain common characteristics*

Identifying Market Segments. It is obvious that you need to segment the jeans market but not the gasoline market, but the decision is not always so clear. Computer makers struggle with these questions all the time: Do home buyers and business buyers want different kinds of machines? What do "power users" want that beginners might not want? Are there "economy" and "luxury" segments? Here are the major factors marketers can use to identify market segments (see Exhibit 12.5):

demographics *Study of the statistical characteristics of a population*

- *Demographics.* Age is one of the issues in the area of **demographics,** the statistical analysis of population. Demographic segmentation uses objective, external factors, including gender, income, composition of household, occupation, education, and ethnic background, in addition to age. Kodak's "life stages" strategy uses age to divide the photography market into the youth, new-parent, and senior segments.[21] Many consumer marketers are pondering the issue of ethnic segments, as they try to find the right mix of products and promotions for African Americans, Asian Americans, Hispanic Americans, and other groups. Budgets for ads aimed at specific ethnic groups are expected to reach $900 million by the turn of the century.[22]

Exhibit 12.5
Common Bases for Segmenting Markets

Category	Segmentation variable	
Demographic	Age Sex Buying power Occupation	Education Race and nationality Family life cycle
Geographic	Global regions Nations National regions States Counties Cities Neighborhoods	Climate Terrain Population density Market density
Psychographic	Social class Personality Lifestyle	
Behavioral	Amount of usage Type of usage Brand loyalty Benefits sought	

Exhibit 12.5
Common Bases for Segmenting Markets
The purpose of segmenting a market is to identify a group of customers who are likely to value the same things in a particular product or service. (Note: Geo-demographic segmentation combines demographic and geographic data.)

- *Geography.* When differences in buying behavior are influenced by where people live, it makes sense to use **geographic segmentation** (see Exhibit 12.6). More snow shovels are bought in Detroit than in Miami, and more surfboards in Honolulu than in Manhattan. Campbell Soup manufactures two types of nacho cheese sauce—a spicy one for customers in the Southwest and West and

geographic segmentation *Categorization of customers according to their geographic location*

Merchandise purchased	Best market	Worst market
Beer and ale (percentage of drinkers who consume)	Milwaukee (67.9)	Dallas/Fort Worth (44.2)
Canned chili (percentage of homemakers who use)	Dallas/Fort Worth (72.7)	Boston (6.0)
Insecticides (percentage of homemakers who use at least once a month)	Houston (61.9)	New York (26.4)
Life insurance (percentage of adults who currently have)	Pittsburgh (80.3)	Miami (53.4)
Lipstick (percentage of women using at least twice a day)	Seattle/Tacoma (58.2)	Cincinnati (35.6)
Panty hose (percentage of women who bought in past month)	Houston (61.1)	Miami (39.7)
Popcorn (percentage of adults who buy for home use)	Minneapolis/St. Paul (54.3)	Miami (26.5)
Scotch whiskey (percentage of drinkers who consume)	New York (35.9)	Cincinnati (9.6)

Exhibit 12.6
Geographic Markets for Selected Products
Regional differences in tastes and needs provide a useful basis for segmenting the market for many products.

a mild one for everyone else.[23] For metropolitan areas, in which city and county boundaries aren't always meaningful for segmentation purposes, marketers can use a system created by the U.S. government that characterizes urban areas according to where people live and work (as opposed to where the official boundaries are). The government's definition of the Seattle, Washington, metropolitan area, for instance, covers not only the city of Seattle but also numerous smaller towns and cities in a two-county region.[24]

psychographics Classification of customers on the basis of their psychological makeup

- *Psychographics.* Whereas demographic segmentation is the study of people from the outside, **psychographics** is the analysis of people from the inside, focusing on consumers' psychological makeup, including social roles, activities, attitudes, interests, opinions, and lifestyle. Psychographic analysis focuses on why people behave the way they do by examining such issues as brand preferences, radio and TV preferences, reading habits, values, and self-concept. Whereas demographics can define such segments as "18- to 34-year-old women," psychographics lead to segments with names like "adventurers" or "self-actualizers." A common psychographic model used to segment consumer markets is called Values and Life-Styles (VALS). The latest version, VALS 2, combines the psychographic dimension of self-orientation (how one views oneself in relation to the world in general) with the demographic issue of resources (one's income, employment, education, and so on).[25]

geodemographics Method of combining geographic data with demographic data to develop profiles of neighborhood segments

- *Geodemographics.* Think about your neighborhood: Does it have a distinct character, with people of fairly similar income levels, lifestyles, and other characteristics? In most cases, the answer is yes. Segmenting the country by neighborhoods is the goal of **geodemographics,** combining geographic data with demographic data. The pioneering geodemographic system, developed by Claritas Corporation, divides the United States into 40 neighborhood types, with such labels as "Blue Blood Estates" and "Old Yankee Rows." This system uses postal zip codes for the geographic segmentation part, making it easy to reach individual neighborhoods with specialized marketing programs.[26] The U.S. zip code system is sometimes too coarse for accurate neighborhood segmentation, but marketers in England can identify geodemographic segments as small as 15 households.[27]

behavioral segmentation Categorization of customers according to their relationship with products or response to product characteristics

- *Behavior.* Another way to segment a market is to classify customers on the basis of their knowledge of, attitude toward, use of, or response to products or product characteristics. This approach is known as **behavioral segmentation.** Imagine that you are in the hotel business. You might classify potential customers according to when and why they stay in hotels, making a distinction between business travelers and vacationers. You could then tailor your services and promotion for one group or the other. The business traveler might be attracted by ads in *The Wall Street Journal,* and the tourist might respond to ads in *Condé Nast Traveler* magazine.

Companies that market to organizational customers use a slightly different set of segmentation variables. The equivalent set of demographic variables, for instance, includes number of employees, sales volume, and type of product manufactured. Psychographics doesn't play a significant role in organizational marketing, but *operational* variables, such as the type of manufacturing process in use, can be very useful.

Choosing Your Market Segments. After you've identified the various segments in a market, the next step is to decide which *target segments* or **target markets** you'll focus on. The criteria include such factors as the size of the segment, the strength of the competition already in the segment, the risks of new competitors or restrictive government regulations, and the amount of time and money needed to reach potential buyers. Depending on the results of your segmentation search, you have a variety of target-marketing alternatives, which fall into four basic categories (see Exhibit 12.7):

target markets *Specific groups of customers to whom a company wants to sell a particular product*

- *Undifferentiated marketing.* **Undifferentiated marketing** (commonly known as mass marketing) does not subdivide the market at all. Rather, it concludes that all the buyers have similar needs and can be served with the same standardized product. The biggest advantage is minimizing production and marketing costs, since you can market the same product to everyone using the same promotional programs.

undifferentiated marketing *Marketing program that offers a single standard product to all consumers; commonly known as mass marketing*

- *Concentrated marketing.* With a **concentrated marketing** approach, you acknowledge that different segments exist in a market and choose to aim at just one of them. Gymboree has built a multi-million-dollar retail chain by targeting only the toddler segment of the clothing market.[28] The biggest advantage of concentrated marketing is that it allows you to focus all your time and resources on a single type of customer, so you can potentially do a better job of attracting customers. The strategy can be risky, however, since you've staked your company's future on just one segment.

concentrated marketing *Marketing program aimed at a single market segment*

- *Differentiated marketing.* You can minimize the risk of concentrated marketing by using the **differentiated marketing** approach, in which you select several target customer groups (perhaps even covering the entire market) and develop marketing programs for each one. This is the approach Nike takes when it designs shoes for basketball, running, aerobics, and other segments. Differentiated mar-

differentiated marketing *Marketing program aimed at several market segments, each of which receives a unique marketing mix*

Exhibit 12.7
Comparison of the Four Basic Segmentation Strategies
Various types of products and markets lend themselves to different segmentation strategies.

Target customer	Marketing approach	Advantage	Disadvantage
Undifferentiated (entire market)	Sell single product to everyone, using same pricing, promotion, and distribution	Minimizes costs	Makes company vulnerable to competitors who focus on specific niches
Concentrated (one homogeneous group)	Tailor marketing mix to needs of specific group	Gives company competitive advantage in serving target segment; is relatively economical	Limits growth potential; makes company vulnerable to shifting tastes of segment and competitive attack
Differentiated (several distinct customer groups)	Create separate mix of product, price, distribution, and promotion to serve each of the distinct customer groups	Enables company to achieve competitive advantage in several segments in order to maximize its market share	Increases production and marketing costs
Customized (individual buyer)	Tailor elements of marketing mix to needs of each individual buyer	Enables company to satisfy each customer's needs	Increases production and marketing costs

CAN UNIVERSAL APPEAL OVERCOME CULTURAL DIFFERENCES?

You've got a great product that's been selling like hotcakes in the United States. Now you want to market it in other countries. How do you go about it? Do you go into each country and conduct extensive market research so that you can adapt—or even create—the product, the packaging, and the promotion specifically for that culture? Do you keep everything essentially the same for all countries, changing only the language on the package and in the advertising? In other words, do you go local or do you go global?

According to Harvard marketing professor Theodore Levitt, global is the only way to go. He argues that, thanks to telecommunications and cheap, easy travel, consumers the world over are becoming more and more alike. People everywhere share certain needs and desires, which allows marketers to sell standardized products at low prices the same way around the world. He points to Coca-Cola as the perfect example of a global product. In Levitt's view, adopting a global marketing perspective not only saves time and money in production and advertising outlays but also helps a company clarify its focus and objectives, making operations easier to manage and coordinate.

When Levitt's controversial ideas were first published in the early 1980s, many companies thought he made a lot of sense and jumped on the global bandwagon. However, many more were wary of the whole idea. They saw numerous barriers to worldwide product standardization, including problems in technology (disparate electrical systems), packaging (colors, for example, can have different meanings in different cultures), consumer habits (it's difficult to sell cereal to Brazilians, who tend not to eat breakfast), and even physical characteristics of consumers (Japanese, on average, have smaller frames than Western people, and some products are too big or heavy for them).

Of course, some products are certainly global. On the streets of any major city in the world, you'll be able to stop for a snack at McDonald's or Pizza Hut. You'll see people wearing Levi's jeans and driving Hondas and Volkswagens, shooting pictures with Canon cameras containing Kodak film, and then heading home to watch U.S. programming on their Sony TVs.

Many products can be standardized globally, but many need to reflect local conditions in terms of positioning and promotion. One marketing authority has summarized this approach as "thinking global, acting local." Thinking global refers to looking for something that people in many countries have in common and appealing to that common need with a universal product or service or one that is easily modified. Acting local means basing marketing strategies on knowledge of consumer behavior and desires in specific target areas.

---

keting is probably the most popular segmentation approach, particularly for consumer products. However, it requires substantial resources because you have to tailor products, prices, promotional efforts, and distribution arrangements for each segment.

- *Customized marketing.* Companies that use a **customized marketing** approach view each customer as a separate segment and customize marketing programs to that individual's specific requirements. This approach is necessary in certain types of industrial markets where the product cannot be standardized. Civil-engineering firms, for example, must design each bridge, road, or sewer system to meet the specific requirements of the customer. This approach is also used for many consumer services such as interior design and home repairs. Thanks to computer databases, more and more consumer marketers can identify the needs and purchase habits of individual consumers and create individualized products and promotions.

customized marketing Marketing program in which each individual customer is treated as a separate segment

Market Position
The second element of marketing strategy is the position a product holds or tries to hold in the minds of buyers and potential buyers. A

market **position** is how these people view a product in relation to their needs and the products offered by competitors. When someone mentions a product category that you're familiar with, say sports cars or hamburgers, you probably have a ranking in your mind. You might rank Wendy's as the best burger, followed by a local restaurant, then by McDonald's, and then by Burger King. If Wendy's holds the top position in your mind, you'll compare other burgers with Wendy's burgers when you make a purchase decision.

Now turn the situation around and assume you're a marketing manager at Burger King, and lots of consumers say you're the number 4 burger. Your goal is to be number 1; what should you do? The first step would be some marketing research to figure out why people rank you at number 4; then you would make the necessary changes. Maybe you need to change the product, increase your advertising, or put your restaurants in better locations. This process of achieving a desired position in the mind of the market is called **positioning.**

Most companies would like to be first in the minds of their target segments, but the simple fact is that most companies aren't first. So what should you do if you're not at the top? You have three choices. First, you can try to dislodge the leader in a direct competitive assault. Second, you can acknowledge that the leader already has that position and try to find a comfortable position lower down the chain. Price is a common way to do this, when companies present themselves as lower-cost alternatives to the leader. Third, you can try to change the way the market thinks about the product category. For example, mouthwashes have traditionally competed on the basis of effectiveness, but some brands have started to tout plaque-removal capabilities, which might make consumers change the way they think about mouthwashes.

It's important to define the position you want to occupy before proceeding with product development and other activities, because this positioning goal should drive all your activities. At the Inn at Spanish Bay, a resort in Pebble Beach, California, everything the company does aims to position it as a world-class facility. From the way the resort is designed to the way it advertises, everything supports this single positioning goal. Whether you're shooting for the top of the market or offering an economy product, consistency is critical. If customers aren't sure what you're trying to offer, the confusion will hurt your ability to reach your marketing objectives.

The Marketing Mix

The third and final part of marketing strategy is your **marketing mix,** which is a combination of four major ingredients: product, price, distribution, and promotion (see Exhibit 12.8). The marketing mix is often referred to as the **four Ps** (with "place" used to mean distribution). These are the elements from which you build marketing programs:

- *Product.* The product is whatever bundle of value you offer potential customers. It can be as simple and tangible as an ice cream cone or as complex and intangible as negotiating the purchase of an entire company. Today companies are realizing that customers

position Place a product holds in the mind of buyers, relative to their needs and the product's competitors

positioning Process of achieving a desired market position

marketing mix Blend of elements satisfying a chosen market

four Ps Marketing elements—product, price, distribution (place), and promotion

Exhibit 12.8

The Marketing Mix

The right decisions about product, price, distribution, and promotion yield the marketing mix that best meets the needs of the customers.

Decision area	Component	Definition
Product	The product	The set of tangible and intangible attributes of the good, service, person, or idea that is being exchanged
	Brand name	Portion of a brand (words, letters, or numbers) that may be expressed orally
	Packaging	The activities that involve designing and producing the container or wrapper for a product
	Services	Activities, benefits, or satisfactions that are offered for sale or are provided in connection with the sale of goods
	Warranty	A manufacturer's promise that the product is fit for the purpose intended
	Postexchange servicing	Activities, such as warranty services, that ensure customer satisfaction
Price	Pricing	Activities concerned with setting the price of a product
	Discount	A reduction from the asked price of a product
Distribution (place)	Channels of distribution	The route taken by a product as it moves from the producer to the final consumer
	Physical distribution	The physical movement of goods from the point of production to the point of consumption
Promotion	Advertising	Nonpersonal communication that is paid for by an identified marketer to promote a product or service
	Personal selling	Person-to-person communication between a marketer and members of the market.
	Public relations	Any communication created primarily to build prestige or goodwill for an individual or an organization
	Sales promotion	Promotional activities other than advertising, personal selling, and publicity that stimulate consumer purchases and dealer effectiveness

price *Amount of money asked in exchange for products; amount needed to cover the marketer's costs plus provide a profit*

expect more than just the basic product. Consultation, installation, training, and repair may all be parts of the bundle of value customers expect from you—and that you need to offer in order to be competitive.

- *Price.* Having made basic decisions about products, you need to decide how to price them. **Price** is the amount of money asked for products in a marketing exchange, and it needs to cover all the marketer's costs plus provide some level of profit. Sometimes low prices maximize profits, as the discussion of supply and demand in Chapter 1 demonstrated. On the other hand, the desirability of some products—like Nike shoes—depends on a high-quality image, which a high price helps confer.

- *Distribution.* The third element in the marketing mix is distribution, which encompasses the strategies and processes for getting products from the point of production to the point of purchase. Distribution decisions range from basic transportation and storage issues to the types of wholesalers and retailers that should be used.

- *Promotion.* Often the most important decision a company makes is how it should inform prospective customers about its products. The alternatives are many, and the choice may determine the success of a marketing effort. Some companies, such as Avon and Mary Kay Cosmetics, emphasize direct selling and spend most of their promotion dollars training and paying salespeople. Others, including the many producers of soap and headache remedies, promote their products through advertising, mainly on television. Department stores also spend heavily on advertising, but they choose local newspapers as the most effective medium.

BUYING BEHAVIOR

Organizations put a great deal of effort into analyzing their markets for one basic reason: They want to know why the customer selects one product and rejects another (or one store or restaurant, in the case of retailing). Armed with this information, companies can tailor their marketing efforts to appeal to the buyer's motives. The motives of individual consumers generally differ from those of organizational buyers.

Consumer Buying Behavior

In the study of **consumer buying behavior,** marketers attempt to explain what it is that induces individuals to buy products. One way to look at the psychology of buying is in terms of how consumers make decisions. A simple formula sums up the decision-making process that nearly everyone goes through when making a purchase:

Choice = want + ability to buy + attitude toward the brand

The following sections take a closer look at this process and at the factors that influence it.

consumer buying behavior *Behavior exhibited by consumers as they consider and purchase various products*

The Buyer's Decision Process

The consumer buying process begins when you become aware of a problem. Your next step is to look for a solution. Possibilities occur to you on the basis of your past experience (your prior use of certain products) and on your exposure to marketing messages. If none of the obvious solutions seems satisfying, you gather additional information. The more complex the problem, the more information you are likely to seek. You may turn to friends or relatives for advice, read articles in magazines, talk with salespeople, compare products and prices in stores, and study sales literature and advertisements.

After satisfying your information needs, you are ready to make a choice. You may select one of the alternatives, postpone the decision, or decide against making any purchase at all, depending on the magnitude of your desire, the outside pressure to buy, and your financial resources.

Once you have made your purchase decision, you will evaluate the wisdom of your choice. If the item you bought is satisfying, you will tend to buy the same thing again under similar circumstances, thus developing a loyalty to the brand. If not, you will probably not re-peat the purchase. Often, if the purchase was a major one, you will suffer from **cognitive dissonance,** commonly known as buyer's re-morse. You will think about all the alternatives you rejected and won-der whether one of them might have been a better choice. At this stage, you're likely to seek reassurance that you have done the right thing. Realizing this tendency, many marketers try to reinforce their sales with guarantees, phone calls to check on the customer's satis-faction, user hot lines, follow-up letters, and so on. When Infiniti (the luxury-car division of Nissan) tied for first place (with Lexus) in the J. D. Powers Car Customer Satisfaction Index Study, it sent a letter to owners announcing the fact, trying to reinforce the notion that they had made a smart choice.[29] Such efforts help pave the way for repeat business.

Factors That Influence Buyer Behavior

Throughout the buying process, various factors may influence the buyer. A person's culture, social class, reference groups, perceptions, attitudes, and self-image all have a bearing on the purchase decision, as do situational factors like the presentation of the product, the events in the buyer's life, and the person's mood at the time of the purchase.

Culture. We are all members of particular cultures and subcultures. As residents of the United States, for example, we attend school and study certain subjects. We learn to admire people such as George Washington, Abraham Lincoln, and Martin Luther King, Jr. Because of our cultural heritage, we share certain values, attitudes, and beliefs that shape our response to the world around us. In contrast, other cultures (and cultural subgroups within the United States), often have different values, heroes, attitudes, and purchase behavior patterns. Un-derstanding culture is therefore an important step in international business and an increasingly important step in diverse countries such as the United States.

Consumers who move here from other countries usually bring ele-ments of their native cultures to their new lives in the United States, and marketers need to be aware of these important influences.

Social Class. In addition to being members of a particular culture, we also belong to a certain social class that affects our attitudes and buying behavior. Membership in a particular class—be it upper, middle, lower, or something in between—is based primarily on educational level, occupation, and family history. In general, the members of the various classes enjoy different activities, buy different goods, shop in different places, and react to different media. Take sports. Upscale consumers prefer golf, tennis, skiing, and sailing, whereas downscale buyers go bowling, hunting, fishing, and waterskiing.[30] An awareness of these preferences enables companies to tailor the elements of the marketing mix to appeal to the group most likely to respond to its products or services.

Reference Groups. Although culture and social class exert an important influence on purchasing patterns, reference groups carry perhaps an even greater weight. A reference group consists of people who have a good deal in common—family members, friends, coworkers, fellow students, teenagers, sports enthusiasts, music lovers, computer buffs. We are all members of many such reference groups, and we use the opinions of the appropriate group as a benchmark when we buy certain types of products or services. For example, our friends influence our choice of clothes, books, music, and movies. We consult our families in choosing cars, homes, food, investments, and furniture.

In every reference group, one or two people are especially important. These are the "influentials," the 10 percent of the population who are the first to try new products and embrace new ideas and who then share their opinions with everyone else. They tend to be more assertive than the average person and are an important source of advice on everything from hairstyles to financial investments. Because their opinions carry so much weight, these are the people that marketers especially want to reach.[31]

Self-Image. Our picture of ourselves is also a key determinant of our purchasing behavior. We all have an image of who we are, and we reinforce this image through our purchases. The tendency to believe that "you are what you buy" is especially prevalent among young people. In a recent study on the meaning of possessions, researchers discovered that students consider possessions the most important aspect of their lives. They attach personal meaning to such objects as stereos, cars, and clothing.[32] Marketers capitalize on our need to express our identity through our purchases by emphasizing the image value of products and services. That's why professional athletes and musicians are used so frequently as product endorsers; we want to incorporate part of their public image into our own self-image.

Situational Factors. Every purchase decision is influenced by a person's cultural, social, and personal identity, but factors of a more circumstantial nature also come into play. When we shop for bread, for example, we may choose one brand instead of another because we have a coupon or because one variety is displayed more prominently than another. A special sale may entice us to buy something that we would ordinarily resist. Important events in our lives, such as weddings, birthdays, and Valentine's Day, also trigger buying decisions.

Even our mood has a bearing on what we buy and how we make our choices. We turn to sweets, alcohol, and cigarettes when we are depressed.[33] We shop to alleviate boredom, dispel loneliness, escape reality, and fulfill our fantasies. For many people, shopping is a leading form of recreation, although in recent years, more and more people have found shopping to be more stressful and less enjoyable, and many have become "shopping dropouts."[34]

Organizational Buying Behavior

Although Nike is concerned with the buying behavior of consumers, Nike itself is an organizational customer with a buying behavior all its own. Organizational buying behavior is similar in some ways to consumer buying behavior, but it is quite different in other ways. These differences fall into two general categories: (1) the kinds of products marketed and how they are purchased and (2) the nature of the buyer-seller relationship.

Differences in Products and Purchasing

The products sold to organizational markets include both raw materials (grain, steel, fabric) and highly technical and complex products (printing presses, telecommunications systems, management consulting). Between these two extremes, organizations buy many products also found in consumer markets; food, paper products, cleaning supplies, and landscaping services are some examples. Federal Express, for instance, sells its services to both organizational customers and individual consumers. However, even though the products may look the same, the quantities purchased and the buying processes are different.

Although both consumers and organizational customers buy Compaq computers, the quantities and purchasing methods vary considerably between the two groups.

Many industrial products are purchased in massive quantities—often by the ton or truckload. Also in contrast to consumer buying, organizational purchases tend to have large dollar values. Even the average consumer's biggest purchases, such as a home, can pale in comparison with the sorts of purchases that industrial giants make, from blast furnaces to skyscrapers.

Because orders are large, organizations tend to make purchases less often than consumers do. In addition, the purchase planning period is longer. A consumer who decides to buy a new toaster simply goes to the store and picks one up, but an organizational buyer in need of machine tools usually has to get input from various departments, select both product and supplier, negotiate the deal, place a purchase order, arrange for delivery, and so on. In complicated situations, the buying process can stretch out over several years.

The motivations behind consumer and organizational purchases are also different. In a general sense, consumer purchases are driven by a desire for personal satisfaction, whereas organizational purchases are driven by economic motives. As a consumer, you purchase airline tickets to visit relatives or to escape to the beach during spring break. As a businessperson, you purchase airline tickets so that you can make sales calls, service customers' equipment, negotiate with suppliers, or perform a variety of other business functions—all of which are motivated by money.

Finally, many organizational purchases entail much greater risks to the buyer than consumer purchases do. Choosing the wrong equipment or suppliers can cripple a business. Critical purchase decisions involve the commitment of huge amounts of money, affect the daily operations of the company, and influence the long-term profitability and survival of the business. If you choose a United Airlines flight that turns out to be late, the consequences aren't usually disastrous. On the other hand, if United chooses the wrong computers for its reservations and ticketing system, it could lose millions of dollars. Because of this risk, organizational buyers make more of a commitment to the important products and suppliers they select.[35]

Differences in the Buyer-Seller Relationship

Unlike consumer households, many organizations have people specially trained to make informed purchases. They have titles such as purchasing agent, and they may be certified by a professional organization. Because organizational buyers number far fewer than consumer buyers, they are often approached individually, rather than through mass marketing. These buyers are constrained by standardized purchasing procedures and by company guidelines concerning suppliers, prices, and negotiations.

Once established, relationships between organizational buyers and their suppliers tend to be stable and long-term. Most buyers will choose two or three suppliers for a frequently purchased item. That way, the buyer ensures a smooth, regular supply and price competition while preventing overdependence.[36] Buyers prefer to stick with tried-and-true sources—if those sources continue to perform to expectations. This source loyalty results in part from the amount of time and effort spent choosing the supplier, especially if the buyer has had to make a major commitment by modifying plant equipment in order to use the supplier's product, by training employees on the equipment, or by taking other risks. Source loyalty may also stem from the fear of taking risks or from lack of desire to make the effort to locate new sources.[37] Source loyalty benefits the buyer by improving communication flow, providing better customization (adapting a product to fit a single customer's needs) of products, and giving preferred status in case of shortages or other crises.[38]

A final significant difference between organizational buying and consumer buying is that many more people are involved in the organizational decision process. Whereas consumers make decisions by themselves or with the input of a few other household members, as many as 50 organizational members may contribute to a single buying decision. This multiple buying influence is perhaps the most important aspect of organizational purchasing behavior.

MARKETING RESEARCH

In one sense, marketing is a series of decisions, from which products to make to how they should be advertised. The quality of every one

marketing research *Process of gathering information about marketing problems and opportunities*

of these decisions depends to a large degree on the quality of the information that a manager has at hand when making the decision. **Marketing research** is the process of gathering data about marketing issues and transforming that raw data into meaningful information that can improve the quality of these decisions and reduce the risks inherent in every marketing action.

How Research Can Help the Marketing Effort

Research can help with nearly every phase of marketing. Marketers rely on research when they set goals for market share, profitability, or a program's sales results. They also use marketing research when developing new products, when segmenting markets, and when planning future marketing programs. During a marketing campaign, marketers use research to monitor the program's effectiveness by answering such questions as how many people have seen a particular ad, how many consumers are using a product, and how many consumers buy a product more than once. They also use marketing research to keep an eye on the competition and to measure customer satisfaction.

When heavy-equipment manufacturer Caterpillar set out to make a new tractor, the company hired an independent research agency to handle the initial study of farmers' tractor needs, using mail surveys and personal interviews. Meanwhile, Caterpillar managers fanned out to interview dealers personally and to understand their sales and service requirements for the new product. Later, Caterpillar put prototypes into the field to test their operation and sent its own technicians and product-development team into the field to visit the test sites. The technicians interviewed users in person and by phone, and they videotaped field tests at dozens of locations. When the product was launched, it was very successful, thanks to the extensive marketing research and attention to customer needs.[39]

However, conducting marketing research is no guarantee of success. You have to collect the right data and use it appropriately. Coca-Cola's experience with New Coke is a classic example of how marketing research can lead a company astray when it's not used correctly. In an effort to stem the growth of archcompetitor Pepsi, Coca-Cola conducted extensive taste tests to find a cola taste consumers liked better than either Coke or Pepsi. On the basis of this research, the company launched New Coke, replacing the 100-year-old Coca-Cola formula. New Coke simply didn't sell, and Coca-Cola had to mount an expensive marketing effort to salvage the new brand. At the same time, the public outcry drove the company to bring back the original formula, renamed Coke Classic.

What went wrong? Coca-Cola's researchers focused only on taste and failed to look at the emotional attachment consumers had to the traditional Coke soft drink. By changing a product many consider to be a part of our culture, Coca-Cola stirred up strong feelings in its customers, who reacted by shunning the new product and demanding the return of the original. If the company had used marketing research to investigate how consumers felt about losing Coke—not

362

just which taste they prefer—the rocky course of New Coke's introduction might have been smoother.[40]

Types of Marketing Research

The type of research you should conduct varies from situation to situation. If you're trying to figure out what's happening in a market, you might choose *exploratory research,* a series of initial research steps that help clarify the problem. If sales have dropped 10 percent in the last month, for instance, you'd do some exploratory research to identify the source of the problem.

A second type of research is *descriptive research,* which seeks to describe a market, a competitor, or other issue. This type of research often follows exploratory research because you must have a good understanding of the problem to be able to conduct research that will describe it in detail. The majority of marketing research is descriptive and is designed to help marketers get a better picture of their customers and their markets.

The third type of research is *causal research,* used to identify the factor that causes a particular effect in the marketplace. You would use causal research, for example, when you want to understand what could happen to sales if you lower prices or how a heavier advertising schedule might affect customer awareness of your product.

The Research Process

Successful researchers follow a careful plan when they set out to answer marketing problems. In general, this plan involves four stages:

- *Define the problem.* This first stage often sounds more obvious than it turns out to be, but you need to define the research problem. In other words, you can't look for answers until you're sure you have the right questions. In the case of New Coke, Coca-Cola apparently assumed that the reason for Pepsi's growth was the product itself; hence it needed to do some research to find the right replacement product. In fact, Pepsi's growth was probably attributable more to effective positioning and advertising than to the product. Coca-Cola wound up finding the right answer to the wrong question.
- *Design the research.* Once you're sure you've figured out the question, the next step is to design a research program that will find the answer. You've already read about the first issue here, which is picking the right type of research (exploratory, descriptive, or causal). Next, you identify where you can get the data that will lead you to an answer. Potential data sources range from libraries and computer databases to retailers and customers. Some research can be done without collecting any new data, but when you do need to collect data, the next step is to identify the *sample.* This is a portion of the overall population to whom you'll pose your research questions. Your sample might be every tenth high-school teacher in the city or the first 500 people you can flag down at the nearest mall, for instance.

Right now, even as you're reading this, your name and your life are part of dozens and dozens of databases. Your bank knows your account balance, where you used to bank, probably even your mother's maiden name (it's requested on most account applications). Your government knows how much money you made last year, the kind of car you own, and how many speeding tickets you've gotten. The list goes on and on, from video stores to insurance companies.

There's nothing unethical about maintaining a database, and there's certainly nothing unethical about using a computer to manage the database. The ethical problems arise when marketers buy, borrow, rent, or exchange information, usually without your knowledge or permission. Most of the time, you won't even know that your records are being seen or used by others, people you never imagined would or should be able to put together a big file on your life.

That's the first question: Who should have the right to see your records? The Selective Service Ad-

YOUR RIGHT TO PRIVACY VERSUS THE MARKETING DATABASES

ministration once wanted to find men of draft age who hadn't yet registered. Among other databases, they bought a list of names and birthdays from an ice cream parlor, a list developed as a promotion to recognize children's birthdays in some special way.

Here's the second question: Should you have the right to know who wants your records and be able to refuse access? What happens when you apply for health insurance and you're asked to sign a statement that allows the insurer to search a medical-records database for your

history and to provide information on you to others? Despite some state laws, a lot of personal information about U.S. citizens can still be disclosed, information that may embarrass people or in some other way have a negative impact on their lives. Denmark, on the other hand, has strict laws that prohibit marketers from exchanging information about substance abuse, criminal activities, or sexual inclinations.

A debate is raging between marketers and those who are concerned about privacy. On the one hand, privacy advocates argue that people should have the right to be left alone. On the other, marketers argue that they should have the right to freedom of speech, the right to inform customers about their offers. Thus the ultimate dilemma: Does a marketer's freedom of speech outweigh the consumer's right to privacy? Some argue that although the freedom of speech is guaranteed in the U.S. Constitution, the right to privacy is not. As the number of comprehensive databases continues to grow, this issue promises to be a central topic in marketing.

---

internal data *Research data that the company already has or can extract from some internal source*

external data *Research data acquired from sources outside the company*

- *Collect the data.* The data used in marketing research can include both **internal data,** which the company already has in its files or sales records, and **external data,** which come from sources outside the company. You have three general options when it comes to collecting data (assuming you need to), and the choice depends on the questions you're trying to answer. The first is *observation,* which is observing the behavior of the people in your sample. "Observing" here means more than just watching, however; the data collected by supermarket scanners are also considered part of observational research. The second method, *interviewing,* involves asking people questions, using a variety of techniques, including mail or telephone surveys, focus groups, and the so-called mall intercepts, where researchers stop people in shopping malls and ask questions. The third method is *experimentation,* in which you alter one or more variables in a marketing situation and observe the results. For instance, you might change the headline in your ad and see what effect such a modification has on sales. The newest experimental techniques involve computer-simulated stores, in which shoppers make choices based on what they see on a computer screen.

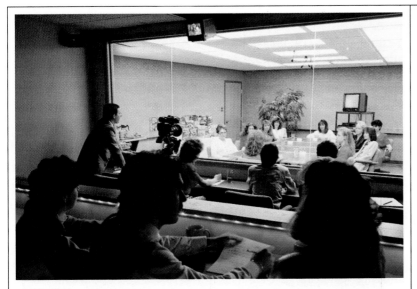

The focus group is a common research technique that collects ideas and opinions from small groups of customers.

- *Analyze the data.* Most research projects collect huge amounts of data, but by themselves, these data points don't help very much. The final and sometimes most crucial step is analyzing the collected data in a search for meaningful information. This effort ranges from simple analysis done with spreadsheets on personal computers to the latest techniques in "data mining" done with advanced supercomputers.[41] Whatever the approach, the goal is to find connections and patterns in the data that lead to new insights about customers and competitors.

It's important to remember the appropriate role of marketing research. It's not a substitute for judgment, and using it inappropriately can lead to expensive mistakes. On the other hand, good research can identify new opportunities and potential hazards, helping managers make profitable decisions. In addition, because the business environment is constantly changing, research should be an ongoing process, not just a one-time event.

1 **Explain what marketing is.**
Marketing is the process of planning and executing the conception, pricing, promotion, and distribution of ideas, goods, and services to create exchanges that satisfy individual and organizational objectives.

2 **Describe the four forms of utility created by marketing.**
Form utility is created when the characteristics of a product or service are made more functionally and psychologically satisfying. Time utility is created by making the product available when the consumer wants to buy it. Place utility is created when a product is made available at a location that is convenient for the consumer. Possession utility is created by facilitating the transfer of ownership from seller to buyer.

3 **Explain the importance of quality and customer service in competitive marketing.**
Delivering quality products backed with good customer service gives a company four advantages over its competitors: building customer loyalty, differentiating its products, decreasing marketing costs, and increasing prices and profits.

4 **Outline the three steps in the strategic planning process.**
The three steps in the strategic planning process are reviewing your current performance, assessing your opportunities, and developing a marketing strategy to capitalize on those opportunities.

5 **Define market segmentation and list the methods most often used to segment markets.**
Market segmentation is the process of subdividing a market into homogeneous groups in order to identify potential customers and to devise marketing approaches geared to their needs and interests. The most common types of segmentation are demographic, geographic, psychographic, geodemographic, and behavioral.

6 **Specify the four basic components of the marketing mix.**
The marketing mix consists of the four Ps: product, price, distribution (place), and promotion.

7 **Describe the five steps in the buyer's decision process.**
The buyer recognizes a need, searches for solutions, gathers information, makes a decision, and then evaluates that decision.

8 **List the four steps in the marketing research process.**
The four steps are to define the problem, design the research program, collect data (if needed), and analyze the data to reach conclusions that can be used in marketing decisions.

Phil Knight's company was facing a formidable challenge launched by an upstart company in a newly emerging market segment. The high-fashion world of aerobic exercise was quite different from Nike's world of high-performance athletics. Reebok's chairman, Paul Fireman, was among the first to spot the trend, and he had his designers create a unique shoe for aerobics workouts. However, even Fireman wasn't prepared for what happened next. As running and sport shoes caught on as fashionable footwear, Reebok's sales shot past those of its older competitor.

The result was that Nike slipped into the runner-up position in 1986, and Knight knew he had to act. He examined the company's marketing mix and made key adjustments in products, distribution, and promotions. Before taking drastic action, however, he took the all-important step of getting a better understanding of his target customers. One of the key insights he gained was that, although technology and performance were vitally important to customers, so too were fashion and style.

As a result, Nike fine-tuned its product strategy by adding stylish accents and more colors. This move soon helped it compete more effectively against Reebok and newcomer L.A. Gear, both successful in combining fashion and technology. Performance remained a top priority for many customers, so Knight poured money into product research and development. A key result was the Nike Air technology, soon featured in many Nike shoes.

Knight had always been adept at using promotion effectively, but this element became even more important as competition heated up. The slogan "Just Do It," which first appeared in ad campaigns in 1989, has become the cornerstone of the company's advertising strategy. Nike ads have been winning industry awards for years, and they catapulted a once-obscure Portland, Oregon, ad agency to prominence. In fact, Wieden & Kennedy's former creative director, Dan Wieden, says that Nike taught him and partner David Kennedy how to advertise.

Knight also raised the stakes on celebrity endorsements, the industry's major marketing technique. Ever since Adidas and Puma pioneered the concept, success in the athletic-footwear industry has depended on attaching the image of a sports star to a line of products. Nike's endorsers include many of the top names in professional sports, including former basketball superstar Michael Jordan, hockey player Wayne Gretzky, tennis pro Andre Agassi, and Russian track and field star Sergei Bubka. Knight explains that you can't say much in a 60-second commercial, but "when you have Michael Jordan, you don't have to."

As the new products and new ads drew new customers, Nike learned how important it is to maintain good relations with the distribution channel. Back when aerobics shoes were all the rage, Nike had mountains of unsold running shoes. The company turned to discount stores to empty its warehouses, which alienated the 12,000 sporting-goods dealers and department stores that carried Nike's regularly priced shoes. Fortunately for Knight, he was able to win the retailers back with Nike Air.

Reebok wasn't sitting still all this time, of course, and its moves included introducing The Pump technology in 1989 and signing the NBA's newest superstar, Shaquille O'Neal, as an endorser. However, Nike learned well from its challenges in the 1980s and now in the mid-1990s maintains the lead over Reebok. Nike's sales are running around $4 billion a year, with the help of expanded product offerings (most notably clothing) and growing markets in Asia and Europe. The race goes on.

Your Mission: You have been hired as a student marketing assistant at Nike headquarters in Beaverton, Oregon. You are assigned to the staff of Jody Rubin, children's marketing manager, to make a special four-week study of the children's shoe industry. This is a relatively new market segment for Nike, and Rubin must strengthen the firm's position. Use your knowledge of the marketing mix and your experience as a consumer to help identify potential winning strategies, to suggest effective competitive approaches, and to plan creative marketing programs.

1. Another competitor entering the children's shoe market is Kanga-ROOS USA, best known for the pockets in its adult sports shoes. The first ad used by KangaROOS in the kids market was "ROOS: Shoes for your feet, pockets for your stuff." Although Nike has no pockets in its kids' shoes, you feel the high-performance fashion statement made by Nike shoes will attract kids. You know you need to open up your thinking and consider all kinds of product possibilities, however. Evaluate the following new-product ideas. Which one has the greatest chance of success?

a. Develop a longer-lasting sports-style shoe for kids, with double soles and reinforced toes to keep the shoes intact long after competitive products have worn out. Don't worry if they look a little goofy; the important thing is to make sure they last a long time.

b. Manufacture current top sellers from the adult line in smaller sizes for kids, making adjustments for differences in children's feet. This idea will work because younger kids like to copy the styles worn by adults, and they'll feel grown-up in their miniature Nikes.

c. Just wait and copy whatever KangaROOS USA does. Let that company spend all its money on marketing research and product design. After it introduces new shoes, wait and see whether the shoes are successful. If a particular model of shoe does take off, copy the design and come out with your own version. Of course, you'll have to make sure you don't violate any trademarks or patents, but this strategy eliminates all the risk.

2. As part of the marketing plan for this year, Rubin wants to expand the distribution channels for the Nike children's shoe line. She has asked you to examine all feasible choices and make recommendations, based on Nike's image as a high-performance, fashion-oriented shoe interpreted for children. Which of the following types of stores would be the best choice for Nike?

a. Department stores such as Bloomingdale's and Nordstrom would be the best choice for selling Nike shoes. Parents will like the fact that they can buy all their kids' clothing and shoes in one place. In addition, Nikes "belong" in upscale department stores; they're too expensive to fit in other types of stores.

b. You need to have specialized outlets, and sporting-goods dealers would work best. After all, Nike started out as a shoe for serious athletes, so it only makes sense that customers should come to buy them at a place that sells athletic products.

c. The best choice would be to sell the shoes through mail-order catalogs. Parents don't have to fight traffic or drag their kids through the mall. They simply make a phone call, and the shoes show up on the doorstep in several weeks.

3. You are attending a meeting at which Nike executives are considering how to make the product more attractive to consumers without changing the shoe itself. One executive suggests offering a lifetime warranty, guaranteeing that the shoes will last until outgrown by the children. Another proposes a money-back 30-day trial period, to give parents an opportunity to see whether the shoes perform as well as expected. You are asked for your opinion. Which of the following ideas would you present as the strongest product enhancement?

a. Give customers a trade-in allowance with their next purchase of Nike kids' shoes. They would take advantage of this offer when buying a replacement for the original Nike pair, and they would be asked to bring in one of the original shoes to get the trade-in allowance.

b. Package a permanent-color marker with each pair of Nike kids' shoes sold. The marker can be used to write the owner's name inside each shoe, and it might even be used to decorate the shoe to suit the wearer.

c. Package the shoes in an inexpensive plastic carrying case with the Nike logo, which can be used to bring shoes to school or along on a trip.

4. To get new products out in front of adult audiences, Nike uses a network of professionals, such as aerobics trainers, who are given shoes in exchange for appearing in trade shows and for fulfilling other promotional duties. These professionals are frequently asked for advice on athletic apparel and shoes. You would like to have a similar panel of people who are in a position to recommend Nike kids' shoes to purchasers. Which of the following groups of people would have the most influence on children's shoe purchasers?

a. Podiatrists, doctors who specialize in care and treatment of foot problems, would be your best choice. They understand feet, and parents will trust their opinions.

b. Scholarship winners from local schools would make the best spokespersons. They will be respected for their scholastic achievements, so parents and children will put faith in what these students have to say.

c. Young celebrities would make the best representatives because children look up to them. Young athletes, musical performers, and television and movie stars will have the visibility to grab the children's attention and get their loyalty.[42]

behavioral segmentation (352)
buyers' markets (343)
cognitive dissonance (358)
competitive advantage (344)
concentrated marketing (353)
consumer buying behavior (357)
consumer market (349)
customer service (345)
customized marketing (354)
demographics (350)
differentiated marketing (353)
exchange process (341)
external data (364)
form utility (342)
four Ps (355)
geodemographics (352)

geographic segmentation (351)
idea marketing (340)
internal data (364)
market (349)
marketing (340)
marketing concept (343)
marketing mix (355)
marketing research (362)
marketing strategy (349)
market segmentation (350)
market segments (350)
market share (349)
need (341)
organizational market (349)
place marketing (340)
place utility (342)

position (355)
positioning (355)
possession utility (342)
price (356)
product differentiation (344)
psychographics (352)
quality (345)
relationship marketing (345)
sellers' markets (342)
target markets (353)
time utility (342)
transaction (342)
undifferentiated marketing (353)
utility (342)
wants (341)

REVIEW QUESTIONS

1. What is marketing, and why is it important to the U.S. economy?
2. How has marketing evolved over time?
3. How does organizational buying differ from consumer buying?

4. What are the main ingredients in the marketing mix?
5. What are the three components of a marketing strategy?
6. What factors influence the consumer in making purchasing decisions?

7. What factors are commonly considered in a demographic approach to market segmentation?
8. How does an undifferentiated approach to market segmentation differ from a concentrated approach?

A CASE FOR CRITICAL THINKING

HOMEBUILDER FINDS A PROFITABLE WAY TO SATISFY CUSTOMERS

A home is the most complex purchase most consumers will ever make. The decision spans the entire spectrum of behavioral influences, from the legal and practical to the social and emotional. From traditional and cozy to sleek and futuristic, practical to extravagant, homes reflect their owners' sense of style, activities, and personal values. Because of this deep connection with self-image and lifestyle, many buyers want their homes to be unique, to have special touches that meet their personal needs and distinguish them from all other houses in the neighborhood.

Unfortunately, this desire to create unique houses collides with the cold

realities of homebuilding economics. Customized houses cost more money, and the more custom a house is, the more it's likely to cost. The reasons range from the need to hire an architect to draw up the plans to the builder's cost of buying specialized materials in small quantities. For the vast majority of new-home buyers, creating a one-of-a-kind masterpiece is simply too expensive. In the typical suburban planned neighborhood, one or more homebuilders offer a few different models from which buyers can choose. Builders can construct these models quickly and cost-effectively, but the result is often cookie-cutter houses that look nearly identical. Consumers who'd love to have a unique house built to satisfy their dreams and demands can look up and down the street and find

other people with practically the same house. It's a little like showing up for a party in some splendid new outfit, only to find a dozen other people wearing the same thing—except that you're stuck with your house for years, not just for an evening.

In this buyer frustration, homebuilder Donald Horton saw opportunity. He realized that it doesn't take much to give most buyers a sense of uniqueness. It could be a marble entryway to impress guests, an enlarged kitchen window to let parents keep a better eye on their children playing in the yard, or a whirlpool bathtub in the master bedroom. Horton offers perhaps 10 basic home models in each of his developments; then he lets people make choices to customize from those standardized starting points. Horton still gets much of the cost-efficiency of mass production, and buyers get to feel a little more special about their new homes. Many cost-conscious builders, in contrast, calculate their costs for each model down to the penny and refuse to budge when buyers ask for changes.

Options such as whirlpool baths and fancy windows have a strong emotional pull for buyers, who often don't think twice about the additional cost. If they do think about the cost, a smart salesperson can remind them that over the life of the typical 30-year mortgage, a few indulgences barely create a financial blip. Adding a $1,000 whirlpool bath to a $200,000 house with a 10 percent, 30-year mortgage, for instance, works out to less than $.30 a day. For $5 a day, you could add about $17,000 worth of custom goodies—enough to add a lot of personal touches to a standard-issue structure.

Being flexible enough to let consumers add all these options pays off handsomely for Horton. First, the profit margin on options is often higher than on the basic structure of the house, so the more options people buy, the higher Horton's profit margin. Second, letting people choose the personal details often leads to faster sales. The faster he can sell homes, the less money he has tied up in inventory.

Having the flexibility to respond to customers' unique requests looks like good business to Horton. His company's profit margin is more than twice that of his nearest competitors, and sales continue to grow. He'd be the first to tell you that listening to customers is just basic good business.

1. How does Donald Horton apply the marketing concept?

2. Because of his willingness to customize the details, would Horton be able to attract all home buyers, regardless of price category? Why or why not?

3. How does Horton's flexibility relate to the definition of quality used in this chapter?

4. Identify at least three other consumer purchase choices that, like houses, reflect the buyer's self-image and lifestyle.

BUILDING YOUR COMMUNICATION SKILLS

Either individually or in a group of three or four, select a consumer product with which you are familiar, and identify the elements that make up the marketing mix: product, price, distribution, and promotion. Use personal observation of print ads, television commercials, radio spots, and information from periodicals and books (available in the library) that focus on advertising and marketing.

• Describe how the elements of the marketing mix create a marketable product.

• Compare your product with similar products to determine which elements of the marketing mix make one product more successful than others.

• Share your findings with the members of your class in a brief presentation. To support your findings, include examples such as print ads and information obtained as a result of your library search.

KEEPING CURRENT USING *THE WALL STREET JOURNAL*

From recent issues of *The Wall Street Journal,* select an article that describes in some detail a particular company's marketing strategy (either in general or for a particular product or product line).

1. Describe the company's market. What geographic, demographic, behavioral, or psychographic segments of the market is the company targeting?

2. What factors influenced the company's decisions about its marketing strategy?

3. According to the article, how successful has this strategy been? What marketing problems or opportunities can you foresee if the company continues to follow this strategy?

MCDONALD'S COVERS THE WORLD WITH FAST FOOD AND GOOD TIMES

Synopsis

The field of marketing covers quite a range of topics, from understanding your customers and designing products that they will find appealing to promoting your products in a persuasive manner and delivering them in ways that are convenient and satisfying. McDonald's is a superb example of the challenges and rewards of contemporary marketing, and this videotape gives you a guided tour of marketing according to McDonald's. You'll see that the marketing exchange offered by McDonald's is more than just food and beverages; it also includes a pleasant social and family experience, convenience, consistency, and value. You'll also see how McDonald's addresses the issue of social responsibility and the complexities of international business.

Exercises

ANALYSIS

1. How does McDonald's apply the four Ps?

2. What factors shown in the video influence the buying behavior of McDonald's customers?

3. What types of utility does McDonald's provide its customers?

4. How has McDonald's responded to changing consumer demands in recent years?

5. Does McDonald's do any market segmentation for its products?

APPLICATION

Identify a business you've seen or patronized and figure out whether franchising would make sense for this business (assuming it's not already franchised).

DECISION

If you were purchasing a new McDonald's franchise and had the choice between locating next to a high school or a minor-league baseball field, which would you choose?

COMMUNICATION

Pick an item from McDonald's menu and create a print (magazine or newspaper) ad for it. Think about the image you want to project, the graphical elements you'll want to use, and the words that will get your point across. (Rough sketches are fine in place of finished artwork.)

INTEGRATION

Refer to Chapter 5 to identify the advantages and disadvantages of buying a McDonald's franchise relative to the idea of creating a new restaurant from the ground up.

ETHICS

One of the issues McDonald's has had to grapple with in recent years is the healthiness of its foods. Some would say that McDonald's can't possibly be a good member of the community if it is feeding people high-calorie and high-cholesterol foods. Others say that McDonald's has made efforts to offer healthy foods and besides, each consumer has the right to decide what he or she is going to eat. What's your opinion?

DEBATE

Many people favor one fast-food chain over another. Option A: In a formal debate format, support either McDonald's or a well-known competitor operating in your area. Option B: Take either side and state your case in a brief report. With either option, consider how points in the cases for and against McDonald's could be used to improve its marketing strategy.

TEAMWORK

In a team of three or four students, identify a business that one or more of you is familiar with, a business that has established a strong relationship with its customers. This business can be anything from a restaurant to the college bookstore. Decide what it is that makes the place special to its customers, and write a list of general guidelines that other businesses could follow.

RESEARCH

Do the research necessary to write a one-paragraph summary on either (a) McDonald's menu changes in recent years or (b) the effect of any recent government regulation on the marketing of fast food.

ROLE PLAYING

One student plays the role of a McDonald's franchise owner trying to explain to his or her employees why it is a good idea to help out with a local charity event. Several other students can play employees with varying attitudes toward helping out. Some agree to do it on their own time, a few others demand to be paid while doing it, and one or two don't want to participate at all.

Chapter

13

Product and Pricing Decisions

Personality with a Pop

It's a funny name for a food product, but Orville Redenbacher has been laughing all the way to the bank since 1970. In just five years, his Orville Redenbacher Gourmet Popping Corn surpassed 82 brands to become the market leader. Before Orville Redenbacher, there was no such thing as "gourmet" popcorn. In fact, before Redenbacher energized the entire category, popcorn production in the United States languished at under 350 million pounds a year. Only after Redenbacher's product became a hit did production pop up past 675 million pounds. However, it was a long way from the corn crib to the store shelf.

As a boy, Redenbacher had grown corn for popping as part of a 4-H project to devise a better strain. He majored in agronomy (soil management and field crops) at Purdue University in the 1920s, and after graduation, he served as an agricultural agent. Then he managed a large Indiana farm where he became involved in growing hybrid corn and processing popcorn seed. That's when Redenbacher met Charlie Bowman, who ran a seed program at Purdue. In 1951 the two entrepreneurs bought a small company that raised and sold corn seed, renamed it Chester Inc., and started to experiment with popcorn seed.

By 1965 Redenbacher had crossbred 40 generations of corn and come up with what he considered the consummate corn for popping. The new corn popped up fluffier than other varieties, and a higher percentage of individual kernels popped.

He now faced the challenge of producing and marketing his newfangled snack. Farmers weren't exactly lining up to grow the new corn. It cost more to harvest than other popping corns, and crop yields were lower per acre than with traditional corns. Moreover, retailers weren't eager to stock the new popcorn, which had been dubbed Red Bow. Merchants told Redenbacher that people just wouldn't pay more for a new popcorn, even popcorn that was of higher quality.

Strong brand identities help distinguish the many brands of popcorn available today.

By 1970 Redenbacher realized he needed a new approach. He traveled to Chicago to meet with a team of marketing specialists, and he spent hours talking about popcorn. He was astonished when they advised changing the product name to Orville Redenbacher's

Gourmet Popping Corn. Moreover, the marketers wanted Redenbacher to put his own picture on the label. Finally, they suggested the new popcorn be positioned as unabashedly upscale, packaged appropriately, and tagged with a premium price.

Although he was skeptical, Redenbacher decided to try these ideas. Put yourself in Redenbacher's shoes: How would you create and support the new brand? What packaging and labeling decisions would you have to make as you introduce the new product? How would you encourage people to try your popcorn, and then buy it again? How would you sustain sales after the product was established?[1]

PRODUCTS: THE BASIS OF COMMERCE

Orville Redenbacher's Gourmet Popping Corn has been a highly successful product. If you were asked to name three other popular products off the top of your head, you might think of Snickers, Levi's, and Pepsi— or three similar products. You might not think of the Boston Celtics, Disneyland, or the television show "60 Minutes." That's because when we're on the buying side of an exchange, we tend to think of products as *tangible* objects that we can actually touch and possess. Basketball teams, amusement parks, and TV programs provide an *intangible* service for our use or enjoyment, not for our ownership; nevertheless, they are products just the same. From a marketing standpoint, a **product** is anything that is offered for the purpose of satisfying a want or need in a marketing exchange.

Types of Products

Marketers have a variety of ways to categorize products as they develop a marketing strategy. You wouldn't market a garden tractor the same way you'd market accounting services; the buyer behavior, product characteristics, market expectations, competition, and other elements of the equation are all different. The two most significant categorizations involve the degree of tangibility and the nature of the customer.

Tangible and Intangible Products

It's convenient to group products as tangible goods or intangible services and ideas, but in reality, things aren't quite so simple. Nearly all products are combinations of tangible and intangible components. Some products are predominantly tangible, whereas others are mostly intangible; however, most products fall somewhere between these two extremes. When you eat in a restaurant, you're paying for more than just food; the total product includes service and atmosphere, too. The *product continuum* graphically indicates the relative amounts of tangible and intangible components in a product (see Exhibit 13.1). Po-

Consider an NBA basketball game such as the McDonald's Open in Munich, Germany: Although it's intangible, it's still a product.

product *Good or service used as the basis of commerce*

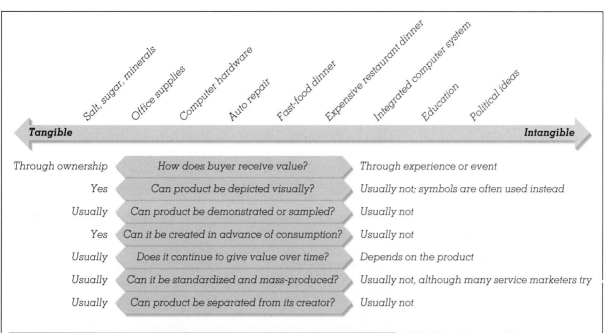

	How does buyer receive value?	
Through ownership	How does buyer receive value?	Through experience or event
Yes	Can product be depicted visually?	Usually not; symbols are often used instead
Usually	Can product be demonstrated or sampled?	Usually not
Yes	Can it be created in advance of consumption?	Usually not
Usually	Does it continue to give value over time?	Depends on the product
Usually	Can it be standardized and mass-produced?	Usually not, although many service marketers try
Usually	Can product be separated from its creator?	Usually not

Exhibit 13.1
The Product Continuum
All products are made up of both tangible and intangible components, and the particular mix in a given product has a lot to do with the way it should be marketed.

litical ideas are an example of products at the intangible extreme, whereas salt and sugar represent the tangible extreme. Dinner in a restaurant falls somewhere in the middle because customers get both tangible components (food and beverages) and intangible components (the food is cooked and served, the dishes are washed, and so on). Dinner in an expensive restaurant, where you're likely to have several servers, live music, and other amenities, has a greater degree of intangibility than dinner at McDonald's or Burger King. Auto repair, on the other hand, can range all over the continuum, depending on the particular problem being repaired.

As the product continuum indicates, service products have some special characteristics that affect the way they are marketed. The most important of these is the fundamental intangibility of services. You can't usually show a service in an ad, demonstrate it for customers before they buy it, or give customers anything tangible to show for their purchase. Successful services marketers often compensate for intangibility by using tangible symbols or by adding tangible components to their products. Prudential Insurance uses the Rock of Gibraltar in its logo and talks about having "a piece of the rock." Gibraltar is a symbol of solid stability, and Prudential wants you to think the same about its services.

Another unique aspect of service products is that they can't usually be created in advance and stored until people want to buy them. This aspect presents big challenges in terms of staffing, pricing, and other management issues. It is this *perishability* of services that leads movie theaters to offer cheaper tickets during the day. The theaters want to shift some of the customer demand from the busy evening and weekend times, and they want to use their service capacity as much as possible.

Because services are performances or experiences, the people providing the service are an important part of the equation. If a computer company received orders for more computers than it could build, it could pay someone else to build the extra computers; customers who received those particular products would never know the difference and would probably not care if they did. On the other hand, you can't separate a service such as live music from its provider. Robert Cray can't put on a B. B. King concert, for instance, even though both are blues guitarists. If King were unable to perform because of illness, the concert would have to be canceled.

In addition to considering the tangible and intangible makeup of a product, marketers need to take into account the intended buyer of the product. As discussed in Chapter 12, consumers and organizations have different purchasing patterns, and these differences have important implications for companies trying to optimize their marketing mixes.

Consumer Products

Although some products are sold to both consumer and organizational markets, those known as **consumer products** are sold exclu-

consumer products *Products sold exclusively to consumers, including convenience products, shopping products, and specialty products*

THINKING ABOUT ETHICS

ARE COMPANIES RESPONSIBLE WHEN CONSUMERS GET HURT?

Have you ever spilled coffee on yourself? Have you ever been awarded $2.9 million after spilling coffee on yourself? That's the amount Stella Liebeck was awarded when she sued McDonald's after spilling a cup of the fast-food giant's steaming java on herself.

The public howled when the news broke. Opinion polls indicated that a majority of people thought this was yet another case of somebody suing a big company when the consumer was in fact to blame. After years of hearing about people receiving huge product-liability awards for such incidents as walking into traffic while wearing headphones or being burned after pouring perfume on a lit candle, the public's response was certainly understandable.

A closer look at the McDonald's case reveals a more complicated situation, however. To begin with, this was not an everyday coffee spill; Liebeck received third-degree burns that required skin grafts and seven days of hospitalization. This was no isolated incident. In the decade leading up to Leibeck's award in 1994, McDonald's had received over 700 complaints about coffee burns. The company had settled some for more than a half million dollars. Jurors say

what really capped the case for them was McDonald's attitude, however. The company knew about coffee-burn dangers but considered them statistically insignificant and said it had more important safety concerns in its restaurants.

Liebeck's case is a good example of the debate raging over product liability. After all, McDonald's didn't spill the coffee; Liebeck did. In addition, the temperature of McDonald's coffee (generally 180 to 190 degrees) meets industry guidelines. The company's own market research indicates that consumers want their coffee steaming hot.

The number of product-liability claims in the United States has ballooned in recent years, and the sizes

of the awards have increased dramatically as well. However, things may be shifting back in the other direction. In 1987 liability plaintiffs won 54 percent of the cases they brought to trial. By 1992, though, that figure had dropped to just 41 percent.

Aside from the issue of who's to blame in individual cases, the tide of litigation has three important effects. First, the court awards raise companies' costs (in both the awards themselves and in increased insurance premiums), and those costs must be accommodated in higher prices to consumers or lower profits. Second, the threat of liability lawsuits may be forcing companies to be less innovative and to offer fewer choices to consumers. In one survey, 39 percent of CEOs of large companies reported deciding against introducing new products and 47 percent discontinued product lines because of the liability issue. Third, liability concerns have clearly encouraged companies overall to design safer products. Thanks to product-liability suits, cars now have air bags, explosive-resistant fuel tanks, and roll bars, and thousands of other safety features have been incorporated into all types of products that otherwise might never have been introduced.

sively to consumers. Most marketing specialists divide the broad category of consumer products into three subgroups according to the approach people take when shopping for them.

Convenience Products. The goods and services that people buy frequently, without much conscious thought, are called **convenience products**—inexpensive items such as toothpaste, soda, and razor blades. Routine personal services like dry cleaning, film developing, and photocopying are convenience products, too. Because the buyer is already familiar with these products, habit is a strong influence in the purchase decision. People buy the same brand or go to the same shop because it is easy to do so. Unless something has made them particularly conscious of price, they don't often even think about the relative cost of alternatives that could serve their purpose just about as well.

convenience products *Products that are readily available, low-priced, and heavily advertised and that consumers buy quickly and often*

Shopping Products. Purchases that require more thought fall into the category of **shopping products.** These are fairly important goods and services that a person doesn't buy every day: a stereo, a suit, an interior decorator, or a college. Such purchases require more thought about price, features, quality, or reputation. These brand differences prompt comparison shopping. Thus the shopping process is a form of education; the more unusual and expensive the product, the more the buyer checks around to compare models, features, and prices. Most buyers consult a variety of information sources, including advertisements, salespeople, friends, and relatives.

shopping products *Products for which a consumer spends a lot of time shopping in order to compare prices, quality, and style*

Specialty Products. People use a different approach when they are shopping for **specialty products,** items that have been mentally chosen in advance and for which there is no acceptable substitute to the consumer. These are things like Chanel perfume, Brooks Brothers suits, and Suzuki violin lessons—particular brands that the buyer especially wants and will seek out, regardless of location or price. The buyer is attracted mainly by the features of the product, although advertising may have helped create an aura of special value. Not all specialty products are expensive, however. Consider your own shopping behavior when you purchase a six-pack of soda: If you're like many people, you want only your favorite brand, and you won't readily accept a substitute.

specialty products *Products that a consumer will make a special effort to locate*

Organizational Products

Organizational buyers tend to base their selection of goods and services on objective criteria such as performance, support services, warranty, and *cost of ownership,* the total cost of buying and owning a product. However, buying approaches vary, depending on the purpose and price of the item being procured. **Organizational products** fall into two general categories (which are based on cost and life span). **Expense items** are relatively inexpensive goods and services that are generally used within a year of purchase. Those that are more expensive and have a longer useful life are considered **capital items.** Most organizations, in fact, have a specified purchase amount, above which a product is classified as a capital item.

Aside from dividing products into expense and capital items, organizational buyers and sellers often classify products according to their intended usage.

organizational products *Products sold exclusively to organizations, including expense items and capital items*

expense items *Relatively inexpensive organizational products that are generally consumed within a year of their purchase*

capital items *Relatively expensive organizational products that have a long life and are used in the operations of a business*

raw materials *Resources used in manufacturing and processing goods, from iron ore and crude petroleum to lumber and chemicals*

components *Parts that go into a manufacturer's final product*

supplies *Items that keep a company's operations going, including maintenance, repair, and operating (MRO) items*

MRO items *Common term for supply products purchased by organizational customers; it stands for maintenance, repair, and operating items*

installations *Organizational goods such as buildings and large stationary equipment, including factories, milling machines, and mainframe computer systems*

brand *Any name, term, sign, symbol, design, or combination used to identify the products of a firm and to differentiate them from competing products*

brand names *Portion of a brand that can be expressed orally, including letters, words, or numbers*

brand marks *Portion of a brand that cannot be expressed verbally*

trademark *Brand that has been given legal protection so that its owner has exclusive rights to its use*

- *Raw materials.* Manufacturing and processing companies have to buy a variety of **raw materials,** ranging from iron ore and crude petroleum to lumber and chemicals.
- *Components.* In addition to raw materials, most manufacturers also buy **components,** which are parts that go into the manufacturers' final products.
- *Supplies.* Organizational customers of all types need **supplies** to keep their operations going. A common term for supplies is **MRO items,** which refers to maintenance, repair, and operating items. Depending on the customer, supplies can mean anything from pencils to nails to floor wax.
- *Equipment.* Even if it's only a desk and a telephone, organizational customers need equipment. For a small service provider, such as an independent consultant, the equipment needs are fairly modest. At the other extreme, the U.S. government, Citicorp, and General Motors have mammoth equipment needs, including robots, computers, vehicles, and thousands of pieces of office furniture.
- *Installations.* **Installations** are among the most complicated organizational goods. They are composed of buildings and large, stationary equipment such as production lines, milling machines, and semiconductor fabrication machinery. Some examples of complete installations include factories, power plants, airports, and mainframe computer systems. Such purchases hold a great deal of risk for the buyer because there are so many ways things can go wrong with major projects such as these. In addition, the location itself is an important part of an installation. Various cities, states, and countries promote themselves as ideal places to build factories and other business facilities. For instance, the French Industrial Development Agency advertises in U.S. magazines, hoping to catch the attention of companies looking to expand their European operations.[2]
- *Business services.* Business services range from simple and fairly risk-free services such as landscaping and cleaning to complex services such as management consulting and auditing, which can strongly affect an organization's success or failure.

Product Brands and Trademarks

Regardless of what type of product a company sells, it usually wants to create a **brand** identity by using a unique name or design that sets the product apart from those offered by competitors. Acura, Mossimo, and Bic are **brand names,** the portion of a brand that can be spoken, including letters, words, or numbers. McDonald's golden arches and the Prudential rock are **brand marks,** the portion of a brand that cannot be expressed verbally. The choice of a brand name and any associated brand marks can be a key success factor. The Hong Kong-based Swank brand of eyeglasses has been a big seller in China, in part because Chinese consumers like the European-sounding name.[3]

Brand names and brand symbols may be registered with the Patent and Trademark Office as trademarks. A **trademark** is a brand that has been given legal protection so that its owner has exclusive rights

Consider how the visual imagery in this ad conveys the message for Levi's Loose Fit jeans; the model and the pennant fluttering in the wind get the point across as well as any headline could.

to its use. Coming up with an effective trademark that hasn't already been used is getting very difficult, however. The Patent and Trademark Office received 125,237 trademark registration applications in 1992 alone.[4]

Because a well-known name is a valuable asset and generates more sales than an unknown name, manufacturers zealously protect their trademarks. White-Westinghouse, for example, runs advertisements to remind people that Laundromat and Frigidaire are registered trademarks, not generic terms. When a name becomes too widely used, it no longer qualifies for protection under trademark laws. Cellophane, kerosene, linoleum, escalator, zipper, shredded wheat, trampoline, and raisin bran are just a few of the many brand names that have passed into the public domain, much to their creators' dismay.

Brand names may be owned by wholesalers, by retailers, and by producers of a product. A & P, the supermarket chain, purchases canned fruits, jellies, rice, household cleaning products, and frozen foods from hundreds of suppliers and offers them under the Jane Parker, A & P, and Ann Page brand names. Brands owned by national manufacturers such as Procter & Gamble are called **national brands.** Brands owned by wholesalers and retailers such as A & P are **private brands.**

The relationship between national brands and private brands has been changing in recent years. In many product categories, the perceived difference between national and private brands has narrowed, prompting more and more consumers to make the switch to the often cheaper private brands. From 1991 to 1993, private brands' share of the disposable-diaper market rose from 21 to 31 percent, a huge jump in just two years. Perrigo, a company that specializes in producing private-label nonprescription drugs that are the functional equivalent of well-known national brands, watched sales grow nearly 300 percent in a recent five-year period.[5]

The trend isn't confined to the United States, either; private brands now account for 24 percent of all supermarket sales in France and

national brands *Brands owned by a manufacturer and distributed nationally*

private brands *Brands that carry the label of a retailer or wholesaler rather than a manufacturer*

32 percent in Great Britain. Aggressive cost reductions on private-label brands in Japan in recent years have caused many consumers to switch from well-known U.S. and Japanese national brands.[6]

As an alternative to branded products, some retailers also offer **generic products,** which are packaged in plain containers that bear only the name of the product. These products are most often standard rather than premium quality. They cost up to 40 percent less than brand-name products because of uneven quality, plain packaging, and lack of promotion. Generic goods have found a definite market niche, as a look at your local supermarket shelves will confirm. However, sales of generics have declined in recent years, partly because inflation has moderated, partly because consumers are disappointed with the uneven quality, and partly because brand-name producers have fought back with cents-off coupons that reduce the generics' cost advantage.[7]

generic products Products in plain packaging that bear only the name of the item, not of its producer

Brand Loyalty

Some of the most popular brands of consumer products have been popular for decades, providing convincing evidence of the strength of **brand loyalty,** or commitment to a particular brand.[8] Nevertheless, a company has to think carefully about the benefits before spending $20 million to $40 million or more on a huge promotion campaign to establish a national brand name.[9] The cost of such a campaign may drive up the price of the product, making it possible for other companies to sell unbranded or lesser-known brand products at a substantially lower price. Additionally, just because consumers recognize the brand name is no guarantee they will buy the product. Surveys have shown that some of the best-known brands are among the least-respected products.[10]

brand loyalty Commitment to a particular brand

Before deciding to build a brand, marketers evaluate whether the payoff will be worth the investment. Often the answer depends on the type of product. People are more loyal to some types of branded products than others (see Exhibit 13.2). Mundane products designed to handle tedious chores are less likely to inspire loyalty than products associated with an individual's personal image.[11]

Brand loyalty can be measured in degrees. The first level is **brand awareness,** which means that people are familiar with the product; they are likely to buy it because they recognize it. The next level is **brand preference.** At this level, people adopt the product—that is, they habitually buy it if it is available. However, they may be willing to experiment with alternatives if they have some incentive to do so.

brand awareness Level of brand loyalty at which people are familiar with a product—they recognize it

brand preference Level of brand loyalty at which people habitually buy a product if it is available

Exhibit 13.2
Brand Loyalty and Product Type
Some types of products inspire more brand loyalty than others. A study conducted by the J. Walter Thompson ad agency found that consumers were relatively unwilling to switch brands of products that they associated with their self-image—even when they were offered an alternative brand at half-price.

High-Loyalty Products	Medium-Loyalty Products	Low-Loyalty Products
Cigarettes	Cola drinks	Crackers
Cold remedies	Furniture polish	Facial tissues
Laxatives	Hand lotion	Paper towels
35-mm film	Margarine	Plastic trash bags
Toothpaste	Shampoo	Scouring powder

The ultimate in brand loyalty is **brand insistence,** the stage at which buyers accept no substitute.

Remember the anecdote in Chapter 12 about Coca-Cola's attempt to replace Coke with New Coke? In addition to being a great example of marketing research, it's a good reminder of the potential strength of brand loyalty. The company was deluged with protests when it made the switch. People were incensed that anyone would tamper with Coke. As it turned out, the incident eventually worked to Coke's advantage. With two main products, it now has almost twice the shelf space in supermarkets.[12]

Brand Equity

A brand is often an organization's most valuable asset because it provides customers with a way of recognizing and specifying a particular product so that they can choose it again or recommend it to others. A brand also enables marketers to develop specific images and interrelated marketing strategies for a particular product. In addition, a brand can command a premium price in the marketplace, and it is often the only element of a product competitors can't copy—although sometimes they try. Agricultural specialists may eventually be able to duplicate Orville Redenbacher's popcorn, but they'll have to search far and wide for a name that could match his. Rather than building brands from scratch, some firms simply buy established brand names. Highly successful brands can be worth millions of dollars in the acquisition marketplace. Cadbury Schweppes calculated that the $220 million it paid for Hires and Crush included $20 million for physical assets and $200 million for "brand value."[13] This notion of the value of a brand is also called **brand equity,** which can be defined to include five components: brand loyalty, brand awareness, perceived quality, brand associations (the perceptions and images that people link with a brand), and other brand assets such as patents.[14]

Brand Strategies

Companies take various approaches to building brands. The traditional approach is to create a separate identity for each product a company sells so that if a problem develops with that product, the other items in the line will not suffer. This approach has the added advantage of allowing a company to create separate product images for various market segments. Take the U.S. automobile companies with their varied product lines aimed at various types of buyers. The person who likes a Corvette and the person who wants a Cadillac are looking for completely different things, even though both want a General Motors car. Among more recent car introductions, Nissan, Toyota, and Honda all opted to create separate brand names for their luxury-car divisions (Infiniti, Lexus, and Acura, respectively). Mitsubishi and Mazda, on the other hand, decided to keep the company brand name for their luxury models.

Although individual branding has its advantages, in the past few years an increasing number of companies have been using **family branding** (or using a brand name on a variety of related products) to add to their product lines. Frito-Lay, for example, launched Cool Ranch Doritos and Cajun Spice Ruffles, extending the brand by

brand insistence *Level of brand loyalty at which people will accept no substitute for a particular product*

brand equity *Overall strength of a brand in the marketplace and its value to the company that owns it; increasingly, companies are trying to assign financial value to brand equity*

family branding *Using a brand name on a variety of related products*

building on the reputations of regular Doritos Tortilla Chips and Ruffles potato chips. Of course, Frito-Lay isn't alone. Around 75 percent of new products introduced by the largest consumer food companies are brand extensions.[15] Building on the name recognition of an existing brand enables companies to cut both costs and risks associated with introducing new products. However, there are limits to how far a brand name can be stretched to accommodate new products. Snickers ice cream bars, Rubbermaid feed bins (for farm use), and Dr. Scholl's socks and shoes worked as brand extensions, but Bic perfume, Rubbermaid computer accessories, and Playboy men's suits did not. The secret is in extending with products that fit the buyer's perception of what the brand stands for.[16]

Delrina obtained a license to use the Opus and Bill characters in a computer-software product.

Another way to reduce the cost of building a new brand is to buy the rights to specific names and symbols that are already well known and then to use these licensed labels to help sell products. **Licensing** is common among manufacturers of children's products, who license popular cartoon or movie characters and affix them to everything from toys to clothing to breakfast cereals. However, the approach may backfire if the popularity of the licensed property declines. Despite this risk, however, licensing is on a roll. Major league sports provide a great example: Combined retail sales of licensed logo merchandise for Major League Baseball, the National Football League, the National Basketball Association, and the National Hockey League are pushing $7 billion a year. Sales are booming outside the United States and Canada as well. Basketball-crazy fans in Turkey, Taiwan, Mexico, and other countries buy millions of dollars' worth of NBA merchandise.[17]

licensing *Giving rights to a company to use a well-known name or symbol in marketing its products*

Packaging

With annual sales of more than $50 billion, the packaging business is the third largest industry in the United States, providing everything from tin cans to airtight boxes.[18] Because most consumer buying decisions are made in the store, product manufacturers consider the money they pay for packaging well spent.[19] Effective packaging not only protects products from damage or tampering but also promotes a product's benefits through shape, composition, and design.

Packages serve other purposes as well. They make products easier to display, attract customers' attention, and reduce the temptation to steal small products. Also, packages provide convenience. For example, more and more frozen foods are being packaged in cardboard rather than aluminum so that they can be used in microwave ovens. In addition, clever packaging can give a manufacturer a real cost advantage against competitors. The packaging for The Budget Gourmet, a popular line of frozen foods, is 30 to 40 percent cheaper than traditional frozen-dinner packaging, allowing the firm to offer a low price on its entrées without skimping on the quality of the food.[20] In many cases, packaging is an essential part of the product itself.

Consider microwave popcorn or toothpaste in pump dispensers. Innovative packages like these may give a company a powerful marketing boost, whereas a poor package may drive consumers away.

Apart from performing practical functions, packaging also acts as a form of communication. Consumers see certain colors and draw conclusions about a product even before they read the label. A red soft-drink can means cola; green means lemon-lime. Dishwashing liquid in a yellow container is lemony; a household cleaner in a green package is associated with pine. Many things packaged in black project an image of elegance. These packaging choices are conscious decisions made to support marketing strategy. As well-known designer Primo Angeli puts it: "A successful design cannot be a conglomeration of whims."[21]

Packaging has become a hot environmental issue. You've probably noticed that compact discs are now sold without the "long box" cardboard packages they used to be packaged in, in response to complaints from environmentally concerned consumers and musicians. Recyclability tends to get the most attention when it comes to packaging and the environment, but this mind-set often oversimplifies the situation. The drink boxes often used to package fruit drinks are a good example. They may not yet be as recyclable as other materials, but the fact that they store and ship more efficiently and don't need refrigeration—and all the energy consumption and air pollution that refrigeration systems involve—may in fact make them more environmentally sensitive than other packages.

Labeling

Labeling is an integral part of packaging. Whether the label is a separate element attached to the package or a printed part of the container, it serves to identify a brand. Sometimes the label also gives grading information about the product or information about ingredients, operating procedures, shelf life, or risks.

The labeling of foods, drugs, cosmetics, and many health products is regulated under a variety of federal regulations. The Food, Drug and Cosmetic Act of 1938 gives the Food and Drug Administration the authority to monitor the accuracy of the list of ingredients on labels. For example, a fruit drink cannot be labeled and sold as a fruit *juice* unless it contains an established minimum fruit content. Labels are also regulated by the Fair Packaging and Labeling Act of 1966, which mandates that every label must carry the product name as well as the name and address of the manufacturer or distributor, and it must conspicuously show the net quantity. The Nutrition Education and Labeling Act of 1990 forced marketers to use standardized terms and amounts when they specify serving size, calories, fat content, and so on.[22]

In addition to communicating with consumers, labels may also be used by manufacturers and retailers as a tool for monitoring product

The new nutrition labels are designed to help consumers make informed choices when buying food products.

performance. **Universal Product Codes (UPCs),** those black stripes on packages, give companies a cost-effective method of tracking the movement of goods. The lines on the code, which are read by laser scanners, identify the product and allow a computer to record what happens to it. In addition to simply recording sales, scanner data can help measure the effectiveness of promotional efforts, such as coupon programs and sale prices.

The Growing Importance of Service

Robots might have an exotic image to most people, but not to Eric Mittelstadt. The head of Fanuc Robotics North America says that "the robot itself has become something of a commodity. The one place you can differentiate yourself is in the service you provide."[23] That last sentence is one of the most important messages you can learn about business today. When the basic product you are offering is not all that different from those offered by competitors, taking better care of your customers is one of the best ways to gain a competitive advantage. When products as complex as robots are starting to look alike, it's a safe bet that this parity situation is happening in many simpler product categories.

Businesses can add valuable services to any kind of product, including both goods and services. Hundreds of companies offer auto insurance, and all of them settle your claim by writing you a check if your car gets totaled. A company called Progressive stands out from the crowd, however, by settling up on the spot. Claims adjusters travel around in mobile offices inside vans, driving wherever their customers have been involved in accidents. Rather than waiting for days or weeks, Progressive's policyholders get instant results.[24]

PRODUCT DEVELOPMENT AND THE PRODUCT LIFE CYCLE

When you buy a package of laundry soap, you get more than a detergent—you get the results of hundreds of small decisions about brand image, packaging, pricing, distribution, and promotion. Although the soap you buy next year may look and smell just like the soap you buy today, over time the product will evolve as the manufacturer adjusts these decisions to respond to changing circumstances.

The Product-Development Process

The possibility of developing a big winner is so alluring that U.S. companies spend billions of dollars a year trying to create new products or improve old ones.[25] Over 10,000 new consumer products are introduced every year.[26] Foods, drugs, beverages, and cosmetics account for most of the "new" products. Actually, some of these products are not really new; only about 5 percent are true innovations.[27] The rest are variations of familiar products, created by changing the packaging, improving the formula, or modifying the form or flavor.

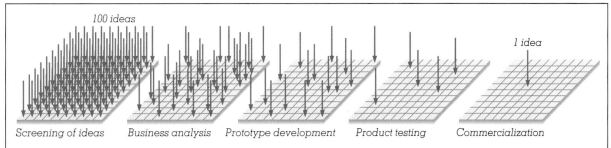

100 ideas   1 idea

Screening of ideas   Business analysis   Prototype development   Product testing   Commercialization

Exhibit 13.3
The Product-Development Process

Exhibit 13.3
The Product-Development Process
For every hundred ideas generated, only one or two salable products may emerge from the lengthy and expensive process of product development.

How many of the new products created every year will endure? Nobody knows for sure, but the odds are that most will disappear within a few years. According to one authority on new products: "To be a real success, a product should be both better and different—a lot better and a little different."[28]

Coming up with a winning product requires both research and creativity. The **product-development process** involves analysis of the marketplace, the buyer, the company's capabilities, and the economic potential of new-product ideas. This process (see Exhibit 13.3) may be both expensive and time-consuming. To accelerate the process, many companies create multidisciplinary teams so that manufacturing and marketing plans can be developed in tandem while the product is being designed.

product–development process *Stages through which a product idea passes—from initial conceptualization to actual appearance in the marketplace*

Generation and Screening of Ideas

The first step is to come up with ideas that will satisfy unmet needs. A producer may get new product ideas from its own employees or from outside consultants, it may simply adapt a competitor's idea, or it may buy the rights to someone else's invention. Customers are often the best source of new-product ideas. Smith & Hawken, a world-famous supplier of gardening tools, once received a suggestion for a new rake design from a customer named Alan Rothenberg. The company took him up on the idea and even named its new product the "Rothenberg Rake."[29]

From the mass of ideas suggested, the company culls a few that appear to be worthy of further development, applying broad criteria such as whether or not the product can use existing production facilities and the amount of technical and marketing risks involved. In the case of industrial or technical products, this phase is often referred to as a "feasibility study," in which the product's features are defined and its workability is tested. In the case of consumer products, marketing consultants and advertising agencies are often called in to help evaluate new ideas. In fact, a new-products industry is growing, made up of consultants who handle all aspects of product development. In some cases, potential customers are asked what they think of a new product idea—a process known as **concept testing.**

concept testing *Process of getting reactions about a proposed product from potential customers*

Business Analysis

A product idea that survives the screening stage is subjected to a business analysis. At this point the question is: Can the company make enough money on the product to justify the investment? To answer this question, companies forecast the probable sales of the product, assuming various pricing strategies. In addition, they estimate the costs associated with various levels of production. Given these projections, the company calculates the potential cash flow and return on investment that will be achieved if the product is introduced.

Prototype Development

prototypes *Working samples of a proposed product*

The next step is generally to create and test a few samples, or **prototypes,** of the product, including its packaging. During this stage, the various elements of the marketing mix are put together. In addition, the company evaluates the feasibility of large-scale production and specifies the resources required to bring the product to market.

Product Testing

test marketing *Product-development stage in which a product is sold on a limited basis*

During the product-testing stage, a small group of consumers actually use the product, often in comparison tests with existing products. If the results are good, the next step is **test marketing,** introducing the product in selected areas of the country and monitoring consumer reactions. This process is expensive and time-consuming. Testing a new product in a supermarket may cost $1 million and take nine months or more. In addition, the test may give competitors a chance to find out about a company's newest ideas.[30] Test marketing

---

UNDERSTANDING THE HIGH-TECH REVOLUTION

COMPUTERIZED CREATIVITY IN NEW-PRODUCT DESIGN

An artistic endeavor such as jewelry design sounds like a great example of traditional craftsmanship, using techniques handed down through the ages. Lately, however, these age-old techniques have been getting some contemporary high-tech help. Jewelry designers can now use computer models to simulate their designs before moving to the expensive and often time-consuming production stage.

If you've ever tried to create accurate three-dimensional (3D) drawings, you know how difficult this can be. Even if you do have the skills to draw a precise 3D picture, what if you (or your customer) would like to see the design from a different angle? You'd have to draw the whole thing all over again. Many people find it hard to visualize in three dimensions, and a customer's idea of what a new product will look like might be very different from what you have in mind.

By creating a 3D model of your design on a computer first, you can move it around to look at all sides and change colors, dimensions, and shapes until the design is right. Dan Harding, of the renowned product-design firm Frogdesign, says that the computer gives him a "liquid model" that he can pull and twist and shape until he gets it just right.

RPD, a firm that specializes in designing new products for other companies, uses models to show customers what products will look like—while it's still easy and inexpensive to make changes. Plus, the models help RPD transform a customer's idea into a finished design more faithfully, boosting customer satisfaction while minimizing expensive rework.

Another key advantage of using computers to design new products is speed. In many industries, from computer parts to clothes, companies must respond to changing customer demands quickly if they are to stay competitive. Computer modeling helped RPD reduce its typical design time from one month to five days.

Jewelry is just one of dozens of industries that have turned to high technology to improve the product-development process. The Boeing 777 jetliner was designed entirely on computers. From home appliances to spacecraft to commemorative coins, computers help product designers create more desirable products in less time. In fact, computer-based product design is rapidly becoming necessary to even compete in many cases. As one leading designer put it, if you're not designing on computer by now, you're probably making a mistake.

386

makes the most sense in cases where the cost of marketing a product far exceeds the cost of developing it.

One way to reduce the cost of test marketing is to test the product in a so-called electronic minimarket, which consists of several thousand consumers monitored by computers that are operated by market-research companies. Each consumer has a plastic identification card that she or he uses to make purchases in local stores. Computers in the stores track their purchases. In addition, each household's television set is equipped with a meter so that the market-research company can monitor the family's TV viewing habits and record the commercials they are exposed to. Using all these data, companies can evaluate consumer responses to new products and to pricing and promotion alternatives. Many argue that computer simulations are less reliable than traditional test marketing. However, simulations cost only about half as much.[31]

Commercialization

The final stage of development is **commercialization,** the large-scale production and distribution of those products that have survived the testing process. This phase requires the coordination of many activities—manufacturing, packaging, distribution, pricing, and promotion. A classic mistake is letting marketing get out of phase with production: The consumer is ready to buy the product before the company can supply it in adequate quantity. A mistake of this sort can be costly, because competitors may be able to jump in quickly. Many companies roll out their new products gradually, going from one geographic area to the next. This plan enables them to spread the costs of launching the product over a longer period and to refine their strategy as the rollout proceeds.

commercialization Large-scale production and distribution of a product

The Product Life Cycle

After launching a new product, the company is naturally eager for it to have a long and profitable life. However, few products last forever. Most go through a **product life cycle,** passing through four distinct stages in sales and earnings: introduction, growth, maturity, and decline (see Exhibit 13.4). As the product passes from stage to stage, various marketing approaches become appropriate.

product life cycle Stages of growth and decline in sales and earnings

The amount of time that elapses during any one of the stages depends on customer needs and preferences, economic conditions, the nature of the product, and the manufacturer's marketing strategy, among other factors. A basic product that serves a real need is likely to show steady growth for quite a few years before leveling off. In contrast, some high-technology items and many fashions and fads generally have relatively short life cycles. Products such as electric hot dog cookers sell for a season or two and then fall out of favor. Baking soda and safety pins, on the other hand, have been around for a long time.

Introduction

The first stage in the product life cycle is the *introductory stage,* during which the producer tries to stimulate demand. Typically, this stage

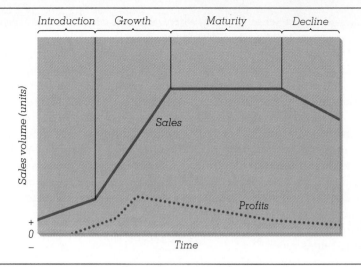

Exhibit 13.4
Stages in the Product Life Cycle
Almost all products and product categories have a life cycle like the one shown by the curve in this diagram. However, the duration of the life cycle varies widely from product to product. A business must introduce new products periodically to balance sales losses as older products decline.

involves an expensive advertising and promotional campaign, plus research-and-development costs. Products in the introductory phase generally require large investments to cover the costs of developing the product, building distribution systems, and educating the public about the product's benefits. The producer isn't likely to make a great deal of profit during this phase and, in many cases, won't make any profit for some time to come. Still, these costs are a necessary investment if a product is to succeed.

Growth

Next comes the *growth stage,* marked by a rapid jump in sales—and, usually, in the number of competitors—as the introductory effort starts paying off. As the product enters the growth phase, competition usually increases and the struggle for market share begins, creating pressure to maintain large promotional budgets and reduce prices. This competitive warfare is expensive, and often the small, weak firms do not survive. For the remaining participants, prices stabilize, and as sales volume increases, per-unit costs decline. The combination of stable prices and lower costs creates better profits, and producers begin to reap the rewards of their investment.

Of course, the right conditions have to exist in the market for this rapid growth to occur. When Indian entrepreneur Venugopal Dhoot started Videocon International to build television sets, sales started out rather slowly. At the time, programming was controlled by the government of India and wasn't very exciting, so few consumers had the incentive to buy their own sets. In 1994 Australian media magnate Rupert Murdoch began beaming a package of six satellite channels (including MTV) to India, and television sales took off. Dhoot sold over 1 million sets that same year. Also, true to form, competition showed up, including Philips India (a subsidiary of the giant Dutch electronics firm) and manufacturers from Japan and Korea.[32]

Maturity

During the *maturity stage,* sales begin to level off or show a slight decline. This slowdown may result in overcapacity in the industry, prompting producers to cut prices to fill their plants. The maturity phase is typically the longest phase in the product life cycle, and the costs of introduction and growth have diminished. Companies count on the profits generated by mature-phase products to fund development of new products, so they work hard to keep products competitive.

One key to success in the maturity phase is to stimulate consumption of the existing product by broadening its appeal or making minor improvements. When Cheez Whiz sales leveled off, the marketers at Kraft General Foods decided not to let their product fade into the sunset. With the help of a $6 million advertising budget, they began promoting Cheez Whiz as a cheese sauce for the microwave oven, and sales climbed by 35 percent.[33]

Decline

Although maturity can be extended for many years, eventually most products enter the *decline phase,* when sales and profits begin to slip and eventually fade away. Declines occur for several reasons: changing demographics, shifts in popular taste, and advances in technology.

When a product reaches this phase, the company must decide whether to remain in the game or to discontinue the product and focus on newer items. Products sold through retail outlets can also get crowded off store shelves if they don't bring retailers enough revenue, even if the manufacturer would like to keep the products alive. Brands such as Ovaltine, Brylcreem, Aqua Velva, and Lifebouy are among the many consumer products that were once leaders in their categories but are now in danger of being dropped.[34]

PRODUCT-MIX AND PRODUCT-LINE DECISIONS

Anticipating the impact of product life cycles, most companies continually add and drop products to ensure that declining items will be replaced by growth products. In this way, they develop a **product mix,** a collection of goods or services offered for sale. The broad product groups within the product mix are called **product lines,** which consist of groups of products that are similar in terms of use or characteristics (see Exhibit 13.5).

product mix Complete list of all products that a company offers for sale

product lines Groups of products that are physically similar or that are intended for similar markets

Width and Depth of Product Mix

Product mixes vary in terms of their width and depth. The simplest product mix is not really a mix at all, but rather a single product. Most companies, however, find that they need more than one product to sustain their sales growth. Many of the largest companies offer thousands of different products.

When deciding on the width of its product mix, a company weighs the risks and rewards associated with various approaches. Some companies limit their product offerings because this method is economical: They can keep production costs per unit down and also limit selling expenses to a single sales force. Other companies follow the philosophy that a broad product mix is insurance against shifts in technology, taste, and economic conditions.

Width of product mix				
Ready-to-Eat Cereals	**Convenience Foods**	**Snack Foods**	**Baking Products**	**Dairy Products**
Clusters	Betty Crocker Cake Mixes	Pop Secret Popcorn	Gold Medal Flour	Yoplait Yogurt
Total		The Berry Bears	Bisquick	
Wheaties	Creamy Deluxe Frosting	Shark Bites	Bac-Os	
Raisin Nut Bran	MicroRave Dessert Mixes	Fruit Roll-Ups		
Oatmeal Raisin Crisp		Fruit Wrinkles		
	Hamburger Helper	Squeezit Fruit Drink		
Oatmeal Swirlers	Potato Medleys Side Dishes	Nature Valley Granola Bars		
Cinnamon Toast Crunch	Suddenly Salad	Bugles Corn Snacks		
Cheerios				
Kix				
Benefit				

Depth of product mix (vertical axis label)

Exhibit 13.5

The Product Mix at General Mills
Selected products from General Mills show a product mix that is fairly wide but is of varying depth inside each product line.

Product-Line Strategies

Within each product line, a company once again confronts decisions about the number of goods and services to offer. How many sizes and flavors of popcorn products should Orville Redenbacher offer? A full-line strategy involves selling a wide number and variety of products, whereas a limited-line strategy focuses on selling a few selected items.

Product lines have a tendency to grow over time as companies look for new ways to boost sales. A line can be expanded in a number of ways:

- *Line filling* is developing items to fill gaps in the market that have been overlooked by competitors or that have emerged as consumers' tastes and needs shift.
- *Line extensions* are new variations of a basic product, such as Tartar Control Crest.
- *Brand extensions* occur when the brand name for an existing product category is extended to a new category, as in the case of Jell-O Pudding Pops.
- *Line stretching* involves the addition of higher- or lower-priced items at either end of the current product line, thus extending its appeal to new economic groups.

PRICING

Once a company has developed a product, it has to decide how to price it. Unfortunately, there are no easy answers. Deciding on a price is tricky, and the stakes are high. If the company charges too much, it will make fewer sales; if it charges too little, it will sacrifice profits that it might have gained. How much is just right? That question is one of the most important ones a business faces. Consider the example of Mazda's RX-7 sports car. In 1985 the price was $16,000, and the company sold 54,000, for revenue on the product of $864 million. In 1993, when the price had soared to $36,000, Mazda sold only 5,000, for a revenue figure of $180 million—an 80 percent drop.[35] Clearly, businesses need to make pricing decisions with great care.

Factors That Affect Pricing Decisions

A company's pricing decisions are influenced by a variety of internal and external factors. The firm's marketing objectives and costs provide a rough indication of what it should charge for its goods or services. Before establishing a final price, however, the firm also considers government regulations, the level of demand, the nature of the competition, and the needs of wholesalers and retailers who distribute the product to the final customer.

Marketing Objectives

The first step in setting a price is to decide what you are trying to accomplish with a particular good or service. Some of the most common objectives are

- To achieve a certain overall profit target
- To increase sales
- To get a bigger share of the market
- To achieve high profits on a particular product
- To discourage competition
- To promote a particular product image
- To accomplish social or ethical goals[36]

Sometimes several objectives are pursued simultaneously.

A major goal for most companies is to reach overall profit targets. To measure their success in hitting those targets, most companies calculate their **return on investment (ROI),** which is profit expressed as a percentage of capital investment.

return on investment (ROI) Profit equal to a certain percentage of a business's invested capital

In addition to its general pricing policy, a company may also have specific objectives for individual products. It may want to maximize sales or gain market share. It may want to achieve high returns on each unit sold, although this objective may conflict with the desire to build sales volume, because the price required to earn a high return may be so high that it discourages customers.

Other objectives might relate to the competitive environment. To eliminate competition or discourage new companies from becoming competitors, a company might charge an extremely low price for its product. Later, when the company has established control of the market, it might then raise the price to improve its own profits.

Some pricing decisions are based on a desire to achieve a particular image or reputation. Rolex watches, for example, are priced at a premium partly to convey the message that they are superior products and partly to cover the higher costs associated with high-quality materials. An organization's pricing objective might also be related to public relations or to social and ethical considerations. Many hospitals adjust their prices to accommodate people who are unable to pay the full rate.

Often a company's pricing goals for a product vary over time, depending on the product's stage in its life cycle. During the introductory phase, the objective might be to recover development costs as quickly as possible. To achieve this goal, the manufacturer might charge a high initial price—a practice known as **skimming**—and then drop the price later, when the product is no longer a novelty and competition heats up. Alternatively, a company might try to build sales volume by charging a low initial price, a practice known as **penetration pricing.** The objective would be to reach a high volume of sales quickly in order to achieve economies of scale and reduce per-unit costs. This approach might have the added advantage of discouraging competitors, because the low price (which the competition would be pressured to match) limits the profit potential for everyone.

Later, during the maturity phase, the goal might be to attract additional customers or to maximize the cash provided by the product. As the product enters its decline, the company's objective might be to get out of the business quickly. To accomplish this, it might establish a low price that will clear out the inventory.

Costs

Every company must translate its own particular objectives into specific prices for specific products. To do so, it must first analyze its costs, since costs establish the minimum acceptable price. To survive over the long term, the company must charge a price that will cover the costs incurred in producing and selling the product.

Two types of costs are associated with producing a product: fixed costs and variable costs. **Fixed costs**—including rent payments, utility bills, insurance premiums, and administrative expenses—are not affected by the number of products sold. Regardless of whether a company sells 10 units or 100 units, the rent on the building must be paid on time. **Variable costs,** on the other hand, do depend on the volume sold. They include raw materials, labor used in production, and supplies consumed during production. The total cost of operating the business is the sum of the fixed and variable costs.

In general, costs decline as volume increases. The more units you produce, the lower the cost per unit tends to be, since the fixed costs are spread over a larger number of units. In addition, as you produce more units, you achieve economies of scale in production, distribution, and promotion. Also, as employees become more skilled at their jobs, production and marketing costs decline even more. This phenomenon, referred to as the **experience curve,** gives companies an incentive to price their products relatively low in order to build volume.

Government Regulations

The U.S. government plays a big role in pricing, as do the governments of many other countries. In an effort to protect consumers and encourage fair competition, the government has enacted various price-related laws over the years, and all marketers need to be aware

---

skimming *Charging a high price for a new product during the introductory stage and lowering the price later*

penetration pricing *Introducing a new product at a low price in hopes of building sales volume quickly*

fixed costs *Business costs that must be covered no matter how many units of a product a company sells*

variable costs *Business costs that increase with the number of units produced*

experience curve *Predictable decline of all costs associated with a product as the total number of units produced increases*

---

of their ramifications. Three important classes of price regulations are price fixing, price discrimination, and deceptive pricing.

Price Fixing. When two or more companies supplying the same type of products agree on the prices they charge or on the formulas they use to set prices, they are engaging in a practice known as **price fixing.** In nearly all cases, price fixing is illegal; two exceptions are when the government itself fixes prices or when regulated public utilities set prices for their services (which they can do only after government approval).[37]

Price Discrimination. One of the most important pieces of pricing-related legislation in the United States is the Robinson-Patman Act of 1936. A key part of this legislation outlaws **price discrimination,** the practice of unfairly offering attractive discounts to some customers but not to others. Price discrimination applies only to tangible goods of the same grade and quality; it doesn't apply to services. Furthermore, the difference in prices must be proven to adversely affect competition. Robinson-Patman was originally passed to protect small retailers who weren't able to command the same discounts from food producers as their large chain-store competitors could; nearly all the defendants in Robinson-Patman cases are large companies.[38]

Deceptive Pricing. The Federal Trade Commission (FTC) has the authority to investigate and stop pricing schemes that it considers misleading; the term normally used in such cases is **deceptive pricing.** The problem being addressed is not so much a pricing issue; rather, it's the way prices are promoted. The FTC's guidelines describe several practices considered deceptive pricing, including (1) comparisons with old prices that weren't in effect for a substantial length of time, (2) comparisons with competitive prices that aren't really being charged by competitors, (3) comparisons with manufacturers' suggested retail prices, and (4) bargains with strings attached.[39]

Laws against deceptive pricing are common throughout the world. Germany, France, Japan, Finland, New Zealand, Norway, Sweden, Switzerland, the United Kingdom, and other countries all have laws

price fixing *Illegal cooperation between two or more companies that agree on prices in order to reduce competition*

price discrimination *Offering a discount to one customer but not to another, with the intention of restraining competition*

deceptive pricing *Range of pricing and promotion practices that are considered misleading by government regulators*

Pricing laws lay out specific rules that marketers must follow when promoting discounts.

that regulate the promotion of prices. Concern is growing in many countries about the way prices are advertised, so all marketers operating internationally must learn about the price regulations of each country in which they do business.[40]

Price and Demand

Whereas a company's costs establish a floor for prices, demand for the product establishes a ceiling. Theoretically, if the price for an item is too high, demand falls and the producers reduce their prices to stimulate demand. As prices fall, profits decline, thereby discouraging further production. Conversely, if the price for an item is too low, demand increases and the producers are motivated to raise prices. As prices climb and profits improve, producers boost their output until supply and demand are in balance and prices stabilize.

The relationship between price and demand isn't always this clear-cut, however. Some goods and services are relatively insensitive to changes in price. Marketers refer to this insensitivity as **inelastic demand**—meaning that demand does not stretch or contract with changes in price. Conversely, a market that is highly responsive to price changes exhibits **elastic demand.** Undifferentiated goods and services typically fall into this category (see Exhibit 13.6).

Generally speaking, when people go shopping, they have a rough price range in mind. If the item they seek is available within that range, they are likely to buy it. If the price is either too low or too high, they hesitate.[41] An unexpectedly low price triggers fear that the item is inferior in quality, whereas an unexpectedly high price makes buyers question whether the product is worth the money.

Competitive Conditions

Because many customers compare prices before buying, companies need to consider the competition when making their pricing decisions. Orville Redenbacher wants his namesake popcorn to be perceived as top-quality, so it is generally priced above the market—that is, at prices higher than those of competitors. His choice is appropriate because he wants consumers to perceive a price-quality relationship. A premium price is also appropriate when the producer wants to appeal to a status-conscious buyer. The expense of owning a Rolls-Royce is part of its appeal.

---

inelastic demand *Situation in which a percentage change in price produces no percentage change in the quantity sold*

elastic demand *Situation in which a percentage change in price produces a distinct percentage change in the quantity sold*

Exhibit 13.6
Price Elasticity
The two general categories of price-demand relationships are elastic demand, in which a given change in price creates a disproportionately larger change in demand, and inelastic demand, in which a price change generates a proportionately smaller demand change. In other words, when prices are elastic, customers are more sensitive to price changes.

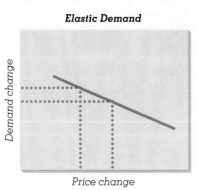

Elastic Demand

(y-axis: Demand change; x-axis: Price change)

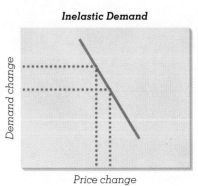

Inelastic Demand

(y-axis: Demand change; x-axis: Price change)

Other firms follow the practice of pricing below the market. Sometimes this policy of underselling the competition is used as a way of breaking into an established market. Volkswagen initially priced its automobiles in this manner. Some firms rely totally on lower prices to attract customers. Discount stores use this approach. Pricing below the market is a particularly effective way to capture a larger share of the market.

A third alternative is pricing with the market. Generally, this means following the pricing policy of a major company in the industry. This company is known as the **price leader.** By pricing with the market, companies avoid the effort required to find out what the consumer would actually pay. Instead, they assume that the price leader has done this research and has established the right price. In this way, they also avoid the unpleasantness of price competition. Companies almost always prefer to compete by attracting customers with their product's features rather than by waging a pricing war.

price leader Major producer in an industry that tends to set the pace in establishing prices

Pricing Methods

After considering all the internal and external factors that have a bearing on price, the company must establish a specific price for its goods or services. Two common methods for setting prices are markup pricing and break-even analysis.

Markup Pricing

Department stores and other retailers often use this method of setting prices. **Markup** is usually defined as the difference between the cost of an item and its selling price. In modern merchandising, firms generally express this difference in terms of the **markup percentage.** For example, if an item costs a firm $50 and is sold for $75, the markup is $25; the markup is $33\frac{1}{3}$ percent of the selling price. This markup percentage has two purposes: It must cover all the expenses of the firm (including both the cost of the item and the cost of selling it), and it must be high enough to allow some profit.

markup Amount added to the cost of an item to create a selling price that produces a profit

markup percentage Difference in percentage between the cost of an item and its selling price

Many businesses offer a large number of products; department stores, for example, can handle over 100,000 items. In cases like this, calculating the markup percentage for each single item is difficult. Thus, many businesses use an **average markup** when setting prices—that is, the same markup percentage is used for each item in a given product line.

average markup Constant markup percentage used in setting prices for all products in a product line

Markups vary by type of store. Take an item costing retailers 50 cents. The markup might range from a low of 22 percent for a supermarket to a high of 55 percent for a florist, and thus the retail price might vary from a low of 61 cents to a high of $1.11. Florists have a high markup percentage because they deal in extremely perishable goods that are sold to a relatively small market. Another factor in the wide range of markup percentages is **turnover,** the number of times the firm's average inventory is sold during a given period. If a firm's average inventory is $1,000 and sales for a month amount to $3,000, the firm can surmise that the average inventory has turned over three times. The slower the rate of turnover, the higher the markup must be to yield a given amount of profit.

turnover Number of times that average inventory is sold during a given period

break-even analysis *Method of calcu-lating the minimum volume of sales needed at a given price to cover all costs*

break-even point *Sales volume at a given price that will cover all of a company's costs*

Break-Even Analysis

Another approach to pricing involves the use of **break-even analy-sis,** which enables a company to determine how many units of a product it would have to sell at a given price in order to cover all costs, or to break even. The **break-even point** is the minimum sales volume the company needs in order to keep from losing money. Sales above that point produce a profit; sales below that point result in a loss. You can determine the break-even point with this simple calcu-lation:

$$\text{Break-even point (in units)} = \frac{\text{fixed costs}}{\text{selling price per unit} - \text{variable costs per unit}}$$

If you wanted to price haircuts at $20 and you had fixed costs of $60,000 and variable costs per haircut of $5, you would need to sell 4,000 of them to break even:

$$\text{Break-even point (in units)} = \frac{\$60,000}{\$20 - \$5} = 4,000 \text{ units}$$

However, $20 isn't your only pricing option. Why not charge $30 in-stead? When you charge the higher price, you need to give only 2,400 haircuts to break even (see Exhibit 13.7). Before you raise your hair-cut prices to $30, however, bear in mind that a lower price may at-tract more customers and enable you to make more money in the long run.

Break-even analysis by itself won't indicate exactly what price a company should charge, but it will provide some insight into the number of units that will have to be sold at a given price to make a profit. This form of analysis is also useful if the price of an item may be set at various levels. The airlines, for example, offer a variety of fares. Once a certain number of seats are filled at the standard price, the airline breaks even. Beyond that point, any additional ticket sales are nearly all profit because variable costs per unit are so low. The airline can afford to offer super-low fares for these seats because fill-ing them doesn't cost the airline much extra.

Exhibit 13.7
Break-Even Analysis
The break-even point is the point at which revenues will just cover costs. After fixed costs and vari-able costs are met, any additional income represents profit. The chart shows that at $20 per hair-cut, the break-even point is reached at 4,000 haircuts; charg-ing $30 per haircut yields a break-even point at only 2,400 haircuts.

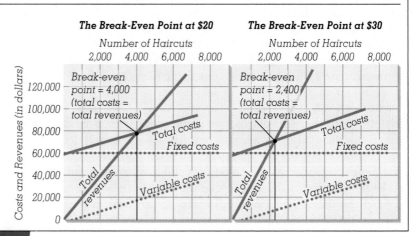

Pricing Strategies

Fine-tuning the price of a product may mean the difference between success and failure in a business. Companies use a variety of **pricing strategies,** or systematic approaches to setting prices, to optimize their pricing decisions. Three of these approaches are price lining, odd-even pricing, and discount pricing.

Many companies follow a policy called **price lining,** offering their products at a limited number of set prices. Companies marketing audiocassettes may offer a $6 line, a $9 line, and a $12 line. Price lining has two advantages: It simplifies the job of selling the products, and it makes the consumer's choice easier by limiting the number of alternatives.

In many industries, prices tend to end in numbers slightly below the next dollar figure, such as $3.95, $4.98, or $7.99. This method is known as **odd-even pricing.** The assumption here is that a customer sees $3.98 as being significantly lower than $4.00; thus, the company will sell more at only 2 cents less. Few studies have tested the effectiveness of such pricing, but those that have been done suggest that customers are more rational than odd-even pricing assumes.

With **discount pricing,** companies offer various types of temporary price reductions, depending on the type of customer and the type of item being offered. A **trade discount** is offered by the producer to the wholesaler or retailer. An interior decorator, for example, may buy furniture from a manufacturer at a discount and then resell it to a client. A **quantity discount** gives customers a break on price if they purchase specified quantities of goods or services. Theoretically, these buyers deserve a price break because they are cheaper to serve; they reduce the cost of selling, storing, and shipping products and of billing customers. A **cash discount** is a price reduction offered to people who pay in cash or who pay promptly. The designation "2/10, net 30" means that the bill is due in 30 days, but if payment is received within 10 days, the customer is eligible for a 2 percent discount.

pricing strategies Systematic approaches to setting price

price lining Offering merchandise at a limited number of set prices

odd-even pricing Setting a price at an odd amount slightly below the next highest dollar figure

discount pricing Offering a reduction in price

trade discount Discount offered to a wholesaler or retailer

quantity discount Discount offered to buyers of large quantities

cash discount Discount offered to buyers who use cash instead of credit

SUMMARY OF LEARNING OBJECTIVES

1 List three types of consumer products and two types of organizational products.
Consumer products may be subdivided into convenience products, shopping products, and specialty products, depending on the approach that the buyer uses when shopping for the item. Organizational products may be subdivided into expense items, which are lower-cost products normally consumed within a year of purchase, and capital items, which cost more and typically last longer.

2 Cite the three levels of brand loyalty and explain the concept of brand equity.
The first level of brand loyalty is brand awareness, in which the buyer is familiar with the product. The next level is brand preference, in which the buyer will select the product if it is available. The final level is brand insistence, in which the buyer will accept no substitute. Brand equity is a measure of the value a brand represents to the company that owns it; more and more companies are trying to assign financial values to their brands, just as they do to their tangible assets.

3 Discuss the functions of packaging.
Packaging provides protection, makes products easier to display, attracts attention, and discourages theft. In addition, packaging enhances the convenience of the product and communicates its attributes to the buyer.

4 Describe the five stages of product development.

The first stage of product development involves generating and screening ideas to isolate those with the most potential. The promising ideas are analyzed to determine their likely profitability. Those that appear worthwhile enter the prototype-development stage, in which a limited number of the products are created. In the next stage, the product is subjected to a market test to determine buyer response. Products that survive market testing are then commercialized.

5 Specify the four stages in the life cycle of a product.

Products move from the introductory phase through a growth phase; then they pass into maturity and eventually decline.

6 Identify four ways of expanding a product line.

A product line can be expanded by filling gaps in the market, by extending the line to include new varieties of existing products, by extending the brand to new product categories, and by stretching the line to include lower- or higher-priced items.

7 List seven common pricing objectives.

Through their pricing tactics, companies attempt to achieve a particular return on investment, increase sales, gain market share, earn a high profit on a product, discourage competition, promote a particular image, or accomplish social or ethical goals.

8 Distinguish between two methods for setting prices.

When setting prices, companies often apply a markup percentage that sets the price at some level above costs. Another approach is to conduct a break-even analysis that indicates how many units of a product a company would have to sell at a given price in order to cover its costs.

ON THE JOB: MEETING BUSINESS CHALLENGES AT ORVILLE REDENBACHER

Popcorn marketers divide time into two distinct eras: pre-Redenbacher and post-Redenbacher. The pre-Redenbacher period in the United States stretches back centuries. At the first Thanksgiving celebration in Plymouth, the Indians treated the colonists to the taste of corn popped over the fire. In the years to come, people sometimes popped corn in a wire basket held over the fire in the fireplace, but popcorn never even came close to being a food fad.

The popcorn business started to heat up late in the nineteenth century, when agricultural experts discovered how to grow hybrid corns that produced better-tasting, fluffier popcorn. By the turn of the century, the industry had its first brand-name product. The pioneer was Cracker Jack, the caramel-covered popcorn-and-peanut confection packaged with a prize inside. In the twentieth century, unflavored pop-at-home corn products appeared regionally on store shelves, primarily in the South and the Midwest. Products such as Jolly Time employed modest advertising claims. Then Orville Redenbacher arrived in 1970 with his hybrid gourmet brand, Orville Redenbacher's Gourmet Popping Corn, and the post-Redenbacher period was set to begin.

Even after changing the name from Red Bow (a combination of his and partner Charlie Bowman's names), Redenbacher wasn't sure his product would be a hit. Consumers still thought of popcorn as a commodity good. The challenge was to encourage people to sample his popcorn and to begin thinking of it as a specialty product so that they would ask for it by name and pay a premium price. Redenbacher differentiated his product in a variety of ways. Whereas competitors packaged their corn kernels in cans or in plastic bags, Redenbacher packaged his corn in glass jars that were vacuum-sealed to keep the kernels fresh. Another twist was in the labeling. The label sported a picture of Redenbacher himself, portraying the co-founder as the sincere popping-corn expert and enthusiast he is.

Redenbacher also went to work on distribution and promotion. He decided that Marshall Field's, the illustrious Chicago department store, would be an appropriate retail outlet. So he sent a case of his popcorn to the manager of the gourmet-food department, waited a month, and then called to ask whether he liked it. The manager was very enthusiastic and placed an order immediately. Redenbacher drove his truck to the store's loading dock and hung around, offering to autograph jars for purchasers. That was the start of a promotional strategy that worked wonders for the fledgling product. Marshall Field's ran newspaper ads about the product and the offer, Redenbacher signed countless jars over the course of three days, and television reporters recounted the story of "the popcorn with a personality."

Next Redenbacher drove a shipment up to Byerly's, an upscale Minnesota supermarket, and looked for other retailers who wanted fancier foods. By this time, the product was catching on, bolstered by the personal promotion. Redenbacher and his partner Charlie Bowman could barely keep up with the flood of orders. In late 1971, Redenbacher turned over distribution in the South and the Southeast to Blue Plate Foods, a subsidiary of Hunt-Wesson Foods. The following year, when Blue Plate launched Orville Redenbacher's Gourmet Popping Corn across the country, Redenbacher traveled almost nonstop for six months to promote his product on radio, on television, in newspapers, and in magazines.

Redenbacher's strategy was paying off: More people were buying the notion of a gourmet popcorn and buying his brand. The product sold 365,000 pounds in 1970–1971, 1 million pounds in 1972–1973, and more than 5 million pounds in 1975–1976. In 1976 Redenbacher and Bowman sold their business to Hunt-Wesson, and Redenbacher agreed to continue his popcorn pilgrimages as brand spokesperson. New parent Hunt-Wesson promptly plunked down several million dollars to promote its popcorn sensation, a figure that was reportedly 10 times larger than the annual ad budgets of all competitors combined. This advertising onslaught sealed Redenbacher's fate as the most famous name—and face—in popcorn.

Of course, it didn't hurt that the product was top-quality and hit the market at the right time. In an increasingly weight-conscious, health-conscious society, a snack low in calories and high in fiber was appealing. Other brands began to chime in with their own claims, some stressing quality, some stressing economy, all riding the crest of the popcorn revolution that Redenbacher had spawned.

The post-Redenbacher boom continues, with new popcorn products (the most successful being microwavable popcorn) capturing the imagination and the pocketbooks of consumers everywhere. The Orville Redenbacher brand is still the best-selling popcorn brand in the world, and Hunt-Wesson intends to keep it that way, no matter how competitors try to turn up the heat.

Your Mission: You're the product manager for Orville Redenbacher's Gourmet Popping Corn. You've been delighted with the sales results of the Orville Redenbacher brand to date, but you've noticed that the number of competitors in the gourmet-popcorn market has multiplied. Also, you're concerned that premium popcorn is losing its appeal as a specialty product. Hunt-Wesson wants you to consider additional ways to increase the product's appeal, based on the product life cycle and the product's own elements. In the following situations, use your knowledge of product concepts to select the answers that will best support your product:

1. As the product manager, you are responsible for recommending new product ideas. Marketing research tells you that the Orville Redenbacher brand is the best-known name in the popcorn business, thanks to your extensive advertising and the personal promotion efforts of Redenbacher himself. You are thinking about using the brand loyalty your customers feel for Orville Redenbacher's Gourmet Popping Corn to create new products under the same brand name. You've checked out your competitors, and you've also gone into the field to take a look at other snacks and related products. Of the brand extension ideas you got when you were doing your research, which of these would you recommend?

a. A line of Orville Redenbacher salty snacks, including pretzels and potato chips

b. A line of Orville Redenbacher popcorn accessories, including popcorn popping oil, popcorn butter, and popcorn salt

c. A line of Orville Redenbacher baked corn products, such as corn muffins and cornbread

2. There's no doubt that the supermarket shelves are overflowing with premium home-popping competitors such as Borden's Cracker Jack Extra Fresh Popping Corn, Old Capital Popcorn, and Yoder's T. T. Popcorn. Although Orville Redenbacher sales have been going up steadily, the pace of growth has slowed. You suspect that the rate of adoption for all gourmet popcorns has increased as consumers learn more about this type of product, but that increased competition is cutting into the sales momentum for your own product. In effect, gourmet popcorns have become a convenience product again because the novelty has worn off. How can you persuade consumers to see the Orville Redenbacher product as a shopping product (or even as a specialty product) so that they will purchase by brand? At the same time, how can you keep competitors in the convenience-product category?

a. Remove Orville Redenbacher popcorn from supermarkets and distribute the product only through gourmet food shops, mail-order fancy-food catalogs, and upscale department stores.

b. Hold in-store demonstrations of Orville Redenbacher popcorn being popped alongside the leading brands. Prove to consumers that your brand pops up fluffier, tastes better, and produces more popcorn per jar than any competitor.

c. Change the packaging and the label. Use a classier-looking label in black and gold foil that emphasizes the premium nature of the product, and put the popcorn into a jar that's shaped like a champagne glass. This approach will convey upscale quality to the consumer.

3. Now that your product is in the mature stage of the product life cycle and has attracted a bucketful of competitors, it may be time to rethink the premium-pricing aspect. Even the consumers who are laggards have probably tried gourmet popcorn by now. It may not be feasible to continue promoting Orville Redenbacher as an expensive but high-quality popcorn product when other brands are making similar quality claims. However, you know that your brand is differentiated from non-gourmet products by a variety of elements, including higher price. Which of these price-related actions can you take (1) to keep customers coming back for more and (2) to maintain the image of a gourmet-popcorn product?

a. Offer a limited-time two-for-one promotion that encourages customers to stock up on Orville Redenbacher. When they have two jars of your product, customers are less likely to buy another package of a competing product.

b. Offer a rebate coupon. When consumers send in two labels from Orville Redenbacher products, send them a coupon good for $1 off their next Orville Redenbacher purchase.

c. Place 25-cent coupons for Orville Redenbacher in upscale newspapers and magazines (such as *Money*). Emphasize the gourmet taste and encourage trial and comparison against other brands.

4. Another way to boost sales in the maturity phase is to stimulate additional sales to current customers. At this point, you believe that all the consumers who plan to adopt your product have already given it a try and made a decision. However, popcorn's status as a healthy snack has been underexploited, and you think that people who like gourmet popcorn will buy and eat more if they become aware of the nutritional benefits of the product. You can approach this challenge from many angles. Of the following ideas, which do you think will help sell more Orville Redenbacher Gourmet Popping Corn to current customers?

a. Enhance the product by adding nutritional flavorings to the popcorn. For example, use vitamin-fortified flavorings to boost the level of nutrients. Then advertise the extra nutritional value in a special campaign, and develop new labels that highlight the added nutritional value.

b. Have Weight Watchers endorse Orville Redenbacher popcorn as the perfect snack for people who want to lose weight and who care about nutrition. Give Weight Watchers a free supply of your popcorn to serve during meetings, and provide Weight Watchers groups with signs that reinforce the Orville Redenbacher name as the official popcorn of the Weight Watchers program.

c. Write articles for nutritional journals and health magazines. The articles should explain why popcorn is nutritious, comparing Orville Redenbacher's nutritional value with that of other snacks such as pretzels and chocolate bars.[42]

KEY TERMS

average markup (395)
brand (378)
brand awareness (380)
brand equity (381)
brand insistence (381)
brand loyalty (380)
brand marks (378)
brand names (378)
brand preference (380)
break-even analysis (396)
break-even point (396)
capital items (377)
cash discount (397)
commercialization (387)
components (378)
concept testing (385)
consumer products (376)
convenience products (377)
deceptive pricing (393)
discount pricing (397)
elastic demand (394)

expense items (377)
experience curve (392)
family branding (381)
fixed costs (392)
generic products (380)
inelastic demand (394)
installations (378)
licensing (382)
markup (395)
markup percentage (395)
MRO items (378)
national brands (379)
odd-even pricing (397)
organizational products (377)
penetration pricing (392)
price discrimination (393)
price fixing (393)
price leader (395)
price lining (397)
pricing strategies (397)
private brands (379)

product (374)
product-development process (385)
product life cycle (387)
product lines (389)
product mix (389)
prototypes (386)
quantity discount (397)
raw materials (378)
return on investment (ROI) (391)
shopping products (377)
skimming (392)
specialty products (377)
supplies (378)
test marketing (386)
trade discount (397)
trademark (378)
turnover (395)
Universal Product Codes (UPCs) (384)
variable costs (392)

1. What is the difference between expense items and capital items?
2. What are the advantages and disadvantages of establishing a brand name?
3. Why would a marketer want to use a licensed label?

4. Why do businesses continually introduce new products, given the risks and high rate of failure of new products?
5. What function do mature products play in a company's product mix?
6. What are the advantages and disadvantages of having a wide product mix as opposed to a narrow product mix?

7. What role does the government play in pricing?
8. What three alternatives are available to companies that take a market-based approach to pricing?

A CASE FOR CRITICAL THINKING

MINIVANS: FAMILIES LOVE THE CONVENIENCE; CHRYSLER LOVES THE PROFITS

With millions of minivans chugging down the nation's highways, it's easy to forget what a radical idea the minivan was when it was introduced in 1984. In fact, the minivan was the first truly new idea in automobiles since the Jeep was adapted for civilian use at the end of World War II, nearly 40 years earlier. The story of the minivan highlights the high-stakes gamble that product development often represents—and the tremendous profits that a winning idea can produce.

Boxy utility vehicles and vans of various designs began to appear as far back as the 1930s, but they didn't see much commercial success until the 1960s, when General Motors and Ford began pushing their utilitarian vans. These utility vans found fans among tradespeople, who could carry tools, supplies, and a small crew. (The other van to appear in this era, VW's Microbus, gained a strong association with hippies and didn't make much of a dent in the overall market.)

The utility vans weren't seen as family vehicles, however. They were associated with painters and

plumbers, and they didn't handle as well as passenger cars, either. If you had a crew of kids to haul around, you bought a station wagon, the one-time king of family vehicles. Not only could they carry quite a few people, they handled better and rode smoother than the utility vans. Then again, the station wagons didn't offer nearly as much cargo room as the vans offered, so it wasn't easy to carry lots of camping gear, lumber, or the myriad other things that families need to move around.

What people really wanted, even though few probably ever envisioned it, was a vehicle that combined the practicality of a utility van with the handling and comfort of a car. By the 1970s, both GM and Ford were tinkering with such a vehicle. GM, in fact, had one designed by the late 1970s. However, the company was focused on redesigning its passenger cars and pulled the plug on the minivan. (Many people inside GM didn't even know about the project until 1994, when somebody found a photograph of a prototype in some old files.) Over at Ford, then-president Lee Iacocca was battling with his boss, Henry Ford II, over building a minivan, too. Mr. Ford wanted nothing to do with the pro-

ject, and when Iacocca quit to move to Chrysler in 1978, his old employer thought so little of the minivan idea that Ford let him take all the customer research Ford had done on minivans.

When Iacocca arrived at Chrysler, he took over a company that was in serious financial trouble. In fact, desperation probably had a lot to do with Iacocca's decision to push ahead with a minivan—if you're sinking, you might as well try something dramatic. This time, dramatic measures paid off in a dramatic way. After pulling money from other programs and taking a huge gamble on the minivan, Iacocca and his team probably leapt for joy as their innovative creation turned the auto market upside down. In its first 10 years, Chrysler sold 3.7 million minivans and left both GM and Ford in the dust. Not only does Chrysler sell lots of minivans, it makes lots of money on each one, too—as much as $6,000 in gross profit on a $19,000 vehicle.

GM and Ford, meanwhile, are still struggling to catch up. Their first minivans were designed by their truck divisions and didn't have the carlike ride that most minivan drivers demand. Ford didn't make a minivan comparable to Chrysler's until 1992. GM didn't attack the minivan market aggressively at first because it didn't want to hammer sales of its own station wagons. Unfortunately for GM, its wagon owners switched to Chrysler's minivans, and the station wagon market went into a nosedive. Thanks to a gutsy gamble and close attention to customer needs, Chrysler built a huge head start and remains the number 1 minivan supplier by a wide margin.

1. How are the concepts of brand awareness and brand loyalty going to come into play as Chrysler continues to fend off emerging competitors?
2. How did product-mix concerns hamper GM's efforts to become a competitive force in the minivan market?
3. Why is Chrysler able to continue making such a healthy profit on its minivans? Explain your answer in terms of both competition and consumer demand.

BUILDING YOUR COMMUNICATION SKILLS

Examine the life cycle of a product with which you are familiar. Locate an article in a magazine or book that describes the life cycle of that product. Note the factors affecting its introduction, its growth, and the strategies that have been used to maintain sales as it reached maturity. If this product has experienced a decline, identify the causes, and describe the manufacturer's attempts to revive the product.

• As directed by your instructor, prepare a brief presentation describing the life cycle of the product.
• In a class discussion, identify the factors contributing to the various stages in your chosen product's life cycle, and compare them with those of products examined by other students. Identify common elements in the life cycles of all the products evaluated by class members.

KEEPING CURRENT USING *THE WALL STREET JOURNAL*

Scan recent issues of *The Wall Street Journal* for an article related to one of the following:

• New-product development
• The product life cycle
• Pricing strategies
• Packaging

1. Does this article report on a development in a particular company, several companies, or an entire industry? Which companies or industries are specifically mentioned?
2. If you were a marketing manager in this industry, what concerns would you have as a result of reading the article? What questions do you think companies in this industry (or related ones) should be asking? What would you want to know?
3. In what ways do you think this industry, other industries, or the public might be affected by this trend or development in the next five years? Why?

SO WHY DO TEXTBOOKS COST SO MUCH?

Synopsis

This program addresses a marketing topic that is near and dear to every one of you: the price of textbooks. You can view this video at two levels. First, as a potential marketing manager, you can gain insights into the risks of developing a new product and the challenge of setting prices. Second, as a consumer of textbooks, you would undoubtedly like to know why college texts cost as much as they do. This program answers that question by showing you the steps in the development process for textbooks and pointing out the costs behind the prices. When you realize that college bookstores see a profit of only 5 cents on the dollar, look at the expenses publishers incur as they develop books, and then compare book prices with increases in tuition and other expenses, you'll realize that textbooks are a better deal than is commonly thought.

Exercises

ANALYSIS

1. What sort of buyer behavior is associated with a college's or instructor's decision to adopt a new textbook?

2. If the fixed costs of producing a textbook are $350,000, the variable costs are $10 per book, and the price the publisher receives from the bookstore is $25, what is the publisher's break-even point?

3. Would your business textbook have the same product life-cycle curve as a basic math text? A classic work of literature?

4. How does the notion of product testing apply to textbooks?

5. How does the idea of packaging apply to textbooks?

APPLICATION

Can you think of any ways to reduce the cost and/or risks of producing textbooks?

DECISION

If you were a successful textbook author and wanted to apply brand extension to create another product (your highly regarded name is basically the "brand" in this case), would you pick a textbook in a related field (e.g., go from a business text to a business-law text) or a book aimed at professional managers?

COMMUNICATION

Assume you write a column in the student newspaper and your new assignment is to explain why textbooks cost what they do. In two or three paragraphs, express the information presented in the video in your own words.

INTEGRATION

Considering the issues of international business described in Chapter 2, do you think textbooks could be exported?

ETHICS

Do you think it is fair for authors and publishers to make a profit from students?

DEBATE

Some upper-level and specialized classes are taught without regular textbooks. The instructor instead collects relevant articles from magazines, journals, and books and then makes copies available for students. Do you think such an approach would work for this introduction to business course? Option A: In a formal debate format, support or reject the idea. Option B: Take either side and state your case in a brief report.

TEAMWORK

With a team of three other students, survey prices in your college bookstore. Make a list of all the texts that all team members are using during the current term; then identify the range of prices. Speculate on why there is a range of prices, on the basis of relative demand and product costs (e.g., a book with color photographs is more expensive to print than one with black-and-white photos or no photos at all).

RESEARCH

Do the research necessary to write a one-page update on the financial health of either a single publishing company or one of these three industry segments: textbooks, trade books (books for the population in general), or magazines.

ROLE PLAYING

One student plays the role of a college bookstore manager, and several others play themselves—students faced with purchasing expensive textbooks. The manager explains why the books cost as much as they do.

Chapter

14

Distribution

LEARNING OBJECTIVES

After studying this chapter, you will be able to

1 List nine functions performed by marketing intermediaries

2 Name the alternative distribution channels for consumer goods, organizational goods, and services

3 Differentiate between intensive, selective, and exclusive market-coverage strategies

4 Describe the three types of wholesalers

5 Identify at least 10 types of retailers

6 Explain what is meant by the wheel of retailing

7 Specify the activities included in physical distribution

8 List the five most common ways of transporting goods

Power-Tool Maker Has a Remodeling Project of Its Own

Nolan Archibald had a bit of a mess on his hands. He had recently been promoted to chairman and CEO of Black & Decker, a multibillion-dollar power-tool manufacturer that was having profit problems, losing market share, and generally annoying many of the wholesalers and retailers it relied on to sell products to consumers and construction professionals.

The problem with wholesalers and retailers was particularly acute. The company was considered rather arrogant, to put it mildly. In the words of a former Black & Decker employee, referring to Archibald's predecessors: "Management seemed to think it had the answer to every question and would generously impart its wisdom to the masses." Such an attitude nearly got Black & Decker kicked out of Wal-Mart, the largest retailer in the United States. Not the best plan for selling products, to say the least.

Inventory shortages plagued retailers. If a Black & Decker product turned out to be popular with the public, there was a pretty good chance that retailers would run out of it because Black & Decker put a lot of emphasis on meeting its internal financial goals. The company restrained production toward the end of its fiscal year to make sure its inventory levels dropped quite low. This practice made Black & Decker's balance sheet look good, but it was driving retailers away.

Moreover, Archibald's predecessors had recently purchased General Electric's entire line of small household appliances (at the time, the biggest brand transfer in history), and although the new line of products provided a strong stream of revenue, it gave Black & Decker yet another distribution headache. Before the acquisition, most Black & Decker products were sold through hardware stores, home-improvement centers, mail-order retailers, and discount stores. To be successful, small appliances had to be sold through department stores as well, and Black & Decker had little experience in this area. Unfortunately, the company tried to use the same approach it had used with power tools, which served only to alienate the department stores that had grown used to good treatment from General Electric.

How could Nolan Archibald repair the bad reputation that Black & Decker had gained with wholesalers and retailers? How could

Black & Decker is one of the many manufacturers whose products are sold to both consumers and professionals, making its distribution challenge more complicated.

he combat the pressure from competitors who were trying to push Black & Decker off the shelf? How could he handle the new small appliances, given the company's lack of experience? In short, what steps could he take to ensure Black & Decker's survival and continued success?[1]

THE DISTRIBUTION MIX

Black & Decker's Nolan Archibald had to figure out some way to balance inventory while regaining the support of wholesalers and retailers. Whether the product is a power tool, a haircut, toothpaste, or insurance, it needs to be conveyed from the producer to the ultimate user. The systems used to move goods and services from producers to customers are called **distribution channels,** or *marketing channels.* Some channels are short and simple; others are complex and involve many people and organizations. An organization's decisions about which combination of channels to use—the **distribution mix**— and its overall plan for moving products to buyers—the **distribution strategy**—play major roles in the firm's success.

The Role of Marketing Intermediaries

Stop and think about all the products you buy: food, cosmetics, toiletries, clothing, sports equipment, airplane tickets, haircuts, gasoline, stationery, appliances, cassettes, videotapes, books, magazines, and all the rest. How many of these products do you buy directly from the producer? If you're like most people, the answer is probably less than 3 percent.[2] For the other 97 percent of your purchases, you rely on **marketing intermediaries.** In some cases, these "go-betweens" sell on behalf of the producers; in others, they actually own the products they sell to you.

Without these intermediaries, the buying and selling process would be an expensive, time-consuming experience (see Exhibit 14.1). Intermediaries are instrumental in creating three forms of utility mentioned in Chapter 12: place utility, time utility, and possession utility. By transferring products from the producer to the customer, intermediaries ensure that goods and services are available at a convenient time and place. They also simplify the exchange process.

In addition, intermediaries perform a number of specific functions that make life easier for both producers and customers:

1. *Providing a sales force.* Many producers, like Black & Decker, would find it expensive and inefficient to employ their own salespeople to sell directly to final customers. Instead, they rely on intermediaries to perform this function.
2. *Providing market information.* Intermediaries often sell dozens of competing or complementary lines to hundreds of buyers. Thus, they are in an ideal position to give producers useful marketing information, such as which products are currently popular.
3. *Providing promotional support.* Intermediaries often help a producer by advertising certain product lines to boost their own sales. In-

---

distribution channels Systems for moving goods and services from producers to customers; also known as marketing channels

distribution mix Combination of intermediaries and channels that a producer uses to get a product to end users

distribution strategy Firm's overall plan for moving products to intermediaries and final customers

marketing intermediaries Businesspeople and organizations that channel goods and services from producers to consumers

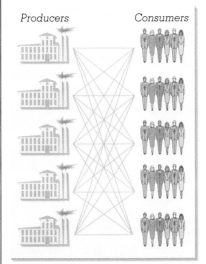

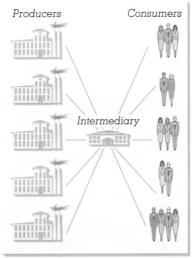

Producers   Consumers   Producers   Consumers

Intermediary

Number of transactions required when consumers buy directly from manufacturers

Number of transactions required when buying is conducted via intermediary

Exhibit 14.1
How Intermediaries Simplify Commerce

Despite the common assumption that buying directly from the producer saves money, intermediaries actually reduce the price we pay for many goods and services. Intermediaries eliminate many of the contacts between producers and consumers that would otherwise be necessary. At the same time, they create place, time, and possession utility.

termediaries also design and distribute eye-catching store displays and other promotional devices for some products.

4. *Sorting, standardizing, and dividing.* Intermediaries break large shipments from producers into more convenient units, sorting bulk quantities into smaller packages and grading products for quality and uniformity.

5. *Carrying stock.* Most intermediaries maintain an inventory of merchandise, which they acquire from a manufacturer in the hope of eventually selling it to other intermediaries or final customers. Without the intermediary, a manufacturer would have to provide storage space and wait for payment until the ultimate customer made a purchase decision.

6. *Delivering the product.* By keeping stock on hand in convenient locations, intermediaries can speed up deliveries to customers. Some intermediaries assume complete responsibility for transporting the producer's goods to widely scattered buyers.

7. *Assuming risks.* By transferring goods to intermediaries, manufacturers can avoid the risks associated with damage, theft, product perishability, and obsolescence.

8. *Providing financing.* Sometimes an intermediary that is much larger than the producers it represents can provide them with loans.

9. *Buying.* Intermediaries relieve the ultimate user of part of the buying responsibility. By consolidating a variety of goods in one place, they save people the trouble and expense of going out and finding separate sources of supply for every product they purchase.

This sounds like a paradox, but the services performed by intermediaries may actually reduce the price that consumers pay for many goods and services, even though intermediaries make a profit (or are paid a fee) on the items they handle. Intermediaries exist because they are able to distribute products more efficiently and economically than manufacturers could. Every transaction costs money, and by reducing the number of transactions required to move goods and services from producers to end users—and increasing the efficiency of all the steps involved—intermediaries often reduce the total cost of distribution. One notable exception to this notion is the distribution system in Japan, which is so complex that most consumer goods can travel through the hands of as many as six intermediaries. This tradition-bound system adds to the price consumers pay, but it is showing signs of becoming more efficient.[3]

Channel Alternatives

The number and type of intermediaries involved in a distribution mix depend on the kind of product and the marketing practices of a particular industry. An arrangement that might be appropriate for a power-tool and appliance manufacturer like Black & Decker would not necessarily work for an insurance company, a restaurant, a steel manufacturer, or a movie studio. Important differences exist between the distribution channels for consumer goods, organizational goods, and services (see Exhibit 14.2).

Channels for Consumer Goods

Channels for consumer goods are generally the most complex distribution channels, although they can be categorized:

- *Producer to consumer.* The most direct way to market a product is for the producer to sell directly to the consumer. Artisans who sell their leather goods or jewelry at crafts fairs or on the street are using this simple distribution channel. Large companies may also prefer to sell directly to the consumer, because this approach gives them more control over sales and eliminates the intermediary's cut of the profit. The problem with direct distribution is that it forces producers to engage in a wide array of marketing functions, and not all producers are up to the task.

Exhibit 14.2
Alternative Channels of Distribution
Consumer goods, organizational goods, and services each have characteristic types of distribution channels. Consumer-goods channels tend to require the most intermediaries, and channels for services tend to require the fewest.

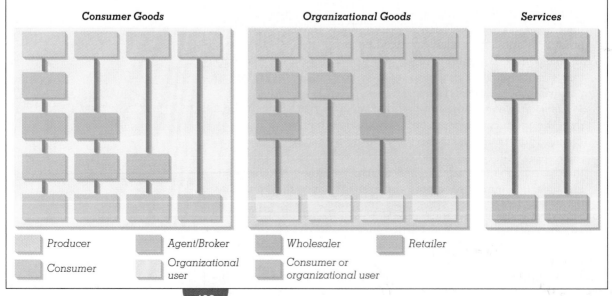

| Consumer Goods | Organizational Goods | Services |

| Producer | Agent/Broker | Wholesaler | Retailer |
| Consumer | Organizational user | Consumer or organizational user | |

- *Producer to retailer to consumer.* Some producers sell their products to retailers, who then resell them to consumers. Automobiles, paint, gasoline, and clothing are typical of the many products distributed in this way.
- *Producer to wholesaler to retailer to consumer.* The most common channel for consumer products is for the producer to sell to a wholesaler who in turn sells to a retailer. Most of the items you buy in supermarkets and drugstores are distributed through this type of channel. This approach is generally the most advantageous alternative for small producers who cannot afford to employ their own sales forces.
- *Producer to agent/broker to wholesaler to retailer to consumer.* Another wholesaling level is typical in certain industries, such as agriculture, where specialists are required to negotiate transactions or perform such functions as sorting, grading, or subdividing the merchandise.

Channels for Organizational Goods
The most common approach for organizational products is direct distribution from producer to user. However, in industries composed of many small producers or many widely scattered buyers, one or more levels of intermediaries may be required to simplify the distribution process. The more fragmented the industry, the more likely it is to rely on the services of intermediaries.

Channels for Services
Most services are distributed directly by the producer to the user because the nature of the service usually requires direct contact between the customer and the service provider. A hairstylist or lawyer, for example, would not be likely to use an intermediary to deal with clients. In addition, because of the intangible nature of many services, such functions as storing, sorting, grading, and transporting goods are needed less frequently.

Some service businesses, however, do employ intermediaries. The travel industry, for example, relies on agents to package vacations and sell tickets. Insurance companies market their policies through insurance brokers, and entertainers book engagements through agents who negotiate deals for them.

Technology provides an increasing number of options for the distribution of services as well. It allows the service provider to reach customers spread over a wide area. Automated teller machines, for instance, allow a bank to distribute its services all over the world. Writers, industrial designers, advertising specialists, consultants, and other "knowledge workers" can deliver their services over long distances using computer networks.

Reverse Channels
Although most marketing channels move products from producers to customers, **reverse channels** move them in the opposite direction. The two most common reverse channels are those used for recycling and for product recalls and repairs. Recycling channels continue to

reverse channels Distribution channels designed to move products from the customer back to the producer grow in importance as consumers and businesses become more sensitive to solid-waste-disposal problems. Local, state, and federal government agencies also contribute to the growth of recycling channels as they pass tighter and tighter restrictions on disposal of glass, paper products, plastics, and recyclable organic materials, such as grass clippings and Christmas trees.

The channels for some recycled goods use traditional intermediaries, which is the case for returnable soft-drink bottles, for which retailers and bottlers form the reverse channel. In other cases, recycling collection centers have been established to funnel material from consumers back to processors. More and more, local governments are creating recycling channels, often in cooperation with waste-management companies.

Another common reverse channel is used for product repairs and recalls. Any firm selling products that need to be recalled for maintenance or repair should establish a channel to direct goods from customers back to an appropriate service facility. Depending on the complexity of the products involved and the financial return on the repair business, companies can establish their own service centers or rely on independent repair and maintenance centers.

Channel Selection

Should a producer sell directly to end users or rely on intermediaries? Which intermediaries should be selected? Should the company try to sell its products in every available outlet or limit its distribution to a few exclusive shops? Should more than one channel be employed? Should distribution be revised over time?

The answers to such questions depend on a number of factors, some related to the product and the market, others to the company—its strengths, weaknesses, and objectives. In general, however, choosing one channel over another is a matter of making trade-offs among three factors: the number of outlets where the product is available, the cost of distribution, and the control of the product as it moves through the pipeline to the final customer. With a short distribution chain, the producer gets the most control but generally gets thinner market coverage and bears more of the expense of warehousing, transportation, and marketing. A longer chain increases market coverage and minimizes the producer's costs but introduces more complexity and thus less control.

Market Coverage

The question of market coverage has to do with the availability of a product. Should a manufacturer blanket the market so that people can find the item anywhere, or should distribution be limited to create an exclusive image or to ensure topnotch customer service? The answer depends primarily on the type of product. Inexpensive convenience goods or organizational supplies—such as bread, toothpaste, cleaning products, and typing paper—sell best if they are available in as many outlets as possible. To achieve this type of **intensive distribution,** where the market is saturated with a product, a producer will almost certainly need a long distribution chain. Trying to cover

intensive distribution *Approach to distribution that involves placing the product in as many outlets as possible*

In Coral Gables, Florida, this Chic Parisien store is the type of retailer likely to have exclusive distribution for selected luxury products.

every outlet without intermediaries would be a major undertaking, one that only the largest, best-financed producers could handle.

A different approach to market coverage might work better for a producer that specializes in shopping goods, such as apparel, appliances, or certain types of organizational products. When the buyer is likely to compare features and prices, the best strategy is usually **selective distribution,** in which a limited number of outlets are capable of giving the product adequate support. With fewer outlets, the distribution chain for shopping goods is generally shorter than it is for convenience goods.

When a company produces expensive specialty or technical products, it may opt for direct sales or **exclusive distribution,** in which the product is available in only one outlet in each market area. Here again, exclusive distribution normally involves simpler and shorter distribution systems.

Cost

Costs play a major role in determining a firm's distribution mix. It takes money to perform all the functions that are handled by intermediaries. Small or new companies often cannot afford to hire a sales force large enough to sell directly to end users or to call on a host of retail outlets. Neither can they afford to build large warehouses and distribution centers or buy trucks to ship their goods. These firms need the help of intermediaries who can spread the cost of these activities across a number of noncompeting products. With time and a larger sales base, a producer may build enough strength to take over some of these functions and reduce the length of the distribution chain.

Control

Another important issue to consider when selecting distribution channels is control. As soon as dealers buy the product, they own it; they can do anything they want with it. A manufacturer cannot force

selective distribution *Approach to distribution that relies on a limited number of outlets*

exclusive distribution *Approach to distribution in which intermediaries are given the exclusive right to sell a product within a given market*

Roses are red,
Violets are blue.
Go after our market share
And we'll destroy you.

Greeting-card companies send some awfully sweet messages to their customers, but they're more likely to send aggressive lawyers to each other. Three giants, Hallmark Cards, American Greetings, and Gibson Greetings, control this market, with a combined share of about 80 percent. Dozens of smaller companies struggle to stay in the battle, a battle that increasingly centers on control of the distribution channel.

Greeting cards are sold through a variety of retail outlets, including grocery, drug, discount, and specialty stores. None of the producers has a commanding legal authority over the channel; for instance, most of the 21,000 stores that carry Hallmark cards and sometimes bear the Hallmark name are ostensibly free to

HEALTHY COMPETITION OR UNHEALTHY CONTROL?

carry anybody's products. Lacking any legal power over retailers, producers use a mixture of sweet talk and strong arm to move their goods through the channel.

Sometimes the struggle for control gets downright nasty. In a highly publicized case, Blue Mountain Arts accused Hallmark of copying the look of its cards, pressuring retailers into dropping (and in some cases allegedly destroying) Blue Mountain cards, and then filling the vacant shelf

space with products from its new Personal Touch line, which looked nearly identical to Blue Mountain cards. After several rounds of complicated legal action, the case was settled when Hallmark promised not to exert pressure on retailers and to redesign the product line that was similar to Blue Mountain's.

In any competitive market, battles over distribution are almost assured. When entrepreneur Mary Ann Jackson hit on the hot idea of microwavable meals for children, competitors were so worried that some allegedly went into grocery stores and took her products off shelves and threw them in the stores' damaged-goods bins.

Aside from the specific legal and ethical issues, some people worry that these fights over distribution hurt consumers by limiting their products choices. Whatever the case, it's an issue that an increasing number of businesses will have to watch in the years ahead.

the intermediaries to promote the product aggressively. The longer the distribution chain, the bigger the problem, since the manufacturer becomes increasingly distant from the ultimate seller.

For certain types of products, control is particularly important because the product can be cheapened if it falls into the wrong hands. A designer of high-priced clothing might want to limit distribution to exclusive boutiques, since the clothing would lose some of its appeal if it were available in discount stores. The company's entire merchandising strategy could be undercut if an intermediary sold some of the fashions to the wrong retailers. Similarly, producers of complex technical products don't want their products handled by unqualified intermediaries who can't provide adequate customer service.

Other Factors

Coverage, cost, and control are the three big issues to consider when selecting a distribution channel, but they aren't the only issues involved. Manufacturers must also take into account a host of other factors, including the dollar value of the item, the market's growth rate, the geographic concentration of the customers, the buyer's need for service, and the importance of rapid delivery (see Exhibit 14.3).

Often the best solution is to use multiple channels to reach various target markets. Say that you have invented a new board game.

Factor	Explanation
Number of transactions	When many transactions are likely, the channel should provide for many outlets, which suggests that several levels of intermediaries will be required. If only a few transactions are likely, the number of outlets can be limited, and the channel can be relatively short.
Value of transactions	If the value of each transaction is high, the channel can be relatively short and direct, since the producer can better absorb the cost of making firsthand contact with each customer. If each transaction has a low value, a long channel is used to spread the cost of distribution over many products and outlets.
Market growth rate	In a rapidly growing market, many outlets and a long channel of distribution may be required to meet demand. In a shrinking market, fewer outlets are required.
Geographic concentration of market	If customers are clustered in a limited geographic area, the channel can be short, since the cost of reaching each account is relatively low. If customers are widely scattered, a multilevel channel with many outlets is preferable.
Need for service and sales support	Complex, innovative, or specialized products require sophisticated outlets where customers can receive information and service support; short, relatively direct channels are generally used. If the product is familiar and uncomplicated, the consumer requires little assistance; long channels with many self-serve outlets can be used.
Speed of delivery	Perishable products or products that must be delivered quickly to the customer generally require relatively short channels, which are quicker than long channels.

You might sell your product through department stores, discount outlets, specialty stores, direct-mail catalogs, or some combination of these outlets.

Over time the optimum distribution arrangement for a product is likely to change. When a product is introduced, buyers may need help making a purchase decision, particularly if the item is technical or unusual. At this stage, the most efficient channel consists of a few highly specialized dealers who can spot trends and identify leading-edge customers. As the product enters the growth stage, distribution must be expanded to handle higher sales volume, but dealers should continue to provide extensive selling support. When the product reaches maturity, the distribution emphasis should shift from service and support to economy, since most customers will already be familiar with the item and will be interested in getting the best price. At this point, producers can rely on advertising as opposed to dealer support to persuade the consumer to buy. During the product's decline phase, cost becomes an even more important issue in the distribution decision, since the manufacturer's objective is usually to extract the maximum profit from the item before phasing it out entirely.[4]

Channel Conflict

Channel conflict can occur when one channel member places its own success above the success of the entire channel. In an effort to increase its own market share, for instance, a producer sometimes forces intermediaries into situations that work well for the producer but not for individual intermediaries. Here are several common sources of channel conflict:

- *Bypassing channels.* If a producer bypasses existing channels in the hope of increasing business, conflict is inevitable. When Taco Bell opened two experimental low-cost burger chains called Hot 'n Now, Taco Bell franchisers began to worry that they'd have to

Exhibit 14.3
Factors Involved in Selecting Distribution Channels
The choice of distribution channel depends on the product, the customer, and the company's capabilities.

compete with their own company.[5] The grocery business is experiencing industrywide conflict between traditional supermarkets and producers. An increasing portion of U.S. grocery products now moves to consumers through warehouse clubs, discount stores, and convenience stores. Not surprisingly, this new route creates friction between the manufacturers and their traditional allies in the supermarket channel.[6]

- *Oversaturating markets.* Some people who purchased franchises in the Subway Sandwich Shops chain charge that the company has sold too many operations too close to each other. Indeed, the company has grown rapidly, increasing fourfold from 1987 to 1992, and some new stores have been placed as close as one mile away from existing stores.[7]
- *Providing inadequate support.* In return for distributing a manufacturer's products, intermediaries expect a certain level of support. This support might include advertising, training, or managerial assistance. If intermediaries are not properly supported, they won't be content, and they won't be as effective as they might be.
- *Behaving inconsistently.* Erratic behavior is likely to disrupt life for everybody in the channel. The best way to avoid this problem is to establish clear guidelines and policies and make sure that discipline is maintained. When changes are necessary, they should be executed with the clear understanding and support of channel partners.[8]

vertical marketing systems *Planned distribution channels in which members coordinate their efforts to optimize distribution activities*

channel captain *Channel member that is able to influence the activities of the other members of the distribution channel*

This Liz Claiborne Outlet Store is part of a corporate vertical marketing system; both the store and the manufacturing operation that creates the clothes are owned by the same company.

Vertical Marketing Systems

One way to reduce conflicts in the distribution system is to plan and control it more carefully. Thus **vertical marketing systems** have evolved, in which members work together to conduct distribution activities.

Vertical marketing systems vary in their level of formality. The most controlled form is the *corporate vertical marketing system,* in which both production and distribution operations are owned by the same organization. In some cases, the entire distribution chain is controlled by a single firm, but often the channel contains a mix of independently owned and corporate-controlled operations.

An *administered vertical marketing system* is a less formal arrangement in which one member of the distribution chain has enough power to influence the behavior of the others. The dominant company, known as the **channel captain,** performs functions that work to the mutual benefit of the entire chain. Toys "R" Us, for instance, has developed computer software that spots emerging trends in toy sales. By passing on this information to toy manufacturers, Toys "R" Us helps the industry balance its production volume.[9] Often the channel captain is the manufacturer as opposed to the retailer. Companies like Procter & Gamble, Kraft General Foods, and Gillette are the dominant forces in the distribution of their products.

A *contractual vertical marketing system* is a compromise between a corporate system and an administered system. With this approach, the members of the channel are legally bound by a contractual agreement that spells out their respective responsibilities. Franchising is the most common form of the contractual vertical marketing system. Many of the world's best-known retail outlets, from McDonald's to Radio Shack, rely on franchising to cover attractive markets.

International Distribution

International distribution adds its own set of complexities to the management of marketing channels. If a U.S. company wants to market its goods in Austria, for example, it has to abide by (1) the export laws of the United States, (2) the import and general business laws of Austria, and (3) the applicable laws of any countries the goods pass through on their way. Such legal requirements and constraints add to the differences inherent in doing business in foreign countries, ranging from language barriers to diverse government policies to local customs.

In addition to legal issues, marketers need to consider the tremendous diversity in distribution channels from country to country. For instance, Colombia has one retail store for every 56,000 people, whereas Italy has a retailer for every 66 people according to one estimate. (The figure in the United States is 127 people per store, by the way.) To reach consumers in Italy, in other words, you have to deal with a mind-boggling number of small retailers.[10]

Sometimes even the simplest assumption doesn't apply when a company considers international distribution. Procter & Gamble, which sells through wholesalers and retailers here in the United States and in most other countries, resorted to selling and distributing its products door-to-door in the Philippines because of that country's inadequate transportation system.[11]

TYPES OF INTERMEDIARIES

Basically, intermediaries are of two main types: wholesalers and retailers. **Wholesalers** sell primarily to retailers, other wholesalers, and organizational users such as governments, institutions, and commercial operations (all of which either resell the product or use it in making products of their own). Wholesalers that sell to organizational customers are often called **industrial distributors** to distinguish them from wholesalers that supply retail outlets. **Retailers** sell to individuals who buy products for ultimate consumption.

Wholesalers and Industrial Distributors

Because wholesalers seldom deal directly with consumers, many people are unfamiliar with this link in the distribution chain. However, roughly 70 percent of all manufactured goods travel through whole-

wholesalers Firms that sell products to other firms for resale or for organizational use

industrial distributors Wholesalers that sell to industrial customers, rather than to retailers

retailers Firms that sell directly to the public

salers on the way to final customers—a total of $2 trillion worth of merchandise annually.[12] The wholesaling sector also employs thousands of business and marketing specialists, making it a prime target for college graduates seeking employment.

Before exploring specific types of wholesalers, it's helpful to consider the differences between industrial distributors and wholesalers that sell to retailers. Although they are technically wholesalers, industrial distributors face a set of marketing challenges different from those of other wholesalers. The first major difference is that the purchasers themselves use the products, rather than reselling them as quickly as possible, as retailers do. Whereas the retailer's primary concern is how much money can be made reselling an item, the industrial buyer considers a range of criteria, from technical performance to cost of ownership. In this sense, industrial buyers have more in common with individual consumers than they have with retailers.

The second major difference is the role consumers play. Assume you're a manufacturer who sells both to retailers and to industrial companies. In other words, you function as both a wholesaler and as an industrial distributor. Consumer purchasing will directly influence the purchasing behavior of your retailers, but not the behavior of your industrial customers. If consumer spending is up, you'll probably see an immediate increase in demand from the retailers. On the industrial side, this change in consumer spending may have a delayed effect or possibly even no effect on demand from your industrial customers.

Merchant Wholesalers

Roughly 80 percent of all wholesalers are **merchant wholesalers,** independently owned businesses that take title to merchandise (become the owners of it) and then resell it to retailers or organizational buyers. **Full-service merchant wholesalers** provide a wide variety of services to their customers, such as storage, delivery, and marketing support. **Rack jobbers,** for example, set up displays in retail outlets, stock inventory, and mark prices on merchandise displayed in a particular section of a store. **Limited-service merchant wholesalers,** on the other hand, provide fewer services. Natural resources such as lumber, grain, and coal are usually marketed through a class of wholesaler called **drop shippers,** who take ownership but not physical possession of the goods they handle.

Agents and Brokers

The big difference between merchant wholesalers and **manufacturer's agents** is that agents never actually own the merchandise they sell. Producers retain title to the product and pay the agents a commission (a percentage of the money received) for any transaction they handle. One of the most common types of agent is the manufacturer's representative. The rep calls on customers in a specific territory, takes orders, and arranges for delivery of the products. By representing several products at once, the sales rep can achieve enough volume to justify the cost of a direct sales call.

merchant wholesalers *Independent wholesalers that take legal title to products*

full-service merchant wholesalers *Wholesaling intermediaries that provide a wide variety of services to their customers, such as storage, delivery, and marketing support*

rack jobbers *Merchant wholesalers that are responsible for setting up and maintaining displays in a particular store area*

limited-service merchant wholesalers *Merchant wholesalers that offer fewer services than full-service wholesalers; they often specialize in particular markets, such as agriculture*

drop shippers *Merchant wholesalers that assume ownership of goods but don't take physical possession; commonly used to market agricultural and mineral products*

manufacturer's agents *Wholesalers that do not take title to products but that receive a commission for selling products*

Brokers are similar in many respects to agents but are usually distinguished by the fact that they don't work for sellers for an extended period of time. In agriculture, for instance, commodity brokers arrange sales for clients who grow the crop, and they receive a commission for this service. Brokers also operate in the financial field. Real estate brokers, insurance brokers, and securities brokers all are paid a commission for providing information and arranging transactions—sometimes by the seller, sometimes by the buyer, and sometimes by both.

Producer-Owned Wholesalers

Two types of wholesale businesses are owned by the producer. The first is the **branch office,** or *sales branch,* an establishment that carries inventory and performs a full range of marketing and business activities. The second type is the **sales office,** which often conducts the same range of marketing and business functions but doesn't carry inventory.

Retailers

In contrast to wholesalers, retailers are a visible element in the distribution chain. On average, each of us spends over $6,500 per year in retail establishments that sell everything from safety pins to Rolls-Royces and from hot dogs to haute cuisine. Although large multiunit chain stores account for over half of all retail sales, most retail stores are very small. In fact, of the roughly 1.5 million retail stores in the United States, nearly 1.3 million employ 20 or fewer people.[13]

By nearly every measure, retailing makes an important contribution to the economy. Retailers employ more than one in six U.S. employees, or over 19 million workers. In fact, retailing is the third largest employer in the United States. Also, retailers continue to create job opportunities; government estimates put the number of retail employees as high as 25 million by 2005.[14]

Today's retail landscape has changed from what it was just a decade ago. Highly specialized stores are cropping up to cater to every taste. At the same time, distinctions between one type of retailer and another are blurring. You can order videotapes along with your pizza or buy clothes at the grocery store. Department stores, bargain stores, specialty shops, supermarkets, convenience stores, and nonstore retailers are all experimenting with new ways to appeal to the consumer (see Exhibit 14.4). Competition among retailers is fierce, particularly since the country has significantly more retail selling capacity than it needs.[15] This competition leads retailers to pay special attention to such factors as atmospherics, a combination of sensory effects designed to put the customer in a particular mood. Atmospherics include not only the way a place looks but also the sounds and even the smells. Consultants charge up to $50,000 to design a signature scent for upscale retailers.[16]

Department Stores

Department stores are large retail establishments that bring together a vast variety of merchandise under one roof and departmentalize

---

brokers *Agents that specialize in a particular commodity but not usually for an extended period of time*

branch office *Producer-owned operation that carries stock and sells it; also called a* sales branch

sales office *Producer-owned operation that markets products but doesn't carry any stock*

department stores *Large retail stores that carry a wide variety of merchandise*

Strategy	Explanation
Value	Retailer offers greater overall value, lower prices than competitors. Holds down costs by eliminating alterations, delivery, exchanges, credit, gift wrapping. Stores are spartan; service is minimal.
Efficiency	Retailer caters to customers who have little time for shopping. Convenience stores are situated in handy locations, remain open long hours. Superstores offer one-stop shopping. Mail-order shopping, telemarketing, and TV shopping all allow customers to shop at home.
Service	Retailer emphasizes personal contact, expert assistance with purchase, postsale service.
Ambience	Retailer creates exciting shopping environment, caters to customer's fantasies with special effects such as theme décor, music, special events, imaginative architecture.
Portfolio	Retailer has a mix of several outlets, each of which caters to a specific segment.

both their merchandising activities and their operating functions. Department stores usually enjoy a reputation for the highest quality, fashion, and service, providing such amenities as credit, delivery, personal service, and in most cases, a pleasant atmosphere. Some, like Sears and J. C. Penney, operate coast to coast; others, like Marshall Field and Nordstrom, focus on narrower geographic territories.

Until fairly recently, most department stores were in downtown locations. In the last several decades, many chains enjoyed steady growth as they opened outlet after outlet in suburban shopping malls across the country. Today, however, the rush to build new malls is slowing, and department-store chains are focusing on increasing the profitability of their current locations.

Marketplace changes in the last decade have left many department stores struggling. For one thing, the same merchandise is generally available in other types of outlets, which has encouraged consumers to shop around for the best price. Sears, once the nation's largest retailer, is in a double squeeze between discounters on the low end and upscale department stores like Nordstrom on the high end. In order to compete, retailers have taken to having more and more sales, which cut into profit margins. Consumers, meanwhile, have learned to expect to get everything at reduced prices, and they often wait for markdowns before buying.

Department stores are dealing with competitors in a variety of ways. Selling merchandise not available anywhere else is one approach. In many cities, department stores are the fashion leaders. They are usually the first retailers to carry a variety of the newest merchandise, and some, like Bloomingdale's and Neiman-Marcus, offer unusual and one-of-a-kind items as well as goods bearing their own labels. Many are also attempting to build traffic via **scrambled merchandising,** stocking goods that are ordinarily handled by another type of retailer. Many big department stores, for example, now sell food items.

Another approach is to maximize the profit that the store makes per square foot of selling space by focusing sales efforts in the areas where they will be most successful. Some department stores have

scrambled merchandising Policy of carrying merchandise that is ordinarily sold in a different type of outlet

eliminated major appliances and furniture from their inventories, concentrating instead on fashion goods. Technology is also helping stores reduce costs and improve operations. When redesigning its stores recently, Sears installed computerized checkout points similar to those used in supermarkets, which enable the company to monitor sales more closely. Such systems are also important in helping control costs.

Some department stores are also emphasizing service to lure customers. One of the leaders in this effort is Seattle-based Nordstrom, with a strong presence in the West and a growing presence in the East and Midwest. Salespeople gift wrap purchases at no charge and have been known to make personal deliveries to customers' homes. Some Nordstrom employees in Alaska even warm up customers' cars while the drivers finish shopping.[17] Nordstrom, Parisian, and other retailers known for great service are still in the minority, however; consumers don't think much of the service they receive at many so-called full-service retailers. Nearly two-thirds of U.S. consumers now consider shopping drudgery, and poor service is frequently listed as the main reason.[18]

Bargain Stores

Retailers that compete on price usually can't afford to offer extensive customer service, nor do their customers expect such service. By keeping their facilities lean and their services at a minimum, bargain retailers are able to offer a variety of nationally advertised and private-brand goods at prices significantly below traditional department-store prices. Sales growth in these outlets is outpacing that of department stores. The general category of bargain stores includes discount stores, off-price stores, warehouse clubs, and factory outlets.

Discount Stores. **Discount stores** such as Kmart and Wal-Mart initiated the movement toward cut-rate pricing after World War II by opening bare-bones facilities in inexpensive locations. They offer a mix of merchandise that is weighted toward relatively inexpensive items but also carry nationally advertised brands that are sold at a discount.

Gradually, many discounters have upgraded their operations and become more like department stores in appearance, merchandise, and price. This process of store evolution, known as the **wheel of retailing,** follows a predictable pattern: An innovative company with low operating costs attracts a following by offering low prices and limited service (see Exhibit 14.5). Over time management adds more services to broaden the appeal of the store. In the process, however, prices creep upward, opening the door for lower-priced competitors. Eventually, these competitors also upgrade their operations and are replaced by still other lower-priced stores.

Off-Price Stores. In contrast to discounters, **off-price stores** sell name-brand merchandise that rivals department-store quality, but they buy their goods at below-wholesale prices. They are able to do this by taking advantage of other people's mistakes—buying overstocked merchandise, irregulars, end-of-season items, and production overruns. In addition, they obtain merchandise at cut rates directly from manufacturers by agreeing to do without some of the privileges ac-

discount stores *Retailers that sell a variety of goods below the market price by keeping their overhead low*

wheel of retailing *Evolutionary process by which stores that feature low prices are gradually upgraded until they forfeit their appeal to price-sensitive shoppers and are replaced by new competitors*

off-price stores *Retailers that offer bargain prices on quality merchandise by maintaining low overhead and acquiring merchandise at below-wholesale costs*

Exhibit 14.5
The Wheel of Retailing
The wheel of retailing is one of several theories explaining the continuous evolution in the world of retailing.

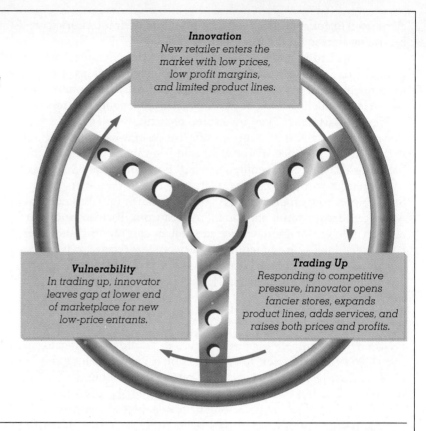

Innovation
New retailer enters the market with low prices, low profit margins, and limited product lines.

Vulnerability
In trading up, innovator leaves gap at lower end of marketplace for new low-price entrants.

Trading Up
Responding to competitive pressure, innovator opens fancier stores, expands product lines, adds services, and raises both prices and profits.

corded to department stores, such as help with promotions, extended payment terms, and return privileges.[19] An off-price store such as T. J. Maxx or Burlington Coat Factory features the same type of merchandise typically found in more luxurious department stores but sells it at substantial discounts.

The off-price phenomenon poses dilemmas for businesses in many parts of the clothing industry. Manufacturers enjoy increased sales through the popular new off-price outlets, but some fear that their carefully nurtured brand-name image will be ruined by association with a lower-priced store. Meanwhile, department stores, which have been losing business to the off-price competition, have threatened to stop buying from manufacturers that sell to these outlets. Some lawyers contend that these measures may violate antitrust laws if they are aimed at keeping retail prices high. Yet even as they try to isolate the off-pricers from their suppliers, department stores themselves are entering the game by acquiring or creating their own off-price subsidiaries and running sales to keep shoppers coming in.[20]

Warehouse Clubs. The latest thing in bargain shopping is **warehouse clubs,** big, bare outlets similar to storage warehouses with merchandise stacked to the ceiling on steel shelving and moved around by forklift trucks. Although warehouse stores are often referred to as "clubs," many don't require (or no longer require) annual memberships, and they offer the same prices to all customers. Shoppers are flocking to take advantage of the bargains. These operations, which include such big names as Price/Costco and Sam's Club, have carved

warehouse clubs *Low-priced stores that sell memberships to small retailers and consumer members*

out a big slice of the retailing industry, with annual sales approaching $40 billion in 1993.[21]

Factory and Retailer Outlets. In contrast to the other types of bargain stores, factory outlets are owned and operated by manufacturers and sell only the manufacturer's goods. Facilities are generally spartan, but the prices are attractive because manufacturers rely on these outlets to rid themselves of closeouts, discontinued merchandise, irregulars, and canceled orders. Retailer outlets, such as the Nordstrom Rack, operate on the same principle but are owned by retailers and can therefore carry many different brands of merchandise.

Specialty Shops and Category Killers

At the same time that shoppers are hunting for bargains, they are also hunting for other things—excitement, ambiance, unusual merchandise, personalized service, convenience. (Looking for lessons from a golf pro while you get fitted for a new suit? Visit the Bergdorf Goodman Men shop in New York City.)[22] In many cases, customers are

---

TOYS "R" US STORES PLAY SANTA INTERNATIONALLY

Imagine 18,000 toys in a 45,000-square-foot toy store—sounds more like Santa's distribution center at the North Pole. Charles Lazarus has put Santa-size Toys "R" Us stores in over 400 locations around the world. Starting with a single discount store in 1957, the company has grown into an international juggernaut selling over $4 billion worth of toys each year. The first expansion beyond U.S. borders was into Canada in 1984, and then into Great Britain in 1985. Today shoppers in Japan, Singapore, Hong Kong, Germany, and France can also buy dolls, trucks, video games, even disposable diapers at discount prices.

The Toys "R" Us international marketing strategy combines a clearly defined target market (parents) with unambiguous positioning (the largest possible year-round selection of toys, offered self-service style in a convenient location at discount prices). Toys "R" Us buyers buy in quantity from manufacturers around the world and tailor the merchandise assortment in each store to local market tastes, which is an important advantage Lazarus uses as he expands globally. Each country's merchandise assortment is fine-tuned individually, with as much as 20 percent of the merchandise geared toward local preferences. In Great Britain, cricket bats are sold alongside Louisville Sluggers. However, just because local kids aren't familiar with a particular item doesn't mean it won't sell. Singapore children have learned to play street hockey, thanks to the hockey sticks and pucks available in Toys "R" Us stores. Also, when Toys "R" Us buyers toured Germany to research local toy tastes before opening the first stores there, they found wooden toys, trains, and blocks that were so appealing they're now part of the Toys "R" Us merchandise assortment in the United States.

Toys "R" Us faces various competitors in each foreign market. Generally, the competition is similar to that in the United States: small neighborhood mom-and-pop toy stores, department stores, and discount and variety chains. However, as the toy-superstore concept catches on outside the United States, foreign competitors are challenging Toys "R" Us head-on. In Britain a major competitor is Woolworth, a variety-store chain based in the United States. Keenly aware of the Toys "R" Us invasion, Woolworth has developed a very different competitive strategy. As the country's leading toy retailer, Woolworth launched a new chain called Kidstore in 1987. Located in urban areas rather than the suburban freestanding locations that Toys "R" Us prefers, Kidstore stocks toys in addition to a wide variety of children's goods. Nevertheless, the Toys "R" Us concept of a discount superstore devoted exclusively to toys is a strong differentiator.

The Lazarus strategy is clearly paying off. The company continues to expand internationally, and sales in 1993 were up in every country except Germany, which was stuck in a lingering recession. Toys "R" Us Stores have sprung up in Belgium, the Netherlands, Switzerland, Portugal, Austria, and Australia. Plans for the second half of the 1990s include several hundred new stores for the United States and expansion into Scandinavia.

A "category killer" is a large retail store that tries to dominate in a particular product category. This Toys "R" Us store in Paramus, New Jersey, is a good example.

specialty shops *Stores that carry only particular types of goods*

supermarkets *Large departmentalized food stores*

finding what they want in **specialty shops,** which carry only particular types of goods. The basic merchandising strategy of a specialty shop is to offer a limited number of product lines but an extensive selection of brands, styles, sizes, models, colors, materials, and prices within each line that is stocked. Specialty shops are particularly strong in certain product categories—books, children's clothing, fast food, and sporting goods.

Although many specialty stores are individually owned and operated, a significant number are chain operations with several outlets, such as Crown Books, The Limited, B. Dalton, PlayCo, and Baskin-Robbins. Franchising is a common format for specialty stores, particularly those in the restaurant business.

Toys "R" Us, Office Depot, and Circuit City represent another class of retailer that grew out of the specialty-store concept. These stores focus on specific product areas but do so on a giant scale. They are often called "category killers" because they tend to dominate retail sales in their respective product categories.

Supermarkets

The large departmentalized food stores known as **supermarkets** range in size from those with annual sales of less than half a million dollars to giant, block-long stores with annual sales of several million dollars. Regardless of size, they rely on high volume to stay in business; the average supermarket has a profit margin of less than 1 percent.[23] Supermarkets carry nationally branded merchandise, private brands, and generic products. Self-service is an important characteristic, but many supermarkets offer separate delicatessen or bakery departments employing their own salespeople.

In recent years, competitive pressures have forced supermarkets to adopt many changes. The *hypermarket* takes one approach: It combines the merchandise of a typical discount store with a full range of grocery products. Slightly smaller variations, known as superstores or combo stores, also stock an assortment of nonfood items, ranging from children's pajamas to small appliances. Although there are more than 2,500 hypermarkets across Europe, the concept has had limited success in the United States.[24] (The Meijer chain in the Midwest is one exception.) The future of hypermarkets in this country appears uncertain, partly because consumers find them overwhelming to shop in and partly because so many other types of retail outlets already exist in this country.[25]

Convenience Stores

As the name implies, **convenience stores** are food stores whose chief stock in trade is time and place utilities. They are typically open 24 hours a day, seven days a week. They can operate in fringe locations that do not have an adequate population base for a supermarket. They control expenses and profits by carrying only a limited selection of brands and sizes and charging higher prices to their customers—who may be too late to get to the supermarket or may simply want to pick up some milk, soft drinks, or bread without standing in a long checkout line.

convenience stores *Food stores that offer convenient locations and hours but stock a limited selection of goods*

Nonstore Retailers

Nonstore retailers do not sell in the traditional store setting. These marketing efforts can involve telemarketing, mail order, vending machines, door-to-door selling, and a variety of electronic methods that include direct-response television and computer shopping.

Telemarketing. You are probably familiar with telephone retailing, or **telemarketing.** No doubt you have been called by insurance agents, newspaper circulation departments, and assorted nonprofit organizations, all trying to interest you in their goods, services, and causes. Advances in telephone technology are partly responsible for the barrage. With low-cost WATS lines and computer-dialing systems, firms can economically deliver their sales message to a large, dispersed audience.

telemarketing *Sale of goods and services by telephone*

Mail-Order Firms. **Mail-order firms** provide customers with a wide variety of goods ordered from catalogs and shipped by mail. Many of the most successful mail-order firms are more like specialty stores, focusing on a narrow range of merchandise; they include J. Crew, L. L. Bean, Lands' End, and Banana Republic, to name a few. Some companies use mail order to supplement and promote their base business, which is conducted primarily through retail stores. Others, such as Harry and David's Fruit-of-the-Month Club, rely almost entirely on mail-order sales. Still others, including J. Crew, view retail stores as a logical expansion from their mail-order businesses.[26]

mail-order firms *Companies that sell products through catalogs and ship them directly to customers*

Vending Machines. For certain types of products, vending machines are an important retail outlet. This is particularly true in Japan, where a wide variety of products are available from vending machines. Soda pop, coffee, candy, sandwiches, and cigarettes are all commonly sold this way. From the consumer's point of view, the chief attraction of vending machines is their convenience: They are open 24 hours a day and may be found in a variety of handy locations such as college dormitories. On the other hand, vending-machine prices are usually no bargain. Because the cost of servicing the machines is relatively high and vandalism is a factor, high prices are required to provide the vending-machine company and the product manufacturer with a reasonable profit.

Door-to-Door Retailers. A door-to-door retailer relies on a large sales force to call directly on customers in their homes or offices, demonstrate merchandise, take orders, and make deliveries. The famous names in door-to-door selling—and its variant, the party plan—include Tupperware, Fuller Brush, Avon, and Electrolux. With more and more women working outside the home, this method of retailing is diminishing in importance.

Electronic Retailing. Some of the most dramatic changes in retailing these days are going on in the field of electronic retailing, a diverse group of methods that rely on some form of electronic communication. You've seen some of these already, and more are on the way. Club Med has used 30-minute infomercials on the Arts & Entertainment cable network to show viewers footage of its vacation resorts, interspersed with frequent sales pitches mentioning the toll-free number to call for more information. More than 20,000 viewers responded in the first eight months the infomercial was shown. Elsewhere on the television dial, home shopping channels now ring up more than $2 billion in sales every year, as this mode of retail outgrows its image for cheap products and expands in major brand-name merchandise. In one 70-minute stretch recently, the QVC shopping channel sold $1.4 million worth of a new Kodak camera model.[27] Computer-interactive retailing is now available on a number of major computer networks, including Prodigy, America Online, CompuServe, and the Internet. Perhaps the most exciting development under way in electronic retailing is the marriage of television and computer technologies, leading to potentially lucrative possibilities on the information superhighway.

PHYSICAL DISTRIBUTION

physical distribution *All the activities required to move finished products from the producer to the consumer*

Physical distribution encompasses all the activities required to move finished products from the producer to the consumer (see Exhibit 14.6). It may not seem at first glance to be one of the most glamorous or exciting aspects of business, but it is definitely one of the most important. Nothing else really matters if you can't deliver your products to customers, and many companies use physical distribution

---

Exhibit 14.6
Steps in the Physical-Distribution Process
The phases of a distribution system should mesh as smoothly as the cogs in a machine. Because the steps are interrelated, a change in one phase can affect the other phases. The objective of the process is to provide a target level of customer service at the lowest overall cost.

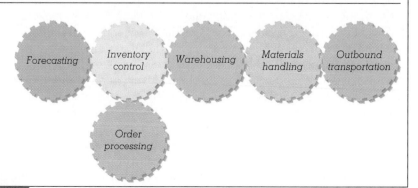

Forecasting | Inventory control | Warehousing | Materials handling | Outbound transportation

Order processing

to gain an edge on their competitors. Wal-Mart raced past Kmart and Sears to become the nation's largest retailer largely on the strength of its physical-distribution capabilities. By treating the movements of goods as a strategic part of the business, Wal-Mart enjoys distribution costs that are half as much as its competitors. Such savings in turn enable the company to offer lower prices while still maintaining healthy profits.[28]

PC Connection, a mail-order retailer of personal-computer hardware and software, uses physical distribution to maintain an edge in customer service. Computer owners can place orders as late as 3:00 A.M. and receive the goods later that same day, nearly anywhere in the United States. PC Connection achieves this remarkable level of service by maintaining a warehouse at the Ohio airport used by its shipping partner, Airborne Express. When an order arrives by phone or fax, the merchandise can be loaded on the next Airborne flight. This dedication to customer service pays off for PC Connection in increased sales and a loyal customer base.[29]

Some of today's most advanced physical-distribution systems employ satellite navigation and communication, voice-input computers, machine vision, robots, on-board computer logbooks, and planning software relying on artificial intelligence. OTR Express, a Kansas-based trucking firm, operates almost as if it were a giant computer system that just happens to use trucks to get the job done. By using custom software to track everything from the location of trucks to the best places in the country to buy tires, OTR squeezes impressive profits while keeping the firm's prices competitive.[30]

Regardless of the technology a company uses, the key to success in managing physical distribution is to coordinate the activities of everyone involved, from the sales staff that is trying to satisfy demanding customers to the product staff that is trying to manage fac-

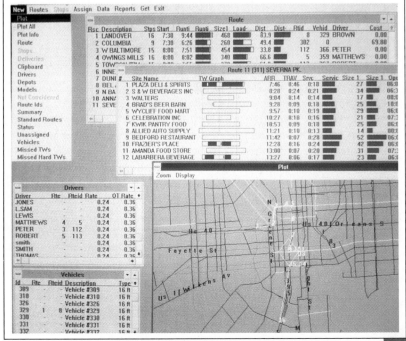

Computer technology, such as this Roadnet route-optimization software, is helping marketers locate new customers, simplify distribution routes, arrange efficient sales territories, and take other steps to boost profitability.

tory workloads. The overriding objective of all concerned should be to achieve a competitive level of **customer-service standards** (the goals that apply to specific issues in product distribution) at the lowest total cost. Generally speaking, as the level of service improves, the cost of distribution increases. A producer must analyze whether it is worthwhile to deliver the product in, say, three days as opposed to five, if doing so increases the price of the item.

This type of trade-off can be difficult to make because the steps in the distribution process are all interrelated. A change in one affects the others. For example, if you use slower forms of transportation, you reduce your shipping costs, but you probably increase your storage costs. Similarly, if you reduce the level of inventory to cut your storage costs, you run the risk of being unable to fill orders in a timely fashion. The trick is to optimize the *total* cost of achieving the desired level of service. This effort requires a careful analysis of each step in the distribution process in relation to every other step.

In-House Operations

The steps in the distribution process can be divided into in-house operations and transportation. The in-house steps in the process include forecasting, order processing, inventory control, warehousing, and materials handling.

Forecasting

To control the flow of products through the distribution system, a firm must have an accurate estimate of demand. To some degree, historical data can be used to project future sales; however, the firm must also consider the impact of unusual events, such as special promotions, that might temporarily boost demand. For example, if Black & Decker decided to offer a special discount price on electric drills during the month of September, management would need to ship additional drills to the dealers during the latter part of August to satisfy the extra demand.

Order Processing

Order processing involves a number of activities, such as checking the customer's credit, recording the sale, making the appropriate accounting entries, arranging for the item to be shipped, adjusting the inventory records, and billing the customer. Because order processing involves direct interaction with the customer, it affects a company's reputation for customer service. Most companies establish standards for filling orders within a specific time period. PC Connection's guarantee of same-day shipping for orders received up to 3:00 A.M. is a good example.

Computers are playing an increasingly important role in processing orders. In some cases, customers and suppliers are connected electronically. Wal-Mart established a computerized ordering system between its warehouses and its suppliers.[31] Using a method called electronic data interchange (EDI), in which computers can send and receive orders automatically, such systems can place orders automatically as stocks are depleted in stores.

Inventory Control

In an ideal world, a company would always have just the right amount of goods on hand to fill the orders it receives. In reality, however, inventory and sales are seldom in perfect balance. Most firms like to build a supply of finished goods so that they can fill orders in a timely fashion. The question is: How much inventory is enough? If your inventory is too large, you incur extra expenses for storage space, handling, insurance, and taxes; you also run the risk of product obsolescence. On the other hand, if your inventory is too low, you may lose sales when the product is not in stock. The objective of **inventory control** is to resolve these issues. Inventory managers decide how much product to keep on hand and when to replenish the supply of goods in inventory. They also decide how to allocate products to customers if orders exceed supply.

inventory control Process of maintaining inventories at a level that prevents stockouts and minimizes holding costs

Warehousing

Products held in inventory are physically stored in a **warehouse.** Warehouses may be owned by the manufacturer, by an intermediary, or by a private company that leases warehouses. Some warehouses are almost purely holding facilities in which goods are stored for relatively long periods. Others, known as **distribution centers,** serve as command posts for moving products to customers. In a typical distribution center, goods produced at a company's various locations are collected, sorted, coded, and redistributed to fill customer orders.

warehouse Facility for storing backup stocks of supplies or finished products

distribution centers Warehouse facilities that specialize in collecting and shipping merchandise

Materials Handling

Materials handling, the movement of goods within and between physical-distribution facilities, is an important part of warehousing activities. One of its main areas of concern is storage methods—whether to keep supplies and finished goods in individual packages, large boxes, or sealed shipping containers. The choice of storage method depends on how the product is shipped, in what quantities, and to which location; a firm that typically sends small quantities of goods to widely scattered customers, for example, probably wouldn't want to use large containers. Materials handling also involves keeping track of inventory so that the company knows where in the distribution process its goods are located and when they need to be moved.

materials handling Activities involved in moving, packing, storing, and inventorying goods

---

Exhibit 14.7
Physical-Distribution Costs
Although the cost of physical distribution varies widely by product, in some cases it adds as much as 20 percent to the retail price of an item. Transportation is the single biggest factor in physical-distribution costs.

Transportation

For any business, the cost of transportation is normally the largest single item in the overall cost of physical distribution (see Exhibit 14.7). It doesn't necessarily follow, however, that a manufacturer should simply pick the cheapest available form of transportation. When a firm chooses a type of transportation, it has to bear in mind its other marketing concerns—storage, financing, sales, inventory size, and the like. The trick is to maximize the efficiency of the entire distribution process while minimizing its cost. Transportation, in fact, may be an especially important sales tool. As PC Connection demonstrates, a firm that can supply its customers' needs more quickly and reliably than competitors gains a key advantage. Thus, it may be more

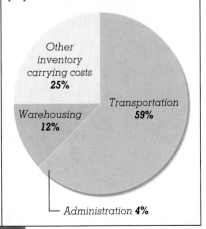

Other inventory carrying costs **25%**

Warehousing **12%**

Transportation **59%**

Administration **4%**

profitable in the long run to pay higher transportation costs rather than risk the loss of future sales.

Companies that move freight are called *carriers,* and they fall into three basic categories: **Common carriers** offer their services to the general public, **contract carriers** haul freight for selected companies under written contract, and **private carriers** are company-owned systems that move their own company's products. Some firms use a combination, relying on common or contract carriers to help out when their own resources are stretched to the limit. In addition, specialized transportation companies help firms in particular areas of distribution. **Freight forwarders,** for instance, help improve shipping efficiency for many companies by pooling several small shipments bound for the same general location. Because of the high cost of international air and ocean freight, consolidation is particularly attractive when shipping goods overseas.

Modes of Transportation

Each mode of transportation has distinct advantages and disadvantages:

- *Trucking.* Trucks are the most frequently used form of transportation for two reasons: convenient door-to-door delivery and operation on public highways that do not require an expensive terminal or right of way, as airlines and railroads do. The main drawback of trucks is that they cannot carry all types of cargo cost-effectively, for example, bulky commodities such as steel or coal.
- *Rail.* Railroads can carry heavier and more diverse cargoes and in fact carry a larger volume of goods than any other mode of transportation. However, they have the big disadvantage of being constrained to railroad tracks, so they can seldom deliver directly to the customer.
- *Water.* The cheapest form of transportation, water is widely used for such low-cost bulk items as oil, coal, ore, cotton, and lumber. However, the disadvantages make it unsuitable for most businesses. Ships are slow, and service to any given location is infrequent. Furthermore, like rail, another form of transportation is usually needed to complete delivery; reloading may add substantial cost because of extra handling, theft, and spoilage caused by weather.
- *Air.* Although airplanes offer the fastest form of transportation, they have numerous disadvantages. Many areas of the country are still not served by conveniently located airports. Airplanes can carry only certain types of cargo because of size and shape limitations. Furthermore, airplanes are the least dependable and most expensive form of transportation. Weather may cause flight cancellations, and even minor repairs may lead to serious delays. However, when speed is paramount, air is usually the only way to go.
- *Pipelines.* For certain types of products, such as gasoline, natural gas, and coal and wood chips (suspended in liquid), pipelines are quite useful. Although they are expensive to build, they are extremely economical to operate and maintain. On the other hand, transportation via pipeline is slow (three to four miles per hour), and routes are not flexible.

Environmental Impact of Transportation

Transportation has an undeniable effect on the natural and human environments. Its effects range from the noise of aircraft to the wildlife hazards posed by railways in remote areas. The negative impact could be reduced in many cases, but often at the trade-off of higher costs. Double-hulled oil tankers, for instance, are less vulnerable to punctures that cause oil spills, but they cost substantially more to build. The oil companies would have to pass all or part of this cost on to consumers. How many consumers are ready to pay higher gas prices in order to decrease the risk of oil spills?

There is a sizable cloud on the horizon for trucking as well. Trucks rely heavily on the nation's 42,798-mile interstate highway system, and that system is in bad shape. In some states, as much as 30 or 40 percent of the interstate miles are considered deficient. Potholes and other problems plague a system that was designed more than 30 years ago to last only 20 years and to carry only one-third the traffic. Trucking surely suffers from bad roads, but it is also a big part of the problem. The U.S. Transportation Department estimates that one 80,000-pound truck causes as much damage to an interstate as 9,600 automobiles. It's not surprising that proposals to increase the size of truck-trailer combinations are meeting with stiff opposition. Railroads are joining the antitruck protests, and their position is supported by the fact that trucks generate four times as much pollution per ton hauled as railroads.[32]

1 List nine functions performed by marketing intermediaries.

Intermediaries provide a sales force, market information, and promotional support. They also sort, standardize, and divide merchandise; carry stock; and deliver products. In addition, they assume risks and provide financing for producers. Finally, they perform a preliminary buying function for users.

2 Name the alternative distribution channels for consumer goods, organizational goods, and services.

Four distribution channels are used for consumer goods: from producer to consumer, from producer to retailer to consumer, from producer to wholesaler to retailer to consumer, and from producer to agent/broker to wholesaler to retailer to consumer. For organizational goods, the channels may be from producer to user, from producer to one or more agent/brokers or wholesalers to user, or from producer to agent/broker to wholesaler to user. Most services are distributed directly from the producer to the user; however, in a few cases, an agent or a broker intervenes.

3 Differentiate between intensive, selective, and exclusive market-coverage strategies.

With an intensive distribution strategy, a company attempts to saturate the market with its products by offering them in every available outlet. Companies that use a more selective approach to distribution choose a limited number of retailers that can adequately support the product. Firms that use exclusive distribution grant a single wholesaler or retailer the exclusive right to sell the product within a given geographic area.

4 Describe the three types of wholesalers.

The three types of wholesalers are merchant wholesalers, agents and brokers, and producer-owned wholesalers. Merchant wholesalers take title to the goods they sell; agents and brokers do not. Producer-owned wholesalers include branch offices and sales offices.

5 Identify at least 10 types of retailers.

Some of the most common types of retail stores are department stores, discount stores, off-price stores, warehouse clubs, factory outlets, specialty stores, supermarkets, and convenience stores. Nonstore retailers include telemarketers, mail-order firms, vending machines, door-to-door retailers, and computer networks.

6 Explain what is meant by the wheel of retailing.

Wheel of retailing is a term used to describe the evolution of stores from low-priced, limited-service establishments to higher-priced outlets that provide more services. As stores are upgraded, lower-priced competitors move in to fill the gap.

7 Specify the activities included in physical distribution.

Physical distribution encompasses not only transportation but also such in-house operations as forecasting, order processing, inventory control, warehousing, and materials handling.

8 List the five most common ways of transporting goods.

Trucks, railroads, airplanes, ships, and pipelines are the most common methods of moving goods.

It's hard to say which is more impressive: the speed at which Nolan Archibald and his colleagues turned around the corporate culture, or the thoroughness of the results. Black & Decker used to be a manufacturer driven by financial measurements; it is now well on its way to being Archibald's vision of a worldwide marketing powerhouse. The company's approach to managing its marketing channels is a central component of the new Black & Decker.

The change started with strategic planning, as it should. In Archibald's own words: "You analyze the problems that are unique to the company and the industry and then determine what the strengths and weaknesses are. Then you develop a plan to leverage the strengths and correct the weaknesses." Archibald and his colleagues made sure that marketing channels were a part of that strategic plan. Moreover, the new approach manages channels as a vital marketing resource, rather than simply as a pipeline for pumping products to customers.

The analysts who have observed Black & Decker's remarkable turnaround point out several aspects of channel management that have been a vital part of the success. The first change was simple but most important: more respect for marketing intermediaries. Black & Decker had a tough act to follow when it acquired General Electric's small-household-appliance line. Known as "Generous Electric" in some circles, GE went out of its way to be a good supplier. This effort included ample support of retailer promotions, deep inventories to ensure no shortage of products in the stores, and a general level of respect for the people and organizations on the front line. Black & Decker's efforts to improve relations started by emulating this regard for retailers.

Out of this new respect flowed assistance. Black & Decker made several important moves to help its channel partners. One of these was a segmented channel strategy that focuses specialized sales assistance on the company's two major groups of customers: industrial/professional and retailers. This strategy allows Black & Decker to give each kind of intermediary the unique help it needs. Another key move was to train its sales force thoroughly, not only in terms of product performance but also in helping retailers with inventory management, purchasing, and in-store product displays. Also, the promotional budget was beefed up to help pull customers into retail stores.

The assistance is mutual. Black & Decker established a number of dealer advisory panels, which retailers can use to give the company feedback on new products customers would like to see. By using its channel as a source of marketing-research information, Black & Decker benefits by getting a better picture of customer needs, and the retailers benefit by being able to deliver the right products.

Coordinated physical distribution is another change that helps both the company and its intermediaries. To better mesh its delivery systems with the needs of distributors and retailers, Black & Decker changed virtually every aspect of its physical distribution. This overhaul included new locations for distribution centers, modified transportation policies, and more powerful systems for managing and coordinating information.

Increasing the number of products held in inventory is another important step. Maintaining a deeper inventory gives retailers the confidence that they'll be able to keep up with demand, particularly during the Christmas shopping season, when many tools and small appliances are purchased.

Yet another element in Black & Decker's strategic plan is growth through acquisition, which has been tied closely to marketing channel management. The recent $2.8 billion purchase of Emhart is a good example. Some observers criticized the move, which gave Black & Decker a big presence in hardware. However, the logic was clear after a second look: Some of Emhart's products fit in perfectly with Black & Decker's existing consumer-goods channels, and others mesh well with the industrial channels. The units of Emhart that didn't align with the existing marketing channels were put up for sale.

Black & Decker's dramatic turnaround is convincing evidence of the importance of effectively managing marketing channels. Its sales are growing in every channel of distribution it uses. In fact, the company is starting to be praised as a strong marketing organization that helps create demand for retailers.

Your Mission: Nolan Archibald faces some tough issues in the selection and management of Black & Decker's marketing channels. However, he knows he can rely on you for help. In your role as the manager in charge of marketing channels, examine the following situations and make your recommendations from the available choices:

1. Archibald knows that marketing channels can perform a wide array of functions, ranging from gathering marketing information to providing physical distribution. He also knows that Black & Decker should identify the most crucial functions that the company would like to see its intermediaries perform. He's asked you to identify these crucial functions. Which of the following combinations of marketing intermediary functions would be most important to Black & Decker?

a. Most of the vital channel functions required of intermediaries by Black & Decker occur after the sale. Keeping customers satisfied is an absolute necessity, and to do that, you need to be in direct contact. Black & Decker can't be there for every single customer. The functions of most interest here are providing product service and helping customers use products successfully.

b. Black & Decker's products are not terribly complicated, so customers don't need much help. The most important channel functions are at the beginning of the sales process, not at the end. Providing feedback from customers is the best place to start because market information like this is necessary if the company is going to design and manufacture the right products for its customers. With that information in place, the intermediaries should all have a say in Black & Decker's strategic planning process; after all, they are quite dependent on the decisions made during the company's planning process.

c. Alleviating discrepancies and matching buyers and sellers are definitely the most important tasks Black & Decker should ask of its channel partners. It simply isn't economical for the company to deliver individual products to each customer; marketing intermediaries need to fill the gap by rearranging quantities and assortments so that customers can get the right number and selection of products. Also, Black & Decker wouldn't necessarily know where to go to find potential customers, so it must rely on retailers to get the products to customers. Standardized transactions wouldn't hurt, either.

2. Customer service is, of course, a vital ingredient in all successful marketing transactions. Archibald knows this and also realizes that customer service is not all that easy to define and execute in a multichannel system like the one Black & Decker relies on. Which of the following definitions of and approaches to customer service best fits the company's situation?

a. Customer-service efforts focus on the final purchasers of the product. Black & Decker can accomplish this objective in several ways. The first is simply to make it easier to be successful with Black & Decker products. This step includes designing for ease of use, providing helpful user guides, and perhaps offering a toll-free number that customers can call with specific questions about using products. A second way to help customers might be to sponsor seminars at places like woodworking shows (for the power-tool and hardware lines) and home shows (for all three lines). For organizational customers in the power-tool segment, another way to help would be to send Black & Decker specialists to customer sites to help them solve specific problems.

b. Black & Decker's real customers are the thousands of marketing intermediaries that buy and then resell its tools, appliances, and hardware. These are the customers that the company should worry about servicing. The intermediaries will, in turn, satisfy the final customers. Black & Decker can help the intermediaries in a number of ways, including promotions, pricing advice, product selection, and display help.

c. The concept of customer service is irrelevant in this case because Black & Decker doesn't sell to final customers. It is the job of intermediaries to satisfy customers. That is, after all, the number 1 purpose of intermediaries and the reason they make money on the products manufactured by Black & Decker.

3. Black & Decker's engineers have developed a new tool that cuts concrete. Unfortunately, it doesn't really fit in the marketing channels that you already have in place, so it's time for you to design a new channel. Here are some important variables you'll need to consider:

Customer type: Organizational, ranging in size from one-person contractors to multinational construction firms.

Geography: Customers are all over the place; the geographic distribution roughly mirrors the population distribution, with concentrations in large cities and widely dispersed customers elsewhere.

Market size: Big; the saw costs around $2,000, and Black & Decker expects to sell thousands every month; it makes sense to put a sizable investment into the distribution channel.

Life cycle: Somewhere between the growth and maturity phases; most customers have a pretty good idea of how to use them and what they're all about.

Support needs: These customers don't need a lot of help, but they do need to be assured of fast service when things go wrong; downtime is critical, and customers would prefer on-site delivery of loaner units in the event of a breakdown.

On the basis of these variables, what's the best channel system for this product?

a. Consider the purchase habits of the people likely to use these products. Even though they are industrial customers, they are human beings, after all. As such, they need to do personal shopping as much as the rest of us. Because of that, the retail stores where they do their other shopping remain a good choice. That way they can combine their personal shopping with their business shopping.

b. The market is large and geographically diverse, and customers don't need much in the way of support. Therefore, mail order would be the perfect channel for this new product. It reaches every corner of the country, and it costs less because retail-store space and salespeople are not needed.

c. This new product should be restricted to tool stores and masonry-supply stores that cater exclusively to professionals. These stores should be able to deliver superior customer service, including on-site delivery of replacement and loaner units. The biggest drawback of using this channel is that these outlets are not as widespread as homeowner-oriented retail stores, but professional builders in out-of-the way locations are accustomed to a little travel time when it comes to shopping for tools and supplies.

4. A new product has just been designed by the small-home-appliance division. This new device is a combination coffee-bean grinder and espresso machine. What is the best channel system for this product? Here are some factors to consider, and this time consider the problem of product and brand image:

Customer type: Consumer.

Geography: Again, customers are all over the place, but they are concentrated primarily in and around large cities and, for the time being, are found mostly on the West Coast.

Market size: Not terribly large because of the price, which is around $700; many people like espresso made from freshly ground coffee beans, but only the most avid connoisseurs are willing to pay that much for the quality and convenience of the combination grinder/coffeemaker.

Life cycle: Espresso machines have been around for years, but their move into consumer markets is fairly new; in the past, most were sold to restaurants.

Support needs: The machine is fairly easy to use and clean, and you don't expect much in the way of repair trouble, but some customers will initially need help and advice in order to brew the perfect demitasse of espresso.

a. Specialty kitchen stores, particularly those that cater to upscale urban consumers, would be the best choice. These stores carry other kitchen and household products of similar quality and price, so it's a natural that the new espresso machine will fit in here as well. The customers who shop at such stores enjoy buying quality products, and some like to boast that they purchase such goods only from specialty stores, never from department or discount stores.

b. No self-respecting connoisseur is going to buy an espresso machine from a manufacturer of power drills. Even the most astute channel selection isn't going to rescue this project; recommend to your managers that they abandon the product entirely or sell the design to another company. You'll need more than just a good marketing channel to make this miracle happen.

c. The existing channels are fine. A $700 coffee maker might look a little out of place in Kmart, but its presence will raise the image of the entire Black & Decker product family.[33]

branch office (417)
brokers (417)
channel captain (414)
common carriers (428)
contract carriers (428)
convenience stores (423)
customer-service standards (426)
department stores (417)
discount stores (419)
distribution centers (427)
distribution channels (406)
distribution mix (406)
distribution strategy (406)
drop shippers (416)
exclusive distribution (411)
freight forwarders (428)

full-service merchant wholesalers (416)
industrial distributors (415)
intensive distribution (410)
inventory control (427)
limited-service merchant wholesalers (416)
mail-order firms (423)
manufacturer's agents (416)
marketing intermediaries (406)
materials handling (427)
merchant wholesalers (416)
off-price stores (419)
order processing (426)
physical distribution (424)
private carriers (428)

rack jobbers (416)
retailers (415)
reverse channels (409)
sales office (417)
scrambled merchandising (418)
selective distribution (411)
specialty shops (422)
supermarkets (422)
telemarketing (423)
vertical marketing systems (414)
warehouse (427)
warehouse clubs (420)
wheel of retailing (419)
wholesalers (415)

REVIEW QUESTIONS

1. What forms of utility do intermediaries create?
2. How does the presence of intermediaries affect the price of products?
3. How does the length of the distribution chain tend to vary for convenience goods, shopping goods, and specialty goods?

4. What is the difference between a merchant wholesaler and an agent?
5. What are some of the strategies that department stores have begun using to compete with stores that offer lower prices?
6. How do off-price stores function, and what are the advantages they offer?

7. What is the goal of inventory management?
8. What are the advantages and disadvantages of truck, rail, air, ship, and pipeline transportation?

HUB-AND-SPOKE IS WHEEL OF FORTUNE FOR FEDERAL EXPRESS

Back in the 1960s, Frederick W. Smith was sure that his innovative physical-distribution ideas could increase efficiency and decrease the cost of moving packages around the United States. Against the advice of numerous skeptics, he implemented the radical concept of hub-and-spoke distribution, and by 1988 he was flying high with $4 billion in revenues. As he continued to expand, however, Smith faced obstacles that hub-and-spoke couldn't solve: air-transport regulations and the challenge of international operations.

The air-express industry that Smith envisioned would fly packages from around the country to a central location to be sorted and then shipped to their final destinations. He reasoned that a company using this system would be able to optimize its airplane and trucking resources and provide fast and efficient package handling for shippers anywhere in the country.

Smith chose his hometown, Memphis, as the hub; it is centrally located and the airport is rarely closed by bad weather. Despite his high hopes, the first night of service was anything but encouraging. Federal Express handled a grand total of eight shipments, seven of which were sent by its own employees to employees in other locations.

One year later, the fledgling company was losing $1 million a month, and Smith realized that he needed a new marketing approach to reach organizational buyers. After a couple of false starts, Federal Express aired an ad campaign based on the slogan "When it absolutely, positively has to be there overnight," and sales soared.

By the mid-1980s, Federal Express was delivering nearly half of the overnight packages sent within the United States. However, because he knew the market was maturing,

Smith began to look beyond U.S. borders for additional growth. In 1985 Federal Express crossed the oceans with a new international service and quickly got caught in the mire of overseas competitors and foreign aviation regulations.

Over a three-year period, Smith lost about $74 million trying to compete internationally. Finally, in 1989 he won government approval to purchase Tiger International, which gave Federal Express access to the Flying Tiger Line air-cargo organization, with its 40 years of international experience and well-established routes. Moreover, Smith could now use Tiger's fleet of long-range planes and become a player in the international heavy-freight market. Combining Tiger's strengths with Federal Express's expertise in door-to-door delivery, Smith forged a formidable weapon to shake up the global cargo market.

However, FedEx's international hopes didn't pan out quite as successfully as Smith had hoped. After pumping millions of dollars into establishing a base of operations throughout Europe, FedEx lost money there for five years in a row. Several factors were at work: Europe is already well served by a number of long-established trucking companies, European businesses didn't take to the overnight urgency message that worked so well in the United States, and the short distances and mountainous paperwork in between countries makes air cargo unacceptably expensive in many cases. Finally in mid-1992, Smith pulled the plug. FedEx retains direct service to 16 European cities, but for service between cities inside Europe, he is forced to hand the packages over to competitors for final delivery. In spite of this setback however, FedEx remains on strong footing in North America and in emerging markets in Latin America and Asia.

1. Although Federal Express has taken on the burden of warehousing inventory for clients of its Business Logistics Services (BLS) division, Smith believes he can improve this service by expanding its functions. As a new service, should he offer to accept inventory returns to the BLS warehouse from his clients' customers, or should he offer to prepare customers' goods with price tags, instruction sheets, and packaging?

2. Because there are so many competitors in the air-express business, imagine that Smith wants to expand into a new area. Which of these two options should he implement: (1) a chain of state-of-the-art public warehouses that rent space to numerous companies near the airport in cities with heavy commercial air traffic, or (2) an international water-transportation service that would speed containerized goods between major port cities around the world?

3. The Federal Express hub at Memphis airport is virtually unused starting about 4:30 each morning (when planes leave loaded with packages for destinations around the country) until about 11:30 each night (when the planes arrive bearing packages to be sorted for delivery the next day). Smith might want to make the hub more productive during its idle hours. Would you suggest that he make the hub available to passenger airlines during the daytime hours? Would you suggest that he use the hub during daytime hours to offer a two-day freight consolidation and forwarding service, a lower-cost shipping option that combines packages going to the same general location?

In a group of three or four students, select a consumer product with which you are familiar, and trace its channel of distribution. The product might be fresh foods, processed foods, cosmetics, clothing, or manufactured goods (ranging from something as simple as a fork to something as complex as a personal computer).

• For information, you might contact a business involved in the manufacture or distribution of the product, either by letter or by telephone. As an alternative, you could locate an article in a trade periodical that describes the channel of distribution for your chosen product.

• Examine the various factors involved in the distribution of the product, and prepare a brief summary of your findings. Consider the following:

The role of the intermediary in distribution

The type of distribution: intensive, selective, or exclusive

The amount of control the manufacturer has over the distribution process

The type of channel used in the distribution process and its influence on the cost of the product

Find an article in *The Wall Street Journal* describing changes in methods of distribution or distribution policies used by a company or several companies in the same industry. For example, have they changed from using an in-house sales force to using manufacturer's reps? Have they added local warehouses or centralized their distribution? Eliminated wholesalers and gone directly to dealers? Opened more company stores or eliminated independent retailers? Added a mail-order division to a retail operation or a retail operation to a mail-order firm? Changed discount policies or shipping methods? Closed stores in downtown areas and moved to malls? Added on-line ordering capabilities?

1. What changes in distribution have taken place? What additional changes, if any, are planned?
2. What were the reasons for the changes? How have population, lifestyle, financial, or other factors affected distribution in this industry?
3. If you were a stockholder in a company in this industry, would you be concerned about distribution-related changes hurting the company in the next five years? Why or why not?

MCKESSON INNOVATES THROUGH 150 YEARS OF SUCCESSFUL WHOLESALING

Synopsis

This video profiles the innovations and customer-support services that are offered by McKesson, the nation's largest wholesaler of pharmaceuticals and health and beauty products. You see some of the company's advanced technology in action, such as the "picking" machine that can count individual items (such as bottles of aspirin) and load each drugstore's order correctly and efficiently. Like other major wholesalers in this and other industries, McKesson also offers its customers a variety of services, from store design through special marketing assistance. As a wholesaler, McKesson is very interested in helping its customers, the retail stores, sell more to consumers because the more those consumers buy from retailers, the more those retailers buy from McKesson.

Exercises

ANALYSIS

1. The automation employed by McKesson doesn't come cheap; does it increase or decrease the final price that consumers pay?

2. Could McKesson afford to invest in automation if its competitors didn't?

3. How does McKesson help its customers compete?

4. What are the risks of investing so much money in distribution technology?

5. Could McKesson use its technology by expanding into other areas of wholesaling, such as groceries?

APPLICATION

Name three other industries that could benefit from the sort of high-tech distribution (such as the machines that can collect a variety of small products for shipment to a customer) illustrated by McKesson in the video.

DECISION

Put yourself in the shoes of a pharmacist who has been offered the McKesson Pharmacy Information Center. These computer terminals provide shoppers with information about drug dosages, side effects, and interactions with other medication. You'd like to provide the service for your customers, but you're afraid the terminal might attract a lot of people who don't buy anything from you but come into the drugstore only to get free information. Assuming that the terminal doesn't cost you anything, should you accept McKesson's offer?

COMMUNICATION

Review the points of "The McKesson Advantage" outlined in the video, and draft a one-page sales brochure that McKesson could use to promote itself to drugstores.

INTEGRATION

Referring to Exhibit 12.1, explain how McKesson delivers the four types of utility to its drugstore customers.

ETHICS

A recurring problem for many wholesalers is supplying small, remote retail locations that don't buy much and cost a great deal to serve. However, if these retailers can't get wholesalers to supply them, they can't provide the goods their customers want and need. Does McKesson have a social obligation to serve these retailers, even if it must do so for little or no profit?

DEBATE

The video states that McKesson can satisfy up to 80 percent of the retailer's product needs. Some people might question the wisdom of a retailer's relying to such a great extent on a single supplier, even one with the sterling reputation of McKesson. Option A: In a formal debate format, assume the role of a retailer and argue for or against the notion of relying on a single wholesaler for the vast majority of your product needs. Option B: Take either position and state your case in a brief report.

TEAMWORK

In a team of three or four students, pick several different types of retail stores and make a list of the services that a wholesaler such as McKesson (or similar companies that serve other industries) could offer. Be sure to consider everything from marketing research to store design, and if time allows, visit representative retail stores to get more ideas.

RESEARCH

Do the research necessary to write a one-paragraph summary on either (a) the current status of McKesson and the drug-wholesaling industry or (b) trends in electronic data interchange (EDI).

ROLE PLAYING

One student plays the role of a "customer satisfaction" trainer employed by McKesson to help drugstore employees treat customers better. Several other students play store employees who have been accustomed to retail environments in which the emphasis was on selling, selling, selling. The trainer explains the meaning and importance of customer satisfaction in retailing.

Chapter

15

Promotion

Opening the Door to Sales on Two Coasts

What's yellow and blue, as large as seven football fields, and filled from floor to ceiling with furniture? The answer, as millions of shoppers from Budapest to Burbank have learned, is an Ikea store. Based in Denmark, Ikea operates more than 100 warehouse-sized furniture stores in 24 countries. The retailer opens between 5 and 10 outlets every year, and no two grand-opening advertising campaigns are exactly alike, because no two markets and no two audiences are exactly alike. So when the chain planned a new U.S. store in Elizabeth, New Jersey, followed by a store in Burbank, California, Ikea president Anders Moberg knew that the grand-opening ad campaigns had to be as different as Coney Island hot dogs and avocado salad.

Ikea's international success has been anything but an overnight phenomenon. Founder Ingvar Kamprad came up with the company name in 1943 by combining his own initials with the first letter of his farm, Elmtaryd, and the first letter of his native parish, Agunnaryd (similar to a county in the United States). His first furniture showroom, in Southern Sweden, featured bargain prices and simple but stylishly functional designs. However, it wasn't until he opened his Stockholm store, in 1965, that Kamprad put into practice the marketing concepts that now distinguish Ikea from its competitors: moderate prices, quality products, and a pleasant shopping environment.

Ikea has enjoyed great success in both Europe and North America by making furniture shopping easier.

Going to an Ikea store is like entering a home-furnishings paradise. Customers are invited to wander through each model room and measure, touch, even sit or lie down on any of the hundreds of furniture samples inside each 200,000-square-foot outlet. What's more, hungry shoppers can snack at the in-store cafe, and harried parents can leave their children at the in-store play area while shopping. Prices are low because customers select their own items and carry them home in flat-pack cartons, where they assemble the pieces using simple tools included with every purchase.

To enter two separate markets, Moberg knew that the store would need completely different ad campaigns. If you were in his shoes, how would you use promotion to introduce Ikea to the target audiences in Elizabeth and Burbank? What advertising strategies would you use to develop ads that will attract customers?[1]

THE PROMOTIONAL MIX

Ikea's Anders Moberg knows that effective promotions can make or break his plans to expand across the country. Of the four ingredients in the marketing mix (product, price, distribution, and promotion) promotion is perhaps the one most often associated with marketing. Although it is no guarantee of success, promotion does have a profound impact on a product's performance in the marketplace.

What exactly is **promotion**? Although the term is defined in many ways, it is basically persuasive communication that motivates people to buy whatever an organization is selling—goods, services, or ideas. Promotion may take the form of direct, face-to-face communication or indirect communication through such media as television, radio, magazines, newspapers, direct mail, billboards, and other channels. A company's **promotional strategy** defines the direction and scope of the promotional activities that will be implemented to meet marketing objectives.

Promotional Goals

Promotional activities have three basic goals: to inform, to persuade, and to remind. *Informing* is the first promotional priority, since people cannot buy something until they are aware of it and understand what it will do for them. Potential customers need to know where the item can be found, how much it will cost, and how to use it. *Persuading* is also an important priority, since most people need to be motivated to satisfy their wants in a particular way. Advertising that meets this goal is classified as **persuasive advertising.** If customers

promotion *Wide variety of persuasive techniques used by companies to communicate with their target markets and the general public*

promotional strategy *Statement or document that defines the direction and scope of the promotional activities that a company will use to meet its marketing objectives*

persuasive advertising *Advertising designed to persuade an audience to change its behavior or attitudes*

This Polish ad for the German AEG brand vacuum cleaner vividly demonstrates the machine's suction power.

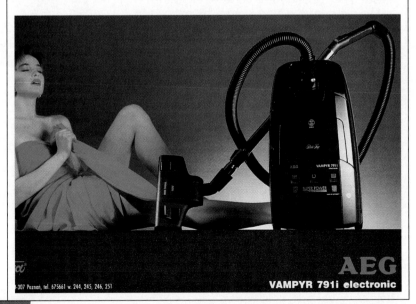

AEG
VAMPYR 791i electronic

have never used the item before, they must be convinced that doing so will be beneficial. If they are using a competing brand, they must be persuaded to switch. *Reminding* the customer of the product's availability and benefits is also important, since such reminders stimulate additional purchases. The term for such promotional efforts is **reminder advertising.**

Informing, persuading, and reminding are the main goals of promotion, but a good promotional effort also seeks to achieve specific objectives. These include attracting new customers, increasing usage among existing customers, aiding distributors, stabilizing sales, boosting brand-name recognition, creating sales leads, and influencing decision makers.

The variety of possible objectives highlights a key point about promotion in general and advertising in particular: Not all promotional efforts are designed to generate sales, at least not directly. That's why promotions experts think in terms of *communications objectives* and *sales objectives*. A communications objective is an interim step toward making a sale. It may be to make an audience aware of a new product or to change negative perceptions of a company. If accomplished, these objectives probably would lead to sales eventually, but the idea with such goals is to focus on a specific step in the process, not the final result.[2]

Promotional Ethics and Regulations

Although promotion serves many useful functions, critics argue that its goals are self-serving. Some contend that sellers use promotional tools to persuade people to buy unnecessary or potentially harmful goods like antiaging creams, baldness "cures," sweetened cereals, liquor, and cigarettes. Others argue that promotion encourages materialism at the expense of more worthwhile values, that it exploits stereotypes, and that it manipulates the consumer on a subconscious level. Still others argue that the money spent on promotion could be put to better use inventing new products or improving the quality of existing items.

Some of these concerns are well founded, and abuses certainly do occur. However, some of the charges leveled at advertising don't stand up to serious logical analysis. Take the charge about materialism. People have been materialistic for centuries, long before advertising as we know it was even invented. It's basic human nature to want to show off and display one's wealth, as a visit to any palace or castle anywhere in the world will confirm.

Perhaps the widest gulf between criticism and reality involves the charge of *subliminal advertising*, the notion that advertisers hide manipulative visual or audio cues in ads. This hysteria started in the late 1950s, when a "researcher" claimed to have increased sales of Coca-Cola in a movie theater by inserting hidden messages in the movie. Everyone seems to remember this side of the story, but few people realize that this supposed experiment in manipulation was a complete fraud, concocted by a man who later admitted he was just trying to sell the projection equipment that inserted the messages into the movie.[3]

reminder advertising *Advertising intended to remind existing customers of a product's availability and benefits*

The most visible critic behind the charge of subliminal manipulation is a man named Wilson Bryan Key, who claims that nude figures, the word *sex,* and other such things are hidden in product photos and sometimes on products themselves. Key even claims that Ritz crackers have the word *sex* embedded on both the top and bottom of the cracker—and he says it makes the crackers taste better. As incredible as all this sounds, he has generated a lot of public mistrust of the advertising profession. However, there is no objective evidence of the existence of this sort of trickery and little psychological evidence to suggest that it would work even if anyone were doing it.[4]

Public concern about potential misuse of promotion has led to the passage of government regulations that limit promotional abuses. The federal government's primary advertising watchdog is the Federal Trade Commission (FTC), which has developed some ground rules for promotion. One rule is that *all statements of fact must be supported by evidence.* This regulation includes words ("Lipton. The Only Naturally Decaffeinated Tea Bags") and demonstrations. Thus, companies cannot use whipped cream in a shaving-cream commercial to create an impression of a firm, heavy lather. Another rule is that *sellers must not create an overall impression that is incorrect.* In other words, they cannot claim that doctors recommend a product if doctors do not; nor can they present an actor who delivers the message dressed in a doctor's white jacket. Most states also regulate promotional practices by individual industries such as liquor stores, stock brokerages, employment agencies, and loan companies.

In response to growing concern and confusion among consumers and health professionals, the Food and Drug Administration and the U.S. Department of Agriculture developed sweeping guidelines and policies for advertising claims and product-label wording. For instance, the word *light* can now be used to describe a product only if it contains at least one-third fewer calories than the regular version of the product; *low-calorie* means no more than 40 calories per standard-sized serving. Similarly, the government now has specific definitions for such terms as *recyclable* and *biodegradable,* and advertisers can't use the terms if they can't meet federal guidelines.[5]

Self-regulation by businesses provides still another vehicle for the restraint of false and misleading promotion. The National Advertising Review Board, whose members include advertisers, agencies, and the general public, has a full-time professional staff that investigates complaints of deceptive advertising. If the complaint appears justified, the board uses both its persuasive power and the threat of referral to governmental agencies to try to get the offending company to stop. Many individual companies and agencies also practice self-regulation.

Four Elements of Promotion

Within the framework of these guidelines, marketers use a mix of four activities to achieve their promotional objectives. The activities are personal selling, advertising, public relations, and sales promotion (see Exhibit 15.1). These elements can be combined in various ways to create a **promotional mix** for a particular product or idea.

promotional mix *Particular blend of personal selling, advertising, public relations, and sales promotion that a company uses to reach potential customers*

442

Activity	Contact mode	Timing	Flexibility	Control	Cost/exposure
Personal selling	Direct personal interaction	Regular, recurrent contact	Message tailored to customer and adjusted to reflect feedback	Sender controls content of message	Relatively high
Advertising	Indirect, no personal interaction	Regular, recurrent contact	Standard, unvarying message	Seller controls content of message	Low to moderate
Public relations	Indirect, no personal interaction	Intermittent, as newsworthy events occur	Standard, unvarying message	Medium usually controls content of message	No direct cost
Sales promotion	Indirect, no personal interaction	Intermittent, based on short-term sales objectives	Standard, unvarying message	Seller controls content of message	Varies

Personal selling involves direct, person-to-person communication, either face-to-face or by phone. It is the only form of promotion that allows for immediate interaction between the buyer and seller. It is also the only form that enables the seller to adjust the message to the specific needs and interests of the individual customer. The chief disadvantage of personal selling is its relatively high cost.

Advertising consists of messages paid for by an identified sponsor and transmitted through a mass communication medium. As we shall see later in the chapter, advertising can take many forms. Its chief advantage lies in its ability to reach a large audience economically. Advertising has several disadvantages, however, starting with the expense of creating an advertising campaign. Second, advertising can't provide direct feedback, as personal selling can, and advertising is also difficult to personalize. Finally, advertising can't always motivate customers to action as effectively as personal selling can.

Public relations encompasses all the nonsales communications that businesses have with their various audiences. Part of the public-relations effort covers general topics, such as responding to journalists' requests for information and helping local schools with educational projects. The other side of the public-relations effort seeks to generate significant news coverage about the company and its products and tries to encourage favorable reviews of products in newspapers and magazines and on radio and television programs.

Sales promotion is the final element in the promotional mix, and it is the most difficult to define. It includes a wide range of events and activities designed to stimulate interest in the product. Coupons, rebates, contests, in-store demonstrations, free samples, trade shows, and point-of-purchase displays all fall into this category.

Many companies are discovering that, over time, their promotional mixes develop into collections of disconnected efforts. Salespeople may visit customers and say one thing about a product, whereas an ad campaign says something different about the product. The result is reduced effectiveness and increased potential for confusing the target buyers. Large companies in particular employ hundreds of marketing people performing a wide variety of promotion activities, and to be as effective as possible, these activities need to be coordinated. An increasingly popular way to ensure such coordination is

Exhibit 15.1
The Four Elements of Promotion
The promotional mix typically includes a blend of various elements. The "right" mix depends on the nature of the market and the characteristics of the item being sold. Over time the mix for a particular product may change.

personal selling *In-person communication between a seller and one or more potential buyers*

advertising *Paid, nonpersonal communication to a target market from an identified sponsor using mass communications channels*

public relations *Nonsales communication that businesses have with their various audiences (includes both communication with the general public and press relations)*

sales promotion *Wide range of events and activities (including coupons, rebates, contests, in-store demonstrations, free samples, trade shows, and point-of-purchase displays) designed to stimulate interest in a product*

integrated marketing communications (IMC), a strategy of co-ordinating and integrating all your communications and promotions efforts with customers.[6]

Promotional Strategies

How do you decide on the right blend of personal selling, advertising, public relations, and sales promotion? That's not an easy question to answer because so many factors must be taken into account. When marketing a product, the seller combines the various elements of the promotional mix, depending on the characteristics of the product and of the market.

Product-Related Factors

Various types of products lend themselves to differing forms of promotion. Simple, familiar items like laundry detergent can be explained adequately through advertising, but personal selling is generally required to communicate the features of unfamiliar and sophisticated goods and services such as office-automation equipment or municipal waste-treatment facilities. Direct, personal contact is particularly important in promoting customized services such as interior design, financial advice, or legal counsel. In general, consumer and organizational goods usually require differing promotional mixes.

The product's price is also a factor in the selection of the promotional mix. Inexpensive items sold to a mass market are well suited to advertising and sales promotion, which have a relatively low per-unit cost. At the other extreme, products with a high unit price lend themselves to personal selling because the high cost of a sales call is justified by the size of the order. Furthermore, the nature of the selling process often demands face-to-face interaction between the buyer and seller.

Another factor that influences both the level and mix of promotional activity is the product's position in its life cycle. Early on, when the seller is trying to inform the customer about the product and build the distribution network, promotional efforts are in high gear. Selective advertising, sales promotion, and public relations are used to build awareness and to encourage early adopters to try the product; personal selling is used to gain the cooperation of intermediaries. As the market expands during the growth phase, the seller broadens the advertising and sales-promotion activities to reach a wider audience and continues to use personal selling to expand the distribution network. When the product reaches maturity and competition is at its peak, the seller's primary goal is to differentiate the product from rival brands. Advertising generally dominates the promotional mix during this phase, but sales promotion is an important supplemental tool, particularly for low-priced consumer products. As the product begins to decline, the level of promotion generally tapers off. Advertising and selling efforts are carefully targeted toward loyal, steady customers.

Market-Related Factors

To some extent, the promotional mix depends on whether the seller plans to focus the marketing effort on intermediaries or final cus-

WE'VE MADE A GREAT CASE FOR INCREASING YOUR PROFITS.

PLEN T PAK

INTRODUCING WRIGLEY'S WHOLESALE CASE.

A Special Case For Special Needs

Wrigley's has created a special case for your unique inventory control and selection needs—a downsized, punch-out, full-faced shipping case that's changing the face of the wholesale gum business.

Reduces Handling Cost

Our new punch-out, perforated design makes stocking easier, reduces handling and helps prevent damaged goods. No case-cutting required. Just punch out the face panel and put the case on the shelf.

Decreases Inventory Cost

Wrigley's new Wholesale Case provides you with an organized, consistent product layout. What's more, our smaller case size lowers your initial out-of-pocket inventory cost. And that increases R.O.I.

Improves Product Visibility And Selection

This full-faced case with color-coded descriptors improves overall category visibility, and facilitates the selection of sugar, sugarfree, and non-stick chewing gums.

Before

After

Call your Wrigley's representative today for more information about our new innovative inventory control system specially designed to meet the challenges of today's wholesale business.

Wrigley's Wholesale Case. A More Profitable Inventory Management System.

---

tomers. If the focus is on intermediaries, the producer uses a **push strategy** to persuade wholesalers and retailers to carry the item. Personal selling and sales promotions aimed at intermediaries dominate the promotional mix. If the marketing focus is on end users, the producer uses a **pull strategy** to appeal directly to the ultimate customer, using advertising, direct mail, contests, discount coupons, and so on. With this approach, consumers learn of the product through promotion and request it from retailers, who respond by asking their wholesalers for it or by going directly to the producer.

The promotional mix is also influenced by the size and concentration of the market. In markets with many widely dispersed buyers, advertising is generally the most economical way of communicating the product's features. In markets with relatively few customers, particularly when they are clustered in a limited area, personal selling is a practical promotional alternative. Many marketers use a combination of methods, often relying on advertising and public relations to build awareness and interest, following up with personal selling to complete the sale. When Cessna introduced its new Citation X business jet, it first got the attention of corporate executives by mailing scale models of the new plane.[7]

International Promotion Decisions

Businesses operating in international markets face another layer of strategic and tactical decisions when it comes to promotion. The *global* and *local* approaches to international advertising represent two extremes. With the global approach, the advertiser tries to keep the strat-

Promoting products to wholesalers and retailers is an important advertising function as well; here Wrigley's tries to persuade retailers that it is helping them succeed.

push strategy *Promotional approach designed to motivate wholesalers and retailers to push a producer's products to end users*

pull strategy *Promotional strategy that stimulates consumer demand, which then exerts pressure on wholesalers and retailers to carry a product*

egy and tactics identical in every country, with necessary exceptions made for local laws and media. With the local approach, the advertiser allows its divisions or representatives in each country to design and implement their own advertising. Most international campaigns fall somewhere between these two extremes. Advertisers who opt for the regional approach strike a compromise between the efficiency of the global approach and the cost and complexity of the local approach by grouping similar countries together under a single campaign.

The controversy surrounding the global approach centers on whether audiences are really similar enough around the world to be effectively reached with a single advertising strategy. Global proponents say that advertisers should seek out and advertise to the similarities they can find. In fact, they should use advertising to shape those similarities. Opponents say there simply aren't that many similarities for the vast majorities of products and that not paying attention to local audience differences leads to mistakes and ineffective advertising. It's a debate that will probably rage on for years, with some companies opting for the global and others deciding to take the local approach.

The Role of Positioning in Promotion

The strategic importance of positioning is discussed in Chapter 12. Although promotion is just one aspect of the positioning process, it is certainly one of the most important. Consequently, positioning strategies should play a key role in the design of every company's promotional mix. The nature of a company's advertising, the type of salespeople it hires, its policy regarding coupons, its support for cultural events—decisions like these have a dramatic effect on the position that a company and its products will occupy in the minds of potential customers. Because so many things influence a product's position, successful businesspeople such as Ikea's Anders Moberg pay attention to the details, from the product selection to the lighting and decor in the stores.

PERSONAL SELLING

By almost any measure, personal selling is the dominant form of promotional activity. Nearly one out of every eight workers in the United States is a salesperson.[8] Also, most companies spend twice as much on personal selling as they do on all other marketing activities combined.[9] The roles these salespeople play can vary widely, however, depending on the product and the market.

Types of Sales Personnel

From the general public's perspective, salespeople are salespeople. However, from a business perspective, salespeople play various roles depending on the size and organization of the company, the type of product it sells, and the nature of its customer base. In general, salespeople can be categorized according to three broad areas of responsibility: (1) order getting, (2) order taking, and (3) sales support services. Although some salespeople focus primarily on one area of responsibility, others may have broader responsibilities that span several areas.

Order Getters

Order getters are responsible for generating new sales and for increasing sales to existing customers. Order getters can range from telemarketers selling bottled water and stockbrokers selling securities to engineers selling computers and nuclear physicists selling consulting services. Order getting is sometimes referred to as **creative selling,** particularly if the salesperson must invest a significant amount of time in determining what the customer needs, devising a strategy to explain how the product can meet those needs, and persuading the customer to buy. This type of creative selling requires a high degree of empathy, and the salesperson takes on the role of consultant in a long-term relationship with the customer.

order getters Salespeople who are responsible for generating new sales and for increasing sales to existing customers

creative selling Selling process used by order getters, which involves determining customer needs, devising strategies to explain product benefits, and persuading customers to buy

Order Takers

Order takers do little creative selling; they primarily process orders. Unfortunately, the term *order taker* has assumed negative overtones in recent years because salespeople often use it to refer to someone too lazy to work for new customers or actively close orders, or they use it to refer to someone whose territory is so attractive that he or she can just sit by the phone and wait for orders to roll in. Regardless of how salespeople use the term, order takers in the true sense play an important role in the sales function.

order takers Salespeople who generally process incoming orders without engaging in creative selling

With the aim of generating additional sales, many companies are beginning to train their order takers to think more like order getters. You've probably noticed that nearly every time you order a meal at McDonald's and don't ask for french fries, the person at the counter will ask, "Would you like an order of fries to go with that?" Such suggestions can prompt customers to buy something they may not otherwise order.

Sales Support Personnel

Sales support personnel generally don't sell products, but they facilitate the overall selling effort by providing a variety of services. Their responsibilities can include looking for new customers, educating potential and current customers, building goodwill, and providing service to customers after the sale. The three most common types of sales support personnel are missionary, technical, and trade salespeople.

sales support personnel Salespeople who facilitate the selling effort by providing such services as prospecting, customer education, and customer service

Missionary salespeople are employed by manufacturers to disseminate information about new products to existing customers (usually wholesalers and retailers) and to motivate them to sell the product to their customers. Manufacturers of pharmaceuticals and medical supplies use missionary salespeople to call on doctors and pharmacists. They leave samples and information, answer questions, and persuade doctors to prescribe their products.

missionary salespeople Salespeople who support existing customers, usually wholesalers and retailers

Technical salespeople contribute technical expertise and assistance to the selling function. They are usually engineers and scien-

technical salespeople Specialists who contribute technical expertise and other sales assistance tists or have received specialized technical training. In addition to providing support services to existing customers, they may also participate in sales calls to prospective customers. Companies that manufacture computers, industrial equipment, and sophisticated medical equipment use technical salespeople to sell their products as well as to provide support services to existing customers.

trade salespeople *Salespeople who sell to and support marketing intermediaries by giving in-store demonstrations, offering samples, and so on*

Trade salespeople sell to and support marketing intermediaries. Producers such as Hormel, Nabisco, and Sara Lee use trade salespeople to give in-store demonstrations, offer samples to customers, set up displays, restock shelves, and work with retailers to obtain more shelf space. Increasingly, producers work to establish lasting, mutually beneficial relationships with their channel partners, and trade salespeople are responsible for building those relationships.

Telemarketing

telemarketing *Selling or supporting the sales process over the telephone*

As the cost of personal sales calls continues to increase, many companies and nonprofit organizations are trying to keep costs down by turning to **telemarketing**—selling over the telephone. Businesses like telemarketing because they can reach a great number of customers, and many customers like it because it saves them time. Telemarketers now sell everything from investment services to computer systems.[10] Sometimes telemarketing is used by itself; in other cases, it is used to supplement door-to-door and other selling methods.

Telemarketing can be broken down into two classes: *Outbound telemarketing* occurs when companies place *cold calls* to potential customers that have not requested a sales call; *inbound telemarketing* establishes phone lines for customers to call in to place orders. Outbound telemarketing can generate a lot of criticism because it interrupts family or business activities and can even pose a threat to safety by tying up a phone line needed in an emergency. If you've been bothered during dinner or roused from a deep sleep just to answer the phone and listen to someone's sales pitch, you understand the criticism. Perhaps the worst abuse comes from computerized dialing systems that call numbers automatically and send a recorded message. Public pressure is leading some states to consider legislation that would regulate or even ban outbound telemarketing.[11]

The Creative Selling Process

Although it may look easy, creative selling is not a simple task. Of course, some sales are made in a matter of minutes. However, other sales, particularly for large organizational purchases, can take months to complete. Salespeople should follow a carefully planned process from start to finish (see Exhibit 15.2).

Step 1: Prospecting

prospecting *Process of finding and qualifying potential customers*

Prospecting is the process of finding and qualifying potential customers. This step involves three activities:

- *Generating sales leads.* Sales leads are names of individuals and organizations that *might* be likely prospects for the company's product.

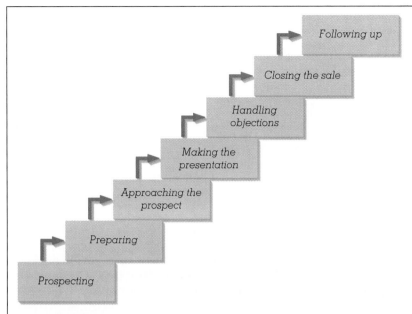

Exhibit 15.2
The Creative Selling Process
The creative selling process can involve up to seven steps, starting with prospecting for sales leads and ending with following up after the sale has been closed.

Steps shown (bottom to top):
- Prospecting
- Preparing
- Approaching the prospect
- Making the presentation
- Handling objections
- Closing the sale
- Following up

- *Identifying prospects.* A prospect is a potential customer who indicates a need or a desire for the seller's product.
- *Qualifying prospects.* Not all prospects are worth investing sales time in. Some may not have the authority to buy, and others won't have enough money. The process of figuring out which ones have both the authority and the available money is called **qualifying,** and the prospects who pass the test are called **qualified prospects.**

Step 2: Preparing

With a list of hot prospects in hand, the salesperson's next step is to prepare for the sales call. Without this preparation, the chances of success are greatly reduced. Preparation starts with creating a prospect profile, which includes the names of key people, their role in the decision-making process, and other relevant information, such as the prospect's buying needs, motive for buying, current suppliers, income/revenue level, and so on.

Next, the salesperson decides how to approach the prospect. Possible options for a first contact include sending a letter or making a cold call in person or by telephone. For an existing customer, the salesperson can either drop by unannounced or call ahead for an appointment, which is generally preferred.

Before meeting with the prospect, the salesperson establishes specific objectives to achieve during the sales call. Depending on the situation, objectives can range anywhere from "getting the order today" to simply "persuading prospects to accept the company as a potential supplier." After establishing the objectives, the salesperson prepares the actual presentation, which can be as basic as a list of points to discuss or as elaborate as a product demonstration or multimedia presentation.

qualifying *Process of identifying potential customers who have both the authority to buy a product and the money to do so*

qualified prospects *Potential buyers who have both the money needed to make the purchase and the authority to make the purchase decision*

In personal selling, the sales representative has an opportunity to build rapport—a sense of psychological connection—with the prospect. Skillful sales reps constantly use body language and verbal directions to get a message to and from the prospect. Here are some hints on how it's done.

Establishing a Bond

Prospects are much more inclined to buy from people who make them feel good and with whom they have developed a personal bond.

- *Try to make yourself seem compatible with the prospect.* Be similar (or seem so) in dress, speaking patterns, and interests.
- *Be sure to set aside a preliminary period to build a feeling of agreement.* Don't plunge into the presentation immediately.
- *Pace your statements and gestures to mirror the customer's observations, experience, or behavior.* "It's been awfully hot these last few days, hasn't it?" "You said you were going to graduate in June."
- *Be sure to use a "probing" period during which you draw out information and identify the prospect's real needs and problems.* A consumer may want status from a car as much as performance; the organizational buyer wants to avoid

STEPS TO AN EFFECTIVE SALES PRESENTATION

looking bad to management. Good sales reps are excellent listeners at the probing stage.

Describing and Demonstrating the Product

Once the prospect's needs have been identified, you should concentrate on relating product features to benefits that may meet the buyer's needs or solve a problem.

- *Focus on benefits.* "This drill will help you make holes faster and more cheaply" is better than a statement about product features ("This drill motor delivers *x* foot-pounds of torque").
- *Use product demonstrations that the prospect can easily see and comprehend.* Say that you have won an appointment with Ms. McCormick to discuss your company's cash-manage-

ment account. You could show Ms. McCormick a sample statement of the type she would receive every month, outlining the activity of an imaginary account and showing how her money will keep earning interest.

Using a Trial Close

Your purpose is ultimately to close the sale by obtaining an order or by getting some other commitment.

- *Try using a "yes" technique.* Use a series of questions or statements that get the prospect to nod or say yes over and over. By the time you finally ask for the order, the prospect may be in the mood to say yes just one more time.

Experienced sales reps know that most prospects won't be entirely satisfied until they've asked questions or posed objections to the sales points. To deal with this very human trait, you may want to launch a trial balloon known as the *trial close*—a maneuver that may not get the order then and there but that will draw out whatever may be standing between the prospect and the sale. The following is a typical trial close:

> *Salesperson:* Would you agree that your money works harder to earn you interest in a cash-manage-

Step 3: Approaching the Prospect

Whether the approach is by telephone, by letter, or in person, a positive first impression results from three elements. The first is an appropriate *appearance*—you wouldn't wear blue jeans to call on a banker, and you probably wouldn't wear a business suit to call on a farmer. Appearance also covers the things that represent you, including business cards, letters, and automobiles. Second, a salesperson's *attitude and behavior* can make or break a sale. A salesperson should come across as professional, courteous, and considerate. Third, a salesperson's *opening lines* should include a brief greeting and introduction, followed by a few carefully chosen words that get the prospect's attention and generate interest. The best way to get a prospect's attention is to focus on a benefit to the customer rather than on the product itself.

ment account than in the money-market fund you're using now?

Customer: I suppose it does.

Salesperson: Then we can open an account for you this week with as little as $1,000 . . . and I can sign you up today with your signature on this acceptance.

Customer: Yes, but what about getting my money if I need it in an emergency? I don't want to tie up my funds or pay a penalty for taking them out.

Now you have a bona fide objection on the table, and you know where the buyer's resistance lies.

Handling Objections

The way to answer objections is *not* to argue with the customer. If you do, you may prove how smart you are by winning the argument, but you will probably lose the sale.

- *Recognize the nature of the objection.* Some objections are rational and product oriented. Others are psychological: They have more to do with the buyer's "hidden agenda" of needs. For instance, the prospect may be afraid of trying something new or may dislike the sales rep.
- *Register agreement.* No matter what the buyer says, the skillful sales rep usually agrees courteously and then shifts the derailed prospect back on the right track. Instead of blurting out, "Oh, no, our service is better than you'd get from your supplier," it's smarter to begin this way: "I can understand why you're concerned about service. These days, you have to be. That's why we offer a seven-point service contract." In other words, answer with a statement that proves your service is better.

- *Probe with a new trial close.* Once the objection has been handled, you may use another trial close to extract new objections. You handle these objections one by one, and eventually you exhaust the buyer's doubts and problems so that you can go to a final close. For instance, a sales rep might say, "I can appreciate your need for 24-hour access to your cash without paying a penalty. That's why we give you this special American Express Gold Card (pulls the card out of portfolio) that lets you get cash from any participating bank whenever you need it."

Moving to the Final Close

The most striking characteristic of a great sales rep is her or his ability to close the sale and walk away with the prospect's signature on an order blank. For some sales reps, the final close is a frightening or an embarrassing moment: It always entails the risk of rejection. Some sales reps botch the sale because they can't stop talking—they effectively sell the product and then buy it back. So be sure that when you end the presentation stage and go for the final close you are able to keep quiet while the customer orders. Here are some useful closing techniques:

- *Summarize the presentation.* Use a simple anecdotal statement that clearly positions the need for the product in the buyer's mind.
- *Make the offer available for a limited time only.* This approach often gets immediate action.
- *Ask for a small "trial" order.* You can reduce the customer's risk this way.
- *Turn the buyer's last objection into a close.* Say, "Then you'd order if I could guarantee a one-year warranty in writing?" This way, you leave the buyer in the position of having run out of valid objections.

Step 4: Making the Presentation

The most crucial step in the selling process is the presentation. It can take many forms, but its purpose never varies: to personally communicate a product message that will persuade a prospect to buy. Most sellers use one of two methods: The **canned approach** is a memorized presentation (easier for inexperienced sellers, but inefficient for complex products or for sellers who don't know the customer's needs). The **need-satisfaction approach** (now used by most professionals) identifies the customer's needs and creates a presentation to specifically address them.

canned approach *Selling method based on a fixed, memorized presentation*

need-satisfaction approach *Selling method that starts with identifying the customer's needs and then creating a presentation that addresses those needs; this is the approach used by most professional salespeople*

Step 5: Handling Objections

No matter how well a presentation is delivered, it doesn't always conclude with an immediate offer that might move the prospect to buy.

Often the prospect will express various types of objections and concerns throughout the presentation. In fact, the absence of objections is often an indication that the prospect is not all that interested. Many successful salespeople look at objections as a sign of the prospect's interest and as an opportunity to develop new ideas that will strengthen future presentations.

Three basic approaches to overcoming objections include asking the prospect a question, giving a response to the objection, or telling the prospect that you will need to look into the matter and address it later. For example, if a prospect objects to the price, you might ask, "Why do you feel the price is too high?" The prospect may then point out underlying problems or objections that you can address, such as perceived shortcomings the product may have when compared with a competing product. Smart salespeople know that objections to price are often a mask for some other issue.

Step 6: Closing

So far, you haven't made a dime. You may have spent weeks or months to bring the customer to this point, but you don't make any money until the prospect decides to buy. This stage of the selling process, when you persuade the customer to place an order, is referred to as **closing.** How should you ask for the order? Closing techniques are numerous; among the more popular are the alternative proposal close, the assumptive close, the silent close, and the direct close. The *alternative proposal close* asks the prospect to choose between some minor details, such as method of shipment. With the *assumptive close,* you simply proceed with processing the order, assuming that the prospect has already decided to buy. Another alternative is the *silent close,* in which you finish your presentation and sit quietly, waiting for the customer to respond with his or her buying decision. Finally, many salespeople prefer the *direct close,* where you just come right out and ask for the order.

These closing techniques might strike you as tricks, and in the hands of unethical salespeople, some closing approaches certainly can be. However, the professional salesperson uses these techniques to make the selling process effective and efficient—not to trick people into buying when they aren't ready.

Step 7: Following Up

Most salespeople depend on repeat sales and referrals from satisfied customers, so it's important that they follow up on all sales and not ignore the customer once the first sale is made. During this follow-up stage of the selling process, you need to make sure that the product has been delivered properly and that the customer is satisfied. Inexperienced salespeople may avoid the follow-up stage because they fear facing an unhappy customer. However, an important part of a salesperson's job is to ensure customer satisfaction and to build goodwill.

US West Cellular, for example, has its service representatives place "Welcome Aboard" calls to new subscribers to thank them for their business and to answer questions. The company has learned that when representatives call customers periodically, the customers perceive im-

closing Point at which a sale is completed

provements in their cellular telephone service—even if there were no technical improvements to the service itself.[12]

In order to improve the odds of keeping a satisfied customer after the sale, salespeople should remember to

- Handle complaints promptly and pleasantly
- Maintain contact with customers
- Keep serving the customer
- Show appreciation[13]

ADVERTISING

You have only to look around to agree with the estimate that the average person in this country is exposed to hundreds of advertising messages, perhaps as many as several thousand, every day.[14] The prevalence of advertising underscores its many advantages. Of the various forms of promotion, it is the best for reaching mass audiences quickly at a low per-person cost. It is also the form of promotion over which the organization has the greatest control. In an advertisement, you can say whatever you want, as long as you stay within the boundaries of the law and conform to the moral and ethical standards of the advertising medium and trade associations. You can promote goods, services, or ideas, using a full range of creative approaches and media to convey your message.

Little wonder then that businesses of all kinds spend large amounts of money on advertising. Four U.S. companies—Procter & Gamble, Philip Morris, General Motors, and Sears—each spend more than a billion dollars a year on advertising. Together, the nation's 100 largest advertisers spend more than $35 billion a year on advertising.[15]

The percentage of income that a company spends on advertising varies according to the product and the market. A cosmetics company like Esteé Lauder may spend 30 percent of total earnings to promote its products in a highly competitive market; a company that manufactures heavy industrial machinery may spend less than 1 percent. In most small businesses, the typical advertising budget is 2 to 5 percent of income.[16]

Types of Advertising

Advertising can be divided into several categories. The most familiar type of advertising is **product advertising,** which tries to sell specific goods or services, such as Kellogg's cereals, Sega video games, or Esteé Lauder cosmetics. Product advertising generally describes the product's features and may mention its price.

Institutional advertising, on the other hand, is designed to create goodwill and build a desired image for a company rather than to sell specific products. Many companies are now spending large sums for institutional advertising that focuses on *green marketing,* creating an image of companies as corporate conservationists. Businesses tout their actions, contributions, and philosophies not only as supporting the environmental movement but as leading the way. Also known as

product advertising *Advertising that tries to sell specific goods or services, generally by describing features, benefits, and occasionally, price*

institutional advertising *Advertising that seeks to create goodwill and to build a desired image for a company rather than to sell specific products*

SONY

ZOOM MIC

SONY

video Hi8
Handycam

10x

STEADY SHOT

AF
Hi-Fi Stereo
PRECISION
CCD

IT'S YOUR LIFE.
IT ONLY GOES AROUND ONCE.

Life races by.
The Sony Handycam® camcorder captures it all with thrilling color and sound.
With five times more recording time than VHS-C™~
2½ hours on a single tape. And direct playback on any TV without a VCR.
These are the memories of a lifetime. It's your life. Isn't it worth a Sony?

This product-oriented ad from Sony promotes the specific features of a single product.

advocacy advertising *Ads that present a company's opinions on public issues such as education and health*

competitive advertising *Ads that specifically highlight how a product is better than its competitors*

comparative advertising *Advertising technique in which two or more products are explicitly compared*

corporate advertising, institutional advertising is often used by corporations to promote an entire line of products. At the same time, institutional ads serve to remind investors that the company is doing well.

Institutional ads that address public issues are called **advocacy advertising.** Mobil and W. R. Grace are well known for running ads that deal with taxation, environmental regulation, and other issues. Advocacy advertising has recently expanded beyond issues in which the organization has a stake. Some companies now run advocacy ads that don't directly benefit their business, such as ads to project opinions and attitudes that support those of their target audiences. Clothing manufacturer Members Only has at times devoted its entire advertising budget to drug-abuse awareness and voter registration.[17]

You can argue that all advertising is competitive in nature, but the term **competitive advertising** is applied to those ads that specifically highlight how a product is better than its competitors. When two or more products are directly contrasted in an ad, the technique being used is **comparative advertising.** In some countries, comparative ads are tightly regulated and in some cases banned, but that is clearly not the case in the United States. Indeed, the Federal Trade Commission started the ball rolling by encouraging advertisers to use direct product comparisons with the intent of better informing customers; 35 to 40 percent of all advertising in this country is comparative.[18]

Comparative advertising is frequently used by competitors vying with the market leader, but it is useful whenever you believe you have some specific product strengths that are important to customers. Burger King used it on McDonald's, Pepsi used it on Coke, and car manufacturers from Ford to Kia (a Korean manufacturer that recently entered the U.S. market) use it. This approach is bare-knuckle marketing, and when done well, it's effective. However, comparative advertising sometimes ends up getting neutralized by look-alike campaigns from the competition. Analgesics (pain killers) is one category cited as an example of comparative advertising taken too far. There are so many claims and counterclaims in this "ad war" that consumers can't keep it all straight anymore.[19]

Comparative advertising can also present a knotty ethical problem: If you are better than a competitor in some respects but not in others, are you obligated to show both your good points and your bad points? Johnson & Johnson once distributed a "safety profile" to doctors, showing that its Tylenol brand exhibited fewer side effects than three of its competitors. However, the company didn't list some other possible side effects, including potential liver damage and greater risk of overdose, in which it lost out to the competition. Several years ago, Congress tightened the laws on comparative advertising to make unfair comparisons illegal, and in 1992 a U.S. district court held that advertising agencies can also be held responsible for misleading comparative claims.[20]

Finally, advertising can be classified according to the sponsor. **National advertising** is sponsored by companies that sell products on a nationwide basis. The term *national* refers to the level of the advertiser, not the geographic coverage of the ad. If a national manufacturer places an ad in only one city, the ad is still classified as a national ad. **Local advertising,** on the other hand, is sponsored by a local merchant. Its objective is to provide details about where a product can be found, at what price, and in what quantity. The grocery store ads in the local newspaper are a good example. **Cooperative advertising** is a cross between local and national advertising in which producers of nationally sold products share the costs of local advertising with local merchants and wholesalers. By one estimate, national producers make as much as $15 billion available for local retailer advertising.[21]

Advertising Appeals

Well-designed ads use a carefully planned appeal to whatever it is that motivates the target audience. Naturally, the best appeal to use depends largely on the target audience. By segmenting along lifestyles and other variables, advertisers try to identify which groups of people can be reached with various kinds of appeals.

Regardless of the specific nature of the appeal, all appeals fall into one of two general categories: logical or emotional. Some ads try to convince you with data, whereas others try to tug at your emotions to get their point across. Even with the most unemotional sort of product, however, emotions play a very big role. When selling to engineers and other technical people, some industrial and high-technology marketers assume that logic is the only way to go. However, people are people, and they all have hopes, fears, desires,

national advertising *Advertising sponsored by companies that sell products on a nationwide basis; refers to the geographic reach of the advertiser, not the geographic coverage of the ad*

local advertising *Advertising sponsored by a local merchant*

cooperative advertising *Joint efforts between local and national advertisers, in which producers of nationally sold products share the costs of local advertising with local merchants and wholesalers*

and dreams, regardless of the job they have or the products they're buying.

Emotional appeals range from the most syrupy and sentimental to the downright terrifying. Fear appeals cover the range: personal and family safety, financial security, social acceptance, and business success or failure. Appeals to fear have to be managed carefully, however. Laying it on too thick can anger the audience or even cause them to block out the message entirely.[22] On the lighter side, some companies try to convince you of how good it will feel to use their products. Flowers, greeting cards, and gifts are among the products usually sold with a positive emotional appeal.

Price or Value Appeal

Promising to give buyers more for their money is one of the most effective appeals you can use, particularly in terms of audience recall.[23] A value appeal can be accomplished in several ways: lowering the price and making people aware of the new price, keeping the price the same but offering more, or keeping the price and the product the same and trying to convince people that the product is worth whatever price you are charging.

Celebrity Appeal

A popular ad approach is the use of celebrities. The theory behind these ads is that people will be more inclined to use products that

This ad from the HIP health-care plan relies on both logical and emotional arguments to convey its message.

What will your employees have to sacrifice next to pay for health care?

The cost of health care is forcing your employees to make some tough choices. Why not make things a little easier on them? Offer HIP. They'll get no deductibles, no hidden costs and no surprises. Just quality health care that's affordable.

HIP is one of the oldest and largest managed health care plans in New York. And we're getting even better by the minute. With tough reviews for doctors. By modernizing medical centers. And by making it faster and easier to get appointments. Plus for almost 50 years, our rates have been among the lowest in the managed care industry. And we're keeping things that way.

To learn more about HIP, please call 1-800-447-2244 right now. Do it for your employees. Do it for their kids.

NEW YORK · NEW JERSEY · FLORIDA

HIP
One Of Medicine's Great Discoveries.

celebrities use themselves and that some of the star's image will rub off on the products they're holding. Celebrity ads do have potential problems, however. First, consumers don't always find them convincing (or at least don't claim to find them convincing). In fact, one survey on the power of various advertising appeals ranked celebrity endorsements as the least convincing, as cited by 70 percent of the respondents. Another big problem is that the public's image of the celebrity can get tangled up with their image of the product, and if the star gets in trouble, the brand can get in trouble too. Madonna, Mike Tyson, O. J. Simpson, Michael Jackson, and Jennifer Capriati are among celebrities who have lost endorsement contracts when aspects of their private lives became public news. Because a celebrity's public image can be frail, animated cartoon characters remain popular as "celebrity" endorsers. Take Bart Simpson, for instance. An executive at Fox Television (producers of "The Simpsons") put it this way: "Bart will never get caught doing crack."[24]

Sex Appeal

Another old standby in the advertising world is selling with sex. The classic technique is to have an attractive, scantily attired model share the page or TV screen with the product. If the model's looks and pose somehow make sense, fine; if they don't, fine. The point is to have the audience associate the product with pleasure. Another standby in advertising is selling with sex or the implied promise of sex. Guess Jeans and Calvin Klein's Obsession perfume are well-known examples of this approach. The sex appeal has to be used with some caution, however. At its extremes, it can keep an ad from running, when print or electronic media refuse to accept it for publication or broadcast. In addition, attempts to present a sexy image may cross the line and offend some readers and viewers as simply sexist, not sexy.[25]

The Power of Novelty

An approach that has taken hold in recent years is trying to catch the audience's attention by making ads really strange. Honda, Reebok, and Infiniti have all tried offbeat approaches in recent years, but with limited results in most cases.[26] Simply making an advertisement "off the wall" doesn't ensure success. Getting people to remember your name doesn't mean they'll buy your product. On the other hand, given the difficulty of getting the audience's attention in today's crowded markets, you shouldn't immediately dismiss the off-the-wall approach. The secret is to not lose sight of your advertising message and to make sure it doesn't get buried by all the strange elements in the ad.

The Elements of an Advertisement

All ads feature two basic elements. The first is **copy,** which is the verbal part of the ad, and the second is **artwork,** which is the visual part of the ad. For a magazine ad, the copy is the words you see on the page. For a radio or TV commercial, the copy is spoken by the actors.

copy *Verbal (spoken or written) part of an ad*

artwork *Visual, graphic part of the ad*

Did you ever look at an ad that has two sentences of copy and then think to yourself, "That looks easy. Anybody could crank out a couple of sentences"? Alas, looks are deceiving. Writing ad copy is part art, part science, and part luck, and few people can do it well. Top copywriters are rewarded handsomely for their ability to create effective copy.

Ad copy has five fundamental purposes:

- Getting the prospect's attention
- Stimulating the prospect's interest
- Building credibility for the product and the company
- Heightening the prospect's desire for the product
- Motivating the prospect toward action[27]

Crafting words that can accomplish all these goals is no easy task. It requires good communications skills, a flair for language, and a thorough knowledge of both the product and the customer.

As powerful as good copy can be, it is usually enhanced by creative artwork. In fact, the artwork is sometimes much more prominent than the copy, with the visual images conveying most or all of the message. The arrangement of copy and artwork in an ad is referred to as the *layout*. Visual elements can be based on a variety of themes, including the product's own package, the product in use, product features, humor, before-and-after comparisons, visual comparisons with other products, and testimonials from users or celebrities.

Advertising Media

To get the message to potential customers, suitable **media,** or channels of communication, must be chosen. The **media plan** specifies the advertising budget, establishes how the money will be divided among the various media, and indicates exactly when the advertisements will appear. The goal of the media plan is to make the most effective use of the company's advertising dollar.

The Media Mix

The critical task in media planning is to select a **media mix,** the combination of print, broadcast, and other media for the advertising campaign. When selecting the media mix, the first step is to determine the characteristics of the target audience and the types of media that will reach the greatest audience at the lowest cost. The choice is also based on what the medium is expected to do (show the product in use, list numerous sale items and prices, and so on). An increasingly popular approach to creating the media mix is the "concentration" strategy, which channels most of the budget into one media type, such as full-page newspaper ads or prime-time TV spots. This strategy allows the advertiser's message to dominate a particular medium in its product class and may help the advertiser obtain better prices on advertising space. The second step in choosing the media mix is to pick specific vehicles in each of the chosen media categories, such as individual magazines (*Time, Rolling Stone, Sports Illustrated*) or individual radio stations (a rock station, a classical station).

media *Communications channels, such as newspapers, radio, and television*

media plan *Written plan that outlines how a company will spend its media budget, including how the money will be divided among the various media and when the advertisements will appear*

media mix *Combination of various media options that a company uses in an advertising campaign*

Whenever you see new computer or communications technology, you can safely assume that somebody, somewhere, is looking for ways to apply it to advertising. Technology is transforming the creation and transmission of just about every kind of traditional advertising, and it has opened up entirely new advertising possibilities. At the same time, however, advertisers may be unchaining a technological force that will turn much of the advertising business upside down.

First, the good news. Both print and broadcast advertising now benefit from the increased productivity and flexibility that technology brings. Take a basic magazine ad, for instance. Just a few years ago, the copywriter sat at a typewriter, and the art director mechanically pasted up typeset copy and whatever visual elements were in the ad. Making even a simple wording change was a slow and expensive process—and forget about something complicated, like moving a photo and surrounding copy.

Today the art director sits at a computer, imports photos and other visuals that have been digitally scanned, grabs the copywriter's words from another computer on the net-

THE MIXED BLESSING OF ADVERTISING TECHNOLOGY

work, and then fits all the pieces together on the screen using a mouse. Photo in the wrong place? No problem; just pick it up with the mouse and move it. Client decides to change the wording of the headline at the last minute? Also not a problem; just type the new words right into the ad, which is sitting there on your screen. When everybody's satisfied, send the file over telephone lines to a service bureau that creates the photographic film ready to drop into a magazine.

For a television spot, computers help with everything from set design to special effects, such as "morphing," a technique that seems to magically transform one product or object into another. When you're ready to edit, digital editing systems make putting the pieces together as easy as moving

paragraphs around in a word processor. Unlike the old system of splicing bits of film together and trying to synchronize the voices, music, and sound effects, these new systems let you work with all the parts on your computer screen; then they create a broadcast-quality videotape when you're finished. The technology gives you more creative flexibility and lets you get more done in less time.

Now for the potentially bad news. The emerging technology of interactive television (in whatever forms it ends up taking) promises to put the audience in control. When television first appeared, you had to sit through commercials. Then came remote controls, which let you mute the sound or switch channels. Even so, the commercials are still there, intruding into the program you're trying to watch. It's hard to tell where interactive television will end up, but one strong possibility is that viewers will be able to choose what they watch and when—and they may be able to avoid traditional ads entirely. Advertisers will have to completely rethink the nature of television advertising if viewers end up in control. Stay tuned; this will be an interesting experiment in technology and advertising creativity.

Media Buying

Sorting through all the media is a challenging task. In fact, many advertisers rely on professional media planners to find the best combinations of media and to negotiate attractive terms. These planners use four important types of data in selecting their media buys. The first is **cost per thousand (CPM),** a standardized ratio that converts the total cost of advertising space to the more meaningful cost of reaching 1,000 people with the ad. CPM is especially useful for comparing media that reach similar audiences.

Two other decision tools are reach and frequency, which represent the trade-off between breadth and depth of communication. **Reach** refers to the total number of audience members that will be exposed to a message at least once in a given time period; it is usually expressed as a percentage of the total number of audience members in a particular population. **Frequency** is the average number of times that each audience member is exposed to the message; it is calculated

cost per thousand (CPM) *Cost of reaching 1,000 people with an ad*

reach *Total number of audience members who will be exposed to a message at least once in a given period*

frequency *Average number of times that each audience member is exposed to the message (equal to the total number of exposures divided by the total audience population)*

by dividing the total number of exposures by the total audience population.

The fourth decision tool is **continuity,** which refers to the period spanned by the media schedule and the timing of ad messages within the period evenly spread over the schedule or heavily concentrated in some periods. Obviously, within a fixed budget, a media plan cannot do everything: If it is important to reach a high percentage of a target group with significant frequency, the cost of doing so on a continuous basis may be prohibitive. Media planners often resort to airing messages in "waves" or "flights"—short periods of high reach and frequency that sacrifice continuity. This strategy is common in the travel industry, which crowds much of its annual media spending into the peak vacation seasons.

Advertising media fall into nine categories (see Exhibit 15.3). Newspapers and television each account for roughly one-quarter of total media spending; direct mail, radio, and magazines together account for about one-third of the total. Other media, including yellow pages, business papers, and outdoor advertising, account for the remaining portion. Each medium has its own strengths and weaknesses for various advertising applications (see Exhibit 15.4).

In the past few years, the distribution of media spending has shifted. Marketers are putting an increasing percentage of their advertising budgets into specialized media directed at selected audiences. The four national TV networks and the national magazines are losing ground to some 10,000 cable stations and to magazines aimed at narrow interest groups. At the same time, alternative media are gaining ground as companies look for fresh ways to get their message through the clutter of competing advertisements.[28] Next time you're out shopping, keep your eyes open for advertisements in unexpected places—in elevators and on shopping carts, for example.

Newspapers. Newspapers offer some definite strengths, including extensive market coverage, low cost, selection of topic areas in which to place ads (sports, home, and so on), and short lead time for placing ads. The downside of newspaper advertising includes short life span, lots of visual competition from other ads, and poor graphic quality.[29]

continuity *Pattern according to which an ad appears in the media; it can be spread evenly over time or concentrated during selected periods*

Exhibit 15.3
How the Advertising Dollar Is Allocated
This chart shows the amounts and percentages of advertising purchased in various media. Despite the prevalence of television in U.S. homes, newspapers remain the most popular advertising medium.

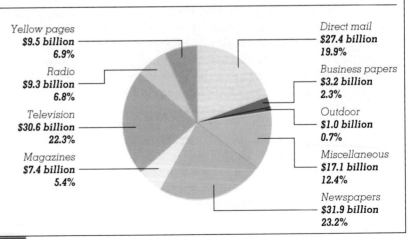

Yellow pages
$9.5 billion
6.9%

Radio
$9.3 billion
6.8%

Television
$30.6 billion
22.3%

Magazines
$7.4 billion
5.4%

Direct mail
$27.4 billion
19.9%

Business papers
$3.2 billion
2.3%

Outdoor
$1.0 billion
0.7%

Miscellaneous
$17.1 billion
12.4%

Newspapers
$31.9 billion
23.2%

PART FOUR | MARKETING

Exhibit 15.4

Medium	Advantage	Disadvantage
Newspapers	Geographic selectivity and flexibility	Limited color availability with variable quality
	Broad reach	Short life span, often with
	Advertising permanence	hasty reading
	Readership not seasonal	Cluttered pages
	Quick response to orders for ads	Little demographic selectivity Little secondary readership
Television	Broad reach	High cost for production
	Frequent messages	and air time
	Creative opportunities for demonstration	Commercial clutter Decreased viewing in
	Appeal to senses of sight and hearing	summer Short life for message
	Entertainment carryover	Long time for preparation
Direct mail	Ability to saturate specific area	High cost per exposure Delivery delays
	Advertising permanence	No editorial matter to
	Ability to target selected prospects	support content Difficulty of obtaining
	Great flexibility in format and style	desired mailing list Consumer resistance
	Excellent control over circulation and quality of message	
Radio	Low cost	No visual possibilities
	High frequency	Short life for message
	Short notice for scheduling	Commercial clutter
	Little seasonal change in audience	Tendency for people to use for background sound
	Highly portable	and ignore commercials
Magazines	Good reproduction	Limited demonstration
	Permanence of message	possibilities
	Demographic selectivity	Less compelling than other
	Local and regional market selectivity	major media Long advance preparation
	Authority and believability	High cost

Exhibit 15.4

Advantages and Disadvantages of Major Advertising Media

When selecting the media mix, marketers attempt to match the characteristics of the media audience with the characteristics of the potential buyers. A typical advertising campaign involves the use of several media.

Television. TV commercials have numerous advantages, starting with the combined impact of sight, sound, and motion. Other strong points include prestige (relative to other media) and the ability to catch people's attention. In addition, television reaches a massive audience—virtually every U.S. home has at least one TV set, and the average set is turned on for six hours a day. The average viewer is exposed to as many as 30,000 commercials a year.[30] The downsides include high cost (both initial and ongoing), short message life, general lack of selectivity, and vulnerability to getting zapped by viewers' remote controls. According to some estimates, viewers zap past 10 to 40 percent of TV commercials that air while they're watching (depending on the time of day and programming), although network executives tend to dispute these numbers. Look for continued changes in television advertising, as syndication, cable, and pay-per-view systems grow. Cable, for instance, offers a high degree of geographic selectivity. BSN Groupe uses cable to reach into the upscale areas most likely to buy its Evian bottled water. In the Miami area, the cable system sends Evian commercials only to wealthier neighborhoods such as Key Biscayne.[31]

Direct Mail. The third largest advertising medium, after newspapers and television, is **direct mail,** which includes both catalog sales and sales of single items marketed through the U.S. Postal Service and private carriers. Its biggest advantage is the ability to deliver large amounts of information to narrowly selected audiences. A promising development in audience selection is **database marketing,** in which the advertiser collects, stores, and uses data about each customer's needs, purchase habits, and so on. This tactic allows precise targeting of advertising messages.[32] The biggest drawbacks to direct mail are high cost per contact, a generally poor image ("junk mail"), and competition from all the other direct-mail pieces in everyone's mailbox.

Radio. Radio advertising has recently experienced a great boost from the renaissance of network radio. Although network TV audiences have begun to shrink, network radio audiences have increased. Yet the cost of network radio advertising has grown more slowly than that of advertising on network TV.[33] One of the main advantages of radio advertising is its large potential audience: More than 500 million radios are in use in the United States, and the average U.S. resident over the age of 12 spends three hours a day tuned in.[34] On the other hand, radio advertising is not without disadvantages. Among them is the fact that listeners, like TV viewers, can easily switch stations to avoid listening to commercials. Most advertisers regard radio primarily as a reminder tool to stimulate the use of already familiar products.

Magazines. Magazines offer some strong benefits, including highly targeted audiences in many cases. Magazines such as *Sound & Vibration* and *Hog Farm Management* are targeted for narrow market niches and are thus efficient ways to reach specialized audiences. Magazines also provide high-quality production, long message life, and the opportunity to reach multiple readers. The biggest drawbacks for magazines are the long lead time between placing and publishing ads (up to several months in some cases) and the absence of motion and sound.[35]

Other Media. Although newspapers, television, direct mail, radio, and magazines account for most of all advertising dollars spent, other media are also effective in reaching certain kinds of customers. Advertisers spend billions of dollars on the familiar yellow pages, for example.[36] A variety of outdoor and transit advertising options (from billboards to ads in subway trains) reach people while they are on the move. Other ways of bringing advertising messages to the public are limited only by the imagination. Free movie magazines are distrib-

Florida Power takes advantage of computer technology to promote the state as an attractive location for businesses.

uted in theater lobbies, commercial airlines carry in-flight advertising, and supermarkets run ads on their shopping bags and shopping carts. Companies are increasingly taking advantage of electronic media, marketing their products through CompuServe, Prodigy, the Internet and other on-line services. Moreover, technological advancements such as in-home video carried by fiber-optic lines promise advertisers entirely new channels of communication.[37]

PUBLIC RELATIONS

Public relations plays a vital role in the success of most companies, and that role applies to more than just the marketing of goods and services. Smart businesspeople know they need to maintain positive relations with their communities, investors, industry analysts, government agencies and officials, and the news media. All these activities fall under the umbrella of public relations. For many companies, public relations is the fastest-growing element of the promotional mix.[38]

A good reputation is one of a business's most important assets. A recent study showed that companies with a good public image have a big edge over less respected companies. Consumers are more than twice as likely to buy new products from companies they admire, which is why smart companies work hard to build and protect their reputations. When PepsiCo began to hear reports of syringes and other dangerous objects in cans of Diet Pepsi during the summer of 1993, the company worked with the Food and Drug Administration to follow up on reports that the syringe stories may have in fact been hoaxes. After taking these actions, PepsiCo president Craig Weatherup took to the airwaves on news programs and talk shows to explain the investigations that the company had conducted. PepsiCo integrated this PR effort with an ad that ran in major newspapers after the investigations, explaining that the company had been the victim of publicity and litigation seekers who had faked their claims.[39]

In addition to customers, investors are willing to invest 50 percent more in "good" companies than in "bad" ones. Highly regarded companies have a three-to-one advantage in attracting talented employees, and their chances are much better of winning community support for new plant construction.[40]

To build and maintain good reputations, many businesses place heavy emphasis on the coverage they receive in the media, both in general news media and in specialized media that cover specific industries. **Press relations** is the process of communicating with newspapers, magazines, and broadcast media. In the personal-computer industry, for example, manufacturers know that many people look to *ComputerWorld, PC, Byte,* and other computer publications as influential sources of information about new products. Editors and reporters often review new products and then make recommendations to their readers, pointing out both strengths and weaknesses. Companies roll out the proverbial red carpet for these media figures, treating them to hospitality suites at conventions, factory tours, and interviews with company leaders. When introducing products, manufacturers often send samples to reporters and editors for review, or they visit the media offices themselves.

press relations *Process of communicating with reporters and editors from newspapers, magazines, and radio and television networks and stations*

The standard tools of press relations are the press release, or news release as it is sometimes called, and the press conference, or press briefing. A **press release** is a short memo sent to the media covering topics that are of potential news interest; some companies send video press releases to television stations.[41] Companies send press releases in the hope of getting favorable news coverage about themselves and their products. A **press conference** is arranged when companies have significant news to announce. They are used in addition to press releases when the news is of widespread interest, when products need to be demonstrated, or when the company wants to be able to answer reporters' questions.

SALES PROMOTION

The fourth element of promotion, sales promotion, covers a wide variety of activities, including coupons, discounts, samples, contests, sweepstakes, and frequent-flyer programs. Depending on how one measures it, sales promotion expenditures in the United States now appear to exceed those for advertising.[42] Sales promotion can be broken down into two basic categories: consumer promotion and trade promotion. Consumer promotion is aimed directly at final users of the product, whereas trade promotion is aimed at retailers and wholesalers. Although shoppers are more aware of consumer promotion, trade promotion actually accounts for a larger share of promotional spending.

Consumer Promotion

Consumer promotions include coupons, specialty advertising, premiums, point-of-purchase advertising, rebates, games and sweepstakes, special events, and other incentives. Such promotions are used to stimulate repeat purchases and to entice new users.

The biggest category of consumer promotion, **couponing,** aims to spur sales by offering a discount through redeemable coupons. In the United States, companies distribute over 300 billion coupons every year. That's more than 1,000 coupons for every woman, man, and child every year (although only 7 or 8 percent are actually redeemed). Coupons work well in several situations, including stimulating trial of new products, reaching out to nonusers of mature products, encouraging repeat purchases, and reducing the price of products without having to enlist the cooperation of retailers. Coupons have several drawbacks, however. The first is encouraging delayed purchases; some customers won't purchase a product until a coupon is available. The second is wasted advertising and lost profits resulting from delivering coupons to people who would buy the product anyway. Third, coupons have been accused of instilling a bargain-hunting mentality in many consumers, which emphasizes the importance of low prices. Fourth, coupons have a tendency to tarnish the brand's image by making it appear cheap.[43]

A **point-of-purchase display** is a device for showing a product in a way that stimulates immediate sales. It may be simple, such as

press release *Brief statement or video program released to the press announcing new products, management changes, sales performance, and other potential news items; also called a* news release

press conference *Gathering of media representatives at which companies announce new information; also called a* press briefing

consumer promotions *Sales promotions aimed at final consumers*

couponing *Distribution of certificates that offer discounts on particular items*

point-of-purchase display *Advertising or other display materials set up at retail locations to promote products to potential customers as they are making their purchase decisions* the end-of-aisle stacks of soda pop in a supermarket or the racks of gum and mints at checkout counters. On the other hand, it may be more elaborate, such as the "computers" Esteé Lauder uses to encourage consumers to buy the Clinique line. Potential buyers enter facts about their skin and makeup problems into a "data bank." On the basis of this information, the Clinique "computer" recommends a complete cosmetics program tailored to the woman's specific needs.

Special-event sponsorship has become one of the most popular sales-promotion tactics. Thousands of companies spend a total of over $1 billion to sponsor 3,000 events ranging from golf to opera. Coca-Cola's recent five-year (1993–1997), $250 million deal with the National Football League ranks as the biggest sports-sponsorship deal ever. Expect to see the various Coke brand names every time you watch NFL games.[44]

Other sales-promotion techniques include rebates, free samples, and **premiums,** which are free or bargain-priced items offered to encourage the consumer to buy a product. Contests and sweepstakes are also quite popular in some industries. Particularly when valuable or unusual prizes are offered, contests and sweepstakes can generate a great deal of public attention. **Specialty advertising,** advertising on coffee mugs, pens, calendars, and so on, helps keep a company's name in front of customers for a long period of time. Advertisers constantly search for ways to display their names and logos. Need boxer shorts with the Domino's Pizza logo, ads made of chocolate, or Christmas ornaments with corporate logos? They're all available from specialty advertising firms.[45]

Trade Promotion

Sales-promotion efforts aimed at inducing distributors or retailers to push a producer's products are known as **trade promotions.** The usual lure is a discount on the price of the merchandise—a **trade allowance**—which enables the distributor or retailer to pass on a price cut to the ultimate consumer.

Many producers would like to see fewer trade allowances because they cut into producers' profit margins. However, according to one specialist, "trade allowances are like opium." Once retailers and distributors get used to receiving such allowances, they become addicted. In some product categories, up to 100 percent of all merchandise sold to retailers is sold on a trade deal.[46]

Trade allowances also create the controversial practice of **forward buying,** in which the retailer takes advantage of a trade allowance by stocking up while the price is low. Say that the producer of Bum-

Motorola gained a lot of public exposure by sponsoring the all-woman America's Cup team known as America³.

premiums Free or bargain-priced items offered to encourage consumers to buy a product

specialty advertising Advertising that appears on various items such as coffee mugs, pens, and calendars, designed to help keep a company's name in front of customers

trade promtions Sales-promotion efforts aimed at inducing distributors or retailers to push a producer's products

trade allowance Discount offered by producers to wholesalers and retailers

forward buying Retailers' taking advantage of trade allowances by buying more products at discounted prices than they hope to sell

ble Bee tuna offers retailers a 20 percent discount for a period of 6 weeks. A retailer might choose, however, to buy enough tuna to last 8 or 10 weeks, which cuts into the producer's profit and increases the retailer's profit.

Experts predicted that the first producer to reduce trade allowances (as a way to lower retail prices) would lose market share, and that appears to be the case. Procter & Gamble, a $30 billion giant whose many national brands include Tide, Clearasil, and Pampers, made the bold move in 1992. The company lost market share in most categories in the year following its decision. Some retailers initially even stopped advertising P&G products, and a few dropped the products altogether. However, some supermarkets are coming around to P&G's way of thinking, in the hope of making the entire distribution system more efficient.[47]

trade show *Gathering where producers display their wares to potential buyers; nearly every industry has one or more trade shows focused on particular types of products*

One of the best promotional tools for many industrial products is the **trade show**, a gathering where producers display their wares to potential buyers. Most of those who attend trade shows are hot prospects. According to one estimate, the average industrial exhibitor can reach 60 percent of all its prospects at a trade show, and some exhibitors do 25 percent or more of annual sales at a single show. Apart from attracting likely buyers, trade shows have the advantage of enabling a producer to demonstrate and explain the product and to compile information about prospects.[48]

In addition to trade allowances and trade shows, producers use several other trade promotion techniques, including display premiums, dealer contests or sweepstakes, and travel bonus programs, all designed to motivate the distributor or retailer to push the producer's merchandise.

SUMMARY OF LEARNING OBJECTIVES

1 Identify the four basic categories of promotion.
The four basic categories of promotion are personal selling, advertising, public relations, and sales promotion.

2 Distinguish between push and pull strategies of promotion.
In the push strategy, the producer "pushes" an item to distributors, who in turn promote the product to end users. The pull approach depends on stimulating enough consumer demand to "pull" a product through the distribution channel. Consumer products are more likely to rely on pull strategies; organizational products are more often pushed.

3 List the seven steps in the personal-selling process.
The seven steps are prospecting (finding prospects and qualifying them), preparing, approaching the prospects, making the sales presentation, handling objections, closing, and following up after the sale has been made.

4 Define institutional, product, and competitive advertising.
Institutional advertising promotes a company's overall image, not any particular products. Product advertising, however, emphasizes the products themselves. Competitive advertising emphasizes the differences between a product and its competitors.

5 Differentiate between logical and emotional advertising appeals.
You can view the difference between logical and emotional appeals as the difference between appealing to the head and appealing to the heart. Logical appeals try to convince the audience with facts, reasons, and rational conclusions. Emotional appeals, as the name implies, persuade through emotion—which can range from heart-warming tenderness to stark fear. It's important to remember, however, that nearly all ads contain a mixture of both logic and emotion; most just lean heavily in one direction or the other.

6 List the five main types of advertising media and at least three less well known types.

Of the total media budget, the largest percentage goes to newspapers. Most of the rest goes to television, direct mail, radio, and magazines. Other media include yellow pages, billboards, ads in subway trains, signs on shopping bags and carts, and on-line computer services.

7 Explain the role of public relations in marketing.

Because consumers and investors support companies with good repu-tations, smart companies use public relations to build and protect their reputations. They communicate with consumers, investors, industry ana-lysts, and government officials through the media. They pursue and maintain press relations so that they can give effective press releases and hold effective press conferences.

8 Distinguish between the two main types of sales promotion, and give at least two examples of each.

The two main types of sales promo-tion are trade promotion and con-sumer promotion. Trade promotions are designed to induce wholesalers and retailers to stimulate sales of a producer's products. Examples in-clude trade allowances, trade shows, display premiums, dealer contests, and travel bonus programs. Consumer promotions are intended to motivate the final consumer to try new prod-ucts or to experiment with the com-pany's brands. Examples include coupons, free samples, specialty advertising, premiums, point-of-purchase displays, and special events.

ON THE JOB: MEETING BUSINESS CHALLENGES AT IKEA

Introducing Ikea to two entirely different markets—five months and 3,000 miles apart—was the promotional challenge facing Anders Moberg. Despite the success of the chain's first four U.S. outlets, Moberg knew that the grand openings in Elizabeth, New Jersey, and Burbank, California, were important stepping stones to the heavily populated New York and Los Angeles metropolitan areas. The advertising had to build awareness of the store name and the retailing concept as well as attract store traffic. The Ikea president also realized that the two grand-opening campaigns could not be clones; each had to be carefully tailored to its lo-cal audience.

The first store opening, in Eliza-beth, was scheduled for May 23, 1990. To reach a target audience of young adults and families, the retailer launched an integrated marketing communications campaign of print, television, billboard, transit, and direct-mail advertising before the store opened. For instance, billboards on the New Jersey Turnpike teased motorists with cryptic messages. One billboard read, "On May 23, find a place to crash on the Jersey Turn-pike." Print ads used lots of copy to explain the headline, "Why thousands will spend their Memorial Day vaca-tion on the Jersey Turnpike." Topping off the ad blitz, Ikea mailed more than 1 million copies of its 200-page catalog to households within 40 miles of the new store.

While the preopening hoopla was going on, Ikea also kicked off a tele-vision campaign to support the chain's overall image. The commer-cials poked fun at the irritations of shopping at traditional furniture stores, such as high prices and deliv-ery hassles. However, the campaign didn't take itself too seriously; its tagline was "It's a big country. Some-one's got to furnish it." The two campaigns started people talking about Ikea, and they helped bring people—by the thousands—to the store on opening day. During the first hour the Elizabeth store was open, 3,000 people surged through the doors; by the end of the first day, 25,000 had visited the store.

Once the Elizabeth store was open, Moberg could concentrate on the Burbank store opening, which was set for November 7. Sticking with a tongue-in-cheek creative ap-proach, the retailer adjusted the me-dia to the local market by relying more heavily on outdoor media, be-cause Southern California is car country. So for six weeks before the new-store opening, slightly irreverent teaser ads appeared on 1,600 bill-boards, buses, and transit shelters around Los Angeles. These intriguing outdoor ads were designed to start people talking about the campaign. Passersby might look at one poster, for example, and wonder what could possibly have "more mass appeal" than the Pope.

The suspense ended two weeks before the Burbank store opened, when Ikea added its store name and opening date to the posters. In addi-tion to mailing catalogs to homes within an hour's drive, the retailer also used radio, television, newspaper, and magazine advertising to give more details about the outlet's prod-ucts, services, and location. Once again, a brief but intense preopening campaign brought results: Burbank's first day was another blockbuster. Despite the results of these new-store openings—which were grand by any standard—Moberg isn't about to take the U.S. market for granted. Af-ter all, it's a big country. Somebody's got to furnish it, and Anders Moberg is determined to see that Ikea gets the job.

Your Mission: Cynthia Neiman, the marketing manager of Ikea West, has hired you to work on advertising campaigns at the Burbank outlet. Your assignment is to battle competitors, to build store traffic, and to sell selected products. Use what you've learned about advertising to choose the best option in each situation:

1. Pier 1 Imports, a major competitor, recently started advertising its wide variety of international products. You wonder whether your audience will be tempted to try Pier 1 because it sells items from many countries, whereas Ikea sells mainly Scandinavian-inspired items. Which advertising strategy would best help you combat this competitive threat?

a. Promote Ikea's key strengths, including huge product selection, without highlighting the store's Scandinavian emphasis.

b. Promote the Scandinavian angle heavily to carve out a clear niche in buyers' minds.

c. Ignore Pier 1 since it doesn't compete with you directly.

2. After years of trying to sell European-sized beds, the chain recently switched to beds in standard U.S. sizes. Which headline do you think would play off the tone of Ikea's image advertising and entice people to the Burbank store to look at the new line of Swedish-style beds?

a. "Now you can sleep with a Swedish king (or a queen, full, or twin)"

b. "Now you can sleep in a bed designed in the land of the midnight sun"

c. "Come see Ikea's new line of Swedish-style beds, the best of the Old World available in the New World"

3. Stor, another competitor, also offers a huge product selection and provides many of the same amenities as Ikea. Watching a television talk show, you notice a commercial inviting viewers to the grand reopening of the newly enlarged Stor outlet near your Burbank location. What should you do?

a. Do nothing; they're not advertising special prices or special products, so you don't have to either. You can save your ad budget for other things.

b. Double the number of times your existing television ads run during the next four weeks, when Stor is likely to be advertising most heavily. This will cost-effectively keep the Ikea name in front of the target audience.

c. Create new commercials showing how Ikea is superior to Stor in terms of prices, assortment, and customer service. This option is more costly than (b), but it's a good way to position Ikea as the market leader once and for all.

4. The average sale at the Burbank store isn't as high as at other Ikea outlets. How can you use advertising to increase the average sales amount?

a. Show complete rooms of home furnishings rather than isolated pieces in your print ads. This will encourage customers to buy more than one of the items they see pictured so that they can get the same "finished" look at home.

b. Advertise large assortments of lower-priced accessories. Because the items aren't expensive, shoppers will be encouraged to buy several.

c. Show only expensive furniture in your ads. This approach will entice customers to buy those items, increasing the average sale amount.[49]

KEY TERMS

advertising (443)
advocacy advertising (454)
artwork (457)
canned approach (451)
closing (452)
comparative advertising (454)
competitive advertising (454)
consumer promotions (464)
continuity (460)
cooperative advertising (455)
copy (457)
cost per thousand (CPM) (459)
couponing (464)
creative selling (447)
database marketing (462)
direct mail (462)
forward buying (465)
frequency (459)
institutional advertising (453)

integrated marketing
  communications (IMC) (444)
local advertising (455)
media (458)
media mix (458)
media plan (458)
missionary salespeople (447)
national advertising (455)
need-satisfaction approach (451)
order getters (447)
order takers (447)
personal selling (443)
persuasive advertising (440)
point-of-purchase display (464)
premiums (465)
press conference (464)
press relations (463)
press release (464)
product advertising (453)

promotion (440)
promotional mix (442)
promotional strategy (440)
prospecting (448)
public relations (443)
pull strategy (445)
push strategy (445)
qualified prospects (449)
qualifying (449)
reach (459)
reminder advertising (441)
sales promotion (443)
sales support personnel (447)
specialty advertising (465)
technical salespeople (447)
telemarketing (448)
trade allowance (465)
trade promotions (465)
trade salespeople (448)
trade show (466)

1. What is promotion?
2. What is the biggest advantage of personal selling over other forms of promotion?
3. What techniques do skilled salespeople employ when closing a sale?

4. What are the advantages and disadvantages of the major advertising media?
5. What are the four chief criteria used in media buying?
6. Why and how do companies seek to foster positive relationships with the general public?

7. What are some common types of consumer promotion?
8. What is the biggest problem with trade allowances, from the producer's perspective?

A CASE FOR CRITICAL THINKING

GM: DRIVING INTO A NEW CHAPTER IN AUTOMOTIVE HISTORY

Back in the mid-1960s, every second car in the United States was a product of General Motors (which includes Chevrolet, Buick, Pontiac, Oldsmobile, and Cadillac). At one point, in fact, some suspected the company of intentionally holding down its sales so that it wouldn't upset government antitrust regulators. Three decades later, no one is likely to accuse GM of acting like a monopoly; the company has laid off tens of thousands of employees, shut numerous plants, racked up billions of dollars in losses, and watched its market share tumble to 35 percent.

GM has tried several times to recover. Perhaps the most intriguing effort was launching an entirely new car company, one that would be free from the old ways of doing business and better positioned to compete with the imports that had been eating up GM's market share. This new company, Saturn, was designed to be much more than a new brand name, though; it was a new way of approaching the automotive business. Don Hudler, vice president of sales, service, and marketing, knew that Saturn needed a new way to approach marketing and advertising as well.

The new approach was based on a rather different kind of marketing objective: making Saturn "the best-liked car company in America." That's an easy thing to say but a difficult goal to achieve. The strategy started with building a reasonably priced car that would satisfy customers, but it didn't stop there. Saturn's strategy touched every aspect of the business, from including employees in decision making to setting fixed prices that consumers don't have to haggle over.

Among the many things Hudler and crew did right was to make a sharp departure from traditional automotive advertising. Saturn ads don't talk about technical details or show cars winding over mountain roads. They talk about real people who drive Saturns and the satisfaction those people derive from the cars. Not only does this approach distinguish Saturn from the pack, it helps build a strong emotional bond between the public, the product, and the company behind the product.

A good example of Saturn's advertising is a magazine ad that tells the story of New Mexico driver Cheryl Silas. Silas was hit from behind while driving her Saturn coupe. The car was totaled, but she walked away unhurt. A police officer at the scene said she was lucky to be alive. The following week, Silas went back to her Saturn retailer and ordered another car. A few days later, so did the police officer. Then one of the officer's friends ordered a Saturn. So did Silas's brother. To top it off, the woman who had run into Silas came in for a test drive. This remarkable story made its way back to Hudler's office and found its way into print as another example of great Saturn advertising.

Advertising Age, the leading trade journal in the advertising industry, calls Saturn "one of the most successful new brands in marketing history." Brand loyalty is so high that Saturn drivers frequently wave at each other as they pass; some even help sell cars in the showrooms. Thousands of owners drove to the factory in Spring Hill, Tennessee, when the company threw itself a birthday party in 1994. Saturn is still selling as many cars as it can make, and creative advertising continues to play a leading role in this automotive success story.

1. Production slowdowns and a commitment to high-quality cars have resulted in occasional product shortages. It's nice to know people are waiting in line to buy your car, but you know you can't satisfy them until they are behind the wheel of their new Saturns. What kind of advertising message would you recommend during these periods of product shortage?
2. Which of the three main goals of advertising (informing, persuading, and reminding) do you think is the objective behind the Cheryl Silas ad?

Select a product you're familiar with, and examine the strategies used to advertise and promote that product. Identify the media (print, television, radio, billboards, and so on) used to advertise the product. Consider the following:

- Where do the ads appear?
- Who is the target audience? Does the company attempt to appeal to a wide variety of people with differing ads?
- What creative theme or appeal is being used?
- Does the company make a large financial investment in advertising? For information about advertising expenditures made by large companies, check the annual special issue of *Advertising Age,* "100 Leading National Advertisers."
- Is the company taking advantage of any emerging technologies for promotion, such as computer-interactive advertising?

In addition to your own observations, you might contact the manufacturer and interview a marketing representative regarding promotional strategies, or you might locate an article in a trade periodical that describes the promotional strategies for a specific product. Prepare a brief summary of your findings as directed by your instructor. Compare your findings with those of other students, and note any differences or similarities in the promotion of various products.

Choose an article from a recent issue of *The Wall Street Journal* that describes the advertising or promotion efforts of a particular company or trade association.

1. Who is the company or trade association targeting?
2. What specific marketing objectives is the organization trying to accomplish?
3. What role does advertising play in the promotion strategy? What other promotion techniques does the article mention? Are any of them unusual or noteworthy? Why?

What's the Best Location for Your New Store?

 You've probably heard the remark that the three most inportant things to look for when buying real estate are location, location, and location. The same basic concern applies to retail stores (although other factors certainly affect your chances of success). Where would you put a store in your city or town?

Assume you're going to start a new business (choose a computer store, restaurant, or service station). Outline the basic business you'd like to start, including target customers and the general goods or services you'll offer. Next, using a street map and the yellow pages, work through the following questions (if you're in a large city, you may want to restrict yourself to one particular section of the city):

1. Where do your target customers work, live, or travel regularly? For instance, if you've defined your business as an expensive restaurant, most of your customers are likely to come from business districts and affluent neighborhoods.
2. How will these people reach you? Can they walk? Will they have to drive? Will they use public transportation? Depending on the business you choose to start, you'll encounter different transportation needs. Think about how far people are willing to drive to eat at a special restaurant, shop at a computer store, or fill up at a service station.
3. Where do your competitors seem to be? You can get a good idea from the yellow pages. Identify the companies you'll compete with and mark their locations on your map. (Again, you may want to restrict the geographic scope of this project; you don't want to track down a thousand restaurants!)
4. Narrow your location choices to two or three, and then visit each one if time permits. How does each area look and feel, with respect to the type of business you want to start?
5. On the basis of the answers to these questions, where would you put your store?

ACUVUE COMMERCIAL GIVES CONSUMERS A NEW LOOK AT CONTACT LENSES

Synopsis

This video gives you a backstage view of the development of a television commercial. In this case, the commercial is for Acuvue, an innovative disposable contact lens recently introduced by a subsidiary of Johnson & Johnson. Acuvue differs from traditional contact lenses in that there is no cleaning involved. Acuvue wearers simply sign up to receive new pairs at regular intervals and toss out each pair as it gets dirty. The video shows how the company and its ad agency identify the single most important benefit to consumers (no cleaning) and how they develop a commercial to communicate that benefit. You'll see how the company combines visual, verbal, and musical elements to create a distinct message.

Exercises

ANALYSIS

1. What type of advertising does the Acuvue commercial represent?

2. What role does the advertising agency play in this process?

3. What role do the clients play?

4. Why did the company choose a simple visual presentation, with just the lens, a blue background, and a collection of cleaning solutions that represent the competition?

5. Why did the company pick the particular music that was used?

APPLICATION

Identify another product that could benefit from the sort of advertising created for Acuvue, and explain how that product benefits customers. You can search back in time for a good example if you like.

DECISION

Would you have put some people in the commercial? If so, who?

COMMUNICATION

Suppose Acuvue's marketers want to back up the TV campaign with radio ads. Write 15 seconds of advertising copy that could be read in a radio commercial.

INTEGRATION

Consider the product life cycle described in Chapter 13. Where was Acuvue at the time this commercial was being created? Where were regular contact lenses?

ETHICS

Suppose the commercial had mentioned competitors by name, as many commercials now do. Do you think it is fair to mention competitors, since they don't have a chance to defend themselves in your ad?

DEBATE

One might argue that the complex photography required to shoot the lens falling in slow motion didn't add much to the ad's effectiveness. Option A: In a formal debate format, argue for or against this notion. Option B: Take either side and state your case in a brief report.

TEAMWORK

With a team of three other students, design a print ad that communicates the same message as the TV commercial you saw in the video. (Rough sketches are fine in place of finished artwork.)

RESEARCH

Do the research necessary to write a one-paragraph update on the success or failure of Acuvue.

ROLE PLAYING

Use one of the ads created in the Teamwork exercise. One student plays the role of a representative of the ad agency and "pitches" the ad idea to several other students who play the role of clients.

PART FIVE

TOOLS OF BUSINESS

Chapter 16
**Computers and
Information Technology**

Chapter 17
Accounting

Chapter

16

Computers and Information Technology

LEARNING OBJECTIVES
After studying this chapter,
you will be able to

1 Distinguish between data
and information and explain
the characteristics of useful
information

2 Identify the major ways
companies can use
information systems

3 Describe the five classes
of computers

4 Identify the major
elements of a computer
system

5 Name the main
categories of application
software

6 Describe the four
generations of computer
languages

7 Explain the purpose of
computer networks

8 Discuss the privacy
and security concerns that
come with extensive
computerization

Information Has Its Privileges

Day after day, week after week, more than 30 million people around the world tell Harvey Golub all about themselves: what they eat, where they travel, when they are likely to buy luxuries, how busy their lifestyles are, and a host of other facts. That's the problem. They are giving him facts—tons of them. In a hotly competitive market, he couldn't afford to lose customer loyalty because of the inefficient management of information.

American Express used to have a microfiche system for storing images of transaction receipts, but processing the millions of pieces of paper for their return to cardholders was cumbersome and caused inaccuracies. Hundreds of employees were required to film receipts for storage, to enter charge amounts into a mainframe computer for billing, to sort receipts and match them with others in the same accounts, to process billing statements, and to insert the receipts and their corresponding statements into envelopes for mailing. Mistakes were made; time was wasted. Some receipts were mangled. Account numbers were misread. Receipts were inserted into the wrong envelopes, so some customers received no receipts while others received those of strangers. Nearly 200 people were employed just to resolve errors that had been made during the initial processing —and those employees also had to shuffle piles of paper. Answering a cardholder's query about a single transaction could take hours while employees searched through long cartridges of film for a record of the appropriate receipt.

The more American Express knows about the likes and lifestyles of its cardholders, the more successfully it can market goods and services to these people.

The cost of doing business this way was more than excess wages and low productivity. American Express did not grant credit for partial or late payment, so a "float" of cash had to be maintained to pay merchants for purchases while awaiting payment from cardholders. The longer it took to process receipts and to bill customers, the longer it took for American Express to get paid, which forced the company to keep more money in its float.

Even if the paper mountain could be flattened with a more efficient system, that would still leave the question of how to manage all those data describing the wants and behaviors of American Express cardholders. Golub's goal is to make American Express into a service-industry giant by offering a wide variety of services, from charge cards to financial planning to travel to entertainment. Those 30 million customers are telling Golub a lot about themselves, and he needs to use their data to gain a competitive advantage, build customer loyalty, and enter new markets. How can Golub get a grip on the mountain of paper? How can he transform the data into useful business information?[1]

COMPUTERS IN TODAY'S BUSINESS ENVIRONMENT

Harvey Golub and his management team at American Express recognize two vital aspects of contemporary business: the importance of information and the usefulness of computers. Most businesses rely on computers and information technology to at least a small degree; many simply couldn't get by without them. In addition to computers, other information technologies play important roles, including fax machines, voice mail (phone systems that can store messages and route calls), and videoconferencing (communicating with television images between two or more locations). Before exploring computers in detail, however, it's important to understand the difference between data and information and to grasp information's role in business management.

From Data to Information to Insight

The receipts that pour into American Express offices every day are an example of **data,** which are recorded statistics, facts, predictions, and opinions. A **database** is a collection of data (usually computerized). However, without further analysis, such data have little meaning. A stack of receipts from restaurants in Boise won't tell Harvey Golub very much. What he needs is **information,** a specific collection of data that are relevant to a particular decision or problem. Information is such an important strategic resource for most companies that many of them now have a top-level executive, sometimes called the **chief information officer (CIO),** who focuses on information and information systems.

Every aspect of a business operation depends on the successful collection, storage, and application of data and information (see Exhibit 16.1). The marketing department needs to know about customers and their needs; the accounting department needs to know how much products cost to make and how much they are selling for; the human resources department needs to keep track of employees and their salaries, benefits, and performance—every department needs particular data and information.

Information is valuable only if it is useful. You can have a never-ending supply of interesting, amusing, and even shocking information, but if it's not useful, it won't help you manage better. For information to be useful, it must meet five criteria:[2]

data *Recorded statistics, facts, predictions, and opinions; data need to be converted to information before they can help people solve business problems*

database *Collection of related data that can be cross-referenced in order to extract information*

information *Specific collection of data that pertain to a particular decision or problem*

chief information officer (CIO) *Top corporate executive with responsibility for information and information systems*

474

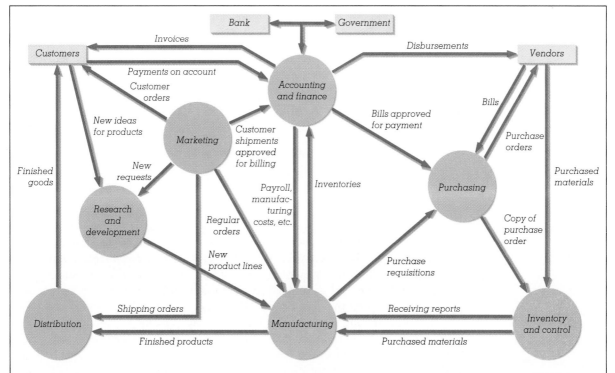

Exhibit 16.1
Information Flow in a Typical Manufacturing Company
Many kinds of manipulations and transfers of information support daily operations and decision making in a manufacturing company.

- *It must be accurate.* Just how accurate information needs to be depends on the situation. If you're trying to size up the market for toothpaste in North America, a population figure within a few hundred thousand people would probably be just fine. On the other hand, if your checkbook balance is getting down toward zero, you need to know the exact amount you have left in the bank, down to the last cent.
- *It must be timely.* Any manager will tell you that decisions must be made, with or without "necessary" information. Most business decisions need to be made within a finite period, and if the information that sheds light on the decision comes a week or a month later, it is of little use. Similarly, unless a manager has a good storage-and-retrieval system, giving him or her information months ahead of time probably won't be much help either.
- *It must be complete.* A manager facing a decision needs information that covers all areas affecting that decision. If you're studying the records of your employees in order to choose a new production supervisor, you need to see the records of all qualified employees, or you won't be able to make an optimum decision.
- *It must be relevant.* Have you ever taken an exam and discovered that some of the clues apply to the question asked whereas other clues don't? One of the most difficult aspects of information management is deciding what is relevant and what isn't and then providing the relevant information only.
- *It must be concise.* Finally, information must be in a form that is efficient for the decision maker to use. Handing your boss a 50-page

report when he or she asks for a single figure is an inefficient way to convey the information.

Of course, information in the real world is rarely perfect, and managers must often make do with whatever information they can get. However, the closer information comes to meeting the five criteria, the more it will improve the management process.

Using Information in Business

Businesses both large and small rely on quality information for just about everything they do. Here's a quick overview of the many ways companies use information:[3]

- *Increasing organizational efficiency.* Companies from Wal-Mart to Reebok have made themselves more efficient through the smart use of information. Wal-Mart uses computerized feedback from its stores to manage inventory levels in regional distribution centers. The goal is to make sure the right products are in the right stores when they are needed. Don't get the idea that computers are reducing paperwork, however; the so-called paperless office is nowhere in sight. In fact, shipments of office paper have nearly doubled in the last 10 years.[4]
- *Staying ahead of competitors.* From gathering data on consumer trends to snooping out potential takeover targets, companies can use information to boost their competitive positions.
- *Finding new customers—and keeping current customers.* Companies can use a variety of information sources, from newspaper stories to telephone directories, to find new customers. Once they have those customers in the fold, the companies use information about their needs and satisfaction levels to keep them coming back for more. For example, American Express analyzes your purchasing patterns to find out which new products you might be interested in.
- *Planning, organizing, leading, and controlling the organization.* Information is at the core of the management process, whether it's charting a new strategy, restructuring an organization, analyzing employees' performance to determine their salaries, or using process feedback to control a product line.

Putting Computers to Work

If you've spent any time at all around computers, you know that data and information can pile up fast. If you're not organized, you'll be swimming in printouts, disks, notes, programs, and all the other elements of computing. Now imagine the mess American Express would be in if it didn't have information systems to help it take care of business. Businesses use computer-based systems to process transactions, automate office tasks, design and manufacture products, market goods and services to customers, and help make management decisions.

Transaction Processing

Much of the daily flow of data into and out of the typical business organization is handled by a **transaction processing system (TPS),**

transaction processing system (TPS)
Computerized information system that processes the daily flow of customer, supplier, and employee transactions, including inventory, sales, and payroll records

Let's say that you spent, oh, around a trillion dollars on an investment. You'd probably like to get some kind of measurable financial return, right? The question sounds rather silly, but if you're a business manager, it's downright troublesome. A trillion dollars is about what businesses have spent on computer equipment in the decade since the personal computer started to become popular (roughly 1984 to 1993). During that time, however, business productivity increased by a measly 2 percent per year. Was the huge investment in computers worth it?

Actually, the $1 trillion investment figure makes for interesting conversation, but one really needs to look at individual industries and even individual companies to see whether the investments make sense. For every spectacular, multimillion-dollar computer-investment failure (usually caused by poor planning or poor management), you can probably find a long list of successes. It's the vast middle ground that is the real concern. Why didn't computers have a bigger impact on business productivity? Put it this way: Would companies have been better off to just sit back and invest all that money in the stock market? Experts can find plenty of blame to spread around:

- *Overpromising and underdelivering.* The computer industry is notorious

LOOKING FOR A RETURN ON OUR $1 TRILLION INVESTMENT

for delivering products months and sometimes even years late. Part of this delay is due to the difficulty inherent in developing software; it's often hard to predict when you'll be finished. However, at least some of the delay is caused by deliberately premature product announcements designed to "freeze" the market while a company scrambles to finish a product. When products do arrive, they sometimes don't do everything they're supposed to do. Such delays all add up to lost time and money for customers. It's not fly-by-night companies that overpromise and underdeliver, either. Some of the biggest in the business, including Apple, IBM, and Microsoft, have committed some of the biggest mistakes.

- *Buying too much and thinking too little.* The businesspeople who buy all this stuff aren't exactly blameless, however. Too often they rush into purchases because something or other is all the rage and every suc-

cessful company simply must have it. They keep stacking layer upon layer of successive generations of hardware and software, with too little thought given to how it all ties together for the good of the organization. At one point in the early 1990s, the insurance company Aetna found itself with 108 different types of word processors, 19 incompatible e-mail systems, and three dozen different networks. It was a logistical nightmare.

- *Being slaves to the past.* As much as 60 percent of the effort in an average software project goes into building links to old computer systems. In other words, instead of focusing on creating solutions for the future, too many companies spend too much time making things fit their old and possibly obsolete systems.

- *Finding new ways to spend—or waste—time and money.* A key point that doesn't receive enough attention in the computer industry or among users is that computers can create a lot of work that simply didn't exist before. Using some personal information managers (PIMs), you can scan in photos of all your employees and display their faces along with their work history and personal data. It's a nice touch, but why do you need computerized photos of the people you work with? If you can't remember what your employees look like, you have bigger problems than a computer can solve.

which takes care of customer orders, billing, employee payroll, and other essential transactions. Sometimes a TPS interacts directly with another computer system, as when a drugstore's computers transmit orders to a drug wholesaler's computers. In most cases, however, human beings are involved. When you check in for a flight and the airline representative checks with the computer to assign you a seat, a TPS is the type of system at work. When you get a seat assignment, the computer updates its database by taking that seat off the available list and confirming your name on the passenger log.

Office Automation

An **office automation system (OAS)** helps people execute typical office tasks more efficiently, whether the job is producing a re-

office automation system (OAS)
Computer system that assists with the tasks that people in a typical business office face regularly, such as drawing graphs or processing documents

Transaction processing systems help retailers and other businesses manage thousands of purchases every day.

Internet *Worldwide collection of computer networks owned by universities, government agencies, and commercial businesses*

port or calculating next year's budget. Office automation systems range from a single personal computer with word-processing software to networks of computers that allow people to communicate using electronic mail to share work among computers. Important recent advances in office automation include "groupware," which lets a team of people work on a single document without getting in each other's way or enables them to schedule meetings by checking everyone's electronic calendars.

Design and Manufacturing

Business can also use computers to automate the work of architects, engineers, and other technical professionals. In many instances, computer-aided design (CAD) systems are replacing the drafting boards and mechanical instruments that engineers and architects traditionally used to lay out designs for new products and projects. Instead of sketching a circle with a compass, an engineer using a CAD system can tell the computer to draw a circle with a certain diameter at a certain spot on the drawing. Advanced systems let designers perform such tasks as creating three-dimensional models or estimating a product's response to shock and vibration. Computer-aided manufacturing (CAM) systems, on the other hand, automate a wide variety of tasks on the factory floor. Some manufacturers have successfully linked CAD and CAM, automatically transferring product specifications from the engineering department to the manufacturing department. These combined CAD/CAM systems can be of great help in a company's efforts to get new products on the market faster.

Marketing

The entire spectrum of marketing, from researching customer needs to supporting customers after the sale, is fertile ground for computerization. Computers are now employed in all kinds of marketing-research activities, including interviewing, database research, and statistical analysis. When it's time to find those new customers and new markets, a *geographic information system (GIS)* helps companies with tasks ranging from identifying target markets to analyzing the petrochemical potential of geological formations. A GIS is essentially a computerized map, upon which marketers can superimpose data from a variety of sources.

Computers help throughout the distribution process, from routine transaction processing for retailers and wholesalers to automatic ordering, in which a customer's computer senses the need for more products and places an order with the supplier's computer. Such exchanges are made possible by *electronic data interchange (EDI),* a standardized way of sending and receiving ordering and shipping information.

Some of the most exciting advances in computer-based marketing are happening in the area of promotions. The **Internet,** a collection of some 30,000 academic, government, and commercial computer networks connecting millions of users worldwide, is giving companies a fast, efficient way to promote themselves to potential buyers. Although it started as a strictly noncommercial service, and remains so to a large extent, the Internet is being used as a promotional channel by thousands of companies large and small. Within a few months of opening shop on the Internet in 1994, Michigan florist Larry Grant was getting as many orders through that channel as he was through traditional means. In the mood for some music? You can download song clips and buy merchandise from groups ranging from the Rolling Stones to Chainsaw Kitten. At the other end of the corporate spectrum, giants such as as IBM, Mitsubishi, and AT&T also use the Internet to market their goods and services. Marketing conducted over the Internet already represents over $10 billion in sales, and it's growing rapidly.[5]

Analysis, Planning, and Decision Making

In addition to function-specific systems for marketing and other parts of the business, companies can employ a variety of systems that help managers make better decisions. A **management information system (MIS)** usually supplies reports and statistics, such as monthly sales figures, employee records, and production schedules for factories. In doing so, it often takes data from a transaction processing system and transforms them into useful information. In addition, in cases involving routine decision making (such as how many tires to order to build a certain number of cars), an MIS can go beyond simple report generation and provide answers to management questions.

Whereas a management information system provides structured, routine information for managerial decision making, a **decision support system (DSS)** assists managers in solving highly unstructured and nonroutine problems. In other words, a DSS gives managers the tools they need to create their own information. Note that DSSs *support* managerial decisions; the systems don't make decisions on their own. Compared with an MIS, a DSS

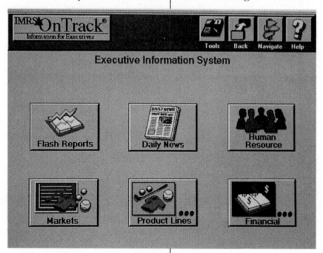

is more interactive (allows the user to interact with the system, as opposed to simply receiving information) and usually relies on both internal and external information (marketing conditions, competitive activity, and so on).[6] Group decision support systems are the most recent innovation in this area; they allow teams of people to work on problems simultaneously and make decisions with each others' input. In the top ranks of the organization, an **executive information system (EIS)** helps executives make the necessary decisions to keep the organization moving forward. Although an EIS is similar in concept to a DSS, it usually has a more strategic focus.

management information system (MIS) *System that supplies periodic, predefined reports to assist in managerial decision making*

decision support system (DSS) *Extension of a management information system that provides managers with the tools and data they need for decision making*

Executive information systems give top managers quick access to the information they need for decision making.

executive information system (EIS) *Similar to a decision support system, but customized to the strategic needs of executives*

From Working to Thinking: The Pursuit of Artificial Intelligence

Powerful systems raise an interesting question: Can computers really think like managers do? Efforts to create computers that mimic human thought processes fall under the heading of **artificial intelligence.**[7] Although the question about whether computers can truly duplicate human thought processes is likely to be debated for many years, artificial intelligence has yielded some important advances that are already making an impact on the business world. One of these is the **expert system,** a computer system that mimics the thought process of a human expert who is adept at solving particular problems.[8]

Expert systems are typically built to solve fairly narrow problems in which the knowledge of one expert can benefit less experienced employees. For instance, the troubleshooting methods used by an experienced auto mechanic could be programmed into an expert system. A beginning mechanic could describe a sick engine's symptoms to the system, which would then apply the expert mechanic's facts and rules to suggest which troubleshooting methods might reveal the cause of the problem. American Express uses an expert system to help with credit-card authorizations, a risky and time-consuming part of the credit-card business.

A second advance in artificial intelligence to make its way into business is the **natural-language processor,** which lets a user communicate with a computer using his or her own "natural" language (English, French, and so on) rather than using a computer language.[9] Even on a simple level, natural-language processing can be a boon to computer users by helping them avoid arcane "computerspeak."

INFORMATION-PROCESSING TECHNOLOGY

With an idea of the scope of computers in business, it's time to take a closer look at computers themselves. In just a few decades, computers have grown from technical curiosities to everyday business tools that every business relies on, either directly or indirectly.

Types of Computer Systems

In increasing order of processing power, today's computers can be grouped into five classes: microcomputers, workstations, minicomputers, mainframes, and supercomputers. Keep in mind that lines between the various classes aren't always clear; as technology continues to advance, the computers in one class can start to behave like their higher-performing cousins in the next category.

Microcomputers

Microcomputers are the machines that most people are familiar with; the Apple Macintosh and the IBM Personal Computer (PC) were among the forerunners here. A **microcomputer,** often referred to generically as a *personal computer,* represents the smallest and least-expensive class of computers. A microcomputer is built around a

---

artificial intelligence Use of computers to mimic human thought processes

expert system Computer system that mimics the thought processes of a human expert who is adept at solving particular problems

natural-language processor System or software program that converts a natural language to a computer language

microcomputer Smallest and least-expensive class of computers; often generally referred to as a personal computer

---

single microprocessor. Computers in this category are now available in several sizes, designated by *desktop, laptop, notebook,* and even *palm-top* (for computers that fit in your hand). The leading manufacturers of microcomputers include Compaq, IBM, and Apple, but there are hundreds of companies fighting for a share of this market.

Workstations

The **workstation** is a relatively recent development that marries the speed of minicomputers with the desktop convenience of micro-computers. Workstations are used primarily by designers, engineers, scientists, and others who need fast computing and powerful graphics capabilities to solve mathematically intense problems. A typical application in this segment is the *computer-aided design (CAD)* function already discussed. An engineer for Rockwell International might use a CAD system to design a part for the space shuttle; the system could perform such tasks as predicting responses to stress and calculating the amount of steel required to make the part. Three of the leading manufacturers of workstations are Sun Microsystems, Hewlett-Packard, and Digital Equipment Corporation (DEC).

Workstations are just as "personal" as microcomputers, in that they are typically used by a single person. However, the term *workstation* is used to separate this more powerful class of computers from microcomputers. Traditionally, the term *workstation* was applied to any terminal at which a computer user works, but the computer industry is increasingly using the term to describe this particular class of computers.

workstation Class of computers with the basic size and shape of microcomputers but with the speed of traditional minicomputers (traditionally, the term was applied to any terminal at which computer users work)

Minicomputers

Minicomputers have the same general capabilities as mainframes (such as supporting multiple users simultaneously), but they are smaller, cheaper, and less powerful. Typical applications of minicomputers include controlling a manufacturing process in a factory, managing a company's payroll, and helping a wholesaler keep track of sales and inventory. Some important applications that were once handled by minicomputers (particularly in scientific research and engineering) are now handled by workstations, whose power has increased in recent years. Leading makers of minicomputers include Hewlett-Packard, DEC, and IBM.

minicomputers Computers that fall between workstations and mainframes in terms of cost, size, and performance

Mainframe Computers

Until the arrival of the microcomputer in the late 1970s and early 1980s, the most common image of a computer was the **mainframe computer,** a large and powerful system capable of handling vast amounts of data. Those refrigerator-sized units that you've seen whirring away in computer rooms and on movie sets are mainframes. They handle a variety of transaction processing tasks, particularly finance and accounting activities, which require a lot of repetitive calculations. The traditional way for users to gain access to mainframe computing power is through *dumb terminals,* devices that look like desktop computers but that don't have the processing power to operate on their own. Today's major mainframe manufacturers include IBM, Control Data, Hitachi, Siemens, Unisys, and Amdahl.[10] As you'll

mainframe computer With the exception of a supercomputer, the largest and most powerful computer

read later in the chapter, many mainframes are being replaced by *client-server systems* composed of groups of smaller computers.

Supercomputers

Supercomputers represent the leading edge in computer performance. A **supercomputer** is capable of handling the most complex processing tasks, with speeds in excess of a billion calculations per second. For a certain class of engineering and scientific problems, a supercomputer is the only tool that can do the job. Seismic analysis, weather forecasting, complex engineering modeling, and genetic research are among the common uses of supercomputers. As you might expect, only a handful of companies are in this arena; Cray Research has two-thirds of the market.[11] Reductions in defense spending in the late 1980s and early 1990s cooled off the market for supercomputers, but *virtual reality* design simulators and other commercial applications show some promise for supercomputer growth. Caterpillar, for instance, designs new tractors and earth movers using virtual reality that lets engineers see how the machines will look and operate before they ever build physical prototypes.[12]

Hardware

To understand what makes all these computers tick, the first step is to distinguish hardware from software. **Hardware** represents the physical equipment used in a computer system—the **integrated circuits** (small pieces of silicon containing thousands of transistors), keyboards, disk drives, and so on. **Software,** on the other hand, encompasses the instructions, or **programs,** that direct the activity of the hardware.

Whether it's a palmtop computer keeping track of your appointment schedule or a supercomputer modeling the structure of a DNA molecule, every computer is made up of a basic set of hardware components. Of course, the hardware in a Cray supercomputer differs greatly from the hardware in a handheld unit, but the concepts are similar. Hardware can be divided into four basic groups: input devices, the central processing unit, output devices, and storage (see Exhibit 16.2).

Input Devices

Before it can perform any calculations, a computer needs data, and it gets those data from one or more input devices. The *keyboard* is the

---

supercomputer *Computer with the highest level of performance, often boasting speeds greater than a billion calculations per second*

hardware *Physical components of a computer system, including integrated circuits, keyboards, and disk drives*

integrated circuits *Electronic components that contain thousands of transistors and can therefore perform complicated tasks, such as arithmetic and data storage*

software *Instructions that drive the activity of computer hardware*

programs *Organized sets of instructions, written in a computer language, that perform designated tasks such as word processing*

Exhibit 16.2
Hardware Elements in a Computer System
The primary elements of computer hardware are the central processing unit, input devices, output devices, and storage.

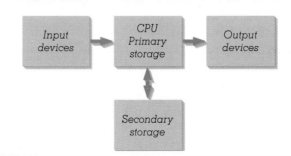

most obvious input device, but other devices used to feed data to computers include the *mouse,* which can be used to select commands based on a pointer's position on the computer screen; the *computer pen,* which lets you write on special tablets that translate your handwriting or drawings into computer-compatible data; the *scanner,* which essentially takes a picture of a piece of paper and sends the computer a graphic image that can be incorporated directly or converted to regular text using *optical character recognition (OCR);* and the *bar code reader,* which reads the black-and-white Uniform Product Codes you see on packages in the supermarket. One of the most intriguing possibilities is *speech recognition,* in which a computer will respond to your spoken commands. Systems capable of recognizing several thousands words are already on the market.[13]

Central Processing Unit

A computer's calculations are made in the **central processing unit (CPU),** which performs the three basic functions of arithmetic, logic, and control/communication.[14] Actually, computer arithmetic is nothing more than addition; subtraction is performed through negative addition, multiplication is repetitive addition, and division is repetitive negative addition.[15] Computer logic is also a simple operation, nothing more than comparing two numbers. For instance, when a person calls PaperDirect, a New Jersey paper-supply company, the salesperson first asks for the caller's phone number so that the company's computer system can compare that phone number with those it has on file to see whether the caller is already a customer. The control/communication function of the CPU keeps the computer working in a rational fashion. This function includes deciding when to accept data from the keyboard, when to perform arithmetic and logic operations, and when to display characters or graphics on the screen.

In microcomputers and workstations, the CPU is composed of a single **microprocessor** (and some associated support circuitry). In minicomputers, mainframes, and supercomputers, the CPU can be either a single processing unit made of multiple integrated circuits or multiple processing units operating in parallel, a scheme known as **parallel processing.** Each processor takes one part of the problem—rather like 10 students working on 10 parts of a homework problem at the same time.

Batch Versus Real-Time Processing. Up until the 1960s (and for many years after that in some organizations), one didn't just walk up to the computer and go to work. Computer use at the time was characterized by **batch processing,** in which users prepared data and programs and then submitted their "jobs" to the computer center, where operators collected the jobs and fed them to the computer in "batches" at regular intervals. Users had no choice but to sit and wait for the results. It isn't hard to imagine the impact that such delays would have on organizational performance.

Batch processing is still the appropriate choice for many computing applications, including payrolls, customer billings, and statistical analysis. In many data-processing situations, however, anything more than a modest amount of delay is intolerable. What if a bank's customers tried to get cash from an ATM, and the machine responded

central processing unit (CPU) *Core of the computer, performing the three basic functions of arithmetic (addition, etc.), logic (comparing numbers), and control/communication (managing the computer)*

microprocessor *Advanced integrated circuit that combines most of the basic functions of a computer onto a single chip*

parallel processing *Use of multiple processors in a single computer unit, with the intention of increasing the speed at which complex calculations can be completed*

batch processing *Computing method in which "jobs" are submitted to the computer in "batches" at regular intervals, so users must wait for their results*

with the message, "I'm working on your request; please come back tomorrow for your cash"? In such cases, the computer has to respond nearly instantaneously in order for the information it provides to be useful. This requirement leads to the idea of **real-time processing,** in which the computer's files are updated as soon as new information arrives.[16]

Bits, Bytes, and Business Productivity. In a sense, even the most complex electronic circuit is nothing more than a collection of switches. Each switch can be either on or off, representing either a 1 or a 0. This switch position represents one **bit** of information, which is shorthand for *binary digit.* The binary number system uses strings of 1's and 0's to represent all numbers (see Exhibit 16.3). For example, the regular decimal number 1 is expressed in binary as 1, the number 2 is expressed as 10, 3 is 11, 4 is 100, 5 is 101, and so on. Bits are usually packaged in groups of eight, which makes up a **byte** of information. The number 5, for instance, would be expressed in a byte of information as 00000101.

Every CPU is designed around a certain number of bits simultaneously. The earliest microcomputers, for instance, could handle 8 at a time, whereas current top-end microcomputers can handle 32 bits at a time. Why would a businessperson care about this technical detail? Because the number of CPU bits influences the speed of the computer. If you ask an 8-bit computer to do something with the number 300, you may be surprised to find out how long it takes. When converted to binary, the number 300 needs 9 bits (1 0010 1100), but your 8-bit CPU can't handle the entire number at once, so it has to deal with half the number at a time. The process of shuffling parts of numbers back and forth is time-consuming, and the result is lower performance. (The total picture of computer performance is a lot more complicated than this, but this example addresses one of the fundamental issues.) To get an instant impression of the importance of CPU bits, just ask microcomputer users with 32-bit machines to trade them for 16- or 8-bit machines. They'll probably chase you out of the room.

Output Devices

Once the data have been successfully entered and the CPU has successfully processed them, they won't be of any use unless they are sent back to the outside world. The first place a computer's output usually goes is the *display,* or monitor, as it is often called. The display acts in the same basic manner as a television and provides the user with text, graphics, or a combination of both.

When you need a permanent record or when you need to share *hard copy* with someone, you probably need a printer. Laser printers have become the output device of choice in many offices, since they provide sharp, clear reports, memos, and graphs. Newer laser printers can even print in color. For less money, inkjet printers can provide hard copy of slightly lower quality. An alternative often used by engineers and scientists is a *plotter,* a device that uses pens to reproduce a displayed image by drawing it on paper.

As with input devices, specialized equipment can provide output for particular applications. The traditional way to develop a business

Decimal	Binary equivalent
5	0 0 0 0 0 1 0 1
10	0 0 0 0 1 0 1 0
46	0 0 1 0 1 1 0 0
73	0 1 0 0 1 0 0 1
127	0 1 1 1 1 1 1 1

Exhibit 16.3
Binary Representations of Data
Various combinations of the binary digits 0 and 1 make it possible for a computer to process and store any type of information that can be represented as, or converted into, numbers, letters, or symbols. This example shows how various decimal numbers are represented in binary format.

presentation involves using some special software to create pictures that you then print as overhead transparencies or 35 mm slides. The process is slow and expensive, and it generates a lot of plastic that needs to be disposed of or recycled (with overheads) or uses harsh chemicals to develop the film (35 mm slides). An increasingly popular alternative is to use a *projection panel,* which is a special display device that connects to your computer and sits on top of a regular overhead projector. These panels can display everything from regular computer screens to videotape from a VCR.

Storage

Input, processing, and output complete the basic computing cycle, but this cycle can't happen without some form of storage for the data being processed and for the software that is in charge of the operation. A **primary storage device** stores data and programs while they are being used in the computer. This device usually involves a set of semiconductor devices known as **random-access memory (RAM),** so called because the computer can access any piece of data in such memory at random. Computers use RAM for temporary storage of programs and data during input, processing, and output operations. Unless it is provided with special back-up circuitry, RAM is erased when electrical power is removed from the computer. (That's why you hear cries of anguish from computer users when the electricity goes out.) RAM's counterpart is called **read-only memory (ROM),** which keeps its contents even when power is cut off. ROM is used for programs such as the start-up routines that computers go through when they are first turned on, which involves checking for problems and getting ready to go to work.

 Secondary storage takes care of data and programs that aren't needed at the moment, and it also provides a permanent record of those data and programs. For instance, if you've finished work on a report that you might need to modify in a month, you put it in secondary storage, which gets it out of the CPU's way and keeps it until you need to go back to work. The most common mechanism for secondary storage is the **disk drive,** which can be of two types: *hard disk drives* are usually enclosed inside the computer and can store data internally on rigid magnetic disks. *Floppy disk drives,* on the other hand, are accessible to the user and store data externally on removable magnetic disks. These removable disks are called *floppy* disks because they are flexible—most computers use $3\frac{1}{2}$-inch floppies encased in stiff plastic. Floppy disks are easily portable, but they can store far less information than hard disks. **CD-ROMs,** which are based on the same technology as music compact discs (CDs), have gained widespread popularity in recent years because of their low cost and large storage capacity. CD-ROM is a key component in **multimedia** computing, which combines regular computer data with audio, computer animation, photography, and full-motion video.[17]

Software

The hardware components just described can be assembled to create impressive computer systems. However, the hardware isn't much good

---

primary storage device Storage for data and programs while they are being processed by the computer

random-access memory (RAM) Primary storage devices allowing a computer to access any piece of data in such memory at random

read-only memory (ROM) Special circuits that store data and programs permanently but don't allow users to record their own data or programs; a common use of ROM is for the programs that activate start-up routines when the computer is turned on

secondary storage Computer storage for data and programs that aren't needed at the moment

disk drive Most common mechanism for secondary storage; includes both hard disk drives and floppy disk drives

CD-ROMs Storage devices that use the same technology as music CDs; popular because of their low cost and large storage capacity

multimedia Computer activity that involves sound, photographic images, animation, or video in addition to traditional computer data

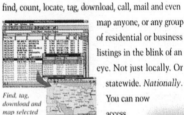

CD-ROMs are particularly useful for business applications that require massive amounts of data, such as the 80 million names on this nationwide phone directory.

operating systems *Class of software that controls the computer's hardware components*

application software *Programs that perform specific functions for users, such as word processing or spreadsheet analysis*

proprietary operating systems *Operating systems that run on only one brand of computer; they offer users a limited selection of hardware and software choices*

open systems *Operating systems (such as UNIX) that run on a wide variety of computers and don't restrict users to a single company's hardware*

without software telling it what to do and how to behave. Software can be divided into two general categories. *Systems software* is perhaps the most important category because it includes **operating systems,** which control the computer's most basic overall functions. An operating system controls such fundamental actions as storing data on disk drives and displaying text or graphics on monitors. **Application software** encompasses programs that perform specific user functions, such as word processing, drawing, organizing, scheduling, and so on.

Systems Software

As mentioned, operating systems make up the most important category of systems software. Other major categories include utilities, shells, and languages. The following material briefly describes the first three types of systems software; languages are discussed later in the chapter.

- *Operating systems.* As already stated, languages and applications need operating systems to accomplish their designated tasks. A word-processing program can't read the disk or write text to the display by itself; it relies on the operating system to direct the computer's hardware and to manage the flow of data into, around, and out of the system. Operating systems that are unique to one particular computer are usually called **proprietary operating systems.** Increasingly, customers demand the freedom of choice that comes with **open systems,** which run on computers from various man-

486

ufacturers. One of the most popular open systems for workstations and minicomputers is **UNIX,** which can run on a wide variety of machines from microcomputers all the way up to mainframes and supercomputers.[18] This flexibility means that programs can be moved from computer to computer and that a business can have several brands and classes of computers all running the same software package. Proprietary operating systems often have the advantage of better performance, since the software can be "tuned" to take maximum advantage of a particular hardware configuration. On the other hand, these proprietary systems may force customers to choose from a narrower range of hardware and software options.

- *Utilities.* Composing one of the biggest software categories are utilities, which help computer users take care of the daily business of being in business. Many of these packages focus on the computer itself, helping users manage the files on hard disks or running performance checks to make sure everything is working properly. The Norton Utilities, a popular utility product for personal computers, provides such capabilities as "unerasing" files that a user accidentally deletes and reorganizing data on a hard disk to speed access.

- *Shells.* One of the frustrations many computer users experience is dealing with operating systems. Even if a person's only intention is to use a word processor, for example, he or she still has to use some basic operating-system commands to start the word-processing program, to copy files to other disks, and even to find the word-processing program in order to get it running. Even though application software has become increasingly user-friendly in recent years, no one will accuse the typical operating system of being overly nice. To insulate users from operating systems and to make their computing lives easier, programmers have created a variety of *shells,* which essentially work between the operating system and the application software. One of the best-known shells is Microsoft Windows, a package that runs on IBM-compatible microcomputers. Windows lets you point a mouse at a picture of an application program; it then finds the program and gets it running for you.

Application Software

Application software performs the business tasks that people need to do their jobs. (The term *application* refers both to an application software product, such as a word processor, and to the actual task for which the software is used, such as preparing reports and memos.) Application software can be either *custom* (developed specifically for a single user or set of users and not sold to other users) or *general-purpose* (developed with the goal of selling it to multiple users). Commercially available general-purpose software products are commonly referred to as *packages,* as in a *word-processing package.*

In today's business-software market, the array of software packages is vast, including products that can prepare books and newspapers, monitor the stock market, locate potential customers on a map, track employee records, and produce sales reports, to name just a few. Here's a quick look at the major categories of application software:

- *Accounting/finance.* Computers got their start in business doing accounting and financial tasks, and these remain a fundamental business application. In fact, nearly all the activities discussed in the next four chapters—on accounting, money and banking, financial management, and securities markets—can be managed faster and more effectively with software.

- *Spreadsheets.* A **spreadsheet** is a program designed to let users organize and manipulate data in a row-column matrix (see Exhibit 16.4). The intersection of each row-and-column pair is called a *cell,* and every cell can contain a number, a mathematical formula, or text used as a label. Among the spreadsheet's biggest strengths is the ability to quickly update masses of calculations when conditions change. For instance, if you have a spreadsheet that calculates profit sharing for your employees, and the profit-sharing percentage changes, you don't have to go through each employee's record and change the number by hand. You simply update the percentage in one place, and the spreadsheet will do all the updating for you (assuming you've programmed it to do so). Although spreadsheets were originally designed to replace the ledger books of accountants, businesspeople now use them to solve a wide variety of problems, ranging from statistical analysis to simulation models used in decision support systems.

- *Word processing.* Word processing is another fundamental business application of computers. Although word processing is frequently described as an enhanced alternative to the typewriter, today's word processors go far beyond anything imaginable on a typewriter. You've probably received a promotional letter that had your name

spreadsheet *Program that organizes and manipulates data in a row-column matrix*

Exhibit 16.4
Sample Spreadsheet Analysis
*Setting up a spreadsheet by hand takes time—especially to do the calculations. A spreadsheet program prepares the computer to accept values in preestablished spreadsheet cells. Paula Chang's hourly wage, for example, is entered in the cell where the "Paula Chang" row intersects the "Wage" column. A spreadsheet program also performs basic mathematical operations, given the proper instructions. To compute an employee's regular pay (**X**), the computer must multiply that employee's wage (**W**) by his or her regular hours worked (**R**).*

EMPLOYEE'S NAME	WAGE (W)	REGULAR HOURS (R)	OVERTIME HOURS (0)	REGULAR PAY (X = WR)	OVERTIME PAY [Y = 1.5(WO)]	TOTAL PAY (Z = X + Y)
Paula Chang	$10.00	40	6	$400.00	$90.00	$490.00
Lewis Bond	$7.50	32	5	$240.00	$56.25	$296.25

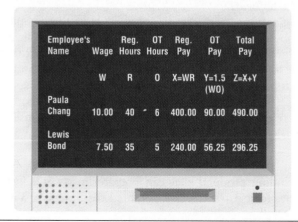

inserted into it to give the appearance that it wasn't a form letter. Word-processing programs can do this with a function called *mail merge,* in which a single generic letter is merged with a list of names at printing time. When each letter is printed, the software picks a name from the list and inserts it into the letter.

- *Publishing.* Publishing software goes a step beyond typical word processors by helping designers lay out printer-ready pages that incorporate artwork, photos, and a large variety of typographic elements. Together with scanners and other specialized input devices, publishing programs let businesspeople create sophisticated documents in a fraction of the time it once took. Publishing software that runs specifically on microcomputers, such as Aldus Pagemaker, gives rise to the term **desktop publishing (DTP).**

- *Business graphics.* Businesspeople need to produce quite a variety of graphic materials, including charts, graphs, and diagrams. Together with specialized output devices such as plotters and color printers, business graphics software can produce overhead transparencies, 35 mm slides, posters, and signs. In addition, the graphic images created with these packages can be imported into publishing programs for incorporation into books and reports or into the projection panels described earlier.

- *Communications.* With communications software, a computer can exchange information with other computers, which opens up an entirely new spectrum of business capabilities. **Electronic mail,** or *e-mail,* is the transmission of written messages in electronic format between computers. A **bulletin board system (BBS)** is an electronic version of traditional bulletin boards, allowing users to exchange ideas, news, and other information. Communications software also gives business users access to an eye-popping array of business information services, from the Internet to specialized databases. Dialog Information Services, for instance, gives users access to over 450 databases, containing data ranging from government statistics to newspaper articles.[19]

- *Drafting and CAD.* Drafting and CAD are the technical counterparts of business graphics. Included in this category are programs that help architects prepare blueprints, programs that let technical illustrators create schematic drawings, and CAD programs that help engineers design new products.

- *Production and process control.* These packages, typically running on minicomputers and mainframes, help manage the production of goods and services by controlling production lines, robots, and other machinery and equipment. In some cases, manufacturing software is linked with design software to automate the entire design-and-production cycle. For instance, an engineer designing a new component for a car engine can electronically transfer the design to the production department, which will then control a milling machine that automatically carves the part from a block of steel.

- *Project management.* Gantt and PERT charts (introduced in Chapter 8) are often computerized in today's business environment. This management capability helps businesspeople in two important ways. First, it helps them create and update schedules much more

desktop publishing (DTP) *Ability to prepare documents using computerized typesetting and graphics-processing capabilities*

electronic mail *Transmission of written messages in electronic format between computers; also known as e-mail*

bulletin board system (BBS) *Electronic equivalents of traditional bulletin boards; users can "post" messages, data, and programs for other people to access*

database management software
Programs designed to create, store, maintain, rearrange, and retrieve the contents of databases

quickly than could be done by hand. Some scheduling packages, for instance, can automatically adjust each employee's work load to make sure no one works more than eight hours a day. Second, scheduling software helps businesspeople communicate with their employees, peers, and managers. Most programs can create attractive printouts that can be used in reports or presentations.

- *Database management.* As the American Express example at the beginning of the chapter points out, businesses often have massive amounts of data on their hands. This situation represents two important challenges: first, how to store all that information in a way that is safe while still making it accessible to the employees who need it, and second, how to transform the data from a database into useful information when such information is needed. It is the job of **database management software** to create, store, maintain, rearrange, and retrieve the contents of databases.[20] Almost anywhere you find a sizable amount of data in electronic format, you'll find a database management package at work, whether it's on a microcomputer or a supercomputer. Such software helps users produce useful information through its ability to look at data from various perspectives. Say that your business class has quizzes every week, that the class has 100 students, and that a helpful assistant logs all the quiz results into the computer every week, along with some basic data about each student. If your instructor wants to know how the class did on the last quiz, he or she can *query* the database for a printout of all 100 scores or for a simple average of the scores. To show how the class has done throughout the course, the instructor could "look back through time" and get a list of the weekly averages since the course began. The same could be done for a single student. If enough data were in the database, the instructor could look only at the scores of students who've taken courses in business before or of those students who are majoring in journalism. Alternatively, if the scores on one quiz were unexpectedly low, the instructor could compare your class's performance on that quiz with the performance of previous classes to see whether the quiz was too difficult. Even in this simple example, you can see that database management can provide a great deal of information from a single stack of data.

- *Industry-specific solutions.* The application categories just described can be used in many industries. In addition to those already noted, many other application packages have been designed to meet the needs of specific industries and types of businesses. A package called Associate helps real estate agents track sales leads, property listings, escrow companies, inspectors, and other important information.[21] Specialized packages are used to help manage dentists' offices, retail stores, law firms, hospitals, and just about every other business institution in existence.

- *Integrated software.* The category of integrated software contains programs that perform multiple functions. The Works product from Microsoft combines spreadsheet, business graphics, word processing, and other capabilities into one package. Doing so makes it easier to take care of multiple business tasks, and it simplifies the job of moving data back and forth between applications.

490

In addition to these major categories, software developers have produced packages for a wide array of specialized business applications, ranging from marketing research to math solvers.

Computer Languages

The final category of information technology covered in this chapter concerns the way software is created. All software is created by another special class of software, **computer languages,** which are sets of rules and conventions for communicating with a computer. Just as human beings communicate with each other using designated languages, human beings communicate with computers using designated languages. The term **programming** describes the steps involved in giving a computer the instructions necessary to perform a desired task.

Computer languages have evolved over several generations. However, each new generation of language hasn't replaced the existing generation. Instead, each generation builds on the previous generation. The four language generations are machine language, assembly language, high-level languages, and fourth-generation languages.[22]

Machine Language

No matter how sophisticated or powerful, every computer communicates in machine language at its lowest level for the simple reason that computer hardware understands only 1's and 0's, and that is the stuff of **machine language.** A machine-language program consists of pages and pages of nothing but 1's and 0's. Every CPU has a unique machine language, unless the CPU is designed specifically to be compatible with another CPU.

Assembly Language

Although machine language is absolutely necessary for a computer to operate, it is not something that humans are naturally conversant in. One of the most significant advances introduced with the computers of the 1950s was **assembly language,** which still didn't look like any language people spoke but was at least composed of mnemonic code words that people could read and write more easily. Instead of the 1's and 0's of machine language, programmers could write programs using commands such as "ST" (for "store") and "M" (for "multiply"). Keep in mind that even when assembly language is used to develop a program, the computer still operates using machine language. Programmers need to convert their assembly-language program to machine language, which is done automatically with a special software tool called an *assembler.*

High-Level Languages

Assembly language was a big advance over machine language, but it still had two big drawbacks: It required a lot of instructions to accomplish even simple tasks, and each CPU had its own assembly language, which meant that you couldn't write a program for one computer and then run it unmodified on another computer. Using **high-level languages,** programmers could use a single command to

---

computer languages *Sets of programmable rules and conventions for communicating with computers*

programming *Process of creating the sets of instructions that direct computers to perform desired tasks*

machine language *"Lowest" level of computer language, consisting entirely of 1's and 0's; the only level of computer language that hardware understands*

assembly language *One level above machine language; it consists of fairly cryptic low-level commands that initiate CPU commands*

high-level languages *Computer languages most people are familiar with, such as BASIC, FORTRAN, and C; single commands accomplish the equivalent of several assembly-language commands, and the language is easier for humans to read and write*

accomplish the equivalent of several assembly-language commands. Moreover, these new languages were not restricted to a single model of computer, so programmers could move their programs from machine to machine much more easily. Once again, high-level languages didn't replace assembly or machine languages but merely provided an easier way to write programs. High-level languages must first be converted to assembly language (and then to machine language) before they can be run, which is done with either a *compiler* (if the entire program is converted before it is run) or an *interpreter* (if each line in the program is converted and then run before the next line is converted). Chances are you've already heard the names of some of the more popular high-level languages: BASIC, COBOL, FORTRAN, Ada, Pascal, and C.

Fourth-Generation Languages

High-level languages helped make the computer revolution fast and pervasive, but they also have some disadvantages. One of the most significant (in the eyes of many computer users) is that people still have to learn a computer language. It may be easier to read and write than assembly language was, but it is another language nonetheless. Also, high-level languages still focus on what the computer should do, rather than focusing on what the user wants done. For instance, you can't use a high-level language to tell a computer to "summarize travel expenses for last month." You have to walk through the process step by step, telling the computer where to get the relevant data, how to process them, and what to do with the results.

In response to these limitations, computer scientists have begun to develop so-called **fourth-generation languages (4GLs),** which is a collective name applied to languages designed to make it easier for people to interact with computers. In many instances, users can give instructions to computers in a language that is remarkably similar to English, French, or another natural language (the natural-language-processing capability referred to earlier in the chapter). It is hard to define 4GLs precisely because various manufacturers have taken unique approaches to the problem, so no industrywide standards or conventions exist for 4GLs, as they do for high-level languages. However, 4GLs are still attractive. In the hypothetical example presented in Exhibit 16.5, a manager wants a list of her employees, together with their performance ranking and current monthly salary. Rather than writing a lengthy program, she merely provides the instructions shown, and the table is generated without a hitch.[23] Such 4GL capabilities have become common in database-management software.

Computer Networks

The brief discussion of communications software hinted at one of the most im-

fourth-generation languages (4GLs)
Collective name applied to a variety of software tools that ease the task of interacting with computers; some let users give instructions in natural languages such as English

Visually oriented programming languages, such as Microsoft's Visual Basic, make it easier for people to create custom business software.

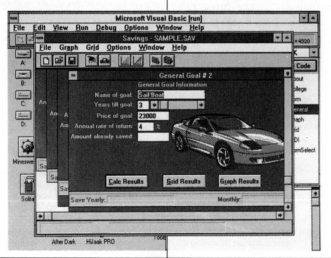

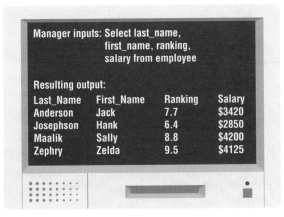

Exhibit 16.5
Benefits of Fourth-Generation Languages

If the manager in this hypothetical example wants an employee list that compares performance rankings and current monthly salaries, she doesn't have to write a program (as she would have to do with a high-level language); she can use a fourth-generation language to query the employee database.

portant issues in business computing: connecting multiple computers in one fashion or another and allowing them to send data back and forth, a process known as **data communications.** Data communications systems allow users not only to communicate with each other but also to gain access to centralized databases and expensive resources such as supercomputers and high-speed laser printers.

Data communication is quite complex and involves many variations in hardware and software. However, it can be divided into four general categories:

- *Long-distance networks.* In general, a **network** is a collection of hardware, software, and communications media that allow computers to communicate. The primary components are the computers themselves, communications software, and some sort of transmission medium. In a *wide area network,* computers at different geographic locations are linked through regular telephone lines, private telephone lines established just for data communication purposes, or radio-frequency connections such as microwave stations or satellites.[24] To communicate over telephone lines, a computer must be equipped with a **modem** (modulator-demodulator), which can be either a stand-alone unit or a circuit board that is plugged into the computer.
- *Local area networks.* A **local area network (LAN),** as its name implies, meets data communications needs within a small area, such as an office or a university campus. LANs can consist entirely of microcomputers or workstations communicating with one another, or they can have a special computer called a *file server.* The file server can provide common data-storage facilities, electronic mail, access to laser printers, and other resources that all the LAN users can share. The proliferation of LANs has created the opportunity for **workgroup computing,** in which teams of employees can more easily work together on projects such as writing books or developing software.
- *Micro-to-mainframe links.* Many business offices have a central mainframe computer (to handle important databases such as customer records and employee records) along with an array of microcom-

data communications *Process of connecting computers and allowing them to send data back and forth*

network *Collection of computers, communications software, and transmission media lines (such as a telephone) that allows computers to communicate*

modem *Hardware device that allows a computer to communicate over a regular telephone line*

local area network (LAN) *Computer network that encompasses a small area, such as an office or a university campus*

workgroup computing *Computing arrangement in which teams can easily work together on projects*

puters (used by individual employees). Some of the computing tasks that employees do can be handled entirely on their microcomputers, such as word processing and preparing charts and graphs. In other cases, however, such as analyzing sales trends or accessing some electronic-mail systems, the employee needs to tap into the central mainframe system. To accomplish this, each microcomputer is wired directly to the mainframe, and employees activate special communications software that makes their micros act like the dumb terminals traditionally associated with mainframes. When the employee is finished accessing the mainframe, he or she signs off the communications software and returns to normal microcomputer operation.

- *Client-server systems.* Many businesses are replacing their traditional mainframes with **client-server systems,** in which a *server* contains software and data used by a number of attached computers, called *clients.* (Technically speaking, client-server setups are really just special versions of LANs, but they're generating enough interest and controversy in the computer industry to warrant extra attention.) Advocates of the client-server approach say the flexibility it offers is more in tune with the needs of companies in today's fast, chaotic business world. In fact, client-server systems are often the foundation of *reengineering* efforts, in which companies try to redesign their operations for peak effectiveness and flexibility. Advocates of mainframes say that the "big iron" still does the big jobs more efficiently. Both technologies are bound to be around for a long time to come.[25]

client-server systems Computer system design in which one computer (the server) contains software and data used by a number of attached computers (the clients); unlike traditional mainframe systems, the clients are full-blown computers themselves

The Information Superhighway

Vice President Al Gore helped popularize the so-called **information superhighway,** a vague term used to describe a nationwide computer network connecting homes, businesses, government offices, and schools. In reality, the closest thing we have at this point is the Internet, and any eventual superhighway is likely to be a patchwork of computer networks, cable television systems, telephone systems, and wireless communication systems.

Some huge technical and financial hurdles stand in the way of the information superhighway as it is popularly envisioned. Some components, such as the "video servers" that would replace video stores and provide movies on demand, require computational power that doesn't exist yet. Other technologies, such as the fiber-optic cables likely to form at least a part of any nationwide network, are ready to go but very expensive. It would cost $100 billion to string fiber optics to every home in the country, for instance. When something finally does reach your home, no one is yet sure what kind of equipment you'll use to access all these nifty offerings. Two things are sure, however: Lots of companies are working hard to realize some form of a superhighway, and it's impossible to predict what the superhighway may eventually look like.[26]

information superhighway Abstract term used to describe a nationwide computer network connecting homes, businesses, government offices, and schools; in reality, the information superhighway is an evolving patchwork of computer networks, cable television systems, telephone systems, and wireless communication systems

Centralized Versus Decentralized Networks

Communications networks can be centralized or decentralized in much the same way as business organizations themselves can be. In

494

CUTTING THE CABLES WITH WIRELESS COMMUNICATIONS

*W*ireless used to be a rather old-fashioned-sounding term. It's what our electronic ancestors called their newfangled radios, which didn't need the wires that tied telegraph stations together. Well, guess what? Wireless is back on the leading edge of technology, and it's anything but old-fashioned. *Wireless* still refers to devices that don't need wires, but it's not telegraph wires this time around. Instead, it's the modern telephone system that these new wireless devices can live without.

The market demand for wireless falls into three categories: (1) people communicating with people, (2) people communicating with machines, and (3) machines communicating with machines. The second and third categories provide some of the more interesting possibilities. How about a car that calls you if it gets stolen? Vending machines that call for help when they need more candy bars? Computers that monitor the location and performance of thousands of freight trucks? All these technologies are in place today.

Wireless comes in several flavors now, with more devices and systems rolling down the pike every year. Some systems transmit only voice or only computer data, whereas others transmit combinations of data, voice communications, and possibly video. All rely on some type of radio transmission, involving either land-based transmitters and receivers, communications satellites, or some combination of the two.

You're already familiar with pagers and cellular phones, which were really the first widespread technologies in the "new" wireless revolution. The next move for cellular is to offer data transmissions. Personal digital assistants (PDAs) are combining paging, voice, and computer capabilities in small, handheld devices. Personal communications services (PCSs) will offer an alternative to cellular phone services. Satellite phone systems, in which your phone communicates directly with a network of low-orbit satellites, will cover vast areas that aren't economical to blanket with cellular or PCS equipment. In other words, you and your equipment (computer, fax, pager, PDA, and so on) will be able to stay in touch just about everywhere on earth.

All this technology does raise an important human question, however. Who wants or needs to be connected all the time? Moreover, is it really all that productive to never get away from your work? Imagine sitting in class all day, all evening, and all weekend long. At some point, your poor brain just overloads and starts to shut down. The same thing might be happening to businesspeople who use wireless to stay in constant touch. By never disappearing—both physically and electronically—employees run the risk of burnout and weariness, and they don't have the chance to stop and get a fresh perspective on things. Wireless is likely to take a toll on family and friends as well, as loved ones and pals never seem quite able to give them their undivided attention.

Whatever the right answer is to these quality-of-life issues, businesspeople had better figure something out soon. The wireless revolution isn't waiting for anybody, and the number of ways to stay connected is only going to increase.

---

a traditional system, the mainframe has all the processing power, and the terminals merely act as communication ports to give users access to the mainframe. This system mirrors a centralized organization in which top management makes all the decisions and employees simply do as they're told.

The alternative is **distributed processing,** in which some, occasionally all, of the processing power is spread out among the various computers attached to the network. In a client-server setup, for instance, users have complete computing capabilities on their own, and the network is more of a support system to help them work efficiently. This system resembles a decentralized organization in which various teams manage their own affairs, and the central organization exists mainly to support the more or less independent teams.

distributed processing *Approach to computer network design in which processing power is spread out among the various computers attached to the network*

PRIVACY AND SECURITY IN THE INFORMATION AGE

Computers are machines, and most machines can be used either well or poorly. Just as automobiles are both convenient and dangerous, computers can be both a help and a hindrance. Thanks to computers, a retired couple may receive Social Security checks rapidly, but they may also get hundreds of pieces of computer-generated direct mail that they don't want. A computer can enable a criminal to break into a bank and steal thousands of dollars while safely sitting at a PC miles away. Also, an amazing amount of information will become part of your permanent file, and you can only hope it will be entered correctly: Mistakes such as typos and transposed numbers are far easier to make than to find and fix.

Data Privacy

One of computerization's most dangerous drawbacks is the unethical use of data processing and databases, which may lead to invasion of privacy. Never before have so many organizations known so much about so many individuals. Nothing is inherently wrong with this; your credit-card company has a right to know what you've charged and whether you're late in paying your bills. (You gave them that right when you accepted the card.)

However, two questions are cause for concern: (1) Do organizations know more about you than they need to? (2) Are they telling anyone else? If you apply for a loan, it makes sense for creditors to check your bank balance or credit history. However, what if, like some organizations, they also interview your neighbors in an attempt to determine your character? Is it relevant to your financial affairs that you once threw a party that kept your next-door neighbor awake or that you have frequent domestic disputes? Once the information is in place, relevant or not, a great many people will be able to read it, from the bored worker or prankster who reads people's files at lunchtime to the companies that sell their databases to, or share them with, other institutions—companies that you may never have heard of or that have no legitimate right to know everything about you.

Employees' privacy inside their own companies is another big concern. In one survey, 22 percent of corporate executives admitted to reviewing communications between their employees, particularly computer files and electronic mail. Employees were told in advance in only a third of these cases that managers would be taking a peek. On the other hand, 34 percent of the executives say they find it unacceptable to look at employees' files or e-mail transmissions.[27]

Data Security

Even firms that don't share their databases are subject to lack of data security. Besides everything else, companies with valuable or sensitive information stored in a computer worry about competitors or thieves raiding the database simply by dialing in through a modem. In fact, security concerns are one of the biggest issues holding back the development of the information superhighway as a full-scale commerce link. Nobody is going to be comfortable sending millions of credit-

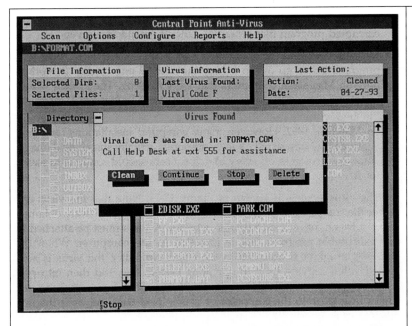

card numbers across the Internet until it can be proven that hackers can't steal them at will. Much of the information available on-line is valuable just for the content, as well, whether it's music, video, or business and technical information vulnerable to unauthorized copying.

Several well-publicized incidents of teenage hackers breaking into bank, hospital, and government computer systems have dramatized the data-security risks that hamper networks. **Computer viruses,** hidden programs that can work their way into computer systems and erase or corrupt data and programs, present another critical security challenge. The problem is that security often conflicts with convenient, decentralized computer use. Safer systems are possible, but a Pentagon-style system with passwords that change daily and special keys for hardware and peripheral devices could bring business to a stop—an ironic turn for a technology that became popular because of the increased convenience and access it offered.

computer viruses *Computer programs that can work their way into a computer system and erase or corrupt data or programs*

SUMMARY OF LEARNING OBJECTIVES

1 Distinguish between data and information and explain the characteristics of useful information.

Data are recorded statistics, facts, predictions, and opinions; information is created when data are arranged in such a manner as to be meaningful for a particular problem or situation. In order to be useful, information needs to be accurate, timely, complete, relevant, and concise.

2 Identify the major ways companies can use information systems.

The chapter discusses five major categories: transaction processing, office automation, design and manufacturing, marketing, and the managerial tasks of analysis, planning, and decision making.

3 Describe the five classes of computers.

Microcomputers, such as the Apple Macintosh and the IBM PC, are the smallest and cheapest computers. Workstations are a step up in price and performance; similar in size and shape to microcomputers, they approach or equal the performance of minicomputers. Minicomputers are a price and performance compromise between the lower-end micros and workstations and the higher-end mainframes; they aren't as powerful as mainframes, but they don't cost as much either. Mainframes represent the traditional notion of big computers, and they are the largest and most powerful, with the exception of supercomputers. This final class contains the fastest and most expensive computers available today.

4 Identify the major elements of a computer system.

Hardware and software are the two major aspects of a computer. Hardware includes input devices (such as keyboards), central processing units, output devices (such as printers), and primary and secondary storage. Software is divided into operating systems, application software, and computer languages.

5 Name the main categories of application software.

The categories mentioned in the chapter are accounting/finance, spreadsheets, word processing, publishing, business graphics, communications, drafting and CAD, produc-tion and process control, project management, database management, industry-specific solutions, and integrated software packages.

6 Describe the four generations of computer languages.

Although computer languages evolved over several generations, each new generation of languages did not replace the previous generation. Instead, new generations made programming easier. The four generations start with machine language, which consists of the 1's and 0's that actually drive the hardware. Assembly language, the next level up, consists of simple instructions that can be read by humans. High-level languages do more with fewer commands than assembly language and are much easier for humans to read and write. Fourth-generation languages attempt to let users communicate in their natural languages as much as possible.

7 Explain the purpose of computer networks.

Networks provide computer users with two important benefits: (1) the ability to share data, programs, messages, and so on; and (2) common access to centralized resources such as databases, printers, mainframes, and supercomputers.

8 Discuss the privacy and security concerns that come with extensive computerization.

Many people are concerned that businesses may know too much about consumers and may share their data and information illegitimately; for businesses, maintaining computer security (including guarding against hackers and viruses) poses an important problem.

ON THE JOB: MEETING BUSINESS CHALLENGES AT AMERICAN EXPRESS

Harvey Golub has the distinct advantage of having one of the world's most advanced information management systems at his fingertips. It took the company six years and $80 million to create, but it provides a powerful set of competitive advantages.

Today more than 3 million charge receipts are received every day at American Express, and they are sent through a unique transaction process-ing system that converts data from paper into digitized images and stores them on disk. All those pieces of paper are shredded and buried in secret locations (for security), so American Express processes images of receipts. Computers index and sort the images according to billing cycle and zip code, collate the images with their appropriate billing statements, print more readable and useful copies of the images on perforated paper, and insert those sheets of paper along with billing statements into envelopes, which are then presorted for mailing. All of this is done so quickly that 100,000 pages of billing statements are printed in only one hour at two processing sites in the United States. Customer queries can be processed within minutes now that the images are stored on optical disks.

Nearly 400 people were once employed only to process, correct, and retrieve the millions of paper receipts received each day, but they have been replaced by the transaction processing system, which is operated by three people who are able to do more work in less time and with greater accuracy. Billing costs have been reduced by 25 percent, with nearly half of that saving coming from a reduction in the cash American Express needs to have available to pay merchants for charged purchases.

The system has enabled the company to gain a competitive advantage in two ways. First, of the three major card companies, American Express is the only one that still returns copies of receipts to its customers for recordkeeping—a service that is especially useful for businesspeople. Second, Golub now knows his customers very well because the purchasing data on each receipt are transformed into useful information. Each cardholder is categorized and profiled according to 450 attributes derived from his or her purchasing patterns, age, gender, and other data.

498

These continually updated portraits are augmented with surveys that are targeted to that cardholder's income and lifestyle.

All these data, and the information that can be derived from them, have allowed American Express to enter a booming business: direct-mail merchandising, its fastest-growing subsidiary. This information has also prevented the company from providing costly services to the wrong cardholders; for example, only holders of platinum cards are greeted with limousine service at airports. The information is also used to find new subscribers to magazines owned by the company's publishing subsidiary—periodicals that, again, are appropriate to each cardholder's lifestyle.

What began with a transaction processing system has been used to help Golub make better strategic decisions. He has a wealth of information useful in making decisions about new products, new services, new markets, and new ways to further innovate for a competitive advantage.

Your Mission: American Express is considered an industry leader in its use of technology, as evidenced by its unique transaction processing system. You are the CIO, responsible for considering tactical and strategic issues to ensure the best use of information throughout American Express subsidiaries, which include IDS Financial Services (a financial-planning firm) and Travel Related Services (American Express's best-known business, which includes the green, gold, and platinum American Express cards and the Optima card).

1. You know that organizing the right data is crucial to providing useful information to decision makers in the company. Assume that each of the following pieces of data is available to the people who make approval decisions for new customers for the classic green American Express card. Although you want to provide sufficient data, you don't want to overload the decision makers with irrelevant or unnecessary data. Which of the following pieces of data would be most useful for the card-approval decision?

a. The applicant's past history with credit, specifically, whether or not the applicant pays bills on time

b. The applicant's income, since people with more income are likely to use their cards more often, which increases American Express's revenue

c. The applicant's educational background, so that you can pick the people who have graduated from the best universities

2. Suppose that several dozen customers called to complain about the system that delivers processed images of their receipts, not the actual receipts themselves. Your customer-service staff tried to convince them that the processed images contain the same data and information as the original and that, in fact, they offer even more. These customers are adamant, however; if they can't get the receipts back, they'll cancel their cards. What should you do?

a. Explain to the customers that American Express needs to use the new system in order to stay competitive.

b. For these customers only, circumvent the new system and provide them with their actual receipts.

c. You hate to lose customers, but your calculations show that circumventing the system for these few customers will cost you more than the revenue that these customers represent. Thank them graciously for their past use of American Express cards, and explain that you won't be able to cater to their particular needs, that you hope they'll reconsider, and that you understand if they want to go ahead and turn in their cards.

3. Like nearly all other credit customers, American Express cardholders are concerned about database privacy. They worry that hackers will get access to their card numbers, and they fear that companies are building profiles of them that say more than they are comfortable revealing, such as what kinds of videos they like to rent or which hotels they prefer to stay in. How could American Express best calm the fears of its customers?

a. The company should institute security measures to minimize the risk of people's breaking into its databases, but it can't restrict access so much that employees are unable to access the data; in addition, the company should give customers control over how their personal data are used and by whom.

b. To be completely secure, the company should never use any of the data it collects, should never sell data to anyone, and should restrict access to a handful of top executives.

c. Simply by using their cards, American Express customers forfeit their right to privacy, since there is no way to process a transaction without the customer's name being involved; if customers are worried about their privacy, they should use cash instead.

4. As an information-technology pioneer, American Express keeps a close eye on such developments as the Internet and the rest of the information superhighway. Which of the following possibilites would you recommend as a potentially lucrative business for the Travel Related Services division?

a. Mailing credit-card applications to everyone who uses the Internet.

b. A "virtual reality" travel-agency service, in which vacation shoppers could experience the look and feel of various travel destinations before making their travel choices through American Express.

c. A "home page" display on the Internet, which would provide computer users with a detailed look at each of the company's credit- and charge-card offerings.[28]

application software (486)
artificial intelligence (480)
assembly language (491)
batch processing (483)
bit (484)
bulletin board system (BBS) (489)
byte (484)
central processing unit (CPU) (483)
CD-ROMs (485)
chief information officer (474)
client-server systems (494)
computer languages (491)
computer viruses (497)
data (474)
database (474)
database management software (490)
data communications (493)
decision support system (DSS) (479)
desktop publishing (DTP) (489)
disk drive (485)
distributed processing (495)
electronic mail (489)

executive information system (EIS)
  (479)
expert system (480)
fourth-generation languages (4GLs)
  (492)
hardware (482)
high-level languages (491)
information (474)
information superhighway (494)
integrated circuits (482)
Internet (478)
local area network (LAN) (493)
machine language (491)
mainframe computer (481)
management information system
  (MIS) (479)
microcomputer (480)
microprocessor (483)
minicomputers (481)
modem (493)
multimedia (485)
natural-language processor (480)
network (493)

office automation system (OAS)
  (477)
open systems (486)
operating systems (486)
parallel processing (483)
primary storage device (485)
programming (491)
programs (482)
proprietary operating systems (486)
random-access memory (RAM)
  (485)
read-only memory (ROM) (485)
real-time processing (484)
secondary storage (485)
software (482)
spreadsheet (488)
supercomputer (482)
transaction processing system (TPS)
  (476)
UNIX (487)
workgroup computing (493)
workstation (481)

REVIEW QUESTIONS

1. Would employee records be considered data or information? Explain your answer.

2. How do transaction processing systems, management information systems, and executive information systems differ?

3. How has artificial intelligence been applied to business?

4. What does real-time processing mean, and when is it important?

5. How do workstations differ from microcomputers and minicomputers?

6. What are the functions of a central processing unit?

7. How do the purposes of primary and secondary storage differ?

8. How are companies taking advantage of networks such as the Internet?

HIGH-TECH TIME BOMB: THE SPREAD OF COMPUTER VIRUSES—AND THEIR PREVENTION

A competitor's raid on a database is only one security problem faced by information managers. Another potential nightmare is a wipeout of their data as a result of some unforeseen natural disaster such as an earthquake or flood. However, losses from this kind of catastrophe stand to be overshadowed by damage from computer viruses. Viruses are small fragments of software that make copies of themselves and spread those copies from computer to computer. Some viruses carry program instructions that can destroy data, damage computer hardware, or monopolize computer communications lines.

According to Philip McKinney of Thumb Scan, a computer-security firm in Illinois, the first viruses were devised in the 1970s by software companies trying to protect their profits. Like most published books, most commercial software is copyrighted. The copyright holder has the right to sell the software or to give it away. The first viruses were used to track the spread of programs being copied illegally in violation of copyright. The viruses never showed their presence. They just kept track of what computer systems they had passed through. Software authors who knew how to read them hoped that the virus programs could be used to trace the routes of the piracy.

Today viruses are often created by pranksters or vandals. Some amateur programmers (hackers) enjoy introducing viruses just to show how vulnerable computer systems are. Disgruntled employees or former employees, competitors, and creditors could also introduce viruses. Some

viruses are designed to act as time bombs, sitting quietly until a specified time and then activating themselves and wreaking havoc.

The wide-open exchange of data and ideas promised by the information age is threatened by viruses. Because so many computers are interconnected, viruses can spread quickly. They can infect all the computers linked on a local area network and then spread over telephone lines to other computers linked in national and even international networks. One virus infected 350,000 computers in the United States and Europe.

Even viruses created accidentally or with no intent of harm can interfere with business by tying up computers and operators. Some viruses use a computer's CPU to copy themselves without restraint. The normal information-processing operations of a business slow as more and more of the computer's processing capacity and memory are used by the renegade programs. Operators must spend time removing viruses, checking to see whether programs or data have been destroyed, and rechecking to make sure that no new infections have taken hold.

One unintentional infection was caused by a Christmas message naively sent over a local network by a German student. The message automatically forwarded itself to everyone on each recipient's regular outgoing electronic-mail list. The message swamped the local network and eventually moved through interconnecting links to IBM's international network, attaching itself to every mailing list it contacted.

Besides originating in business networks, viruses sometimes spread through the electronic bulletin boards that allow computer users to share public-domain (noncopy-

righted) programs. To protect users of his Manhattan-based electronic bulletin board, Ross Greenberg carefully screens for computer viruses before he posts any new programs. Besides contaminating their own microcomputers at home, users who download a virus along with useful public-domain programs might carry them into the office on disk. Such a virus could quickly infect a corporate network.

Just as with biological diseases, experts are scrambling to devise preventives for computer viruses. Greenberg uses these "vaccines" to spot invading viruses and to render them harmless. In an attempt to protect computer systems, vaccines are used by all kinds of businesses, from home-based sole proprietorships to IBM and the Internal Revenue Service.

Although some experts downplay the danger of viruses, others consider them a serious threat. Suppose that a vandal learned how to confuse the computers that manufacturers use to set specifications or those of a country's military, banking system, or air traffic control. Michael Peckman, systems analyst at George Washington University, recommends a combination of computer-security tools and safeguard practices that can limit the risk of virus infection. For example, using a write-protect tab on program disks prevents the addition of anything, including viruses, to a disk while it's being used in a disk drive. Regularly backing up (copying) data and programs to disks or tapes that are safely stored at a distance provides a fallback if some virus causes destruction within the computer system.

Requiring users to enter a password limits access to the computer system by unauthorized personnel. An audit system allows a computer-system manager to track who accessed data, when it was accessed, and what kinds of things were done to it. Policies that limit and control the movement of data, programs, and hardware among microcomputers within an organization can help control the spread of viruses. Restricting the use of public-domain software, bulletin boards, and on-line services can also reduce the risk of infection. Finally, using a vaccine program regularly can help detect viruses that have slipped through other lines of defense.

1. Like the viruses that cause biological diseases, computer viruses come in many varieties with many "disease" strategies. They can be designed to seek out various sites in the computer. What are some of the problems inherent in "vaccinating" computer systems against viruses?

2. What sorts of business information stored in computers would be most painful to lose?

3. Why do you think a bank might go under after a computer disaster? If you were a bank president, how would you plan for such a disaster?

4. Some computer experts say that media coverage of computer viruses should be toned down or stopped because it only encourages publicity-seeking hackers to generate more viruses. What are some advantages and disadvantages of press reports about viruses?

BUILDING YOUR COMMUNICATION SKILLS

Select a local business that uses computers in its management operations, and examine how those operations are affected by technology. Contact a member of the management team, and ask about the applications of computers in that business. If that option isn't possible, locate an article in a periodical that describes the implementation of computer technology in a particular business.

• Consider any changes or improvements in the efficiency of information processing that were made possible by computer technology, including management information systems, data processing, and desktop publishing. Have jobs been enhanced or eliminated by computers?

• Prepare a brief written or oral summary of your investigation, as directed by your instructor. Compare the applications of computer technology in the business you examined with those in businesses examined by other students.

KEEPING CURRENT USING *THE WALL STREET JOURNAL*

Scan recent issues of *The Wall Street Journal* for an article showing how computers or other office-technology advances have helped a company improve its competitive advantage or its profitability.

1. What advantage did technology give the company? Are other companies in the same industry using the same technology as effectively? If the information is available, comment on why or why not.

2. Did the article mention any problems the company had implementing its new technology? What were they? Do you think the problems could have been avoided? How?

3. How do you think employees feel about this technology? How would you feel if your job required you to use it?

ARTIFICIAL INTELLIGENCE

Synopsis

In one sense, artificial intelligence (AI) has been one of the great myths of the computer age. Science-fiction writers, overzealous researchers, and an uncritical media teamed up to set all kinds of fantastic expectations for what computers would be doing by now. As this video points out, delivering on those expectations turned out to be much harder than most people expected. Indeed, the program refers to one promising area of AI, natural-language processing, as "spectacularly unsuccessful." (However, researchers have progressed since this video was made, and rudimentary voice-recognition systems are now on the market.) In another sense, though, AI is making some important contributions in many fields, including science, education, and industry. This video highlights progress in those areas.

Exercises

ANALYSIS

1. Can small businesses apply computers in the same way that aerospace giant Boeing applies them? Explain your answer.

2. What did the Boeing executive mean when he said that computers represent the last remaining opportunity for productivity improvements?

3. Is it possible for computers to slow down, rather than speed up, business operations? Explain your answer.

4. Why did the expert on computer security advise that computers should never be relied on to make judgment calls in important matters?

5. Is computer phobia still a problem for businesses today? Aren't all the young people joining companies aware of and experienced in operating computers? Explain your responses to these two questions.

APPLICATION

Pretend you own a baseball memorabilia shop. Your customer database consists of names, addresses, favorite players, favorite teams, and spending history. Speculate on some of the ways you could use such data to increase sales.

DECISION

Would you buy a computer for your small business even if you had no computer experience? Explain your answer.

COMMUNICATION

List several ways that computers can help with business communication both inside and outside the company.

INTEGRATION

Refer to the discussion of segmentation in Chapter 12 to determine how you could use computerized customer lists to segment your markets.

ETHICS

As the world revolves more and more around computer technology, some experts fear that we'll evolve into a society of information haves and have-nots. Is it fair to develop such concepts as the information superhighway, knowing that many people won't be able to afford the access to them? Why or why not?

DEBATE

You've probably received direct mail that the sender has tried to personalize by inserting your name into the letter, putting your name in the caption of a cartoon, and so on. Option A: In a formal debate format, argue for or against the suggestion that computer-personalized mailings are effective, on the basis of your own response to such letters. Option B: Take either position and state your case in a brief report.

TEAMWORK

In a team of four students, research the respective competitive strengths of Macintosh-compatible computers using Apple's operating system, IBM-compatible computers running Microsoft Windows, computers running IBM's OS/2, and computers running UNIX. From these four options, recommend the one you think is best for small-business owners.

RESEARCH

Do the research necessary to write a one-paragraph update on the progress made by voice-recognition systems. Are they becoming common business tools, or are they still on the fringe? Also, compare the progress made by voice-recognition computing with that of pen-based computing—another promised alternative to typing.

ROLE PLAYING

Divide into small groups, each of which consists of members with varying degrees of computer experience; at least one member of each group should be a highly skilled computer user. The experienced user will play the role of a company trainer trying to overcome the rest of the group's fear of computers (if the other group members aren't afraid of computers, they can pretend to be).

Chapter

17

Accounting

LEARNING OBJECTIVES
After studying this chapter,
you will be able to

1 Describe the importance
of accounting information to
managers, investors,
creditors, and government
agencies

2 Distinguish between
public and private
accountants

3 State the basic
accounting equation

4 Explain the purpose of
the balance sheet and
identify its three main
sections

5 Explain the purpose of an
income statement and
identify its three main
components

6 Explain the purpose of
the statement of cash flows

7 Identify five areas in
which accountants have
discretion in their methods
and assumptions

8 List the four main
categories of financial ratios

Company Accountants— Friends or Foes?

When people get together to make business decisions about their company, their products, and their costs, they need information they can trust and rely on. At Roseville Networks Division (RND) of Hewlett-Packard, however, such meetings often ended in heated arguments and emotional discord. During decision-making sessions, representatives from marketing, manufacturing, product design, and accounting could not agree on the right way to find a product's "real" cost. Each department would come up with a different cost, would defend the method used to determine that cost, and would argue about which number was right.

Hewlett-Packard's RND produces about 250 products, mostly printed-circuit assemblies and mechanical devices used with central processing units (the brains of computers). Debbie Berlant is cost accounting supervisor, and she recalls that people began to resent the accounting department, because no matter how individual departments calculated costs, the "official" accounting-department numbers were invariably the numbers used for the company's internal cost accounting. Production people were especially sensitive, looking at accountants as opponents, not as team members. Moreover, it seemed that many of the measurements required by accounting were wasteful.

Every time an assembly worker put a part on a circuit board, the amount of time spent on the task had to be recorded. Technicians tracked the time they spent on each test, and they charged that time to a particular work order. Manufacturing (and other departments such as product design) tracked a lot of information just for accounting and then used different data to estimate production costs for themselves. Clearly, the accounting department's cost figures did not provide what other departments needed.

Procurement people complained that accounting's estimated cost of purchasing and handling inexpensive parts was not realistic. Product designers complained that because of accounting they were being forced to design products that could be assembled without direct labor, even when manufacturing those products without direct labor would be more difficult. Production people complained that direct-

As a leader in computer technology, Hewlett-Packard looks to its accounting professionals for accurate information on costs and profits.

CHAPTER 17 | ACCOUNTING

labor hours did not reflect the manufacturing resources actually consumed by a product. Marketing accused accounting of overestimating the costs of certain products.

Although RND's traditional system for internal cost accounting had been in place for years, Debbie Berlant knew that changes had to be made. If you were the cost accounting supervisor at RND, what would you do to bring the various departments to agreement? How could you adapt the accounting methods to the information needs of other departments? Should the people from product design, manufacturing, and marketing simply accept the guidelines and information from accounting? How does accounting information actually affect the business decisions that must be made by companies?[1]

THE NATURE OF ACCOUNTING

accounting *Process of recording, classifying, and summarizing the financial activities of an organization*

Accounting is the system a business uses to measure its financial performance by recording and classifying sales, purchases, and other transactions. Accounting also summarizes this information in statements that make it possible to evaluate a company's past performance, present condition, and future prospects. Armed with accounting information, managers are better equipped to make business decisions. Exhibit 17.1 presents the process for putting all of a company's financial data into standardized formats that can be used for decision making, analysis, and planning.

Functional Areas of Accounting

Exhibit 17.1
The Accounting Process
The traditional printed accounting forms are shown here. Today nearly all companies use the computer equivalents of these forms.

Accounting is important to business for two reasons. First, it helps managers plan and control a company's operations, as it did at Hewlett-Packard's RND. Second, it helps outsiders evaluate the business. Because these two audiences use accounting information in dif-

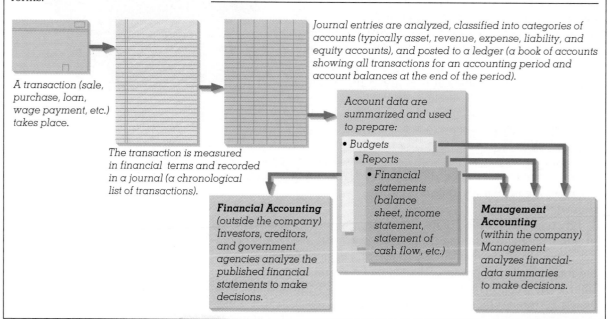

A transaction (sale, purchase, loan, wage payment, etc.) takes place.

The transaction is measured in financial terms and recorded in a journal (a chronological list of transactions).

Journal entries are analyzed, classified into categories of accounts (typically asset, revenue, expense, liability, and equity accounts), and posted to a ledger (a book of accounts showing all transactions for an accounting period and account balances at the end of the period).

Account data are summarized and used to prepare:
• Budgets
  • Reports
    • Financial statements (balance sheet, income statement, statement of cash flow, etc.)

Financial Accounting (outside the company) Investors, creditors, and government agencies analyze the published financial statements to make decisions.

Management Accounting (within the company) Management analyzes financial-data summaries to make decisions.

PART FIVE | TOOLS OF BUSINESS

ferent ways, accounting has two distinct facets. **Financial accounting** is concerned with preparing information for the outside world; **management accounting** is concerned with preparing information for internal use by managers who must make decisions.

Financial Accounting

The outsiders who use accounting information have a variety of interests. Suppliers, banks, and other lenders want to know whether a business is creditworthy; investors and shareholders are concerned with a company's profit potential. Government agencies regulate and tax businesses; they are interested in a business's *tax accounting.* These users need information that is objective, consistent over time, and comparable to information supplied by other companies. Thus, financial accounting statements must be prepared according to **generally accepted accounting principles** (GAAP), basic standards and procedures that have been agreed on by the accounting profession.

Management Accounting

Management accounting, in contrast, is tailored to the needs of managers in a particular company. Its overall purpose is to help the managers evaluate results and make informed decisions. In a typical company, the management-accounting system covers a wide range of financial activities, from recording sales and billing customers to helping management evaluate expenditures on buildings, equipment, and payroll. A particular kind of accounting, *cost accounting,* helps managers understand and control product costs. This is the kind of accounting that Debbie Berlant does for Hewlett-Packard's RND.

In general, a company's accounting department performs many functions. One of the biggest jobs that accounting employees handle is financial planning, which involves forecasting sales, costs, expenses, and profits. These forecasts enable management to spot problems and opportunities and to allocate resources intelligently. Part of the process includes developing a **budget,** a financial blueprint for a given period (often one year) that structures financial plans in a framework of estimated revenues, expenses, and cash flows. Because working out a budget forces a company to determine how much money will be coming in and how much will be going out, budgeting becomes simultaneously a controlling as well as a planning operation. The master (or operating) budget—the overall estimate of revenues, costs, expenses, and cash flow—is based on several other budgets, including the sales budget and the production budget.

In addition to preparing a budget, company accountants help analyze production costs so that management will know what the company spends to make a given product; Debbie Berlant was on the team that developed a new cost accounting system at Hewlett-Packard's RND. Management uses this information on production costs to control expenses and to make pricing and product decisions.

Types of Accountants

The distinction between financial accounting and management accounting is reflected in the professional orientation of the accoun-

financial accounting *Area of accounting concerned with preparing financial information for users outside the organization*

management accounting *Area of accounting concerned with preparing data for use by managers within the organization*

generally accepted accounting principles (GAAP) *Professionally approved standards used by the accounting profession in preparing financial statements*

budget *Financial plan for a company's future activities that estimates revenues and proposed expenditures and that forecasts how expenditures will be financed*

Public accountants' responsibilities	**Private accountants' responsibilities**
Auditing: Provide independent analysis of financial statements, which is used in reports to shareholders, investors, and purchasers of businesses	**General accounting:** Record all business transactions and prepare reports and financial statements
Management consulting: Provide objective evaluations of decisions in such areas as finance, marketing, and manufacturing for large and small businesses; offer advice on meeting special requirements for accounting, taxes, and reporting in other countries	**Management accounting:** Use reported data to help managers plan operations, price new products, select alternative methods of financing, and make other decisions
Tax accounting: Provide tax planning, tax preparation, and representation in case of tax audit	**Internal auditing:** Check the accuracy of company records and accounting methods; police errors and possible employee larceny
	Cost accounting: Provide information to help management control the cost of manufactured products and their distribution; help management estimate future costs
	Installing accounting systems: Design systems for recording and reporting financial data and for cross-checking record keeping

Exhibit 17.2
Public Versus Private Accounting
Accountants who sell their services to a variety of individuals and businesses have responsibilities that are different from those of accountants who are employed privately.

public accountants *Independent outsiders who provide accounting services for businesses and other organizations*

audit *Accountant's evaluation of the fairness and reliability of a client's financial statements*

creditors *People or organizations that have loaned money or extended credit*

debtors *People or organizations who have to repay money they have borrowed*

certified public accountants (CPAs) *Professionally licensed accountants who meet certain requirements for education and experience and who pass an examination*

tants themselves. They may be divided into two groups: public accountants and private, or corporate, accountants (see Exhibit 17.2).

Public Accountants
Public accountants are independent of the businesses, organizations, and individuals they serve. They are retained to prepare financial statements, prepare taxes, and provide consultation for individuals and organizations. For larger companies, they are also retained to prepare reports on the fairness of those statements. Sometimes such a report is based on an **audit,** a formal evaluation of the fairness and reliability of financial statements. The report accompanies the client's published financial statements and indicates (1) whether the statements have been prepared in accordance with GAAP and (2) whether it's necessary to include any disclosures about uncertainties that would materially affect the client's financial position.

Public accountants' detached position obligates them to be objective and, when necessary, critical. Their reports are valuable to anyone who needs an unbiased picture of the financial standing of a particular business, such as creditors, shareholders, investors, and even government agencies. **Creditors** are people or organizations that have loaned money or extended credit to an individual or a business; those who borrow money are known as **debtors.**

Public accountants become **certified public accountants** (CPAs) by meeting a state's requirements for education and experience and by passing an examination prepared by the American Institute of Certified Public Accountants. Some 44 percent of the CPAs in the United States are in private practice, working in accounting firms that range in size from one-person shops to partnerships employing hundreds of CPAs. The profession is dominated by a small number of giant firms that audit more than 95 percent of the Fortune 500 companies and take in a good portion of the profession's annual revenues.[2]

The six largest U.S. accounting firms, known as the "Big Six," are Arthur Andersen and Company, Coopers & Lybrand, Deloitte & Touche, Ernst and Young, KPMG Peat Marwick, and Price Waterhouse & Company. These megafirms are able to service global customers, offer broader services, and provide both auditing and consultation in one convenient location. Competition for clients is increasing, and the smaller firms have difficulty competing against the giants. In addition, some observers worry that higher prices will be passed along to consumers, that clients will have more difficulty switching auditors, and that more competitors will share the same accountant.[3]

Some of the Big Six have been in the news in connection with business failures and frauds. Coopers & Lybrand paid $20 million to the Federal Deposit Insurance Corporation (FDIC) in a case related to the failure of its client Silverado Banking, Savings & Loan Association. Lenders and suppliers who were owed money by Laribee Wire Manufacturing, a troubled New York company, charged auditor Deloitte & Touche with failing to detect inventory fraud. Litigation against public accounting firms has focused attention on the accounting profession's responsibility for identifying client fraud during their audits.[4]

Are accountants adequately protecting the public against financial fraud? Some legislators want to require auditors to report client fraud to regulators. Accountants, on the other hand, maintain that such a role would cause their clients to mistrust them, possibly resulting in client lawsuits for libel, negligence, or misrepresentation. Although the accounting profession has proposed voluntary guidelines to help businesses prevent fraud, some observers believe that the guidelines fall short of what is needed.[5]

These developments, along with increased competition resulting from the shrinking pool of clients as more and more companies merge, have prompted many accounting firms to diversify into other areas. As consultants, accountants are designing computer systems for businesses, giving financial advice, and setting up personnel plans. Such activities, often referred to as *management advisory services (MAS),* have been especially valuable for small and midsized businesses. For example, the accounting firm of Friedman & Fuller in Rockville, Maryland, offers specialized services in profit improvement, risk management, and systems training. Accountants are also expanding their services to include *personal financial planning (PFP).* In fact, they were already performing a number of these services when involved in income-tax planning, estate-tax planning, retirement planning, and profit sharing.[6] These additional services cause some to worry that as accountants become more involved in their clients' business and personal finances, they may lose some of the objectivity they need as independent auditors.

Private Accountants
Private accountants, sometimes called corporate accountants, are those employed by a business (like Debbie Berlant of Hewlett-Packard's RND), a government agency, or a nonprofit corporation to

Ernst and Young, one of the Big Six accounting firms, offers a broad array of accounting and consulting services to clients around the world.

private accountants *In-house accountants employed by organizations and businesses; also called* corporate accountants

certified management accountants (CMAs) *Accountants who have fulfilled the requirements for certification as specialists in management accounting*

bookkeeping *Record keeping, clerical phase of accounting*

controller *Highest-ranking accountant in a company, responsible for overseeing all accounting functions*

internal auditors *Employees who analyze and evaluate the operation of company departments to determine their efficiency*

supervise the accounting system and the bookkeeping staff. They are also responsible for generating and interpreting financial reports. Many private accountants are CPAs; however, a growing number are **certified management accountants (CMAs),** a designation that indicates they have passed a two-day exam given by the Institute of Management Accountants that is comparable in difficulty to the CPA exam.[7]

The work of an in-house accounting staff is varied, ranging from routine **bookkeeping,** the clerical function of recording transactions, to high-level decision making. The highest-ranking private accountants typically have the title of **controller** or financial vice president. They oversee virtually every aspect of a company's financial operations and usually report directly to the president. The controller of a medium or large corporation monitors and cross-checks all financial data, usually with the help of a computer, in order to evaluate the company's financial health at any given point. The controller also supervises the preparation of financial analyses, budgets, forecasts, tax returns, and internal auditing. **Internal auditors** are employees assigned to investigate and evaluate the company's departments to determine whether they are operating efficiently.

An increasingly urgent ethical issue is how and when to disclose any involvement in costly pollution problems. To identify operations or locations that may not be environmentally sound or may not comply with government rules, company internal auditors need to regularly examine all business activities. If certain environmental problems are found, government regulations in Canada and the United States require that they be disclosed as part of the financial information that shareholders, investors, bankers, and others receive.[8] However, the cost of cleaning up environmental problems can vary, so accounting experts often face difficult decisions about how to estimate

Consolidated Papers meets pollution-control problems head-on. As soon as managers become aware of any problems, they release the information to the public and budget for cleanup costs.

the cost, how to explain the problem, and how early to announce potential problems. Consolidated Papers, a paper manufacturer based in Wisconsin, has taken an unusually candid approach by disclosing pollution-control problems—and setting aside money to cover cleanup costs—as soon as the company becomes aware of them.[9]

The Reliability of Accounting Information

As important as accounting is to the smooth operation of any business, it's not an exact science. Using the same financial data, honest accountants may legitimately come up with a wide range of results, depending on the assumptions they make and the way they interpret the accounting rules. Many companies prepare two sets of financial records—one for external reporting purposes and one for income-tax-assessment purposes. Accountants present shareholders with a fair picture of the company's financial position and the results of operations. However, for the tax collector, accountants use all the legal options the tax code allows to minimize the income subject to taxes.

The "creativity" an accountant can exercise is limited by generally accepted accounting principles. Although these principles are not legally binding on nonpublic companies, most accountants apply them to all financial statements and report any deviations from GAAP in published financial statements. Moreover, financial statements that do not conform to current GAAP are not acceptable to the Securities and Exchange Commission in the filings required for issuing and trading stock. Nevertheless, it is important to realize that to a large extent, accounting numbers represent human judgment.

KEY ACCOUNTING CONCEPTS

In their work with financial data, accountants are guided by two fundamental concepts: the accounting equation and double-entry book-keeping. Both were developed centuries ago but remain central to the accounting process.

The Accounting Equation

For thousands of years, businesses and governments have kept records of their **assets**—valuable things they own or lease, such as equipment—and their **liabilities**—what they owe to others. When it was said of ancient princes that they were "as rich as Croesus" (a wealthy king of Lydia), it was not just because they had much gold and grain. It was because they owned these treasures almost outright and had few debts or creditors' claims on their assets. In other words, wealth does not consist of assets alone. What remains after liabilities have been deducted from assets is **owners' equity**:

Assets	*$100,000*	
Liabilities	*− 30,000*	
Owners' equity	*$ 70,000*	

assets Physical objects and intangible rights that have economic value to the owner

liabilities Debts or obligations that are owed to individuals or organizations

owners' equity Portion of a company's assets that belongs to the owners after obligations to all creditors have been met

This simple observation is the basis for the all-important **accounting equation:**

$$Assets = liabilities + owners'\ equity$$
$$\$100,000 = \$30,000 + \$70,000$$

The company's liabilities are placed before owners' equity in the accounting equation because creditors have first claim on assets. After liabilities are paid, anything left over belongs to the owners or, in the case of a corporation, to the shareholders. However, to emphasize the amount of owners' equity, the accounting equation may be written as

$$Assets - liabilities = owners'\ equity$$
$$\$100,000 - \$30,000 = \$70,000$$

Whichever form is used, the relationship of assets, liabilities, and owners' equity remains in balance; in other words, one side of the equation always equals the other side.

Double-Entry Bookkeeping

To keep the accounting equation in balance, companies use a double-entry system that records every transaction affecting assets, liabilities, or owners' equity. This system dates back to 1494 and an Italian monk, Fra Luca Pacioli, who immediately caught the attention of the merchants and princes of his day. Fra Luca explained that every transaction—a sale, a payment, a collection—had two offsetting sides. No matter what kinds of transactions are made, the accounting equation remains in balance if the transactions are properly recorded. **Double-entry bookkeeping** requires a two-part, "give-and-get" entry for every transaction.

double-entry bookkeeping *Way of recording financial transactions that requires two entries for every transaction so that the accounting equation is always kept in balance*

Say that you're opening a videocassette-rental shop. You'll stock 1,000 cassettes, which cost $30 each, for a total of $30,000 in capital. If you have $20,000 of your own to invest, your accounting equation would show

$$Assets = liabilities + owners'\ equity$$
$$\$20,000\ (cash) = 0 + \$20,000$$

In other words, $20,000 in cash is equal to your owners' equity of $20,000. As yet, your business has no liabilities.

Next, imagine that you do three things:

1. You borrow from the bank the additional $10,000 you need. That $10,000 is added both to your cash account under "Assets" and to your bank-loan account under "Liabilities." This double entry keeps your accounting equation in balance.
2. You spend $30,000 on videocassettes. Your assets are thus converted from cash into videocassettes, $10,000 worth of which your creditor, the bank, has a claim on. The other $20,000 worth of cassettes represents owners' equity. The right side of the accounting equation is not affected by the conversion of assets from one form (cash) into another (cassettes).
3. In the first month, you rent each of the 1,000 cassettes once, charging $2 per rental. Your total revenue is $2,000. You spend $1,500

Transaction	Cash	Inventory (cassettes)	=	Bank loan	Stock	Profit (retained earnings)
Investment	20,000	—	=	—	+ 20,000	—
Loan	+10,000	—	=	+10,000	+ —	—
	30,000	—	=	10,000	+ 20,000	—
Inventory purchase	−30,000	+30,000	=	—	+ —	—
	—	30,000	=	10,000	+ 20,000	—
Rental revenue	+ 2,000	—	=	—	+ —	+2,000
Expenses	− 1,100	−400	=	—	+ —	−1,500
	900	29,600	=	10,000	+ 20,000	500

Assets = Liabilities + Owners' equity

30,500 = 30,500

Exhibit 17.3

An Example of Double-Entry Bookkeeping

In double-entry bookkeeping, the sum of the numbers on both sides of the equal sign must always be in balance. In this example, the equation in each row balances, as does the "bottom-line" equation.

retained earnings *Net increase in assets (cash and outstanding receivables) for an accounting period; part of owners' equity*

to run the store, including salaries, rent, and $400 in wear and tear on your cassettes. The $500 profit (rental revenues minus expenses) is plowed back into the business, becoming **retained earnings** and part of your owners' equity. Earnings retained by the business consist of the increase in assets (cash and amounts due from others) for an accounting period.

These transactions might be recorded as shown in Exhibit 17.3. Note that the two sides of the accounting equation are—and must always be—equal.

FINANCIAL STATEMENTS

After a few months, the transactions recorded by a bookkeeper will accumulate, making it difficult for management to sort out what is going on. To simplify the picture, accountants prepare financial statements that summarize the transactions. Three of the most important are the balance sheet, the income statement, and the statement of cash flows.

The Balance Sheet

A **balance sheet,** also known as a statement of financial position, is a kind of "snapshot" of where a company is, financially speaking, at one moment in time. It includes all the elements in the accounting equation, showing the balance between assets on the one hand and liabilities and owners' equity on the other. Exhibit 17.4 is a balance sheet for Sweet Dreams Ice Cream, a small corporation that makes ice cream and sells it through its own shop. Most detailed balance sheets classify assets, liabilities, and owners' equity into categories like those shown in the Sweet Dreams balance sheet.

However, no business can stand still while its financial condition is being examined. A business may make hundreds of transactions of various kinds every working day. Even during a holiday, office fixtures grow older and decrease in value, and interest on savings accounts accumulates. Yet the accountant must set up a balance sheet

balance sheet *Financial statement that shows assets, liabilities, and owners' equity on a given date; also known as a statement of financial position*

SWEET DREAMS ICE CREAM, INC.
Balance Sheet
December 31, 1995

ASSETS

Current Assets

Cash		$22,790	
Marketable securities		4,200	
Accounts receivable	$19,780		
Less: Allowance for uncollectible accounts	430	$19,350	
Notes receivable		21,500	
Merchandise inventory		12,685	
Prepaid expenses		4,400	
TOTAL CURRENT ASSETS			$ 84,925

Fixed Assets

Factory equipment	$64,919		
Less: Accumulated depreciation	11,706	$53,213	
Leasehold improvements	$77,030		
Less: Accumulated amortization	14,308	62,722	
TOTAL FIXED ASSETS			115,935

Intangible Assets

Organization costs		$ 420	
Trademark		6,405	
Goodwill		5,000	
TOTAL INTANGIBLE ASSETS			11,825
TOTAL ASSETS			$212,685

LIABILITIES AND SHAREHOLDERS' EQUITY

Current Liabilities

Accounts payable		$23,790	
Note payable (short-term)		15,115	
Salaries payable		7,452	
Taxes payable		6,318	
TOTAL CURRENT LIABILITIES			$ 52,675

Long-Term Liabilities

Long-term note payable @ 12%			53,750
TOTAL LIABILITIES			$106,425

Shareholders' Equity

Common stock, 10,000 shares		$43,000	
Retained earnings		63,260	
TOTAL SHAREHOLDERS' EQUITY			106,260
TOTAL LIABILITIES AND SHAREHOLDERS' EQUITY			$212,685

Exhibit 17.4
A Sample Balance Sheet
The categories used on Sweet Dreams Ice Cream's year-end balance sheet are typical.

calendar year *Twelve-month accounting period that begins on January 1 and ends on December 31*

fiscal year *Any 12 consecutive months used as an accounting period*

so that managers and other interested parties can evaluate the business's financial position as if it were not ever-changing.

Every company prepares a balance sheet at least once a year, most often at the end of the **calendar year,** covering from January 1 to December 31. However, many business and government bodies use a **fiscal year,** which may be any 12 consecutive months. A business may choose a fiscal year that runs from June 1 to May 31 because its peak selling season ends in May. Its fiscal year would then correspond to its full annual cycle of manufacturing and selling. Some companies prepare a balance sheet more often than once a year, perhaps at the end of each month or quarter. Thus, every balance sheet is dated to show when the financial snapshot was taken.

Instead of using a calendar year for their balance sheets, retailers often use a fiscal year that ends after their peak selling seasons. So that it can include results from the all-important winter holiday selling season, the J. C. Penney fiscal year ends on the last Saturday in January.

Assets

Most often, the asset section of the balance sheet is divided into three types of assets—current, fixed, and intangible—listed in order of the ease with which the assets can be turned into cash. The balance sheet gives a subtotal for each type of asset and then a grand total for all assets.

Current Assets. **Current assets,** which include cash and other items that will or can become cash within the following year, are always listed first.

current assets Cash and other items that can be turned back into cash within one year

- *Cash:* Funds on hand in checking and savings accounts. Not included are funds in special deposits or in any other form not readily available for use.
- *Marketable securities:* Stocks, bonds, and other investments that can quickly be turned into cash when needed. Such investments are temporary and do not represent any long-term control over the company that issued the securities.
- *Accounts receivable:* Amounts due from customers. Often accountants deduct from accounts receivable an allowance for bad debts (uncollectible accounts). This deduction alerts creditors and shareholders that some of the receivables may not be collectible.
- *Notes receivable:* Written and signed promises by customers to pay a definite sum, plus interest, usually on a certain date and at a certain place. They are generally collected routinely through customers' banks.
- *Inventories:* Usually merchandise on hand. Manufacturers may have inventories of raw materials, goods in process, and finished goods ready for sale.
- *Prepaid expenses:* Supplies on hand and services paid for but not yet used. An example is prepaid insurance, the unexpired portion of insurance purchased by a business. It is considered a current asset because it can be turned into cash if canceled or because it will be used and thus reduce cash outlay in the next year.

Fixed Assets. **Fixed assets**—sometimes referred to as *property, plant, and equipment*—are long-term investments in buildings, equipment, furniture and fixtures, transportation equipment, land, and any

fixed assets Assets retained for long-term use, such as land, buildings, machinery, and equipment; also referred to as property, plant, and equipment

other tangible property used in running the business. They have a useful life of more than one year and are not expected to be directly converted into cash.

A long-lived asset such as a machine or a truck slowly wears out or becomes obsolete and at some point will become useless. The accounting procedure for systematically spreading out the cost of such an asset over its estimated useful life is known as **depreciation** if the asset is a tangible asset such as a building or **amortization** if the asset is an intangible asset such as a patent. Depreciation (or amortization) allocates the cost of a long-lived asset to those accounting periods in which it is used to produce revenue. When the balance sheet is prepared, the accountant records the depreciation for the period. Of the various kinds of fixed assets, only land does not depreciate.

Intangible Assets. **Intangible assets** include the costs of organizing the business, obtaining patents on a process or invention, obtaining copyrights on written or reproducible material, and registering trademarks. Even though patents, copyrights, and trademarks are not physical assets like chairs or desks, they are valuable because they can be licensed or sold outright to others. For example, the song "Happy Birthday to You," one of the most popular songs in the English language, was sold not long ago for $25 million.

Least tangible of all but no less valuable is **goodwill,** which consists mainly of a company's reputation, especially in its relations with customers. Goodwill is not entered as an asset unless the business has been purchased. In that case, the purchaser records goodwill as the difference between the cost of the purchased company as reflected in its financial statements and the price that the purchaser is willing to pay. This goodwill premium paid by the purchaser may range from a single token dollar to several million dollars.

Liabilities

The debts that a business has incurred represent claims against the assets, and they come next on the balance sheet. Liabilities may be current or long-term, and they are listed in the order in which they will come due. The balance sheet gives subtotals for current and long-term liabilities and then a grand total for all liabilities.

Current Liabilities. Obligations that will have to be met within a year of the date of the balance sheet are **current liabilities.**

- *Accounts payable:* Generally due in 30 days or less and often listed first. Such liabilities usually result from buying goods or services on credit.
- *Notes payable:* Written and signed promises to pay a certain sum plus interest at a definite time and place. Unlike notes receivable, these liabilities represent money owed rather than money coming in. Notes payable generally come due after a much longer time than accounts payable. Because notes usually require payment of interest as well as repayment of the principal, this item in the balance sheet represents both.
- *Accrued expenses:* Expenses that have been incurred but for which bills have not yet been received. Wages, interest, and taxes are ex-

depreciation *Accounting procedure for systematically spreading the cost of a tangible asset over its estimated useful life*

amortization *Accounting procedure for systematically spreading the cost of an intangible asset over its estimated useful life*

intangible assets *Assets having no physical existence but having value because the owner can license or sell them to others*

goodwill *Value assigned to a business's reputation, calculated as the difference between the price paid for the business and the underlying value of its assets*

current liabilities *Obligations that must be met within a year*

amples of expenses that will be payable in the near future. If such expenses and their associated liabilities were not recorded, the business's financial statements would be misleading because some debts and costs of earning revenue would not be shown.

Long-Term Liabilities. Obligations that are due a year or more after the date of the balance sheet are categorized as **long-term liabilities.** They are similar to owners' equity because they are claims on the business that may go unpaid for a long time (though interest on such debts must be paid when due). When a company goes out of business, the claims of long-term creditors are normally paid before those of the owners. Other liabilities may fall into the long-term category, including many types of leases (agreements that enable their holders to use assets without legally owning them) and mortgages (agreements that pledge property owned by a business—such as land, buildings, or machines—to creditors as security).

long-term liabilities *Obligations that fall due more than a year from the date of the balance sheet*

Owners' Equity

The owners' investment in a business is listed on the balance sheet under owners' equity. Sole proprietorships list owner's equity under the owner's name with the amount (assets minus liabilities). Small partnerships list each partner's share of the business separately, and large partnerships list the total of all partners' shares. Owners' equity for a corporation (referred to as shareholders' equity, as in Exhibit 17.4) is presented in terms of the amount of common stock that is outstanding, meaning the amount that is in the hands of shareholders. The amount shown represents the investment that was paid into the corporation by the shareholders when the stock was issued. This is also the section that shows a corporation's retained earnings —the total earnings of all previous periods minus the amount distributed as dividends.

The Income Statement

The **income statement** reflects the results of operations over a period of time, typically one year. If the balance sheet is a snapshot, the income statement is a movie. It summarizes all **revenues** (or sales), the amounts that have been or are to be received from customers for goods or services delivered to them, and all **expenses,** the costs that have arisen in generating revenues. Expenses are then subtracted from revenues to show the actual profit or loss of a company, a figure known as **net income**—profit or the *bottom line.* Exhibit 17.5 is an income statement for Sweet Dreams Ice Cream.

income statement *Financial statement showing how a business's revenues compare with expenses for a given period of time*

revenues *Amount of sales of goods or services and inflow from miscellaneous sources such as interest, rent, and royalties*

expenses *Costs created in the process of generating revenues*

net income *Profit or loss of a company, determined by subtracting expenses from revenues; also called the* bottom line

Revenues

The revenues of a business usually come from sales to customers, fees for services, or both. Other kinds of revenue include rents, commissions, interest, and fees paid by other firms to use the company's patents.

Two Methods of Recording Revenues. In an ice cream store like Sweet Dreams, the shopkeeper receives revenue the moment a customer hands over a dollar for a cone. In a business that sells more expen-

SWEET DREAMS ICE CREAM, INC.
Income Statement
For the Year Ended December 31, 1995

Revenues			
Gross sales		$478,293	
Less: Returns and allowances		3,079	
Less: Discounts		1,200	
NET SALES			$474,014
Cost of Goods Sold			
Beginning inventory		$ 10,473	
Purchases for the year	$198,267		
Less: Purchase discounts	5,300		
Net purchases		192,967	
Cost of goods available for sale		$203,440	
Less: Ending inventory		12,685	
COST OF GOODS SOLD			190,755
Gross Profit			$283,259
Operating Expenses			
Selling expenses			
Wages	$101,700		
Advertising	18,075		
Store supplies	24,016		
Payroll taxes	10,170		
Rent	31,142		
Repairs and maintenance	7,418		
Auto and truck	11,697		
Insurance	4,068		
Utilities	8,700		
Depreciation and amortization	13,245		
Miscellaneous	400		
TOTAL SELLING EXPENSES		$230,631	
General Expenses			
Professional services	$ 3,916		
Office supplies	1,354		
Miscellaneous	300		
TOTAL GENERAL EXPENSES		5,570	
TOTAL OPERATING EXPENSES			236,201
OPERATING INCOME			$ 47,058
Other Income and Expenses			
Interest expense		$ 4,750	
Interest income		(986)	
TOTAL OTHER INCOME AND EXPENSES			3,764
NET INCOME			$ 43,294
INCOME TAXES			6,494
NET INCOME AFTER TAXES			$ 36,800

Exhibit 17.5

A Sample Income Statement

An income statement summarizes the company's financial operations over a particular accounting period, usually a year.

accrual basis *Accounting method in which revenue is recorded when a sale is made and expense is recorded when incurred*

sive products—business computers, for example—some time passes between the moment the salesperson and the customer make a deal and the day the customer pays for the merchandise. At what point has the vendor actually made a sale? If a company records its sales on an **accrual basis,** the company puts the revenue on its books as soon as the deal is made and the product is delivered, even if the customer does not pay until the following year. If a business is run on a **cash basis,** however, the company records revenue only when money from the sale is actually received.

Although most companies use the accrual method, some small companies prefer to avoid that method of recording revenue because then they have to pay taxes on the revenue before they actually collect the money. For businesses that have to borrow money to pay their tax bills, the advantages of cash-based accounting are obvious. However, accrual-based accounting benefits the government, because the Internal Revenue Service gets its tax money sooner. Since 1982 the IRS has required manufacturers and retailers to use the accrual method and has allowed only farmers and certain service businesses to use the cash method. The Tax Reform Act of 1986 further limits the use of the cash method.

cash basis Accounting method in which revenue is recorded when payment is received and expense is recorded when cash is paid

Gross Sales Versus Net Sales. **Gross sales,** the total dollar amount of products sold, doesn't give the entire revenue picture. In the normal course of business, deductions are made from gross sales. Customers may return the goods they have bought and get full refunds. Cash discounts, offered to customers who pay early, also reduce gross sales. After such discounts are deducted from gross sales, the remaining amount is called **net sales.** Exhibit 17.5 shows the impact of returns and discounts on the gross sales of Sweet Dreams.

gross sales All revenues received from the sale of goods or services

net sales Amount remaining after cash discounts, refunds, and other allowances are deducted from gross sales

Expenses

Expenses, the costs of doing business, include both the costs directly associated with creating products and general operating expenses.

Cost of Goods Sold. For any products that a producer or distributor sells, it must pay certain costs. A manufacturer like Hewlett-Packard's RND must take into account the expense of producing its goods, whereas a retailer must allow for the expense of buying merchandise. **Cost of goods sold** is calculated differently for these two kinds of businesses.

cost of goods sold Cost of producing or acquiring a company's products for sale during a given period

Manufacturers must first total the costs of producing goods, including expenses for labor, raw materials, and factory operations. These costs are then added to the value of the inventory of finished goods on hand at the beginning of the year. The value of the inventory (finished goods not sold) at the end of the year is then subtracted, yielding the cost of goods sold.

In contrast, wholesalers and retailers start by evaluating inventory on hand at the beginning of the year. Purchases made during the year (less discounts) are then added to this figure. These sums make up the total cost of goods available for sale. To find out the cost of goods sold, the cost of inventory still on hand at the end of the period is deducted. As shown for Sweet Dreams in Exhibit 17.5, cost of goods sold is then deducted from net sales to arrive at gross profit.

operating expenses All costs of operation that are not included under cost of goods sold

Operating Expenses. In addition to the costs directly associated with producing their goods or services, companies must account for two types of **operating expenses. Selling expenses** are operating expenses incurred through marketing and distributing the company's products. These expenses include wages or salaries of salespeople, advertising, supplies, insurance for the sales operation, depreciation of the store and sales equipment, and other sales-department expenses such as utilities. **General expenses** are operating expenses incurred in the overall administration of a business. They include professional

selling expenses All the operating expenses associated with marketing goods or services

general expenses Operating expenses, such as office and administrative expenses, not directly associated with creating or marketing a good or service

WHAT'S YOUR NET WORTH?

How much do you think you are really worth? Take a guess. Now get ready for what may be a pleasant surprise. At the very least, filling out the personal balance sheet included here will help you evaluate your resources and plan for the future. Wouldn't you like to know whether you're too deeply in debt? What the value of your possessions is? The amount you can expect from your pension and retirement accounts?

Net worth is simply the difference between assets and liabilities. The first step in calculating your net worth, then, is to assess your assets. How much would you receive for your investments, your home, and your automobile if you were to convert them to cash today? Be realistic. For personal property, be especially

conservative; it's easy to let sentiment inflate the value of your prized possessions. Now write down only a quarter of the amount you have estimated as the value of your personal property, because it is difficult to sell used household goods. Be similarly tough-minded about money other people owe you: How much are you really likely to collect?

The liabilities section of your personal balance sheet includes all your current financial obligations: what you owe on your home, car, credit cards, furniture, college education, and so on. It also includes any taxes you owe for which money has not already been withheld.

Once you're sure you haven't overlooked any of your assets or liabilities, total each column. Then subtract your liabilities from your assets. The result is your net worth today. Keep in mind, however, that a year from now—even a month from now—your net worth will be different. So to keep up-to-date on your financial status, plan to revise your personal balance sheet a year from now and every year after that.

ASSETS		LIABILITIES	
Checking account	$_____	Installment loans (and interest charges)	$_____
Savings account	_____	Other loans (and interest charges)	_____
Money-market fund	_____	Charge accounts (and interest charges)	_____
Time deposits and certificates	_____	Mortgage	_____
House (market value)	_____	Current bills outstanding	_____
Other real estate	_____	Taxes due	_____
Securities (bonds, stocks, other)	_____	Other debts	_____
Life insurance cash value	_____	TOTAL	$_____
Investments	_____		
Annuities	_____		
Company or union pension	_____	**NET WORTH**	
Individual Retirement Account or Keogh Plan	_____	Subtract your total liabilities from your total assets to find your net worth	
Interest in business	_____	TOTAL ASSETS	$_____
Automobile	_____	TOTAL LIABILITIES	$_____
Personal property (clothing, jewelry, furniture, cameras, and the like)	_____	NET WORTH	$_____
Loans receivable (debts owed to you)	_____		
Other	_____		
TOTAL	$_____		

services (accounting and legal fees), office salaries, depreciation of office equipment, insurance for office operations, supplies, and so on.

Net Income or Loss
Once you have calculated your revenues and expenses for a period, you are ready to determine your net income, which shows whether

you made a profit or loss. The first step is to deduct the cost of goods sold from net sales (gross sales minus returns and allowances and discounts) to obtain the **gross profit** (or *gross margin*). The next step is to deduct the total operating expenses from gross profit. The remainder is the **operating income.**

Once you know your operating income, you add to it any other revenues received by the business (such as interest income). Then you deduct any other expenses (such as income taxes). The balance shows the company's *net income* for the period. Owners, creditors, and investors can evaluate the company's past performance and future prospects by comparing net income for one year with net income for previous years. Ideally, the net income figure should go up every year as the company becomes more profitable.

The Statement of Cash Flows

In addition to preparing a balance sheet and an income statement, all public companies and many privately owned companies prepare a **statement of cash flows** to show how a company's cash has increased or decreased in a period. The Financial Accounting Standards Board (FASB, the chief rule-making body for U.S. accountants) requires public companies to include this statement among their annual financial statements.[10] The statement of cash flows summarizes how cash was received and spent in three areas: operations, investments, and financing. An analysis of cash flows provides a good idea of a company's *liquidity,* or ability to pay its short-term obligations when they become due; the cash-flow status is thus one good indicator of financial health.

FINANCIAL ANALYSIS

Organizations and individuals use financial statements—balance sheets, income statements, statements of cash flows, and others—to spot problems and opportunities and make business decisions. When analyzing financial statements, managers and outsiders try to evaluate a company's performance in relation to the economy as a whole and to the company's competitors, taking into account the methods the company has used to make various accounting disclosures. To perform this analysis, most users look at historical trends and certain key ratios that indicate how the company is performing.

Reviewing the Economic and Competitive Context

Local, regional, national, and international economic conditions have a significant influence on most industries and companies. Consider the housing industry. When times are tough, people tend to put off buying a new house, and homebuilders' sales drop. Hard times may make even the best-run companies look weak. The converse is also true: Good times are likely to improve the earnings of even the worst-run businesses.

When gauging a company's financial health, take into account these uncontrollable economic forces and then examine how the company

gross profit Amount remaining when the cost of goods sold is deducted from net sales; also known as gross margin

operating income Amount remaining when operating expenses are deducted from gross profit

statement of cash flows Financial statement that summarizes receipts and disbursals of cash in three areas: operations, investments, and financing

has responded compared with its competitors. Sales growth may slow during a recession for all companies in an industry. However, a company that maintains large profit margins while its competitors struggle may be assumed to be doing well.

Allowing for Different Accounting Methods

Comparing one company with another may be tricky because of the subjectivity involved in accounting techniques. Some accountants—like some professors—are tough graders, taking the most conservative approach to everything. Others allow a more liberal interpretation of the rules. Thus, a company that gets the equivalent of a B on its financial report card may well be better managed than a competitor that gets an A using less rigorous accounting methods. To be sure you aren't comparing apples with oranges, you must question how various accounting matters have been handled.

When Are Revenues Recorded?

Companies have some discretion in deciding when to record a sale on their books. Therefore, when evaluating an income statement, you would have to ask, "Are these sales really firm?" Some manufacturers load up their distributors with supplies well before payments are due and create the impression that sales are booming. In fact, these producers have not generated revenue but have merely transferred inventory to their distributors. If the product does not sell well, the producer may have to accept sizable returns from distributors; at that point, the producer will have to revise the sales figures downward. IBM records revenue when it ships computers to its dealers, even though the dealers can return them later, and it makes allowances for returns. This practice, critics charge, is too aggressive.[11] A more conservative approach is to record revenues only after products have been received by customers and all potential returns can reasonably be projected.

Congress and the IRS have taken the guesswork out of determining the depreciable life of some assets by assigning depreciable lives and indicating the percentage of the asset's cost that may be deducted each year. Tractors, for example, have a 3-year depreciable life, whereas farm buildings have a 20-year depreciable life.

Which Depreciation Method Is Used?

Accountants may use any of several methods of calculating depreciation expenses. However, various depreciation methods require different procedures. All the methods are based on the accountant's estimate of the useful life of each fixed asset. Estimates of useful life may vary—can a delivery truck be expected to last 10 years, or is 5 years more realistic? Nevertheless, GAAP forbid accountants from deliberately overestimating a fixed asset's useful life, so users of financial statements may assume that such estimates are reasonable. The method chosen to depict the pattern of a fixed asset's depreciation, however, can make financial statements trickier to analyze. One commonly used method allocates an equal amount of depreciation expense to every year of the asset's estimated useful life, whereas another method permits more depreciation expense to be deducted in the early years of the asset's life than in its later years. Thus, the depreciation method used can make a company look more or less profitable.

How Is Cost of Goods Sold Calculated?

A company can also raise or lower its earnings by changing the way it calculates the cost of goods sold. Say that you own a motorcycle dealership, and you buy motorcycles from the manufacturer for re-sale to customers. During the year, the manufacturer might raise its prices, so your inventory would consist of machines that had cost you different amounts. You might have five motorcycles that you bought several months ago for $2,000 each and five that you just bought for $2,200 apiece. If you sell five bikes for $3,000 each, your revenues are $15,000—But which five bikes did you sell? If you assume that you sold the oldest bikes first, your gross profit is $5,000 ($15,000 in revenues less $10,000, or five bikes at $2,000 each). If you assume that you sold the newest bikes first, your gross profit is $4,000 ($15,000 less $11,000, or five bikes at $2,200 each).

Whether your gross profit is $4,000 or $5,000 depends on the method you use to determine the cost of inventory. The "first in, first out" method, or **FIFO,** treats inventory costs as if they were on a conveyor belt traveling through the balance sheet to the income statement. The costs you enter in your books as the units are purchased are assigned in the same order to the units as they are sold. This is the method you're using if you figure that you have sold the five $2,000 "old" bikes. The "last in, first out" method, or **LIFO,** is like stacking inventory costs in a box. When a layer of costs is at the bottom, it can't be reached until all the layers above it are removed. This is the method you're using if you figure that you have sold the five $2,200 "new" bikes.

In times of high inflation, the LIFO method produces a higher cost of goods sold, a lower value for remaining inventory, and lower profits. This arrangement usually results in lower taxes, as Exhibit 17.6 shows. In contrast, FIFO produces a higher value for ending inventory and a lower cost of goods sold. Because the profit—the difference between that lower cost and the inflated selling price—is greater, taxes are higher. Many executives believe that FIFO taxes their companies on "phantom" profits—earnings that are not really profits but that merely represent money needed to restock the shelves at tomorrow's prices. In inflationary times, executives often opt for LIFO to lower their paper profits and thus their cash tax payments.

In general, however, neither FIFO nor LIFO is necessarily better. The point to remember is that during periods of price changes in an industry, two companies (doing equally well in most respects) could legitimately report differing levels of profit. After a fast look at the financial statements, a person unfamiliar with accounting might con-

FIFO *"First in, first out" method of pricing inventory under which the costs of the first goods acquired are the first ones charged to the cost of goods sold*

LIFO *"Last in, first out" method of pricing inventory under which the costs of the last goods acquired are the first ones charged to the cost of goods sold*

	FIFO	LIFO
Sales	$15,000	$15,000
Cost of goods sold	10,000	11,000
Gross profit	$ 5,000	$ 4,000
Taxes (at 30 percent)	1,500	1,200
Net income	$ 3,500	$ 2,800

Exhibit 17.6
How Different Methods of Costing Inventory Affect Taxes
Note that in this example, the tax is 25 percent higher with the FIFO method than with the LIFO method.

clude that the company using FIFO was more profitable. However, the company using LIFO might actually be better managed because its use of that method would reduce its tax bill. Because the inventory costing method has such a powerful effect on net income, a company must state in the footnotes to its financial statements which method it used.

How Are Allowances Made?

Whatever the business, certain debts are uncollectible and some loans incur losses. Also, pension funds must be available if payments have been promised to retiring employees. Preparing for these events is sound business practice, and many companies put aside allowances to cover such situations. Although a company may look less profitable when it sets aside these allowances, it will be better off than its less cautious competitors if things go wrong.

Consider uncollectible accounts receivable. For almost every company, some accounts receivable will go uncollected. The question is which ones—and how much will the bad debts amount to? Accountants may allow for uncollectible accounts by basing their estimates either on a percentage of credit sales or on a percentage of outstanding accounts receivable. Both of these percentages are determined on the basis of the company's past experience with uncollectible accounts and on its expectations about future uncollectibles. Again, depending on what percentage is used, the company will look more or less profitable.

Savings and loan companies must allow for loan losses, but insufficient allowances have been cited as one factor in the failures of many savings and loan institutions. In fact, creative accounting procedures and overestimated real estate appraisals allowed S&Ls to ignore mounting problems while their executives drew high salaries and fees.[12]

Investment funds for pensions are another type of allowance that may be handled in various ways. How much will companies need in order to pay employees when they retire? This is a difficult question because no one is sure how long a retired employee will actually draw a pension. Nevertheless, if readers of a balance sheet are to get a true and total picture of the company's financial position, they need to see the total of **unfunded pension liabilities,** the difference between how much a company estimates its pension obligations will be and how much it has already allowed for that expense. Accounting rules now require unfunded pension liabilities to be displayed in the liability section of the balance sheet, which doesn't materially affect a company's cash flow but does make its liabilities look larger.

What Are the Effects of Extraordinary or Unusual Items?

Sometimes a company will boost its earnings through extraordinary or unusual measures — selling off assets, for example, or changing the way it accounts for various items. These one-time events have nothing to do with revenues from the company's regular operations, but they do make the bottom line look better. When Eastman Kodak sold off its clinical-diagnostics unit, its prescription-drug business, and its over-the-counter-medicine business during a single year,

unfunded pension liabilities *Amount by which a company's estimated future pension obligations exceed the funds set aside to cover those obligations*

the money from those one-time events helped the company reduce its debt and look more profitable.[13]

Although a business can legitimately make money on such transactions, a well-run company can't sustain a record of earnings growth using this practice over a number of years. A seemingly healthy track record may be an illusion if it is based on selling off assets or switching accounting methods from one accounting period to the next. Thus, analysts and creditors look closely at a company's earnings to determine whether extraordinary measures are involved.

Calculating Trends and Ratios

Besides summarizing business transactions, financial statements provide information that can be analyzed for further clues to the health and future prospects of a business. Information in financial statements is most often analyzed in terms of trends and ratios.

Trend Analysis

The process of comparing financial data from year to year in order to see how they have changed is known as **trend analysis.** You can use trend analysis to uncover shifts in the nature of the business over time and to compare your company with others in its industry or with the economy as a whole. Most large companies provide data for trend analysis in their annual reports. Their balance sheets and income statements typically show three to five years or more of data (making comparative statement analysis possible); changes in other key items—such as revenues, income, earnings per share, and dividends per share—are usually presented in tables and graphs.

When you analyze trends, look closely to see whether the results have been distorted by inflationary trends. During the late 1970s, when the inflation rate was in double digits, every company in the United States could automatically increase its sales revenue by at least 10 percent annually without achieving any real improvement in its basic business. By simply raising prices to keep up with inflation, a company could give at least a superficial appearance of growth. When inflation slowed in the 1980s, many companies' sales growth slowed as well—not because their business was bad, but because the built-in inflation kicker had diminished.

To correct for this potential distortion, the Securities and Exchange Commission requires the largest public companies to supplement their financial statements with footnotes showing what their historical costs would look like when adjusted for inflation. Now that inflation has abated, the accounting profession has put this sort of inflation-adjusted accounting on the back burner. However, accountants may return to it if inflation rises again.

Ratio Analysis

In **ratio analysis,** two elements from the same year's financial figures are compared. For example, sales might be compared with assets or with income. The result of such a comparison is stated as a percentage or a ratio, which can be compared with the company's past ratios or with those of competitors.

trend analysis *Comparison of a company's financial data from year to year to see how they have changed*

ratio analysis *Comparison of two elements from the same year's financial results, stated as a percentage or a ratio*

*S*pring is the time of year for blue-
birds to sing, flowers to bloom,
baseball players to take the field,
and annual reports to pour off the printing presses. The nation's 10,000 publicly
traded corporations "tell all" in these financial reports to shareholders, but finding
the important information in them isn't
easy. More and more companies are turning out glossy magazine-style reports
filled with color photos and glowing accounts of the company's accomplishments.
The real story about the company's financial health is often buried in footnotes
and dense tables. You'll need to know
how to read annual reports in your career,
whether you're thinking of investing in
companies, becoming a supplier for them,
or applying for a job with them. Thus, it's
worth your while to consider the advice of
Newsweek *columnist Jane Bryant*
Quinn, *who provided the following*
pointers in an ad created for International
Paper Company as part of its "The
Power of the Printed Word" campaign.
Using as her example the annual report
of the fictional Galactic Industries, Quinn
tells you how to find the important
information.

Start at the Back
First, turn back to the report of the
Certified Public Accountant. This
third-party auditor will tell you right
off the bat if Galactic's report con-

HOW TO READ
AN ANNUAL REPORT

forms with "generally accepted accounting principles." What else
should you know before you check
the numbers? First, stay in the back
of the book and go to the footnotes.
Yep! The whole profits story is
sometimes in the footnotes. Second,
check to see whether earnings are up
or down. If they're down only because of a change in accounting,
maybe that's good! The company
owes less tax and has more money in
its pocket. If earnings are up, maybe
that's bad. They may be up because
of a special windfall that won't happen again next year. The footnotes
know.

For What Happened and Why
Now turn to the letter from the
chairman. Usually addressed "to our

shareholders," it's up front—and
should be in more ways than one.
The chairman's tone reflects the personality, the well-being of the company.

In this letter, the chairman should
tell you how the company fared this
year. But more important, the letter
should tell you why. Keep an eye out
for sentences that start with "Except
for . . ." and "Despite the . . . ."
They're clues to problems.

Insights into the Future
On the positive side, a chairman's
letter should give you insights into
the company's future and its stance
on economic or political trends that
may affect it.

While you're up front, look for
what's new in each line of business.
Is management getting the company
in good shape to weather the tough
and competitive [years ahead]?

Now—and no sooner—should
you dig into the numbers!

One source is the balance sheet. It
is a snapshot of how the company
stands at a single point in time. On
the top are assets—everything the
company owns. Things that can
quickly be turned into cash are current assets. On the bottom are liabilities—everything the company owes.
Current liabilities are the debts due

---

profitability ratios *Financial ratios*
that indicate to what extent a company
is making a profit

return on investment (ROI) *Ratio*
between the net income earned by a
company and total owners' equity; also
known as return on equity

Like trend analysis, ratio analysis reveals how the company's performance compares with that of similar companies in its industry, but
it focuses on certain areas of current performance instead of on comparisons of performance over time. Every industry tends to have its
own "normal" ratios, which act as yardsticks for individual companies. The average statistics for various industries, grouped by company size, are available in published sources. One such report is published by Dun & Bradstreet, a credit-rating firm.

Profitability Ratios. You can analyze how well a company is conducting its ongoing operations by computing **profitability ratios,**
which show the state of its financial performance. Three of the most
common profitability ratios are return on investment, return on sales,
and earnings per share.

Return on investment (ROI), also known as *return on equity,* is
the income a business generates per dollar of owner or shareholder
investment. Consider Sweet Dreams Ice Cream, which made $43,294

in one year, which are paid out of current assets.

The difference between current assets and current liabilities is working capital, a key figure to watch from one annual (and quarterly) report to another. If working capital shrinks, it could mean trouble. One possibility: The company may not be able to keep dividends growing rapidly.

Look for Growth Here

Owners' or shareholders' equity is the difference between total assets and liabilities. It is the presumed dollar value of what the owners or shareholders own. You want it to grow.

Another important number to watch is long-term debt. High and rising debt, relative to equity, may be no problem for a growing business. But it shows weakness in a company that's leveling out. (More on that later.)

The second basic source of numbers is the income statement. It shows how much money Galactic made or lost over the year.

Most people look at one figure first. It's in the income statement at the bottom: earnings per share. Watch out. It can fool you. Galactic's management could boost earnings by selling off a plant. Or by cutting the budget for research and advertising. (See the footnotes!) So don't be smug about earnings until you've found out how they happened—and how they might happen next year.

Check Net Sales First

The number you should look at first in the income statement is net sales. Ask yourself: Are sales going up at a faster rate than the last time around? When sales increases start to slow, the company may be in trouble. Also ask: Have sales gone up faster than inflation? If not, the company's real sales may be behind. And ask yourself once more: Have sales gone down because the company is selling off a losing business? If so, profits may be soaring.

(I never promised you that figuring out an annual report was going to be easy!)

Get Out Your Calculator

Another important thing to study is the company's debt. Get out your pocket calculator, and turn to the balance sheet. Divide long-term liabilities by owners' or shareholders' equity. That's the debt-to-equity ratio.

A high ratio means the company borrows a lot of money to spark its growth. That's okay—if sales grow, too, and if there's enough cash on hand to meet the payments. A company doing well on borrowed money can earn big profits for its shareholders. But if sales fall, watch out. The whole enterprise may slowly sink. Some companies can handle high ratios; others can't.

You Have to Compare

That brings up the most important thing of all: One annual report, one chairman's letter, one ratio won't tell you much. You have to compare. Is the company's debt-to-equity ratio better or worse than it used to be? Better or worse than the industry norms? Better or worse after this recession than it was after the last recession? In company-watching, comparisons are all. They tell you if management is staying on top of things.

Financial analysts work out many other ratios to tell them how the company is doing. You can learn more about them from books on the subject. Ask your librarian.

Each year, companies give you more and more information in their annual reports. Profiting from that information is up to you. I hope you profit from mine.

---

in net income on an equity base of $106,260. (These amounts and those used in calculating the following ratios are taken from Exhibits 17.4 and 17.5.) The ratio (expressed as a percentage) would be

$$\frac{Net\ income}{Owners'\ equity} = \frac{\$43,294}{\$106,260} = 40.74\%$$

In this case, for every dollar of equity, the company made about 40 cents in net income in 1995. How good is this particular return on investment? Very high, although there is no agreed-on ideal. For the most part, managers and investors evaluate return on investment by comparing it with the ratios for similar businesses and with the company's own past performance.

Return on sales, or net profit margin—the net income a business makes per unit of sales—is another important indicator of profitability. It is determined by comparing net income to net sales. For Sweet Dreams, the ratio would be set up as follows:

return on sales *Ratio between net income and net sales; also known as* net profit margin

$$\frac{Net\ income}{Net\ sales} = \frac{\$43,294}{\$474,014} = 9.13\%$$

Sweet Dreams's return on sales of 9.13 percent indicates that just over 9 cents of every dollar earned is profit. When compared with the percentages of other companies in the same business, this figure may give a potential investor a valuable warning of inefficiency—or reassurance that the business is doing well. In this case, Sweet Dreams is above average. Most companies in the ice cream business average a return on sales of only 2.0 to 3.5 percent.[14]

Earnings per share is a measure of how much profit a company earns for each share of stock outstanding. Managers and investors are particularly interested in this ratio because it shows the company's ability to build up the business and pay dividends. The earnings per share for Sweet Dreams is calculated as follows:

$$\frac{Net\ income\ after\ taxes}{\substack{Number\ of\ shares\ of \\ common\ stock\ outstanding}} = \frac{\$36,800}{10,000\ shares} = \$3.68\ per\ share$$

In other words, if the company were to distribute all its earnings to shareholders, each one would get $3.68 per share for 1995.

You may have difficulty comparing one company's earnings per share with another's because the figure depends on both net income after taxes and the number of shares of stock outstanding. The best way to compare is to look at the growth in earnings per share over the past five years. If company A's earnings per share have grown at an annual rate of 10 percent and company B's have grown by only 6 percent, you may conclude that company A's profit growth is stronger, even if company B's earnings per share show a higher absolute number.

Liquidity Ratios. A company's ability to pay its short-term obligations is indicated by **liquidity ratios.** As you might expect, lenders and creditors are keenly interested in liquidity measures. Liquidity can be judged on the basis of working capital, the current ratio, and the quick ratio.

earnings per share *Measure of a company's profitability for each share of outstanding stock, calculated by dividing net income after taxes by shares of common stock outstanding*

liquidity ratios *Financial ratios that indicate how quickly a company can repay short-term obligations*

Bankers are particularly interested in the financial results of the companies that have borrowed money from them. They regularly meet with company owners and executives to assess the borrower's financial performance through ratio analysis.

A company's **working capital**—current assets minus current liabilities—reflects the resources (provided by investors and long-term creditors) that the company has invested in its current assets. Because it represents current assets remaining after payment of all current liabilities, working capital is an indicator of liquidity. The dollar amount of working capital can be misleading, however. For example, it may include the value of slow-moving inventory items that cannot be used to help pay a company's short-term debts.

A different picture of the company's liquidity is provided by the **current ratio**—current assets divided by current liabilities. On December 31, 1995, Sweet Dreams had current assets of $84,925 and current liabilities of $52,675. The current ratio would be calculated as follows:

$$\frac{Current\ assets}{Current\ liabilities} = \frac{\$84,925}{\$52,675} = 1.61$$

Sweet Dreams has $1.61 of current assets to meet every dollar of short-term liabilities. How safe is this ratio? To answer the question, analysts compare a company's current ratio with the average for the particular type of business. As a rule, however, a company with a current ratio of at least 2.0 is considered a safe risk for short-term credit. If the ratio is less than 1.5, a company may have to stretch so far to pay its debts that it won't have anything left to reinvest in the business.

The **quick ratio,** also called the *acid-test ratio,* is another, more conservative measure of a company's ability to meet its short-term debts with cash, marketable securities, and receivables. Some analysts consider it a better indicator of the ability to pay immediate debts than the current ratio because the quick ratio leaves out inventories. The quick ratio for Sweet Dreams would be calculated as follows:

$$\frac{Cash + marketable\ securities + accounts\ receivable + notes\ receivable}{Current\ liabilities}$$

$$= \frac{\$22,790 + \$4,200 + \$19,350 + \$21,500}{\$52,675} = \frac{\$67,840}{\$52,675} = 1.29$$

Analysts consider a quick ratio of 1.0 to be reasonable, so Sweet Dreams is in good shape. If the company needed cash and inventory was moving slowly, this ratio shows that it would have $1.29 to meet each dollar of current debt.

Activity Ratios. A number of **activity ratios** may be used to analyze how well a company is managing its assets. The most commonly used is the **inventory turnover ratio,** which tells potential investors how fast the company's inventory is turned into sales. The quicker the better is the general rule. This ratio is computed by dividing the cost of goods sold by the average value of inventory for a period. Where inventories are fairly constant, an average of the beginning inventory and the ending inventory would be accurate enough. If inventories fluctuate widely during the year, all month-end inventories for the year should be averaged. Sweet Dreams's inventory is more or less constant, so its turnover ratio is calculated as follows:

working capital *Current assets minus current liabilities*

current ratio *Measure of a company's short-term liquidity, calculated by dividing current assets by current liabilities*

quick ratio *Measure of a company's short-term liquidity, calculated by adding cash, marketable securities, and receivables, and then dividing that sum by current liabilities; also known as the acid-test ratio*

activity ratios *Financial ratios that indicate how well a company is managing its assets*

inventory turnover ratio *Measure of the time a company takes to turn its inventory into sales, calculated by dividing cost of goods sold by the average value of inventory for a period*

$$\frac{Cost\ of\ goods\ sold}{(Beginning\ inventory\ +\ ending\ inventory)/2}$$

$$= \frac{\$190,755}{(\$10,473 + \$12,685)/2} = \frac{\$190,755}{\$11,579} = 16.47$$

This ratio means that Sweet Dreams's average inventory is converted (turned over) into sales 16.47 times per year, or approximately once every 22 days (365 days divided by 16.47). A potential investor would be interested in this information because it demonstrates that the company converts its average monthly inventory into receivables fairly quickly. This information, combined with the turnover ratio for accounts receivable, enables users of financial statements to analyze the company's cash flow (liquidity) and its managerial efficiency. The "ideal" turnover ratio varies with the type of operation. A grocery store's turnover ratio, for example, would be around 16. A yarn shop, in contrast, would turn over its inventory about 3.0 to 3.5 times per year.

Debt Ratios. You can measure a company's ability to pay its long-term debts by calculating the **debt ratios,** or coverage ratios. Lenders look at these ratios to determine whether the potential borrower has put enough money into the business to serve as a protective cushion for the loan.

The **debt-to-equity ratio** indicates the extent to which a business is financed by debt as opposed to invested capital (equity). From the lender's standpoint, the lower this ratio, the safer the company, because the company has less existing debt and may be able to repay additional money it wants to borrow. However, a company that is conservative in its long-term borrowing is not necessarily well managed; often a low level of debt is associated with a low growth rate. The debt-to-equity ratio for Sweet Dreams is

$$\frac{Total\ liabilities}{Stockholders'\ (owners')\ equity} = \frac{\$106,425}{\$106,260} = 1.00$$

In other words, creditors have lent the company one dollar for each dollar of equity. A debt-to-equity ratio above 1.0 indicates that debts exceed equity and thus the business may be relying too heavily on debt.

The **debt-to-total-assets ratio** also serves as a simple measure of a company's ability to carry long-term debt. As a rule of thumb, the amount of debt should not exceed 50 percent of the value of total assets. For Sweet Dreams, this ratio is

$$\frac{Total\ liabilities}{Total\ assets} = \frac{\$106,425}{\$212,685} = 0.50$$

For every dollar of assets, then, the company carries only 50 cents of debt—which matches the 50 percent debt-to-assets guideline.

However, this ratio, like the others, is not a magic formula. Even companies whose financial ratios indicate straight A's may suddenly develop unexpected problems. Like grades on a report card, ratios are clues to performance. Managers, creditors, lenders, and investors can use them to get a fairly accurate idea of how a company is doing.

debt ratios *Financial ratios that indicate the extent of a company's burden of long-term debt; (sometimes called coverage ratios)*

debt-to-equity ratio *Measure of the extent to which a business is financed by debt as opposed to invested capital, calculated by dividing the company's total liabilities by owners' equity*

debt-to-total-assets ratio *Measure of a company's ability to carry long-term debt, calculated by dividing total liabilities by total assets*

1 Describe the importance of accounting information to managers, investors, creditors, and government agencies.

Accounting information helps managers make business decisions and spot problems and opportunities; provides investors, suppliers, and creditors with the means to analyze a business; and supports the government's efforts to collect taxes and regulate business.

2 Distinguish between public and private accountants.

Public accountants operate independently of the businesses they serve, and they monitor the businesses' financial statements. Private accountants serve a single business in one of a number of specialized areas.

3 State the basic accounting equation.

Assets = liabilities + owners' equity is the basic accounting equation.

4 Explain the purpose of the balance sheet and identify its three main sections.

The balance sheet provides a snapshot of the business at a particular point in time. Its main sections are assets, liabilities, and owners' equity.

5 Explain the purpose of an income statement and identify its three main components.

The income statement reflects the results of operations over a period of time. Its main components are revenues, expenses, and net income or loss.

6 Explain the purpose of the statement of cash flows.

The statement of cash flows summarizes how a company's cash was received and spent in three areas: operations, investments, and financing.

7 Identify five areas in which accountants have discretion in their methods and assumptions.

The five areas where accountants have the most latitude are in the timing of revenue recognition, the choice of a depreciation method, the choice of an inventory-valuation method, the determination of allowances, and the method of disclosing extraordinary or unusual items.

8 List the four main categories of financial ratios.

Most of the important ratios fall into one of four categories: profitability ratios, liquidity ratios, activity ratios, and debt ratios.

When people at Roseville Networks Division of Hewlett-Packard began resenting the accounting department, it was because they weren't getting the information from accounting that they needed and because they had to give so much seemingly useless information back to accounting. However, Debbie Berlant and RND's cost accounting manager, Reese Browning, refused to let things stay as they were. Initially motivated to eliminate unnecessary measurements, Berlant and Browning decided to rethink their internal cost accounting system to provide the other departments with information that would be useful.

They agreed on three goals. They wanted their new system to (1) reflect manufacturing costs accurately, (2) use data that manufacturing and other departments could collect easily, and (3) meet the legal and practical needs of the accounting function. The key was learning what truly drives costs.

First, they had to decide which costs to trace. Eventually, they eliminated direct labor as a separate category and combined it with overhead. They discovered that direct labor made up only 2 percent of total manufacturing costs, but the old system had spent a lot of time tracking it.

They also found that they didn't really need production to track and charge its time on every task. They

had to decide which categories of manufacturing overhead they would use, ending up with procurement overhead, production overhead, and support overhead. Then, within these categories, they separated the important activities and, with the help of people in every department, narrowly defined each activity.

Finally, they had to decide what factors were actually driving the costs for the various activities they had defined, which was "really just a matter of talking to the people on the factory floor," say Berlant and Browning. "We recognize that costs cannot be traced with surgical precision. But we're convinced that at least for now, we have found cost drivers that produce more accurate product costs than before."

With the new accounting system in place, RND's personnel understand more fully the processes of manufacturing as well as what drives the related costs. People no longer argue about how cost is determined, and they continue to suggest ways for improving the accounting system, which means it just gets better and better. In RND's competitive computer market, accurate and timely cost information is crucial. Finally, accounting and every other department at RND are getting numbers and information they can trust.

Your Mission: As a member of Roseville Networks Division accounting department, you are expected to contribute your own ideas on how to continue fine-tuning the cost accounting system and all activities of your department.

1. Management wants to find the best way to record the revenues from a new line of customized software products. The marketing department says customers shouldn't pay for the software until they are satisfied that it meets their needs. If it turns out that the software can't meet their needs, customers don't have to pay at all. When should you record the revenue

from these sales? Choose the best answer from the following proposals:

a. It's your job to make the financial picture look as bright as possible. As soon as a sale looks likely, you should record it. If the customer decides not to order, you can just go back and erase that sale.

b. You should wait until after the customer has ordered and the software installation team is confident that the product is going to work. This method is less risky than (a), and you can always set aside a small reserve to cover those situations that don't work out.

c. You don't want to mislead management or stockholders, so you should not record a sale until you actually have the customer's money. There is too much risk of accounting errors caused by customers who decide not to pay.

2. In an effort to optimize the effect of inventory on cost, Berlant is considering changing the way the cost of goods is currently calculated. She asks you to evaluate the FIFO and LIFO methods. Which method should RND use?

a. If Berlant wants to change the method of calculating cost of goods sold, she must want to lower the company's earnings to save tax dollars. You recommend the LIFO method because it results in less profit and saves taxes.

b. Berlant's interest in changing the method of pricing inventory must mean that she's worried about showing the highest profits possible. Inflation is low, so you don't have to worry about RND being taxed on "phantom" profits. You conclude that RND should use FIFO so that profits will be higher.

c. Your research reveals that neither FIFO nor LIFO is really better. However, using one or the other can affect what profits look like and how much RND must pay in taxes. You recommend that Berlant use LIFO if she believes that saving money in taxes is more important than showing the highest profit possible. However, if Berlant believes that profits are more important than saving money on taxes, you recommend that FIFO be used.

3. RND wants to make an acquisition, and you are asked to evaluate the financial results of the three companies under consideration. You find the following negative information in the firms' annual reports going back several years. Which company do you think is in the *worst* financial shape?

a. Company A didn't grow at all in the last year. The report says that this lack of growth was the result of a short-term recession in the company's major markets. However, the company didn't lose any market share and was able to keep sales strong.

b. Company B grew in the last year by dropping prices 10 percent below those of the competition to build sales, even though this strategy caused a loss for the year. You discover that the company has reported losses for many years, even when its prices were higher than average.

c. Company C's sales grew slightly faster than inflation, and its market share grew slightly as well. However, you note that both of these increases resulted from a key competitor's bankruptcy a year and a half earlier.

4. Berlant wants you to analyze current financial records to discover how efficiently RND is using its assets. Which method should you use?

a. Use trend analysis because it allows you to compare your figures over time. If you allow for corre-

sponding changes in the value of the dollar, you should come up with a good picture of how RND uses its assets.

b. Use return on investment because it will show the income RND generates per dollar of investment. By comparing your figures with those of other companies, you can estimate how well RND is using its assets.

c. Use the inventory turnover ratio because it shows how fast the company's inventory is turned into sales. Depending on how inventories fluctuate, you can either average the beginning and ending inventory or average all month-end inventories for the year.[15]

KEY TERMS

accounting (506)
accounting equation (512)
accrual basis (518)
activity ratios (529)
amortization (516)
assets (511)
audit (508)
balance sheet (513)
bookkeeping (510)
budget (507)
calendar year (514)
cash basis (519)
certified management accountants (CMAs) (510)
certified public accountants (CPAs) (508)
controller (510)
cost of goods sold (519)
creditors (508)
current assets (515)
current liabilities (516)
current ratio (529)
debt ratios (530)

debt-to-equity ratio (530)
debt-to-total-assets ratio (530)
debtors (508)
depreciation (516)
double-entry bookkeeping (512)
earnings per share (528)
expenses (517)
FIFO (523)
financial accounting (507)
fiscal year (514)
fixed assets (515)
general expenses (519)
generally accepted accounting principles (GAAP) (507)
goodwill (516)
gross profit (521)
gross sales (519)
income statement (517)
intangible assets (516)
internal auditors (510)
inventory turnover ratio (529)
liabilities (511)
LIFO (523)

liquidity ratios (528)
long-term liabilities (517)
management accounting (507)
net income (517)
net sales (519)
operating expenses (519)
operating income (521)
owners' equity (511)
private accountants (509)
profitability ratios (526)
public accountants (508)
quick ratio (529)
ratio analysis (525)
retained earnings (513)
return on investment (ROI) (526)
return on sales (527)
revenues (517)
selling expenses (519)
statement of cash flows (521)
trend analysis (525)
unfunded pension liabilities (524)
working capital (529)

1. What is the difference between financial accounting and management accounting? Between a public accountant and a private accountant?
2. What factors affect the reliability of accounting information?
3. Why is it important that the two sides of the accounting equation be kept in balance?
4. What are the three types of assets and the two types of liabilities listed on a balance sheet?
5. What is the difference between an income statement and a balance sheet?
6. How is net income calculated?
7. What is the difference between FIFO and LIFO, and which produces the lower profit figure in times of high inflation?
8. What are the three main profitability ratios, and how is each calculated?

A CASE FOR CRITICAL THINKING

GOING TO THE CLEANERS

After years of dreaming about owning your own business, you decide that a dry-cleaning business would be perfect. Luckily for you, two establishments happen to be for sale—at the same price and in equally attractive locations. You manage to get enough financial data to compare the year-end condition of the two companies, as shown in Exhibit 17.7. Study the numbers carefully; your livelihood depends on choosing wisely between the two.

1. What factors should you consider before deciding which company to buy? What additional data might be helpful to you? (Note that net income is implied.)

2. What questions should you ask about the methods used to record revenues and equipment depreciation?

3. On the basis of the data provided, which company would you purchase? Detail the process you use to make your decision.

Exhibit 17.7
Financial Data for Two Companies
December 31, 1995, year-end balance sheet.

	Ajax Services, Inc.	Mallard Cleaners, Inc.
ASSETS		
Cash	$10,000	$ 25,000
Accounts receivable	2,000	4,000
Cleaning equipment	50,000	80,000
Office equipment	11,000	18,000
Supplies	22,000	34,000
TOTAL ASSETS	$95,000	$161,000
LIABILITIES AND OWNERS' EQUITY		
Accounts payable	$21,000	$ 38,000
Bank loans payable	49,000	68,000
Owners' equity	25,000	55,000
TOTAL LIABILITIES AND OWNERS' EQUITY	$95,000	$161,000
Personal withdrawals from cash during 1995	$40,000	$ 38,000
Owners' investments in business during 1995	$16,000	$ 32,000
Capital balances for each business on January 1, 1995	$30,000	$ 12,000

Obtain a copy of the annual report of a business, and with three or four other students, examine what the report shows about finances and current operations. In addition to other chapter material, use the information in "How to Read an Annual Report" on pages 526–527 as a guideline for understanding the annual report's content.

• Consider the statements made by the CEO regarding the past year: Did the company do well, or are changes in operations necessary to its future well-being? What are the projections for future growth in sales and profits?

• Examine the financial summaries for information about the fiscal condition of the company: Did the company show a profit?
• If possible, obtain a copy of the company's annual report from the previous year, and compare it with the current report to determine whether past projections were accurate.
• Prepare a brief written summary of your conclusions.

Select an article from *The Wall Street Journal* that discusses the quarterly or year-end performance of a company that industry analysts consider notable for either positive or negative reasons.

1. Did the company report a profit or a loss for this accounting period? What other performance indicators were reported? Did the company's performance represent an improvement over previous accounting periods?
2. What, according to the article, was the significance of this performance? Did it match industry analysts' expectations, or was it a surprise?
3. What reasons were given for the company's improvement or decline in performance?

Expanding the World of Computers

 You are the president of a desktop-publishing company that provides services to small businesses across the United States. You've risen to the top of a fragmented market by offering quality service at reasonable prices. One key to those reasonable prices has been your policy of hiring people who own home computers and are active users of their machines. These employees cost less for you to train, and they tend to keep up on current technology without much prodding from you. Part of the money you save on training goes back into bet-

ter benefits and higher wages. In short, their personal interests overlap your business interests, so everybody wins.

An international business consultant has warned you not to expect the same scenario as you expand overseas. So far, computer companies have had less success penetrating the home market of many other countries, so you'll find fewer experienced home-computer users to hire as employees. In addition, businesses in some companies have not been as quick to adopt personal computers, so many people aren't getting on-the-job training either.

The strategy you've adopted for expansion is simple. Rather than change your business model and switch to more intensive (and expen-

sive) employee training, you decide to expand only as quickly as the numbers of experienced computer users increase from country to country.

Find as much information as you can about home and business use of personal computers in the following countries:

- Japan
- Hong Kong
- India
- England

Now, strictly on the basis of your information about the home and business use of personal computers, decide the order in which you will expand into these countries.

JUST HOW ACCOUNTABLE ARE THOSE ACCOUNTING NUMBERS, ANYWAY?

Synopsis

One of the most important issues in corporate finance is placing a value on a company. Managers inside the company need to know how much the company is worth for several reasons, including judging how well they're handling the company's assets. People outside the company, particularly investors, need to know how much the company is worth so that they have some idea of exactly what it is that they're investing in. As this video shows, valuing a company isn't quite as simple as you might think; you can't just walk around with the calculator and add up the value of the company's buildings, machinery, office furniture, and so on—the machinery might be gasping its last breath, for instance, making it far less valuable than brand new equipment. You can't just add up the price of all the company's stock, either; the video points out that stock prices usually far outpace book value, which represents the best estimate of the company's tangible value.

Exercises

ANALYSIS

1. What role should intangibles, such as brand names and customer goodwill, play when you are placing a value on a company?

2. Does computing book value fall under the umbrella of financial accounting or management accounting?

3. If a company paid off its debts with cash that it had sitting in the bank, would this action change the shareholders' equity?

4. Why do companies usually try to keep their debt burdens as low as possible?

5. You saw in the video that Gillette had a large portion of its total assets tied up in inventory; shouldn't it try to reduce the size of this inventory?

APPLICATION

Compute your own net worth, using the process shown in the video: add up all your assets; then subtract all your liabilities (debts). (For the sake of privacy, feel free to omit any items that you might not want discussed in class; but don't worry about the magnitude of your net worth—nobody expects college students to be wealthy.)

DECISION

When you computed your net worth in the Application exercise, how did you arrive at figures for clothes, car, and other personal belongings?

COMMUNICATION

Find a recent article that describes a stock that has dropped in price dramatically. Pretend that you're the CEO of this company, and write a letter to shareholders explaining the sudden drop.

INTEGRATION

Referring to the discussion of insider trading in Chapter 3, list some situations in which company insiders could be in a position to benefit from insider trading.

ETHICS

In terms of disclosing your company's financial health to investors, how far is far enough? For instance, suppose you know that a major customer is about to switch to one of your competitors. Would you be obligated to tell your shareholders?

DEBATE

When people buy shares in a company, they are basically betting that management will follow a sensible plan for reaching the company's goals. Option A: In a formal debate format, argue for or against the suggestion that management should have to reveal its strategic plans to investors. Option B: Take either position and state your case in a brief report.

TEAMWORK

In a team of three or four students, obtain a company's annual report and compare the chairperson's letter to shareholders with both the financial data contained in the report (see "How to Read an Annual Report" in the chapter) and any recent news that you can find about the company. Does the chairperson's letter reflect what you've seen elsewhere?

RESEARCH

Do the research necessary to write a one-paragraph update on either (a) recent news that has affected Gillette's stock price or (b) any recent changes in accounting rules that have affected what information companies must tell shareholders.

ROLE PLAYING

Two students play the role of an investment-adviser team, and two others play customers who just received a "great tip" from a friend about a certain stock. The advisers should explain to the customers what they need to do in order to evaluate the stock.

Chapter

18

Money and Banking

LEARNING OBJECTIVES
After studying this chapter, you will be able to

1 Name three functions of money

2 Differentiate between demand deposits and time deposits

3 Distinguish M1 from the total money supply

4 Identify nine members of the banking system

5 Explain the effects of bank deregulation and interstate banking legislation

6 Discuss the responsibilities and insurance methods of the FDIC

7 Describe the organization of the Federal Reserve System

8 Cite the four ways the Federal Reserve System regulates the money supply

Building the Bank of the Future

Hugh L. McColl, Jr., the CEO of North Carolina–based NCNB, didn't need a crystal ball to see that the future of the U.S. banking system would be quite different from its past. For decades bankers and financiers had operated according to federal and state laws and regulations that defined neat cubbyholes for all players: Savings and loans made home loans, commercial banks made business and consumer loans, investment banks financed the stock offerings of public companies, and securities brokerages sold stocks and bonds. They were all regulated, with ceilings on interest paid and fees charged, and in return, they were safe from competition.

This well-ordered system was thrown into chaos when deregulation, globalization, and technological innovation forced everyone to compete. No one was better prepared for the new climate than McColl, a brusque ex-Marine who loved a good fight and approached his job as if he were leading troops into battle. In his view, the banking industry would eventually be dominated by a few superbanks with branch systems spread coast to coast. These superbanks, he believed, would make money by reducing costs through economies of scale and by providing a wide array of services to customers of all types. They would court a broad customer base—foreign corporations, mom-and-pop businesses, wealthy individuals, and blue-collar families—with a sweeping range of banking and financing services. Within this vision of the future, McColl could see his bank's role not as NCNB, a strong regional bank, but as NationsBank, a superbank prepared to do business throughout the country.

Once a regional Southern bank, NCNB has been transformed into NationsBank, a nationwide bank.

At the time, the prospect of NCNB's becoming a superbank seemed unlikely, even though it was a strong regional bank with branches in North Carolina, South Carolina, and Florida. McColl tried for years to acquire crosstown rival Citizens and Southern (C&S), but C&S escaped by merging with Sovran Financial Corporation of Virginia. Although NCNB continued to buy small Southern banks, it still wasn't ready to move into the ranks of the superbanks.

McColl's challenge was to find a way to make NCNB into one

of the nation's largest banks—or watch it disappear into the structure of an even more aggressive competitor during the next major wave of mergers and acquisitions. How could he transform his bank from NCNB, a regional bank serving the South, into NationsBank, a national institution? Would he be able to take advantage of the financial woes of other industry players by buying a troubled bank or thrift cheaply so that he could build a larger customer base? How could he make the most of the turmoil caused by deregulation and the desire of regulators to keep commercial banks from buckling under the weight of bad loans, which had toppled so many savings and loan institutions?[1]

THE NATURE OF MONEY

NationsBank is only one of many banks that are changing with the times. As never before, the business of money has entered a new era. **Money** is anything generally accepted as a means of paying for goods and services. Before it was invented, people got what they needed by trading their services or possessions; in some primitive societies, this system of trading, or bartering, still prevails. However, barter is inconvenient and impractical in a modern industrial society, where many of the things we want are intangible or require the combined work of many people. For example, how would you buy an airplane ticket if all you had to offer in exchange was milk from the family cow? How much milk would the ticket cost? Of the many people involved in running an airline, who would you pay? What if none of them liked milk? What if the milk spoiled before you saved enough to pay for the ticket?

Functions and Characteristics of Money

Completing an exchange between buyer and seller is easier when money is used. No matter what the exchange, money performs three main functions:

- *Money serves as a medium of exchange.* Money is a tool for simplifying transactions between buyers and sellers. With money in your pocket, you can go to a travel agent or an airline counter and buy a ticket.
- *Money serves as a measure of value.* You don't have to negotiate the relative worth of dissimilar items every time you buy something, as you would if you were bartering milk for airline tickets. The value of the ticket is stated in dollars, and what you exchange is measured in the same terms. Because of this common denominator, you can easily compare your ability to pay with the price of the item.
- *Money serves as a store of value.* Unlike many goods, it will keep. You can put it in your pocket until you need it, or you can deposit it in a bank.

Any object can be used as money, but some items serve better than others. Societies using cattle as money have had problems with purchases costing half a cow and with savings being wiped out by hoof-

money *Anything used by a society as a token of value in buying and selling goods and services*

and-mouth disease. Salt served well as money for the Romans because it was hard to come by in those times (the word *salary* comes from the Latin word for salt). To be used as a medium of exchange, money should be relatively durable—able to be passed between many buyers and sellers without quickly falling apart. It should also be easy to divide into smaller amounts to make purchases of various sizes. Another important characteristic of money is that it should be easy to carry. Unlike a cow or a gallon of milk, paper money and coins can easily be brought along to make a purchase.

In addition, most societies have designed and produced money so that it is difficult to copy, or counterfeit. One of the reasons money is valuable is that it is scarce (it would lose value if people could simply make more of it whenever they wanted), and making it difficult to counterfeit helps assure the money's legitimacy. Also, money must have the characteristic of liquidity, enabling people to convert it into other forms of wealth relatively quickly.

Finally, the value of money needs to be fairly stable. If it fluctuates wildly, or loses value because of extremely high inflation, people may turn to other items, such as precious metals, as a more stable store of value. Another way people respond to instability in the value of money is to switch to barter. Soaring inflation in Russia since the breakup of the Soviet Union has pushed many individuals and companies to trade for goods or services rather than accept money in payment. As inflation slows—it dropped to 4.6 percent a month recently, compared with 29 percent a month during the year before—people will return to money as the medium of exchange.[2]

The Money Supply

In the United States today, the money supply consists of three major components that each fulfill the functions of money as described above. These components are currency, demand deposits, and time deposits.

Currency

currency *Bills and coins that make up the cash money of a society*

Currency refers to both bills (paper money) and coins. One study, completed a few years ago, estimated that roughly $171 billion in U.S. currency is floating around, although officials don't know exactly where it all is. At any given time, most adults have about $100 in cash, for a total of $18 billion, which is only a fraction of all the currency believed to be in circulation. Businesses also keep cash on hand, and children hoard coins in their piggy banks. The rest of the currency—about 75 percent—is officially unaccounted for, although some has certainly made its way overseas. Undoubtedly, part of it is circulating in the underground economy, the segment of the economy that is not reflected in official GDP reports.[3]

checks *Written orders that tell the customer's bank to pay a specific amount to a particular individual or business*

Cashier's checks, money orders, and traveler's checks are also considered currency. They may be purchased from a bank for their face value plus a small fee. These checks differ from a customer's business or personal checks because checks purchased from a bank are payable from the funds of the bank itself, rather than from a business or personal account.

payee *Person or business a check is made out to*

demand deposit *Money in a checking account that can be used by the customer at any time*

Demand Deposits

debit cards *Plastic cards that allow the bank to take money from the user's demand-deposit account and transfer it to a retailer's account*

Although cash has its advantages, businesses and individuals alike appreciate the convenience of **checks,** written orders that direct the customer's bank to pay the stated amount of money to the check writer or to someone else. The idea of checks originated in the Middle Ages, when gold was the only widely accepted form of payment. Because traveling merchants found gold bulky and dangerous to carry, banks emerged to issue documents that would be honored abroad against a gold deposit that would remain at home.

automated teller machines (ATMs) *Electronic terminals that permit people with plastic cards to perform simple banking transactions 24 hours a day without the aid of a human teller*

With the checking accounts of today, a customer deposits money in an account and is given a book of checks. When the customer wants to pay someone, he or she writes and signs a check, making it out to the **payee,** the business or person indicated. Because the money in the customer's account is available immediately (on demand), this type of account is known as a **demand deposit.** (However, the bank may refuse to honor the check if the account is overdrawn—that is, if the customer's account lacks sufficient funds.)

Automated teller machines (ATMs) allow customers to perform certain bank transactions 24 hours a day in places other than a branch. This ATM, installed in the food court of a shopping mall, offers customers the convenience of banking where they shop.

Demand deposits are widely used: Eighty-three percent of all U.S. households have checking accounts. Companies and individuals draw on the funds in these accounts by writing approximately 55 billion checks every year.[4] In addition, people can pay for purchases at many stores and gasoline stations by using **debit cards,** plastic cards that authorize the bank to transfer money from the customer's demand deposit account to the retailer's account. Another convenient way to move money into or out of a demand deposit account at any time is through **automated teller machines (ATMs),** electronic self-service terminals that allow customers to handle simple banking transactions at any hour of the

day or night, using a plastic card. These ATMs can do about 60 percent of a teller's job at less than half the cost of a human teller.[5]

Time Deposits

A large portion of the money supply is held in **time deposits,** accounts that pay interest and restrict the owner's right to withdraw funds on short notice. They include savings accounts, certificates of deposit (CDs), and money-market deposit accounts. The rate of interest for CDs is fixed for specified periods, whereas money-market accounts pay interest that may fluctuate daily for as long as the money remains on deposit. Banks require some advance notice before a customer is allowed to withdraw money from these accounts, which is why they are called time deposits. Because a time deposit is not payable on demand (although some money-market accounts offer limited check-writing privileges), it's less liquid than a demand deposit.

time deposits Bank accounts that pay interest and require advance notice before money can be withdrawn

Measures of the Money Supply

Oddly enough, nobody knows precisely how much money there is, although the federal government has a rough idea. When it measures the money supply, it looks at various combinations of currency, demand deposits, and time deposits (see Exhibit 18.1). The narrowest commonly used measure of money, known as **M1,** consists of currency and demand deposits. All the money defined as M1 can be used as a medium of exchange. **M2,** a broader measure of the money supply, includes time deposits as well. As discussed later in the chapter, the money supply is regulated by the Federal Reserve Board.

M1 That portion of the money supply consisting of currency and demand deposits

M2 That portion of the money supply consisting of currency, demand deposits, and time deposits

THE U.S BANKING SYSTEM

No matter where in the world you live, work, or travel, you'll find that a banking system has developed to provide individuals and businesses with a wide range of financial services. In the United States, the banking system consists of more than 25,000 institutions.

Members of the System

Money goes round and round: Individuals receive money in the form of salaries and wages, which they spend on goods and services. This

Currency $321 billion

Demand deposits $807 billion

Time deposits $2,438 billion

Currency $321 billion + Demand deposits $807 billion = Total M1 $1,128 billion

Total M1 $1,128 billion + Time deposits $2,438 billion = Total M2 $3,566 billion

Exhibit 18.1
The Total Money Supply
M1 is a measure of the U.S. money supply that includes currency and demand deposits. M2 is a broader measure that also includes time deposits.

Bank	Assets*
Citicorp	$216,574.0
BankAmerica Corp.	186,933.0
NationsBank Corp.	157,686.0
Chemical Banking Corp.	149,888.0
J.P. Morgan & Co.	133,888.0
Chase Manhattan Corp.	102,103.0
Bankers Trust N.Y. Corp.	92,082.0
Banc One Corp.	79,918.6
First Union Corp.	70,787.0
PNC Bank Corp.	62,080.0

*1993 data.

Exhibit 18.2
The 10 Largest U.S. Banks
These 10 U.S. banks provide deposit and loan functions for millions of businesses and individuals. NationsBank and several other institutions have gained a wider base of customers and deposits by merging with other banks or taking over the operations of troubled banks.

---

commercial banks *Traditional banks offering savings, checking, and loan services*

national banks *Banks chartered by the federal government*

state banks *Banks chartered by a state government*

savings and loan associations (S&Ls) *Banks offering savings, interest-bearing checking, and mortgages*

savings banks *Mostly in New England, banks offering interest-bearing checking, savings, and mortgages*

credit unions *Cooperative financial institutions that provide loan and savings services to their members*

finance companies *Companies that specialize in making loans*

process of moving money from person to person and business to business is facilitated by a network of financial institutions. Commercial banks are the main source of banking services for many businesses and individuals.

Commercial Banks

Commercial banks are profit-making organizations that accept deposits and use these funds to make loans. As long as the return on loans exceeds both expenses and the interest paid on deposits, banks make a profit. Commercial banks have traditionally been a key source of capital for businesses, but finance companies and other nonbank lenders have taken much of the banks' share of short-term business loans.[6] Commercial banks also provide loans and checking, time deposit, and credit-card accounts to individuals.

Commercial banks are of two types: **national banks** chartered by the federal government and **state banks** chartered by state governments. Competitive pressures have been reducing the number of both types, but currently some 4,065 national banks and 8,445 state banks operate in the United States. All national banks are members of the Federal Reserve System, whereas about 90 percent of state banks are members.[7] The 10 largest U.S. commercial banks are shown in Exhibit 18.2.

Thrift Institutions

Savings and loan associations, commonly known as S&Ls, are financial institutions that offer personal checking and savings accounts and use these deposits as the basis of home mortgage loans. **Savings banks,** which are located mostly in New England, generally provide the same services as S&Ls. Both types of "thrift" institutions have historically encouraged people to put money into savings accounts. They have also served as the primary source of home loans. However, changes in banking laws and the rash of S&L failures during the late 1980s provoked a large-scale consolidation of the industry that continues today. Today, only about 2,240 thrifts remain in business.[8]

Credit Unions

Credit unions are nonprofit, member-owned cooperatives that offer personal checking and savings accounts, credit cards, and consumer loans. All 13,500 credit unions were formed by people with a "common bond," usually an employer, union, or similar organization.[9] Some of these institutions are able to provide credit on favorable terms, mainly because of their nonprofit status.

Other Financial Institutions

A variety of other institutions provide selected banking services to businesses and individuals:

- *Finance companies* are companies that offer short-term loans to businesses or individuals but do not accept deposits. In general, finance companies charge high rates of interest because they are willing to provide loans to higher-risk customers who cannot obtain financing elsewhere. Led by General Motors Acceptance Corporation (GMAC), GE Capital, and Ford Motor Credit, finance companies have increasingly taken market share from banks. Finance companies now provide nearly 80 percent of all commercial business loans and 20 percent of all car loans and credit-card loans made to individuals.[10]

- *Limited-service banks,* also known as nonbank banks, are hybrid organizations that mix other businesses with certain banking functions. Despite their name, they are anything but limited, often offering a mix of stock-brokerage, insurance, real estate, mortgage, banking, and credit services. They are limited in only one respect: They may make commercial loans or they may accept demand deposits, but they may not do both.
- *Large brokerage houses* such as Merrill Lynch have joined the club by expanding beyond the business of selling securities and moving into related financial services. Many now offer personal loans as well as combination savings and checking accounts paying attractive interest rates.
- *Insurance companies* use part of the money they receive in premiums from policyholders to provide long-term financing for corporations and commercial real estate developers.
- *Pension funds* are large pools of money created to provide retirement income for an organization's members. Pension-fund managers invest the money in various ways: business loans, commercial real estate mortgages, government bonds, and corporate securities.
- **Investment banks,** also known as underwriters, are specialized institutions that help corporations raise capital. When a company decides to issue new stocks or bonds, the investment bank buys the entire issue and then resells the securities to the public.

What Banks Do

The U.S. banking system provides both businesses and individuals with a wide variety of services. Financial institutions differ in the specific services they provide, but most do two things: They attract deposits and then lend some of the money to other customers. In addition, many offer other money-handling services, for which customers usually pay a fee.

Deposit Functions

Thanks to changes in U.S. banking regulations, the line between checking and savings accounts has blurred. Banks and thrifts now vie for depositors by offering a bewildering array of options featuring various combinations of privileges, fees, and interest rates. Even though banks are feeling increased competition from nonbanks eager to make loans, they still hold nearly all deposits in the United States.

Regular checking accounts pay little or no interest, and many banks charge a monthly service fee as well as a small fee for every check cashed. Basic savings accounts pay a modest interest rate and do not allow check writing. Several types of hybrid accounts combine fea-

investment banks *Financial institutions that specialize in helping companies or government agencies raise funds;* *also known as* underwriters

NOW account *Interest-bearing negotiable order of withdrawal account with a minimum-balance requirement*

super NOW account *Interest-bearing negotiable order of withdrawal account with a relatively high minimum-balance requirement*

money-market deposit accounts *Bank accounts that pay money-market interest rates and permit the depositor to write a limited number of checks*

certificate of deposit (CD) *Note issued by a bank that guarantees to pay the depositor a specific interest rate for a fixed period of time*

individual retirement account (IRA) *Type of savings account that provides tax advantages to depositors who are building a fund for retirement*

Keogh account *Type of retirement savings account for the self-employed that provides tax advantages*

tures of these two traditional accounts. To earn interest on a checking account, for example, you may open a **NOW account,** or negotiable order of withdrawal account, which allows unlimited check writing and pays interest but requires customers to leave a minimum balance in the account. A variation, known as the **super NOW account,** requires an even larger minimum balance but pays higher interest. Funds in **money-market deposit accounts** earn higher rates of interest than demand deposits. However, because these accounts are technically considered time deposits, banks usually limit the number of checks that may be written.

If you are willing to invest more money and lose some liquidity, you may earn higher interest by buying a **certificate of deposit,** or CD, a type of time deposit that requires you to leave your money in the bank for a specified period. The longer you're willing to lock up your money, the higher the interest you'll earn. Bear in mind that nearly every bank will require you to pay a penalty if you want to withdraw your money before the end of the period.

You may also invest up to $2,000 a year ($2,250 for married, single-income couples) in an **individual retirement account,** or IRA, which earns interest that is not taxed until you retire. Some people (depending on their income and pension coverage) can deduct all or part of their IRA contribution from their income taxes. A similar account for self-employed people—a **Keogh account**—has a ceiling of $30,000 a year. However, you'll pay a penalty if you withdraw your money from an IRA or a Keogh account prematurely.

Loan Functions

Once the banks have your money, they combine it with all their other deposits and use it to make loans. Because banks know that all their depositors will not withdraw their funds at one time, they can lend a majority of those funds to borrowers and keep the remainder on reserve. The smaller the percentage of deposits a bank keeps on reserve, the more loans it can make.

In the process of making loans, banks create new money. Say that you apply for a $1,000 business loan. If the bank grants the loan, it permits you to withdraw up to $1,000 from a checking account into which you haven't made any deposits. This loan is in a sense "new" money created by the bank. The government allows banks to create money in this fashion as long as they keep enough cash on hand to meet expected withdrawals by depositors.

What level of reserves is safe? That depends on how many people draw on their accounts at the same time. If many depositors rush to withdraw cash on the same day, the bank may not be able to meet the demand. Such bank runs occurred on a massive scale in the early 1930s. In response, President Franklin D. Roosevelt declared a *bank holiday,* closing all U.S. banks temporarily to avoid widespread panic. Some individual banks have experienced runs since then, but the federal government has guarded against another national catastrophe by requiring banks to hold in reserve a specified portion of their deposits. The reserve requirement for demand deposits varies depending on a particular bank's total amount of demand deposits.

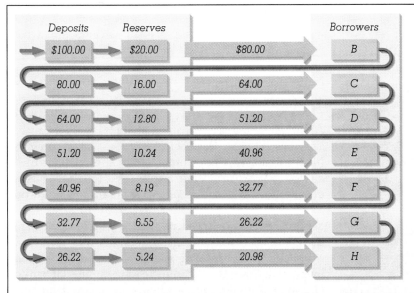

Deposits	Reserves	Borrowers
$100.00	$20.00	$80.00 → B
80.00	16.00	64.00 → C
64.00	12.80	51.20 → D
51.20	10.24	40.96 → E
40.96	8.19	32.77 → F
32.77	6.55	26.22 → G
26.22	5.24	20.98 → H

Exhibit 18.3
How Banks Create Money
Banks stay in business by earning more on interest from loans than they pay out in the form of interest on deposits; they can increase their earnings by "creating" money. When customer A deposits $100, the bank must keep some in reserve but can lend, say, $80 to customer B (and earn interest on that loan). If customer B deposits the borrowed $80 in the same bank, the bank can lend 80 percent of that amount to borrower C. The initial $100 deposit, therefore, creates a much larger pool of funds from which customer loans may be made.

The impact of the reserve requirement is greater than meets the eye. Imagine an island with only one bank, which has a 20 percent reserve requirement. Someone deposits $100 in the bank. The bank could make a loan of $80 from that deposit. Now say that the borrower of that $80 deposits it in a checking account at the bank (see Exhibit 18.3). The bank would be required to reserve 20 percent of that new account, or $16, but could lend the other $64. If the second borrower deposited the full $64 in the bank, once again 80 percent of that amount, or $51.20, could be lent. If the process continues, the bank will lend about three times the original amount by the time it makes six loans—assuming that all the borrowers eventually deposit their loans in the bank.

Financial institutions generally loan money for real estate mortgages, home improvement, and business expansion, earning money on the interest they charge for the use of the borrowed money. Most banks also offer a **line of credit,** which makes money available to a person or business for use at any time after the loan has been approved. The customer can borrow as much or as little of the money specified in this credit line. Many banks link a line of credit to a customer's checking account. When customers write checks that exceed the amount of money on deposit, they can conveniently draw on the prearranged credit line without any delay or extra paperwork.

Another way to loan money is to offer a **credit card,** a plastic card that entitles the customer to make purchases now and repay the loaned amount later. Visa and MasterCard are two types of credit cards that many financial institutions offer. The largest Visa and MasterCard issuer in the United States is Citibank, which has nearly 16 million accounts and more than $33 billion in credit-card loans. The second largest issuer is AT&T, which serves 9 million customers.[11] When a customer uses a Visa or MasterCard credit card to pay for a restaurant meal, for example, the card issuer repays the restaurant for the price of the meal (less a small fee) and then adds the purchase to

line of credit Arrangement in which the financial institution makes money available for use at any time after the loan has been approved

credit card Plastic card that allows the customer to buy now and pay back the loaned amount at a future date

Customers who use credit cards can make purchases and then repay the loaned amount later.

electronic funds transfer systems (EFTS) *Computerized systems for performing financial transactions*

the customer's monthly bill. The customer can either pay the full amount or pay a small percentage of what is due, making additional monthly payments until the entire amount—including the interest charged for the loan—has been repaid.

Other Services

Although taking deposits and making loans are the main activities of most financial institutions, banks such as NationsBank also offer other services, for which they charge a fee. Most operate a trust department that handles money on behalf of people who are unable to do so directly (such as children). Many also provide safe-deposit boxes, issue traveler's checks, wire funds around the globe, exchange currencies, and offer other services. More and more banks are selling various insurance and investment options.[12] At an increasing number of banks, customers can also take advantage of discount brokerage and mutual fund offerings and gain access to electronic banking.

Discount Brokerage and Mutual Funds. In the early 1980s, many banks added discount brokerage to their service package. The Glass-Steagall Act of 1933 forbids banks from underwriting stocks and from giving customers advice on stocks, but discount brokers do neither of these things (the main reason they are able to charge lower fees than full-service brokers). Although the securities industry challenged this invasion of its turf, the U.S. Supreme Court has ruled that banks are allowed to expand into discount brokerage.[13] NationsBank, for example, has approval to go beyond discount-brokerage services and offer its customers investment advice.

Some banks also offer customers the opportunity to buy shares of *mutual funds,* pools of investments in stocks or bonds. Citibank and other banks sell mutual funds managed by Fidelity Investments and other investment companies. In addition, a number of banks, including Chase Manhattan in New York, have launched their own mutual funds.[14]

Electronic Banking. Banking with the aid of computerized equipment takes many forms. **Electronic funds transfer systems (EFTS)** were designed to offer something for everyone: convenience for customers and cost savings for financial institutions. One of the most popular electronic-banking options allows employers to transfer wages directly from the company bank account to employee accounts. More than one-third of all U.S. workers take advantage of this direct-deposit service, which saves both employer and employee the worry and headaches of handling large amounts of cash.[15]

Electronic banking now allows customers to withdraw money from their demand-deposit accounts using automated teller machines located all over the United States and around the world. By linking their ATMs with regional, national, and international ATM networks, banks can offer you the convenience of drawing out cash from an ATM that's hundreds or thousands of miles from home. To use an ATM, you insert a plastic card into the terminal and then enter a code, known as a personal identification number (PIN). The machine responds by dispensing cash, taking deposits, or handling other simple banking transactions; outside your home state, however, you're limited to withdrawing cash and checking balances.

A more complex variation of electronic banking involves the use of *point-of-sale terminals* located at retailers' checkout counters and tied electronically to a bank computer. When a store customer presents a debit card, the point-of-sale terminal automatically transfers the money for the purchase from the customer's demand deposit account to the store's account. Yet another variation enables a person to pay bills by pushing buttons on a telephone or by using a personal computer linked by telephone to the bank computer. Once the customer enters the required information about the bill and the amount, the bank computer automatically transfers money from the customer's account to the biller's account.

The Evolving Banking Environment

Technological advances are but a small part of the forces influencing the evolving U.S. banking system. Before 1980, banks, finance companies, and other financial institutions operated within well-defined boundaries in a highly regulated environment. Commercial banks made business loans, thrifts lent money for home mortgages, investment banks underwrote corporate stock and bond issues, brokerage firms sold those securities, and insurance companies insured businesses and individuals. The government set a ceiling on the amount of interest that could be paid on savings accounts, which limited competition for depositors' dollars.

This approach worked well until double-digit inflation hit the U.S. economy in the late 1970s. Depositors seeking higher returns increasingly moved their money out of banks and thrifts and into money-market mutual funds offered by Merrill Lynch and other brokerage firms, which could offer higher interest rates because they were not regulated.[16] In turn, banks and thrifts persuaded Congress to deregulate the banking industry so that they could compete for deposits. The resulting deregulation brought a new set of challenges and opportunities.

Deregulation and Competition

The Depository Institutions Deregulation and Monetary Control Act of 1980, legislation supported by the banking industry, deregulated banking and paved the way for financial institutions to offer a wider range of services and to pay higher rates on savings. Banks were now allowed to sell stocks and bonds—and brokerage firms could offer checking and credit-card accounts—which blurred the lines between banks and other financial institutions.

As they searched for higher profits in this competitive environment, some banks and thrifts invested heavily in real estate and oil-drilling activities, loaned money to foreign governments, and financed company buyouts. Then the real estate market collapsed, oil prices plummeted, developers went bankrupt, and countries and companies hit hard by economic woes slowed or stopped payments on their

Merger mania among financial institutions has created larger banks that serve customers over wider geographic areas. One such merger, between NCNB and C&S–Sovran, created one of the largest banks in the United States.

loans. More than 1,000 banks and thrifts failed as a result of these and other risky investments.[17]

Seeking strength, efficiency, and access to more customers and markets, U.S. banks undertook a series of mergers, acquisitions, and takeovers during the 1980s and early 1990s. In many cases, banks and thrifts that were about to fail were involuntarily taken over by stronger banks. During one year, 500 bank mergers were announced—including three giant deals involving $440 billion in bank assets. The creation of megabanks covering wide geographic areas could trim an estimated $10 billion a year from the industry's operating costs (since mergers and acquisitions often lead to layoffs and other cost-cutting steps). Even independent banks are cutting costs by combining departments and closing branches.

However, not everyone thinks bank consolidation is necessarily good. Economists at the Federal Reserve found that the merged banks weren't able to cut more from their costs than independent banks. Moreover, depositors earn less interest and borrowers pay more interest in states having highly concentrated banks.[18]

The institutions that could fare the best in this evolving environment are small community banks. They have two characteristics that larger banks want to duplicate: personal relationships with customers and the ability to serve local needs. "We're really focused on the community," says A. Pierce Stone, president of Virginia National Bank. "We financed a lot of businesses that would not have been otherwise. It's good for the town, and it's good for us because we live here." Small businesses, which often have difficulty obtaining loans from big banks squeezed by competition and regulation, are turning to small or start-up banks in many U.S. communities. Although many community banks, particularly the weaker ones, will be swallowed up in the wave of consolidation, many are expected to remain viable institutions with less than $100 million in assets.[19]

Business lending remains a sore topic. As discussed earlier, finance companies have become the primary source of business loans as U.S. banks keep a tight rein on business lending. This credit crunch has also made foreign banks attractive sources of loans and expertise. Bank of Tokyo, for example, lends money to multinational corporations based in the United States, and it offers specialized services to help customers trade with Pacific Rim companies.[20] Companies unable to borrow when banks are reluctant to lend—or when rates are too high—can instead issue **commercial paper,** an IOU backed by the corporation's reputation, which is used to raise short-term capital.

commercial paper *An IOU, backed by the corporation's reputation, issued to raise short-term capital*

Interstate Banking

The banking environment changed again when Congress passed the Interstate Banking and Efficiency Act of 1994. This law removes barriers to interstate banking by 1997, so banks can open or acquire branches anywhere in the United States. Customers will be able to make deposits, cash checks, or handle any banking transaction in any branch of their banks, regardless of location. This easing of restric-

---

EXPLORING GLOBAL BUSINESS

ONE CONTINENT, ONE BANKING MARKET

If you do business in the United States, Mexico, and Canada, you still have to think in terms of U.S. dollars, pesos, and Canadian dollars. Now, however, you can ask just one bank to provide all the financial services you need to operate anywhere on the North American continent. Since 1988, banks in Canada and the United States have been allowed to hop national borders to open branch offices and offer any financial services that they are permitted to provide in their home countries. Then the North American Free Trade Agreement (NAFTA) expanded the borderless market to include Mexico, paving the way for a continentwide market in financial services.

Both U.S. and Canadian financial institutions are starting to enter the Mexican market. One of the appeals of opening shop in Mexico is the ability to combine banking, insurance, and stock brokerage operations under one corporate umbrella, a combination outlawed in the United States. Another appeal is the change in policy that allows foreign banks to own subsidiaries in Mexico for the first time in 50 years. Although the government will be phasing out rules

that limit the ability of U.S. and Canadian banks to acquire many small and medium-sized Mexican banks, restrictions will continue to protect Mexico's largest financial institutions from takeovers.

Already, U.S. stock-brokerage firms are applying to join the Mexican Stock Exchange, known as the Bolsa. Bank of Boston has set up a bank subsidiary in Mexico to finance environment projects. Banc One, based in Ohio, has formed an alliance with Banamex, the largest bank in Mexico, to process credit cards in Mexico. New York–based Citibank has been active in Mexico since 1929, and it is expanding into insurance and securities underwriting activities.

Canadian banks have also begun marching toward Mexico. The Bank of Nova Scotia owns a share of the financial group that controls Mexico's largest stock-brokerage house as well as a share of a large commercial bank in Mexico. The Royal Bank of Canada is taking a different approach. It has decided to concentrate its North American banking operations in one city, New York, and work from that location to serve the business banking needs of U.S. companies that operate across the continent.

U.S. businesses that have crossed the border to operate in Canada or Mexico—or both—are delighted by borderless banking. "It'll mean we'll be able to get seamless service from one institution, whether it's based in the U.S., Canada, or Mexico," says Anthony Sommer, executive vice president and chief financial officer for Spartan Motors in Charlotte, Michigan. As more U.S. and Canadian companies swing south to take advantage of free trade across North America, they'll also be able to reap the benefits of a single market for financial services.

tions is especially convenient for travelers and for the 60 million people who live and work in metropolitan areas that cross state lines. Customers who move from one state to another will also benefit. "You can keep your same checking and savings accounts when you move from Bakersfield to Phoenix or Phoenix to Sacramento," says Luke Helms, vice chairman of BankAmerica.[21]

Of course, the banks benefit as well: BankAmerica, for example, was forced to operate separate banking systems in 10 states until this bill allowed it to bring all its banks under a single system.[22] Because banks won't need separate systems or headquarters offices when operating branches in several states, bank efficiency will improve. That's good news for NationsBank and other institutions that want to expand by crossing state lines.

Bank Safety

Bank failures are nothing new. As many as 9,000 U.S. banks failed during the depression years of 1929 to 1934 (see Exhibit 18.4). After several decades with few problems, a series of spectacular failures again rattled the banking industry, creating public doubt about bank safety. From 1980 through 1990, 1,228 banks failed, and much of the thrift industry had to be salvaged by the largest taxpayer-financed bailout in history.[23] However, the crisis seemed under control by the mid-1990s. From January to June 1994, only four banks, two thrifts, and 30 credit unions failed. The number of troubled banks and thrifts

Exhibit 18.4
Bank Failures

The number of bank failures in the United States peaked in 1933. However, banks that failed during the 1980s and 1990s held many billions of dollars more than the failed banks of the 1920s and 1930s. These larger failures presented more risk to depositors and to the entire banking system.

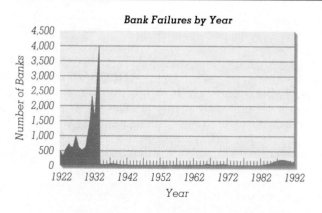

Bank Failures by Year

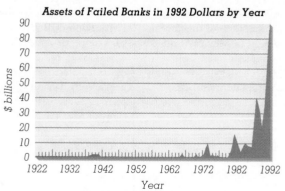

Assets of Failed Banks in 1992 Dollars by Year

stood at 433, a major improvement from the 1,305 considered troubled just two years earlier.[24]

In response to concerns about bank safety during the depression years, the government established the Federal Deposit Insurance Corporation (FDIC) to protect money in customer accounts. Today FDIC insurance covers customers' funds on deposit with a particular bank to a maximum of $100,000. Under FDIC supervision are two funds that insure depositors' money. The Bank Insurance Fund (BIF) covers customer deposits at nearly 13,000 commercial banks and savings banks. The Savings Association Insurance Fund (SAIF) covers customer deposits at more than 2,000 savings and loan associations. In addition, deposits in more than 13,000 credit unions are insured by the National Credit Union Share Insurance Fund, a separate agency.

The FDIC collects insurance premiums from banks and sends the money to the Treasury, where it is put in the general fund to finance everything from defense needs to highway construction. When a bank fails, the Treasury borrows money in the financial markets on behalf of the FDIC, which keeps track of how much money it has collected and how much it has spent. Thus, the FDIC fund is really nothing more than a balance sheet.[25]

The FDIC BIF was ahead by about $2 billion at the end of 1990, but it dropped into the red in 1991 as it repaid depositors who had accounts in failed banks. To keep the fund going, Congress voted to allow it up to $30 billion if needed. However, an improved economic environment and higher insurance premiums paid by banks helped the FDIC repay the additions provided by Congress—and build a cushion of nearly $7 billion—by mid-1993.[26]

One reason many savings and loan associations failed was their need to boost profits. The S&Ls had made mortgage loans at low rates but found themselves having to pay higher interest rates on savings accounts after deregulation sparked more intense competition. Regulators therefore allowed these institutions to seek higher returns by diversifying into other activities, such as investing directly in real estate. With the government insuring all deposits up to $100,000, thrift managers felt free to seek out increasingly speculative deals. Then real estate markets crashed, leaving taxpayers to bail out the industry.

The rescue had a steep price. The Federal Savings and Loan Insurance Corporation, which formerly insured depositors' accounts at S&Ls, was declared insolvent, and its successor, the SAIF, was brought under the supervision of the FDIC. Congress moved to avert higher losses in 1989 by authorizing interested banks to buy thrifts and merge their branch systems. It also set new financial requirements so rigorous that many thrifts may go out of business because of this measure alone. In all, the S&L crisis is estimated to have cost more than $150 billion.[27]

Keeping the FDIC funded is a prime concern, but paying for failures can be costly. Insurance premiums paid by banks skyrocketed 277 percent between 1989 and 1991 alone, and bankers warn that further increases might cause more failures.[28] Currently, healthy banks pay lower premiums than troubled banks, which gives problem banks a financial reason for improving their health.

Everyone from members of Congress to members of the financial community worries about the FDIC's having to bail out a giant bank, which by itself would bankrupt the fund. For decades everyone believed that the federal government would never let a major bank fail. The FDIC took over when the giant Bank of New England was threatened with collapse in 1991, and it quickly arranged a takeover by Fleet–Norstar Financial Group. BNE was an institution considered too large to let fail, so all deposits, even those of more than $100,000, were protected. In reality, the "too big to fail" doctrine has been extended to all but the smallest community banks, which is a major reason for concern about the FDIC's financial situation.[29]

The Federal Reserve System functions as a clearinghouse for business and personal checks that are presented for payment at member banks throughout the United States.

THE FEDERAL RESERVE SYSTEM

The Federal Reserve System was created in 1913 and is commonly known as the Fed. It is the most powerful financial institution in the United States, serving as the country's central bank. The Fed's primary role is to supply us with the "right" amount of money so that we avoid both recession and inflation. It also supervises and regulates banks and serves as a clearinghouse for checks.

The Federal Reserve's Structure

The Fed is a network of 12 regional banks that controls the country's banking system. Each regional bank is owned by the participating commercial banks within its district. Almost 5,500 banks are members of the system, including all the national banks and 90 percent of the state banks. (The rest of the state banks are regulated chiefly by state governments, which tend to have more liberal policies than the Fed.)[30]

The overall policy of the Fed is established by a seven-member board of governors in Washington, D.C. To preserve their political independence, the members are appointed by the president to 14-year terms, staggered at 2-year intervals. The Fed's regulatory authority was strengthened in 1980 by the Depository Institutions Deregulation and Monetary Control Act, which, among other things, extended some of the Fed's regulatory powers to cover nonmember banks, savings banks, and savings and loans. In addition, the Fed can often persuade nonmember banks to follow its policies simply by jawboning, or threatening to use its considerable power.

The Federal Reserve's Functions

The Fed's main job is to establish and implement *monetary policy*, which is a set of guidelines for handling the nation's economy and the money supply. It aims to make certain that enough money and credit are available to allow the economy to expand, increasing the country's supply of goods, services, and jobs. It must also be careful not to release too much money and credit into the economy at any one time because a surplus has historically produced inflation.

554

The Federal Reserve System has three major functions: regulating the money supply, supplying currency, and clearing checks. The most important of these is regulating the money supply.

Regulating the Money Supply

The Fed uses monetary policy in an attempt to stimulate economic growth and employment while suppressing inflation. However, complications may arise. When the money supply increases and there is more money to go around, banks can charge lower interest to borrowers. However, an increased money supply may lead to more spending and thus more inflation. During inflationary periods, the dollars that borrowers repay to lenders have less purchasing power than they had when the loan was made. To offset this loss of purchasing power, lenders must add a certain percentage—corresponding to the rate of inflation—to the interest rates they would otherwise charge. So a growth in the money supply, if it fans inflation, may lead to higher interest rates.

The Federal Reserve has an additional responsibility: The Fed is the official banker of the federal government—specifically, the U.S. Department of the Treasury. When the federal budget is running a deficit, the Treasury must raise money to fill the gap. If the Treasury borrows from the public, it competes with consumer and business borrowing, which may push up interest rates. To avoid such pressure on interest rates, the Fed might choose to lend money to the Treasury itself. However, the cash (or demand deposits) that the Fed supplies to the Treasury is new money pumped into the economy. This increase in the money supply may lead to inflation, thus conflicting with other aspects of monetary policy.

To implement its monetary policy, the Fed has four basic tools: It can change reserve requirements; it can change the interest rate that member banks must pay to borrow from the Fed (the discount rate); it can buy or sell government securities (open-market operations); and it can set the terms of credit for certain types of loans (selective credit controls). Exhibit 18.5 summarizes the effects of using these tools.

Reserve Requirements. The Fed requires all member banks and financial institutions to set aside **reserves,** sums of money equal to a certain percentage of their deposits. The percentage of deposits that

reserves *Funds a financial institution keeps on tap to meet projected withdrawals*

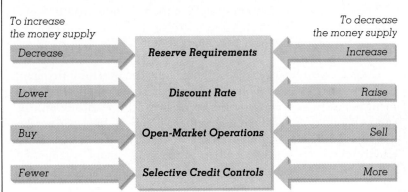

To increase the money supply		To decrease the money supply
Decrease	**Reserve Requirements**	Increase
Lower	**Discount Rate**	Raise
Buy	**Open-Market Operations**	Sell
Fewer	**Selective Credit Controls**	More

Exhibit 18.5
Controlling the Money Supply
The Federal Reserve manipulates the money supply in various ways as it attempts to stimulate economic growth and keep both inflation and interest rates at acceptable levels.

reserve requirement *Percentage of a bank's deposits that must be set aside*

Fed funds rate *Interest rate charged for overnight loans between banks*

discount rate *Interest rate charged by the Federal Reserve on loans to member banks*

prime interest rate *Lowest rate of interest charged by banks for short-term loans to their most creditworthy customers*

open-market operations *Activity of the Federal Reserve in buying and selling government bonds on the open market*

banks must set aside is called the **reserve requirement.** The bank keeps this money on deposit with the Federal Reserve Bank in its district.

Changing the reserve requirement is a powerful tool that can be used for occasional adjustments to the money supply. By increasing the reserve requirements, the Fed forces banks to set more of its deposits aside, which means they cannot lend as much to their customers. Conversely, by reducing the reserve requirements, the Fed allows banks to make more money available for loans to businesses and consumers. However, the Fed rarely uses this technique because it can have such a far-reaching effect on the money supply.

Some banks find that they have more reserves on deposit at the Fed than they need for the short term; others find that their reserves are insufficient for the short term and that they must make up the difference. If a bank with a surplus wishes to lend its excess reserves to a bank with a deficit, the Fed conveniently makes the bookkeeping entries for the two banks so that the funds never actually need to be moved around. The interest rate that banks charge each other for overnight loans is called the **Fed funds rate.**

The Discount Rate. Banks can obtain extra funds to lend to their customers by borrowing from their regional Federal Reserve Bank, which in a sense is banker to the banks. The interest rate that the Fed charges member banks for loans is called the **discount rate.** Discounting is often attractive to commercial banks because they can charge their customers a substantially higher rate for the loans made from the funds that they themselves have borrowed from the Fed, thereby earning a nice profit. However, discounting has disadvantages too: When a bank borrows from the Fed, the Fed typically imposes conditions on the bank's operations.

Here again is a way the Fed can control the economy. When the Fed raises the discount rate, member banks tighten the availability of loans to customers and raise their lending rates. This action slows economic growth and helps keep inflation in check. On the other hand, when the Fed lowers the discount rate, member banks feel encouraged to make more loans and lower their lending rates, which fuels economic growth. Changes in the discount rate may indirectly affect the **prime interest rate**—the lowest rate at which banks will make short-term loans to their most creditworthy business customers. The prime interest rate is also directly affected by supply and demand for loans.

The power of interest rates to affect the economy may be significant. Overall, each percentage-point drop in average interest rates adds about one-third of a percentage point to the nation's annual economic growth.

Open-Market Operations. The tool that the Fed uses most frequently to carry out monetary policy is its power to buy and sell government bonds (which are promises to repay a debt, with interest). Because anyone can buy these government bonds on the open market, this tool is known as **open-market operations.** The bonds are attractive purchases because lending to the government is considered a risk-free way of earning interest.

SPEEDING BANK-TO-BANK MONEY TRANSFERS

How can a bank move millions of dollars to another bank quickly and safely? The answer, for more than 7,500 financial institutions in the United States, is FedWire. Operated by the Federal Reserve System, FedWire is an electronic communications system that speeds the transfer of money between participating banks.

Whether the two banks are miles apart or just down the street from each other, FedWire streamlines the movement of money by eliminating the headaches of doing paperwork and physically transporting cash. Imagine that a company with an account at BankAmerica in California is paying $35 million to buy a factory from a company with an account at Chase Manhattan Bank in New York. One way to get the money across the country would be to truck cash from one bank vault to the other. Another way would be to send a check in the mail or by overnight delivery service. However, because both banks have accounts at the Federal Reserve, the simplest (and most secure) way to transfer the money is to issue instructions electronically to FedWire.

At BankAmerica, the computer operator types instructions into the computer terminal specifying the amount, naming Chase as the receiving bank, and providing the security code that authorizes the transfer. Within a minute or so, the Fed computer responds with a confirmation that $35 million has been transferred from BankAmerica's Federal Reserve account to Chase's account. The Fed computer immediately notifies Chase's computer that $35 million has been transferred into the bank's account. The transfer is complete.

Not only are Fedwire transfers fast and convenient, they also avoid the risk of theft or loss posed by checks or cash. Little wonder, then,

that FedWire is kept busy moving money between banks all over the United States. On an average day, FedWire processes 220,000 transactions totaling $790 billion. In addition to paying a monthly fee to use the service, participating banks pay to link up with the FedWire computer and then pay $10 for every transfer.

Smaller banks generally don't make many large transfers, so they may not be willing to go to the expense of hooking up with FedWire. These banks can still move money electronically by using Fedline, a Fed service that allows banks to use personal computers to transfer money and complete other transactions without paperwork. FedWire and Fedline have been so successful in cutting through the paper logjam associated with money transfers that the Fed has started electronic communications systems for bidding and buying government securities, collecting corporate taxes, and processing savings bonds. Within a few years, the Fed expects these computerized systems to have squeezed virtually all the paperwork out of moving money and government securities through the Federal Reserve System.

If the Federal Open Market Committee, which directs open-market operations, is concerned about inflation and wants to reduce the amount of money available, it can move to sell U.S. government bonds to the public and to banks. The money paid for the bonds immediately goes out of circulation. Conversely, when the Fed wants to get the economy moving again, the committee can move to buy back the government bonds, thus putting additional cash back into the economy. Because the money supply increases, interest rates drop, so businesses can borrow more money at a lower cost and expand their opportunities for growth and competition.

The Fed also uses a type of open-market operation when it influences the price that the dollar brings in exchange for another country's currency. The dollar's value goes up when the Fed buys dollars on the foreign-exchange market, and it goes down when the Fed sells dollars. These buying and selling actions change the level of U.S. reserves.[31] To offset the effect on the money supply, the Fed uses open-market purchases or sales of U.S. government bonds. When the Fed buys a foreign currency, it completes an open-market sale of an equal amount of U.S. government bonds at the same time to replenish the reserves; when it sells a foreign currency, the Fed simultaneously buys bonds of an equal amount using those reserves.

Selective Credit Controls. The Fed also has the power to set credit terms for various kinds of loans. By exercising this power, known as **selective credit controls,** it can exert great influence on business activity.

The Fed may set **margin requirements,** which limit the amount of money that stockbrokers and banks may lend a customer for buying stocks. When government economists feel that there is too much stock-market speculation for the economy's good, the Fed simply sets margin requirements at levels that will prevent financial institutions from lending much money for stock purchases.

Supplying Currency

In addition to regulating the money supply, the Fed performs other functions that help keep the financial system running smoothly. For example, individual Federal Reserve Banks are responsible for providing member banks with adequate amounts of currency.

The demand for coins and paper money is seasonal. As you might expect, many people withdraw some of their savings from the banks in the form of cash during the winter holidays. In addition, retailers need bills and coins so that they can make change for customers during busy shopping periods. The Federal Reserve has to supply the extra currency that banks need at such times.

Clearing Checks

Another function of the Fed is to act as a clearinghouse for checks. Banks use the Fed's check-processing system to clear checks drawn on banks outside their Federal Reserve districts (see Exhibit 18.6). For example, a check written against an account in a Boston bank may be deposited in a bank in Dallas. The Dallas bank forwards the check to the Federal Reserve Bank in Dallas, which collects the funds from the Boston Federal Reserve Bank and credits the account of the local bank. For a high-value check, the Dallas bank may do a "direct send," forwarding the check to the Federal Reserve Bank in Boston.

Not all checks are sent to the Fed for clearance. Many rural banks simply pay larger banks to perform this service for them. Transactions among banks in the same area are handled locally and then reported to the Federal Reserve, which charges and credits the appropriate accounts. Imagine that, on a particular day, checks written on accounts at the Tallahassee National Bank total $550 and have been deposited in accounts at the First Miami Bank. At the same time, the Federal Reserve Bank in Atlanta notes that First Miami's depositors have written $400 worth of checks that have been deposited at Tallahassee. The Federal Reserve Bank balances out the difference, crediting First Miami with $150 and subtracting the same amount from Tallahassee National's account.

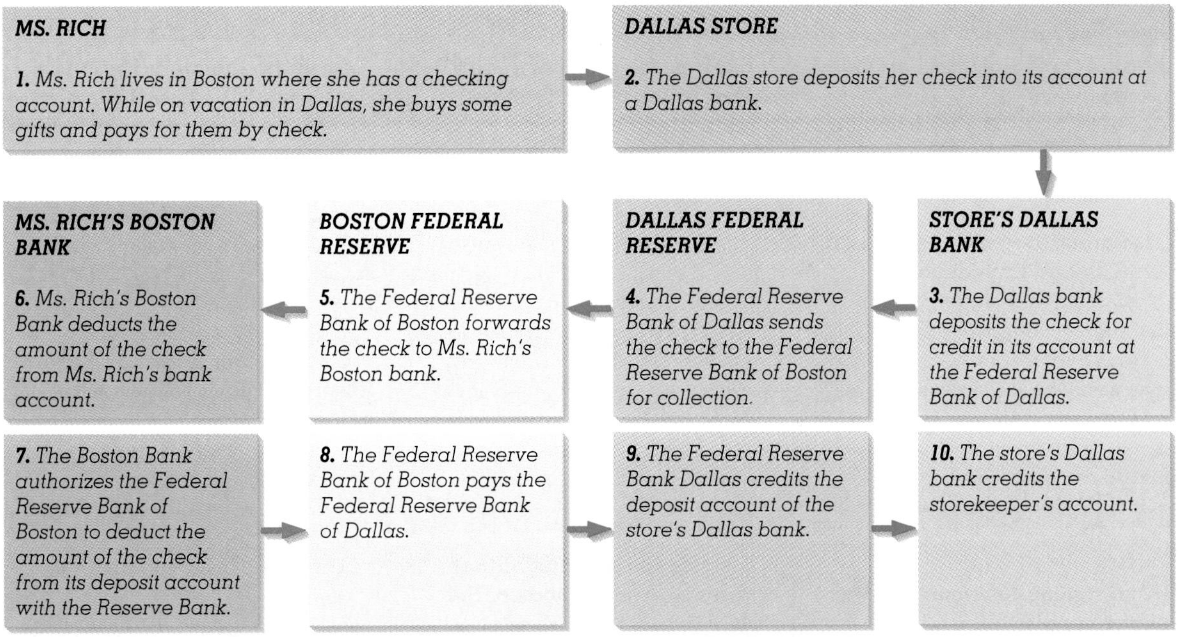

MS. RICH		DALLAS STORE	
1. Ms. Rich lives in Boston where she has a checking account. While on vacation in Dallas, she buys some gifts and pays for them by check.		**2.** The Dallas store deposits her check into its account at a Dallas bank.	

MS. RICH'S BOSTON BANK	BOSTON FEDERAL RESERVE	DALLAS FEDERAL RESERVE	STORE'S DALLAS BANK
6. Ms. Rich's Boston Bank deducts the amount of the check from Ms. Rich's bank account.	**5.** The Federal Reserve Bank of Boston forwards the check to Ms. Rich's Boston bank.	**4.** The Federal Reserve Bank of Dallas sends the check to the Federal Reserve Bank of Boston for collection.	**3.** The Dallas bank deposits the check for credit in its account at the Federal Reserve Bank of Dallas.
7. The Boston Bank authorizes the Federal Reserve Bank of Boston to deduct the amount of the check from its deposit account with the Reserve Bank.	**8.** The Federal Reserve Bank of Boston pays the Federal Reserve Bank of Dallas.	**9.** The Federal Reserve Bank Dallas credits the deposit account of the store's Dallas bank.	**10.** The store's Dallas bank credits the storekeeper's account.

However, the checks written by the customers of Tallahassee National and First Miami are actually deposited in banks all over the district during the normal course of business. That's why the debits and credits from all the banks in the district have to be added up before the proper amounts can be added to or subtracted from Tallahassee National's and First Miami's accounts with their Federal Reserve district bank.

Exhibit 18.6
How a Check Clears
The Fed processes more than 55 billion checks every year. In this example, a customer who lives in Boston pays by check for a purchase made in a Dallas store. The check passes through the Federal Reserve Banks in Dallas and Boston before reaching the customer's bank and the store's bank.

1 Name three functions of money.

Money functions as a medium of exchange, a measure of value, and a store of value.

2 Differentiate between demand deposits and time deposits.

Demand deposits are more liquid than time deposits. Customers can get to the money in a demand deposit, such as a checking account, more quickly and easily than they can get to the money in time deposits (savings accounts, money-market deposit accounts, and certificates of deposit).

3 Distinguish M1 from the total money supply.

The total money supply comprises currency, demand deposits, and time deposits. M1 is that part of the money supply slated to be spent fairly soon, and it consists of currency and demand deposits.

4 Identify nine members of the banking system.

The participants in the banking system include commercial banks, thrift institutions, credit unions, finance companies, limited-service banks, brokerage houses, insurance companies, pension funds, and investment banks.

5 Explain the effects of bank deregulation and interstate banking legislation.

Deregulation has enabled banks to compete with other financial institutions by diversifying their offerings, paying higher interest rates on savings, and expanding their geographic base of operations. Interstate banking allows banks to take customer deposits, cash checks, or handle any banking transaction in any branch, regardless of location. Banks also benefit because they can consolidate their state operations to improve efficiency.

6 Discuss the responsibilities and insurance methods of the FDIC.

The Federal Deposit Insurance Corporation is a federal insurance program that protects deposits in member banks. Banks pay premiums to the FDIC, which insures funds on deposit with a particular bank for up to $100,000 in case of bank failure. The FDIC supervises the Bank Insurance Fund, which covers deposits in commercial banks and savings banks, and the Savings Association Insurance Fund, which covers deposits in savings and loan associations.

7 Describe the organization of the Federal Reserve System.

The Federal Reserve System consists of almost 5,500 member banks and 12 regional banks. The overall system is administered by a seven-member board of governors whose members are appointed to 14-year terms, at 2-year intervals.

8 Cite the four ways the Federal Reserve System regulates the money supply.

The Fed regulates the money supply by changing reserve requirements, changing the discount rate, carrying out open-market operations, and setting selective credit controls.

Hugh L. McColl, Jr., had spent years extending his NCNB's presence throughout the Southeast, first in its home state of North Carolina and then in South Carolina and Florida. NCNB was a strong regional bank, but McColl knew that the time had come to take some huge steps: Either NCNB would become one of the nation's largest and most powerful banks by making major acquisitions, or it would be gobbled up by an even more aggressive national competitor.

McColl started by acquiring First RepublicBank, the largest and most financially troubled bank in Texas. This acquisition brought NCNB a good share of the market in four of the state's five largest cities. However, McColl did not buy the acquired bank's bad loans; about $10 billion in nonperforming loans was taken over by the Federal Deposit Insurance Corporation (FDIC), which wanted to keep First RepublicBank afloat. With the government essentially assuming the risk of the bad loans, NCNB was able to acquire the solid assets of the troubled institution with little risk. To increase his branch network in Texas, McColl bought 18 other failing banks and thrifts across the state.

Now McColl turned his attention to banks closer to home. Citizens and Southern's merger with Sovran had burdened the bank with a sizable load of bad real estate loans.

C&S–Sovran needed help, and McColl came to the rescue. NCNB's acquisition of C&S–Sovran was actually made possible by its buyout of First RepublicBank: Because the FDIC had assumed the risk of the bad loans in Texas, NCNB was in a good position to withstand the risks of taking over C&S–Sovran's problem loans. The merger of NCNB and C&S–Sovran created the fourth largest bank in the United States, eclipsed only by Citicorp, BankAmerica, and Chemical Banking Corporation. McColl named his new institution after the vision of the future he had championed for years: NationsBank.

With more than 1,900 branches from Chesapeake Bay to the Rio Grande, from the Blue Ridge of Virginia to Miami Beach, McColl was ready to add a variety of new products to attract consumers and businesses alike. He forged an alliance with the securities firm of Dean Witter Reynolds to place brokers in hundreds of NationsBank branches. Then he created a new unit dedicated to making loans for mobile homes, pianos, recreational vehicles, and other major purchases. Finally, to better serve large corporate customers, he expanded the bank's trading operations by acquiring the Chicago Research and Trading Group.

Now that McColl has transformed NCNB into NationsBank, he faces new challenges. "The next test will be to prove that we can run this huge enterprise we've created, and run it better than anyone else," he says. "After doing that, we would fully expect to continue building a national company."

Your Mission: Hugh McColl has appointed you his special assistant in charge of growth strategy. It is your job to advise McColl on issues facing NationsBank as it grows ever larger.

1. Many customers want to earn higher returns on their savings.

NationsBank can give its customers access to mutual funds, stocks, and other nonbank investments, but the bank earns more profit when customers leave their money in a savings account or a CD. How should NationsBank resolve this problem?

a. Promote your full range of savings and investments options, and be sure customers understand the benefits and risks of each choice. If you don't offer these options, customers will eventually move their money to a financial institution that is willing to help them earn higher returns.

b. Promote savings accounts and CDs as safe investments, and stress the benefits of keeping savings in a convenient, local bank. You can arrange for customers to invest in mutual funds or other investments if they threaten to move their funds to another financial institution.

c. Tell your customers that NationsBank is planning an extensive study of the benefits and risks of various savings accounts and investments. This study will help customers see the advantages of savings and CD accounts.

2. One of the problems NationsBank is experiencing in its aggressive growth strategy is having enough qualified managers to oversee the increasing number of branches and services. What should NationsBank do?

a. Hire seasoned managers whose jobs have been eliminated by the merging and consolidation of other banks.

b. In addition to (a), improve NationsBank's training program for midlevel managers so that the bank's culture won't be diluted by managers who have grown used to other, and possibly less aggressive, management styles.

c. In addition to (b), raid BankAmerica to find experienced managers who can work without close supervision to set up and run global banking operations in other countries.

3. Small-business customers have fled a number of larger banks because they feel lost in the shuffle after a merger or acquisition. They often lose a long-term relationship when their banker is replaced by a succession of managers or loan officers. What compounds the problem is the debate within many banks over who should serve the small-business community: commercial divisions that are usually housed in centralized locations, or branch managers who are closer to their communities but don't always have the experience or support they need to meet the needs of small-business customers. How can NationsBank prevent small-business owners from moving to smaller banks?

a. Add small-business loan officers to each branch, regardless of the added cost and loss of centralization.

b. Establish small-business units that would be attached to branches on the basis of geographical areas so that branch managers would have direct support in their banking relations with the small-business community.

c. Let branch managers handle all small-business services. They can get to know local businesses better than the people in a central office can.

4. Building and staffing branch offices can be costly. McColl wants you to think about how to give more customers better service without expanding or burdening the branch system. Which one of these ideas would you recommend?

a. Join a national ATM network. Your customers will be able to use ATMs around the area for making deposits, withdrawing money, checking balances, and handling other simple transactions, thereby visiting your branches less often. In addition, when traveling, they will be able to withdraw money or check balances at the ATM machines of nearly any bank in the country.

b. Allow customers to bank via personal computer. Under this system, customers with personal computers could transfer money, check balances, and pay bills without leaving their homes or offices. Customers would enjoy the convenience, and they would visit the branches less often.

c. Start a real estate division to sell homes and, of course, offer mortgages to home buyers. The real estate brokers could work in a corner of each branch, saving the expense of renting office space elsewhere.[32]

KEY TERMS

automated teller machines (ATMs) (542)
certificate of deposit (CD) (546)
checks (542)
commercial banks (544)
commercial paper (551)
credit card (547)
credit unions (544)
currency (542)
debit cards (542)
demand deposit (542)
discount rate (556)
electronic funds transfer systems (EFTS) (548)

Fed funds rate (556)
finance companies (544)
individual retirement account (IRA) (546)
investment banks (545)
Keogh account (546)
line of credit (547)
M1 (543)
M2 (543)
margin requirements (558)
money (540)
money-market deposit accounts (546)
national banks (544)

NOW account (546)
open-market operations (556)
payee (542)
prime interest rate (556)
reserve requirement (556)
reserves (555)
savings and loan associations (S&Ls) (544)
savings banks (544)
selective credit controls (558)
state banks (544)
super NOW account (546)
time deposits (543)

1. What is the difference between M1 and M2?
2. How are demand deposits created?
3. How does a limited-service bank differ from a commercial bank?

4. What advantages do electronic funds transfer systems offer banks and consumers?
5. How has banking deregulation changed competition among financial institutions?
6. What is the main objective of the Federal Reserve System?

7. What are three of the Federal Reserve's functions?
8. What role do the 12 Federal Reserve Banks play in clearing checks drawn on commercial banks?

A CASE FOR CRITICAL THINKING

CAN AN INNER-CITY COMMUNITY BANK THRIVE?

Ronald Grzywinski, Mary Houghton, Milton Davis, and James Fletcher believed that doing good could mean doing well for a bank with a conscience. That's the philosophy behind South Shore Bank, the bank they bought to help revitalize a decaying downtown Chicago neighborhood. The bank serves the South Shore community, which is home to a population of 78,000. In the 1970s, this district was suffering from economic depression, with struggling small businesses and deteriorating homes and apartment houses. Like the area it served, South Shore Bank was ailing when Grzywinski, Houghton, Davis, and Fletcher took over in 1973.

Despite the neighborhood problems, the four were able to build South Shore Bank into a successful local institution. Their efforts have so revitalized the community that today it is a model for community banking. How was an inner-city bank able to make itself profitable *and* reverse the downward spiral of its community? By redirecting capital the way all banks do—only with a twist.

A bank's depositors don't necessarily see their money reinvested in their communities. This is particularly true of national banks, which make loans where the risk is lowest. South Shore Bank's new owners redirected capital also, but *into* South Shore instead of out of it. They created "Development Deposits"—savings accounts, certificates of deposit, and

checking accounts with one thing in common: The deposits came from people and institutions around the country who wanted their money to help an inner-city community. In turn, the bank loaned this money to small-business owners and real estate developers, supporting the local economy and improving neighborhood housing.

Keith Banks was one of the first developers to apply for a loan. With the $43,000 he received, Banks renovated a South Shore apartment building. After the first project, he went on to successfully—and profitably—restore 11 other buildings, all with the bank's lending support. More real estate–development loans followed and, within 20 years, South Shore Bank had provided the financing for roughly one-third of the houses and apartment buildings in its community.

All this activity has begun transforming the entire South Shore community and has even prompted banks from outside the area to once again make home loans there. South Shore Bank has grown to more than $250 million in assets, earning $2 million in annual profits. In the process, it has proven how important a bank can be to its community. The bank now lends $33 million every year, of which more than 99 percent is repaid, a good record. It also runs a business training and development center and a consulting firm to support local businesses. Just as important, the bank provides jobs for more than 300 people.

Ronald Grzywinski, who serves as

chairman of the bank's corporate parent, wants to provide economic opportunity and better housing in other states and in developing nations. The bank is already involved in community redevelopment efforts in rural Arkansas, northern Michigan, Bangladesh, Finland, and Poland. Profit is involved, but the main motivation is to promote a social agenda of urban redevelopment. "Our forefathers invested in things like hospitals and universities to take care of public needs," he says. "I think our generation is figuring out that it has to create permanent development institutions to take care of today's needs."

1. If you were the head of a big-city bank who agreed with South Shore's philosophy of banking, what policies would you establish to support community redevelopment?
2. Does the federal government have a role, through its laws and regulations, in encouraging more banks to support inner-city redevelopment, or should such efforts be left to the marketplace? If the government's influence is necessary, what would you recommend it do?
3. Why would people from California or Massachusetts deposit money in checking and savings accounts held in a Chicago bank? Would you deposit your money in South Shore Bank? Explain your answer.

Learn more about how FDIC insurance protects depositors by talking with an officer in a neighborhood bank or by writing the regional Federal Reserve Bank in your area. Prepare a brief report (as directed by your instructor) describing the answers you received.

• Which bank accounts are protected by FDIC insurance?
• Does the bank offer investments that are not FDIC-insured? Why aren't these investments covered by FDIC insurance?
• What can depositors with more than $100,000 on deposit in a particular bank do if they want to be fully covered by the FDIC?

From recent issues of *The Wall Street Journal*, choose an article that explains in some detail the problems facing a particular bank or an entire category of banks (such as thrift institutions).

1. What are the problems faced by the bank or group of banks? Be as specific as possible.
2. To what degree are these problems related to specific economic developments? To the pressures of deregulation and competition? List all the major reasons given in the article.
3. How are bank officials dealing with these problems? Have regulatory agencies or officials either taken or threatened to take action? What are they doing or proposing to do?

HOW MUCH LONGER CAN TRADITIONAL BANKS SURVIVE?

Synopsis

This video explores the current plight of traditional banks in this country. Banking boils down to two primary functions: attracting depositors who like the interest rates that you'll pay them and then attracting borrowers who like the interest rates they'll have to pay you. The difference between the rates a bank pays its depositors and earns from its borrowers, minus expenses, is the bank's profit. As this video points out, however, traditional banks are getting squeezed on both fronts. On the deposit side, mutual fund companies such as Fidelity Investments often provide better returns for investors. On the borrowing side, consumers are increasingly turning to car companies for car loans and to specialized mortgage bankers for home loans, taking away two of the bank's biggest traditional customers. Large businesses often bypass regular banks as well, using specialized investment banks instead.

Exercises

ANALYSIS

1. How can Ford afford to offer such attractive rates on its car loans?
2. Why would a consumer decide to build, say, a retirement fund through Fidelity, rather than through a regular bank account?
3. How does Fidelity keep its costs so low?

4. With better rates elsewhere, why do consumers bother with traditional banks at all?
5. How much sympathy do you have for troubled banks?

APPLICATION

What are your options for financing your college education (assuming you aren't able to pay as you go and didn't receive a full scholarship)? Does your financing involve banks?

DECISION

Let's say IBM was considering getting into the credit-card business, as Sears and AT&T have done. What issues

should IBM consider first?

COMMUNICATION

Write a brief description of investment banking, differentiating it from consumer banking and commercial banking.

INTEGRATION

Referring to the discussion of the business environment in Chapter 1, what are the environmental forces causing so much trouble for banks?

ETHICS

Is it fair to tie banks' hands, as the banking executive explains the government is doing?

DEBATE

Should taxpayers foot the bill for bailing out failed banks and savings and loan institutions? Option A: In a formal debate format, argue for or against the suggestion that taxpayers should pay. Option B: Take either position and state your case in a brief report.

TEAMWORK

With a team of three or four students, find out why banks were excluded from certain financial services back in the Great Depression; then decide if you think the exclusions are still necessary or fair.

RESEARCH

Do the research necessary to find out whether banks are still prohibited from selling mutual funds and other securities.

ROLE PLAYING

One student plays a taxpayer advocate who is testifying to Congress that taxpayers shouldn't have to foot the bill for bank bailouts. Several other students play members of Congress.

Chapter

19

Financial Management

Finding Financial Fuel for a Food Firm

What filling food can boast no fat, high fiber, and only eight calories per ounce? The answer, as Jim Kilmer found out when he joined the Weight Watchers program, is spaghetti squash, a little-known vegetable that can be substituted for pasta. Relying on spaghetti squash and other healthy foods, Kilmer had lost 62 pounds following the Weight Watchers program. Now he wanted to make spaghetti squash a key ingredient in his recipe for entrepreneurial success.

Kilmer worked for H. J. Heinz, the parent company of Weight Watchers, for more than 13 years, including a stint as the product manager for Weight Watchers ice cream and frozen novelties. When Heinz eliminated a number of jobs, including his own, Kilmer gladly accepted severance pay and started his own food-manufacturing firm, which he called Remlik (Kilmer spelled backward). He considered many ideas, but he was particularly intrigued by the idea of selling prepared spaghetti squash.

From personal experience, he knew that foods low in calories but high in nutritional value weren't always the fastest or most convenient to cook. Preparing fresh spaghetti squash is a job that takes 30 minutes or more. Kilmer believed that people would flock to the refrigerator case to buy precooked spaghetti squash that was ready to be heated and sauced. To emphasize the cooked vegetable's similarity to pasta, the entrepreneur named his product Nature's Pasta.

One immediate problem was the product's shelf life: Refrigerated, precooked squash tended to spoil after seven days. Because his product had such a short shelf life, Kilmer would be forced to work out an especially speedy delivery system, and he would be limited to selling only to nearby stores. Finding a way to extend the squash's shelf life was essential if the company was to grow, but the cost of this research was beyond Kilmer's reach.

Expensive research wasn't his only financial concern. To avoid buying a manufacturing plant, Kilmer rented space and a part-time crew from a caterer. He kept costs low by buying used equipment and overhauling it himself. Rather than pay a salesperson, he visited gro-

Jim Kilmer believed that weight-conscious people would enjoy the convenience of the low-cal, precooked spaghetti squash offered by Nature's Pasta.

cery stores himself, persuading seven to buy the new product as a test. The initial sales were more than twice what he had expected. "I was giddy," he remembers. "But I woke up overwhelmed with the things I had to do to get through each day."

Working more than 80 hours a week to meet the unexpected demand wasn't enough. Where would Kilmer find the money to outfit a manufacturing plant, hire employees, and buy a large refrigerator truck? How could he finance the research he needed to extend the squash's shelf life? How would he pay his suppliers when the money from selling products didn't come in quickly enough?[1]

FINANCE: A COMPANY'S LIFEBLOOD

Jim Kilmer wants his new business to survive, but he's also looking ahead to expansion. The key to both of these efforts is money. Every company, from the little corner store to General Motors, worries about money—how to get it and how to use it. This area of concern, known as **financial management,** or finance, is tremendously complex.

financial management *Effective acquisition and use of money*

The Goals of Financial Management

All companies need to pay their bills and still have some money left over to improve the business. Furthermore, a key goal is to increase the business's value to its owners (and other stakeholders) by making it grow. Maximizing the owners' wealth sounds simple enough: Just sell a good product for more than it costs to make. Before you can earn any revenue, however, you need money to get started. Once the business is off the ground, your need for money continues—whether

Financial managers help their companies determine how much money they need for operations and for expansion. They're also responsible for identifying the right combination of funding sources at the lowest cost.

it's to see you through a slow season or to buy or renovate facilities and equipment, as Jim Kilmer needed to do.

Because companies have to start with money to make money, they often need to borrow additional funds. The use of borrowed money to make more money is called **leverage** because the loan acts like a lever: It magnifies the power of the borrower to generate profits. If you combine your own funds (the equity you have in the company) with borrowed money, you have a bigger pool of money to work with. As long as you earn a greater rate of return on the borrowed money than the interest you pay, you stay ahead (see Exhibit 19.1). However, leverage works both ways: Borrowing may magnify your losses as well as your gains.

Borrowing is complicated by the fact that many sources of funding exist, each with advantages and disadvantages, costs and benefits. The financial manager's task is to find the combination of funding sources with the lowest cost. This process is dynamic because changing economic conditions affect the cost of borrowing.

In addition to obtaining funds, the financial manager needs to make sure those funds are used efficiently. In most companies, the number of potential expenditures is large, but the amount of available funds is limited. To choose the best expenditures, the financial manager needs a selection process that highlights the options that are best able to meet the company's objectives.

leverage *Use of borrowed funds to finance a portion of an investment*

The Process of Financial Management

When you prepare a financial plan for a company, you have two objectives in mind: achieving positive cash flow and efficiently investing any excess cash flow to make your company grow. The process consists of five basic steps:

1. Estimate the month-by-month flow of funds into the business from all sources, including gains on external investments.
2. Estimate the month-by-month flow of funds out of the business, including both operating expenses and capital investments.

Equity (total funds) = $10,000

Annual earnings = $10,000 funds × 15% return = $1,500 profit

$$\text{Return on equity} = \frac{\$1,500 \text{ profit}}{\$10,000 \text{ equity}} = 15\%$$

Equity = $10,000
+ Debt = $30,000
Total funds = $40,000

Annual earnings = $40,000 funds × 15% return = $6,000
− Annual interest cost = $30,000 debt × 10% interest = $3,000
Profit = $3,000

$$\text{Return on equity with borrowed funds} = \frac{\$3,000 \text{ profit}}{\$10,000 \text{ equity}} = 30\%$$

Exhibit 19.1
How Leverage Works
If you invest $10,000 of your own money in a business venture and it yields 15 percent (or $1,500), your return on equity is 15 percent. However, if you borrow an additional $30,000 at 10 percent interest and invest a total of $40,000 with the same 15 percent yield, the ultimate return on your $10,000 equity is 30 percent (or $3,000). The key to using leverage successfully is to try to make sure that your profit on the total funds is greater than the interest you must pay on the portion of it that is borrowed.

3. Compare inflows and outflows. If cash flow is negative, determine how to make it positive, either by reducing outflows or increasing inflows. If cash flow is positive, determine how to invest excess funds most productively.
4. Choose which capital investments should be made for continued growth. Determine the most cost-effective combination of inside and outside sources of financing.
5. Establish a system for tracking the flow of funds and measuring the return on investment.

In smaller companies like Jim Kilmer's Remlik, the owner is directly involved in financial management. In larger operations, financial planning is the responsibility of a department that reports to a vice president of finance. In addition to overseeing the inflow and outflow of money, financial managers often handle other related functions (see Exhibit 19.2).

The Sources and Uses of Funds

Where can a firm obtain the money it needs? The most obvious source would be revenues—cash received from sales, rentals of property, interest on short-term investments, and so on. Another likely source would be suppliers who may be willing to do business on credit, thus enabling the company to postpone payment. Most firms also obtain money in the form of loans from banks, finance companies, or other commercial lenders. In addition, public companies can sell shares of stock, and large corporations can sell bonds.

The money obtained from these sources is used to cover the expenses of the business and to acquire new assets (see Exhibit 19.3). Some financing needs are related to day-to-day operations, such as meeting the payroll and buying inventory. Money is also needed to buy land, production facilities, and equipment. As you might imagine, finding money to take care of next month's payroll is different

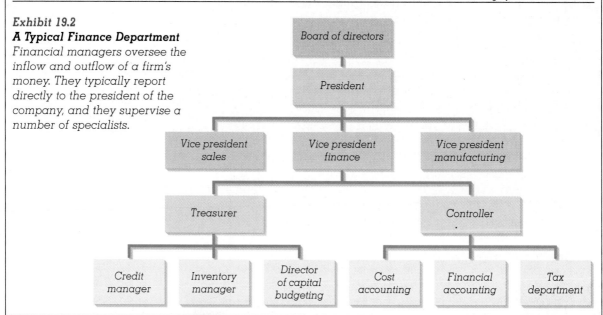

Exhibit 19.2
A Typical Finance Department
Financial managers oversee the inflow and outflow of a firm's money. They typically report directly to the president of the company, and they supervise a number of specialists.

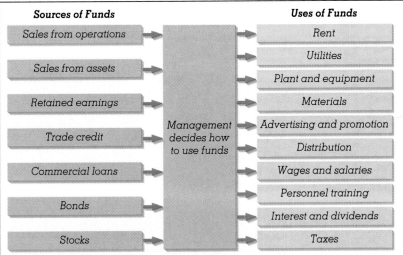

Exhibit 19.3
The Flow of a Company's Funds
Financial management involves both finding suitable sources of funds and deciding on the most appropriate uses for those funds.

Sources of Funds

- Sales from operations
- Sales from assets
- Retained earnings
- Trade credit
- Commercial loans
- Bonds
- Stocks

Management decides how to use funds

Uses of Funds

- Rent
- Utilities
- Plant and equipment
- Materials
- Advertising and promotion
- Distribution
- Wages and salaries
- Personnel training
- Interest and dividends
- Taxes

from arranging the financing for a new manufacturing plant that will be operational three years from now. For this reason, financial matters are often discussed in terms of time periods: short-term (less than one year) and long-term (over one year).

The Cost of Capital

Generally speaking, a company wants to obtain money at the lowest cost and risk. However, lenders and investors want to receive the highest possible return on their investment at the lowest risk. Therefore, a company's **cost of capital,** the price it must pay to raise money, depends on the risk associated with the company, the prevailing level of interest rates, and management's selection of funding vehicles.

cost of capital Average rate of interest a firm pays on its combination of debt and equity

Risk

Lenders and investors who provide money to businesses expect their returns to be in proportion to the two types of risk they face: the quality of the venture and time. Obviously, the more financially solid a company is, the less risk investors face. However, time plays a vital role. The longer a lender or investor must wait to receive an expected return, the greater the risk; a dollar is worth less tomorrow than it is today, so lenders need to be compensated for waiting to be repaid. As a result, long-term loans or investments cost a company more than short-term loans or investments.

Generally speaking, a company with a sound financial position can obtain capital for short-term needs more cheaply than less secure rivals. A company that is seeking capital for long-term needs (such as building a new manufacturing plant) will pay more if lenders and investors are concerned about the borrower's financial health.

Interest Rates

Regardless of how solid a company is, its cost of money will vary over time because interest rates fluctuate. The prime rate is the lowest interest rate offered on short-term bank loans to preferred bor-

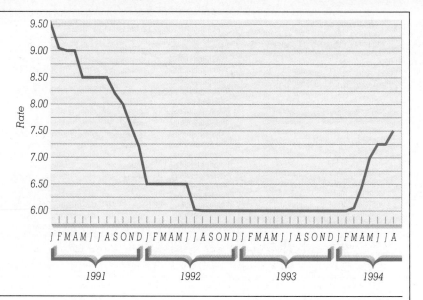

Exhibit 19.4
Average Prime Rate by Month
The prime rate is the rate of interest charged on loans that banks make to their largest, most creditworthy business customers. Fluctuations in the prime rate are tied closely to the interest rates that banks pay the Federal Reserve.

rowers. The prime changes irregularly and, at times, quite frequently (see Exhibit 19.4). A financial manager planning a short-term project when the prime rate is 8.5 percent would want to reevaluate the project if the prime rose to 10 percent a few months later. The company might not be able to afford the project after the higher prime rate increased the cost of borrowing.

Financial managers try to time their borrowing to take advantage of drops in interest rates, but this option is not always possible. A firm's need for money doesn't always coincide with a period of favorable rates. At times, a company may be forced to borrow when rates are high and then renegotiate the loan when rates drop.

Mix of Funding Vehicles

Apart from timing their borrowing properly, financial managers must choose from an array of funding vehicles. When deciding how to balance these options, financial managers analyze the pros and cons of internal versus external financing, short- versus long-term funding, and debt versus equity.

Internal Versus External Financing. Using a company's own money to finance its growth has one chief attraction: No interest payments are required. For this reason, many companies rely on *retained earnings,* the money kept by the firm after meeting its expenses and taxes. Some companies also raise money internally by *selling assets.* However, internal financing is not free; this money has an opportunity cost. That is, a company might be better off investing retained earnings in external opportunities rather than using those earnings as internal financing. Most companies depend on some degree of external financing. The issue is not so much *whether* to use outside money; rather, it's a question of how much should be raised, by what means, and when. The answers to such questions determine the firm's **capital structure,** its mix of debt and equity.

capital structure Financing mix of a firm

Short- Versus Long-Term Funding. When choosing between short- and long-term financing, companies are guided by the **matching principle**—the concept that the timing of a company's borrowing should roughly match the timing of its spending. If you borrow money for short-term purposes, you should plan to pay it back in that time frame so that the flow of money into and out of the business is balanced. At the same time, when you undertake a project that will last for some time, you should fund it with long-term financing that will stretch your repayment over an extended period. Short-term interest rates are typically lower than long-term interest rates, but they're also more volatile. To avoid sudden rate changes that might affect the company's financial health, managers usually avoid short-term financing for long-term projects.

Debt Versus Equity. When choosing between debt and equity, companies consider various elements (see Exhibit 19.5). Generally speaking, debt is cheaper than equity for two reasons: (1) companies can deduct the interest on debt from their taxes, whereas dividend payments on stock (earnings distributed to shareholders) are not deductible; (2) bondholders and lenders must always be paid before shareholders, and because they assume less risk than stockholders, the company can pay them a lower rate of return over time.

Although debt has its advantages, it also has one major disadvantage: Too much of it causes a high degree of risk. A company that sells stock can survive rough times by omitting dividends, but one that can't meet its loan and bond commitments could be forced into

matching principle *Concept that long-term projects should be funded with long-term sources of capital, whereas short-term expenditures should be funded from current income*

Characteristic	Debt	Equity
Claim on income	Company must pay interest on debt held by bondholders and lenders before paying any dividends to shareholders. Interest payments must be met regardless of operating results.	Shareholders may receive dividends after creditors have received interest payments; however, company is not required to pay dividends.
Claim on assets	If company fails, bondholders and lenders have a claim on company assets, which are sold and used to reimburse the creditors.	After all creditors have been paid, shareholders can claim any remaining assets.
Repayment terms	Company must repay lenders and retire bonds on a specific schedule.	Company is not required to repay shareholders for their investment in the enterprise.
Tax treatment	Company can deduct interest payments from its corporate income tax.	Company must pay dividends from after-tax income.
Influence over management	Creditors can impose limits on management only if interest payments are not received.	As owners of the company, shareholders can vote on some aspects of corporate operations. Shareholder influence varies, depending on whether stock is widely distributed or closely held.

Exhibit 19.5
Debt Versus Equity
The cost of debt is generally lower than the cost of equity, largely because the interest paid on debt is tax-deductible. However, too much debt can increase the risk that a company will be unable to meet its interest and principal payments.

Company	Dollar value of IPO
British Sky Broadcasting	1,300,000,000
Nabisco	1,000,000,000
Telewest	615,000,000
Southern Peru Copper	370,000,000
Bridas	140,000,000

bankruptcy. Many U.S. companies got into trouble by taking on too much debt during the 1980s. As their interest payments ballooned, they had to dip into profits to cover repayments. All this debt effectively canceled out the tax advantages of leveraging, and the financial condition of many companies became so weak that they paid higher interest on new debt because of the added risk.[2]

Offering stock to the public for the first time, a process known as *going public,* involves other advantages and disadvantages. Dividend payments can be omitted and, unlike creditors, stockholders do not have to be repaid later. However, equity financing is more costly than debt financing because dividends are paid with dollars that remain after the company has paid income tax. In addition, the original company owners have to share control of the company and the rights to future earnings with stockholders. Still, an *initial public offering,* called *IPO* for short, is a good option for many companies (see Exhibit 19.6). "The war chest of new capital dramatically improves the balance sheet," says Professor Jeffrey Timmons of Harvard Business School. "The company now has cash and liquidity."[3]

Capital Budgeting

Stockholders, of course, invest in public companies for more than just dividends. They're speculating on a company's ability to grow and compete. For that to happen, a company makes **capital investments,** such as a new or renovated plant, new equipment, or even major personnel training programs. Before any move can be made, however, each company faces crucial questions, including which of the many possible capital investments to make, how to finance those that are undertaken, and even whether to make any capital investments at all. This process is called **capital budgeting.**

capital investments Money paid to acquire something of permanent value in a business

capital budgeting Process for evaluating proposed investments in select projects that provide the best long-term financial return

All divisions within a company might issue capital requests—essentially, "wish lists" of investments that would make the company more profitable and thus more valuable to its owners over time. The financial manager first decides which investments need evaluation and which don't. The routine replacement of old equipment probably wouldn't need evaluation; however, a new manufacturing facility would. The purpose of a financial evaluation is to determine whether the amount of money required for a particular investment will be greater than, equal to, or less than the amount of revenue it will generate. On the basis of this analysis, the financial manager can determine which projects should be approved.

Northwest Airlines canceled a $3.5 billion order for new jet aircraft as part of a recent drive to control long-term expenses. The company had been having cash-flow problems, and its financial managers determined that canceling the 74 airplanes—and postponing other airplane purchases—would strengthen its financial situation. Although this move helped Northwest get through a difficult period, some industry analysts warned that the airline needed the new planes to keep up with Japan Airlines, Singapore Airlines, and other competitors.[4] As Northwest's financial executives know, weighing immediate results against potential future results is a delicate but necessary balancing act.

Possible capital investments are not only evaluated but also ranked according to the standards that are considered most important to the company. If the firm is growing, then projects that would produce the greatest growth rates would receive highest priority. However, if the company is trying to reduce costs, those projects that enhance the company's efficiency and productivity would be ranked toward the top.

In fact, the financial manager may decide that, given the company's strategy, the financial risks of all proposed investments are much greater than alternative uses for that money. So instead of buying new equipment, a company may choose to invest in short-term certificates of deposit, or it may choose to repurchase shares of stock from investors. In addition, one company may be able to finance projects at a lower cost than another, which is an important element in any decision to spend or invest money. That's why some companies increase their capital spending more than others, even though economic conditions are the same for both.

Before Mead Paper decided to build a new mill in Phoenix City, the company used capital budgeting to determine the value of this capital investment.

SHORT-TERM FINANCING

Short-term debt is any debt that will be repaid within one year. The three primary categories of short-term debt are

- Trade credit from suppliers
- Loans from a commercial bank or some other type of short-term lending institution
- Money from the sale of commercial paper to outside investors or other businesses

Exhibit 19.7 gives an overview of these three sources.

short-term debt Borrowed funds used to cover current expenses (generally repaid within a year)

Trade Credit

Trade credit is the most widespread source of short-term financing for business. Rather than borrowing money to pay for products or supplies, a company buys on credit from the supplier. The degree of

trade credit Credit obtained by the purchaser directly from the supplier

Exhibit 19.7
Major Sources of Short-Term Funds

Although companies of all types and sizes use short-term debt, these financing vehicles are particularly important for small businesses, which typically do not have the option of selling bonds or stock.

Arrangement	Example
Trade credit	
Open-book account	EverFresh Grocery Store buys display racks from Reliable Retail Equipment and agrees to pay the debt in full in 30 days or with a 2 percent discount in 10 days.
Promissory note	EverFresh signs a note promising payment in 30 days.
Loans from financial institutions	
Unsecured bank loan	EverFresh borrows from First National Bank on its good name and repays with interest.
Secured loan	
Pledge of accounts receivable	EverFresh borrows from a bank or commercial finance company on the bills owed it and repays with interest.
Pledge of inventory	EverFresh borrows from a bank or finance company on its marketable groceries and repays with interest.
Pledge of other property	EverFresh borrows from a commercial lender on its delivery truck and repays with interest.
Sales of accounts receivable	EverFresh sells what is owed it for less than the amount owed.
Loans from investors	
Commercial paper	EverFresh borrows money from First National and Reliable at a lower interest rate solely on the promise to repay.`

formality in such arrangements ranges from a simple handshake to an ironclad written agreement. Two of the most common forms of trade credit are open-book credit and promissory notes.

Open-Book Credit

open-book credit *Payment terms that allow the purchaser to take possession of goods and pay for them later; also referred to as an* open account

A majority of all business transactions involving merchandise are financed through **open-book credit,** sometimes referred to as an "open account." This is an informal arrangement whereby a purchaser may obtain products before paying for them. Say that you own a men's-clothing store. You place an order for men's suits with the manufacturer, who agrees to let you have them on credit. Later, when you begin to sell the suits, you pay the manufacturer's bill. This arrangement enables you to minimize the mismatch between cash outflows and inflows.

The suit manufacturer also benefits. By offering you 60 days to pay your bills, as opposed to the more customary 30 days, the manufacturer persuades you to buy from him or her rather than from a rival supplier. In addition, to encourage you to pay promptly, most suppliers will give you a discount. For example, an invoice that shows payment terms of "2/10, net 30" is offering a 2 percent discount if you pay the bill within 10 days. You can also choose to wait up to 30 days to pay this bill, but then you'll have to pay in full, losing the chance to deduct 2 percent from your payment.

Promissory Notes

Not all businesspeople are comfortable with the relative informality of open-book credit. They prefer the security of a written agreement to repay, signed in advance by the customer they're supplying. One such agreement is a **promissory note,** an uncondi-tional written commitment drawn up by the borrower, who promises to pay the creditor a fixed sum of money on a specified date in return for immediate credit. Promissory notes often include an interest rate, which is indicated on the note itself.

Loans

As important as trade credit may be to a business, a time may come when other sources of short-term fund-ing are required. Perhaps the business finds itself unable to pay its own debts because customers have not yet paid theirs. The managers of the business may want to make a purchase for which they have to pay cash. In either case, the business may turn to a commercial bank or other financial institution for short-term credit.

The interest charged on a short-term loan may be either fixed or floating. With a fixed-rate loan, interest payments are constant throughout the life of the loan. With a variable-rate loan, loan payments fluctuate, de-pending on increases and decreases in prevailing inter-est rates. Banks charge their largest corporate customers the most favorable rate—the prime rate. They charge all other businesses the prime rate plus a given num-ber of percentage points. Assume that the prime rate is 6.5 percent. The interest rate for a large borrower might match that prime rate, but the interest rate for a smaller borrower might be prime plus 3 percentage points, for a total of 9.5 percent.

Secured Loans

Secured loans are those backed by something of value, known as **collateral,** which may be seized by the lender in the event that the borrower fails to repay the loan. The three main types of collateral are accounts receivable, inventories, and other property.

When a business loan is secured with *accounts receivable,* its cus-tomers' outstanding balances on open-book accounts are used as col-lateral. Suppose the Global Gadget Company has sold $100,000 worth of gadgets to various customers on open-book credit. Global may borrow about $75,000 from its bank by promising that all open-book credit payments will be paid to the bank.

Another alternative is to sell accounts receivable, at a discount, to a finance company instead of using them for collateral, a procedure known as **factoring** accounts receivable. The factor charges a dis-count, so the company receives less than the full amount of its ac-counts receivable. Generally, a company receives a cash payment of about 80 percent of the value of its accounts. Customers are directed

promissory note *Unconditional writ-ten promise to repay a certain sum of money on a specified date*

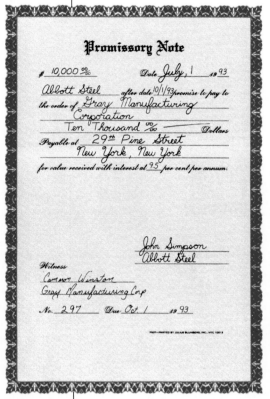

A promissory note gives the credi-tor a written guarantee of pay-ment for goods obtained on credit.

secured loans *Loans backed up with something of value that the lender can claim in case of default, such as a piece of property*

collateral *Tangible asset a lender can claim if a borrower defaults on a loan*

factoring *Sale of a firm's accounts re-ceivable, at a discount, to a finance company, known as a factor*

to pay their bills directly to the *factor,* a finance company that specializes in this type of loan. Retailers often use factoring because it reduces the headaches of trying to collect unpaid bills. Although the retailer doesn't receive the full value of the receivables, it does get cash immediately, which leaves it free to concentrate on selling merchandise instead of trying to collect bills. This technique, which usually costs the company more than a secured loan, is also used by electronics manufacturers, health-care companies, and other fast-growing businesses in need of financing (see Exhibit 19.8).[5]

In some industries, businesses commonly borrow by pledging their *inventories* (generally finished goods rather than raw materials) as security for a loan. If a firm has an excellent credit rating and valuable inventories, its bank or finance company may simply accept the firm's signed statement that the inventories are pledged to the lender in the event of nonpayment. More often, the lender insists that the borrower place the inventory in a separate warehouse for safekeeping.

Appliance dealers, car dealers, and other businesses often finance their inventory by using *floor-planning,* a short-term borrowing arrangement in which the lender pays for the merchandise, turns it over to the borrower, and is repaid as the borrower sells each item out of the inventory. Using the serial numbers on the television sets, cars, or stoves, the lender can identify each piece of merchandise that has been pledged as collateral on such loans.

Many other forms of collateral are used to secure loans. If something has value, chances are that some bank or financial institution will lend on it. Short-term loans are commonly made against *movable property,* including automobiles, trucks, and agricultural machines. When a business takes out a loan to buy such an item, the bank or finance company will sometimes require the borrower to sign a **chattel mortgage** agreement in addition to a loan agreement. Under the terms of the chattel mortgage, the movable property—along with

chattel mortgage *Agreement that the movable property purchased through a loan belongs to the borrower, although the lender has a legal right to the property if payments are not made as specified in the loan agreement*

Exhibit 19.8
Factoring Becomes More Popular
The volume of factoring nearly doubled between 1983 and 1993 as more companies used this form of financing to fuel growth in the United States and abroad.

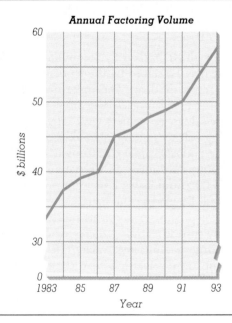

Annual Factoring Volume

You have an idea for an item or a service that you are convinced has a market just waiting to be tapped. However, you need money—to get started, to purchase inventory, to train employees, or to build a plant. Here are the steps you take to obtain a business loan.

Define Your Project

Be as specific and as accurate as possible. Ask yourself whether it is money (and not some sort of management action) that is needed. Once your project is clearly defined, prepare a financial forecast of what will happen as a result of obtaining a loan. This forecast must show precisely where the money will go, how it will affect your business, when it will show a return, how much of a return can reasonably be expected, and when and how you will repay the loan. Three formats for this information include the profit-and-loss statement, the balance sheet, and the cash flow. If you cannot do this forecast yourself, you can hire an accountant.

Identify Possible Lenders

Talk with a variety of lenders—for example, a commercial bank, a savings and loan association, a finance company, and a private investor. Ask neighbors and local businesspeople or your own suppliers, customers, and business colleagues for the names of lenders and loan officers. You are looking not only for competitive services and rates but also for a loan officer who is competent and easy to work with.

Once you have an idea about the institution and the person you would like to work with, contact that person and request an initial interview. At your first meeting, talk in detail about your project, your financial forecast, your background, and your experience. Also indicate the amount and the duration of the credit you are seeking. Ask what papers you will need to prepare, which documents must accompany those papers, and

HOW TO PLAN AND NEGOTIATE A BUSINESS LOAN

what terms the bank can offer on your type of loan. Postpone any discussion of collateral, existing debts, mortgages, or personal assets, because you are only gathering information at this point.

Find out about the lending institution's approval process—how long it takes and what mechanics are involved. Carefully note the answers you get from each lender you contact. If you feel uneasy or vague about anything discussed, call that lender for clarification (being sure to make note of the time, the date, and the person who gives you the information).

Prepare a Persuasive Application

This is the time to promote yourself, your project, and your loan to the bank. Even a weak balance sheet may be overlooked if the bank has confidence in you and in your project. The best way to highlight key information relating to your loan application is use your own financial statement rather than the bank's preprinted form to present the figures.

Above all, your project must be creditworthy. You will need adequate equity and available assets to back up the business. (If you are not sure how much equity you must have, compare your business with similar existing businesses.) Show earning power or cash flow sufficient to repay the loan (preferably both), and provide a wide margin of safety. Most important, project confidence in the business ability of the management of your company.

Negotiate the Best Terms and Conditions Possible

Negotiating your loan involves two areas: terms and conditions. *Terms* refer to the rate of interest for your loan and the maturity schedule—when and how much you will pay the lender on a regular basis in order to repay the loan. Request a "skip-payment" plan so that, if needed, payments can be suspended for a time. If the lender will not accept a repayment schedule that you know you can make, go elsewhere.

Conditions refer to lender requests for collateral, additional equity, or other covenants (meaning any other restrictions the lender wants to attach to your loan). Try not to pledge more collateral than necessary. If possible, insist that you be notified at least 15 business days in advance if the lender decides to demand immediate repayment. Read everything in the loan papers. Better yet, have an attorney review them as well.

Learn from Rejection

If your application is rejected, get a clear statement of exactly what the lender needs for approval, and ask for suggestions about alternative ways to finance your project. If that fails, go to another lender.

Maintain a Positive Relationship with Your Lender

Pay on time, not one day late. If you find that you cannot comply with any condition or payment schedule, call the lender immediately and follow up with a letter. Give the lender periodic progress reports about your business. If you have any setbacks, explain the circumstances in person, and take a detailed written report with you. The annual review of your loan presents an opportunity for requesting a lower rate and better loan conditions. If you become dissatisfied with your lender, you may want to find an additional lender to handle part of your business. Such action can spark competitive spirit among the lenders and also provide you with another source of credit.

the risk of loss—belongs to the borrower, but the lender can take possession of the property if payments are not made as specified in the loan agreement.

Unsecured Loans

An **unsecured loan** is one that requires no collateral. Instead, the lender relies on the general credit record and the earning power of the borrower. To increase the returns on such loans and to obtain some protection in case of default, most lenders insist that the borrower maintain some minimum amount of money on deposit at the bank—a **compensating balance**—while the loan is outstanding. Although the borrower pays interest on the full amount of the loan, a substantial portion of it remains on deposit in the bank.

Another important type of unsecured loan eliminates the need to negotiate with the bank each time a business needs to borrow. The line of credit is an agreed-on maximum amount of money the bank is willing to lend the business during a specific period of time, usually a year. Once a line of credit has been established, the business may obtain unsecured loans for any amount up to that limit, provided the bank has funds. The line of credit can be canceled at any time, so companies that want to be sure of obtaining credit when needed should arrange a **revolving line of credit,** which guarantees that the bank will honor the line of credit up to the stated amount. An extra fee is usually charged for this legal commitment, which can extend up to three years.

Commercial Paper

A short-term financing option that has become increasingly popular for a company with a good credit standing and reputation is to borrow from other businesses and investors. The company borrowing money issues *commercial paper,* which represents a promise to pay back a stated amount of money within a stated number of days (legally, 1 to 270 days). The business or investor generally buys commercial paper at a price lower than the face value; then at the end of the period, the buyer receives the face value. The difference between the discounted price and the face value is the equivalent of interest on a loan. For example, a 90-day, $1 million offering of Exxon commercial paper is a promise by Exxon to repay $1 million to the holder of the paper 90 days from the date of the loan. The buyer would give Exxon less than $1 million, perhaps $970,000. The $30,000 difference is the interest earned by the holder during the 90 days.

The market for commercial paper has grown steadily in recent years (see Exhibit 19.9). The appeal of commercial paper is threefold: (1) it doesn't require a compensating balance, as unsecured loans do; (2) it allows a borrower to lock in an acceptable interest rate for up to 270 days; and (3) it's easier for a company to sell commercial paper for short-term financing than to receive a commercial loan at a bank (because companies don't have to "qualify" to sell commercial paper). More than any other, this last feature is what has made commercial paper increasingly popular for the larger, more stable companies that can use this financing method.

---

unsecured loan Loan requiring no collateral but a good credit rating

compensating balance Portion of an unsecured loan that is kept on deposit at the lending institution to protect the lender and increase the lender's return

revolving line of credit Guaranteed line of credit that can be used over a specified period

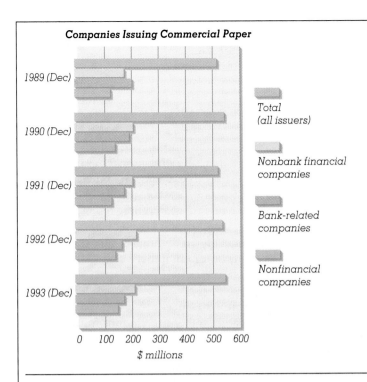

Companies Issuing Commercial Paper

1989 (Dec)

1990 (Dec)

1991 (Dec)

1992 (Dec)

1993 (Dec)

0   100   200   300   400   500   600
$ millions

Total (all issuers)

Nonbank financial companies

Bank-related companies

Nonfinancial companies

Exhibit 19.9
The Market for Commercial Paper
As competition for loan services grew during the past decade, the market for commercial paper enjoyed tremendous growth. U.S. corporations could more easily find buyers for their commercial paper than find a bank willing to approve a traditional short-term loan.

LONG-TERM FINANCING

When it comes to financing long-term projects—such as major construction, acquisition of other companies, and research and development—most companies rely on a combination of internal and external funding sources (see Exhibit 19.10). The four main sources of external funding are loans, leases, bonds, and equity.

Long-Term Loans and Leases

Long-term loans are repaid over a period of one year or more and may be either secured or unsecured. The most common type of secured loan is a mortgage, in which a piece of property is used as collateral. Commercial banks traditionally made most of the long-term loans to businesses, but pension funds and insurance companies have increased the number of long-term corporate loans they make. In-

long-term loans *Debt that must be repaid over a period of more than a year*

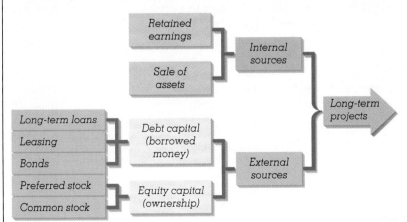

Retained earnings

Sale of assets

Internal sources

Long-term loans

Leasing

Bonds

Preferred stock

Common stock

Debt capital (borrowed money)

Equity capital (ownership)

External sources

Long-term projects

Exhibit 19.10
Sources of Long-Term Funds
To finance long-term projects, financial managers rely on both internal and external sources of capital.

terest rates on long-term loans are generally higher than those on short-term loans because the lenders demand a greater return for giving up the use of their money for a longer period.

Rather than borrowing from a commercial lender to buy a piece of property or equipment, a firm may enter into a **lease,** under which the owner of an item allows another party to use it in exchange for regular payments. Under certain conditions, leasing provides tax advantages for both lessor and lessee. Leasing may also be a good alternative for a company that has difficulty obtaining loans because of a poor credit rating. Creditors are more willing to provide a lease than a loan because, should the company fail, the lessor need not worry about a default on loan payments; it can simply repossess equipment it legally owns. Some firms use leases to finance up to 35 percent of their total assets, particularly in industries such as airlines, where assets are mostly large pieces of equipment.

Bonds

When a company—or a government—needs to borrow a large sum of money, it may not be able to get the entire amount from a single source. Under such circumstances, it may borrow from many individual investors by issuing bonds. A **bond** is a certificate that obligates the company (or government agency) to repay a certain sum, plus interest, to the bondholder.

A bond is like a loan certificate indicating that its issuer has borrowed a sum of money from the bondholder. Each bond has a **denomination,** the amount of the loan represented by one bond. Bonds sold by corporations are usually available in $1,000 denominations, but they also come in denominations of $5,000, $10,000, $50,000, and $100,000. A bond usually shows the date when the full amount of the bond, or the **principal,** must be repaid. Bonds typically have maturity dates of 10 years or more.

Secured and Unsecured Bonds

Like loans, corporate bonds may be either secured or unsecured. **Secured bonds** are backed by specific property of one kind or an-

lease Legal agreement that obligates the user of an asset to make payments to the owner of the asset in exchange for using it

bond Certificate of indebtedness that is sold to raise funds

denomination Face value of a single bond

principal Amount of a debt, excluding any interest

secured bonds Bonds backed by specific assets

Bonds are transferable long-term securities that pay interest regularly for the term of the loan.

other that will pass to the bondholders if the issuer does not live up to the terms of the agreement. The security may be a mortgage on a piece of real estate or a claim to other assets, such as freight cars, airplanes, or plant equipment owned by a company. **Unsecured bonds,** also called *debentures,* are backed not by collateral but by the general good name of the issuing company. If the bond-issuing company fails, the bondholders have a claim on the assets—but only after creditors with specific collateral have been paid.

unsecured bonds Bonds backed only by the reputation of the issuer; also called debentures

Bond Interest Rates

A bond provides interest, stated in terms of an annual percentage rate but paid at six-month intervals. For example, the holder of a $1,000 bond that pays 8 percent interest due January 15 and July 15 could expect to receive $40 on each of those dates.

A look at the financial section of any newspaper will show that some corporations sell new bonds at an interest rate two or three percentage points higher than that offered by other companies. Yet the terms of the bonds seem similar. These variations in interest rates reflect the level of risk associated with the bond. A corporation with excellent prospects of earning enough money in future years to pay both the interest on the bonds and the principal at maturity can afford to offer a relatively low interest rate. A less secure borrower has to offer a higher interest rate in order to attract buyers. Bond-rating agencies rate bonds on the basis of the financial stability of issuing companies. Bonds that are rated investment grade are considered the safest bonds for investors. Bonds rated below investment grade are popularly known as **junk bonds.**

junk bonds Bonds that pay high interest because they are below investment

Retirement of Debt

A company that sells bonds must repay its debt to the bondholders. Normally, this is done when the bonds mature—say, 10, 15, or 20 years after the bond is issued. The cost of retiring the debt can be staggering because bonds are generally issued in quantity—perhaps thousands of individual bonds in a single issue. To ease the burden of redeeming its bonds, companies sometimes issue **serial bonds,** which mature at various times, as opposed to **term bonds,** which all mature at the same time.

serial bonds Bonds from a single issue that must be repaid at intervals

term bonds Bonds from a single issue that must be repaid simultaneously

Another way of relieving the financial strain of retiring many bonds all at once is to set up a **sinking fund.** When a corporation issues a bond payable by a sinking fund, it must set aside a certain sum of money each year to pay the debt. This money is either used to retire a few bonds each year or set aside to accumulate until the issue matures.

sinking fund Account into which a company makes annual payments for use in redeeming its bonds in the future

With most bond issues, a corporation retains the right to pay off the bonds before maturity. Bonds containing this provision are known as **callable bonds,** or redeemable bonds. If a company issues bonds when interest rates are high and interest rates fall later on, it may want to pay off its high-interest bonds and sell a new issue at a lower rate. However, this feature carries a price tag: Investors must be offered a higher interest rate to encourage them to buy callable bonds. The portion of the percentage rate that is above market rates is actually a "call premium."

callable bonds Bonds that a company can redeem before the stated maturity date; also known as redeemable

Another way for a company to pay off bonds is to repay them with stock rather than with money. Bonds that may be paid off with stock are called *convertible bonds.* The actual decision to accept stock or money is left up to the bondholder. Suppose a company sold an issue of $1,000 convertible bonds with an interest rate of 10 percent and a maturity date of 1999. A purchaser would receive $100 a year and get back the original $1,000 in 1999. But at any time before 1999, the bondholder could exchange each bond for an agreed-on number of shares of common stock in the company. If the value of the stock rose appreciably after the date on which the bonds were first issued, the investor might decide to convert the bond to common stock. Because investors have two options for making money with them, convertible bonds generally carry lower interest rates—a feature that reduces the company's costs.

Equity

Unlike debt, which must be repaid, equity represents a "piece of the action." When a company raises capital by increasing equity, it expands the ownership of the business. Each investor becomes a part owner of the company, with the expectation of sharing in its profits through dividends and the capital gain that results when the stock is sold at a price higher than its purchase price. In a small company, the source of equity is generally a single individual or a limited number of investors. The owner might personally invest more money in the business or might seek outside funding through a venture capitalist. If the firm is a partnership, a new partner might be brought in. In a larger business, when the need for funds exceeds the resources of a few people, equity may be obtained by selling stock to many individual investors on the open market.

stock certificate *Document that proves stock ownership*

Stocks are simply shares of ownership in a company, and the **stock certificate** that a shareholder receives is evidence of ownership. Each certificate shows the name of the shareholder, the number of shares of stock owned, and the special characteristics of the stock. Many stock certificates also bear a **par value,** an arbitrary face value that is usually less than the stock's estimated market value and that may be used (for certain kinds of stock) as the basis for figuring dividends.

par value *Arbitrary value assigned to a stock that is shown on the stock certificate*

The number of stock shares a company sells depends on the amount of equity capital the company will require and on the price of each share it sells. A corporation's board of directors sets a maximum number of shares into which the business can be divided. In theory, all these shares—called **authorized stock**—may be sold at once. What often happens, however, is that the company sells only part of its authorized stock. The part sold and held by shareholders is called **issued stock;** as yet unsold stock is called **unissued stock.**

authorized stock *Shares that a corporation's board of directors has decided to sell eventually*

issued stock *Authorized shares that have been released to the market*

unissued stock *Authorized shares that are to be released in the future*

Well-established companies distribute part of their profits to shareholders in the form of **dividends.** Dividends may be paid in cash, but rapidly growing companies often issue dividends in the form of stock. By doing so, they conserve the firm's cash for capital investment, research and development, and similar types of expenditures.

dividends *Payments to shareholders from a company's earnings*

Preferred Stock

A company may issue two classes of stock. **Preferred stock** gives its holders certain preferences, or special privileges, that holders of common stock do not have:

- *They are preferred as to dividends.* Dividends on preferred stocks must be paid before any dividends are paid on common stocks.
- *They are preferred as to assets.* If a company fails, preferred shareholders have the right to receive their share of whatever assets are left (after the company's debts have been paid) before common shareholders receive anything.

The amount of the dividend on preferred stock is shown on the stock certificate. It may be expressed either as a percentage of the par value or as a dollar amount. Most preferred stock accumulates dividends if the corporation does not pay them in a given period. The company must pay this accumulation before it can pay any dividends on its common stock.

Generally, preferred shareholders play a smaller role in company affairs than do the common shareholders. In some companies, preferred shareholders have no voting power at all. More commonly, they receive limited voting privileges, usually on matters that directly concern their rights, such as a decision to sell off a major part of the company or to change a provision of the charter that involves the preferred stock.

Common Stock

In spite of its name, preferred stock is far less popular as a funding vehicle than **common stock,** which gives shareholders voting rights and the last claim on dividends and assets. Their voting rights mean that holders of common stock can participate in the selection of the company's board of directors and speak out on other issues, such as mergers, acquisitions, and takeovers. However, common shareholders enjoy no special privileges as far as dividends or assets are concerned.

preferred stock *Shares that give their owners first claim on a company's dividends and assets*

common stock *Shares whose owners have voting rights and have the last claim on distributed profits and assets*

Stock certificates represent a share of the ownership of a company.

The claims of preferred shareholders and bondholders take precedence over those of common shareholders. Also, common stock never carries a stated dividend, nor are its dividends cumulative.

Why do people buy common stock when they could have more security with preferred stock? Because, in addition to receiving dividends, the profits that owners of common stock can enjoy isn't limited, the way it is for preferred stock. Preferred stock is dependable and stable; dividends are assured, but the value of the shares does not usually change much. Common stock, on the other hand, is less predictable but potentially more valuable if shares are sold for much more than their purchase price when the share price goes up.

A special type of common stock is *targeted stock,* which refers to shares linked to the performance of one unit of a public corporation. If the unit is profitable, the corporation may pay a special dividend to holders of the targeted stock—but it can also choose not to pay a dividend if the money is needed for other corporate obligations. The corporation has the right to do what it wishes with the unit's assets, so holders of targeted stock may not benefit from the unit's success. From the corporation's perspective, targeted stock is a good way of showing market watchers and investors what a particular unit can do on its own—without actually selling the unit. The first targeted stock was issued by General Motors in 1984; the handful that have been issued since have had mixed performance.[6]

Common-Stock Dividends. There is no law that requires a corporation to pay dividends on common stock. The decision is up to the board of directors, who may decide—for good reasons—to omit the dividend or keep it to a minimum. In the case of a small, young company, for instance, the best course is usually to put all the profits back into the business. This practice enables the company to grow without using expensive outside financing. In the long run, the shareholders benefit more from the growth of the company and the resulting increase in the value of their stock than they do solely from the dividend.

In addition to paying a dividend, another option for increasing shareholder value is to repurchase outstanding common stock. This option reduces the amount of issued stock, thus increasing the value of each share.

When large, well-established companies cut or omit dividends, the reason is usually a decline in profits. Dividends theoretically represent a share of the profits; when profits fall, there is less to share. The company hangs on to its cash in order to cover operating expenses. Unfortunately, shareholders not only lose out on their dividends in such situations but frequently lose out on the value of the stock as well. When a big company cuts its dividend, the price of its stock generally falls—at least temporarily.

Stock Splits. A dividend is not the only benefit a company can offer its common shareholders. Another alternative is a **stock split,** a procedure whereby the company doubles (or triples, or whatever) the number of shares that each stock certificate represents. In a 2-for-1 stock split, for example, a company whose stock was selling for $50 per share would double the number of shares outstanding, giving each shareholder two shares instead of one. Initially, these shares would

stock split *Increase in the number of shares of ownership that each stock certificate represents*

each be worth only $25, but as the market price of the stock increased, the shareholder could realize a handsome profit. Companies generally use a stock split to keep the share price at a relatively affordable level for investors.

New Issues and the Secondary Market

When a company issues new stock through an initial public offering, it is offering more slices of the profit pie. The amount of money a company can raise for each new slice depends on what the market expects the size of the total earnings pie to be. Not surprisingly, corporations often react to a rise in share prices by deciding to issue new stock.

Investors generally buy stocks from other investors rather than directly from corporations. After stock has been issued, it is bought and sold in organized markets known as **stock exchanges,** where investors trade their individual shares (see Chapter 20). The actual trading is completed by **stockbrokers,** people who buy and sell stocks on behalf of investors. As shares move back and forth, any gain or loss in value goes to the shareholders—not to the companies that issued the stock. Even though corporations do not make any money on stock traded in the secondary market, they are concerned about the fluctuations in the price of their shares, because the "going rate" establishes what a company can raise through a new issue. Companies try to buoy their stock price by paying dividends, achieving ambitious performance goals, promoting the company's reputation with investors, and buying back their shares when the price is low.

stock exchanges *Facilities where shares of stock are bought and sold*

stockbrokers *People who buy and sell shares of stock on behalf of investors*

INTERNAL FINANCIAL PLANNING AND CONTROL

Although raising money is important, using that money wisely is an equally vital task. The goal of cash management is to have as little as possible tied up in excess cash, uncollected accounts receivable, and inventory. Instead, the money should be used productively to help build the business.

Managing Cash and Marketable Securities

How much cash do you carry in your wallet? If you have more than you need to cover your immediate expenses, you're not thinking like an aggressive financial manager. Although excess cash might make you feel secure, it isn't earning any interest for you. An underlying concept of financial management is that all money should be used productively.

Still, companies occasionally find themselves with more cash on hand than they need. A seasonal business may experience a quiet period between the time when revenues are collected from the last busy season and the time when suppliers' bills are due. Department stores, for example, may have excess cash during a few weeks in January and February. A firm may also have excess cash if it is holding funds to meet a large commitment in the near future. It may be about to reach the next stage in the construction of a new plant, or it may be waiting for a special bargain on supplies. Finally, every firm keeps some surplus cash on hand as a cushion in case its needs are greater than expected.

Part of the financial manager's job is to make sure that this cash is invested so that it earns interest. The task is to find a good "parking place" for the funds, some sort of investment that will yield the highest possible return but will create no problem if the firm needs to liquidate the investment for instant cash. A number of short-term investments, called **marketable securities,** meet these needs. They are said to be "marketable" because they can easily be converted back to cash.

The financial manager has many varieties of marketable securities to choose from. Banks sell large-denomination *certificates of deposit,* which are time deposits at that bank. The federal government issues *Treasury bills,* which work like commercial paper; they are bought at a discount and redeemed by the U.S. Treasury for the face value on a specific maturity date (the date on which they must be repaid—in this case, less than a year from the date of purchase). Other businesses offer commercial paper that may be appropriate short-term investments.

When selecting a portfolio of marketable securities, financial managers must make trade-offs between safety/liquidity and maximum rate of return. Because marketable securities are generally viewed as contingency funds, most financial managers take a reasonably conservative approach to the management of these securities.

Managing Receivables and Payables

One of the big problems in managing working capital is that a company's revenues don't always come in at exactly the same rate that bills have to be paid. Financial managers must therefore carefully monitor *cash flow,* the total amount of money acquired and spent to keep the business running. The goal is to create a better match between money outflow and inflow.

One important aspect of this task is to keep a sharp eye on accounts receivable—the money owed to the firm by its customers. The volume of receivables depends on the financial manager's decisions regarding several issues. For example, who qualifies for credit and who does not? How long do customers have to pay their bills? How aggressive is the firm in collecting its debts? In addition to answering questions of this type, the financial manager analyzes the firm's receivables to identify patterns that might indicate problems.

Careful management of accounts receivable was one of the strategies that chief financial officer George Robson used to return the computer maker Unisys to profitability. The company needed to generate more cash, so Robson set out to speed up collection of the accounts receivable. Customers were asked to pay their bills a few days early—and those that were willing to pay cash instead of buying on credit received preferential treatment. Within three years, the company had slashed its accounts receivable by half, which dramatically improved the company's cash flow.[7]

---

marketable securities *Stocks, bonds, and other investments that can be turned into cash quickly*

How do you proceed after an overseas buyer places an order for the first time? Selling an item for export brings its own set of unique financial challenges. When you've never dealt with a buyer before—and the buyer is hundreds or thousands of miles away in another country—you may have difficulty determining that buyer's ability to pay your bill. What's more, you may want your money more quickly than your buyer wants to pay. How can you arrange the financial details of this sale?

Most exporters begin a new relationship with an overseas buyer by asking for a *letter of credit,* a written promise by the buyer's bank to pay a specified amount to the exporter after ordered goods have been shipped. In effect, the letter of credit substitutes the bank's credit standing for the buyer's credit standing. Of course, before it issues the letter of credit, the bank checks the buyer's credit standing to be sure that the company can afford to pay for the ordered goods.

Once the buyer's bank has approved the letter of credit, it sends it

EXPORTING MEANS FINANCING, TOO

to the exporter's bank. The exporter then ships the goods and gives its bank proof that the shipment has been made. The exporter's bank sends these documents to the buyer's bank, which pays the exporter's bill.

Using a letter of credit takes much of the worry and risk out of the first sale to a new buyer. It can also speed up payment, especially when information is sent back and forth by computer. Once you've established a relationship with a buyer, however, you may move away from requiring a letter of credit and set payment terms as you would for any other customer.

Of course, collecting bills from

overseas buyers takes time and paperwork that many companies don't want to handle. Instead, they can get immediate cash for their accounts receivable from banks or trading companies that act as factors for global transactions. Scubi Sea Fashions in Richmond, Virginia, turns to Exim Corporation, a trading company in Virginia, to finance sales of swimwear sold throughout North and South America. In addition to receiving its money more quickly, the company enjoys the convenience and safety of having the trading company check customers' credit records and collect payment.

Similarly, Blaw Knox Rolls, a West Virginia steelmaker, arranged a sale to a buyer in Brazil. Then the company sold its accounts receivables to ABN AMRO Bank, a Dutch bank with U.S. branches. The bank bought the receivables at a 7 percent discount—and approved the transaction in just 10 days, with a minimal amount of paperwork. Not every global transaction will run so smoothly, but smart exporters take the time to plan their cross-border financial moves carefully.

The flip side of managing receivables is managing payables—the bills that the company owes to its creditors. Here the objective is generally to postpone paying bills until the last moment, since accounts payable represent interest-free loans from suppliers. However, the financial manager also needs to weigh the advantages of paying promptly if doing so entitles the firm to cash discounts. In addition, paying on time is a good way to maintain the company's credit standing, which in turn influences a lender's decision to approve a loan.

More and more businesses are streamlining their accounts payable process by using **electronic data interchange (EDI),** the computerized exchange of order and payment information between companies and their suppliers. Using EDI cuts down on the mountain of paperwork and number of people needed to check orders, on shipping instructions, and on inventory details. More important, it speeds the company's order through the supplier's system—and it speeds the company's payment to the supplier. Instead of writing a check and putting it in the mail, the company uses its computer system to send payment instructions to the bank. For example, when financial managers at Chevron need to pay a supplier that ships parts to the com-

electronic data interchange (EDI)
Computerized exchange of order and payment details between businesses and suppliers

pany's oil refineries, their EDI system can direct their bank to send payment directly to the supplier's bank. More than 35 million invoices are paid through EDI every year, a number that is fast increasing as firms discover the convenience and control that EDI gives them.[8]

Managing Inventory

Inventory is another area where financial managers can fine-tune the firm's cash flow. Inventory sitting on the shelf represents capital that is tied up without earning interest. Furthermore, the firm incurs expenses for storage and handling, insurance, and taxes. In addition, there is always a risk that the inventory will become obsolete before it can be converted into finished goods and sold.

The firm's goal is to maintain enough inventory to fill orders in a timely fashion at the lowest cost. To achieve this goal, the financial manager tries to determine the **economic order quantity (EOQ),** or quantity of raw materials that, when ordered regularly, results in the lowest ordering and storage costs. The problem is complicated by the fact that minimizing ordering costs tends to increase storage costs and vice versa. The best way to cut ordering costs is to place one big order for parts and materials once a year, while the best way to cut storage costs is to order small amounts of inventory frequently. The challenge facing the financial manager is to find a compromise that minimizes total costs.

Businesses can minimize the investment in inventory by using just-in-time systems to bring supplies into the production process when and where they're needed. Lifeline Systems, a maker of personal-response communication devices, uses JIT to minimize the level of raw materials on hand and to speed up shipment time. Parts are used within four days of their receipt, which lowers the investment in raw materials; just as important, finished products are sent to customers within 24 hours, which reduces the amount of inventory that is on hand.[9]

The most efficient JIT systems use computer links to connect businesses with their customers and suppliers. By coordinating their production schedules with their customers' delivery dates and their suppliers' delivery schedules, companies can automatically order only as much as is necessary for a given period of time.

economic order quantity (EOQ)
Optimal, or least-cost, quantity of inventory that should be ordered

1 List the five steps involved in the financial-planning process.

When developing a financial plan, the financial manager estimates the monthly inflow of funds, estimates the monthly outflow of funds, compares them to determine whether cash flow is negative or positive and how to use or create excess funds, chooses which capital investments should be made, and establishes a system for monitoring cash flows and return on investments.

2 Identify the three elements that influence a company's cost of capital.

The cost of capital depends on the risk associated with the company, the prevailing level of interest rates, and management's selection of funding vehicles.

3 State the matching principle.

The timing of a company's borrowing should roughly match the timing of its spending so that the flow of cash out of the company balances the flow of cash into the company.

4 Explain the main advantage and disadvantage of financing through debt rather than equity.

The main advantage of debt is that it is cheaper than equity: (1) Debt payments can be deducted from a company's income tax, whereas dividend payments on stock are paid with after-tax dollars; (2) companies can pay bondholders and lenders a lower rate of return over time. The main disadvantage is that too much debt causes a high degree of risk.

5 Name three major types of short-term debt.

The three major types of short-term debt are trade credit, loans, and commercial paper.

6 List four major long-term financing options.

The four major long-term financing options are loans, leases, bonds, and equity.

7 Explain the guiding principle of cash management.

The guiding principle of cash management is to limit the amount of money in excess cash, accounts receivable, and inventory to the minimum necessary to cover immediate expenses so that all available money is used productively in building the business.

8 State the financial manager's primary goal in handling receivables and payables.

The financial manager's goal is to collect amounts due from accounts receivable as quickly as possible. At the same time, the company needs to balance prompt payment of accounts payable with the possibility of receiving discounts for early payment and the maintenance of good credit standing.

As sales of Nature's Pasta increased and Jim Kilmer stood on the brink of success, he learned the hard way that a new business needed money to grow—lots of money. From product research to storage space to transportation, everything cost more than the entrepreneur was prepared to spend. Nature's Pasta was being sold in 21 stores, including some Giant Eagle supermarkets, so Kilmer knew that his product was viable. Now the challenge was to obtain financing without going too far into debt or giving away too much control.

One of Kilmer's first steps was to find money for research into ways of extending the shelf life of spaghetti squash. He solved this problem by applying for a research grant from the Ben Franklin Technology Center. Within a few months, the grant was approved—but for $50,000, not the $84,000 he had requested. Using the grant money, scientists at the Pennsylvania State University Food Science Department started work on the problem.

Next he had to find a way to fix his cash flow. Although he enjoyed a good profit margin, he found that collecting on his accounts receivable was a slow process. What's more, he had underestimated the storage and labor costs, so the money he did collect went right back out to pay urgent bills.

Fortunately, Kilmer had kept his bankers informed of his progress. "I had forwarded newspaper articles about me, called them often to tell them where I stood and told them that by November I *might* need a loan," he says. Because the bankers were aware of his needs and understood his plans, they were better able to evaluate his financial situation. The bank soon approved a $20,000 *demand loan,* which meant that Kilmer would pay interest but not have to repay the principal right away. Another advantage was that the loan did not have to be secured by his home or his other assets, so the bank wouldn't be able to take those assets from Kilmer if he didn't repay the loan.

Kilmer then began to search for investors who would put up $500,000 so that he could move his growing operation into a suitable plant. He found that few venture-capital groups would invest in start-ups. Instead, he turned to the Fay-Penn Economic Development Corporation, a nonprofit organization, for help in arranging additional financing and in locating a plant site. In the meantime, the cash crunch had become so severe that Remlik had to be temporarily shut down, even though the Penn State scientists had just succeeded in extending the shelf life of Nature's Pasta to 21 days.

Through Fay-Penn, Kilmer met several potential investors, and within a few months, he had negotiated a $500,000 deal that gave him the cash he needed. His investors gained partial ownership and seats on his board of directors, but Kilmer retained majority control of the company and the board.

Cash in hand, Kilmer started to pay himself a small salary. He also hired an office assistant to handle the administrative duties. Fay-Penn had found a suitable plant near Uniontown, but Kilmer needed more than $1 million to buy the plant and production equipment. He applied for and received several low-interest loans from state agencies and other sources and then geared up for expansion throughout Pittsburgh—and beyond.

Your Mission: Jim Kilmer has hired you as chief financial officer of Remlik. You are responsible for financial planning and reporting for the company, and Kilmer relies on you for sound advice. Consider the following problems and select the best solution to each:

1. As Remlik expands, you have to balance your cash-flow requirements with the need for higher inventory levels. You can't order huge quantities of squash at one time to get a volume discount, because it may spoil before it is processed. If you order too frequently, you will have a lot of paperwork and your transportation costs will go up. What is your best approach?

a. Install just-in-time inventory control. Every time a package of Nature's Pasta is purchased, suppliers will be electronically advised to deliver the right amount of squash to Remlik's plant.

b. Calculate the economic order quantity to determine how much squash should be on hand. Take into account how much storage space is available in the Remlik plant, how long fresh squash can be stored before it spoils, and how much money you save by ordering various large quantities.

c. Calculate the company's monthly cash flow, deduct monthly payables, and then use some of the balance to buy and store additional inventory.

2. Sales have been strong and you have reported positive cash flow for six consecutive months. As you prepare to expand into two new markets, Kilmer asks your advice on what to do with the money. What is your best response?

a. Tell him to immediately buy back some of the equity he sold when he started Remlik. This action will allow Kilmer to keep more of the money the company earns, rather than paying dividends to investors.

b. Tell him to give himself and his key workers a raise, since all have been drawing low salaries for many months.

c. Tell him to invest in promotional activities that will build demand for Nature's Pasta in Pittsburgh and in the two new markets you will enter.

3. After expanding into two new markets, you need more cash to finance higher inventory levels because of the fast-growing demand. Which of the following ways of arranging short-term financing best suits your situation?

a. Talk your supplier into letting you pay in 90 days instead of 30 days so that you can buy more without having to pay for it right away. By the time the bills come due, you will have collected your own accounts receivable.

b. Talk your supplier into letting you sign a promissory note instead of paying cash for the next shipment. To persuade the supplier to agree, offer to pay a higher interest rate than you would pay to your bank.

c. Talk a finance company into buying your accounts receivable at a discount. This strategy will relieve you of the problem of collecting when bills come due, and you will get cash that you can use to buy more squash when needed.

Your Mission: You are a loan officer at a commercial bank that does a lot of business with new companies, not just Remlik. In this position, you are expected to make good decisions regarding loans and lines of credit, on the basis of the financial information you receive from your customers.

4. Which of the following would be the most important financial information for you to obtain when doing business with entrepreneurs?

a. Determining how much of each company's revenue is devoted to repaying loans and how much is devoted to current operations

b. Determining whether each company's cash flow is positive or negative, and what the company intends to do if cash flow is negative

c. Both (a) and (b)[10]

authorized stock (584)
bond (582)
callable bonds (583)
capital budgeting (574)
capital investments (574)
capital structure (572)
chattel mortgage (578)
collateral (577)
common stock (585)
compensating balance (580)
cost of capital (571)
denomination (582)
dividends (584)
economic order quantity (EOQ) (590)

electronic data interchange (EDI) (589)
factoring (577)
financial management (568)
issued stock (584)
junk bonds (583)
lease (582)
leverage (569)
long-term loans (581)
marketable securities (588)
matching principle (573)
open-book credit (576)
par value (584)
preferred stock (585)
principal (582)

promissory note (577)
revolving line of credit (580)
secured bonds (582)
secured loans (577)
serial bonds (583)
short-term debt (575)
sinking fund (583)
stockbrokers (587)
stock certificate (584)
stock exchanges (587)
stock split (586)
term bonds (583)
trade credit (575)
unissued stock (584)
unsecured bonds (583)
unsecured loan (580)

REVIEW QUESTIONS

1. What is the primary goal of financial management?
2. What are the two main types of trade credit?
3. What are some of the assets a business can pledge as collateral for a loan?

4. What is the function of commercial paper?
5. What are the four ways to pay back the debt that bonds incur?
6. Why would a company consider going public through an initial public offering?

7. What are marketable securities, and what purpose do they serve?
8. What types of projects are typically considered in the capital-budgeting process?

A SELLER OF BEST-SELLERS GOES PUBLIC

How does a nationwide bookseller finance a shift from small mall bookstores to huge discount stores? That was the challenge facing Leonard Riggio, chairman and CEO of Barnes & Noble. Riggio's New York–based company owned the B. Dalton, Doubleday, Scribner's, and Barnes & Noble book chains, which together sold more than $1 billion worth of books in a year. Already the company operated some 900 stores in shopping centers and downtown locations across 48 states.

Riggio saw that more and more of the book battles were being fought in "superstores," gigantic stores with up to 150,000 titles on the shelf (compared with 15,000 to 25,000 in the typical mall store). Where the mall stores had only about 3,000 square feet in which to sell books, superstores could sell books in spacious, attractive surroundings that ranged from roughly 10,000 to 40,000 square feet. Superstores had the space for a coffee bar or a children's corner (or both), which encouraged customers to stay for an hour or two. Also, once a superstore was open for a few years, it was more economical to operate than a mall store.

Superstores were the future, and Barnes & Noble already operated more than 100 superstores, but its competitors weren't standing still. The Crown chain had more than 60 superstores, and the Borders chain had more than 44 superstores—and these rivals were expanding into more superstores. At the same time, independent booksellers were fighting back by offering specialized books and individualized customer service. In short, competition was becoming more intense.

To compete more effectively, Riggio planned to shut down some less productive mall bookstores and push ahead with a string of new superstores. Although Barnes & Noble's cash flow was strong, financing this rapid expansion required more long-term debt, which raised the amount of money spent on interest. Plowing so much money into expansion didn't help the company's profit picture: It posted a loss two years in a row. Despite the lack of profits, the CEO saw a brighter future ahead, and he was determined to stay on the road to fast expansion.

As he searched for another source of financing, Riggio tried an initial public offering of common stock in 1992. This offering was postponed because the market for new stocks wasn't favorable. By 1993, however, the market was more interested in new stocks, so the company went ahead and offered shares at $20 each, to be traded on the New York Stock Exchange. This initial public offering sold more than 9 million shares of common stock and raised more than $160 million. It also lowered the ratio of long-term debt to stockholders' equity, which improved the company's financial health.

As Riggio had forecast, superstores soon began bringing in an ever-larger share of Barnes & Noble's revenues, and they now account for about half the company's sales. Going public helped Riggio expand superstore operations, but it had another important consequence as well: It added shareholders to the list of company stakeholders. Although Riggio is the largest individual investor in Barnes & Noble, he still has to be sure that any actions he takes are in the best interests of his fellow shareholders. One measure of shareholder response to company actions is in the stock price, and Riggio is bound to watch this indicator as closely as his competitors follow the pace of his superstore expansion.

1. How is the company's financial health improved by lowering the ratio of long-term debt to stockholders' equity?

2. Why would Riggio choose to issue common stock rather than issuing bonds?

3. Each superstore has as many as 150,000 books in inventory. What are the implications for Barnes & Noble's financial managers?

When a new business is formed, its owners usually try to defray their initial expenses by obtaining a business loan. Call or write to a loan officer in a nearby financial institution or in a local Small Business Administration office to find out how a company qualifies for a small-business loan. Ask about the following:

- The materials that must be presented to show the company's creditworthiness
- How the loan-approval process works
- What information is requested on the loan application
- The terms and conditions of such loans

As directed by your instructor, prepare a brief summary of the information you have obtained regarding the small-business loan policies of that financial institution. Compare your findings with the information obtained by other students. Are the terms and conditions of the various institutions similar? Are the loan-approval processes similar? What do these differences mean for small businesses seeking loans from these institutions?

Choose a recent article from *The Wall Street Journal* that deals with the financing arrangements or strategies of a particular company.

1. What form of financing did the company choose? Did the article indicate why the company selected this form of financing?
2. Who provided the financing for the company? Was this arrangement considered unusual, or was it routine?
3. What does the company intend to do with the arranged financing—purchase equipment or other assets, finance a construction project, finance growth and expansion, or do something else?

ARCHER DANIELS MIDLAND MIXES BONDS AND VEGGIE BURGERS

Synopsis

A self-described "supermarket to the world," Archer Daniels Midland (ADM) is a global giant in agricultural products. Dwayne Andreas, ADM's CEO, wants to continue expanding his company's operations; one of his pet projects is the veggie burger, made from soy protein. However, expansion requires capital, which ADM borrows on a long-term basis by selling bonds. When bond rates are high, the payback from borrowing to build new plants or create new products is lower, because the company has to include the cost of borrowing when it figures its profits. ADM's profit opportunities look brighter when bond rates are low, however, so when bond rates go down, Andreas quickly authorizes the sale of $250 million in corporate bonds.

Exercises

ANALYSIS

1. Why don't all companies adopt a "pay as you go" approach and finance their expansion through current sales, rather than selling bonds?

2. Would you buy ADM's corporate bonds, knowing that your investment doesn't allow you any say in how the company is run?

3. If you were Dwayne Andreas, would you issue secured or unsecured bonds? Which is better for the company? For the investor?

4. Considering ADM's long record of profits and growth, do you think its bonds would be rated as junk bonds? Explain.

5. Why wouldn't ADM sell commercial paper to raise money for new plants and equipment?

APPLICATION

Could you sell unsecured bonds to help launch your own computer-repair business?

DECISION

What would you have to know before deciding whether to buy ADM's bonds?

COMMUNICATION

Imagine that you're a broker trying to sell ADM's bonds. Write a letter to a customer explaining why you think they are a good investment.

INTEGRATION

If Sweet Dreams Ice Cream used bonds to borrow, where on the balance sheet shown in Chapter 17 would this transaction appear?

ETHICS

How far should ADM have to go in terms of explaining risks to potential investors who buy its bonds? For example, should the company have to disclose every legal or regulatory problem it has or anticipates in the near future?

DEBATE

Should junk bonds be outlawed because of the potential risks to investors, who may lose their investments if a troubled company fails? Option A: In a formal debate format, argue for or against outlawing junk bonds. Option B: Take either position and summarize your case in a brief report.

TEAMWORK

Team up with two or three other students and together decide how you would invest $10,000 in the bond market. Be prepared to explain your reasoning to the class.

RESEARCH

Do the research necessary to write a summary of either (a) the price movement of ADM bonds over the past month or (b) overall trends in interest rates on investment-grade corporate bonds over the past three months.

ROLE PLAYING

Using the bond picks your team made in the Teamwork exercise, play the role of a stockbroker trying to persuade customers to make those same investments. One or more students can play potential investors.

Chapter

20

Securities Markets

Searching for Growth Beneath a Mountain of Debt

I t was a heavy responsibility: managing millions of dollars invested by clients so that their wealth would continue to grow. Moreover, clients expected their wealth to grow regardless of prevailing economic or stock market conditions. As a vice president at Landes Associates (a Delaware-based investment management firm), William A. Francis could choose among a wide array of investments, including commodities futures, common and preferred stock, corporate and government bonds, and mutual funds. The challenge was knowing when to buy which products, how long to hold them, and when to sell them.

His challenge was made more difficult by the investment needs of his clients. Primarily wealthy individuals, these investors didn't need extra income. They wanted their investments to grow steadily and without a high degree of risk. Francis decided to avoid commodities, the riskiest of available investments. He also decided against preferred stock, corporate bonds, and government bonds, because such investments are usually designed to produce reliable income (something his clients didn't need). Finally, he ruled out mutual funds, because such funds are intended for small investors who lack the financial means to create their own portfolios. His analysis showed that the best investment for his clients would be common stocks.

To pick the right companies to invest his clients' money in, Francis had to know three things: (1) the major forces at work in the economy that could affect a particular industry or company, (2) the general investment climate of the securities markets, and (3) the performance of particular companies. Francis knew that purchasing stock isn't like buying products in a store, where prices are clearly marked and where value is relatively easy to recognize. Investors buy expectations. They are always asking: "What's going to attract other investors to this stock? Why should somebody else be willing to pay a higher price for this stock than I'm paying now?" The answer to both questions is the company's expected growth.

However, the recessionary economy of the early 1990s had slowed many a company's growth, which presented Francis with a tremen-

Brokers at Landes Associates pay close attention to their clients' investment objectives so they can recommend appropriate stocks and bonds.

dous challenge. He had to find the few companies worth investing in. Then he had to decide the best time to invest in them: immediately, after the economy improved, or once the stock market was on the way up. Finally, he had to determine the best time to sell stocks—both those his clients were currently invested in and those he would recommend. Where would Francis find the information he needed to make these decisions? How could he determine which companies his clients could invest in to make their wealth grow without undue risk? How would he know when to sell a client's stock?[1]

INVESTORS AND INVESTING

As an investment adviser and broker, William A. Francis is part of a multitrillion-dollar industry that spans the globe. Investments are the foundation of most of the world's financial systems, whether in the United States, in Europe, in Japan, or in any of the Third World nations that have their own stock exchanges. Governments and businesses invite investments so that they can raise the capital necessary to finance their operations; investors use these investments to earn a return in the form of interest, dividends, or capital gains.

Institutional and Private Investors

Two types of investors buy and sell **marketable securities** (investments that can easily be converted to cash): institutions and individuals. **Institutional investors**—such as pension funds, insurance companies, investment companies, and colleges and universities—dominate U.S. securities markets. A study by the Securities Industry Association found that institutions and large securities firms constitute nearly 82 percent of all trading on the New York Stock Exchange, whereas individual investors account for only 18 percent.[2] Institutions hire professional money managers to handle their accounts, and these managers increasingly use computers to make instantaneous trades based on hundreds of financial and economic factors. Because institutions have such large pools of money to work with, their investment decisions have a major impact on the market, increasingly in the form of *volatility*—that is, the securities markets tend to gain or lose more in shorter periods of time than in the past.

Individuals can invest either directly (in securities) or indirectly (through mutual funds, insurance products, or employee pension plans). Because of the security market's increasing volatility, many individual investors are changing from direct investments (such as common stocks) to indirect investments (such as mutual funds). Although the

marketable securities *Securities that can be bought and sold easily in an organized market*

institutional investors *Companies that invest money entrusted to them by others*

Many individual investors have turned away from bank time deposits and invested in mutual funds. This Fidelity Stock Investment Center in Boston handles mutual fund investment accounts and makes instantaneous stock trades.

migration is a 20-year-old trend, it has intensified dramatically since the stock market crash of October 19, 1987.[3]

Investment Objectives

Many institutions seek the highest return in the quickest period possible, so they trade large amounts of securities frequently. Others want a steady return over a long period so that they can meet long-term obligations such as funding retirement benefits. Similarly, the majority of individual investors have traditionally made long-term investments, trading their securities only when they felt it necessary to do so, whether because of market conditions or changes in their personal lives. Their objectives include funding retirement activities and providing money to send their children to college, among others. In general, people make investment decisions on the basis of five criteria: *income, growth, safety, liquidity,* and *tax consequences.*

If an investor wants a steady, reasonably predictable flow of cash, he or she will seek an investment that provides income. Fixed-income investments include certificates of deposit, government securities, corporate bonds, and preferred stocks. A retired person wanting to supplement Social Security or pension benefits would be a customer for this type of investment.

Many investors are concerned with wealth accumulation, or growth. Their objective is to maximize **capital gains**—the return made by selling a security for a price that is higher than its purchase price. Common stock is generally known as *equity* because it represents an ownership position in a company and because common stock is the primary investment instrument for achieving growth. Over 20 years or more, stocks usually offer higher returns than bank time deposits or bonds, for example.[4] Other instruments include options and commodities futures. Some nonfinancial assets such as fine art, horses, and real estate may be able to achieve the same goal, but usually, a much longer period is needed.

Safety is another concern. Generally, the higher the potential for income or growth, the greater the risk of the investment. **Speculators** are investors who accept high risks in order to realize large capital gains. Of course, every investor must make some kind of trade-off. This is true for all investments. Government bonds are safer than corporate bonds, which are safer than common stocks, which are safer than futures contracts, which are safer than commodities. Still, experts caution that investors who stick only to the safest instruments— which return less than riskier instruments—face the risk that their holdings will not provide good returns, let alone guard against losses.[5]

Even within the bond and stock markets, an investor will face varying degrees of risk. Investment-grade corporate bonds are safer than speculative-grade corporate bonds, commonly known as junk bonds. Likewise, the common stock of a major, established corporation such as Wal-Mart is safer than that of a technology company that's less than six months old. This assumption doesn't mean that Wal-Mart's stock will never decline in value, but it does mean that Wal-Mart's stock is more likely to climb in price and provide dividends over a longer

capital gains Difference between the price at which a financial asset is sold and its original cost (assuming the price has gone up)

speculators Investors who seek large capital gains through relatively risky investments

period than the stock of a small technology company with an unproven product.

Two final factors that investors take into consideration are liquidity and tax consequences. Liquidity is the measure of how quickly an investor can change an investment into cash. For example, common stock is more liquid than real estate; most financial assets can be changed into cash within a day. Some, like certificates of deposit, can be cashed in before maturity, but only after paying a penalty. All investors must consider the tax consequences of their decisions. Historically, dividend and interest income have been taxed heavily, and capital gains have been taxed relatively lightly. However, in 1986 Congress eliminated the tax advantage associated with long-term gains. A consideration for individual investors is that the income from some government securities is not taxed at the federal or state levels.

The Investment Portfolio

No single investment instrument will provide income, growth, and a high degree of safety. For this reason, all investors—whether institutions or individuals—build **investment portfolios,** or collections of various types of investments. Money managers and financial advisers, like William Francis, are often asked (1) to determine which investments should be in an investor's portfolio and (2) to buy and sell securities and maintain the client's portfolio.

A major concern for these managers is **diversification**—reducing the risk of loss in a client's total portfolio by investing funds in several different securities so that a loss experienced by any one will not hurt the entire portfolio. One way to diversify is by investing in securities from unrelated industries. Another way is by investing in securities from other countries, which can balance lower returns in one country with higher returns from faster-growing areas.[6] "When the U.S. market isn't doing so well, the foreign markets may rise and vice versa," says Gary P. Brinson, who heads a Chicago money-management firm.[7] By diversifying, investors can reap the rewards when some securities increase in value and minimize the damage when some decrease in value.

A portion of a portfolio might be in investment-grade corporate bonds, and a portion might be in common stocks. Likewise, owning stock in ten established companies provides greater safety through diversification than owning the stock of only one small technology company. That way, a loss in one stock might be offset by gains in one or more other stocks. A portfolio might also be structured to provide a desired **rate of return,** the percentage gain or interest yield on investments. For example, an investment-grade corporate bond might pay 7 percent interest but provide an expected capital gain of only 2 percent, whereas a growth stock might be expected to return a capital gain of 14 percent but pay no dividend.

Asset Allocation

Managing a portfolio to gain the highest rates of return while reducing risk as much as possible is known as **asset allocation.** A por-

investment portfolios Assortment of investment instruments

diversification Assembling investment portfolios in such a way that a loss in one investment won't cripple the value of the entire portfolio

rate of return Percentage increase in the value of an investment

asset allocation Method of shifting investments within a portfolio to adapt them to the current investment environment

tion of the portfolio might be devoted to cash instruments such as money-market mutual funds, a portion to income instruments such as government and corporate bonds, and a portion to equities (mainly common stock). The money manager then determines how much each portion should be, on the basis of economic and market conditions—not an easy task. If the economy is booming and the stock market is performing well, the money manager might take advantage of the good environment by shifting 75 percent of the total portfolio into stocks, 20 percent into bonds, and 5 percent into cash. If the economy turns bad, the stock market heads downward, and inflation heats up, the money manager might readjust the portfolio and invest 30 percent in stocks, 40 percent in short-term government securities, and 30 percent in cash. This adjustment helps protect the value of the portfolio during poor investment conditions.[8]

Market Indexes

Individual stocks are bought and sold every business day, and their values fluctuate minute to minute, hour to hour, day to day, depending on what buyers and sellers think of each company's investment potential. Investors, brokers, and others who trade stocks are careful to follow the thousands of bits of information that affect each company, its stock, and the economy (everything from revenues and profits to interest rates and currency exchange rates). Because of this variation in stock prices, the overall market can be up or down on any given day.

Some institutional investors try to do at least as well as the market itself. **Market indexes** such as Standard & Poor's 500 use a selection of securities as a model to gauge the activity of the market as a whole. Institutional investors can tie the performance of their investments to the overall performance of the market by **indexing,** which involves building a portfolio of securities that are selected because together they reflect the profile of the market as a whole.

INVESTMENT CHOICES

As William Francis knows well, various investment instruments serve different purposes. Government securities raise money for federal, state, and local governments to fund public expenses, from national defense to road improvements. Corporate bonds finance business operations and are debt obligations of the issuing companies. Stocks also finance business operations, but they are certificates of ownership that let the investor reap the benefits—and suffer the losses—of the issuing companies. These and other securities are all traded in organized markets, and they are cyclical in their performance: Sometimes they rise in value; sometimes they fall.

market indexes *Measures of security markets calculated from the prices of a selection of securities*

indexing *Assembling investment portfolios by selecting securities that together reflect the profile of the market as a whole*

As this ad from BA Investment Services indicates, investors have a wide variety of objectives and can choose among a diverse array of investment choices.

Government Securities

The least risky investments are U.S. government securities, which are of two basic types: those backed by the U.S. Treasury and those backed by agencies of the government. State and local governments also raise money through bond issues. Although government securities pay less interest than corporate bonds, they do provide advantages in terms of safety and tax consequences.

Federal Government Issues

The three principal types of U.S. government issues are **Treasury bills** for short-term debt, **Treasury notes** for debt obligations of 1 to 10 years, and **Treasury bonds** for long-term debt. All three are generally the most liquid investments available and are traded in an organized market. Investors trade government securities with each other, except for savings bonds, which can be bought and sold only through the U.S. Treasury.

Treasury bills (also referred to as T-bills) come in maturities of 13 weeks, 26 weeks, or 52 weeks. Unlike many other income-oriented investments, T-bills do not pay interest. Instead, they are sold at a discount from their face value and then redeemed at full face value when they mature. The difference between the purchase price and the redemption price is, in effect, interest. T-bills require a minimum investment of $10,000. Treasury notes and Treasury bonds, which have maturities of 1 to 30 years, are available for a minimum investment of $1,000. Twice a year they pay a fixed amount of interest, which is exempt from state and local income taxes.

U.S. savings bonds are debt instruments issued by the U.S. government that are available in denominations ranging from $50 to $10,000. These are sold to individual investors, and unlike other Treasury instruments, they are nonmarketable, which means that they can't be traded among investors. Investors can choose between two types of U.S. savings bonds. One pays a fixed rate of return. The other pays an interest rate that is tied to the returns on Treasury bills and notes.[9]

Some 20 other government agencies also issue debt, including the Student Loan Marketing Association and the Farm Credit System. The two largest and most important are the Government National Mortgage Association (Ginnie Mae) and the Federal National Mortgage Association (Fannie Mae). These agencies raise money to help finance mortgages for U.S. homeowners, so their issues are known as mortgage-backed securities. Although the U.S. government doesn't guarantee investments in Ginnie Maes and Fannie Maes, these are considered relatively safe investments because the government is unlikely to allow these agencies to **default**—that is, to not meet their interest payments. They are also highly liquid; the market for these securities is huge and active.

Municipal Bonds

Municipal bonds are issued by states, cities, and special government agencies such as the Tennessee Valley Authority, port authorities, and airports to finance public services. They come in two forms, general obligation bonds and revenue bonds. Governments pay off their prin-

---

Treasury bills *Short-term debt issued by the federal government; also referred to as T-bills*

Treasury notes *Debt securities issued by the federal government that mature within 1 to 10 years*

Treasury bonds *Debt securities issued by the federal government that mature in 10 to 30 years*

U.S. savings bonds *Debt instruments sold by the federal government in small denominations*

default *Failure of issuers to meet their contractual principal and interest obligations*

municipal bonds *Debt issued by a state or a local agency; interest earned on municipal bonds is exempt from federal income tax and from taxes in the issuing jurisdiction*

cipal and interest obligations to the buyers of **general obligation bonds** through tax receipts. The principal and interest on **revenue bonds** are paid from the revenues raised by the issuer. For example, bonds issued by a city airport are paid from revenues raised by the airport's operation.

To encourage investment, the federal government doesn't tax the interest that investors receive from municipal bonds. Also, many states do not tax the interest paid on bonds issued by governments within those states. However, capital gains made on the sale of municipal bonds are taxed at the federal and state levels.

general obligation bonds *Municipal bonds backed by the issuing agency's general taxing authority*

revenue bonds *Municipal bonds backed by revenue generated from the projects financed with the bonds*

Corporate Bonds

When you look in the business section of your daily newspaper, you'll see that the stock market gets most of the attention. The bond market, which is actually several times larger, operates with less fanfare, even though nearly as many individual investors own bonds as own common stock.[10] For years bonds just quietly earned interest for investors, but that changed during the 1980s when the junk bond market ballooned and then burst. Corporations all across the United States found themselves in default on their bond issues.

Corporations issue three principal types of bonds. **Mortgage bonds** are backed by real property owned by the issuing corporation so that if the corporation goes bankrupt, the investor has a greater chance of recouping a portion of the original investment. **Debentures** are unsecured bonds, backed only by the corporation's promise to pay. Because debentures are riskier than other types of bonds, they pay higher interest to the investor. **Convertible bonds** can be exchanged, at the investor's option, for a certain number of shares of the corporation's common stock.

Corporate bonds are rated for their safety by Standard & Poor's Corporation and by Moody's Investors Service. Exhibit 20.1 shows how these two companies rate bonds. The higher the rating on a bond, the safer it is considered, so the less interest it pays; the lower the rating, the riskier it is, so it pays a higher rate of interest to attract investors.

mortgage bonds *Corporate bonds backed by real property*

debentures *Corporate bonds backed by the company's good faith*

convertible bonds *Corporate bonds that can be exchanged at the owner's discretion into common stock of the issuing company*

S&P	Moody's	Rating explanation
AAA	Aaa	Highest rating; strongest capacity to pay principal and interest
AA+	Aa1	
AA	Aa2	Very strong capacity to pay principal and interest
AA–	Aa3	
A+	A1	
A	A2	Strong capacity to pay principal and interest, but more susceptible to the adverse effects of changing business and economic conditions
A–	A3	
BBB+	Baa1	
BBB	Baa2	Adequate capacity to pay principal and interest; any changes in business or economic conditions will likely lead to weakened financial status
BBB–	Baa3	Speculative investment grade; "junk bonds"

Exhibit 20.1
Corporate Bond Ratings
Standard & Poor's Corporation and Moody's Investors Service are the two primary companies that rate the safety of corporate bonds. As ratings decline, investors take on more risk, so they are compensated with higher interest rates.

In addition to receiving interest, bondholders can also realize capital gains on bonds by taking advantage of shifts in interest rates, which trigger increases or decreases in the face value of the bonds. For example, a $1,000 bond with an interest rate of 8 percent will sell for more than $1,000 if interest rates fall to 7 percent, because new bonds will pay annual interest of $70 instead of $80. If investors can sell the 8 percent bond for more than $1,000, they realize a capital gain. In fact, interest rates move up and down every day, and so do the prices at which bonds are traded, but in the opposite direction. The degree of movement in a particular bond depends on its maturity date. In general, the longer the maturity of the bond, the more its price will fluctuate.

Stocks

shareholder Owner of equities

An investor in a company's stock owns a portion of that company and is known as a **shareholder.** As a part owner, the shareholder gets to vote on the members of the company's board of directors as well as on any major policies that will affect ownership. The shareholder also shares in the company's profits or losses in two ways: through capital gains (or losses) and through dividends (or the cancellation of dividends). After a company has paid all expenses and taxes out of revenues, its board of directors can pay a portion of what remains—its earnings—to investors in the form of dividends. The board decides whether to make dividend payments; no law mandates that a company do so. Therefore, a board may decide either to reduce the dividend or to suspend its payment altogether (if the company needs the money to continue operating).

Common Stocks

blue-chip stocks Equities issued by large, well-established companies with consistent records of stock price increases and dividend payments

Most stock issued by corporations is common stock, which generally carries no special privileges and which is the last to be paid off (if any funds remain) when the company liquidates to go out of business. **Blue-chip stocks** are the stocks of established corporations that have paid sizable dividends consistently for years and that have periodically raised their dividends as profits increased. These are considered to be conservative equity investments because, in addition to the dividends they pay, their prices tend to rise slowly over longer periods, and they are generally less susceptible to sudden drops in the market.

growth stocks Equities issued by small companies with unproven products or services

In contrast, **growth stocks** are issued by younger and smaller companies that have strong growth potential. These companies normally pay no dividends because they reinvest earnings in the company to expand operations. Their stock prices tend to rise more quickly, but they can fall just as quickly. For this reason, growth stocks are considered aggressive investments; the investor is hoping to make a capital gain more quickly.

Most shareholders are looking for growth; some, for the income provided by dividends. Others might want to own common stock because of special situations regarding the issuing companies. Three specific examples are turnarounds, cyclical stocks, and plays:

606

- *Turnarounds.* In a *turnaround,* the investor thinks a company that has been close to, or even in, bankruptcy is going to turn itself around and become profitable. The shareholder expects the stock's price to increase as a result.
- *Cyclical stocks.* A *cyclical stock* is one issued by a company whose business reflects the cycles of the economy. Ford and other automakers are an example; consumers buy more cars when the economy booms. If the economy is showing signs of coming out of a recession, an investor might want to invest in cyclical stocks to take advantage of the growing economy.
- *Plays.* A *play* often involves the possibility of two companies merging or one acquiring another. Generally, when a company is "in play," rumors or published reports indicate that it will be acquired by another, and the price of the stock temporarily rises. Also, companies that are in financial trouble and yet hold large salable assets can become plays even without the threat of takeover. Investors buy stock when they believe a company will sell assets to improve its finances or to avoid a takeover; either action can cause the stock price to rise.

Preferred Stocks

Investors who buy preferred stocks do so primarily for the dividends they pay. Preferred stock offers two advantages over common stock: (1) shareholders of preferred stock are guaranteed to receive their dividends before shareholders of common stock, and (2) if the issuing company liquidates its assets to go out of business, holders of preferred stock will be paid off after bondholders but before holders of common stock. For these reasons, preferred stocks are a hybrid of fixed-income securities and equities. Their prices tend to react more

Investors may want to time their purchases of cyclical stocks such as General Motors to coincide with economic recoveries that boost demand. When the U.S. economy moves into a growth phase, workers at General Motors's Willow Run Assembly Plant in Michigan gear up for higher sales of Chevrolet cars.

to changes in interest rates than to changes in the prices of the issuing company's common stock.

Cumulative preferred stock has an additional advantage: If the issuing company suspends dividends, the dividends on these shares will accumulate until shareholders have been paid in full. *Convertible preferred stock* can be exchanged at the shareholder's discretion for a certain number of shares of common stock issued by the company.

Corporations are some of the largest buyers of preferred stock because they receive a 70 percent tax break on dividends received from their preferred stock holdings. So if the investing corporation receives $100,000 in dividend income in a year, it pays taxes on only $30,000 of that income.

Short Selling

Short selling is selling stock that is borrowed from a broker in the hope of buying it back later at a lower price. When the borrowed stock is returned to the broker, the investor keeps the difference between what it sold for and what it was bought back for. Although "shorting" has traditionally been done by specialists, individual investors are increasingly using this method to make money. About $30 billion in stock is sold short these days, compared with $3 trillion in stocks that are owned the common way.[11]

Selling a stock short is something done by an investor who is pessimistic. Suppose you think a company's stock will decline in the near future. You borrow shares of the stock that are selling for $30 per share and then sell short, pledging to deliver the shares you do not own back to the broker from whom you borrowed them. When the stock's price has sunk to $15 per share, you buy the stock on the open market and make $15 a share profit (minus transaction costs).

Selling short is not without its risks. If you had waited for the stock's price to go even lower than $15 a share, you might have wound up owing your broker money. For instance, if the stock had gone back up to $30, you would have had to buy it at the same price you sold it for; after paying the broker's commissions and interest charges, you would have shown a loss.

Mutual Funds

An increasingly popular alternative for investors is to buy shares of **mutual funds,** pools of money drawn from many investors and used by an investment company to buy stocks, bonds, government securities, gold, or other marketable securities. Mutual funds are particularly suited to small investors who do not have the time or experience to search for investment opportunities. However, institutional investors also put money in mutual funds, seeking the same diversification and liquidity that individual investors can enjoy.

The movement of money from bank time deposits into mutual funds has sparked tremendous growth and diversity in the mutual fund business. Nearly $2 trillion is currently invested in U.S. mutual funds. In 1977 investors could choose among 477 mutual funds; today they can choose among more than 5,000.[12] *Load funds* require investors to pay a small percentage of their investment as a commission to the bro-

---

short selling *Selling stock borrowed from a broker with the intention of buying it back later at a lower price, repaying the broker, and pocketing the profit*

mutual funds *Pools of money raised by investment companies and invested in stocks, bonds, or other marketable securities*

kers who sell those funds. Funds without any sales charges are known as *no-load funds.*

Various funds have different investment priorities. Among the more popular mutual funds are **money-market funds,** which seek good returns by investing in short-term securities such as commercial paper, certificates of deposit, Treasury bills, and other liquid investments. *Growth funds* invest in stocks of rapidly growing companies. *Income funds* invest in securities that return high dividends and interest. *Balanced funds* diversify by allocating their investments among common stocks, preferred stocks, and bonds. *Sector funds,* also known as specialty or industry funds, focus on investing in companies within a particular industry.

Investment companies offer two types of mutual funds. An *open-end fund* invests on behalf of as many investors as want to be in it; its size increases or decreases as investors put their money into, or take their money out of, the fund. In essence, the fund's books never close. Shares in an open-end fund aren't traded in a separate market; investors receive shares in the fund when they put money into it, and they can redeem those shares for cash only with the investment company.

Closed-end funds invest on behalf of a fixed number of investors; as soon as a certain number of shares are sold, the fund closes its books. The shares in a closed-end fund are then bought and sold in the same markets in which other securities are traded. Other than this major distinction, they offer the same diversification as open-end funds.

Other Investments

Stocks, bonds, and mutual funds are the most common marketable securities available for investors. However, other securities have been developed. For the most part, these securities—including options, futures, and their variations—are used by money managers and savvy traders. In recent years, some of these securities, particularly options, have been used more by individual investors.

Options

A **stock option** is the purchased right—but not the obligation—to buy or sell a specified number of shares of a stock at a predetermined price during a specified period. By trading options, the investor doesn't have to own shares of stock in a company—only an option to buy or sell those shares. The cost of buying an option on shares of stock is significantly less than the cost of purchasing the stock itself. Also, option sellers receive a premium for the transactions they complete.

A **call option** is the right to buy stock at a specified price and sell at market price. An investor who buys a call option believes the price of the underlying stock will increase, thus making the call more valuable. The investor who sells that call believes just the opposite—that the price of the underlying stock will decline. If the buyer of a call is correct and exercises the right to purchase those shares of stock before the right expires, he or she can buy the stock from the op-

money-market funds Mutual funds that invest in short-term securities

stock option Contract allowing the holder to buy or sell a given number of shares of a particular stock at a given price by a certain date

call option Right to buy shares at a specified price and sell at a market price

tion seller at the option's exercise price and then sell the stock for a capital gain.

On the other hand, a **put option** is the right to buy stock at market price and sell at a specified price. An investor who buys a put option believes the price of the underlying stock will decline, thus making the put more valuable. The buyer usually already owns shares of the underlying stock. The investor who sells that put believes the price of the underlying stock will rise. If the buyer of a put is correct and exercises the right to sell the stock before the right expires, then he or she can sell the shares of stock to the seller of the put option at the higher exercise price.

Options can be used for wild speculation, or they can be used as a way of making an investor's stock portfolio a little safer. For example, investors can **hedge** their position–that is, partially protect against a sudden loss—by selling a call option at the price of the underlying stock that is in the investor's portfolio. That way, the seller receives the premium to help offset a loss if the price of the stock suddenly falls.

Financial Futures

Financial futures are similar to options, but they are *legally binding* contracts to buy or sell a financial instrument (stocks, Treasury bonds, foreign currencies) for a set price at a future date. Like options traders, investors in financial futures are betting that the price of a financial instrument will either rise or fall. More than 250 million futures contracts are traded in the United States every year.[13] Most of these are traded on margin—borrowing a portion of the money needed to purchase a security—which magnifies both the potential risks and the potential rewards. In addition, investors can borrow more money to margin options and futures than they can to option stocks.

Stock Index Futures. Stock market index futures have become a popular type of financial futures investment. With this instrument, traders speculate on the behavior of a certain group of stocks. The cumulative or average prices of the stocks in that group tend to rise and fall with the stock market as a whole. In effect, those who trade stock market index futures are speculating on the behavior of the stock market and the economy. Investing in stock index futures is a way of trying to do at least as well as the overall market.

Stock Index Options. As if investing in financial futures wasn't complicated enough, investors now have stock index options, the right to buy or sell a hypothetical portfolio of stocks at a particular price and time. A small initial cash outlay buys command over stocks worth much more, so the options can provide a quick, cheap capital gain. The seller of these options incurs a greater risk because small downward changes in an index easily produce large dollar losses.

Commodities

For the investor who is comfortable with risky investments, nothing compares with speculating in **commodities**—raw materials and agricultural products, such as petroleum, gold, coffee beans, pork bellies, beef, and coconut oil. Commodities markets originally sprang up as a convenience for buyers and sellers interested in trading the ac-

---

put option *Right to buy shares at market price and sell at a specified price*

hedge *Make an investment that protects the investor from suffering loss on another investment*

financial futures *Legally binding agreements to buy or sell financial instruments at a future date*

commodities *Raw materials used in producing other goods*

tual commodities. A manufacturer of breakfast cereals, for example, must buy wheat, rye, oats, and sugar from hundreds of farmers. The easiest way to arrange these transactions is to meet in a forum where many buyers and sellers come to trade. Since the commodities are too bulky to bring to the marketplace, the traders buy and sell contracts for delivery of a given amount of these raw materials at a given time.

spot trading *Trading in commodities that will be delivered immediately; also called* cash trading

commodities futures *Contracts for commodities that will be delivered at a future date*

Trading contracts for immediate delivery of a commodity is called **spot trading,** or cash trading. Most commodity trading is for future delivery, usually months in advance, sometimes a year or more; this is called trading **commodities futures.** The original purpose of futures trading was to allow producers and consumers of commodities to hedge their position, or protect themselves against violent price swings. For example, farmers might sell futures contracts calling for delivery of some of the wheat they expect to have grown by harvest time to bakers who expect to use the flour milled from that wheat to bake bread. By selling before the crop is in, farmers get operating capital—as well as the assuance that they'll get a certain fixed price for their crops, even if prices collapse later. The bakers, on the other hand, can buy some of the supplies they expect to use and be assured that no matter how bad the crop is or how high the price goes, they'll have enough wheat to stay in business.

Today speculators play an important role in the commodities markets, doing most of the trading and increasing the liquidity of the market. Hoping to profit as prices rise and fall, they voluntarily assume the risk that the hedger tries to avoid. In reality, however, 75 percent of the people who speculate in commodities lose money in the long run.[14] Even seasoned veterans have been known to lose literally millions of dollars within a few days. Despite the risks, many investors see speculation in commodities as a way to reach higher returns.

Trading commodities futures is a convenient way of assuring that farmers will receive operating capital and that bakers will receive wheat for their products when needed.

THE MECHANISMS OF INVESTING

When Wall Street was in its infancy, investors could buy stocks "over the counter," as though they had walked into a store for a loaf of bread. Around 1817 the New York Stock Exchange (NYSE) board organized an indoor market for trading securities. Since the advent of that market, investors must work through a broker, who places the order with a central clearinghouse for trading in that type of security. After 200 years of trading being dominated by the New York Stock Exchange, technology is restoring some of the "over-the-counter" feeling from the past by letting investors trade through their brokers on-screen (via computer). In the next few years, the mechanisms of investing will change as much as the types of investments have changed in the past two decades.

Securities Marketplaces

Investors can trade securities in two types of marketplaces: auction exchanges (the traditional marketplace) and dealer exchanges. In an **auction exchange,** all buy and sell orders (and all information concerning companies traded on that exchange) are funneled onto an auction floor. There, buyers and sellers are matched by a **stock specialist,** a member of a brokerage firm who occupies a post on the trading floor and conducts all the trades in a particular stock. The process is different in **dealer exchanges,** primarily because no central place exists for making transactions. Instead, all buy and sell orders are executed through computers by **market makers,** registered stock and bond representatives who sell securities out of their own inventories and who are spread out across the country—in some cases, even around the world.

The differences have profound implications for the future of securities trading. Advances in computerized trading are occurring so quickly, and its practice is becoming so widespread, that the New York Stock Exchange, the world's most famous auction exchange, is under threat of losing its preeminent place in global capitalism. A senior Wall Street executive has gone so far as to pronounce: "Time is running out for the New York Stock Exchange."[15] Already, more than half of all stocks around the world are traded outside the United States.[16]

Auction Exchanges

The NYSE, also known as the "Big Board," is the largest and most widely known of the stock exchanges in the United States. The stocks and bonds of more than 1,600 companies, whose market values exceed $2.6 trillion, are traded on the exchange's floor.[17] Options, futures, and closed-end funds are also traded there. The other large organized exchange is the American Stock Exchange (AMEX), plus several regional exchanges, which include the Pacific, Boston, Philadelphia, and Chicago exchanges. More than half of the NYSE-listed stocks can be bought and sold at one or more of the regional exchanges. For all of its importance, however, the NYSE is battling a rising tide of critics.

The primary problem that the NYSE and other auction exchanges confront is that the auction process itself is rapidly becoming antiquated. In an auction exchange transaction, the stock specialist occupies a post on the trading floor and conducts all the trades in a particular stock. When brokers send their buy and sell orders to the exchange, the specialist matches them up by acting as an auctioneer.

auction exchange Centralized marketplace where securities are traded by specialists on behalf of investors

stock specialist Intermediary who trades in a particular security on the floor of an auction exchange; "buyer of last resort"

dealer exchanges Decentralized marketplaces where securities are bought and sold by dealers out of their own inventories

market makers Dealers in dealer exchanges who sell securities out of their own inventories so that a market is always available for buyers and sellers

The specialist must fill small public orders before handling large institutional trades, thus ensuring that the small trader gets a fair shake.

Probably the most important duty of the specialist is to act as the buyer or seller if one can't be found. Thus the specialist keeps his or her own inventory of stocks. During the market's crash on October 19, 1987—when 608 million shares were traded on the NYSE—specialists were forced to buy countless stocks for which there were no buyers. As good as this arrangement may sound for investors who want to bail out of a free-falling stock, the specialist's role is one reason for the NYSE's problems. The system worked fine when individual investors accounted for most of the NYSE's business, but matters have changed. Twenty years ago, individual investors held 80 percent of equities in the United States, but today they hold only 55 percent. Institutions trade such huge quantities of securities that some specialists can no longer serve as "buyers of last resort."[18]

Program Trading. The inability of specialists to cover all stock sales could become a major problem because of **program trading,** in which institutional investors use computer programs to buy and sell diversified collections, or "baskets," of shares. Program trading has a number of variations, but the most common approach involves **arbitrage,** the age-old practice of buying something in one market and simultaneously selling its equivalent in another market at a higher price (and pocketing the difference). For example, when the price of a futures contract on the Standard & Poor's 500 rises above the prices of the actual stocks, an institutional investor might sell the futures (which are expensive), buy the actual stocks (which are cheaper), and make a tidy little profit on the transaction.

Institutional investors use computers to make program trades. For the trades to work best, large blocks of stock must be traded instantaneously without causing stock prices to fluctuate sharply. If prices change too much too quickly, the gains that program traders expect may not materialize. By serving as buyers and sellers of last resort, specialists have traditionally prevented prices from making sharp swings. However, institutional investors doubt that specialists will be able to continue doing so as program trading becomes more common. Conceivably, if stock prices fall too much, specialists could run out of capital and be unable to buy stocks from program traders in a rush to sell.

Commodity Exchanges. Not all auction exchanges face such problems. Commodity exchanges continue to operate much as they always have—even though their operations can seem quite confusing. **Commodity exchanges** use their own variation of the auction: Crowds of dealers (who work for companies that are members of the exchanges) stand in auction "pits," buying and selling commodity contracts in a frenzy of activity. Of course, products do not actually change hands at the exchange; contracts are bought and sold to deliver goods at future dates.

Various goods are traded on each exchange. The Chicago Board of Trade handles corn, soybeans, wheat, oats, and plywood as well as gold, silver, and financial futures. At the Chicago Mercantile Exchange, traders deal in cattle, hogs, pork bellies, lumber, potatoes, Treasury

program trading *Investment strategy using computer programs to buy or sell large numbers of securities, thereby taking advantage of price discrepancies between stock index futures or options and the actual stocks represented in those indexes*

arbitrage *Simultaneous purchase in one market and sale in a different market with a profitable price or yield differential*

commodity exchanges *Marketplaces where contracts for raw materials are bought and sold*

bills, gold, foreign currency, and stock market futures. Other exchanges include the Chicago Board Options Exchange; the New York Futures Exchange; the New York Mercantile Exchange; the Commodity Exchange (COMEX); the New York Cotton Exchange; the Minneapolis Grain Exchange; the Kansas City Board of Trade; the MidAmerica Commodity Exchange; and the Coffee, Sugar, and Cocoa Exchange.

Dealer Exchanges

Despite its central position in the U.S. financial system, the NYSE is feeling competitive pressures from many directions. The regional exchanges handle the stocks of many large corporations, as does the NYSE. Because it costs less to trade on the regionals, institutional investors often use them to trade stocks listed on the Big Board.

However, the biggest threat to all auction exchanges comes from dealer exchanges, decentralized marketplaces where securities are bought and sold by dealers out of their own inventories. They come in many forms, the largest and most important of which is the **over-the-counter market (OTC).** Instead of a single trading floor where transactions occur, the OTC market consists of a network of about 415,000 registered stock and bond representatives across the country. Some 420 of these brokers are market makers—meaning they buy and sell securities held in inventory—and they are linked by a nationwide computer network called NASDAQ (National Association of Securities Dealers Automated Quotations).

NASDAQ has grown so much that it now represents a total market value of $462 billion—second only to the NYSE. Because it has been a computerized trading system from the beginning, it enjoys a head start in creating a global, 24-hour securities exchange—which is what many market experts expect will be common in the next decade. NASDAQ also has a branch in Great Britain, called NASDAQ International, that handles trades between 3:30 A.M. and 9 A.M. (eastern standard time) each trading day. Through NASDAQ market makers, U.S. investors can trade the equities of foreign companies listed on NASDAQ International, and foreign investors can trade the equities of U.S. companies.[19]

Nevertheless, NASDAQ must compete with rivals in the computerized securities trading industry. Reuters Holdings PLC, a British media conglomerate, operates Instinet Crossing Network, and U.S. brokerage Jefferies & Company has teamed up with a California consulting firm to offer Posit. Both of these are national services that match buyers and sellers at certain times of the day for trades based on closing NYSE prices. Working with the Chicago Mercantile Exchange, Reuters has also created Globex, a computerized night-trading system that allows traders to buy and sell securities listed on foreign exchanges.

Technology isn't the only advantage dealer exchanges have over auction exchanges; they cost less, too. On auction exchanges, all buy and sell orders are funneled to specialists, who match the closest bidding and asking prices. Therefore, these markets are driven by the volume of orders that are placed. Auction exchanges charge commissions—sometimes very expensive ones—for every trade that is

over-the-counter (OTC) market
Network of dealers who trade securities that are not listed on an exchange

made. In contrast, dealer exchanges are so named because dealers buy and sell out of their own inventory; they don't match buyers and sellers as much as they provide a service for buyers and sellers, and that service is less expensive than the commission structure at auction exchanges.[20]

Foreign Exchanges

New York was once the center of the financial world; today the Tokyo Stock Exchange is second only to the NYSE, followed closely by stock exchanges in London, Frankfurt, Paris, Toronto, and Montreal. In recent years, companies listed on exchanges in Mexico, Spain, and Hong Kong have produced large gains for investors around the world.

As might be expected, U.S. institutional investors, including pension funds, are the main players in foreign stock markets. However, individual investors can easily invest in foreign stocks and bonds through mutual funds. *Global funds* invest in foreign and U.S. securities, whereas *international funds* invest strictly in foreign securities. Because of the potential for growth, many investment advisers recommend global and international funds for individual investors, so these funds are becoming more popular.

Smaller investors can buy shares in companies that are traded on foreign exchanges by investing in *American depository receipts,* or *ADRs,* certificates representing shares of foreign stocks that are held in safe-

The volume of securities trading in other countries has grown tremendously in recent years. The Tokyo Stock Exchange is now the second largest in the world.

keeping by a bank and that can be traded on U.S. stock exchanges.[21] To buy actual shares of common stock, investors have to trade through major U.S. brokerages or through brokerages in other countries. Investing in foreign equities can be problematic, however, because most exchanges around the world require less information from listed companies than U.S. exchanges do, so investors can't easily evaluate a potential investment.[22] Moreover, regulatory standards are looser in overseas markets, which can complicate the process of obtaining good information or enforcing legal rights.[23]

Trading Procedures

If you want to trade in securities on an exchange, your first step is to select a brokerage firm such as Landes Associates to handle the transaction. Next, you choose, or are assigned, a commodities broker or a stockbroker, depending on the type of investment you are planning to make. A **broker** is an expert who has studied the intricacies of the market and has passed a series of examinations on buying and selling securities. Landes Associates's William Francis is a broker and investment adviser.

The Order to Buy or Sell

You have to give your broker specific instructions about how to invest your money. A **market order** gives the broker the go-ahead to make the trade at the best price that can be negotiated at the moment. A **limit order** specifies the highest price at which you are willing to buy, or the lowest price at which you are is willing to sell. Limit orders are good for one day only. You can also place an **open order,** which instructs the broker to leave the order open until canceled by the investor.

If you have special confidence in your stockbroker's ability to judge the trend of market prices, you may place a **discretionary order,** which gives the broker the right to buy or sell the security at his or her discretion. In some cases, discretionary orders can save you from taking a loss, because the broker may have a better sense of when to sell a stock. If the broker's judgment proves wrong, however, you cannot hold him or her legally responsible for the consequences.

Margin Trading

You might want to leverage an investment to magnify the potential for capital gains through **margin trading.** Instead of paying for the stock in full, you borrow money from your stockbroker, paying interest on the borrowed money and leaving the stock with the broker as collateral. The Federal Reserve Board sets margin requirements, dictating the percentage of the stock's purchase price that the customer must place on deposit with the broker. For many years, the margin on most stock trades has been set at 50 percent.

Here's how margin works: With $1,000, only 100 shares could be bought of a stock selling at $10 a share. With a 50 percent margin, however, $2,000 worth of stock can be controlled with $1,000 ($2,000 × 50% = $1,000). Suppose the interest on the amount borrowed from the broker is 10 percent annually, or $100 a year. In ad-

broker *Individual registered to sell securities*

market order *Authorization for a broker to buy or sell securities at the best price that can be negotiated at the moment*

limit order *Market order that stipulates the highest or lowest price at which the customer is willing to trade securities*

open order *Limit order that does not expire at the end of a trading day*

discretionary order *Market order that allows the broker to decide when to trade a security*

margin trading *Borrowing money from brokers to buy stock, paying interest on the borrowed money, and leaving the stock with the broker as collateral*

dition, suppose that, by the end of the year, the stock doubles in price to $20 per share. The investor receives $4,000 if all 200 shares are sold. Subtracting $1,000 for the original investment, and subtracting $1,100 in interest and principal on the loan, the investor has a capital gain of $1,900. Had the investment not been margined, the gain would have been only $1,000 (100 shares × $20 = $2,000 − $1,000 for the original investment).

However, buying on margin increases risk. If the price of a stock falls, investors have to give the broker more money to increase collateral—which increases the probability that the investors will lose more money than if they had simply bought the stock without margin.

The Cost of Trading

As an investor, you pay **transaction costs** for every buy or sell order, to cover the broker's commission and the taxes on a sale. Commissions vary with the size of the trade: The fewer the shares traded, the more it costs; the more the shares traded, the less the cost per share. Trades must be executed in *round lots* of 100s. Fewer than 100 shares are traded in *odd lots*. So if you want to sell 150 shares of a stock, the brokerage actually makes two trades, one of 100 shares and another of 50 shares. Trading in odd lots is more expensive for the broker and the investor.

The nature of the brokerage house also affects transaction costs. **Full-service brokerages,** such as Merrill Lynch, provide research and a variety of proprietary products, such as their own mutual funds. As a result, the commissions they charge are higher than those charged by **discount brokerages,** which provide nothing more than a service to buy or sell. At many discount brokerages, brokers offer no investment advice.

transaction costs *Costs of trading securities, including broker's commission and taxes*

full-service brokerages *Financial-services companies with a full range of services, including investment advice, securities research, and investment products*

discount brokerages *Financial-services companies that sell securities but give no advice*

ANALYSIS OF THE FINANCIAL NEWS

When you're a serious investor, you continually research financial markets. No single source of information is the best, but a good start is with the daily reports on stocks, bonds, mutual funds, government securities, commodities, and financial futures in major city newspapers. Other sources of financial information include newspapers aimed specifically at investors (such as *Investor's Daily* and *Barron's*) and general-interest business publications that not only follow corporate developments but also report news and give hints about investing (such as *The Wall Street Journal, Forbes, Fortune,* and *Business Week*). Standard & Poor's, Moody's Investor Service, and Value Line also publish newsletters and special reports on equities, bonds, and mutual funds. These publications can often be found in large libraries.

Investors with personal computers have even more alternatives, including the Dow Jones News Retrieval Service, Investor's Express, and The Source. These services provide the investor with up-to-the-minute data on financial markets and on the world events that may affect markets. Stock prices can drop quickly in reaction to news of war, sudden political changes, and other important events—but they can also bounce back within hours or days. William LeFevre, a market strategist at a New York brokerage firm, advises investors to wait a bit and get all the details before acting.[24]

Broad Market Indicators

Equity investors always want to know whether now is the time to buy or sell. The most closely watched market is the NYSE, where the performance of stocks generally sets the tone for investor sentiment on all other exchanges. If investors are buying low and selling high—that is, if they are counting on making a profit from rising prices because they are optimistic and believe business is improving—then Wall Street is said to be in a **bull market,** one characterized by a long-term trend of rising prices. Conversely, if investors are selling short—that is, if they are counting on making profits from falling prices because they are pessimistic and believe business is get-

bull market *Rising stock market*

Nancy Richards, who lives in Chattanooga, Tennessee, wants to buy some shares of Eli Lilly common stock because she believes that growth prospects for drug companies are good. She has read the listings of New York Stock Exchange transactions that appear daily in her Chattanooga newspaper, and she knows that Lilly is selling at around $79 a share. She calls her local stock-brokerage firm, Jones & Company, and enters a market order with her broker to buy 100 shares of Lilly.

The broker receives a call from the customer, who requests that a market order be entered.

HOW TO MAKE A STOCK PURCHASE

The order is telephoned to the Jones & Company clerk on the floor of the New York Stock Exchange. The clerk hands it to the New York Stock Exchange member who is a partner in Jones & Company. This member goes to the Lilly trading post (the specific location on the

A clerk calls in an order to a member firm as a broker checks on incoming orders and an ITS operator receives incoming orders from the Intermarket Trading System.

worse—then Wall Street is said to be in a **bear market,** one characterized by a long-term trend of falling prices.

bear market *Falling stock market*

How might you determine whether you should be bullish or bearish? First, look at the broad movements in the markets (see Exhibit 20.2). Has a bull market gone on maybe too long, which would suggest that stocks are overvalued and a *correction* might be imminent? If so, the market will correct itself downward, sometimes slowly and other times quickly, as it did in the crash of October 19, 1987. Second, watch the volume of shares traded each day. If the stock market is down on heavy volume (that is, if prices are moving downward and a lot of trading is going on), you might conclude that investors are trying to sell before prices go down further—a strong bearish sign.

The most common way investors determine whether the market is bullish or bearish is to watch indexes and averages, which use the performance of a representative sampling of stocks, bonds, or com-

floor where that particular stock is traded) and calls out, "How's Lilly?" A specialist in Lilly stock answers, "Seventy-nine to a quarter," meaning that someone is currently bidding $79 a share for 100 shares (or more) of the stock and that someone else is

Brokers trade with each other.

willing to sell at $79.25. The Jones & Company member could buy the stock immediately for Nancy Richards at $79.25 a share, because hers was a market order. More likely, however, the member will bid $79\frac{1}{8}$ for a few minutes, hoping to save a little money.

In Palo Alto, California, mean-

while, Doug Andrews has decided to sell his 100 shares of Lilly stock in order to pay his son's college bills for the year. He has phoned his broker and given him an order to sell 100 shares of Lilly at $79\frac{1}{8}$. The exchange member representing Andrews's brokerage firm reaches the trading post in time to hear the interchange between the Lilly specialist and the Jones & Company member. He hears the Jones & Company member bid $79\frac{1}{8}$ for the stock and shouts out, "Sold at seventy-nine and an eighth." The two exchange members initial each other's order slips. A stock exchange employee, known as a reporter, makes a note of the trade. Within minutes, the transaction is reported back to the brokerage houses and to the two customers.

The trading procedures for over-the-counter stocks are different. Say that Nancy Richards wanted to buy 100 shares of American Greetings, which is not listed on any stock exchange. Her stockbroker would check the NASDAQ quotes via computer to determine the current bidding and asking prices offered by each of the broker-dealers who trade in the stock. Nancy's broker would then use the computer to complete the trade instantaneously at the best price.

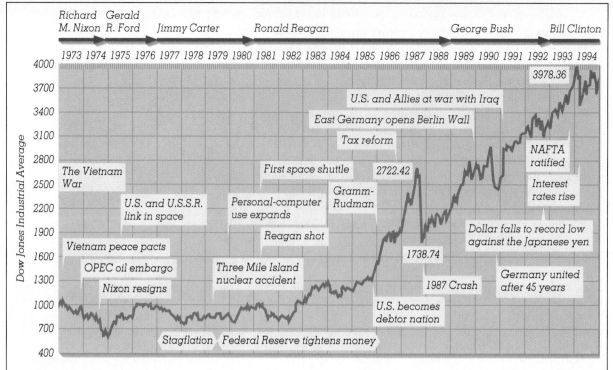

Exhibit 20.2
The Stock Market's Ups and Downs

The performance of the stock market is affected by the state of the economy and other world events. The peaks and valleys on this chart represent swings in the Dow Jones Industrial Average, the most widely used indicator of stock prices.

Chart labels:

Richard M. Nixon — Gerald R. Ford — Jimmy Carter — Ronald Reagan — George Bush — Bill Clinton

1973 1974 1975 1976 1977 1978 1979 1980 1981 1982 1983 1984 1985 1986 1987 1988 1989 1990 1991 1992 1993 1994

Dow Jones Industrial Average: 4000, 3700, 3400, 3100, 2800, 2500, 2200, 1900, 1600, 1300, 1000, 700, 400

The Vietnam War

U.S. and U.S.S.R. link in space

Vietnam peace pacts

OPEC oil embargo

Nixon resigns

Personal-computer use expands

First space shuttle

Reagan shot

Three Mile Island nuclear accident

Stagflation

Federal Reserve tightens money

Gramm-Rudman

Tax reform

East Germany opens Berlin Wall

U.S. and Allies at war with Iraq

2722.42

1738.74

1987 Crash

U.S. becomes debtor nation

Dollar falls to record low against the Japanese yen

Germany united after 45 years

NAFTA ratified

Interest rates rise

3978.36

modities as a gauge of activity in the market as a whole. The most famous is the Dow Jones Industrial Average (DJIA), which tracks the prices of 30 stocks traded on the NYSE. The DJIA is the barometer that captures the headlines. However, money managers and most professional investors are critical of its usefulness; it consists of relatively few stocks, which means a major change in just one stock can move the index. Some investors therefore prefer to follow the Standard & Poor's 500 Stock Average (S&P 500).[25]

Other averages and indexes include the Dow Jones Utility Average of 15 utility stocks; the Dow Jones Transportation Average of 20 transportation stocks; the New York Stock Exchange Index, which covers 1,614 common and preferred stocks listed on the exchange; the NASDAQ Index; and the Wilshire Index, which includes 5,000 stocks and gives the broadest indication of market trends.

The most widely followed indicators for commodities are the Dow Jones commodity indexes, which cover spot and futures trading. Dow Jones also publishes bond averages.

Daily Price Quotations

Once you have some insight into underlying market trends, you can begin to identify specific investments that meet your objectives. This is an important step because the mix of investments you select will have more impact on your overall success than any other factor. Indeed, one consulting firm estimates that deciding where to put your money—in stocks, bonds, cash, or whatever—accounts for about 85 percent of the return on your investment.[26]

Because you can't always be well informed about everything, you may want to focus on one type of investment, such as stocks or commodities. You might narrow your focus even further, specializing in a particular industry or type of commodity. For example, you might decide to specialize in consumer-products companies, because as a consumer you are familiar with the relative strengths of some of those companies.

Stock Exchange Listings

Once you have narrowed your focus, the search for specific stocks becomes easier. You might pick 20 companies that appeal to you and begin to track their daily performance in the newspaper. Exhibit 20.3 is a sample of a stock exchange report in a daily newspaper, showing high and low prices for the past 52 weeks, the number of shares traded (volume), and the change from the closing price of the day before.

Exhibit 20.3
How to Read a Newspaper Stock Quotation
To the uninitiated, the daily stock quotations in the newspapers look like a mysterious code. However, the code, when broken, yields a great deal of information on the performance of a particular stock.

Indicates the highest price of the stock during the preceding 52 weeks plus the current week, but not the latest trading day. Most stocks are quoted in eighths of a dollar: 1/8 is $0.125; 867/8 is $86.875.

Indicates the lowest price of the stock during the preceding 52 weeks plus the current week, but not the latest trading day: 647/8 is $64.875.

Boldface quotations are those issues whose price changed by 5 percent or more if their previous closing price was $2 or higher.

Low price of shares for the day was 697/8, or $69.875.

High price of shares for the day was 703/8, or $70.375.

Number of shares (in hundreds) traded in one day; 422,800 shares of Dayton Hudson were traded on this particular day.

The price/earnings ratio indicates how many dollars investors are willing to pay for one dollar of a company's earnings. It is determined by dividing the closing market price by the company's primary per-share earnings for the most recent four quarters.

| 52 Weeks | | | | | Ytd | | | Vol | | | | Net |
Hi	Lo	Stock	Sym	Div	%	PE	100s	Hi	Lo	Close	Chg
12	65/8	DataGen	DGN	...		dd	1275	101/4	97/8	10	....
71/2	**11/4**	**Datapoint**	**DPT**		...	dd	671	**23/8**	**21/8**	**23/8**	**+ 1/4**
83/4	11/4	Datapoint pfA		.75j	...	...	87	21/8	77/8	21/8	+ 1/4
10	61/4	DavisW&W	DWW	.08e	.8	dd	116	95/8	91/2	91/2	− 1/8
867/8	647/8	DaytnHud	DH	1.68	2.4	12	4228	703/8	697/8	697/8	− 1/8
331/2	251/4	DeanFood	DF	.68	2.4	14	299	283/4	281/2	283/4	− 1/4
87/8	71/4	DeanWtGvTr	GVT	.60	7.9	...	363	73/4	75/8	75/8	− 1/8
431/8	311/2	DeanWtDscvr	DWD	.50	1.4	8	22492	347/8	335/8	347/8	+ 11/4
151/2	13	DebartoloRlty	EJD		...	...	926	145/8	141/2	141/2	− 1/8
907/8	611/4	Deere	DE	2.20	3.4	9	2705	653/4	65	65	− 11/4
147/8	113/8	DE GpDivinco	DDF	1.11e	9.4	...	394	12	113/4	113/4	− 1/8

The percentage yield shows dividends as a percentage of the share price—in this case, 2.4 percent.

Dayton Hudson paid, 1.68 or $1.68 per share, in dividends.

Dayton Hudson's symbol on the New York Stock Exchange ticker tape.

Dayton Hudson is the name of the stock.

Underlined quotations are those stocks with large changes in volume, per exchange, compared with the issue's average trading volume.

At the close of the trading day, Dayton Hudson shares sold for 697/8, or $69.875 each.

The price of each Dayton Hudson share went down 1/8 point, or $0.125, from the price it commanded at the close of business the day before.

price-earnings ratio (p/e ratio)
Comparison of a stock's market price with its annual earnings per share; also known as the price-earnings multiple

One item of information also included in stock listings for the major exchanges is the **price-earnings ratio,** or *p/e* ratio (also known as the price-earnings multiple), which is computed by dividing a stock's market price by its yearly earnings per share. Say that Acme stock sold for $20 a share last year and earned $2 per share. The price-earnings ratio would be 10:

$$\frac{\$20 \; market \; price}{\$2 \; earnings \; per \; share} = 10$$

Stocks in the same industry tend to have *p/e* ratios that are roughly the same. You might expect to see a *p/e* ratio of 20 in a high-tech area like genetic engineering and a *p/e* ratio closer to 5 in the electric-utilities industry. Price-earnings ratios also vary from year to year, depending on corporate profitability and the performance of the stock market. During the 1980s, the average *p/e* ratio for all companies ranged from 8 to 16.[27]

GAINING THE COMPETITIVE EDGE

Inexperienced investors may use some of the same techniques that professional analysts use when deciding whether a stock is worth buying. One tried-and-true method is "fundamental analysis," an approach to stock selection that involves careful examination of a company's history, current financial position, and prospects for the future. Fundamental analysis emerged shortly after the stock market crash of 1929; until then, the most common means of stock selection could have been called the "grapevine method."

Analyzing a company's fundamentals requires careful evaluation of its balance sheet and income statement, making comparisons with benchmarks established by that company in earlier years and by other firms in the industry. The worksheet here is designed to help you make the key comparisons that will tell you whether a stock deserves further consideration. You'll find the basic numbers you need in the stock market listings of your newspaper or *The Wall Street Journal* and in the Value Line Investment Survey, available in well-stocked libraries. Value Line

STOCK ANALYSIS: CALCULATING PROSPECTS FOR GROWTH

makes earnings estimates and compiles some of the industry averages; the others can be calculated from Value Line reports on companies in specific industries. You'll also have to work out the percentage change in earnings. To determine whether the stock is widely held by financial institutions, divide the number of shares they own (listed in Value Line under "Institutional Decisions") by total shares outstanding (found under "Capital Structure"). Check your newspaper to make sure the stock price that Value Line used for such data as the price-earnings ratio is not out of date.

In addition to earnings growth, a company's financial strength shows up in its net profit margin (which is the rate of return on sales), in its return on net worth (another gauge of profit), and in its cash flow per share (which indicates how much money the company is generating to finance further growth). This information is available in Value Line as well. Give the company a plus for each of these values if it is higher than the industry average. The last three measures on the worksheet give you an idea of the relative value of the stock. Give the stock a plus if any of these ratios are below average. When you've scored the company on each item, tally the pluses and minuses. Plus three or better is encouraging.

Once you've isolated a promising stock, more work needs to be done. Dig energetically for clues about the prospects for the firm's industry and the quality of the firm's management. Just before you place an order, check with your broker for late news about the company. Although the company looks rock solid from your perspective, its stock price may be down for an important reason.

A high or low *p/e* ratio is not necessarily good or bad. What you should examine is a company's ratio relative to those of other companies in its industry. If the *p/e* ratio is significantly below the industry norm, you may conclude either that the company is having problems or that it is an undiscovered gem that may soon go up in price.

Listings of Other Investments

Many newspapers carry a report of trading in bonds on the major exchanges (see Exhibit 20.4). When reading bond prices, remember that the high and low are given as a percentage of the bond's face value. For example, a $1,000 bond shown closing at 65 actually sold at $650.

Price quotations for mutual funds, commodities, options, and government securities may also be found in the major newspapers. Exhibit 20.5 illustrates a mutual fund listing, and Exhibit 20.6 is a list-

Example: SmythKellman Beechum
Industry: Drugs

Ticker symbol:	SKB	Your stock			SKB	Your stock
Latest price	$63.75		Last year's per-share earnings		$5.51	
52-week range	$57–$77		This year's estimated earnings		$6.40	
Annual dividend	$2.60		Estimated change		+15.6%	

The Financial Analysis

The following should be above the industry average:	SKB	INDUSTRY AVERAGE	ABOVE OR BELOW AVERAGE	SCORE	YOUR STOCK	INDUSTRY AVERAGE	ABOVE OR BELOW AVERAGE	SCORE
Five-year average annual earnings growth	33%	17%	above	+				
Net profit margin	15.3%	11.4%	above	+				
Return on net worth	24.7%	18%	above	+				
Cash flow per share	$6.58	$3.51	above	+				
The following should be below the industry average:	SKB	INDUSTRY AVERAGE	ABOVE OR BELOW AVERAGE	SCORE	YOUR STOCK	INDUSTRY AVERAGE	ABOVE OR BELOW AVERAGE	SCORE
Price / earnings ratio	11.5	24	below	+				
Ratio of price to book value	311%	474%	below	+				
Institutional stockholdings	61%	46%	above	–				
			Net score:	+5			Net score:	

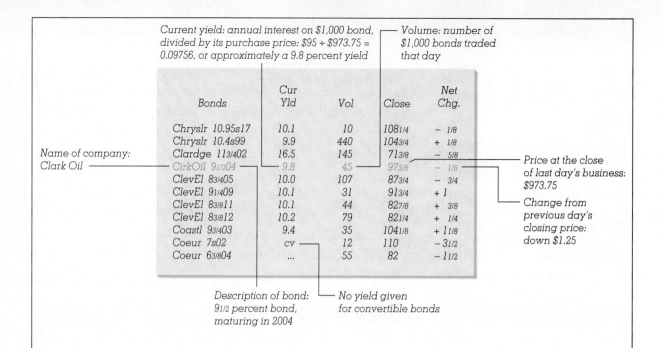

Current yield: annual interest on $1,000 bond, divided by its purchase price: $95 ÷ $973.75 = 0.09756, or approximately a 9.8 percent yield

Volume: number of $1,000 bonds traded that day

Name of company: Clark Oil

Price at the close of last day's business: $973.75

Change from previous day's closing price: down $1.25

Bonds	Cur Yld	Vol	Close	Net Chg.
Chryslr 10.95s17	10.1	10	108 1/4	− 1/8
Chryslr 10.4s99	9.9	440	104 3/4	+ 1/8
Clardge 11 3/4 02	16.5	145	71 3/8	− 5/8
CirkOil 9 1/2 04	9.8	45	97 3/8	− 1/8
ClevEl 8 3/4 05	10.0	107	87 3/4	− 3/4
ClevEl 9 1/4 09	10.1	31	91 3/4	+ 1
ClevEl 8 3/8 11	10.1	44	82 7/8	+ 3/8
ClevEl 8 3/8 12	10.2	79	82 1/4	+ 1/4
Coastl 9 3/4 03	9.4	35	104 1/8	+ 1 1/8
Coeur 7s02	cv	12	110	− 3 1/2
Coeur 6 3/8 04	...	55	82	− 1 1/2

Description of bond: 9 1/2 percent bond, maturing in 2004

No yield given for convertible bonds

Offer price: net asset value plus sales commission, if any ($26.32).

Gain or loss, (in this case, gain of 6¢) based on the previous NAV quotation.

Ranking: Funds are grouped by investment objectives defined by The Wall Street Journal and ranked. "C" means middle 20 percent.

Name of management company.

Name of mutual fund: Fortis Fund Growth A.

Total return: performance calculations, as percentages, assuming reinvestment of all distributions (without sales charges). For year to date: loss of 1.8 percent; for 26 weeks: gain of 7.3 percent; and for 4 years: gain of 14.5 percent.

	Inv. Obj.	NAV	Offer Price	NAV Chg.	−Total Return− YTD	26 wks	4 yrs	R
Fortis Funds:								
AstAIA p	S&B	13.93	14.59	+0.03	−0.7	+4.6	+10.9	C
CaApA p	SML	22.37	23.42	−0.04	−2.3	+8.0	+17.3	C
CaptIA p	G&I	16.68	17.51	+0.02	−1.6	+5.1	+13.8	B
FidcrA p	GRO	27.81	29.20	+0.04	−1.7	+6.8	+14.7	B
GlbGrA p	WOR	13.85	14.54	−0.08	−1.6	+3.4	NS	··
GvTRA p	MTG	7.64	8.00	+0.03	+0.2k	−1.2k	+3.1k	E
GrwthA p	CAP	25.07	26.32	+0.06	−1.8	+7.3	+14.5	C
HiYldA p	BHI	7.62	7.98	...	+0.1k	−3.4k	+20.7k	A
TF MNE	SSM	9.79	10.25	+0.01	0.0k	−0.7k	+6.4k	C
TF NatE	GLM	10.10	10.58	+0.02	0.0k	−0.7k	+7.0k	B
USGvtE	MTG	8.62	9.03	+0.02	+0.1k	−0.2k	+5.1k	E
44 WlEa	CAP	5.55	5.55	+0.06	−0.2	NA	+13.9	C

Investment objective based on stated investment goals, which in this case is capital appreciation (CAP).

Net asset value: the per-share value ($25.07), based on closing quotes, unless noted.

hibit 20.5 illustrates a mutual fund listing, and Exhibit 20.6 is a listing of spot prices on the commodities market (also called cash trading prices).

REGULATION OF SECURITIES TRADING

Since the early days of stock trading, state governments have tried to control the way stocks are bought and sold. Even though almost every state has its own laws governing securities trading, the federal government has the leading role in investment regulation (see Exhibit 20.7). Today trading in stocks and bonds is monitored by the Securities and Exchange Commission (SEC), and trading in commodities is supervised by the Commodity Futures Trading Commission (CFTC).

Of the two federal agencies, the SEC is the older and stronger. Its 2,450 staff members supervise the stock exchanges, over-the-counter markets, 10,500 brokerage houses, 417,000 registered representatives, 19,000 investment advisers, and 21 public-utility holding companies. Every year the SEC screens 14,000 prospectuses, 6,500 proxy statements, 15,200 annual reports, and 40,000 investor complaints. Although the securities industry has mushroomed in the past 10 years, the SEC has not expanded its staff as rapidly. It operates on an annual budget of about $187 million.[28]

Like many other regulatory agencies with a heavy work load and a limited staff, the SEC tries to focus its efforts where they will do

Exhibit 20.4 (opposite, top)
How to Read a Newspaper Bond Quotation
Many newspapers carry bond quotations in addition to stock quotations. Prices represent a percentage of a bond's face value, which is typically $1,000.

Exhibit 20.5 (opposite, bottom)
How to Read a Newspaper Mutual Fund Quotation
A mutual fund listing shows the net asset value of one share (the price at which one share is trading) and the change in trading price from one day to the next.

Exhibit 20.6
Newspaper Listing of Cash Trading Prices on the Commodities Market
The basic information in a listing about the performance of an item on the commodities market—in this case, butter—is its price per unit today and yesterday.

Type of commodity: AA grade — Unit of price: pound — Price per pound on trading day: 65¢ — Price on preceding trading day: 65¢

FOODS			
Beef, Carcass, Equiv.Index Value, choice 1-3,550-700lbs.	104.25	c104.60	104.95
Beef Carcass, Equiv.Index Value, select 1-3,550-700lbs.	97.95	c96.45	102.60
Broilers, Dressed "A" NY lb	x.4894	.4913	.5373
Broilers, 12-Cty Comp Wtd Av	.5074	.5074	.5240
Butter, AA, Chgo., lb.	.65	.65	.64
Cocoa, Ivory Coast, $metric ton	g1,654	1,602	1,535
Coffee, Brazilian, NY lb.	n1.611/4	1.603/4	.611/2
Coffee, Colombian, NY lb.	n1.77	1.77	.79
Eggs, Lge white, Chgo doz.	.58-.63	.59-.64	.691/2
Flour, hard winter KC cwt	10.85	10.75	11.20
Hams, 17-20 lbs, Mid-US lb fob	z	.48	z
Hogs, Iowa-S.Minn. avg. cwt	35.25	35.00	40.75
Hogs, Omaha avg cwt	36.75	35.25	40.00
Pork Bellies, 12-14 lbs Mid-US lb ..	.32-.34	.391/2-.34	.49
Pork Loins, 14-18 lbs. Mid-US lb	.91-.98	.99-1.00	.89
Steers, Tex.-Okla, ch avg cwt	73.00	72.00	72.00
Steers, Feeder, Okl Cty, av cwt	85.75	85.75	89.50
Sugar, cane, raw, world, lb. fob ...	.1574	.1526	.1048

Commodity: butter

Location of commodities market: Chicago

Price one year ago: 64¢

Exhibit 20.7

Major Federal Legislation Governing the Securities Industry

Although you have no guarantee that you'll make money on your investments, you are protected by laws against unfair securities trading practices.

Legislation	Date	Effect
Securities Act	1933	Known as the Truth in Securities Act; requires full disclosure of relevant financial information from companies that want to sell new stock or bond issues to the general public
Securities Exchange Act	1934	Created the Securities and Exchange Commission (SEC) to regulate the national stock exchanges and to establish trading rules
Maloney Act	1938	Created the National Association of Securities Dealers to regulate over-the-counter securities trading
Investment Company Act	1940	Extended the SEC's authority to cover the regulation of mutual funds
Amendment to the Securities Exchange Act	1964	Extended the SEC's authority to cover the over-the-counter market
Securities Investor Protection Act	1970	Created the Securities Investor Protection Corporation (SIPC) to insure individual investors against losses in the event of dealer fraud or insolvency
Commodity Futures Trading Commission Act	1974	Created the Commodity Futures Trading Commission (CFTC) to establish and enforce regulations governing futures trading
Insider Trading and Securities Fraud Enforcement Act	1988	Toughened penalties, authorized bounties for information, required brokerages to establish written policies to prevent employee violations, and made it easier for investors to bring legal action against violators
Securities Market Reform Act	1990	Increased SEC market control by granting additional authority to suspend trading in any security for 10 days, to restore order in the event of a major disturbance, to establish a national system for settlement and clearance of securities transactions, to adopt rules for actions affecting market volatility, and to require more detailed record keeping and reporting of brokers and dealers

the most good. It concentrates on a few big cases and urges brokerage houses and securities exchanges to police themselves. One of the SEC's top priorities is to crack down on *insider trading,* in which a few people with access to nonpublic information (say, a pending merger) buy or sell a company's stock before the information can become public and before the price can change in reaction to the news.

The stock exchanges also play a role in monitoring the securities industry. To be listed on an exchange, a company must file registration papers and fulfill certain requirements. In addition, traders must conform to the rules of the exchange, many of which are designed to protect investors. Generally speaking, the New York Stock Exchange and the American Stock Exchange (AMEX) enforce more

counter companies with assets of more than $1 million and having at least 500 shareholders must file comprehensive annual financial reports with the SEC, just as listed companies must do.

How are investors protected if their brokerage fails? Since 1970, 228 brokerages have gone bankrupt. To cope with such collapses, Congress established the Securities Investor Protection Corporation (SIPC). The SIPC is not a part of the federal government; its operations and insurance fund are financed by the securities industry. It provides up to $500,000 worth of insurance against fraud or bankruptcy for each investor who buys and leaves securities for safekeeping with a brokerage house, and it provides up to $100,000 worth of insurance for cash left with a brokerage house. The SIPC does not cover commodities contracts or limited-partnership investments. Nor does it protect against losses from declines in the price of securities. Of the 330,000 claims filed since 1970, all but 293 have been fully covered by SIPC insurance.[29]

1 Identify five criteria to be considered when making investment decisions.

Investors should consider the income, growth, safety, liquidity, and tax consequences of alternative investments.

2 List five investment options available to the investor and compare them in terms of safety and potential rate of return.

Investors may choose stocks, corporate bonds, government securities, mutual funds, and commodities. Although the performance of these investments varies from year to year and depends on the specific issue selected, they can be characterized in terms of safety and potential rate of return. Government securities are considered the safest investment, followed by corporate bonds, mutual funds, stocks, and commodities, in that order. In terms of potential rate of return, commodities and stocks are ranked highest, followed by mutual funds, corporate bonds, and government securities.

3 Describe asset allocation and how it's used during changing economic conditions.

Asset allocation is a method of shifting investable assets within a portfolio to maximize income and growth while minimizing loss. If economic conditions are good, most of a portfolio tends to be invested in equities; if economic conditions are poor, the majority of a portfolio will be invested in fixed-income instruments, such as cash instruments.

4 Explain the safety and tax advantages of investing in U.S. government securities.

U.S. government securities, including those backed by the U.S. Treasury and those backed by agencies of the government, are relatively safe because the government and its agencies are unlikely to default on interest payments. Interest from Treasury notes and Treasury bonds is exempt from state and local income taxes.

5 Describe two types of securities marketplaces.

Auction exchanges funnel all buy and sell orders, and all information regarding the traded stocks, into one centralized location. There, specialists match buy and sell orders to get the best price for both parties on a given security. Specialists also act as "buyers of last resort" if no investor wants to buy a security that is for sale. Dealer exchanges are decentralized marketplaces in which dealers are connected electronically. Dealers, also known as market makers, carry their own inventory of securities, so they perform a service for buyers and sellers by completing the transactions, instead of by trying to match buyers and sellers to a market price.

6 List at least four sources of information about investments.

Investors may obtain information on investments from newspapers, business magazines, investment-rating services, and electronic-data services (as well as from television shows, brokerage houses, financial planners, and corporations).

7 Discuss six indexes that provide a broad indication of how the stock market is performing.

The Dow Jones Industrial Average is the most widely recognized market indicator; it is limited to selected stocks traded on the New York Stock Exchange. The Standard & Poor's 500 Stock Average and the New York Stock Exchange Index cover a wider cross section of stocks traded on the NYSE. The Dow Jones Utility Average covers 15 utility stocks, and the NASDAQ Index covers shares traded on the over-the-counter market. The Wilshire Index, which covers 5,000 NYSE, AMEX, and OTC stocks, is the broadest market indicator.

8 Name two federal agencies involved in regulating the investment industry.

The Securities and Exchange Commission oversees trading on the stock exchanges, and the Commodity Futures Trading Commission oversees trading on the commodities exchanges.

William A. Francis had to understand the economic trends that affected the stock market. However, no matter how well the economy fared, no matter whether the stock market was moving up or down, his objective remained the same: to steadily increase the wealth of his clients over time. He knew that speculating for a quick gain could lead to an even quicker loss.

Therefore, Francis had to know how *not* to invest. He didn't want to invest in companies just because they were fascinating or just because they were big. Biotechnology might be exciting, but it had yet to realize its promise. Until it did, investing in biotechnology companies carried a heavy risk. As for big firms, a $60 billion giant usually has less growth potential than a company worth $6 million (a 10 percent gain would require $6 billion for the giant firm, but only $600,000 for the smaller one). Neither did Francis want to invest in companies that were unsure of their business. Corporations that are in the headlines tend to be those that are continually changing focus, management structure, or business plans, and their potential is generally uncertain. Well-managed companies that stick to their business might attract less press, but the news is usually much better.

So just what was Francis looking for in a company? Most important, Francis wanted to see companies developing a particular competitive advantage. Whether they developed it through their product, their customer service, or their market share wasn't important, as long as the advantage gave the company a sustainable growth potential. A software firm might specialize in the types of products that businesses are expected to need in the coming years, or a major retailer might be expanding into lucrative new markets. In addition, Francis wanted to see companies that had positive track records: at least two years of rising productivity, falling costs, low debt, and consistent spending for research and development.

Francis was in search of the few companies that were still pursuing long-term growth. He needed information about products and services that were relatively new. He wanted to know about companies that held great promise. He needed information about which companies were satisfying their customers and increasing sales. Even though the times had changed, his methods of searching had not. He turned to business publications such as *The Wall Street Journal, Investor's Daily, Barron's, Business Week, Fortune,* and *Forbes.* He also read industry publications and studied statistical profiles found in *Standard & Poor's Stock Guide* and in Value Line.

To determine when to sell a stock, Francis needed the same information. The only difference was that instead of looking for growth potential, he looked for the likelihood that growth would slow down enough to affect stock prices. Before selling a stock, he asked three questions: (1) Are the stocks, in general, overvalued? (2) Are the profit margins ("the blood pressure of the company") beginning to drop? (3) Is the company making any unnecessary strategic changes? A yes answer to all three questions signaled Francis to consider selling. After all, he invests his clients' money in common stock to realize capital gains, not capital losses.

Your Mission: You have just been hired as an investment adviser at Landes Associates. In addition to your assignment to bring new clients into the firm, you have been assigned to manage a certain number of existing accounts. They include investors who are interested in both growth and income, who are more conservative and less conservative, and who all seek good value in their investments. Your job is to successfully manage the investments for all these clients.

1. A new client has come to you seeking safe income from a long-term investment. Which of the following would be the best investment for her needs?
   a. Buying U.S. Treasury bonds
   b. Short-selling common stocks
   c. Buying pork belly futures

2. One of your best clients is thinking about buying stock in General Motors. He asks for your opinion. Before you give him an answer, you need to find out for yourself whether it's a good investment. What sources would you use to find the latest, most accurate, and most objective information about GM's current business and future prospects?
   a. *Car and Driver* and *Consumer Reports* magazines
   b. Automotive-industry reports and *Standard & Poor's Stock Guide*
   c. GM's annual and quarterly reports

3. A friend has asked you for some advice. She has a small amount of money to invest and is looking for a diverse portfolio of stocks and bonds, mainly for long-term capital gains. Which would be the best investment?

a. A mutual stock fund of common stocks and a mutual bond fund of corporate and government bonds

b. Selected individual common stocks and an investment in both long-term and short-term government bonds

c. Individual common stocks and a mutual bond fund of corporate bonds

4. You have to buy a new battery for your car one Saturday, so you decide to visit the new auto-parts store that just opened on the corner.

When you enter the store, you notice how busy the store is, how large the store's selection of auto parts is, and how well customers (including you) are being served. As you're paying for your battery, you recall reading about the company that owns and operates this chain of auto-parts stores—an article that complimented the company's management and its business strategy. You also believe that, with the economy in its current downturn, more people will be re-

pairing their old cars rather than buying new ones. On the basis of these observations, you think this company might make a good investment, but you aren't sure. What would be the best way for you to find out?

a. Study the company's annual and quarterly reports.

b. Research the company and the industry in business and industry publications.

c. Both (a) and (b)[30]

KEY TERMS

arbitrage (613)
asset allocation (602)
auction exchange (612)
bear market (619)
blue-chip stocks (606)
broker (616)
bull market (618)
call option (609)
capital gains (601)
commodities (610)
commodities futures (611)
commodity exchanges (613)
convertible bonds (605)
dealer exchanges (612)
debentures (605)
default (604)
discount brokerages (617)
discretionary order (616)

diversification (602)
financial futures (610)
full-service brokerages (617)
general obligation bonds (605)
growth stocks (606)
hedge (610)
indexing (603)
institutional investors (600)
investment portfolios (602)
limit order (616)
margin trading (616)
marketable securities (600)
market indexes (603)
market makers (612)
market order (616)
money-market funds (609)
mortgage bonds (605)
municipal bonds (604)
mutual funds (608)
open order (616)

over-the-counter (OTC) market (614)
price-earnings ratio (*p/e* ratio) (622)
program trading (613)
put option (610)
rate of return (602)
revenue bonds (605)
shareholder (606)
short selling (608)
speculators (601)
spot trading (611)
stock option (609)
stock specialist (612)
transaction costs (617)
Treasury bills (604)
Treasury bonds (604)
Treasury notes (604)
U.S. savings bonds (604)

REVIEW QUESTIONS

1. What is an institutional investor?
2. When might an investor sell stock short? What risks are involved in selling short?
3. What are the differences between a Treasury bill, a Treasury note or bond, and a U.S. savings bond?

4. What is the difference between a general obligation bond and a revenue bond?
5. How does a load mutual fund differ from a no-load mutual fund?
6. What are the limitations of the Dow Jones Industrial Average?

7. What is a *p/e* ratio, and what does it signify to an investor?
8. What is the function of the Securities Investor Protection Corporation?

A LEGENDARY INVESTOR NOW PREFERS PREFERREDS

Probably the greatest investor of the late twentieth century is Warren Buffett, a soft-spoken Nebraskan who characterizes his investment strategy as "lethargy bordering on sloth"—meaning that he's perfectly willing to keep a quality investment for years. Buffett is not one to continually buy and sell equities in an attempt to beat the market at every turn. However, he does admit that it's not as easy as it used to be, and he sometimes finds himself in situations he never expected.

Buffett gained his reputation as chairman of Berkshire Hathaway, a Massachusetts textile manufacturer that he transformed into an investment company by acquiring about a dozen insurance companies and using the flow of insurance premiums to make investments. About 80 percent of Berkshire's investments are held by the insurance group. Buffett's investment strategies have increased the value of Berkshire's common stock from a 1980 low of $240 per share to a 1993 high of $16,600.

He began by looking for companies whose assets were undervalued by the market—that is, companies whose stock prices reflected little more than operating profits. In time, the market saw the same value in those companies as Buffett did, and it bid the stock prices up. This action increased the wealth of Berkshire Hathaway and of Buffett, who owns 42 percent of Berkshire's common stock.

During the 1980s, he invested in General Foods, Beatrice, and RJR Nabisco, believing all three to be in play for possible takeovers. When these companies did become involved in mergers and acquisitions, their common stock prices skyrock-eted. By the late 1980s, though, Buffett found it increasingly difficult to identify undervalued stocks or to make quick gains on takeovers. So he started buying convertible preferred stock in companies that were threatened with hostile takeovers. If converted into common shares, the investments were large enough to thwart the intentions of corporate raiders, making Buffett a "white knight." Even so, Buffett's strategy was unusual because preferred stock doesn't usually produce significant capital gains. Moreover, Buffett doesn't consider his strategy aggressive; he calls it "lending money, plus an equity kicker."

Using this strategy, Buffett's Berkshire invested $2 billion in preferred stock of Champion International, USAir Group, Gillette, and Salomon Brothers. The first two investments have underperformed, but Buffett won big on Gillette, earning Berkshire a 50 percent gain after only two years.

Here's how his strategy worked in the case of Salomon. Berkshire invested $700 million in Salomon preferred stock, which could be converted after three years into Salomon common stock at $38 a share. Until the stock was converted, though, Berkshire would receive a 9 percent dividend yield. Because Berkshire got a 70 percent tax break on dividend income from the Salomon preferred stock, Buffett's company received an 8 percent yield after taxes—which at the time was better than the after-tax yield on high-quality corporate bonds. If the preferred stock was converted into common, Berkshire would then own 14 percent of Salomon, more than any other single investor. This investment resulted in Buffett's being named chairman of the company.

The appointment came after Salomon admitted to illegal bidding in the $2.2 trillion U.S. Treasury securities market. Salomon's board of directors named Buffett in an effort to restore the company's credibility, keep it out of court, and most important, retain Salomon's status as a major player in the Treasury securities market.

Berkshire has yet to realize any capital gain on Salomon, whose stock dropped after the firm admitted guilt in the Treasury securities trading scandal. Berkshire can't make a capital gain until the preferred shares are converted into common shares—at $38 per share—and then sold. Even if that never happens, however, it's unlikely Berkshire will lose on the deal. First, it's still receiving dividend income. Second, if Buffett decides against converting the preferred into common shares, Salomon must begin buying the stock back between 1995 and 1999.

1. Buffett prefers to buy and hold investments for long periods. Why do you think he has been called the investor's investor?
2. What do you think is the most important factor in deciding whether to invest in a company's convertible preferred stock: the stock's dividend yield computed on an after-tax basis, the price at which the preferred stock can be converted into common, or the need for income or growth in your portfolio?
3. Do you think the small investor can really learn anything practical from Buffett, or is it impossible because he's such a big investor?

Using this chapter as a resource, investigate the world of securities markets by interviewing a stockbroker. The interview may be conducted either by phone or in person. Prepare for the interview by drafting a list of 8 to 10 questions about current and expected trends in stock and bond prices, methods of working with clients, selection of appropriate investments to meet investors' objectives, and other issues that interest you. Then, as requested by your instructor, write a brief report describing the results of your interview, or give a three-minute oral report to the class.

KEEPING CURRENT USING *THE WALL STREET JOURNAL*

You have $10,000 to invest. Using as much information as your instructor recommends, select a well-known company traded on the New York Stock Exchange, American Stock Exchange, or NASDAQ. Assignment: Begin a stock-transaction journal. On the first page, record the company's name, the stock exchange abbreviation, the exchange on which it is traded, the 52-week high and low, the price/earnings ratio, and your reasons for selecting this stock.

• *Buying.* On the first day of the project, record the number of shares purchased (whole shares only), the price per share, the total purchase price (number of shares × price/share), the commission paid on your purchase (assume 1 percent of the purchase price), and today's Dow Jones Industrial Average. Now add the commission paid to the purchase price to get your *total purchase cost.*

• *Monitoring.* Record and chart the closing price of your stock each day,

and plot it on a graph. Scan *The Wall Street Journal* or other publications regularly for articles on your company to include in your journal. Note any major developments that may affect your stock.

• *Selling.* In this exercise, you select the best time to sell—as long as it meets two requirements: You must sell on or before the day designated by your instructor, and (if your instructor wishes) you must notify your instructor on the day you sell your stock. (This means that you'll probably need to sell on a day that your class meets—unless your instructor posts a sign-up sheet that you can use on other days.) On the day you sell your stock, record the following information: the selling price (the closing price/share that day), the number of shares sold, the total sales price (the number of shares × selling price/share), the commission paid on the sale (assume 1 percent of the total sales price), and that day's Dow Jones Industrial Average. Now subtract the commission paid from the total sales price to arrive at your *sales proceeds.*

• *Analysis.* Subtract your total purchase cost from your sales proceeds to arrive at your *net gain* or *net loss.*

How well did your investment do? How did it compare with gains or losses in the Dow Jones Industrial Average during this period? How close was the selling price to the stock's 52-week high or low? Use the articles you collected during this project to relate recent developments to the performance of your stock.

The Dow Jones Industrial Average (DJIA), the Standard & Poor's 500, the Wilshire Index— these and other such stock market indexes provide good indications of where U.S. markets are headed. Unfortunately, they aren't much help for markets in other countries. You can find similar indexes in all the other major industrialized countries of the world; perhaps the best known of these is Japan's Nikkei index.

Understanding the composition of a market index is vital (1) to interpret the index's movement up or down and (2) to compare it with the DJIA or other U.S. indexes. Select one of the following stock market indexes and answer the questions that follow:

• Nikkei (Japan)
• DAX (Germany)
• FT-SE (Britain)
• CAC (France)
• Hang Seng (Hong Kong)
• Straits Times (Singapore)
• All Ordinaries (Australia)[31]

1. Does the index have more or fewer companies than the DJIA? Than the S&P 500?
2. Over the last 5 or 10 years, how has your chosen index performed, compared with the DJIA?
3. Does the index appear to represent the stock market as a whole or just one sector, as the DJIA does?

THE ABCS OF INVESTING: GETTING SMART IS THE FIRST STEP TOWARD GETTING RICH

Synopsis

This video offers a different sort of program from the others you've seen in this class—this one provides basic advice for anybody who wants to invest money, which presumably applies to just about everyone taking this class. You can use the concepts to improve your current investing skills or to get you started in investing if you haven't already. The video starts with the most important investment decision you have to make: setting your financial goals. Whether it's saving for retirement, a house, or a new car, investing is more successful if you have a clear, realistic goal in mind. The program then outlines the major classes of investments—stocks, bonds, mutual funds—and explains how each one works. It concludes with a look at how you can become a better-informed investor. (The program was produced by CNBC, an all-business cable TV channel, which explains the advice on watching CNBC for investment news.)

Exercises

ANALYSIS

1. Why would you buy mutual funds instead of individual stocks and bonds?

2. Who should be the more aggressive investor: a single 25-year-old or a 50-year-old with two kids in college?

3. If you work or have worked for a publicly traded company, would you buy some of its stock as an investment? Why or why not?

4. If your college or university were a publicly traded company, would you buy some of its stock as an investment? Why or why not?

5. Are bonds always a safer investment than stocks?

APPLICATION

Would it be a good idea to borrow money in order to invest in the stock market?

DECISION

If you were investing both your own money and your parents' retirement fund (let's assume that you're in your 20s and your parents are a dozen years or so from retirement), would you use the same style of investing?

COMMUNICATION

Pretend you just made an investment for a friend (pick any investment you like). Now write your friend a letter, and explain why you made this particular choice.

INTEGRATION

Review the topic of business plans in Chapter 5; then list the points you would consider before investing in a new company.

ETHICS

Should stockbrokers be held responsible for their recommendations to customers?

DEBATE

Some people would never trust their own judgment in the stock market, whereas others always make their own buy and sell decisions. Option A: In a formal debate format, argue for the idea of always (or usually) making your own investment choices or for the idea of letting a professional make those decisions for you. Option B: Take either position and state your case in a brief report.

TEAMWORK

Assume that you and three or four other students are partners in a small company that just received $1 million in a legal settlement. Decide how you should invest it, making up whatever details about the company that you need.

RESEARCH

Do the research necessary to list the latest values of the Dow Jones Industrial Average, the S&P 500, and the NASDAQ Composite.

ROLE PLAYING

Two students play the role of a couple who want to start investing but who are currently overloaded with consumer debt. A third student plays the role of an investment adviser who gives them a plan to get out of debt and into investing.

PART SEVEN

THE ENVIRONMENT OF BUSINESS

Chapter

21

Government Regulation, Taxation, and Business Law

LEARNING OBJECTIVES
After studying this chapter
you will be able to

1 List three roles of
government that affect
business

2 Name five general areas
in which government
regulates business

3 List five revenue-raising
taxes and two regulatory
taxes

4 Explain how business
influences government

5 Describe the three
sources of law

6 Explain the meaning of
product liability

7 State the seven elements
of a valid contract

8 Distinguish between real,
personal, and intellectual
property

W alk into the nearest Wal-Mart store, and you'll be greeted by a friendly employee and given free rein to wander down aisles stacked with bargain-priced products. Particularly when you need to keep your daily expenses in check, Wal-Mart comes across as a great place to buy things for yourself or your family. Now contrast this positive image with some of the things being said about the company:

The Giant Retailer's Opponents Try to Get the Law on Their Side

We're destroying our culture and replacing it with Wal-Mart.
Wal-Mart is the ultimate predator.
A corporate colonialist that moves into distant places and strip-mines them culturally and economically.
You can't buy small-town life at Wal-Mart. You can only lose it there.
Wal-Mart is a metaphor for the American dream run amok.

Why are people saying such negative things about the country's largest retailer? As it marches its way across the continent from its home base in Arkansas, Wal-Mart has gained plenty of fans and a fairly small but very vocal band of opponents.

The opponents fall into two basic groups: small-town retailers who feel threatened by the discount giant's low prices and a less clearly defined group that criticizes the effect Wal-Mart allegedly has on small-town environments. This latter group includes historic preservationists and middle-aged activists, some of whom describe themselves as aging hippies, who are pushing for smaller, community-based businesses.

Wal-Mart faces critics when it moves into some towns, but young families whose needs are growing faster than their incomes usually applaud the big retailer's arrival.

The first group's concerns are primarily economic, whereas the second group's are more esthetic, but they are joined in their opposition to Wal-Mart's plans to move into such small towns as Westford, Massachusetts, and Chestertown, Maryland. One of their basic strategies for keeping Wal-Mart out is drumming up enough public opposition to encourage the company to change its mind. However, when all else fails, Wal-Mart's most committed opponents are more than willing to seek legal remedies. A town council may vote to restrict the size of commercial buildings within city limits. Wal-Mart stores are huge, so size restrictions are a good way to keep them out.

If you were David Glass, president and CEO of Wal-Mart, how would you deal with this opposition? Would you stay out of towns where you aren't openly welcome? Would you forge ahead wherever you can?[1]

BUSINESS AND GOVERNMENT

Over the years, the United States has accumulated laws and regulations that help resolve disputes such as those Wal-Mart faces with activists and small retailers. Although the United States is philosophically committed to the free-enterprise system and its economy is shaped primarily by market forces, the government has often stepped in to solve specific problems. In many ways, therefore, a company's success hinges on its ability to understand the law and to manage its relations with the government.

The process of managing government relations is complicated by the fact that more than one government must be dealt with. In addition to worrying about Uncle Sam, a business has to consider local, county, state, and possibly foreign governments, all of which impose specific and sometimes conflicting laws and restrictions. Furthermore, each government body interacts with business in a variety of ways. On Monday, a business may approach the government as a supporter, partner, or customer; on Tuesday, it may clash with the government over standards and regulations; on Wednesday, the company may interact with the government on a tax matter; and on Thursday, it may be involved in legal actions of a criminal or civil nature, as defined by the government.

Government as Supporter, Partner, and Customer

Although it often seems that business and government are adversaries, the opposite is true. One of government's chief objectives is to foster business prosperity; a nation's, state's, or locality's economic health depends on the success of individual companies. When business is making a profit and creating jobs, citizens benefit. Government support for business takes several forms:

- *Promoting economic growth.* The federal government tries to keep the economy growing at a steady pace by adjusting monetary (money supply) policy; all governments affect the economy through their fiscal (taxing and spending) policies. Theoretically, these actions help the economy avoid high inflation and severe recessions, both of which are harmful to business. By smoothing out the economic cycle, the government creates a climate that is good for business. The federal government also helps promote by negotiating international treaties and trade agreements, such as NAFTA and GATT, that help companies compete and operate more efficiently.
- *Supporting and subsidizing business.* Governments operate countless programs that are specifically designed to help businesses. One of

governments' most valuable functions is simply providing information and training through agencies such as the U.S. Department of Commerce. Governments also provide direct loans, loan guarantees, and subsidies of various types. For companies trying to develop new technologies and new products, some of the federal government's 700 research labs will help, too.[2] In some cases, state and federal agencies step in to help with specific business deals, usually when the buyer is a foreign government.

- *Maintaining the infrastructure.* By building roads, bridges, dams, airports, harbors, and the like, governments indirectly help businesses distribute their products. In addition, governments own and operate power plants that provide energy for business operations. Public schools provide companies with a supply of educated labor.
- *Buying industry's products.* Federal, state, and local government agencies spend over $1 trillion for goods and services provided by private industry.[3] Government procurements range from army uniforms and delivery trucks to consulting services and computers; such products involve companies of every size and description.

Government as Watchdog and Regulator

Although the United States has one of the "freest" free-market systems, various government bodies regulate and monitor nearly every aspect of business to one degree or another. This section discusses five major areas in which government regulates business activities: competition, consumer rights, employee rights, investor rights, and the natural environment.[4] (Note that there is a great deal of overlap across

The U.S. government is a major customer for General Dynamics, whose engineers are shown here testing a cruise missile.

all these categories; laws designed to promote competition often have the ultimate goal of protecting consumers, for instance.) In addition, over time the government has regulated and deregulated a number of specific industries, as you'll see at the end of this section.

Promoting Competition

In most sectors of the economy, state and federal regulators work to ensure that all competitors have an equal chance of producing a product, reaching the market, and making a profit. By setting ground rules and establishing basic standards of proper business behavior, government helps prevent conflicts and facilitates the workings of the economic system. Laws concerning competition make up a huge and complex body of government regulation.

When regulators figure that the public can be best served by limiting competition in certain industries, they will consider restricting entry into those markets. For instance, only two companies are allowed to offer cellular phone service in each city in the United States, in part because of the chaos that would probably result if any company could offer cellular service—the portion of the radio spectrum dedicated to cellular can handle only so many transmissions at a time.

In most industries, however, the government sets ground rules that enable many competitors to compete. Over the last century or so, a number of regulations have been established to help prevent individual companies or groups of companies from gaining control of markets in ways that restrain competition and/or harm consumers.

Some of the earliest government moves in this arena occurred from 1890 to the beginning of World War I. That period saw the passage of such landmark pieces of legislation as the Sherman Antitrust Act, the Clayton Antitrust Act, and the Federal Trade Commission Act, which generally sought to rein in the power of a few huge companies such as Standard Oil. These companies, usually referred to as the **trusts** (hence the label *antitrust legislation,* which you read about in Chapter 1), had financial and management control of a significant number of other companies in the same industry. The trusts thus controlled enough of the supply and distribution in their respective industries to muscle smaller competitors outx of the way.[5]

The Sherman Act got the regulatory ball rolling, and the Clayton Act added specific restrictions against **tying contracts,** which attempted to force buyers to purchase unwanted goods along with goods actually desired; **interlocking directorates,** or boards of directors made up of board members from competing firms; the practice of acquiring large blocks of competitors' stock; and discriminatory prices. The Federal Trade Commission Act set up a watchdog group (the FTC) to monitor specific activities that might be unfair. The FTC's authority was later expanded to cover practices that harmed the public, even if they didn't harm competitors.

Following the Great Depression of the 1930s, the rise of giant retailing firms prompted small retailers to turn to the federal government for protection against the chains, which were able to negotiate big price discounts from suppliers. The government responded by passing the Robinson-Patman Act, which, among other things, made

trusts Companies built by arrangements in which people owning stock in several other companies give control of their securities to trustees who then gain control of and manage these other companies; sometimes used to buy up or drive out smaller companies, thus giving monopolistic powers to the trusts

tying contracts Contracts forcing buyers to purchase unwanted goods along with goods actually desired

interlocking directorates Situation in which members of the board of one firm sit on the board of a competing firm

638

it illegal for manufacturers to sell the same product to two customers at different prices if that would stand in the way of free competition.

Laws regulating competition continue to grow and evolve as the economy itself evolves. A key area of concern to regulators involves mergers and acquisitions. Such deals must pass government approval, and approval won't be granted if regulators think a deal will restrain competition. Regulators also keep an eye on changes in technology that might give companies an unfair advantage. One of the highest-profile antitrust cases of the early 1990s involved the software giant Microsoft, which makes both the operating-system software used by most personal computers and a wide array of application software that runs on those operating systems. The U.S. Justice Department accused Microsoft of using its vast clout with operating systems to give itself an unfair advantage in the application-software business. The Justice Department could have gone as far as splitting the company in two but settled for some relatively minor changes in the demands Microsoft can make on companies that want (or don't want) to buy its operating systems.[6]

Protecting Consumers
Since the 1950s, government regulators have placed a high priority on protecting consumers from unsafe products and unfair business practices. Specific laws include the Fair Packaging and Labeling Act, which mandates specific product and supplier information on consumer-goods labels, and the Fair Credit Reporting Act, which regulates how reporting agencies collect consumer credit information and prescribes how they may use it.[7] The Nutrition Education and Labeling Act of 1990 (which was not finalized until 1994) forced food companies to adopt standardized nutrition labels. The motive beyond this act was to make it easier for consumers to make informed purchases by controlling the use of such terms as *low-fat* and *lite*.[8] The extent of government's role as consumer protector is illustrated in Exhibit 21.1, which shows how regulations relating to food quality affect fast-food hamburgers.

Protecting Employees
In addition to protecting the consumers outside the firm, a host of regulations attempt to protect employees inside the firm. Some laws apply specifically to unionized employees; others apply to employees in both union and nonunion firms. Here are the general categories:[9]

- *A safe work environment.* The Occupational Safety and Health Administration (OSHA) is the primary federal agency charged with keeping employees safe on the job. In addition to establishing safety standards and monitoring adherence to them, the government gives employees the right to refuse to work in unsafe conditions (pending a government investigation).
- *Freedom from discrimination.* At the federal level, the Equal Employment Opportunity Commission (EEOC) guarantees employees freedom from discrimination based on physical handicaps, gender, age, race, or religious affiliation. This protection applies to

Enriched bun: *Must contain at least 1.8 mg of thiamine, at least 1.1 mg of riboflavin, and at least 8.0 but no more than 12.5 mg of iron*

Meat: *Must be fresh or frozen chopped beef without added water, binders, or extenders; must be inspected before and after slaughter and at boning, grinding, fabrication, and packaging stages*

Growth promoters: *Must not be used beyond the time specified by law*

Pesticides: *No more than 5 parts of the pesticide DDT per million parts of fat in the meat*

Fat: *No more than 30 percent fat content*

Pickle slices: *Must be between 1/8 and 3/8 inch thick*

Tomatoes: *Must be mature but not overripe or soft*

Lettuce: *Must be fresh, not soft, overgrown, burst, or "ribby"; no sulfites may be used to preserve a fresh appearance*

Cheese: *Must contain at least 50 percent milk fat and, if made with milk that is not pasteurized, must be cured for 60 or more days at a temperature of at least 35°F*

Ketchup: *To be considered grade A fancy, must flow no more than 14 cm in 30 seconds at 20°C (69°F)*

Mayonnaise: *May be seasoned or flavored as long as the substances do not color it to look like egg yolk*

Exhibit 21.1
Government Regulations Affecting Fast-Food Hamburgers
Each of the government-imposed specifications shown here is intended to ensure that fast-food burgers are both nutritious and safe to eat.

hiring, promotion, termination, pay, and transfer. One of the most significant pieces of legislation in this area in recent years is the Americans with Disabilities Act, which requires businesses to provide disabled employees with compatible work environments.

- *Freedom from harassment.* Whereas discrimination involves denying people the chance to advance in their careers, harassment deals with a variety of negative behaviors, from verbal abuse to physical aggression. Harassment can be related to ethnicity or religion, although sexual harassment usually gets the most attention. Conduct is considered sexual harassment if (1) accepting the conduct is a condition of employment (either explicitly or implicitly), (2) employment decisions are made about employees on the basis of whether they submit to or reject the conduct, and (3) the conduct creates a hostile or intimidating work environment.

- *Protection from unlawful termination.* Government regulators also protect employees from getting fired for reasons not related to job performance. Situations covered here range from blowing the whistle on safety or environmental regulations to implied employment contracts.

- *Certain rights to privacy.* One of the touchiest issues in business today is employee privacy. Several factors are bringing this issue to the forefront, including advances in technology that make it easier to monitor employees and the drive to keep health-care costs as low as possible. For instance, should your employer be allowed to find out whether you bungee jump or have an alcohol problem, since both could lead to higher health-care costs?

- *The right to participate in labor unions.* The Wagner Act, which established the National Labor Relations Board, gives employees the right to organize and to join unions without fear of reprisal from their employers. As long as the activities employees engage in stand to benefit a group of employees and the issues are covered by the Wagner Act (wages and working hours, for instance), employers cannot legally take action against employees.

Protecting Investors

As the owners of publicly traded corporations, shareholders also receive some protection under both state and federal regulations. These rules fall into several categories. The first group includes laws that require corporations to disclose information that affects shareholders' investment decisions, including financial performance and executive pay. The most prominent vehicle for these disclosures is the annual report. Second, shareholders have the right to vote on major mergers, acquisitions, changes to the corporation's founding charter and bylaws, and proposals raised by other shareholders. In addition, shareholders elect the board of directors to keep an eye on the company's strategies and operations. Third, shareholders are entitled to dividend payments if the board declares dividends for the company's stock. Fourth, rules against *insider trading* help prevent some shareholders from gaining an advantage at the expense of other shareholders. If a

The annual shareholders meeting gives RCA a chance to communicate with the people who own the company.

company is about to be acquired in a takeover—the news of which is likely to raise the company's stock price—people on the inside who know about the impending takeover are forbidden to buy shares until the news becomes public. At the federal level, the Securities and Exchange Commission oversees the information-disclosure practices of publicly traded corporations to make sure investors have the information they need to make decisions.[10]

Protecting the Natural Environment

The government doesn't protect just people; a large and complex body of regulations address the environmental practices of businesses, too. From clearing land for new factories to hauling products along interstate highways to disposing of used materials, businesses must comply with numerous environmental regulations. The Clean Air Act amendments of 1990 require manufacturers, dry cleaners, oil refineries, gas stations, bakeries, and a host of other businesses to reduce harmful emissions. The result will be a healthier planet, but these changes cost U.S. business a lot of money, an estimated $25 billion every year. Some of that $25 billion comes out of salaries, profits, and the other financial rewards of being in business, and some of it comes out of consumers' pockets in the form of higher prices. On the other hand, that $25 billion represents business opportunities for the companies that provide goods and services for pollution control.[11]

Regulating and Deregulating Specific Industries

In addition to all these regulations, another layer of regulations applies to specific industries. From mining to retailing to banking to advertising, government officials keep tabs on companies to ensure fair competition, safe working conditions, and generally ethical business practices. For instance, the Federal Aviation Administration sets rules for the commercial airline industry, the Federal Communications Commission oversees telephone services and radio and television broadcasts, and the Federal Reserve Board and the Treasury Department look after the banking industry.[12]

In past years, some industries were under very strict government control. In the most extreme cases, regulators decided who could enter an industry, what customers they had to serve, and how much they could charge. The telecommunications, airline, and banking industries fell under such control until the 1970s and 1980s, when a wave of **deregulation,** the abandonment or relaxation of existing regulations, opened up competition (see Exhibit 21.2). In the telecommunications business, the federal government broke up AT&T in 1982 to allow other companies to compete for long-distance telephone business. Companies such as MCI and Sprint quickly entered the market, and price emerged as a key competitive issue.[13] However, deregulation wasn't all bad for AT&T; the government allowed AT&T to enter the market for computers and other goods at the same time that it lost its monopoly on long-distance phone service.

Deregulation produced some problems, as industries used to government protection and stability struggled to compete. In one three-year period following deregulation, the U.S. airline industry lost more money than it had earned in its entire existence, dating all the way

deregulation Removal or relaxation of rules and restrictions affecting business

1982 *AT&T is broken up, leaving local phone companies on their own.*

1982 *Congress deregulates intercity bus services and allows S&Ls to make commercial real estate loans up to 40% of assets.*

1981 *Sears, Roebuck is allowed to offer one-stop financial shopping ("stocks to socks"): insurance, brokerage services, banking.*

1980 *Congress deregulates trucking and railroads, allows S&Ls to diversify, and increases the level of insured deposits to $100,000.*

1979 *Federal Communications Commission permits AT&T to sell nonregulated services (such as data processing).*

1978 *Congress deregulates airlines.*

1977 *Merrill Lynch (a brokerage firm) is allowed to enter into more direct competition with commercial banks with the debut of its cash-management account.*

1975 *Securities and Exchange Commission stops stockbrokers from charging fixed commissions.*

1974 *Justice Department files antitrust suit against AT&T.*

1970 *Federal Reserve lifts ceiling on interest rates on bank deposits over $100,000 (maturities less than six months).*

1969 *Federal Communications Commission lets MCI connect its long-distance network with local phone systems.*

1968 *Supreme Court allows non-AT&T equipment to be hooked up with the AT&T system (Carterfone decision).*

Exhibit 21.2
The Steps in Deregulation
The move toward deregulation started slowly in the late 1960s and gained momentum in the 1970s and 1980s. Advocates of deregulation claimed it would revitalize the affected industries and give the overall economy a boost. However, the results have been mixed, ranging from a telecommunications industry that's thriving to a savings and loan industry in ruins and an economy struggling to recover from another recession.

back to the Wright brothers. Things got so bad that one airline chairman urged the government to reconsider some form of regulated minimum fares to prevent desperate competitors from dragging the entire industry down.[14]

Understanding the Impact of Government Regulation
It would be hard to overstate the complexity of business regulation. Not only do thousands of federal rules and regulations restrict what companies can do, but the individual states often have overlapping and conflicting rules on the same subjects. Many companies resent the struggle of dealing with 50 "little Washingtons," referring to the rules enacted by every state. On top of that, doing business outside the United States means complying with regulations in other countries and even in regional entities such as the European Union. Regulations keep lots of employees busy in large companies—just keeping track of new regulations is a big job by itself—and they can be an extreme burden to small companies that lack the resources of their larger cousins.

This inconvenience doesn't mean that businesses universally dislike regulations, however. The antitrust laws, for instance, make it possible for many small companies to compete with larger ones. Some regulations designed to help consumers help businesses as well by encouraging an honest business environment. When the Chinese government imposed rules for accuracy and scientific supportability on medical advertising in 1992, legitimate marketers were pleased. Kenny Ho of the Dentsu, Young & Rubicam ad agency explained that the new rules will help stop dishonest advertising and allow his clients to compete more effectively.[15]

Regulators often conduct a **cost-benefit analysis**—comparing the cost of regulations with their potential benefit—when considering whether to propose new regulations (or drop existing ones). If the costs outweigh the benefits, then it probably doesn't make sense to establish or keep the regulations. Unfortunately, this type of analysis isn't as simple as it sounds; many costs and benefits related to social and environmental issues are impossible to quantify.[16]

cost-benefit analysis *Comparison of the costs and benefits of a particular action for the purpose of assessing its desirability*

Government as Tax Collector

From road repair to regulation, running a government is an expensive affair. Like the regulatory structure, tax laws have developed in a hodgepodge fashion over many years. If you've lamented the job of filing a tax return, think about large corporations. Many of their tax-return filings are several feet thick or more. Entire segments of the accounting and legal professions have sprung up to help companies cope with both the burden of taxes themselves and the increasingly complex job of actually paying them.

To fund their operations, cities, counties, states, and the national governments levy a variety of revenue-raising taxes: personal and corporate income taxes, property taxes, sales taxes, and value-added taxes. Governments also levy regulatory taxes such as excise taxes and customs duties (see Exhibit 21.3).

Exhibit 21.3
Sources of Tax Revenues
These two charts show the sources of tax revenues collected by the federal government (left) and by state and local governments (right). The federal government receives 57 percent of all revenues collected.

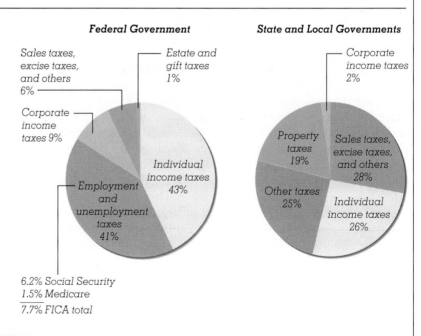

Federal Government

Sales taxes, excise taxes, and others 6%

Estate and gift taxes 1%

Corporate income taxes 9%

Individual income taxes 43%

Employment and unemployment taxes 41%

6.2% Social Security
1.5% Medicare
7.7% FICA total

State and Local Governments

Corporate income taxes 2%

Property taxes 19%

Sales taxes, excise taxes, and others 28%

Other taxes 25%

Individual income taxes 26%

PART SEVEN | THE ENVIRONMENT OF BUSINESS

SHOULD GOVERNMENTS BE IN THE GAMBLING BUSINESS?

Next time you plunk some cash down on the counter to buy lottery tickets, ask yourself this: Why is it that most states outlaw most forms of commercial gambling when the majority of them are in the gambling business themselves? After all, that's what a lottery is. It's gambling, and it's big business for states from coast to coast. In 1993 alone, state lotteries pulled in $25 billion from jackpot dreamers.

On the one hand, that's $25 billion that didn't come out of taxpayers' pockets. Between 1985 and 1994, California's lottery pumped $6 billion into that state's educational system. States feeling the pinch between increased demand for services and reduced federal assistance look at lotteries as their own little jackpot. It's a lot easier to set up a state lottery than it is to raise state taxes to get the same amount of money.

On the other hand, gambling-addiction experts worry that states are profiting off human weaknesses. If gambling is so negative that most states outlaw most forms of it, why are state governments in the business themselves? One response to this question is that most people who play the lottery spend only a few dollars a week. The serious gambling addicts who can't control their spending make up a fairly small fraction of all players, states say. Richard Meyers, a computer specialist with Colorado's state lottery says, "We're not part of the hard-core gambling game. We try to align ourselves as a healthy product that's fun." However, the fact that some states use part of their gambling revenues to fund gambling-addiction programs is strong evidence that a problem exists.

In that unpredictable way it has, technology is about to compound this ethical dilemma many times over. With various pieces of the information superhighway falling into place, all kinds of new gambling options are opening up. Computerized Keno and video poker games, 800 and 900 call-in services, multimedia racetrack systems, and interactive gambling channels are taking this issue far beyond the comparatively simple lotteries. The new technologies give states more ways to raise revenue, to be sure, but worries about gambling addiction are growing with every technological advancement. Arnold Wexler, executive director of New Jersey's Council on Compulsive Gambling, says, "With interactive TV, you'll be able to stay in your house, sell your car and destroy yourself gambling without getting out of bed."

Pay attention to developments on the information superhighway for more on this issue. "Telegambling" is likely to be one of the hottest ethics issues in the coming years.

Personal Income Taxes

Personal income taxes have been the federal government's largest single source of revenue and a major source of state revenues as well.[17] On the federal level, the personal income tax is a graduated tax, which means that as you make more money, the tax you pay is a higher percentage of your income. Although the personal income tax is assessed on individual income, it does affect businesses. In partnerships and sole proprietorships, profits are considered the personal income of the owners and are therefore taxable at personal-income-tax rates.

Corporate Income Taxes

Corporations pay federal taxes on their profits, much as individuals pay taxes on their income. Many state and local governments also impose corporate income taxes. Because most of this country's large corporations also operate abroad, they must pay income taxes in foreign countries as well. (It should be noted that the federal government allows U.S. corporations a *tax credit,* or reduction from their tax obligations, for taxes paid to a foreign government.) The tax system and corporate-income-tax rate of a state or country typically influence a business's decision to operate there.

Property Taxes

Businesses pay property taxes on the land and the structures they own. In some communities, taxes are assessed on the basis of the value of buildings. A 20-story office tower, for instance, is worth far more on the tax rolls than a fast-food restaurant. In addition, commercial property is usually taxed at a higher rate than houses and farms, so businesses often pay a large portion of a community's property tax.

Sales Taxes

In most states and in some cities, merchandise sold at the retail level is subject to a sales tax. Although businesses are exempt from paying a sales tax on merchandise they buy for resale, the sales tax does affect business because it increases the prices customers have to pay. Also, as with personal income taxes, businesses are required to collect the sales tax from their customers and forward it to the government, which involves administrative expense.

Value-Added Taxes

value-added taxes (VATs) *Taxes paid at each step in the distribution chain on the difference between the cost of inputs and the price obtained for outputs at that step*

From time to time, policymakers in this country have considered **value-added taxes (VATs),** which are assessed all along the chain of distribution on the difference in value between the cost of the goods and services used in production (inputs) and the price that the end products (outputs) are sold for. VATs have not yet been adopted in this country, but they do exist in other countries. In the European Union they are the main type of tax on sales of goods and services. U.S. companies operating overseas may therefore be subject to VATs.

Excise Taxes

excise taxes *Taxes intended to help control potentially harmful practices or to help pay for government services used only by certain people or businesses*

A number of items are subject to **excise taxes,** which are regulatory taxes intended to help control potentially harmful practices ("sin taxes") or to help pay for services used only by certain people. The United States imposes excise taxes on products such as gasoline, tobacco, and liquor. Federal excise taxes are also levied on certain services of national scope, such as air travel and telephone calls.

Income from federal excise taxes must be used for a purpose related to the tax. The gasoline tax, for example, goes toward funding road-building projects. Thus, the burden of paying for the roads is in large part borne by those who use them most.

Excise taxes are imposed on the manufacturer, the retailer, or both. Ultimately, however, the consumer pays these taxes, because they are often factored into the prices of products. Because products with these hidden taxes are frequently subject to a general sales tax as well, those who consume the products may be hit twice.

Customs Duties

customs duties *Fees imposed on goods brought into the country; also called import taxes*

Products brought into this country are often subject to import taxes, or **customs duties.** These regulatory taxes are selective; they vary with the product and its country of origin. Designed to protect U.S. businesses against foreign competition, customs duties have the effect of raising the price of imports to a level comparable to the price of similar U.S.-made merchandise. Customs duties have been used with increasing frequency as a weapon in foreign policy: The products of friendly nations are often taxed at lower rates than those of indifferent or openly hostile countries.

Tax Credits and Tax Deductions

In addition to raising revenue, some taxes are designed to encourage or discourage various activities. A **tax credit** is a direct reduction in the amount of income tax that a person or a business owes, granted by a government body in return for engaging or not engaging in selected activities. For instance, the federal government grants tax credits to businesses that sell or use alcohol-based fuels. Other tax-credit activities include hiring people from selected population groups, increasing investments in research, or using recycled motor oil.[18]

Tax credits are direct reductions in the amount of tax you owe, whereas **tax deductions** are reductions in the amount of income on which you must pay taxes. Both have the effect of reducing your taxes, but for businesses, tax deductions are generally designed to help them arrive at *taxable income* figures that reflect their actual net income. For instance, a company with annual sales revenue of $1,000,000 and operating costs of $900,000 will pay less tax than a company with the same revenue but costs of only $750,000, because the latter has more net income.

Business's Influence on Government

Given the impact that government has on business, it is not surprising that business has responded by trying to influence government in various ways. One of the most common approaches is to create **lobbies,** groups of people who try to persuade legislators to vote according to the groups' interests. Industry associations such as the American Bankers Association, the Chamber of Commerce of the United States, and the American Medical Association are typically involved in lobbying. Although the members of such associations are competitors, they often have common objectives when it comes to government action.

Businesses also try to influence government by donating money to politicians. Campaign laws strictly limit businesses' ability to donate money directly to candidates; however, they may funnel contributions through **political action committees (PACs).** Through a PAC, a company can solicit contributions from its employees and then allocate the money to various campaigns. In addition to operating company PACs, many companies also work through trade-association PACs. Opponents of PACs complain that these committees corrupt the democratic process, favor incumbents,

tax credit Direct reduction in the amount of income tax owed by a person or business; granted by a government body for engaging or not engaging in selected activities

The Tobacco Institute, an industry association representing tobacco companies, wants retailers to take a clear stand on selling to minors.

Is This Sign In Your Window?

IT'S THE LAW

WE DO NOT SELL TOBACCO PRODUCTS TO PERSONS UNDER 18

We Think It Should Be.

We can help you if it isn't. Join the thousands of retailers across the country already displaying this sign to demonstrate that they observe state laws prohibiting the sale of tobacco products to minors.

Since the "It's the Law" program was launched in 1990, more than 1.9 million stickers, decals and other materials have been distributed to businesses nationwide through this voluntary effort underwritten by the tobacco industry.

No one wants tobacco products in the hands of young people. This sign on your front window, on product displays and at point-of-purchase reminds customers of your commitment to verify age and obey the law.

Sign up today. Return the coupon, and we will send you the free material you need to get this program in your store.

TOBACCO INSTITUTE
P.O. Box 41169, Washington, DC 20018

PLEASE SEND ME MORE INFORMATION ON THE "IT'S THE LAW" PROGRAM.	The Tobacco Institute P.O. Box 41169 Washington, DC 20018
NAME	
ADDRESS	
CITY	
STATE	ZIP
W5	

tax deductions Direct reductions in the amount of income on which a person or business pays taxes

lobbies Groups who try to persuade legislators to vote according to the groups' interests

political action committees (PACs) Groups formed under federal election laws to raise money for candidates

and drive up the cost of campaigning for everyone. Some employees dislike PACs because they feel pressured to contribute yet have little say in how their money will be allocated.[19]

THE U.S. LEGAL SYSTEM

One of the most pervasive ways that government affects business is through the legal system. The law protects both individuals and businesses against those who threaten society. It also spells out accepted ways of performing many essential business functions—along with the penalties for failure to comply. In other words, like the average person, companies must obey the law or face the consequences. Although this fact limits a company's freedom, it also provides protection from wrongdoers.

Sources of Law

The U.S. Constitution, including the Bill of Rights, is the foundation for our laws. Because the Constitution is a general document, laws offering specific answers to specific problems are constantly embellishing its basic principles. However, law is not static; it develops in response to changing conditions and social standards. Individual laws originate in various ways: through legislative action (statutory law), through administrative rulings (administrative law), and through customs and judicial precedents (common law). To one degree or another, all three forms of law affect businesses.

Statutory Law

statutory law Statute, or law, created by a legislature

Without Congress, there would be no federal **statutory law,** which is law written by legislative bodies. The Constitution, in fact, specifically grants the Senate and the House of Representatives the right "to regulate commerce." States also have legislative bodies that write statutory laws applicable within their boundaries. However, state laws can vary considerably, presenting problems for companies that do business in several states. The problem would be much worse, however, without the **Uniform Commercial Code (UCC),** which provides

Uniform Commercial Code (UCC) Set of standardized laws that govern business transactions and that have been adopted by most states

a nationwide standard in many areas of commercial law, such as the writing of sales contracts and warranties. The UCC has been adopted in its entirety in 49 states and the District of Columbia, and about half of it has been adopted in Louisiana.

Administrative Law

Once laws have been passed by a state legislature or Congress, an administrative agency or commission typically takes responsibility for enforcing them. That agency may be called on to clarify a regulation's intent, often by consulting representatives of the affected industry. The administrative agency may then write more specific regulations, which are considered **administrative law.** For example, the Federal Trade Commission issues regulations and enforces statutory laws concerning such deceptive trade practices as unfair debt collection and false advertising. Governmental agencies cannot, however,

administrative law Rules, regulations, and interpretations of statutory law set forth by administrative agencies and commissions

create regulations out of thin air—they must be linked to specific statutes to be legal.

Administrative agencies also have the power to investigate corporations suspected of breaking administrative laws. A corporation found to be misbehaving may agree to a **consent order,** which allows the company to promise to stop doing something without actually admitting to any illegal behavior. As an alternative, the administrative agency may start legal proceedings against the company in a hearing presided over by an administrative law judge. During the hearing, witnesses are called and evidence is presented to determine the facts of the situation. The judge then issues a decision, which may impose corrective actions on the company. If either party objects to the decision, it may file an appeal to the appropriate federal court.[20]

consent order Settlement in which an individual or organization promises to discontinue some illegal activity without admitting guilt

Common Law

Common law, the sort of law that comes out of courtrooms and judges' decisions, began in England many centuries ago and was transported to America by the colonists. It is applied in all states except Louisiana (which follows a French model). Common law is sometimes called the "unwritten law" to distinguish it from legislative acts and administrative-agency regulations, which are written documents. Instead, common law is established through custom and the precedents set in courtroom proceedings.

common law Law based on the precedents established by judges' decisions

Despite its "unwritten" nature, common law has great continuity, which derives from the doctrine of **stare decisis** (Latin for "to stand by decisions"). What the stare decisis doctrine means is that judges' decisions establish a precedent for deciding future cases of a similar nature. Because common law is based on what has gone before, the legal framework develops gradually.

stare decisis Concept of using previous judicial decisions as the basis for deciding similar court cases

In the United States, common law is applied and interpreted in the system of courts (see Exhibit 21.4). Common law thus develops through the decisions in trial courts, special courts, and appellate courts. The Supreme Court (or the highest court of a state when state laws are involved) sets precedents for entire legal systems; lower courts must then abide by those precedents as they pertain to similar cases.

In legal proceedings, common law, administrative law, and statutory law may all be applicable. If they conflict, statutory law generally prevails. However, the three forms of law overlap to such an extent that the differences between them are often indistinguishable. For instance, if you bought what you thought was a goose-down coat and then found out that it was actually filled with reprocessed polyester, you could sue the coat manufacturer for misrepresentation. Although the basis for this suit is an old concept in common law, it has also been incorporated in state and federal legislation against fraudulent and misleading advertising, which is further interpreted and enforced by the Federal Trade Commission.

Business-Related Law

Regardless of its source, law can also be classified as either public or private. **Private law** concerns itself with relationships between individuals, between an individual and a business, or between two busi-

private law Law that concerns itself with relationships between individuals, between an individual and a business, or between two businesses

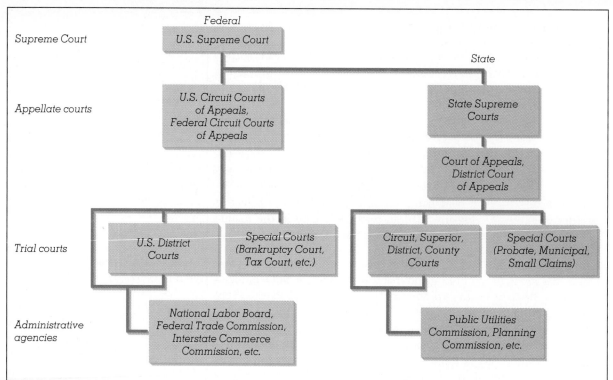

Federal

| Supreme Court | U.S. Supreme Court |

State

| Appellate courts | U.S. Circuit Courts of Appeals, Federal Circuit Courts of Appeals | State Supreme Courts |

| Court of Appeals, District Court of Appeals |

| Trial courts | U.S. District Courts | Special Courts (Bankruptcy Court, Tax Court, etc.) | Circuit, Superior, District, County Courts | Special Courts (Probate, Municipal, Small Claims) |

| Administrative agencies | National Labor Board, Federal Trade Commission, Interstate Commerce Commission, etc. | Public Utilities Commission, Planning Commission, etc. |

Exhibit 21.4
The U.S. Court System
A legal proceeding may begin in a trial court or an administrative agency (examples of each are given here). An unfavorable decision may be appealed to a higher court at the federal or state level. (The court of appeals is the highest court in states that have no state supreme court; some other states have no intermediate appellate court.) The U.S. Supreme

public law *Law that concerns itself with relationships between the government and individual citizens*

tort *Noncriminal act (other than breach of contract) that results in injury to a person or to property*

intentional tort *Willful act that results in injury*

nesses. **Public law** concerns itself with the relationships between the government and individual citizens.[21] Insider trading on Wall Street, forgery of signatures on checks and other documents, unauthorized access to computer databases, negligence in regard to worker safety, and other white-collar crimes are covered by public law. One company's infringing on another company's trademark or copyright is covered by private law.

Torts

A **tort** is a noncriminal act (other than breach of contract) that results in injury to a person or to property.[22] The victim of a tort is legally entitled to some form of compensation, called a *compensatory damage award*. In some cases, the victim may also receive a *punitive damage award* to punish the wrongdoer if the misdeed was glaringly bad. Tort law covers both intentional torts and negligence, which includes the important business topic of product liability.

Intentional Torts. An **intentional tort** is a willful act that results in injury. For example, accidentally knocking a ball through someone's window while you're playing softball is a tort, but purposely cutting down someone's tree because it obscures your view is an intentional tort. Note that *intent* in this case does not mean the intent to cause harm; it is the intent to commit a specific physical act. The most common intentional torts include assault, battery, and intentional communication of false statements that harm another's reputation (if the communication is in writing or on television, it is called *libel*; if it is spoken, it is *slander*).[23]

Negligence and Product Liability. In contrast to intentional torts, torts of **negligence** involve a failure to use a reasonable amount of care necessary to protect others from unreasonable risk of injury.[24] You don't have to read too many issues of your daily newspaper to find mention of a business getting entangled in a negligence lawsuit. Cases of alleged negligence often involve **product liability,** which is a product's capacity to cause damages or injury for which the producer or seller is held responsible. Product-liability lawsuits cost business owners as much as $80 billion every year.[25] In addition to the sheer costs of these lawsuits, such cases are perplexing because of the confusing and often conflicting laws surrounding product liability.

A company may be held liable for injury caused by a defective product even if the company used all reasonable care in the manufacture, distribution, or sale of its product. Such **strict product liability** makes it possible to assign liability without assigning fault. It must only be established that (1) the company is in the business of selling the product, (2) the product reached the customer or user without substantial change in its condition, (3) the product was defective, (4) the defective condition rendered the product unreasonably dangerous, and (5) the defective product caused the injury.[26]

Although few people would argue that individual victims of harmful products are entitled to some sort of compensation, many people question whether such strict interpretation of product-liability laws is good for society. Because of the increasing frequency and size of compensatory and punitive damage awards, many companies are having trouble obtaining product-liability insurance at a reasonable price. As a consequence, they are withdrawing from high-risk businesses such as drug manufacturing. If each product innovation brings on a flood of lawsuits, society could quickly lose the benefits of advancing technology. To forestall that result, some states have instituted reforms designed to control excessive damage awards.[27]

Companies face potential product liability lawsuits for even the simplest products, as McDonald's discovered when it was sued by a woman burned by the fast-food giant's coffee.

Contracts

Broadly defined, a **contract** is an exchange of promises enforceable by law. Many business and personal transactions—including marriage, estate planning (wills), and credit purchases—involve contracts. Contracts may be either express or implied. An **express contract** is derived from the words (either oral or written) of the parties; an **implied contract** is derived from the actions or conduct of the parties.[28]

Elements of a Contract. The law of contracts deals largely with identifying the exchanges that can be classified as contracts. The following factors must usually be present for a contract to be valid and enforceable:

- *An offer must be made.* One party must propose that an agreement be entered into. The offer may be oral or written, but it must be firm, definite, and specific enough to make it clear that someone intends to be legally bound by the offer. Finally, the offer must be communicated to the intended party or parties.
- *An offer must be accepted.* For an offer to be accepted, there must be clear intent (spoken, written, or by action) to enter into the contract. An implied contract arises when a person requests or ac-

contract Exchange of promises enforceable by law

express contract Contract derived from words, either oral or written

implied contract Contract derived from actions or conduct

consideration *Bargained-for exchange necessary to make a contract legally binding*

warranty *Statement specifying what the producer of a product will do to compensate the buyer if the product is defective or if it malfunctions*

Exhibit 21.5
Elements of a Contract
This simple document contains all the essential elements of a valid contract.

The band entitled "XYZ" agrees to provide entertainment at the Club de Hohenzollern on April 30, 1995 between 8:30 P.M. and midnight.

The band will be paid $500.00 for its performance.

Signed on the date of
February 19, 1995

Violetta Harvey
Violetta Harvey,
Manager,
Club de Hohenzollern
and

Ralph Perkins
Ralph Perkins,
Manager, XYZ

cepts something and the other party has indicated that payment is expected. If, for example, your car breaks down on the road and you call a mobile mechanic and ask him or her to repair it, you are obligated to pay the reasonable value for the services even if you didn't agree to specific charges beforehand. However, when a specific offer is made, the acceptance must satisfy the terms of the offer—that is, if someone offers you a car for $18,000, and you say you would take it for $15,000, you have not accepted the offer. Your response is a *counteroffer,* which may or may not be accepted by the salesperson.

- *Both parties must give consideration.* A contract is legally binding only when the parties have bargained with one another and exchanged something of value, which is called the **consideration.** The relative value of each party's consideration does not generally matter to the courts. In other words, if you make a deal with someone and later decide you didn't get enough in the deal, that result is not the court's concern. You entered into the deal with the original consideration in mind, and that fact is legally sufficient as far as the courts are concerned.[29]

- *Both parties must give genuine assent.* To have a legally enforceable contract, both parties must agree to it voluntarily. The contract must be free of fraud, duress, undue influence, and mutual mistake.[30] If only one party makes a mistake, it ordinarily does not affect the contract. On the other hand, if both parties make a mistake, the agreement would be void. For example, if both the buyer and seller of a business believed it was profitable, when in reality it was operating at a loss, their agreement would be void.

- *Both parties must be competent.* The law gives to certain classes of people only a limited capacity to enter into contracts. Minors, people who are senile or insane, and in some cases, those who are intoxicated cannot usually be bound by a contract for anything but the bare necessities: food, clothing, shelter, and medical care.

- *The contract must not involve an illegal act.* Courts will not enforce a promise that involves an illegal act. For example, a drug dealer cannot get help from the courts to enforce a contract to deliver illegal drugs at a prearranged price.

- *The contract must be in proper form.* Most contracts can be made orally, by an act, or by a casually written document; however, certain contracts are required by law to be in writing. For example, the transfer of goods worth $500 or more must be accompanied by a written document. The written form is also required for all real estate contracts. A contract need not be long; all these elements of a contract may be contained in a simple document (see Exhibit 21.5). In fact, a personal check is one type of simple contract.

The Uniform Commercial Code also specifies that everyday sales transactions are a special kind of contract (although this provision applies only to tangible goods, not services), even though they may not meet all the exact requirements of regular contracts. Related to the sales contract is the notion of a **warranty,** which is a statement specifying what the producer of a product will do to compensate the

PART SEVEN | THE ENVIRONMENT OF BUSINESS

buyer if the product is defective or if it malfunctions. Warranties come in several flavors, and those covering sales between companies differ from those covering sales to consumers. One important distinction is between *express warranties,* which are specific, written statements, and *implied warranties,* which are unwritten but involve certain protections under the law. Also, warranties are either *full* or *limited.* The former obligates the seller to repair or replace the product, without charge, in the event of any defect or malfunction, whereas the latter impose restrictions on the defects or malfunctions that will be covered. Warranty laws also address a number of other details, including giving consumers instructions on how to exercise their rights under the warranty.[31]

Contract Performance. Contracts normally expire when the agreed-to conditions have been met, called *performance* in legal terms. However, not all contracts run their expected course. Both parties involved can agree to back out of the contract, for instance. In other cases, however, one party fails to live up to the terms of the contract, a situation called **breach of contract.** The other party has several options at that point:

- *Discharge.* When one party violates the terms of the agreement, generally the other party is under no obligation to continue with his or her end of the contract. In other words, the second party is discharged from the contract.
- *Damages.* A party has the right to sue in court for damages that were foreseeable at the time the contract was entered into and that result from the other party's failure to fulfill the contract. The amount of damages awarded usually reflects the amount of profit lost and often includes court costs as well.
- *Specific performance.* A party can be compelled to live up to the terms of the contract if money damages would not be adequate.

In the past, most businesspeople negotiated informally with each other when there were contract problems. In recent years, however, companies have increasingly resorted to litigation to solve problems. Not surprisingly, this tendency has increased the costs of doing business. In response, some companies are now experimenting with alternatives to the courtroom, including independent mediators who sit down with the two parties and try to hammer out a satisfactory solution to contract problems.

Agency

These days it seems that nearly every celebrity has an agent. Baseball players' agents sign their clients to do cereal commercials and handle their contract negotiations; authors' agents sell manuscripts to the publishers that offer the largest advances; actors' agents try to find choice movie and television roles for their clients. These relationships illustrate a common legal association known as **agency,** which exists when one party, known as the *principal,* authorizes another party, known as the *agent,* to act on his or her behalf and when the principal has the right to control the conduct of the agent in whatever activity is delegated.[32]

breach of contract *Failure to live up to the terms of a contract, with no legal excuse*

agency *Business relationship that exists when one party (the principal) authorizes another party (the agent) to act on her or his behalf, while controlling the agent's conduct*

power of attorney *Written authorization for one party to legally act for another*

All contractual obligations come into play in agency relationships. The principal usually creates this relationship by explicit authorization. In some cases—where a transfer of property is involved, for example—the authorization must be written in the form of a document called **power of attorney,** which states that one person may legally act for another (to the extent authorized).

Usually, an agency relationship is terminated when the objective of the relationship is met or at the end of a period specified in the contract between agent and principal. It may also be ended by a change of circumstances, by the agent's breach of duty or loyalty, or by the death of either party.

Property Transactions

property *Rights held regarding any tangible or intangible object*

real property *Land and everything permanently attached to it*

personal property *All property that is not real property*

Anyone interested in business must know the basics of property law. Most people think of property as some object they own (a book, a car, a house). However, **property** is actually the relationship between the person having rights with regard to any tangible or intangible object and all other persons. The law recognizes two primary types of property: real and personal. **Real property** is land and everything permanently attached to it, such as trees, fences, or mineral deposits. **Personal property** is all property that is not real property; it may be tangible (cars, jewelry, or anything having a physical existence) or intangible (bank accounts, stocks, insurance policies, customer lists). A piece of marble in the earth is real property until it is cut and sold as a block, when it becomes personal property. Some intangible personal property is called **intellectual property,** such as trademarks, trade secrets, patents, and copyrights.[33] Property rights are subject to various limitations and restrictions. For example, the government monitors the use of real property for the welfare of the public, to the point of explicitly prohibiting some property uses and abuses.[34]

intellectual property *Intangible personal property such as ideas, songs, trademarks, trade secrets, patents, or copyrights*

deed *Legal document by which an owner transfers the title to real property to a new owner*

lease *Legal agreement that temporarily transfers the right to use an asset from the owner to another individual or business*

title *Legal ownership of property*

Two types of documents are important in obtaining real property for factory, office, or store space. A **deed** is a legal document by which an owner transfers the title to real property to a new owner. A **lease** is used for a temporary transfer of interest in real property. The party that owns the property is commonly called the landlord; the party that occupies or gains the right to occupy the property is the tenant. The tenant pays the landlord, usually in periodic installments, for the use of the property. Generally, a lease may be granted for any length of time that the two parties agree on.

A permanent transfer of tangible or intangible personal property—such as merchandise or a check—is technically a transfer of **title,** or ownership of the property. Most problems with the transfer of personal property relate to the question of when the sale occurred or who should be responsible for damaged or lost goods. These questions may sound easy to answer, but in a legal sense, their solution is sometimes difficult.

Negotiable Instruments

negotiable instrument *Transferable document that represents a promise to pay a specified amount*

Whenever you write a personal check, you are creating a **negotiable instrument,** a transferable document that represents a promise to pay a specified amount. (*Negotiable* in this sense means that it can be sold or used as payment of a debt; an *instrument* is simply a written

Several forms of legal protection are available for your creations. Which one you should use depends on what you have created.

Copyrights

Copyrights protect the creators of literary, dramatic, musical, artistic, and other intellectual works. Any printed, filmed, or recorded material can be copyrighted. The copyright gives its owner the exclusive right to reproduce (copy), sell, or adapt the work he or she has created. Copyright law covers reproduction by photocopying, videotape, and magnetic storage.

The Copyright Office, Library of Congress, will issue a copyright to the creator or to whomever the creator has granted the right to reproduce the work. (A book, for example, may be copyrighted by the author or the publisher.) Copyrights issued after 1977 are valid for the lifetime of the creator plus 50 years. Copyrights issued through 1977 are good for 75 years.

Technically, copyright protection exists from the moment you create the material. When you distribute a work, place on the copies a notice that includes the term *copyright* or an abbreviation, the name of the author or creator, and the year of publication or production—for example, "Copyright 1986 Jane Doe." Works can be registered with the Copyright Office for $10. For more information, write to the Copyright Office, Library of Congress, Washington, DC 20559. Ask for Copyright Kit 118, which is available free.

Trademarks

A trademark is any word, name, symbol, or device used to distinguish the product of one manufacturer from

THREE WAYS TO PROTECT YOUR IDEAS: COPYRIGHTS, TRADEMARKS, AND PATENTS

those made by others. A service mark is the same thing for services. McDonald's golden arches are one of the most visible of modern trademarks. Brand names can also be registered as trademarks. Examples are Exxon, Polaroid, and Chevrolet.

If properly registered and renewed every 20 years, a trademark generally belongs to its owner forever. Among the exceptions are popular brand names that have become generic terms, meaning that they describe a whole class of products. A brand-name trademark can become a generic term if the trademark has been allowed to expire, if it has been incorrectly used by its owner (as in the case of Borden's ReaLemon lemon juice, which the Federal Trade Commission ruled was being used by Borden to maintain a monopoly in bottled lemon juice), or if the public comes to equate the name with the class of products (for example, zipper and xerox).

It is a good idea to have a patent attorney do a "clearance search" before you begin using a mark in order to be sure it isn't already in use. There's a filing fee of $175 for registration with the Patent and Trademark Office. Registration protects your mark for 20 years, and you may renew every 20 years. For more information and registration forms, request a free copy of the booklet

General Information Concerning Trademarks from the Commissioner of Patents and Trademarks, Patent and Trademark Office, Washington, DC 20231.

Patents

A patent protects the invention or discovery of a new and useful process, an article of manufacture, a machine, a chemical substance, or an improvement on any of these. Issued by the U.S. Patent Office, a patent grants the owner the right to exclude others from making, using, or selling the invention for 17 years. After that time, the patent becomes available for common use. On the one hand, patent law guarantees the originator the right to use the discovery exclusively for a relatively long period of time, thus encouraging people to devise new machines, gadgets, and processes. On the other hand, it also ensures that rights to the new item will be released eventually. Other enterprises may be able to make use of it more creatively than did its originator.

For more information, get a copy of *Introduction to Patents* from the Small Business Administration, P.O. Box 15434, Fort Worth, TX 76119. *Questions and Answers About Patents* is available free from the Commissioner of Patents and Trademarks, Patent and Trademark Office, Washington, DC 20231.

document that expresses a legal agreement.) In addition to checks, negotiable instruments include certificates of deposit, promissory notes, and the commercial paper you read about in Chapter 19. To be negotiable, an instrument must meet several criteria:[35]

- It must be in writing and signed by the person who created it.
- It must have an unconditional promise to pay a specified sum of money.
- It must be payable either on demand or at a specified date in the future.
- It must be payable either to some specified person or organization or to the person holding it (the bearer).

You can see how a personal check meets these criteria—when you write one, you are agreeing to pay the amount of the check to the person or organization to whom you're writing it.

Bankruptcy

Even though the U.S. legal system establishes the rules of fair play and offers protection from the unscrupulous, it can't prevent most businesses from taking on too much debt. The legal system does, however, provide help for businesses that find themselves in deep financial trouble. **Bankruptcy** is the legal means of relief for debtors (either individuals or businesses) who are no longer able to meet their financial obligations.[36]

Voluntary bankruptcy is initiated by the debtor; **involuntary bankruptcy** is initiated by creditors. The law provides for several types of bankruptcy, which are commonly referred to by chapter number of the Bankruptcy Reform Act. In a Chapter 7 bankruptcy,

bankruptcy *Legal procedure by which a person or a business that is unable to meet financial obligations is relieved of debt*

voluntary bankruptcy *Bankruptcy proceedings initiated by the debtor*

involuntary bankruptcy *Bankruptcy proceedings initiated by a firm's creditors*

When companies go bankrupt, their assets are often put up for sale at public auctions; here bidders look at vehicles belonging to the defunct Eastern Airlines.

A receiver is appointed.
The court appoints a temporary custodian of the firm's assets (a receiver).

A referee is appointed.
The court names its representative (a referee).

A trustee is elected.
The creditors elect someone to sell assets and distribute the proceeds as specified by law.

The bankruptcy firm is legally discharged from its obligations.
With its debts discharged, the firm is free to start anew without the weight of past failures.

Exhibit 21.6
Steps in Chapter 11 Bankruptcy Proceedings
Chapter 11 bankruptcy may buy a debtor time to reorganize finances and continue operating. However, using this device to evade financial obligations is extremely risky from a legal standpoint, and declaring bankruptcy may severely damage the reputation and credit rating of a firm or an individual.

the debtor's assets will be sold, and the proceeds will be divided equitably among the creditors. Under Chapter 11 (which is usually aimed at businesses but does not exclude individuals other than stockbrokers), a business is allowed to get back on its feet and continue functioning while it arranges to pay its debts.[37] For the steps involved in a Chapter 11 bankruptcy, see Exhibit 21.6.

By entering Chapter 11, a company gains time to cut costs and streamline operations. Many companies emerge from Chapter 11 as leaner, healthier organizations. Creditors often benefit, too. If the company can get back on its financial feet, creditors may be able to retrieve more of the money they are owed.

1 List three roles of government that affect business.

Government relates to business as a supporter, partner, and customer; as a watchdog and regulator; and as a tax collector.

2 Name five general areas in which government regulates business.

Various government regulations are designed to promote competition, protect consumers, protect employees, protect investors, and protect the natural environment.

3 List five revenue-raising taxes and two regulatory taxes.

Revenue-raising taxes include personal income taxes, corporate income taxes, property taxes, sales taxes, and value-added taxes. Regulatory taxes include excise taxes and customs duties.

4 Explain how business influences government.

Businesses band together to form lobbies that approach politicians in order to influence legislation. They also donate money to political candidates through PACs in order to gain access to the legislative process and to help elect those whose attitudes toward their industry or business are favorable.

5 Describe the three sources of law.

Statutory law is developed through the legislative process. Administrative law arises when administrative agencies issue interpretations of statutory law and specific regulations derived from statutory law. Common law is developed in courts on the basis of statutory law, administrative law, and courtroom precedents.

6 Explain the meaning of product liability.

Product liability, which is part of tort law, is a product's capacity to cause damages or injury for which the producer or seller is held responsible.

7 State the seven elements of a valid contract.

A valid contract consists of a clear offer, a clear acceptance of the offer, consideration from both parties, genuine assent from both parties, competency, legality, and proper form.

8 Distinguish between real, personal, and intellectual property.

Real property is land and anything that is permanently attached to it, such as trees, buildings, and mineral deposits. Personal property is anything that is not real property. Intellectual property is a type of intangible personal property, such as copyrights, trademarks, ideas, songs, or any other product of mental creativity.

David Glass and his colleagues at Wal-Mart have probably heard it all by now, from how Wal-Mart is a visual blight on the landscape to how it destroys small-town business communities. Like many other cases where business interests, community interests, and business law intersect, the reality of Wal-Mart's situation is far more complicated. A look at all sides of the issue will shed some light.

To begin with, the company couldn't have shot out of nowhere to become the nation's largest retailer if more than a few people didn't like shopping there. The company sells more than $60 billion worth of goods every year, and sales continue to climb, so quite a few people must like shopping at Wal-Mart, in fact. Many shoppers in small towns such as Omak, Washington—240 miles from Seattle and 150 miles from Spokane—appreciate the presence of Wal-Mart in their midst. Before Wal-Mart, shoppers had to choose between limited selections at local shops or long drives to larger retailers in larger cities.

Moreover, Wal-Mart's success results largely from simply doing a better job of providing people with the products they want at the lowest possible prices. In fact, late founder Sam Walton started back in 1950 with one of the local stores that his company is sometimes now accused of running out of business. By locating stores in out-of-the-way places that other chains didn't want to bother with, and by using fast, efficient distribution strategies to deliver products to stores, Wal-Mart built a huge nationwide business. It's not as if Wal-Mart rides into town with guns blazing and drives innocent business owners out into the cold. Consumers are making the choice.

Small-business owners aren't automatically crushed when Wal-Mart arrives, either. In the small town of Aberdeen, Washington, shoppers used to pile in the car for a "Costco run" to the big discount warehouses in Olympia, the state capital, about an hour's drive east. After hitting Costco and the discount malls around Olympia, these consumers would frequently make other shopping stops as well. When Wal-Mart moved into Aberdeen, however, many of these long-distance consumers stayed in town and did their major shopping at the new Wal-Mart. With no reason to run to Olympia, they also did all the rest of their shopping in Aberdeen, too, which helped the local retailers.

Across the state in Omak, business leaders noticed another positive result from Wal-Mart's presence—their small town started to show up in computer databases that track business growth across the country. The mayor began to get calls from other companies that might be interested in moving to Omak, all of which would help the local economy.

On the other hand, no one could accuse Wal-Mart of being a wimp when it comes to competition. While company leaders would no doubt like to get along with everybody, they aren't bashful about competing.

In fact, the company has a cheer on the subject:

Stack it deep, sell it cheap,
Stack it high, and watch it fly!
Hear those downtown merchants cry!

Such attitudes, coupled with the company's record of strong growth, might be behind such comments as this one, from a lawyer leading the fight in Chestertown, Maryland: "We are not anti–Wal-Mart. We are anti-pig."

On the issue of esthetics, Wal-Mart's giant, blocky stores stand out in small towns like proverbial sore thumbs. This is particularly true in quaint, historical towns that rely on tourist trade for much of their commerce.

The Wal-Mart situation, in all its complexity, raises some of the same legal issues that U.S. business law has been grappling with for more than a century. Whose rights should take precedence—Wal-Mart's or the local businesses'? Less affluent consumers who like the bargains or more affluent consumers who don't like the traffic or the way the stores look? Should companies that can't compete with Wal-Mart receive special protection under the law (which is effectively what the various legal strategems designed to keep Wal-Marts out of town accomplish)?

Because retail-store siting is by definition a local issue, Wal-Mart is dealing with new stores on a town-by-town basis. In Waterford, Massachusetts, opponents raised such a fuss that the company chose to back off and look for open arms elsewhere in the state. In Chestertown, however, Wal-Mart found itself blocked out through a new law, passed at the urging of the opposition. County commissioners voted to limit the size of any new stores to 50,000 square feet. That size is about half as big as Wal-Mart wants, so it is looking for other sites in a neighboring county. The struggle will continue to play out in towns across the country.

Your Mission: You are a member of Glass's executive team trying to balance community concerns with the company's strategic plans. Consider the following situations and choose the best answer in each case:

1. The city council in a town where one of your stores is located plans to adopt an excise tax for sales at retail stores 100,000 square feet and larger. Your store is the only one in town that big. The council's reasoning is that these stores are responsible for more traffic, which requires more road maintenance, so the store and its customers should foot the extra expense. What is your response?

   a. Lobby the council not to pass the tax on the grounds that everyone in the town uses the roads, so it's unfair to make Wal-Mart customers pay extra.

   b. Do nothing; you don't want to upset the city council.

   c. Propose an alternative, such as helping the city build a new park, that would come out of the company's pockets, not those of its customers.

2. One of Wal-Mart's merchandise buyers has come across a product that she thinks could be a hot seller in company stores: a safety helmet for bungee jumping. Because the product will be used in a dangerous activity, the manager in charge of store operations decided to run the idea past the executive team first. How would you respond?

   a. Product liability shouldn't be a concern because Wal-Mart will only be selling the product; someone else manufactures it.

   b. Even as the seller, Wal-Mart could be held liable in the event someone receives a head injury, so it's best to avoid the product.

   c. The buyer is a specialist in picking products that consumers will want; let her decide.

3. When the owner of a drugstore near a Wal-Mart starts a campaign to provide special protection for small stores that can't match Wal-Mart's low prices, you're asked to appear on a radio talk show to give the company's response. Which of these answers sounds best to you?

   a. Say that Wal-Mart is doing nothing illegal, so giving smaller stores some legal protection wouldn't be fair.

   b. Say that consumers should have the opportunity to buy the products they want at the lowest possible prices, and the best way to achieve that is open and free competition.

   c. Say that the law doesn't guarantee results or success; it simply says all companies should have the chance to compete.

4. In an interview with a local newspaper from a town that Wal-Mart would like to move into, a reporter asks you for the number 1 reason the town should let Wal-Mart in. Which of the following responses would you use?

   a. Consumers will benefit from getting the products they need at lower prices.

   b. Other businesses will benefit because Wal-Mart's presence will encourage them to be more competitive.

   c. It would be unfair and perhaps even illegal to try to stop Wal-Mart.[38]

KEY TERMS

administrative law (648)
agency (653)
bankruptcy (656)
breach of contract (653)
common law (649)
consent order (649)
consideration (652)
contract (651)
cost-benefit analysis (644)
customs duties (646)
deed (654)
deregulation (642)
excise taxes (646)
express contract (651)
implied contract (651)

intellectual property (654)
intentional tort (650)
interlocking directorates (638)
involuntary bankruptcy (656)
lease (654)
lobbies (647)
negligence (651)
negotiable instrument (654)
personal property (654)
political action committees (PACs) (647)
power of attorney (654)
private law (649)
product liability (651)
property (654)
public law (650)

real property (654)
stare decisis (649)
statutory law (648)
strict product liability (651)
tax credit (647)
tax deductions (647)
title (654)
tort (650)
trusts (638)
tying contracts (638)
Uniform Commercial Code (UCC) (648)
value-added taxes (VATs) (646)
voluntary bankruptcy (656)
warranty (652)

1. What are the major areas in which governments regulate business?

2. Do businesses dislike all regulations? Explain your answer.

3. What is precedent, and how does it affect common law?

4. What is the difference between private law and public law?

5. What is the difference between negligence and intentional torts?

6. What are the implications to businesses of the concept of strict product liability?

7. Why is agency important to business?

8. What is the advantage of declaring Chapter 11 bankruptcy? Why is Chapter 11 bankruptcy controversial?

A CASE FOR CRITICAL THINKING

PUBLIC SERVANT OR MAILING MONOPOLY?

You've probably seen the mailboxes designated "For Metered Mail Only." The meters those boxes are referring to—pieces of equipment that stamp the correct amount of postage on mail and packages—are big business these days. They save the government over $500 million annually in reduced handling costs, and the Postal Service itself uses some 40,000 meters at its service windows. Thousands and thousands of meters are used by private businesses. All in all, nearly $20 billion dollars of postage every year is sold through those postage meters.

Most of the meters sold every year (87 percent, to be exact) are made by one company, Pitney Bowes. The manufacturer's dominance began in 1920, when the U.S. Post Office took a liking to the new device presented by Chicago inventor Arthur H. Pitney and his partner, Walter H. Bowes. In subsequent years, as Pitney Bowes seized and controlled the market for its new meters, the company's near-monopoly did not escape the notice of government officials. The Justice Department filed an antitrust suit against Pitney Bowes in 1959. With no admission of guilt on the company's part, the suit was settled out of court, and Pitney Bowes agreed to share its patents, royalty-free, with "qualified manufacturers." However, a decade

later this restriction and others were lifted, and the Justice Department has since determined that Pitney Bowes is operating within the law.

The problem is that postage meters are so efficient that both government and businesses have come to depend on them. The meters store a large amount of postage bought at one time from the Postal Service (which "sets" the meter according to how much postage is purchased). That postage is then doled out slowly as each piece of mail is stamped with the appropriate amount. The fact that the stamping can be done in the customer's own mail room saves time and labor at both ends. Additionally, the Postal Service contends that the ultimate benefactor of this cost saving is the mailing public.

Pitney Bowes's competitors aren't quite as happy with the chummy relations between the manufacturer and the U.S. government. In recent years, German, French, and Swiss manufacturers have managed to grab 13 percent of Pitney Bowes's market share (which used to be 99 percent). Yet because of Pitney Bowes's close relations with the Postal Service, competitors complain that they are at an unfair disadvantage. Because the Postal Service tightly regulates meter design in order to protect its postage revenue, competitors must "design around" Pitney Bowes's patents, risk patent-infringement suits, or wait

until Pitney Bowes sells the rights to use its designs (which, of course, Pitney Bowes won't do until it has already upgraded its own meters, drawing from its heavy investment in research and development).

To keep its edge, Pitney Bowes employs a full-time director of postal regulations in Washington, D.C., just a few steps away from postal headquarters. The director's job is clearly defined: Get all information possible so that Pitney Bowes encounters no surprises in terms of new government regulations. When the Postal Service came out with new requirements regarding large-volume mailings, Pitney Bowes was ready with a high-tech mailing system designed to help mailers meet those regulations *before* the government specifications had been released to the public. Whether or not the fortuitous timing was an "absolute fluke," as claimed by a Pitney Bowes engineer, Pitney Bowes's competitors were left at the starting gate, waiting for the official announcement.

Meanwhile, the Postal Service has logged some millions of dollars in annual savings from the popular new technology. One postal official admitted that the Postal Service has no stomach to fight Pitney Bowes. "Ours is an extensive and wide-ranging cooperative relationship. We don't want to jeopardize it." Another official explained, "The real loser would be the mailers."

Pitney Bowes is not resting, even though it still has a commanding lead in the meter market. The company spent six years and a half billion dollars developing its latest automated mailing equipment. The company hopes to maintain a wide technological edge over its competitors, even if they do manage to keep chipping away at Pitney Bowes's close relationship with the U.S. Postal Service.

1. How has Pitney Bowes controlled the U.S. market for postage meters?
2. How might the government change its policies to allow freer competition among postage-meter manufacturers?
3. Do you think the Postal Service is correct in its contention that consumers would suffer from any attempt to loosen Pitney Bowes's hold over the postage-meter market?

BUILDING YOUR COMMUNICATION SKILLS

Select a business lobby by consulting the *Encyclopedia of Associations,* and examine the influence of that group on the process of government. Prepare a brief report summarizing the information you have obtained about that lobby. As directed by your instructor, share your report with members of your class, and discuss the positive and negative impact of these groups.

KEEPING CURRENT USING *THE WALL STREET JOURNAL*

Choose an article from *The Wall Street Journal* that relates to one of the following topics:

- Deregulation
- Product liability
- Contract disputes
- Business taxation
- Business lobbying and political action committees (PACs)

1. What is the significance of the event reported in the article? Does it point to a new development in this area, or does it relate to a long-standing problem or issue?
2. Who is affected by this development? Is it expected to touch other companies? An entire industry? The general public?
3. Is the local, state, or federal government involved in this situation? If so, what role does government play—watchdog/regulator, tax collector/enforcer, or a combination of these roles?

SIX AMERICANS TAKE ON THE LAWSUIT CRISIS

Synopsis

This video presents two learning opportunities. First, the actual subject of the video is that unreasonable lawsuits (unreasonable both in their number and in the magnitude of damages they seek to recover) threaten our business opportunities and our lifestyles. You'll see six people from different walks of life doing their part to fight today's barrage of lawsuits. Second, the identity of the group sponsoring this video influences the effectiveness of its message. As you watch these six people, they come across as concerned citizens fighting a valiant battle to protect freedoms and privileges that are important to all of us. However, who would go to all the trouble and expense of bringing these stories to our attention? At the very end of the video, you see that these stories are brought to you by the insurance industry. Why? Because insurance companies are the ones who often have to pay the "outrageous" jury awards.

Exercises

ANALYSIS

1. Who decides whether liability lawsuits are truly at a stage of crisis?
2. With so many consumer-protection laws already in place, why do we even need product-liability lawsuits? Shouldn't the laws be enough?
3. What would happen if there were no consumer-protection laws and consumers had to use legal action to force manufacturers and other businesses to deliver safe, effective products? Such a scheme was proposed in Congress in 1995.
4. What does it mean to say that we all pay for the costs of these big product-liability lawsuits?
5. Which industry or professional group(s) would be most likely to produce a video opposing the position maintained in this video? Why?

APPLICATION

Outline a video program that would take the other side of this issue, making the case that consumers deserve the right to sue and that if companies and other organizations would behave responsibly, there wouldn't be so many lawsuits.

DECISION

Pretend you're the producer of this video program. You need to decide where and how to credit the insurance-industry group that sponsored the program (or whether to credit the group at all). Would you put simple logos at the end of the program without explanation (as is done in the actual video), or would you make the industry's role more prominent (perhaps by announcing its sponsorship at the beginning)?

COMMUNICATION

Write a three-paragraph press release that summarizes the message contained in this video program.

INTEGRATION

Refer to Chapter 5 and determine the effect that product-liability lawsuits are likely to have on small or new businesses.

ETHICS

Since the insurance industry could benefit financially if liability lawsuits declined, is it ethical for that industry to sponsor this video without making its support more noticeable?

DEBATE

Find an example of a recent product-liability case that awarded millions of dollars. Have one group of students take the position that the plaintiff deserved the money because of the damage he or she suffered. Have the other group argue that the award was unreasonable.

TEAMWORK

The video mentions that everyone should have the right to sue, but it doesn't explain how to protect that right while avoiding the crisis stage that the liability issue is said to have reached. With three other students, devise a plan that protects consumers and the general public and that is less vulnerable to abuse than the current system.

RESEARCH

How bad is the lawsuit crisis in this country? Do the research needed to uncover trends in liability lawsuits over the last few decades.

ROLE PLAYING

Research a product-liability lawsuit that was settled in the past five years. Have one student play the plaintiff; another, the plaintiff's attorney; another, the defendant; another, the defendant's attorney; and a fifth, the judge. Retry the case (simplify it as needed to fit the available time).

Chapter

22

Risk Management and Insurance

Chairman J. W. Marriott, Jr., didn't like what he was hearing. Operations managers were complaining loudly about runaway insurance costs, and the international lodging and hospitality corporation had to kick another $10 million into a funding reserve for its insurance program. Insurance costs had gotten out of hand, and he wanted to know *why:* Why was the corporation charging each operating unit self-insurance premiums that increased in each of five consecutive years, with annual increases of up to 38 percent for some units over a three-year period? Why were workers' compensation claims rising faster than expected during the company's expansion to more than 209,000 employees and to more than 150,000 hotel rooms worldwide? Why was the cost of controlling risks becoming prohibitive?

Insurance costs had become a problem years earlier in ways that Marriott could not control, when catastrophic fires swept through several competing hotels. In the largest single tragedy, 84 people died and another 700 were injured in a fire at the MGM Grand Hotel in Las Vegas. Newsmaking fires at three other hotels killed 44 and injured 240. Although Marriott's hotels passed unscathed through the series of disasters, the company's liability coverage did not: Commercial insurance (once available to all lodging companies) virtually dried up. In one year alone, Marriott's commercial insurance was cut in half—and that coverage had been pieced together like a patchwork quilt.

However, Marriott's insurance problems weren't caused solely by the fallout from others' misfortunes; the numbers of workers' compensation claims were rising, and medical costs were escalating more rapidly than the general level of inflation. First, the sudden increase of workers' compensation claims from injured employees was coming from companies that Marriott had acquired. Second, escalating medical costs were a problem. Workers' compensation claims were being processed by third-party administrators, which was a common business practice throughout the United States but which was costing more and more as the number of claims increased. Moreover, and probably most troublesome, the costs of

Taking the "Hospital" out of Hospitality

Marriott's focus on prevention is the key to minimizing risks in all areas of its business, from accidents to employee health care.

health care and lost productivity during employee recuperation were increasing.

Marriott faced a serious and perplexing problem: The number of insurance claims being filed against the corporation was increasing, health-care costs were skyrocketing, and commercial insurance coverage was becoming more difficult—and more expensive—to purchase. How could the company reduce the number of workers' compensation claims? How could it lower health-care costs? How could Marriott obtain commercial insurance coverage more easily and more cheaply?[1]

PROTECTION AGAINST RISK

risk *Threat of loss*

Like any other business, Marriott must protect itself from **risk,** the threat of loss. Reasonable or not, risks are inescapable in business because the possibilities for loss are as real as the prospects for profit. Even though managers do everything they can to ensure that their businesses succeed, they cannot guard against every conceivable form of risk. Not only can unforeseen circumstances result in a loss of income and profits, they can cost companies tidy sums in **damages,** the amount a court awards a plaintiff in a successful lawsuit.

damages *Amount a court awards a plaintiff in a successful lawsuit*

Pure Risk Versus Speculative Risk

pure risk *Risk that involves the chance of loss only*

Businesspeople face various kinds of risk. **Pure risk** is the threat of a loss without the possibility of gain. In other words, a disaster such as an earthquake or a fire is costly for the business it strikes, but the fact that no disaster occurs contributes nothing to a firm's profit. It is primarily pure risk that insurance deals with. Such disasters aren't entirely of nonhuman origin; a terrorist bomb that rocked New York's World Trade Center in 1993 caused more than a half-billion dollars in property damage and loss of business.[2]

speculative risk *Risk that involves the chance of both loss and profit*

Speculative risk, on the other hand, is the type of risk that offers the prospect of making a profit; it prompts people to go into business in the first place. Every business accepts the possibility of losing money in order to make money. The idea is to identify the risks and take steps to minimize them as much as possible.

Risk Management

risk management *Process of evaluating and minimizing the risks faced by a company*

loss exposures *Areas of risk in which a potential for loss exists*

The process of reducing the threat of loss from uncontrollable events is called **risk management.** Those areas of risk in which a potential for loss exists are called **loss exposures,** and they fall under four headings: (1) loss of property (due to destruction or theft of tangible or intangible assets); (2) loss of income (either through decreased revenues or through increased expenses resulting from an accidental event); (3) legal liability to others, including employees; and (4) loss of the services of key personnel (through accidental injury or death).[3]

The function of establishing programs and policies to prevent losses is typically performed by the risk manager, whose job has become increasingly complex and critical. Risk managers must be able to implement a program that is cost-effective and that provides maximum risk protection. Thus they must (1) assess the risk, (2) choose the risk-management techniques that provide an appropriate mix of insurance and loss-prevention methods, and (3) implement and monitor those techniques.[4]

Before exploring the details, however, its important to note that although risk management is traditionally tied to specific programs, and insurance coverage in general, risk management is really everybody's job. Businesses face all kinds of risk, and practically every employee can take steps to reduce his or her company's exposure to risk. These steps can range from the small and immediately practical, such as maintaining safer work areas, to such longer-term issues as understanding customer needs more thoroughly in order to increase the chance that investments in new products will pay off.

Avoiding accidents and injuries through such measures as protective clothing is an important step in managing corporate risk.

Risk Assessment

Consider just one of the many loss exposures that a manufacturer of stuffed toys must face: the product-liability exposure. First, the manufacturer must identify the ways a consumer (most likely a child) can be injured by a stuffed toy. Among numerous possibilities, the child might choke on button eyes, get sick from eating the stuffing, or have an allergic reaction to any material in the toy. Second, the company must identify any possible flaws in the production or marketing of the toys that might lead to one of these injuries; for example, a child may have an allergic reaction to the toy if its materials are not carefully tested for allergenic substances, if impurities enter the toy during manufacture, or if the toy is not properly packaged (allowing foreign substances to reach it). Third, the manufacturer must analyze the possibilities in order to compute possible product-liability losses. Because it is often impossible to identify all the ways a product might cause injury or property damage, and because it is often impossible to calculate an exact value for these losses, the risk manager must often be satisfied with rough estimates.

Risk-Management Techniques

Once all risks have been assessed, the risk manager must consider the techniques available to deal with the problems. The two categories of techniques are risk control and risk financing.

Risk Control. Risk managers and others in a business use **risk-control techniques** to minimize an organization's losses:

risk-control techniques *Methods of minimizing losses*

- *Uncertainty reduction.* Much of the speculative risk a company faces stems from lack of information. You can never be sure that a new product will succeed, for instance, and you sometimes have to pump millions of dollars into developing it with no assurance that it will sell. Reducing such uncertainties is a key way to reduce speculative risks. Marketing research and advanced information systems that give decision makers the background data they need are two big steps companies can take to reduce such risks.

- *Risk avoidance.* A risk manager might try to completely eliminate the chance of a particular type of loss. With rare exception, such risk avoidance is extremely difficult. The stuffed-toy manufacturer could avoid being sued for a child's allergic reaction by not making stuffed toys, but, of course, the company would also be out of business.

- *Loss prevention.* A risk manager may try to reduce (but not totally eliminate) the chance of a given loss. The toy manufacturer might reduce the risk of children's having allergic reactions to the stuffed toys by testing the materials before production, by controlling impurities during manufacture, or by carefully packaging each toy to guard against foreign substances. Steps taken for other kinds of loss exposures typically include installing overhead sprinklers to prevent extensive damage from fire, putting safety locks on doors to prevent theft, and checking equipment to prevent accidents.

- *Loss reduction.* A risk manager may try to reduce the severity of the losses that do occur. By adhering to all government regulations, the toy company can avoid the addition of punitive damages to any damages the company may have to pay an injured consumer. Also, by maintaining good relations with consumers whose children do have allergic reactions, and by paying their medical expenses, the toy company can reduce the size of the claims they may have to pay.

- *Risk-control transfer.* A risk manager may try to eliminate risk by transferring to some other person or group either (1) the actual property or activity responsible for the risk or (2) the responsibility for the risk. A firm can sell a building to eliminate the risks associated with ownership, or a contractor already committed to a job can eliminate the risk of cost increases by hiring a subcontractor. Such transfers are closely related to risk avoidance. A risk manager may also try to eliminate risk by transferring responsibility, that is, by transferring the risk itself. A tenant may be able to persuade a landlord to take any responsibility for damage to the landlord's property. A manufacturer may make a retailer take responsibility for any product damage occurring after products leave the manufacturing facility. The idea of transfer also applies in risk-financing techniques, discussed next.

Risk Financing. Risk managers use **risk-financing techniques** to pay (at the least possible cost) to restore losses that occur despite the organization's risk-control efforts:

- *Risk retention.* A risk manager may choose to pay losses with funds that originate within the organization. Many companies draw on current revenues or set aside a contingency fund to cover unexpected losses. Some businesses form their own liability-insurance companies. Actually, the risk-retention programs of various businesses fall along a continuum, and most companies use a combination of techniques. Deciding to **self-insure** with a liability reserve fund means putting aside a certain sum each year to cover

risk-financing techniques *Paying to restore losses*

self-insure *Accumulating funds each year to pay for any losses, rather than buying insurance from another company*

PART SEVEN | THE ENVIRONMENT OF BUSINESS

possible liability losses. However, self-insuring differs greatly from "going bare" (having no reserve funds). In a small company, setting aside enough money to cover catastrophes is virtually impossible. If disaster strikes, companies that cannot afford insurance may have to borrow funds to cover the losses, or they could be forced out of business. Some companies have found a solution in risk-retention groups, collections of companies that band together to self-insure.

- *Risk-financing transfer.* A risk manager may choose to limit risk by paying losses with funds that originate outside the organization. By purchasing **insurance,** companies transfer the risk of loss to an insurance firm, which agrees to pay for certain types of losses. For this service, the insurance firm collects a fee known as a **premium.**

insurance Written contract that transfers to an insurer the financial responsibility for any losses

premium Fee that the insured pays the insurer for coverage against losses

Proper risk management nearly always requires a combination of at least one risk-control technique and at least one risk-financing technique.

Implementing and Monitoring Risk-Management Techniques

Risk managers implement those techniques that contribute to the total value of the organization, which is best measured through the organization's net cash flows. Thus the stuffed-toy manufacturer must decide whether testing materials, controlling impurities during manufacture, or packaging toys individually would best fit the company's cash flow. Of course, the company may choose all three. Risk managers must also decide whether purchasing conventional insurance or establishing some form of self-insurance would have the least impact on the company while providing the best coverage. In the end, the best choice may be a combination of options.

Monitoring the risk-management program determines whether the original choice of techniques was correct and, if so, whether conditions have changed enough to warrant choosing new techniques. Effective monitoring has three aspects: (1) setting standards for defining acceptable performance, (2) comparing actual results with those standards, and (3) correcting any technique to comply more fully with the standards.

Insurable and Uninsurable Risks

Risk managers must distinguish between insurable and uninsurable risks (see Exhibit 22.1). Outside insurers are unwilling to promise they will pay for losses unless they can reasonably expect that they won't have to. Most (but not all) pure risks are insurable; in general, speculative risks are not insurable.

Uninsurable Risks

An **uninsurable risk** is one that no insurance company will agree to cover. It is possible to purchase disaster insurance against such calamities as floods (available from the federal government), hurricanes, tornadoes, and earthquakes. However, insurers are reluctant or unwilling to consider covering potential government actions and gen-

uninsurable risk Risk that few, if any, insurance companies will assume because of the difficulty of calculating the probability of loss

Insurable	Uninsurable
Property risks: Uncertainty surrounding the occurrence of loss from perils that cause 1. Direct loss of property 2. Indirect loss of property Personal risks: Uncertainty surrounding the occurrence of loss due to 1. Premature death 2. Physical disability 3. Old age Legal liability risks: Uncertainty surrounding the occurrence of loss arising out of 1. Use of automobiles 2. Occupancy of buildings 3. Employment 4. Manufacture of products 5. Professional misconduct	Market risks: Factors that may result in loss of property or income, such as 1. Price changes, seasonal or cyclical 2. Consumer indifference 3. Style changes 4. Competition offered by a better product Political risks: Uncertainty surrounding the occurrence of 1. Overthrow of the government or war 2. Restrictions imposed on free trade 3. Unreasonable or punitive taxation 4. Restrictions on free exchange of currencies Production risks: Uncertainties surrounding the occurrence of 1. Failure of machinery to function economically 2. Failure to solve technical problems 3. Exhaustion of raw-material resources 4. Strikes, absenteeism, labor unrest Personal risks: Uncertainty surrounding the occurrence of 1. Unemployment 2. Poverty from factors such as divorce, lack of education or opportunity, loss of health from military service

Exhibit 22.1
Insurable and Uninsurable Risks
Insurance companies consider some pure risks insurable. They usually view speculative risks as uninsurable. (Some pure risks such as flood and strike are also considered uninsurable.)

insurable risk *Risk for which an acceptable probability of loss may be calculated and that an insurance company might therefore be willing to cover*

eral economic conditions. Such uncertainties as changes in the law and economic fluctuations are beyond the realm of insurance.

Sometimes uninsurable risks become insurable when enough data become available to permit accurate estimation of future losses. Insurers were once reluctant to cover passengers on airplanes, but decades of experience have made these risks predictable. Similarly, companies can now buy insurance against the prospect of a foreign country's seizing their overseas factories, mines, or offices.

Insurable Risks

An **insurable risk,** one that an insurance company will cover, generally meets the following requirements:

- *The peril covered must not result from deliberate actions of the insured.* Insurers do not pay for losses that are intentionally caused by the insured, at the insured's direction, or with the insured's collusion. For example, a fire-insurance policy excludes loss caused by the insured's own arson. However, the same policy does cover losses caused by an employee's arson.
- *Losses must be calculable, and the cost of insuring must be economically feasible.* To operate profitably, insurance companies must have data on the frequency and severity of losses caused by a given peril. If this information covers a long period of time and is based on a large number of cases, insurance companies can usually predict how many losses will occur in the future. For example, the death rate per 1,000 people in the United States has been calculated with

great precision, and insurance companies use this information to set policyholders' life-insurance premiums.

- *A large number of similar cases must be subject to the same peril.* The more cases there are in a given category, the more likely it is that future experience will reflect insurance-company predictions. Insurance companies are therefore more willing to issue insurance for risks that many businesses or individuals face. For example, fire is a common danger that threatens virtually all buildings, so insurance for loss by fire is usually easy to come by. Even though Marriott hotels had trouble getting affordable fire insurance, the opportunity to obtain coverage was always there. However, the possibility that Steffi Graf will fracture her serving arm and miss several lucrative tennis matches is an unusual risk because there is only one Steffi Graf. Most insurance companies would not consider issuing this sort of insurance.

- *The peril must be unlikely to affect all insured simultaneously.* Unless an insurance company spreads its coverage over large geographic areas or a broad population base, a single disaster might force it to pay out on all its policies at once.

- *The possible loss must be financially serious to the insured.* An insurance company could not afford the paperwork involved in handling numerous small **claims** (demands by the insured that the insurance company pay for a loss) of a few dollars each, nor would a business be likely to insure such a small loss. As a result, many policies have a clause specifying that the insurance company will pay only that part of a loss greater than an amount stated in the policy. This amount, the **deductible,** represents small losses that the insured has agreed to absorb. Your health insurer, for example, may require you to pay the first $100 of your physician's fees, and the company that insures your car may require you to pay the first $200 of any covered repairs.

claims *Demands for payments from an insurance company due to some loss by the insured*

deductible *Amount of loss that must be paid by the insured before the insurer will pay for the rest*

THE INSURANCE INDUSTRY

In its simplest form, the idea of insurance is probably as old as humankind. Since the days of the cave dweller, groups of people have banded together to help one another in times of trouble. They have stored food in years of plenty so that they would have something to draw on during years of famine. If their neighbor's house burned, they helped rebuild it, with the tacit understanding that the favor would be returned if they were ever in need. Over the years, the informal cooperation between neighbors gradually became institutionalized. Mutual-aid societies were formed, and dues were collected from the members for use in emergencies. Ultimately, modern insurance companies emerged, with professional management.

Basic Insurance Concepts

Private insurance companies are businesses. The product they sell is financial protection. To succeed, they must cover their costs, which

Actuaries try to predict their companies' level of exposure to such natural disasters as earthquakes.

actuaries *People employed by an insurance company to compute expected losses and to calculate the cost of premiums*

underwriters *Insurance-company employees who decide which risks to insure, for how much, and for what premiums*

law of large numbers *Principle that the larger the group on which probabilities are calculated, the more accurate the predictive value*

include payments to cover the losses of policyholders as well as sales and administrative expenses, dividends, and taxes.

To decide how much income they need to generate from premiums, insurance companies must predict the amount they will probably have to pay in claims over a given period. The amount of the premium for a specific type of risk is based mainly on the probability of loss. For example, because fire is a greater risk for wooden than for brick buildings, insurance premiums tend to be higher for wooden structures. The people who figure out how many deaths, illnesses, fires, accidents, natural disasters, and so on are likely to occur over the course of a year are called **actuaries;** they develop actuarial tables of probabilities for various occurrences that can be used to calculate premiums. **Underwriters** then decide which risks to insure and under what terms.

When calculating probabilities, actuaries rely on the **law of large numbers**—that is, the larger the pool of insured parties, the more accurate the predictions of the loss per unit. Insurance companies don't count on making a profit on any particular policy, nor do they count on paying for a single policyholder's losses out of the premium paid by that particular policyholder. Rather, each insurance company pays for a loss by drawing money out of the pool of premiums it has received from all its policyholders (see Exhibit 22.2). In this way, the insurance company redistributes the cost of losses from a single individual to a large number of policyholders.

Exhibit 22.2
How the Law of Large Numbers Works
An insurance company covers the cost of a policyholder's loss out of the premiums paid by a large pool of policyholders. Thus, if 100 policyholders pay $400 each to insure against fire damage, the insurance company can afford to compensate one policyholder who actually suffers fire damage with $40,000.

Insurance Providers

When most people think of insurance, they think of private insurance—the kind purchased from an insurance company. Actually, the largest single source of insurance in the United States is the government, which accounts for nearly half of the total insurance premiums collected for all types of coverage combined. More than a quarter of the federal government's revenue comes from social insurance receipts.[5]

Government Insurance Programs

Most government insurance programs are designed to protect people from loss of income, either because they have reached retirement age or because they have lost their jobs or become disabled. Unlike private insurance, which is voluntarily chosen by the insured, government-sponsored programs are compulsory. The largest of the public insurance programs is Social Security, which was created by the federal government during the Great Depression of the 1930s. Officially known as Old-Age, Survivors, Disability, and Health Insurance, this program covers 9 out of 10 workers.

The basic purpose of the Social Security program is to provide a minimum level of income for retirees, their survivors, and their dependents, as well as for the permanently disabled. The program also provides hospital and medical payments—known as Medicare—for people age 65 and over. Social Security benefits vary, depending on how long a worker has contributed to the system. The program is funded by a tax paid half and half by workers and their employers. In most cases, these taxes are automatically deducted from each paycheck. Self-employed people pay the full amount of tax as part of their regular tax filings. It's important to note that Social Security is not a needs-based program; every eligible person is entitled to the benefits of the system, regardless of his or her financial status.[6]

The Social Security Act of 1935 also provided for federal and state cooperation to insure workers against unemployment. The cost is borne by employers. A worker who becomes unemployed for reasons not related to performance is entitled to collect benefits. The amount of the benefit is usually tied to the employee's total earnings during the previous year, but both the amount and the length of time the benefit is available vary from state to state.

Private Insurance Companies

Thousands of private insurance companies are currently doing business in the United States; most are either stock or mutual companies.[7] A **stock company** is a profit-making corporation with shareholders who expect to receive dividends on their investment in the company. A **mutual company** is a nonprofit cooperative owned by

stock company *Profit-making insurance company owned by shareholders*

mutual company *Nonprofit insurance company owned by the policyholders*

THINKING ABOUT ETHICS

Every business knows that rates for all kinds of insurance continue to climb. The rising costs of coverage have spurred many companies to drop their coverage, move to other states, or get out of certain kinds of businesses. Some reasons for the rate increases are complex and esoteric: shifts in technology, changes in government regulations, vague economic forces.

One key reason is much more down-to-earth, however: it's simple fraud. From property/casualty to automobiles to health care, scams cost insurance companies millions of dollars every year. More precisely, the scams cost taxpayers and businesses million of dollars, since the insurance companies usually pass the costs on in the form of higher premiums.

Property/casualty insurers pay out $200 billion in claims every year, and industry experts say that 10 percent—$20 billion—is bogus. A typical scam involves either faked or exaggerated damage, in which the client, an insurance-company employee, and a third-party adjuster (a person who assesses damage for insurance companies) collaborate. They might hose down the inside of a warehouse to give the impression of extensive water damage, for instance,

IN THE WAR AGAINST INSURANCE FRAUD, THE CROOKS SEEM TO BE WINNING

and then file a claim on the value of all the goods stored in the warehouse, even if the goods aren't damaged. Some fraud teams are so organized that they even have a supply of damaged products and office furniture that they move from site to site. Insurers are hard-pressed to keep up with fraud, although some investigators are making progress by tracking and comparing details from many claim cases.

In the health-care business, insurance fraud is even more serious; estimates range from $50 to $80 billion a year in fake claims. The scams are creative, varied, and increasingly organized by large teams of con artists. One operation in Southern Califor-

nia involved a medical group that performed tests on patients who really didn't need them and then sent the bills to insurers. The 12 crooks earned $50 million before federal authorities shut them down.

The numbers seem staggering in the auto-insurance business, too. At one police precinct in New York, as many as 7 out of every 10 people who come in to report a stolen vehicle wind up getting arrested—for destroying their own cars and trying to collect on the insurance. Along the Merrimack River in Lawrence, Massachusetts, police sometimes wake up to find so many "stolen" cars pushed in the river that the last one in the previous night rests on top of all the others and sticks out above the water.

These insurance scams hurt everybody who buys insurance, whether it's your personal car insurance or coverage for a multinational corporation. Law-enforcement officials and insurance-company investigators are trying to catch the thieves, but every time they plug a hole in the system, con artists find a new way to steal. So far at least, the crooks are winning the war.

the policyholders; excess income may be returned to the policy-holders, either in the form of dividends or as a reduction in their insurance premiums. In terms of premium volume, a firm such as Marriott would probably go to stock companies for property and liability insurance and to mutual companies for medical and life insurance.

Insurance-Industry Problems

Historically, the insurance industry has gone through cycles of profit and loss that depend on financial markets, underwriting practices, and competitive pressures. When interest rates are high, insurance companies make extra money from investment income, and premiums go down. When interest rates fall, investment income diminishes, and companies must rely more heavily on premiums, which then go up. The length of these cycles is usually three years up and three years down, but in the last decade, a seven-year downturn was followed by only two years of upturn before profits began dipping again. Some analysts worry that if rates and premiums drop too sharply or for too long, insurance companies will become insolvent.[8]

In the most tragic cases, insurance companies collapse completely, leaving their customers uncovered. Other insurers experiencing losses or shrinking profits are cutting back on or pulling out of whole areas of insurance. Once insurers such as Aetna, Travelers, and Continental attempted to sell all things to all people: life policies to newlyweds, fire insurance to homeowners, and liability coverage to corporations. That approach has changed, however. Aetna, Travelers, and Cigna are now making major pushes in group health insurance. Chubb is focusing on large companies and wealthy individuals. Continental has sold its life- and health-insurance interests, to concentrate on selling property and casualty insurance.[9]

TYPES OF BUSINESS INSURANCE

If you were starting a business, what type of insurance would you need? To some extent, the answer to that question would depend on the type of business you were in. In general, however, you would probably want to cover your property against losses and protect assets such as cash and securities from loss due to natural or human causes. In the discussion of risk management, four types of loss exposure are listed: loss of property, loss of income, liability, and loss of services of key personnel. Businesses can purchase insurance to cover each of these four areas (see Exhibit 22.3).

Loss of Property

Property can be lost through a variety of causes, including accidental damage, natural disaster, and theft. Property can also be lost through employee dishonesty and nonperformance.

Loss Due to Destruction or Theft

When a cannery in California ships jars of pizza sauce by truck to New York, the goods face unavoidable risks in transit. One wrong

Exhibit 22.3
Business Risks and Protection
Here are some of the more widely purchased types of business insurance.

Risk	Protection
Loss of property	
Due to destruction or theft	Fire insurance
	Disaster insurance
	Marine insurance
	Automobile insurance
Due to dishonesty or nonperformance	Fidelity bonding
	Surety bonding
	Credit life insurance
	Crime insurance
Loss of income	Business-interruption insurance
	Extra-expense insurance
	Contingent business-interruption insurance
Liability	Comprehensive general liability insurance
	Automobile liability insurance
	Workers' compensation insurance
	Umbrella liability insurance
	Professional liability insurance
Loss of services of key personnel	Key-person insurance

property insurance *Insurance that provides coverage for physical damage to or destruction of property*

replacement-cost coverage *Insurance that entitles policyholder to buy new property to replace the old*

depreciated-value coverage *Insurance that assumes that lost or damaged property was worth less than new replacement property*

fidelity bond *Coverage that protects employers from dishonesty on the part of employees*

surety bond *Coverage that protects companies against losses incurred through nonperformance of a contract*

turn could cover a whole hillside with broken glass and sauce, which would represent a sizable loss to the manufacturer. The canning factory itself is vulnerable to fire, flood, and (especially in California) earthquake.

Property insurance covers the insured for physical damage to or destruction of property and also for its loss by theft. When purchasing property insurance, the buyer has two options: replacement-cost coverage or depreciated-value coverage (actual cash value insured). **Replacement-cost coverage** is more expensive but provides more protection because it entitles the policyholder to buy new property to replace the old. **Depreciated-value coverage** assumes that the property that was lost or damaged was worth less than new property because the owner had used it for some period of time.

Loss Due to Dishonesty or Nonperformance

Dishonest employees and criminals outside the company pose yet another threat to business property and assets. Various ways exist for dealing with this problem. One is a **fidelity bond,** which protects the insured business against dishonest acts committed by employees, such as embezzlement, forgery, and theft.

Another is a **surety bond,** a three-party contract in which one party agrees to be responsible to a second party for the obligations of a third party. In public-construction projects, the law requires surety bonds that guarantee the performance of every contract. The insurance company would pay damages for any uncompleted or incompetent work of its insured (a construction company, for example) that had been awarded a contract by a municipality. Similar bonds are required for municipal contracts for garbage collection and snow removal as well as for elected officials, who must be insured against untrustworthiness while in office. Surety bonds are also commonly used in the private sector. Railroads, for example, permit shippers to defer payment of freight charges with the filing of a bond; corporations reissue lost or destroyed securities if there is a satisfactory bond.[10]

INTERNATIONAL INSURANCE— DON'T LEAVE HOME WITHOUT IT

Thousands of small and mid-sized companies doing business overseas could find themselves in for a nasty surprise if disaster strikes. Many of these companies apparently assume that their domestic insurance policies cover their overseas activities, or they figure courts and juries in other countries aren't as prone to award huge damages as U.S. residents are. The companies are often wrong on the first assumption and increasingly wrong on the second. One insurance-industry analyst estimates that 80 to 90 percent of small U.S. exporters don't have enough insurance to cover their foreign operations adequately.

Many domestic policies do offer a level of overseas coverage, but the coverage is often spotty, in terms of both areas of the world and particular categories of damage that the policy will cover. Most don't cover losses due to overseas travel, for instance, and most won't pay off when liability suits are brought in foreign courts.

Although it is true that, in general, U.S. courts are likely to award much higher damages in product-liability lawsuits and other cases, some countries seem to be trying hard to catch up. A court settlement in England recently awarded a man the equivalent of nearly $15 million for the damages he received in a highway accident. Moreover, the European Union is moving in the direction of a policy of strict liability, so companies could be sued for liability even if there is no evidence of negligence.

The risks of doing business in some countries are greater than many businesspeople may suspect. From kidnapping of executives to embezzlement by overseas associates or employees, international business presents all kinds of ways to get into trouble. Even for a midsized manufacturer such as Cordis, which makes medical equipment, the $50,000 it pays every year in international insurance premiums makes sense. As company treasurer Williams James puts it: "The risks are so substantial that they are not something we are willing to fully assume ourselves." All international businesspeople might be wise to follow Cordis's advice.

Another form of insurance against loss due to nonperformance is **credit life insurance,** which guarantees repayment of the amount due on a loan or an installment contract if the borrower dies. Yet another is **crime insurance,** which covers loss from theft of any kind, whether it is burglary or robbery.

Loss of Income

A fire in a supermarket chain's warehouse would result in property loss, but that's only part of the story. Fires also disrupt the business, often costing the company more than repairs or replacement of damaged stock. Expenses continue—salaries, interest payments, rent—but no revenues are coming in. Disruption also results in new expenses: leasing temporary space, paying overtime to meet work schedules with a reduced capacity, or buying additional advertising to assure the public that the business still exists. A prolonged interruption of business could even cause bankruptcy.

For this reason, many companies carry property-insurance protection that goes beyond mere loss of property. Available coverage includes **business-interruption insurance,** which protects the insured against lost profits and continuing expenses when a fire or other disaster causes a company to shut down temporarily; **extra-expense insurance,** which pays the additional costs of maintaining operations in temporary quarters; and **contingent business-interruption**

credit life insurance Coverage that guarantees repayment of a loan or an installment contract if the borrower dies

crime insurance Insurance against loss from theft

business-interruption insurance Insurance that covers losses resulting from temporary business closings

extra-expense insurance Insurance that covers the added expense of operating the business in temporary facilities after an event such as a fire

contingent business-interruption insurance Insurance that protects a business from losses due to an interruption in the delivery of supplies

insurance, which protects against loss of profit due to fire or other disaster that interrupts the operations of an important supplier.

Liability

All licensed drivers are aware that they may be held liable for substantial damages if they cause an auto accident. Similarly, businesses are liable for any injury they cause to a person or to the property of others. **Liability insurance** covers the insured for losses arising from injury to a individual, death due to something the company does, and damage to the property of others.

Sources of Liability

What sorts of accidents or corporate practices might make a company liable for damages? The types of accidents that most commonly result in legal action are injuries received on the company's property, injuries caused by the company's products, injuries to the company's own employees, and injuries from professional malpractice. Injuries received on the company's property may affect employees or outsiders; for instance, an elevator accident may involve either, whereas injury resulting from the collapse of metal shelving in a warehouse is likely to affect employees only. Examples of injuries caused by a company's products are food poisoning and choking on a loose toy part. Malpractice includes bodily injury arising from treatment by doctors and dentists and loss of assets due to mishandling by lawyers and accountants.

Types of Liability Insurance

To accommodate these various forms of liability, the insurance industry has created various types of liability policies.

Comprehensive General Liability. For basic coverage, most companies carry **comprehensive general liability insurance,** which automatically provides protection against all forms of liability not specifically excluded under the terms of the policy. Most comprehensive general liability policies cover liability for operations on the business premises, product liability, completed operations, and operations of independent contractors.[11] **Product-liability coverage** protects insured companies from being threatened financially when someone claims that one of their products caused damage, injury, or death.

When purchasing liability insurance, the buyer has two options. *Occurrence policies* cover losses that occur during the policy period, no matter when the claim is made. *Claims-made policies* cover claims filed during the policy period for losses that occurred on or after some retroactive date, which may be the beginning of the policy period or some earlier date.[12]

liability insurance *Insurance that covers losses arising either from injury to an individual or from damage to other people's property*

comprehensive general liability insurance *Liability insurance that covers a wide variety of losses, except certain losses specifically mentioned in the policy*

product-liability coverage *Insurance that protects companies from claims for injuries or damages that result from use of a product the company manufactures or distributes*

Author Karen Berger was one of the leading authorities in the recent product liability debates over the safety of silicone breast implants.

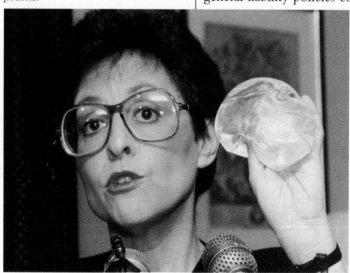

Automobile Liability. Many companies also carry insurance that specifically covers liability connected with any vehicles owned or operated by the company. In states having **no-fault insurance laws,** which limit lawsuits connected with auto accidents, this form of coverage is less important.

Workers' Compensation. Another form of liability coverage, **workers' compensation insurance,** pays the medical bills of employees who are hurt or become ill as a result of their work. It covers loss of income by occupationally injured or diseased workers plus rehabilitation expenses for these workers, and it provides death benefits to the survivors of any employee killed on the job. In most cases, it covers both full- and part-time employees. Workers' compensation insurance is required by law throughout the United States. It can be obtained through adequate self-insurance in some states, from state funds in some states, and from a private insurer in most states.

An employee who is temporarily disabled receives weekly benefits. If the injury is fatal, dependents receive weekly payments for a specified period. In nearly all states, the weekly benefit rate for an injured worker is normally two-thirds of the employee's weekly wage.

Over the years, the courts have interpreted workers' compensation laws broadly, holding employers liable for injuries related even indirectly to an employee's work. In one case, a worker in Rhode Island got angry, punched a coffee machine, and permanently damaged an arm. The worker was awarded $7,500 because the injury was "deemed to have met the requirements for a compensable situation—arising out of and in the course of employment."[13]

The premiums for workers' compensation vary from state to state, depending on the hazards in particular lines of work. Approximately 400 premium-rate classifications range from less than $1 per $100 of payroll for clerical workers to more than $60 per $100 of payroll for bridge workers.[14] You can see how insurance costs can be a huge financial factor for businesses in high-risk industries.

Workers' compensation premiums have more than doubled in recent years, for a variety of reasons: Higher benefits are being paid as wages and living costs rise; employees are not encouraged to control costs through cost sharing; the courts have expanded the definition of "work-related injuries," as we have seen; and lawsuits have opened up new areas of coverage. Work-related illness, especially lung ailments from chemicals and fibers encountered on the job, is an area in which workers' compensation claims seem certain to grow.

To find less expensive alternatives, many businesses are turning to self-insurance programs for workers' compensation coverage. Another way to avoid paying high premiums was taken by Marriott: The company cut down on the number of employee claims by reducing injuries and job-related illnesses. With that aim in mind, many companies are examining their safety programs more closely.

Umbrella Liability Insurance. **Umbrella policies** are designed to give extra protection above and beyond that provided under other liability policies. Because of the unknowns associated with this type of coverage, many insurance companies have recently raised their rates for umbrella coverage by up to 1,000 percent or have refused to issue this form of policy. As a result, some insurance buyers, such as

no-fault insurance laws *Laws limiting lawsuits connected with auto accidents*

workers' compensation insurance *Insurance that partially replaces lost income, medical costs, and rehabilitation expenses for employees who are injured on the job*

umbrella policies *Insurance that provides businesses with coverage beyond what is provided by a basic liability policy*

malpractice insurance *Insurance that covers losses arising from damages or injuries caused by the insured in the course of performing professional services for clients*

key-person insurance *Insurance that provides a business with funds in compensation for loss of a key employee*

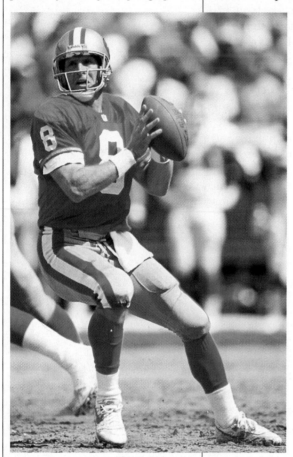

When employers place a high value on the continued job performance of key employees, such as the value the San Francisco 49ers place on quarterback Steve Young, they often consider key-person insurance to protect themselves from losses in the event that the employee can no longer perform.

du Pont, have set up their own insurance companies to obtain additional coverage.

Professional Liability Insurance. Doctors, lawyers, accountants, architects, stockbrokers, and other professionals usually carry some form of **malpractice insurance.** This type of coverage, which protects professionals from financial ruin if they are sued by dissatisfied clients, is another form of insurance that is becoming increasingly—and prohibitively—expensive. For accounting firms, the cost per partner for professional liability has tripled in only five years. Because of the escalating costs of malpractice insurance, thousands of obstetricians decided to stop delivering babies.[15] Estimates are that 1 in 10 CPA firms are going bare (carrying no coverage) because of the high premiums, and most of these are the smaller firms.[16] Going bare saves money in the short term, of course, but it leaves a company vulnerable to major losses in the event it is successfully sued for malpractice.

Loss of Services of Key Personnel

In some businesses, just one executive or employee has expertise or experience that is crucial to the company's operation. **Key-person insurance** can be purchased by a company to protect itself against the financial impact of the death or disablement or such a key employee (in the event of death, the beneficiary is the company, not the employee's survivors). The Charlotte Hornets professional basketball team pays $2 million a year to insure its players. With a player such as Larry Johnson under an $84 million contract, the team wants to be covered in the event Johnson can't play.[17]

TYPES OF EMPLOYEE INSURANCE

Besides insuring their property and assets, most businesses buy coverage for risks to employees. Disease and disability may cost employees huge sums of money unless they are insured. In addition, death carries the threat of financial hardship for an employee's family. Unemployment caused by a slowdown in business threatens *all workers* with loss of income.

Federal law requires employers to pay half the cost of employees' Social Security taxes and to help finance state unemployment-insurance funds. All 50 states mandate benefits for work-related injury, and a few states even require employers to provide disability-income insurance. Beyond these mandatory programs, however, most businesses also provide employees with substantial additional coverage.

Generally, companies are interested in three kinds of employee protection: health insurance, life insurance, and pension plans (discussed in Chapter 10). Protection is usually provided through group policies, which are sold to the company by the insurer. In some cases, the employer pays for the insurance in full; in other cases, employees pay part or all of the cost through a payroll deduction plan.

Health Insurance

There have traditionally been two main types of health insurance—one covering medical expenses, the other guaranteeing income in the event of a disabling illness or injury. That framework still exists, but today there tends to be more coverage for "ordinary" care as well as for serious medical problems. Dental coverage, for example, is more widespread: Some 85 percent of employers now offer some form of dental insurance.[18] As for group disability protection, benefits now last longer and payments are higher. Waiting periods are longer, however; many policies do not begin paying benefits until six months after the disability occurred.

Medical Coverage

Health insurance covers a variety of medical expenses. Although the types of coverage available have increased in the last few years, the vast majority of programs fall into five general areas.

Hospitalization insurance pays the major portion of the cost of a hospital stay. Coverage varies, but most policies pay all or part of the cost of a semiprivate room and the total cost of drugs and services while the insured is in a hospital.

Surgical and medical insurance pays the costs of surgery and of physicians' in-hospital care. Policies usually specify a maximum payment for each surgical procedure covered.

Major-medical insurance covers all the medical expenses that fall outside the coverage limits of hospitalization insurance and surgical and medical insurance. Frequently, the insured must pay at least $250 to $500 of her or his own medical costs per year. A typical major-medical policy may pay 80 percent of all medical expenses up to $1 million; after the employee's own co-payment in a given year has passed $1,500, most plans pick up 100 percent of the rest.[19] This arrangement of sharing costs is referred to as **coinsurance.** In recent years, a trend has developed toward comprehensive medical insurance, which is a variation of major medical.[20]

Dental and vision insurance covers a fixed percentage of an employee's expenses for eyeglasses, medically prescribed contact lenses, and various forms of dental work. The best plans, however, have a "stop-loss" cutoff of about $1,000, after which the insurance company pays the whole tab.[21] These programs are becoming increasingly popular.

Mental-health insurance pays for psychiatric care and psychological counseling. After satisfying the deductible required by the policy, an employee with a mental or nervous disorder is usually eligible for mental-health benefits ranging from 50 to 80 percent of the cost of treatment. However, some companies do not offer mental-health insurance.[22] Substance abuse (drug and alcohol) treatment pro-

hospitalization insurance Health insurance that pays for most of the costs of a hospital stay

surgical and medical insurance Insurance that pays for the costs of surgery and physicians' fees while a person is hospitalized or recovering from hospitalization

major-medical insurance Insurance that covers many medical expenses not covered by other health-insurance plans

coinsurance Share of medical costs the patient picks up to supplement the remaining costs paid by the insurer

dental and vision insurance Insurance that covers a portion of the costs of dental and eye care

mental-health insurance Insurance that covers the costs of psychiatric care, psychological counseling, and substance abuse treatment programs

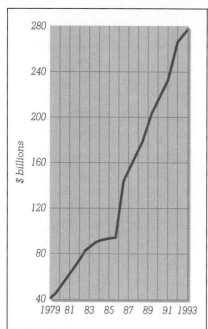

Exhibit 22.4
Employer Spending on Group Health Insurance
Employee health-insurance plans are an increasingly expensive part of the compensation package as health-insurance premiums skyrocket along with health-care costs.

cost shifting *Hospitals' and doctors' boosting their charges to private paying patients to make up for the shortfall in government reimbursements for their Medicare and Medicaid patients*

grams are usually handled on the same terms as mental-health benefits. Mental-health insurance is one of the fastest-rising insurance costs that companies have to shoulder today.[23]

The Costs of Medical Care. The majority of employees in the United States are covered by some form of employer-provided health insurance.[24] Employers typically pay about 80 percent of the premiums; however, as costs rise, employers are shifting more of the cost burden to employees by requiring them to pay a larger portion of their own premiums, larger deductibles, and higher co-payments. Still, it costs employers an average of several thousand dollars per year per employee, and the costs continue to rise.[25] Exhibit 22.4 illustrates the rapid growth in total employer spending for health-insurance protection during the last several years. Premiums have climbed faster for small businesses than for large ones. As a result, many small companies have been forced to drop health insurance altogether.

The health-care crisis has employers and employees alike clamoring for reform, and the problem is getting more and more attention from Congress, which has been struggling with the issue for nearly a decade.[26] One particularly controversial proposal first discussed in Oregon is medical rationing, or spreading limited funds among the greatest number of people by deciding which illnesses can be treated most cost-effectively and by abandoning payments for costly treatments such as organ transplants. Whether medical rationing is workable or even ethical is the subject of heated debate.[27]

Much of the debate on health-care reform focuses on the idea of *national health care,* which is generally interpreted as some form of centralized government support or control. One of the strongest motivations for national health care is the goal of providing coverage for people who either aren't covered by employer programs or can't afford to cover themselves. England, Canada, and many other countries have national health care, but such proposals have met with strong opposition in this country. In fact, with the huge amounts of money involved, any changes to the current system are likely to meet opposition from somebody, whether it's health-care professionals, insurance companies, employers, or employees. Some people want to let free-market forces drive the system; others believe the only way to get everyone covered is through government intervention. Some argue that a centralized, so-called single-payer system is the best way to make health care more efficient and more widely available, but opponents are skeptical that any government program—particularly one as massive as national health care—could ever be efficient.

It's difficult to predict where reform efforts will lead in the next few years, but several things are possible. The burden for coverage may shift from employers to the government, or it may continue to shift toward employees, who are increasingly expected to pay for more of their own coverage. The idea of *pooling,* in which groups of consumers, businesses, or communities band together to buy coverage, may spread. Many states are forging ahead with their own plans, not waiting to see if Congress can resolve the issue on a national level.[28]

Several factors have led to the escalating cost of health care. Some observers assert that the most significant factor is **cost shifting,** hospitals' and doctors' boosting their charges to private paying patients to make up for the shortfall in government reimbursements for their Medicare and Medicaid patients.[29] When hospitals and doctors increase their charges, health-insurance premiums go up. Other factors causing the escalation of insurance premiums include the spread of costly surgical procedures such as organ transplants, the emergence of new medical issues such as AIDS, and the use of expensive high-tech diagnostic equipment, such as computed tomography (CT) and magnetic resonance imaging (MRI) scanners. In addition, more doctors are becoming specialists and thus commanding higher fees.

To help employees cope with costs above and beyond the scope of traditional health-insurance policies, some employers include new types of policies in their insurance packages, offer their workers the option of paying for extra coverage through payroll deductions, or, like Marriott, develop their own hybrid programs for managing health-care costs.

Cost-Containment Measures. Allied-Signal is one example of a company that developed its own program to help control health-insurance costs. Rather than resort to traditional remedies, such as increasing deductibles and asking employees to pay a larger share of their premiums, the high-tech aerospace and automotive-products company chose a managed-care approach. Under **managed care,** employers (usually through an insurance carrier) set up their own networks of doctors and hospitals that agree to discount the fees they charge in return for the flow of patients.[30] Allied-Signal's managed-care program covers its 70,000 nonunion employees nationwide. At the end of the initial three-year contract, Allied-Signal's annual premium increases were less than 10 percent, and the total premium bill was cut nearly in half.[31]

Many companies have also instituted worksite disease-prevention programs, referred to as "wellness programs" or "wellcare." Keeping employees healthy reduces absenteeism and lowers health costs. Johnson & Johnston's version of a wellness program is Live for Life: Employees volunteer for physical checkups to identify health risks, after which they participate in free, professionally run workshops to stop smoking, control weight, improve nutrition, reduce stress, and promote physical fitness. Other companies reward employees for staying well with cash incentives.

Accident-prevention programs are gaining popularity across the country, too. American Property Construction in Alexandria, Virginia, cut its workers' compensation claims from well over $100,000 a year to almost zero by training employees in accident-prevention techniques. Employees who must drive on the job are a special concern, and companies ranging from small family firms to multinational giants such as Hewlett-Packard are training their employees in safer driving techniques.[32]

Some companies are using **health maintenance organizations (HMOs),**

managed care *Health care set up by employers (usually through an insurance carrier) who provide networks of doctors and hospitals that agree to discount the fees they charge in return for the flow of patients*

health maintenance organizations (HMOs) *Prepaid medical plans in which consumers pay a set fee in order to receive a full range of medical care from a group of medical practitioners*

Cutting health-care costs by improving employees' health is the goal of the Xerox Corporate Fitness Center.

which are comprehensive, prepaid, group-practice medical plans in which consumers pay a set fee and in return receive all their health care at little or no additional cost. Unlike hospitals and doctors in private practice, who charge on a fee-for-service basis, HMOs charge a fixed annual fee with which they must cover all their expenses. Forced to operate within each year's "subscription income," they have a strong incentive to limit treatment and to avoid costly hospitalization. HMOs are actually the precursor to managed-care programs, which are sometimes called "open HMOs" because members have the option of using hospitals and doctors outside the network. The advantages of an HMO include lower co-payments, coverage for preventive care, and no claim forms to fill out.[33]

As an alternative to HMOs, some employers are opting for **preferred-provider organizations (PPOs)**, health-care providers that contract with employers, insurance companies, or other third-party payers to deliver health-care services to an employee group at a reduced fee. In most companies, employees are not required to use preferred providers, but they are offered incentives to do so: reduced deductibles, lower co-payments, or wellcare. PPOs not only save employers money but also allow them to control the quality and appropriateness of services provided. However, critics point out that without cost-control incentives, PPOs may be tempted to make up in quantity of services what they lose in reduced fees. Other disadvantages are the restrictions placed on employees' choice of hospitals and doctors, the additional paperwork required to get approval for some services, and the fact that preventive services are not covered.[34]

Disability Coverage

Workers are protected from loss of income while disabled or partially disabled by **disability income insurance.** The insured employee receives monthly payments while disabled, usually after a specified waiting period. The payment and size of benefits normally depend on whether the disability is partial or total, temporary or permanent. Disabled workers generally receive 50 to 60 percent of their salary until retirement, offset by disability payments from Social Security. Some policies even provide partial payments if an employee is able to return to work but unable to maintain the same pace of career advancement or hours of labor per week.

Life Insurance

Life insurance is the closest thing there is to a universal employee benefit: It is offered to roughly 90 percent of the employees in the United States.[35] Life-insurance policies pay predetermined amounts to **beneficiaries** when the covered individual dies. Policies purchased by businesses typically pay an amount equal to two or three times an employee's annual salary to beneficiaries in case of death. A related form of insurance is *credit life insurance,* required by many lending institutions to guarantee that a mortgage or other large loan will be paid off in case of the borrower's death.[36]

Term insurance, as the name implies, covers a person for a specific period of time—the term of the policy. If the insured does not

preferred-provider organizations (PPOs) *Health-care providers offering reduced-rate contracts to groups that agree to obtain medical care through the providers' organization*

disability income insurance *Insurance that protects an individual against loss of income while that individual is disabled as the result of an illness or accident*

beneficiaries *People named in a life-insurance policy who are paid by the insurer when the insured dies*

term insurance *Life insurance that provides death benefits for a specified period*

684

die before the term expires, the policy has no value. Group term insurance usually carries a one-year renewable term but generally cannot be renewed past the age of 65. The older the insured, the higher the insurance premium.

Types of life insurance not usually provided by employers include whole life, endowment, variable, and universal. **Whole life insurance,** which is more expensive than term insurance, provides a combination of insurance and savings. The policy stays in force until the insured dies, provided that the premiums are paid. In addition to paying death benefits, whole life insurance accumulates value, much as a savings account does. A whole life policyholder can take out a low-interest loan against the accumulated value or, when it's time to retire, withdraw the accumulated value either in annual payments or in one lump sum.

whole life insurance Insurance that provides both death benefits and savings for the insured's lifetime, provided that premiums are paid

Endowment insurance is similar to whole life insurance in that it is a form of savings as well as a form of insurance; however, endowment policies are written for a specific term. If the insured dies before the term expires, the insurance company pays the face value of the policy to the beneficiary. If the insured is still alive when the term expires, the insurance company pays the full face value at that time. These policies have become rare.

endowment insurance Life insurance that guarantees death benefits for a specified period, after which the face value of the policy is paid to the policyholder

Variable life insurance was developed in response to the soaring inflation of the late 1970s and early 1980s. Like whole life insurance, it guarantees benefits until the death of the insured (as long as the policy remains in force) and accumulates cash value. The difference is that variable life insurance is most often associated with an investment portfolio. The insured can decide how to invest the cash value, whether in stocks, bonds, or money-market funds. If the insured's investment decisions are good, the policy's cash value and death benefit will increase. On the other hand, if the investments do poorly, the cash value and death benefit may decrease—although usually not below a guaranteed minimum level.

variable life insurance Whole life insurance policy that allows the policyholder to decide how to invest the cash value

Universal life insurance is also a flexible policy, but it is better than variable life insurance for those who are not comfortable making their own investment decisions. Premiums on a universal life-insurance policy are used to fund, in essence, term insurance and a savings account. The interest that accumulates on the savings portion of the policy is pegged to current money-market rates (but generally guaranteed to stay above a certain level). Premium payments may vary too, depending on the insured's preferences, as long as the cash value is large enough to fund the term-insurance portion of the policy. Of course, cash value accumulates more slowly when interest rates or premiums decline. This type of policy has lost popularity during the past few years.

universal life insurance Combination of a term life insurance policy and a savings plan with flexible interest rates and flexible premiums

1 Explain the difference between pure risk and speculative risk.

A pure risk involves only the potential for loss, without any possibility of gain; a speculative risk is one that accompanies the possibility of a profit.

2 Discuss the risk-management techniques available to a risk manager.

Managers use risk-control techniques to minimize organizational losses. These techniques include risk avoidance, loss prevention, and loss reduction. Managers use risk-financing techniques to restore losses that occur. These techniques include risk retention and risk transfer.

3 Distinguish uninsurable risks from insurable risks.

An uninsurable risk is one for which insurance generally is not available, such as losses due to economic and environmental conditions, poor management, and changes in government regulations. Insurable risks are relatively calculable, and insurance companies are willing to cover them.

4 Clarify how insurance companies decide the amount of income they need to generate from premiums.

The insurance companies must predict the amount they will probably have to pay in claims over a given period.

5 List the two main government insurance programs.

The two main government insurance programs are Social Security and unemployment compensation.

6 Name four types of business risks that are often insured.

Businesses run the risk of property loss, losses due to liability, income loss, and loss of key personnel.

7 Identify the two main types of health-insurance coverage.

Health insurance includes medical coverage (hospitalization insurance, surgical and medical insurance, major-medical insurance, dental and vision insurance, and mental-health insurance) and disability coverage.

8 Describe the five main forms of life insurance.

Term life insurance provides death benefits for a specific period. Whole life insurance provides both savings and death benefits throughout the insured's life, as long as premiums are paid. Endowment life insurance (now rare) provides both savings and death benefits for a specified period. Variable life insurance is similar to whole life, except that it allows the policyholder to manage the investment portion of the policy. Universal life insurance is, in effect, a combination of term insurance and a savings account.

Faced with a serious challenge to his company's liability exposure, J. W. Marriott, Jr., found that the best way to hold down costs was to minimize the chances for liability in the first place. In other words, instead of waiting for accidents to happen, he decided to prevent as many accidents as possible. This philosophy guided the company in all its risk-management efforts, from claims processing to medical care. Marriott's managers were so effective that costs were reduced, accident claims were decreased, employee morale was boosted, and the company became a model for other lodging and food-service corporations.

The crucial first step was a multimillion-dollar effort to get as much commercial insurance coverage as possible—beyond the company's own self-insurance program—and to get it at the least possible cost. Coverage had dried up after a series of tragic hotel fires, so in response, Marriott ordered all hotels managed by his company to be retrofitted with quick-response sprinkler systems. What made this program noteworthy throughout the industry (and what impressed fire-safety officials nationwide) was Marriott's use of plastic pipe instead of the traditional black iron pipe. Retrofitting a hotel with iron pipe was prohibitively expensive in many cases because entire floors had to be shut down while the sprinkler system was installed. Fire-safety officials had always avoided plastic piping because they thought it would melt in a fire. However, Marriott managers proved in a $1 million experiment that plastic pipe would do the job. The experiment's success convinced building-safety and fire-safety officials across the country that Marriott's system was more than adequate to prevent major hotel fires. Additionally, it convinced insurance companies that Marriott was worthy of receiving more liability coverage than its competitors.

Marriott's next step was to reduce the number and the cost of workers' compensation claims. It started with a companywide safety program, placing special emphasis on those units that had been acquired by Marriott.

Safety programs became an integral part of all Marriott businesses. The number of workers' compensation claims was halved in two years at Marriott's Great American amusement park—a remarkable achievement considering that the park's workforce swelled by more than 3,000 young employees every summer season. Not only were claims reduced, but the costs of processing those claims were slashed by bringing claim administration in-house and designing a computerized system to manage it. A key benefit of that system was a reduction in lost work time for employees recuperating from accidents; these employees were often able to return to work early by filling positions that would not hamper their recovery.

Finally, Marriott took on the problem of rising health-care costs—a problem so vast that it continues to have a major detrimental effect on all businesses in the United States. Marriott hired a staff of highly competent nurses to review all workers' compensation claims and doctors' reports, ensuring that treatment costs wouldn't get out of hand. The nurses also manage a companywide employee-assistance program that helps injured workers select the appropriate doctors, fill out and manage the paperwork, and speed up recuperative periods. In addition, nurses are available at nearly all of Marriott's business sites, including hotels and food-service facilities, to monitor safety standards and working conditions and, when necessary, to administer first aid quickly. The nursing program has helped boost employee morale and has contributed to reducing costs in another interesting way: Legal costs have come down substantially because fewer claims are filed against the corporation—one more benefit of reducing the risks associated with doing business.

Your Mission: You have just been promoted to vice president for risk management and insurance at Marriott. It is your job to monitor all in-surance programs, internal and external, and to continue reducing costs wherever possible through risk control.

1. Although Marriott manages hotels, the company doesn't own all the properties. Most are owned by outside investors, which has made some risk-management programs difficult to implement companywide. Extra time and effort were required to convince some owners of the benefits of joining Marriott's self-insurance program and of installing plastic pipe sprinklers in their properties. Now some owners are objecting to the cost of adding nurses to their staffs, saying their operations are not large enough to warrant such expense. Of the following, which would be your best response?

a. Conduct a cost-benefit study for each independently owned property; that is, analyze the cost of adding a nurse and compare it with the amount that having a nurse would save in health-claim costs.

b. Increase the responsibilities of nurses working out of corporate-owned hotels by including independently owned hotels in their service areas.

c. Group hotels according to region, size, and room bookings to determine which properties should have nurses on staff and which should be covered by centralized nursing staffs.

2. A number of Marriott properties are in high-risk earthquake zones. Assume that earthquake insurance is available at all the properties. The good news is that these insurance options cover replacement costs; in other words, the value of the policy fluctuates with cost of rebuilding or repairing a hotel. If it costs 25 percent more to replace a hotel in 2003 than it did to build it in 1995, the insurance will pay the additional amount. The bad news is twofold: Earthquake coverage is expensive, and, on average, these coverage options carry a 10 percent deductible (so Marriott would have to pick up the first 10 percent of the replacement or repair costs). What should you do?

a. Earthquakes are such rare occurrences that it really isn't sensible to waste time or money worrying about them. Don't bother with any kind of earthquake coverage.

b.. Yes, earthquakes are rare, but the damage they do is often extensive, and the costs of unexpectedly having to replace a hotel or conduct major repairs could be a big blow to the company's cash flow. It is important to cover all the hotels for earthquake risk, regardless of the expense.

c. Yes, when they do hit, earthquakes are likely to cause serious damage to Marriott properties. However, the risk of earthquakes hitting more than one Marriott property in a given period is rather low, so the company should self-insure for earthquakes, setting aside enough capital to rebuild a hotel quickly if one is damaged or destroyed.

3. Health-care costs used to be dominated by hospitalization cases. However, as employers (including Marriott) have found ways to reduce costs, hospitalization cases have been reduced. Now the problem is with outpatient claims: Their number and costs are rising to unmanageable proportions. Among the following options, which is the best way to reduce corporate medical-insurance costs?

a. Contract with a health maintenance organization, a type of prepaid health-care service that keeps outpatient costs low.

b. Increase the deductible paid by all employees on their medical insurance, thereby providing a financial incentive for them to use outpatient services less.

c. Begin a program for health information and education to be administered by company nurses and physicians, teaching employees how to lead healthier lives in the first place.

4. Liability claims filed by Marriott hotel guests are another source of insurance concern. These claims range from major catastrophes (such as a building collapsing) to individual incidents (such as people tripping on stairs). What's the best way to reduce the costs of these claims (regardless of whether you cover them with commercial insurance or self-insurance)?

a. Build an aggressive legal team

that fights every liability claim and does everything possible to reduce the amounts that the company has to pay.

b. Instead of focusing on insurance, focus on the things and situations in Marriott hotels that cause accidents. Require all properties to provide comprehensive reports on all accidents, and then analyze the causes

and get to work on fixing the highest-priority problems, which might be anything from poor stairway design to inadequate maintenance.

c. These problems are much like the earthquake situation; you can't predict them, and you can't control the actions of guests that might lead to accidents. There is no sense trying to worry about liability claims.[37]

KEY TERMS

actuaries (672)
beneficiaries (684)
business-interruption insurance (677)
claims (671)
coinsurance (681)
comprehensive general liability insurance (678)
contingent business-interruption insurance (677)
cost shifting (682)
credit life insurance (677)
crime insurance (677)
damages (666)
deductible (671)
dental and vision insurance (681)
depreciated-value coverage (676)
disability income insurance (684)
endowment insurance (685)
extra-expense insurance (677)
fidelity bond (676)

health maintenance organizations (HMOs) (683)
hospitalization insurance (681)
insurable risk (670)
insurance (669)
key-person insurance (680)
law of large numbers (672)
liability insurance (678)
loss exposures (666)
major-medical insurance (681)
malpractice insurance (680)
managed care (683)
mental-health insurance (681)
mutual company (674)
no-fault insurance laws (679)
preferred-provider organizations (PPOs) (684)
premium (669)
product-liability coverage (678)
property insurance (676)

pure risk (666)
replacement-cost coverage (676)
risk (666)
risk-control techniques (667)
risk-financing techniques (668)
risk management (666)
self-insure (668)
speculative risk (666)
stock company (674)
surety bond (676)
surgical and medical insurance (681)
term insurance (684)
umbrella policies (679)
underwriters (672)
uninsurable risk (669)
universal life insurance (685)
variable life insurance (685)
whole life insurance (685)
workers' compensation insurance (679)

REVIEW QUESTIONS

1. What are the four types of loss exposure?
2. What is self-insurance, and why is it becoming increasingly popular among large corporations?
3. What are the five characteristics of insurable risks?

4. What is the difference between a stock company and a mutual company?
5. What are the causes of the insurance industry's historical profitability problems?
6. What sorts of business insurance are available to protect against the

four main types of business risks?
7. What is the difference between workers' compensation insurance and disability income insurance?
8. How are the insurance companies and the government responding to the soaring costs of liability insurance?

MANAGING RISK WITHOUT A RISK MANAGER

Many small and midsized companies cannot afford to hire someone whose sole responsibility is managing risk. Without a risk manager, the company's owner, chief executive officer, or controller is likely to inherit the responsibility by default. The main drawback of this arrangement is that the day-to-day responsibilities of running a business leave little or no time for evaluating insurance coverage and developing strategies for controlling losses. Even when there is time, the process is becoming too complex for many managers to handle effectively. Factors contributing to the complexity are inflation, the growth of international operations, more complex technology, and increasing government regulation.

As a result, more companies are turning to outside consultants to help them cost-effectively manage risk. When John Cirigliano became managing director and chief executive of HBSA, a New York–based manufacturer of department-store fixtures, he made overhauling the company's insurance coverage a top priority. However, Cirigliano didn't know much about risk management and insurance, so he went to insurance consultant Paul Gregory for a review that is known in the trade as a *conceptual*.

Because consultants are not in the business of selling policies or giving recommendations about specific insurers, they can provide an unbiased perspective on a company's insurance needs. Gregory's conceptual involved analyzing the premiums, claims records, insurance appraisals and adjustments, and coverage descriptions of all HBSA's insurance policies. His conclusion was bleak. "This was a company," says Gregory, "that had stayed with one insurance broker for 40 years and just kept renewing its policies out of inertia. The kinds of coverage and policy options it had chosen didn't make sense anymore."

The conceptual for HBSA pointed to three problem-ridden insurance areas: workers' compensation, property-casualty coverage, and group health insurance. Using the conceptual as a guide, Cirigliano interviewed several insurance brokers, looking not only for lower prices but also for technical support on issues such as improving worker safety. A year after revamping HBSA's coverage, Cirigliano cut costs by 20 percent. Here's how he did it:

• *Workers' compensation.* Companies don't often bother to see whether their workers' compensation job classifications are current and accurate. In HBSA's case, clerical workers at one of its Southwestern facilities had been incorrectly classified in a costly high-risk manufacturing category for years. Cirigliano applied to the state for a reclassification and not only reduced premiums but earned a retroactive refund as well. In addition, Cirigliano found ways to reduce the frequency and severity of the company's workers' compensation claims. One way was to have HBSA's insurance broker hold employee-safety workshops. Cirigliano also encouraged his managers to consult the broker when they had questions about workers' compensation. The advice was free, and it helped control costs.

• *Property-casualty insurance.* HBSA's conceptual revealed some costly blunders in its property-casualty coverage. The most glaring was the continuation of flood-insurance coverage for a manufacturing facility the company had stopped leasing two years earlier. To further reduce the cost of insuring machinery and inventory at its 13 production sites, Cirigliano switched to a blanket loss policy, which pegs loss limits at the value of the entire company. Since there's vir-

tually no risk that all 13 sites will be damaged simultaneously, premiums remain affordable. In addition, Cirigliano added a 5 percent annual cost-of-living increase to the loss limit to eliminate the need for yearly appraisals. As Cirigliano points out, "If we enter a period of intense growth, we can either raise that figure or start doing some appraisals at that point."

• *Group health insurance.* The primary problem with HBSA's group health-insurance coverage was that the company was providing more generous benefits than other companies in its industry. Instead of paying for 100 percent coverage for his employees, Cirigliano set up a coinsurance scheme requiring employees to pay a $250 deductible as well as 20 percent of the price of their annual premium.

HBSA's consultant recommended that the company update its conceptual every three years. Insurance is one area where a little forethought and planning can produce measurable cash-flow improvement if not actual savings. In fact, Cirigliano said he saved so much money on insurance during the first year that he can actually afford to start thinking about ways to broaden the company's employee benefits.

1. What types of employee insurance are companies required by law to provide?

2. How do job classifications affect workers' compensation rates?

3. What steps do you think small companies can take to manage risk cost-effectively if they can't afford to hire a consultant or a risk manager?

Either individually or in a group of three or four students, develop a risk-management plan for a local business (small or large, from beauty salon to manufacturer). Interview a member of the company's management team, develop a profile of the business, and evaluate the risk factors that should be considered. If that option is not possible, locate a description of a business in a book or periodical that supplies you with enough information to develop the risk-management plan. On the basis of this information, select the types of insurance coverage that would be most appropriate. You might want to contact an insurance broker to help with the selection process.

• As you develop a risk-management plan for the business, consider such factors as contingency funds and self-insurance, uninsurable risks, employee insurance needs, types of liability needs, and types of property risks.
• Prepare a brief presentation that describes the business, the risk-management plan you developed, and the reasons for your choices.
• Discuss the process with other members of your class. Were there any factors that made it more difficult for some and easier for others? What were the major considerations in developing the risk-management plan?

Locate a recent article in *The Wall Street Journal* that describes a company's experience with one of the following risks:

• Product liability
• Professional liability
• Casualty losses and other expenses caused by fire or some other physical disaster
• Losses caused by fraud, theft, or employee dishonesty
• Workers' compensation
• Employee medical coverage

1. What was the company's experience? If the firm suffered a loss, was it the result of a pure risk (over which it had no control) or a speculative risk (part of the anticipated risks of doing business)? Could the company have done anything to avoid or minimize the risk?
2. Was the company insured by an outside company, self-insured (with a reserve fund), or uninsured? Was this coverage adequate?
3. What was the financial impact of this experience on the company? What, if any, major changes did it bring about in the company's business practices?

Managing the Risks of International Transportation

Selecting an international manufacturing location is a complex decision process. You must consider a wide range of benefits and risks, from local politics and economic stability to communication and transportation. The risks can never be eliminated, of course, but they can be managed and minimized.

Imagine that you're the production manager for a company that manufactures office furniture in Phoenix, Arizona. Increased demand for your products has stretched your current manufacturing capacity to the limit, and it's time to expand. You don't have time to build another factory, however, so you plan to buy an existing facility. You've identified three possibilities, all of which are in other countries. All three can handle the basic assembly you need, but you'll have to transport the assembled products to your main factory in Phoenix for finishing, packaging, and shipping to customers. The furniture is too bulky to be transported economically by air, so you'll have to use trucks, railroads, or ships.

The first factory is in Edmonton, Alberta, Canada. The second is in the Dutch port city of Rotterdam. The third is in the Nicaraguan capital, Managua. Disregarding for the moment the issue of cost and other business issues, which of these sites seems the least risky?

Consider such potential risk factors as climate, politics, and distance from Phoenix—anything that might disrupt shipments or endanger your investment in the factory. Learn as much as you can about the three sites (and the challenge of transporting products to Phoenix). Finally, recommend one, and explain your decision.

AFTER THE STORM: THE INSURANCE INFORMATION INSTITUTE RESPONDS

Synopsis

This video starts with a collage of news reports featuring the kind of information the Insurance Information Institute (III) was putting out after and immediately before Hurricane Andrew. It focuses on the Insurance Information Center established on the scene to help everyone: customers, media representatives, and insurance agents. It concludes with a summary of the lessons learned from helping customers during Hurricane Andrew.

Exercises

ANALYSIS

1. In this case, how does the communication of accurate information function as total quality management?

2. Why is the media such an important resource for insurers after and immediately before a hurricane?

3. How might inaccurate or sensationalized news stories hurt clients?

4. Why would setting up an office at the scene of the disaster be such a crucial factor for insurance agents?

5. How would the way the disaster of Hurricane Andrew was handled by individual insurers affect the insurance industry as a whole?

APPLICATION

Unable to reach many customers either because of downed phone lines and debris-blocked roads or because they had fled to temporary shelters, insurers had to be creative. Some insurers even hired airplanes to fly banners with the name of the company and an 800 number to call. List other steps that could be taken in similar emergency situations.

DECISION

If you were the CEO of a large insurance company with your office at company headquarters in a city far from the disaster area, what information would you need before making large-scale decisions concerning disaster relief? How could you ensure you were getting accurate information?

COMMUNICATION

Assume you are employed by the Insurance Information Center. You have been asked by one of the networks to appear on television to explain why, despite the fact that the insurance adjusters are working hard, progress has been slow. This interview is your opportunity to explain how claims are being handled and to provide resource information. Prepare a checklist of topics you want to cover. Practice what you will say in response to criticisms.

INTEGRATION

Refer to Chapter 3 to identify the four stakeholder groups. In the wake of Hurricane Andrew, what specific concerns might arise for an insurer with regard to each stakeholder group? Do different stakeholders' interests conflict?

ETHICS

Assume that a group such as the Insurance Information Institute has set up an office after a natural disaster. It is clear that most insurance companies are on the scene and getting the job done right. A few small companies, however, are struggling and are receiving mounting complaints. One of the objectives of the office is to reassure the public and to avoid panic. Is it ethical to withhold the negative information? Explain.

DEBATE

Organize a debate in which one group of students takes the position that the Insurance Information Center is a waste of resources (which might be better spent on more direct forms of aid to hurricane victims) and a second group argues that the Center is an essential support service.

TEAMWORK

Form teams and assign each member a recent disaster situation (such as the riots in Los Angeles, the fires in Oakland, the earthquake in San Francisco or in Los Angeles, the floods in the Midwest, or Hurricane Iniki in Kauai). Do the research necessary to determine the insurance industry's response. As a team, compare results; look for patterns of industry strengths and weaknesses. Identify not only the characteristics of effective industry response but also the problems that the industry must learn to solve.

RESEARCH

This video depicts the relationship between the insurance industry and society. At your library, look for news articles featuring insurance companies in your state. Do the articles paint a generally positive or negative picture? What conclusions can you reach about the strength of the insurance industry in your state?

ROLE PLAYING

Form a team of three or four students, each of whom plays the role of an insurance agent (each for a different small company) on the scene after a hurricane. All insurance offices are overwhelmed with calls, and all agents are working long hours but still have reached only a small percentage of clients. Discuss how you can work together to reach the remaining clients. Devise a plan for a cooperative effort among your companies; list the steps to be taken in order of priority.

APPENDIX A

CAREER GUIDE: THE EMPLOYMENT SEARCH

THINKING ABOUT YOUR CAREER

Getting the job that's right for you takes more than sending out a few letters and signing up with the college placement office. Planning and research are important if you want to find a company that suits you. Before you limit your job search to a particular industry or functional specialty, analyze what you have to offer and what you hope to get from your work.

Analyze What You Have to Offer

First, examine your marketable skills. One way is to jot down 10 achievements you're proud of, whether they include learning to ski, taking a prize-winning photo, tutoring a child, or editing the school paper. Look carefully at each of those achievements. What specific skills did they demand? For example, leadership, speaking ability, and artistic talent may have been the skills that helped you coordinate a winning presentation to the college administration. As you analyze your achievements, you'll begin to recognize a pattern of skills. Which of them might be valuable to potential employers?

Second, examine your educational preparation, work experience, and extracurricular activities. What kinds of jobs are you qualified to do on the basis of your knowledge and experience? What have you learned from participating in volunteer work or class projects that could benefit you on the job? Have you held any offices, won any awards or scholarships, mastered a second language?

Third, take stock of your personal characteristics so that you can determine the type of job you'll do best. Are you aggressive, a born leader, or would you rather follow? Are you outgoing, articulate, great with people, or do you prefer working alone? Make a list of what you believe are your four or five most important qualities. Ask a relative or friend to rate your traits as well.

If you're having trouble figuring out your interests and capabilities, consult your college placement office or career guidance center. Many campuses administer a variety of tests designed to help you identify your interests, aptitudes, and personality traits. Although these tests won't reveal the "perfect" job for you, they'll help you focus on the types of work that best suit your personality.

Determine What You Want

Knowing what you *can* do is one thing. Knowing what you *want* to do is another. Many students are so accustomed to doing what parents, peers, and instructors expect that they've lost sight of their own values. Choosing a career is a decision you need to make on your own. Get advice and information from everyone you know (family, friends, teachers, professional acquaintances), but remember that you are the only one who can decide which career is best for you. Begin by finding out just what it is you want: the tasks you enjoy, the compensation you expect, and the work environment you prefer.

What Tasks Do You Enjoy?

Basically, you need to decide what you'd like to do every day. If you have a limited range of experience, take part-time jobs, participate in work/study programs, serve as an intern in your particular field, participate in study-abroad programs, do anything you can think of to broaden your career horizons. You can also talk to people in various occupations. When Nathan James was a sophomore in college, he thought he might enjoy a career in sales, marketing research, or advertising, but he didn't know enough about the working lives of people in those fields to make an intelligent choice. So he went to his school's alumni relations office and made a list of former graduates working in the three professions. After making a few phone calls, he knew a lot more. In fact, one alumnus—an account executive with an advertising agency—invited James to spend spring break shadowing him. That experience persuaded James to focus his courses on advertising. He's now interning with a prominent advertising agency in Philadelphia.[1]

Another way to learn about various occupations is to read about them. Your college library or placement office might be a good place to start. One of the liveliest books aimed at college students is Lisa Birnbach's *Going to Work*. Among other things, Birnbach describes test-driving cars for Ford and selling cosmetics at Bloomingdale's. Another useful source is the 13-volume *Career Information Center* encyclopedia of jobs and careers, which is arranged by industry. For each job title, there's a description of the nature of the work, entry requirements, application procedures, advancement possibilities, working conditions, earnings, and benefits.

Apart from looking at specific occupations, also consider general factors, such as how much independence you want on the job, how much variety you like, and whether you prefer to work with products, machines, people, ideas, figures, or some combination. Do you like physical work, mental work, or a mix? Do you prefer constant change or a predictable role?

What Compensation Do You Expect?

Money and opportunities for advancement are also something to think about. Establish some specific compensation targets. What do you hope to earn in your first year on the job? What kind of pay increase do you expect each year? What's your ultimate earnings goal? Would you be comfortable with a job that pays on commission, or would you prefer a steady paycheck? What occupations offer the kind of money you're looking for? Are these occupations realistic for someone with your qualifications? Are you willing to settle for less money in order to do something you really love?

Next, consider your place within the company or profession. Where would you like to start? Where do you want to go from there? What's the ultimate position you would like to attain? How soon after joining the company would you like to receive your first promotion? Your next one? Once you have established these goals, ask yourself what additional training or preparation you'll need to achieve them.

What Work Environment Do You Prefer?

Another factor to consider is the environment you want to work in. Start by thinking in broad terms about the size and type of operation that appeals to you. Do you like the idea of working for a small, entrepreneurial operation, or would you prefer to be part of a large company? How do you feel about profit-making versus non-profit organizations? Are you attracted to service businesses or manufacturing operations? What types of products appeal to you? Do you want regular, predictable hours, or do you thrive on flexible, varied hours? Do you prefer to work from 9:00 A.M. to 5:00 P.M., or are you willing to work evenings and weekends, as in the entertainment and hospitality industries? Would you enjoy a seasonally varied job like education (which may give you summers off) or retailing (with its selling cycles)?

Location can also be important. Would you like to work in a city, a suburb, or a small town? In an industrial area or an uptown setting? Do you favor a particular part of the country? Does working in another country appeal to you? Do you like working indoors or outdoors?

What about facilities? Is it important to you to work in an attractive place, or will simple, functional quarters suffice? Do you need a quiet office to work effectively, or can you concentrate in a noisy, open setting? Would you prefer to work at the company's headquarters or in a small field office? Do such amenities as an in-house gym or handball court matter to you? Is access to public transportation or freeways important?

Perhaps the most important environmental factor is the corporate culture. Would you be happy in a well-defined hierarchy, where roles and reporting relationships are clear, or would you prefer a less structured situation? What qualities do you want in a boss? Are you looking for a paternalistic organization or one that fosters individualism? Do you like a competitive environment or one that rewards teamwork?

SEEKING EMPLOYMENT OPPORTUNITIES

Once you know what you have to offer and what you want, you can start finding an employer to match. If you haven't already committed yourself to any particular career field, first find out where the job opportunities are. Which industries are strong? Which parts of the country are booming, and which specific job categories offer the best prospects for the future? Consult sources in several areas:

- *Business and financial news.* Subscribe to a major newspaper and scan the business pages every day. Watch some of the TV programs that focus on business, such as "Wall Street Week," and read the business articles in popular magazines such as *Time* and *Newsweek.* You might even want to subscribe to a business magazine such as *Fortune, Business Week,* or *Forbes.*
- *Library references.* For information about the future for specific jobs, see *The Dictionary of Occupational Titles* (U.S. Employment Service), *Occupational Outlook Handbook* (U.S. Bureau of Labor Statistics), and the employment publications of Science Research Associates. For an analysis of major industries, see the annual Market Data and Directory issue of *Industrial Marketing,* and look through Standard & Poor's industry surveys.
- *Journals, people, and associations.* Study professional and trade journals in the career fields that interest you. Also, talk to people in these fields; for names of the most prominent, consult *Standard & Poor's Register of Corporations, Directors and Executives.* Find recent books about the fields you're considering by checking *Books in Print.* You may be able to network with executives in your field by joining or participating in student business organizations, especially those with ties to real-world organizations such as the American Marketing Association or the American Management Association.

Once you've identified a promising industry and a career field, compile a list of specific organizations that appeal to you. You can put together a reasonable list by consulting several sources:

- *Directories of employers.* Directories such as *The College Placement Annual* and *Career: The Annual Guide to Business Opportunities* may be helpful. Write to the organizations on your list and ask for an annual report and any descriptive brochures or newsletters they've published. If possible, visit some of the organizations on your list, contact their personnel departments, or talk with key employees.
- *Local and major newspapers.* Businesses often advertise

their products as well as their job openings in newspapers.

- *Trade and professional journals.* For information on journals in career fields that interest you, see *Ulrich's International Periodicals Directory.*
- *Agencies and offices.* Job listings can also be obtained from your college placement office, state employment bureaus, and private employment agencies.
- *Electronic services.* A personal computer and modem can expand your job search opportunities. On-line services such as America Online, Prodigy, and CompuServe all offer help-wanted listings, forums for discussing career issues, and networking groups. Job-seekers' ads can be placed with Dow Jones News Retrieval or Kinexus. The New York Times Company offers an interactive system for employers to advertise jobs and for prospective employees to send résumés.[2]

In any job, your ultimate goal is an interview with potential employers. The fastest way to obtain an interview is to get a referral from someone you know. Some organizations recruit students for job openings by sending representatives to college campuses for interviews (usually coordinated by the campus placement office, which keeps files containing college records, data sheets, and letters of recommendation for all students registered for the service). Employers also recruit candidates through campus publications and the employment bureaus operated by some trade associations. Unsolicited résumés can be vital for obtaining interviews—just remember that for every 100 letters you send out, you can expect to get only about six interviews.[3]

Preparing Your Résumé

A **résumé** is a structured, written summary of a person's education, employment background, and job qualifications. It's a form of advertising, designed to help you get an interview. Your objective is to call attention to your best features and to downplay your disadvantages, without distorting or misrepresenting the facts.[4] A good résumé conveys seven specific qualities that employers seek. It shows that a candidate (1) thinks in terms of results, (2) knows how to get things done, (3) is well-rounded, (4) shows signs of progress, (5) has personal standards of excellence, (6) is flexible and willing to try new things, and (7) possesses strong communication skills. As you put your résumé together, think about how the format, style, and content convey these seven qualities.

Controlling the Format and Style

If your résumé doesn't *look* sharp, chances are nobody will read it carefully enough to judge your qualifications. So it's important to use a clean typeface on high-grade, letter-size bond paper (in white or some light earth tone). Make sure that your stationery and envelope match. Leave

ample margins all around, and be certain any corrections are unnoticeable. Avoid italic typefaces, which can be difficult to read. If you have reservations about the quality of your typewriter or printer (dot-matrix printing is not suitable for most résumés), you might want to turn your résumé over to a professional service. To make duplicate copies, use offset printing or photocopying.

Lay out your résumé so that the information is easy to grasp.[5] Break up the text by using headings that call attention to various aspects of your background, such as your work experience and education. Underline or capitalize key points, or set them off in the left margin. Use indented lists to itemize your most important qualifications. Leave plenty of white space, even if doing so forces you to use two pages rather than one.

Pay attention to mechanics. Be sure that your grammar, spelling, and punctuation are correct. Because your résumé has only seconds to make an impression, keep the writing style simple and direct. Instead of whole sentences, use short, crisp phrases starting with action verbs. You might say, "Coached a Little League team to the regional playoffs" or "Managed a fast-food restaurant and four employees."

In general, try to write a one-page résumé. If you have a great deal of experience and are applying for a higher-level position, you may wish to prepare a somewhat longer résumé. The important thing is to give yourself enough space to present a persuasive but accurate portrait of your skills and accomplishments.

Tailoring the Contents

Most potential employers expect¡ to see certain items in any résumé. The bare essentials are name and address, academic credentials, and employment history. Otherwise, make sure your résumé emphasizes your strongest, most impressive qualifications. It's up to you to combine your experiences into a straightforward message that communicates what you can do for your potential employer.[6] Think in terms of an image or a theme you'd like to project. Are you academically gifted? Are you a campus leader? A well-rounded person? A creative genius? A technical wizard? If you know what you have to sell, you can shape the elements of your résumé accordingly. Don't exaggerate, and don't alter the past or claim skills you don't have, but don't dwell on negatives, either. By focusing on your strengths, you can convey the desired impression without distorting the facts.

Choosing the Organizational Plan

Although you may want to include a little information in all categories, emphasize the information that has a bearing on your career objective and minimize or exclude any that is irrelevant or counterproductive. You focus attention on your strongest points by adopting the most appropriate organizational plan—chronological, functional, or targeted.

Chronological Résumés. The most traditional type of résumé is the **chronological résumé,** in which a person's employment history is listed sequentially in reverse order, starting with the most recent experience. When you organize your résumé chronologically, the "Work Experience" section dominates the résumé and is placed in the most prominent slot, immediately after the name and address and the objective. Under each listing, you describe your responsibilities and accomplishments, giving the most space to the most recent positions. If you're just graduating from college, you can vary the chronological plan by putting your educational qualifications before your experience, thereby focusing attention on your academic credentials. The chronological approach is especially appropriate if you have a strong employment history and are aiming for a job that builds on your current career path (see Exhibit A.1).

Functional Résumés. A **functional résumé** is organized around a list of skills and accomplishments, identifying employers and academic experience in subordinate sections. This pattern stresses individual areas of competence, and it's useful for people who are just entering the job market or those who want to redirect their careers or minimize breaks in employment. Exhibit A.2 illustrates how a recent graduate used the functional approach to showcase her qualifications for a career in public relations.

Targeted Résumés. A **targeted résumé** is organized to focus attention on what you can do for a particular employer in a particular position. Immediately after stating your career objective, you list any related capabilities. This

---

Exhibit A.1
Chronological Résumé

```
                            Roberto Cortez
                         5687 Crosswoods Drive
                        Falls Church, VA 22044
                         Home: (703) 987-0086
                         Office: (703) 549-6624

OBJECTIVE       Accounting manager, with international finance
                emphasis

EXPERIENCE

March 1991      Staff Accountant/Financial Analyst
to present      INTER-AMERICAN IMPORTS  ALEXANDRIA, VA

                Prepare general accounting reports for
                wholesale giftware importer with annual sales
                of $15 million.  Audit all financial
                transactions between company headquarters and
                suppliers in 12 Latin American countries.
                *  Created a computerized model to adjust
                   accounts for fluctuations in currency
                   exchange rates
                *  Represented company in negotiating joint
                   venture agreements with major suppliers in
                   Mexico and Colombia

October 1985    Staff Accountant
to March 1991   MONSANTO AGRICULTURAL CHEMICALS  MEXICO CITY

                Handled budgeting, billing, and credit-
                processing functions for the Mexico City
                branch of Monsanto's Agricultural Chemicals
                division.  Audited travel and entertainment
                expenditures for Monsanto's 30-member Latin
                American sales force.  Assisted in launching
                an on-line computer system (IBM).

EDUCATION       GEORGE MASON UNIVERSITY  FAIRFAX, VA
                1991-1994 M.B.A. with emphasis on
                international business

                UNIVERSIDAD NACIONAL AUTONOMA DE MEXICO
                MEXICO CITY, MEXICO
                1981-1985 B.B.A., Accounting

PERSONAL        Fluent in English, Spanish, and German.  Have
DATA            lived and traveled extensively in Latin
                America.

REFERENCES      Available on request.


                Resume Submitted in Confidence
```

list is followed by a list of your achievements, which provide evidence of your capabilities. Employers and schools are listed in subordinate sections. Targeted résumés are a good choice for people who have a clear idea of what they want to do and who can demonstrate their ability in the targeted area (see Exhibit A.3).

Preparing Your Application Letter

If you're like most job seekers, you'll send your résumé to as many employers as possible, because the chances of getting an interview from each inquiry are relatively slight. To make the process more efficient, use the same résumé repeatedly, and tailor your application for each potential employer by including a cover letter that projects your theme and tells what you can do for that specific organization. Like your résumé, your application letter is a form of advertising. You stimulate the reader's interest before showing how you can satisfy the organization's needs.

Let your letter reflect your personal style. Be yourself, but be businesslike too; avoid sounding cute, using slang, or designing a gimmicky layout. By doing your homework and showing that you know something about the organization, you'll capture the reader's attention and convey your desire to join the organization. The letter in Exhibit A.4 gains attention by referring to a recent magazine article about the company.

Following Up on Your Application

If your application letter and résumé fail to bring a response within a month or so, follow up with a second

```
                        Glenda St. Johns

Box 6671, College Station      Objective:  Corporate public
Iowa City, Iowa 52240          relations officer
(515) 545-9856


WRITING/EDITING:
    *  Wrote arts and entertainment articles for college
       newspaper
    *  Edited University of Iowa Handbook, guidebook mailed to
       all incoming freshmen
    *  Wrote guest editorial on student attitudes for Des
       Moines Register
    *  Wrote prize-winning script for sorority skit in Fall
       Follies talent show

PUBLIC SPEAKING:
    *  Participated in over 100 debates as member of college
       debating team
    *  Led seminars to teach job-search skills to under-
       privileged teenagers as part of campus outreach program
    *  Performed in summer theater productions in Clear Lake,
       Iowa

MANAGING:
    *  Created and administered summer parks and recreation
       program for city of Osage, Iowa
    *  Developed budget, schedule, and layouts for college
       handbook; assigned work to photographers and
       copywriters
    *  Developed publicity campaign for Fall Follies, three-
       hour talent show that raised $7,000 for The University
       of Iowa's Panhellenic Council

EDUCATION:
The University of Iowa, Iowa City, September 1991-June 1995
B.A. Journalism (3.81 GPA on 4.0 scale)
Speech minor; two courses in public relations

EXPERIENCE:
June 1993-April 1994, Editor, University of Iowa Handbook
Summer 1992, Director, Summer Recreation Program, Osage, Iowa
Summer 1991, Actress, Cobblestone Players, Clear Lake, Iowa

PERSONAL DATA:
Willing to relocate; have traveled extensively.

REFERENCES AND SUPPORTING DOCUMENTS:  Available from Placement
Office, The University of Iowa, Iowa City, IA 52242
```

ERICA VORKAMP'S QUALIFICATIONS
FOR SPECIAL EVENTS COORDINATOR
IN THE CITY OF BARRINGTON

993 Church Street
Barrington, IL 60010
(312) 884-2153

CAPABILITIES

* Plan and coordinate large-scale public events
* Develop community support for concerts, festivals, and entertainment
* Manage publicity for major events
* Coordinate activities of diverse community groups
* Establish and maintain financial controls for public events
* Negotiate contracts with performers, carpenters, electricians, and suppliers

ACHIEVEMENTS

* Arranged 1995's weeklong Arts and Entertainment Festival for the Barrington Public Library, which involved performances by 25 musicians, dancers, actors, magicians, and artists

* Supervised the 1994 PTA Halloween Carnival, an all-day festival with game booths, live bands, contests, and food service, which raised $7,600 for the PTA

* Organized the 1993 Midwestern convention for 800 members of the League of Women Voters, which extended over a three-day period and required arrangements for hotels, meals, speakers, and special tours

* Served as chairperson for the 1993 Children's Home Society Fashion Show, a luncheon for 400 that raised $5,000 for orphans and abused children

EDUCATION

* Northwestern University (Evanston, Illinois), September 1975 to June 1980, B.A. Psychology; Phi Beta Kappa

WORK HISTORY

* First National Bank of Chicago, June 1980 to October 1982, Personnel Counselor/Campus Recruiter; scheduled and conducted interviews with graduating M.B.A. students on 18 Midwestern campuses; managed orientation program for recruits hired for bank's management trainee staff
* Northwestern University, November 1977 to June 1980, Part-time Research Assistant; helped Professor Paul Harris conduct behavioral experiments using rats trained to go through mazes

letter to keep your file active. This follow-up letter also gives you a chance to update your original application with any recent job-related information. Even if you have received a letter acknowledging your application and saying that it will be kept on file, don't hesitate to send a follow-up letter three months later to show that you are still interested. Sending such letters demonstrates that you are sincerely interested in working for the organization, that you are persistent in pursuing your goals, and that you continue upgrading your skills to make yourself a better employee—and it might just get you an interview.

Interviewing with Potential Employers

The best way to prepare for a job interview is to think carefully about the job itself. Approach job interviews with a sound appreciation of their dual purpose: The organization's main objective is to find the best person available for the job; the applicant's main objective is to find the job best suited to his or her goals and capabilities.

Organizations approach the recruiting process in various ways, so adjust your job search accordingly. In general, the easiest way to connect with a big company is through your campus placement office; the most efficient way to approach a smaller business is by contacting the company directly. In either case, once you get your foot in the door, you move to the next stage and prepare to meet with a recruiter during an **employment interview,** a formal meeting during which an employer and an applicant ask questions and exchange information to see whether the applicant and the organization are a good match.

Exhibit A.4
Application Letter

```
                                              216 Westview Circle
                                              Dallas, TX 75231
                                              June 16, 1995


        Mr. William DuPage, Managing Partner
        Grant & Grant Financial Planning Associates
        1775 Lakeland Drive
        Dallas, TX 75218

        Dear Mr. DuPage:

        Congratulations on being featured in this month's Fortune
        magazine article about the coming developments in corporate
        tax planning.  After reading about your firm's innovative
        electronic tax-reporting programs, I believe my background
        in computerized accounting and bookkeeping methods would
        benefit Grant & Grant.

        My 42 units of college accounting and courses in electronic
        data processing have equipped me to work with computer-based
        clients like yours.  Training in business writing, human
        relations, and psychology should help me achieve solid
        rapport with them.  My advanced studies in tax accounting
        will enable me to analyze their financial needs from a
        planning perspective.

        Because your company specializes in tax-shelter planning, my
        work experience could also be beneficial.  After two years
        as a part-time bookkeeper for a securities brokerage firm, I
        was promoted to full-time financial analyst intern in the
        corporate investment division.  When making recommendations
        to the firm's corporate clients, I analyzed and selected
        specific tax-shelter programs.  After three months, my
        accomplishments were acknowledged by a substantial salary
        increase.

        Dennis Paul, vice president of Citibank, and other
        references listed on the enclosed résumé will confirm my
        potential for the staff accountant position.

        At a time convenient for you, I would appreciate the oppor-
        tunity to discuss my qualifications for beginning a career
        with your company.  I will phone you early next Wednesday to
        see whether we can arrange a meeting at your convenience.

                                        Sincerely,

                                        Diane Fahey

                                        Diane Fahey


        Enclosure
```

Most employers conduct two or three interviews before deciding whether to offer a person a job. The first interview, generally held on campus, is the **preliminary screening interview,** which helps employers eliminate unqualified applicants from the hiring process. Those candidates who best meet the organization's requirements are invited to visit company offices for further evaluation. Some organizations make a decision at that point, but many schedule a third interview to complete the evaluation process before extending a job offer.

Because these three steps take time, start seeking interviews well in advance of the date you want to start work. It takes an average of 10 interviews to get one job offer. If you hope to have several offers to choose from, you can expect to go through 20 or 30 interviews during your job search.[7] Some students start their job search as early as nine months before graduation. Early planning is even more crucial during downturns in the economy because many employers become more selective when times are tough, and many corporations reduce their campus visits and campus hiring programs, which puts more of the job-search burden on you.

What Employers Look For

In general, employers are looking for two things: proof that a candidate can handle a specific job and evidence that the person will fit in with the organization. Every interviewer approaches these issues a little differently. Employers are usually most concerned with the candidate's experience, intelligence, communication skills, enthusiasm, creativity, and motivation.

- *Qualifications for the job.* When you're invited to interview for a position, the interviewer may already have some idea of whether you have the right qualifications, based on a review of your résumé. During the interview, you'll be asked to describe your education and previous jobs in more depth so that the interviewer can determine how well your skills match the requirements. In many cases, the interviewer will be seeking someone with the flexibility to apply diverse skills in several areas.[8]
- *Personality traits.* A résumé can't show whether a person is lively and outgoing, subdued and low-key, able to take direction, or able to take charge. Each job requires a different mix of personality traits, so the task of the interviewer is to find out whether a candidate will be effective in a particular job.
- *Physical appearance.* Clothing and grooming reveal something about a candidate's personality and professionalism. For example, for an interview with a conservative firm, it would probably be a big mistake to show up in blue jeans. Even in companies where interviewers may dress casually, it's important to show good judgment by dressing (and acting) in a professional manner. Interviewers also consider such physical factors as posture, eye contact, handshake, facial expressions, and tone of voice.
- *Age.* Job discrimination against middle-aged people is prohibited by law, but if you feel your youth could count against you, counteract its influence by emphasizing your experience, dependability, and mature attitudes.
- *Personal background.* You might be asked about your interests, hobbies, awareness of world events, and so forth. You can expand your potential along these lines by reading widely, making an effort to meet new people, and participating in discussion groups, seminars, and workshops.
- *Attitudes and personal style.* Openness, enthusiasm, and interest are likely to impress an interviewer. So are courtesy, sincerity, willingness to learn, and a positive, self-confident style—all of which help a new employee adapt to a new workplace and new responsibilities.

What Applicants Need to Find Out

What things should you find out about the prospective job and employer? By doing a little advance research and asking the right questions during the interview, you can probably find answers to all the following questions and more:

- Are these my kind of people?
- Can I do this work?
- Will I enjoy the work?

- Is this job what I want?
- Does the job pay what I'm worth?
- What kind of person would I be working for?
- What sort of future can I look forward to with this organization?

How to Prepare for a Job Interview

It's perfectly normal to feel a little anxious before an interview. So much depends on it, and you don't know quite what to expect. Don't worry too much, however; preparation will help you perform well:

- *Do some basic research.* Learning about the organization and the job is important because it enables you to review your résumé from the employer's point of view.
- *Think ahead about questions.* Most job interviews are essentially question-and-answer sessions: You answer the interviewer's questions about your background, and you ask questions of your own to determine whether the job and the organization are right for you. By planning for your interviews, you can handle these exchanges intelligently (see Exhibit A.5). Of course, you don't want to memorize responses or sound over-rehearsed.
- *Bolster your confidence.* By overcoming your tendencies to feel self-conscious or nervous during an interview, you can build your confidence and make a better impression. If some aspect of your background or appearance makes you uneasy, correct it or exercise positive traits to offset it, such as warmth, wit, intelligence, or charm. Instead of dwelling on your weaknesses, focus on your strengths so that you can emphasize them to an interviewer.
- *Polish your interview style.* Confidence helps you walk into an interview, and once there, give the interviewer an impression of poise, good manners, and good judgment. In the United States, you're more likely to be invited back for a second interview or offered a job if you maintain eye contact, smile frequently, sit in an attentive position, and use frequent hand gestures. These nonverbal signals convince the interviewer that you're alert, assertive, dependable, confident, responsible, and energetic.[9] Work on eliminating speech mannerisms such as "you know," "like," and "um," which might make you sound inarticulate. Speak in your natural tone, and try to vary the pitch, rate, and volume of your voice to express enthusiasm and energy.
- *Plan to look good.* The best policy is to dress conservatively. Wear the best-quality businesslike clothing you can, preferably in a dark, solid color. Avoid flamboyant styles, colors, and prints. Good grooming makes any style of clothing look better. Make sure your clothes are clean and unwrinkled, your shoes unscuffed and well shined, your hair neatly styled and combed, your fingernails clean, and your breath fresh. If possible, check your appearance in a mirror before entering the

Exhibit A.5
Common Interview Questions

1. **Employers' Questions About College**
   What courses in college did you like most? Least? Why?
   Do you think your extracurricular activities in college were worth the time you devoted to them? Why?
   When did you choose your college major? Did you ever change your major? If so, why?
   Do you feel you did the best scholastic work you are capable of?
   Which of your college years was the toughest? Why?

2. **Employers' Questions About Employment and Jobs**
   What jobs have you held? Why did you leave?
   What percentage of your college expenses did you earn? How?
   Why did you choose your particular field of work?
   What are the disadvantages of your chosen field?
   Have you served in the military? What rank did you achieve? What jobs did you perform?
   What do you think about how this industry operates today?
   Why do you think you would like this particular type of job?

3. **Employers' Questions About Personal Attitudes and Preferences**
   Do you prefer to work in any specific geographic location? If so, why?
   How much money do you hope to be earning in 5 years? In 10 years?
   What do you think determines a person's progress in a good organization?
   What personal characteristics do you feel are necessary for success in your chosen field?
   Tell me a story.
   Do you like to travel?
   Do you think grades should be considered by employers? Why or why not?

4. **Employers' Questions About Work Habits**
   Do you prefer working with others or by yourself?
   What type of boss do you prefer?
   Have you ever had any difficulty getting along with colleagues or supervisors? Other students? Instructors?
   Would you prefer to work in a large or a small organization? Why?
   How do you feel about overtime work?
   What have you done that shows initiative and willingness to work?

5. **Students' Questions for Interviewers**
   What are this job's major responsibilities?
   What qualities do you want in the person who fills this position?
   Do you want to know more about my related training?
   What is the first problem that needs the attention of the person you hire?
   What are the organization's major strengths? Weaknesses?
   Who are your organization's major competitors, and what are their strengths and weaknesses?
   What makes your organization different from others in the industry?
   What are your organization's major markets?
   Does the organization have any plans for new products? Acquisitions?
   What can you tell me about the person I would report to?
   How would you define your organization's managerial philosophy?
   What additional training does your organization provide?
   Do employees have an opportunity to continue their education with help from the organization?
   Would relocation be required, now or in the future?
   Why is this job now vacant?

---

room for the interview. Don't spoil the effect by smoking cigarettes before or during the interview. Finally, remember that one of the best ways to look good is to smile at appropriate moments.

- *Be ready when you arrive.* For the interview, plan to take a small notebook, a pen, a list of the questions you want to ask, two copies of your résumé protected in a folder, an outline of what you have learned about the organization, and any past correspondence about the position. You may also want to take a small calendar, a transcript of your college grades, a list of references, and if appropriate, samples of your work. Be sure you know when and where the interview will be held. The worst way to start any interview is to be late. Then, once you arrive, relax. You may have to wait a little while, so bring along something to read or occupy your time (the less frivolous or controversial, the better).

Following Up After the Interview

Touching base with the prospective employer after the interview, either by phone or in writing, shows that you really want the job and are determined to get it. It also brings your name to the interviewer's attention once again and reminds him or her that you're waiting to know the decision.

The two most common forms of follow-up are the thank-you message and the inquiry. These are generally handled by letter, but a phone call is often just as effective, particularly if the employer seems to favor a casual, personal style. Express your thanks within two days after the interview, even if you feel you have little chance for the job. Keep your message brief. Acknowledge the interviewer's time and courtesy, convey the idea that you continue to be interested, and then ask politely for a decision. If you're not advised of the interviewer's decision by the promised date or within two weeks, you might make an inquiry, particularly if you've received a job offer from a second firm and don't want to accept it before you have an answer from the first. Assume that a simple oversight is the reason for the delay, not outright rejection.

BUILDING YOUR CAREER

At one time in the United States, joining an organization meant you would most likely be employed with that same organization for life. You would start at the bottom step of the hierarchy and, through seniority, climb the ladder to success. Today the average person beginning a career in the United States will probably work in 10 or more jobs for five or more employers before retiring. So getting a job after graduation is only one step toward building your career.[10]

Employers are seeking people who are able and willing to adapt to diverse situations, who thrive in an ever-changing workplace, and who continue to learn throughout their careers. Employers want team players with strong work records. So try to gain skills you can market in various industries. Join networks of professional colleagues and friends who can help you stay abreast of where your occupation, industry, and company are going. As you search for a permanent job that fulfills your career goals, take interim job assignments, consider temporary work or freelance jobs. Employers will be more willing to find (or even create) a position for someone they've learned to respect, and your temporary or freelance work gives them a chance to see what you can do. You might even consider starting your own business.

At the least, work on polishing and updating your skills. While you're waiting for responses to your résumé or to hear about your last interview, take a computer course or use the time to gain some other educational or work experience that would be difficult to get while working full time. Have a plan, but be flexible and ready to take advantage of new opportunities. That's the way you'll build your career and achieve your career goals.[11]

KEY TERMS		
chronological résumé (A4)	functional résumé (A4)	résumé (A3)
employment interview (A6)	preliminary screening interview (A7)	targeted résumé (A4)

APPENDIX B

RESEARCH, STATISTICAL ANALYSIS, AND REPORTS

Businesspeople use sophisticated information-gathering methods and interpretation techniques to get a clear view of many factors affecting the efficiency, productivity, and profits of their businesses. Production managers use statistics in quality control. Human resources managers may use statistics to ensure that test scores reflect the ability to do a job. Marketing managers do a lot of research, measuring the size of markets, the effectiveness of various marketing techniques, and the needs and desires of prospective customers. In accounting, audits are often conducted by analyzing in detail a representative group of accounts. Financial managers analyze the performance of their investment portfolios. Risk managers use statistics to determine risks. Without such research, managers might make some very costly errors.

BASIC RESEARCH

The first step in business research is to decide what needs to be studied. What precisely is the problem, and what are the possible answers? A production manager may know that the quality of a finished product is a problem, but she or he needs to make some educated guesses about the specific components or processes that are faulty in order to pursue solutions. The next step is to seek data that will prove or disprove the possible solutions.

Sources of Data

Staff people and all levels of managers need to know where and how to obtain data; it is an important business skill. They must also understand the two main ways to classify data: (1) according to where they are located and (2) according to the reason they were gathered.

Data grouped according to location are either internal data or external data. **Internal data** are those available in the company's own records—invoices, purchase orders, personnel files, and the like. **External data** are those obtained from outside sources, including government agencies—say, the Census Bureau—and nongovernment sources, such as trade associations and trade periodicals. Internal data are sometimes easier to obtain and more specific to the company, but outside sources often have better resources for gathering data on broad economic and social trends.

Data grouped by purpose are either primary or secondary. **Primary data** consist of information gathered for the study of a specific problem. **Secondary data** consist of information previously produced or collected for a purpose other than that of the moment. Sometimes the collection of secondary data is characterized as "library research." In business research, government and trade organizations are the major sources of secondary data.

Businesspeople usually examine secondary data first because these data often have three advantages over primary data:

- *Speed.* Secondary data sources, such as *A Guide to Consumer Markets,* put out by The Conference Board, provide information at a moment's notice.
- *Cost.* Collecting primary data may be an expensive process. On the other hand, for the cost of membership in an organization, a business can have the results of all the group's research at its disposal.
- *Availability.* The owner of a business can hardly expect the owner of a competing firm to make information available. Trade associations and the government, on the other hand, collect information from all firms and make it available to everyone.

Secondary data do have some drawbacks, however. The information may be out of date, or it may not be as relevant as it first seems. The company or agency that collected the data may not be as impartial as it should be. Furthermore, the source may lack expertise: The survey may not be broad enough to cover the targeted geographic area or income group, or questions may be phrased in such a way that the respondents may guess the "correct answers"—that is, they may say what the researcher wants to hear.

Primary Research Techniques

The best way to overcome the disadvantages of secondary data may be to collect primary data through original research. Although primary data may also be collected ineptly, they are certain to be more relevant to the particular business's needs. To find answers to their questions and problems, businesses of all sizes and types use the following techniques: sampling, observation, surveys, and experimentation.

Sampling

A **sample** is a small part of a large group of people or items. (In statistical language, the group from which a sample is drawn is known as a *population* or *universe*.) Researchers use data collected from a properly selected sample to draw conclusions or to make forecasts about the population from which the sample was drawn, and they are able to do so because of the laws of probability.

Probability. **Probability** is the likelihood, over the long run, that a certain event will occur in one way rather than in another way. For example, if you flip a coin, the likelihood of throwing heads is one-half, or 50 percent (because a coin has only two sides), and the likelihood of throwing tails is also 50 percent. In a series of 10 tosses, you would expect to throw heads about 5 times. You could throw heads 10 times, but that outcome would be unlikely.

How does a businessperson use probability in everyday operations? Suppose the manager of a department store found that out of every 1,000 letters from customers, about 50 letters, or 5 percent, were complaints. The manager would expect that on any day when 100 letters arrive from customers, about 5 of them will be complaints. Of course, there may be more or fewer complaint letters, but if the number suddenly increases to 20 or 30 and stays at that level for a few days, the manager might suspect a problem. Perhaps someone is tampering with the customer correspondence file; perhaps customers don't like something new or different in the store's operations. In either case, a sudden shift that contradicts probability will alert the manager.

Probability is the principle behind sampling. For instance, if 10 out of 100 finished products sampled Monday are found to be defective, it is probably safe to assume that 10 percent of the whole production run is defective, provided that the sample was selected to fairly represent the universe of finished products.

Random Sampling. The most common method of selecting a sample is **random sampling.** A group of items or individuals is chosen from a larger group in a way that gives all items or persons in the group an equal chance of being selected. Simple methods of random selection include drawing names from a hat, taking every hundredth product to come off the production line, and auditing every fifth financial report.

Imagine that a college bookstore in an urban area has ordered 1,000 T-shirts imprinted with the school's name. The T-shirt manufacturer may use sampling to determine whether clothing stores in that city would also like to stock the T-shirts. It is impractical for the manufacturer to call the 200 stores that, according to the yellow pages, carry this kind of merchandise. Instead, the manufacturer may call every twentieth shop listed. The 10 stores that would be called represent a random sample because they are listed alphabetically—not by size, location, type of customer, or any other factor that might affect their interest in the T-shirts. A good response from those 10 stores would indicate that many of the other 190 stores would be interested in the T-shirts, too.

The major limitation of random sampling is that the population to be sampled has to be small enough and sufficiently concentrated geographically so that a list of all the names or items it includes is available or can easily be prepared. To draw a sample from all the clothing stores in the United States would be too large and expensive a task; other sampling techniques may be used in such instances. It's sufficient to note here that random sampling is most effective when used in limited populations.

Observation
Observation is the technique of watching or otherwise monitoring incidents of the particular sort that the investigator wants to study. One example of observation would be an employer's using cameras and videotape to study the way employees do their work. Another example would be a municipal traffic department's using a counting mechanism to record the number of cars that use a given street; the department would then be able to determine whether the street should be widened or whether a traffic light should be installed.

Observation sounds simple enough, but deciding exactly what sort of activity should be measured can be difficult, especially when it comes to observing human behavior. For example, if the purpose of the research is to determine the level of procrastination among office workers, what behavior reveals procrastination? Is gazing into space a sign of procrastination, or is it a necessary pause to reflect and plan? Is someone who makes frequent trips to the water cooler procrastinating? Is the procrastinator the one who industriously writes ten relatively pointless memos instead of writing one important 10-page report?

Surveys
Businesses often need to know why employees or potential customers behave the way they do. The simplest way to find out is to ask them, and that's where **surveys** come in. To conduct a survey, investigators may mail a questionnaire (a list of questions) to the respondents (the people who answer the questions), or they may get their answers via face-to-face or telephone interviews. Respondents may be questioned once or a number of times. The biggest problems in doing surveys are selecting an appropriate sample and phrasing questions objectively.

Experimentation
In an **experiment,** the investigator tries to find out how one set of conditions will affect another set of conditions by setting up a situation in which all factors may be carefully measured. An experiment differs from ordinary observation because the experimenter can deliberately make changes in the situation to see what effect each change has. The conditions that change are called **variables.** The changes that the experimenter makes deliberately are the **independent variables;** those that change in response

are the **dependent variables.** In a taste test, for example, the independent variable would be the various brands sampled; the dependent variable would be the tasters' preferences for particular brands.

Experiments are often conducted in laboratories, where independent variables can be easily controlled. A scientist studying the effects of crowding on mice could, in the laboratory, control the size of the cages, the number of mice in each cage, and so on. On the other hand, some experiments may be performed in an ordinary social setting.

An experimenter usually tries to observe two separate groups made up of similar individuals who are randomly assigned to one group or the other. One group is exposed to a specific independent variable, and the other is not. (The group that is not exposed to the independent variable is called the control group.) To find out whether employees who undergo a certain type of training do better work, a personnel director might put one group of workers through on-the-job training only, while putting the other group through both on-the-job training and classroom training. After a suitable time in the actual work setting, the performance of the two groups of workers could be compared. If the group that underwent both classroom and on-the-job training was doing a significantly better job, the dual-training approach (the independent variable) might be considered worth the expense. However, if the control group (the group that received only on-the-job training) did better or if the two groups did equally well, the dual-training approach would not be considered advantageous.

STATISTICS

Some data obtained through primary and secondary research pertain to people's likes and dislikes, their opinions and feelings; other data are of a more factual nature. Factual data presented in numerical form are referred to as **statistics.** Examples of statistics include the batting averages of ballplayers, the number of highway deaths in a year, and the number of ice cream cones eaten in August. Statistics are often expressed as percentages—an inflation rate of 17 percent, for instance.

Businesspeople rely on statistical information because of its relative precision and analytical value. Although they must be able to understand such statistics, they do not really need to be statisticians. Today many microcomputer software packages are available that allow even those who have little experience with statistics to analyze and interpret data.

Analyzing Data

Raw data—lists and tables of numbers—are of little practical value by themselves. Instead, they must be manipu-lated to bring forward certain key numbers, such as averages, index numbers, and trends.

Averages

One way to present data in an easily understood way is to find an **average,** a number typical of a group of numbers or quantities. A personnel manager may want to know the average wage of workers in each labor classification in order to make a forecast of future labor costs when a new union contract is negotiated. A marketing manager may want to know the average age of potential consumers of a new product in order to slant advertising toward that age group.

The most widely used averages are the mean, the median, and the mode. A single set of data may be used to produce all three. In Exhibit B.1, for example, the mean, median, and mode are different numbers, even though all three have been calculated on one week's performance by a sales force.

The Mean. The statistic most often thought of as an average is the **mean,** the sum of all the items in a group divided by the number of items in the group. The mean is invaluable when comparing one item or individual with a group.

For example, if a sales manager wants to compare the performance of her salespeople during a certain week, the mean would give a simple figure for comparison. She would begin with the basic data in Exhibit II.1 and then divide total sales by the number of salespeople:

$$\frac{\$63,000}{9} = \$7,000 \ mean \ sales \ for \ the \ week$$

Exhibit B.1
Mean, Median, and Mode
The same set of data can be used to produce three kinds of averages, each of which has important business applications.

Salesperson	Sales	
Wilson	$3,000	
Green	5,000	
Carrick	6,000	
Wimper	7,000	—Mean
Keeble	7,500	—Median
Kemble	8,500	
O'Toole	8,500	—Mode
Mannix	8,500	
Caruso	9,000	
Total	$63,000	

By this measure, Wimper's sales were average; the three people with sales below $7,000 were below average; the five with sales above $7,000 were above average. If some of the salespeople needed to be cut, the sales manager could base decisions on figures like these.

The advantages of the mean are ease of comprehension and speed of computation. One disadvantage is that the mean gives a distorted picture when there is an extreme value. For instance, if Caruso's sales for the week were $27,000, the mean for the nine salespeople would be $9,000 ($81,000 divided by 9). Because eight of the nine salespeople would have sold less than the mean, this calculation would be of little help to the sales manager.

The Median. When items or numbers are arranged from lowest to highest, as in Exhibit II.1, it is possible to find the **median**—the midpoint, or the point at which half the numbers are above and half are below. With an odd number of items, the median may be arrived at by inspection. In Exhibit II.1, for example, the median is $7,500. Four figures are above it and four are below. With an even number of items—say, 10 salespeople instead of 9—the midpoint would be the mean of the two central figures. The chief disadvantage of the median is that many people do not understand what it means. Moreover, it is cumbersome to arrange a large number of items in order of size.

With a limited number of items, the median is easy to find, and when items that are difficult to measure can be arranged in order of size, the median is a great time-saver. It also avoids the distortion caused by extreme values and thus gives a more accurate picture of the data. For example, if Caruso's sales were $27,000 instead of $9,000, the median would not be affected. If it were necessary to know the average amount spent on advertising by retail grocers, the figure used would probably be the median because the amounts spent by the big chains would not distort the average. In business, therefore, the median is a useful measure.

The Mode. The **mode** is the number that occurs most often in any series of data or observations. The mode answers the question, How frequently? or What is the usual size or amount? In the sales manager's study, the mode is $8,500.

One important use of the mode is to supply marketing information about common sizes of shoes and clothing. If you were the owner of a shoe store, you would not want to stock four pairs of every shoe size in each style. You might find that for every 40 pairs of size 8 sold, only 2 of size 12 were sold.

Like the median, the mode is not influenced by extreme values. The mode should not be used, however, when the total number of observations is small or when a large group is subdivided into many small groups. In such cases, a significantly repeated value may not exist, and there is no mode if a number does not appear more than once.

Index Numbers

In business, it is often important to know how results in one period compare with those of another. To express this comparison conveniently, an index number is used. An **index number** is a percentage that represents the amount of fluctuation between a base figure, such as a price or cost at one period, and the current figure.

Say an oil company wants to keep an index on the number of workers it employs. It chooses as a base year 1993, when it employed 5,000 workers. In 1994, employment slipped to 4,900 workers. In 1995, it surged to 5,300. The index numbers for the years 1994 and 1995 are obtained by dividing the base-year figure into the current-year figure and then multiplying by 100 to change the resulting decimal into a percentage:

$$\frac{\textit{Current-year employment (1994)}}{\textit{Base-year employment}} = \frac{4,900}{5,000} = 0.98, \textit{or } 98\%$$

$$\frac{\textit{Current-year employment (1995)}}{\textit{Base-year employment}} = \frac{5,300}{5,000} = 1.06, \textit{or } 106\%$$

These figures tell us that employment was off 2 percent in 1994 but up 6 percent in 1995.

One of the best-known index numbers is the Consumer Price Index, which is used by economists to track inflation. Others include the Dow Jones Industrial Average (which gauges ups and downs in the stock market), the Index of Industrial Production, and the Wholesale Price Index.

Trend Analysis

Managers must often determine whether the variations in business activity indicated by statistics have any regular pattern. Suppose that a department store's monthly index of sales shows an increase of 6 percent for December. Before the manager can decide whether to increase the number of sales clerks, the amount of inventory, and the advertising budget, he or she must know whether the increase in sales will continue into January and February and beyond.

Trend analysis, also known as time-series analysis, is the examination of data over a sufficiently long time so that regularities and relationships can be detected, interpreted, and used as the basis for forecasts of business activity. Such an analysis generally explains change in terms of three factors: seasonal variations, cyclical variations, and secular (or long-term) trends in business growth.

Seasonal Variations. A **seasonal variation** is a regular, predictable change over the course of a year. For instance, the demand for ice cream is always higher in August than in February. Two other examples are increased store sales during the winter holidays and the rise in sales of swimsuits when the temperature rises.

Businesses can sometimes use knowledge of seasonal variations to open up new markets in slack seasons. Mak-

APPENDIX B | RESEARCH, STATISTICAL ANALYSIS, AND REPORTS

ers of tea, for example, noticed that tea drinking fell off sharply at the end of winter. However, they wanted to maintain a constant labor and sales force; they wanted to avoid hiring extra workers in peak seasons and laying off workers in slack periods. So they successfully promoted iced tea to keep sales (and thus production) more evenly distributed throughout the year.

Cyclical Variations. Over a period of several years (often four), the economy goes through a fluctuation known as the business cycle, which is a familiar example of medium-term **cyclical variation.** The business cycle begins with prosperity, a period of high income and employment in which businesses grow and construction activity is high. Then follows a recession, during which income, employment, and production all fall. If sufficient corrective measures (usually by government regulation) are not taken, depression sets in. A depression is a radical drop in business activity with consequent high unemployment and frequent business failures. Generally, a depression is followed by recovery, which is characterized by a rise in production, construction, and employment. The cycle usually begins again. Government spending, wars, and inflation may temporarily disrupt this pattern, but eventually the cycle's phases are likely to return to normal.

An understanding of this cycle is important in financial management because investments yield various results in various economic climates. Cycles are also important in manufacturing and other capital-intensive businesses. Building an expensive new plant just before the economy hits a recession phase is dangerous because orders for the goods produced in it may not reach necessary levels for several years. If the plant is built at the tail end of a recession, however, the manufacturer will be ready to take advantage of the surge in demand that accompanies the recovery phase.

Secular Trends. A **secular trend** (or *long-term trend*) is a pattern of growth or decline in a particular industry or in a national economy over a long period, usually 20 or 30 years. Secular trends may result from changes in population, availability of capital, new technology and production methods, consumer habits and spending patterns, and so on. One familiar secular trend has been the decline in the demand for rail travel since the development of the automobile and airplane. Another is the upward trend the drug companies have been enjoying because of increased interest in health care. Managers study secular trends to plan for the long term, to compare their company's growth with that of other firms in the same industry, and to set standards for their own performance.

Interpreting Data

As useful as key numbers are in making business decisions, more sophisticated techniques may produce even more valuable statistics. Further calculations can reveal relationships between sets of data, suggest predictions, and help uncover the underlying factors that contribute to a wider range of findings. In effect, data analysis yields a picture; data interpretation yields a story.

One of the most common types of data interpretation is the calculation of a **correlation,** which is a relationship between two or more variables (changeable factors in a situation or experiment). Imagine that analysis has shown a decrease in worker productivity over the past year. It is possible, but not efficient, to think of all the variables that might have caused the change and then, one by one, construct experiments to test their relationship to the decrease. It costs far less and takes far less time to statistically compare the trends for all those variables with the trend in productivity to see whether any of them exhibit a similar pattern.

Correlations may be positive or negative. A **positive correlation** is one in which the trends travel in the same direction simultaneously. The decrease in productivity, for instance, may be positively correlated with workers' experience levels or with incentive pay scales; in other words, as experience levels or incentive pay scales go down, so does productivity. A **negative correlation,** on the other hand, is like a mirror image: The trends travel in opposite directions. If productivity goes down as the number of accidents goes up, the two variables are negatively correlated.

Correlations may point the way toward solutions, but remember that correlations do not indicate cause-and-effect relationships. They merely show that two variables change at the same time, not that change in one actually causes change in the other. Even though productivity drops when the number of accidents goes up, for instance, there is no evidence that accidents cause productivity declines or vice versa.

To predict or control business activity, it may be foolish to rely on a correlation without further interpretation. For example, a large department store noticed that its sales seemed to be positively correlated with the Dow Jones Industrial Average: An increase in the stock price index was regularly followed by a similar increase in the store's sales. After several years, however, the correlation suddenly turned negative: When the stock price index went up, store sales went down. Statisticians soon found the reason. The Dow Jones Industrial Average and the store's sales were both dependent variables related to a third variable, the state of the economy as a whole. When the economy started to decline, so did the store's sales (a positive correlation). However, the economy's health and stock prices were not so clearly correlated. Stock prices sometimes rose temporarily during periods of low prosperity. So the store managers realized that watching stock prices would not help them predict how well the business would do; there was no real cause-and-effect relationship between the two.

REPORTS

Even the most carefully planned and painstakingly prepared statistical research project may be a waste of time if the information is poorly presented. Written reports that highlight key research results must be clear and easy to follow. Tables and graphs help, and such visual aids may even be crucial to giving readers a clear picture of the situation.

Business-Report Format

A good business report has six parts:

- The *title* should be a brief description of the report as a whole rather than a catchy headline. The names of the authors and the date go under the title.
- The *introduction* should briefly state the subject of the report, the research techniques used, and the nature of the specific problem to be solved.
- The *conclusions*—the answers to the problem outlined in the introduction—should be presented concisely.
- *Recommendations*—suggestions on how the company might deal with the problem—should be practical, specific, and derived from the conclusions.
- The *body of the report* should present data to back up the conclusions and recommendations.

- *Appendixes* (which contain data not directly related to the problem), *notes* (which give additional information on points made in the body), and *sources* (which tell the reader where the information in the report was obtained) all go at the end of the report.

Sometimes the conclusions and recommendations follow the body of the report.

Tables and Diagrams

With all the graphics software available for computers, there is little reason not to present data in a form that has visual impact. Several types of diagrams are used to display relationships between data (see Exhibit B.2):

- A *line graph* is a line connecting points. Line graphs show trends, such as an increase in profits.
- A *bar chart* uses either vertical or horizontal bars to

Exhibit B.2
Diagrams Used in Business Reports

These types of diagrams—pie chart, line graph, bar chart, pictograph, and statistical map—are most often used to present business data.

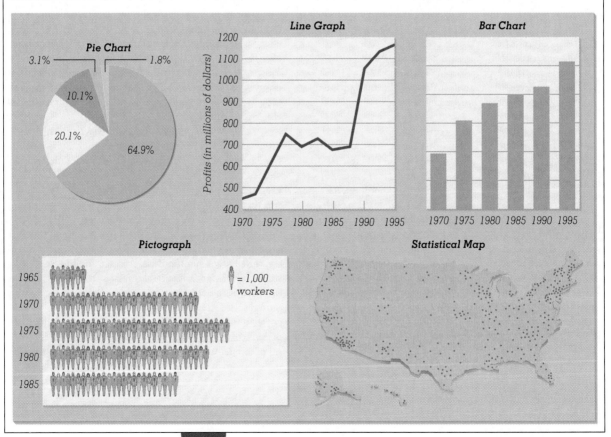

Gross Revenues by Source (in thousands of dollars)	1992*	1993	1994	1995
Entertainment and recreation	445,165	508,444	571,079	643,380
Motion pictures	118,058	152,135	134,785	161,400
Consumer products and other	66,602	80,564	90,909	109,725
TOTAL REVENUES	629,825	741,143	796,773	914,505

*Reclassified for comparative purposes and to comply with reporting requirements adopted in 1992.
Source: Company Annual Reports, 1992, 1993, 1994, 1995.

Exhibit B.3
The Parts of a Table
All tables, whether long or short, simple or complicated, contain a title, column heads (across the top), line heads (down the left side), and entries to complete the matrix. They may also include footnotes and a source note.

compare information. Because of its simplicity, the bar chart is frequently used in business reports.

- A *pictograph* is a variation of the bar chart, with symbols or pictures instead of bars used to represent data. Pictographs are good attention-getters, but using them can often mean sacrificing some accuracy.
- A *pie chart* is a circle divided into slices. The slices are labeled as percentages of the whole circle, or 100 percent. A pie chart provides a vivid picture of relationships, but it is not good for showing precise data.
- A *statistical map* shows both locations and quantities by variations in color, texture, or shading or by a concentration of dots. Like the pie chart, it shows general relationships better than it shows specifics.

A **table,** a grid of words and numbers, is commonly used to present data when there is a large amount of precise numerical information to convey. Exhibit B.3 shows the standard parts of a table.

Statistics and Honesty

Numbers don't lie, as the saying goes. However, it's also true that the people who collect and present numbers are not always as straightforward as they might be. Statistical findings are sometimes manipulated or juggled to make them appear in the best possible light. One of many such tactics is the use of precise, impressive-sounding statistics that may actually prove very little. An advertising agency may claim that half an ounce of an antiseptic killed 31,108 germs in a test tube in 11 seconds. However, an antiseptic that kills germs in a test tube may not work in the human body. Even if it does work in the human body, there may be so many thousands of germs in a comparable portion of the human anatomy that the ability to kill 31,108 is woefully inadequate.

Another juggling technique is the "shifting base." Suppose a store offers $10 Christmas gifts in October and urges customers to buy right away to save 50 percent. Save 50 percent of what? The store plans to increase the price to $20 in November, so the saving would be 50 percent of the coming markup, not of the advertised price. In neglecting to say what base the percentage was figured on, the store is being less than honest.

The people who misuse statistics cannot take all the blame, however. There are so many ways to analyze, interpret, and report numbers that judgment naturally becomes a big factor. Anyone in business (and, for that matter, any consumer) should therefore take some responsibility for understanding what the numbers are saying before making decisions that are based on those numbers.

KEY TERMS

average (B3)
correlation (B5)
cyclical variation (B5)
dependent variables (B3)
experiment (B2)
external data (B1)
independent variables (B2)
index number (B4)
internal data (B1)

mean (B3)
median (B4)
mode (B4)
negative correlation (B5)
observation (B2)
positive correlation (B5)
primary data (B1)
probability (B2)
random sampling (B2)

sample (B1)
seasonal variation (B4)
secondary data (B1)
secular trend (B5)
statistics (B3)
surveys (B2)
table (B7)
trend analysis (B4)
variables (B2)

REFERENCES

NOTES

CHAPTER 1

1. Carolyn M. Brown, "Coming Through in the Clutch," *Black Enterprise,* June 1994, 108–122.

2. U.S. Bureau of the Census, *Statistical Abstract of the United States: 1993,* 113th ed., (Washington, D.C.: U.S. Government Printing Office, 1993), 437.

3. U.S. Bureau of the Census, *Statistical Abstract of the United States: 1993,* 445, 841, 852.

4. Karen Pennar and Christopher Farrell, "Notes from the Underground Economy," *Business Week,* 15 February 1993, 98–101; Tibbett L. Speer, "Digging into the Underground Economy," *American Demographics,* February 1995, 15–16; Louis Winnick, "Invisible, Outlawed, and Untaxed: America's Underground Economy," *Public Interest,* Winter, 1995, 123.

5. Robert L. Heilbroner and Lester C. Thurow, *Economics Explained,* updated ed. (New York: Simon & Schuster, 1987), 27.

6. David Satter, "End of the Road in Magnitogorsk," *Wall Street Journal,* 6 May 1991, A12.

7. Jane Perlez, "Poland's New Entrepreneurs Push the Economy Ahead," *New York Times,* 20 June 1993, sec. f, 7; Michael Muth, "Marketing Still Inconsistent in Poland," *Marketing News,* 2 January 1995, 5; Anthony Robinson, "Portrait of an Entrepreneur," *Financial Times,* 28 March 1995, S5.

8. Bruce W. Nelan, "Watch Out for China," *Time,* 29 November 1993, 36–39; Clement K. W. Chow, "Evaluating Small Business Development in China's Retail Sector: An Empirical Analysis," *Journal of Small Business Management,* January 1995, 87–92; "Business Outlook: China," *Crossborder Monitor,* 5 April 1995, 7.

9. Richard Ringer, "Open Accounts: Bank of Montreal Trust Co. Offers Financial Haven for Hong Kong Émigrés," *North American International Business,* June 1992, 22.

10. Richard A Melcher, "Sweden Fights to Come in from the Cold," *Business Week,*

2 November 1992, 46–47; Christopher Knowlton, "The Triumph of the Market," *Fortune,* 14 January 1991, 14; Jeremy Main, "How Latin America Is Opening Up," *Fortune,* 6 April 1991, 84–88.

11. Andrew E. Serwer, "How to Escape a Price War," *Fortune,* 13 June 1994, 82–90; Courtland L. Bovée, Michael J. Houston, and John V. Thill, *Marketing* 2d ed. (New York: McGraw-Hill, 1995), 372; Deborah Gage, "Decisive Battle Has Yet to be Fought in Brutal Price Wars," *Computer Reseller News,* 13 February 1995, 79–84; Neal McGrath, "Parlaying Price Wars into Profit," *Asian Business,* January 1995, 10.

12. Serwer, "How to Escape a Price War," 82–90.

13. Serwer, "How to Escape a Price War," 82–90.

14. Robert F. Black, Don L. Boroughs, Sara Collins, and Kenneth Sheets, "Heavy Lifting," *U.S. News & World Report,* 6 May 1991, 54–55.

15. James F. Peltz, "Down but Not Out," *Los Angeles Times,* 26 September 1993, D1, D4.

16. Robert Pear, "In Bush Presidency, the Regulators Ride Again," *New York Times,* 28 April 1991, sec. 4, 5.

17. Gary Hoover, Alta Campbell, and Patrick J. Spain, eds., *Hoover's Handbook of American Business, 1994* (Austin, Tex.: Reference Press, 1994), 190, 752.

18. Alfred L. Malabre, Jr., "Business-Cycle Lens Helps Focus Slump," *Wall Street Journal,* 20 May 1991, A1.

19. Black et al., "Heavy Lifting," 52–61.

20. Patrick Bloomfield, "When Not Enough Looks Like Too Much: Increase in Short-Term Interest Rates by U.S. Federal Reserve Fails to Eliminate Inflationary Tendencies," *Financial Post,* 19 November 1994, 24.

21. Serwer, "How to Escape a Price War," 82–90.

22. Bovée, Houston, and Thill, *Marketing,* 133.

23. See note 1.

CHAPTER 2

1. Adapted from Seth Lubove, "We Have a Big Pond to Play In," *Forbes,* 13 September 1993, 216–218, 220, 222, 224; Subrata N. Chakravarty, "Victualler to the Resistance," *Forbes,* 9 December 1991, 172, 173; Allen R. Myerson, "Setting Up an Island in the Soviet Storm," *New York Times,* 30 December 1990, sec. 3, 1, 6; Anthony Ramirez, "Soviet Pizza Huts Have Local Flavor," *New York Times,* 11 September 1990, sec. C, 18; Mark Berniker, "Pizza Hut Succeeds in Soviet Challenge," *Journal of Commerce,* 10 September 1990, 1A, 5A; Stuart Elliot, "Pizza Hut Managers Drill Soviets in Art of Service," *USA Today,* 2 October 1990, 2B; "Red Tape Greets Moscow Pizza Hut," *USA Today,* 2 October 1990, 2B; Interview with Donald Kendall, "Go There and Get the Business," *Directors-Boards,* Winter 1991, 15–19; Mary E. Tomzack, "Ripe New Markets," *Success,* April 1995, 73–77; John R. Engen, "The Hole Story," *World Trade,* January-February 1995, 22–26; Mark L. Levine, "Risk and Reward: Russian Roulette or Different Paradigms?" *Appraisal Journal,* January 1995, 111–116.

2. Adapted from Barry Schiller, *The Economy Today,* 5th ed. (New York: McGraw-Hill, 1991) 856–857.

3. Michael E. Porter, "The Competitive Advantage of Nations," *Harvard Business Review,* March–April 1990, 73–93; Michael E. Porter, *Competitive Advantage of Nations* (New York: Free Press, 1990), 71; Elisabeth Farrell, "Flower Power," *Europe,* November 1993, 8–10; "Developing Competitive Advantage," *Business Africa,* 1 April 1995, 47; John H. Frair, "Competitive Advantage through Performance Innovation in a Competitive Market," *Journal of Product Innovation Management,* January 1995, 33–42; Kenneth B. Ackerman, Michael A. McGinnis, C.M. Kochunny, "Who Provides Competitive Advantage?" *Transportation & Distribution,* January 1995, 66–86.

4. Yves Doz, "International Industries: Fragmentation Versus Globalization," in

Global Strategic Management: The Essentials, 2d ed., edited by Heidi Vernon-Wortzel and Lawrence Wortzel (New York: Wiley, 1991), 20–34; Porter, *Competitive Advantage of Nations,* 14.

5. Robert Collison, "How Bata Rules the World," *Canadian Business,* September 1990, 28–34.

6. Louis Uchitelle, "Dollar's Decline as Export Engine," *New York Times,* 26 February 1991, sec. D, 2; Andrews E. Serwer, "The Dollar's Decline," *Fortune,* 3 April 1995, 16; Marjorie Coeyman, "Dollar's Decline Could Boost Earnings and Production in U.S.," *Chemical Week,* 15 May 1995, 8.

7. Robert B. Reich, "Who Is Us?" *Harvard Business Review,* January–February 1990, 53–64.

8. Paul Hofheinz, "Yes, You *Can* Win in Eastern Europe," *Fortune,* 16 May 1994, 110–112; "The Russian Investment Dilemma," *Harvard Business Review,* May–June 1994, 35–37, 40–44; Robert J. Bowman, "Are You Covered?" *World Trade,* March 1995, 100–104.

9. John J. Curran, "China's Investment Boom," *Fortune,* 7 March 1994, 116–118, 120, 122, 124; Pete Engardio, "Rising from the Ashes: Can Free Markets Turn Vietnam into a Tiger?" *Business Week,* 23 May 1994, 44–46, 48; J. Robert Warren, "Phillips Weighs China Investment," *Chemical Marketing Reporter,* 27 February 1995, 24.

10. Jim Powell, "Who Owns the U.S. and Does It Matter?" *World Monitor,* June 1990, 58–64.

11. Robert H. Bork, Jr., "'New Protectionism' to Fit the Times," *U.S. News & World Report,* 6 April 1987, 44; Caspar W. Weinberger, "The New Europe—Sovereignty, Protectionism, Politics," *Forbes,* 13 March 1995, 35; "Protectionism Won't Protect U.S." *Business Week,* 6 March 1995, 128.

12. Steven Greenhouse, "Trade Curbs: Do They Do the Job?" *New York Times,* 16 April 1992, sec. C, 1, 20.

13. Robert J. Shapiro, "A Battle Royal over Food," *U.S. News & World Report,* 23 May 1988, 56; Benjamin Fulford, "Rice Maneuvers," *Business Tokyo,* 1 September 1991, 28; Howard La Franchi, "Officials Hope to Resolve GATT," *The Christian Science Monitor,* 26 August 1991, 4; Robert J. Samuelson, "The Absurd Farm Bill," *Newsweek,* 6 August 1990, 51; Cindy Tursman, "GATT Revisited: Key Provisions of the Trade Pact," *Business Credit,* March 1995, 21–22.

14. Keith Bradsher, "As U.S. Urges Free Markets, Its Trade Barriers Are Many," *New York Times,* 7 February 1992, sec. A, 1, 11.

15. Nick Cumming-Bruce and James Popkin, "Apparatchiks and Entrepreneurs," *U.S. News & World Report,* 14 February 1994, 23–25.

16. Bork, "'New Protectionism' to Fit the Times," 45.

17. Robert L. Rose, "Latin Squeeze: Brazil's Moves to Curb Its Inflation Also Curb U.S. Concerns' Profits," *Wall Street Journal,* 25 July 1990, A1, A9.

18. F. Amanda DeBusk, "Dumping Laws Still Endanger the Deal," *New York Times,* 17 April 1994, sec. 3, 13.

19. Clemens P. Work and Robert F. Black, "Uncle Sam as Unfair Trader," *U.S. News and World Report,* 12 June 1989, 42–44.

20. Barbara Rudolph, "Megamarket," *Time,* 10 August 1992, 43–44; Hubert B. Herring, "Business Diary: Believe It or Not, a GATT Agreement (with Some Holes)," *New York Times,* 19 December 1993, sec. 3, 2; Peter Passell, "Adding Up the Trade Talks: Fail Now, Pay Later," *New York Times,* 16 December 1990, sec. 4, 3.

21. Robert J. Shapiro, "A Hidden Tax on All Our Houses," *U.S. News & World Report,* 21 March 1988, 52.

22. Edwin A. Finn, Jr., and Kathleen Healy, "We've Met the Enemy and They Are Us?" *Forbes,* 9 February 1987, 83.

23. Work and Black, "Uncle Sam as Unfair Trader," 42–44.

24. Roger Cohen, "After 7 Years, a Trade Accord: A Success, Although a Limited One," *New York Times,* 16 December 1993, sec. C, 1, 6; Clyde H. Farnsworth, "Trade Focus Has Changed," *New York Times,* 28 May 1991, sec. C, 1, 9.

25. Bernard Weinraub, "Clinton Spared Blame by Hollywood Officials," *New York Times,* 16 December 1993, sec. C, 1, 7; Cohen, "After 7 Years, a Trade Accord," *New York Times,* 16 December 1993, sec. C, 1, 6.

26. Tim Lang and Colin Hines, "GATT: The Pitfalls Amid the Promise," *New York Times,* 17 April 1994, sec. 3, 13; R. C. Longworth, "World Trade System Won't Be the Same After Failure of GATT Talks," *San Diego Union,* 9 December 1990, A-2, A-19.

27. Bruce Barnard, "GATT Succeeds," *Europe,* February 1994, 20–21.

28. Keith Bradsher, "As Global Talks Stall, Regional Trade Pacts Multiply," *New York Times,* 23 August 1992, sec. A, 3, 5; "Ambition Giving Way to Reality," *San Diego Union,* 23 June 1991, I-1, I-8; Mark M. Nelson and Martin Du Bois, "Pact Extends Europe's Common Market," *Wall Street Journal,* 23 October 1991, A12.

29. Anthony DePalma, "G.M. Coloring Mexico with Chevys," *New York Times,* 12 May 1994, sec. C, 1, 4.

30. "CEO Survey: North America Inc.," *Across the Board,* March 1994, 13–14; Geri Smith, "NAFTA: Green Light for Red Tape," *Business Week,* 25 July 1994, 48.

31. Bob Davis, "Global Paradox: Growth of Trade Binds Nations, But It Also Can Spur Separatism," *Wall Street Journal,* 20 June 1994, A1, A6; Rudolph, "Megamarket," 43–44; Peter Truell, "Free Trade May Suffer from Regional Blocs," *Wall Street Journal,* 1 July 1991, A1; "Grand Illusions," *Economist,* 4 March 1995, 87.

32. John W. Wright, ed., *The Universal Almanac, 1991* (Kansas City, Mo.: Andrews and McMeel, 1990), 322; "To Him That Hath Not," *The Economist,* 27 April 1991, 82; "Poor Countries Victim of U.S. Budget Deals," *Forbes,* 2 September 1991, 37.

33. Mark Robichaux, "Federal Export Programs Overlap Despite Changes," *Wall Street Journal,* 26 June 1991, B1.

34. Michael R. Czinkota, Ilkka A. Ronkainen, and Michael H. Moffett, *International Business,* 3d ed. (Fort Worth, Tex.: Dryden Press, 1994), 223.

35. Robert Keatley, "U.S. Firms Bemoan Their Disadvantage Vying for Foreign Work Without Bribes," *Wall Street Journal,* 10 June 1994, A7.

36. James Bennet, "Mercedes Selects Alabama Site," *New York Times,* 30 September 1993, sec. C, 1, 6.

37. Robert W. Casey, "Should You Be Competing in the Global Marketplace?" *Working Woman,* October 1988, 58–66.

38. Susan Dentzer, "The Coming Global Boom," *U.S. News & World Report,* 16 July 1990, 22–28.

39. Press release, Export Now, 1988.

40. Rob Norton, "Strategies for the New Export Boom," *Fortune,* 22 August 1994, 124–127, 129–130.

41. Carol Steinberg, "Franchise Fever," *World Trade,* July 1992, 86, 88, 90–91; John O'Dell, "Franchising America," *Los Angeles Times,* 25 June 1989, sec. IV, 1, 5; "Padgett Surveys Franchise/Small Business Sectors," *Franchising World,* March/April 1995, 46; John Stansworth, "Penetrating the Myths Surrounding Franchise Failure Rates— Some Old Lessons for New Businesses," *International Small Business Journal,* January– March 1995, 59–63; Laura Koss-Feder, "Building Better Franchise Relations," *Hotel & Motel Management,* 6 March 1995, 18.

42. Mel Mandell, "Get It Together!" *World Trade,* July 1993, 36-38, 40; Carla Kruytbosch, "Let's Make a Deal," *International Business,* March 1993, 92–94, 96.

43. Maria Shao, Robert Neff, and Jeffrey Ryser, "For Levi's, a Flattering Fit Overseas," *Business Week,* 5 November 1990, 76–77.

44. Kerry Pechter, "Buying America," *International Business,* December 1993, 57–58, 60, 62, 64, 66.

45. William C. Symonds, "High-Tech Star," *Business Week,* 27 July 1992, 54–58.

46. Floris A. Maljers, "Inside Unilever: The Evolving Transnational Company," *Harvard Business Review,* September–October 1992, 46–51; "Re-engineering a Unilever Unit with HR Help," *Business Europe,* March 20, 1995, 7; David Teather, "Does Unilever's Move Mean Direct Success?" *Marketing,* 23 February 1995, 9.

47. Hiroto Oyama, "No Competition?" *Look Japan,* January 1993, 4–8.

48. Maljers, "Inside Unilever," 46–51.

49. See note 1.

CHAPTER 3

1. Adapted from Emily DeNitto, "Ben & Jerry's & Spike & Smooth," *Advertising Age,* 21 March 1994, 3, 42; *Ben & Jerry's Homemade 1993 Annual Report;* Suein L. Hwang, "While Many Competitors See Sales Melt, Ben & Jerry's Scoops Out Solid Growth," *Wall Street Journal,* 25 May 1993, B1, B5; Betsy Wiesendanger, "Ben & Jerry Scoop Up Credibility," *Public Relations Journal,* August 1993, 20; Carolyn Friday, "Cookies, Cream 'n' Controversy," *Newsweek,* 5 July 1993, 40; Leonard L. Drey, "Making a Difference: Ice Cream Meets Charity in Harlem," *New York Times,* 21 February 1993, sec. 3, 13; Justin Burke, "Russia Gets a Triple Dip of 'Caring Capitalism,'" *Christian Science Monitor,* 5 March 1993, 8; Suzanne Alexander, "Life's Just a Bowl of Cherry Garcia for Ben & Jerry's," *Wall Street Journal,* 15 July 1992, B3; Erik Larson, "Forever Young," *Inc.,* July 1988, 50; Steven S. Ross, "Green Groceries," *Mother Jones,* February–March 1989, 48; Mark Bittman, "Ben & Jerry's Caring Capitalism," *Restaurant Business,* 20 November 1990, 132; Bill Kelley, "The Cause Effect," *Food and Beverage Marketing* 9 (2 March 1990): 20; Ellie Winninghoff, "Citizen Cohen," *Mother Jones,* January 1990, 12; Jeanne Wegner, "This Season, Sharp-Dressed Dairy Products Are Wearing Green," *Dairy Foods,* September 1990, 72; Therese R. Welter, "Industry and the Environment: A Farewell to Arms," *Industry Week,* 20 August 1990, 36; Warren Thayer, "Ben & Jerry's New CEO Eyes Global Expansion," *Frozen Food Age,* March 1995, 1, 38; "Ben & Jerry's," *Marketing Week,* 3 February 1995, 46; Pat Sloan, "Yo! Ben & Jerry's Finds a CEO with Taste for Verse," *Advertising Age,* 6 February 1995, 4.

2. Marjorie Kelly, "Musings: A Copernican Revolution in Corporate Governance," *Business Ethics,* March–April 1994, 6.

3. Frank Edward Allen, "McDonald's to Reduce Waste in Plan Developed with Environmental Group," *Wall Street Journal,* 17 April 1991, B1, B2; Joan S. Lublin, "'Green' Executives Find Their Mission Isn't a Natural Part of Corporate Culture," *Wall Street Journal,* 5 March 1991, B1, B8.

4. William H. Miller, "Those Stingy American Companies," *Industry Week,* 21 January 1991, 48–53.

5. See letters in *New York Times,* 25 August 1918, and *New York Herald,* 1 October 1918.

6. Louis Harris, *Inside America* (New York: Vintage, 1987), 235.

7. Marjorie Kelly, "Business and the Decline of Kings," *Business Ethics,* October 1993, 6–7.

8. John McCormick and Marc Levinson, "The Supply Police," *Newsweek,* 15 February 1993, 48–49.

9. Peter F. Drucker, *The Age of Discontinuity* (New York: Harper Torchbooks, 1978), 206–207.

10. "U.S. Spends Big to Clean Up Pollution," *San Diego Union,* 23 December 1990, A-1, A-18; "$40 Billion Reported Spent on Illegal Drugs," *San Diego Union,* 20 June 1991, A-2.

11. Amal Kumar Naj, "Can $100 Billion Have 'No Material Effect' on Balance Sheets?" *Wall Street Journal,* 11 May 1988, A1.

12. Gregg Easterbrook, "Cleaning Up," *Newsweek,* 24 July 1989, 27–42.

13. Rose Gutfeld, "For Each Dollar Spent on Clean Air Someone Stands to Make a Buck," *Wall Street Journal,* 29 October 1990, A1; "Clean Air Car Fight Will Hit Fleet Buy," *Purchasing,* 6 April 1995, 21–23.

14. Sam Atwood, "Superfund: Boon or Bust? Debate Rages On," *USA Today,* 22 April 1991, 9E; John F. Spisak, "Superfund's Second Chance," *Environment Today,* 32 March 1995, 4; Catherine Cooney, "Superfund Heads for Front Burner," *Environment Today,* March 1995, 3, 14.

15. Timothy Noah, "EPA Declares 'Passive' Smoke a Human Carcinogen," *Wall Street Journal,* 6 January 1993, B1, B5.

16. *The World Almanac and Book of Facts, 1991* (New York: Pharos Books, 1990), 249.

17. Jeremy Main, "The Big Cleanup Gets It Wrong," *Fortune,* 20 May 1991, 95–96, 100–101.

18. Barbara Rosewicz, "Americans Are Willing to Sacrifice to Reduce Pollution, They Say," *Wall Street Journal,* 20 April 1990, A1.

19. Dick Thompson, "Giving Greed a Chance," *Time,* 12 February 1990, 67–68.

20. Linda Himelstein, "A Warning Shot to Scare Polluters Straight," *Business Week,* 22 November 1993, 60.

21. David Kirkpatrick, "Environmentalism: The New Crusade," *Fortune,* 12 February 1990, 44–53; Bradford A. McKee, "Environmental Activists Inc.," *Nation's Business,* August 1990, 27–29.

22. Faye Rice, "Next Steps for the Environment," *Fortune,* 19 October 1992, 98–99; Philip Shabecoff, "In Search of a Better Law," *New York Times,* 14 May 1989, sec. 4, 1, 5.

23. Barbara Rosewicz, "Price Tag Is Producing Groans Already," *Wall Street Journal,* 29 October 1990, A6.

24. Easterbrook, "Cleaning Up," 27–42.

25. Gutfeld, "For Each Dollar Spent," A1, A6.

26. "Life Ever After," *Economist,* 9 October 1993, 77; Emily T. Smith, "Growth vs. Environment," *Business Week,* 11 May 1992, 66–75; "Jobs versus Environment: Is There Really a Trade-off?" *Occupational Hazards,* March 1995, 67–68; Evan Goldstein, "Jobs or the Environment? No Trade-Off," *Challenge,* January/February 1995, 41–45.

27. Easterbrook, "Cleaning Up," 27–42.

28. Barnaby J. Feder, "In the Clutches of the Superfund Mess," *New York Times,* 16 June 1991, sec. 3, 1, 6.

29. Peter Hong, "The Toxic Waste Called Superfund," *Business Week,* 11 May 1992, 32–33.

30. Feder, "Superfund Mess," sec. 3, 6; Atwood, "Superfund," 9E; "Throwing Good Money After Bad Water Yields Scant Improvement," *Wall Street Journal,* 15 May 1991, A1, A6.

31. John H. Sheridan, "Pollution Prevention Picks Up Steam," *Industry Week,* 17 February 1992, 36–37, 40, 42–43.

32. Bobbi Igneizi, "The Enforcer," *San Diego Union,* 9 May 1989, C-1, C-2.

33. James R. Healey, "Audi Drives to Polish Its Image," *USA Today,* 23 March 1988, 1B, 2B.

34. Steven Waldman, "Kids in Harm's Way," *Newsweek,* 18 April 1988, 48.

35. Laura Shapiro, "The War of the Labels," *Newsweek,* 5 October 1992, 63, 66.

36. John Carey and Zachary Schiller, "The FDA Is Swinging 'a Sufficiently Large Two-by-Four,'" *Business Week,* 27 May 1991, 44; Barbara Presley Noble, "After Years of Deregulation, a New Push to Inform the Public," *New York Times,* 27 October 1991, sec. f, 5; Marian Burros, "F.D.A. Plans to Take the Fantasy out of Labels," *New York Times,* 18 September 1991, sec. b, 1, 6.

37. Patricia Sellers, "How to Handle Customers' Gripes," *Fortune,* 24 October 1988, 88–100.

38. "Denny's Does Some of the Right Things," *Business Week,* 6 June 1994, 42; "Making Amends at Denny's," *Business Week,* 21 November 1994, 47; Mark Lowery, "Denny's New Deal Ends Blackout," *Black Enterprise,* 20 February 1995, 43.

39. Joel Russel, "Mentor-Protégé: A Difficult Birth," *Hispanic Business,* September 1991, 26, 28, 30.

40. Alan Farnham, "Holding Firm on Affirmative Action," *Fortune,* 13 March 1989, 87, 88; Don Munro, "The Continuing Evolution of Affirmative Action Under Title VII: New Directions After the Civil Rights Act of 1991," Virginia Law Review, March 1995, 565–610; "Congress to Review Affirmative Action," *HRMagazine,* 4 April 1995, 12; "Affirmative Football," *Economist,* 14 January 1995, 78; Alfred Edmond, "25 Years of Affirmative Action," *Black Enterprise,* February 1995, 156–157.

41. Alice Cuneo, "Diverse by Design," *Business Week Reinventing America 1992,* 72; Jo McIntyre, "They Just Did It," *Business Ethics,* March–April 1994, 14.

42. "Burger King Plan," *New York Times,* 7 December 1993, sec. C, 7.

43. Sylvia Nasar, "Women's Gains Will Keep Coming," *U.S. News & World Report,* 2 April 1990, 45; Charlene Marmer Solomon, "Careers Under Glass," *Personnel Journal,* April 1990, 97–105.

44. James Aley, "The Pay Gap Narrows, But . . . .," *Fortune,* 19 September 1994, 32.

45. Amy Saltzman, "Trouble at the Top," *U.S. News & World Report,* 17 June 1991, 40–48.

46. Saltzman, "Trouble at the Top," 40–48.

47. Susan E. Tifft, "Board Gains," *Working Woman,* February 1994, 37–39, 70, 74.

48. Amy Saltzman, "Family Friendliness," *U.S. News & World Report,* 22 February 1993, 59–60, 63–66.

49. Susan Crawford, "A Wink Here, a Leer There: It's Costly," *New York Times,* sec. C, 28 March 1993, 17; Elizabeth Kolbert, "Sexual Harassment at Work Is Pervasive, Survey Suggests," *New York Times,* 11 October 1991, sec. a, 1, 11.

50. Helen Winternitz, "Anita Hill: One Year Later," *Working Woman,* September 1992, 21.

51. Joann S. Lublin, "Companies Try a Variety of Approaches to Halt Sexual Harassment on the Job," *Wall Street Journal,* 11 October, 1991, B1, B10; Stephanie Strom, "Many Companies Assailed on Sex Harassment Rates," *New York Times,* 20 October 1991, sec. C, 1, 15; Gerald D. Bloch, "Avoiding Liability for Sexual Harassment," *HRMagazine,* April 1995, 91–97; Janice A. Huebner, "How to Avoid Sexual Harassment Traps," *HR Focus,* March 1995, 15–16; Sharon Nelton, "Sexual Harassment: Reducing the Risks," *Nation's Business,* March 1995, 24–26.

52. Robert Pear, "U.S. Proposes Rules to Bar Obstacles for the Disabled," *New York Times,* 22 January 1991, sec. a, 1, 12.

53. Otto Johnson, ed., *The 1991 Information Please Almanac* (Boston: Houghton Mifflin, 1990), 818; Ron Winslow, "Safety Group Cites Fatalities Linked to Work," *Wall Street Journal,* 31 August 1990, B8.

54. Milo Geyelin, "Study Faults Federal Effort to Enforce Worker Safety," *Wall Street Journal,* 28 April 1989, B1.

55. Dana Milbank, "Companies Turn to Peer Pressure to Cut Injuries as Psychologists Join the Battle," *Wall Street Journal,* 29 March 1991, B1, B3.

56. Jane Bryant Quinn, "Why Tele-Crooks Are Still on the Line," *Washington Post,* 25 March 1990, H11.

57. Earl C. Gottschalk, Jr., "Con Artists Charged in California Sting," *Wall Street Journal,* 26 April 1991, C1, C16.

58. Kent Hodgson, "Adapting Ethical Decisions to a Global Marketplace," *Management Review,* May 1992, 53–57.

59. Kevin Kelly and Joseph Weber, "When a Rival's Trade Secret Crosses Your Desk . . . ," *Business Week,* 20 May 1991, 48.

60. Lynn Sharp Paine, "Managing for Organizational Integrity," *Harvard Business Review,* March–April 1994, 106–117; Gregory A. Patterson, "Sears Gets a Harsh Lesson from States in Handling of Auto-Repair Inquiries," *Wall Street Journal,* 2 October 1992, A7A.

61. Susan Gaines, "Handing Out Halos," *Business Ethics,* March–April 1994, 20–24.

62. Timothy D. Schellhardt, "What Bosses Think About Corporate Ethics," *Wall Street Journal,* 6 April 1988, B25.

63. Christopher Caggiano, "The Inc. Fax-Poll: Can You Afford to Be Ethical?" *Inc.,* December 1992, 16.

64. Manuel Velasquez, Dennis J. Mober, and Gerald F. Cavanagh, "Organizational Statesmanship and Dirty Politics: Ethical Guidelines for the Organizational Politician," *Organizational Dynamics,* Autumn 1983, 67–74.

65. Margaret Kaeter, "The 5th Annual Business Ethics Awards for Excellence in Ethics," *Business Ethics,* December 1993, 26–29.

66. Stanley J. Modic, "Corporate Ethics: From Commandments to Commitment," *Industry Week,* 14 December 1987, 34.

67. Janet Bamford, "Changing Business as Usual," *Working Woman,* November 1993, 62-65, 99, 106, 108–110.

68. Gaines, "Handing Out Halos," 20–24.

69. See note 1.

CHAPTER 4

1. Alan Chai, Alta Campbell, and Patrick J. Spain, eds., *Hoover's Handbook of American Business, 1994* (Austin, Tex.: Reference Press, 1994), 242–243, 334–335; Anne B. Fisher, "How to Make a Merger Work," *Fortune,* 24 January 1994, 66–78.

2. John S. McClenahen and Perry Pascarella, "America's New Economy," *Industry Week,* 26 January 1987, 30.

3. James L. Heskett, "Lessons in the Service Sector," *Harvard Business Review,* March–April 1987, 118–126; Mohammed F. Khayum, "The Impact of Service Sector Growth on Intersectoral Linkages in the United States," *Service Industries Journal,* January 1995, 35–49; David F. Burgess, "Is Trade Liberalization in the Service Sector in the National Interest?" *Oxford Economic Papers,* January 1995, 70–78.

4. *Statistical Abstract of the United States, 1993* (Washington, D.C.: GPO, 1993), 410.

5. *Statistical Abstract of the United States, 1993,* 410.

6. "The Fitness Market Follows Consumers into Middle Age," *Market: Europe,* November 1991, 8–9.

7. *Statistical Abstract of the United States, 1990* (Washington, D.C.: GPO, 1990), 380; "Labor Force Status of the Population: 1870 to 1970," *Historical Statistics of the United States: Colonial Times to 1970,* Pt. 1 (Washington, D.C.: GPO, 1975), 127–128.

8. Courtland L. Bovée, Michael J. Houston, and John V. Thill, *Marketing,* 2d ed. (New York: McGraw-Hill, 1995), 301.

9. *Statistical Abstract of the United States, 1988* (Washington, D.C.: GPO, 1987), 385.

10. Steven Solomon, *Small Business USA* (New York: Crown, 1986), 28.

11. Felicity Barringer, "What America Did After the War: A Tale Told by the Census," *New York Times,* 2 September 1990, sec. 4, 5.

12. Chai, Campbell, and Spain, eds., *Hoover's Handbook of American Business, 1994,* 96.

13. Walter Guzzardi, "Big Can Still Be Beautiful," *Fortune,* 25 April 1988, 50.

14. Solomon, *Small Business USA,* 27.

15. Lamar James, "Farmers Appear to Be Dwindling," *Arkansas Gazette,* 4 August 1991, 10F; "Farmers Speak Out," *Agri Marketing,* March 1995, 6; Owen Roberts, "I've Never Met So Many Real Farmers," *Agri Marketing,* February 1995, 20–22.

16. *Statistical Abstract of the United States, 1993,* 531.

17. Chai, Campbell, and Spain, eds., *Hoover's Handbook of American Business, 1994,* 544–545; Nina Barnett, "All Set to Bounce Back," *Fortune,* 22 April 1991, 281; *Census and You* (Washington, D.C.: GPO, March 1991), 3.

18. Brain L. Schorr, "LLCs: A New Form of Ownership," *Small Business Reports,* October 1991, 43–46; George Livanos, "LLCs: The Entity of the Future?" *CPA Journal,* March 1995, 66–67.

19. Brett Duval Fromson, "The Big Owners Roar," *Fortune,* 30 July 1990, 67.

20. Judith H. Dobrzynski, Michael Schroeder, Gregory L. Miles, and Joseph Weber, "Taking Charge," *Business Week,* 3 July 1989, 66.

21. Michael Galen, "A Seat on the Board Is Getting Hotter," *Business Week,* 3 July 1989, 72; "Boards Should Get Their Hands Dirty," *Business Week,* 20 April 1992, 126; Robert J. McCartney, "GM Shift May Signal Surge of Outside Director Activism," *Washington Post,* 8 April 1992, C1+; Melissa Schoor and Lisa Kalis, "Corporate Boards: The Way They Still Are," *Working Woman,* April 1995, 11.

22. Chai, Campbell, and Spain, eds., *Hoover's Handbook of American Business, 1994,* 544–545, 640–641; Dobrzynski et al., "Taking Charge," 66.

23. John Forbis and William Adams, "Corporate Victims of the Eighties," *Across the Board,* December 1990, 16.

24. John S. McClenahen, "Alliances for Competitive Advantage," *Industry Week,* 24 August 1987, 34.

25. Michael W. Miller, "Race to Develop HDTV Narrows to Five Plans," *Wall Street Journal,* 24 March 1992, B1; Philip Elmer-Dewitt, "The Picture Suddenly Gets Clearer," *Time,* 30 March 1992, 54–55.

26. Robert England, "The Takeover Tug-of-War Continues," *Insight,* 28 December–4 January 1988, 40; Dennis C. Meuller, "Corporate Takeovers and Productivity," *Journal of Finance,* March 1995, 383–387.

27. Thomas McCarroll and William McWhirter, "The Proxy Punch-Out," *Time,* 16 April 1990, 41; Vineeta Anand, "Shareholders Switch Proxy Battle Tactics," *Pensions & Investments,* 3 April 1995, 25, 26.

28. Fisher, "Make a Merger Work," 66–78.

29. Michael Oneal, Brian Bremner, Jonathan B. Levine, Todd Vogel, Zachary Schiller, and David Woodruff, "The Best and Worst Deals of the '80s," *Business Week,* 15 January 1990, 52.

30. Dave Savona, "The Crossborder M&A Rush," *International Business,* April 1994,

28–30; Joseph Weber, Joan O'C. Hamilton, Gail Edmondson, and Paul Dwyer, "Drug-Merger Mania," *Business Week,* 16 May 1994, 30–31; Linda Grant, "The Decade of Strategic Mergers," *U.S. News & World Report,* 28 March 1994, 16.

31. William M. Bulkeley, "Comglonerates Make a Surprising Comeback—With a '90s Twist," *Wall Street Journal,* 1 March 1994, A1, A11.

32. Chai, Campbell, and Spain, eds., *Hoover's Handbook of American Business, 1994,* 282–283, 300–301, 560–561, 724–725.

33. See note 1.

CHAPTER 5

1. Adapted from Patrick J. Spain, Alta Campbell, and Alan Chai, eds., *Hoover's Handbook of Emerging Companies, 1993–1994* (Austin, Tex.: Reference Press, 1993), 335; *Staples, Inc., Annual Report 1992;* Steven Flax, "Perils of the Paper Clip Trade," *New York Times Magazine,* 11 June 1989, 65; "Staples Inc.," *Boston Business Journal,* 8 October 1990, 26; Stephen D. Solomon, "Born to Be Big," *Inc.,* June 1989, 94; Michael Barrier, "Tom Stemberg Calls the Office," *Nation's Business,* July 1990, 42; David Rottenberg, "Staples' Top Gun," *Boston Magazine,* December 1987, 91–97; "Staples Inc.," *New York Times,* 25 February 1992, sec. c, 4; "Staples Moves to Purchase 10 Workplace Stores in Fla.," *HFD-The Weekly Home Furnishings Newspaper,* 2 March 1992, 6; "Staples Inc.," *Wall Street Journal,* 3 February 1992, B4; James A. McConville, "Staples Head Still Sees Growth," *HFD-The Weekly Home Furnishings Newspaper,* 18 October 1993, 103–104; Dave Schwzb, "Office Supply Megastores Stick Staples in Little Guys," *San Diego Business Journal,* 20 March 1995, 1–2.

2. Rod Riggs, "Getting Business off the Ground Is Not a Small Job," *San Diego Union,* 31 May 1994, C1.

3. "Matters of Fact," *Inc.,* April 1985, 32.

4. *Statistical Abstract of the United States, 1993,* 113th ed., (Washington D.C.: U.S. GPO, 1993), 396, 402.

5. Steven Solomon, *Small Business USA* (New York: Crown, 1986), 18.

6. Maria Zate, "On a Course of Prosperity," *Hispanic Business,* April 1994, 50–56; Wendy Zellner, "Women Entrepreneurs," *Business Week,* 18 April 1994, 104–110.

7. Brian O'Reilly, "The New Face of Small Business," *Fortune,* 2 May 1994, 82–88; "Small Business Group Continues to Press Its Agenda," *CPA Journal,* March 1995, 8; Peter Crawford, "Some Myths about Small Business," *New Zealand Manufacturer,* February 1995, 13.

8. O'Reilly, "New Face," 82–88.

9. Lisa J. Moore and Sharon F. Golden, "You Can Plan to Expand or Just Let It Happen," *U.S. News & World Report,* 23 October 1989, 78; John Case, "The Origins of Entrepreneurship," *Inc.,* June 1989, 56.

10. Mark Robichaux, "Business First, Family Second," *Wall Street Journal,* 12 May 1989, B1.

11. Roger Ricklefs, "Road to Success Becomes Less Littered with Failures," *Wall Street Journal,* 10 November 1989, B2.

12. Case, "The Origins of Entrepreneurship," 54, 62.

13. David Wessel and Buck Brown, "The Hyping of Small-Firm Job Growth," *Wall Street Journal,* 8 November 1988, B1.

14. Edward O. Welles, "It's Not the Same America," *Inc.,* May 1994, 82–98.

15. Solomon, *Small Business USA,* 74–75.

16. Janice Castro, "Big vs. Small," *Time,* 5 September 1988, 49; Solomon, *Small Business USA,* 124.

17. Stuart Gannes, "America's Fastest-Growing Companies," *Fortune,* 23 May 1988, 30.

18. Shelly Branch, "How Hip-Hop Fashion Won Over Mainstream America," *Black Enterprise,* June 1993, 111–120.

19. Joseph W. Duncan, "The True Failure Rate of Start-Ups," *D&B Reports,* January–February 1994; Maggie Jones, "Smart Cookies," *Working Woman,* April 1995, 50–52+.

20. Zellner, "Women Entrepreneurs," 104–110.

21. Briane Dumaine, "America's Smart Young Entrepreneurs," *Fortune,* 21 March 1994, 34–48.

22. Ricklefs, "Road to Success" B2.

23. J. Tol Broome, Jr., "How to Write a Business Plan," *Nation's Business,* February 1993, 29–30; Albert Richards, "The Ernst & Young Business Plan Guide," *R & D Management,* April 1995, 253; David Lanchner, "How Chitchat Became a Valuable Business Plan," *Global Finance,* February 1995, 54–56; Marguerita Ashby-Berger, "My Business Plan—and What Really Happened," *Small Business Forum,* Winter 1994/1995, 24–35.

24. Amar Bhide, "How Entrepreneurs Craft Strategies That Work," *Harvard Business Review,* March–April 1994, 150–161.

25. "The 1990 Guide to Small Business," *U.S. News & World Report,* 23 November 1989, 78.

26. Ronaleen R. Roha, "Raising Money for Your Small Business," *Changing Times,* May 1990, 47.

27. Ronaleen R. Roha, "Big Loans for Small Businesses," *Changing Times,* April 1989, 105–109; "Small Loans, Big Problems," *Economist,* 28 January 1995, 73; Elizabeth Kadetsky, "Small Loans, Big Dreams," *Working Woman,* February 1995, 46–49; Reid Rutherford, "Securitizing Small-Business Loans: A Banker's Action Plan," *Commercial Lending Review,* Winter 1994/1995, 62–74.

28. Roha, "Big Loans for Small Businesses," 105.

29. Monua Janah, "'Angels' Find Financing Start-Ups Isn't So Heavenly," *Wall Street Journal,* 4 June 1990, B2.

30. Caryne Brown, "The Best Ways to Finance Your Business," *Black Enterprise,* June 1993, 270–278.

31. Udayan Gupta, "How Big Companies Are Joining Forces with Little Ones for Mutual Advantage," *Wall Street Journal,* 25 February 1991, B1.

32. Martha E. Mangelsdorf, "Inc.'s Guide to 'Smart' Government Money," *Inc.,* August 1989, 51.

33. David Riggle, "Great Places to Grow a Business," *In Business,* September–October 1990, 20–22.

34. Data provided by the National Business Incubation Association, 153 South Hanover Street, Carlisle, PA 17013.

35. David L. James, "When the Going Gets Public," *Small Business Reports,* October 1989, 31; Moore and Golden, "You Can Plan to Expand," 77; Udayan Gupta, "The Art of Going Public," *Black Enterprise,* June 1985, 191.

36. Courtland L. Bovée, John V. Thill, Marian B. Wood, and George P. Dovel, *Management,* (New York: McGraw-Hill, 1993), 393.

37. Jeremy Main, "Why Franchising Is Taking Off," *Fortune,* 12 February 1990, 124; Meg Whittemore, "Four Paths to Franchising," *Nation's Business,* October 1989, 1; Echo Montgomery Garrett, "The Game Plan: Jack-Rabbit Growth versus Slow and Steady Franchising," *Inc.,* April, 1995, 121+; Laura Koss-Feder, "Consultants Offer Opinions on Franchising," *Hotel & Motel Management,* March 6, 1995, 33; Laura Koss-Feder, "Looking at Franchising's Future," *Hotel & Motel Management,* 6 March 1995, 17; Meg Whittemore, "New Directions in Franchising," *Nation's Business,* January 1995, 45.

38. Nancy Croft Baker, "Franchising into the '90s," *Nation's Business,* March 1990, 61.

39. Eric S. Hardy, "Franchise Primer," *Forbes,* 15 August 1994, 141.

40. Meg Whittemore, *Growth Opportunities in Franchising* (Washington, D.C.: International Franchise Association).

41. Buck Brown, "Franchisers Now Offer Direct Financial Aid," *Wall Street Journal,* 6 February 1989, B1.

42. Kevin McDermott, "The Hard Facts About Franchising," *D&B Reports,* September–October 1993, 36–38.

43. Constance Mitchell, "Franchising Fever Spreads," *USA Today,* 13 September 1985, 4B.

44. See note 1.

45. "United States of America," Microsoft® Encarta. Copyright © 1994 Microsoft Corporation. Copyright © 1994 Funk & Wagnall's Corporation.

CHAPTER 6

1. Adapted from "How Bill Gates Sees the Future," *Fortune,* 28 June 1993, 10; T. R. Reid, "The Future According to Gates: Reign and Sunshine for Microsoft," *Washington Post,* 9 March 1992, WB18; Rich Karlgaard, "Bill Gates," *Forbes ASAP,* 7 December 1992, 63–64, 66, 70–72, 74; Brenton R.

Schlender, "Bill Gates Sets a New Target," *Fortune,* 25 February 1991, 12–13; *Microsoft Corporation 1990 Annual Report,* 1–18; *Microsoft Corporation 1992 Annual Report,* 3–7; Evelyn Richards, "A Hard-Nosed Businessman with a Certain Boyish Charm," *Washington Post,* 30 December 1990, H3; Carrie Tuhy and Greg Couch, "Software's Old Man Is 30," *Money,* July 1986, 54–55; Brenton R. Schlender, "How Bill Gates Keeps the Magic Going," *Fortune,* 18 June 1990, 82–86, 88–89; G. Pascal Zachary, "Operating System: Opening of 'Windows' Shows How Bill Gates Succeeds in Software," *Wall Street Journal,* 21 May 1990, A1, A4; Mary Jo Foley, "Boy Wonder: Microsoft's Bill Gates," *Electronic Business,* 15 August 1988, 54–56; D. Ruby, S. Kanzler, R. Glitman, and T. Pompili, "Can Microsoft Blend Blue Jeans and Gray Flannel?" *PC Week,* 21 October 1986, 57, 59, 72–74; "Microsoft's Network Is a Model for Corporate Communications Systems," *PC Week,* 21 October 1986, 73; Richard A. Chafer, "The Growth of Microsoft," *Personal Computing,* June 1986, 29; Jonathan B. Eleven, "Microsoft: Recovering from Its Stumble over 'Windows,'" *Business Week,* July 22, 1985, 107–108; Eric Nee, "Interviews with Microsoft Executives," *Upside,* April 1995, 66, 87; "Why Microsoft (Mostly) Shouldn't Be Stopped," *Upside,* April 1995, 34–53; G. Pascal Zachary, "The Once and Future Microsoft," *Upside,* April 1995, 16–32.

2. David H. Holt, *Management: Principles and Practices,* 2d ed. (Englewood Cliffs, N.J.: Prentice Hall, 1990), 10–12; James A. F. Stoner, *Management,* 4th ed. (Englewood Cliffs, N.J.: Prentice Hall, 1989), 15–18.

3. Gilbert Fuchsberg, "Chief Executives See Their Power Shrink," *Wall Street Journal,* 15 March 1993, B1, B3; "Avon Finishes Executive Shift," *New York Times,* 17 November 1992, sec. c, 5.

4. Brian S. Moskal and Thomas M. Rohan, "A Much Tougher Line Faces Line Managers," *Industry Week,* 18 April 1988, 29–30.

5. Robert L. Katz, "Skills of an Effective Administrator," *Harvard Business Review,* September–October 1974. Reprinted in *Paths Toward Personal Progress: Leaders Are Made, Not Born* (Boston: Harvard Business Review, 1983), 23–35; Mike Dawson, "Leaders versus Managers," *Systems Management,* March 1995, 32; R. S. Dreyer, "Do Good Bosses Make Lousy Leaders?" *Supervision,* March 1995, 19–20; Michael Maccoby, "Teams Need Open Leaders," *Research-Technology Management,* January/February 1995, 57–59.

6. Alan M. Webber, "What's So New About the New Economy?" *Harvard Business Review,* January–February 1993, 24–32, 41–42.

7. Webber, "What's So New?" 24–32, 41–42.

8. Robert H. Lengel and Richard L. Daft, "The Selection of Communication Media as an Executive Skill," *Academy of Management Executive* 11, no. 3 (1988): 225–232.

9. Gary A. Yukl, *Leadership in Organizations,* 2d ed. (Englewood Cliffs, N.J.: Prentice Hall, 1989), 58.

10. Lengel and Daft, "Selection of Communication Media," 225–232.

11. Kathryn M. Bartol and David C. Martin, *Management* (New York: McGraw-Hill, 1991), 268–272; Richard L. Daft, *Management,* 2d ed. (Chicago: Dryden, 1991), 188–195; Ricky W. Griffin, *Management,* 3d ed. (Boston: Houghton Mifflin, 1990), 131–137.

12. Bill Saporito, "How Quaker Oats Got Rolled," *Fortune,* 8 October 1990, 131–138; Gary Hoover, Alta Campbell, and Patrick J. Spain, *Hoover's Handbook of American Business 1994* (Austin, Tex.: Reference Press, 1993), 906–907.

13. Paul C. Nutt, *Making Tough Decisions* (San Francisco: Jossey-Bass, 1989), 3.

14. Nutt, *Making Tough Decisions,* 6–7; Daft, *Management,* 180–184.

15. James J. Darazsdi, "Mission Statements Are Essential," *Personnel Journal,* February 1993, 24–25; Mark B. Roman, "The Mission," *Success,* June 1987, 54–57; Fred R. David, "How Companies Define Their Mission," *Long Range Planning* 22, no. 1 (February 1989): 90–97; Charles A. Rarick and John Vitton, "Mission Statements Make Cents," *Journal of Business Strategy,* January/February 1995, 11–12.

16. David L. Calfee, "Get Your Mission Statement Working!" *Management Review,* January 1993, 54–57.

17. Daft, *Management,* 128; Bartol and Martin, *Management,* 157–159.

18. Daft, *Management,* 132–136; Bartol and Martin, *Management,* 172–173.

19. Daft, *Management,* 130.

20. Daft, *Management,* 460.

21. Alan M. Weber, "Corporate Egotists Gone with the Wind," *Wall Street Journal,* 15 April 1991, A14.

22. Yukl, *Leadership in Organizations,* 9, 175–176.

23. Yukl, *Leadership in Organizations,* 210.

24. Bartol and Martin, *Management,* 506–508.

25. Susan Diesenhouse, "Harvard Law '55 (Pre-Ginsburg); Now, Alone at the Top," *New York Times,* 10 October 1993, sec. 3, 7.

26. Yukl, *Leadership in Organizations,* 83.

27. Ricardo Semler, "Managing Without Managers," *Harvard Business Review,* September–October 1989, 76–84.

28. Harry Bacas, "Who's in Charge Here?" *Nation's Business,* May 1985, 57.

29. Mark Frohman, "Participative Management," *Industry Week,* 2 May 1988, 37–42.

30. Joani Nelson-Horchler, "The Magic of Herman Miller," *Industry Week,* 18 February 1991, 11–17.

31. Greg Bounds, Lyle Yorks, Mel Adams, and Gipsie Ranney, *Beyond Total Quality Management: Toward the Emerging Paradigm* (New York: McGraw-Hill, 1994), 29–30, 678–704.

32. Peter Nulty, "The National Business Hall of Fame," *Fortune,* 11 March 1991, 98–102.

33. William B. Werther, Jr., and Keith Davis, *Human Resources and Personnel Management,* 4th ed. (New York: McGraw-Hill, 1993), 359–360.

34. Ronald Grover, "Boxed In at Jack in the Box," *Business Week,* 15 February 1993, 40; Kathy Tyrer, "Jack in the Box Keeps Cool in Crisis," *Adweek,* 1 February 1993, 6; "Jack in the Box Settles Suit Over E. Coli Infection," *Supermarket News,* 3 April 1995, 20; Richard Martin, "Foodmaker Revives 'Jack' to Aid Turnaround Efforts," *Nation's Restaurant News,* 30 January 1995, 20.

35. Christine M. Pearson, "From Crisis Prone to Crisis Prepared: A Framework for Crisis Management," *Academy of Management Executive* 7, no. 1 (1993): 48–59; Wayne Durham, Steve Johnson, Julian Winston, "Crisis in the Wind—Why Action Is Needed Now to Prepare for Tomorrow's 'Killer Hurricanes,'" *CPCU Journal,* March 1995, 17–34; Martyne Warwick, "Painful Lessons in Crisis Mismanagement," *Communications International,* March 1995, 4–5.

36. Joanne R. Piersall, "Contingency Planning: Facing Disaster & Surviving," *Nonprofit World,* May–June 1993, 35–38; Mark Hofman, "Planning for Catastrophes," *Business Insurance,* 27 March 1995, 2; Paul Schoemaker, "Scenario Planning: A Tool for Strategic Thinking," *Sloan Management Review,* Winter 1995, 25–40.

37. Carla Lazzareschi, "How 2 Firms Coped with Riots," *Los Angeles Times,* 11 May 1992, D1, D6.

38. See note 1.

CHAPTER 7

1. Patrick Flanagan, "IBM One Day, Lexmark the Next," *Management Review,* January 1994, 38–44; Mary Kathleen Flynn, "Inside Lexmark: A Taste of the New IBM?" *PC Magazine,* 25 February 1992, 30–31; Paul B. Carroll, "Culture Shock: Story of an IBM Unit that Split Off Shows Difficulties of Change," *Wall Street Journal,* 23 July 1992, A1, A5; "Lexmark: The Typing on the Wall," *Economist,* 3 October 1992, 74–75.

2. James E. Grunig, "Communication Is Not Enough," *Communications Briefings,* July 1987, 4; John H. Sheridan, "Aligning Structure with Strategy," *Industry Week,* 15 May 1989, 15–23; Richard L. Daft, *Management,* 2d ed. (Chicago: Dryden, 1991), 246.

3. Jim Brokaw, "Dr. Pepper, Sealtest and the Wood Brothers," *Motor Trend,* March 1974, 102.

4. Nancy K. Austin, "Reorganizing the Organization Chart," *Working Woman,* September 1993, 23–24, 26.

5. "Bubble Chart Sends Message," *The Pryor Report,* July 1990, 4.

6. Henry Mintzberg, *The Structuring of Organizations* (Englewood Cliffs, N.J.: Prentice Hall, 1979), 9, 81–84; Kathryn M. Bartol and David C. Martin, *Management* (New York: McGraw-Hill, 1991), 336.

7. Bartol and Martin, *Management,* 345.

8. Tom Brown, "Future Organizations," *Industry Week,* 1 November 1993, 22–24, 26, 28; William B. Werther, Jr., and Keith Davis, *Human Resources and Personnel Management,* 4th ed. (New York: McGraw-Hill, 1993), 155.

9. James Bennet, "At G.M. Parts Plants, Painful Change," *New York Times,* 4 January 1994, C1, C5.

10. Janet Houser Carter, "Minimizing the Risks from Delegation," *Supervisory Management,* February 1993, 1–2.

11. Robert B. Nelson, *Empowering Employees Through Delegation* (Burr Ridge, Ill.: Irwin, 1994), as summarized by Soundview Executive Book Summaries, 4; Jeffery C. Kennedy, "Empowering Employees through the Performance Appraisal Process," *International Journal of Public Administration,* May 1995, 795–811; Roland A. Foulkes, "Globalizing Organizations and Empowering People for High Performance Leadership of Our Multicultural World: Or, Behold, the Demise of Business-as-Usual Is At Hand," *Equal Opportunities International,* Volume 14, 1995, 37–46; Lin Standke, "Managing the Hidden Organization: Strategies for Empowering Your Behind-The-Scenes Employees," *Training,* March 1995, 100.

12. Jay T. Knippen and Thad B. Green, "Delegation," *Supervision,* March 1990, 7–9, 17.

13. John S. McClenahen, "Flexible Structures to Absorb the Shocks," *Industry Week,* 18 April 1988, 41, 44.

14. Oren Harari, "Imperatives for Deflating the Fat Organization," *Management Review,* June 1992, 61–62.

15. Bartol and Martin, *Management,* 349.

16. John S. McClenahen, "Managing More People in the '90s," *Industry Week,* 20 March 1989, 30–38.

17. Bartol and Martin, *Management,* 352.

18. Barbara Hetzer, "Pushing Decisions Down the Line at Campbell Soup," *Business Month,* July 1989, 62–63.

19. Richard T. Pascale, "Fit or Split?" *Across the Board,* June 1990, 48–52.

20. Bartol and Martin, *Management,* 345.

21. Bartol and Martin, *Management,* 370–371.

22. Daft, *Management,* 256–259.

23. Daft, *Management,* 259–262; Bartol and Martin, *Management,* 373–377.

24. Daft, *Management,* 260.

25. John A. Byrne, "The Horizontal Corporation," *Business Week,* 20 December 1993, 76–81; "Is a Horizontal Organization for You?" *Fortune,* 3 April 1995, 96; Rahul Jacob, "The Struggle to Create an Organization for the 21st Century," *Fortune,* 3 April 1995, 90–96.

26. Daft, *Management,* 261; Bartol and Martin, *Management,* 376.

27. Daft, *Management,* 262; Bartol and Martin, *Management,* 376.

28. Thomas A. Stewart, "The Search for the Organization of Tomorrow," *Fortune,* 18 May 1992, 92–98; Jenny C. McCune,

"More Power to Them," *Small Business Reports,* November 1992, 51–59.

29. Austin, "Reorganizing the Organization Chart," 23–24, 26; John Hoerr, "Work Teams Can Rev Up Paper-Pushers, Too," *Business Week,* 28 November 1988, 64–68, 72.

30. Daft, *Management,* 266.

31. Daft, *Management,* 264; Jolie B. Solomon and John Bussey, "Pressed by Its Rivals, Procter & Gamble Co. Is Altering Its Ways," *Wall Street Journal,* 20 May 1985, 1, 16; Tom Peters, *Thriving on Chaos* (New York: Harper & Row, 1987), 428.

32. Joseph Weber, "A Culture That Just Keeps Dishing Up Success," *Business Week Innovation,* 1989, 120–123.

33. Jan Shaw, "Galoob Regroups After President Leaves Toymaker," *San Francisco Business Times,* 5 July 1991, 3; John W. Wilson, "And Now, the Post-Industrial Corporation," *Business Week,* 3 March 1986, 64–71; "Digital Equipment Moves to Speed Its Reaction Time," *New York Times,* 23 December 1992, sec. c, 4.

34. Daft, *Management,* 272–273.

35. Daft, *Management,* 280–281; Bartol and Martin, *Management,* 357–358.

36. Daft, *Management,* 282.

37. Neal Boudette, "Networks to Dismantle Old Structures," *Industry Week,* 16 January 1989, 27–31.

38. Thomas M. Rohan, "Whitecollar Wisdom," *Industry Week,* 3 September 1990, 32–34.

39. Daft, *Management,* 282; Bartol and Martin, *Management,* 360–361.

40. Paul R. Lawrence and Jay W. Lorsch, "New Management Job: The Integrator," *Harvard Business Review,* November–December 1967, 142–150; Saroja Girishankar, "Integrator's Road to Success," *Communications Week,* 27 March 1995, 120, 125.

41. Daft, *Management,* 284.

42. Keith H. Hammonds, "Rethinking Work," *Business Week,* 17 October 1994, 74–77, 80–81, 84–87.

43. William Bridges, "The End of the Job," *Fortune,* 19 September 1994, 52–64, 68, 72, 74.

44. David Krackhardt and Jeffrey R. Hanson, "Informal Networks: The Company Behind the Chart," *Harvard Business Review,* July–August 1993, 104–111; Charles Hall, "The Informal Organization Chart," *Supervisory Management,* January 1986, 41; Ronald J. Burke, Mitchell G. Rothstein, Julia M. Bristor, "Interpersonal Networks of Managerial and Professional Woman and Men," *Women in Management Review,* Volume 10, 1995, 21–27.

45. Fred Luthans, "Successful vs. Effective Real Managers," *Academy of Management Executive* 2, no. 2 (1988): 130.

46. Princess Jackson Smith, "Networking: What It Is, What It Can Do for You, How You Do It," *Vital Speeches of the Day,* 15 September 1983, 712–713.

47. "The Advantage of Female Mentoring," *Working Woman,* October 1991, 104; Michelle N. Martinez, "Mentoring with an 'Equality' Twist," *HRMagazine,* January 1995, 16.

48. Daniel R. Denison, *Corporate Culture and Organizational Effectiveness* (New York: Wiley, 1990), 2, 33; Terence E. Deal and Allan A. Kennedy, *Corporate Cultures: The Rites and Rituals of Corporate Life* (Reading, Mass.: Addison-Wesley, 1982); Paul S. Nadler, "Corporate Culture in a Changing World," *Secured Lender,* March/April 1995, 45; Stan Glaser, "Why Your Corporate Culture Change Isn't Working . . . and What To Do About It," *Management Decision,* Volume 33, 1995, 33–34.

49. Lawrence A. Bossidy, "Why Do We Waste Time Doing This?" *Across the Board,* May 1991, 17, 20–21.

50. See note 1.

CHAPTER 8

1. Adapted from *Harley-Davidson 1993 Annual Report;* Brian S. Moskal, "Born to Be Real," *Industry Week,* 2 August 1993, 14–18; Martha H. Peak, "Harley-Davidson: Going Whole Hog to Provide Stakeholder Satisfaction," *Management Review,* June 1993, 53–55; Gary Slutsker, "Hog Wild," *Forbes,* 24 May 1993, 45–46; Kevin Kelly and Karen Lowry Miller, "The Rumble Heard Round the World: Harleys," *Business Week,* 24 May 1993, 58, 60; James B. Shuman, "Easy Rider Rides Again," *Business Tokyo,* July 1991, 26–30; Holt Hackney, "Easy Rider," *Financial World,* 4 September 1990, 48–49; Roy L. Harmon and Leroy D. Peterson, "Reinventing the Factory," *Across the Board,* March 1990, 30–38; John Holusha, "How Harley Outfoxed Japan with Exports," *New York Times,* 12 August 1990, sec. F, 5; Peter C. Reid, "How Harley Beat Back the Japanese," *Fortune,* 25 September 1989, 155–164.

2. Gene Bylinsky, "The Race to the Automatic Factory," *Fortune,* 21 February 1983, 51+.

3. Wickham Skinner, *Manufacturing: The Formidable Competitive Weapon* (New York: Wiley, 1985), 216.

4. George Stalk, Jr., and Thomas M. Hout, *Competing Against Time* (New York: Free Press, 1990), 2, 52, 58; "Speeding to the Hospital," CAD/CAM Planning 1992 supplement to *Penton Publications,* 1992, CC-6.

5. Alex Taylor III, "How Toyota Copes with Hard Times," *Fortune,* 25 January 1993, 78–81.

6. Dwight B. Davis, "Apple: Harvesting the Macintosh," *High Technology,* May 1985, 39–40.

7. "Could a Robot Do That Job?" *Industry Week,* 10 June 1985, 5.

8. Kathryn M. Bartol and David C. Martin, *Management* (New York: McGraw-Hill, 1991), 688.

9. Shawn Tully, "Can Boeing Reinvent Itself?" *Fortune,* 8 March 1993, 66–68, 72–73; Doris Jones Yang, "Boeing Knocks Down the Wall Between the Dreamers and the Doers," *Business Week,* 28 October 1991, 120–121; Robert J. Bowlby, "How Boeing Tracks Costs, A to Z," *Financial Executive,* November/December 1995, 20–23; J.P. Donlon, "Boeing's Big Bet," *Chief Executive,* November/December 1995, 40–44.

10. Joel Kotkin, "The Great American Revival," *Inc.,* February 1988, 52–63; Bob Davis, "Computers Speed the Design of More Workaday Products," *Wall Street Journal,* 18 January 1985, sec. B, 19.

11. Bartol and Martin, *Management,* 687.

12. Stephen Kreider Yoder, "Putting It All Together," *Wall Street Journal,* 4 June 1990, R24.

13. "Creating a 21st-Century Business," *Industry Week,* 19 April 1993, 38.

14. Bylinsky, "The Race to the Automatic Factory," 51+.

15. Moskal, "Born to Be Real," 14–18.

16. Bylinsky, "The Race to the Automatic Factory," 51+.

17. John H. Sheridan, "Agile Manufacturing: Stepping Beyond Lean Production," *Industrial Week,* 19 April 1993, 30–33, 36–38, 40–41, 44, 46.

18. James O'Toole, "Eli Whitney, You've Met Your Waterloo," *Across the Board,* November 1985.

19. John H. Sheridan, "Manufacturing: Lessons from the Best," *Industry Week,* 15 February 1993, 54–56, 58–60, 63; Gary S. Vasilash, "A Working FMS!" *Production,* December 1990, 50–52.

20. James B. Dilworth, *Production and Operations Management: Manufacturing and Nonmanufacturing,* 3d ed. (New York: Random House, 1986), 566.

21. Wickham Skinner, "The Focused Factory," *Harvard Business Review,* May–June 1974, 115.

22. Robert H. Hayes and Gary P. Pisano, "Beyond World-Class: The New Manufacturing Strategy," *Harvard Business Review,* January–February 1994, 77–86; Jenny McCune, "Tomorrow's Factory," *Management Review,* January 1993, 19–23.

23. Roger W. Schmenner, *Production/Operations Management: Concepts and Situations,* 2d ed. (Chicago: Science Research Associates, 1981), 281.

24. Dilworth, *Production and Operations Management,* 356.

25. Milt Freudenheim, "Removing the Warehouse from Cost-Conscious Hospitals," *New York Times,* 3 March 1991, sec. c, 5.

26. "Production Problems Become More Manageable," *Business Week,* 25 April 1983, 70+; Ranjit Rebello, "Specialized Inspection Problems in Serial Production Systems," *European Journal of Operational Research,* January 19, 1995, 277–296.

27. Schmenner, *Production/Operations Management,* 618.

28. Glenn Rifkin, "'What If . . .' Software for Manufacturers," *New York Times,* 18 October 1992, sec. 3, 9.

29. "Quality: The U.S. Drives to Catch Up," *Business Week,* 1 November 1982, 66+; Peter Adrian, "Cost-Cutting, Quality Improvement Insufficient to Ensure Manufacturing Success," *Manufacturing Automation,* November 1991, 2; Candice Goodwin, "The Stamp of Quality Approval," *Accountancy,* December 1991, 114+.

30. David A. Garvin, "Product Quality: Profitable at Any Cost," *New York Times,* 3 March 1985, sec. 3, 3; Maurice Jeffrey, "Quality in Product Development," *Candy Industry,* November 1991, 49.

31. Richard T. Schonberger and E. M. Knod, *Operations Management,* 4th ed. (Homewood, Ill.: Irwin, 1991), 872.

32. Schmenner, *Production/Operations Management,* 209.

33. Jeremy Main, "Ford's Drive for Quality," *Fortune,* 18 April 1983, 62+.

34. Courtland L. Bovée and John V. Thill, *Marketing* (New York: McGraw-Hill, 1992), 729.

35. Amy Borrus, "The Navy Tries to Get Its Ship in Shape," *Business Week Quality 1991,* 25 October 1991, 134.

36. Greg Bounds, Lyle Yorks, Mel Adams, and Gipsie Ranney, *Beyond Total Quality Management: Toward the Emerging Paradigm* (New York: McGraw-Hill, 1994), 87.

37. Michael E. Raynor, "Worldwide Winners," *Total Quality Management,* July–August 1993, 43–48; Bounds et al., *Beyond Total Quality Management,* 212; Bonnie G. Mani, "Old Wine in New Bottles Tastes Better: A Case Study of TQM Implementation in the IRS," *Public Administration Review,* March/April 1995, 147–158; Louis E. Boone and Dianne Wilkins, "The Role of Benchmarking in Total Quality Management," *International Journal of Management,* March 1995, 123–131.

38. Raynor, "Worldwide Winners," 43–48; Theodore R. Marra, "The States of Excellence," *Total Quality Management,* July–August 1993, 27–31.

39. Schmenner, *Production/Operations Management,* 209.

40. Dilworth, *Production and Operations Management,* 618.

41. Marilyn Joyce, "An Ergonomics Primer Part 1: Office Considerations," *Management Solutions,* April 1988, 38–45; Stephen A. Dawkins, "Does Ergonomics Work?" *Managing Office Technology,* March 1995, 12–14; "OSHA Considers Guidelines for Ergonomics," *Occupational Hazards,* March 1995, 13; "Facilities and Ergonomics," *Managing Office Technology,* February 1995, 30; Kathryn G. Parker, "Why Ergonomics is Good Economics," *Industrial Engineering,* February 1995, 41–46.

42. Dilworth, *Production and Operations Management,* 608–609.

43. Main, "Ford's Drive for Quality," 62+; "Ford Uses Employee-Involvement Groups to Improve Quality," *Automotive News,* 28 February 1983, 4; John N. Younker, "Selecting Your Organization's Employee Involvement and Empowerment Strategy," *Tap-ping the Network Journal,* Winter 1995, 19–22; Denis Collins, "Self-interests and Group Interests in Employee Involvement Programs: A Case," *Journal of Labor Research,* Winter 1995, 57–79.

44. Peter F. Drucker, "The Emerging Theory of Manufacturing," *Harvard Business Review,* May–June 1990, 94–102.

45. Gilbert Fuchsbert, "Gurus of Quality Are Gaining Clout," *Wall Street Journal,* 27 November 1990, B1.

46. John H. Sheridan, "World-Class Manufacturing," *Industry Week,* 2 July 1990, 36, 38, 40–46.

47. Jonathan P. Hicks, "Making Steel Cheaper and Faster," *New York Times,* 27 February 1991, sec. d, 7.

48. Amil Kumar Naj, "Industrial Switch: Some Companies Cut Pollution by Altering Production Methods," *Wall Street Journal,* 24 December 1990, 1, 21.

49. Keith H. Hammonds and Monica Roman, "Itching to Get onto the Factory Floor," *Business Week,* 14 October 1991, 62, 64.

50. Dilworth, *Production and Operations Management,* 551–556.

51. Bartol and Martin, *Management,* 307–308.

52. See note 1.

53. Gary Hoover, Alta Campbell, and Patrick J. Spain, eds. *Hoover's Handbook of American Business 1994* (Austin, Tex.: Reference Press, 1994), 268–269, 712–713, 1092–1093; U.S. Bureau of the Census, *Statistical Abstract of the United States: 1993,* 113th ed. (Washington, D.C.: G.P.O., 1993), 750–751, 696–697.

CHAPTER 9

1. Adapted from Suzanne Wittebort, "Some Like It Hot: John Correnti Has Been Through the Mill," *Business-North Carolina,* 1994, 20+; Shawn Tully, "Your Paycheck Gets Exciting," *Fortune,* 1 November 1993, 83–84, 95, 98; *Nucor Corporation 1993 Annual Report,* 3–5; Thomas M. Rohan, "Maverick Remakes Old-Line Steel," *Industry Week,* 21 January 1991, 26–30; Richard Preston, "Annals of Enterprise; Hot Metal-I," *The New Yorker,* 25 February 1991, 43–71; "Nucor's Ken Iverson on Productivity and Pay," *Personnel Administrator,* October 1986, 46–52, 106–108; John Merwin, "People, Attitudes and Equipment," *Forbes,* 8 February 1988, 68–72; "Empowering Employees," *Chief Executive,* March–April 1989, 44–49; Michael A. D'Amato and Jeremy H. Silverman, "How to Make Money in a Dull Business," *Across the Board,* December 1990, 54–59; Stephen Baker, "The Brutal Brawl Ahead in Steel," *Business Week,* 13 March 1995, 13; Harlow G. Unger, "David and Goliath Forge Bond of Steel," *Purchasing and Supply Management,* 12 January 1995, 34, El Hoeffer, "How Nucor and David Joseph Avoid Disrupting the Scrap Market," *Iron Age New Steel,* February 1995, 27; Stephen

Baker, "Nucor," *Business Week,* 13 February 1995, 70.

2. Bernard M. Bass, *Leadership and Performance Beyond Expectations—Executive Book Summaries* 8, no. 6 (June 1986): 6; Kathy Rebello, "Microsoft," *Business Week,* 24 February 1992, 60–64.

3. "New Findings About What Makes Workers Happy," *Working Woman,* February 1985, 22.

4. Dennis C. Kinlaw, "What Employees 'See' Is What Organizations 'Get,'" *Management Solutions,* March 1988, 38–41.

5. Claude S. George, Jr., *The History of Management Thought,* 2d ed. (Englewood Cliffs, N.J.: Prentice-Hall, 1972), 62–63; Daniel A. Wren, *The Evolution of Management Thought,* 2d ed. (New York: Wiley, 1979), 70–75.

6. F. J. Roethlisberger and William J. Dickson, *Management and the Worker* (Cambridge, Mass.: Harvard University Press, 1939), 14–18; Elton Mayo, *The Human Problems of an Industrial Civilization* (New York: Macmillan, 1933), 55–76.

7. Roethlisberger and Dickson, *Management and the Worker,* 412–426; Allen C. Bluedorn, ed., "Special Book Review Section on the Classics of Management," *Academy of Management Review,* 11 April 1968, 461–463.

8. Berkeley Rice, "The Hawthorne Defect: Persistence of a Flawed Theory," *Psychology Today,* February 1982, 70–74; John G. Adair, "The Hawthorne Effect: A Reconsideration of the Methodological Artifact," *Journal of Applied Psychology* 69, no. 2 (1984): 334–345.

9. Abraham H. Maslow, "A Theory of Human Motivations," *Psychological Review,* July 1943, 370; *Motivation and Personality,* 2d ed. (New York: Harper & Row, 1970).

10. Frederick Herzberg, *Work and the Nature of Man* (New York: World, 1971).

11. David A. Nadler and Edward E. Lawler III, "Motivation—A Diagnostic Approach," in *Perspectives on Behavior in Organizations,* edited by Richard Hackman, Edward E. Lawler III, and Lyman W. Porter (New York: McGraw-Hill, 1977).

12. Robert C. Beck, *Motivation: Theories and Principles,* 3d ed. (Englewood Cliffs, N.J.: Prentice-Hall, 1990), 153.

13. W. Clay Hamner, "Reinforcement Theory and Contingency Management in Organizational Settings," in *Motivation and Work Behavior,* 5th ed., edited by Richard M. Steers and Lymon W. Porter (New York: McGraw-Hill, 1991), 61–87.

14. Adi Ignatius, "Now If Ms. Wong Insults a Customer, She Gets an Award," *Wall Street Journal,* 24 January 1989, A1, A17.

15. Hamner, "Reinforcement Theory and Contingency Management," 74–75; Dawn Gunsch, "Award Programs at Work," *Personnel Journal,* September 1991, 85–89.

16. Douglas McGregor, *The Human Side of Enterprise* (New York: McGraw-Hill, 1960).

17. Christopher Byron, "An Attractive Japanese Export: The XYZs of Management Theory Challenge American Bosses," *Time,*

2 March 1983, 74; William G. Ouchi, *Theory Z: How American Business Can Meet the Japanese Challenge* (Reading, Mass.: Addison-Wesley, 1981).

18. U.S. Department of Labor Statistics, *Statistical Abstract of the United States, 1993* (Washington, D.C.: GPO, 1993), 394; Robert J. Paul and James B. Townsend, "Managing the Older Worker—Don't Just Rinse Away the Grey," *Academy of Management Executive* 7, no. 3 (1993): 67–74.

19. Anne B. Fisher, "The Downside of Downsizing," *Fortune,* 23 May 1988, 42; Martin S. Tamaren, "How to Survive a Downsizing," *Telecommunications,* March 1995, 84–86; Jay Dial and Kevin J. Murphy, "Incentives, Downsizing, and Value Creation at General Dynamics," *Journal of Financial Economics,* March 1995, 261–314; Robert Carey, "Downsizing Becomes the Norm," *Incentive Performance Supplement,* March 1995, 11; David Burda, "Sensible Downsizing Can Lower Costs, Improve Quality," *Modern Healthcare,* 27 February 1995, 42; Jeffrey Marshall, "Downsizing's Double-Edged Sword," *United States Banker,* February 1995, 8.

20. Sharon Nelton, "Golden Employees—In Their Golden Years," *Nation's Business,* August 1993, 34–35; John Case, "The Real Age Wave," *Inc.,* July 1989, 23; Paul and Townsend, "Managing the Older Worker," 67–74; Rod Davies, "Third Age Careers: Meeting the Corporate Challenge," *International Journal of Career Management,* Volume 7, 1995, v–vi.

21. Julia Lawlor, "Busters Have Work Ethic All Their Own," *USA Today,* 20 July 1993, 1B–2B.

22. *Statistical Abstract of the United States, 1993* (Washington, D.C.: GPO, 1993), 400; Kathleen McKay-Rispoli, "Small Children: No Small Problem," *Management World,* March–April 1988, 15.

23. Joseph F. McKenna and Brian S. Moskal, "The Plight of the Seasoned Worker," *Industry Week,* 7 June 1993, 12–14, 18–19, 22.

24. "Workforce 2000 Is Welcome Today at Digital," *Business Ethics,* July–August 1990, 15–16.

25. "12 Companies That Do the Right Thing," *Working Woman,* January 1991, 57–59.

26. Fisher, "The Downside of Downsizing," 42; Daniel Goleman, "When the Boss Is Unbearable," *New York Times,* 28 December 1986, sec. 3, 29.

27. Janice Castro, "Where Did the Gung Ho Go?" *Time,* 11 September 1989, 53.

28. Brian S. Moskal, "Company Loyalty Dies, a Victim of Neglect," *Industry Week,* 1 March 1993, 11–12.

29. Karen Matthes, "Job Placement: Redefining the Fast Track," *Management Review,* November 1992, 5.

30. Carol R. Riggs, "Hardwired for Success," *D&B Reports,* September–October 1993, 24–25.

31. Alan Deutschman, "What 25-Year-Olds Want," *Fortune,* 27 August 1990, 43.

32. Andrew Pollack, "Assembly-Line Amenities for Japan's Auto Workers," *New York Times,* 20 July 1992, sec. a, 1, sec. c, 2.

33. Edwin A. Locke and Gary P. Latham, *Goal Setting: A Motivational Technique That Works!* (Englewood Cliffs, N.J.: Prentice-Hall, 1984).

34. Robert W. Goddard, "Well Done!" *Management World,* November–December 1987, 14–15.

35. Ronald Whipple, "Rewards Have Value," *Personnel Journal,* September 1990, 92–93; Barbara Dewey, "Aligning Work and Rewards," *Management Review,* February 1995, 19–23.

36. Helene Cooper, "The New Educators: Carpet Firm Sets Up an In-House School to Stay Competitive," *Wall Street Journal,* 5 October 1992, A1, A6.

37. John W. Newstrom and Keith Davis, *Organizational Behavior: Human Behavior at Work,* 9th ed. (New York: McGraw-Hill, 1993), 345.

38. Laurie M. Grossman, "Truck Cabs Turn Into Mobile Offices as Drivers Take On White-Collar Tasks," *Wall Street Journal,* 3 August 1993, B1, B5.

39. "A Work Revolution in U.S. Industry," *Business Week,* 16 May 1983, 100+.

40. "A Work Revolution," 100+.

41. "USA Snapshots," *USA Today,* 20 November 1990, 1D.

42. Hewitt Associates, reported in Cathy Trost and Carol Hymowitz, "Careers Start Giving In to Family Needs," *Wall Street Journal,* 18 June 1990, 9E.

43. Sharon Nelton, "A Flexible Style of Management," *Nation's Business,* December 1993, 24–25, 28–29, 31.

44. Dennis J. Kravitz, *The Human Resource Revolution—Executive Book Summaries* 11, no. 7 (July 1989): 4.

45. Sue Shellenbarger, "Work & Family," *Wall Street Journal,* 10 February 1993, B1.

46. Julie A. Cohen, "Managing Tomorrow's Workforce Today," *Management Review,* January 1991, 19; Bob Cohn, "A Glimpse of the 'Flex' Future," *Newsweek,* 1 August 1988, 39.

47. Tracy E. Benson, "Empowered Employees Sharpen the Edge," *Industry Week,* 19 February 1990, 18.

48. Kevin M. Paulsen, "Gain Sharing: A Group Motivator," *MW,* May–June 1989, 24–25.

49. "Where Ducks and Fun Mean Success," *Industry Week,* 18 March 1991, 29.

50. See note 1.

CHAPTER 10

1. Adapted from Sally Roberts, "Balancing Work, Family," *Business Insurance,* 27 September 1993, 3, 20; Julie Cohen Mason, "Healthy Equals Happy Plus Productive," *Management Review,* July 1992, 33–37; Monica Battagliola, "Making Employees Better Health Care Consumers," *Business & Health,* June 1992, 22, 24, 26–28; "Changing a Corporate Culture," *Business Week,* 14 May 1984, 130–138; *The Johnson & Johnson 1990 Annual Report*; "Shrinking, Changing Labor Force Prompts Johnson & Johnson Family Issues Policies," *Employee Benefit Plan Review,* September 1989, 57–60; "What Makes Sales Forces Run?" *Sales & Marketing Management,* 3 December 1984, 24–26; Susan Dentzer, "Excessive Claims," *Business Month,* July 1990, 52–63; Evelyn Gilbert, "Benefits No 'Soft' Issue: J&J Official," *National Underwriter,* 10 December 1990, 15, 21; Christopher Power, "At Johnson & Johnson, a Mistake Can Be a Badge of Honor," *Business Week,* 26 September 1988, 126–128; Lee Smith, "J&J Comes a Long Way from Baby," *Fortune,* 1 June 1981, 58–66; Neal Templin, "Johnson & Johnson 'Wellness' Program for Workers Shows Healthy Bottom Line," *Wall Street Journal,* 21 May 1990, B1, B6; Barbara Scherr Trenk, "Corporate Fitness Programs Become Hearty Investments," *Management Review,* August 1989, 33–37; Michael A. Verespej, "A Ticket to Better Health," *Industry Week,* 4 February 1991, 24–25; Joseph Weber, "No Band-Aids for Ralph Larsen," *Business Week,* 28 May 1990, 86–87; Rhona L. Ferling, "Johnson & Johnson on How to Sell Wellness," *Financial Executive,* March/April 1995, 28.

2. Ellen Brandt, "Global HR," *Personnel Journal,* March 1991, 40; Dawn Anfuso, "Colgate Aligns HR with Its Global Vision," *Personnel Journal,* January 1995, 74; Leon Rubis, "Cultivating the Human Side of Business," *HRMagazine,* January 1995, 68–74.

3. Harvey Gittler, "Name Change Not Enough," *Industry Week,* 7 March 1994, 14.

4. James W. Walker, *Human Resource Planning* (New York: McGraw-Hill, 1980), 4.

5. Joel Dreyfuss, "Get Ready for the New Work Force," *Fortune,* 23 April 1990, 172.

6. "Job Puzzle: Skilled Workers Scarce Even as Layoffs Mount," *San Diego Tribune,* 1 October 1991, A-1, Edward Gubman, "People Are More Valuable than Ever," *Compensation & Benefits Review,* January/February 1995, 7–14.

7. Lori Ionannou, "It's a Small World After All," *International Business,* February 1994, 82–84, 86–88.

8. Mark Henricks, "It's Not Just Academic," *Small Business Reports,* May 1994, 24–31.

9. Neal Templin and Joseph B. White, "GM Goes to Great Lengths to Match Workers and Work," *Wall Street Journal,* 21 April 1994, B4.

10. Brian Tarcy, "Contingent Workers: Where's the Fit?" *Across the Board,* April 1994, 36–40; Peter T. Kilborn, "Part-Time Hirings Bring Deep Changes in U.S. Workplaces," *New York Times,* 17 June 1991, sec. a, 1.

11. Lisa Genasci, "Companies Increase Hiring of Temps," *The News-Times* (Danbury, Conn.), 24 July 1994, D12; Michael A. Verespej, "Temporary Temps," *Industry Week,* 6 February 1995, 45–46; "Working with Temps, Part-timers, and Freelancers," *Supervisory Management,* February 1995, 6–7.

12. Max Messmer, "Strategic Staffing for the '90s," *Personnel Journal,* October 1990, 94.

13. David Kirkpatrick, "Smart New Ways to Use Temps," *Fortune,* 15 February 1988, 110–116.

14. "The Interviewing Process," *Small Business Reports,* December 1987, 61–66; Kelley M. Barrett, "The Smart Woman's Guide to Interviewing and Salary Negotiation," *Personnel Psychology,* Spring 1995, 227–231.

15. Thomas J. Burns, "Tests to Target Dependability," *Nation's Business,* March 1989, 26, 28–29.

16. "Drug Testing," *Wall Street Journal,* 19 March 1991, A1.

17. Carl Camden and Bill Wallace, "Job Application Forms: A Hazardous Employment Practice," *Personnel Administrator,* March 1983, 31+.

18. Jean Sensel and Dianne MacDonald, "Dragging Employers into Child Support," *Nation's Business,* October 1991, 34–35.

19. Daniel Weisberg, "Preparing for the Unthinkable," *Management Review,* March 1994, 58–61.

20. Jenny C. McCune, "Companies Grapple with Workplace Violence," *Management Review,* March 1994, 52–57; Lawrence R. Murphy, "Managing Job Stress: An Employee Assistance/Human Resource Management Partnership," *Personnel Review,* Volume 24, 1995, 41–50; Carlo Wolff, "Danger at the Front Desk," *Lodging Hospitality,* March 1995, 34–36; Michael H. Covanes, "Ticking Bombs: Defusing Violence in the Workplace," *Security Management,* March 1995, 81–82; Louis P. DiLorenzo and Darren J. Carroll, "Screening Applicants for A Safer Workplace," *HRMagazine,* March 1995, 55–58.

21. Marj Charlier and Wade Lambert, "McDonald's Told to Pay $210,000 Damages in Negligent-Hiring Case," *Wall Street Journal,* 15 March 1991, B4.

22. "New-Employee Orientation," *Small Business Reports,* April 1984, 37–40.

23. Robin Bergstrom, "Hard Times," *Production,* July 1990, 50.

24. "The Three R's on the Shop Floor," *Fortune,* Education 1990, 87.

25. Susan E. Kuhn, "How Business Helps Schools," *Fortune,* Education 1990, 91.

26. "The Three R's," 88.

27. Kevin Kelly, "Motorola: Training for the Millennium," *Business Week,* 28 March 1994, 158–161; Brian S. Moskal, "Just a Degree of Confidence," *Industry Week,* 19 February 1990, 65–66.

28. A. Nicholas Komanecky, "Developing New Managers at GE," *Training and Development Journal,* June 1988, 62.

29. William B. Werther, Jr., and Keith Davis, *Human Resources and Personnel Management,* 4th ed. (New York: McGraw-Hill, 1993), 102.

30. *Statistical Abstract of the United States,* 1993 (Washington, D.C.: GPO, 1993), 425.

31. Joann S. Lublin, "Looking Good," in *Executive Pay* special section of *Wall Street Journal,* 13 April 1994, R1–R2.

32. Janice Castro, "How's Your Pay?" *Time,* 15 April 1991, 40; John A. Byrne, "The Flap over Executive Pay," *Business Week,* 6 May 1991, 90; Jenny C. McCune, "Up and Away," *Management Review,* January 1995, 20–25; Paul E. Gobat, "Measuring the Internal Equity of Executive Pay," *Journal of Compensation & Benefits,* March/April 1995, 20–25; Bruce Walters, Tim Hardin, James Schick, "Top Executive Compensation: Equity or Excess? Implications for Regaining American Competitiveness," *Journal of Business Ethics,* March 1995, 227–234.

33. Kerry Hannon, "Variable-Pay Programs: Where the Real Raises Are," *Working Woman,* March 1994, 48–51, 72, 96.

34. "Chrysler Will Pay $28 Million in Bonuses," *New York Times,* 20 January 1994, sec. c, 4.

35. Edward C. Baig, "The Great Earnings Gamble," *U.S. News & World Report,* 17 September 1990, 65, 68.

36. John Greenwald, "Workers: Risks and Rewards," *Time,* 15 April 1991, 42–43.

37. Greenwald, "Workers: Risks and Rewards," 42–43; Hannon, "Variable-Pay Programs," 48–51, 72, 96.

38. Earl Ingram, "Compensation: The Advantages of Knowledge-Based Pay," *Personnel Journal,* April 1990, 138–140.

39. Dawn Gunsch, "Benefits Leverage Hiring and Retention Efforts," *Personnel Journal,* November 1992, 91–92, 94–97.

40. U.S. Chamber of Commerce, *Employee Benefits* (Washington, D.C.: GPO, 1991), 34–36.

41. David J. Jefferson, "Family Matters: Gay Employees Win Benefits for Partners at More Corporations," *Wall Street Journal,* 18 March 1994, A1, A6.

42. Richard A. Wolfe and Donald F. Parker, "Employee Health Management: Challenges and Opportunities," *Academy of Management Executive* 8, no. 2 (1994): 22–31.

43. Roger Thompson, "The Threat to Pension Plans," *Nation's Business,* March 1991, 18–24.

44. Christopher Power, "Pension Raiding, 1983 Style," *Forbes,* 20 June 1983, 130; Julie Rohrer, "IBM Rethinks Pensions," *Institutional Investor,* March 1995, 141–142; Kathleen Utgoff and Theodore R. Groom, "The Regulation of Pensions: Twenty Questions after Twenty Years," *Journal of Pension Planning and Compliance,* Spring 1995, 1–13.

45. John Hoerr, "ESOPs: Revolution or Ripoff?" *Business Week,* 15 April 1985, 94–108; William Smith, Harold Lazarus, and Harold Murray Kalkstein, "Employee Stock Ownership Plans: Motivation and Morale Issues," *Compensation and Benefits Review,* 1 September 1990, 37; Carol Cheatham, Leo R. Cheatham, and Michelle McEacharn, "ESOPs Fable: The Goose that Laid the Golden Eggs," *National Public Accountant,*

April 1995, 33–35; Ed Carberry, "Ins and Outs of Employee Stock Ownership," *Editor & Publisher*, 25 February 1995, 31, 44.

46. "Taking Baby Steps Toward a Daddy Track," *Business Week*, 15 April 1991, 90.

47. Carol A. Perkin, "Help for Workers Who Care for Their Parents," *New York Times*, 4 June 1989, sec. 3, 19.

48. Sue Shellenbarger, "Work & Family: Elderly Relatives Part of Relocation Deals," *Wall Street Journal*, 11 May 1994, B1.

49. Barbara Presley Noble, "At Work: We're Doing Just Fine, Thank You," *New York Times*, 20 March 1994, 25.

50. "Flexible Benefit Plans Popular with Small Companies," *Small Business Reports*, November 1985, 34.

51. Barbara Marsh, "Workers at Risk: Chance of Getting Hurt Is Generally Far Higher at Smaller Companies," *Wall Street Journal*, 3 February 1994, A1, A8.

52. "Why We Should Invest in Human Capital," *Business Week*, 17 December 1990, 89.

53. Templin, "Johnson & Johnson 'Wellness' Program," B1.

54. Julie A. Cohen, "Managing Tomorrow's Workforce Today," *Management Review*, January 1991, 21.

55. Michael J. Major, "Employee Assistance Programs: An Ideal Whose Time Has Come," *Modern Office Technology*, March 1990, 76.

56. Maria Helene Sekas, "Dual-Career Couples—A Corporate Challenge," *Personnel Administrator*, April 1984, 37–45.

57. "Workplace Trends: Alternatives to Promotions," *Small Business Reports*, August 1991, 25–26; William McWhirter, "Major Overhaul," *Time*, 30 December 1991, 56–58.

58. Survey Research Center, Economic Policy Division, Chamber of Commerce of the United States, *Employee Benefits 1981* (Washington, D.C.: Chamber of Commerce of the United States, 1981).

59. "Helping Squeezed Executives When the Belt Gets Tighter," *Insight*, 26 November 1990, 39.

60. Kirkland Ropp, "Downsizing Strategies," *Personnel Administrator*, February 1987, 61–64.

61. Audrey Choi, "VW Trimming Workers' Week to Four Days," *Wall Street Journal*, 26 November 1993, A4.

62. Daniel Forbes, "The No-Layoff Payoff," *Dun's Business Month*, July 1985, 64–66.

63. Bill Saporito, "Cutting Costs Without Cutting People," *Fortune*, 25 May 1987, 27–32.

64. Donald C. Bacon, "See You in Court," *Nation's Business*, July 1989, 17.

65. Joann S. Lublin, "Firing Line: Legal Challenges Force Firms to Revamp Ways They Dismiss Workers," *Wall Street Journal*, 13 September 1983.

66. Robert A. Snyder and Billie Brandon, "Riding the Third Wave: Staying on Top of ADEA Complaints," *Personnel Administrator*,
February 1983, 41–47; Arnold H. Lubasch, "U.S. Court Decides Cases on Age Bias," *New York Times*, 16 December 1982; Aaron Bernstein, "Putting Mandatory Retirement Out to Pasture," *Business Week*, 10 June 1985, 104–105.

67. Irene Pave, "They Won't Take It Anymore," *Across the Board*, November 1990, 20.

68. Sandra Evans, "Today's Elderly: Healthier, Happier," *Washington Post*, 9 March 1986, A1.

69. See note 1.

CHAPTER 11

1. Adapted from James Bennet, "Saturn, G.M.'s Big Hope, Is Taking Its First Lumps," *New York Times*, 29 March 1994, sec. a, 1, 12; Phil Frame, "Saturn Status Report," *Automotive News*, 31 May 1993, 8; Lindsay Chappell, "UAW Beats the Drums for War on Saturn Labor Rules," *Automotive News*, 31 May 1993, 8; Liz Pinto, "Simplicity Is Key to Labor Tranquillity at Saturn," *Automotive News*, 7 September 1992, 42; Morgan O. Reynolds, "Unions and Jobs: The U.S. Auto Industry," *Journal of Labor Research*, Spring 1986, 103–126; William A. Nowlin, "Restructuring in Manufacturing: Management, Work, and Labor Relations," *Industrial Management*, November–December 1990, 5–9, 30; Anne B. Fisher, "Behind the Hype at GM's Saturn," *Fortune*, 11 November 1985, 34–49; Donald Ephlin, "Saturn's Strategic Role in Industrial Relations," *Survey of Business*, Summer 1986, 23–25; Alex Taylor III, "Back to the Future at Saturn," *Fortune*, 1 August 1988, 63–72; "GM–Auto Workers Saturn Contract," *Monthly Labor Review*, October 1985, 48–50; James B. Treece, "Here Comes GM's Saturn," *Business Week*, 9 April 1990, 56–62; Maralyn Edid, "How Power Will Be Balanced on Saturn's Shop Floor," *Business Week*, 5 August 1985, 65–66; Ben Fischer, "Finishing Out the Century," *Journal for Quality and Participation*, March 1991, 48–52; Doron P. Levin, "Reality Comes to G.M.'s Saturn Plant," *New York Times*, 14 November 1991, sec. c, 1, 5; "Saturn Unit's Workers Pass Labor Pact by 72% to 28%," *Wall Street Journal*, 15 November 1991, A2; Jay C. Thomas, "Quality Wars: The Triumphs and Defeats of American Business," *Personnel Psychology*, Spring 1995, 182–185; David Mayes, Matthew N. Murray, "The Automobile Industry and the Economic Development of Tennessee and the Southeast: New Investment Has Increased Production Capacity," *Survey of Business*, Winter 1995, 41–52.

2. Peter F. Drucker, "Peter Drucker Asks: Will Unions Ever Again Be Useful Organs of Society?" *Industry Week*, 20 March 1989, 18–19; "Getting Their Dues: Trade Unions in America," *Economist*, 25 March 1995, 68.

3. William B. Werther, Jr., and Keith Davis, *Human Resources and Personnel Management*, 4th ed. (New York: McGraw-Hill, 1993), 560–561.

4. Clemens P. Work, "Making It Clear
Who's Boss," *U.S. News & World Report*, 8 September 1986, 43.

5. James R. Healy and Micheline Maynard, "New Spirit of Partnership Driving Force," *USA Today*, 23 June 1993, B1–B2.

6. Barbara Presley Noble, "Reinventing Labor: An Interview with Union President Lynn Williams," *Harvard Business Review*, July–August 1993, 115–125.

7. James Cook, "Collision Course," *Forbes*, 13 May 1991, 81.

8. David Moberg, "Like Business, Unions Must Go Global," *New York Times*, 19 December 1993, sec. 3, 13.

9. Thomas A. Kochan and Harry C. Katz, *Collective Bargaining and Industrial Relations* (Homewood, Ill.: Irwin, 1988), 165.

10. Kochan and Katz, *Collective Bargaining and Industrial Relations*, 166.

11. Barry Schiffman, "Tougher Tactics to Keep Out Unions," *New York Times*, 3 March 1991, sec. 3, 8.

12. Ephraim Lewis, "BW/Harris Poll: Confidence in Unions Is Crumbling," *Business Week*, 8 July 1985, 76. Reprinted by special permission, copyright © 1985 by McGraw-Hill, Inc.

13. Dan Callahan, "Difficult Labor," *Business Ethics*, July–August 1993, 28–31.

14. Kochan and Katz, *Collective Bargaining and Industrial Relations*, 173.

15. Terry Schraeder, "Decertification Elections: An Opportunity for Employers," *PIMA Magazine*, October 1990, 10; Thomas G. Pearce, James E. Groff, John R. Wingender, "Union Decertification's Impact on Shareholder Wealth," *Industrial Relations*, January 1995, 58–72.

16. Daniel Quinn Mills, *Labor-Management Relations*, 5th ed. (New York: McGraw-Hill, 1994), 366.

17. Kochan and Katz, *Collective Bargaining and Industrial Relations*, 176, 238.

18. Louis Uchitelle, "Labor Draws the Line in Decatur," *New York Times*, 13 June 1993, sec. 3, 1, 6.

19. *World Almanac and Book of Facts* (New York: Scripps Howard, 1989), 161.

20. Aaron Bernstein, "The Secondary Boycott Gets a Second Wind," *Business Week*, 27 June 1988, 82; Michael H. Cimini, Charles J. Muhl, "Labor-Management Bargaining in 1994," *Monthly Labor Review*, January 1995, 23–39.

21. David Benjamin/Jay, "Labor's Boardroom Guerrilla," *Time*, 20 June 1988, 50.

22. Facts on File, 15 July 1988, 514; Personal communication, Ben Albert of COPE.

23. "Next!" *Forbes*, 18 July 1983, 149; "Paper Avoids a Replay of J. P. Stevens," *Business Week*, 27 June 1983, 33+.

24. Bob Baker, "Riding Out the Strike," *Los Angeles Times*, 26 August 1990, D1–D3; Peter T. Kilborn, "Ban on Replacing Strikers Faces Veto Threat," *New York Times*, 7 March 1991, sec. a, 10.

25. "Telescabbing: The New Union Buster," *Newsweek*, 29 August 1983, 53–54; Peggy Stuart, "Labor Unions Become Business Partners," *Personnel Journal,* August 1993, 54–63.

26. "NLRB Permits Replacements During Legal Lockout," *Personnel Journal,* January 1987, 14–15.

27. Dennis Farney, "To End an Impasse: Workers at Caterpillar Hope Against Hope Clinton Will Be True," *Wall Street Journal,* 26 July 1993, A1, A4; Kevin Kelly, "A New Life for Cat?" *Business Week,* 6 February 1995, 28–29.

28. "Timex Closes Scottish Plant," *New York Times,* 30 August 1993, 2.

29. Daniel D. Luria, "New Labor–Management Models for Detroit?" *Harvard Business Review,* September–October 1986, 27.

30. "Strikes and Lockouts in U.S. Now on Rise," *New York Times,* 12 March 1987, sec. a, 28.

31. Louis Uchitelle, "Blue-Collar Compromises in Pursuit of Job Security," *New York Times,* 19 April 1992, 1, 13.

32. U.S. Department of Labor, Bureau of Labor Statistics, *Current Wage Developments* (Washington, D.C.: GPO, February 1991), 4.

33. Clarence R. Deitsch and David A. Dilts, "The COLA Clause: An Employer Bargaining Weapon?" *Personnel Journal,* March 1982, 220–223; Kenneth B. Noble, "Workers Aren't Betting on Inflation," *New York Times,* 27 April 1986, sec. e, 4.

34. John J. Lacombe II and Fehmida R. Sleemi, "Wage Adjustments in Contracts Negotiated in Private Industry in 1987," *Monthly Labor Review,* May 1988, 23; U.S. Department of Labor, Bureau of Labor Statistics, *Compensation and Working Conditions* (Washington, D.C.: GPO, August 1991), 49.

35. Edward M. Coates III, "Profit Sharing Today: Plans and Provisions," *Monthly Labor Review,* April 1991, 19; Barry Gerhart, "Profit Sharing: Does It Makes a Difference?" *Industrial & Labor Relations Review,* January 1995, 366–367.

36. Gary W. Florkowski, "Profit Sharing and Public Policy: Insights for the United States," *Industrial Relations,* Winter 1991, 98; "Pension Plan Is Scrapped in Favor of Profit Sharing," *New York Times,* 8 April 1995, 21; "Profit-sharing Based on Productivity," *HRMagazine,* April 1995, 71.

37. Florkowski, "Profit Sharing and Public Policy," 98.

38. "Bell System's Breakup Is Jarring the Unions," *Business Week,* 30 May 1983, 76+; "The Sudden Uncertainties of Working for Bell," *Business Week,* 20 June 1983, 26.

39. Gregory A. Patterson, "Blue Collar Boon: Hourly Auto Workers Now on Layoff Have a Sturdy Safety Net," *Wall Street Journal,* 29 January 1991, A1; Gregory A. Patterson and Joseph B. White, "GM–UAW Pact Allows Company to Cut Payroll in Return for Worker Buy-Outs," *Wall Street Journal,* 19 September 1990, A3.

40. James Bennet, "Ford Reaches Accord on U.A.W. Pact," *New York Times,* 16 October 1993, 19; James Bennet, "G.M.'s Pact Disappoints Wall Street," *New York Times,*

26 October 1993, sec. c, 1, 6.

41. Jeremy Main, "Anatomy of an Auto-Plant Rescue," *Fortune,* 4 April 1983, 108+.

42. Mills, *Labor-Management Relations,* 201.

43. Mills, *Labor-Management Relations,* 199.

44. Dawn Anfuso, "Peer Review Wards Off Unions and Lawsuits," *Personnel Journal,* January 1994, 64; Daniel Seligman, "Who Needs Unions?" *Fortune,* 12 July 1982, 54+; Joyce Parks and Christine W. Lindstrom, "Taking the Fear Out of Peer Review," *Nursing Management,* March 1995, 40–48.

45. Donald Thompson, "New Role for Labor Unions," *Industry Week,* 9 February 1987, 35.

46. Richard Leonard, "ESOPs Bring Participation Home," *Management Review,* November 1990, 45–49. Ed Carberry, "Ins and Outs of Employee Stock Ownership," *Editor & Publisher,* 25 February 1995, 31, 44.

47. Robert L. Rose and Erle Norton, "ESOP Fables: UAL Worker-Owners May Face Bumpy Ride if the Past Is a Guide," *Wall Street Journal,* 23 December 1993, A1, A4; Aaron Bernstein, "Move Over Boone, Carl, and Irv—Here Comes Labor," *Business Week,* 14 December 1987, 125.

48. Stuart, "Labor Unions Become Business Partners," 54–63.

49. Philip A. Miscimarra and Jeffrey C. Kauffman, "Keeping Teamwork Legal," *Small Business Reports,* May 1993, 16–20; Michael A. Verespej, "New Rules on Employee Involvement," *Industry Week,* 1 February 1993, 55–56.

50. Michael A. Verespej, "Unions Seize Opportunity," *Industry Week,* 2 May 1988, 22.

51. David Pauly, "2001: A Union Odyssey," *Newsweek,* 5 August 1985, 40.

52. Dana Milbank, "Labor Broadens Its Appeal by Setting Up Associations to Lobby and Offer Services," *Wall Street Journal,* 13 January 1993, B1, B4.

53. Seligman, "Who Needs Unions?" 54+; *Fortune* Panel, "Are the Unions Dead?"

54. "Next a Valet with Each Job?" *Time,* 2 March 1987, 55.

55. See note 1.

56. *Culturgram for the '90s: Egypt* (Provo, Utah: Brigham Young University, 1991).

CHAPTER 12

1. Adapted from "Richard Donahue, President of Nike Inc.," *Europe,* July–August 1993, 30–33; Dan Wieden and Fleming Meeks, "Be Ferocious," *Forbes,* 2 August 1993, 40–41; "A Sense of Cool: Nike's Theory of Advertising," *Harvard Business Review,* July–August 1992, 97; Dori Jones Yang and Robert Buderi, "Step by Step with Nike," *Business Week,* 13 August 1990, 116–117; "The '80s: What a Decade!" *Advertising Age,* 1 January 1990, 34; Kate Fitzgerald, "Nike Flexes Muscle for Kids," *Advertising Age,* 10 July 1989, 51; PRNewswire, 3 October 1989; "The Billboard Is Back! Nike Captures Award as Decade's Best," PRNewswire, 5 December 1989; Sheryl Franklin, "The Other Side," *Bank Marketing,* August 1987,

62; "Nike Outdoes Competition in Delivery to Customers," *Global Trade,* March 1988, 8; Ellen Benoit, "Lost Youth," *Financial World,* 20 September 1988, 28–31; Robert F. Hartley, *Marketing Successes, Historical to Present Day: What We Can Learn* (New York: Wiley, 1985), 214–224; Marcy Magiera, "Nike Edges Reebok; L.A. Gear Sprinting," *Advertising Age,* 25 September 1989, 93; Douglas C. McGill, "Nike Is Bounding Past Reebok," *New York Times,* 11 July 1989, sec. d, 1, 4; Barbara Buell, "Nike Catches Up with the Trendy Frontrunner," *Business Week,* 24 October 1988, 88; Pat Sloan, "Reebok Runs Harder to Keep Lead," *Advertising Age,* 24 July 1989, 6; G. Christian Hill, "Nike Posts Big Gains in Sales and Profit; Reebok Hopes Pump Will Help It Keep Up," *Wall Street Journal,* 19 December 1989, B10; Pat Sloan, "Reebok Gets Pumped for 1990," *Advertising Age,* 20 November 1989, 35; Bruce Horovitz, "Athletes Team Up for New Nike Campaign," *Los Angeles Times,* 27 June 1989, sec. 4, 6; Marcy Magiera, "Nike: Bo's Still an All-Star," *Advertising Age,* 20 May 1991, 8; Meg Rottman, "Nike Plans to Put Muscle in Product, Marketing," *Footwear News,* 25 February 1991, 34; Noreen O. Leary, "Will the Shoe Fit?" *Adweek,* 3 April 1995, 12–13.

2. "AMA Board Approves New Marketing Definition," *Marketing News,* 1 March 1985, 1.

3. Franklin S. Houston, "The Marketing Concept: What It Is and What It Is Not," *Journal of Marketing,* April 1986, 81–87.

4. George S. Day and Robin Wensley, "Assessing Advantage: A Framework for Diagnosing Competitive Superiority," *Journal of Marketing,* April 1988, 1–20.

5. Janice Castro, "Mr. Sam Stuns Goliath," *Time,* 25 February 1991, 62–63.

6. Michael E. Porter, *Competitive Advantage* (New York: Free Press, 1985), 14.

7. Ron Zemke and Dick Schaaf, *The Service Edge: 101 Companies That Profit from Customer Care* (New York: New American Library, 1989), 50.

8. William H. Davidow and Bro Uttal, *Total Customer Service: The Ultimate Weapon* (New York: Harper & Row, 1989), 21–22.

9. Milind M. Lele, *The Customer Is Key* (New York: Wiley, 1987), 39–41; Albert G. Canen, Normal L. Lawrie, "Looking at Customer Service in a Drinks Company," *Logistics Information Management,* Volume 8, 1995, 13–16; Jo McHale, "Giving Power to Staff Leads to Better Customer Service," *People Management,* 9 February 1995, 50; Marc Hequet, "Customer Service or Else," *Training,* February 1995, 77; Susan Greco, "Customer-Service Audit," *Inc.,* February 1995, 100; Robert Grimes, "Technology's Impact on Customer Service," *Nation's Restaurant News,* 23 January 1995, 22, 60.

10. Davidow and Uttal, *Total Customer Service,* 34–35.

11. Davidow and Uttal, *Total Customer Service,* 8; Valarie A. Zeithaml, A. Parasuraman, and Leonard L. Berry, *Delivering Quality Service* (New York: Free Press, 1990), 9; George J. Castellese, "Customer Service . . . Building a Winning Team," *Supervision,* January 1995, 9–13; Erica G. Sorohan and Catherine M. Petrini, "Dumpsters, Ducks, and Customer Service," *Training and Development,* January 1995, 9.

12. Suzanne Taylor, "Intuit Focuses on Creating Wow!" *QuickNews,* Spring 1994, 1.

13. Malcolm H. B. McDonald, "Ten Barriers to Marketing Planning," *Journal of Product and Brand Management,* Fall 1992, 51–64.

14. Malcolm McDonald and John W. Leppard, *Marketing by Matrix* (Lincolnwood, Ill.: NTC, 1993), 10; H. Igor Ansoff, "Strategies for Diversification," *Harvard Business Review,* November–December 1957, 113–124; H. Igor Ansoff, *Corporate Strategy* (New York: McGraw-Hill, 1965).

15. Eben Shapiro, "Food Labs Gaze Hungrily at Potential in Labeling Rules," *Wall Street Journal,* 10 December 1992, B2; "Research Targets Food Labeling," *Retail World,* 27 February 1995, 9; Scott Hample, "The Marketing King: A Modern Fable," *American Demographics,* Marketing Tools Supplement, March/April 1995, 76.

16. Kari Huus, "Look Out, Chinese Love Solution," *Advertising Age International,* 28 September 1992, I-6.

17. Mike Brennan, "Business Gets Rainy Day Blues," *The Herald* (Everett, Wash.), 1 August 1993, B1.

18. Elaine Underwood, "Just Plane Hot," *Brandweek,* 24 August 1992, 16–17.

19. Alex Taylor III, "How to Murder the Competition," *Fortune,* 22 February 1993, 87, 90.

20. Courtland L. Bovée and John V. Thill, *Marketing* (New York: McGraw-Hill, 1992), 188.

21. Gerry Khermouch, "Kodak Focuses on 'Life Stages,'" *Brandweek,* 15 February 1993, 4.

22. Thomas McCarroll, "It's Mass Market No More," *Time,* Fall 1993, 80–81.

23. Larry Carpenter, "How to Market to Regions," *American Demographics,* November 1987, 45.

24. *Statistical Abstract of the United States, 1990* (Washington, D.C.: GPO, 1990), 908, 916.

25. Martha Farnsworth Riche, "Psychographics for the 1990s," *American Demographics,* July 1989, 53–54.

26. Michael J. Weiss, *The Clustering of America* (New York: Harper & Row, 1988), 41.

27. Peter Sleight, "Where They Live," *Admap,* May 1992, 17–22.

28. "Gymboree Is More Than Just Child's Play: Toddler Activity Classes Grow into Lifestyle Concept Retail Stores," *Chain Store Age Executive,* November 1987, 115, 118, 120, 122.

29. Letter to owners, from Infiniti Division of Nissan Motor Corporation, 23 July 1991.

30. Robert B. Settle and Pamela Alreck, "How to Be Class Conscious," *Success,* June 1987, 8, 10.

31. "Roper's America: A Small, Outspoken Group Forms Majority of Opinions," *Adweek,* 25 April 1988, 16.

32. "The Customer Isn't Always Rational," *Adweek,* 7 December 1987, 36.

33. "The Customer Isn't Always Rational," 37.

34. Francine Schwadel, "Shoppers' Blues: The Thrill Is Gone," *Wall Street Journal,* 13 October 1989, B1–B2; Betsy Morris, "As a Favored Pastime, Shopping Ranks High with Most Americans," *Wall Street Journal,* 30 July 1987, 1, 16; "Not Shopping but Dropping," *Economist,* 11 March 1995, 67.

35. Michael H. Morris and Jeanne L. Holman, "Source Loyalty in Organizational Markets: A Dyadic Perspective," *Journal of Business Research* 16, no. 2 (1988): 117–131.

36. Ernest F. Cooke, "What Is Business and Industrial Marketing?" *Journal of Business and Industrial Marketing,* Fall 1986, 9–17.

37. Morris and Holman, "Source Loyalty in Organizational Markets," 118; Cooke, "What Is Business and Industrial Marketing?" 11.

38. Haken Hakansson, ed., *International Marketing and Purchasing of Industrial Goods* (New York: Wiley, 1984).

39. "Caterpillar: Challenging a 'Soft' Market," *Business Marketing,* August 1988, 40, 42; Tracy E. Benson, "Caterpillar Wakes Up: Corporate Excavation Uncovers a Hidden Gold Mine," *Industry Week,* 20 May 1991, 33.

40. Pamela G. Hollie, "What's New in Market Research," *New York Times,* 15 June 1986, sec. 3, 19; Phyllis M. Thornton, "Linking Market Research to Strategic Planning," *Nursing Homes,* January/February 1995, 34–37.

41. Laurie Hays, "Using Computers to Divine Who Might Buy a Gas Grill," *Wall Street Journal,* 16 August 1994, B1, B4.

42. See note 1.

CHAPTER 13

1. Brian K. Burton, "Tops in Popcorn: Indiana Is the World's Largest Producer," *Indiana Business,* October 1987, 18–24; Robert Runde, "Fortunes from Scratch: A Popcorn King Who's in the Chips," *Money,* November 1979, 106, 108, 110, 112, 114; Orville Redenbacher, "The Funny-Looking Farmer with the Funny-Sounding Name," *Guideposts,* January 1990, 2–5; Frazier Moore, "A Corn for Connoisseurs," *Madison Avenue,* May 1985, 14, 16–18; Bernice Kanner, "Kernel Knowledge," *New York,* 11 January 1988, 14–15; Lori Kesler, "Personalities Pitching Products," *Advertising Age,* 3 May 1984, M30, M34, M38; Laura Klepacki, "Popping Up: Light Microwave Popcorn May Be Low in Fat and Low in Salt, but Sales Are Airborne," *Supermarket News,* 9 March 1992, 13+; Betsy Spethmann, "General Mills Pops Corn Snack, Redenbacher Tests Counterpart," *Brandweek,* January 1995, 10.

2. Advertisement for the French Redevelopment Agency, *Electronic Business,* 17 September 1990, 1.

3. Drew Wilson and Helen Deal, "To Brand, or Not to Brand," *Asian Advertising & Marketing,* 10 September 1993, 12–13.

4. "Choosing a Product Name Is a High Stakes Game," Prodigy Services Company, 19 July 1993.

5. Gabriella Stern, "Cheap Imitation: Perrigo's Knockoffs of Name-Brand Drugs Turn into Big Sellers," *Wall Street Journal,* 15 July 1993, A1, A9; Zachary Schiller, "Procter & Gamble Hits Back," *Business Week,* 19 July 1993, 20–22.

6. Patrick Oster, Gabrielle Saveri, and John Templemann, "The Eurosion of Brand Loyalty," *Business Week,* 19 July 1993, 22; Yumiko Ono, "The Rising Sun Shines on Private Labels," *Wall Street Journal,* 26 April 1992, B1, B5; Cyndee Miller, "Big Brands Fight Back Against Private Labels," *Marketing News,* 16 January 1995, 1, 8+.

7. Ronald Alsop, "What's in a Name? Ask Supermarket Shoppers," *Wall Street Journal,* 9 May 1988, 21.

8. "How to Break Loyalty to the Competition" (interview with Andrew Parsons and James Schroer), *Boardroom Reports,* 1 April 1987, 3.

9. Bill Saporito, "Has-Been Brands Go Back to Work," *Fortune,* 28 April 1986, 124; Christine Donahue, "Marketers Restore Old Masters," *Adweek,* 14 September 1987, 4.

10. Ronald Alsop, "To Know a Brand Is Not to Love It," *Wall Street Journal,* 15 June 1988, 25.

11. Anne B. Fisher, "Coke's Brand-Loyalty Lesson," *Fortune,* 5 August 1985, 46.

12. Fisher, "Coke's Brand-Loyalty Lesson," 44, 45.

13. Howard Schlossberg, "Brand Value Can Be Worth More Than Physical Assets," *Marketing News,* 5 March 1990, 6.

14. David A. Aaker, *Managing Brand Loyalty* (New York: Free Press, 1991), 19–21.

15. John Bissell, "What's in a Brand Name? Nothing Inherent to Start," *Brandweek,* 7 February 1994, 16.

16. Steven Flax, "The Big Brand Stretch," *The Marketer,* September 1990, 32–35; Michael McDermott, "Too Much of a Good Thing?" *Adweek's Marketing Week,* 4 December 1989, 20–25; Tom Bunday, "Capitalizing on Brand Extensions," *Journal of Consumer Marketing,* Fall 1989, 27–30; Joshua Levine, "But in the Office, No," *Forbes,* 16 October 1989, 272–273.

17. Elizabeth Lesly, "What's Next, Raiders' Deodorant?" *Business Week,* 30 November 1992, 65.

18. "The Packaging Investment," *In Business,* March–April 1988, 40.

19. Jack G. Vogler and Steven Lawrence, "Packaging Better," *Boardroom Reports,* 1 June 1987, 10.

20. "Budget Gourmet's Downscale Look (and Its Upscale Taste) Whetted Consumers' Appetites," *Adweek,* 3 August 1987, 30; Re-

becca Fannin, "The Right Stuff: The Budget Gourmet," *Marketing & Media Decisions,* Winter 1986, 14+; "Good and Cheap," *Packaging Digest,* November 1984, 62+.
21. Roberta Maynard, "What a Difference a Package Makes," *Nation's Business,* February 1994, 8; Pamela G. Hollie, "Importance of Color Packaging," *New York Times,* 20 August 1985, 55; Jim Oppenheimer, "CD-ROM Sales: It's All in the Packaging," *CD–ROM Professional,* March 1995, 33–39.
22. Eben Shapiro, "Food Labs Gaze Hungrily at Potential in Labeling Rules," *Wall Street Journal,* 10 December 1992, B2.
23. Ronald Henkoff, "Service Is Everybody's Business," *Fortune,* 27 June 1994, 48–56.
24. Henkoff, "Service Is Everybody's Business," 48–56.
25. Jacob M. Schlesinger, "Firms Strive to Improve Basic Products," *Wall Street Journal,* 8 October 1985, B1.
26. James Cox, "Boom Year for New Products," *USA Today,* 12 January 1988, 1B; Thomas T. Semon, "Forecasting Demand for New Products Always Difficult," *Marketing News,* March 27, 1995, 10; "New Products," *Rough Notes,* March 1995, 78–81; Sam Bradley, "New Products at Record Pace," *Brandweek,* 13 February 1995, 37.
27. "New Product Winners—And Losers," *In Business,* April 1985, 64.
28. Anna Sobczynski, "New Product Success Can Be All in the Timing," *Advertising Age,* 3 May 1984, M15.
29. *Tools of the Trade* catalog from Smith & Hawken, 1990, 17.
30. Toni Mack, "Let the Computer Do It," *Forbes,* 10 August 1987, 94.
31. Nancy Madlin, "Streamlining the Test-Marketing Process," *Adweek,* 11 November 1985, 10; Robert Mendenhall, "Ways to Sidestep New-Product Traps," *Advertising Age's Business Marketing,* April 1995, 23.
32. Peter Fuhrman, "Thank You, MTV," *Fortune,* 6 June 1994, 48.
33. Ronald Alsop, "Giving Fading Brands a Second Chance," *Wall Street Journal,* 24 January 1989, B1.
34. Stuart Elliot, "The Famous Brands on Death Row," *New York Times,* 7 November 1994, sec. 3, 1, 6.
35. Faye Rice, "Sports Cars Low on Gas," *Fortune,* 27 June 1994, 16.
36. "The Pricing Decision: Part I—The Cornerstone of the Marketing Plan," *Small Business Reports,* May 1985, 73; Eunsup Shim and Ephraim F. Sudit, "How Manufacturers Price Products," *Management Accounting,* February 1995, 37–39.
37. Christine Ammer and Dean S. Ammer, *Dictionary of Business and Economics* (New York: Free Press, 1977), 327.
38. Norton E. Marks and Neely S. Inlow, "Price Discrimination and Its Impact on Small Business," *Journal of Consumer Marketing,* Winter 1988, 31–38.
39. Thomas T. Nagle, *The Strategy and Tactics of Pricing* (Englewood Cliffs, N.J.: Prentice-

Hall, 1987), 335–336.
40. Kent B. Monroe, *Pricing: Making Profitable Decisions* (New York: McGraw-Hill, 1990), 406.
41. Charles D. Schewe, *Marketing Principles and Strategies* (New York: Random House, 1987), 336.
42. See note 1.

CHAPTER 14
1. Joseph Weber, "Black & Decker Cuts a Neat Dovetail Joint," *Business Week,* 31 July 1989, 52–53; Janet Meyers, "Black & Decker Ups Share in Hardware," *Advertising Age,* 24 July 1989, 28; Rebecca Fannin and Laura Konrad Jereski, "Black & Decker Powers into Housewares," *Marketing & Media Decisions,* August 1985, 34–40, 109; Bill Kelley, "Black & Decker Rebuilds," *Sales & Marketing Management,* June 1987, 49; Christopher S. Eklund, "How Black & Decker Got Back in the Black," *Business Week,* 13 July 1987, 86, 90; James A. Constantin and Robert F. Lusch, "Discover the Resources in Your Marketing Channel," *Business,* July–September 1986, 19–26; Paula Schnorbus, "B&D Turns On the Power," *Marketing & Media Decisions,* May 1988, 57–58, 62, 64; John Huey, "The New Power in Black & Decker," *Fortune,* 2 January 1989, 89–91, 94; "Winning Turnaround Strategies at Black & Decker," *Journal of Business Strategy,* March–April 1988, 30–33; "Black & Decker to Send Sales Specialists into Industrial and Construction Markets," *Industrial Distribution,* April 1987, 4; Deborah Schondorf, "Home Appliance Industry," *Value Line Investment Survey,* 20 March 1992, 128+; Kurt Kleiner, "Black & Decker Takes Aim at Japanese with New Tool Line," *Baltimore Business Journal,* 7 February 1992, 3; Debra Sparks, "Black & Decker: Back and Tougher," *Financial World,* 28 March 1995, 20–22; Thomas Jaffe, "The Black & Decker Drill," *Forbes,* 13 March 1995, 188; "B&D Powers Up Tools," *Marketing,* 16 February 1995, 34.
2. Rom Markin, *Marketing Strategy and Management,* 2d ed. (New York: Wiley, 1982), 297.
3. Emily Thornton, "Revolution in Japanese Retailing," *Fortune,* 7 February 1994, 143–146.
4. Milind Lele, "Matching Your Channels to Your Product's Life Cycle," *Business Marketing,* December 1986, 64.
5. Matthew Grimm, "Taco Bell Franchisees Want It Hot 'n Later," *Brandweek,* 7 September 1992, 3; Matthew Grimm, "Franchisees Fret over 'Conflict,'" *Brandweek,* 24 August 1992, 1, 6.
6. Howard Schlossberg, "Manufacturers Fighting Back with Alternative Retail Outlets, *Marketing News,* 2 August 1992, 9, 11.
7. Barbara Marsh, "Franchise Realities: Sandwich-Shop Chain Surges, but to Run One Can Take Heroic Effort," *Wall Street Journal,* 16 September 1992, A1, A10.
8. Allan J. Magrath and Kenneth G. Hardy,

"Avoiding the Pitfalls in Managing Distribution Channels," *Business Horizons,* September–October 1987, 29–33; Robert E. Weigand, "Fit Products and Channels to Your Markets," *Harvard Business Review,* January–February 1977, 95–105; Brett A. Boyle, F. Robert Dwyer, "Power, Bureaucracy, Influence, and Performance: Their Relationships in Industrial Distribution Channels," *Journal of Business Research,* March 1995, 189–200.
9. Joseph Pereira, "Toys 'R' Us: Big Kid on the Block, Won't Stop Growing," *Wall Street Journal,* 11 August 1988, B6.
10. Philip R. Cateora, *International Marketing,* 7th ed. (Homewood, Ill.: Irwin, 1990), 587.
11. Brian Dumaine, "P & G Rewrites the Marketing Rules," *Fortune,* 6 November 1989, 34–48.
12. Joseph Weber, "It's 'Like Somebody Shot the Postman,'" *Business Week,* 13 January 1992, 82; Louis Rukeyser, John Cooney, and George Winslow, *Louis Rukeyser's Business Almanac* (New York: Simon & Schuster, 1988), 649; Steven P. Galante, "Distributors Switch Strategies to Survive Coming Shakeout," *Wall Street Journal,* 20 July 1987, B21; *Statistical Abstract of the United States, 1989* (Washington, D.C.: GPO, 1989), 779.
13. *Statistical Abstract of the United States, 1993* (Washington, D.C.: GPO, 1993), 538.
14. *Statistical Abstract of the United States, 1993,* 409–410.
15. Janice Castro, "No Holds Barred," *Time,* 11 April 1988, 46.
16. Cyndee Miller, "Scent as a Marketing Tool," *Marketing News,* 18 January 1993, 1, 2.
17. "Nordstrom Teams with Facconnable to Open New York Store," PRNewswire, 15 June 1993; "Why Rivals Are Quaking as Nordstrom Heads East," *Business Week,* 15 June 1987, 99–100.
18. Michael Dotson and W. E. Patton III, "Consumer Perceptions of Department Store Service: A Lesson for Retailers," *Journal of Services Marketing,* Spring 1992, 15–28.
19. Jack G. Kaikati, "Don't Discount Off-Price Retailers," *Harvard Business Review,* May–June 1985, 86.
20. Kaikati, "Don't Discount Off-Price Retailers," 91.
21. Julie Liesse, "Welcome to the Club," *Advertising Age,* 1 February 1993, S3, S6; *Value Line Investment Survey,* 30 November 1990, 1650; Howard C. Gelbtuck, "The Warehouse Club Industry," *The Appraisal Journal* 58 (April 1990): 153–159.
22. Deirdre Fanning, "Only the Best for the Bergdorf Man?" *New York Times,* 16 September 1990, sec. 3, 23.
23. "Supermarkets' Lean Margins," *USA Today,* 18 December 1990, 1B.
24. Anthony Ramirez, "Will American Shoppers Think Bigger Is Really Better?" *New York Times,* 1 April 1990, sec. f, 11.
25. Jack Hitt, "More and More and More and More," *New York Times Magazine,* 23 January 1994, 34–35.

26. N. R. Kleinfield, "Even for J. Crew, the Mail-Order Boom Days Are Over," *New York Times,* 2 September 1990, sec. 3, 5; Howard Rudnitsky, "Growing Pains," *Forbes,* 27 February 1995, 32; Sigmund Kiener, "The Future of Mail Order," *Direct Marketing,* 15 February 1995, 17.

27. Don L. Boroughs, "Purchasing Power," *U.S. News & World Report,* 31 January 1994, 56–69; Kathy Haley, "The Infomercial Begins a New Era as a Marketing Tool for Top Brands," *Advertising Age,* Special Advertising Section, 25 January 1993, M3–M4; "Club Med Guests Star in Its 'Paradise Found,'" *Advertising Age,* Special Advertising Section, 25 January 1993, M9; Mark Landler, "The Infomercial Inches Toward Respectability," *Business Week,* 4 May 1992, 175; Howard Schlossberg, "Once Fodder and Filler, Infomercials Now Attract Mainstream Advertisers," *Marketing News,* 20 January 1992, 1, 6–7.

28. Howard Rudnitsky, "Play It Again, Sam," *Forbes,* 10 August 1987, 48.

29. PC Connection catalog, vol. 4, no. 6B, 1994, 2–3.

30. Edward O. Welles, "Riding the High-Tech Highway," *Inc.,* March 1993, 72–85.

31. "Wal-Mart Computers Talk to Vendors," *Chain Store Age,* January 1985, 20.

32. John Yoo, "Bad Trip: As Highways Decay, Their State Becomes Drag on the Economy," *Wall Street Journal,* 30 August 1989, A1, A8; Daniel Machalaba, "Push for Long Trucks Hits Bumpy Road," *Wall Street Journal,* 9 May 1990, B1–B2; Debra Lynn Dadd and Andre Carothers, "A Bill of Goods? Green Consuming in Perspective," *Greenpeace,* May–June 1990, 8–12.

33. See note 1.

CHAPTER 15

1. Richard W. Stevenson, "Ikea's New Realities: Recession and Aging Consumers," *New York Times,* 25 April 1993, sec. 3, 4; "Ikea Blasts into L.A. Marketplace with Record-Bashing Outdoor Blitz," *Adweek Western Advertising News,* 22 October 1990, 1, 4; Cara Appelbaum, "How IKEA Blitzes a Market," *Adweek's Marketing Week,* 11 June 1990, 18–19; Michael Winerip, "Shopping Siren Sings This Song: IKEA! IKEA!" *New York Times,* 25 May 1990, sec. b, 1; Judith Newman, "Swede Deal," *Adweek,* 20 July 1992, 16; Randall Rothenberg, "Deutsch's Campaign for Ikea Furniture," *New York Times,* 4 May 1990, sec. d, 17; Mary Krienke, "IKEA's Anders Moberg," *Stores,* January 1992, 98–100, 102; "Shoppers at IKEA Go Bonkers," *HFN The Weekly Newspaper for the Home Furnishing Network,* 9 January 1995, 8.

2. Courtland L. Bovée, John V. Thill, George P. Dovel, and Marian B. Wood, *Advertising Excellence* (New York: McGraw-Hill, 1995), 177–182.

3. Mark Crispin Miller, "Hollywood: The Ad," *Atlantic,* April 1990, 41–54.

4. Timothy E. Moore, "Subliminal Advertising: What You See Is What You Get," *Journal of Marketing,* Spring 1982, 38–47; Jack Haberstroh, "Can't Ignore Subliminal Ad Charges," *Advertising Age,* 17 September 1984, 3, 42, 44.

5. Keith Schneider, "Guides on Environmental Ad Claims," *New York Times,* 29 July 1992, sec. c, 3; Jeanne Saddler, "FTC Issues a 'Green-Marketing' Guide to Help Prevent Deceptive-Ad Charges," *Wall Street Journal,* 29 July 1992, B5; Nanci Hellmich, "Big Changes Proposed for Food Labels," *USA Today,* 6 November 1991, 1D.

6. Courtland L. Bovée, John V. Thill, George P. Dovel, and Marian Burk Wood, *Advertising Excellence* (New York: McGraw-Hill, 1994), 16.

7. "Cessna Lands on CEO's Desks: A Big, Bold, Beautiful Campaign," *Business Marketing,* January 1993, 42.

8. *Statistical Abstract of the United States, 1993* (Washington, D.C.: GPO, 1993), 405–406.

9. "Sales Costs Higher for Small Firms," *Small Business Reports,* November 1990, 18.

10. Lynn Asinof, "Telemarketing Makes Rapid Strides at U.S. Corporations," *Wall Street Journal,* 21 July 1988, A1; Roger Reece, "The New Generation of Integrated Inbound/Outbound Telemarketing Systems," *Telemarketing,* March 1995, 58–65; Malynda H. Madzel, "Outsourcing Telemarketing: Why It May Work for You," *Telemarketing,* March 1995, 48–49; "Despite Hangups, Telemarketing a Success," *Marketing News,* 27 March 1995, 19.

11. Courtland L. Bovée, Michael J. Houston, and John V. Thill, *Marketing,* 2d ed. (New York: McGraw-Hill, 1995), 475.

12. George R. Walther, "Reach Out to Accounts," *Success,* May 1990, 24.

13. Eugene Johnson, David Kurtz, and Eberhard Scheuing, *Sales Management Concepts, Practices, and Cases* (New York: McGraw-Hill, 1986), 81–82.

14. Kenneth R. Sheets, "3-D or Not 3-D? That's the Question for Advertisers," *U.S. News & World Report,* 25 January 1988, 59; Authors' estimates.

15. "100 Leading National Advertisers," *Advertising Age,* 29 September 1993, 1.

16. "Down to Business, Chapter VII: Everything You Always Wanted to Know About Advertising—Cheap!" *Entrepreneur,* May 1985, 84.

17. "Not for Members Only," *Marketing Management,* vol. 1, no. 4, 1993, 6–7; Herb Goldsmith, "Members Only Fashions a Unique Selling Strategy," *Journal of Business Strategy,* May–June 1989, 8–11.

18. Janet Neiman, "The Trouble with Comparative Ads," *Adweek's Marketing Week,* 12 January 1987, 4–5.

19. Kia national television advertising, September 1994; Neiman, "The Trouble with Comparative Ads," 4–5; Joseph B. White, "Ford Decides to Fight Back in Truck Ads," *Wall Street Journal,* 28 February 1989, B1, B6.

20. Steven W. Colford, "Agencies Feel More Heat on Comparative Claims," *Advertising Age,* 31 August 1992, 39; Jeffrey A. Trachtenberg, "New Law Adds Risk to Comparative Ads," *Wall Street Journal,* 1 June 1989, B6; Bruce Buchanan and Doron Goldman, "Us vs. Them: The Minefield of Comparative Ads," *Harvard Business Review,* May–June 1989, 38–40, 42, 44, 48, 50; William T. Neese, "Comparative Ads Work Well Even for 'Help Wanted': Strategy Is Best for Mature Markets," *Marketing News,* 20 January 1992, 13; Milton Bordwin, "Don't Bad-Mouth Your Competition," *Management Review,* March 1995, 45–47; Gene Koprowski, "Theories of Negativity," *Brandweek,* February 1995, 20–22.

21. William Panczak, "Co-Op Advertising: Cutting Through the Confusion," *Discount Store News,* 21 October 1991, 10, 14; Ed Crimmins, "Automation: Co-Op's Secret Weapon," *Sales & Marketing Management,* May 1990, 100–102; "Manufacturer Support—and How to Get It," *Restaurant Business Brand Power Supplement,* March 1995, 14–15; Hashi Syedain, "Co-operative Advertising," *Marketing,* 26 January 1995, 33.

22. Paul Duke, Jr., and Ronald Alsop, "Advertisers Beginning to Play Off Worker Concern over Job Security," *Wall Street Journal,* 1 April 1988, A11; Ronald Alsop, "More Food Advertising Plays on Cancer and Cardiac Fears," *Wall Street Journal,* 8 October 1987, 33; George E. Belch and Michael A. Belch, *Introduction to Advertising and Promotion Management* (Homewood, Ill.: Irwin, 1990), 186.

23. Thomas R. King, "Pitches on Value Stick in Consumers' Minds," *Wall Street Journal,* 4 June 1990, B1.

24. "American Voice," *American Demographics,* December 1990, 14; "USA Snapshots: Ads We Find Least Convincing," *USA Today,* 9 March 1988, 1D; Alix Freedman, "Marriages Between Celebrity Spokesmen and Their Firms Can Be Risky Ventures," *Wall Street Journal,* 22 January 1988, A23; Christian Ryssel and Erich Stamminger, "Sponsoring World-Class Tennis Players," *European Research,* May 1988, 110–116.

25. Joshua Levine, "Fantasy, Not Flesh," *Forbes,* 22 January 1990, 118–120.

26. James Cox, "Infiniti's Epiphany," *USA Today,* 15 January 1990, 6B; Joanne Lipman, "Ads of the '80s: The Loved and the Losers," *Wall Street Journal,* 28 December 1989, B1, B4; Ronald Alsop, "Surreal Ads Startle—But Do They Sell?" *Wall Street Journal,* 20 October 1988, B1; Stuart Elliott, "Eternal Wait for Infiniti," *USA Today,* 29 August 1989, 2B; Ronald Alsop, "Can Honda Scooter Ads Get Any More Offbeat Than This?" *Wall Street Journal,* 4 June 1987, B25.

27. Courtland L. Bovée and William F. Arens, *Contemporary Advertising* (Homewood, Ill.: Irwin, 1989), 259–261.

28. Joanne Lipman, "Ad Industry's Health Draws Mixed Prognoses," *Wall Street Journal,* 23 September 1987, B7.

29. Warren Berger, "We're So Sorry," *Inside Print,* January 1988, 34–36, 38, 40, 44.

30. David Ogilvy, *Ogilvy on Advertising* (New York: Vintage Books, 1983), 112.

31. Mark Robichaux, "Cable Operators Refine 'Micro-Marketing,'" *Wall Street Journal,* 16 April 1992, B10; Marcy Magiera, "Cable Network Tunes In Ad Sales After Slow Start," *Advertising Age,* 27 April 1992, 12; Cabletelevision Advertising Bureau, *1991 Cable TV Facts,* 28; Robichaux, "Cable Operators Refine 'Micro-Marketing,'" B10; Dennis Kneale, "'Zapping' of TV Ads Appears Pervasive," *Wall Street Journal,* 25 April 1988, 21.

32. William R. Morrissey, "Gain Competitive Edge with Data-Based Direct Marketing," *Marketing News,* 15 March 1985, 22–23; Jeffery D. Zbar, "Database Marketing Tips Offered," *Advertising Age's Business Marketing,* 23 February 1995, 23; "Database Marketing Goes Mainstream, Says Survey," *Chain Store Age Executive,* January 1995, 82–84; Donald R. Farr, "Database Marketing: From Promise to Practice," *Credit World,* January/February 1995, 17–21.

33. Richard P. Kern, "1984 Survey of Selling Costs: Something Old, Something New," *Sales & Marketing,* 20 February 1984, 12+.

34. Louis Rukeyser, ed., *Louis Rukeyser's Business Almanac* (New York: Simon & Schuster, 1988), 580.

35. Paragraphs on media adapted from Belch and Belch, *Introduction to Advertising and Promotion Management,* 311; Tom Eisenhart and Sue Kapp, "Orchestrating Your Media Options," *Business Marketing,* April 1990, 38–41, 44–47.

36. Kristine Stiven, "Leading Media Companies 1988 Edition," *Advertising Age,* 27 June 1988, S4.

37. Hanna Rubin, "Home Video," *Adweek's Marketing Week,* 11 September 1989, 166, 168; Amy Zipken, "Direct Marketing," *Adweek's Marketing Week,* 11 September 1989, 228, 230; "Calculators on Shopping Carts Can Add Up to Good Business," *San Diego Union,* 23 December 1991, A-22.

38. Paul Holmes, "Public Relations," *Adweek's Marketing Week,* 11 September 1989, 234–235.

39. Gerry Khermouch, "Pepsi Flack Attack Nips Hoax in the Bud," *Brandweek,* 21 June 1993, 5.

40. "To the Winners Belong the Spoils," *Marketing News,* 10 October 1986, 1, 13.

41. Cyndee Miller, "VNRs Are Still Hot, but They're Drawing Fire," *Marketing News,* 12 November 1990, 6.

42. "Sales Promotions—Annual Report 1989: Growing Up & Out," *Marketing & Media Decisions,* July 1990, 20–21.

43. Howard Schlossberg, "Coupons Likely to Remain Popular," *Marketing News,* 29 March 1993, 1, 7; Scott Hume, "Coupons Set Record, but Pace Slows," *Advertising Age,* 1 February 1993, 25; John Philip Jones, "The Double Jeopardy of Sales Promotions," *Harvard Business Review,* September–October 1990, 145–152; Laurie Petersen, "The Pavlovian Syndrome," *Adweek's Marketing Week,* 9 April 1990, P6–P7; Belch and Belch, *Introduction to Advertising and Promotion Management,* 524–526; Fiona Plant, "Smart Card Supersedes Coupons?" *International Journal of Retail & Distribution Management Retail Insights,* Spring 1995, xi; "Coupons—Still the Shopper's Best Friend," *Progressive Grocer,* February 1995, SS11.

44. Terry Lefton and Matthew Grimm, "Coca-Cola Cuts $250 Mil NFL Deal," *Brandweek,* 8 March 1993, 1, 6; "Coke Tops in Backing Big Events," *Advertising Age,* 7 December 1992, 10.

45. Richard Gibson, "Latest in Corporate Freebies Try to Be Classy Instead of Trashy," *Wall Street Journal,* 7 August 1989, B4.

46. Monci Jo Williams, "Trade Promotion Junkies," *The Marketer,* October 1990, 30–33; Margaret Littman, "The Death of Advertising?" *Prepared Foods,* February 1992, 25; Anil Jagtiani, "How to Make Money on Trade Promotions," *Foods & Beverage Marketing,* February 1992, 21+; Michael McCarthy, "The Empire Strikes Back," *Adweek,* 24 February 1992, 1+; Al Urbanski, "Blame It on the Trade," *Food & Beverage Marketing,* January 1992, 28+; Betsy Spethmann, "Trade Promotion Redefined," *Brandweek,* 13 March 1995, 25–32.

47. Seema Nayyar, "Stores Concede on EDLP with a Slashing Passion," *Brandweek,* 2 November 1992, 1, 6; Zachary Schiller, "Procter & Gamble Hits Back," *Business Week,* 19 July 1993, 20–22; Richard Gibson, "Broad Grocery Price Cuts May Not Pay," *Wall Street Journal,* 7 May 1993, B1, B4; Jon Berry, "So How Is P&G's Share? Lagging, New Study Says," *Brandweek,* 19 April 1993, 16.

48. "Trade Shows: An Alternative Method of Selling," *Small Business Reports,* January 1985, 67; Kate Bertrand, "Trade Shows Can Be Global Gateways," *Advertising Age's Business Marketing,* March 1995, 19–20.

49. See note 1.

CHAPTER 16

1. Adapted from Harvey P. Newquist, "AI at Amex," *AI Expert,* January 1993, 39–40; *American Express Annual Report, 1993;* Dennis Livingston, "American Express Reins in the Paper," *Systems Integration,* May 1990, 52–58; James A. Rothi and David C. Yen, "Why American Express Gambled on an Expert Data Base," *Information Strategy,* Spring 1990, 16–22; Patrick Lyons and Anthony Fabiano, "Using Expert System Technology to Foster Innovation," *Review of Business,* Fall 1990, 33–38; John Paul Newport, Jr., "American Express: Service That Sells," *Fortune,* 20 November 1989, 80–94; Steve Fluty, "American Express Goes the Distance," *Inform,* January 1987, 34–36; Eva Kiess-Moser, "Customer Satisfaction," *Canadian Business Review,* Summer 1989, 43–45; "American Express: Focus on Management," *Incentive Marketing,* January 1989, 32–33; Jill Andresky Fraser, "James D. Robinson III: Member Since 1969," *Inc.,* September 1990, 159; Robert Teitelman, "Image vs. Reality at American Express," *Institutional Investor,* February 1992, 36+; Bruce Caldwell, "Amex's Data Center Shuffle: Unloading an Overbuilt Facility Has Proven Daunting," *Information Week,* 10 February 1992, 30+; Phil Britt, "Travelers Checks: An Uncertain Future?" *Savings & Community Banker,* March 1995, 31–34.

2. Kathryn M. Bartol and David C. Martin, *Management* (New York: McGraw-Hill, 1991), 703–705.

3. Courtland L. Bovée, John V. Thill, Marian B. Wood, and George P. Dovel, *Management* (New York: McGraw-Hill, 1993), 572–578.

4. Thomas A Stewart, "The Information Age in Charts," *Fortune,* 4 April 1994, 75–79.

5. David C. Churbuck, "Dial-a-Catalog," *Forbes,* 10 October 1994, 126–130; John W. Verity, "The Internet: How It Will Change the Way You Do Business," *Business Week,* 14 November 1994, 80–88; Peter H. Lewis, "Getting Down to Business on the Net," *New York Times,* 19 June 1994, sec. 3, 1, 6; Paul Wiseman, "The Internet Snares More Businesses," *USA Today,* 7 July 1994, B1, B2; Albert Fried-Cassorla, "Successful Marketing on the Internet: A User's Guide," *Direct Marketing,* March 1995, 39–42; David Taylor, "Digital Dreaming: The Internet Marketing Primer," *Marketing Computers,* March 1995, 24, 36+.

6. Bartol and Martin, *Management,* 709–710.

7. Donald H. Sanders, *Computers Today* (New York: McGraw-Hill, 1988), 118.

8. Sanders, *Computers Today,* 122.

9. Sanders, *Computers Today,* 121–122.

10. Gary Hoover, Alta Campbell, and Patrick J. Spain, eds., *Hoover's Handbook of American Business 1994* (Austin, Tex.: Reference Press, 1993), 161.

11. Hoover, Campbell, and Spain, *Hoover's Handbook of American Business 1994,* 408–409.

12. Gene Bylinksy, "The Digital Factory," *Fortune,* 14 November 1994, 92–110.

13. William M. Bulkeley, "Speech Recognition Gets Cheaper and Smarter," *Wall Street Journal,* 6 June 1994, B1, B6; Mike Sharman, "Speech Recognition Technology Helps Banks Enhance Customer Service," *Bankers Magazine,* March/April 1995, 60–62; Eric E. Cohen and Cliff Beshers, "Making Automated Speech Recognition Work," *CPA Journal,* February 1995, 72–74.

14. Timothy Trainor and Diane Krasnewich, *Computers!* (New York: McGraw-Hill, 1989), 90.

15. Trainor and Krasnewich, *Computers!,* 90–91.

16. Charles S. Parker, *Management Information Systems, Strategy and Action* (New York: McGraw-Hill, 1989), 54.

17. Laurie Flynn, "CD-ROMs: They're Not Just for Entertainment," *New York Times,* 24 April 1994, sec. f, 10; Nancy K. Herther, "CD-ROM at Ten Years: The Technology and the Industry Mature," *Online,* March/April 1995, 86–93.

18. Stephen G. Kochan and Patrick H. Wood, *Exploring the UNIX System* (Indianapolis: Hayden, 1989), 1.

19. *Database Catalog* (Palo Alto, Calif.: Dialog Information Services, 1994).

20. Sanders, *Computers Today,* 406.

21. Information on Associate obtained from Business Software Database.

22. The section on languages is adapted from Sanders, *Computers Today,* 501–517.

23. Adapted from an example in Trainor and Krasnewich, *Computers!,* 41.

24. Trainor and Krasnewich, *Computers!,* 161–163.

25. L. John Severson, "Junk My Mainframe? You Bet!" *Computerworld,* 30 May 1994, 92, 96; Joe Vincent, "Junk My Mainframe? No Way!" *Computerworld,* 30 May 1994, 93, 97.

26. Bart Ziegler, "Building the Highway: New Obstacles, New Solutions," *Wall Street Journal,* 18 May 1994, B1; Geraldine Cronin, "Marketability and Social Implications of Interactive TV and the Information Superhighway," *IEEE Transactions on Professional Communication,* March 1995, 24–32; "Groups Crowd the on Ramp for the Information Superhighway," *Medical Economics,* 13 March 1995, 170; Valencia Roner, "Lost on the Information Superhighway?" *Black Enterprise,* April 1995, 45; Nobilangelo Ceramalus, "Glimpses Down the Information Superhighway: A Kaleidoscope," *Management-Auckland,* March 1995, 26–27; Lawrence Watt and Polly Stewart, "Cashing in on the Information Superhighway," *Management-Auckland,* February 1995, 58–65; Peter Meyer, "Information Superhighway," *Business & Economic Review,* January-March 1995, 26–27.

27. Frank Jossi, "Eavesdroppers in Cyberspace," *Business Ethics,* May–June 1994, 22–25.

28. See note 1.

CHAPTER 17

1. Adapted from Debbie Berlant, Reese Browning, and George Foster, "How Hewlett-Packard Gets Numbers It Can Trust," *Harvard Business Review,* January–February 1990, 178–183.

2. Personal communication, American Institute of Certified Public Accountants, New York, 1992; Spencer Phelps Harris, ed., *Who Audits America?* (Menlo Park, Calif.: Data Financial Press, 1990), 283.

3. Paul Schneider, "'Til Retirement Do Them Part," *Business Month,* July 1990, 14–15; "Less Is More Among the Bean Counters," *U.S. News & World Report,* 17 July 1989, 11; David Greising, Leah J. Nathans, and Laura Jereski, "The New Numbers Game in Accounting," *Business Week,* 24 July 1989, 20–21; "The Big Eight, Seven, Six . . . ," *Time,* 17 July 1989, 77.

4. Suzanne Woolley, "These White Shoes Are Splattered with Mud," *Business Week,* 7 September 1992, 32; Lee Berton, "Convenient Fiction: Inventory Chicanery Tempts More Firms, Fools More Auditors," *Wall Street Journal,* 14 December 1993, A1, A5; Ellen Benoit, "The Bean-Counter Blues," *Financial World,* 22 January 1991, 38–39.

5. Lee Berton, "Accountants Issue Guidelines to Prevent Manager Fraud; Legislator Assails Them," *Wall Street Journal,* 13 March 1991, A2; Lee Berton, "Guides to Prevent Fraud in Business Are Slated Today," *Wall Street Journal,* 12 March 1991, C21; Alison Leigh Cowan, "Accountants Fear S. & L. Backlash," *New York Times,* 31 July 1990, sec. c, 1; Richard H. Franke, "Fraud: Bringing Light to the Dark Side of Business," *Academy of Management Executive,* February 1995, 93–95.

6. Susan Goodwin and Edward W. Younkins, "How the Expanding Scope of CPA Services Threatens Accountants' Claim to Independence," *Practical Accountant,* September 1990, 92–99; March Leepson, "Taking Off by the Numbers," *Nation's Business,* August 1987, 49.

7. Jack L. Smith, Robert M. Keith, and William L. Stephens, *Accounting Principles, 4th ed.* (New York: McGraw-Hill, 1993), 16–17.

8. Wayne Tusa, "A Proactive Approach to Environmental Risks," *Risk Management,* January 1994, 12–13; Dennis L. Kimmell, "Readings," *Internal Auditor,* June 1993, 16; Jo-Ann Longworth and Karen Montano, "Cleaning Up the Books," *CA Magazine,* June–July 1993, 55–58.

9. Bill Birchard, "The Right to Know," *CFO: The Magazine for Senior Financial Executives,* November 1993, 28–38.

10. Lee Berton, "FASB Rule Requires Public Companies to Issue Annual Cash-Flow Statements," *Wall Street Journal,* 23 November 1987, 10.

11. Michael W. Miller and Lee Berton, "Softer Numbers: As IBM's Woes Grew, Its Accounting Tactics Got Less Conservative," *Wall Street Journal,* 7 April 1993, A1, A4.

12. Steven Waldman and Rich Thomas, "How Did It Happen?" *Newsweek,* 21 May 1990, 27–28, 32; Jonathan Beaty, "Running with a Bad Crowd," *Time,* 1 October 1990, 36–40; Howard Rudnitsky, "Good Timing, Charlie," *Forbes,* 27 November 1989, 140–144.

13. Suein L. Hwang, "J & J to Acquire Unit of Kodak for $1.01 Billion," *Wall Street Journal,* 7 September 1994, A3, A4.

14. Robert Mulligan, "Ice Cream," *Starting Out Series,* no. 142, U.S. Small Business Administration, September 1980 (republished 1983).

15. See note 1.

CHAPTER 18

1. Adapted from Linda Grant, "A Rebel Banker Battles On," *U.S. News & World Report,* 7 March 1994, 59, 61; "Here Comes Hugh (Again)," *United States Banker,* July 1993, 6; Yvette Kantrow, "NationsLender," *American Banker,* 4 March 1992, 2; Rob Levin, "Birth of a NationsBank," *Business Atlanta,* December 1991, 30–32, 34; Allen M. Myerson, "Nationsbank Will Create a Firm with Dean Witter," *New York Times,* 27 October 1992, sec. c, 1, 6; Peter Nulty, "America's Toughest Bosses," *Fortune,* 27 February 1989, 40–46, 50, 54; Robert Bruce Slater, "The Architect of NCNB's First Republic Buyout," *Bankers Monthly,* May 1989, 26–27; James Srodes, "A Tale of Two Banks: East Coast Wisdom . . . ," *Financial World,* 6 February 1990, 26–30; Gary Hector, "The Brash Banker Who Bought Texas," *Fortune,* 27 August 1990, 54–62; Mary Colby, "Southeast Superregionals Go to the Mat," *Bank Marketing,* November 1990, 40–45; Betsy Morris, Fred Bleakley, and Martha Brannigan, "Power Shift: In New Merger Wave, Superregional Banks Are Grabbing the Lead," *Wall Street Journal,* 28 June 1991, A1–A6; Kenneth Cline and James R. Kraus, "C&S–Sovran Forced to Play a Weak Hand," *American Banker,* 9 July 1991, 1, 7; Martha Brannigan, "NCNB C&S–Sovran Agree to a $4.26 Billion Merger," *Wall Street Journal,* 22 July 1991, A3; Martha Brannigan, "NCNB–C&S Merger Will Stir Up South," *Wall Street Journal,* 23 July 1991, A2; Marilyn Sczech and Dennis Attenello, "NationsBank Reengineers to Achieve Leadership in International Services," *National Productivity Review,* Spring 1995, 89–96.

2. Amy Borrus and Peter Galuszka, "Russia: 'The Fears Are Gone,'" *Business Week,* 26 September 1994, 76–77; Laurie Laird, "Notebook: Foreign Banks in Russia," *Europe,* March 1995, SS2-SS3; Ben Edwards, "Why Russia's Banks Want Tougher Regulation," *Euromoney,* January 1995, 45–52.

3. Thomas McCarroll, "No Checks. No Cash. No Fuss?" *Time,* 9 May 1994, 60–61; "88% of U.S. Currency Unaccounted For, Study Says," *San Diego Union,* 11 February 1986, A-2; Paul W. Cockerham, "Verify or Guarantee? Check Dilemma: Retailers Reassess Ways to Protect Against Bad Checks," *Stores,* January, 1995, 94.

4. Carol Boyd Leon, "Why Americans Are Writing More Checks," *American Demographics,* February 1987, 35; McCarroll, "No Checks. No Cash. No Fuss?" 60–61.

5. Margaret Mannix, "Checks Made of Plastic," *U.S. News & World Report,* 14 March 1994, 72–74; "Spreading Financial Networks," *Nation's Business,* June 1985, 42.

6. Terence P. Pare, "Tough Birds That Quack Like Banks," *Fortune,* 11 March 1991, 79–84.

7. Nyra Krstovich, Reference Librarian at Federal Reserve Bank of San Francisco, personal communication, 28 September 1991.

8. "Banks Regaining Health, Government Says," *The News Times* (Danbury, Conn.), 16 June 1994, D-8; John Meehan, Mike McNamee, Gail DeGeorge, and Joan O'C.

Hamilton, "Is There Any Bottom to the Thrift Quagmire?" *Business Week,* 4 March 1991, 62–63.

9. Desiree French, "Credit Unions Giving Banks a Fierce Fight," *USA Today,* 16 November 1992, B1; March Scanlin, "How Small Credit Unions Can Market 'Big,'" *Credit Union Executive,* January/February 1995, 18–22; Nicolette Lemmon, "Credit Unions—The Next Generation: What the Future Holds," *Credit Union Executive,* January/February 1995, 14–17.

10. Shlomo Maital, "What Business Are Banks In?" *Across the Board,* April 1992, 47–48; Bernard Baumohl, "Are Banks Obsolete?" *Time,* 28 June 1993, 49–50; Pare, "Tough Birds That Quack Like Banks," 79–84; Catherine Yang, Howard Gleckman, Mike McNamee, Chuck Hawkins, and Peter Coy, "The Future of Banking: Banks Must Be Free—and Willing—to Change, or They May Die," *Business Week,* 22 April 1991, 72–76.

11. G. Bruce Knecht, "Era of Lush Profits Ends as Card Issuers Face Increased Competition, Savvy Users," *Wall Street Journal,* 22 June 1994, B1, B2.

12. Leonard Sloane, "Banks Expand Their Range of Services," *New York Times,* 2 May 1992, 18.

13. Vicky Cahan, "Banks Are on the Brink of Breaking Loose," *Business Week,* 7 March 1988, 99.

14. Marc Levinson, "Lenders Out on a Limb," *Newsweek,* 7 June 1993, 40; John Meehan, "Fewer Pieces, a Better Fit," *Business Week Reinventing America 1992,* 126–128, 132.

15. McCarroll, "No Checks. No Cash. No Fuss?" 60–61.

16. Michael Siconolfi, "Widening Reach: Merrill Lynch, Pushing into Many New Lines, Expands Bank Services," *Wall Street Journal,* 7 July 1993, A1, A9.

17. John Meehan, "America's Bumbling Bankers: Ripe for a New Fiasco," *Business Week,* 2 March 1992, 86–87.

18. Mike McNamee, "Are Fewer Banks Better?" *Business Week,* 17 August 1992, 92–93; Steve Lohr, "Recasting the Big Banks: Weakened Giants, in Humbling Mergers, Are Fighting to Regain Their Dominance," *New York Times,* 17 July 1991, sec. a, 1, sec. c, 6; Michael Quint, "Bigger Banks, but Better Banking?" *New York Times,* 23 August 1991, sec. c, 1, 4.

19. Michael Allen and Peter Pae, "Feisty Small Fry: Despite the Mergers of Many Big Banks, Tiny Ones May Thrive," *Wall Street Journal,* 9 October 1991, A1, A7; Pamela J. Podger, "Bank Start-Ups Draw Interest of Small Firms," *Wall Street Journal,* 28 December 1990, B1–B2; "Despite Changing Market, Banks Still Urge to Merge," *CFO Alert,* January 30, 1995, 1; Steven Lipin and Timothy L. O'Brien, "Mergers Between U.S Banks Seem to be Heating Up Again," *Wall Street Journal—Europe,* 23 February 1995, 11.

20. Lori Ioannou, "Friendly Invaders: Foreign Banks Score Big with U.S. Companies," *International Business,* November 1992, 29–30, 32.

21. Robert A. Rosenblatt, "Border Crossing," *Los Angeles Times,* 5 June 1994, D1, D4.

22. Rosenblatt, "Border Crossing," D1, D4.

23. Julie Stacey, "USA Snapshots: Bank Failures," *USA Today,* 23 May 1991, 1B; Fred R. Bleakley, "Bank Industry Had Dismal '90, Survey Shows," *Wall Street Journal,* 11 February 1991, A3, A6; Kenneth H. Bacon, "Big Banks Would Get Vastly Broader Powers Under Treasury's Plan," *Wall Street Journal,* 6 February, 1991, A1–A4; Stephen Labaton, "Top U.S. Auditor Predicts Banks May Be Headed for Large Bailout," *New York Times,* 12 June 1991, sec. a, 1, sec. c, 3; Leonard Silk, "The Argument over Banks," *New York Times,* 8 February 1991, sec. d, 2; David T. Llewellyn, "The Future Business of Banking," *Banking World,* January 1995, 16–19.

24. "Banking Business on the Rebound," *The News Times* (Danbury, Conn.), 23 September 1994, C-8.

25. William M. Isaac, "Wrong Time to Soak the Banks," *Wall Street Journal,* 29 January 1991, A16.

26. Meir Kohn, *Financial Institutions and Markets* (New York: McGraw-Hill, 1994), 761.

27. Mark D. Fefer, "Time to Speed Up the S&L Cleanup," *Fortune,* 16 November 1992, 116–118, 120; Don Moehrke, Liam Carmody, Tony Matera, and Joseph Pendleton, "Service Variety Seen Key to Home Banking's Future," *EFT Report,* 29 March 1995, 4.

28. Associated Press, "47% of Bankers Have Doubts About FDIC," *Arizona Republic,* 8 October 1991, 14; Stephen Labaton, "Bank Deposit Fund Nearly Insolvent, U.S. Auditor Says," *New York Times,* 27 April 1991, sec. 1, 31; Stephen Labaton, "Bank Fund Outlook Is Bleaker," *New York Times,* 28 June 1991, sec. c, 1, 9.

29. Paul Duke, Jr., "S&L Mess May Spark a Thorough Overhaul of Deposit Insurance," *Wall Street Journal,* 3 July 1990, A1, A10.

30. "A Guide Through the Banking Maze," *USA Today,* 25 February 1985, 3B.

31. Roland I. Robinson and Dwayne Wrightsman, *Financial Markets: The Accumulation and Allocation of Wealth* (New York: McGraw-Hill, 1974), 214–215.

32. See note 1.

CHAPTER 19

1. Adapted from Ronaleen R. Roha, "Starting a New Business: The Scary First Year," *Kiplinger's Personal Finance Magazine,* February 1993, 75–78, 80.

2. John J. Curran, "Hard Lessons from the Debt Decade," *Fortune,* 18 June 1990, 76–81; Robert F. Black, Don L. Boroughs, Sara Collins, and Kenneth Sheets, "Heavy Lifting," *U.S. News & World Report,* 6 May 1991, 52–61.

3. Stephen J. Negrotti, "Going for the Gold," *Enterprise '92,* advertising supplement to *New York Times Magazine,* 21 June 1992, 4A, 8A.

4. Agis Salpukas, "Northwest Cancels Jet Order," *New York Times,* 8 December 1992, sec. c, 1, 5.

5. Monika Guttman, "Fishing for Financing," *U.S. News & World Report,* 8 August 1994, 48.

6. Stephanie Strom, "It's Called Targeted Stock: Shun It, Some Experts Say," *New York Times,* 12 July 1994, sec. c, 1, 5; Tom Pratt, "First 'Targeted Stock' Issue to Unwind in Continental Sale," *Investment Dealers Digest,* 16 January 1995, 14.

7. Dana Wechsler Linden, "The Bean Counter as Hero," *Forbes,* 11 October 1993, 46–48.

8. Fred R. Bleakley, "Fast Money: Electronic Payments Now Supplant Checks at More Firms," *Wall Street Journal,* 13 April 1994, A1, A8; Daniel J. Biby, "Who Really Needs EDI?" *Industry Week,* 2 November 1992, 45–46; Clay Youngblood, "Standards and EDI," *Industry Week,* 2 November 1992, 47–48; Vince Schoon, "Integrating EDI into the Procurement Cycle," *TMA Journal,* March/April 1995, 50–52; Geoff Tyler, "Unravelling EDI, E-mail & Internet," *Management Services,* March 1995, 26–30; Linda Cole and Jake W. Windham, "A Bank's Role in EDI Implementation," *Healthcare Financial Management,* March 1995, 52–53.

9. Julie Candler, "Just-in-Time Deliveries," *Nation's Business,* April 1993, 64–65; Bill Bailey, "Distributor Wants to Rid Materials Management Vocabulary of 'Just-in-Time' and 'Stockless,'" *Hospital Materials Management,* April 1995, 9; Jayanta J. Bandyopadhyay and Mulumudi J. Jayaram, "Implementing Just-in-Time Production and Procurement Strategies," *International Journal of Management,* March 1995, 83–90.

10. See note 1.

CHAPTER 20

1. Adapted from William A. Francis, vice president, Landes Associates, Inc., Wilmington, Delaware, personal communication, 7 October 1991.

2. William Power, "Small Investors Are Punier Than Many Think," *Wall Street Journal,* 28 March 1989, C1, C10; Jordan E. Goodman, "Small Investors Reach for Rising Rates," *Money,* March 1995, 63; T. Carter Hagaman, "A Sure-Footed Path for Small Investors," *Management Accounting,* January 1995, 14.

3. Anise C. Wallace, "How the Little Guy Is Playing the Market," *New York Times,* 3 September 1989, sec. 3, 1, 10.

4. John Waggoner, "Hot Line Tackles Today's Financial Quandries," *USA Today,* 4 October 1993, 3B.

5. Jonathan Clements, "For a Calmer Portfolio: Just Add a Little Risk," *Wall Street Journal,* 24 June 1994, C1.

6. Ellen E. Schultz, "How to Build a Stock Portfolio Even If You Aren't a Moneybags," *Wall Street Journal,* 10 April 1992, C1, C11; Debbie Galant, "How Safe Are Stocks?" *Institutional Investor,* March 1995, 133; "Mark Hulbert, "The Bear Growls," *Forbes,* 27 March 1995, 154.

7. Michael R. Sesit, "Why It's Time for Investors to Think Globally," *Wall Street Journal,* 23 April 1993, C1, C5.

8. Martin L. Leibowitz and Stanley Kogelman, "Asset Allocation Under Shortfall Constraints," *Journal of Portfolio Management,* Winter 1991, 18–23.

9. Gordon J. Alexander, William F. Sharpe, and Jeffery V. Bailey, *Fundamentals of Investments,* 2d ed. (Englewood Cliffs, N.J.: Prentice Hall, 1993), 540–542.

10. Jeffrey B. Little and Lucien Rhodes, *Understanding Wall Street,* 2d ed. (Blue Ridge Summit, Pa.: Liberty House, 1987), 128.

11. Gary Weiss, "The Long and Short of Short-Selling," *Business Week,* 10 June 1991, 106–108; Mack Gracian, "Selling Short, an Adventure in Risk," *Black Enterprise,* April 1995, 47–48; Andrew Marshall, "New Arrangements for Short Selling Disclosure During Secondary Offers," *Financial Regulation Report,* February 1995, 12–13.

12. John Greenwald, "The Siren Call of Mutual Funds," *Time,* 8 November 1993, 58–60; David H. Bugen, "Your Best Assets: Individual Securities or Mutual Funds?" *Financial Executive,* January/February 1995, 57–58; "What Clients Need to Know about Mutual Funds," *Canadian Banker,* January/February 1995, 28.

13. Barnaby J. Feder, "Chicago's Exchanges Look Toward an Electronic Salvation," *New York Times,* 29 November 1992, sec. 3, 5.

14. Sumner N. Levine, ed., *The Dow Jones–Irwin Business and Investment Almanac* (Homewood, Ill.: Dow Jones–Irwin, 1988), 453.

15. William E. Sheeline, "Who Needs the Stock Exchange?" *Fortune,* 19 November 1990, 119–124.

16. John Waggoner, "Funds a Solid, Low-Cost Bet," *USA Today,* 4 October 1993, 3B.

17. Sheeline, "Who Needs the Stock Exchange?" 119–124.

18. Craig Torres and William Power, "Big Board Is Losing Some of Its Influence over Stock Trading," *Wall Street Journal,* 17 April 1990, A1, A6.

19. Robert Ferri, National Association of Securities Dealers, New York, personal communication, December 1991; "NASDAQ International to Start Up in January," press release, National Association of Securities Dealers Automated Quotation System, 10 October 1991.

20. Sheeline, "Who Needs the Stock Exchange?" 119–124; Richard L. Stern, "A Dwindling Monopoly," *Forbes,* 13 May 1991, 64–66; Torres and Power, "Big Board Is Losing Influence," A1, A6.

21. Susan Antilla, "New Shaker in the A.D.R. Business," *New York Times,* 1 August 1993, sec. 3, 13; Jack Clark Francis, *Management of Investments,* 3d ed. (New York: McGraw-Hill, 1993), 664.

22. Catherine Friend White, "At Home in the Global Marketplace," *Business Ethics,* September–October 1993, 39–40.

23. Diana B. Henriques, "In World Markets, Loose Regulation," *New York Times,* 23 July 1991, sec. c, 1, 6–7.

24. Susan Antilla, "Why Stocks Swing on World Events," *New York Times,* 23 September 1993, C1, C4.

25. Kathy M. Kristof, "The Dow Jones Industrial Average," *Los Angeles Times,* 7 August 1994, D1, D6.

26. John J. Curran, "Finding a Path Between Greed and Fear," *Fortune 1986 Investor's Guide,* Fall 1985, 9.

27. Louis Rukeyser, ed., *Louis Rukeyser's Business Almanac* (New York: Simon & Schuster, 1988), 305.

28. John Heine, deputy director of the office of public affairs, Securities and Exchange Commission, Washington, D.C., personal communication, December 1991; Susan Antilla, "Wall Street: A Watchdog from the Other Side," *New York Times,* 10 October 1993, sec. c, 13.

29. Theodore Focht, president and general counsel at the Securities Investors Protection Corporation, Washington, D.C., personal communication, December 1991.

30. Adapted from William A. Francis, vice president, Landes Associates, Inc., Wilmington, Delaware, personal communication, 7 October 1991.

31. Index names from Alan Chai, Alta Campbell, and Patrick J. Spain, eds., *Hoover's Handbook of World Business, 1993* (Austin, Tex.: Reference Press, 1993), 90–97.

CHAPTER 21

1. Richard Buck, "Living with Wal-Mart," *Seattle Times,* 14 November 1994, E1, E6; Eugene L. Meyer, "Up Against the Wal-Mart," *Washington Post,* 28 February 1993, F1, F3; Bob Ortega, "Ban the Bargains," *Wall Street Journal,* 11 October 1994, A1, A6; Suzanne Alexander, "Feisty Yankees Resist Wal-Mart's Drive to Set up Shop in New England Towns," *Wall Street Journal,* 16 September 1993, B1, B7; John L. Gann, Jr., "Main Street vs. Wal-Mart," *Wall Street Journal,* 30 August 1993, A10; Jeffrey Pfeffer, Toru Hatano, Timu Santalainen, "Producing Sustainable Competitive Advantage through the Effective Management of People," *Academy of Management Executive,* February 1995, 55–72; "Building Around the World," *Chain Store Age Executive,* February 1995, 88–92.

2. Jacqueline Davidson and Barbara Ettorre, "Need R&D Help? Ask the Feds," *Small Business Reports,* May 1994, 48–54.

3. *Survey of Current Business* (Washington, D.C.: GPO, September 1991), 3, 8.

4. William C. Frederick, Keith Davis, and James E. Post, *Business and Society,* 6th ed. (New York: McGraw-Hill, 1990), 154–166.

5. Richard M. Steuer, *A Guide to Marketing Law: What Every Seller Should Know* (New York: Harcourt Brace Jovanovich, 1986), 4–6.

6. Elizabeth Corcoran, "Deal: How Microsoft Settled," *Seattle Times,* 18 July 1994, A1.

7. Steuer, *A Guide to Marketing Law,* 21, 143, 157.

8. Eben Shapiro, "Food Labs Gaze Hungrily at Potential in Labeling Rules," *Wall Street Journal,* 10 December 1992, B2.

9. Anne Scott Daughtrey and Betty Roper Ricks, *Contemporary Supervision* (New York: McGraw-Hill, 1989), 532–540.

10. Frederick, Davis, and Post, *Business and Society,* 243–258.

11. Vicky Cahan, "A Clean-Air Bill Is Easy; Clean Air Is Hard," *Business Week,* 5 November 1990, 50; Richard C. Scherr, Allan G. Smalley, Jr., and Michael E. Norman, "Clean Air Amendments Put Big Burden on Refinery Planners," *Oil and Gas Journal,* 10 June 1991, 35; "Clean Air: Where It Hurts," *Economist,* 4 March 1995, 26–31; Anthony J. Sadar, "Demand to Curb Pollution is Getting Everyone in on the Act —The Clean Air Act," *Plant Engineering,* 6 March 1995, 101, 104; Vincent A. Rocco, "New Requirements Under the Clean Air Act," *Risk Management,* March 1995, 25–28.

12. Frederick, Davis, and Post, *Business and Society,* 158.

13. "Ma Bell's Family Leaves Home, 1982," *Wall Street Journal,* 1 December 1989, B1; Laura Evenson, "MCI Cuts Intrastate Telephone Call Rates," *San Francisco Chronicle,* 9 January 1990, sec. c, 1, 12.

14. "New TWA Chairman Calls for Price Controls," Prodigy Services Company, 7 July 1993.

15. Kari Huus, "Look Out, Chinese Love Solution," *Advertising Age International,* 28 September 1992, I-6.

16. Frederick, Davis, and Post, *Business and Society,* 168–169.

17. *Survey of Current Business,* 7.

18. Internal Revenue Service, Form 1040 Instructions for 1993, 25.

19. Richard L. Berke, "Donors to Parties Sidestepped Rules," *New York Times,* 18 May 1991, sec. b, 7.

20. George A. Steiner and John F. Steiner, *Business, Government, and Society* (New York: McGraw-Hill, 1991), 149.

21. Bartley A. Brennan and Nancy Kubasek, *The Legal Environment of Business* (New York: McGraw-Hill, 1991), 17.

22. Thomas W. Dunfee, Frank F. Gibson, John D. Blackburn, Douglas Whitman, F. William McCarty, and Bartley A. Brennan, *Modern Business Law* (New York: Random House, 1989), 164.

23. Brennan and Kubasek, *The Legal Environment of Business,* 183.

24. Brennan and Kubasek, *The Legal Environment of Business,* 184.

25. Gail Greco, "Product Liability Bill on Its Way," *Entrepreneur,* October 1990, 192–193.

26. Dunfee et al., *Modern Business Law,* 569.
27. Brennan and Kubasek, *The Legal Environment of Business,* 198–199.
28. Dunfee et al., *Modern Business Law,* 236.
29. Dunfee et al., *Modern Business Law,* 284–297; Brennan and Kubasek, *The Legal Environment of Business,* 125–127; Douglas Whitman and John William Gergacz, *The Legal Environment of Business,* 2d ed. (New York: Random House, 1988), 196–197; *The Lawyer's Almanac* (Englewood Cliffs, N.J.: Prentice Hall Law & Business, 1991), 888.
30. Brennan and Kubasek, *The Legal Environment of Business,* 128.
31. Steur, *A Guide to Marketing Law,* 151–152.
32. Dunfee et al., *Modern Business Law,* 745, 749.
33. Brennan and Kubasek, *The Legal Environment of Business,* 152–153; Whitman and Gergacz, *The Legal Environment of Business,* 252.
34. Brennan and Kubasek, *The Legal Environment of Business,* 160; Whitman and Gergacz, *The Legal Environment of Business,* 260.
35. Jerry M. Rosenberg, *Dictionary of Business and Management* (New York: Wiley, 1983), 340.
36. Ronald A. Anderson, Ivan Fox, and David P. Twomey, *Business Law* (Cincinnati: South-Western Publishing, 1987), 635.
37. Brennan and Kubasek, *The Legal Environment of Business,* 516–517.
38. See note 1.

CHAPTER 22

1. Adapted from *Marriott International 1993 Annual Report;* Kathryn J. McIntyre, "1991 Risk Manager of the Year: Growing with Marriott," *Business Insurance,* 29 April 1991, 142–156; Pamela Taulbee, "Corralling Runaway Workers' Comp Costs," *Business & Health,* April 1991, 46–55; Carol Cain, "No Kidding About Safety: Great American Keeps Comp Losses Down, Despite Very Young, Seasonal Workforce," *Business Insurance,* 8 August 1983, 3, 37; Mary Jane Fisher, "Informed Workers Make Wise Health Care Users," *National Underwriter,* 2 May 1988, 10–11; Kathy Seal, "Marriott Hotels Get Green Light from EPA," *Hotel & Motel Management,* 24 February 1992, 26.
2. William D. Harrel and John S. DeMott, "Business Lessons from a Disaster," *Nation's Business,* May 1993, 38–40.
3. George L. Head, "The Steps in Risk Management," in *The Risk Management Process* (New York: Risk and Insurance Management Society, 1978), 12.
4. Much of the material related to the three steps of the risk-management process is adapted from Head, "The Steps in Risk Management," 12–15.
5. "The Budget Dollar," *San Diego Union,* 30 January 1992, A-7; Mark R. Greene and James S. Trieschmann, *Risk and Insurance* (Cincinnati: South-Western Publishing, 1988), 81.

6. Mark S. Dorfman, *Introduction to Risk Management and Insurance,* 5th ed. (Englewood Cliffs, N.J.: Prentice Hall, 1994), 376.
7. "America's Insurers: No Thrift Crisis, This," *The Economist,* 20 April 1991, 78, 80, 82.
8. Beatrice E. Garcia, "Insurers Slip into Cyclical Downturn," *Wall Street Journal,* 14 February 1989, A1.
9. Eric N. Bert, "Insurance Giants No Longer Ask to Be All Things to All People," *New York Times,* 7 February 1991, sec. a, 1.
10. John D. Long and Davis W. Gregg, eds., *Property and Liability Insurance Handbook* (Homewood, Ill.: Irwin, 1965), 829+.
11. Greene and Trieschmann, *Risk and Insurance,* 530.
12. C. Arthur Williams, Jr., and Richard M. Heins, *Risk Management and Insurance,* 6th ed. (New York: McGraw-Hill, 1989).
13. Leonard Sloane, "Worker Insurance Evolution," *New York Times,* 6 December 1983, sec. c, 1.
14. "Controlling Insurance Costs," *Inc.,* April 1988, 128.
15. American Institute of Certified Public Accountants; George J. Church, "Sorry, Your Policy Is Canceled," *Time* 24 March 1986, 20; Lee Berton, "The CPA Jungle: Accounting Profession, Once a Staid Field, Is Torn by Incivility," *Wall Street Journal,* 24 July 1991, A1.
16. Stephen H. Collins, ed., "Practitioner's Update: Liability Crisis Ahead?" *The Practical Accountant,* November 1990, 19.
17. Randall Lane, "Dangerous Games," *Forbes,* 31 January 1994, 88.
18. Martha Glaser, "Managed Care Bites Benefit!" *Business and Health,* May 1991, 71–72, 74, 76, 78; "Managed Care Resources Update," *Medical Marketing & Media,* March 1995, 78; Jill Wechsler, "Reaching Out to Managed Care," *Managed Healthcare,* April 1995, 52–54; "Managed Care Answer Book," *Employee Benefit Plan Review,* March 1995, 48; "How One Group Expects to Dazzle Managed-Care Plans," *Medical Economics,* 13 March 1995, 52.
19. Jennell Patterson, Public Relations Office, Health Insurance Association of America, personal communication, 1989.
20. Greene and Trieschmann, *Risk and Insurance,* 298.
21. Patterson, personal communication, 1989.
22. Patterson, personal communication, 1989.
23. Ellen Paris, "Sigmund Freud, Meet Jean-Baptiste Say," *Forbes,* 19 February 1990, 148.
24. Maureen Weiss, "The High Cost of Klutzmanship," *Across the Board,* May 1991, 59.
25. Milt Freudenheim, "Health Care a Growing Burden," *New York Times,* 29 January 1991, sec. c, 1.
26. Philip J. Hilts, "Say Ouch: Demands to Fix U.S. Health Care Reach a Crescendo,"

New York Times, 19 May 1991, sec. 4, 1; Paul Dwyer and Susan B. Garland, "A Roar of Discontent," *Business Week,* 25 November 1991, 28–30.
27. U.S. to Meet with Major Health Insurers," *New York Times,* 24 September 1991, sec. a, 19; Medical Rationing," *U.S. News & World Reports,* 7 January 1991, 85.
28. David Azevedo, "California Rejects Single-Payer; Oregon Adopts Aid-in-Dying," *Medical Economics* 71, no. 22 (1994): 40; Barbara A. Grumet, "Health Policy Reform in America: Innovations from the States," *American Review of Public Administration* 24, no. 3 (1994): 331–332.
29. Sidney Marchasin, "Cost Shifting: How One Hospital Does It," *Wall Street Journal,* 9 December 1991, A10.
30. Ron Winslow, "Medical Experiment: Some Companies Try 'Managed Care' in Bid to Curb Health Costs," *Wall Street Journal,* 1 February 1991, A1; Sally Berger and John Abendshien, "Questions to Mull on Managed-Care Pacts," *Modern Heathcare,* 16 March 1992, 54; Christine Woolsey, "Risks of Managed Care," *Business Insurance,* 23 March 1992, 2; Lauren Haworth, "Traditional Health Plans Give Way to Managed Care," *The Business Journal—Portland,* 24 February 1992, 9.
31. Joyce E. Santora, "Allied-Signal's Network Cuts Health Care Costs," *Personnel Journal,* May 1991, 41.
32. Julie Candler, "Safe Driving Saves Money," *Nation's Business,* March 1993, 60–62; Roger Thompson, "Taking Charge of Workers' Comp," *Nation's Business,* October 1993, 18–24.
33. Edmund Faltermayer, "Strong Medicine for Health Costs," Fortune, 23 April 1990, 221, 226; Michelle Neely Martinez, "Dramatic Slowdown in Health-Care Costs," *HRMagazine,* April 1995, 25–26; Joseph V. Vincenzino, "Health Care Costs: Market Forces and Reform," *Statistical Bulletin–Metropolitan Life Insurance Company,* January–March 1995, 45.
34. Faltermayer, "Strong Medicine for Health Costs," 224, 226.
35. *Employee Benefits* (Washington, D.C.: U.S. Chamber of Commerce, 1991), 28.
36. *1991 Life Insurance Fact Book, Update* (Washington, D.C.: American Council of Life Insurance, 1991), 4.
37. See note 1.

APPENDIX A

1. Sewell Whitney, "On-Line Résumés Put Job Candidates in Line," *Advertising Age,* 7 March 1985, 48.
2. Kathleen Murray, "Plug In. Log On. Find a Job." *New York Times,* 2 January 1994, sec. c, 23; "Times to Offer Résumé Service," *New York Times,* 4 November 1993, sec. c, 17.
3. Carol M. Barnum, "Writing Résumés That Sell," *MW,* September–October 1987, 11.

4. Pam Stanley-Weigand, "Organizing the Writing of Your Resume," *The Bulletin of the Association for Business Communication* LIV, no. 3 (September 1991): 11–12.
5. Janice Tovey, "Using Visual Theory in the Creation of Resumes: A Bibliography," *The Bulletin of the Association for Business Communication* LIV, no. 3 (September 1991): 97–99.
6. Sal Divita, "If You're Thinking Résumé, Think Creatively," *Marketing News,* 14 Sep-

tember 1992, 29.
7. Sylvia Porter, "Your Money: How to Prepare for Job Interviews," *San Francisco Chronicle,* 3 November 1981, 54.
8. Joel Russell, "Finding Solid Ground," *Hispanic Business,* February 1992, 42–44, 46.
9. Robert Gifford, Cheuk Fan Ng, and Margaret Wilkinson, "Nonverbal Cues in the Employment Interview: Links Between Applicant Qualities and Interviewer Judg-

ments," *Journal of Applied Psychology* 70, no. 4 (1985): 729.
10. Louis S. Richman, "How to Get Ahead in America," *Fortune,* 16 May 1994, 46–51; Bruce Nussbaum, "I'm Worried About My Job," *Business Week,* 7 October 1991, 94–97.
11. Lee Smith, "Landing That First Real Job," *Fortune,* 16 May 1994, 58–60; Richman, "How to Get Ahead," 46–51; Russell, "Finding Solid Ground," 42–46.

ILLUSTRATION AND TEXT CREDITS

CHAPTER 1
3 George Dovel, founder, Dovel Group, Seattle, Wash., personal communication, 5 October 1994. Reprinted by permission.
5 Exhibit 1.1, *The 1994 Information Please Almanac* (Boston: Houghton Mifflin, 1994), 144–287; *The Statistical Abstract of the United States, 1994* (Washington, D.C.: GPO, 1994), 864.
6 Exhibit 1.2, adapted from Samuel C. Certo, Max E. Douglas, and Stewart W. Husted, *Business,* 2d edition. Copyright © 1984 by Allyn & Bacon, Inc. Reprinted with permission; William F. Schoell and Joseph P. Guiltinan, *Marketing: Contemporary Concepts and Practices,* 5th edition, 215. Copyright © 1992 by Allyn & Bacon, Inc. Reprinted with permission.
8 Adapted from World Resources Institute, "Managing Earth's Resources," Special Advertising Supplement, *Business Week,* 18 June 1990, 5, 6, 56, 57; Emily T. Smith, Vicki Cahan, Naomi Freundlich, James E. Ellis, and Joseph Weber, "The Greening of Corporate America," *Business Week,* 23 April 1990, 96–103; Thomas DiLorenzo, "Does Free Enterprise Cause Pollution?" *Across the Board,* January–February 1991, 35–41; Gretchen Morgenson and Gale Eisenstodt, "Profits Are for Rape and Pillage," *Forbes,* 5 March 1990, 94–100.
21 Exhibit 1.6, From "21st Century Capitalism." Reprinted from *Business Week,* November 18, 1994 by special permission, copyright © 1994, McGraw-Hill, Inc., 194.
28 Courtland L. Bovée, John V. Thill, Marian G. Wood, and George P. Dovel, *Management* (New York, McGraw-Hill, 1993), 30–31; Gary Hoover, Alta Campbell, and Patrick J. Spain, eds. *Hoover's Handbook of American Business, 1994* (Austin, Tex.: Reference Press, 1994), 778–779; Judith Hodges and Deborah Melewski, "Software Magazine's 1994 Top 100," *Software Magazine,* July 1994, 80; Elizabeth Corcoran, "Deal: How Microsoft Settled," *Seattle Times,* 18 July 1994, A1.

CHAPTER 2
35 Exhibit 2.1, adapted from *1995 Information Please Almanac,* 48th ed. (Boston:

Houghton Mifflin, 1994), 72.
35 Exhibit 2.2, adapted from Christopher Farrell, Michael J. Mandel, Keith Hammonds, Dori Jones Yang, and Paul Magnusson, "At Last, Good News," reprinted from June 3, 1991 issue of *Business Week,* by special permission copyright © 1991 by McGraw-Hill, Inc. Updated from *Survey of Current Business,* November 1992, pp. 6–7; *Survey of Current Business,* September 1993, vol. 73, no. 9, p. 7; *Survey of Current Business,* September 1994, vol. 74, no. 9, p. 79.
36 Exhibit 2.3, adapted from Sylvia Nasar, "U.S. Trade Benefits From War," *New York Times,* 13 March 1991, C1. Copyright © 1991 by The New York Times Company. Reprinted by permission.
45 Exhibit 2.4, adapted from John Labate, "The World Economy in Charts: Special Report—Gearing Up for Steady Growth," *Fortune,* 29 July 1991, 99 © 1991 the Time Inc. Magazine Company. All rights reserved. Updated from *Federal Reserve Bulletin,* December 1994, Table 3.28, p. A66.
47 Adapted from Nathaniel Gilbert, "The Case for Countertrade," *Across the Board,* May 1992, 43–45; John S. DeMott, "Soviet Promise: Bets on a Bartering Revival," *International Business,* October 1991, 17–19; Matt Schaffer, *Winning the Countertrade War* (New York: Wiley, 1989), 73.
48 Exhibit 2.5, *Survey of Current Business,* August 1994, 137.
51 Exhibit 2.6, adapted from Kerry Pechter, "Buying America," *International Business,* December 1993, 56–58, 60, 62, 64, 66. 1993 data updated from "Foreign Direct Investment in the United States: Industry Detail for Selected Items," *Survey of Current Business,* August 1994, Table 17, pp. 124–125.
53 Adapted from David Ricks, "How to Avoid Business Blunders Abroad," *Business,* April–June 1984, 3–11.
57 Adapted from Jerry Flint, "One World, One Ford," *Forbes,* 20 June 1994, 40–41; Paul Ingrassia and Jacqueline Mitchell, "Ford to Realign with a System of Global Chiefs," *Wall Street Journal,* 31 March 1994, A3; Steve Kichen, "Will the Third Time Be the Charm?" *Forbes,* 15 March 1993, 54; Miche-

line Maynard, "Ford Stalls in Europe," *USA Today,* 29 October 1992, 8B.

CHAPTER 3
80 Exhibit 3.5, adapted from Diane Harris, "Does Your Pay Measure Up?" *Working Woman,* January 1994, 27–32.
83 Exhibit 3.6, adapted from National Safety Council, *Accident Facts, 1994 edition* (Chicago: National Safety Council, 1994), 36.
85 Adapted from Marlene C. Piturro, "Just Say . . . Maybe," *World Trade,* June 1992, 87–88, 90–91; Kent Hodgson, "Adapting Ethical Decisions to a Global Marketplace," *Management Review,* May 1992, 53–57; Jeffrey A. Fadiman, "A Traveler's Guide to Gifts and Bribes," *Harvard Business Review,* July–August 1986, 122–136.
89 Adapted from Lowell G. Rein, "Is Your (Ethical) Slippage Showing?" *Personnel Journal,* September 1980, 740–743.
93 Adapted from Jane Gross, "Laura S. Scher: She Took One Look at the Age of Greed and Made a Quick Left," *New York Times,* 7 November 1993, sec. 3, 8; Ann Hornaday, "Making Money While Making a Difference," *Working Woman,* February 1992, 31, 34; James W. Crawley, "Phone Business Isn't All Business," *San Diego Union-Tribune,* 1 November 1992, I1–I2.

CHAPTER 4
98 Exhibit 4.1 *The World Almanac and Book of Facts, 1995* (New York: St. Martin's Press), 124.
99 Exhibit 4.2 adapted from *Survey of Current Business* (Washington, D.C.: GPO, July 1994), Table 6.4c, 89.
102 Exhibit 4.3 adapted from *Statistical Abstract of the United States, 1990* (Washington, D.C.: GPO, 1990), 522, 523.
103 Exhibit 4.4 Reprinted with the permission of Simon & Schuster, Inc. from the Macmillan College text *The Legal Environment of Business,* 2d ed., by Charles R. McGuire. Copyright © 1986, 1989 by Merrill Publishing, an imprint of Macmillan College Publishing Company, Inc., 216.
107 Adapted from Sharon G. Hadary,

"Think Big," *National Business Employment Weekly, Managing Your Career,* Spring, 1990, 11–12; Kevin Gudgridge and John A. Byrne, "A Kinder, Gentler Generation of Executives," *Business Week,* 23 April 1990, 86–87; Jerry Buckley, "The New Organization Man," *U.S. News & World Report,* 16 January 1989, 41–43.

112   Lori Ioannou, "It's a Small World After All," *International Business,* February 1994, 82–88.

117   Exhibit 4.7 adapted from Greg Steinmetz, "Mergers and Acquisitions Set Records, but Activity Lacked That '80s Pizazz," *Wall Street Journal,* 3 January 1995, R8.

123   Adapted from Brent Bowers and Udayan Gupta, "Shareholder Suits Beset More Small Companies," *Wall Street Journal,* 9 March 1994, B1–B2.

CHAPTER 5

130   Exhibit 5.1, *Handbook of Small Business Data, 1994* (Washington, D.C.: GPO, 1994), 252–253, 263–264.

131   Exhibit 5.2, adapted from Ellen Graham, "The Truth About Start Ups." Reprinted with permission, *Inc.* Magazine, January 1988. Copyright 1988 by *Inc.* Publishing Company, 38 Commercial Wharf, Boston MA 02110; adapted from Ellen Graham, "The Entrepreneurial Mystique," in *The Wall Street Journal Special Report on Small Business,* May 20, 1985. Reprinted by permission of *The Wall Street Journal Special Report on Small Business,* © 1985 Dow Jones & Company, Inc. All Rights Reserved Worldwide, sec. 3, p. 4C.

132   Exhibit 5.3, adapted from John Case, "Disciples of David Birch," *Inc.,* January 1989, 41. Reprinted with permission, *Inc.* Magazine, January 1989. Copyright © 1989 by Goldhirsch Group, Inc., 38 Commercial Wharf, Boston, MA 02110.

132   Exhibit 5.4, adapted from Geoffrey N. Smith and Paul B. Brown, "Sweat Equity." Excerpted in *Macmillan Executive Summary Program,* December 1986, 3, 4.

137   Exhibit 5.6, adapted from "The 1990 Guide to Small Business," *U.S. News & World Report,* November 23, 1989, 78, copyright, 1989, U.S. News & World Report, reprinted by permission; "How to Bankroll Your Venture," reprinted by permission from the September 1985 issue of *Changing Times Magazine,* copyright © 1985 The Kiplinger Washington Editors, Inc., 41.

140   Exhibit 5.7, adapted from Carrie Dolan, "Entrepreneurs Often Fail as Managers," *The Wall Street Journal,* May 15, 1989. Reprinted by permission of *The Wall Street Journal,* © 1989 Dow Jones & Company, Inc. All Rights Reserved Worldwide, B1.

144   Exhibit 5.8, *Statistical Abstract of the United States, 1994* (Washington, D.C.: GPO), 790.

145   Adapted from Martin Mendelsohn, "International Franchising—The Financial Dilemma," *Franchising World,* September–October 1994, 62; Carol Steinberg, "Mating Game," *World Trade,* April 1993, 147–158.

147   Exhibit 5.9, adapted from Alfred Edmond, Jr., "The B. E. Franchise Start-Up Guide," *Black Enterprise,* September 1990. Reprinted by permission of Earl G. Graves Publishing Co., 75.

150   Adapted from Eric S. Hardy, "Franchise Primer," *Forbes,* 15 August 1994, 141; Harlan S. Byrne, "Mail Boxes Etc.," *Barron's,* 5 April 1993, 50–52; "Etc., etc., etc.," *Franchising World,* November–December 1993, 12; *1991 Mail Boxes Etc. Annual Report.*

CHAPTER 6

161   Adapted from Andrew S. Grove, "What's the Right Thing? Everyday Ethical Dilemmas," *Working Woman,* June 1990, 16–18; John Case, "Honest Business," *Inc.,* January 1990, 59–65; Kenneth R. Andrews, "Ethics in Practice," *Harvard Business Review,* September–October 1989, 99–104.

164   Exhibit 6.2, adapted from *Management,* Second Edition, by Richard L. Daft, copyright © 1991 by The Dryden Press, reprinted by permission of the publisher. Based on information in Christie Brown, "Sweat Chic," *Forbes,* 5 September 1988, 130.

166   Adapted from Karen Lowry Miller, "Overhaul in Japan," *Business Week,* 21 December 1992, 80–83, 86; Bradley A. Stertz, "Importing Solutions: Detroit's New Strategy to Beat Back Japanese Is to Copy Their Ideas," *Wall Street Journal,* 1 October 1992, A1, A6; Doron P. Levin, "At Saturn Plant, a Vote on Innovation," *New York Times,* 14 November 1991, sec. d, 1, 9; S. C. Gwynne, "The Right Stuff," *Time,* 29 October 1990, 74–77, 81, 84; Louis Kraar, "Japan's Gung-Ho U.S. Car Plants," *Fortune,* 30 January 1989, 98–100, 104, 106, 108; John Hoerr, "The Payoff from Teamwork," *Business Week,* 10 July 1989, 56–62; Marguerite Michaels, "Hands Across the Workplace," *Time,* 26 December 1988, 14–15, 17.

168   Exhibit 6.3, adapted and reprinted by permission of *Harvard Business Review,* an exhibit from "How to Choose a Leadership Pattern" by Robert Tannenbaum and Warren H. Schmidt, May–June 1973. Copyright © 1973 by the President and Fellows of Harvard College; all rights reserved.

175   Adapted from *General Electric 1993 Annual Report,* 3–5; "Jack Welch's Lessons for Success," *Fortune,* 25 January 1993, 86–89, 92–93; Linda Grant, "The Management Model That Jack Built," *Los Angeles Times Magazine,* 9 May 1993, 20+; James C. Hyatt and Amal Kumar Naj, "GE Is No Place for Autocrats, Welch Decrees," *Wall Street Journal,* 3 March 1992, B1, B10; Noel Tichy and Ram Charan, "Speed, Simplicity, Self-Confidence: An Interview with Jack Welch," *Harvard Business Review,* September–October 1989, 112–120; Stratford P. Sherman, "Today's Leaders Look to Tomorrow," *Fortune,* 26 March 1990, 30–32; Martha H. Peak, "Anti-manager Named Manager of the Year," *Management Review,* October 1991, 7.

CHAPTER 7

185   Adapted from Carla Rapoport, "A Tough Swede Invades the U.S.," *Fortune,* 29 June 1992, 76–79; Paul Klebnikov, "The Powerhouse," *Forbes,* 2 September 1991, 46–52; Jules Arbose, "ABB the New Energy Powerhouse," *International Management,* June 1988, 24–30.

189   Adapted from A. J. Vogl, "Reengineering," *Across the Board,* June 1993, 26–33; Thomas Vollmann, "Downsizing," *European Management Journal* 11, no. 1 (March 1993): 18–28; Ronald Henkoff, "Cost Cutting: How to Do It Right," *Fortune,* 9 April 1990, 40–53; Andrall E. Pearson, "Tough-Minded Ways to Get Innovative," *Harvard Business Review,* May–June 1988, 99–106; John H. Sheridan, "Aligning Structure with Strategy," *Industry Week,* 15 May 1989, 15–23; Patricia Sellers, "Pepsi Keeps on Going After No. 1," *Fortune,* 11 March 1991, 62–70; Amanda Bennett, "Downsizing Doesn't Necessarily Bring an Upswing in Corporate Profitability," *Wall Street Journal,* 6 June 1991, B1.

191   Exhibit 7.5, © 1984 Time, Inc. Reprinted by permission.

191   Exhibit 7.6, adapted from *Campbell Share Owner,* First Quarter Fiscal 1994.

192   Exhibit 7.7, adapted from *Time Warner 1993 Annual Report.*

193   Exhibit 7.9, adapted from *Johnson & Johnson 1993 Annual Report.*

193   Exhibit 7.10, adapted from *Quaker Oats 1993 Annual Report.*

203   Adapted from Stuart Rock, "Swissair: New Routes to Staying on Top," *Director,* November 1988, 185–188.

CHAPTER 8

214   Adapted from Gene Bylinksy, "The Digital Factory," *Fortune,* 14 November 1994, 92–110; John S. DeMott, "Look, World, No Hands!" *Nation's Business,* June 1994, 41–42; Ron Pidgeon, "Getting to Grips with High-Speed Product Handling," *Packaging Week,* 12 May 1994, 24–25.

221   Adapted from Richard W. Stevenson, "Auto Aristocrat Trims Down," *New York Times,* 8 March 1994, C1, C4; Brian S. Moskal, "The Rescue of the Gilded Lady," *Industry Week,* 17 January 1994, 15–16, 18.

223   Exhibit 8.4, adapted from Mark L. Goldstein, "Choosing the Right Site," *Industry Week,* 15 April 1985, 58. Reprinted with permission from *Industry Week,* 15 April 1985. Copyright, Penton Publishing, Inc., Cleveland, Ohio.

229   Exhibit 8.7, adapted from Gerald H.

Graham, *The World of Business* (Reading, Mass.: Addison-Wesley, 1985), 199.

234 Adapted from Greg Bounds, Lyle Yorks, Mel Adams, and Gipsie Ranney, *Beyond Total Quality Management: Toward the Emerging Paradigm* (New York: McGraw-Hill, 1994), 449; Robert H. Hayes, Steven C. Wheelwright, and Kim B. Clark, *Dynamic Manufacturing: Creating the Learning Organization* (New York: Free Press, 1988), 256–257; John Teresko, "Making CIM Work with People," *Industry Week,* 2 November 1987, 50–65; Thomas M. Rohan, "Whipping Resistance," *Industry Week,* 2 November 1987, 68–84; Therese R. Welter, "Getting Set for Implementation," *Industry Week,* 2 November 1987, 86–92; Kenneth R. Sheets with Robert F. Black, "America's Blue Collars Get Down to Business," *U.S. News & World Report,* 29 February 1988, 52–53; Alan Halcrow, "Employee Participation Is a Sign of the Times in L.A.," *Personnel Journal,* January 1988, 10–11.

CHAPTER 9

245 **Exhibit 9.3,** adapted from *Management,* 2d ed. by Richard L. Daft, copyright © 1991 by The Dryden Press, reproduced by permission of the publisher, 406.

246 **Exhibit 9.4,** adapted from Richard M. Steers and Lyman W. Porter, *Motivation and Work Behavior* (New York: McGraw-Hill, 1991), 65–72.

251 **Exhibit 9.5,** adapted from *Statistical Abstract of the United States, 1994,* 114th ed. (Washington, D.C.: GPO, 1994), 395, 627.

251 **Exhibit 9.6,** U.S. Census Bureau, personal communication, 1995.

252 Adapted from Dawn Gunsch, "Games Augment Diversity Training," *Personnel Journal,* June 1993, 78–83; Mary J. Winterle, "Toward Diversity, with Carrots and Sticks," *Across the Board,* January–February 1993, 50; "Diversity: Managing Diversity for Competitive Advantage," *Management Review,* April 1993, 6; Lena Williams, "Scrambling to Manage a Diverse Workforce," *New York Times,* 15 December 1992, sec. a, 1, sec. c, 2; Audrey Edwards, Suzanne B. Laporte, and Abby Livingston, "Cultural Diversity in Today's Corporations." First appeared in *Working Woman* Magazine. Copyright © 1991 by W. W. T. Partnership.

254 Adapted from Joseph D'Obrian, "Only English Speakers Need Apply," *Management Review,* January 1991, 41–45; Seth Mydans, "Pressure for English-Only Job Rules Stirring a Sharp Debate Across U.S.," *New York Times,* 8 August 1990, sec. a, 12; L. Erik Bratt and Fred Alvarez, "English-Only Memo Outrages Employees," *San Diego Union,* 15 September 1990, C-1.

255 **Exhibit 9.7,** adapted from Suzy Parker, "A Look at Statistics That Shape Your Finances," *USA Today,* 24 January 1990, 1B. Copyright 1990, *USA Today,* reprinted with permission.

265 Adapted from Donald J. Vlcek, Jr.,

with Jeffrey P. Davidson, *The Domino Effect* (Homewood, Ill.: Business One Irwin, 1992), as summarized by *Soundview Executive Book Summaries,* 14, no. 6, pt. 2 (June 1992): 2–3; Alan Halcrow, "A Gold Medal Boost to Morale at Domino's Pizza," *Personnel Journal,* August 1987, 23, 25.

CHAPTER 10

273 **Exhibit 10.2,** adapted from John C. Szabo, "Finding the Right Workers," *Nation's Business,* February 1991, 16–22. Copyright 1991, U.S. Chamber of Commerce, copyright 1990 Towers Perrin, from Workforce 2000, Competing in a Sellers Market: Is Corporate America Prepared? A Survey Report on Corporate Responses to Demographic and Labor Force Trends.

276 **Exhibit 10.3,** Louis E. Boone and David L. Kurtz, *Management,* 4th ed. (New York: McGraw-Hill, 1992), 278. Reprinted by permission of the publisher.

278 **Exhibit 10.4,** adapted from "The Interview Process," *Small Business Reports,* December 1987, 64.

280 Adapted from Tony Mauro and Julia Lawlor, "More Bosses Set Rules for After Hours," *USA Today,* 13 May 1991, 1A; Jane Easter Bahls, "Checking Up on Workers," *Nation's Business,* December 1990, 29–31; Patricia Amend, "High-Tech Surveillance: The Boss May Be Watching," *USA Today,* 14 March 1990, 11B; John S. McClenahen, "The Privacy Invasion: In a Job Setting, How Personal Is Too Personal?" *Industry Week,* 11 November 1985, 50–53; John Corbett O'Meara, "The Emerging Law of Employees' Right to Privacy," *Personnel Administrator,* June 1985, 159–165.

283 Lewis J. Perelman, "Kanban to Kanbrain," *Forbes ASAP,* April 1994, 85–95.

288 **Exhibit 10.6,** adapted from National Institute of Business Management, "Compensation and Benefits," *Small Business Reports,* October 1990, 49. Reprinted by permission.

288 **Exhibit 10.7,** adapted from *Statistical Abstract of the United States, 1993* (Washington, D.C.: GPO, 1993), 430.

290 **Exhibit 10.8,** adapted from *Statistical Abstract of the United States, 1993* (Washington, D.C.: GPO, 1993), 430.

294 **Exhibit 10.9,** adapted from Katherine C. Naff and Paul van Rijn, "The Next Generation: Why Are They Leaving?" *The Bureaucrat,* Summer 1990, 39–43. Reprinted by permission of the Bureaucrat, Inc.

302 Adapted from Seth H. Lubove, "Pivotal People," *Wall Street Journal,* 3 August 1987, 1. Reprinted by permission of The Wall Street Journal, © Dow Jones & Company, Inc., 1987. All Rights Reserved Worldwide.

CHAPTER 11

306 Peggy Stuart, "Labor Unions Become Business Partners," *Personnel Journal,* August 1993, 54–63.

309 **Exhibit 11.2,** adapted from Bureau of Labor Statistics, Bureau of National Affairs, reported in *Business Week,* 8 July 1985, 72; Peter Fullam, "Organized Labor at Crossroads," *Indianapolis Star,* 2 September 1991, CO4; *Statistical Abstract of the United States, 1993* (Washington, D.C.: GPO, 1993), 436.

312 Adapted from Dana Milbank, "Labor Broadens Its Appeal by Setting Up Associations to Lobby and Offer Services," *Wall Street Journal,* 13 January 1993, B1, B4; John Hoerr, "What Should Unions Do?" *Harvard Business Review,* May–June 1991, 44–45; "Labor Letter," *Wall Street Journal,* 26 January 1991, A1; Dana Milbank, "Far from the Mill," *Wall Street Journal,* 23 May 1991, A1.

317 Adapted from "Roadway Express Says Strike May Mean Layoffs," *News-Times* (Danbury, Conn.) 14 April 1994, D-8; Barbara Loecher, "Hospital Nurses Ready to Picket," *News-Times* (Danbury, Conn.), 15 April 1994, B-1; Linda Greenhouse, "High Court Eases Rule on Unionizing Hospital Workers," *New York Times,* 24 April 1991, sec. a, 1; "High Court Ruling to Help Hospital Unions Organize," *San Diego Union,* 24 April 1991, A-2; Frank Swoboda, "Greyhound Declares Strike Over," *Washington Post,* 8 May 1990, A8; Peter T. Kilborn, "Small Towns Grow Lonelier as Bus Stops Stopping," *New York Times National,* 11 July 1991, A8; James R. Healey and Mark Memmott, "Businesses Felt Rail Strike Most," *USA Today,* 18 April 1991, 1A; "Casey Jones Walks Out," *Time,* 29 April 1991, 65.

322 **Exhibit 11.6,** U.S. Department of Labor, Bureau of Labor Statistics, *Compensation and Working Conditions* (Washington, D.C.: GPO, June 1991, June 1992, June 1993, June 1994); *Statistical Abstract of the United States, 1994* (Washington, D.C.: GPO, 1994), 448.

327 **Exhibit 11.7,** adapted from John Hoerr, "Beyond Unions: A Revolution in Employee Rights Is in the Making." Reprinted from July 8, 1985 issue of *Business Week* by special permission, copyright © 1985 by McGraw-Hill, Inc.; Joan Biskopic, "Bush Signs Anti-Job Bias Bill Amid Furor over Preferences," *The Congressional Quarterly Weekly Report,* 23 November 1991, 3463.

334 Adapted from Gregory A. Patterson, "Nordstrom Inc. Sets Back-Pay Accord on Suit Alleging 'Off the Clock' Work," *Wall Street Journal,* 12 January 1993, A2; "Union Leaves Nordstrom Store to Avoid Vote," *Women's Wear Daily,* 6 August 1992, 14; Francine Schwadel, "Nordstrom Workers Reject Their Union in Voting at Five Seattle-Area Stores," *Wall Street Journal,* 22 July 1991, B4; "Briefly: Employees Want Nordstrom Union Booted," *Los Angeles Times,* 4 May 1991, D2; "NLRB Clears Nordstrom of Unfair Labor Practices," *Women's Wear Daily,* 10 April 1991, 22; Charlene Marmer Solomon, "Nightmare at Nordstrom," *Personnel Journal,* September 1990, 76–83;

Linda Darnell Williams, "Nordstrom Pact Aims to Resolve Labor Dispute," *Los Angeles Times,* 18 August 1990, D1, D2; Francine Schwadel, "Irate Nordstrom Straining in Labor Fight," *Wall Street Journal,* 5 April 1990, B1, B6; Stuart Silverstein, "Taking On Nordstrom," *Los Angeles Times,* 12 March 1990, D1, D4.

CHAPTER 12

343 Exhibit 12.2, adapted from Charles D. Schewe, *Marketing Principles and Strategies.* Copyright © 1987, reprinted by permission of McGraw-Hill, Inc., 35.

344 Exhibit 12.3, adapted from Courtland L. Bovée and John V. Thill, *Marketing* (New York: McGraw-Hill, 1992), 14.

351 Exhibit 12.5, adapted from William F. Schoell and Joseph P. Guiltinan, *Marketing: Contemporary Concepts and Practices,* 3d ed. (Boston: Allyn & Bacon, 1988), 215. Copyright © by Allyn & Bacon. Reprinted with permission; adapted from Samuel C. Certo, Max E. Douglas, and Stewart W. Husted, *Business,* 2d ed., Allyn & Bacon, 1988.

351 Exhibit 12.6, adapted from "More Bang for the Ad Dollar," Niles Howard, *Dun's Review,* November 1978. Reprinted with the permission of *Dun's Business Month,* November 1978. Copyright 1978, The Goldhirsch Group, Inc.

353 Exhibit 12.7, adapted from William Zikmund and Michael D'Amico, *Marketing,* 2d ed. (New York: Wiley, 1986), 99. Reprinted by permission of John Wiley & Sons, Inc.

354 Adapted from Courtland L. Bovée, John V. Thill, George P. Dovel, and Marian B. Wood, *Advertising Excellence* (New York: McGraw-Hill, 1995), 205–210; John Thackray, "Much Ado About Global Marketing," *Across the Board,* April 1985, 38–46; Perry Pascarella, "In Search of Universal Designs," *Industry Week,* 11 July 1985, 47–52; William W. Locke, "The Fatal Flaw: Hidden Cultural Differences," *Business Marketing,* April 1986, 64, 72–76; Alice Rudolph, "Standardization Not Standard for Global Marketers," *Advertising Age,* 27 September 1985, 3–4.

356 Exhibit 12.8, adapted from Charles D. Schewe, *Marketing Principles and Strategies.* Copyright © 1987, reprinted by permission of McGraw-Hill, Inc., 35.

364 Adapted from R. C. Baker, Roger Dickinson, and Stanley Hollander, "Big Brother 1994: Marketing Data and the IRS," *Journal of Public Policy & Marketing* 5 (1986): 213; "Is Nothing Private?" *Business Week,* 4 September 1989, 74–82; "Privacy vs. Free Speech," *Direct Marketing,* May 1989, 42; Robert J. Posch, Jr., "Can We Have à la Carte Constitutional Rights?" *Direct Marketing,* July 1989, 76.

369 R. Lee Sullivan, "Just Say Yes," *Forbes,* 28 February 1994, 84

CHAPTER 13

375 Exhibit 13.1, adapted from Courtland L. Bovée and John V. Thill, *Marketing* (New York, McGraw-Hill, 1992), 253. Reprinted with the permission of Simon & Schuster, Inc. from the Macmillan College Publishing text *Marketing,* 6th ed., by Joel R. Evans and Barry Berman. Copyright © 1994 by Macmillan College Publishing Company, Inc., 615.

376 Andrea Gerlin, "A Matter of Degree: How a Jury Decided That a Coffee Spill Is Worth $2.9 Million," *Wall Street Journal,* 1 September 1994, A1, A6; Milo Geyelin, "Product-Liability Suits Fare Worse Now," *Wall Street Journal,* 12 July 1994, B7; Tracy E. Benson, "Product Liability: Deep Waters to Debate," *Industry Week,* 6 August 1990, 46–63; "Limits to Liability," *San Diego Union,* 1 October 1990, B6; Marisa L. Manley, "Controlling Product Liability," *Inc.,* February 1987, 103–107.

380 Exhibit 13.2, adapted from Anne B. Fisher, "Coke's Brand-Loyalty Lesson," *Fortune,* 5 August 1985, 46; © 1985, Time Inc. All rights reserved. Reprinted by permission. John Koten, "Why Do Hot Dogs Come in Packs of 10 and Buns in 8s and 12s?" *Wall Street Journal,* 21 September, 1984, A1, 15.

386 "High-Tech Jewelry Design," *Industry Week,* 18 July 1994, 18; Jack R. Harkins, "Originality Sacrificed by CAD?" *Appliance Manufacturer,* June 1994, 11; Chris Williams, "Vibration Technology for Quality Products," *Quality,* June 1994, 26–28; Lisa Kempfer, "CAD Captures Creative Expression," *Computer-Aided Engineering,* June 1994, 28–34.

388 Exhibit 13.4, adapted from Charles D. Schewe, *Marketing: Principles and Strategies* (New York: McGraw-Hill, 1987), 294. Reprinted by permission of the publisher.

390 Exhibit 13.5, adapted from Courtland L. Bovée and John V. Thill, *Marketing* (New York: McGraw-Hill, 1992), 290. Reprinted by permission of the publisher.

394 Exhibit 13.6, adapted from Thomas C. Kinnear and Kenneth L. Bernhardt, *Principles of Marketing,* 3rd ed. (Glenview, Ill.: Scott, Foresman/Little, Brown, 1990), 610. Reprinted by permission; *Principles of Marketing,* Third Edition, by Thomas C. Kinnear and Kenneth L. Bernhardt, p. 610. Copyright © 1990, 1986, 1983 Scott, Foresman and Company. Reprinted by permission of HarperCollins Publishers.

401 Adapted from Raymond Serafin, "Windstar Tosses Gauntlet at the Minivan Segment," *Advertising Age,* 28 September 1994, 16; David Woodruff, "Chrysler Is Burning Up the Minivan Lane," *Business Week,* 5 September 1994, 31; Alex Taylor, "Iacocca's Minivan," *Fortune,* 30 May 1994, 56–66.

CHAPTER 14

407 Exhibit 14.1, adapted from Theodore Beckman, William Davidson, and W. Wayne Talarzyk, *Marketing,* 9th ed. (New York: Ronald Press, 1973), 307.

412 Adapted from Gregory Stricharchuk, "Card Makers' Tough Tactics Belie Sweet Verse as Competition Rises," *Wall Street Journal,* 24 December 1987, 11; Denise M. Topolnicki, "Greetings from the Rack Race," *Venture,* February 1988, 44–48; Hallmark Cards press release, 24 October 1988; Michael Booth, "Sweet Talk, Tough Tactics," *New York Times,* 22 January 1989, sec. f, 6; Suzanne Oliver, "The Shiksa Chef," *Forbes,* 24 May 1993, 66, 68.

413 Exhibit 14.3, adapted from Charles D. Schewe, *Marketing Principles and Strategies* (New York: McGraw-Hill, Inc., 1987), 399. Reprinted with permission of McGraw-Hill, Inc.

418 Exhibit 14.4, adapted from Charles D. Schewe, *Marketing Principles and Strategies* (New York: McGraw-Hill, Inc., 1987), 435–436. Reprinted with permission of McGraw-Hill, Inc.

420 Exhibit 14.5, adapted from Courtland L. Bovée and John V. Thill, *Marketing* (New York: McGraw-Hill, 1992), 455. Reprinted by permission of the publisher. Adapted from *Retail Management* by Avigit Ghosh, copyright © 1990 by the Dryden Press, reprinted by permission of the publishers.

421 Adapted from "Toys 'R' Us Reports Third Quarter Results," PRNewswire, 15 November 1993; Kathryn Graven, "For Toys 'R' Us, Japan Isn't Child's Play," *Wall Street Journal,* 7 February 1990, B1; "Toys 'R' Us Goes Overseas—And Finds That Toys 'R' Them, Too," *Business Week,* 26 January 1987, 71–72; Michael Salter, "Big Stores, Bigger Sales: Canada," *McLean's,* 15 December 1986, 42–43; Joseph Pereira, "Toys 'R' Us, Big Kid on the Block, Won't Stop Growing," *Wall Street Journal,* 11 August 1988, B6

427 Exhibit 14.7, adapted from Thomas A. Foster, "Logistics: Our Economy's Engine," *Chilton's Distribution,* July 1991, 6–14.

435 Adapted from Mark B. Solomon, "Losses in Europe Left Carrier with Little Choice but to Leave," *Journal of Commerce,* 18 March 1992, A1; Douglas MacDonald, "Overnight Success (or Failure)," *New England Business,* 21 April 1986, 57–64; Dean Foust, "Mr. Smith Goes Global," *Business Week,* 13 February 1989, 66–72; "Federal Express Spreads Its Wings," *Journal of Business Strategy,* July–August 1988, 15–19; Carl Williams, "A Company Study: The Challenge of Retail Marketing at Federal Express," *Journal of Services Marketing,* Summer 1987, 25–38; Dean Foust, "Why Federal Express Has Overnight Anxiety," *Business Week,* 9 November 1987, 66; Peter Bradley, "Good Things Come in Small Packages," *Purchasing,* 9 November 1989, 61, 64.

CHAPTER 15

443 Exhibit 15.1, adapted from William

Zikmund and Michael D'Amico, *Marketing,* 2d ed. (New York: Wiley, 1986), 479. Reprinted by permission of John Wiley & Sons, Inc.

449 Exhibit 15.2, adapted from Courtland L. Bovée and John V. Thill, *Marketing,* (New York: McGraw-Hill, 1992), 590. Reprinted by permission of the publisher.

459 Adapted in part from Courtland L. Bovée, John V. Thill, George P. Dovel, and Marian B. Wood, *Advertising Excellence* (New York: McGraw-Hill, 1995), 277–283, 320–326.

460 Exhibit 15.3, *Facts About Newspapers* (Reston, Va.: Newspaper Association of America, 1994), 11.

461 Exhibit 15.4, adapted from Christopher Gilson and Harold W. Berkman, "Advantages and Disadvantages of Major Advertising Media," in *Advertising: Concepts and Strategies* (New York: McGraw-Hill, 1980), 274–275.

469 Adapted from Kathleen Kerwin, "Forget Woodstock — These Folks Are Headin' to Spring Hill," *Business Week,* 27 June 1994, 36; Carol J. Loomis, "Dinosaurs?" *Fortune,* 3 May 1993, 36–42; Raymond Serafin, "The Saturn Story," *Advertising Age,* 16 November 1992, 1, 8, 13, 16; Fara Warner, "The Marketers of the Year: Donald Hudler," *Brandweek,* 16 November 1992, 21; "Saturn Gears Up Another Blockbuster Ad," *Adweek,* 4 January 1993, 8.

CHAPTER 16

475 Exhibit 16.1, reprinted with the permission of Simon & Schuster, Inc. from the Macmillan College text *Systems and Design: A Case Study Approach* 2nd ed. by Robert J. Thierauf and George W. Reynolds. Copyright © 1986 by Merrill Publishing, an imprint of Macmillan College Publishing Company, Inc., 69.

477 Adapted in part from Dennis Kneale, "Unleashing the Power," *Wall Street Journal,* 27 June 1994, R1, R6–R7; William Brandel, "Product Propaganda Battle Rages On," *Computerworld,* 30 May 1994, 41. Reprinted by permission of the publisher.

493 Exhibit 16.5, adapted from Timothy Trainor and Diane Krasnewich, *Computers!* (New York: McGraw-Hill, 1989), 40.

495 Adapted from G. Christian Hill, "Look! No Wires!" *Wall Street Journal,* 11 February 1994, R1–R6; Dennis Kneale, "Leave Me Alone," *Wall Street Journal,* 11 February 1994, R26.

501 Adapted from Eliot Marshall, "The Scourge of Computer Viruses," *Science,* 8 April 1988, 133–134; Philip Elmer-De-Witt, "Invasion of the Data Snatchers!" *Time,* 26 September 1988, 62–67; Asra Q. Nomani, "Byteing Back: Bug Busters Devise Electronic Vaccines for Computer Viruses," *Wall Street Journal,* 17 June 1988, 1.

CHAPTER 17

508 Exhibit 17.2, adapted from "As

Many of the Big Eight Centralized, Price Waterhouse Bucked the Trend," reprinted from October 24, 1983 issue of *Business Week* by special permission, copyright © 1983 by McGraw-Hill, Inc.

520 Adapted from Elizabeth S. Lewin, "How Much Are You Really Worth?" *Sylvia Porter's Personal Finance Magazine,* February 1986, 66, 68; *Sylvia Porter's Money Book* (New York: Avon, 1976), 36–37; M. Herbert Freeman and David K. Graf, *Money Management* (Indianapolis: Bobbs-Merrill, 1980), 10–11; Desmond A. Jolly, *Personal Financial Statement,* University of California, Division of Agricultural Sciences, February 1979, 2–3.

522 Photo caption information adapted from Pamela P. Peterson, *Financial Management and Analysis* (New York: McGraw-Hill, 1994), 78–79.

526 Adapted from Manual Schiffres, "All the Good News That Fits," *U.S. News & World Report,* 14 April 1986, 50–51.

534 Jack E. Kiger, Stephen E. Loeb, and Gordon S. May, *Accounting Principles,* 2d ed. (New York: Random House, 1987), 148.

CHAPTER 18

543 Exhibit 18.1, adapted from *Statistical Abstract of the United States, 1994* (Washington, D.C.: GPO, 1994), 523.

544 Exhibit 18.2, from 1995 *Information Please Almanac.* Copyright © 1994 by Houghton Mifflin Co. Reprinted by permission of Houghton Mifflin Co. All rights reserved.

551 Adapted from Lori Ioannou, "Better Banking with NAFTA," *International Business,* January 1994, 40, 42, 44; William C. Gruben, John H. Welch, and Jeffrey W. Gunther, "U.S. Banks, Competition, and the Mexican Banking System: How Much Will NAFTA Matter?" *Federal Reserve Bank of Dallas Financial Industry Studies,* October 1993, 11–22; "Eight Key Banking Provisions of NAFTA," *ABA Banking Journal,* November 1993, 56.

552 Exhibit 18.4, adapted from Meir Kohn, *Financial Institutions and Markets* (New York: McGraw-Hill, 1994), 758–759. Reprinted by permission of the publisher.

557 William Roberds, "The Rise of Electronic Payments Networks and the Future Role of the Fed with Regards to Payment Finality," *Economic Review,* March–April 1993, 1–22; Gerald D. Manypenny and Michael L. Bermudez, "The Federal Reserve Banks as Fiscal Agents and Depositories of the United States," *Federal Reserve Bulletin,* October 1992, 727–737; Meir Kohn, *Financial Institutions and Markets* (New York: McGraw-Hill, 1994), 347; Benjamin Geva, "FedWire Transfer of Funds," *The Banking Law Journal,* September–October 1987, 412–446.

563 Adapted from Catherine Friend White, "Social Investing: Put Your Money Where the Need Is," *Business Ethics,*

March–April 1994, 38, 40; Mary Scott and Howard Rothman, *Companies with a Conscience* (New York: Citadel Press, 1994), 62–75; John Huey, "Finding New Heroes for a New Era," *Fortune,* 25 January 1993, 62–65, 68–69; Michael Quint, "A Bank Shows It Can Profit and Follow a Social Agenda," *New York Times,* 24 May 1992, sec. c, 1, 14; Ronald Grzywinski, "The New Old-Fashioned Banking," *Harvard Business Review,* May–June 1991, 87–98; Jo David and Karen File, "Saintly Companies That Make Heavenly Profits," *Working Woman,* October 1989, 72–78, 122–124, 126; Kevin T. Kane, "Banking on Better Neighborhoods," *Mortgage Banking,* May 1993, 58–62, 65–67, 69; Amy Bodwin, "Banking on the Future: Chicago Idea Could Aid City," *Crain's Detroit Business,* 30 September 1991, 13–14; Robert Reed, "Thinking Small," *Crain's Chicago Business,* 16 July 1990, 17–19; David Osborne, "Bootstrap Banking," *Inc.,* August 1987, 69; Steve Mills, "South Shore Turns Itself Around While Showing How a Bank Can Help," *The American Banker,* 16 April 1986, 24.

CHAPTER 19

572 Exhibit 19.4, adapted from "Prime Rate Charged by Banks," Table 1.33, *Federal Reserve Bulletin,* October 1994, A25.

573 Exhibit 19.5, adapted from Louis E. Boone and David L. Kurtz, *Contemporary Business,* 5th ed. (Chicago: Dryden, 1987), 562.

574 Exhibit 19.6, adapted from " 'Tis the Season for IPO Fever." Reprinted from December 5, 1994 issue of *Business Week,* by special permission, copyright © 1994 by McGraw-Hill, Inc.

578 Exhibit 19.8, adapted from Monika Guttman, "Fishing for Financing," *U.S. News & World Report.* Copyright, August 8, 1994, U.S. News & World Report. Reprinted by permission.

579 Adapted from Kenneth W. Sparks, "Successful Business Borrowing: How to Plan and Negotiate a Loan," *Macmillan Executive Summary Program,* December 1986, 2–8.

581 Exhibit 19.9, adapted from "Commercial Paper and Bankers Dollar Acceptances Outstanding," Table 1.32, *Federal Reserve Bulletin,* October 1994, A24.

589 Adapted from Stephen W. Quickel, "Providing Credit Where Due," *International Business,* January 1993, 26–28; Kerry Pechter, "Enjoying Dutch Treats," *International Business,* July 1993, 25–26; "How to Obtain Export Capital," *Nation's Business,* May 1994, 24.

595 Adapted from Myron Magnet, "Let's Go for Growth," *Fortune,* 7 March 1994, 60, 62, 64, 68, 70, 72; Richard Phalon, "A Bold Gamble," *Forbes,* 28 February 1994, 90–91; *Barnes & Noble 1993 Annual Report;* Stephanie Strom, "Barnes & Noble Goes Public: Vol. 2," *New York Times,* 3 September

1993, sec. c, 1, 2; John Mutter, "A Chat with Bookseller Len Riggio," *Publishers Weekly,* 3 May 1992, 33–34, 36, 38.

CHAPTER 20

605 Exhibit 20.1, based on information from Kate Ennis, communications coordinator, Standard & Poor's Corporation, New York, personal communication, December 1991; David M. Blitzer, "GNP Benchmark Revisions," *Standard & Poor's Industry Surveys: Trends and Projections,* 14 November 1992, 5; Marc Levinson, "Living on the Edge," *Newsweek,* 4 November 1991, 22–25.
620 Exhibit 20.2, Standard & Poor's, Telescan, Inc. 1995; "A Centennial View: Dow Jones Industrial Average," *Wall Street Journal,* centennial edition, B15, and reprinted by permission of *The Wall Street Journal,* © 1991 Dow Jones & Company, Inc. All Rights Reserved Worldwide.
621 Exhibit 20.3, From *Wall Street Journal,* 5 January 1995, C4. Reprinted by permission of *The Wall Street Journal.* © 1995 Dow Jones & Company, Inc. All Rights Reserved Worldwide.
622 Adapted from Jordan E. Goodman, "Stock Analysis Checklist," *Money,* September 1983, 69. Excerpted from the September 1983 issue of *Money* magazine by special permission. © 1983, Time, Inc.
624 Exhibit 20.4, From *Wall Street Journal,* 5 January 1995, C16. Reprinted by permission of *The Wall Street Journal.* © 1995 Dow Jones & Company, Inc. All Rights Reserved Worldwide.
624 Exhibit 20.5, From *Wall Street Journal,* 5 January 1995, C20. Reprinted by permission of *The Wall Street Journal.* © 1995 Dow Jones & Company, Inc. All Rights Reserved Worldwide.
625 Exhibit 20.6, From *Wall Street Journal,* 5 January 1995, C14. Reprinted by permission of *The Wall Street Journal.* © 1995 Dow Jones & Company, Inc. All Rights Reserved Worldwide.
631 Adapted from Robert Lenzner, "Warren Buffett's Idea of Heaven: 'I Don't Have to Work with People I Don't Like,'" *Forbes 400,* 18 October 1993, 40, 42–45; Judith H. Dobrzynski, "Warren's World," *Business Week,* 10 May 1993, 30, 32; Anne B. Fisher, "Sa-

lomon Inc: Buffett's School of Management" *Fortune,* 14 June 1993, 116, 118; Floyd Norris, "Forcing Salomon into Buffett's Conservative Mold," *New York Times,* 29 September 1991, sec. 3, 8; Linda Sandler, "For Buffett, Salomon Isn't Sole Worry," *Wall Street Journal,* 22 August 1991, C1–C2; Tatiana Pouschine and Carolyn Torcellini, "Will the Real Warren Buffett Please Stand Up?" *Forbes,* 19 March 1990, 92–98; Joshua Hammer, Joanna Stone, and Marc Levinson, "'I Will Be Ruthless,'" *Newsweek,* 9 September 1991, 62; Thomas McCarroll, "Salvaging Salomon Brothers," *Time,* 2 September 1991, 59; John Train, *The Money Masters* (New York: Harper & Row, 1980), 1–41.

CHAPTER 21

640 Exhibit, 21.1, based on information from *Code of Federal Regulations,* Titles 9, 21, Pts. 100–169, 200-N, Superintendent of Documents, GPO, Washington, D.C., 1994.
643 Exhibit, 21.2, adapted from "Deregulating America," *Business Week,* 28 November 1983, 80–81; Donald L. Bartlett and James B. Steele, "Deregulation Decimated Airlines, Truck Industry — Are the Banks Next?" *San Diego Union,* 19 November 1991, A-1, A-4; George A. Steiner and John F. Steiner, *Business, Government, and Society* (New York: McGraw-Hill, 1991), 307–309.
644 Exhibit, 21.3, adapted from *Facts and Figures on Government Finance,* 23rd ed. (Washington, D.C.: Tax Foundation, 1986).
645 Adapted from Joseph Maglitta, "High-Tech Wagering: Jackpot or Jeopardy?" *Computerworld,* 7 February 1994, 28; E. Bernadette McKinney and John W. Swain, "State Lotteries: Explaining Their Popularity," *International Journal of Public Administration* 16, no. 7 (1993): 1015–1033.
650 Exhibit, 21.4, adapted from Bartley A. Brennan and Nancy Kubasek, *The Legal Environment of Business* (New York: Macmillan, 1988), 24; Douglas Whitman and John Gergacz, *The Legal Environment of Business,* 2d ed. (new York: Random House, 1988), 22, 25.
655 Adapted from "Howto Find Your Market," *Changing Times,* September 1985, 36, 67. Adapted with permission from

Changing Times Magazine. © Kiplinger Washington Editors, Inc., 1985; David A. Westenberg, "What's in a Name? Establishing and Maintaining Trademark and Service," *Business Lawyer,* November 1986, 65–89; Ernest E. Helms, "Protecting Your Ideas — And Your Money," *Black Enterprise,* September 1986, 65–69.
661 Adapted from Alan Chai, Alta Campbell, and Patrick J. Spain, eds., *Hoover's Handbook of American Business, 1994* (Austin, Tex.: Reference Press, 1993), 880–881; Johnnie L. Roberts, "Pitney Bowes Thrives from Close Relations with Postal Service," *Wall Street Journal,* 4 April 1991, A1, A6; Niels Erich, "The Mail Must Go Through," *D&B Reports,* March–April 1989, 56–57; Alan Farnham, "What Goes On in Your Mailroom?" *Fortune,* 27 February 1989, 105–108; Gary Slutsker, "Mail Smart," *Forbes,* 12 December 1988, 246, 248.

CHAPTER 22

670 Exhibit 22.1, adapted from Mark R. Greene and James S. Trieschmann, *Risk and Insurance* (Cincinnati: South-Western Publishing, 1984), 25.
674 Adapted from Carolyn T. Geer, "Inside Jobs," *Forbes,* 23 May 1994, 52–57; Peter Kerr, "Blatant Fraud Pushing Up the Cost of Car Insurance," *New York Times,* 6 February 1992, sec. a, 1, sec. c, 4; "Health Care Fraud," *U.S. News & World Report,* 24 February 1992, 34–39.
677 Rosalind Resnick, "Overseas Cover," *International Business,* June 1994, 39–42.
682 Exhibit 22.4, adapted from "Pinned Down by Medical Bills," *Time,* 30 June 1986, 64; Joseph Carey, "Health Benefits for Employees Enter New Era," *U.S. News & World Report,* 22 July 1985, 73; Employee Benefit Research Institute, Washington, D.C., personal communication, 1989.
661 Adapted from Jill Andresky Fraser, "A Fresh Look at Insurance," *Inc.,* December 1990, 153–154; Henry A. Revzan, "Controlling Insurance Costs," *Small Business Reports,* April 1991, 62–67; Mark R. Greene and James S. Trieschmann, *Risk and Insurance* (Cincinnati: South-Western Publishing, 1984), 44.

CHAPTER 1

Opposite page 1 James Rudnick/Stock, Boston
1 Kirk Schlea/Zephyr
4 Courtesy Dell Computer
9 Cary Wolinsky/Stock, Boston
11 Bob Daemmrich/Stock, Boston
18 Courtesy Boeing Corporation
23 Lawrence Migdale/Stock, Boston
26 Kirk Schlea/Zephyr

CHAPTER 2

30 Anthony Cassidy/Tony Stone
31 Courtesy Round Table
32 Andy Snow/Zuma Images
38 Greg Girard/Contact Press Images
42 Chris Davies/Network/Matrix
49 James H. Simon/Picture Cube
50 R. Lord/Image Works
55 Courtesy Round Table

CHAPTER 3

60 Jon Riley/Tony Stone
61 Zephyr
65 Courtesy American Red Cross
67 AP/Wide World
75 Courtesy ConAgra Frozen Foods
81 Nelvin Cepeda/San Diego Union Tribune
86 Courtesy Northrop Grumman
91 Zephyr

CHAPTER 4

96 Jeffrey Sylvester/FPG
97 Alan Orling/Black Star
101 Les Moore/Uniphoto
105 Frank Siteman/Monkmeyer
108 Elena Rooraid/PhotoEdit
113 Courtesy Sony Corporation of America
118 Lawrence Migdale/Photo Researchers
120 Alan Orling/Black Star

CHAPTER 5

126 Uniphoto
127 Robin Landholm
128 William Johnson/Stock, Boston
130 Courtesy ACN Franchise Systems
135 Susan Holtz
139 Courtesy Seattle Business Incubator
143 Cameramann/Image Works
148 Robin Landholm

CHAPTER 6

154 Gabe Palmer/Stock Market
155 Uniphoto
156 Nik Kleinbert/Stock, Boston
159 Allen Green/Photo Researchers
163 Joseph Nettis/Photo Researchers
165 Courtesy Rockwell International
172 Tom Ebenhoh/Black Star
174 Uniphoto

CHAPTER 7

178 Jon Feingersh/Stock Market

179 Spencer Grant/Stock, Boston
181 Michael Dodge/White Flower Farm
183 Bob Daemmrich/Image Works
186 Alison Scott
187 Chuck Keeler/Tony Stone
200 William Hubbell/Woodfin Camp
201 Spencer Grant/Stock, Boston

CHAPTER 8

206 Dick Luria/FPG
207 Oli Tennent/Tony Stone
211 Courtesy Ford Motor Company
216 Paul Chesley/Photographers Aspen
218 Holt Confer/Image Works
220 Peter Menzel/Stock, Boston
227 Andy Sachs/Tony Stone
232 Oli Tennent/Tony Stone

CHAPTER 9

238 Uniphoto
239 C. J. Allen/Stock, Boston
240 Courtesy The Body Shop
248 Courtesy Pacific Crest Outward Bound School
256 Bob Daemmrich/Stock, Boston
259 Michael Newman/PhotoEdit
260 Charlie Archambault
263 C.J. Allen/Stock, Boston

CHAPTER 10

268 Stephen Simpson/FPG
269 Uniphoto
271 Russ Gilbert/The San Diego Union
274 Crandall/Image Works
278 Bob Daemmrich/Stock, Boston
282 Bob Daemmrich/Image Works
293 Billy Barnes/PhotoEdit
300 Uniphoto

CHAPTER 11

304 Uniphoto
305 Robin Landholm
306 Courtesy The Document Company, Xerox
314 Courtesy *Solidarity Magazine,* photo by Karl Mantyla
319 Duane Burleson/Sygma
324 Courtesy GM Cadillac
328 Courtesy United Airlines
332 Robin Landholm

CHAPTER 12

338 Stacy Pickerell/Tony Stone
339 Tom King/Image Bank
341 David Wells/Image Works
348 Okonewski/Image Works
358 Lester Sloan/Woodfin Camp
360 James Lukoski/Black Star
365 Courtesy Focus Suites
367 Tom King/Image Bank
369 Susan Holtz

CHAPTER 13

372 AP/Wide World

373 Robin Landholm
374 Courtesy National Basketball Association
379 Courtesy Levi Strauss & Co.
382 © 1995 Delrina (Washington) Corporation, © 1995 Berkeley Breathed. All Rights Reserved.
383 John Lei/Stock, Boston
393 Elena Rooraid/PhotoEdit
398 Robin Landholm

CHAPTER 14

404 Martin Rogers/Tony Stone
405 Bob Daemmrich/Stock, Boston
411 Starr/Stock, Boston
414 Maggie Porter
422 Steve Winter/Black Star
425 Courtesy Roadnet Technologies
429 Bruce Hands/Image Works
431 Bob Daemmrich/Stock, Boston

CHAPTER 15

438 Uniphoto
439 Denise de Luise/Zephyr
440 Courtesy AEG
445 Courtesy Wm. J. Wrigley Co.
454 Courtesy Sony Electronics, Inc.
456 Courtesy HIP
462 Courtesy Florida Power Corporation
465 Courtesy Motorola Cellular Subscriber Group
467 Denise de Luise/Zephyr

CHAPTER 16

472 David Joel/Tony Stone
473 Zephyr
478 Jeff Zaruba/Tony Stone
479 Courtesy OnTrack
486 Courtesy ProPhone
492 Reprinted with permission from Microsoft Corporation
497 Courtesy Central Point Software
498 Zephyr

CHAPTER 17

504 Gabe Palmer/Stock Market
505 Flip Chalfant/Image Bank
509 Courtesy Ernst & Young LLP
510 Courtesy Consolidated Paper
515 Courtesy J.C. Penney
522 Roy Roper/Zuma Images
528 Terry Vine/Tony Stone
532 Flip Chalfant/Image Bank

CHAPTER 18

538 Zephyr
539 Billy Barnes/Stock, Boston
541 Jeffrey MacMillan/U.S. News & World Report
542 Cathlyn Melloan/Tony Stone
548 Palmer Kane Inc./Stock Market
550 AP/Wide World
554 David Wells/Image Works
561 Billy Barnes/Stock, Boston

CHAPTER 19
566 Uniphoto
567 Zephyr
568 Gabe Palmer/Stock Market
575 Clemmer/Zuma Images
577 Courtesy Julius Blumberg
582 Courtesy Julius Blumberg
585 O.G.S. Inc./Picture Cube
592 Zephyr

CHAPTER 20
598 Uniphoto
599 D. Mason/Zephyr
600 Courtesy Fidelity Investments
603 Courtesy BA Investments

607 UPI/Bettmann
611 Andy Sachs/Tony Stone
615 Roger Tully/Tony Stone
618 *left* Don Spiro/Tony Stone
618 *right* AP/Wide World
619 C. J. Pickerell/Image Works
629 D. Mason/Zephyr

CHAPTER 21
634 Chad Ehlers/International Stock
635 Sepp Seitz/Woodfin Camp
637 Ken Whitmore/Tony Stone
641 Catherine Ursillo/Photo Researchers
647 Courtesy Tobacco Institute
651 Susan Holtz

656 AP/Wide World
659 Sepp Seitz/Woodfin Camp

CHAPTER 22
664 Bruce Ayres/Tony Stone
665 G. K. & Vikki Hart/Image Bank
667 Philip Habib/Tony Stone
672 Susan Holtz
678 Reuters/Bettmann
680 Peter Brouillet/NFL Photos
683 Ken Kerbs/DOT
686 G. K. & Vikki Hart/Image Bank
691 UPI/Bettmann

GLOSSARY

A

absolute advantage Nation's ability to produce a particular product with fewer resources (per unit of output) than any other nation

accountability Necessity to report results to supervisors and justify outcomes that fall below expectations

accounting Process of recording, classifying, and summarizing the financial activities of an organization

accounting equation Assets = liabilities + owners' equity

accrual basis Accounting method in which revenue is recorded when a sale is made and expense is recorded when incurred

acquisition Combination of two companies in which one company purchases the other and remains the dominant corporation

activity ratios Financial ratios that indicate how well a company is managing its assets

actuaries People employed by an insurance company to compute expected losses and to calculate the cost of premiums

administrative law Rules, regulations, and interpretations of statutory law set forth by administrative agencies and commissions

administrative skills Technical skills in information gathering, data analysis, planning, organizing, and other aspects of managerial work

advertising Paid, nonpersonal communication to a target market from an identified sponsor using mass communications channels

advocacy advertising Ads that present a company's opinions on public issues such as education and health

affirmative action Activities undertaken by businesses to recruit and promote minorities, based on an analysis of the work force and the available labor pool

agency Business relationship that exists when one party (the principal) authorizes another party (the agent) to act on her or his behalf, while controlling the agent's conduct

agency shop Workplace requiring nonunion employees who are covered by agreements negotiated by the union to pay service fees to that union

amortization Accounting procedure for systematically spreading the cost of an intangible asset over its estimated useful life

analytic system Production process that breaks incoming materials into various component products

antitrust laws Federal regulations that prohibit most monopolies

arbitrage Simultaneous purchase in one market and sale in a different market with a profitable price or yield differential

arbitration Process for resolving a labor-contract dispute in which an impartial third party studies the issues and makes a binding decision

artwork Visual, graphic part of the ad

assembly line Series of workstations at which each em-ployee performs a specific task in the production process

assembly-line layout Method of arranging equipment in which production is a flow of work proceeding along a line of workstations

asset allocation Method of shifting investments within a portfolio to adapt them to the current investment environment

assets Physical objects and intangible rights that have economic value to the owner

auction exchange Centralized marketplace where securities are traded by specialists on behalf of investors

audit Accountant's evaluation of the fairness and reliability of a client's financial statements

authority Power granted by the organization to make decisions and take actions to accomplish goals

authorization cards Sign-up cards designating a union as the signer's preferred bargaining agent

authorized stock Shares that a corporation's board of directors has decided to sell eventually

autocratic leaders Managers who do not involve others in decision making

automated teller machines (ATMs) Electronic terminals that permit people with plastic cards to perform simple banking transactions 24 hours a day without the aid of a human teller

automation Process of performing a mechanical operation with the absolute minimum of human intervention

average Number typical of a group of numbers or quantities

B

balance of payments Sum of all payments one nation has made to other nations minus the payments it has received from other nations during a specified period of time

balance of trade Relationship between the value of the products a nation exports and those it imports

balance sheet Financial statement that shows assets, liabilities, and owners' equity on a given date; also known as a *statement of financial position*

bankruptcy Legal procedure by which a person or a business that is unable to meet financial obligations is relieved of debt

barriers to entry Factors that make it difficult to launch a business in a particular industry

bartering Trading by exchanging goods or services directly rather than through a medium such as money

bear market Falling stock market

behavior modification Systematic use of rewards and punishments to change human behavior

behavioral segmentation Categorization of customers according to their relationship with products or response to product characteristics

benchmarking Process of comparing a company's processes and products with standards set by the world's best and then matching or exceeding those standards

beneficiaries People named in a life-insurance policy who are paid by the insurer when the insured dies

bill of materials Listing of all parts and materials in a product that are to be made or purchased

blacklist Secret list circulated among employers to keep people such as union organizers from getting jobs

blue-chip stocks Equities issued by large, well-established companies with consistent records of stock price increases and dividend payments

board of directors Group of people, elected by the shareholders, who have the ultimate authority in guiding the affairs of a corporation

bonus Cash payment in addition to the regular wage or salary, which serves as a reward for achievement

bond Certificate of indebtedness that is sold to raise funds

bookkeeping Record keeping, clerical phase of accounting

boycott Union activity in which members and sympathizers refuse to buy or handle the product of a target company

branch office Producer-owned operation that carries stock and sells it; also called a *sales branch*

brand Any name, term, sign, symbol, design, or combination used to identify the products of a firm and to differentiate them from competing products

brand awareness Level of brand loyalty at which people are familiar with a product—they recognize it

brand equity Overall strength of a brand in the marketplace and its value to the company that owns it; increasingly, companies are trying to assign financial value to brand equity

brand insistence Level of brand loyalty at which people will accept no substitute for a particular product

brand loyalty Commitment to a particular brand

brand marks Portion of a brand that cannot be expressed verbally

brand names Portion of a brand that can be expressed orally, including letters, words, or numbers

brand preference Level of brand loyalty at which people habitually buy a product if it is available

breach of contract Failure to live up to the terms of a contract, with no legal excuse

break-even analysis Method of calculating the minimum volume of sales needed at a given price to cover all costs

break-even point Sales volume at a given price that will cover all of a company's costs

broker Individual registered to sell securities

brokers Agents that specialize in a particular commodity but not usually for an extended period of time

budget Financial plan for a company's future activities that estimates revenues and proposed expenditures and that forecasts how expenditures will be financed

bull market Rising stock market

business agent Full-time union staffer who negotiates with management and enforces the union's agreements with companies

business cycle Fluctuations in the rate of growth that an economy experiences over a period of several years

business-interruption insurance Insurance that covers losses resulting from temporary business closings

buyers' markets Situations in which supply exceeds demand and marketers need to pay close attention to customers' needs

C

calendar year Twelve-month accounting period that begins on January 1 and ends on December 31

call option Right to buy shares at a specified price and sell at a market price

callable bonds Bonds that a company can redeem before the stated maturity date; also known as *redeemable bonds*

canned approach Selling method based on a fixed, memorized presentation

capital The physical, human-made elements used to produce goods and services, such as factories and computers; can also refer to the money invested in, or available to invest in, a business

capital budgeting Process for evaluating proposed investments in select projects that provide the best long-term financial return

capital gains Difference between the price at which a financial asset is sold and its original cost (assuming the price has gone up)

capital-intensive businesses Businesses that require large investments in capital assets

capital investments Money paid to acquire something of permanent value in a business

capital items Relatively expensive organizational products that have a long life and are used in the operations of a business

capital structure Financing mix of a firm

capitalism Economic system based on economic freedom and competition

cartel Association of producers that attempts to control a market and keep prices high by limiting output and dividing market shares among the members

cash basis Accounting method in which revenue is recorded when payment is received and expense is recorded when cash is paid

cash discount Discount offered to buyers who use cash instead of credit

centralization Concentration of decision-making authority at the top

certificate of deposit (CD) Note issued by a bank that guarantees to pay the depositor a specific interest rate for a fixed period of time

certification Process by which a union is officially recognized by the National Labor Relations Board as the bargaining agent for a group of employees

certified management accountants (CMAs) Accountants who have fulfilled the requirements for certification as specialists in management accounting

certified public accountants (CPAs) Professionally licensed accountants who meet certain requirements for education and experience and who pass an examination

chain of command Pathway for the flow of authority from one management level to the next

channel captain Channel member that is able to influence the activities of the other members of the distribution channel

chattel mortgage Agreement that the movable property purchased through a loan belongs to the borrower, although the lender has a legal right to the property if payments are not made as specified in the loan agreement

checks Written orders that tell the customer's bank to pay a specific amount to a particular individual or business

chief executive officer (CEO) Person appointed by a corporation's board of directors to carry out the board's policies and supervise the activities of the corporation

chief information officer (CIO) Top corporate executive with responsibility for information and information systems

chronological résumé Traditional résumé in which a person's employment history is listed sequentially in reverse order

circular flow Continuous exchange of goods and services for money among the participants in an economic system

claims Demands for payments from an insurance company due to some loss by the insured

closed shop Workplace in which union membership is a condition of employment

closing Point at which a sale is completed

code of ethics Written statement setting forth the principles that should guide an organization's decisions

cognitive dissonance Anxiety following a purchase that prompts buyers to seek reassurance about the purchase; commonly known as *buyer's remorse*

coinsurance Share of medical costs the patient picks up to supplement the remaining costs paid by the insurer

collateral Tangible asset a lender can claim if a borrower defaults on a loan

collective bargaining Process used by unions and management to negotiate work contracts

commercial banks Traditional banks offering savings, checking, and loan services

commercial paper An IOU, backed by the corporation's reputation, issued to raise short-term capital

commercialization Large-scale production and distribution of a product

commissions Payments to employees who achieve a certain percentage of sales made

commodities Raw materials used in producing other goods

commodities futures Contracts for commodities that will be delivered at a future date

commodity business Business in which products are undifferentiated, with the result that price becomes the chief competitive weapon; usually applied to basic goods such as minerals and agricultural products

commodity exchanges Marketplaces where contracts for raw materials are bought and sold

common carriers Transportation companies that offer their services to the general public

common law Law based on the precedents established by judges' decisions

common stock Shares whose owners have voting rights and have the last claim on distributed profits and assets

communication Exchange of information

communication media Channels of communication

communism Economic system in which all productive resources are owned and operated by the government, to the elimination of private property

comparable worth Concept of equal pay for jobs that are equal in value to the organization and require similar levels of education, training, and skills

comparative advantage Nation's ability to produce an item more efficiently than other nations because of its natural and human resources

comparative advertising Advertising technique in which two or more products are explicitly compared

compensating balance Portion of an unsecured loan that is kept on deposit at the lending institution to protect the lender and increase the lender's return

compensation Payment to employees for their work

competition Rivalry between two or more suppliers who are pursuing the same customers

competitive advantage Quality that makes a product more desirable than similar products offered by the competition

competitive advertising Ads that specifically highlight how a product is better than its competitors

components Parts that go into a manufacturer's final product

comprehensive general liability insurance Liability insurance that covers a wide variety of losses, except certain losses specifically mentioned in the policy

computer-aided design (CAD) Use of computer graphics in the development of products or processes

computer-aided engineering (CAE) Use of computers to test products without building an actual model

computer-aided manufacturing (CAM) Use of computers to control production machines

computer-integrated manufacturing (CIM) Computer-based systems that coordinate and control all the elements of design and production, including CAD and CAM

concentrated marketing Marketing program aimed at a single market segment

concept testing Process of getting reactions about a proposed product from potential customers

conceptual skills Ability to understand the relationship of parts to the whole

conglomerate mergers Combinations of companies that are in unrelated businesses, designed to augment a company's growth and diversify risk

consent order Settlement in which an individual or organization promises to discontinue some illegal activity without admitting guilt

consideration Bargained-for exchange necessary to make a contract legally binding

consortium Group of companies working jointly to promote a common objective or engage in a project of benefit to all members

consumer buying behavior Behavior exhibited by consumers as they consider and purchase various products

consumer market Individuals who buy goods or services for personal use

consumer products Products sold exclusively to consumers, including convenience products, shopping products, and specialty products

consumer promotions Sales promotions aimed at final consumers

consumerism Movement that pressures businesses to consider consumer needs and interests

contingency leadership Leadership style promoting the flexibility to adopt the style most appropriate to current business conditions; also called situational management

contingency plans Actions the company can take to cope with unforeseen events

contingent business-interruption insurance Insurance that protects a business from losses due to an interruption in the delivery of supplies

continuity Pattern according to which an ad appears in the media; it can be spread evenly over time or concentrated during selected periods

contract Exchange of promises enforceable by law

contract carriers Specialized freight haulers that serve selected companies under written contract

controller Highest-ranking accountant in a company, responsible for overseeing all accounting functions

controlling Process of measuring progress against goals and objectives and correcting deviations if results are not as expected

convenience products Products that are readily available, low-priced, and heavily advertised and that consumers buy quickly and often

convenience stores Food stores that offer convenient locations and hours but stock a limited selection of goods

conversion process Sequence of events (input → transformation → output) for transforming materials into goods and services

convertible bonds Corporate bonds that can be exchanged at the owner's discretion into common stock of the issuing company

cooling-off period Eighty-day period allowed by the Taft-Hartley Act during which a strike is suspended by order of the president of the United States and the courts to protect public health and safety

cooperative advertising Joint efforts between local and national advertisers, in which producers of nationally sold products share the costs of local advertising with local merchants and wholesalers

cooperatives Associations of people or small companies with similar interests, formed to obtain greater bargaining power and other economies of scale

copy Verbal (spoken or written) part of an ad

corporate culture Set of values and norms that guides and influences the attitudes and behavior of employees and managers within a company

corporation Legally chartered enterprise with most of the legal rights of a person, including the right to conduct a business, to own and sell property, to borrow money, and to sue or be sued

correlation Statistical relationship between two or more variables

cost-benefit analysis Comparison of the costs and benefits of a particular action for the purpose of assessing its desirability

cost of capital Average rate of interest a firm pays on its combination of debt and equity

cost of goods sold Cost of producing or acquiring a company's products for sale during a given period

cost-of-living adjustment (COLA) Clause in a union contract ensuring that wages will rise in proportion to inflation

cost per thousand (CPM) Cost of reaching 1,000 people with an ad

cost shifting Hospitals' and doctors' boosting their charges to private paying patients to make up for the shortfall in government reimbursements for their Medicare and Medicaid patients

countertrade Trading practice in which local products are offered instead of cash in exchange for imported products

couponing Distribution of certificates that offer discounts on particular items

craft unions Unions made up of skilled artisans belonging to a single profession or practicing a single craft

creative selling Selling process used by order getters, which involves determining customer needs, devising strategies to explain product benefits, and persuading customers to buy

credit card Plastic card that allows the customer to buy now and pay back the loaned amount at a future date

credit life insurance Coverage that guarantees repayment of a loan or an installment contract if the borrower dies

credit unions Cooperative financial institutions that provide loan and savings services to their members

creditors People or organizations that have loaned money or extended credit

crime insurance Insurance against loss from theft

crisis management System for minimizing the harm that might result from some unusually threatening situations

critical path method (CPM) Scheduling method that estimates the smallest amount of time in which a project can be completed by projecting the time needed for com-pletion of the longest sequence of tasks (the critical path)

currency Bills and coins that make up the cash money of a society

current assets Cash and other items that can be turned back into cash within one year

current liabilities Obligations that must be met within a year

current ratio Measure of a company's short-term liquidity, calculated by dividing current assets by current liabilities

customer divisions Divisional structure that focuses on customers or clients

customer service Efforts a company makes to satisfy its customers and to help them realize the greatest possible value from the products they are purchasing

customer-service standards In physical distribution, goals a company sets for its performance in on-time delivery, cost, convenience, and other factors related to customer satisfaction

customized marketing Marketing program in which each individual customer is treated as a separate segment

customs duties Fees imposed on goods brought into the country; also called *import taxes*

cyclical variation Change that occurs in a regularly repeating pattern

D

damages Amount a court awards a plaintiff in a successful lawsuit

data Recorded statistics, facts, predictions, and opinions; data need to be converted to information before they can help people solve business problems

database Collection of related data that can be cross-referenced in order to extract information

database marketing Direct marketing in which advertisers take advantage of comprehensive information on customers, including purchase behavior, demographics, and lifestyle

dealer exchanges Decentralized marketplaces where securities are bought and sold by dealers out of their own inventories

debentures Corporate bonds backed by the company's good faith

debit cards Plastic cards that allow the bank to take money from the user's demand-deposit account and transfer it to a retailer's account

debt Funds obtained by borrowing

debt-to-equity ratio Measure of the extent to which a business is financed by debt as opposed to invested capital, calculated by dividing the company's total liabilities by owners' equity

debt ratios Financial ratios that indicate the extent of a company's burden of long-term debt; (sometimes called *coverage ratios*)

debt-to-total-assets ratio Measure of a company's ability to carry long-term debt, calculated by dividing total liabilities by total assets

debtors People or organizations who have to repay money they have borrowed

decentralization Delegation of decision-making authority to employees in lower positions

deceptive pricing Range of pricing and promotion practices that are considered misleading by government regulators

decertification Process employees use to take away a union's official right to represent them

decision making Process of identifying a decision situa-tion, analyzing the problem, weighing the alternatives, arriving at a decision, taking action, and evaluating the results

deductible Amount of loss that must be paid by the insured before the insurer will pay for the rest

deed Legal document by which an owner transfers the title to real property to a new owner

default Failure of issuers to meet their contractual principal and interest obligations

delegation Assignment of authority and responsibility to lower-level managers and employees

demand Specific quantity of a product that consumers are willing and able to buy at various prices at a given time

demand curve Series of points on a graph showing the relationship between price and quantity demanded

demand deposit Money in a checking account that can be used by the customer at any time

democratic leaders Managers who delegate authority and involve employees in decision making

demographics Study of the statistical characteristics of a population

denomination Face value of a single bond

dental and vision insurance Insurance that covers a portion of the costs of dental and eye care

department stores Large retail stores that carry a wide variety of merchandise

departmentalization Grouping people within an organization according to function, division, teams, matrix, or network

departmentalization by division Grouping departments according to similarities in product, process, customer, or geography

departmentalization by function Grouping workers ac-cording to their similar skills, resource use, and expertise

departmentalization by matrix Permanently assigning employees to both a functional group and a project team (thus using functional and divisional patterns simultaneously)

departmentalization by network Electronically connecting separate companies that perform selected tasks for a small headquarters organization

departmentalization by teams Assigning functional employees to teams that handle specific work tasks

dependent variables Events that change as the independent variables change

depreciated-value coverage Insurance that assumes that lost or damaged property was worth less than new replacement property

depreciation Accounting procedure for systematically spreading the cost of a tangible asset over its estimated useful life

deregulation Removal or relaxation of rules and restrictions affecting business

differentiated marketing Marketing program aimed at several market segments, each of which receives a unique marketing mix

direct mail Advertising sent directly to potential customers, usually through the U.S. Postal Service

disability income insurance Insurance that protects an individual against loss of income while that individual is disabled as the result of an illness or accident

discount brokerages Financial-services companies that sell securities but give no advice

discount pricing Offering a reduction in price

discount rate Interest rate charged by the Federal Reserve on loans to member banks

discount stores Retailers that sell a variety of goods below the market price by keeping their overhead low

discretionary order Market order that allows the broker to decide when to trade a security

discrimination In a social and economic sense, denial of opportunities to individuals on the basis of some characteristic that has no bearing on their ability to perform in a job

disinflation Economic condition in which the rate of inflation declines

dispatching Issuing work orders and routing papers to department heads and supervisors

distribution centers Warehouse facilities that specialize in collecting and shipping merchandise

distribution channels Systems for moving goods and services from producers to customers; also known as *marketing channels*

distribution mix Combination of intermediaries and channels that a producer uses to get a product to end users

distribution strategy Firm's overall plan for moving products to intermediaries and final customers

diversification Assembling investment portfolios in such a way that a loss in one investment won't cripple the value of the entire portfolio

divestiture Sale of part of a company

dividends Payments to shareholders from a company's earnings

division of labor Specialization in or responsibility for some portion of an organization's overall work tasks; also called work specialization

double-entry bookkeeping Way of recording financial transactions that requires two entries for every transaction so that the accounting equation is always kept in balance

downsizing Laying off employees in an effort to become more profitable

drop shippers Merchant wholesalers that assume ownership of goods but don't take physical possession; commonly used to market agricultural and mineral products

due process System of procedures and mechanisms for ensuring equity and justice on the job

dumping Charging less than the actual cost or less than the home-country price for goods sold in other countries

E

earnings per share Measure of a company's profitability for each share of outstanding stock, calculated by dividing net income after taxes by shares of common stock outstanding

ecology Relationship among living things in the water, air, and soil, as well as the nutrients that support them

economic order quantity (EOQ) Optimal, or least-cost, quantity of inventory that should be ordered

economic system Means by which a society distributes its resources to satisfy its people's needs

economies of scale Savings from manufacturing, marketing, or buying large quantities

effectiveness Increasing competitiveness through efficiency, quality, and improved human relations

efficiency Minimizing cost by maximizing the level of output from each resource

elastic demand Situation in which a percentage change in price produces a distinct percentage change in the quantity sold

electronic data interchange (EDI) Computerized exchange of order and payment details between businesses and suppliers

electronic funds transfer systems (EFTS) Computerized systems for performing financial transactions

embargo Total ban on trade with a particular nation or in a particular product

employee assistance program (EAP) Company-sponsored counseling or referral plan for employees with personal problems

employee benefits Compensation other than wages, salaries, and incentive programs

employee stock-ownership plan (ESOP) Program enabling employees to become owners or part owners of a company

employment at will Employer's right to keep or terminate employees as it wishes

employment interview Formal meeting in which an employer and an applicant ask questions and exchange information to see whether the applicant and the organization are a good match

empowerment Giving employees more say in the day-to-day workings of a company

endowment insurance Life insurance that guarantees death benefits for a specified period, after which the face value of the policy is paid to the policyholder

entrepreneurs People who accept the risk of failure to organize the other three factors of production in order to produce goods and services more efficiently

equilibrium price Point at which quantity supplied and quantity demanded are in balance

equity Capital funds obtained by selling shares of ownership in the company

ergonomics Study of human performance in relation to the tasks performed, the equipment used, and the environment

ethical dilemma Situation in which both sides of an issue can be supported with valid arguments

ethical lapse Situation in which an individual makes an unethical decision

ethics Study of individual choices made in the framework of certain rules of conduct or moral standards

exchange process Act of obtaining a desired object from another party by offering something in return

exchange rate Rate at which the money of one country is traded for the money of another

excise taxes Taxes intended to help control potentially harmful practices or to help pay for government services used only by certain people or businesses

exclusive distribution Approach to distribution in which intermediaries are given the exclusive right to sell a product within a given market

expectancy theory Idea that the amount of effort an employee expends will depend on the expected outcome

expense items Relatively inexpensive organizational products that are generally consumed within a year of their purchase

expenses Costs created in the process of generating revenues

experience curve Predictable decline of all costs associated with a product as the total number of units produced increases

experiment Data-collection method in which the investigator tries to find out how one set of conditions will affect another set of conditions by setting up a situation in which all factors and events involved may be carefully measured

exporting Selling and shipping goods or services to another country

express contract Contract derived from words, either oral or written

external data Research data acquired from sources outside the company

extra-expense insurance Insurance that covers the added expense of operating the business in temporary facilities after an event such as a fire

F

factoring Sale of a firm's accounts receivable, at a discount, to a finance company, known as a factor

factors of production Resources that a society uses to produce goods and services, including natural resources, labor, capital, and entrepreneurship

family branding Using a brand name on a variety of related products

featherbedding Practice of requiring employees to be kept on the payroll for work they don't do or for work that isn't necessary

Fed funds rate Interest rate charged for overnight loans between banks

fidelity bond Coverage that protects employers from dishonesty on the part of employees

FIFO "First in, first out" method of pricing inventory under which the costs of the first goods acquired are the first ones charged to the cost of goods sold

finance companies Companies that specialize in making loans

financial accounting Area of accounting concerned with preparing financial information for users outside the organization

financial futures Legally binding agreements to buy or sell financial instruments at a future date

financial management Effective acquisition and use of money

first-line managers Those at the bottom of the management hierarchy, who supervise the operating employees; also called supervisory managers

fiscal policy Use of government revenue collection and spending to influence the business cycle

fiscal year Any 12 consecutive months used as an accounting period

fixed assets Assets retained for long-term use, such as land, buildings, machinery, and equipment; also referred to as *property, plant, and equipment*

fixed costs Business costs that must be covered no matter how many units of a product a company sells

fixed-position layout Method of arranging equipment in which the product is stationary and equipment and personnel come to it

flat structure Organization structure having a wide span of management and few hierarchical levels

flexible manufacturing Production use of computer-controlled machines that can adapt to various versions of the same operation; also called *soft manufacturing*

flextime Scheduling system in which employees are allowed certain options regarding time of arrival and departure

floating exchange rate system World economic system in which the values of all currencies are determined by supply and demand

focused factory Manufacturing facility that deals with only one narrow set of products

for-profit corporations Companies formed to earn money for their owners

foreign exchange Trading one currency for the equivalent amount of another currency

foreign sales corporations (FSCs) Tax-sheltered subsidi-aries of U.S.-based corporations that engage in exporting

form utility Consumer value created when a product's characteristics are made more satisfying

forward buying Retailers' taking advantage of trade allowances by buying more products at discounted prices than they hope to sell

four Ps Marketing elements—product, price, distribution (place), and promotion

franchise Business arrangement in which an individual obtains rights from a larger company to sell a well-known product or service

franchisee Person or group to whom a corporation grants an exclusive right to the use of its name in a certain territory, usually in exchange for an initial fee plus monthly royalty payments

franchiser Corporation that grants a franchise to an individual or group

free enterprise The nature of business in a free-market system

free-market system Economic system in which the way people spend their money determines which products will be produced and what those products will cost

free trade International trade unencumbered by restrictive measures

freight forwarders Specialized companies that pool small shipments bound for the same general location, thereby increasing cost efficiencies for shippers

frequency Average number of times that each audience member is exposed to the message (equal to the total number of exposures divided by the total audience population)

full-service brokerages Financial-services companies with a full range of services, including investment advice, securities research, and investment products

full-service merchant wholesalers Wholesaling intermediaries that provide a wide variety of services to their customers, such as storage, delivery, and marketing support

functional résumé Résumé in which focus is on a list of skills and accomplishments; employment and academic experience are covered in subordinate sections

G

gain sharing Motivational program that offers monetary rewards based on short-term team performance

Gantt chart Bar chart used to control schedules by showing how long each part of a production process should take and when it should take place

general expenses Operating expenses, such as office and administrative expenses, not directly associated with creating or marketing a good or service

general obligation bonds Municipal bonds backed by the issuing agency's general taxing authority

general partnership Partnership in which all partners have the right to participate as co-owners and are individually liable for the business's debts

generally accepted accounting principles (GAAP) Professionally approved standards used by the accounting profession in preparing financial statements

generic products Products in plain packaging that bear only the name of the item, not of its producer

geodemographics Method of combining geographic data with demographic data to develop profiles of neighborhood segments

geographic divisions Divisional structure based on location

geographic segmentation Categorization of customers according to their geographic location

givebacks Concessions made by union members to give up promised increases in wages or benefits because the company believes the higher costs will hurt its competitive position

glass ceiling Invisible barrier of subtle discrimination that keeps women out of the top positions in business

goal Broad, long-range target or aim

going public Act of raising capital by selling company shares to the public for the first time

golden parachute Generous compensation packages guaranteed to executives in the event they lose their jobs after a takeover

goods-producing businesses Businesses that produce tangible products

goodwill Value assigned to a business's reputation, calculated as the difference between the price paid for the business and the underlying value of its assets

government-owned corporations Corporations formed and owned by a government body for a specific public purpose

grapevine Communication network of the informal organization

grievances Employee complaints about management's violating some aspect of a labor contract

gross domestic product (GDP) Dollar value of all the final goods and services produced by an economy during a specified period (usually a year); includes profits from foreign-owned businesses within a nation's borders, and excludes receipts from overseas operations of domestic companies

gross national product (GNP) Total value of all the final goods and services produced by an economy over a given period of time; includes receipts from overseas operations of domestic companies, and excludes profits from foreign-owned businesses within a nation's borders

gross profit Amount remaining when the cost of goods sold is deducted from net sales; also known as *gross margin*

gross sales All revenues received from the sale of goods or services

group norms Standards of behavior that all members of a given group accept

growth stocks Equities issued by small companies with unproven products or services

H

hard manufacturing Use of specialized production equipment that cannot readily be moved

Hawthorne effect Improvement in performance as a by-product of attention, a theory developed during the Hawthorne studies of productivity

health maintenance organizations (HMOs) Prepaid medical plans in which consumers pay a set fee in order to receive a full range of medical care from a group of medical practitioners

hedge Make an investment that protects the investor from suffering loss on another investment

hierarchy Pyramidlike organizational structure comprising top, middle, and lower management

high-growth ventures Small businesses intended to achieve rapid growth and high profits on investment

holding company Company that owns most, if not all, of another company's stock but that does not actively participate in the management of that other company

horizontal mergers Combinations of companies that are direct competitors in the same industry

horizontal organization Structure to coordinate activity by facilitating communication and information exchange across departments

hospitalization insurance Health insurance that pays for most of the costs of a hospital stay

hostile takeovers Situations in which an outside party buys enough stock in a corporation to take control against the wishes of the board of directors and corporate officers

human relations Ways two or more people interact with one another

human relations skills Skills required to understand other people and to interact effectively with them

human resources management Specialized function of planning how to obtain employees, oversee their training, evaluate them, and compensate them

hygiene factors Aspects of the work environment that are associated with dissatisfaction

I

idea marketing Marketing of concepts that provide intellectual or spiritual benefits

implied contract Contract derived from actions or conduct

importing Purchasing goods or services from another country and bringing them into one's own country

incentives Cash payments to employees who produce at a desired level or whose unit (often the company as a whole) produces at a desired level

income statement Financial statement showing how a business's revenues compare with expenses for a given period of time

incubator Facility set up to nurture businesses during their early growth phases

independent variables Events that are controlled by outside factors

index number Percentage used to compare such figures as prices or costs in one period with those in a base or standard period

indexing Assembling investment portfolios by selecting securities that together reflect the profile of the market as a whole

individual retirement account (IRA) Type of savings account that provides tax advantages to depositors who are building a fund for retirement

individual rights Philosophy used in making ethical decisions that aims to protect human dignity

industrial distributors Wholesalers that sell to industrial customers, rather than to retailers

industrial unions Unions representing both skilled and unskilled employees from all phases of a particular industry

inelastic demand Situation in which a percentage change in price produces no percentage change in the quantity sold

inflation Economic condition in which prices rise steadily throughout the economy

informal organization Interactions that are not defined by the formal structure but that influence how the organization accomplishes its goals

information Specific collection of data that pertain to a particular decision or problem

information systems All written and electronic forms of sharing information, processing data, and communicating ideas

injunction Court order directing someone to do something or not do something

insider trading Employee's or manager's use of unpublicized information gained in the course of his or her job to benefit from fluctuations in the stock market

installations Organizational goods such as buildings and large stationary equipment, including factories, milling machines, and mainframe computer systems

institutional advertising Advertising that seeks to create goodwill and to build a desired image for a company rather than to sell specific products

institutional investors Companies that invest money entrusted to them by others

insurable risk Risk for which an acceptable probability of loss may be calculated and that an insurance company might therefore be willing to cover

insurance Written contract that transfers to an insurer the financial responsibility for any losses

intangible assets Assets having no physical existence but having value because the owner can license or sell them to others

integrated marketing communications (IMC) Strategy of coordinating and integrating communications and promotions efforts with customers to ensure greater efficiency and effectiveness

intellectual property Intangible personal property such as ideas, songs, trademarks, trade secrets, patents, or copyrights

intensive distribution Approach to distribution that involves placing the product in as many outlets as possible

intentional tort Willful act that results in injury

interlocking directorates Situation in which members of the board of one firm sit on the board of a competing firm

internal auditors Employees who analyze and evaluate the operation of company departments to determine their efficiency

internal data Research data that the company already has or can extract from some internal source

Internet Worldwide collection of computer networks owned by universities, government agencies, and commercial businesses

intrapreneurs Employees who have the entrepreneurial spirit to develop innovative ideas within the organization

inventory Goods held on hand for the production process or for sales to final customers

inventory control Method of determining the right quantity of various items to have on hand and of keeping track of their location, use, and condition

inventory turnover ratio Measure of the time a company takes to turn its inventory into sales, calculated by dividing cost of goods sold by the average value of inventory for a period

investment banks Financial institutions that specialize in helping companies or government agencies raise funds; also known as *underwriters*

investment portfolios Assortment of investment instruments

involuntary bankruptcy Bankruptcy proceedings initiated by a firm's creditors

issued stock Authorized shares that have been released to the market

J

job analysis Process by which jobs are studied to determine the tasks and dynamics involved in performing them

job description Statement of the tasks involved in a given job and the conditions under which the holder of the job will work

job enrichment Reducing work specialization and making work more meaningful by adding to the responsibilities of each job

job sharing Splitting a single full-time job between two employees for their convenience

job shop Firm that produces dissimilar items or that produces its goods or services at intervals

job specification Statement describing the kind of person who would be best for a given job—including the skills, education, and previous experience that the job requires

joint venture Enterprise supported by the investment of two or more parties for mutual benefit

junk bonds Bonds that pay high interest because they are below investment grade

justice Philosophy used in making ethical decisions that aims to ensure the equal distribution of burdens and benefits

just–in–time (JIT) system Continuous process of inventory control that, through teamwork, seeks to deliver a small quantity of materials where and when they are needed

K

Keogh account Type of retirement savings account for the self-employed that provides tax advantages

key-person insurance Insurance that provides a business with funds in compensation for loss of a key employee

knowledge-based pay Pay keyed to an employee's acquisition of skills; also called *skill-based pay*

L

labor Generally, the human resources used to produce goods and services; also used in a specific sense to refer to organized union workers

labor federation Umbrella organization of national unions and unaffiliated local unions that undertakes large-scale activities on behalf of their members and that resolves conflicts between unions

labor-intensive businesses Businesses in which labor costs are more important than capital costs

labor unions Organizations of employees formed to protect and advance their members' interests

laissez-faire leaders Managers who lead by taking the role of consultant, leaving the actual decision making up to employees

law of large numbers Principle that the larger the group on which probabilities are calculated, the more accurate the predictive value

layoffs Termination of employees for economic or business reasons

lead times Periods that elapse between placement of a purchase order and receipt of materials from the supplier

leadership Skill of persuading others to achieve organizational goals by showing how things are done and by setting an example in behavior and spirit

leading Process of influencing and motivating people to work toward organizational goals

lease Legal agreement that obligates the user of an asset to make payments to the owner of the asset in exchange for using it

leverage Use of borrowed funds to finance a portion of an investment

leveraged buyouts (LBOs) Situations in which individuals or groups of investors purchase companies with the debt secured by the companys' assets

liabilities Debts or obligations that are owed to individuals or organizations

liability insurance Insurance that covers losses arising either from injury to an individual or from damage to other people's property

licensing Giving rights to a company to use a well-known name or symbol in marketing its products

lifestyle businesses Small businesses intended to provide the owner with a comfortable livelihood

lifetime security Arrangement that gives employees some protection against temporary layoffs during an economic slowdown and against job loss during a downsizing or plant closing

LIFO "Last in, first out" method of pricing inventory under which the costs of the last goods acquired are the first ones charged to the cost of goods sold

limit order Market order that stipulates the highest or lowest price at which the customer is willing to trade securities

limited liability companies (LLCs) Organizations that combine the benefits of S corporations and

limited partnerships without the drawbacks of either

limited partnership Partnership composed of one or more general partners and one or more partners whose liability is usually limited to the amount of their capital investment

limited-service merchant wholesalers Merchant wholesalers that offer fewer services than full-service wholesalers; they often specialize in particular markets, such as agriculture

line of credit Arrangement in which the financial institution makes money available for use at any time after the loan has been approved

line organization Chain-of-command system that establishes a clear line of authority flowing from the top down

line-and-staff organization Organization system that has a clear chain of command but that also includes functional groups of people who provide advice and specialized services

liquidity Asset's ease of conversion to cash

liquidity ratios Financial ratios that indicate how quickly a company can repay short-term obligations

lobbies Groups who try to persuade legislators to vote according to the groups' interests

local advertising Advertising sponsored by a local merchant

locals Relatively small union groups, usually part of a national union or a labor federation, that represent members who work in a single facility or in a certain geographic area

lockouts Management activities in which union members are prevented from entering a business during a strike, to force union acceptance of management's last contract proposal

long-term liabilities Obligations that fall due more than a year from the date of the balance sheet

long-term loans Debt that must be repaid over a period of more than a year

loss exposures Areas of risk in which a potential for loss exists

M

M1 That portion of the money supply consisting of currency and demand deposits

M2 That portion of the money supply consisting of currency, demand deposits, and time deposits

macroeconomics Study of the economy as a whole

mail-order firms Companies that sell products through catalogs and ship them directly to customers

major-medical insurance Insurance that covers many medical expenses not covered by other health-insurance plans

malpractice insurance Insurance that covers losses arising from damages or injuries caused by the insured in the course of performing professional services for clients

managed care Health care set up by employers (usually through an insurance carrier) who provide networks of doctors and hospitals that agree to discount the fees they charge in return for the flow of patients

management Process of coordinating organizational resources to meet a goal

management accounting Area of accounting concerned with preparing data for use by managers within the organization

management by objectives (MBO) Control method in which managers are motivated to achieve results by the opportunity to structure personal objectives and make plans that mesh with the organization's goals

management information system (MIS) System that supplies periodic, predefined reports to assist in managerial decision making

managerial integrator Manager who coordinates activities of several functional departments but belongs to none

mandatory retirement Required dismissal of an employee who reaches a certain age

mandatory subject Topic that must be discussed in collective bargaining

manufacturer's agents Wholesalers that do not take title to products but that receive a commission for selling products

manufacturing resource planning (MRP II) Computer-based system that integrates data from all departments to manage production planning and control

margin requirements Limits set by the Federal Reserve on the amount of money that stockbrokers and banks may lend customers for the purpose of buying stocks

margin trading Borrowing money from brokers to buy stock, paying interest on the borrowed money, and leaving the stock with the broker as collateral

market People who need or want a product and who have the money to buy it

market economies Economic systems in which goals are achieved by the action of the free market, with a minimum of government intervention

market indexes Measures of security markets calculated from the prices of a selection of securities

market makers Dealers in dealer exchanges who sell securities out of their own inventories so that a market is always available for buyers and sellers

market order Authorization for a broker to buy or sell securities at the best price that can be negotiated at the moment

market segments Groups of individuals or organizations within a market that share certain common characteristics

market share Measure of a firm's portion of the total sales in a market

marketable securities Stocks, bonds, and other investments that can be turned into cash quickly

marketing Process of planning and executing the conception, pricing, promotion, and distribution of ideas, goods, and services to create exchanges that satisfy individual and organizational objectives

marketing concept Approach to business management that stresses not only customer needs and wants but also long-term profitability and the integration of marketing with other functional units within the organization

marketing intermediaries Businesspeople and organizations that channel goods and services from producers to consumers

marketing mix Blend of elements satisfying a chosen market

marketing research Process of gathering information about marketing problems and opportunities

marketing strategy Overall plan for marketing a product

market segmentation Division of a market into subgroups of buyers that are likely to respond in consistent ways

markup Amount added to the cost of an item to create a selling price that produces a profit

markup percentage Difference in percentage between the cost of an item and its selling price

mass production Manufacture of uniform products in great quantities

master limited partnership (MLP) Business partnership that acts like a corporation, trading partnership units on listed stock exchanges; if 90 percent of income is passive, MLPs are taxed at individual rates

matching principle Concept that long-term projects should be funded with long-term sources of capital, whereas short-term expenditures should be funded from current income

material requirements planning (MRP) Method of getting the correct materials where they are needed for production and doing it on time and without unnecessary stockpiling

materials handling Activities involved in moving, packing, storing, and inventorying goods

mean Sum of all the items in a group, divided by the number of items in the group

mechanization Use of machines to do work previously done by people

media Communications channels, such as newspapers, radio, and television

media mix Combination of various media options that a company uses in an advertising campaign

media plan Written plan that outlines how a company will spend its media budget, including how the money will be divided among the various media and when the advertisements will appear

median Midpoint, or the point in a group of numbers at which half are higher and half are lower

mediation Process for resolving a labor-contract dispute in which a neutral third party meets with both sides and attempts to steer them toward a solution

mental-health insurance Insurance that covers the costs of psychiatric care, psychological counseling, and substance abuse treatment programs

mentor Experienced member of an organization who serves as a guide and protector to a lower-level employee

merchant wholesalers Independent wholesalers that take legal title to products

merger Combination of two or more companies in which the old companies cease to exist and a new enterprise is created

methods improvement Examining all aspects of a job or task in order to improve efficiency levels

microeconomics Study of specific entities in the economy, such as households, companies, or industries

middle managers Those in the middle of the management hierarchy, who implement the goals of top managers and coordinate the work of first-line managers

minorities In a social and economic sense, categories of people that society at large singles out for discriminatory, selective, or unfavorable treatment

mission Overall purpose of an organization

mission statement Putting the organization's mission into words

missionary salespeople Salespeople who support existing customers, usually wholesalers and retailers

mixed capitalism Economic system in which operation of the free market is influenced to some degree by government involvement

mode Number that occurs most often in any series of data or observations

monetary policy Actions taken by the Federal Reserve Board to influence the economy by controlling the money supply; the Fed's primary tool is the manipulation of interest rates

money Anything used by a society as a token of value in buying and selling goods and services

money-market deposit accounts Bank accounts that pay money-market interest rates and permit the depositor to write a limited number of checks

money-market funds Mutual funds that invest in short-term securities

monopolistic competition Situation in which many sellers offer products that differ from competing products in at least some small way

monopoly Market in which there are no direct competitors so that one company dominates

morale How an employee sees the job or the organization

mortgage bonds Corporate bonds backed by real property

motivating Giving employees a reason to do the job and to perform at their peak

motivation Force that moves someone to take action

motivators Factors of human relations in business that may increase motivation

MRO items Common term for supply products purchased by organizational customers; it stands for maintenance, repair, and operating items

multinational corporations (MNCs) Companies with operations in more than one country

multiplier effect Chain reaction whereby a change in one economic variable affects other variables, resulting in a ripple of changes throughout an economic system

municipal bonds Debt issued by a state or a local agency; interest earned on municipal bonds is exempt from federal income tax and from taxes in the issuing jurisdiction

mutual company Nonprofit insurance company owned by the policyholders

mutual funds Pools of money raised by investment companies and invested in stocks, bonds, or other marketable securities

N

national advertising Advertising sponsored by companies that sell products on a nationwide basis; refers to the geographic reach of the advertiser, not the geographic coverage of the ad

national banks Banks chartered by the federal government

national brands Brands owned by a manufacturer and distributed nationally

national competitive advantage Ability of a nation's industries to be innovative and move to a higher level of technology and productivity

national union Nationwide organization made up of locals that represent employees in locations around the country

natural resources Land, forests, minerals, water, and other tangible assets usable in their natural states

need Difference between a person's actual state and his or her ideal state; provides the basic motivation to make a purchase

need-satisfaction approach Selling method that starts with identifying the customer's needs and then creating a presentation that addresses those needs; this is the approach used by most professional salespeople

negative correlation Statistical relationship in which a change in one variable is associated with the other variable's change in the opposite direction

negligence Failure to observe a reasonable standard of care in order to protect others from unreasonable risk of injury

negotiable instrument Transferable document that represents a promise to pay a specified amount

net income Profit or loss of a company, determined by subtracting expenses from revenues; also called the *bottom line*

net sales Amount remaining after cash discounts, refunds, and other allowances are deducted from gross sales

networking Seeking to broaden one's effectiveness in an organization or industry by forming relationships with others in the same and related fields

no-fault insurance laws Laws limiting lawsuits connected with auto accidents

not-for-profit corporations Incorporated institutions whose owners have limited liability and that exist to provide a social service rather than to make a profit

not publicly traded corporations Corporations that withhold their stock from public sale; also called *closed corporations*

NOW account Interest-bearing negotiable order of withdrawal account with a minimum-balance requirement

O

objective Specific, short-range target or aim

observation Technique of watching or otherwise monitoring all incidents of the particular sort that the investigator wants to study

odd-even pricing Setting a price at an odd amount slightly below the next highest dollar figure

office automation system (OAS) Computer system that assists with the tasks that people in a typical business office face regularly, such as drawing graphs or processing documents

off-price stores Retailers that offer bargain prices on quality merchandise by maintaining low overhead and acquiring merchandise at below-wholesale costs

oligopoly Market dominated by a few producers

open-book credit Payment terms that allow the purchaser to take possession of goods and pay for them later; also referred to as an *open account*

open-market operations Activity of the Federal Reserve in buying and selling government bonds on the open market

open order Limit order that does not expire at the end of a trading day

open shop Workplace in which union membership is voluntary and employees need not join or pay dues

operating expenses All costs of operation that are not included under cost of goods sold

operating income Amount remaining when operating expenses are deducted from gross profit

operational objectives Objectives that focus on short-term issues and describe the results needed to achieve tactical objectives and strategic goals

operational plans Actions designed to achieve operational objectives and to support tactical plans, usually defined for less than one year and developed by first-line managers

opportunity cost Value of using a resource; measured in terms of the value of the next best alternative for using that resource

order getters Salespeople who are responsible for generating new sales and for increasing sales to existing customers

order processing Functions involved in receiving and handling an order

order takers Salespeople who generally process incoming orders without engaging in creative selling

organization Group of people whose interactions are structured into goal-directed activities

organization chart Diagram showing how employees and tasks are grouped and where the lines of communication and authority flow

organization structure Formal patterns designed by managers to define work tasks and individual jobs, to establish reporting relationships, and to coordinate all organizational tasks

organizational market Customers who buy goods or services for resale or for use in conducting their own operations

organizational products Products sold exclusively to organizations, including expense items and capital items

organizing Process of arranging resources to carry out the organization's plans

orientation Session or procedure for acclimating a new employee to the organization

outplacement Job-hunting and other assistance that a company provides to laid-off employees

over-the-counter (OTC) market Network of dealers who trade securities that are not listed on an exchange

owners' equity Portion of a company's assets that belongs to the owners after obligations to all creditors have been met

P

par value Arbitrary value assigned to a stock that is shown on the stock certificate

parent company Company that owns most, if not all, of another company's stock and that takes an active part in managing that other company

participative management System for involving employees in a company's decision making

partnership Unincorporated business owned and operated by two or more persons under a voluntary legal association

pattern bargaining Negotiating similar wages and benefits for all companies within a particular industry

pay for performance Accepting a lower base pay in exchange for bonuses based on meeting production or other goals

payee Person or business a check is made out to

penetration pricing Introducing a new product at a low price in hopes of building sales volume quickly

pension plans Company-sponsored programs for providing retirees with income

performance appraisal Evaluation of an employee's work according to specific criteria

perks Special class of employee benefits made available to a company's most valuable employees

permissive subject Topic that may be omitted from collective bargaining

personal property All property that is not real property

personal selling In-person communication between a seller and one or more potential buyers

persuasive advertising Advertising designed to persuade an audience to change its behavior or attitudes

physical distribution All the activities required to move finished products from the producer to the consumer

picketing Strike activity in which union members march before company entrances to persuade non-striking employees to walk off the job and to persuade customers and others to cease doing business with the company

piecework system Practice of paying employees a certain amount for each unit produced

place marketing Efforts to market neighborhoods, cities, states, regions, and even entire countries

place utility Consumer value added by making a product available in a convenient location

plan Systematic set of actions designed to achieve goals and objectives

planned economy Economic system in which resource-allocation decisions are made by the central government

planning Establishing objectives and goals for an organization and determining the best ways to accomplish them

point-of-purchase display Advertising or other display materials set up at retail locations to promote products to potential customers as they are making their purchase decisions

poison pill Defense against hostile takeovers; the basic idea is to make the company less attractive in some way to the potential raider

political action committees (PACs) Groups formed under federal election laws to raise money for candidates

pollution Threats to the physical environment caused by human activities in an industrial society

Ponzi scheme Form of fraud in which money received from later investors is used to pay off the earlier investors

position Place a product holds in the mind of buyers, relative to their needs and the product's competitors

positioning Process of achieving a desired market position

positive correlation Statistical relationship in which an increase or decrease in one variable is associated with another variable's change in the same direction

possession utility Consumer value created when someone takes ownership of a product

power of attorney Written authorization for one party to legally act for another

preferred-provider organizations (PPOs) Health-care providers offering reduced-rate contracts to groups that agree to obtain medical care through the providers' organization

preferred stock Shares that give their owners first claim on a company's dividends and assets

preliminary screening interview First of several interviews conducted by employers; usually held on campus, it helps employers eliminate unqualified applicants from the hiring process

premium Fee that the insured pays the insurer for coverage against losses

premiums Free or bargain-priced items offered to encourage consumers to buy a product

press conference Gathering of media representatives at which companies announce new information; also called a *press briefing*

press relations Process of communicating with reporters and editors from newspapers, magazines, and radio and television networks and stations

press release Brief statement or video program released to the press announcing new products, management changes, sales performance, and other potential news items; also called a *news release*

price Amount of money asked in exchange for products; amount needed to cover the marketer's costs plus provide a profit

price discrimination Offering a discount to one customer but not to another, with the intention of restraining competition

price-earnings ratio (*p/e* ratio) Comparison of a stock's market price with its annual earnings per share; also known as the *price-earnings multiple*

price fixing Illegal cooperation between two or more companies that agree on prices in order to reduce competition

price leader Major producer in an industry that tends to set the pace in establishing prices

price lining Offering merchandise at a limited number of set prices

pricing strategies Systematic approaches to setting price

primary data Facts gathered for the study of a specific problem

prime interest rate Lowest rate of interest charged by banks for short-term loans to their most credit-worthy customers

principal Amount of a debt, excluding any interest

private accountants In-house accountants employed by organizations and businesses; also called *corporate accountants*

private brands Brands that carry the label of a retailer or wholesaler rather than a manufacturer

private carriers Transportation operations owned by a company to move its own products and not those of the general public

private corporations Companies owned by private individuals or companies

private law Law that concerns itself with relationships between individuals, between an individual and a business, or between two businesses

probability Likelihood, over the long run, that a certain event will occur in one way rather than in another way

process divisions Divisional structure based on the major steps of a production process

process layout Method of arranging equipment so that production tasks are carried out in discrete locations containing specialized equipment and personnel

product Good or service used as the basis of commerce

product advertising Advertising that tries to sell specific goods or services, generally by describing features, benefits, and occasionally, price

product-development process Stages through which a product idea passes—from initial conceptualization to actual appearance in the marketplace

product differentiation Features that distinguish one com-pany's product from another company's similar product

product divisions Divisional structure based on products

product liability Product's capacity to cause damages or injury for which the producer or seller is held responsible

product-liability coverage Insurance that protects companies from claims for injuries or damages that result from use of a product the company manufactures or distributes

product life cycle Stages of growth and decline in sales and earnings

product lines Groups of products that are physically similar or that are intended for similar markets

product mix Complete list of all products that a company offers for sale

production Transformation of resources into forms that people need or want

production control Production planning, routing, scheduling, dispatching, and follow-up and control in an effort to achieve efficiency and high quality

production forecasting Estimating how much of a company's goods and services must be produced in order to meet future demand

production and operations management (POM) Coordination of an organization's resources in order to manufacture its goods or produce its services

productivity How efficiently available factors of production are used

professional corporations Companies whose shareholders offer professional services (medical, legal, engineering) and set up beneficial pension and insurance plans

profit Money left over after expenses and taxes have been deducted from revenue generated by selling goods or services

profit sharing System for distributing a portion of the company's profits to employees

profitability ratios Financial ratios that indicate to what extent a company is making a profit

program evaluation and review technique (PERT) Scheduling method similar to the critical path method but relying on statistical estimates of how long each task should take

program trading Investment strategy using computer programs to buy or sell large numbers of securities, thereby taking advantage of price discrepancies between stock index futures or options and the actual stocks represented in those indexes

project management Assigning employees to a functional group but also temporarily assigning them to a specific project

promissory note Unconditional written promise to repay a certain sum of money on a specified date

promotion Wide variety of persuasive techniques used by companies to communicate with their target markets and the general public

promotional mix Particular blend of personal selling, advertising, public relations, and sales promotion that a company uses to reach potential customers

promotional strategy Statement or document that defines the direction and scope of the promotional activities that a company will use to meet its marketing objectives

property Rights held regarding any tangible or intangible object

property insurance Insurance that provides coverage for physical damage to or destruction of property

prospecting Process of finding and qualifying potential customers

protectionism Government policies aimed at shielding a country's industries from foreign competition

prototypes Working samples of a proposed product

proxy Document authorizing another person to vote on behalf of a shareholder in a corporation

proxy fight Attempt to gain control of a takeover target by urging shareholders to vote for directors favored by the acquiring party

psychographics Classification of customers on the basis of their psychological makeup

public accountants Independent outsiders who provide accounting services for businesses and other organizations

public goods Goods or services that can be supplied more efficiently by government than by individuals or businesses

public law Law that concerns itself with relationships between the government and individual citizens

public relations Nonsales communication that businesses have with their various audiences (includes both communication with the general public and press relations)

publicly traded corporations Corporations that actively sell stock on the open market; also called *open corporations*

pull strategy Promotional strategy that stimulates con-sumer demand, which then exerts pressure on wholesalers and retailers to carry a product

pure capitalism Capitalism in its ideal state, in which all resource allocations are controlled by the unfettered operation of the free market

pure competition Situation in which so many buyers and sellers exist that no single buyer or seller can control the price of a product or the number of units sold

pure risk Risk that involves the chance of loss only

push strategy Promotional approach designed to motivate wholesalers and retailers to push a producer's products to end users

put option Right to buy shares at market price and sell at a specified price

Q

qualified prospects Potential buyers who have both the money needed to make the purchase and the authority to make the purchase decision

qualifying Process of identifying potential customers who have both the authority to buy a product and the money to do so

quality Degree to which a product meets customer expectations and requirements

quality assurance System of policies, practices, and procedures implemented throughout the company to create and produce quality goods and services

quality circles Regularly scheduled meetings of a small group of employees to come up with solutions to quality, safety, and production problems

quality control Routine checking and testing of a finished product for quality against some standard

quality of work life (QWL) Overall environment that results from job and work conditions

quantity discount Discount offered to buyers of large quantities

quasi-government corporations Public utilities having a monopoly to provide basic services

quick ratio Measure of a company's short-term liquidity, calculated by adding cash, marketable securities, and receivables, and then dividing that sum by current liabilities; also known as the *acid-test ratio*

quotas Fixed limits on the quantity of imports a nation will allow for a specific product; fixed numbers of minority-group members to be hired

R

rack jobbers Merchant wholesalers that are responsible for setting up and maintaining displays in a particular store area

random sampling Selecting a sample in a way that gives all items or persons in the larger group an equal chance of being selected

rate of return Percentage increase in the value of an investment

ratification Process by which union members vote on a contract negotiated by union leaders

ratio analysis Comparison of two elements from the same year's financial results, stated as a percentage or a ratio

raw materials Resources used in manufacturing and processing goods, from iron ore and crude petroleum to lumber and chemicals

reach Total number of audience members who will be exposed to a message at least once in a given period

real property Land and everything permanently attached to it

recession Period during which national income, employment, and production all fall

recruiters Members of the human resources staff who are responsible for obtaining new job candidates

recruiting Process of attracting appropriate applicants for an organization's jobs

reinforcement theory Theory that people repeat actions that produce pleasant outcomes and do not repeat actions that produce unpleasant outcomes

relationship marketing Focus on fostering long-term customer loyalty

reminder advertising Advertising intended to remind existing customers of a product's availability and benefits

repetitive manufacturing Repeated, steady production of identical goods or services

replacement-cost coverage Insurance that entitles policy-holder to buy new property to replace the old

reserve requirement Percentage of a bank's deposits that must be set aside

reserves Funds a financial institution keeps on tap to meet projected withdrawals

responsibility Obligation to perform the duties and to achieve the goals and objectives associated with a particular position

résumé Structured, written summary of a person's edu-cation, employment background, and job qualifications; a form of advertising designed to get you an interview

retailers Firms that sell directly to the public

retained earnings Net increase in assets (cash and outstanding receivables) for an accounting period; part of owners' equity

return on investment (ROI) Ratio between the net income earned by a company and total owners' equity; also known as *return on equity*

return on sales Ratio between net income and net sales; also known as *net profit margin*

revenue bonds Municipal bonds backed by revenue generated from the projects financed with the bonds

revenues Amount of sales of goods or services and inflow from miscellaneous sources such as interest, rent, and royalties

reverse channels Distribution channels designed to move products from the customer back to the producer

revolving line of credit Guaranteed line of credit that can be used over a specified period

right-to-work laws Laws giving employees the explicit right to keep a job without joining a union

risk Threat of loss

risk-control techniques Methods of minimizing losses

risk-financing techniques Paying to restore losses

risk management Process of evaluating and minimizing the risks faced by a company

robots Programmable machines that can complete a variety of tasks by working with tools and materials

roles Behavioral patterns

routing Specifying the sequence of operations and the path the work will take through the production facility

S

S corporation Corporations with no more than 35 shareholders that may be taxed as a partnership; also known as a subchapter S corporation

salaries Weekly, monthly, or yearly cash compensation for work

sales office Producer-owned operation that markets products but doesn't carry any stock

sales promotion Wide range of events and activities (including coupons, rebates, contests, in-store demon-strations, free samples, trade shows, and point-of-purchase displays) designed to stimulate interest in a product

sales support personnel Salespeople who facilitate the selling effort by providing such services as prospecting, customer education, and customer service

sample Small part of a large group

savings and loan associations (S&Ls) Banks offering savings, interest-bearing checking, and mortgages

savings banks Mostly in New England, banks offering interest-bearing checking, savings, and mortgages

scarity Shortage of desirable resources

scheduling Process of determining how long each production operation takes and then setting a starting and ending time for each

scientific management Management perspective that focuses on the scientific study of work situations to improve efficiency

scrambled merchandising Policy of carrying merchandise that is ordinarily sold in a different type of outlet

seasonal variation Regular, predictable change over a year's time

secondary data Facts previously produced or collected for a purpose other than that of the moment

secular trend Pattern of growth or decline in a particular business, industry, or economy that occurs over a long period of time—say, 20 or 30 years; also called a *long-term trend*

secured bonds Bonds backed by specific assets

secured loans Loans backed up with something of value that the lender can claim in case of default, such as a piece of property

selective credit controls Federal Reserve's power to set credit terms on various types of loans

selective distribution Approach to distribution that relies on a limited number of outlets

self-insure Accumulating funds each year to pay for any losses, rather than buying insurance from another company

self-managing teams Teams in which members are responsible for an entire process or operation

sellers' markets Situations in which demand for products exceeds supply, which may tempt marketers to pay less attention to customer satisfaction

selling expenses All the operating expenses associated with marketing goods or services

seniority Longevity in a position or company, frequently used as a basis for making human resources decisions (compensation, termination, and so on)

serial bonds Bonds from a single issue that must be repaid at intervals

service businesses Businesses that provide intangible products or perform useful labor on behalf of another

setup costs Expenses incurred each time a producer organizes resources to begin producing goods or services

sexism Discriminating against a person on the basis of gender

sexual harassment Unwelcome sexual advance, request for sexual favors, or other verbal or physical conduct of a sexual nature within the workplace that affects a person's job prospects or job performance

shareholder Owner of equities

shareholders Owners of a corporation

shark repellent Direct takeover defense in which the company's board requires a large majority of voting shares to approve any takeover attempt

shop steward Union member and employee who is elected to represent other union members and who attempts to resolve employee grievances with management

shopping products Products for which a consumer spends a lot of time shopping in order to compare prices, quality, and style

short selling Selling stock borrowed from a broker with the intention of buying it back later at a lower price, repaying the broker, and pocketing the profit

short-term debt Borrowed funds used to cover current expenses (generally repaid within a year)

sinking fund Account into which a company makes annual payments for use in redeeming its bonds in the future

skimming Charging a high price for a new product during the introductory stage and lowering the price later

slowdown Decreasing employee productivity to pressure management

small business Company that is independently owned and operated, that is not dominant in its field, and that meets certain criteria for number of employees or annual sales revenue

social audit Periodic assessment and reporting of what a business is doing to be socially responsible

social responsibility Concept that a business needs to look beyond its own goals and recognize other obligations to society

socialism Economic system characterized by public ownership and operation of key industries combined with private ownership and operation of less vital industries

sole proprietorship Business owned by a single individual

span of management Number of people under one manager's control; also known as *span of control*

specialty advertising Advertising that appears on various items such as coffee mugs, pens, and calendars, designed to help keep a company's name in front of customers

specialty products Products that a consumer will make a special effort to locate

specialty shops Stores that carry only particular types of goods

speculative risk Risk that involves the chance of both loss and profit

speculators Investors who seek large capital gains through relatively risky investments

spot trading Trading in commodities that will be delivered immediately; also called *cash trading*

staff Functional experts who supplement the line organization by providing advice and specialized services

staffing Process of matching the right people with the right jobs

stakeholders Individuals or groups to whom business has a responsibility

standardization Uniformity in goods or parts, making them interchangeable

standards Criteria against which performance may be measured

stare decisis Concept of using previous judicial decisions as the basis for deciding similar court cases

start-up companies New ventures

state banks Banks chartered by a state government

statement of cash flows Financial statement that summarizes receipts and disbursals of cash in three areas: operations, investments, and financing

statistical process control (SPC) Monitoring the production process using control charts

statistical quality control (SQC) Use of random sampling to test the quality of production output

statistics Factual data that can be presented in numerical form

statutory law Statute, or law, created by a legislature

stock Shares of ownership in a corporation

stock certificate Document that proves stock ownership

stock company Profit-making insurance company owned by shareholders

stock exchanges Facilities where shares of stock are bought and sold

stock option Contract allowing the holder to buy or sell a given number of shares of a particular stock at a given price by a certain date

stock specialist Intermediary who trades in a particular security on the floor of an auction exchange; "buyer of last resort"

stock split Increase in the number of shares of ownership that each stock certificate represents

stockbrokers People who buy and sell shares of stock on behalf of investors

strategic goals Goals focusing on broad organizational issues

strategic plans Actions designed to accomplish strategic goals, usually defined for periods of two to five years and developed by top managers

strict product liability Concept that assigns product liability even if the company used all reasonable care in the manufacture, distribution, or sale of its product

strike Temporary work stoppage by employees who want management to accept their union's demands

strikebreakers People who cross a picket line to work

subsidiary corporations Corporations whose stock is owned entirely or almost entirely by another corporation

super NOW account Interest-bearing negotiable order of withdrawal account with a relatively high minimum-balance requirement

supermarkets Large departmentalized food stores

supplies Items that keep a company's operations going, in-cluding maintenance, repair, and operating (MRO) items

supply Specific quantity of a product that the seller is able and willing to provide at various prices at a given time

supply curve Series of points on a graph showing the relationship between price and quantity supplied

surety bond Coverage that protects companies against losses incurred through nonperformance of a contract

surgical and medical insurance Insurance that pays for the costs of surgery and physicians' fees while a person is hospitalized or recovering from hospitalization

surveys Data-collection method in which the subjects are asked questions to determine their attitudes and opinions

synthetic system Production process that combines two or more materials or components to create finished products; the reverse of an analytic system

T

table Grid for displaying relationships between words and numbers, particularly many precise numbers

tactical objectives Objectives that focus on departmental issues and describe the results necessary to achieve the organization's strategic goals

tactical plans Actions designed to achieve tactical objectives and to support strategic plans, usually defined for a period of one to three years and developed by middle managers

tall structure Organization structure having a narrow span of management and many hierarchical levels

target markets Specific groups of customers to whom a company wants to sell a particular product

targeted résumé Résumé that focuses attention on what a person can do for a particular employer in a particular position

tariffs Taxes levied on imports

task force Group of people from several departments who are temporarily brought together to address a specific issue

tax credit Direct reduction in the amount of income tax owed by a person or business; granted by a government body for engaging or not engaging in selected activities

tax deductions Direct reductions in the amount of income on which a person or business pays taxes

team Two or more people working together to achieve a specific objective

technical salespeople Specialists who contribute technical expertise and other sales assistance

technical skills Ability and knowledge to perform the mechanics of a particular job

telecommuting Working from home and communicating with the company's main office via computer and other devices

telemarketing Selling or supporting the sales process over the telephone

tender offer Invitation made directly to shareholders by an outside party who wishes to buy a company's stock at a price above the current market price

term bonds Bonds from a single issue that must be repaid simultaneously

term insurance Life insurance that provides death benefits for a specified period

termination Act of getting rid of an employee through layoffs or firing

test marketing Product-development stage in which a product is sold on a limited basis

Theory X Set of managerial assumptions about employee motivations focusing on lower-level needs

Theory Y Set of managerial assumptions about employee motivations focusing on higher-level needs

Theory Z Human relations approach that emphasizes involving employees at all levels and treating them like family

time deposits Bank accounts that pay interest and require advance notice before money can be withdrawn

time utility Consumer value added by making a product available at a convenient time

title Legal ownership of property

top managers Those at the top of an organization's management hierarchy, having the most power and responsibility in the organization

tort Noncriminal act (other than breach of contract) that results in injury to a person or to property

total quality management (TQM) Comprehensive management approach that builds quality into every organizational process as a way of improving customer satisfaction; also called total quality control

trade allowance Discount offered by producers to wholesalers and retailers

trade credit Credit obtained by the purchaser directly from the supplier

trade deficit Negative trade balance created when a country imports more than it exports

trade discount Discount offered to a wholesaler or retailer

trade promotions Sales-promotion efforts aimed at in-ducing distributors or retailers to push a producer's products

trade salespeople Salespeople who sell to and support marketing intermediaries by giving in-store demonstrations, offering samples, and so on

trade show Gathering where producers display their wares to potential buyers; nearly every industry has one or more trade shows focused on particular types of products

trade surplus Positive trade balance created when a country exports more than it imports

trademark Brand that has been given legal protection so that its owner has exclusive rights to its use

trading blocs Organizations of nations that remove barriers to trade among their members and that establish uniform barriers to trade with nonmember nations

transaction Exchange between parties

transaction costs Costs of trading securities, including broker's commission and taxes

transaction processing system (TPS) Computerized information system that processes the daily flow of customer, supplier, and employee transactions, including inventory, sales, and payroll records

transactional leadership Traditional view of management involving motivating employees to perform at expected levels, structuring employee roles and tasks, and linking rewards with goal achievement

transfer payments Payments by government to individuals that are not made in return for goods and services

transformational leadership Beyond the traditional view of management, involving motivating performance above expected levels, inspiring employee concern for broader issues, and spurring employees to work toward a challenging future vision

Treasury bills Short-term debt issued by the federal government; also referred to as *T-bills*

Treasury bonds Debt securities issued by the federal government that mature in 10 to 30 years

Treasury notes Debt securities issued by the federal government that mature within 1 to 10 years

trend analysis Examination of data over a sufficiently long period so that regularities and relationships may be detected, analyzed, and used as the basis for forecasts; also known as *time-series analysis*

trusts Monopolistic arrangements established when one company buys a controlling share of the stock of competing companies in the same industry

turnover Number of times that average inventory is sold during a given period

two-tier wage plans Compensation agreements in

which new employees are put on a wage scale lower than that of veteran employees

tying contracts Contracts forcing buyers to purchase unwanted goods along with goods actually desired

U

umbrella policies Insurance that provides businesses with coverage beyond what is provided by a basic liability policy

underground economy Economic activity that is not reported, even though it is generated by legal activities

underwriters Insurance-company employees who decide which risks to insure, for how much, and for what premiums

undifferentiated marketing Marketing program that offers a single standard product to all consumers; commonly known as *mass marketing*

unemployment insurance Government-sponsored program for assisting employees who are laid off or, to a lesser extent, who quit their jobs

unfunded pension liabilities Amount by which a company's estimated future pension obligations exceed the funds set aside to cover those obligations

Uniform Commercial Code (UCC) Set of standardized laws that govern business transactions and that have been adopted by most states

uninsurable risk Risk that few, if any, insurance companies will assume because of the difficulty of calculating the probability of loss

union shop Workplace in which the employer may hire new people at will but only for a probationary period, after which they must join the union

unissued stock Authorized shares that are to be released in the future

universal life insurance Combination of a term life insurance policy and a savings plan with flexible interest rates and flexible premiums

Universal Product Codes (UPCs) Black stripes on packages that can be scanned by lasers to identify a product and track it by computer

unlimited liability Legal condition under which any damages or debts attributable to the business can also be attached to the owner, because the two have no separate legal existence

unsecured bonds Bonds backed only by the reputation of the issuer; also called *debentures*

unsecured loan Loan requiring no collateral but a good credit rating

U.S. savings bonds Debt instruments sold by the federal government in small denominations

utilitarianism Philosophy used in making ethical decisions that aims to achieve the greatest good for the greatest number

utility Power of a good or service to satisfy a human need

V

value-added taxes (VATs) Taxes paid at each step in the distribution chain on the difference between the cost of inputs and the price obtained for outputs at that step

variable costs Business costs that increase with the number of units produced

variable life insurance Whole life insurance policy that allows the policyholder to decide how to invest the cash value

variables Changeable factors in an experiment

venture capitalists (VCs) Investment specialists who provide money to finance new businesses or turnarounds in exchange for a portion of the ownership, with the objective of making a considerable profit on the investment

vertical marketing systems Planned distribution channels in which members coordinate their efforts to optimize distribution activities

vertical mergers Combinations of companies that participate in different phases of the same industry

vertical organization Structure linking activities at the top of the organization with those at the middle and lower levels

voluntary bankruptcy Bankruptcy proceedings initiated by the debtor

W

wages Cash payment based on a calculation of the number of hours the employee has worked or the number of units the employee has produced

wants Things that are desirable in light of a person's experiences, culture, and personality

warehouse Facility for storing backup stocks of supplies or finished products

warehouse clubs Low-priced stores that sell memberships to small retailers and consumer members

warranty Statement specifying what the producer of a product will do to compensate the buyer if the product is defective or if it malfunctions

wheel of retailing Evolutionary process by which stores that feature low prices are gradually upgraded until they forfeit their appeal to price-sensitive shoppers and are replaced by new competitors

NAME/ORGANIZATION/BRAND/ COMPANY INDEX

BankAmerica, 116, 120, 552, *544*, 557, 561
Bankers Trust, *48, 544*
Banks, Keith, 563
Barnes & Noble, 595
Barnes, Peter, 93
Barnevik, Percy, 185
Barron's, 617, 629
Baskin-Robbins, 144, 422
Bata, 34
Bata shoes, 34
Baty, W. Mark, Jr., 161
Baxter International, 216
Beatrice, 631
Bell Atlantic, 17
BellSouth, 17
Ben & Jerry's Homemade, 61–62, 63, 91
Ben Franklin Technology Center, 592
Benefit, *390*
Bentley cars, 221
Bergdorf Goodman Men, 420
Berkshire Hathaway, 631
Berlant, Debbie, 505–506, 507, 509, 532
Berry Bears, The, *390*
Best Buy, 11–12
Bethlehem Steel, 221, 242
  Burns Harbor plant, 221
Betty Crocker Cake Mixes, *390*
Bic, 378, 382
Bierman, Christine, 172
BIF (Bank Insurance Fund), 553
Bildt, Carl, 9
Birnbach, Lisa, A1
Bisquick, *390*
Black & Decker, 405–406, 408, 425, 431
Blaw Knox Rolls, 589
Bloomingdale's, 117, 418
Blue Cross and Blue Shield of Michigan, 297
Blue Mountain Arts, 412
Blue Plate Foods, 399
BMW, 51
Body Shop, The, 240
Boeing, 18, 211, 282, 429
Boeing 777, 211, 386
Bofors Nobel, 66
Bok, Joan T., 167
Bolsa (Mexican Stock Exchange), 551
Borden, 117, 655
Boston Celtics, 374
Boston Stock Exchange, 612
Bowerman, Bill, 339
Bowes, Walter H., 661
Bowman, Charlie, 373, 398, 399

Brandeis, Louis D., 280
Brennan, Edward, 86
Brinson, Gary P., 602
British Petroleum, 344
Brooks Brothers suits, 377
Brown Boveri, 185
Browning, Reese, 532
Brylcreem, 389
BSN Groupe, 462
Bubka, Sergei, 367
Budget Gourmet, 382
Buffett, Warren, 631
Bugles Corn Snacks, *390*
Buick, 469
Bumble Bee tuna, 465–466
Bumpus, Bruce, 235
Burger King, 79, 145, 252, 347, 355, 375, 455
Burke, James E., 269, 300
Burlington Coat Factory, 420
Burlington Industries, 117
Burrows, Roger, 73–74
Business Week, 617, 629, A2
Byerly's, 399
Byte, 463

C

Cadbury Schweppes, 381
Cadillac, 469
Cadillac automobile, 324, 381
Cajun Spice Ruffles, 381
Calloway, Wayne, 189
Calvin Klein's Obsession, 457
Campbell Soup, 189, *191,* 351
  Biscuit and Bakery Division, *191*
  International Division, *191*
  U.S.A. Division, *191*
Campbell's soups, *191*
Campeau, 117
C&S-Sovran, 550, 561
Canon, 201
Capriati, Jennifer, 457
Carlton, Don, 256
Carnegie, Andrew, 64
Carter, Jimmy, 320
Carterfone, *643*
Casey, James E., 170
Caterpillar, 42, 319, 362, 482
Ceasar, Sherita, 214
Central Point Software, 497
Cessna, 445
Chainsaw Kitten, 479
Chamber of Commerce of the United States, 647
Champion International, 631

Chanel perfume, 377
Chappell, Kate, 105
Chappell, Tom, 105
Charlotte Hornets, 680
Chase Brass & Copper, 329
Chase Manhattan, 297, *544,* 548, 557
Chávez, César, 316–317
Cheerios, *390*
Cheez Whiz, 389
Chemical Bank, 97, 98, 101, 114, 120, 121
Chemical Banking Corporation, *544,* 561
Cherry Point Naval Aviation Depot, 218
Chevrolet, 469, 655
Chevron, 589
Chic Parisien, 411
Chicago Board of Trade, 613
Chicago Board Options Exchange, 614
Chicago Mercantile Exchange, 613–614
Chicago Research and Trading Group, 561
Chicago Stock Exchange, 612
Chicago Tribune, 319
Chrysler, 42, 57, 166, 221, 287, 309, 321, 324, 401–402
Chubb, 675
Ciba-Geigy, 218
Cigna, 675
Cinnamon Toast Crunch, *390*
CIO (Congress of Industrial Organizations), 307, 308
Circuit City, 12, 422
Cirigliano, John, 689
Citation X, 445
Citibank, 547, 548, 551
Citicorp, 378, *544,* 561
Citizens and Southern (C&S), 539, 561
Clairol, 222
Claritas Corporation, 352
Clark, Jacqueline, 130
Clark Oil, *624*
Clearasil, 466
Clinique, 465
Club Med, 424
Clusters, *390*
CNBC, 632
CNN, 253
Coca-Cola, 37, *110,* 144, 354, 362, 363, 381, 441, 455, 465
Coffee, Sugar, and Cocoa Exchange, 614
Coffey, Allana M., 256
Cohen, Ben, 61–62, 91

SUBJECT INDEX

Branch office, 417
Brand(s), 378
    creating, 373–374, 398–399
    "family branding," 381–382
    national, 379
    private, 379–380
    trademarks and, 378–382
Brand awareness, 380
Brand equity, 381, 397
Brand extensions, 390
Brand insistence, 381
Brand loyalty, 380–381, *380, 397*
Brand marks, 378
Brand names, 378, 655
Brand preference, 380
Brand strategies, 381–382
"Brand value," 381
Brazil, 31, 39, 95, 117, 167
Breach of contract, 653
Break-even analysis, 396, *396*
Break-even point, 396, *396*
Bribery, gift-giving and, 85
Broad market indicators, 618–620, *620*
Brokerage houses, 545
Brokers, 416–417, *417,* 616
Brunei, 42
Budget, 507
Budget deficit (federal), 19–20
Bulgaria, 8, 52
Bull market, 618
Bulletin board system (BBS), 489
Business (*See* American business; International business)
Business agents, 310–311, 314
Business analysis, in product development, 385–386
Business cycle, 19, 675
Business-format franchises, 143
Business graphics software, 489
Business-interruption insurance, 677
Business law, 649–657
    agency law, 653–654
    bankruptcy, 656–657, *657*
    contracts, 651–653
    hiring practices, 279
    negotiable instruments, 654, 656
    property transactions, 654
    torts, 650–651
Business loans and lending (*See* Loans)
Business ownership (*See* Ownership forms)
Business plan:
    development for new ventures, 135–136, 147

topics in, 135–136, 147
Business publications, 617
Business reports, B6–B7
    format of, B6
    statistics in, B7
    tables and diagrams in, B6–B7, *B6, B7*
Business services, 378
Business subsidy, 636–637
"Buy American" policy, 153
Buyer, pricing and, 13, *13*
Buyer response, 350
Buyers' markets, 342–343
Buyer's remorse, 358
Buyer-seller relationship, 361
Buying behavior, 357–361
    of consumers, 357–360
    of organizations, 360–361
Buying responsibility, 407
Bytes, 484

C

C (computer language), 492
CAD (computer-aided design), 211, 478, 481, 489
CAD/CAM systems, 478
CAE (computer-aided engineering), 211
"Cafeteria" approach to benefits, 292
Calendar year, 514
Call option, 609–610
Call premium, 583
Callable bonds, 583
CAM (computer-aided manufacturing), 211, 478
Canada, 3, 5, *5,* 7, 15, 34, 38, 42, 44, *48,* 51, 52, 66, *193,* 219, 382, 421, 510, 551, 682, 690
Canada Awards for Business Excellence, 219
Canned approach, *449,* 451
Capital, 2
    for business start-up, 137
    cost of, 571-574, 591
    working, 529
Capital budgeting, 574–575
Capital gains (or losses), 601, 606
Capital-intensive businesses, 101
Capital investments, 574–575
Capital items, 377
Capitalism, 6–7, *6*
    "me first" nature of, 64–65
Career choice, A1–A2
Career guidance center (college), A1
Career Information Center Encyclopedia of Jobs and Careers, A1

Career: The Annual Guide to Business Opportunities, A2
Carriers, 428
Carterfone decision, *643*
Cash, as current asset, 515
Cash basis, 518–519
Cash discount, 397
Cash flow, 569–570, 588
Cash flow per share, 622
Cash instruments, 603
Cash management, 587–588
Casualty insurance, fraud in, 674
"Category killers," 422
Causal marketing research, 363
Cause-related marketing, 63
Caveat emptor, 63
CD-ROMs, 485, 486
CDs (certificates of deposit), 543, 546, 588
Celebrity endorsements, 367, 456–457
Central America, 42
Central processing unit (CPU), 483–484, 491
Centralization, 188, 190
Centralized networks, 494–495
CEO (chief executive officer), 111, 157, 286
CERCLA (1980), *69,* 71
Certificate of deposit (CD), 543, 546, 588
Certification election, 311, *311*
Certified management accountants (CMAs), 510
Certified public accountants (CPAs), 508, 526
CFCs (chlorofluorocarbons), 67, 70
CFTC (Commodity Futures Trading Commission), 625
Chain of command, delegation and, 186
Chain stores, 422
Chairman's letter, 526
Channel captains, 414–415
Channels of distribution, 1, 406, 410–411, 430
    alternatives in, 408–409, *408,* 430
    conflict in, 413–414
    control and, 411–412
    management of, 431
    market coverage and, 410–411
    marketing intermediaries in, 406–408, *407,* 430
    reverse channels in, 409–410
    selection of, 410–413
    vertical marketing systems and, 414–415

Chapter 7 bankruptcy, 656–657
Chapter 11 bankruptcy, 657, *657*
Chattel mortgage, 578, 580
Checks (checking accounts), 542, 545
    clearing of, 558–559
Chief executive officer (CEO), 111,
    157, 286
Chief information officer (CIO), 474
Child care, 250
Child-care assistance, 291
Child Protection and Toy Safety Act
    (1969), *73*
China, *5,* 8–9, 15, 29, 33, 37, 41, 50, 59,
    117, 152, 246, 348, 378, 644
Chlorofluorocarbons (CFCs), 67, 70
Chronological résumé, A4, *A4*
Cigarette Labeling Act (1965), *72*
CIM (computer-integrated
    manufacturing), 211, 234
CIO (chief information officer), 474
Circular flow, 14–15, *14*
Civil Rights Act (1964), 78
Civil Rights Act (1991), 78, *327*
Claims-made policies, 678
Classroom training, 282
Clayton Antitrust Act (1914), *64,* 638
Clean Air Act (1963), 16
    amendments to, 68–69, *68,* 70, 642
    EPA implementation costs of, 70
Clean Water Act (1977), *69*
Clearance searches, 655
Client-server systems, 482, 495
Closed corporations, 108
Closed-end fund, 609
Closed shop, 320
Closed-loop recycling systems, 125
Closing, in sales presentations, *449,*
    451, 452
CMAs (certified management
    accountants), 510
Coal emissions, 66–67
COBOL, 492
Code of ethics, 88
Cognitive dissonance, 358
Coinsurance, 681
COLA (cost-of-living adjustment), 322
Cold calls, 448
Collateral, 577
Collective bargaining, 64, 313–315,
    313, 331
    breakdown in, 316–320
    process of, 313–315
Collective-bargaining agreement,
    320–325
    administration of, 325
    basic contract issues in, 320–324, 331

flexibility in, 332
College placement office, A1
College Placement Annual, The, A2
Color Additives Amendment (1962), *72*
Colorado Department of Social
    Services, 281
Combo stores, 422–423
Commercial banks, 544, *544*
Commercial farms, 102
Commercial paper, 551, 580, *581*
Commercialization, 386–387
Commissions, 286
Commodities, 610–611
Commodities futures, 611
Commodity businesses, 102
Commodity exchanges, 613–614
Commodity Futures Trading Commis-
    sion (CFTC), 625
Commodity Futures Trading Commis-
    sion Act (1974), *626, 628*
Common carriers, 428
Common law, 649
Common stock, 585–587, 606–607
    dividends on, 586
    public offering of, 595
    stock splits, 586–587
    (*See also* Preferred stock; Stock[s])
Communication(s), 155–156, 159
    cultural differences and, 52–53, 54
    between divisions, 193
    electronic, 196, 489
    in horizontal organization, 196
    in human relations, 240–241
    between levels of management, 174
    matrix departmentalization and,
        194–195
    objectives of, 441
    oral, 159–160
    packaging as, 383
    during restructuring, 254
    with shareholders, 123
    written, 160, B6–B7
Communication media, 159, 458
Communications software, 489
Communications technology, 3, 141,
    459, 495
Communism, *6,* 7–9
Community banks, 550, 563
Company PACs, 647
Company valuation, 537
Comparable worth, 285–286
Comparative advantage, 32–33, 54
Comparative advertising, 454–455
Compensating balance, 580
Compensation, 285–293, 299
    benefits and services, 287–293, *288*

COLAs, 322
collective bargaining for, 321–323
    goals for, A2
    gender discrimination and, 79, *80*
    incentive programs for, 286–287
    salaries, 285–286
    wages, 321–322, *322*
Compensatory damage awards, 650
Competence, 652
Competition, 10–12, 17–19, 25
    in banking, 549–551
    changing bases of, 25
    in financial analysis, 522
    government regulation of, 638–639,
        659
    industrial spying and, 86
    innovation and, 12
    international, 22
    marketing objectives and, 391
    marketing planning and, 347–348
    monopolistic, 12
    planning for, 141
    pricing decisions and, 11, 394–395
    in product life cycle, 388
    quality/service and, 11–12
    use of information and, 476
Competitive advantage:
    computer technology and, 498–499
    customer satisfaction and, 344–346
    in investing, 629
    in union organization, 312
    of working for large companies, 107
Competitive advertising, 454
Competitiveness, 208–222, *208*
Compiler, 492
Completeness, of information, 475
Components, 378
Comprehensive Environmental Re-
    sponse, Compensation, and Liabil-
    ity Act (CERCLA, 1980), *69,* 71
Comprehensive general liability
    insurance, 678
Compulsory arbitration, 315
Computer-aided design (CAD), 211,
    217, 478, 481, 489
Computer-aided engineering (CAE),
    211
Computer-aided manufacturing
    (CAM), 211, 478
Computer-integrated manufacturing
    (CIM), 211, 234
Computer hardware, 482–485, *482*
    central processing unit (CPU),
        483–484, 491
    input devices, 482–483
    output devices, 484–485

Foreign competition, wage rates and, 321–322
Foreign corporation, 109
Foreign Corrupt Practices Act, 45, 85
Foreign exchanges, 46, 54, 615–616
Foreign investments in United States, 36–37, 50–51, *51*
Foreign sales corporations (FSCs), 44
Foreign trade, 41–45
Form utility, 342
FORTRAN, 492
Fortune 500 companies, 107–108, 110, 114, *131, 282*, 508
Forward buying, 465–466
"Four Ps," 355–357, *356*
Fourth-generation computer languages (4GLs), 492, *493*
France, 31, 39, 42, 44, *48,* 59, 112, 378, 379, 393, 421, 651
Franchisee, 143, 145
Franchiser, 143, 145
Franchises and franchising, 49, 143–147, *144,* 148
    advantages of, 144–146, 148
    disadvantages of, 146, 148
    evaluation of, 146–147, *147*
    in global marketplace, 145
    to reduce potential for competition, 150–151
    of specialty stores, 422
Fraud, 509
Free enterprise, 7
Free-market system, 2–9, 7
    capitalism and, 6–7, *6*
    communism and, 6, 7–9
    economic goals and measurements in, 3–6, *5*
    factors of production in, 2–3
    socialism and, *6,* 9
Free trade, 41
Freight forwarders, 428
Frequency, 459–460
FSCs (foreign sales corporations), 44
FTC (*See* Federal Trade Commission)
Full-line strategy, 390
Full-service brokerage, 617
Full-service merchant wholesalers, 416
Full warranty, 653
Functional departmentalization, 190–191, *191*
Functional résumé, A4, *A5*
Funding vehicles, 572–574
Funds, sources and uses of, 570–571, *571*
Future-favors system, 85
Futures, 610, 611

G

GAAP (*See* Generally accepted accounting principles)
Gain sharing, 261, 286, 287
Gantt charts, 228, *229,* 489
GATT (*See* General Agreement on Tariffs and Trade)
Gay employees, benefit coverage for, 288
GDP (*See* Gross domestic product)
Gender, job discrimination and, 79–81, *80,* 90
    (*See also* Women)
General Agreement on Tariffs and Trade (GATT), 37, 41, 54, 636
General expenses, 519–520
General obligation bonds, 604–605
General partnership, 105, 119
General-purpose software, 487
Generally accepted accounting principles (GAAP), 507, 508, 511, 522, 526
Generic products, 380
Geodemographics, 352
Geographic divisions, 192–193, *193*
Geographic information system (GIS), 478
Geographic patterns, of business, 236
Geographic segmentation, 351–352, *351*
Germany, 7, 15, 31, 39, 42, 44, *45, 48,* 51, 53, 59, 112, 185, 234, 326, 393, 421, 651
Gift-giving, 85
GIS (geographic information system), 478
Givebacks, 314, 321–322
Glass ceiling, 79
Global business issues:
    borderless banking, 551
    countertrade (barter), 47
    craftsmanship and advanced technology, 221
    financing for exports, 589
    franchising, 145
    gifts versus bribes, 85
    insurance, 677
    marketing of toys, 421
    organization structure, 185
    training in cultural diversity, 252
Global corporations, 46–53, *48, 57*
    countertrade and, 46, 47
    forms of business activity by, 47–50, 54
    franchising and, 49, 145

handling of cultural differences by, 52–53, 54, 59
    human resources in, 270
    importing and exporting by, 48
    joint ventures and strategic alliances of, 49–50
    licensing by, 48–49
    management of, 51–52
    training and development in, 283
    wholly owned facilities of, 50
Global economy, 23
    growth of service sector and, 100
    labor unions and, 309
Global funds, 615
Global marketing perspective, 354
Globalization, of banking, 539
GNP (gross national product), 4
Goal setting, 255–256
Goals, 162
    coordination between levels of, 163–164, *164*
    departmentalization and, 201
    in economic systems, 3–6, *5*
    objectives and, 162–163, 174, 175
    in promotional mix, 440–441
Going public, 140, 574
Golden parachute, 118–119
Goods, 98–99
Goods-producing businesses, 98, *98*
Goods-producing sector, *98,* 101–102, 119
Goodwill, 516
Government:
    deregulation by, 642-643, *643*
    protectionist measures of, 37–41
    role of, 15–20, 26, 636–644
    small businesses and, 142–143
Government insurance programs, 673–674
Government market, 349
Government-owned corporations, 108, *110*
Government procurement, 637
Government regulation(s), 16–17, 348, 378, 392–394, 636–648
    of banking, 539
    of competition, 17–19, 638–639
    of computer industry, 28
    consumer protection and, 639, *640*
    for corporations, 112–113
    of currency, 45–46, *45,* 54
    of economic stability, 19–20
    for employee protection, 639–641
    for environmental protection, 642
    of foreign trade, 44–45
    impact of, 643–644

Occurrence policies, 678
OCR (optical character recognition), 483
Odd-even pricing, 397
Odd lots, 617
Off-price stores, 419–420
Offer, 651
Office automation system (OAS), 477–478
Office politics, 199–200
Officers, of corporations, 111, *111,* 119
Oil Pollution Act (1990), *69*
Old-Age Survivors, Disability, and Health Insurance (*See* Social Security)
Oligopoly, 17
Open accounts, 576
Open-book credit, 576
Open-end fund, 609
Open-market operations, 555, *555,* 556–558
Open order, 616
Open (publicly traded) corporations, 108
Open shop, 321
Open systems, 486–487
Operating budget (master budget), 507
Operating expenses, 519–520
Operating income, 521
Operating systems, 486–487
Operational objectives, 163
Operational plans, 163, 173
Operations plan, 136, 147
Opportunities:
   in large corporations, 107
   for new ventures, 133–134, *134*
Opportunity cost, 10
Optical character recognition (OCR), 483
Optional benefits, 288, *288*
Oral communication, 159–160
Order getters, 447
Order of Administrative Reorganization (1970), *68*
Order processing, 426
Order takers, 447
Organization:
   horizontal, 195–197
   informal, 198–200, *198*
   new approaches to, 197–198
   office politics and, 199–200
   vertical, 182–190
Organization chart, 180, *180,* 181, *181,* 194
Organization structure, 180–182, *180, 181*

changing, 179–180, 201–202
   of global company, 185
   production improvement and, 234
   purposes of, 201
Organizational buying behavior, 360–361
Organizational customers, 352–353
Organizational efficiency, 476
Organizational market, 349
Organizational products, 377–378, 397, 409
Organizing function, 164–165
Organizations, 178–201
   building of, 179–180, 201–202
   corporate culture in, 200
   defining structure of, 180–182, *180, 181*
   departmentalization of, 190–195
   formal design of, 182–198
   grapevines in, 199
   human relations in, 240–241
   restructuring of, 189
Orientation programs, 281
Orphan Drug Act (1983, 1985), *72*
OSHA (Occupational Safety and Health Administration), 82, 292, 639
OTC (over-the-counter) market, 611, 614, 619
Out-of-state corporation, 109
Outbound telemarketing, 448
Outdoor and transit advertising, *460,* 462–463
Outplacement assistance, 295–296
Output devices, for computers, 484–485
Outside directors, 110
Oversaturated markets, 414
Over-the-counter market (OTC), 611, 614, 619
Owners' equity, 511, 517
Ownership forms, 102–113, *102, 103,* 119
   corporations, 106–113
   of new ventures, 134–135, *135*
   partnerships, 105–106
   sole proprietorships, 104
Ozone layer, 67

P

Pacific Rim countries, 37, *193,* 551
Packaging, 397
   cultural differences and, 53
   of products, 382–383
PACs (political action committees), 318, 647–648

Palmtop computers, 481
Par value, 584
Parallel processing, 483
Parent company, 109, *110*
Participative management, 168, 176, 310
Partnerships, *102, 103,* 105–106, 119
   advantages of, 105–106
   disadvantages of, 106
   owners' equity in, 517
   starting, 134, *135*
Part-time employees, 273, 274
Pascal (computer language), 492
Patent and Trademark Office, 378, 379, 655
Patents, 655
Pattern bargaining, 321
Pay for performance (gain sharing), 287
Payables (*See* Accounts payable)
Payee, 542
PCS (personal communications service), 495
PDAs (personal digital assistants), 495
p/e ratio (price/earnings ratio), 622
Peer-review system, 326
Penetration pricing, 392
Pension funds, 545
Pension guarantees, 289–290
Pension plans, 289, *290*
People's Republic of China (PRC), 29
Perceived conditions, morale and, 241
Performance appraisal, 283–285, *284*
Performance measures, 170
Perishability, of services, 375
Perks, 287, *288,* 292
"Permanent" employees, 296–297
Permissive subjects, in collective bargaining, 314–315
Personal communications service (PCS), 495
Personal computers (microcomputers), 480–481
Personal digital assistants (PDAs), 495
Personal financial planning (PFP), 509
Personal identification number (PIN), 549
Personal income taxes, 645
Personal information manager (PIM), 477
Personal objectives, 170
Personal property, 654
Personal selling, 443, *443,* 444, 446–453, 466
Persuading, as promotional goal, 440–441

Small businesses *(cont.)*
    trends affecting, 129–130, *130*
"Smart factories," 214
Smog, 66, 70
Smoke-free workplace, 67
Smoking, 67, 300
Social audit, 62–63
Social causes, donation to, 61, 93
Social class, buying behavior and, 359
Social concerns, 24
Social considerations, in marketing, 391–392
Social needs, *243,* 244
Social responsibility, 62–66
    as company policy, 90, 93
    consumerism and, 72–76, *72–73*
    as corporate philosophy, 61–62, 91
    in environmental issues, 66–72
    ethical behavior and, 86–90
    evolution of, 63–65, *64*
    investors and, 83–86
    practical limitations on, 65–66
    stakeholders and, 62–63
    toward workforce, 76–83
Social Security, 17, 673, 684
Social Security Act (1935), 289, 674
Social Security system, 64
Social trends, marketing planning and, 347
Socialism, *6, 9*
Society:
    relationship with business, 62
    as stakeholder, 62
Soft manufacturing, 212
Software, 485–491
    applications, 487–491
    development of, 477
    systems, 486–487
Sole proprietorships, *102, 103,* 104, 119
    owners' equity in, 517
    starting, 134, *135*
Solid Waste Disposal Act (1965, 1984), *68*
Sorting, by intermediaries, 407
South Africa, 50
South America, 42, 589
South Korea, 36, 185
Southeast Asia, 112
Soviet Union, 8, 23, 31–32, 36–37, 50, 541
S&P 500 (Standard & Poor's 500 average), 613, 620, 628, 632
Spain, 39, 42
Span of control, 186–188, *188*
Span of management, delegation and, 186–188, *188*

Specialization:
    international trade and, 33
    problems in, 183, 201
Specialty advertising, 465
Specialty products, 377
Specialty shops, 421–422
Specific performance, 653
Speculative-grade corporate bonds, 583, 601–602
Speculative risk, 666
Speculators, 601, 611
Speech recognition (computer), 483
Spokespeople, 156
Spot prices, 623, 625, *625*
Spot trading, 611
Spreadsheets, 488, *488*
SQC (statistical quality control), 218
Stability, of monetary value, 541
Staffing, 164–165
Stakeholders, 62–63, 90
Standard & Poor's 500 average (S&P 500), 613, 620, 628, 632
Standard & Poor's Stock Guide, 629
Standardization, 209, 354
    in flexible manufacturing, 213
    by intermediaries, 407
    production improvement and, 232
Standards, 169–170
Stare decisis, 649
Start-up companies, 131
State banks, 544
State court systems, *650*
State ownership, under communism, 7
Statement of cash flows, 521, 531
States, government regulation by, 643
Statistical map, *B6,* B7
Statistical process control, 218
Statistical quality control (SQC), 218
Statistics, B3–B5
    analysis of, B3–B5
    interpretation of, B5
Statutory law, 648
Stock(s), 107, 606–608
    selling to finance new ventures, 140
    short selling of, 608
    value of, 123
    (See also Common stock; Preferred stock)
Stock analysis, 622, *623*
Stock certificates, 584
Stock company, 674
Stock exchange listings, 621–623, *621*
Stock exchanges, 587
    monitoring function of, 626
Stock index futures, 610

Stock index options, 610
Stock options, 609–610
Stock price quotations, 620–625
Stock specialists, 612–613
Stock splits, 586–587
Stockbrokers, 587
Stockless distribution, 216
Strategic alliances, 49–50
Strategic goals, 163, 170
Strategic mergers, 117, 120
Strategic plans, 163, 173
Strict product liability, 651
Strike vote, 314
Strikebreakers, 318–319
Strikes, 316
Subliminal advertising, 441–442
Subsidiary corporations, 109, *110*
Subsidies, 39
Summary, in business plan, 135–136, 147
Summit meetings, economic, 43–44
Super NOW account, 546
Superbanks, 539–540, 561
Supercomputers, 482
Superfund, 71
"Superfund Act" (CERCLA), *69,* 71
Supermarkets, 422–423
Superstores, 422–423
Supervision, effectiveness of, 187
Supervisory managers (*See* First-line managers)
Supplemental unemployment benefits, 289
Supplies, 378
Supply and demand, 12–14
    in computer industry, 28
    in human resources planning, 272
    prices and, 25
    pricing decisions and, 394, *394*
Supply-and-demand relationships, 102
Supply curve, 13, *13*
Surety bond, 676
Surface Mining and Reclamation Act (1976), *68*
Surgical and medical insurance, 681
Surveys, B2
Sweden, 9, 42, 44, 112, 185, 393, 439
Switzerland, 42, 44, *48,* 112, 185, 203–204, 393, 651
Synthetic system of conversion, 209

T

Tables, in business reports, B6, B7, *B7*
Tactical objectives, 163
Tactical plans, 163, 173

Business Around the World

(Continued from front endpapers)

23. South Korea
Hyundai Corporation produces steel, metal, energy, machinery, and transportation vehicles, including Hyundai automobiles.

24. Kuwait
Kuwait Pharmaceutical Industries manufactures medicinal products.

25. Mexico
Petróleos Mexicanos (PEMEX) explores, drills, and produces petroleum and petrochemicals.

26. The Netherlands
Philips Electronics manufactures electrical equipment, medical apparatus, scientific equipment, and household appliances.

27. New Zealand
Fletcher Challenge manufactures forest, agricultural, and petroleum products.

28. Norway
Norsk Hydro produces oil, gas, metals, and petrochemicals.

29. Philippines
Tagumpay Manufacturing and Integrated Leather makes equine and bovine leather goods.

30. Poland
Konsbud manufactures musical instruments and accessories.

31. Russia
Palekh Union of Artists is an international trader in works of art, collectors' pieces, and antiques.

32. Saudi Arabia
Saudi Marble Company produces granite, marble, travertine, alabaster, and other stones.

33. Singapore
Cheng Meng Furniture manufactures custom-made furniture for industrial use.

34. South Africa
DeBeers Consolidated Mines is the world's leading producer of diamonds.

35. Spain
Elosua manufactures olive oil and other food products, including Star olive oil and Golden Gate pickled specialties.

36. Sweden
Ikea Svenska manufactures and (through its retail outlets) sells Ikea furniture.

37. Switzerland
SMH Société Suisse DeMicro-Electron Hologerie manufactures Swatch, Hamilton, Omega, Rado, Tissot, and Movamatic watches and microelectronic products.

38. Taiwan
Intex Corporation manufactures PVC inflatable products and furniture, including Stoneville furniture and Intex Recreation products, such as waterbeds, inflatables, and sporting goods.

39. Thailand
Unicord Company produces canned and frozen food products, including Bumble Bee seafoods.

40. Turkey
Koc Holding operates Koc Amerikan Bank and Bekoteknik electronic appliances and is in a joint venture with Fiat of Italy to manufacture Tofas trucks.

41. United Kingdom
Body Shop manufactures and (through its own retail outlets) sells cosmetics and cleaning preparations.

42. United States
Microsoft Corporation manufactures computer software.

43. Venezuela
Corporation Grupo Químico manufactures paints, resins, and pigments, including Chemsouth paints.

44. Vietnam
Shell Exploration and Production has a joint venture with Royal Dutch/Shell Group of companies, Netherlands, to produce petroleum.